W9-ASI-486

THE
GUINNESS
BOOK OF RECORDS
32ND EDITION 1986

Editor and Compiler
NORRIS D. McWHIRTER

Assistant General Editor
COLIN SMITH

Assistant Sports Editor
JULIAN FARINO

Art Editor
DAVID L. ROBERTS

GUINNESS BOOKS

The Story Behind The Guinness Book

On Saturday 10 Nov 1951, Sir Hugh Beaver (1890–1967) was out shooting on The North Slob, by the river Slaney in County Wexford in the south-east of Ireland. Some golden plover were missed by the party. That evening at Castlebridge House it was realized that it was not possible to confirm in reference books whether or not the golden plover was Europe's fastest game bird.

In August 1954 argument arose as to whether grouse were even faster. Sir Hugh, managing director of Guinness, thought that there must be numerous other questions debated nightly in the 81,400 pubs in Britain and in Ireland, but there was no book with which to settle arguments about records.

On 12 September 1954, Sir Hugh invited Norris and Ross McWhirter to see if their fact and figure agency in London could help. An office was set up at 107 Fleet Street and intense work began on the first slim 198 page edition. The printers bound the first copy on 27 August 1955. Well before Christmas the Guinness Book was No. 1 on the bestsellers list. It has occupied this position every year since except 1957 and 1959 when it was not republished.

The first US edition appeared in New York in 1956 followed by editions in French (1962) and German (1963). In 1967 there were first editions in Japanese, Spanish, Danish and Norwegian, while the following year editions were published in Swedish, Finnish and Italian. In the 'seventies there followed Dutch (1971); Portuguese (1974); Czechoslovak (1976); Hebrew, Serbo-Croat and Icelandic (all in 1977) and Slovenian (1978). In the 1980's translations into Greek, Indonesian, Chinese, Turkish, Hindi, Malay and Arabic brought the total to 220 editions in 25 languages.

In November 1974 the *Guinness Book* earned its own place in the *Guinness Book*. It had become the top selling copyright book in publishing history with sales of 23·9 million. By 1985 the global sales had risen to more than 51 million, which is equivalent to 114 stacks each as high as Mount Everest.

CHAIRMAN
ARTHUR GUINNESS & SONS PLC
OCTOBER 1985

Iveagh

No part of this book may be reproduced or transmitted in any form or by any means electronic, chemical or mechanical, including photocopying, any information storage or retrieval system without a licence or other permission in writing from the copyright owners. Reviewers are welcome to quote brief passages should they wish.

World Copyright Reserved
Copyright © 1985
Guinness Superlatives Ltd

This book is sold subject to the Standard Conditions of Sale of Net Books and may not be resold in the United Kingdom below the net price fixed by the publishers and ascertainable from their 1985 Catalogue.

British Library Cataloguing in Publication Data

Guinness book of records.—32
1. Curiosities and wonders—Periodicals
032'.02   AG243

ISBN 0–85112–433–X

Standard Book Number ISBN: 0–85112–433–X
Standard Book Number ISBN: 0–85112–434–8 (*Australian Edition*)

'Guinness' is a registered trade mark of Guinness Superlatives Ltd.

Printed in England. Produced by William Clowes Limited, Beccles, Suffolk.
Printed by Jarrold Printing, Norwich, Norfolk.
Litho origination by East Anglian Engraving, Norwich, Norfolk.

Notes On The Acceptability Of Records

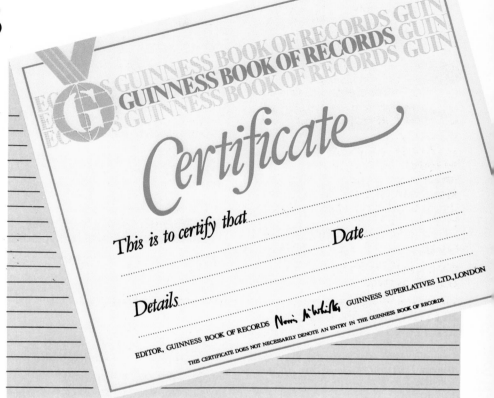

We are inclined to publish only those records which improve upon previous records or which are newly significant in having become the subject of widespread and preferably international competitiveness. However, in no circumstances will we *undertake* to publish any record.

It should be stressed that unique occurrences, interesting peculiarities or 'firsts' are not in themselves necessarily records. Records in our sense essentially have to be both measurable and comparable. Records which are *qualified* in some way, for example, by age, day of the week, county, etc, cannot be accommodated in a reference work so general as *The Guinness Book of Records*.

The publishers do *not* normally supply personnel to invigilate record attempts but reserve the right to do so. The name Guinness is a registered trade mark and should not be used in publicity for, or otherwise in the context of, a record attempt without our prior written consent.

Claimants should send independent *written* corroboration in the form of local or national press coverage and signed authentication by independent adult witnesses or representatives of

Editor Norris McWhirter presents Mr Izumi (born 1865), seen here also with the Mayor of Asan, Tokunoshima, Japan, with an additional supply of that other 'elixir of life'—Guinness stout (see page 13–14).

organisations of standing in their community. Signed log books should show there has been unremitting surveillance in the case of endurance events. Action photographs (*preferably* colour transparencies) should also be supplied.

Five minute rest intervals (optional but aggregable) are *permitted* after each completed hour in marathon events except for those very few 'nonstop' categories in which minimal intervals may be taken only for purposes other than for resting. All record attempts are undertaken at the sole risk of the (potential) claimant. The publishers cannot be held in any way responsible for any (potential) liability, howsoever arising out of any such attempt, whether to the claimant or any third party.

The publishers do not publish gratuitously dangerous categories such as the lowest height for a handcuffed free-fall parachutist or the thinnest burning rope suspending a man in a straitjacket from a helicopter.

If an activity is one controlled by a recognised world or national governing body, that body should be consulted and involved in ratifying it. Guidance and authentication notes are available from the publishers upon postal application and receipt of prepaid postage.

EDITOR & COMPILER

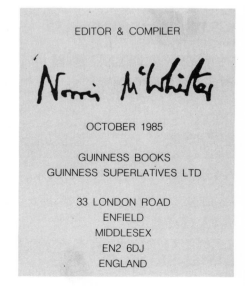

Norris McWhirter

OCTOBER 1985

GUINNESS BOOKS
GUINNESS SUPERLATIVES LTD

33 LONDON ROAD
ENFIELD
MIDDLESEX
EN2 6DJ
ENGLAND

CONTENTS

CONTENTS CONTENTS CONTEN

The world's longest car—the 10 wheeled Ultra Limo fifty footer built in 1985 by Vini Bergeman and Kraig Kavanagh of Ultra Limo, La Palma, California, USA. There is a 12 foot *3,65 m* swimming bath at the aft end for water lovers. *Franklin Berger, Northridge, CA*

Extra GIFT OFFER

A year's Club membership makes a great extra gift.

The GUINNESS RECORD BREAKERS Club

I bet you didn't know that you can join the new Guinness Record Breakers Club for only £2.75.. Is this a record?

If you and your friends are fascinated by records and record breaking, and if you'd like to have a better understanding of the courage, dedication and character that makes a record breaker, then you'll be interested in joining the exciting new Guinness Record Breakers Club.

On joining, you get your own Record Breakers Club package which consists of a membership card, club badge, personal record book and a full year's subscription to the Guinness Record Breakers magazine published six times a year exclusively for members.

And that's not all, included is a voucher worth 50p off admission to the superb Guinness World of Records exhibition in London's Piccadilly.

Your own copy of the exciting Club magazine.

This is the magazine that gives you the real inside stories. It's bright, full of colour pictures and news. In it you can read the dramatic stories behind records past and present. There will be sections on Pop, Sport, The Human World, The Natural World and all the other record breaking categories you will find in this book.

As well as publishing your letters, there will be lots of competitions for you, your friends and your school to enter. There will be lots of prizes to be won and – who knows – you may even get into the world-famous Guinness Book of Records!

In addition, there will be quizzes, puzzles and exciting special offers as well as details of record attempts in the pipeline and an update on the exciting Guinness World of Records exhibition. In fact, everything to make it the most action-packed magazine around.

Your own records to make and break.

Each club member gets their own personal record log book. It's pocket sized to go with you anywhere and it's laid out so as to help you keep a track of your own achievements and assess how your performance is improving.

Whether it's swimming, football, or even standing on one leg – keeping a record can make it all the more fun.

How to Join.

If the Guinness Record Breakers Club sounds like your kind of action, or you know someone who would really enjoy being a member, don't delay, send a crossed cheque or postal order for £2.75 made out to the Guinness Record Breakers Club with full name, address and age details to Guinness Record Breakers Club, FREEPOST, PO Box 109, Penn, High Wycombe, Buckinghamshire HP10 8BR.

Alternatively use the special application form between pages 32 and 33.

If you are paying for a gift subscription, this special form allows you to enclose a personal greeting and nominate a delivery date for the membership starter pack.

Please note that membership of the Record Breakers Club is restricted at present to United Kingdom and Republic of Ireland residents only.

Why not apply now?

CHAPTER ONE

The Human Being

A masterpiece of organisation of the human race—the first ever assemblage of one hundred people aged from 1 to 100 years. *(John Fox, Tony Tree; Evening Argus, Brighton. Organised by Max le Grand)*

1. DIMENSIONS

TALLEST GIANTS

The true height of human giants is frequently obscured by exaggeration and commercial dishonesty. The only admissible evidence on the actual height of giants is that collected this century under impartial medical supervision. Unfortunately medical papers themselves are not guiltless in including fanciful, as opposed to measured, heights.

The assertion that Goliath of Gath (*c.* 1060 BC) stood 6 cubits and a span (9 ft 6½ in *290 cm*) suggests a confusion of units or some over-zealous exaggeration by the Hebrew chroniclers. The Jewish historian Flavius Josephus (born AD 37/38, died *c.* AD 100) and some of the manuscripts of the Septuagint (the earliest Greek translation of the Old Testament) attribute to Goliath the wholly credible height of 4 Greek cubits and a span (6 ft 10 in *208 cm*).

Extreme mediaeval data, taken from bone measurements, invariably refer to specimens of extinct whale, giant cave bear, mastodon, woolly rhinoceros or other prehistoric non-human remains.

Giants exhibited in circuses and exhibitions are routinely under contract not to be measured and are, almost traditionally, billed by their promoters at heights up to 18 in *45 cm* in excess of their true heights. There are many notable examples of this, and 23 instances were listed in the *Guinness Book of Records* (14th edition). The acromegalic giant Eddie Carmel (b. Tel Aviv, Israel, 1938), formerly 'The Tallest Man on Earth' of Ringling Bros. and Barnum & Bailey's Circus (1961–8) was allegedly 9 ft 0⅝ in *275 cm* tall (weighing 38 st 3 lb *242 kg*), but photographic evidence suggests that his true height was about 7 ft 6⅝ in *230 cm*. He died in New York City on 14 Aug 1972 when his standing height, due to severe kyphoscoliosis, (two dimensional spinal curvature), was *c.* 7 ft *213 cm*.

An extreme case of exaggeration concerned Siah Khān ibn Kashmir Khān (b. 1913) of Bushehr (Bushire), Iran. Prof. D. H. Fuchs showed photographs of him at a meeting of the Society of Physicians in Vienna, Austria, in January 1935, claiming that he was 320 cm *10 ft 6 in* tall. Later, when Siah Khān entered the Imperial Hospital in Teheran for an operation, it was revealed that his actual height was a full metre less at 220 cm *7 ft 2.6 in.*

World *All-time*

Modern opinion is that the tallest recorded man of whom there is irrefutable evidence was the pre-acromegalic giant Robert Pershing Wadlow, born at 6.30 a.m. on 22 Feb 1918 in Alton, Illinois, USA.

He was born to Harold F. and Addie Mae Wadlow (1896–1980) weighing 8 lb 6 oz *3,79 kg* in Monroe St., Alton. His abnormal growth started at the age of 2 following a double hernia operation. His height progressed as follows:

Age in Years	Height		Weight	
			lb	kg
5	5' 4"	*163 cm*	105	*48*
8	6' 0"	*183 cm*	169	*77*
9	6' 2½"	*189 cm*	180	*82*
10	6' 5"	*196 cm*	210	*95*
11	6' 7"	*200 cm*	—	—
12	6' 10½"	*210 cm*	—	—
13	7' 1¾"	*218 cm*	255	*116*
14	7' 5"	*226 cm*	301	*137*
15	7' 8"	*234 cm*	355	*161*
16	7' 10½"	*240 cm*	374	*170*
17	8' 0½"	*245 cm*	315[1]	*143*
18	8' 3½"	*253 cm*	—	—
19	8' 5½"	*258 cm*	480	*218*
20	8' 6¾"	*261 cm*	—	—
21	8' 8½"	*265 cm*	491	*223*
22.4[2]	8' 11"	*272 cm*	439	*199*

[1] *Following severe influenza and infection of the foot.*
[2] *Wadlow was still growing during his terminal illness.*

Dr C. M. Charles, Associate Professor of Anatomy at Washington University's School of Medicine in St Louis, Missouri and Dr Cyril MacBryde measured Robert Wadlow at 272 cm *8 ft 11.1 in* in St Louis on 27 June 1940. Wadlow died 18 days later in a hotel, at 1.30 a.m. on 15 July 1940, in Manistee, Michigan as a result of cellulitis (inflammation of cellular tissue) of the right ankle aggravated by a brace, which had been poorly fitted only a week earlier.

He was buried in Oakwood Cemetery, Alton, Illinois in a coffin measuring 10 ft 9 in *328 cm* in length, 32 in *81 cm* wide and 30 in *76 cm* deep. His greatest recorded weight was 35 st 1 lb *222,71 kg*, on his 21st birthday. He weighed 31 st 5 lb *199 kg* at the time of his death. His shoes were size 37AA (18½ in *47 cm* long) and his hands measured 12¾ in *32,4 cm* from the wrist to the tip of the middle finger (*cf.* the depth of this page at 11¼ in *28,5 cm*). He wore a size 25 ring.

GIANT LEAGUE

The only other men for whom heights of 8 ft *244 cm* or more have been reliably reported are the nine listed below. In seven cases, gigantism was followed by acromegaly, a disorder which causes an enlargement of the nose, lips, tongue, lower jaw, hands and feet, due to renewed activity by an already swollen pituitary gland, which is located at the base of the brain.

John F. Carroll (1932–69) of Buffalo, New York State, USA [1] 8 ft 7¾ in *263,5 cm*.

John William Rogan (1871–1905), a Negro of Gallatin, Tennessee, USA [2] 8 ft 6 in *259,1 cm*.

Don Koehler (1925–81) of Denton, Montana, USA [3] 8 ft 2 in *248,9 cm*, latterly lived in Chicago.

Bernard Coyne (1897–1921) of Anthon, Iowa USA [4] 8 ft 2 in *248,9 cm*.

Väinö Myllyrinne (1909–63) of Helsinki, Finland [5] 8 ft 1.2 in *246.8 cm*.

Patrick Cotter O'Brien (1760–1806) of Kinsale, County Cork, Ireland [6] 8 ft 1 in *246 cm*.

'Constantine' (1872–1902) of Reutlingen, West Germany [7] 8 ft 0.8 in *245,8 cm*.

Gabriel Estevao Monjane (b. 1944–*fl.* 1984) of Monjacaze, Mozambique [8] *c.* 8 ft 0¾ in *245,7 cm*.

Sulaimān 'Ali Nashnush (b. 1943–*fl.* 1984) of Tripoli, Libya [9] 8 ft 0.4 in *245 cm*.

[1] *Severe kypho-scoliosis (two dimensional spinal curvature). The figure represents his height with assumed normal spinal curvature, calculated from a standing height of 8 ft 0 in 244 cm, measured on 14 Oct 1959. His standing height was 7 ft 8¼ in 234 cm shortly before his death.*
[2] *Measured in a sitting position. Unable to stand owing to ankylosis (stiffening of the joints through the formation of adhesions) of the knees and hips. Weighed only 175 lb 79 kg.*
[3] *Spinal curvature reduced his standing height to c. 7 ft 10 in 238,4 cm. Abnormal growth started at the age of 10. He had a twin sister who is 5 ft 9 in 175 cm tall. His father was 6 ft 2 in 187 cm and his mother 5 ft 10 in 177 cm.*
[4] *Eunuchoidal giant (Daddy long-legs syndrome). Rejected by Army in 1918 when 7 ft 9 in 236 cm. Still growing at time of death.*
[5] *Stood 7 ft 3¼ in 222 cm at the age of 21 years. Experienced a second phase of growth in his late thirties and may have stood 8 ft 3 in 251 cm at one time.*
[6] *Revised height based on skeletal remeasurement in 1975.*
[7] *Eunuchoidal. Height estimated, as both legs were amputated after they turned gangrenous. He claimed a height of 8 ft 6 in 259 cm.*
[8] *Eunuchoidal. Measured 7 ft 5 in 226 cm at the age of 16 and 7 ft 10 in 238,7 cm in Dec 1965. Latest measurement taken in May 1967. Has not been anthropometrically assessed since joining a Portuguese circus (billed height 265 cm 8 ft 8¼ in). Now suffering from scoliosis.*
[9] *Operation to correct abnormal growth successfully carried out in Rome in 1960.*

Alton, Illinois's tallest police officer Raymond Galloway (6 ft 2 in *188 cm*) being dwarfed by the Mayor's son Robert Wadlow—the tallest human of all time at 8 ft 11.1 in *2,72 m. (Alton Telegraph)*

His arm span was 9 ft 5¾ in *288 cm* and his peak daily consumption attained 8000 calories. At the age of 9 he was able to carry his father, Harold F. Wadlow (d. Sept 1967) later Mayor of Alton, who stood 5 ft 11 in *180 cm* and weighed 170 lb *77 kg*, up the stairs of the family home. His last words were 'The doctor says I won't get home for the ... celebrations' (a reference to his paternal grandparents golden wedding).

A table of the tallest giants of all-time in the 31 countries with men taller than 7 ft 4 in *223,5 cm* was listed in the 15th edition of the *Guinness Book of Records* (1968) at page 9.

Muhammad Aalam Channa (b. Sehwan, 1956), who works as an attendant at the shrine of Lal Shahbaz Qalandar in Pakistan assumed the role of the world's tallest man in 1981 with the death of Don Koehler (see left). A height of 8 ft 2¾ in *251 cm* attributed to him by news agencies and the international press was proved in 1984 to be exaggerated by some 15 cm *5.9 in*. The tallest living humans are thus Monjane and Nashnush (see left).

The tallest teenage giant still growing is Kazim Hussein (b. 1968) of Baghdad, Iraq, who was 2,26 m *7 ft 5 in* in Feb 1985. He had grown 7,6 cm *3 in* in the previous 12 months.

England

The tallest Englishman ever recorded was William Bradley (1787–1820), born in Market Weighton, Humberside. He stood 7 ft 9 in *236 cm*. John Middleton (1578–1623), the famous Childe of Hale, from near Liverpool, was credited with a height of 9 ft 3 in *282 cm* but a life-size impression of his right hand (length 11½ in *29,2 cm*, *cf.* Wadlow's 12¾ in *32,4 cm*) painted on a panel in Brasenose College, Oxford indicates his true stature was nearer 7 ft 8 in *233,6 cm*. James Toller (1795–1819) of St Neots, Cambridgeshire was alleged to be 8 ft 6 in *259 cm* but was actually 7 ft 6 in *229 cm*. Albert Brough (1871–1919), a publican of Nottingham, reached a height of 7 ft 7½ in *232 cm*. Frederick Kempster (1889–1918) of Bayswater, London, was reported to have measured 8 ft 4½ in *255 cm* at the time of his death, but photographic evidence suggests that his height was 7 ft 8½ in *235 cm*. He measured 234 cm *7 ft 8.1 in* in 1913. Henry Daglish, who stood 7 ft 7 in *231 cm* died in Upper Stratton, Wiltshire, on 16 March 1951, aged 25. The much-publicised Edward (Ted) Evans (1924–58) of Englefield Green, Surrey, was reputed to be 9 ft 3 in *282 cm* but actually stood 7 ft 8½ in *235 cm*. The tallest fully mobile man now living in Great Britain is Christopher Paul Greener (b. New Brighton, Merseyside, 21 Nov 1943) of Hayes, Kent, who measures 7 ft 6¼ in *229 cm* (weight 26 st *165 kg*). Terence Keenan (b. 1942) of Rock Ferry, Merseyside measured 7 ft 6 in *229 cm* in 1968, but is confined to a wheelchair owing to a leg condition. His abnormal growth began at the age of 17 when he was only 5 ft 4 in *163 cm* tall.

Scotland

The tallest Scotsman, and the tallest recorded 'true' (non-pathological) giant, was Angus Macaskill (1825–63), born on the island of Berneray, in the Sound of Harris, in the Western Isles. He stood 7 ft 9 in *236 cm* and died in St Anns', on Cape Breton Island, Nova Scotia, Canada. Lambert Quételet (1796–1874), a Belgian anthropometrist, considered that a Scotsman named MacQuail, known as 'the Scotch Giant', stood 8 ft 3 in *251 cm*. He served in the famous regiment of giants of Frederick William I (1688–1740), King of Prussia. His skeleton, now in the Staatliche Museum zu Berlin, East Germany, measures 220 cm *7 ft 2.6 in*. Sam McDonald (1762–1802) of Lairg in Sutherland, was reputed to be 8 ft *244 cm* tall but actually stood 6 ft 10 in *208 cm*. William Olding (b. 1914–*fl.* 1942) of Glasgow measured 7 ft 6½ in *230 cm* (weight 366 lb *166 kg*). The tallest Scotsman now living is George Gracie (b. 1938) of Forth, Strathclyde. He stands 7 ft 3 in *221 cm* and weighs 32 st *203 kg*. His brother Hugh (b. 1941) is 7 ft 0½ in *215 cm*.

Wales

The tallest Welshman on record was William Evans (1599–1634) of Gwent, then Monmouthshire, who was porter to King James I. He stood 7 ft 6 in *228,6 cm*.

Ireland

The tallest Irishman was the 8 ft 1 in *246 cm* tall Patrick Cotter O'Brien (1760–1806), born in Kinsale, County Cork. He died at Hotwells, Bristol (See Table p. 9).

Twins

The tallest twins (identical) ever recorded were the Knipe brothers (b. 1761–*fl.* 1780) of Magherafelt, near Londonderry, Northern Ireland, who both measured 7 ft 2 in *218,4 cm*. The world's tallest living twins (also identical) are Dan and Doug Busch (b. 12 Aug 1961) of Flagstaff, Arizona, USA who both measure 6 ft 11 in *210,8 cm*. Britain's tallest twins are Jonathan and Mark Carratt (b. 11 June 1955) of Maltby, South Yorkshire who are 6 ft 8 in *203,2 cm* and 6 ft 9 in *205,7 cm* respectively. David and John Moore (b. 29 Mar 1963) of Erith, Kent both measure 6 ft 8¼ in *203,8 cm*.

TALLEST GIANTESSES

World *All-time*

Giantesses are rarer than giants but their heights are still spectacular. The tallest woman in history was the acromegalic giantess Zeng Jinlian (pronounced San Chung Lin) (b. 26 June 1964) of Yujiang village in the Bright Moon Commune, Hunan Province, central China. She could not stand erect, due to scoliosis, but was 247 cm *8 ft 1¼ in* long when she died on 13 Feb 1982. She began to grow abnormally from the age of 4 months and stood 156 cm *5 ft 1½ in* before her 4th birthday and 217 cm *7 ft 1½ in* when she was 13. Her hands measured 25,5 cm *10 in* and her feet 35,5 cm *14 in* in length. She suffered from both scoliosis and diabetes. Her parents are 163 cm *5 ft 4 in* and 156 cm *5 ft 1½ in* while her brother was 158 cm *5 ft 2¼ in* aged 18.

United Kingdom

The tallest woman in British medical history has been Jane ('Ginny') Bunford, born on 26 July 1895 at Bartley Green, Northfield, Birmingham, England. Her abnormal growth started at the age of 11 following a head injury, and on her 13th birthday she measured 6 ft 6 in *198 cm*. Shortly before her death on 1 April 1922 she stood 7 ft 7 in *231 cm* tall, but she had severe kyphoscoliosis and would have measured about 7 ft 11 in *241 cm* with assumed normal spinal curvature. Her skeleton, now preserved in the Anatomical Museum in the Medical School at Birmingham University, has a mounted height of 7 ft 4 in *223,5 cm*.

Living

The tallest living woman is Sandy Allen (b. 18 June 1955, Chicago) of Niagara Falls, Ontario, Canada. On 14 July 1977 she underwent a pituitary gland operation, which inhibited further growth at 7 ft 7¼ in *231,7 cm*. A 6½ lb *2,95 kg* baby, her acromegalic growth began soon after birth. She now weighs 33 st *209,5 kg* and takes a size 16EEE American shoe (=14½ UK or 50PP Continental).

Tallest couple

Anna Hanen Swan (1846–88) of Nova Scotia, Canada, was billed at 8 ft 1 in *246 cm* but actually measured 7 ft 5½ in *227 cm*. In London on 17 June 1871 she married Martin van Buren Bates (1845–1919) of Whitesburg, Letcher County, Kentucky, USA, who stood 7 ft 2½ in *219 cm* making them the tallest married couple on record.

SHORTEST DWARFS

The strictures which apply to giants apply equally to dwarfs, except that exaggeration gives way to understatement. In the same way as 9 ft *274 cm* may be regarded as the limit towards which the tallest giants tend, so 23 in *58 cm* must be regarded as the limit towards which the shortest mature dwarfs tend (*cf.* the average length of new-born babies is 18–20 in *46–50 cm*). In the case of child dwarfs their *ages* are often enhanced by their agents or managers.

There are many forms of human dwarfism, but those suffering from ateleiosis (midgets) are generally the shortest. They have essentially normal proportions but suffer from growth hormone deficiency. Such dwarfs tended to be even shorter at a time when human stature was generally shorter due to lower nutritional standards.

World *All-time*

The shortest mature human of whom there is independent evidence was Pauline Musters ('Princess Pauline'), a Dutch midget. She was born at Ossendrecht, on 26 Feb 1876 and measured 30 cm *11.8 in* at birth. At the age of 9 she was 55 cm *21.65 in* tall and weighed only 1,5 kg *3 lb 5 oz*. She died, at the age of 19, of pneumonia, with meningitis, her heart weakened from alcoholic excesses, on 1 Mar 1895 in New York City, NY, USA. Although she was billed at 48 cm *19 in*, she had earlier been medically measured to be 59 cm *23.2 in* tall. A *post mortem* examination showed her to be exactly 61 cm *24 in* (there was some elongation after death). Her mature weight varied from 3,4–4 kg *7½–9 lb* and her 'vital statistics' were 47–48–43 cm *18½–19–17 in*, which suggests she was overweight.

In 1938 a height of 19 in *48 cm* was attributed to Paul Del Rio (b. Madrid, Spain, 1920) by *Life Magazine* when he visited Hollywood, but the fact that his presence created no great impression among other dwarfs in the film capital and that he weighed as much as 12 lb *5,4 kg* suggests that he was closer to 26 in *66 cm* tall.

In 1979 a height of 50 cm *19.68 in* and a weight of 4 lb 6 oz *1,98 kg* were reported for a nine-year-old Greek girl named Stamatoula being cared for at the Lyrion Convent, Athens. The child, believed to be the survivor of twins, is suffering from Seckel's 'bird-face' syndrome and growth had allegedly ceased, but in a similar case from Corsica the girl eventually reached a height of 34 in *86,3 cm* and a weight of 26 lb *11,8 kg*.

Male All-time

The shortest recorded adult male dwarf was Calvin Phillips, born on 14 Jan 1791 in Bridgewater, Massachusetts, USA. He weighed 2 lb *907 g* at birth and stopped growing at the age of 5. When he was 19 he measured 26½ in *67 cm* tall and weighed 12 lb *5,4 kg* with his clothes on. He died two years later, in April 1812, from progeria, a rare disorder characterised by dwarfism and premature senility.

The most famous midget in history was Charles Sherwood Stratton, *alias* 'General Tom Thumb', born on 4 Jan 1838. When he got into the clutches of the circus proprietor Mr Barnum his birth date was changed to 4 Jan 1832 so that when billed at 30½ in *77 cm* at the age of 18 he was in fact 12. He died in his birthplace of Bridgeport, Connecticut, USA of apoplexy on 15 July 1883 aged 45 (not 51) and was 3 ft 4 in *102 cm*.

William E. Jackson, *alias* 'Major Mite', born on 2 Oct 1864 in Dunedin, New Zealand, measured 9 in *23 cm* long and weighed 12 oz *340 g* at birth. In November 1880 he stood 21 in *53 cm* and weighed 9 lb *4 kg*. He died in New York City, NY, USA, on 9 Dec 1900, when he measured 27 in *69 cm*.

Living

The world's shortest known mobile living adult human is Antonio Ferreira (b. 1943), a rachitic dwarf of Arcozelo, Portugal who measures 75 cm *29½ in*. He is a professional drummer. In July 1982 an unconfirmed height of 28 in *71 cm* was reported for a chicken farmer named Ghucam Ahmed Dar living near Srinagar in Kashmir, India.

United Kingdom

The shortest mature human ever recorded in Britain was Miss Joyce Carpenter (b. 21 Dec 1929), a rachitic dwarf of Charford, Hereford & Worcester, who stood 29 in *74 cm* tall and weighed 30 lb *13,60 kg*. She died on 7 Aug 1973 aged 43. Hopkins Hopkins (1737–54) of Llantrisant, Mid Glamorgan who suffered from progeria, was 31 in *79 cm* tall. He weighed 19 lb *8,62 kg* at the age of 7 and 13 lb *6 kg* at the time of his death. There are an estimated 2000 people of severely restricted growth (i.e. under 4 ft 8 in *142 cm*), living in Britain today.

The shortest adult living in Britain is Michael Henbury-Ballan (b. 26 Nov 1958) of Bassett, Southampton, who is 37 in *94 cm* tall and weighs 5½ st *35 kg*. A 5 lb 14 oz *2,66 kg* baby, he stopped growing at the age of 13 years. His fraternal twin brother Malcolm is 5 ft 9 in *175 cm* tall and weighs 11 st 7 lb *73 kg*.

Twins shortest

The shortest twins ever recorded were the primordial dwarfs Matjus and Bela Matina (b. 1903–*fl.* 1935) of Budapest, Hungary who later became naturalised Americans. They both measured 30 in *76 cm*. The world's shortest living twins are John and Greg Rice (b. 1952) of Palm Beach, Florida, USA who both measure 34 in *86,3 cm*.

Oldest

There are only two centenarian dwarfs on record. The older was Hungarian-born Miss Susanna Bokoyni ('Princess Susanna') of Newton, New Jersey, USA who died aged 105 years on 24 Aug 1984. She was 3 ft 4 in *101 cm* tall and weighed 37 lb *16,78 kg*. The other was Miss Anne Clowes of Matlock, Derbyshire, who died on 5 Aug 1784 aged 103 years. She was 3 ft 9 in *114 cm* tall and weighed 48 lb *21,7 kg*.

Most variable stature

Adam Rainer, born in Graz, Austria, in 1899, measured 118 cm *3 ft 10.45 in* at the age of 21. But then he suddenly started growing at a rapid rate, and by 1931 he had reached 218 cm *7 ft 1¾ in*. He became so weak as a result that he was bed-ridden for the rest of his life. At the time of his death on 4 Mar 1950 aged 51 he measured 234 cm *7 ft 8 in* and was the only person in medical history to have been both a dwarf and a giant.

Most disparate couple *Britain*

Nigel Wilks (6 ft 6 in *198 cm*) of Kingston upon Hull, Humberside married Beverly Russell (4 ft *122 cm*) on 30 June 1984.

TRIBES

Tallest

The tallest major tribe in the world is the Tutsi (also known as Watussi) (pop. *c.* 10,000), Nilotic herdsmen of Rwanda and Burundi, Central Africa where the average adult height (males) is more than 6 ft *183 cm*. The Tehuelches of Patagonia, long regarded as of gigantic stature (*i.e.* 7–8 ft *213–244 cm*), have in fact an average height (males) of 5 ft 10 in *177 cm*. The Montenegrins of Yugoslavia, with a male average of 5 ft 10 in *177 cm* (in the town of Trebinje the average height is 6 ft *183 cm*), compare with the men of Sutherland, at 5 ft 9½ in *176,5 cm*. In 1912 the average height of the men living in Balmaclellan, in the Kircudbright district of Dumfries and Galloway was reported to be 5 ft 10.4 in *179 cm*.

Shortest

The smallest pygmies are the Mbuti, with an average height of 4 ft 6 in *137 cm* for men and 4 ft 5 in *135 cm* for women, with some groups averaging only 4 ft 4 in *132 cm* for men and 4 ft 1 in *124 cm* for women. They live in the forests near the river Ituri in Zaïre, Africa.

WEIGHT

Heaviest men *World*

The heaviest human in recorded medical history was alleged to be Jon Brower Minnoch (b. 29 Sept 1941) of Bainbridge Island, Washington, USA, who was carried on planking by a rescue team into the University Hospital, Seattle in March 1978. Dr Robert Schwartz, the endocrinological consultant, estimated, by extrapolating his intake and elimination rates, that he was 'probably more' than 1400 lb *635 kg* (100 st). His highest actually recorded bodyweight was 975 lb *442 kg* in September 1976. To roll him over in his hospital bed it took 13 attendants. After nearly 2 years on a 1200 calorie per day diet he was discharged at 476 lb *216 kg* (34 st). He had to be readmitted in October 1981 having

The only others for whom weights of more than 60 st (840 lb) *381 kg* have been reported are the 10 listed below:

	lb	st	lb	kg
Michael Walker *née* Francis Lang (b. 1934) USA (6 ft 2 in *188 cm*)[1] ...... est.	1187	84	11	*538*
Robert Earl Hughes (1926–58) USA (6 ft 0½ in *184 cm*)	1069	76	5	*485*
Mohamed Naaman (b 1946) Kenya (6 ft 0 in *182 cm*)[2]	1055	75	5	*478*
Mills Darden (1798–1857) USA (7 ft 6 in *229 cm*)	1020	72	12	*462*
John Hanson Craig (1856–94) USA (6 ft 5 in *195 cm*)[3]	907	64	11	*411*
Arthur Knorr (1914–60) USA (6 ft 1 in *185 cm*)[4]	900	64	4	*408*
Albert Pernitsch (b. 1956) of Grafkorn, Austria (5 ft 9 in *175 cm*)[5]	880	62	12	*399*
T. J. Albert Jackson (b. 1941) Canton, Mississippi, USA[6]	872	62	4	*395*
Toubi (b. 1946) Cameroon	857½	61	3½	*389*
T. A. Valenzuela (1895–1937) Mexico (5 ft 11 in *180 cm*)	850	60	10	*385*

[1] *Reduced to 369 lb 167 kg by Feb. 1980. Peak weight was only estimated in 1971.*
[2] *Reported in Aug 1984 to have reduced to 770 lb 349 kg.*
[3] *Won $1000 in a 'Bonny Baby' contest in New York City in 1858.*
[4] *Gained 300 lb 136 kg in the last 6 months of his life.*
[5] *Believed to be heaviest living human. His left arm tattoo proclaims 'Nobody is perfect'. In July 1984 his girth was 200 cm 78¾ in.*
[6] *A French press report attributed a weight of 470 kg 1036 lb to him in 1979. He stands 6 ft 4 in 1,93 m.*

Five of the attendants at the Guinness World of Records at the Trocadero, Piccadilly, London prove themselves hopelessly inadequate in trying to match the weight of a model of America's super-heavyweight 76 stone *485 kg* Robert Earl Hughes (1926–58).

reportedly gained 200 lb *91 kg* (over 14 st) in 7 days. He died *c.* 10 Sept 1983. This former taxicab driver stood 6 ft 1 in *1,85 m* tall. He was 400 lb *181 kg* in 1963, and 700 lb *317 kg* in 1966.

Great Britain

The heaviest recorded man in Great Britain was Peter Yarnall of East Ham, London, who died on 30 March 1984 aged 34 years. He was 5 ft 10 in *177,8 cm* tall and weighed 59 st *374 kg*. His coffin measured 7 ft 4 in *2,23 m* in length, 4 ft *1,22 m* across and had a depth of 2 ft 9 in *83,8 cm*.

Only two other British men had a recorded weight of more than 50 st *317,5 kg*. One of them

was William Campbell (b. Glasgow 1856) who died on 16 June 1878 when a publican at High Bridge, Newcastle upon Tyne, Tyne and Wear. He was 6 ft 3 in *190 cm* tall and weighed 53 st 8 lb *340 kg* with an 85 in *216 cm* waist and a 96 in *244 cm* chest. The other was the celebrated Daniel Lambert (1770–1809) of Stamford. He stood 5 ft 11 in *180 cm* tall and weighed 52 st 11 lb *335 kg* shortly before his death and had a girth of more than 92 in *233 cm*.

Britain's heaviest man is the 6 ft 11 in *210,8 cm* tall professional wrestler Martin Ruane ('Giant Haystacks') (b. Camberwell, London 1946) of Manchester. A 14 lb *6,35 kg* baby he weighed

Britain's topmost 19th-century heavyweights who both exceeded 50 stone *317,5 kg: top* William Campbell of Glasgow; *above* Daniel Lambert of Stamford, Lincolnshire. *(The Leicester Museum)*

25 st *158,7 kg* at the age of 18 years and 32 st *203 kg* when he was 25. His weight now fluctuates between 41 st *260 kg* and 43 st *273 kg* but he once claimed to have tipped the scales at 50 st *317 kg*.

Ireland

The heaviest Irishman is reputed to have been Roger Byrne, who was buried in Rosenallis, County Laoighis (Leix), on 14 Mar 1804. He died in his 54th year and his coffin and its contents weighed 52 st *330 kg*. Roly McIntyre (b. 1955) of Kesh, Fermanagh, Northern Ireland scaled a peak 42 st 4 lb *268,5 kg* in April 1983 (see slimming below).

Heaviest women *World*

The heaviest woman ever recorded was the late Mrs Percy Pearl Washington, 46 who died in hospital in Milwaukee, on 9 Oct 1972. The hospital scales registered only up to 800 lb (57 st 2 lb) *362,8 kg* but she was believed to weigh about 880 lb (62 st 12 lb) *399,1 kg*. The previous

feminine weight record had been set 84 years earlier at 850 lb (60 st 10 lb) *385 kg* although a wholly unsubstantiated report exists of a woman Mrs Ida Maitland (1898–1932) of Springfield, Mississippi, USA, who reputedly weighed 65 st 1 lb (911 lb) *413,2 kg*.

A more reliable and better documented case was that of Mrs Flora Mae Jackson (*née* King), a 5 ft 9 in *175 cm* Negress born in 1930 at Shuqualak, Mississippi, USA. She weighed 10 lb *4,5 kg* at birth, 19 st 1 lb (267 lb) *121 kg* at the age of 11, 44 st 5 lb (621 lb) *282 kg* at 25 and 60 st (840 lb) *381 kg* shortly before her death in Meridian, Mississippi, on 9 Dec 1965. She was known in show business as 'Baby Flo'.

Great Britain and Ireland

The heaviest woman ever recorded in Great Britain was a patient admitted to the Royal Free Hospital in Hampstead, London in *c.* 1975. After her death the intrigued undertaker took the hearse over a weighbridge, loaded and unloaded, so revealing, after making an allowance for the coffin, a weight of 46 stone *292 kg*.

Heaviest twins

The heaviest twins in the world were Billy Leon (1946–79) and Benny Loyd (b. 7 Dec 1946) McCrary *alias* McGuire of Hendersonville, North Carolina, USA, who in November 1978 were weighed at 743 lb *337 kg* (Billy) and 723 lb *328 kg* (Benny) and had 84 in *213 cm* waists. As professional tag wrestling performers they were *billed* at weights up to 770 lb *349 kg*. Billy died at Niagara Falls, Ontario, Canada on 13 July 1979 after a mini-motorcycle accident.

Lightest *World*

The lightest adult human on record was Lucia Zarate (b. San Carlos, Mexico 2 Jan 1863, d. October 1889), an emaciated Mexican ateleiotic dwarf of 26½ in *67 cm*, who weighed 2,125 kg *4.7 lb* at the age of 17. She 'fattened up' to 13 lb *5,9 kg* by her 20th birthday. At birth she weighed 2½ lb *1,1 kg*. The lightest adult ever recorded in the United Kingdom was Hopkins Hopkins (Shortest dwarfs, see p. 10).

The thinnest recorded adults of normal height are those suffering from Simmonds' Disease (Hypophyseal cachexia). Losses up to 65 per cent of the original body-weight have been recorded in females, with a 'low' of 3 st 3 lb *20 kg* in the case of Emma Shaller (b. St Louis, Missouri 8 July 1868, d. 4 Oct 1890), who stood 5 ft 2 in *157 cm*. Edward C. Hagner (1892–1962), *alias* Eddie Masher (USA) is alleged to have weighed only 3 st 6 lb *22 kg* at a height of 5 ft 7 in *170 cm*. He was also known as 'the Skeleton Dude'. In August 1825 the biceps measurement of Claude-Ambroise Seurat (b. 10 Apr 1797, d. 6 Apr 1826) of Troyes, France was 4 in *10 cm* and the distance between his back and his chest was less than 3 in *7.6 cm*. According to one report he stood 5 ft 7½ in *171 cm* and weighed 5 st 8 lb *35 kg*, but in another account was described as 5 ft 4 in *163 cm* and only 2 st 8 lb *16 kg*. It was recorded that the American exhibitionist Rosa Lee Plemons (b. 1873) weighed 27 lb *12 kg* at the age of 18.

In July 1977 the death was reported of an 83 year old woman in Mexborough, South Yorkshire who scaled only 2 st 5 lb *15 kg* (height not recorded).

Lightest Great Britain

Robert Thorn (b. 1842) of March, Cambridgeshire weighed 49 lb *22 kg* at the age of 32. He was 4 ft 6 in *137 cm* tall and had a 27 in *68 cm* chest (expanded) and 4½ in *11.4 cm* biceps.

Slimming

The greatest recorded slimming feat was that of

William J. Cobb (b. 1926), *alias* 'Happy Humphrey', a professional wrestler of Macon, Georgia, USA. It was reported in July 1965 that he had reduced from 57 st 4 lb *364 kg* to 16 st 8 lb *105 kg*, a loss of 40 st 11 lb *259 kg* in 3 years. His waist measurement declined from 101 to 44 in *256 to 112 cm*. In October 1973 it was reported that 'Happy' was back to his normal weight of 46½ st or 651 lb *295 kg*. By July 1979 Jon Brower Minnoch (1941–83) (see p. 11) had reduced to 476 lb *216 kg* (34 st); if his estimated peak weight was authentic, this indicated a weight loss of 924 lb *419 kg* (66 st) in 2 years, a speed record of 8.8 lb *3,99 kg* per week.

The US circus fat lady Mrs Celesta Geyer (b. 1901), *alias* Dolly Dimples, reduced from 553 lb *251 kg* to 152 lb *69 kg* in 1950–51, a loss of 401 lb *182 kg* in 14 months. Her vital statistics diminished *pari passu* from 79–84–84 in *200–213–213 cm* to a *svelte* 34–28–36 in *86–71–91 cm*. Her book 'How I lost 400 lbs' was not a best-seller because of the difficulty of would-be readers identifying themselves with the dress-making and other problems of losing more than 28 st *178 kg* when 4 ft 11 in *150 cm* tall. In December 1967 she was reportedly down to 7 st 12 lb *50 kg*. In February 1951 Mrs Gertrude Levandowski (b. 1893) of Burnips, Michigan, USA successfully underwent a protracted operation for the removal of a cyst which subsequently reduced her weight from 44 st *280 kg* to 22 st *140 kg* (See also p. 23).

Ron Allen (b. 1947) sweated off 21½ lb *9,7 kg* of his 250 lb *113,4 kg* in Nashville, Tennessee, USA in 24 hr in Aug 1984. Roly McIntyre, 29, (see above) reduced from 42 st 4 lb *268,5 kg* to 13 st 5 lb *84,8 kg* from April 1983 to Feb 1985.

The feminine champion in Britain was Mrs Dolly Wager (b. 1933) of Charlton, London, who, between September 1971 and 22 May 1973 reduced from 31 st 7 lb *200 kg* to 11 st *69,8 kg* so losing 20 st 7 lb *130 kg* with Weight Watchers.

Weight gaining

The reported record for gaining weight was set by Jon Minnoch (see p. 11 and above) when in October 1981 he was readmitted to University Hospital, Seattle, Washington State, USA having re-gained 200 lb *91 kg* in 7 days. Miss Doris James of San Francisco, California, USA is alleged to have gained 23 st 3 lb *147 kg* in the 12 months before her death in August 1965, aged 38, at a weight of 48 st 3 lb *306 kg*. She was only 5 ft 2 in *157 cm* tall.

Greatest differential

The greatest weight differential recorded for a married couple is 65 st 12 lb *418 kg* in the case of Mills Darden (72 st 12 lb *462 kg*—see p. 11) and his wife Mary (7 st *44,5 kg*). Despite her diminutiveness, however, Mrs Darden bore her husband three (perhaps five) children before her death in 1837. The UK record is held by Martin Ruane (see p. 11) and his 7½ st *47,6 kg* wife Rita, where their weight differential was at times 42½ st *270 kg*. They have three sons.

2. ORIGINS

EARLIEST MAN

SCALE OF TIME
If the age of the Earth-Moon system (latest estimate 4450 million years) is likened to a single year, Hominids appeared on the scene at about 4.15 p.m. on 31 December, Britain's earliest known inhabitants arrived at about 11.10 p.m., the Christian era began about 14 seconds before midnight and the life span of a 119-year-old person (pp. 13 & 14) would be about three-quarters of a second. Present calculations indicate that the Sun's increased heat, as it becomes a 'red giant' will make life insupportable on Earth in about 10,000 million years. Meanwhile there may well be colder epicycles. The period of 1000 million years is sometimes referred to as an aeon.

Man (*Homo sapiens*) is a species in the sub-family Homininae of the family Hominidae of the super-family Hominoidea of the sub-order Simiae (or Anthropoidea) of the order Primates of the infra-class Eutheria of the sub-class Theria of the class Mammalia of the sub-phylum Vertebrata (Craniata) of the phylum Chordata of the sub-kingdom Metazoa of the animal kingdom.

Earliest *Primate*

The first primates appeared in the Palaeocene epoch about 69,000,000 years ago. The earliest members of the sub-order Anthropoidea are known from both Africa and South America in the early Oligocene, 34–30 million years ago, when the two infra-orders, Platyrrhini and Catarrhini from the New and Old Worlds respectively were already distinct.

Earliest *Hominid*

Characteristics typical of the Hominidae such as the large brain and bipedal locomotion do not appear until much later. The earliest undoubted hominid relic found is an Australopithecine jaw bone with two molars 2 in *5 cm* in length found by Kiptalam Chepboi near Lake Baringo, Kenya in Feb 1984 and dated at 4 million years by associated fossils and 5.6–5.4 million years by rock correlation by K-Ar dating.

The most complete of the earliest hominid skeletons is that of 'Lucy' (forty per cent complete) found by Dr Donald C. Johanson and T. Gray at Locality 162 by the Awash river, Hadar, in the Afar region of Ethiopia on 30 Nov 1974. She was estimated to be *c.* 40 years old when she died 3 million years ago, and she was 3½ ft *106 cm* tall.

Parallel tracks of hominid footprints extending over 80 ft *24 m* were discovered at Laetoli, Tanzania in 1978, first by Paul Abell, in volcanic ash dating to 3.5 million years ago. The height of the smallest of the seemingly 3 individuals was estimated to be 120 cm *4 ft 7 in*.

Earliest genus *Homo*

The earliest species of the genus *Homo* is *Homo habilis* or 'Handy Man' named by Dr Louis Leakey in 1964. The greatest age attributed to fossils of this genus is for the skull KNM-ER (Kenya National Museum-East Rudolf) 1470 discovered in 1972 by Bernard Ngeneo at Koobi Fora by Lake Turkana, North Kenya. It is dated to 1.9 million years old and was reconstructed by Mrs Meave Leakey.

The earliest stone tools are between 2 and 2.4 million years old. They have been excavated from two sites in Ethiopia, one at the Omo Valley and the other at Hadar. On 25 Oct 1984 *Komsomolskaya Pravda* reported the discovery of more than 1800 stone artefacts from the permafrost of Yakutskaya, Siberia. These possibly dated back 2,000,000 years.

Earliest *Homo erectus*

The earliest *Homo erectus* (upright man), the species directly ancestral to *Homo sapiens*, was discovered by Bernard Ngeneo at Koobi Fora, North Kenya. It is also the most complete skull known of this species and is about 1.5 million years old.

Great Britain

The earliest but disputed evidence for the presence of hominids in Great Britain dates from *c.* 400,000 BC. Five worked flint artefacts showing features normally attributed to human workmanship were found in cave deposits near Westbury-sub-Mendip, Somerset, and described in 1975 by Michael J. Bishop. The oldest human remains ever found in Britain are pieces of a brain case from a specimen of *Homo sapiens*, recovered in June 1935 and March 1936 by Dr Alvan T. Marston from the Boyn Hill terrace in the Barnfield Pit, near Swanscombe, northern Kent. The remains were associated with a middle Acheulian tool culture and probably date to the Holsteinian interglacial (230,000 BC). Three hominid teeth, mandible fragments and a vertebra were found in Pontnewydd Cave, Lower Elwy Valley, North Wales from October 1980. They were dated by the Thorium/Uranium disequilibrium method to a little over 200,000 years.

3. LONGEVITY

No single subject is more obscured by vanity, deceit, falsehood and deliberate fraud than the extremes of human longevity. Extreme claims are generally made on behalf of the very aged rather than *by* them. The 1970 US Census disclosed 106,441 self-reported centenarians of

AUTHENTIC NATIONAL LONGEVITY RECORDS

	Years	Days		Born		Died	
Japan	120	—	Shigechiyo Izumi	29 June	1865	*fl.* 31 July	1985
United States[1]	113	273	Fannie Thomas	24 Apr	1867	22 Jan	1981
Canada[2]	113	124	Pierre Joubert	15 July	1701	16 Nov	1814
Spain[3]	112	228	Josefa Salas Mateo	14 July	1860	27 Feb	1973
France	112	66	Augustine Teissier (Sister Julia)	2 Jan	1869	9 Mar	1981
United Kingdom[4]	112	40	Anna Williams (Mrs) (*née Davies*)	2 June	1873	*fl.* 12 July	1985
Morocco	>112		El Hadj Mohammed el Mokri (Grand Vizier)		1844	16 Sept	1957
Poland	112	+	Roswlia Mielczarak (Mrs)		1868	7 Jan	1981
Ireland	111	327	The Hon. Katherine Plunket	22 Nov	1820	14 Oct	1932
Australia	111	235	Jane Piercy (Mrs)	2 Sept	1869	3 May	1981
South Africa[5]	111	151	Johanna Booyson	17 Jan	1857	16 June	1968
Czechoslovakia	111	+	Marie Bernatkova	22 Oct	1857	*fl.* Oct	1968
Channel Islands (Guernsey)	110	321	Margaret Ann Neve (*née Harvey*)	18 May	1792	4 April	1903
Northern Ireland	110	234	Elizabeth Watkins (Mrs)	10 Mar	1863	31 Oct	1973
Sweden	110	200+	Wilhelmine Sande (Mrs)	24 Oct	1874	*fl.* 12 May	1985
Yugoslavia	110	150+	Demitrius Philipovitch	9 Mar	1818	*fl.* Aug	1928
Netherlands[6]	110	141	Gerada Hurenkamp-Bosgoed	5 Jan	1870	25 May	1980
Greece[7]	110	+	Lambrini Tsiatoura (Mrs)		1870	19 Feb	1981
USSR[8]	110	+	Khasako Dzugayev	7 Aug	1860	*fl.* Aug	1970
Italy	110	+	Dimiana Sette (Sig)		1884	25 Feb	1985
Norway[9]	109	208	Marie Olsen (Mrs)	1 May	1850	24 Nov	1959
Tasmania (State of)	109	179	Mary Ann Crow (Mrs)	2 Feb	1836	31 July	1945
Scotland[10]	109	14	Rachel MacArthur (Mrs)	26 Nov	1827	10 Dec	1936
Belgium	108	327	Mathilda Vertommen-Hellemans	12 Aug	1868	4 July	1977
Germany[11]	108	128	Luise Schwarz	27 Sept	1849	2 Feb	1958
Iceland	108	45	Halldóra Bjarndóttir	14 Oct	1873	28 Nov	1981
Portugal[12]	108	+	Maria Luisa Jorge	7 June	1859	*fl.* July	1967
Finland	109	182	Andrei Akaki Kuznetsoff	17 Oct	1873	*fl.* 17 Apr	1983
Malaysia	106	+	Hassan Bin Yusoff	14 Aug	1865	*fl.* Jan	1972
Luxembourg	105	228	Nicolas Wiscourt	31 Dec	1872	17 Aug	1978

[1] Ex-slave Mrs Martha Graham died at Fayetteville, North Carolina on 25 June 1959 reputedly aged 117 or 118. Census researches by Eckler show that she was seemingly born in Dec 1844 and hence aged 114 years 6 months. Mrs Rena Glover Brailsford died in Summerton, South Carolina, USA on 6 Dec 1977 reputedly aged 118 years. Mrs Rosario Reina Vasquez who died in California on 2 Sept 1980 was reputedly born in Sonora, Mexico on 3 June 1866, which would make her 114 years 93 days. The 1900 US Federal Census for Crawfish Springs Militia District of Walker County, Georgia, records an age of 77 for a Mark Thrash. If the Mark Thrash (reputedly born in Georgia in December 1822) who died near Chattanooga, Tennessee on 17 Dec 1943 was he, and the age attributed was accurate, then he would have survived for 121 years.

[2] Mrs Ellen Carroll died in North River, Newfoundland, Canada on 8 Dec 1943, reputedly aged 115 years 49 days. Research is underway on the Ontario 1881 Census records on the claim of David Trumble to have been b. 15 Dec 1867.

[3] Snr Benita Medrana of Avila died on 28 Jan 1979 allegedly aged 114 years 335 days.

[4] London-born Miss Isabella Shepheard was allegedly 115 years old when she died at St Asaph, Clwyd, North Wales, on 20 Nov 1948, but her actual age was believed to have been 109 years 90 days. Charles Alfred Nunez Arnold died in Liverpool on 15 Nov 1941 reputedly aged 112 years 66 days based on a baptismal claim (London, 10 Sept 1829). Mrs Elizabeth Cornish (*née Veale*) who was buried at Stratton, Cornwall on 10 Mar 1691/2 was reputedly baptized on 16 Oct 1578, 113 years 4 months earlier.

[5] Mrs Susan Johanna Deporter of Port Elizabeth, South Africa, was reputedly 114 years old when she died on 4 Aug 1954. Mrs Sarah Lawrence, Cape Town, South Africa was reputedly 112 on 3 June 1968.

[6] Thomas Peters was recorded to have been born on 6 Apr 1745 in Leeuwarden and died aged 111 years 354 days on 26 Mar 1857 in Arnhem.

[7] The claim that Liakon Efdokia died 17 Jan 1982 aged 118 years 13 days is not substantiated by the censuses of 1971 or 1981. Birth registration before 1920 was fragmentary.

[8] There are allegedly 21,700 centenarians in USSR (cf. 7000 in USA). Of these 21,000 are ascribed to the Georgian SSR i.e. one in every 232. In July 1962 it was reported that 128, mostly male, were in the one village of Medini.

[9] Mrs W. Sande was born in present-day Norway.

[10] Lachlen McDonald died 7 June 1858 in Harris, Outer Hebrides, was recorded as being '110 years' on his death certificate.

[11] West Germany: An unnamed female died in 1979 aged 112 years and an unnamed male died, aged also 112 years in 1969. The Austrian record is 108 years (female d. 1975) and the Swiss record is also 108 years (female d. 1967).

[12] Senhora Jesuina da Conceicao of Lisbon was reputedly 113 years old when she died on 10 June 1965.

Note: *fl* is the abbreviation for *floruit*, Latin for he (or she) was living at the relevant date.

whom 100,241 were disallowed by the US Department of Health and Human Services.

Many hundreds of claims throughout history have been made for persons living well into their second century and some, insulting to the intelligence, for people living even into their third. Centenarians surviving beyond their 113th year are in fact of the extremest rarity and the present absolute proven limit of human longevity does not yet admit of anyone living to celebrate any birthday after their 120th.

The most reliably pedigreed large group of people in the world, the British peerage, has, after ten centuries, produced only three centenarian peers, but only one reached his 101st birthday. However, this is possibly not unconnected with the extreme draughtiness of many of their residences and the amount of lead in their game.

In the 30 year period 1950–1979 the deaths of 6 men and 10 women were recorded in England and Wales aged 110, 111 and in one case 112 (see Table). The 1971 Census showed 65 citizens of 108 and over. The odds of surviving from one birthday to the next are only worse than 50–50 after a 105th birthday.

Scientific research into extreme old age reveals that the correlation between the claimed density of centenarians in a country and its regional illiteracy is 0.83 ± 0.03. In late life, very old people often tend to advance their ages at the rate of about 17 years per decade. This was nicely corroborated by a cross analysis of the 1901 and 1911 censuses of England and Wales. Early claims must necessarily be without the elementary corroboration of birth dates. England was among the earliest of all countries to introduce compulsory local registers (September 1538) and official birth registration (1 July 1837) which was made fully compulsory only in 1874. Even in the United States, 45 per cent of births occurring between 1890 and 1920 were unregistered.

Several celebrated super-centenarians (over 110 years) are believed to have been double lives (father and son, relations with the same names or successive bearers of a title). The most famous example is Christian Jakobsen Drackenberg allegedly born in Stavanger, Norway on 18 Nov 1626 and died in Aarhus, Denmark aged seemingly 145 years 326 days on 9 Oct 1772. A number of instances have been commercially sponsored, while a fourth category of recent claims are those made for political ends, such as the 100 citizens of the Russian Soviet Federative Socialist Republic (population about 132,000,000 at mid-1967) claimed in March 1960 to be between 120 and 156. From data on documented centenarians, actuaries have shown that only one 115-year life can be expected in 2100 million lives (cf. world population was estimated to be 4575 million at mid-1982).

The height of credulity was reached on 5 May 1933, when a news agency solemnly filed a story from China with a Peking date-line that Li Chung-yun, the 'oldest man on Earth', born in 1680, had just died aged 256 years (sic). It was solemnly announced on 29 July 1982 that one of China's 5,000,000 census enumerators had unearthed in the Guangxi Region, Lan Buping, whose birthdate was entered as 13 Apr 1848. The French anthropologist Jean Rauch recorded in 1969 the death of Anai Dollo of the Auris subgroup of the Dogon people in the village of Bongo in Mali at the reputed age of 122. The tribe's oral tradition was that he had participated in their most sacred rite (held strictly at 60 year intervals) three times—as a baby in 1847, in 1907 and in 1967. The most extreme case of

longevity recently claimed in the USSR has been 168 years for Shirali 'Baba' Mislimov of Barzavu, Azerbaijan, who died on 2 Sept 1973 and was reputedly born on 26 Mar 1805. No interview of this man was ever permitted to any Western journalist or scientist. He was said to have celebrated the 100th birthday of his third wife Hartun, in 1966, and that of one of his grandchildren in August 1973. It was reported in 1954 that in the Abkhasian Republic of Georgia, USSR, where aged citizens are invested with an almost saint-like status, 2.58 per cent of the population was aged over 90—24 times the proportion in the USA.

Official Soviet insistence in 1961 on the unrivalled longevity of the country's citizenry is curious in view of the fact that the 592 persons in their unique 'over 120' category must have spent at least the first 78 years of their prolonged lives under Tsarism. It has recently been suggested that the extreme ages claimed by some men in Georgia, USSR, are the results of attempts to avoid military service when they were younger, by assuming the identities of older men.

Dr Zhores A. Medvedev, the expelled Soviet gerontologist, in Washington DC, on 30 Apr 1974 referring to USSR claims stated 'The whole phenomenon looks like a falsification' adding 'He [Stalin] liked the idea that [other] Georgians lived to be a 100 or more.' 'Local officials tried hard to find more and more cases for Stalin.' He points out (a) the average life-span in the regions claiming the highest incidence of centenarians is lower than the USSR average and (b) that, contrary to the rest of the world the incidence of centenarians claimed in the Caucasus had declined rapidly from 8000 in 1950 to 4500 in 1970. Dr Medvedev, in December 1977, put the proven limit in the USSR as low as 108 years.

It was announced in February 1984 that the 1982 Census in China revealed only 3765 centenarians of whom two thirds were women. In the US the mid-1983 figure was 32,000. Birth and death registration however became complete only in 1933 and was only 30.9 per cent by 1915.

Oldest authentic centenarian World

The greatest authenticated age to which any human has ever lived is a unique 120th birthday in the case of Shigechiyo Izumi of Asan on Tokunoshima an island 820 miles 1320 km SW of Tokyo, Japan. He was born where he lives on 29 June 1865 and recorded as a 6-year-old in Japan's first census of 1871. He watches television and says the best way to a long life is 'not to worry' and to leave things to 'God, the Sun, and Buddha'. He was visited by the Editor on 3 Apr 1980. The word 'anamelanism' has been suggested as a name for the unexplained phenomenon of his white hair returning to black at his temples. In 1984 his blood pressure was recorded as 60/170 and his pulse as 84. He stands 4 ft 8 in 1,42 m and weighs 43 kg 94.8 lb.

Oldest authentic centenarian Great Britain

The United Kingdom has an estimated population of some 4000 centenarians of whom only 22 per cent are male. The only UK citizens with birth and death certificates more than 112 years apart have been Miss Alice Stevenson (1861–1973) (112 years 39 days), Miss Janetta Jane Thomas (1869–1982) (112 years 35 days) and Mrs Anna Williams who surpassed them both (see Table, page 13). Britain's oldest proven man has been John Mosley Turner (b. 15 June 1856), who died on 22 Mar 1968 aged 111 years 281 days. In April 1706 a John Bailes was buried at All Saints Church, Northampton, having apparently been baptised on 20 Aug 1592. If these two

John Bailes were the same person, he would have been 113 years 8 months. The oldest living person born in Britain is Mrs Anna Eliza Williams (b. 2 June 1873) of Tuxedo Old People's Home, Swansea, West Glamorgan (see Table, page 13).

The first recorded case in the UK of three siblings being centenarians occurred on 26 Nov 1982 when Miss Frances Adams MSc became 100. Her brother was Dr John Andrew Adams (1867–1967) and her sister Dr Elizabeth Hart (née Adams) (1876–1977). The family came from Omagh, Co Tyrone, Northern Ireland.

Oldest quadruplets

The world's oldest quads are the Ottman quads of Munich, West Germany—Adolf, Anne-Marie, Emma and Elisabeth. They celebrated their 72nd birthday on 5 May 1984.

Oldest triplets

The longest-lived triplets on record were Faith, Hope and Charity Caughlin born at Marlboro, Massachusetts, USA on 27 Mar 1868. The first to die was Mrs (Ellen) Hope Daniels aged 93 on 2 Mar 1962.

Oldest twins World and Great Britain

The oldest recorded twins were Eli Shadrack and John Meshak Phipps (b. 14 Feb 1803, Affington, Virginia, USA). Eli died at Hennessey, Oklahoma on 23 Feb 1911 aged 108 years 9 days on which day John was still living in Shenandoah, Iowa. The chances of identical twins both reaching 100 are said to be one in 700 million. On 17 June 1984, identical twin sisters, Mildred Widman Philippi and Mary Widman Franzini of St. Louis, Missouri, USA celebrated their 104th birthday. The oldest twins on record in Great Britain have been the Bean twins Robert, of Birkenhead, Merseyside and Mary (later Mrs Simpson) of Etton, Cambridgeshire who celebrated their 100th birthday on 19 Oct 1973. Robert died before the end of 1973.

Most reigns

The greatest number of reigns during which any English subject could have lived is ten. A person born on the day (11 April) that Henry VI was deposed in 1471 had to live to only the comparatively modest age of 87 years 7 months and 6 days to see the accession of Elizabeth I on 17 Nov 1558. Such a person could have been Thomas Carn of London, reputedly born in 1471 and died 28 Jan 1578 in his 107th year.

Last 18th-century link

The last Briton with 18th-century paternity was Miss Alice J. Grigg of Belvedere, Kent (d. 28 Apr 1970) whose father William was born on 26 Oct 1799.

Oldest mummy

Mummification (from the Persian word mām, wax) dates from 2600 BC or the 4th dynasty of the Egyptian pharaohs. The oldest surviving mummy is of Wati, a court musician of c. 2400 BC from the tomb of Nefer in Saqqâra, Egypt found in 1944.

4. REPRODUCTIVITY

MOTHERHOOD

Most children World

The greatest officially recorded number of children produced by a mother is 69 by the first of the two wives of Feodor Vassilyev (b. 1707–fl. 1782), a peasant from Shuya, 150 miles 241 km east of Moscow. In 27 confinements she gave birth to 16 pairs of twins, 7 sets of triplets and 4 sets of quadruplets. The case was reported by the Monastery of Nikolskiy on 27 Feb 1782 to Moscow. At least 67 survived infancy. Empress Ekaterina II (The Great) (1762–96) was reputed to have evinced interest. The children, of whom almost all survived to their majority, were born in the period c. 1725–65.

Currently the world's most prolific mother is reported to be Leontina Albina (née Espinosa) (b. 1925) of San Antonio, Chile, who in 1981 produced her 55th and last child. Her husband Gerardo Secunda Albina (variously Alvina) (b. 1921) states that he was married in Argentina in 1943 and they had 5 sets of triplets (all boys) before coming to Chile. 'Only' 40 (24 boys and 16 girls) survive. Eleven were lost in an earthquake thus indicating the truth about the many other children born earlier than those born in Chile.

Great Britain

The British record is seemingly held by Elizabeth, wife of John Mott married in 1676 of Monks Kirby, Warwickshire, who produced 42 live-born children. She died in 1720, 44 years later. According to an inscription on a gravestone in Conway Church cemetery, Gwynedd, North Wales, Nicholas Hookes (d. 27 Mar 1637) was the 41st child of his mother Alice Hookes, but further details are lacking. It has not been possible to corroborate or refute this report. Mrs Elizabeth Greenhille (d. 1681) of Abbot's Langley, Hertfordshire is alleged to have produced 39 children (32 daughters, 7 sons) in a record 38 confinements. Her son Thomas was author of 'Art of Embalming' (1705).

Great Britain's champion mothers of today are believed to be Mrs Margaret McNaught (b. 1923), of Balsall Heath, Birmingham (12 boys and 10 girls, all single births) and Mrs Mabel Constable (b. 1920), of Long Itchington, Warwickshire who also has had 22 children including a set of triplets and two sets of twins.

Ireland's champion is Mrs Catherine Scott (b. 4 July 1914), who bore an authenticated total of 24 children.

Oldest mother *World*

Medical literature contains extreme but unauthenticated cases of septuagenarian mothers, such as Mrs Ellen Ellis, aged 72, of Four Crosses, Clwyd, who allegedly produced a still-born 13th child on 15 May 1776 in her 46th year of marriage. Many very late maternities will be cover-ups for illegitimate grandchildren. The oldest recorded mother for whom the evidence satisfied medical verification was Mrs Ruth Alice Kistler (née Taylor), formerly Mrs Shepard (1899–1982), of Portland, Oregon, USA. A birth certificate indicates that she gave birth to a daughter, Suzan, at Glendale, near Los Angeles, California, on 18 Oct 1956, when her age was 57 years 129 days. After her death a person purporting to be a relative alleged for an unknown motive that Mrs Kistler had 'changed the birth date'.

Great Britain

The oldest British mother reliably recorded is Mrs Winifred Wilson (née Stanley) of Eccles, Greater Manchester. She was born in Wolverhampton on 11 Nov 1881 or 1882 and had her tenth child, a daughter Shirley, on 14 Nov 1936, when aged 54 or 55 years and 3 days. She died aged 91 or 92 in January 1974. At Southampton, on 10 Feb 1916, Mrs Elizabeth Pearce gave birth to a son when aged 54 years 40 days. According to a report in the *Lancet* (1867) a woman aged 62 gave birth to triplets. She had previously had 10 children.

Ireland

The oldest Irish mother recorded was Mrs Mary Higgins of Cork, County Cork (b. 7 Jan 1876) who gave birth to a daughter, Patricia, on 17 Mar 1931 when aged 55 years 69 days.

MULTIPLE BIRTHS

Lightest twins

The lightest recorded birthweight for a pair of surviving twins has been 2 lb 3 oz *992 g* in the case of Mary 16 oz *453 g* and Margaret 19 oz *538 g* born to Mrs Florence Stimson, Queens Road, Old Fletton, Peterborough, England, delivered by Dr Macaulay on 16 Aug 1931. Margaret is now Mrs M. J. Hurst.

The Walton sextuplets—first Christmas at home together. From left to right: Hannah, Lucy, Jenny, Sarah, Kate and Ruth. *(Robert Ettinger)*

MULTIPLE BIRTHS

	World	United Kingdom
HIGHEST NUMBER REPORTED AT SINGLE BIRTH	10 (decaplets) (2 male, 8 female) Bacacay, Brazil, 22 Apr 1946 (also report from Spain, 1924 and China, 12 May 1936)	
HIGHEST NUMBER MEDICALLY RECORDED[1]	9 (nonuplets) (5 male, 4 female) to Mrs Geraldine Brodrick at Royal Hospital, Sydney, Australia on 13 June 1971. 2 males stillborn. Richard (12 oz *340 g*) survived 6 days 9 (all died) to patient at University of Pennsylvania, Philadelphia 29 May 1972 9 (all died) reported from Bagerhat, Bangladesh, *c.* 11 May 1977 to 30-year-old mother	6 (sextuplets) (all female) to Mrs Janet Walton (b. 1952) at Liverpool Maternity Hospital on 18 Nov 1983. All survive. 6 (4 male, 2 female) to Mrs Jane Underhill (b. 1957) at Rosie Maternity Hospital, Cambridge, on 2 May 1985. 3 boys and 2 girls survive. 6 (2 male, 4 female) to Mrs Sheila Ann Thorns (*née* Manning) at New Birmingham Maternity Hospital on 2 Oct 1968. Three survive. 6 (1 male, 5 female) to Mrs Rosemary Letts (*née* Egerton) at University College Hospital, Greater London, on 15 Dec 1969. One boy and 4 girls survive
HIGHEST NUMBER SURVIVING[2]	6 out of 6 (3 males, 3 females) to Mrs Susan Jane Rosenkowitz (*née* Scoones) (b. Colombo, Sri Lanka, 28 Oct 1947) at Mowbray, Cape Town, South Africa on 11 Jan 1974. In order of birth they were: David, Nicolette, Jason, Emma, Grant and Elizabeth. They totalled 24 lb 1 oz *10,915 kg* 6 out of 6 (4 males, 2 females) to Mrs Rosanna Giannini (b. 1952) at Careggi Hospital, Florence, Italy on 11 Jan 1980. They are Francesco, Fabrizio, Giorgio Roberto, Letizia and Linda 6 out of 6 (all female) see also above right: Mrs Janet Walton	6 out of 6 (see above)

	Heaviest (World and UK)	*Most Sets* (World and UK)
QUINTUPLETS World	25 lb 11,*35 kg* Mrs Lui Saulien, Chekiang, China, 7 June 1953 25 lb 11,*35 kg* Mrs Kamalammal, Pondicherry, India, 30 Dec 1956	No recorded case of more than a single set
QUADRUPLETS World	10,*35 kg 22 lb 13 oz* Mrs Ayako Takeda, Tsuchihashi Maternity Hospital, Kagoshima, Japan, 4 Oct 1978 (4 girls)	4 Mde Feodor Vassilyev, Shuya, Russia (d. *ante* 1770)
TRIPLETS[3] World UK	26 lb 6 oz 11,*96 kg* (unconfirmed) Iranian case (2 male, 1 female) 18 Mar 1968 24 lb 0 oz *10,886 kg* Mrs Mary McDermott, of Bearpark, Co Durham, 18 Nov 1914	15 Maddalena Granata (1839–*fl.* 1886)
TWINS World UK	27 lb 12 oz *12,590 kg* (surviving) Mrs J. P. Haskin, Fort Smith, Arkansas, USA, 20 Feb 1924 The 35 lb 8 oz, *16,1 kg* reported in the *Lancet* from Derbyshire, England, on 6 Dec 1884 for the Warren Case (2 males liveborn) is believed to have been a misprint for 25 lb 8 oz 11,*6 kg*	16 Mde Vassilyev (see above). *Note also* Mrs Barbara Zulu of Barbeton, South Africa bore 3 sets of girls and 3 mixed sets in 7 years (1967–73) 15 Mrs Mary Jonas of Chester (d. 4 Dec 1899)—all sets were boy and girl

[1] Mrs Edith Bonham (d. 1469) of Wishford Magna, Wiltshire reportedly had septuplets. [2] The South African press were unable to verify the birth of 5 babies to Mrs Charmaine Craig (*née* Peterson) in Cape Town on 16 Oct 1980 and a sixth on 8 Nov. The reported names were Frank, Salome, John, Andrew, William and belatedly Deborah. [3] Mrs Anna Steynvaait of Johannesburg, South Africa produced 2 sets within 10 months in 1960.

'Siamese' twins

Conjoined twins derived the name 'Siamese' from the celebrated Chang and Eng Bunker (known in Thailand as Chan and In) born at Meklong, on 11 May 1811 of Chinese parents. They were joined by a cartilaginous band at the chest and married in April 1843 the Misses Sarah and Adelaide Yates of Wilkes County, North Carolina, USA and fathered ten and twelve children respectively. They died within three hours of each other on 17 Jan 1874, aged 62. The only known British example to reach maturity were the pygopagus twins Daisy and Violet Hilton born in Brighton, East Sussex, on 5 Feb 1908, who were joined at the buttocks. They died in Charlotte, North Carolina, USA, on 5 Jan 1969, aged 60 from Hong Kong flu. The earliest successful separation of Siamese twins was performed on xiphopagus girls joined at the sternum at Mt Sinai Hospital, Cleveland, Ohio by Dr Jac S. Geller on 14 Dec 1952.

The rarest form of conjoined twins is Dicephales tetrabrachius dipus (two heads, four arms and two legs) of which only three examples are known today. They are the pair Masha and Dasha born in the USSR on 4 Jan 1950, an unnamed pair separated in a 10-hour operation in Washington, DC, USA on 23 June 1977, and Fonda Michelle and Shannon Elaine Beaver of Forest City, North Carolina, USA born on 9 Feb 1980. The only known British example were the 'Scottish brothers', who were born near Glasgow in 1490. They were brought to the Court of King James IV of Scotland in 1491, and lived under the king's patronage for the rest of his reign. They died in 1518 aged 28 years, one brother succumbing five days before the other, who 'moaned piteously as he crept about the castle gardens, carrying with him the dead body of the brother from whom only death could separate him and to whom death would again join him'.

The oldest surviving unseparated twins are the craniopagus pair Yvonne and Yvette Jones (b. 1949) of Los Angeles, California, USA whose heads are fused together at the crown. They have turned down an operation to separate them.

Most twins *Geographically*

In Chungchon, South Korea it was reported in September 1981 that there was unaccountably 38 pairs in only 275 families—the highest ever recorded ratio.

Fastest triplet birth

The fastest recorded natural birth of triplets has been 2 minutes in the case of Mrs James E. Duck of Memphis, Tennessee (Bradley, Christopher and Carmon) on 21 Mar 1977.

Quindecaplets

It was announced by Dr Gennaro Montanino of Rome that he had removed the foetuses of 10 girls and 5 boys from the womb of a 35-year-old housewife on 22 July 1971. A fertility drug was responsible for this unique and unsurpassed instance of quindecaplets.

Longest and shortest pregnancy

Claims up to 413 days have been widely reported but accurate data are bedevilled by the increasing use of oral contraceptive pills which is a cause of amenorrhoea. *The US Medical Investigator* of 27 Dec 1884 reported a case of 15 months 20 days and the *Histoire de l'Academie* of 1751 the most extreme case of 36 months. In the pre-pill era English law has accepted pregnancies with extremes of 174 days (*Clark* v. *Clark*, 1939) and 349 days (*Hadlum* v. *Hadlum*, 1949). Ernestine Hudgins was born weighing 17 oz *482 g* 18 weeks premature in San Diego, California, USA on 8 Feb 1983.

DESCENDANTS

In polygamous countries, the number of a person's descendants can become incalculable. The last Sharifian Emperor of Morocco, Moulay Ismail (1672–1727), known as 'The Bloodthirsty', was reputed to have fathered a total of 525 sons and 342 daughters by 1703 and a 700th son in 1721.

In April 1984 the death was reported of Adam Borntrager, aged 96, of Medford, Wisconsin, USA who had had 707 direct descendants of whom all but 32 were living. The total comprised 11 children, 115 grand, 529 great-grand and 20 great-great grandchildren. The family is of the Amish Mennonite sect who eschew cars, telephones, electric light, jewellery and higher education.

Mrs Sarah Crawshaw (d. 25 Dec 1844) left 397 descendants according to her gravestone in Stones Church, Ripponden, Halifax, West Yorkshire.

Multiple great-grandparents

The report in 1983 that Jane Kau Pung (1877–1982) had left 4 great-great-great-grandchildren has proved to be incorrect. She in fact proved to be one of many cases of great-great-great-grandparents. Of these cases the youngest person to learn that their great-granddaughter had become a grandmother was Mrs Ann V. Weirick (1888–1978) of Paxtonville, Pennsylvania, USA, who received news of her great-great-great-grandson Matthew Stork (b. 9 Sept 1976) when aged only 88. She died on 6 Jan 1978. Britain's youngest 3 greats grandmother is Mrs Violet Lewis (b. June 1885) of Southampton.

Most living ascendants

Jesse Jones Werkmeister (b. 27 Oct 1979) of Tilden Nebraska, USA, had a full set of grandparents and great-grandparents and four great-great-grandparents, making 18 direct ascendants. This was equalled on 21 Oct 1980 on the birth of Kendel Shenner, at Big Beaver, Saskatchewan, Canada.

BABIES

Heaviest *World*

The heaviest viable babies on record, of normal parentage, were boys of 22 lb 8 oz *10,2 kg* born to Sig Carmelina Fedele of Aversa, Italy in September 1955 and by caesarian section to Mrs Christina Samane at Sipetu Hospital, Transkei, South Africa on 24 May 1982. The latter boy named Sithandive weighed 77 lb *34,9 kg* at 16 months. Mrs Anna Bates *née* Swan (1846–88), the 7 ft 5½ in *227 cm* Canadian giantess (see also p. 10), gave birth to a boy weighing 23 lb 12 oz *10,77 kg* (length 30 in *76 cm*) at her home in Seville, Ohio, USA on 19 Jan 1879, but the baby died less than 24 hours later. Her first child, an 18 lb *8,16 kg* girl (length 24 in *61 cm*) was still-born when she was delivered in 1872. On 9 Jan 1891 Mrs Florentin Ortega of Buenos Aires, Argentina produced a still-born boy weighing 25 lb *11,3 kg*. In May 1939 a deformed baby weighing 29 lb 4 oz *13,26 kg* was born in a hospital at Effingham, Illinois, USA, but died two hours later.

Heaviest *United Kingdom*

The greatest recorded live birth weight in the United Kingdom is 21 lb *9,53 kg* for a child born on Christmas Day, 1852. It was reported in a letter to the *British Medical Journal* (1 Feb 1879) from a doctor in Torpoint, Cornwall. The only other reported birth weight in excess of 20 lb *9,07 kg* is 20 lb 2 oz *9,13 kg* for a boy born to a 33-year-old schoolmistress in Crewe, Cheshire, on 12 Nov 1884 with a 14½ in *36,8 cm* chest.

Most bouncing baby

The most bouncing baby on record was probably James Weir (1819–21) who, according to his headstone in Cambushnethan, Old Parish Cemetery, Wishaw, Strathclyde, Scotland was 8 st or 112 lb *50,8 kg* at 13 months, 3 ft 4 in *1,01 m* in height and 39 in *99 cm* in girth. Brazil's 'super-baby' Veridiano dos Santos (b. 1978) weighed 143 lb *64,8 kg* aged 5. Therese Parentean, who died in Rouyn, Quebec, Canada on 11 May 1936 aged 9 years, weighed 24 st 4 lb *154 kg*. (*cf.* 27 st *171 kg* for Robert Earl Hughes at the age of ten [see Table p. 11 and Chest measurements, right]).

Lightest

The lowest birth weight recorded for a surviving infant, of which there is definite evidence, is 10 oz *283 g* in the case of Mrs Marian Taggart *née* Chapman (b. 5 June 1938, d. 31 May 1983) who was born six weeks premature in South Shields, Tyne and Wear. She was born unattended (length 12¼ in *31 cm*) and was nursed by Dr D. A. Shearer, who fed her hourly for the first 30 hours with brandy, glucose and water through a fountain-pen filler. At three weeks she weighed 1 lb 13 oz *821 g* and by her first birthday 13 lb 14 oz *6,29 kg*. Her weight on her 21st birthday was 7 st 8 lb *48,08 kg*. The smallest viable baby reported from the United States has been Jacqueline Benson born at Palatine, Illinois, on 20 Feb 1936, weighing 12 oz *340 g*.

A weight of 8 oz *227 g* was reported on 20 Mar 1938 for a baby born prematurely to Mrs John Womack, after she had been knocked down by a lorry in East St Louis, Illinois, USA. The baby was taken alive to St Mary's Hospital, but died a few hours later. On 23 Feb 1952 it was reported that a 6 oz *170 g* baby only 6½ in *17 cm* long lived for 12 hours in a hospital in Indianapolis, Indiana, USA. A twin was still-born.

Coincident birthdates

The only verified example of a family producing five single children with coincident birthdays is that of Catherine (1952); Carol (1953); Charles (1956); Claudia (1961) and Cecilia (1966), born to Ralph and Carolyn Cummins of Clintwood, Virginia, USA, all on 20 February. The random odds against five single siblings sharing a birthdate would be one in 17,797,577,730—almost 4 times the world's population.

The three children of the Henriksen family of Andenes, Norway, Heidi (b. 1960); Olav (b. 1964) and Lief-Martin (b. 1968) all celebrate their birthday infrequently, because these all fall on Leap Day – February 29. Ralph Bertram Williams was born on 4 July 1982 in Wilmington, North Carolina, USA. His father, grandfather and, in 1876, his great-grandfather were also born on 4 July.

Most southerly birth

Emilio Marcos Palma (Argentina) born 7 Jan 1978 at the Sargento Cabral Base, Antarctica is the only infant who can claim to be the first born on any continent. The mother was flown from Argentina at governmental expense.

Test tube baby *Earliest*

Louise Brown (5 lb 12 oz *2,6 kg*) was delivered by Caesarian section from Lesley Brown, 31, in Oldham General Hospital, Lancashire, at 11.47 p.m. on 25 July 1978. She was externally conceived on 10 Nov 1977.

5. PHYSIOLOGY AND ANATOMY

Hydrogen (63 per cent) and oxygen (25.5 per cent) constitute the commonest of the 24 elements in the human body. In 1972 four more trace elements were added—fluorine, silicon, tin and vanadium. The 'essentiality' of nickel has not yet been finally pronounced upon.

BONES

Longest

Excluding a variable number of sesamoids, there are 206 bones in the human body. The thigh bone or *femur* is the longest. It constitutes usually 27½ per cent of a person's stature, and may be expected to be 19¾ in *50 cm* long in a 6 ft *183 cm*-tall man. The longest recorded bone was the femur of the German giant Constantine, who died in Mons, Belgium, on 30 Mar 1902, aged 30 (see p. 9). It measured 76 cm *29.9 in*. The femur of Robert Wadlow, the tallest man ever recorded, measured an estimated 29½ in *75 cm*.

Smallest

The *stapes* or stirrup bone, one of the three auditory ossicles in the middle ear, is the smallest human bone, measuring from 2,6 to 3,4 mm *0.10 to 0.17 in* in length and weighing from 2,0 to 4,3 mg *0.03 to 0.065 g*.

MUSCLES

Largest

Muscles normally account for 40 per cent of the body weight and the bulkiest of the 639 muscles in the human body is the *gluteus maximus* or buttock muscle, which extends the thigh.

Smallest

The smallest muscle is the *stapedius*, which controls the *stapes* (see above), an auditory ossicle in the middle ear, and which is less than 1/20th of an inch *0,127 cm* long.

Smallest waists

Queen Catherine de Medici (1519–89) decreed a waist measurement of 13 in *33 cm* for ladies of the French Court. This was at a time when females were more diminutive. The smallest recorded waist among women of normal stature in the 20th century is a reputed 13 in *33 cm* in the case of Mlle Polaire (1881–1939) and Mrs Ethel Granger (1905–82) of Peterborough who reduced from a natural 22 in *56 cm* over the period 1929–39.

Largest chest measurements

The largest chest measurements are among endomorphs (those with a tendency towards globularity). In the extreme case of Hughes (see Table p. 11) this was reportedly 124 in *315 cm*, but in the light of his known height and weight a figure of 104 in *264 cm* would be more supportable. George Macaree (formerly Britain's heaviest man) has a chest measurement of 75 in *190,5 cm* (waist 70 in *177,8 cm*), at a bodyweight of 31 st *196,8 kg* (height 5 ft 10 in *177,8 cm*) and Martin Ruane (see p. 11) has a chest measurement of 73 in *185,4 cm* (waist 68 in *172,7 cm*). Among muscular subjects (mesomorphs) of normal height *expanded* chest measurements above 56 in *142 cm* are extremely rare.

The diameter of the biceps of America's strongman Gary Aprahamian, at 25 in *63,5 cm* outstrip the waist measurements of some Miss Americas.

Vasili Alexeyev (b. 1942), the 6 ft 1¼ in *186 cm* Russian super-heavyweight weight-lifting champion, had a 60½ in *153,6 cm* chest at his top weight of 350 lb *158,7 kg*. Arnold Schwarzenneger (b. 1948) of Graz, Austria, the 6 ft 1 in *185 cm* former Mr Universe and 'the most perfectly developed man in the history of the world', had a chest measurement of 57 in *145 cm* (bicep 22 in *55,8 cm*) at his best bodyweight of 235 lb *107 kg*. The American power lifter Gary Aprahamian (b. 2 Feb 1962) the first man to achieve a cold (not pumped) bicep measurement over 25 in *63,5 cm* with 25⅜ in *64,4 cm* has a normal chest measurement of 61 in *155 cm*. He weighs 365 lb *165 kg*.

Longest necks

The maximum measured extension of the neck by the successive fitting of copper coils, as practised by the Padaung or Kareni people of Burma, is 15¾ in *40 cm*.

BRAIN AND BRAIN POWER

Largest

The brain of an average adult male (*i.e.* 20–55 years) weighs 1424 g *3 lb 2.2 oz*, decreasing gradually to 1395 g *3 lb 1.1 oz* with advancing age. The heaviest non-diseased brain on record was that of Ivan Sergeyvich Turgenev (1818–83), the Russian author. His brain weighed 2012 g *4 lb 6.9 oz*.

Human brains are getting heavier. Examination of post-mortem records shows that the average male brain weight has increased from 1372 g *3 lb 0.4 oz* in 1860 to 1424 g *3 lb 2.2 oz* today. Women's brains have also put on weight, from 1242 g *2 lb 11.8 oz* to 1265 g *2 lb 12.6 oz* and in recent years have been growing almost as fast as men's.

Brains and Beauty combine superlatively in the form of IQ record-breaker Marilyn Mach vos Savant. (See Highest IQ)

Smallest

The lightest 'normal' or non-atrophied brain on record was one weighing 1096 g *2 lb 6.7 oz* reported by Dr P. Davis and Prof E. Wright of King's College Hospital, London in 1977. It belonged to a 31 year old woman.

Highest IQ

Intelligence quotients or IQ's comprise the subject's mental age divided by his chronological or actual age multiplied by 100 such that an 8 year old more gifted than an average 16 year old would have an IQ of $\frac{16}{8} \times 100 = 200$. The highest childhood score has been achieved by Marilyn Mach vos Savant of St. Louis, Missouri, USA who as a 10-year-old achieved a ceiling score for 23-year-olds thus giving her an IQ of 230.

In adult High IQ clubs admission requirements are not on IQ points but are gauged in percentiles. An IQ exhibited by 1 person in 10,000 for instance coincides with 158 on the Stanford-Binet scale but 187 on the Cattell scale. The most elite ultra High IQ Society is the Mega Society with 26 members with percentiles of 99.9999 or 1 in a million. The topmost scorer in the Mega admission test, devised by its founder Ronald K. Hoeflin, has been 46 out of 48 by Mach vos Savant superceding the 43 of Jeff Ward.

The three members who have scored 197 are Christopher Philip Harding (born Keynsham, England, 1944) of Rockhampton, Queensland, Australia, Dr Ferris Eugene Alger (b. Des Moines, Iowa, 1913) of New Hope, Pa, USA and Dr Johannes Dougles Veldhuis (b. Hamilton, Ontario, Canada, 1949) of Charlottesville, Virginia, USA.

The highest IQ published for a national population is 111 for the Japanese. For those born in 1960–61 a figure of 115 has been published. At least 10 per cent of their whole population has an IQ > 130.

Human computer

The fastest extraction of a 13th root from a 100 digit number is in 1 min 28.8 sec by Willem Klein (b. 1912, Netherlands) on 7 Apr 1981 at the National Laboratory for High Energy Physics (KEK), Tsukuba, Japan. Mrs Shakuntala Devi of India demonstrated the multiplication of two 13-digit numbers 7,686,369,774,870 × 2,465,099,745,779 picked at random by the Computer Department of Imperial College, London on 18 June 1980, in 28 sec. Her correct answer was 18,947,668,177,995,426,462,773,730. An eminent mathematical writer has questioned the conditions under which this was apparently achieved and predicts that it would be impossible for her to replicate such a feat under highly rigorous surveillance.

Some experts on calculating prodigies refuse to give credence to the above—largely on the grounds that it is so vastly superior to the calculating feats of any other invigilated prodigy.

Human memory

Bhandanta Vicitsara recited 16,000 pages of Bhuddist canonical texts in Rangoon, Burma in May 1974. Rare instances of eidetic memory— the ability to re-project and hence 'visually' recall material—are known to science.

Creighton Carvello memorised a random sequence of 6 packs (312) of cards on a single sighting with only 4 errors including an all correct straight run of 139 cards at the New Marske Institute Club, Cleveland, England on 21 Mar 1985.

The greatest number of places of π

All India Radio broadcast in its *Weekly Roundup* on 5 July 1981 part of a recording made earlier that day of Rajan Srinivasen Mahadevan, 23, in the process of reciting 'pi' from memory (in English) to 31,811 places in 3 hr 49 min (incl. 26 min of breaks) at the Lion Seva Mandir, Mangalore. His rate was 156.7 digits per minute. Mr Mahadevan has explained to the Editor that he learns each digit separately and acquires a 'feeling', when he is able to recall the number at will. The British record is 20,013 by Creighton Carvello on 27 June 1980 in 9 hr 10 min at the Saltscar Comprehensive School, Redcar, Cleveland, England. Note: It is only the *approximation* of π at $^{22}/_7$ which recurs after its sixth decimal place and can, of course, be recited *ad nauseam*. The true value is a string of random numbers fiendishly difficult to memorise. The average ability for memorizing random numbers is barely more than 7.

HANDS, FEET AND HAIR

Touch sensitivity

The extreme sensitivity of the fingers is such that a vibration with a movement of 0.02 of a micron can be detected.

Most fingers and toes

At an inquest held on a baby at Shoreditch, East London on 16 Sept 1921 it was reported that the boy had 14 fingers and 15 toes.

Least toes

The 'lobster claw syndrome' exhibited by the two-toed Wadomo tribe of the Zambesi valley, Zimbabwe and the Kalanga tribe of the eastern Kalahari desert, Botswana is hereditary *via* a single mutated gene.

Longest finger nails

The longest finger nails ever reported are those of Shridhar Chillal, (b. 1937) of Poona, India. The aggregate measurement, on 8 Apr 1985, was 143 in *363 cm* for the 5 nails on his left hand (thumb 34½ in *86,4 cm*). He last cut his nails in 1952.

Longest hair

Swami Pandarasannadhi, the head of the Tirudaduturai monastery, Tanjore district, Madras, India was reported in 1949 to have hair 26 ft *7,92 m* in length. From photographs it appears that he was afflicted with the disease Plica caudiformis, in which the hair becomes matted and crusted as a result of neglect. The length of hair of Miss Skuldfrid Sjorgren (b. Stockholm) was reported from Toronto, Canada in 1927 to have reached twice her height at 10 ft 6 in *3,20 m*.

Strongest hair

In a test on BBC TV *Record Breakers* on 9 Sept 1984 a hair from the head of Miss Pham Thy Lan broke at a strain of 178 g *6¼ oz*.

Longest beard

The longest beard preserved was that of Hans N. Langseth (b. 1846 near Eidsroll, Norway) which measured 17½ ft *5,33 m* at the time of his burial at Kensett, Iowa in 1927 after 15 years residence in the United States. The beard was presented to the Smithsonian Institution, Washington, DC in 1967. Richard Latter (b. Pembury, Kent, 1831) of Tunbridge Wells, Kent, who died in 1914 aged 83, reputedly had a beard 16 ft *4,87 m* long but contemporary independent corroboration is lacking and photographic evidence indicates this figure was exaggerated. The beard of the bearded lady Janice Deveree (b. Bracken Co., Kentucky, USA, 1842) was measured at 14 in *36 cm* in 1884. The beard of Mlle Helene Antonia of Liège, Belgium, a 17th century exhibitionist was said to have reached her hips.

West Germany's Georgia Sebrantke: contender for today's title for having the world's longest tresses at 289 cm *9 ft 5¼ in.*

Longest moustache

The longest moustache on record was that of Masuriya Din (b. 1908), a Brahmin of the Partabgarh district in Uttar Pradesh, India. It grew to an extended span of 8 ft 6 in *2,59 m* between 1949 and 1962. Karna Ram Bheel (b. 1928) was granted permission by a New Delhi prison governor in February 1979 to keep his 7 ft 10 in *238 cm* moustache grown since 1949 during his life sentence. Birger Pellas (b. 21 Sept 1934) of Malmö, Sweden has a 2,216 m *7 ft 3¼ in* moustache grown since 1973. The longest moustache in Great Britain has been that of Mr John Roy (b. 14 Jan 1910), of Weeley, near Clacton, Essex. It attained a peak span of 68½ in *174 cm* between 1939 and when measured on the BBC TV 'Nationwide' programme on 2 Apr 1976. The current UK champion is Mike Solomons of Long Ditton, Surrey with 31 in *78,7 cm* as of 21 Mar 1985.

DENTITION

Earliest

The first deciduous or milk teeth normally appear in infants at 5–8 months, these being the mandibular and maxillary first incisors. There are many records of children born with teeth, the most distinguished example being Prince Louis Dieudonné, later Louis XIV of France, who was born with two teeth on 5 Sept 1638. Molars usually appear at 24 months, but in Pindborg's case published in Denmark in 1970, a 6-week premature baby was documented with 8 natal teeth of which 4 were in the molar region.

Most

Cases of the growth in late life of a third set of teeth have been recorded several times. A reference to a case in France of a fourth dentition, known as Lison's case, was published in 1896. A triple row of teeth was noted in 1680 by Albertus Hellwigius.

Most dedicated dentist

Brother Giovanni Battista Orsenigo of the Ospedale Fatebenefratelli, Rome, Italy, a religious dentist, conserved all the teeth he extracted in three enormous cases during the time he exercised his profession from 1868 to 1904. In 1903 the number was counted and found to be 2,000,744 teeth.

Most valuable tooth

In 1816 a tooth belonging to Sir Isaac Newton (1643–1727) was sold in London for £730. It was purchased by a nobleman who had it set in a ring which he wore constantly.

OPTICS

Smallest visible object

The resolving power of the human eye is 0.0003 of a radian or an arc of one minute ($\frac{1}{60}$th of a degree), which corresponds to 100 microns at 10 in. A micron is a thousandth of a millimetre, hence 100 microns is 0.003937, or less than four thousandths, of an inch. The human eye can, however, detect a bright light source shining through an aperture only 3 to 4 microns across. In October 1972 the University of Stuttgart, W. Germany reported that their student Veronica Seider (b. 1951) possessed a visual acuity 20 times better than average. She could identify people at a distance of more than a mile *1,6 km.* The Russians are reputedly working on a new type of lens implant which will give the wearer super-human sight.

Colour sensitivity

The unaided human eye, under the best possible viewing conditions, comparing large areas of colour, in good illumination, using both eyes, can distinguish 10,000,000 different colour surfaces. The most accurate photo-electric spectrophotometers possess a precision probably only 40 per cent as good as this. About 7.5 per cent of men and 0.1 per cent of women are colour blind. The most extreme form, monochromatic vision, is very rare. The highest recorded rate of redgreen colour blindness is in Czechoslovakia and the lowest rate among Fijians and Brazilian Indians.

VOICE

Highest and lowest

The highest and lowest recorded notes attained by the human voice before this century were a staccato E in *alt altissimo* (e^{iv}) by Ellen Beach Yaw (US) (1869–1947) in Carnegie Hall, New York, on 19 Jan 1896, and an A$_1$ (55 Hz (cycles per sec)) by Kasper Foster (1617–73). Madeleine Marie Robin (1918–60) the French operatic coloratura could produce and sustain the B above high C in the Lucia mad scene in *Lucia di Lammermoor*. Since 1950 singers have achieved high and low notes far beyond the hitherto accepted extremes. However, notes at the bass and treble extremities of the register tend to lack harmonics and are of little musical value. Frl Marita Gunther, trained by Alfred Wolfsohn, has covered the range of the piano from the lowest note, A$_{II}$ to c^v. Of this range of 7¼ octaves,

Madeleine Marie Robin whose crystalcracking 'B above high C' was long the toast of France's operaphiles.

six octaves are considered to be of musical value. Mr Roy Hart, also trained by Wolfsohn, has reached notes below the range of the piano. Barry Girard of Canton, Ohio in May 1975 reached the e (4340 Hz) above the piano's top note. The highest note put into song is G^{iv} first occurring in *Popoli di Tessaglia* by Mozart. The lowest vocal note in the classical repetoire is in Mozart's *Il Seraglio* by Osmin who descends to low D (73.4 Hz). Dan Britton reached the 4th E below middle C at 20.6 Hz at Anoka County Fair, Maryland, USA on 31 July 1984. Stefan Zucker sang A in *alt altissimo* for 3.8 sec in the tenor role of Salvini in the première of Bellini's *Adelson e Salvini* in New York, USA on 12 Sept 1972.

Greatest range

The normal intelligible outdoor range of the male human voice in still air is 200 yd *180 m*. The *silbo*, the whistled language of the Spanishspeaking Canary Island of La Gomera, is intelligible across the valleys, under ideal conditions, at five miles *8 km*. There is a recorded case, under freak acoustic conditions, of the human voice being detectable at a distance of 10½ miles *17 km* across still water at night. It was said that Mills Darden (see table page 8) could be heard 6 miles *9 km* away when he bellowed at the top of his voice.

Because of their more optimal frequency, female screams register higher readings on decibel meters than male bellows. The annual World Shouting Championship record is 112.4 dBA by Anthony Fieldhouse on 9 Sept 1984 at Scarborough. The highest scientifically measured emission has been one of 123.2 dBA by the screaming of Neil Stephenson of Newcastle-upon-Tyne, Tyne and Wear on 18 May 1985.

Lowest detectable sound

The intensity of noise or sound is measured in terms of pressure. The pressure of the quietest sound that can be detected by a person of normal hearing at the most sensitive frequency of *c.* 2750 Hz is 2×10^{-5} pascal. One tenth of the logarithm to this standard provides a unit termed a decibel (dBA). Prolonged noise above 150 decibels will cause immediate permanent deafness while above 192 dBA a fatal over-pressure shock wave can be formed. A noise of 30 decibels is negligible.

Highest detectable pitch

The upper limit of hearing by the human ear has long been regarded as 20,000 Hz (cycles per sec), although children with asthma can often detect a sound of 30,000 Hz. Bats emit pulses at up to 90,000 Hz. It was announced in February 1964 that experiments in the USSR had conclusively proved that oscillations as high as 200,000 Hz can be heard if the oscillator is pressed against the skull.

Fastest talker

Few people are able to speak *articulately* at a sustained speed above 300 words per min. The fastest broadcaster has been regarded as Gerry Wilmot (b. Victoria, BC, Canada, 6 Oct 1914) the ice hockey commentator in the post-World War II period. Raymond Glendenning (1907–74), the BBC horseracing commentator, once spoke 176 words in 30 sec while commentating on a greyhound race. In public life the highest speed recorded is a 327 words per min burst in a speech made in December 1961 by John Fitzgerald Kennedy (1917–63), then President of the United States. Tapes of attempts to recite Hamlet's 262-word Soliloquy in under 24 sec (655 w.p.m.) have proved unintelligible. Results of tests by a radio station on John Moschitta (USA) in March 1983 indicate intelligibility at a rate of 534 in 58 sec or 552 words per min.

BLOOD

Blood groups

The preponderance of one blood group varies greatly from one locality to another. On a world basis Group O is the most common (46 per cent), but in some areas, for example Norway, Group A predominates.

The full description of the commonest sub-group in Britain is O MsNs, P+, Rr, Lu(a−), K−, Le(a−b+), Fy(a+b+), Jk(a+b+), which occurs in one in every 270 people.

The rarest blood group on the ABO system, one of 14 systems, is AB, which occurs in less than 3 per cent of persons in the British Isles. The rarest type in the world is a type of Bombay blood (sub-type A-h) found so far only in a Czechoslovak nurse in 1961 and in a brother (Rh positive) and sister (Rh negative) named Jalbert in Massachusetts, USA reported in February 1968. The American male has started a blood bank for himself.

Richest natural resources

Joe Thomas of Detroit, Michigan, USA was reported in August 1970 to have the highest known count of Anti-Lewis B, the rare blood antibody. A US biological supply firm pays him $1500 per quart *1,13 l*. The Internal Revenue regard this income as a taxable liquid asset.

Champion plasmapheresis blood donor

Since 1966 Allen Doster, a self-employed beautician, has (to 1 Jan 1983) donated 1508 US pints at Roswell Park Memorial Institute, New York, USA as a plasmapheresis donor. The present-day normal limit on donations is 5 pints per annum. A 50-year-old haemophiliac Warren C. Jyrich required 2400 donor units *1080 l* of blood when undergoing open heart surgery at the Michael Reese Hospital, Chicago, USA in December 1970.

Largest vein

The largest vein in the human body is the *inferior vena cava*, which returns most of the blood from the body below the level of the heart.

Most alcoholic subject

California University Medical School, Los Angeles reported in December 1982 the case of a confused 24-year-old female, who was shown to have a blood alcohol level of 1510 mg per 100 ml—nearly 19 times the UK driving limit and triple the normally lethal limit. After two days she discharged herself.

The United Kingdom's legal limit for motorists is 80 mg of alcohol per 100 ml of blood. The hitherto recorded highest figure in medical literature of 656 mg per 100 ml was submerged when the late Samuel Riley (b. 1922) of Sefton Park, Merseyside, was found by a disbelieving pathologist to have a level of 1220 mg on 28 Mar 1979. He had expired in his flat and had been an inspector at the plant of a well-known motor manufacturer.

BODY TEMPERATURE

Highest body temperature

Willie Jones, a 52 year old black, was admitted to Grady Memorial Hospital, Atlanta, Georgia on 10 July 1980 with heat stroke on a day when the temperature reached 90° F *32,2° C* with 44% humidity. His temperature was found to be 46,5° C *115.7° F*. After 24 days he was discharged 'at prior baseline status'.

Lowest body temperature

There are two recorded cases of patients surviving body temperatures as low as 60.8° F *16,0° C*.

Publican Paul Braddon back behind the bar with his wife after he had recovered from being Britain's first malaria victim for 35 years. (See Rarest Disease)

Dorothy Mae Stevens, (1929–74) was found in an alley in Chicago, Illinois on 1 Feb 1951 and Vickie Mary Davis aged 2 years 1 month in an unheated house in Marshalltown, Iowa on 21 Jan 1956, both with this temperature. People may die of hypothermia with body temperatures of 95.0° F *35,0° C.*

ILLNESS AND DISEASE

Commonest disease
The commonest non-contagious disease in the world is periodontal disease, such as gingivitus, which afflicts some 80 per cent of the US population. In Great Britain 13 per cent of people have lost all their teeth before they are 21 years old. During their lifetime few completely escape its effects. Infestation with pinworm (*Enterobius vermicularis*) approaches 100 per cent in some areas of the world.

The commonest contagious disease in the world is coryza (acute nasopharyngitis) or the common cold. Only 872,000 working days were reportedly lost as a result of this illness in Great Britain between mid-1981 and mid-1982, since absences of less than three days were not reported. The greatest reported loss of working time in Britain is from neurotic disorders, which accounted for 27,384,700, or 7.59 per cent, of the total of 361,015,100 days lost from mid 1982 to mid 1983.

The most resistant recorded case to being infected at the Medical Research Council Common Cold Unit, Salisbury, Wiltshire is J. Brophy, who has had one mild reaction in 24 visits.

Rarest disease
Medical literature periodically records hitherto undescribed diseases. A disease as yet undescribed but predicted by a Norwegian doctor is podocytoma of the kidney—a tumour of the epithelial cells lining the glomerulus of the kidney. The last case of endemic smallpox was recorded in Ali Maow Maalin in Merka, Somalia on 26 Oct 1977. In Britain Paul Braddon of Rusper, West Sussex was reported on 2 Aug 1983 to be the first case to contract malaria for more than 35 years.

Kuru, or laughing sickness, afflicts only the Fore tribe of eastern New Guinea and is 100 per cent fatal. This was formally attributed to the cannibalistic practice of eating human brains. The rarest fatal diseases in England and Wales have been those from which the last deaths (all males) were all recorded more than 40 years ago—yellow fever (1930), cholera nostras (1928) and bubonic plague (1926).

Most infectious disease
The most infectious of all diseases is the pneumonic form of plague, which also has a mortality rate of about 99.99 per cent. This is matched by rabies and AIDS (Acquired immune-deficiency syndrome), which was first recorded from African swine in 1909. Leprosy, transmissible by coughing, sneezing or spitting, is the most bacilliferous of communicable diseases. The bacillus is *Mycobacterium leprae* discovered by G. H. A. Hansen (Norway) (1841–1912) in 1871.

Highest mortality
Rabies in humans has been regarded as uniformly fatal when associated with the hydrophobia symptom. A 25-year-old woman Candida de Sousa Barbosa of Rio de Janeiro, Brazil, after surgery by Dr Max Karpin, was believed to be the first ever survivor of the disease in November 1968, though some sources give priority to Matthew Winkler, 6, who, on 10 Oct 1970, was bitten by a rabid bat.

Leading cause of death
The leading cause of death in industrialised countries is arteriosclerosis (thickening of the arterial wall) which underlies much coronary and cerebrovascular disease.

Most notorious carrier
The most publicised of all typhoid carriers has been Mary Mallon, known as Typhoid Mary, of New York City, NY, USA. She was the source of nine outbreaks, notably that of 1903. She was placed under permanent detention from 1915 until her death in 1938. A still anonymous dairy farmer from Camden, N.Y. was the source of 409 cases (40 fatal) in August 1909.

Parkinson's disease
The most protracted case of Parkinson's disease (named after Dr James Parkinson's essay of 1817) for which the earliest treatments were not published until 1946, is 56 years in the case of Frederick G. Humphries (d. 23 Feb 1985) of Croydon, Greater London whose symptoms became detectable in 1923.

MEDICAL EXTREMES

Heart stoppage
The longest recorded heart stoppage is a minimum of 3 hr 40 min in the case of Miss Jean Jawbone, 20, who was revived by a team of 26, using peritoneal dialysis, in the Health Sciences Centre, Winnipeg, Manitoba, Canada on 8 Jan 1977. A 'Mammalian diving reflex' can be triggered in humans falling into water cooler than 70° F *21° C.* In February 1974 Vegard Slettmoen, 5, fell through the ice on the river Nitselv, Norway. He was found 40 min later 2,5 m *8 ft* down but was revived in Akershus Central Hospital without brain-damage.

The longest recorded interval in a *post mortem* birth was one of 84 days in the case of a baby girl delivered on 5 July 1983 from a clinically dead woman in Roanoke, Virginia, who had been kept on life support since suffering a seizure in April.

Pulse rates
A normal adult pulse rate is 70–72 beats per min at rest for males and 78–82 for females. Rates increase to 200 or more during violent exercise and drop to as low as 12 in the extreme cases of Dorothy Mae Stevens (see Lowest body temperature, p. 20), and Jean Hilliard (b. 1962) of Fosston, Minnesota, USA on 20 Dec 1980.

Longest coma
The longest recorded coma was that undergone by Elaine Esposito (b. 3 Dec 1934) of Tarpon Springs, Florida, USA. She never stirred since an appendicectomy on 6 Aug 1941, when she was 6, in Chicago, Illinois, USA, and she died on 25 Nov 1978 aged 43 years 357 days, having been in a coma for 37 years 111 days.

Longest dream
Dreaming sleep is characterised by rapid eye movements known as REM discovered in 1953 by William Dement of the University of Chicago. The longest recorded period of REM is one of 2 hr 23 min on 15 Feb 1967 at the department of Psychology, University of Illinois, Chicago on Bill Carskadon, who had had his previous sleep interrupted. In July 1984 The Sleep Research Centre, Haifa, Israel recorded nil REM in a 33-year-old male who had a shrapnel brain injury.

Largest stone
The largest stone or vesical calculus reported in medical literature was one of 13 lb 14 oz *6,29 kg* removed from an 80-year-old woman by Dr Humphrey Arthure at Charing Cross Hospital, London, on 29 Dec 1952.

Longest in iron lung
The longest recorded survival by an 'iron lung' patient is that of Mrs Laurel Nisbet (b. 17 Nov 1912) of La Crescenta, California, USA. She has been in an 'iron lung' continuously since 25 June 1948. The longest survival in an 'iron lung' in Britain has been 30 years by Denis Atkin in Lodge Moor Hospital, Sheffield, South York-

shire. Mr John Prestwich (b. 24 Nov 1938) of Kings Langley, Hertfordshire has been dependent on a negative pressure respirator since 24 Nov 1955. Paul Bates of Horsham, West Sussex, was harnessed to a mechanical positive pressure respirator on 13 Aug 1954. From continuous respiration, he has received an estimated 230,016,128 respirations into his lungs *via* his trachea up to 1 May 1985.

Fastest nerve impulses
The results of experiments published in 1966 have shown that the fastest messages transmitted by the human nervous system travel as fast as 180 mph *288 km/h*. With advancing age impulses are carried 15 per cent more slowly.

Fastest reactions
The fastest recorded reaction times recorded for sprinters at the 1980 Olympic Games were 120/1000ths of a second for Romy Müller (GDR) in the women's 200 metre semi-final and 124/1000ths for Wilbert Greaves (GB) in the 110 m hurdles heats. These compare with 11/1000ths for the cockroach *Periplaneta americana*.

Hiccoughing
The longest recorded attack of hiccoughs or singultus is that which afflicted Charles Osborne (b. 1894) of Anthon, Iowa, USA, for 60 years from 1922. He contracted it when slaughtering a hog and has hiccoughed about 430 million times in the interim period. He was unable to find a cure, but led a reasonably normal life in which he had two wives and fathered eight children. He did admit, however, that he could not keep in his false teeth.

Sneezing
The most chronic sneezing fit ever recorded is that of Donna Griffiths (b. 1969) of Pershore, Hereford & Worcester. She started sneezing on 13 Jan 1981 and surpassed the previous duration record of 194 days on 27 July 1981. She sneezed an estimated million times in the first 365 days. She achieved her first sneeze-free day on 16 Sept 1983—the 978th day. The highest speed at which expelled particles have ever been measured to travel is 103.6 mph *167 km/h*.

Snoring *Loudest*
The highest measured sound level recorded by any chronic snorer is a peak of 87.5 decibels at Hever Castle, Kent in the early hours of 28 June 1984. Melvyn Switzer of Hampshire was 1 ft *30 cm* from the meter. His wife Julie is deaf in one ear.

Yawning
In Lee's case, reported in 1888, a 15-year-old

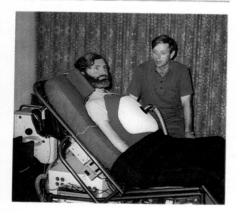

John Prestwich, whose life has been prolonged by 30 years by dint of a negative pressure respirator. (See above, Longest in Iron Lung)

female patient yawned continuously for a period of 5 weeks.

Sleeplessness
Researches indicate that on the Circadian cycle for the majority peak efficiency is attained between 8 and 9 p.m. and the low point comes at 4 a.m. The longest recorded period for which a person has voluntarily gone without sleep is 449 hr (18 days 17 hr) by Mrs Maureen Weston of Peterborough, Cambridgeshire in a rocking chair marathon on 14 Apr–2 May 1977. Though she tended to hallucinate toward the end of this surely ill-advised test, she surprisingly suffered no lasting ill-effects. Victims of the very rare condition chronic colestites (total insomnia) have been known to go without definable sleep for many years. An example has been Jesus de Frutos (b. 1925) of Segovia, Spain who claims only to have dozed since 1954.

Motionlessness
The longest that anyone has continuously remained motionless is 13 hr by Willie Nugent, 37, at *The Guinness World of Records* permanent exhibition at the Trocadero, Piccadilly, London, on 24 June 1985. The longest recorded case of involuntarily being made to stand to attention was when Staff Sgt Samuel B. Moody USAF, was so punished in Narumi prison camp, Nagoya, Japan for 53 hr in the spring of 1945. He survived to write *Reprieve from Hell*.

Most voracious fire breathers and extinguishers
Reg Morris blew a flame from his mouth to a distance of 27 ft *8,23 m* igniting a bonfire, at The Castle Working Men's Club, Brownhills, West Midlands on 5 Nov 1983. On 11 May 1985, Gerry Mawdsley of Westhoughton, Lancashire, extinguished 13,115 torches of flame successively in his mouth in 2 hr at Blackrod, Lancashire. On 13 Feb 1982 at the 'Six Bells' Stoke Poges, Bucks, Jean Leggett set a female record of 6607.

Human salamanders
The highest dry-air temperature endured by naked men in the US Air Force experiments in 1960 was 400° F *204,4° C* and for heavily clothed men 500° F *260° C*. Steaks require only 325° F *162,8° C*. Temperatures of 140° C *284° F* have been found quite bearable in *Sauna* baths.

The highest temperature recorded by pyrometer for the coals in any fire walk was 1494° F *812° C* for a walk by 'Komar' (Vernon E. Craig) of Wooster, Ohio at the International Festival of Yoga and Esoteric Sciences, Maidenhead, England on 14 Aug 1976.

Thirty five people from the Sawau tribe on the island of Beqa in the Fijian group participated in a firewalk with the temperature over 1000° F *537° C* on 18 May 1982. There is an annual fire walk during the feast of St Constantine each May in Aghia Eleni, northern Greece.

Swallowing
The worst reported case of compulsive swallowing was an insane female Mrs H. aged 42, who complained of a 'slight abdominal pain'. She proved to have 2533 objects, including 947 bent pins, in her stomach. These were removed by Drs Chalk and Foucar in June 1927 at the Ontario Hospital, Canada. The heaviest object extracted from a human stomach has been a 5 lb 3 oz *2,53 kg* ball of hair in Swain's case from a 20-year-old female compulsive swallower in the South Devon and East Cornwall Hospital, England on 30 Mar 1895.

Sword
Edward Benjamin 'Count Desmond' (b. 1941 of Binghamton, NY, USA) swallowed thirteen 23 in *58,4 cm* long blades to below his xiphister-

num and injured himself in the process. *This category has now been retired and no further claims will be entertained.*

Fasting
Most humans experience considerable discomfort after an abstinence from food for even 12 hr but this often passes off after 24–48 hr. Records claimed unless there is unremitting medical surveillance are inadmissible. The longest period for which anyone has gone without solid food is 382 days by Angus Barbieri (b. 1940) of Tayport, Fife, who lived on tea, coffee, water, soda water and vitamins in Maryfield Hospital, Dundee, Angus, from June 1965 to July 1966. His weight declined from 33 st 10 lb *214,1 kg* to 12 st 10 lb *80,74 kg*.

Hunger strike
The longest recorded hunger strike was one of 94 days by John and Peter Crowley, Thomas Donovan, Michael Burke, Michael O'Reilly, Christopher Upton, John Power, Joseph Kenny and Seán Hennessy in Cork Prison, Ireland, from 11 Aug to 12 Nov 1920. These nine survivors from 12 prisoners owed their lives to expert medical attention and an appeal by the nationalist leader Arthur Griffith (1872–1922). The longest recorded hunger strike in a British gaol is 385 days from 28 June 1972 to 18 July 1973 by Denis Galer Goodwin in Wakefield Prison, West Yorkshire protesting his innocence of a rape charge. He was fed by tube orally.

The longest recorded case of survival without food *and* water is 18 days by Andreas Mihavecz, 18, of Bregenz, Austria who was put into a holding cell on 1 Apr 1979 in a local government building in Höchst, Austria but was totally forgotten by the police. On 18 Apr 1979 he was discovered close to death having had neither food nor water. He had been a passenger in a crashed car.

Underwater
The world record for voluntarily staying underwater is 13 min 42.5 sec by Robert Foster, aged 32, an electronics technician of Richmond, California, who stayed under 10 ft *3,05 m* of water in the swimming pool of the Bermuda Palms Motel at San Rafael, California, USA, on 15 Mar 1959. He hyperventilated with oxygen for 30 min before his descent. (See also Heart Stoppage, above.)

g forces
The acceleration g, due to gravity, is 32 ft 1.05 in per sec per sec *978,02 cm/sec²* at sea-level at the Equator. A *sustained* acceleration of 25 g was withstood in a dry capsule during astronautic research by Dr Carter Collins of California, USA. The highest g value endured on a water-braked rocket sled is 82.6 g for 0.04 of a sec by Eli L. Beeding Jr. at Holloman Air Force Base, New Mexico, USA, on 16 May 1958. He was put in hospital for 3 days. A man who fell off a 185 ft *56,39 m* cliff (before 1963) has survived a *momentary* g of 209 in decelerating from 68 mph *109 km/h* to stationary in 0.015 of a sec.

The racing driver David Purley GM survived a deceleration from 108 mph *173 km/h* to zero in 26 in *66 cm* in a crash at Silverstone on 13 July 1977 which involved a force of 179.8 g. He suffered 29 fractures, 3 dislocations and 6 heart stoppages.

A land diver of Pentecost Island, New Hebrides dived from a platform 81 ft 3 in *24,76 m* high with liana vines attached to his ankles on 15 May 1982. The body speed was 50 ft *15,24 m* per sec 34 mph *54 km/h*. The jerk transmitted a momentary g force in excess of 110.

Electric shock *Highest voltage*
People in aircraft in thunder clouds may be at

30 million volts relative to the earth without harm. In some 'bare hand' laboratory work in France experimenters in insulated cabins have experienced 5 million volts. People walking on nylon carpets on dry days may go up to 10,000 volts relative to earth and yet experience only mild shocks. Contact with exposed high tension power lines with system voltages of 765,000 have occurred in the US and at up to 400,000 in the UK. A person in contact with earth via ladders, dinghy masts, crane jibs etc, normally suffer instant death due to a heavy current arc or flashover flowing through the body. That shocks received from high tension cables by Brian Latasa (230,000 volts in Griffith Park, Los Angeles on 9 Nov 1967) and Harry F. McGrew (340,000 volts in Huntington Canyon, Utah on 7 Oct 1977) were non-lethal underlines their idiosyncratic nature when compared with the mere 2,500 volts used since 1890 in judicial electrocution.

Isolation
The longest recorded period for which any volunteer has been able to withstand total deprivation of all sensory stimulation (sight, hearing and touch) is 92 hr, recorded in 1962 at Lancaster Moor Hospital, Lancashire.

The farthest that any human has been isolated from all other humans has been the lone pilots of lunar command modules when antipodal to their Apollo missions, two lunar explorers 2200 miles *3540 km* distant.

Pill-taking
The highest recorded total of pills swallowed by a patient is 414,134 between 9 June 1967 and 1 Jan 1983 by C. H. A. Kilner (b. 1926) of Bindura, Zimbabwe, following a successful operation to remove a cancerous pancreas on 26 May 1966.

Most injections
The diabetic Mrs Evelyn Ruth Winder (b. 1921) of Invercargill, New Zealand gave an estimated 57,108 insulin injections to herself over 54 years to May 1985.

Most tattoos
The seeming ultimate in being tattooed is represented by Wilfred Hardy of Huthwaite, Nottinghamshire, England. Not content with a perilous approach to within 4 per cent of totality, he has been tattooed on the inside of his cheek, his tongue, gums and eyebrows. Walter Stiglitz of North Plainfield, New Jersey, USA in March 1984 claimed 5457 separate tattoos by six artists. Britain's most decorated woman is Rusty Field (b. 1944) of Aldershot, Hampshire, who after 12 years under the needle of Mr Skuse, has come within 15 per cent of totality. He stated he always had designs on her. Both the 1980 and 1981 World's Most Beautiful Tattooed Lady Contest in the US were won by Susan Jones (GB) (b. 1959).

OPERATIONS

Longest
The most protracted reported operation, for surgical as opposed to medical control purposes, has been one of 96 hr performed on Mrs Gertrude Levandowski (see also p. 12) during the period 4–8 Feb 1951. The patient suffered from a weak heart and the surgeons had to exercise the utmost caution during the operation. The 'slowest' operation on record is one on the feet of Mrs Doreen Scott of Derby, England on 20 Nov 1981. She had been waiting since 10 March 1952.

Most
Padmabhushan Dr M. C. Modi, a pioneer of mass eye surgery in India since 1943, has performed 833 cataract operations in a single working day.

Dr Robert B. McClure (b. 1901) of Toronto, Canada performed 20,423 major operations in 1924–78.

Joseph Ascough (b. 1935) of Nottingham, England underwent his 327th operation (for the removal of papillomas from his wind pipe) on 20 Mar 1985. These wart-like growths which impede breathing first formed when he was 18 months old.

Oldest subject
The greatest recorded age at which a person has been subjected to an operation is 111 years 105 days in the case of James Henry Brett, Jr (b. 25 July 1849, d. 10 Feb 1961) of Houston, Texas, USA. He underwent a hip operation on 7 Nov 1960. The oldest age established in Britain was the case of Miss Mary Wright (b. 28 Feb 1862) who died during a thigh operation at Boston, Lincolnshire on 22 Apr 1971 aged 109 years 53 days.

Heart transplant *Earliest and longest surviving*
The first human heart transplant operation was performed on Louis Washkansky, aged 55, at the Groote Schuur Hospital, Cape Town, South Africa, between 1.00 a.m. and 6 a.m., on 3 Dec 1967, by a team of 30 headed by Prof. Christiaan Neethling Barnard (b. Beaufort West, South Africa, 8 Oct 1922). The donor was Miss Denise Ann Darvall, aged 25. Washkansky died on 21 Dec 1967. The longest surviving heart transplantee has been Emmanuel Vitra, of Marseilles, France (b. 1921) who received the heart of a 20 year old man on 28 Nov 1968 and entered the 17th year of his new life in 1984. Britain's longest-surviving heart transplant patient was Keith Castle (1927–85) of Battersea, London who died 5 years 310 days after his transplant on 18 Aug 1979 at Papworth Hospital, Cambridge.

Hollie Roffey (b. 20 July) underwent a heart transplant aged a record 10 days in a 5½ hr operation by Mr Magdi Yacoub at the National Heart Hospital, London on 30 July 1984. She died after 18 days, aged 28 days, on 17 August.

The first transplantee to give birth was Betsy Sneith, 23, with a baby girl Sierra (7 lb 10 oz *3,45 kg*) at Stanford University, California on 17 Sept 1984. She had received a donor heart in February 1980.

Artificial heart
On 1–2 Dec 1982 at the Utah Medical Center, Salt Lake City, Utah, USA, Dr Barney B. Clark, 61 of Des Moines, Wisconsin, USA received an artificial heart. The surgeon was Dr William C. De Vries. The heart was a Jarvik Mark 7 designed by Dr Robert K. Jarvik. Dr Clark died on 23 Mar 1983, 112 days later.

Earliest kidney transplant
R. H. Lawler (b. 1895) (USA) performed the first homo transplantation of the kidney in the human in 1950. The longest survival, as between identical twins, has been 20 years.

Earliest appendicectomy
The earliest recorded successful appendix operation was performed in 1736 by Claudius Amyand (1680–1740). He was Serjeant Surgeon to King George II (reigned 1727–60).

Earliest anaesthesia
The earliest recorded operation under general anaesthesia was for the removal of a cyst from the neck of James Venable by Dr Crawford Williamson Long (1815–78), using diethyl ether ($C_2H_5)_2O$, in Jefferson, Georgia, USA, on 30 Mar 1842. The earliest amputation under an anaesthetic in Great Britain was by Dr William Scott and Dr James McLauchlan at the Dumfries and Galloway Infirmary, Scotland on 19 Dec 1846.

Most durable cancer patient
The most extreme recorded case of survival from diagnosed cancer is that of Mrs Winona Mildred Melick (*née* Douglass) (b. 22 Oct 1876) of Long Beach, California. She had four cancer operations in 1918, 1933, 1966 and 1968 but died from pneumonia on 28 Dec 1981, 67 days after her 105th birthday.

Laryngectomy
On 24 July 1924 John I. Poole of Plymouth, Devon after diagnosis of carcinoma, then aged 33 underwent total laryngectomy in Edinburgh. He died on 19 June 1979 after surviving nearly 55 years as a 'neck-breather'. Mr F. B. Harvey of Plymouth, Devon has been a neck-breather since 1929.

Fastest amputation
The shortest time recorded for a leg amputation in the pre-anaesthetic era was 13–15 sec by Napoleon's chief surgeon Dominique Larrey. There could have been no ligation.

Largest tumour
The largest tumour ever recorded was Spohn's case of an ovarian cyst weighing 328 lb *148,7 kg* from a woman in Texas, USA in 1905. She recovered fully. The most extreme case reported in Britain was of a cyst weighing 298 lb *135 kg* removed from a woman in England in 1846. The patient did not survive.

Surgical instruments
The largest surgical instruments are robot retractors used in abdominal surgery introduced by Abbey Surgical Instruments of Chingford, Essex in 1968 and weighing 11 lb *5 kg*. Some bronchoscopic forceps measure 60 cm *23⅝ in* in length. The smallest are Elliot's eye trephine, which has a blade 0.078 in *0,20 cm* in diameter and 'straight' stapes picks with a needle-type tip or blade of 0,3 mm *0.013 in* long.

PSYCHIC FORCES

Extra-sensory perception
The two most extreme published examples of ESP in scientific literature have been those of the Reiss case of a 26 year old female at Hunter College, New York State, USA in 1936 and of Pavel Stepánek (Czechoslovakia) in 1967–68. The importance which might be attached to their cases was diminished by subsequent developments. The Reiss subject refused to undergo any further tests under stricter conditions. When Stepánek was retested at Edinburgh University with plastic cards he 'failed to display any clairvoyant ability'. Much smaller departures from the laws of probability have however been displayed in less extreme cases carried out under strict conditions.

Most durable ghosts
Ghosts are not immortal and, according to the *Gazetteer of British Ghosts*, seem to deteriorate after 400 years. The most outstanding exception to their normal 'half-life' would be the ghosts of Roman soldiers thrice reported still marching through the cellars of the Treasurer's House, York Minster after nearly 19 centuries. The book's author, Peter Underwood, states that Britain has more reported ghosts per square mile than any other country with Borley Rectory near Long Melford, Suffolk the site of unrivalled activity between 1863 and its destruction by fire in 1939. Andrew M. Green, author of *Ghost Hunting, A Practical Guide* claims to possess the only known letter from a *poltergeist*.

CHAPTER TWO

The Living World

A life size sand sculpture of the world's mightiest animal, the Blue whale of which today only 12,000 survive. (See General and Mammalia records below)

ANIMAL KINGDOM GENERAL RECORDS

Note—Guinness Superlatives Ltd has published a specialist volume entitled *The Guinness Book of Animal Facts and Feats* (3rd Edition) by Gerald L. Wood (price £8.95). This work treats the dimensions and performances of the Classes of the Animal Kingdom in greater detail, giving also the sources and authorities for much of the material in this chapter.

Largest and heaviest

The largest and heaviest animal in the world is the female Blue or Sulphur-bottom whale (*Balaenoptera musculus*), also called Sibbald's rorqual (see table). The longest specimen ever recorded was a female landed at the Compania Argentina de Pesca, Grytviken, South Georgia some time in the period 1904–20 which measured 107 Norwegian fot *33,58 m 110 ft 2½ in* in length. A nursing cow whale may generate up to 1300 lb *590 kg* of milk per day. During summer months an average-sized specimen consumes up to 3 million calories per day. The tongue and heart of the 190 tonne *187 ton* female (see Table p. 26) taken by the *Slava* whaling fleet in the Southern Ocean on 20 Mar 1947 weighed 4.22 tons *4,29 tonnes* and 1540 lb *698,5 kg* respectively.

The low frequency pulses made by blue whales when communicating with each other have been measured up to 188 dB making them the loudest sounds emitted by any living source. They have been detected 850 km *530 miles* away.

Heaviest brain

The Sperm whale (*Physeter macrocephalus*) has the heaviest brain of any living animal. The brain of a 49 ft *14,93 m* bull processed aboard the Japanese factory ship *Nissin Maru No. 1* in the Antarctic on 11 Dec 1949 weighed 9,2 kg *20.24 lb* compared with 6,9 kg *15.38 lb* for a 90 ft *27 m* Blue whale. The heaviest brain recorded for an elephant was an exceptional 16.5 lb *7,5 kg* in the case of a 1.94 ton *1957 kg* Asiatic cow. The brain of the adult bull African elephant is normally 9¼–12 lb *4,2–5,4 kg*.

Largest eye

The Giant squid (*Architeuthis* sp.) has the largest eye of any living animal. The ocular diameter may exceed 38 cm *15 in* (*cf.* 30 cm *11.81 in* for a 33⅓ long-playing record).

Largest egg

The largest egg laid by any known animal was that of the Elephant bird (*Aepyornis maximus*) which lived in southern Madagascar until *c.* AD 900. One example preserved in the British Museum (Natural History) measures 85,6 cm *33.7 in* round the long axis with a circumference of 72,3 cm *28.5 in*, giving a capacity of 8,88 litres *2.35 gal* or equivalent to 180–185 hen's eggs. It weighed about 27 lb *12,2 kg* when full.

The largest egg of any living animal is that of the Whale shark (*Rhincodon typus*). One egg case measuring 12 in by 5.5 in by 3.5 in *30 × 14 × 9 cm* was picked up on 29 June 1953 at a depth of 31 fathoms (186 ft *56,6 m*) in the Gulf of Mexico 130 miles *209 km* south of Port Isabel, Texas, USA. The egg contained a perfect embryo of a Whale shark 13.78 in *35 cm* long.

Longest gestation

The viviparous Alpine black salamander (*Salamandra atra*) has a gestation period of up to 38 months at altitudes above 1400 m *4600 ft* in the Swiss Alps, but this drops to 24–26 months at lower altitudes.

Fastest and slowest growth

The fastest growth in the Animal Kingdom is that of the Blue whale calf (see Table and above). A barely visible ovum weighing a fraction of a milligramme (*0.000035 oz*) grows to a weight of *c.* 26 tons *26 tonnes* in 22¾ months, made up of 10¾ months gestation and the first 12 months of life. This is equivalent to an increase of 30,000 million-fold. The slowest growth is that of the deep-sea clam *Tindaria callistiformis* of the North Atlantic, which takes *c.* 100 years to reach a length of 8 mm *0.31 in*.

Highest altitude

The highest altitude attained by any non-human animal is by turtles aboard the USSR Zond 5 in circumlunar flight. In April 1967 NASA reported that bacteria had been discovered at an altitude of 135,000 ft (25.56 miles) *41 100 m*.

Greatest size difference between sexes (Dimorphism)

The largest female marine worms of the species *Bonellia viridis* are at least 100 million times heavier than the smallest males. The female is up to 100 cm *39.3 in* long against the miserable 1,0 mm *0.04 in* of the male.

Most monogamous

Male Klipspringers (*Oreotragus oreotragus*) rarely stray more than 5 metres *16¼ ft* from their mate during their lifetime.

Highest g force

The highest force encountered in nature is the 400 g *averaged* by the Click beetle *Athous haemorrhoidalis* (a common British species) when 'jack-knifing' into the air to escape predators. One example measuring 12 mm *0.47 in* in length and weighing 40 mg *0.00014 oz* which jumped to a height of 30 cm *11¾ in* was calculated to have 'endured' a peak brain deceleration of 2300 g at the end of the movement.

Internal temperatures

The highest average mammalian blood temperature is that of the Xoloitzcuintli or Mexican hairless dog with 104° F *40,0° C*. That of the dromedary *Camelus dromedarius* reaches 41° C *105.8° F* at the end of a hot day. The lowest mammalian blood temperature is that of the Spiny anteater (Echidna), (*Tachyglossus aculeatus*), a monotreme found in Australia and New Guinea, with a normal range of 72°–87° F *22,2°–24,4° C*. The ice worm of Alaska has an internal temperature of − 10° C *14° F*.

Most prodigious eater

The most phenomenal eating machine in nature is the larva of the Polyphemus moth (*Antheraea polyphemus*) of North America which, in the first 48 hours of its life, consumes an amount equal to 86,000 times its own birthweight. In human terms, this would be equivalent to a 7 lb *3,17 kg* baby taking in 269 tons *273 tonnes* of nourishment!

Most valuable furs

The highest-priced animal pelts are those of the Sea otter (*Enhydra lutris*), also known as the Kamchatka beaver, which fetched up to $2700 (*then £675*) before their 55-year-long protection started in 1912. The protection ended in 1967, and at the first legal auction of Sea otter pelts at Seattle, Washington, USA on 31 Jan 1968, Neiman-Marcus, the famous Dallas department store, paid $9200 (*then £3832*) for four pelts from Alaska. In 1983 a price of $100,000 (*then £67,000*) was quoted for a full-length Russian lynx fur coat manufactured by Ben Kahn and Maximilian of New York City.

Heaviest ambergris

The heaviest piece of ambergris (a fatty deposit in the intestine of the Sperm whale) on record was a 1003 lb *455 kg* lump recovered from a Sperm whale (*Physeter macrocephalus*) caught off Tasmania on 24 Dec 1912. It was later sold in London for £23,000, equivalent in 1985 to more than £500,000.

Most valuable

The most valuable animals in cash terms are thoroughbred racehorses. It was announced in October 1980 that *Easy Jet* (see Chap. 12 Horseracing) had been syndicated for $30 million (*£14.2 million*). The most valuable zoo exhibit is the Giant panda (*Ailuropoda melanoleuca*), 'Chu-Lin' (b. Sept 1982) of Madrid Zoo, Spain. It was the first cub in Europe to be valued at more than £1 million. The most valuable marine exhibits are 'Orky' and 'Corky', the world's only captive breeding pair of killer whales (*Orcinus orca*) at Marineland, Palos Verdes, Los Angeles. In 1985 they were valued at $2,000,000 (*then £1,650,000*).

Newest phylum

The 35th and only second new Phylum since 1900 was added to taxonomy in Sept 1983 with the confirmation of the minute *Loricifera* first found by R. M. Kristensen at Helsingør, Denmark in Oct 1975.

1. MAMMALS (Mammalia)

Largest and heaviest *British waters*

The largest Blue whale ever recorded in the waters of Great Britain was probably an 88 ft *26,8 m* specimen killed near the Bunaveneader station in Harris in the Western Isles, Scotland in 1904. In Dec 1851 the carcase of a blue whale measuring 94 ft 9 in *28,87 m* in length (girth 42 ft *13,7 m*) was brought into Bantry harbour, Co. Cork, Ireland after it had been found floating dead in the sea. A specimen stranded on the west coast of Lewis, Western Isles, Scotland in *c.* 1870 was credited with a length of 105 ft *32 m* but the carcase was cut up by the local people before the length could be verified. The length was probably exaggerated or taken along the curve of the body instead of in a straight line from the tip of the snout to the notch in the flukes. Four Blue whales have been stranded on British coasts since 1913, at least two of them after being harpooned by whalers. The last occurrence (*c.* 60 ft *18 m*) was at Wick, Highland, Scotland on 15 Oct 1923.

Blue whales inhabit the colder seas and migrate to warmer waters in the winter for breeding.

Above An artist's impression of the aptly named but extinct Elephant bird *Aepyornis maximus*. Before their extinction *c.* AD 900 they laid eggs larger than those of any dinosaur or the Whale shark. *Below* a portion of the egg, actual size, from the British Museum (Natural History).

Observations made in the Antarctic in 1947–8 showed that a Blue whale can maintain a speed of 20 knots (23 mph *37 km/h*) for 10 min when frightened. It has been calculated that a 90 ft *27 m* Blue whale travelling at 20 knots *37 km/h* would develop 520 hp *527 cv*. Newborn calves measure 6,5–8,6 m *21 ft 3¼ in–28 ft 6 in* in length and weigh up to 3000 kg *2.95 tons*.

It has been estimated that there were about 12,000 Blue whales living throughout the oceans today. This compares with a peak estimate of *c.* 220,000 in the past. The species has been protected *de jure* since 1967, although non-member countries of the International Whaling Commission, *e.g.* Panama and Taiwan, are not bound by this agreement. A world-wide ban on commercial whaling is due to come into effect in 1986 though both the USSR and Norway will exempt themselves and Japan will only agree to cease in 1988.

Deepest dive

The greatest *recorded* depth to which a whale has dived is 620 fathoms (3720 ft *1134 m*) by a 47 ft *14,32 m* bull Sperm whale (*Physeter macrocephalus*) found with its jaw entangled with a submarine cable running between Santa Elena, Ecuador and Chorillos, Peru, on 14 Oct 1955. At this depth the whale withstood a pressure of 1680 lb/in² *11583 kPa* of body surface. On 25 Aug 1969 another bull Sperm whale was killed 100 miles *160 km* south of Durban after it had surfaced from a dive lasting 1 hr 52 min, and inside its stomach were found two small sharks which had been swallowed about an hour earlier. These were later identified as *Scymnodon* sp., a species found only on the sea floor. At this point from land the depth of water is in excess of 1646 fathoms (10,476 ft *3193 m*) for a radius of 30–40 miles *48–64 km*, which now suggests that the Sperm whale sometimes descends to a depth of over 10,000 ft *3000 m* when seeking food and is limited by pressure of time rather than by pressure of pressure.

Largest on land *World*

(*See also Table*) The largest living land animal is the African bush elephant (*Loxodonta africana*). The average adult bull stands 10 ft 6 in *3,2 m* at the shoulder and weighs 5.6 tons *5,7 tonnes*. The largest specimen ever recorded, and the largest land animal of modern times, was a bull shot 25 miles *40 km* north-northeast of Mucusso, southern Angola on 7 Nov 1974. Lying on its side this elephant measured 13 ft 8 in *4,16 m* in a projected line from the highest point of the shoulder to the base of the forefoot, indicating that its standing height must have been about 13 ft *3,96 m*. Other measurements included an overall length of 35 ft *10,67 m* (tip of extended trunk to tip of extended tail) and a forefoot circumference of 5 ft 11 in *1,80 m*. The weight was computed to be 26,998 lb (12.05 tons, *12,24 tonnes*) (see also Shooting, Ch. 12).

Largest on land *Britain*

The largest wild mammal in the British Isles is the Red deer (*Cervus elaphus*). A full-grown stag stands 3 ft 8 in *1,11 m* at the shoulder and weighs 230–250 lb *104–113 kg*. The heaviest ever recorded was probably a stag killed at Glenfiddich, Banff, Scotland in 1831, which weighed 525 lb *238 kg*. The heaviest park Red deer on record was a stag weighing 476 lb *215 kg* (height at shoulder 4 ft 6 in *1,37 m*) killed at Woburn, Bedfordshire in 1836. The so-called wild pony (*Equus caballus*) may weigh up to 700 lb *320 kg* but there are no truly feral populations living today.

SUPERLATIVES OF THE ANIMAL KINGDOM

	Largest/Heaviest	Longest/Tallest	Smallest/Lightest	Fastest
WHOLE ANIMAL KINGDOM	190 tonnes Blue whale (*Balaenoptera musculus*); female 27,6 m *90½ ft* long caught by Soviet ship *Slava* in Antarctica, 1947	180 ft *55 m* Bootlace worm (*Lineus longissimus*); St Andrews, Fife, Scotland, 1864	0.008 in *0,2 mm* long Hairy-winged beetles (family *Ptiliidae*) and battledore-wing fairy flies (family *Myrmaridae*)	350 km/h *217 mph* Peregrine falcon (*Falco peregrinus*) during stoop. Germany 1963–7
MAMMALS	Land Mammal: est. 12,24 tonnes African bush elephant (*Loxodonta africana*) Angola, 1974	20 ft *6,09 m* Giraffe (*Giraffa camelopardalis tippelskirchi*) from Kenya. 'George' d. Chester Zoo, 22 July 1969	0.062–0.071 oz *1,75–2,0 g* Kitti's hog-nosed bat (*Craseonycteris thonglongyai*), Thailand	60–63 mph *96–101 km/h* Cheetah (*Acionyx jubatus*)
BIRDS	345 lb *156,5 kg* Ostrich (*Struthio c. camelus*). Up to 9 ft *2,7 m* tall North Africa	Largest wing span 11 ft 11 in *3,63 m* Wandering albatross (*Diomedea exulans*) Tasman Sea, 18 Sept 1965	0.056 oz *1,6 g* male Bee humming-bird (*Mellisuga helenae*) Cuba, Caribbean. Overall length 57 mm *2¼ in*	*Level flight (air speed): 106.2 mph 171 km/h* White throated spinetail swift (*Hirundapus caudacutus*) USSR, 1942
REPTILES	>2 tonnes, 28 ft 4 in *8,63 m* Norman River, Australia, July 1957, Salt-water crocodile (*Crocodylus porosus*)	10 m *32 ft 9 in* Reticulated python (*Python reticulatus*) Celebes, 1912	*0.7 in* 18 mm Gecko (*Sphaerodactylus parthenopion*) British Virgin Islands, 1964	On land: 18 mph *29 km/h* Six-lined racerunner (*Cnemidophorus sexlineatus*) South Carolina, 1941
SNAKES	Nearly 500 lb *227 kg* Anaconda (*Eunectes murinus*) girth 44 in *111 cm*, length 27 ft 9 in *8,45 m* Brazil, c. 1960	Of venomous species 18 ft 9 in *5,71 m* King Cobra (*Ophiophagus hannah*) or Hamadryad, Malaya 1937 (d. London Zoo)	4.7 in *11,9 cm* Thread snake (*Leptotyphlops bilineata*), West Indies	7 mph *11 km/h* Black mamba (*Dendroaspis polylepis*) Tanzania April 1906
AMPHIBIANS	143 lb *65 kg* Chinese giant salamander (*Andrias davidianus*) Hunan Province	5 ft 11 in *180 cm* length (see left)	8,5–12,4 mm *0.33–0.48 in* Arrow-poison frog (*Smithnillus limbatus*) Cuba	c. 18 mph *29 km/h* take-off speed by champions in frog leaping contests
FISHES	42.4 tons *43 tonnes* Whale shark (*Rhincodon typus*) Koh Chik, Gulf of Siam 1919. Length 60¾ ft *18,5 m*	(Of freshwater fish) 720 lb *327 kg* European catfish (*Siluris glanis*) 15 ft *4,6 m*, Dneiper River, USSR, c. 1856.	0.00014 oz *4 mg* Dwarf pygmy goby (*Pandaka pygmaea*) Luzon, Philippines. Males *7,5–9,9 mm 0.28–0.38* long. Up to 7150 per oz.	Est. 68 mph *109 km/h* Sailfish *Istiophorus platypterus*, Long Key, Florida
SPIDERS	'Nearly 3 oz *85 g*' *Lasiodora klugi*; Manaos, Brazil 1945	10.6 in *270 mm* legspan. *Lasiodora* sp.; Puraque, W. Brazil 1973	0.016 in *0,43 mm* male *Patu marplesi*; Western Samoa, 1956	1.17 mph *1,88 km/h* female *Tegenaria gigantea*
CRUSTACEANS	44 lb 6 oz *20,14 kg* North Atlantic lobster (*Homarus americanus*) overall length 3½ ft *1,06 m* Nova Scotia, 11 Feb 1977	>12 ft *3,65 m* claw span Giant spider crab (*Macrocheira kaempferi*) Eastern Japan	0.01 in *0.25 mm*, Water flea (genus *Alonella*) northern Europe	18 mph *28 km/h* Lobsters *H. vulgaris* and *Polinurus vulgaris* when leaping backwards
INSECTS	3.5 oz *100 g* Goliath beetle (*Goliathus giganteus*) equatorial Africa	13 in *330 mm* female Giant stick insect (*Pharnacia serratipes*) Indonesia	See above: Smallest in Whole Animal Kingdom	36 mph *58 km/h* Deer bot-fly (*Cephenemyia pratti*)
MOLLUSCS	2 tons/*tonnes* Atlantic Giant squid (*Architeuthis dux*) Thimble Tickle Bay, Newfoundland, 2 Nov 1878	57 ft (*17,37 m* Giant squid (*Architeuthis longimanus*) Tentacle 49 ft *14,93 m*, New Zealand, 1887	0.02 in *0,5 mm* diameter univalve shell *Ammonicera rota*; British waters	(Of snails) 55 yd *50,3 m* per hour. Common garden snail *Helix aspersa*. Some species 23 in *58 cm* per hour

The world's largest land animal: the African bush elephant *Loxodonta africana*. Males occasionally surpass 10 and even 12 tons.

Smallest *Land*

(*See also Table*) The Kitti's hog-nosed bat (*Craseonycteris thonglongyai*) or Bumblebee bat, is now restricted to a few caves near the forestry station at Ban Sai Yoke on the Kwae Noi River, Kanchanaburi, Thailand. A new hydro-electric project is endangering the species. Mature specimens (both sexes) have a wing span of *c.* 160 mm *6.29 in* and weigh 1,75–2 g *0.062–0.071 oz*. The smallest mammal found in the British Isles is the European pygmy shrew (*Sorex minutus*). Mature specimens have a head and body length of 43–64 mm *1.69–2.5 in*, a tail length of 31–46 mm *1.22–1.81 in* and weigh between 2,4 and 6,1 g *0.084 and 0.213 oz*.

Smallest *Marine*

The smallest totally marine mammal in terms of weight is probably Commerson's dolphin (*Cephalorhynchus commersoni*) also known as Le Jacobite, which is found in the waters off the southern tip of South America. In one series of six adult specimens the weights ranged from 23 kg *50.7 lb* to 35 kg *77.1 lb*. The Sea otter (*Enhydra lutris*) of the north Pacific is of comparable size (55–81.4 lb *25–38,5 kg*), but this species sometimes comes ashore during storms.

Rarest

A number of mammals are known only from a single (holotype) specimen. An example is Garrido's hutia (*Capromys garridoi*) known only from a single specimen collected on the islet of Cayo Maja, off southern Cuba in April 1967. In 1979 zoologists uncovered the first evidence that the Bali leopard (*Panthera pardus balica*) still existed on the island. On 19 Jan 1984 the Wild Life Service in Tasmania announced that a Tasmanian wolf had been sighted in July 1982.

Britain's rarest native mammal is the Large mouse-eared bat (*Myotis myotis*) (see p. 30).

Fastest *World*

(*See also Table*) The fastest of all land animals over a short distance (*i.e.* up to 600 yd *549 m*) is the Cheetah or Hunting leopard (*Acinonyx jubatus*) of the open plains of East Africa, Iran, Turkmenia and Afghanistan, with a probable maximum speed of 60–63 mph *96–101 km/h* over suitably level ground. Speeds of 71, 84 and even 90 mph, *114, 135 and 145 km/h* have been claimed for this animal, but these figures must be considered exaggerated. Tests in London in 1937 showed that on an oval greyhound track over 345 yd *316 m* a female cheetah's average speed over three runs was 43.4 mph *69,8 km/h* (*cf.* 43.26 mph *69,6 km/h* for the fastest racehorse), but this specimen was not running flat out and had great difficulty negotiating the bends. The fastest land animal over a sustained distance (*i.e.* 1000 yd *914 m* or more) is the Pronghorn antelope (*Antilocapra americana*) of the western United States. Specimens have been observed to travel at 35 mph for 4 miles *56 km/h for 6 km*, at 42 mph for 1 mile *67 km/h for 1,6 km* and 55 mph for half a mile *88,5 km/h for 0,8 km*.

Fastest *Britain*

The fastest British land mammal over a sustained distance is the Roe deer (*Capreolus capreolus*), which can cruise at 25–30 mph *40–48 km/h* for more than 20 miles *32 km*, with occasional bursts of up to 40 mph *64 km/h*. On 19 Oct 1970 a frightened runaway Red deer (*Cervus elaphus*) registered a speed of 42 mph

Longest Lived	Commonest	Rarest
c. 220 years Ocean quahog (*Arctica islandica*). Example with 220 annual growth rings reported from mid-Atlantic, 1982	Nematodes sea worms. Est. populaton 4×10^{25} *cf.* Est. total of all living things on Earth of 3×10^{33}	A member of species known only from a single specimen or holotype.
120 years Man (see p 11) *Homo sapiens* 1865–*fl.* 1985	House mouse (*Mus musculus*): distribution embraces all continents	Single Tasmanian wolf or thylacine (*Thyalacine cynocephalus*) positively identified after a 21 year void, Tasmania, July 1982 by a wildlife ranger. Last captured specimen d. 7 Sept. 1936.
72+ years male Andean Condor (*Vultur gryphus*) Moscow Zoo, *fl.* 1892–1964	In the wild: 10,000 million Red-billed quelea (*Quelea quelea*) sub-Saharan Africa	Yellow-fronted bowerbird (*Amblyornis flavifrons*) one male sighting from 1895 to 1981
152+ years male Marion's tortoise *Geochelone sumeiriei*; Mauritius, d. 1918	Sea snake (*Astrotia stokesii*) found *en masse* from Arabia sea to south western Pacific	Holotype—Dwarf chameleon (*Evoluticanda tuberculata*), Madagascar
40 years 3 months, Common Boa (*Boa c. constrictor*) named 'Popeye', Philadelphia Zoo, USA, d. April 1977	(see above) In May 1929 a coiled mass of these sea snakes in the Malacca Straits measured 60 miles *96 km*	Keel-scaled boa (*Casarea dussumieri*) of Round Island, western India Ocean has total population of 58 (1982).
c. 55 years Japanese giant salamander (*Andrias japonicus*) 1826–1881, Amsterdam Zoo, Netherlands	Marine toad (*Bufo marinus*) world-wide distribution. Female may ovulate 35,000 eggs in a year	Israel painted frog (*Discoglossus nigriventer*) Lake Huleh—5 since 1940
82 years Lake sturgeon (*Acipenser fulvescens*) based on annuli; Lake Winnebago, Wisconsin, USA, 1951–54	Deep-sea bristlemouth (*Cyclothone elongata*) 3 in *76 mm* long; world-wide	Holotypes (see above)
c. 28 years female *Mygalomorphae* (tarantula) Mexico c. 1923–1951	Crab spiders (family *Thomisidae*) are common with worldwide distribution	Trapdoor spider (genus *Liphistius*) south-east Asia
c. 50 years North American lobster (see left)	>500 million tonnes krill (*Euphausia superba*) of the southern oceans. A 10 million tonne swarm was tracked in March 1981	Holotypes (see above)
47 years Splendour beetle (*Buprestidae aurulenta*) Prittlewell, Essex 1936–83	Springtails (Order Collembola) attain densities of 5000 per ft² or *54 000/m²*	(Butterfly) Only 2 specimens of the Eight spotted skipper (*Dalla octomaculata*) of Costa Rica, found since 1900. Many holotypes exist
See above: Longest lived Whole Animal Kingdom	Sea hare (*Tethys californicus*) can lay a million eggs in a day	Prices up to $12,000 have been offered by conchologists for examples of *Conus cypraea*

67,5 km/h on a police radar trap as it charged through a street in Stalybridge, Greater Manchester.

Slowest and sleepiest

The slowest moving land mammal is the Ai or Three-toed sloth (*Bradypus tridactylus*) of tropical America. The average ground speed is 6–8 ft *1,83–2,44 m* a minute (0.068–0.098 mph *0,109–0,158 km/h*), but in the trees it can 'accelerate' to 15 ft *4,57 m* a minute (0.17 mph *0,272 km/h*) (*cf.* these figures with the 0.03 mph *0,05 km/h* of the common garden snail and the 0.17 mph *0,27 km/h* of the giant tortoise). The slowest swimming marine mammal is the Sea otter (*Enhydra lutris*) which has a top speed of *c.* 6 mph *9,6 km/h*. Some armadillos (*Dasypodidae*) and opossums sleep more than two thirds of their life.

Longest lived

No other mammal can match the extreme proven 119 years attained by Man (*Homo sapiens*) (see pp. 10 and 11). It is probable that the closest approach is made by the Asiatic elephant (*Elephas maximus*). The greatest age that has been verified with absolute certainty is 78 years in the case of a cow named 'Modoc', who died at Santa Clara, California, USA on 17 July 1975. She was imported into the USA from Germany in 1898 at the age of two. The longest lived marine mammal is Baird's beaked whale (*Berardius bairdii*) which has a maximum life-span of *c.* 70 years.

Highest living

The highest living wild mammal in the world is probably the Yak (*Bos grunniens*), of Tibet and the Szechwanese Alps, China, which occasionally climbs to an altitude of 20,000 ft *6100 m* when foraging. There are also reliable records of the Woolly hare (*Lepus oiostolus*) and the Woolly wolf (*Canis lupus chanco*) being seen at 19,800 ft *6035 m* and 19,000 ft *5790 m* respectively on the Tibetan Plateau.

Largest herds

The largest herds on record were those of the Springbok (*Antidorcas marsupialis*) during migration across the plains of the western parts of southern Africa in the 19th century. In 1849 John (later Sir John) Fraser observed a *trekbokken* that took three days to pass through the settlement of Beaufort West, Cape Province. Another herd seen moving near Nels Poortje, Cape Province in 1888 was estimated to contain 100,000,000 head, although 10,000,000 is probably a more realistic figure. A herd estimated to be 15 miles *24 km* wide and more than 100 miles *160 km* long was reported from Karree Kloof, Orange River, South Africa in July 1896.

The largest concentration of wild mammals found living anywhere in the world today is that of the Mexican free-tailed Bat (*Tadarida brasiliensis*) in Bracken Cave, San Antonio, Texas, USA, where up to twenty million animals assemble after migration.

Longest and shortest gestation periods

The longest of all mammalian gestation periods is that of the Asiatic elephant (*Elephas maximus*), with an average of 609 days or just over 20 months and a maximum of 760 days—more than two and half times that of a human. By 1981 only *c.* 35,000 survived. The gestation period of the American opossum (*Didelphis marsupialis*), also called the Virginian opossum, is normally 12–13 days but may be as short as 8 days.

The gestation periods of the rare Water opossum or Yapok (*Chironectes minimus*) of central and northern South America (average 12–13 days) and the Eastern native cat (*Dasyurus viverrinus*) of Australia (average 12 days) may also be on occasion as short as 8 days.

Largest litter

The greatest number of young born to a *wild* mammal at a single birth is 31 (30 of which survived) in the case of the Tail-less tenrec (*Tenrec ecaudatus*) found in Madagascar and the Comoro Islands. The normal litter size is 12–15, although females can suckle up to 24.

Youngest breeder

The Streaked tenrec (*Hemicentetes semispinosus*) of Madagascar is weaned after only 5 days, and females can breed 3–4 weeks after birth.

CARNIVORES

Largest land *World*

The largest living terrestrial carnivore is the Kodiak bear (*Ursus arctos middendorffi*), which is found on Kodiak Island and the adjacent Afognak and Shuyak islands in the Gulf of Alaska, USA. The average adult male has a nose to tail length of 8 ft *2,4 m* (tail about 4 in *10 cm*), stands 52 in *132 cm* at the shoulder and weighs between 1050 and 1175 lb *476–533 kg*. In 1894 a weight of 1656 lb *751 kg* was recorded for a male shot at English Bay, Kodiak Island, whose *stretched* skin measured 13 ft 6 in *4,11 m* from the tip of the nose to the root of the tail. This weight was exceeded by a 'cage-fat' male in the Cheyenne Mountain Zoological Park, Colorado Springs, Colorado, USA which scaled 1670 lb *757 kg* at the time of its death on 22 Sept 1955. In 1981 an unconfirmed weight of over 2000 lb *907 kg* was reported for an Alaskan brown bear on exhibition at the Space Farms Zoological Park at Beemerville, New Jersey, USA.

Weights in excess of 1600 lb *725 kg* have also been reported for the Polar bear (*Ursus maritimus*), but the average adult male weighs 850–900 lb *386–408 kg* and measures 7¾ ft *2,4 m* nose to tail. In 1960 a Polar bear allegedly weighing 2210 lb *1002 kg* before skinning was shot at the polar entrance to Kotzebue Sound, north-west Alaska. The mounted specimen has a standing height of 11 ft 1¼ in *3,38 m*.

Largest land *Britain*

The largest land carnivore found in Britain is the Badger (*Meles meles*). The average adult boar (sows are slightly smaller) measures 3 ft *90 cm* in length—including a 4 in *10 cm* tail—and weighs 27 lb *12,3 kg* in the early spring and 32 lb *14,5 kg* at the end of the summer when it is in 'grease'. In December 1952 a boar weighing exactly 60 lb *27,2 kg* was killed near Rotherham, South Yorkshire.

Largest marine

The largest toothed mammal ever recorded is the Sperm whale (*Physeter macrocephalus*), also called the Cachalot. The average adult bull measures 47 ft *14,3 m* in length and weighs about 33 tons *33,5 tonnes*. The largest accurately measured specimen on record was a 67 ft 11 in *20,7 m* bull captured off the Kurile Islands, north-west Pacific, by a USSR whaling fleet in the summer of 1950. Thirteen cachalots have been stranded on British coasts since 1913. The largest, a bull measuring 61 ft 5 in *19 m*, was washed ashore at Birchington, Kent on 18 Oct 1914. Another bull estimated at 65 ft *19,8 m* but badly decomposed was stranded at Ferryloughan, Co. Galway, Ireland on 2 Jan 1952.

Smallest

The smallest living member of the order Carnivora is the Least weasel (*Mustela rixosa*), also called the Dwarf weasel, which is circumpolar in distribution. Four races are recognised, the smallest of which is *M. r. pygmaea* of Siberia. Mature specimens have an overall length of 177–207 mm *6.96–8.14 in* and weigh between 35 and 70 g *1¼–2½ oz*.

Largest feline

The largest member of the cat family (Felidae) is the protected long-furred Siberian tiger (*Panthera tigris altaica*), also called the Amur or Manchurian tiger. Adult males average 10 ft 4 in *3,15 m* in length (nose to tip of extended tail), stand 39–42 in *99–107 cm* at the shoulder and weigh about 585 lb *265 kg*. In 1950 a male weighing 384 kg *846.5 lb* was shot in the Sikhote Alin Mts, Maritime Territory, USSR. In November 1967 David H. Hasinger of Philadelphia, USA shot an outsized Indian tiger (*Panthera tigris tigris*) in northern Uttar Pradesh which measured 10 ft 7 in *3,22 m* between pegs (11 ft 1 in *3,37 m* over the curves) and weighed 857 lb *388,7 kg* (*cf.* 9 ft 3 in *2,82 m* and 420 lb *190 kg* for average adult male). It is now on display in the US Museum of Natural History, Smithsonian Institution, Washington, DC.

The largest 'Big Cat' presently in captivity is an adult male Litigon (an Indian lion/Tigon cross) named 'Cubanacan' at Alipore Zoological Gardens, Calcutta, India, who is believed to weigh at least 800 lb *363 kg*. This animal stands 52 in *1,32 m* at the shoulder (*cf.* 44 in *1,11 m* for the lion 'Simba') and measures a record 11 ft 6 in *2,5 m* in total length.

The average adult African lion (*Panthera leo*) measures 9 ft *2,7 m* overall, stands 36–38 in *91–97 cm* at the shoulder and weighs 400–410 lb *181–185 kg*. The heaviest wild specimen on record was one weighing 690 lb *313 kg* shot by Mr Lennox Anderson just outside Hectorspruit in the eastern Transvaal, South Africa in 1936. In July 1970 a weight of 826 lb *375 kg* was reported for a black-maned lion named 'Simba' (b. Dublin Zoo, 1959) at Colchester Zoo, Essex. He died on 16 Jan 1973 at Knaresborough Zoo, North Yorkshire, where his stuffed body is currently on display.

Smallest feline

The smallest member of the cat family is the Rusty-spotted cat (*Felis rubiginosa*) of southern India and Sri Lanka. The average adult male has an overall length of 25–28 in *64–71 cm* (tail 9–10 in *23–25 cm*) and weighs about 3 lb *1,35 kg*.

PINNIPEDS (Seals, Sea-lions and Walruses)

Largest *World*

The largest of the 34 known species of pinniped is the Southern elephant seal (*Mirounga leonina*), which inhabits the sub-Antarctic islands. Adult bulls average 16½ ft *5 m* in length (tip of inflated snout to the extremities of the outstretched tail flippers), 12 ft *3,7 m* in maximum bodily girth and weigh about 5000 lb (2.18 tons *2268 kg*). The largest accurately measured specimen on record was a bull killed in Possession Bay, South Georgia on 28 Feb 1913 which measured 21 ft 4 in *6,5 m* after flensing (original length about 22½ ft *6,85 m*) and probably weighed at least 4 tons/*tonnes*. There are old records of bulls measuring 25–30 ft *7,62–9,14 m* and even 35 ft *10,66 m* but these figures must be considered exaggerated.

Largest *British*

The largest pinniped among British fauna is the Grey seal (*Halichoerus grypus*), also called the Atlantic seal. In one sample taken during the breeding season at the Farne Islands, Northumberland the heaviest (a male) weighed 310 kg *683½ lb* (length from nose to tip of flippers 2,45 m *8 ft 0½ in.*)

Smallest *World*

The smallest pinnipeds are the Ringed seal (*Phoca hispida*) of the Arctic and the closely-related Baikal seal (*P. sibirica*) of Lake Baykal

This illustration shows the comparative sizes of some of the pinnipeds mentioned on pages 28 and 30.
Artwork Matthew Hillier

Largest—Southern elephant seal *Mirounga leonina*

Fastest—Californian sea-lion *Zalophus californianus*

Most abundant—Crabeater seal *Lobodon carcinophagus*

Rarest—Monk seal *Monachus tropicalis*

Deepest—Weddell seal *Leptonychotes weddelli*

Smallest—Ringed seal *Phoca hispida*

and the Caspian seal (*P. caspica*) of the Caspian Sea, USSR. Adult specimens (males) measure up to 5 ft 6 in *1,67 m* in length and reach a maximum weight of 280 lb *127 kg*. Females are about two-thirds this size.

Smallest *British*
Britain's smallest pinniped is the Common seal (*Phoca vitulina*). Adult males measure 1,5–1,85 m *4 ft 11 in–6 ft 0¼ in* in length and weigh up to 105 kg *231 lb*. Females are four-fifths this size.

Most abundant
The most abundant species of pinniped is the Crabeater seal (*Lobodon carcinophagus*) of Antarctica. In 1978 the total population was believed to be nearly 15,000,000.

Rarest
The last reliable sighting of the Caribbean or West Indian monk seal (*Monachus tropicalis*) was on Serranilla Bank off the coast of Mexico's Yucatan peninsula in 1952. In 1974 two seals were sighted near Cay Verde and Cay Burro, SE Bahamas, but a search in 1979 found nothing. It has been suggested that they may have been Californian sea-lions which had escaped from captivity and have been recorded in the Gulf of Mexico on several occasions.

Fastest and deepest
The highest swimming speed recorded for a pinniped is a 25 mph *40 km/h* spurt by a Californian sea-lion (*Zalophus californianus*). The deepest dive recorded for a pinniped is 600 m *1960 ft* for a bull Weddell seal (*Leptonychotes weddelli*) in McMurdo Sound, Antarctica in March 1966. At this depth the seal withstood a pressure of 875 lb/in² *6033 kPa* of body area. The Northern elephant seal (*Mirounga angustirostris*) has in experiments recorded a dive of 300 m *984 ft* while unconfirmed measurements down to 2000 ft *609 m* have been claimed for the Southern elephant seal (*Mirounga leonina*).

Longest lived
A female Grey seal (*Halichoerus grypus*) shot at Shunni Wick in the Shetland Islands on 23 Apr 1969 was believed to be 'at least 46 years old' based on a count of dentine rings. The captive record is an estimated 43 years for a bull grey seal 'Jacob' held in Skansen Zoo (1901–42).

BATS

Largest *World*
The only flying mammals are bats (order

A Great vampire bat from Venezuela whose ultrasonic echolocation system inspired the pre-war invention of radar. (*Stephen Dalton, Oxford Scientific Films*)

Chiroptera), of which there are about *c.* 950 living species. That with the greatest wing span is the Bismarck flying fox (*Pteropus neohibernicus*) of the Bismarck Archipelago and New Guinea. One specimen preserved in the American Museum of Natural History has a wing spread of 165 cm *5 ft 5 in* but some unmeasured bats probably reach 183 cm *6 ft*.

Largest *Britain*
The largest bat found in Britain (15 species) is the very rare Large mouse-eared bat (*Myotis myotis*). Mature specimens have a wing span of 355–450 mm *13.97–17.71 in* and weigh up to 45 g *1.58 oz* in the case of females).

Smallest *World*
For details of Kitti's hog-nosed bat see p. 26 and 27.

Smallest *Britain*
The smallest native British bat is the Pipistrelle (*Pipistrellus pipistrellus*). Mature specimens have a wing span of 190–250 mm *7.48–9.84 in* and weigh between 3 and 8 g *0.1–0.28 oz*.

Rarest *World*
At least three species of bat are known only from the single or type specimen. They are: the Small-toothed fruit bat (*Neopteryx frosti*) from Tamalanti, West Celebes (1938/39); *Paracoelops megalotis* from Vinh, Vietnam (1945); and *Latidens salimalii* from the High Wavy Mountains, southern India (1948).

Rarest *Britain*
The rarest bat on the British list is now the Large mouse-eared bat (*Myotis myotis*) of Southern England. In 1982 only two males were known to survive.

Fastest
Because of the great practical difficulties few data on bat speeds have been published. The greatest velocity attributed to a bat is 32 mph *51 km/h* in the case of a Mexican free-tailed bat (*Tadarida brasiliensis*), but this may have been wind-assisted. In one American experiment using an artificial mine tunnel and 17 different kinds of bat, only four of them managed to exceed 13 mph *20,8 km/h* in level flight.

Longest lived
The greatest age reliably reported for a bat is 31 years 5 months for an Indian flying fox (*Pteropus giganteus*) which died at London Zoo on 11 Jan 1979.

Highest detectable pitch
Because of their ultrasonic echolocation bats have the most acute hearing of any terrestrial animal. Vampire bats (*Desmodontidae*) and Fruit bats (*Pteropodidae*) can hear frequencies as high as 120–210 kHz (*cf.* 20 kHz for the adult human limit.

PRIMATES

Largest
The largest living primate is the Mountain gorilla (*Gorilla gorilla berengei*) of the volcanic mountain ranges of W Rwanda, SW Uganda and E Zaïre. The average adult male stands 5 ft 9 in *1,75 m* tall (including crest) and weighs about 430 lb *195 kg*. The greatest height (top of crest to heel) recorded for a gorilla is 195 cm *6 ft 4¾ in* for a male collected by a German expedition at Alimbongo, N Kivu on 16 May 1938.

The heaviest gorilla ever kept in captivity was a male of the mountain race named 'N'gagi', who died in San Diego Zoo, California, USA on 12 January 1944 aged 18 years. He scaled 683 lb *310 kg* at his heaviest in 1943, and weighed

636 lb *288 kg* at the time of his death. He was 5 ft 7¾ in *1,72 m* tall and boasted a record chest measurement of 78 in *198 cm*. The heaviest gorilla living in captivity today is a Western lowland (*Gorilla g. gorilla*) male called 'Zaak', who was received at Kobe Oji Zoo, Japan in December 1962. He tipped the scales at 628 lb *285 kg* in June 1976, but has not been weighed since.

Smallest
The smallest known primate is the rare Pen-tailed shrew (*Ptilocercus lowii*) of Malaysia, Sumatra and Borneo. Adult specimens have a total length of 230–330 mm *9–13 in* (head and body 100–140 mm *3.93–5.51 in*, tail 130–190 mm *5.1–7.5 in*) and weigh 35–50 g *1.23–1.76 oz*. The Pygmy marmoset (*Cebuella pygmaea*) of the Upper Amazon Basin and the Lesser mouse-lemur (*Microcebus murinus*) of Madagascar are also of comparable length but heavier, adults weighing 50–75 g *1.76–2.64 oz* and 45–80 g *1.58–2.82 oz* respectively.

Rarest
The rarest primate is the Hairy-eared dwarf lemur (*Allocebus trichotis*) of Madagascar which, until fairly recently, was known only from the holotype specimen and three skins. In 1966, however, a live example was found on the east coast near Mananara.

Longest lived
The greatest irrefutable age reported for a non-human primate is *c.* 59 years in the case of a male Orang-utan (*Pongo pygmaeus*) named 'Guas', who died in Philadelphia Zoological Garden, Pennsylvania, USA on 9 Feb 1977. When he was received on 1 May 1931 he was at least 13 years of age. The world's oldest living primate is a male Chimpanzee (*Pan troglodytes*) named 'Jimmy' at Seneca Zoo, Rochester, N.Y., USA, who was still alive in March 1985 aged 54 years 9 months. The famous Western Lowland gorilla 'Massa' (b. July 1931) died on 30 Dec 1984 aged 53 years 5 months.

Strength
In 1924 'Boma', a 165 lb *74,80 kg* male chimpanzee at Bronx Zoo, New York, NY, USA recorded a right-handed pull (feet braced) of 847 lb *384 kg* on a dynamometer (*cf.* 210 lb *95 kg* for a man of the same weight). On another occasion an adult female chimpanzee named 'Suzette' (estimated weight 135 lb *61 kg*) at the same zoo registered a right-handed pull of 1260 lb *572 kg* while in a rage. A record from the USA of a 100 lb *45 kg* chimpanzee achieving a two-handed dead lift of 600 lb *272 kg* with ease suggests that a male gorilla could with training raise 1800 lb *816 kg*.

MONKEYS

Largest
The only species of monkey reliably credited with weights of more than 100 lb *45 kg* is the Mandrill (*Mandrillus sphinx*) of equatorial West Africa. The greatest reliable weight recorded is 119 lb *54 kg* for a captive male but an unconfirmed weight of 130 lb *59 kg* has been reported. (Adult females are about half the size of males).

Smallest
The smallest known monkey is the Pygmy marmoset (*Cebuella pygmaea*) of the Upper Amazon Basin (see Primate Smallest).

Oldest
The world's oldest living monkey is a male White-throated capuchin (*Cebus capucinus*) called 'Bobo' owned by Dr Raymond T. Bartus of the American Cyanamid Company in Pearl River, NY, USA, which celebrated his 49th birthday in 1984.

Rarest

The rarest living monkey is the Golden lion tamarin (*Leontopithecus rosalia*) of south-east Brazil. In 1980 there were less than 100 of these animals left, all of them in the São João basin in the State of Rio de Janeiro, and the species could well be extinct in the wild by 1985–90.

RODENTS

Largest

The world's largest rodent is the Capybara (*Hydrochoerus hydrochaeris*), also called the Carpincho or Water hog, which is found in tropical South America. Mature specimens have a head and body length of 3¼–4½ ft *0,99–1,4 m* and weigh up to 250 lb *113 kg* (cage-fat specimen). Britain's largest rodent is now the Coypu (*Myocastor coypus*) also known as the Nutria, which was introduced from Argentina by East Anglian fur-breeders in 1929. Three years later, the first escapes were recorded and by 1960 at least 200,000 coypus were living in East Anglia. About 80 per cent were killed by the winter of 1963 and a government campaign of extermination has reduced the population to *c.* 4000 animals and a target date of 1990 has been set for the complete eradication of the species in Britain. Adult males measure 30–36 in *76–91 cm* in length (including short tail) and weigh up to 28 lb *13 kg* in the wild state (40 lb *18 kg* in captivity).

Smallest

The smallest known rodent is the Northern Pygmy mouse (*Baiomys taylori*) of central Mexico and southern Arizona and Texas, USA, which measures up to 109 mm *4.3 in* in total length and weighs 7–8 g *0.24–0.28 oz*. Britain's smallest rodent is the Old World harvest mouse (*Micromys minutus*), which measures up to 135 mm *5.3 in* in total length and weighs 7–10 g *0.24–0.35 oz*.

Rarest

The rarest rodent in the world is probably the Little earth hutia (*Capromys sanfelipensis*) of Juan Garcia Cay, an islet off southern Cuba. It has not been recorded since its discovery in 1970.

Longest lived

The greatest reliable age reported for a rodent is 27 years 3 months for a Sumatran crested porcupine (*Hystrix brachyura*) which died in National Zoological Park, Washington DC, USA, on 12 Jan 1965.

Fastest breeder

The female Meadow vole (*Microtus agrestis*) found in Britain, can reproduce from the age of 25 days and have up to 17 litters of 6–8 young in a year.

INSECTIVORES

Largest

The largest insectivore is the Moon rat (*Echinosorex gymnurus*), also known as Raffles' gymnure, which is found in Burma, Thailand, Malaysia, Sumatra and Borneo. Mature specimens have a head and body length of 265–445 mm *10.43–17.52 in*, a tail measuring 200–210 mm *7.87–8.26 in* and weigh up to 1400 g *3.08 lb*. Although the much larger Anteaters (family Tachyglossidae and Myrmecophagidae) feed on termites and other soft-bodied insects they are not insectivores, but belong to the orders Monotremata and Edentata, ('without teeth').

Smallest

The smallest insectivore is Savi's white-toothed pygmy shrew (*Suncus etruscus*), also called the Etruscan shrew, which is found along the coast of the northern Mediterranean and southwards to Cape Province, South Africa. Mature specimens have a head and body length of 36–52 mm *1.32–2.04 in*, a tail length of 24–29 mm *0.94–1.14 in* and weigh between 1,5 and 2,5 g *0.052 and 0.09 oz*.

Longest lived

The greatest reliable age recorded for an insectivore is 17+ years for a Lesser hedgehog-tenrec (*Echinops telfairi*), which was born in Amsterdam Zoo, Netherlands in 1966 and was later sent to Jersey Zoo. It was still alive in March 1985.

ANTELOPES

Largest

The largest of all antelopes is the rare Giant eland (*Tragelaphus derbianus*), of West and Central Africa, which may surpass 2000 lb *907 kg*. The Common eland (*T. oryx*) of East and South Africa has the same shoulder height of up to 5 ft 10 in *1,78 m* but is not quite so massive, although there is one record of a 5 ft 5 in *1,65 m* bull shot in Nyasaland (now Malawi) in *c.* 1937 which weighed 2078 lb *943 kg*.

Smallest

The smallest known antelope is the Royal antelope (*Neotragus pygmaeus*) of West Africa. Mature specimens measure 10–12 in *25–31 cm* at the shoulder and weigh only 7–8 lb *3–3,6 kg* which is the size of a large Brown hare (*Lepus europaeus*). Salt's dik-dik (*Madoqua saltina*) of NE Ethiopia and Somalia weighs only 5–6 lb *2,2–2,7 kg* when adult, but this species stands about 14 in *35,5 cm* at the withers.

Rarest

The rarest antelope is the Arabian oryx (*Oryx leucoryx*) which has not been reported in the wild since 1972 when 3 were killed and 4 others captured on the Jiddat-al Harasis plateau, South Oman. On 31 Jan 1982 ten specimens, nine of

Above The most massive of all antelopes the 17½ cwt *900 kg* eland found in Africa. (*Mark Boulton, Bruce Coleman Ltd*).

them born and bred at San Diego Zoo, California, USA, were released into the open desert in South Oman under the protection of a nomadic tribe. By Jan 1985 there were 25 animals in the herd.

Oldest

The greatest reliable age recorded for an antelope is 25 years 4 months for an Addax (*Addax nasomaculatus*) which died in Brookfield Zoo, Chicago, Illinois, USA on 15 Oct 1960.

Below The rarest of all antelopes, the Arabian oryx of which only 25 now survive in deserts of south Oman. Here is shown a calf recently born in London Zoo. (*Zoological Society of London*)

DEER

Largest

The largest deer is the Alaskan moose (*Alces alces gigas*). Adult bulls average 6 ft *1,83 m* at the shoulder and weigh *c.* 1100 lb *500 kg*. A bull standing 7 ft 8 in *2,34 m* between pegs and weighing an estimated 1800 lb *816 kg* was shot on the Yukon River in the Yukon Territory, Canada in September 1897. Unconfirmed measurements up to 8 ft 6 in *2,59 m* at the shoulder and estimated weights up to 2600 lb *1180 kg* have been claimed. The record antler span or 'rack' is 78½ in *199 cm*.

Smallest

The smallest true deer (family Cervidae) is the Northern pudu (*Pudu mephistopheles*) of Ecuador and Colombia. Mature specimens measure 13–14 in *33–35 cm* at the shoulder and weigh 16–18 lb *7,2–8,1 kg*. The smallest ruminant is the Lesser Malay chevrotain (*Tragulus javanicus*) of SE Asia, Sumatra and Borneo. Adult specimens measure 8–10 in *20–25 cm* at the shoulder and weigh 6–7 lb, *2,7–3,2 kg*.

Rarest

The rarest deer in the world is Fea's muntjac (*Muntiacus feae*), which until recently, was known only from two specimens collected on the borders of S Burma and W Thailand. In December 1977 a female was received at Dusit Zoo, Bangkok, since followed by 8 more examples from Tibet.

Oldest

The greatest reliable age recorded for a deer is 26 years 8 months for a Red deer (*Cervus elaphus scoticus*) which died in Milwaukee Zoo, Wisconsin, USA on 28 June 1954.

MARSUPIALS

Largest

The largest of all marsupials is the Red kangaroo (*Macropus rufus*) of central, southern and eastern Australia. Adult males stand up to 7 feet *2,13 m* tall, weigh up to 175 lb *79 kg* and measure up to 9 ft 6 in *2,9 m* along the curves of the body.

Smallest

The smallest known marsupial is the very rare Ingram's planigale (*Planigale ingrami = P. subtilissima*), a flat-skulled mouse found only in north-west Australia. Adult males have a head and body length of 45 mm *1.77 in*, a tail length of 50 mm *2 in* and weigh about 4 g *0.14 oz*.

Longest lived

The greatest reliable age recorded for a marsupial is 26 years 0 months 22 days for a Common Wombat (*Vombatus ursinus*) which died in London Zoo on 20 Apr 1906.

Fastest speed, highest and longest jumps

The highest speed recorded for a marsupial is 40 mph *64 km/h* for a young female Eastern grey kangaroo (*Macropus giganteus*). The greatest height cleared by a hunted kangaroo is 10 ft 6 in *3,20 m* over a pile of timber and during the course of a chase in January 1951 a female Red kangaroo made a series of bounds which included one of 42 ft *12,80 m*. There is also an unconfirmed report of an Eastern grey kangaroo jumping nearly 13,5 m *44 ft 8½ in* on the flat.

TUSKS

Longest

The longest recorded elephant tusks (excluding prehistoric examples) are a pair from Zaïre preserved in the National Collection of Heads and Horns kept by the New York Zoological Society in Bronx Park, New York City, NY, USA. The right tusk measures 11 ft 5½ in *3,49 m* along the outside curve and the left 11 ft *3,35 m*. Their combined weight is 293 lb *133 kg*. A single tusk of 11 ft 6 in *3,5 m* has been reported. Ivory rose from $2.30 to $34/lb in 1970–80.

Heaviest

The heaviest recorded tusks are a pair in the British Museum (Natural History) which were collected from an aged bull shot by an Arab with a muzzle-loading gun at the foot of Mt Kilimanjaro, Kenya in 1897. They originally weighed 240 lb *109 kg* (length 10 ft 2½ in *3,11 m*) and 225 lb *102 kg* (length 10 ft 5½ in *3,18 m*) respectively, giving a total weight of 465 lb *211 kg*, but their combined weight today is 440½ lb *200 kg*.

The greatest weight ever recorded for an elephant tusk is 117 kg *258 lb* for a specimen collected in Benin, West Africa and exhibited at the Paris Exposition in 1900.

HORNS

Longest

The longest horns grown by any living animal are those of the Water buffalo (*Bubalus arnee = B. bubalis*) of India. One huge bull shot in 1955 had horns measuring 13 ft 11 in *4,24 m* from tip to tip along the outside curve across the forehead. The longest single horn on record was one measuring 81¼ in *206 cm* on the outside curve found on a specimen of domestic Ankole cattle (Bos taurus) near Lake Ngami, Botswana. The largest spread recorded for a Texas longhorn steer is 9 ft 9 in *2,97 m*.

Longest *Rhinoceros*

The longest recorded anterior horn for a rhinoceros is one of 62¼ in *158 cm* found on a female southern race White rhinoceros (*Ceratotherium simum simum*) shot in South Africa in *c.* 1848. The posterior horn measured 22¼ in *57 cm*. There is also an unconfirmed record of an anterior horn measuring 81 in *206 cm*.

HORSES AND PONIES

The world's horse population is estimated to be 75,000,000.

Largest

The largest horse ever recorded was a 19.2 hand (6 ft 6 in *1,98 m*) pure-bred red-roan Belgian (Brabant) stallion named 'Brooklyn Supreme' (1928–48) owned by C. G. Good of Ogden, Iowa, USA which weighed 3200 lb 1.42 tons *1,44 tonnes* at his heaviest in 1938 and had a chest girth of 102 in *259 cm*.

Detail from a painting of the renowned canal horse Old Billy. He worked on the Mersey at Irwell canal in England for over 55 years in the 18th and 19th centuries. He died aged 62 in 1822. *(Manchester Museum)*

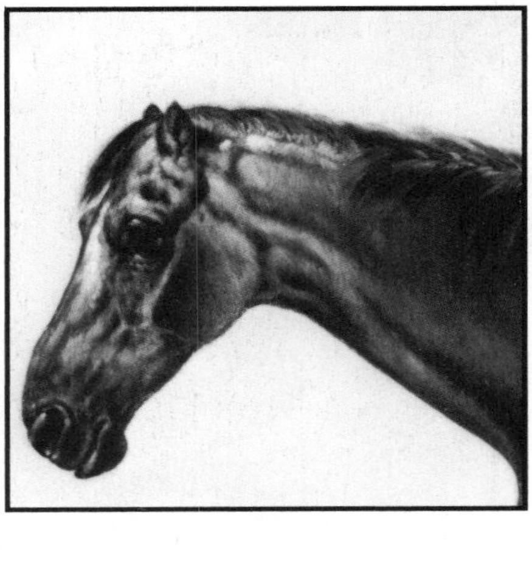

In April 1973 the Belgian mare 'Wilma du Bos' (foaled 15 July 1966), owned by Mrs Virgie Arden of Reno, Nevada, USA was reported to weigh slightly in excess of 3200 lb *1451 kg* when in foal and being shipped from Antwerp. The normal weight of this 18.2-hand *1,88 m* mare is about 2400 lb *1088 kg*. The British weight record is held by the 17.2-hand (5 ft 10 in *1,78 m*) Shire stallion 'Honest Tom 5123' (foaled in 1884), owned by James Forshaw of Littleport, Cambridgeshire, which scaled 2912 lb *1325 kg* in 1891. This poundage may have been exceeded by another huge Shire stallion named 'Great Britain 978', bred by Henry Bultitaft of Ely, Cambridgeshire in 1876, but no weight details are available. In 1888 this horse was sold to Phineas T. Barnum, the American showman, for exhibition purposes.

The heaviest horse living in Britain today is the 17.2 hands (5 ft 10 in *1,78 m*) champion Percheron stallion 'Pinchbeck Union Crest' (foaled 27 Jan 1964), owned by Mr. George Sneath of Pinchbeck, Spalding, Lincs., which has weighed up to 23½ cwt *1194 kg*.

Tallest

The tallest documented horse on record was the Shire gelding named 'Sampson' (later renamed 'Mammoth') bred by Thomas Cleaver of Toddington Mills, Bedfordshire. This horse (foaled in 1846) measured 21.2½ hands (7 ft 2½ in *2,19 m*) in 1850 and was later said to have been 30 cwt 3360 lb *1524 kg*. Britain's tallest living horse is the 19 hand Shire gelding 'Goliath' (foaled 1977) owned by Young & Company's Brewery of Wandsworth, London.

Smallest

The smallest breed of horse is the Falabella of Argentina which was developed over a period of 70 years by inbreeding and crossing a small group of undersized horses originally discovered in the southern part of the country. Most adult specimens stand less than 30 in *76 cm* and average 80–100 lb *36–45 kg*. The smallest mature horse bred by Julio Falabella of Recco de Roca before he died in 1981 was a mare which stood 15 in *38 cm* and weighed 26¼ lb *11,9 kg*. Dr T. H. Hamison of the Circle Veterinary Center, Spartenburg, South Carolina on 30 Nov 1975 certified that the stallion 'Little Pumpkin' (foaled 15 Apr 1973) owned by J. C. Williams Jr. of Della Terra Mini Horse Farm, Inman, South Carolina, USA stood 14 in *35,5 cm* and weighed 20 lb *9,07 kg*.

Oldest

The greatest reliable age recorded for a horse is 62 years in the case of 'Old Billy' (foaled 1760), believed to be a cross between a Cleveland and Eastern blood, who was bred by Mr Edward Robinson of Wild Grave Farm in Woolston, Lancashire. In 1762 or 1763 he was sold to the Mersey and Irwell Navigation Company and remained with them in a working capacity (*i.e.* marshalling and towing barges) until 1819 when he was retired to a farm at Latchford, near Warrington, where he died on 27 Nov 1822. The skull of this horse is preserved in the Manchester Museum, and his stuffed head is now on display in the Bedford Museum. The greatest reliable age recorded for a pony is 54 years for a stallion owned by a farmer in Central France (*fl.* 1919). The greatest age recorded for a thoroughbred racehorse is 42 years in the case of the bay gelding 'Tango Duke' (foaled 1935), owned by Mrs Carmen J. Koper of Barongarook, Victoria, Australia. The horse died on 25 Jan 1978.

Strongest *draught*

The greatest load ever hauled by a pair of draught-horses was allegedly one weighing 144 short tons (130.9 tonnes) which two Clydesdales with a combined weight of 3500 lb *1587 kg* pulled on a sledge litter for a distance of 440 yd *402 m* along a frozen road at the Nester Estate near Ewen, Michigan, USA on 26 Feb 1893, but this tonnage was exaggerated. The load, which comprised 50 logs of white pine scaling 36 055 board feet, actually weighed in the region of 53 short tons *42,3 tonnes*. On 23 April 1924 a Shire gelding named 'Vulcan', owned by Liverpool Corporation, registered a pull equal to a starting load of 29 tons *29,47 tonnes* on a dynamometer at the British Empire Exhibition at Wembley, and a pair of Shires *easily* pulled a starting load of 50 tons *51 tonnes*, the maximum registered on the dynamometer.

DOGS

Guinness Superlatives has published a more specialist book *The Guinness Book of Pet Records* (£7.95) by Gerald L. Wood.

UK dog population 5,800,000 (1984 estimate) compared with 46,000,000 for the USA).

Largest

The heaviest breed of domestic dog (*Canis familiaris*) is the St Bernard. The heaviest recorded example is 'Benedictine Jr Schwarzwald Hof', owned by Thomas and Anne Irwin of Grand Rapids, Michigan, USA. He was whelped in 1982 and weighed 22 st 2 lb *140,6 kg* on 3 Dec 1984 (height at shoulder 39 in *99 cm*). The heaviest dog ever recorded in Britain is 'Heidan Dark Blue' (whelped 23 Apr 1978) also called 'Jason', a St Bernard owned by Nicol Plummer of Skeffington, Leics. In December 1981 he reached a peak 21 st 10¾ lb *138,23 kg* (shoulder height 34 in *86,3 cm*) but by January 1983 he was down to 15 st *95,25 kg* after being put on a diet. Shortly before his death on 4 Nov 1983 he scaled 14 st 10 lb *93,4 kg.*

Tallest

The tallest breeds of dog are the Great Dane and the Irish wolfhound, both of which can exceed 39 in *99 cm* at the shoulder. In the case of the Great Dane the extreme recorded example is 'Shamgret Danzas' (whelped in 1975), owned by Mr and Mrs Peter Comley of Milton Keynes, Bucks. He stood 41½ in *105,4 cm* or 42 in *106,6 cm* when his hackles went up and weighed up to 17 st *108 kg*. He died on 16 Oct 1984. The Irish Wolfhound 'Broadbridge Michael' (1920–29), owned by Mrs Mary Beynon of Sutton-at-Hone, Kent, stood 39½ in *100,3 cm* at the age of 2 years.

Smallest

The world's smallest breeds of dog are the Yorkshire terrier, the Chihuahua and the Toy poodle, *miniature* versions of which have been known to weigh less than 16 oz *453 g* when adult.

The smallest mature dog on record was a matchbox-sized Yorkshire terrier owned by Mr Arthur F. Marples of Blackburn, Lancs, a former editor of the magazine *Our Dogs*. This tiny atom, which died in 1945 aged nearly two years, stood 2½ in *6,3 cm* at the shoulder and measured 3¾ in *9,5 cm* from the tip of its nose to the root of its tail. Its weight was an incredible 4 oz *113 g!*

Oldest

Most dogs live between 8 and 15 years, and authentic records of dogs living over 20 years are rare. The greatest reliable age recorded for a dog is 29 years 5 months for an Australian cattle-dog named 'Bluey', owned by Mr Les Hall of Rochester, Victoria, Australia. The dog was obtained as a puppy in 1910 and worked among cattle and sheep for nearly 20 years. He was put to sleep on 14 Nov 1939. The British record is 27 years 313 days for a Welsh collie named 'Taffy' owned by Mrs Evelyn Brown of Forge

Farm, West Bromwich, W. Midlands. He was whelped on 2 Apr 1952 and died on 9 Feb 1980.

Strength and endurance

The greatest load ever shifted by a dog was 6400½ lb *2905 kg* of railroad steel pulled by a 176 lb *80 kg* St Bernard named 'Ryettes Brandy Bear' at Bothell, Washington, USA on 21 July 1978. The 4-year-old dog, owned by Douglas Alexander of Monroe, Washington, pulled the weight on a four-wheeled carrier across a concrete surface for a distance of 15 ft *4,57 m* in less than 90 sec. Ten days earlier the same dog had moved 6600 lb *2993 kg*, but was 5 in *12,7 cm* short of the 15 ft *4,5 m* minimum distance when the 90 seconds were up. The strongest dog in the world in terms of most proportionate weight hauled is 'Barbara-Allen's Dark Hans', a 97 lb *44 kg* Newfoundland, who pulled 5045½ lb *2289 kg* (= 52 lb *23,5 kg* per lb *0,45 kg* body weight) across a cement surface at Bothell on 20 July 1979. The dog, owned by Miss Terri Dickinson of Kenmore, Washington, was only 12 months old when he made the attempt. The record time for the annual 1049 mile *1688 km* sled race from Anchorage to Nome, Alaska (inaugurated 1973) is 12 days 7 hr 45 min by Rick Swenson's team of dogs in the 1981 race.

Rarest

The world's rarest breed of dog is the Tahltan bear dog, which was formerly used by the Tahltan Indians of western Canada for hunting big game. Until February 1984 it was thought that only two examples of this hound still survived, both of them spayed bitches, one in Atler and one in Carcross in British Columbia, Canada. Paul C. Szabo of Cambden, Maine, USA reported ownership of a 2-year-old dog—a claim not yet fully authenticated.

Guide dog

The longest period of *active service* reported for a guide dog is 13 years 2 months in the case of a Labrador-retriever bitch named 'Polly' (whelped 10 Oct 1956), owned by Miss Rose Resnick of San Rafael, California, USA. The dog was put to sleep on 15 Dec 1971.

Largest litter

The largest recorded litter of puppies is one of 23 thrown on 19 June 1944 by 'Lena', an American foxhound bitch owned by Commander W. N. Ely of Ambler, Pennsylvania, USA. All survived. On 6–7 Feb 1975 'Careless Ann', a St Bernard, owned by Robert and Alice Rodden of Lebanon, Missouri, USA also produced a litter of 23, 14 of which survived. The British record is held by 'Settrina Baroness Medina', (d. 1983) an Irish Red Setter owned by Mgr M. J. Buckley, Director of the Wood Hall Centre, Wetherby, West Yorkshire. The bitch gave birth to 22 puppies, 15 of which survived, on 10 Jan 1974.

Most prolific

The greatest sire of all time was the champion greyhound 'Low Pressure', nicknamed 'Timmy', whelped in September 1957 and owned by Mrs Bruna Amhurst of Regent's Park, London. From December 1961 until his death on 27 Nov 1969 he fathered 2414 registered puppies, with at least 600 others unregistered.

Most valuable

In 1907 Mrs Clarice Ashton Cross of Ascot, Berkshire turned down an offer of £32,000 (equivalent to £865,000 today!) from the American financier and industrialist J. Pierpont Morgan for her famous Pekingese 'Ch. Ch'êrh of Alderbourne' (1904-fl. 1914). Mr Morgan then came back with an 'open' cheque, but again she turned him down.

The largest legacy devoted to dogs was by the oil heiress Eleanor Ritchey who 'left' her 161 dogs $4.3 million in 1968.

Highest and longest jump

The canine 'high jump' record for a leap and a scramble over a smooth wooden wall (without any ribs or other aids) is held by a German shepherd dog named 'Max of Pangoula', who scaled an 11 ft 5⅛ in *3,48 m* wall, at Chikurubi prison's dog training school near Harare, Zimbabwe on 18 Mar 1980. His trainer was Chief Prison Officer Alec Mann. 'Young Sabre', another German shepherd dog, handled by Cpl David Smith scaled a ribbed wall with regulation shallow slats to a height of 11 ft 8 in *3,55 m* at RAF Newton, Nottinghamshire on 17 July 1981. The longest recorded canine long jump was one of 30 ft *9,14 m* by a greyhound named 'Bang' made in jumping a gate in coursing a hare at Brecon Lodge, Gloucestershire in 1849.

Ratting

The greatest ratter of all time was a 26 lb *11,8 kg* 'bull and terrier' dog named 'Billy'. During the five-year period 1820–24 he despatched 4000 rats in 17 hr in matches, a remarkable feat considering that he was blind in one eye. His most notable feat was the killing of 100 rats in 5 min 30 sec at the cockpit in Tufton St, Westminster, London on 23 Apr 1825. He died on 23 Feb 1829 aged 13 yrs. James Searle's famous 'bull and terrier' bitch 'Jenny Lind' was another outstanding ratter. On 12 July 1853 she was backed to kill 500 rats in under 3 hr at 'The Beehive' in Old Crosshall St, Liverpool, and completed the job in 1 hr 36 min.

Tracking

The greatest tracking feat on record was performed by a Dobermann Pinscher named 'Sauer', trained by Detective-Sergeant Herbert Kruger. In 1925 he tracked a stock-thief 100 miles *160 km* across the Great Karroo, South Africa by scent alone. In 1923 a collie dog named 'Bobbie', lost by his owners while they were out on holiday in Wolcott, Indiana, USA, turned up at the family home in Silverton, Oregon 6 months later, after covering a distance of some 2000 miles *3200 km*. The dog, later identified by householders who had looked over him along the route, had apparently travelled back through the states of Illinois, Iowa, Nebraska and Colorado, before crossing the Rocky Mountains in the depths of winter.

Top show dogs

The greatest number of Challenge Certificates won by a dog is the 78 compiled by the famous chow chow 'Ch. U'Kwong King Solomon' (whelped 21 June 1968). Owned and bred by Mrs Joan Egerton of Bramhall, Cheshire, 'Solly' won his first CC at the Cheshire Agricultural Society Championship Show on 4 June 1969, and his 78th CC was awarded at the City of Birmingham Championship Show on 4 Sept 1976. He died on 3 April 1978. The greatest number of 'Best-in-Show' awards won by any dog in all-breed shows is the 158 compiled by the Scottish terrier bitch 'Ch. Braeburn's Close Encounter' (whelped 22 Oct 1978) up to the end of Oct 1984. She is owned by Sonnie Novick of Plantation Acres, Florida, USA.

Show Largest World

At the Ladies Kennel Association Show (LKA) held at the Birmingham National Exhibition Centre on 14–15 Dec 1984 there were 21,212 entries and a total of 14,611 dogs exhibited.

Top trainer

The most successful dog trainer in the world is Mrs Barbara Woodhouse of Rickmansworth, Hertfordshire, who has trained 19,000 dogs to obey the basic commands during the period 1951 to her retirement in 1985. The fastest dog trainer is Mr Armand Rabuttinio of Aston, Pennsylvania, USA. His highest total for a single day (9 am–6 pm) is 132 dogs at a training marathon held at Upland, Pennsylvania on 12 June 1982.

Drug sniffing

The greatest drug-sniffing dog on record was a golden retriever named 'Trep' (whelped 1969), owned by former policeman Tom Kazo of Dade County, Miami, Florida, USA. During the 5-year period 1973–77 'Agent K9–3', as he was also known, sniffed out $63 million (*then £36 million*) worth of narcotics. His owner said he would retire his pet, who could detect 16 different drugs, when he reached the magic $100 million (*then £57 million*) mark, but it is not known whether Trep achieved this target. The only drug-sniffing dog with a 100 per cent arrest record was a German shepherd of the US Army called 'General'. During the period April 1974 to March 1976 this canine detective and his handler, SP4 Michael R. Harris of the 591st Military Police Company in Fort Bliss, Texas, carried out 220 searches for narcotiocs, arrested 220 people for possession and uncovered 330 caches of drugs.

CATS (*UK cat population 4,897,000 (1982 estimate) compared with 42,000,000 for the USA*)

Largest

In the majority of domestic cats (*Felis catus*), the average weight of the male (tom) at maturity is 6.2 lb *2,81 kg*, compared to 5.4 lb *2,45 kg* for the adult female or queen. Neuters and spays average out somewhat heavier. The heaviest domestic cat on record is an eight year old neutered male tabby named 'Himmy' owned by Thomas Vyse of Redlynch, Cairns, Queensland, Australia. On 12 Jan 1985 he weighed 21,3 kg *46 lb 15¼ oz* (neck 15 in *38,1 cm*, waist 33 in *83,8 cm*, length 38 in *96,52 cm*). The heaviest cat ever recorded in Britain is an 11-year-old male tabby called 'Poppa' owned by Miss Gwladys Cooper of Newport, Gwent, S. Wales. He scaled 44½ lb *20,19 kg* in Nov 1984. The largest of the 330 breeds of cat is the ragdoll with males weighing 15–20 lb *6,8–9,07 kg*.

The largest of the 330 known types of domestic breeds of cat—a ragdoll cat which is often triple the weight of the average cat (see above).

LARGEST PET LITTERS

Animal/Breed	Date	No.	Owner
CAT *Burmese/Siamese*	7.8.1970	**15***	Mrs Valerie Gane, Church Westcote, Kingham, Oxfordshire.
DOG *Foxhound*	19.6.1944	**23****	Cdr W. N. Ely, Ambler, Pennsylvania, USA.
DOG *St Bernard*	6/7.2.1975	**23**	R. and A. Rodden, Lebanon, Missouri, USA.
RABBIT *New Zealand White*	1978	**24**	Joseph Filek, Sydney, Cape Breton, Nova Scotia, Canada.
GUINEA PIG (CAVY)	1972	**12**	Laboratory Specimen.
HAMSTER *Golden*	28.2.1974	**26**†	L. and S. Miller, Baton Rouge, Louisiana, USA.
MOUSE *House*	12.2.1982	**34**‡	Marion Ogilvie, Blackpool, Lancs.
GERBIL *Mongolian*	5.1983	**14**	Sharon Kirkman, Bulwell, Nottingham.
GERBIL *Mongolian*	1960's	**15**§	George Meares, genetecist-owner gerbil breeding farm, St Petersburg, Florida, USA.

*4 still born   ** all survived   † 18 killed by mother   ‡ 33 survived   § Uses special food formula

CAGED PET LONGEVITY
The greatest recorded ages for commonly kept pets

Animal/Species	Name, Owner etc.	Years	Months
HAMSTER *Golden*	Reported 1984 Cambridge, England	**19**	—
RABBIT	*Flopsy* caught 6 Aug 1964 d. 29 June 1983 (owner Mrs. L. B. Walker) Longford, Tasmania	**18**	**10¾**
GUINEA PIG	*Snowball* Died: 14 Feb 1979 (owner, M. A. Wall) Bingham, Notts.	**14**	**10½**
GERBIL *Mongolian*	Reported from Longford, Tasmania	**18**	**11**
MOUSE *House*	*Fritzy fl.* Apr 1985 (owner West House School, Edgbaston, Birmingham)	**7**	**6**
RAT *Common*	Died: *c.* 1924 Philadelphia, Pennsylvania, USA.	**5**	**8**

Note: A report of 10 years 2 months for a hamster has been published but details are lacking.

Smallest

The smallest breed of domestic cat is the Singapura or 'Drain Cat' of Singapore. Adult males average 6 lb *2,72 kg* in weight and adult females 4 lb *1,81 kg*. A male Siamese cross named 'Ebony-Eb-Honey Cat' owned by Miss Angelina Johnston of Boise, Idaho, USA tipped the scales at only 1 lb 12 oz *0,79 kg* in February 1984 when aged 23 months.

Oldest

Cats are generally longer-lived than dogs. Information on this subject is often obscured by two or more cats bearing the same nickname in succession. The oldest cat ever recorded was probably the tabby 'Puss', owned by Mrs T. Holway of Clayhidon, Devon who celebrated his 36th birthday on 28 Nov 1939 and died the next day. A more recent and better-documented case was that of the female tabby 'Ma', owned by Mrs Alice St George Moore of Drewsteignton, Devon. This cat was put to sleep on 5 Nov 1957 aged 34.

Largest kindle

The largest litter ever recorded was one of 19 kittens (4 stillborn) delivered by Caesarean section to 'Tarawood Antigone', a 4-year-old brown Burmese, on 7 Aug 1970. Her owner, Mrs Valerie Gane of Church Westcote, Kingham, Oxfordshire, said the result was a mis-mating with a half-Siamese. Of the 15 survivors, 14 were males and one female.

The largest live litter (all of which survived) was one of 14 kittens born in December 1974 to a Persian cat named 'Bluebell', owned by Mrs Elenore Dawson of Wellington, Cape Province, South Africa.

Most prolific

The greatest number of kittens produced by a cat during her breeding life was 420 in the case of a tabby named 'Dusty' (b. 1935) living in Bonham, Texas, USA. She gave birth to her last kindle (a single kitten) on 12 June 1952. The British record is held by another tabby named 'Tippy' of Kingston-upon-Hull, Humberside, who produced her 343rd kitten in June 1933 when aged 21 years.

Richest and most valuable

When Mrs Grace Alma Patterson of Joplin, Missouri, USA died in January 1978 she left her entire estate worth $250,000 (*then £131,000*) to her 18 lb *8,16 kg* white alley cat 'Charlie Chan'. When the cat dies the estate, which includes a three-bedroom house, a 7 acre *2,9 ha* pet cemetery and a collection of valuable antiques, will be auctioned off and the proceeds donated to local and national humane societies. In 1967 Miss Elspeth Sellar of Grafham, Surrey turned down an offer of 2000 guineas (£2100) from an American breeder for her international champion copper-eyed white Persian tom 'Coylum Marcus' (b. 28 Mar 1965) who died on 14 Apr 1978.

Best climber

On 6 Sept 1950 a four-month-old kitten belonging to Josephine Aufdenblatten of Geneva, Switzerland, followed a group of climbers up to the top of the 14,691 ft *4,478 m* Matterhorn in the Alps.

Mousing Champion

The greatest mouser on record is a female tortoiseshell named 'Towser' (b. 21 Apr 1963) owned by Glenturret Distillery Ltd near Crieff, Tayside, Scotland who notched up her 24,621st kill by her 22nd birthday. She averages 3 mice per day.

RABBITS

Largest

The largest breed of domestic rabbit (*Oryctolagus cuniculus*) is the Flemish Giant. Adults weigh 7–8,5 kg *15.4–18.7 lb* (average toe to toe length when fully stretched 36 in *91 cm*), but weights up to 25 lb *11,3 kg* have been reliably reported for this breed. The largest British breed is the Giant Rabbit (British). Adults regularly weigh 12–15 lb *5,4–6,8 kg*, and examples over 20 lb *9 kg* have been recorded. In April 1980 a five month old French lop doe weighing 12 kg *26.45 lb* was exhibited at the Reus Fair, NE Spain.

The heaviest recorded wild rabbit (av. weight 3½ lb *1,58 kg*) was one of 8 lb 4 oz *3,74 kg*, killed by Norman Wilkie of Markinch, Fife, Scotland while ferreting on 20 Nov 1982.

Smallest

In April 1980 a five-month-old French Lop (Belier Francais) doe weighing 12 kg *26.45 lb* was exhibited at the Reus Fair, NE Spain. It was bred and raised on a farm in Omellions (Lerida Province). The ideal weight for this breed is said to be 5,5 kg *12.12 lb*.

Most prolific

The most prolific domestic breeds are the New Zealand white and the Californian. Does produce 5–6 litters a year, each containing 8–12 kittens during their breeding life (*cf.* five litters and three to seven young for the wild rabbit).

HARES

Largest

In November 1956 a Brown hare (*Lepus europaeus*) weighing 15 lb 1 oz *6,83 kg* was shot near Welford, Northamptonshire. The average adult weight is 8 lb *3,62 kg*

2. BIRDS (*Aves*)

Largest *Ratite*

The largest living bird is the North African ostrich (*Struthio camelus camelus*), which is found in reduced numbers south of the Atlas Mountains from Upper Senegal and Niger across to the Sudan and central Ethiopia (*see Table* pp. 26–7).

Largest *Carinate*

The heaviest flying bird or carinate is the Kori bustard or Paauw (*Otis kori*) of East and South Africa. Weights up to 40 lb *18 kg* have been reliably reported for cock birds shot in South Africa. The Mute swan (*Cygnus olor*), which is resident in Britain, can also reach 40 lb *18 kg* on occasion, and there is a record from Poland of a cob weighing 22,5 kg *49.5 lb* which could not fly. The heaviest bird of prey is the Andean condor

(*Vultur gryphus*), adult males averaging 20–25 lb *9,09–11,3 kg*. A weight of 31 lb *14,1 kg* has been claimed for an outsize male Californian condor (*Gymnogyps californianus*) now preserved in the California Academy of Sciences, Los Angeles. This species is appreciably smaller than the Andean condor and rarely exceeds 23 lb *10,4 kg*.

Largest wing span

The Wandering albatross (*Diomedea exulans*) of the southern oceans has the largest wing span of any living bird (*see Table*). The only other bird reliably credited with a wingspread in excess of 11 ft *3,35 m* is the vulture-like Marabou stork (*Leptoptilus crumeniferus*) of Africa. In 1934 a freakish measurement of 13 ft 4 in *4,06 m* was reported for a male shot in Central Africa, but this species rarely exceeds 9 ft *2,43 m*.

Smallest *World*

The smallest bird in the world in the male Bee

The largest of all the 8733 known species of birds—the North African ostrich. They stand up to 9 ft *2,7 m* tall and their eggs take 40 minutes to boil. (*Dr Alan Beaumont*)

One land and one sea bird contest the title for the bird with the largest wing span:

Above the Marabou stork of Africa and *left* the Wandering albatross of the Southern oceans. Uniquely both these two species have been recorded with spans in excess of 11 ft *3,35 m.*

Artwork: Pat Gibbon

Artwork: Eddie Botchway/Matthew Hillier

The bird with a range thousands of miles beyond that of any airliner. A ringed Arctic tern in 1955 was proved to have made a 14,000 miles *22 530 km* flight.

hummingbird (*Mellisuga helenae*) of Cuba and the Isle of Pines (*see Table*). The smallest bird of prey is the 35 g *1.23 g* White-fronted falconet (*Microhierax latifrons*) of NW Borneo which is sparrow-sized. The smallest sea bird is the Least storm petrel (*Halocyptena microsoma*), which breeds on many of the small islands in the Gulf of California, NW Mexico. Adult specimens average 140 mm *5½ in* in total length and weigh *c*. 28 g *1 oz*.

Smallest *Great Britain*

The smallest regularly-breeding British bird is the Goldcrest (*Regulus regulus*), also known as the Golden crested wren or Kinglet. Adult specimens measure 90 mm *3.5 in* total length and weigh between 3,8 and 4,5 g *0.108 and 0.127 oz*.

Most abundant *Wild*

The most abundant species of wild bird is the Red-billed quelea (*Quelea quelea*) (*see Table*). The most abundant sea bird is probably Wilson's storm-petrel (*Oceanites oceanicus*) of the Antarctic. No population estimates have been published, but the number must run into hundreds of millions. Britain's most abundant sea-bird is the Common guillemot (*Uria aalge*) with an estimated 577,000 breeding pairs in 1969–70.

Most abundant *Domestic*

The most abundant species of domesticated bird is the Chicken, the domesticated form of the wild Red jungle fowl (*Gallus gallus*) of south-east Asia. In 1984 there were believed to be about 4,500,000,000 in the world, or about one chicken for every member of the human race. The fowl stock in Britain was estimated at 120,826,000 in 1984, producing 469,150,000 chicks annually.

Most abundant *Great Britain*

The commonest nesting birds found in Great Britain are the House sparrow (*Passer domesticus*), the starling (*Sturnus vulgaris*) and the chaffinch (*Fringilla coelebs*), all of which have a peak breeding population in excess of 5 million pairs. Between 1964 and 1974 the population of the Wren (*Troglodytes troglodytes*) increased tenfold after a series of mild winters, and at the end of this period there were an estimated 10 million pairs. This bird, however, is severely affected by very cold weather and suffered heavy losses during bad winters of 1981–2 and 1984–5. It was estimated in 1984 that 250,000 pigeon fanciers owned an average of 40 racing pigeons per loft, making a population of *c*. 10 million in Great Britain.

Rarest *World*

Because of the practical difficulties involved in assessing bird populations in the wild, it is virtually impossible to establish the identity of the world's rarest living bird (*see Table*). The strongest contenders must be the Ooaa (*Moho braccatus*) of Kauai, Hawaiian Islands, which was down to a single pair in 1980 and the protected Dusty seaside sparrow (*Ammospiza nigrescens*) of Titus Marshes, Florida, USA with only 4 males known in 1984. The world's rarest bird of prey is the Madagascar fish eagle (*Heliaeetus vociferoides*) now down to *c*. 10 pairs.

Rarest *Great Britain*

According to the British Ornithologists' Union there are more than 40 species of birds which have been recorded only once in the British Isles—most of them since the end of the Second World War in 1945. That which has not recurred for the longest period is the Black-capped petrel (*Pterodroma hasitata*), of the West Indies. A specimen was caught alive on a heath at Southacre, near Swaffham, Norfolk in March or April 1850. On 28–29 May 1979 an Aleutian tern (*Sterna aleutica*) was sighted on the Farne Islands, Northumberland. This bird breeds on the coasts of Alaska and eastern Siberia, and until then had never been recorded outside the N. Pacific. The most tenuously established British bird is the Snowy owl (*Nyctea scandiaca*). During the period 1967–75 one pair bred regularly on Fetlar, Shetland Isles and reared a total of 21 young, but soon afterwards the old male took off for an unknown destination, having driven off all the young males, and left the females without a mate. On 19–22 April 1979 an adult male was seen on Fair Isle some 80 miles *129 km* further south, but it did not find its way to Fetlar. A vagrant female was spotted near Walsingham, Durham on 26 Nov 1981. An English vicar stole the eggs of the last White-tailed sea eagle (*Haliaeetus albicilla*) in 1916 on Skye. There are now at least 40 following their re-introduction from Norway to Rhum in 1975.

Fastest and slowest flying

The fastest flying bird in level flight is the White-throated spine-tailed swift (*Hirundapus caudacutus*) (*see Table*). The slowest flying bird is the American woodcock (*Scolopax minor*), which has been timed at 5 mph *8 km/h* without sinking.

The bird which presents the hunter with the greatest difficulty is the Red-breasted merganser (*Mergus serrator*). On 29 May 1960 a specimen flushed from the Kukpuk River, Cape Thompson, northern Alaska, USA by a light aircraft recorded an air speed of 80 mph *128 km/h* in level flight for nearly 13 sec before turning aside. The Spur-winged goose (*Plectropterus gambiensis*) has been timed at 88 mph *142 km/h* in an escape dive.

Fastest and slowest wing beat

The fastest recorded wing beat of any bird is that of the Horned sungem (*Heliactin cornuta*) of tropical South America with a rate of 90 beats a second. Large vultures (Vulturidae) sometimes exhibit a flapping rate as low as one beat per sec, and condors can cruise on air currents for up to 60 miles *96 km* without beating their wings once.

Longest lived

The greatest irrefutable age reported for any bird is 72+ years (*see Table*). The British record is 68+ years in the case of a female European eagle-owl (*Bubo bubo*) which was still alive in 1899. On 28 Oct 1982 the death occurred however of London zoo's famous Greater sulphur crested cockatoo (*Cacatua galerita*) 'Cocky' after spending 57 years in the parrot house. He was already a mature bird when he was acquired by a Mr R. Stevens at the turn of the century, and was thus probably at least 26 years of age when he was presented to the zoo in 1925.

Eggs *Largest*

The largest egg produced by any living bird is that of the ostrich (*Struthio camelus*). The average example measures 6–8 in *15–20 cm* in length, 4–6 in *10–15 cm* in diameter and weighs 3.63–3.88 lb *1,65–1,78 kg* (equal to the volume of two dozen hen's eggs). It requires about 40 min for boiling. The shell, though ¹⁄₁₆ in *1,5 mm* thick, can support the weight of a 20 st *127 kg* man. The largest egg laid by any bird on the British list is that of the Mute swan (*Cygnus olor*), which measures 4.3–4.9 in *109–124 mm* in length and between 2.8 and 3.1 in *71–78,5 mm* in diameter. The weight is 12–13 oz *340–368 g*.

Eggs *Smallest*

The smallest egg laid by any bird is that of the Vervain hummingbird (*Mellisuga minima*) of Jamaica. Two specimens measuring less than 10 mm *0.39 in* in length weighed 0,365 g *0.0128 oz* and 0,375 g *0.0132 oz* respectively (*cf*

0,5 g *0.017 oz* for the Bee hummingbird). The smallest egg laid by a bird on the British list is that of the Goldcrest (*Regulus regulus*), which measures 12,2–14,5 mm *0.48–0.57 in* in length and between 9,4 and 9,9 mm *0.37 and 0.39 in* in diameter with a weight of 0,6 g *0.021 oz.* Eggs emitted from the oviduct before maturity, known as 'sports', are not reckoned to be of significance in discussion of relative sizes.

Incubation *Longest and shortest*
The longest normal incubation period is that of the Wandering albatross (*Diomedea exulans*), with a normal range of 75–82 days. There is an isolated case of an egg of the Mallee fowl (*Leipoa ocellata*) of Australia taking 90 days to hatch against its normal incubation of 62 days. The shortest incubation period is the 10 days of the Great spotted woodpecker (*Dendrocopus major*) and the Blackbilled cuckoo (*Coccyzus erythropthalmus*). The idlest of cock birds include hummingbirds (family Trochilidae), Eider duck (*Somateria mollissima*) and Golden pheasant (*Chrysolophus pictus*) among whom the hen bird does 100 per cent of the incubation, whereas the female Common kiwi (*Apteryx australis*) leaves this to the male for 75–80 days.

Longest flights
The greatest distance covered by a ringed bird is 14,000 miles *22 530 km* by an Arctic tern (*Sterna paradisea*), which was banded as a nestling on 5 July 1955 in the Kandalaksha Sanctuary on the White Sea coast and was captured alive by a fisherman 8 miles *13 km* south of Fremantle, Western Australia on 16 May 1956. The bird had flown south via the Atlantic Ocean and then circled Africa before crossing the Indian Ocean. It did not survive to make the return journey.

Highest flying
The highest acceptable altitude recorded for a bird is just over 27,000 ft *8230 m* for 30 Whooper swans (*Cygnus cygnus*) flying in from Iceland to winter at Lough Foyle, Northern Ireland. They were spotted by an airline pilot over the Outer Hebrides on 9 Dec 1967, and the height was also confirmed by air traffic control in Northern Ireland after the swans had been picked up on radar.

Most airborne
The most aerial of all birds is the Sooty tern (*Sterna fuscata*) which, after leaving the nesting grounds, remains continuously aloft for 3 or 4 years before returning to the breeding grounds. The most aerial land bird is the Common swift (*Apus apus*) which remains 'airborne' for 2–3 years until it is mature enough to breed.

Fastest swimmer
The fastest swimming bird is the Gentoo penguin (*Pygoscelis papua*) which has a maximum burst speed of *c.* 17 mph *27,4 km/h.* The deepest diving bird is the Emperor penguin (*Aptenodytes forsteri*) of the Antarctic which can reach a depth of 265 m *870 ft* and remain submerged for up to 18 min.

Most acute vision
Birds of prey (Falconiformes) have the keenest eyesight in the avian world, and their visual acuity is at least 8–10 times stronger than that of human vision. The Golden eagle (*Aquila chrysaetos*) can detect an 18 in *46 cm* long hare at a range of 2 miles *3,2 km* in good light and against a contrasting background, and a Peregrine falcon (*Falco peregrinus*) can spot a pigeon at a range of over 5 miles *8 km.*

Highest g force
Recent American scientific experiments have revealed that the beak of the Red-headed woodpecker (*Melanerpes erythrocephalus*) hits the bark of a tree with an impact velocity of 13 mph *20,9 km/h.* This means that when the head snaps back the brain is subject to a deceleration of about 10 g.

Feathers *Longest*
The longest feathers grown by any bird are those of the Phoenix fowl or Onagadori (a strain of Red junglefowl *Gallus gallus*) which has been bred in south-western Japan since the mid 17th century. In 1972 a tail covert measuring 10,6 m *34 ft 9½ in* was reported for a rooster owned by Masasha Kubota of Kochi, Shikoku. Among flying birds the two central pairs of tail feathers of Reeve's pheasant (*Syrmaticus reevesi*) of central and northern China can exceed 8 ft *2,43 m.* They serve as an escape brake.

Feathers *Most*
In a series of 'feather counts' on various species of bird a Whistling swan (*Cygnus columbianus*) was found to have 25,216 feathers, 20,177 of which were on the head and neck. The Ruby-throated hummingbird (*Archilochus colubris*) has only 940.

Earliest and latest cuckoo
It is unlikely that the Cuckoo (*Culculus canorus*) has ever been *heard and seen* in Britain earlier than 2 Mar, on which date one was observed under acceptable conditions by Mr William A. Haynes of Trinder Road, Wantage, Oxfordshire in 1972. The two latest dates are 16 Dec 1912 at Anstey's Cove, Torquay, Devon and 26 Dec 1897 or 1898 in Cheshire.

Champion bird-spotter
The world's leading bird-spotter or 'twitcher' is Norman Chesterfield (b. 8 Mar 1913) of Wheatley, Ontario, Canada. By 5 Apr 1984 he had logged exactly 6000 of the 8733 known species. The British life list record is 450 by Ron Johns and the British year list record is 330 by Stephen Webb of Chelmsford, Essex in 1980. On 23–24 Nov 1984 three Kenyan birdwatchers spotted 290 species.

Nests *Largest*
The largest bird's nest on record is one 9½ ft *2,9 m* wide and 20 ft *6 m* deep built by a pair of Bald eagles (*Haliaeetus leucocephalus*) and possibly their successors near St Petersburg, Florida, USA reported in 1963. It weighed more than 3 tons/*tonnes.* The Golden eagle (*Aquila chrysaetos*) also constructs huge nests, and one 15 ft *4,57 m* deep was reported from Scotland in 1954. It had been in use for 45 years. The incubation mounds built by the Mallee fowl (*Leipoa ocellata*) of Australia are much larger, having been measured up to 15 ft *4,57 m* in height and 35 ft *10,6 m* across. The nest site may involve the mounding of matter weighing 300 tonnes *295 tons.*

DOMESTICATED BIRDS

Chicken *Heaviest*
The heaviest breed of chicken is the White Sully which Mr Grant Sullens of West Point, California, USA developed over a period of 7 years by crossing and re-crossing from large Rhode Island Reds with other varieties. One monstrous rooster named 'Weirdo' reportedly weighed 22 lb *10 kg* in January 1973, and was so aggressive that he had already killed two cats and crippled a dog which came too close. The largest chicken reported in Britain was a 17 lb 3 oz *7,78 kg* Cobb capon bred by Mr Henry Ransom of Brancaster Staithe, Dorset and weighed in December 1982.

Chicken flying *for distance*
The record distance flown by a chicken is 310 ft 6 in *94,64 m* by *Shorisha* owned by Morimitzu Meura at Hammatzu, Japan on 8 Mar 1981. Hens are better fliers than cocks.

Turkey *Heaviest*
The greatest dressed weight recorded for a turkey (*Meleagris gallapavo*) is 78 lb 14¾ oz *35,8 kg* for a stag reared by Dale Turkeys of Caynham, Shropshire. It won the annual 'heaviest turkey' competition in London on 15 Dec 1982. Turkeys were introduced into Britain *via* Spain from Mexico in 1549.

Most expensive
The highest price reached at auction (auctioneers Michael Denison CBE and Dulcie Gray CBE) for a turkey was the £3100 paid by Royston Hine of Matthews Butchers, London for a 75 lb *34 kg* stag at Smithfield Market, London on 11 Dec 1984.

Longest lived
The longest lived domesticated bird (excluding the ostrich) is the domestic goose (*Anser anser domesticus*) which normally lives about 25 years. On 16 Dec 1976 a gander named 'George' owned by Mrs Florence Hull of Thornton, Lancashire, died aged 49 years 8 months. He was hatched out in April 1927. The longest lived small cagebird is the canary (*Serinus canaria*). The oldest example on record was a 34-year-old cock bird named 'Joey' owned by Mrs K. Ross of Hull. The bird was purchased in Calabar, Nigeria in 1941 and died on 8 Apr 1975. The oldest budgerigar (*Melopsittacus undulatus*) was a hen bird named 'Charlie' owned by Miss J. Dinsey of Stonebridge, London. She died on 20 June 1977 aged 29 years 2 months.

Most talkative
The world's most talkative bird is a male African grey parrot (*Psittacus erythacus*) named 'Prudle', owned by Mrs Lyn Logue of Golders Green, London, which won the 'Best talking parrot-like bird' title at the National Cage and Aviary Bird Show in London each December for 12 consecutive years (1965–76). Prudle, who has a vocabulary of nearly 800 words, was taken from a nest at Jinja, Uganda in 1958. He retired undefeated.

3. REPTILES *(Reptilia)*

(Crocodiles, snakes, turtles, tortoises and lizards.)

Largest and heaviest
The largest reptile in the world is the Estuarine or Salt-water crocodile (*Crocodylus porosus*) of south-east Asia, northern Australia, New Guinea, the Malay archipelago and the Solomon Islands (*see Table* pp. 26–7).

Smallest
The smallest known species of reptile is believed to be *Sphaerodactylus parthenopion*, a tiny gecko found only on the island of Virgin Gorda, one of the British Virgin Islands, in the West Indies (*see Table*). It is possible that another gecko, *Sphaerodactylus elasmorhynchus*, may be even smaller. The only known specimen was an apparently mature female with a snout-vent length of 17 mm *0.67 in* and a tail the same measurement found on 15 March 1966 among the roots of a tree in the western part of the Massif de la Hotte in Haiti.

The smallest reptile found in Britain is the Viviparous or Common lizard (*Lacerta vivipara*). Adult specimens have an overall length of 118–178 mm *4.64–7.01 in* weighing 8–15 g *0.28–0.53 oz.*

Fastest
The highest speed measured for any reptile on land is 18 mph *29 km/h* for a Six-lined racerunner

(*Cnemidophorus sexlineatus*) (*see Table*). The highest speed claimed for any reptile in water is 22 mph *35 km/h* by a frightened Pacific leatherback turtle (see below).

Lizards *Largest*

The largest of all lizards is the Komodo monitor or Ora (*Varanus komodoensis*), a dragonlike reptile found on the Indonesian islands of Komodo, Rintja, Padar and Flores. Adult males average 225 cm *7 ft 5 in* in length and weigh about 59 kg *130 lb*. Lengths up to 30 ft *9,14 m* (*sic*) have been claimed for this species, but the largest specimen to be accurately measured was a male presented to an American zoologist in 1928 by the Sultan of Bima which taped 3,05 m *10 ft 0.8 in*. In 1937 this animal was put on display in St Louis Zoological Gardens, Missouri, USA for a short period. It then measured 10 ft 2 in *3,10 m* in length and weighed 365 lb *166 kg*. The longest lizard in the world is the slender Salvadori monitor (*Varanus salvadori*) of New Guinea which has been reliably measured up to 15 ft 7 in *4,75 m*.

Lizards *Oldest*

The greatest age recorded for a lizard is more than 54 years for a male Slow worm (*Anguis fragilis*) kept in the Zoological Museum in Copenhagen, Denmark from 1892 until 1946.

Chelonians *Largest*

The largest living chelonian is the Pacific leatherback turtle (*Dermochelys coriacea schlegelii*). The average adult measures 6–7 ft *1,83–2,13 m* in overall length (length of carapace 4–5 ft *122–152 cm*) and weighs up to 1000 lb *453 kg*. The greatest weight reliably recorded is 1908 lb *865 kg* for a male captured off Monterey, California, USA on 29 Aug 1961 measuring 8 ft 4 in *2,54 m* overall. The largest chelonian found in British waters is the Atlantic leatherback turtle (*Dermochelys coriacea coriacea*). A male which drowned off Crail, Fifeshire, Scotland measured 6 ft 4 in *1,93 m* in total length and weighed 772 lb *350 kg*.

The largest living tortoise is *Geochelone gigantea* of the Indian Ocean islands of Aldabra, Mauritius, and the Seychelles (introduced 1874). Adult males in the wild can exceed 450 lb *200 kg* but much heavier specimens have been recorded. A male named 'Marmaduke' received at London Zoo in 1951 recorded a peak weight of 616 lb *279 kg* before his death on 27 Jan 1963.

Chelonians *Longest lived*

The greatest authentic age recorded for a tortoise is 152+ years for a male Marion's tortoise (*Testudo sumeirii*) brought from the Seychelles to Mauritius in 1766 by the Chevalier de Fresne, who presented it to the Port Louis army garrison. This specimen (it went blind in 1908) was accidentally killed in 1918. When the famous Royal Tongan tortoise 'Tu'malilia' (believed to be a specimen of *Testudo radiata*) died on 19 May 1966 it was reputed to be over 200 years old, having been presented to the then King of Tonga by Captain James Cook (1728–79) on 22 Oct 1773, but this record may well have been conflated between two (or more) overlapping residents. The greatest proven age of a continuously observed tortoise is 116+ years for a Mediterranean spur-thighed tortoise (*Testudo graeca*) (*see Table*).

Chelonians *Slowest moving*

In a recent 'speed' test carried out in the Seychelles a male giant tortoise (*Geochelone gigantea*) could only cover 5 yd *4,57 m* in 43.5 sec (0.23 mph *0,37 km/h*) despite the enticement of a female tortoise. The National Tortoise Championship record is 18 ft *5,48 m* up a 1 : 12 gradient in 43.7 sec, 0.28 mph *0,45 km/h* by 'Charlie' at Tickhill, South Yorkshire on 2 July 1977.

SNAKES

Longest *World*

The longest of all snakes (average adult length) is the Reticulated python (*Python reticulatus*) of south-east Asia, Indonesia and the Philippines (*see Table*).

Longest *In captivity*

The longest (and heaviest) snake ever held in captivity was a female Reticulated python (*Python reticulatus*) named 'Colossus' who died in Highland Park Zoo, Pennsylvania, USA on 15 Apr 1963. She measured 28 ft 6 in *8,68 m* in length, and scaled 320 lb *145 kg* at her heaviest. Another female reticulated python 'Cassius', owned by Mr. Adrian Nyoka of Knaresborough Zoo, North Yorkshire measured about 25 ft 6 in *7,77 m* at the time of her death on 3 Apr 1980. She yielded a 29 ft *8,84 m* skin.

Longest *British*

The longest snake found in Britian is the Grass snake (*Natrix natrix*), which is found throughout southern England, parts of Wales and in Dumfries and Galloway, Scotland. Adult males average 660 mm *26 in* in length and adult females 760 mm *29.92 in*. The longest accurately measured specimen was probably a female killed in South Wales in 1887 which measured 1775 mm *5 ft 10 in*.

Shortest

The shortest known snake is the Thread snake *Leptotyphlops bilineata*, which is found on the islands of Martinique, Barbados and St Lucia in the West Indies (*see Table*). The shortest venomous snake is the Spotted dwarf adder (*Bitis paucisquamata*) of Little Namaqualand, South West Africa, with adults averaging 9 in *228 mm* in length.

Heaviest

The heaviest snake is the Anaconda (*Eunectes murinus*) (*see Table*). The heaviest venomous snake is the Eastern diamond-back rattlesnake (*Crotalus adamanteus*) of the south-eastern United States. One specimen measuring 7 ft 9 in *2,36 m* in length weighed 34 lb *15 kg*. Less reliable lengths up to 8 ft 9 in *2,66 m* and weights up to 40 lb *18 kg* have been reported. In February 1973 a posthumous weight of 28 lb *12,75 kg* was reported for a 14 ft 5 in *4,39 m* long King cobra (*Ophiophagus hannah*) at New York Zoological Park (Bronx Zoo).

Venomous *Longest and Shortest*

The longest venomous snake in the world is the King cobra (*Ophiophagus hannah*) (*see Table*).

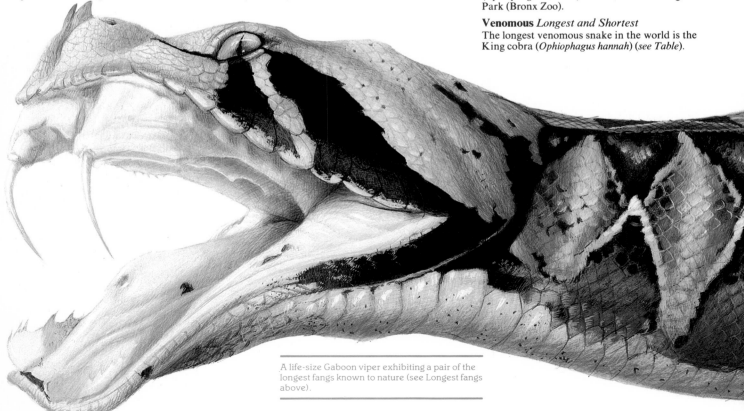

A life-size Gaboon viper exhibiting a pair of the longest fangs known to nature (see Longest fangs above).

Oldest

The greatest irrefutable age recorded for a snake is 40 years 3 months and 14 days for a male Common boa (*Boa constrictor constrictor*) (*see Table*).

Fastest moving

The fastest moving land snake is probably the slender Black mamba (*Dendroaspis polylepis*) (*see Table*). A speed of 10–12 mph *16–19 km/h* may be possible for short bursts over level ground. The British grass snake (*Natrix natrix*) has a maximum speed of 4.2 mph *6,8 km/h.*

Most venomous *World*

The world's most venomous snake is the sea snake *Hydrophis belcheri* which has a venom one hundred times as toxic as that of the Australian taipan (*Oxyuranus scutellatus*). The snake abounds round Ashmore Reef in the Timor Sea, off the coast of North West Australia. The most venomous land snake is the Small scaled or Western taipan (*Oxyuranus microlepidotus*) of the Diamantina River and Cooper's Creek drainage bases in Channel County, Queensland which has a venom nine times as toxic as that of the Tiger snake (*Notechis scutatus*) of South Australia and Tasmania. One specimen yielded 110 mg *0.00385 oz* of venom after milking, a quantity sufficient to kill 125,000 mice. On the Amami Islands in the Ryukyu group, SW Japan there is an incidence of one snakebite case per 500 people per annum from the aggressive Okinawa habu (*Trimeresurus flavavirdes*). With modern treatments mortality is now only 3 per cent.

Most venomous *Britain*

The only venomous snake in Britain is the adder (*Vipera berus*). Since 1890 ten people have died after being bitten by this snake, including six children. The most recently recorded death was on 1 July 1975 when a 5-year-old was bitten at Callander, Central Scotland and died 44 hr later. The longest-recorded specimen was a female measuring 43½ in *110,5 cm* which was killed by Graham Perkins of Paradise Farm, Pontrilas, Hereford & Worcester in August 1977.

Rarest

The rarest snake in the world is the Keel-scaled boa (*see Table*). The rarest snake of Britain's 3 indigenous species is the Smooth snake (*Coronella austriaca*) of southern England. A localised population of the harmless *Elaphe longissima* found in southern Europe and Asia Minor has established itself in the Colwyn Bay area, North Wales following the escape of a gravid female in the early 1960s.

Longest fangs

The longest fangs of any snake are those of the highly venomous Gaboon viper (*Bitis gabonica*) of tropical Africa. In a 6 ft *1,83 m* long specimen they measured 50 mm *1.96 in*. On 12 Feb 1963 a Gaboon viper bit itself to death in the Philadelphia Zoological Gardens, Philadelphia, Pennsylvania, USA. Keepers found the dead snake with its fangs deeply embedded in its own back.

4. AMPHIBIANS (*Amphibia*)

Largest *World*

The largest species of amphibian is the Chinese giant salamander (*Andrias davidianus*), which lives in the cold mountain streams and marshy areas of north-eastern, central and southern China (*see Table* pp. 26–7).

Largest *Britain*

The heaviest British amphibian is the Common toad (*Bufo bufo*) of which a female has been weighed at 118 g *4.16 oz.*

The longest is the Warty or Great crested newt (*Triturus cristatus*). One female specimen collected at Hampton, Greater London measured 162 mm *6.37 in* in total length.

Smallest *World and Britain*

The smallest species of amphibian is the frog *Sminthillus limbatus*, found only in Cuba (*see Table*). The smallest amphibian found in Britain is the Palmate newt (*Triturus helveticus*). Adult specimens measure 7,5–9,2 cm *2.95–3.62 in* in total length and weigh up to 2,39 g *0.083 oz*. The Natterjack or Running toad (*Bufo calamita*) has a maximum snout-vent length of only 80 mm *3.14 in* (female) but it is a bulkier animal.

Longest lived

The greatest authentic age recorded for an amphibian is 55 years for a Japanese giant salamander (*Andrias japonicus*) (*see Table*).

Rarest *World and Britain*

The rarest amphibian in the world is the Israel painted frog (*Discoglossus nigriventer*) (*see Table*). Britain's rarest amphibian is the Natterjack toad (see above). In 1983 the total population was estimated at 20,000, a third of them living among the sand dunes between Southport and Liverpool.

Highest and lowest

The greatest altitude at which an amphibian has been found is 8000 m *26,246 ft* for a Common toad (*Bufo vulgaris*) collected in the Himalayas. This species has also been found at a depth of 340 m *1115 ft* in a coal mine.

Most poisonous

The most active known poison is the batrachotoxin derived from the skin secretions of the Golden dart-poison frog (*Phyllobates terribilis*) of western Colombia, South America, which is at least 20 times more toxic than that of any other known dart-poison frog. An average adult specimen contains enough poison (1100 mg *0.038 oz*) to kill 2200 people.

Newt *Largest world*

The largest newt in the world is the Pleurodele or Ribbed newt (*Pleurodeles waltl*), which is

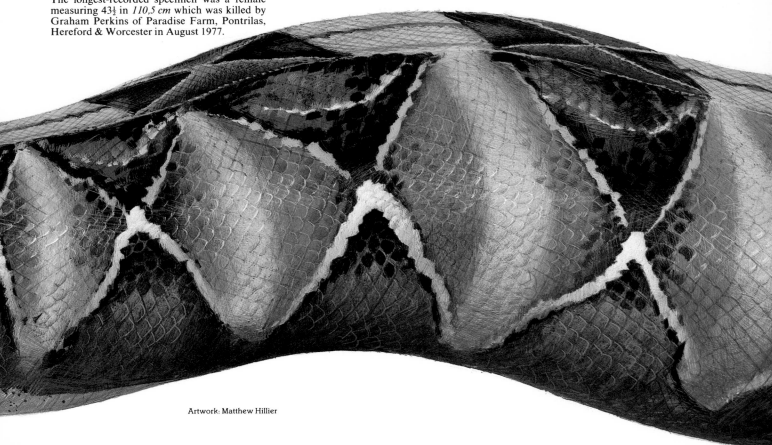

Artwork: Matthew Hillier

found in Morocco and on the Iberian Peninsula. Specimens measuring up to 40 cm *15.74 in* in total length and weighing over 1 lb *450 g* have been reliably reported.

Newt *Smallest world*
The smallest newt in the world is believed to be the Striped newt (*Notophthalmus perstriatus*) of the south-eastern United States. Adult specimens average 51 mm *2.01 in* in total length.

Frog *Largest World*
The largest known frog is the rare Goliath frog (*Rana goliath*) of Cameroun and Equatorial Guinea. A female weighing 3306 g *7 lb 4.5 oz* was caught in the River Mbia, Equatorial Guinea on 23 Aug 1960. It had a snout–vent length of 34 cm *13.38 in* and measured 81,5 cm *32.08 in* overall with legs extended.

Frog *Largest Britain*
The largest frog found in Britain is the *introduced* Marsh frog (*Rana r. ridibunda*). Adult males have been measured up to 96 mm *3.77 in* snout to vent, and adult females up to 133 mm *5.25 in*, the weight ranging from 60 to 95 g *1.7–3 oz*.

Longest jump
(*Competition Frog Jumps are invariably triple jumps*). The record for three consecutive leaps is 10,3 m *33 ft 5½ in* by a female South African sharp-nosed frog (*Rana oxyrhyncha*) named 'Santjie' at a frog Derby held at Lurula Natal Spa, Paulpietersburg, Natal on 21 May 1977. The record at the famous annual Calaveras Jumping Jubilee at Angels Camp, California is 20 ft 3⅜ in by Bruce Hamilton's 'Johnny Jumper'. 'Santjie' would have been ineligible because Calaveras entrants must measure at least 4 in *10,16 cm* 'stem to stern'.

Tree frog *Largest*
The largest species of Tree frog is *Hyla vasta*, found only on the island of Hispaniola (Haiti and the Dominican Republic) in the West Indies. The average snout–vent length is about 9 cm *3.54 in* but a female collected from the San Juan River, Dominican Republic, in March 1928 measured 14,3 cm *5.63 in*.

Tree frog *Smallest*
The smallest tree frog in the world is the Least tree frog (*Hyla ocularis*), found in the south-eastern United States. It has a maximum snout–vent length of 15,8 mm *0.62 in*.

Though the largest of all frogs the Goliath frog of the Cameroun is too massive to leap record distances. (*Jorge Sabaterpi*)

Toad *Largest World*
The most massive toad in the world is probably the Marine toad (*Bufo marinus*) of tropical South America. An enormous female collected on 24 Nov 1965 at Miraflores Vaupes, Colombia and later exhibited in the Reptile House at Bronx Zoo, New York City, USA had a snout–vent length of 23,8 cm *9.37 in* and weighed 1302 g *2 lb 11¼ oz* at the time of its death in 1967.

Toad *Largest Britain*
The largest toad and heaviest amphibian found in Britain is the Common toad (*Bufo bufo*). An outsized female collected in Kent with a snout–vent length 99 mm *3.89 in* weighed 118 g *4.16 oz*.

Toad *Smallest World*
The smallest toad in the world is the sub-species *Bufo taitanus beiranus*, first discovered in *c.* 1906 near Beira, Mozambique, East Africa. Adult specimens have a maximum recorded snout–vent length of 24 mm *0.94 in*.

5. FISHES (*Agnatha, Gnathostomata*)

Largest marine *World*
The largest fish in the world is the rare plankton-feeding Whale shark (*Rhincodon typus*), which is found in the warmer areas of the Atlantic, Pacific and Indian Oceans. The taxonomic name has been variously spelt Rhiniodon; Rhineodon; Rhincodon (1829) and Rhinodon (1840). It is not, however, the largest marine animal, since it is smaller than the larger species of whales (mammals) (*see Table* pp. 26–7). The largest carnivorous fish (excluding plankton eaters) is the comparatively rare Great white shark (*Carcharodon carcharias*), also called the 'Maneater', which ranges from the tropics to temperate zone waters. Adult specimens (females are larger than males) average 14–15 ft *4,3–4,6 m* in length and generally scale between 1150–1700 lb *522–771 kg* but larger individuals have been recorded. A 21 ft *6,4 m* specimen caught off Castillo de Cojimar, Cuba in May 1945 weighed 7302 lb *3312 kg*. A 21 ft 4 in *6,5 m* female was caught near Hobart, Tasmania in June 1983 but weighed 4500 lb *2040 kg*.

The longest of the bony or 'true' fishes (Pisces) is the Oarfish (*Regalecus glesne*), also called the 'King of the Herrings', which has a worldwide distribution. In *c.* 1885 a 25 ft *7,6 m* long example weighing 600 lb *272 kg* was caught by fishermen off Pemaquid Point, Maine, USA. Another oarfish, seen swimming off Asbury Park, New Jersey by a team of scientists from the Sandy Hook Marine Laboratory on 18 July 1963, was estimated to measure 50 ft *15,2 m* in length. The heaviest bony fish in the world is the Ocean sunfish (*Mola mola*), which is found in all tropical, sub-tropical and temperate waters. On 18 Sept 1908 a huge specimen was accidentally struck by the SS *Fiona* off Bird Island about 40 miles *65 km* from Sydney, New South Wales, Australia and towed to Port Jackson. It measured 14 ft *4,26 m* between the anal and dorsal fins and weighed 4927 lb *2235 kg*.

Britain
The largest fish ever recorded in the waters of the British Isles was a 36 ft 6 in *11,12 m* Basking shark (*Cetorhinus maximus*) washed ashore at Brighton, East Sussex in 1806. It weighed an estimated 8 tons/*tonnes*. The largest bony fish found in British waters is the Ocean sunfish (*Mola mola*). A specimen weighing 800 lb *363 kg* stranded near Montrose, Scotland on 14 Dec 1960 was sent to the Marine Research Institute in Aberdeen.

Largest freshwater *World*
The largest fish which spends its whole life in fresh or brackish water is the rare Pa beuk or Pla buk (*Pangasianodon gigas*) (*see Table*). This size *was* exceeded by the European catfish or Wels (*Silurus glanis*) in earlier times (in the 19th century lengths up to 15 ft *4,57 m* and weights up to 720 lb *336,3 kg* were reported for Russian specimens), but today anything over 6 ft *1,83 m* and 200 lb *91 kg* is considered large. The Arapaima (*Arapaima glanis*), also called the Pirarucu, found in the Amazon and other South American rivers and often claimed to be the largest freshwater fish, averaged 6½ ft *2 m* and 150 lb *68 kg*. The largest 'authentically recorded' measured 8 ft 1½ in *2,48 m* in length and weighed 325 lb *147 kg*. It was caught in the Rio Negro, Brazil in 1836. In September 1978, a Nile perch (*Lates niloticus*) weighing 416 lb *188,6 kg* was netted in the eastern part of Lake Victoria, Kenya.

Largest freshwater *Britain*
The largest fish ever caught in a British river was a Common sturgeon (*Acipenser sturio*) weighing 507½ lb *230 kg* and measuring 9 ft *2,74 m*, which was accidentally netted in the Severn at Lydney, Gloucestershire on 1 June 1937. Larger specimens have been taken at sea—notably one weighing 700 lb *317 kg* and 10 ft 5 in *3,18 m* long netted by the trawler *Ben Urie* off Orkney and landed on 18 Oct 1956.

Smallest
The shortest and lightest freshwater fish is the Dwarf pygmy goby (*Pandaka pygmaea*) (*see table*). The shortest recorded marine fish—and the shortest known vertebrate—is the Dwarf goby *Trimmatom nanus* of the Chagos Archipelago, central Indian Ocean. In one series of 92 specimens collected by the 1978–9 Joint Services Chagos Research Expedition of the British Armed Forces the adult males averaged 8,6 mm *0.338 in* in length and the adult females 8,9 mm *0.35 in*. The lightest of all vertebrates and the smallest catch possible for any fisherman is the Dwarf goby *Schindleria praematurus* from Samoa which measures 12–19 mm *0.47–0.74 in*. Mature specimens have been known to weigh only 2 mg, which is equivalent to *17,750 to the oz*. The smallest British marine fish is Guillet's goby (*Lebutus guilleti*) which does not exceed 24 mm *0.94 in*. It has been recorded from the English Channel, the west coast of Ireland and the Irish Sea. The smallest known shark is the Long-faced dwarf shark (*Squaliolus laticaudus*) of the western Pacific which does not exceed 150 mm *5.9 in*.

The world's smallest commercial fish is the now endangered Sinarapan (*Mistichthys luzonensis*), a goby found only in Lake Buhi, Luzon. Adult males measure 10–13 mm *0.39–0.51 in* in length, and a dried 1 lb *454 g* fish cake contains about 70,000 of them!

Fastest
The Cosmopolitan sailfish (*Istiophorus platypterus*) is generally considered to be the fastest species of fish, although the practical difficulties of measurement make data extremely difficult to secure. A figure of 68 mph *109 km/h* (100 yd *91 m* in 3 sec) has been cited for one off Long Key, Florida, USA. The swordfish (*Xiphias gladius*) has also been credited with very high speeds, but the evidence is based mainly on bills that have been found deeply embedded in ships' timbers. A speed of 50 knots (57.6 mph *92,7 km/h*) has been calculated from a penetration of 22 in *56 cm* by a bill into a piece of timber, but 30–35 knots (35–40 mph *56–64 km/h*) is the most conceded by some experts. A Wahoo (*Acantho-cybium solandri*), 1,1 m *43 in* in length is capable of attaining a speed of 77 km/h *47.8 mph*.

Longest lived

Aquaria are of too recent origin to be able to establish with certainty which species of fish can be regarded as being the longest lived. Early indications are, however, that it may be the Lake sturgeon (*Acipenser fulvescens*) of North America (*see Table*). In July 1974 a growth ring count of 228 years (*sic*) was reported for a female Koi fish, a form of fancy carp, named 'Hanako' living in a pond in Higashi Shirakawa, Gifu Prefecture, Japan, but the greatest authoritatively accepted age for this species is 'more than 50 years'. In 1948 the death was reported of an 88-year-old female European eel (*Anguilla anguilla*) named 'Putte' in the aquarium at Halsingborg Museum, southern Sweden. She was allegedly born in the Sargasso Sea, North Atlantic in 1860, and was caught in a river as a three year old elver.

Oldest goldfish

Goldfish (*Carassius auratus*) have been reported to live for over 40 years in China. The British record is held by a specimen named 'Fred' owned by Mr A. R. Wilson of Worthing, Sussex, which died on 1 Aug 1980, aged 41 years.

Shortest lived

The shortest-lived fishes are probably certain species of the sub-order Cyprinodontei (Killifish) found in Africa and South America which normally live about eight months.

Most abundant

The most abundant species of fish in the world is the 3 in *76 mm* long deep-sea Bristlemouth *Cyclothone elongata* which has a worldwide distribution.

Deepest

The greatest depth from which a fish has been recovered is 8300 m *27,230 ft* in the Puerto Rico Trench (27,488 ft *8366 m*) in the Atlantic by Dr Gilbert L. Voss of the US research vessel *John Elliott* who took a 6½ in *16,5 cm* long *Bassogigas profundissimus* in April 1970. It was only the fifth such brotulid ever caught. Dr Jacques Picard and Lieutenant Don Walsh, US Navy, reported they saw a sole-like fish about 1 ft *33 cm* long (tentatively identified as *Chascanopsetta lugubris*) from the bathyscaphe *Trieste* at a depth of 35,810 ft *10 915 m* in the Challenger Deep (Marianas Trench) in the western Pacific on 24 Jan 1960. This sighting, however, has been questioned by some authorities, who still regard the brotulids of the genus *Bassogigas* as the deepest-living vertebrates.

Most and least eggs

The Ocean sunfish (*Mola mola*) produces up to 300,000,000 eggs, each of them measuring about 0.05 in *1,3 mm* in diameter at a single spawning. The egg yield of the Tooth carp *Jordanella floridae* of Florida, USA is only *c.* 20 over a period of several days.

Most valuable

The world's most valuable fish is the Russian sturgeon (*Huso huso*). One 2706 lb *1227 kg* female caught in the Tikhaya Sosna River in 1924 yielded 541 lb *245 kg* of best quality caviare.

Dr Takayaki Hosogi, the owner of a 7 year old 35 in *89 cm* long fancy carp called 'Fujitavo', which won the All-Japan Koi Championship on 1 Mar 1982, has since refused an offer of £69,400 for this specimen.

Most venomous

The most venomous fish in the world are the Stonefish (*Synanceiidae*) of the tropical waters of the Indo-Pacific, and in particular *Synanceja horrida* which has the largest venom glands of any known fish. Direct contact with the spines of its fins, which contain a strong neurotoxic poison, often proves fatal.

Most electric

The most powerful electric fish is the Electric eel (*Electrophorus electricus*), which is found in the rivers of Brazil, Colombia, Venezuela and Peru. An average sized specimen can discharge 400 volts at 1 ampere, but measurements up to 650 volts have been recorded.

6. STARFISHES (*Asteroidea*)

Largest

The largest of the 1600 known species of starfish in terms of total arm span is the very fragile Brisingid *Midgardia xandaros*. A specimen collected by the Texas A & M University research vessel *Alaminos* in the southern part of the Gulf of Mexico in the late summer of 1968, measured 1380 mm *54.33 in* tip to tip, but the diameter of its disc was only 26 mm *1.02 in*. Its dry weight was 70 g *2.46 oz*. The heaviest species of starfish is the five-armed *Thromidia catalai* of the Western Pacific. One specimen collected off Ilot Amedee, New Caledonia on 14 Sept 1969 and later deposited in Noumea Aquarium weighed an estimated 6 kg *13.2 lb* (total arm span 630 mm *24.8 in*). The largest starfish found in British waters is the Spiny starfish (*Marthasterias glacialis*). In January 1979 Jonathon MacNeil of the Isle of Barra, Western Isles, found a specimen on the beach which originally spanned 30 in *76,2 cm*.

Smallest

The smallest known starfish is *Asterina phylactica*, found in the Adriatic and the Mediterranean as well as waters off south-western Britain, which is not known to exceed 15 mm *0.58 in* in diameter.

Deepest

The greatest depth from which a starfish has been recovered is 7584 m *24,881 ft* for a specimen of *Porcellanaster ivanovi* collected by the USSR research ship *Vityaz* in the Marianas Trench, in the West Pacific *c.* 1962.

7. ARACHNIDS (*Arachnida*)

SPIDERS (order Araneae)

Largest *World*

The world's largest known spiders in terms of leg-span are the bulky theraphosid spiders of the genera *Lasiodora* and *Grammostola* of Brazil, and *Theraphosa* of NE South America, all of which have been credited with leg spans in excess of 10 in *250 mm* (*see Table* pp. 26–7).

Largest *Britain*

Of the 617 known British species of spider covering an estimated population of over 500,000,000,000, the Cardinal spider (*Tegenaria gigantea*) of Southern England has the greatest leg span. On 24 Sept 1983 Mr Craig Stangroom of Little Odell, Bedfordshire collected an outsized female in his garden which had a span of at least 143 mm *5.63 in*. The well-known 'Daddy Longlegs' spider (*Pholcus phalangioides*) rarely exceeds 4½ in *114 mm* in leg span, but one outsized specimen collected in England measured 6 in *15,2 cm* across. The heaviest spider found in Britain is the Orb weaver *Araneus quadratus*. On 10 Sept 1979 a female weighing 2,25 g *0.079 oz*

Jonathon from the MacNeil family of Barra with the 2½ ft *76,2 cm* span star fish he found in 1979. (*BBC TV Record Breakers*)

was collected at Lavington, Sussex by J. R. Parker.

Smallest *World and Britain*

The smallest known spider is *Patu marplesi* (family Symphytognathidae) of Western Samoa (*see Table*).

Britain's smallest spider is the extremely rare Money spider *Clyphesis cottonae* found only in a swamp near Beaulieu Road Station, Hampshire and on Thursley Common, Surrey. Adult specimens of both sexes have a body length of 1 mm *0.039 in*.

Rarest

The most elusive of all spiders are the rare Trapdoor spiders of the genus *Liphistius*, which are found in south-east Asia (*see Table*). The most elusive spiders in Britain are the four species which are known only from the holotype specimen. These are the jumping spiders *Salticus mutabilis* (1 male Bloxworth, Dorset, 1860) and *Heliophanus melinus* (1 female Bloxworth, 1870); the Crab spider *Philodromus buxi* (1 female Bloxworth pre-1879); and the Cobweb spider *Robertus insignis* (1 male Norwich, 1906).

Commonest *World and Britain*

For world's commonest see Table. The commonest spider in Britain is the Orb weaver *Araneus diadematus*, which has been recorded from all but four counties of Great Britain and Ireland.

Fastest

The highest speed recorded for a spider on a level surface is by *Tegenaria gigantea* (*see Table*). This is 33 times her body length per sec compared with the human record of 5½ times.

Longest lived

The longest lived of all spiders are the primitive *Mygalomorphae* (tarantulas and allied species) (*see Table*). The longest-lived British spider is probably the Purse web spider (*Atypus affinis*). One specimen was kept in a greenhouse for nine years.

Largest and smallest webs

The largest webs are the aerial ones spun by the tropical orb weavers of the genus *Nephila*, which have been measured up to 18 ft 9¾ in *573 cm* in circumference. The smallest webs are spun by spiders such as *Glyphesis cottonae*, (see above) which cover about 0.75 in² *480 mm²*.

Most venomous

The most venomous spiders in the world are the Brazilian wandering spiders of the genus *Phoneutria*, and particularly *P. fera*, which has the most active neurotoxic venom of any living spider. These large and highly aggressive creatures frequently enter human dwellings and hide in clothing or shoes. When disturbed they bite furiously several times, and hundreds of accidents involving these species are reported annually. Fortunately an effective antivenin is available, and when deaths do occur they are usually children under the age of seven.

8. CRUSTACEANS
(Crustacea)

(Crabs, lobsters, shrimps, prawns, crayfish, barnacles, water fleas, fish lice, woodlice, sandhoppers, krill, etc.)

Largest *World*

The largest of all crustaceans (although not the heaviest) is the Sanschouo or Giant spider crab (*Macrocheira kaempferi*), also called the Stilt crab, which is found in deep waters off the south-eastern coast of Japan (*see Table* pp. 26–7).

Largest *Britain*

The largest crustacean found in British waters is the Common or European lobster (*Homarus vulgaris*), which averages 2–3 lb *900–1360 g*. In June 1931 an outsized specimen weighing 20½ lb *5,80 kg* and measuring 4 ft 1½ in *1,26 m* in total length, was caught in a caisson during the construction of No. 3 jetty at Fowey, Cornwall. Its crushing claw weighed 2 lb 10 oz *1188 g* after the meat had been removed. The largest crab found in British waters is the Edible or Great crab (*Cancer pagurus*). In 1895 a crab measuring 11 in *279 mm* across the shell and weighing 14 lb *6,35 kg* was caught off the coast of Cornwall.

Smallest

The smallest known crustaceans are water fleas of the genus *Alonella*, which may measure less than 0,25 mm *0.0098 in* in length (*see Table*). They are found in British waters.

Longest lived

The longest lived of all crustaceans is the American lobster (*Homarus americanus*) (*see Table*).

Vertical distribution

The greatest depth from which a crustacean has been recovered is 10 500 m *34,450 ft* for *live* amphipods from the Challenger Deep, Marianas Trench, West Pacific by the US research vessel *Thomas Washington* in November 1980. Amphipods and isopods have also been collected in the Ecuadorean Andes at a height of 13,300 ft *4053 m*.

9. INSECTS *(Insecta)*

Heaviest *World*

The heaviest insects in the world are the Goliath beetles (family *Scarabaeidae*) of equatorial Africa. The largest members of the group are *Goliathus regius* and *Goliathus goliathus* (= *giganteus*) (*see Table* pp. 26–7).

Heaviest *Britain*

The heaviest insect found in Britain is the Stag beetle (*Lucanus cervus*) which is widely distributed over southern England. The largest specimen on record was a male collected at Sheerness, Kent, in 1871 and now preserved in the British

BRITAIN'S RAREST BUTTERFLIES

The rarest of Britain's 59 species of indigenous butterflies. *Top*, the Chequered Skipper (*Carternocephalus palaemon*) found only in Fort William and, *below*, the Heath fritillary (*Melitaea athalia*) found only in Kent and in Cornwall.

Artwork: Eddie Botchway / Matthew Hillier

Museum (Natural History), London, which measures 87,4 mm *3.04 in* in length (body plus mandibles) and probably weighed over 6000 mg *0.21 oz* when alive.

Rarest

It was estimated by Dr Erwin (USA) in 1982 that there may be 30 million species of insect—more than all other classes put together. Many are single holotypes.

BUTTERFLIES AND MOTHS (order Lepidoptera)

Largest *World*

The largest known butterfly is the protected Queen Alexandra's birdwing (*Ornithoptera alexandrae*) which is restricted to the Popondetta Plain in Papua New Guinea. Females may have a wing span exceeding 280 mm *11.02 in* and weigh over 5 g *0.176 oz*. The largest moth in the world (although not the heaviest) is the Hercules moth (*Cosdinoscera hercules*) of tropical Australia and New Guinea. A wing area of up to 40.8 in² *263,2 cm²* and a wing span of 280 mm *11 in* have been recorded. In 1948 an unconfirmed measurement of 360 mm *14.17 in* was reported for a female captured near the post office at the coastal town of Innisfail, Queensland, Australia now in the Oberthur collection. The rare Owlet moth (*Thysania agrippina*) of Brazil has been measured up to 12.16 in *308 mm* wing span in the case of a female taken in 1934 and now in the collection of John G. Powers in Ontario, Canada.

Largest *Britain*

The largest (but not the heaviest) of the 21,000 species of insect found in Britain is the very rare Death's head hawkmoth (*Acherontia atropos*). One female found dead in a garden at Tiverton, Devon, in 1931 had a wing span of 5.75 in *145 mm* and weighed nearly 3 g *0.10 oz*. The largest butterfly found in Britain is the Monarch butterfly (*Danaus plexippus*), also called the Milkweed or Black-veined brown butterfly, a rare vagrant which breeds in the southern United States and Central America. It has a wing span of up to 5 in *127 mm* and weighs about 1 g *0.04 oz*. The largest *native* butterfly is the Swallowtail (*Papilio machaon britannicus*), females of which have a wing span up to 100 mm *3.93 in*. This species is now confined to a few fens in Suffolk, Cambridgeshire and the Norfolk Broads.

Smallest *World and Britain*
The smallest of the 140,000 known species of Lepidoptera are the moths *Johanssonia acetosea* found in Britain, and *Stigmella ridiculosa* from the Canary Islands, which have a wing span of *c.* 2 mm *0.08 in* with a similar body length. The world's smallest known butterfly is the Dwarf blue (*Brephidium barberae*) of South Africa. It has a wing span of 14 mm *0.55 in*. The smallest butterfly found in Britain is the Small blue (*Cupido minimus*), which has a wing span of 19–25 mm *0.75–1.0 in*.

Rarest *World and Britain*
The birdwing butterfly *Ornithopteria* (= *Troides*) *allottei* of Bougainville, Solomon Islands is known from less than a dozen specimens. A male from the collection of C. Rousseau Decelle was auctioned for £750 in Paris on 24 Oct 1966.

The rarest British butterfly (59 species) is the Chequered Skipper (*Carterocephalus palaemon*) now confined to a single site near Fort William, Inverness, Scotland. The Large blue (*Maculinea arion*) was officially declared extinct in 1979 but was re-introduced from stocks in France and Sweden in June 1983.

Most acute sense of smell
The most acute sense of smell exhibited in nature is that of the male Emperor moth (*Eudia pavonia*) which, according to German experiments in 1961, can detect the sex attractant of the virgin female at the almost unbelievable range of 11 km *6.8 miles* upwind. This scent has been identified as one of the higher alcohols ($C_{16}H_{29}OH$), of which the female carries less than 0,0001 mg.

Longest
The longest insect in the world is the giant stick-insect *Pharnacia serratipes* of Indonesia (*see Table*). The longest known beetles (excluding antennae) are the Hercules beetles (*Dynastes hercules* and *D. neptunus*) of Central and South America, which have been measured up to 190 mm *7.48 in* and 180 mm *7.08 in* respectively. More than half the length however, is taken up by the prothoracic horn.

Smallest *World*
The smallest insects recorded so far are the 'Hairy-winged' beetles of the family *Ptiliidae* (= *Trichopterygidae*) and the 'Battledore-wing fairy flies' (parasitic wasps) of the family *Myrmaridae* (*see Table*). They are smaller than some of the protozoa (single-celled animals). The male Bloodsucking banded louse *Enderleinellus zonatus*, ungorged, and the parasitic wasp (*Caraphractus cinctus*) may each weigh as little as 0,005 mg, or *5,670,000 to an oz*. The eggs of the latter each weigh 0,0002 mg, *or 141,750,000 to an oz*.

Commonest
The most numerous of all insects are Springtails (Order Collembola), which have a wide geographical range (*see Table*).

Fastest flying
Experiments have proved that the widely publicised claim by an American entomologist in 1926 that the Deer bot-fly *Cephenemyia pratti* could attain a speed of 818 mph *1316 km/h* (*sic*) was wildly exaggerated. If true it would have generated a supersonic 'pop'! Acceptable modern experiments have now established that the

highest maintainable airspeed of any insect, including the Deer bot-fly, is 24 mph *39 km/h*, rising to a maximum of 36 mph *58 km/h* for short bursts (*see Table*).

Longest lived
The longest-lived insects are the Splendour beetles (*Buprestidae*) (*see Table*). On 27 May 1983 a *Buprestis aurulenta* appeared from the staircase timber in the home of Mr W. Euston of Prittlewell, Southend-on-Sea, Essex after 47 years as a larva.

Loudest
The loudest of all insects is the male cicada (family Cicadidae). At 7400 pulses/min its tymbal organs produce a noise (officially described by the United States Department of Agriculture as 'Tsh-ee-EEEE-e-ou') detectable more than a quarter of a mile *400 m* distant. The only British species is the very rare Mountain cicada (*Cicadetta montana*), which is confined to the New Forest area in Hampshire.

Southernmost
The farthest south at which any insect has been found is 77° S (900 miles *1450 km* from the South Pole) in the case of a springtail (order Collembola).

Largest locust swarm
The greatest swarm of Desert locusts (*Schistocera gregaria*) ever recorded was one covering an estimated 2000 miles² *5180 km²* observed crossing the Red Sea in 1889. Such a swarm must have contained about 250,000,000,000 insects weighing about 500,000 tons *508 000 tonnes*. In 1958 in Somalia a swarm of *c* 60,000 million covering a measured 1000 km² *400 miles²* was estimated to be devouring *c* 120,000 tons of biomass daily.

Fastest wing beat
The fastest wing beat of any insect under natural conditions is 62,760 per min by a tiny midge of the genus *Forcipomyia*. In experiments with truncated wings at a temperature of 37° C *98.6° F* the rate increased to 133,080 beats/min. The muscular contraction–expansion cycle in 0.00045 or 1/2218th of a sec, further represents the fastest muscle movement ever measured.

Coming out of the woodwork in fully fledged splendour after 47 years as a larva—Britain's and the world's senior beetle. (*Southend Museum*)

Slowest wing beat
The slowest wing beat of any insect is 300 per min by the Swallowtail butterfly (*Papilio machaon britannica*). The average is 460–636 per min.

Hive record
The greatest reported amount of wild honey ever extracted from a single hive is 549 lb *249,02 kg* recorded by A. D. Wilkes of Cairns, Queensland, Australia in the 11 months Feb–Dec 1983.

Dragonflies *Largest and smallest*
The largest dragonfly in the world is *Megaloprepus caeruleata* of Central and South America, which has been measured up to 191 mm *7.52 in* across the wings and 120 mm *4.72 in* in body length. The largest dragonfly found in Britain is *Anax imperator*, which has a wing span measurement of up to 106 mm *4.17 in*. The smallest British dragonfly is *Lestes dryas*, which has a wing span of 20–25 mm *0.78–0.98 in*.

Flea *Largest*
The largest known flea is *Hystrichopsylla schefferi schefferi*, which was described from a single specimen taken from the nest of a Mountain beaver (*Aplodontia rufa*) at Puyallup, Washington, USA in 1913. Females measure up to 8 mm *0.31 in* in length which is the diameter of a pencil. The largest flea (61 species) found in Britain is the Mole and Vole flea (*H. talpae*)—females measured to 6 mm *0.23 in*.

Flea *Longest jump*
The champion jumper among fleas is the Common flea (*Pulex irritans*). In one American experiment carried out in 1910 a specimen allowed to leap at will performed a long jump of 13 in *330 mm* and a high jump of 7¾ in *197 mm*. In jumping 130 times its own height a flea subjects itself to a force of 200 g. Siphonapterologists recognise 1830 varieties.

10. CENTIPEDES (*Chilopoda*)

Longest
The longest known species of centipede is a large variant of the widely distributed *Scolopendra morsitans*, found on the Andaman Islands, Bay of Bengal. Specimens have been measured up to 13 in *330 mm* in length and 1½ in *38 mm* in breadth. The longest centipede found in Britain is *Haplophilus subterraneus*, which has been measured up to 70 mm *2.75 in* in length and 1,4 mm *0.05 in* across the body. On 1 Nov 1973 Mr Ian Howgate sighted an uncollected specimen on the run in St Albans, Herts, estimated to be at least 4½ in *114 mm* long.

Shortest
The shortest recorded centipede is an unidentified species which measures only 5 mm *0.19 in*. The shortest centipede found in Britain is *Lithobius dubosequi*, which measures up to 9,5 mm *0.374 in* in length.

Most legs
The centipede with the greatest number of legs is *Himantarum gabrielis* of southern Europe which has 171–177 pairs when adult.

Fastest
The fastest centipede is probably *Scrutigera coleoptrata* of southern Europe which can travel at 1.1 mph *1,8 km/h*.

11. MILLIPEDES (*Diplopoda*)

Longest
The longest known species of millipede are *Graphidostreptus gigas* of Africa and *Scaphistos-*

treptus seychellarum of the Seychelles in the Indian Ocean, both of which have been measured up to 280 mm *11.02 in* in length and 20 mm *0.78 in* in diameter. The longest millipede found in Britain is *Cylindroiulus londinensis* which measures up to 50 mm *1.96 in*.

Shortest

The shortest millipede in the world is the British species *Polyxenus lagurus*, which measures 2,1–4,0 mm *0.082–0.15 in*.

Most legs

The greatest number of legs reported for a millipede is 355 pairs (710 legs) for an unidentified South African species.

12. SEGMENTED WORMS (Annelida)

Longest

The longest known species of giant earthworm is *Microchaetus rappi* (= *M. microchaetus*) of South Africa. An average-sized specimen measures 136 cm *4 ft 6 in* in length (65 cm *25½ in* when contracted), but much larger examples have been reliably reported. In *c.* 1937 a giant earthworm measuring 22 ft *6,70 m* in length when naturally extended and 20 mm *0.78 in* in diameter was collected in the Transvaal, and in November 1967 another specimen measuring 11 ft *3,35 m* in length and 21 ft *6,40 m* when naturally extended was found reaching over the national road (width 6 m *19 ft 8¼ in*) near Debe Nek, eastern Cape Province. The longest segmented worm found in Britain is the King rag worm (*Nereis virens*). On 19 Oct 1975 a specimen measuring 44 in *111,7 cm* when fully extended was collected by Mr James Sawyer in Hauxley Bay, Northumberland. On 5 Nov 1982 the mutilated body of an earthworm measuring 5 ft 1 in *155 cm* in length was found in a garden in Herne Bay, Kent, but it was discarded before it could be identified.

Shortest

The shortest known segmented worm is *Chaetogaster annandalei*, which measures less than 0,5 mm *0.019 in* in length.

Worm charming

The record for attracting (by vibrations) earthworms to the surface of a 9 square metre plot in 30 minutes is 511 by Tom Shufflebotham in 1980 at Willaston CP School, Northwich, Cheshire.

13. MOLLUSCS (Mollusca)

(Squids, octopuses, shellfish, snails, etc.)

Largest squid

The largest known invertebrate is the Atlantic giant squid *Architeuthis dux* (*see Table* pp. 26–7). The largest squid ever recorded in British waters was an *Architeuthis monachus* found at the head of Whalefirth Voe, Shetland on 2 Oct 1959 which measured 24 ft *7,31 m* in total length.

Largest octopus

The largest octopus known to science is *Octopus apollyon* of the coastal waters of the North Pacific which regularly exceeds 12 ft *3,7 m* in radial spread and 55 lb *25 kg* in weight. One huge individual caught single-handed by skindiver Donald E. Hagen in Lower Hoods Canal, Puget Sound, Washington, USA on 18 Feb 1973 had a relaxed radial spread of 23 ft *7,01 m* and weighed 118 lb 10 oz *53,8 kg*. In November 1896

the remains of an unknown animal weighing an estimated 6–7 tons/*tonnes* were found on a beach near St Augustine, Florida, USA. Tissue samples were later sent to the US National Museum in Washington, DC, and in 1970 they were *positively* identified as belonging to a giant form of octopus (*Octopus giganteus*). Some experts, however, do not agree with this assessment because there was no evidence of tentacles or a beak and believe the decomposing carcase was more probably that of a large whale or shark. The largest octopus found in British waters is the Common octopus (*Octopus vulgaris*). It may span 7 ft *2,13 m* and weigh more than 10 lb *4,5 kg*.

Longest lived mollusc

The longest lived mollusc is the Ocean Quahog (*Artica islandica*) (*see Table*).

A giant Giant clam—the only shell which can weigh more than ¼ of a ton. Its pearls are also outsize (see Chapter 5).

SHELLS

Largest

The largest of all existing bivalve shells is the marine Giant clam *Tridacna gigas*, which is found on the Indo-Pacific coral reefs. A specimen measuring 110 cm *43.3 in* in length and weighing 333 kg *734 lb* collected off Ishigaki Island, Okinawa, Japan, was found in 1956 but not formally measured until Aug 1984 by Dr Shomei Shirai. Another specimen in the American Museum of Natural History, New York City measures 52 in *132 cm* in length (weight 507 lb *230 kg*). The largest bivalve shell found in British waters is the Fan mussel (*Pinna fragilis*). One specimen found at Tor Bay, Devon measured 37 cm *14.56 in* in length and 20 cm *7.87 in* in breadth at the hind end.

Smallest

The smallest shell is the univalve *Ammonicera rota*, which measures 0,5 mm *0.02 in* in diameter (*see Table*). The smallest bivalve shell also found in British waters is the coinshell *Neolepton sykesi*, which has an average length of 1,2 mm *0.047 in*. This species is only known from a few examples collected off Guernsey, Channel Islands and West Ireland.

Most Expensive Shell

For details of most expensive shell see table.

GASTROPODS

Largest

The largest known gastropod is the Trumpet or Baler conch (*Syrinx aruanus*) of Australia. One outsized specimen collected off Western Australia in 1979 and now owned by Don Pisor (who

bought it from a fisherman in Kaoh-siung, Taiwan in November 1979) of San Diego, California, USA measures 77,2 cm *30.39 in* in length and has a maximum girth of 101 cm *39.76 in*. It weighed nearly 40 lb *18,14 kg* when alive.

The largest known land gastropod is the African giant snail (*Achatina* sp.). An outsized specimen 'Gee Geronimo' found by Christopher Hudson (1955–79) of Hove, E. Sussex, measured 15½ in *39,3 cm* from snout to tail, (shell length 10¾ in *27,3 cm*) in December 1978 and weighed exactly 2 lb *900 g*. The snail was collected in Sierra Leone in June 1976 where shell lengths up to 14 in *35,5 cm* have been reliably reported.

The largest land snail found in Britain is the Roman or Edible snail (*Helix pomatia*), which measures up to 4 in *10 cm* in overall length and weighs up to 3 oz *85 g*. The smallest British land snail is *Punctum pygmaeum*, which has a shell measuring 0.023–0.035 in *0,6–0,9 mm* by 0.047–0.059 in, *1,2–1,5 mm*.

Speed

The fastest-moving species of land snail is probably the common garden snail (*Helix aspersa*) (*see Table*).

14. RIBBON WORMS (Nemertina)

Longest

The longest of the 550 recorded species of ribbon worms, also called nemertines (or nemerteans), is the 'Boot-lace worm' (*Lineus longissimus*), which is found in the shallow waters of the North Sea (*see Table* pp. 26–7).

15. JELLYFISHES (Scyphozoa)

Largest and smallest

The largest jellyfish is the Arctic giant jellyfish (*Cyanea capillata arctica*) of the north-western Atlantic. One specimen washed up in Massachusetts Bay had a bell diameter of 7 ft 6 in *2,28 m* and tentacles stretching 120 ft *36,5 m*. The largest cnidarian found in British waters is the rare 'Lion's mane' jellyfish (*Cyanea capillata*), also known as the Common sea blubber. One specimen measured at St Andrew's Marine Laboratory, Fife, Scotland had a bell diameter of 91 cm *35.8 in* and tentacles stretching over 13,7 m *45 ft*. Some true jellyfishes have a bell diameter of less than 20 mm *0.78 in*.

Most venomous

The most venomous cnidarian is the Australian sea wasp (*Chironex fleckeri*) which carries a cardio-toxic venom similar in strength to that found in the Asiatic cobra. These box jellyfish have caused the deaths of 66 people off the coast of Queensland, Australia since 1880. Victims die within 1–3 min if medical aid is not available. A most effective defence is women's panty hose, outsize versions of which are now worn by Queensland lifesavers at surf carnivals.

16. SPONGES (Porifera)

Largest

The largest known sponge is the barrel-shaped Loggerhead sponge (*Spheciospongia vesparium*) of the West Indies and the waters off Florida,

USA. Single individuals measure up to 3 ft 6 in *105 cm* in height and 3 ft *91 cm* in diameter. Neptune's cup or goblet (*Poterion patera*) of Indonesia grows to 4 ft *120 cm* in height, but it is a less bulky animal. In 1909 a Wool sponge (*Hippospongia canaliculatta*) measuring 6 ft *183 cm* in circumference was collected off the Bahama Islands. When first taken from the water it weighed between 80 and 90 lb *36 and 41 kg* but after it had been dried and relieved of all excrescences it scaled 12 lb *5,44 kg* (this sponge is now preserved in the US National Museum, Washington, DC, USA).

Smallest
The smallest known sponge is the widely distributed *Leucosolenia blanca*, which measures 3 mm *0.11 in* in height when fully grown.

Deepest
Sponges have been recovered from depths of up to 18,500 ft *5637 m*.

Coral
The world's greatest stony coral structure is the Great Barrier Reef off Queensland, north east Australia. It stretches 1260 miles *2028 km* and covers 80,000 miles² *207 000 km²*.

The world's largest reported discrete coral is a stony colony of *Galaxea fascicularis* found in Sakiyama Bay off Irimote Island, Okinawa on 7 Aug 1982 by Dr Shohei Shirai. It measured more than 16 m *52¼ ft* overall.

The largest hunk of coral yet found—measuring more than 16 m *52¼ feet* round the curve. (Note the scuba diver for scale).

17. EXTINCT ANIMALS

Longest *World*
A huge diplodocid scapula-coracoid bone measuring 8 ft 10 in *2,69 m* in length was found in the Dry Mesa Quarry in western Colorado, USA in 1979. This presupposes a diplodicus from the Middle to Late Jurassic (135–160 million years ago) with an overall length of 147–164 ft *45–50 m* and a weight of 50–55 tonnes *49–54 tons*. It was dubbed the 'ultrasaurus'. The remains of an Ultrasaurus-type brachiosaurid of comparable size has since been discovered in Korea. Rebbachisaurus with a back vertebrae measuring up to 5 ft *1,52 m* from Morocco and Tunisia was probably equally large.

Longest and heaviest *Britain*
Britain's longest (and heaviest) land vertebrate was the sauropod *Cetiosauriscus oxoniensis* ('whale lizard'), which roamed across southern England about 150 million years ago. It measured up to 68 ft 6 in *20,88 m* in total length and weighed about 25 tonnes *24.5 tons*.

Largest land predator
The largest of the flesh-eating dinosaurs was probably the 5,7 tonne *5.6 ton Tyrannosaurus rex* ('king tyrant lizard') which stalked over what are now the states of Montana and Wyoming in the USA about 75,000,000 years ago. No complete single skeleton of this dinosaur has ever been discovered, but a composite skeleton in the American Museum of Natural History, New York City has a bipedal height of 18 ft *5,5 m*. It has been estimated that the overall length was about 40 ft *12,0 m*. *Tarbosaurus efremovi* ('alarming lizard'), its Mongolian counterpart, measured up to 46 ft *14 m* in length but had a longer tail and was less heavily built. An upper jaw bone (maxilla) of another *T. rex* preserved at the University of California, Berkeley is nearly 30 per cent more massive than that in New York and must have belonged to a tyrannosaurid weighing closer to 12 tonnes/*tons*.

Fastest dinosaurs
Trackways can be used to estimate dinosaur speeds, and one from the Lower Cretaceous of Texas discovered in 1981 indicated that a carnivorous dinosaur had been moving at 40 km/h *25 mph*. Some of the Ornithomimids (ostrich dinosaurs) were even faster, and the 220 lb *100 kg Dromiceiomimus* could probably out-sprint an ostrich, which has a top speed of 45 mph *72 km/h*.

Smallest dinosaurs
The smallest dinosaurs so far recorded are the chicken-sized *Compsognathus* ('pretty jaw') of southern West Germany and south-east France, and an undescribed plant-eating fabrosaurid from Colorado, USA, both of which measured 75 cm *29.5 in.* from the snout to the tip of the tail.

Most brainless
Stegosaurus ('plated reptile'), which measured up to 30 ft *9 m* in total length had a walnut-sized brain weighing only 2½ oz *70g*, which represented 0.004 of 1 per cent of its computed body

EARLIEST OF THEIR TYPES

Type	Scientific name and year of discovery	Location	Estimated years before present
Ape	Unnamed species (May 1979)	Padaung Hills, Burma	40,000,000
Primate	Tarsier-like	Indonesia	70,000,000
	Lemur	Madagascar	70,000,000
Social insect	*Sphecomyrma freyi* (1967)	New Jersey, USA	110,000,000
Bird	*Archaeopteryx lithographica* (1861)	Bavaria, W. Germany	150,000,000
Moth	*Archaeolepis* (1985)	Dorset coast, England	180,000,000
Mammal	*Megazostrodon* (1966)	Thaba-ea-Litau, Lesotho	190,000,000
Reptiles	*Hylonomus, Archerpeton, Protoclepsybrops Romericus*	all in Nova Scotia	290,000,000
Amphibian	*Ichthyostega* (first quadruped)	Greenland	350,000,000
Spider	*Palaeostenzia crassipes*	Tayside, Scotland	370,000,000
Insect	*Rhyniella procursor*	Tayside, Scotland	370,000,000
Vertebrates (Fish scales)	*Anatolepis*	Crook County, Wyoming, USA	510,000,000
Crustacean	*Karagassiema* (12 legged)	Sayan Mts, USSR	c. 650,000,000
Metazoans	Bore hole tracks	Zambia	1,000,000,000
Eukaryotes	(c. Sept 1983)	Tianjin, China	1,800,000,000
Microfossils	Carbonaceous microspheroids	'North Pole', Western Australia	3,500,000,000

Note: Free Oxygen began forming in the Earth's atmosphere about 2300 million years ago.

weight of 1¾ tons/tonnes. (cf. 0.074 of 1 per cent for an elephant and 1.88 per cent for a human). It roamed widely across the Northern Hemisphere about 150,000,000 years ago.

Largest dinosaur eggs

The largest known dinosaur eggs are those of *Hypselosaurus priscus*, ('high ridge lizard'), a 40 ft *12,19 m* long titanosaurid which lived about 80,000,000 years ago. Some examples found in the valley of the Durance near Aix-en-Provence, southern France in October 1961 would have had, uncrushed, a length of 12 in *300 mm* and a diameter of 10 in *255 mm* (capacity 5.8 pints *3,3 l*).

Largest flying creature

The largest flying creature is the pterosaur *Quetzalcoatlus northropi* which glided over what is now the state of Texas, USA about 65 million years ago. Partial remains discovered in Big Bend National Park, West Texas in 1971 indicate that this reptile must have had a wing span of 11–12 m *36–39 ft* and weighed about 190 lb *86 kg*.

Largest marine reptile

The largest marine reptile ever recorded was *Stretosaurus macromerus*, a short-necked pliosaur from the Kimmeridge Clay of Stretham, Cambridgeshire and Oxfordshire.

A mandible found at Cumnor, Oxfordshire and now in the University Museum, Oxford has a restored length of over 3 m *9 ft 10 in* and must have belonged to a reptile measuring at least 46 ft *14 m* in total length.

Kronosaurus queenslandicus, another pliosaur, was also of comparable size, and a complete skeleton in the Museum of Comparative Zoology at Harvard University, Cambridge, Massachusetts, USA measures 42 ft *12,8 m* in total length.

Largest crocodile

The largest known crocodile was *Deinosuchus riograndensis*, which lived in the lakes and swamps of what is now the state of Texas, USA about 75,000,000 years ago. Fragmentary remains discovered in Big Bend National Park, West Texas, indicate a hypothetical length of 16 m *52 ft 6 in*, compared with the 12–14 m *39.3–45.9 ft* of the *Sarcosuchus imperator* of Niger. The huge gavial *Rhamphosuchus*, which lived in what is now northern India about 2,000,000 years ago, was even longer reaching 60 ft *18,3 m*, but it was not so heavily built.

Largest chelonians

The largest prehistoric chelonian was *Stupendemys geographicus*, a pelomedusid turtle which lived about 5,000,000 years ago. Fossil remains discovered by Harvard University palaeontologists in Northern Venezuela in 1972 indicate that this turtle had a carapace (shell) measuring 218–230 cm *7 ft 2 in–7 ft 6½ in* in mid-line length and measured 3 m *9 ft 10 in* in overall length. It had a computed weight of 4500 lb *2041 kg* in life.

Largest tortoise

The largest prehistoric tortoise was probably *Geochelone* (= *Colossochelys*) *atlas*, which lived in what is now northern India, Burma, Java, the Celebes and Timor about 2 million years ago. In 1923 the fossil remains of a specimen with a carapace 5 ft 11 in *180 cm* long (7 ft 4 in *223 cm* over the curve) and 2 ft 11 in *89 cm* high were discovered near Chandigarh in the Siwalik Hills. This animal had a total length of 8 ft *2,44 m* and is computed to have weighed 2100 lb *852 kg* when it was alive. Recently the fossil remains of other giant tortoises (*Geochelone*) have been found in Florida and Texas, USA.

Longest snake

The longest prehistoric snake was the python-like *Gigantophis garstini*, which inhabited what is now Egypt about 55,000,000 years ago. Parts of a spinal column and a small piece of jaw discovered at Fayum in the Western Desert indicate a length of *c*. 37 ft *11 m*.

The Cretaceous Age's answer to the Harrier Jump Jet (wing span 25¼ ft *7,70 m*)—the pterosaur with a wing span of 36 ft *11 m*.

Artwork: Matthew Hillier

Another fossil giant snake, *Madtsoia bai* from Patagonia, S. America, measured *c*. 10 m *33 ft* in length, comparable with the longest constrictors living today.

Largest amphibian

The largest amphibian ever recorded was the gharial-like *Prionosuchus plummeri* which lived 230,000,000 years ago. In 1972 the fragmented remains of a specimen measuring an estimated 9 m *30 ft* in life, were discovered in North Brazil.

Largest fish

No prehistoric fish larger than living species has yet been discovered. The claim that the Great shark (*Carcharodon megalodon*), which abounded in Miocene seas some 15,000,000 years ago, measured 80 ft *24 m* in length, based on ratios from fossil teeth has now been shown to be in error. The modern estimate is that this shark did not exceed 43 ft *13,1 m*.

Largest insect

The largest prehistoric insect was the dragonfly *Meganeura monyi*, which lived about 280,000,000 years ago. Fossil remains (*i.e.* impressions of wings) discovered at Commentry, central France, indicate a wing extending up to 70 cm *27.5 in*.

Britain's largest dragonfly was *Typus* sp. (family *Meganeuridae*), which is only known from a wing impression found on a lump of coal in Bolsover colliery, Derbyshire in July 1978. It had an estimated wing span of 50–60 cm *19.68–23.62 in* and lived about 300,000,000 years ago, making it the oldest flying creature so far recorded.

Most southerly

The most southerly creature yet found is a freshwater salamander-like amphibian *Labyrinthodont*, represented by a 2½ in *63,5 mm* piece of jawbone found near Beardmore Glacier Antarctica, 325 miles *532 km* from the South Pole, dating from the early Jurassic of 200,000,000 years ago. This discovery was made in December 1967.

Largest bird

The largest prehistoric bird was the flightless *Dromornis stirtoni*, a huge emu-like creature which lived in central Australia 11,000,000 years ago. Fossil leg bones found near Alice Springs in 1974 indicate that the bird must have stood *c*. 10 ft *3 m* in height and weighed *c*. 1100 lb *500 kg*. The Giant moa *Dinornis maximus* of New Zealand was even taller, attaining a maximum height of 12 ft *3,6 m* but it only weighed about 500 lb *227 kg*.

The largest known flying bird was the giant teratorn *Argentavis magnificens* which lived in Argentina about 6 million years ago. Fossil remains discovered at a site 100 miles *160 km* west of Buenos Aires in 1979 indicate that this gigantic vulture had a wing span of 7,0–7,6 m *23–25 ft* and weighed about 120 kg *265 lb*.

Largest mammals

The largest land mammal ever recorded was *Baluchitherium* (= Indricotherium, Pristinotherium and Benaratherium), a long-necked horn less rhinoceros which roamed across western Asia and Europe (Yugoslavia) about 35 million years ago. A restoration in the American Museum of Natural History, New York measures 17 ft 9 in *5,41 m* to the top of the shoulder hump and 37 ft *11,27 m* in total length, and this particular specimen must have weighed about 20 tonnes/*tons* in the flesh. The bones of this gigantic browser were first discovered in the Bugti Hills in east Baluchistan, Pakistan in 1907–08.

The largest marine mammal was the serpentine *Basilosaurus* (*Zeuglodon*) *cetoides*, which swam in the seas over what are now the American states of Arkansas and Alabama 50 million years ago. It measured up to 70 ft *21,3 m* in length.

Largest mammoth

The largest prehistoric elephant was the Steppe mammoth *Mammuthus* (*Parelephas*) *trogontherii*, which roamed over what is now central Europe a million years ago. A fragmentary skeleton found in Mosbach, West Germany indicates a shoulder height of 4,5 m *14 ft 9 in*.

Tusks *Longest*

The longest tusks of any prehistoric animal were those of the Straight-tusked elephant *Palaeoloxodom antiquus germanicus*, which lived in northern Germany about 300,000 years ago. The average length in adult bulls was 5 m *16 ft 5 in*. A single tusk of a Woolly mammoth (*Mammuthus primigenius*) preserved in the Franzens Museum at Brno, Czechoslovakia measures 5,02 m *16 ft 5¼ in* along the outside curve. In *c.* August 1933, a single tusk of an Imperial mammoth (*Mammuthus imperator*) measuring 16 + ft *4,87 + m* (anterior end missing) was unearthed near Post, Gorza County, Texas, USA. In 1934 this tusk was presented to the American Museum of Natural History in New York City, NY, USA.

Tusks *Heaviest*

The heaviest single fossil tusk on record is one weighing 150 kg *330 lb* with a maximum circumference of 35 in *89 cm* now preserved in the Museo Civico di Storia Naturale, Milan, Italy. The specimen (in two pieces) measures 11 ft 9 in *3,58 m* in length.

The heaviest recorded fossil tusks are a pair belonging to a 13 ft 4 in *4,06 m* tall Columbian mammoth (*Mammuthus columbi*) in the State Museum, Lincoln, Nebraska, USA which have a combined weight of 498 lb *226 kg* and measure 13 ft 9 in *4,21 m* and 13 ft 7 in *4,14 m* respectively. They were found near Campbell, Nebraska in April 1915.

Antlers *Greatest span*

The prehistoric Giant deer (*Megaceros giganteus*), which lived in northern Europe and northern Asia as recently as 8000 BC, had the longest horns of any known animal. One specimen recovered from an Irish bog had greatly palmated antlers measuring 14 ft *4,3 m* across.

PLANT KINGDOM (Plantea)

PLANTS

The medicinal value of plants was known to Neanderthal man *c.* 60,000 BC. The world's oldest garden has yet to be identified but is probably that of a Chinese temple. The world's oldest Botanical Garden is that at Pisa dating from 1543. Britain's oldest is the Botanic Garden, Oxford founded as a Physic Garden in 1621.

Oldest living thing

'King Clone', the oldest known clone of the creosote plant (*Larrea tridentata*) found in south west California, was estimated in February 1980 by Prof. Frank C. Vasek to be 11,700 years old. It is possible that crustose lichens in excess of 500 mm *19.6 in* in diameter may be as old. In 1981 it was estimated that Antarctic lichens of more than 100 mm *3.9 in* in diameter are at least 10,000 years old. The oldest known pot-plant is the succulent *Fockea crispa* potted by Baron Jacquin (1728–1817) at the Schönbrunn gardens, Vienna *c.* 1801.

Rarest

Plants thought to be extinct are rediscovered each year and there are thus many plants of which specimens are known in but a single locality. The small pink blossoms of *Presidio manzanita* survive in a single specimen reported in June 1978 at an undisclosed site in California. *Pennantia baylisiana*, a tree found in 1945 on Three Kings Island, off New Zealand, only exists as a female and cannot fruit. In May 1983 it was reported that there was a sole surviving specimen of the Lady's slipper orchid (*Cypripedium calceolus*). *Sporastatia cinerea*, a new genus of alpine lichen for Britain was found in Choire Garbh snowfield in the Cairngorm Scotland in 1982.

Northernmost

The Yellow poppy (*Papaver radicatum*) and the Arctic willow (*Salix arctica*) survive, the latter in an extremely stunted form, on the northernmost land (83° N).

Southernmost

Lichens resembling *Rhinodina frigida* have been found in Moraine Canyon in 86° 09′ S 157° 30′ W in 1971 and in the Horlick Mountain area, Antarctica in 86° 09′ S 131° 14′ W in 1965. The southernmost recorded flowering plant is the Antarctic Hair grass (*Deschampsia antarctica*) which was found in latitude 68° 21′ S on Refuge Island, Antarctica on 11 Mar 1981.

Highest

The greatest certain altitude at which any flowering plants have been found is 21,000 ft *6400 m* on Kamet (25,447 ft *7756 m*) by N. D. Jayal in 1955. They were *Ermania himalayensis* and *Ranunculus lobatus*.

Roots

The greatest reported depth to which roots have penetrated is a calculated 400 ft *120 m* in the case of a wild fig tree at Echo Caves, near Ohrigstad, East Transvaal, South Africa. An elm tree root of at least 360 ft *110 m* was reported from Auchencraig, Largs, Strathclyde *c.* 1950. A single Winter rye plant (*Secale cereale*) has been shown to produce 387 miles *622,8 km* of roots in 1.83 ft³ *0,051 m³* of earth.

Worst weeds

The most intransigent weed is the mat-forming water weed *Salvinia auriculata*, found in Africa. It was detected on the filling of Kariba Lake in May 1959 and within 11 months had choked an area of 77 miles² *199 km²* rising by 1963 to 387 miles² *1002 km²*. The world's worst land weeds are regarded as Purple nut sedge, Bermuda grass, Barnyard grass, Jungle-rice, goose grass, Johnson grass, Guinea grass, Cogon grass and lantana. The most damaging and widespread cereal weeds in Britain are the wild oats *Avena fatua* and *A. ludoviciana*. Their seeds can withstand temperatures of 240° F *115,6° C* for 15 min and remain viable.

The largest weed in Britain is the giant hogweed *Heracleum manteggazzianum* which established itself from seeds brought from the Caucasas before 1862. It grows to over 12 ft *3,65 m* in height.

Most spreading plant

The greatest area covered by a single clonal growth is that of the wild Box huckleberry (*Gaylussacia brachyera*), a mat-forming evergreen shrub first reported in 1796. A colony covering 8 acres, *3,2 hectares* was discovered in 1845 near New Bloomfield, Pennsylvania. Another colony, covering about 100 acres, was found on 18 July 1920 near the Juniata River, Pennsylvania. It has been estimated that this colony began 13,000 years ago.

Longest Philodendron

A Philodendron, 619 ft *188,6 m* in length grows in the home of Mr M. J. Linhart in Thornton, Leicestershire.

Longest Passion plant

In November 1974 a Passion plant, fed by a hormone by Dennis and Patti Carlson, was reported to have grown to a length of 600 ft *182 m* at Blaine, Minnesota, USA.

Largest aspidistra

The aspidistra (*Aspidistra elatior*) was introduced to Britain as a parlour palm from Japan and China in 1822. The biggest aspidistra in Britain is one 50 in *127 cm* tall with more than 500 leaves spanning 5 ft *1,52 m* grown by Gertie James in Staveley, Chesterfield. The biggest in the world (*pace* Gracie Fields) is uncertain but Cliff Evans of Kiora, Moruya, NSW, Australia had his measured in April 1983 to be 56 in *142 cm* tall.

Earliest flower

The oldest fossil of a flowering plant with palmlike imprints was found in Colorado, USA, in 1953 and dated about 65,000,000 years old.

Largest cactus

The largest of all cacti is the saguaro (*Cereus giganteus* or *Carnegiea gigantea*), found in Arizona, south-eastern California, USA and Sonora, Mexico. The green fluted column is surmounted by candelabra-like branches rising to a height of 16 m *52 ft 6 in* in the case of a specimen measured on the boundary of the Saguaro National Monument, Arizona. They have waxy white blooms which are followed by edible crimson fruit. An armless cactus 78 ft *24 m* in height was measured in April 1978 by Hube Yates in Cave Creek, Arizona.

Tallest hedge *World*

The world's tallest hedge is the Meikleour beech hedge in Perthshire, Scotland. It was planted in 1746 and has now attained a trimmed height of 85 ft *26 m*. It is 600 yd *550 m* long. Some of its trees now exceed 120 ft *36,5 m*.

Tallest hedge *Yew*

The tallest yew hedge in the world is in Earl Bathurst's Park, Cirencester, Gloucestershire. It was planted in 1720, runs for 170 yd *155 m*, reaches 36 ft *11 m*, is 15 ft *4,5 m* thick at its base and takes 20 man-days to trim.

Tallest hedge *Box*

The tallest box hedge is 35 ft *10,7 m* in height at Birr Castle, Offaly, Ireland dating from the 18th century.

Longest *Seaweed*

Claims made that the seaweed off Tierra del Fuego, South America, grows to 600 ft *182,5 m* and even to 1000 ft *305 m* in length have gained currency. More recent and more reliable records indicate that the longest species of seaweed is the Pacific giant kelp (*Macrocystis pyrifera*), which does not exceed 196 ft *60 m* in length. It can grow 45 cm *18 in* in a day. The longest of the 700 species of British seaweed is the Brown seaweed *Chorda filum* which grows up to a length of 20 ft *6,10 m*. The Japanese *Sargassum muticum* introduced *c.* 1970 can grow to 30 ft *9,0 m*.

Almost a vintage on its own—the record bunch of grapes grown by Bozzolo y Perut Ltda of Chile (see above).

VINES & VINEYARDS

The largest recorded grape vine was one planted in 1842 at Carpinteria, California, USA. By 1900 it was yielding more than 9 tons/*tonnes* of grapes in some years, and averaging 7 tons/*tonnes* per year. It died in 1920. Britain's largest vine (1898–1964) was at Kippen, Stirling with a girth, measured in 1956, of 5 ft *1,52 m.* England's largest vine is the Great Vine, planted in 1768 at Hampton Court, Greater London. Its girth is 85 in *215,9 cm* with branches up to 114 ft *34,7 m* long and an average yield of 703 lb *318,8 kg.* In 1983 Leslie Stringer of Dartford, Kent obtained a yield of 1015½ lb *460,6 kg* from a vine from Banstead, Surrey planted in 1962. A single bunch of grapes (Red Thomson seedless weighing 9400 grammes *20 lb 11½ oz* were weighed in Santiago, Chile in May 1984.

Most northerly and southerly vineyards

A vineyard at Sabile, Latvia, USSR is just north of Lat. 57° N. The most northerly commercial vineyard in Britain is that at Renishaw hall, Derbyshire with 2600 vines. It lies in Lat. 53° 18′ N. The most southerly commercial vineyard is operated by Moorilla Estates Pty Ltd at Berridale, Tasmania in Lat. 42° 47′ S.

Deepest *Seaweed*

The greatest depth at which plant life has been found is 884 ft *269 m* by Mark and Diane Littler (USA) off San Salvadore Island, Bahamas in October 1984. These maroon coloured algae survived though 99.9995 per cent of sunlight was filtered out.

Mosses

The smallest of mosses is the pygmy moss (*Ephemerum*) and the longest is the brook moss (*Fontinalis*), which forms streamers up to 3 ft *91 cm* long in flowing water.

BLOOMS AND FLOWERS

Largest bloom *World*

The mottled orange-brown and white parasitic Stinking corpse lily (*Rafflesia arnoldii*) has the largest of all blooms. These attach themselves to the cissus vines of the jungle in south-east Asia and measure up to 3 ft *91 cm* across and ¾ inch *1,9 cm* thick, and attain a weight of 15 lb *7 kg.* The spathe and spadix of the less massive green and purple flower of *Amorphophallus titanum* of Sumatra may attain a length of more than 1,5 m *5 ft.*

The largest known inflorescence is that of *Puya raimondii*, a rare Bolivian plant with an erect panicle (diameter 8 ft *2,4 m*) which emerges to a height of 35 ft *10,7 m.* Each of these bears up to 8000 white blooms (see also Slowest-flowering plant below). The flower-spike of an agave was in 1974 measured to be 52 ft *15,8 m* long in Berkeley, California.

The world's largest blossoming plant is the giant Chinese wisteria at Sierra Madre, California, USA. It was planted in 1892 and now has branches 500 ft *152 m* long. It covers nearly an acre, weighs 225 tons *228 tonnes* and has an estimated 1,500,000 blossoms during its blossoming period of five weeks, when up to 30,000 people pay admission to visit it.

Largest bloom *Great Britain*

The largest bloom of any indigenous British flowering plant is that of the wild white water lily (*Nymphaea alba*), which measures 6 in *15 cm* across. Other species bear much larger inflorescences such as the 19 in *48 cm* diameter sunflower (*Helianthus annuus*) flower head measured for Mrs Lena Filipchuk of Burnaby, British Columbia, Canada on 15 Oct 1984.

Smallest flowering and fruiting plant

The floating flowering aquatic duckweed *Wolffia angusta* of Australia described in 1980 is only 0,6 mm $\frac{1}{42}$ *of an inch* in length and 0.33 mm $\frac{1}{85}$ *of an inch* in width. It weighs about 0,00015 g *1/190,000 of an oz*, its fruit resembling a miniscule fig weighs 0.00007 g or 400,000 to the oz. The smallest land plant regularly flowering in Britain is the chaffweed (*Cetunculus minimus*), a single seed of which weighs 0,00003 of a gramme.

Smallest plant

The smallest 'plant' is a uni-cellular alga and is listed under Protista smallest (see p. 52).

Most valuable

The Burpee Co $10,000 prize offered in 1954 for the first all-white marigold was won on 12 Aug 1975 by Alice Vonk of Sully, Iowa, USA.

Fastest growth

The case of a *Hesperogucca whipplei* of the family Liliaceae growing 12 ft *3,65 m* in 14 days was reported from Tresco Abbey, Isles of Scilly in July 1978.

Slowest flowering plant

The slowest flowering of all plants is the rare *Puyu raimondii*, the largest of all herbs, discovered in Bolivia in 1870. The panicle emerges after about 150 years of the plant's life. It then dies. (See also above under Largest blooms.) Some agaves, erroneously called Century plants, first flower after 40 years.

Largest wreath

The largest wreath constructed was the wreath built by The Gothenburg Florists at Liseberg Amusement Park, Sweden, completed on 4 Sept 1982. It measured 20,83 m *68 ft 4 in* in diameter and weighed 1980 kg (*1.95 tons*).

Longest daisy chain

The longest daisy chain, made in 7 hr, was one of 4529 ft 6 in *1380,5 m* at the Museum of Childhood, Sudbury, Derbyshire on 6 June 1981. The team is limited to 16.

Orchid *Largest and Tallest*

The largest of all orchids is *Grammatophyllum speciosum*, native to Malaysia. Specimens have been recorded up to 25 ft *7,62 m* in height. The largest orchid flower is that of *Phragmipedium caudatum*, found in tropical areas of America. Its petals are up to 18 in *46 cm* long, giving it a maximum outstretched diameter of 3 ft *91 cm.* The flower is, however, much less bulky than that of the Stinking corpse lily (see above). The tallest free-standing orchid is *Grammatophyllum speciosum* (see above). *Galeola foliata* may attain 49 ft *15 m* on decaying rainforest trees in Queensland, Australia.

The first flowering in Britain of *Grammatophyllum wallisii* from Mindanao, Philippines at Burnham Nurseries, Kingsteignton, Devon in 1982 produced 557 flowers.

Orchid *Smallest*
The smallest orchid is *Platystele Jungermannoides*, found in Central America. Its flowers are 1 mm *0.04 in* across.

Orchid *Highest priced*
The highest price ever paid for an orchid is 1150 guineas (£1,207.50), paid by Baron Schröder to Sanders of St Albans for an *Odontoglossum crispum* (variety *pittianum*) at an auction by Protheroe & Morris of Bow Lane, London, on 22 Mar 1906. A Cymbidium orchid called Rosanna Pinkie was sold in the United States for $4500 (*then £1600*) in 1952.

Largest rhododendron
The largest species of rhododendron is the scarlet *Rhododendron arboreum*, examples of which reach a height of 65 ft *19,8 m* on Mt Japfu, Nagaland, India. The cross-section of the trunk of a *Rhododendron giganteum*, reputedly 90 ft *27,43 m* high from Yunnan, China is preserved at Inverewe Garden, Highland. The largest in the United Kingdom is one 25 ft *7,60 m* tall and 272 ft *82,90 m* in circumference at Government House, Hillsborough, Co. Down. A specimen 35 ft *10,65 m* high and 3 ft 3 in *99 cm* in circumference has been measured at Tregothan, Truro, Cornwall.

Largest rose tree
A 'Lady Banks' rose tree at Tombstone, Arizona, USA, has a trunk 40 in *101 cm* thick, stands 9 ft *2,74 m* high and covers an area of 5380 ft² *499 m²* supported by 68 posts and several thousand feet of piping. This enables 150 people to be seated under the arbour. The cutting came from Scotland in 1884.

FRUITS AND VEGETABLES

Most and least nutritive
An analysis of the 38 commonly eaten raw (as opposed to dried) fruits shows that the one with the highest calorific value is avocado (*Persea americana*), with 741 calories per edible pound or *163 cals per 100 gr*. That with the lowest value is cucumber with 73 calories per pound *16 cals per 100 gr*. Avocados probably originated in Central and South America and contain also vitamins A, C, and E and 2.2 per cent protein.

Chilli
The tallest reported red chilli plant *Capsicum annuum* was one of 4,2 m *13 ft 8 in* grown by Shri Satagopan Nanduri of Hyderabad, India in 1981.

Melon
A watermelon weighing 200 lb *90,7 kg* was reported by Grace's Garden in April 1980. The growers were Ivan and Lloyd Bright of Hope, Arkansas, USA.

Peach *Largest*
The largest peach reported in Britain is one of 14½ oz *411 g* 12 in *30,4 cm* in Aug 1984 from a 26-year-old Italian tree grown by Mrs Jean Bird of London SW6.

Pineapple *Largest*
A pineapple weighing 17 lb 8 oz *7,96 kg* was harvested by Dole Philippines Inc at South Cotabato, Philippines in Nov 1984. Pineapples up to 13 kg *28.6 lb* were reported in 1978 from Tarauaca, Brazil.

Potato
A record display of 369 varieties of potato (*Solanum tuberosum*) was mounted on *BBC Record Breakers* by Donald MacLean on 16 Sept 1984.

HERBS
Herbs are not botanically defined but consist of plants whose leaves or roots are of culinary or medicinal value. The most heavily consumed is coriander *Coriandrum sativum*. It is used in curry powder, confectionery, in bread and in gin.

FERNS

Largest
The largest of all the more than 6000 species of fern is the tree fern (*Alsophila excelsa*) of Norfolk Island, in the South Pacific, which attains a height of up to 60 ft *18,28 m*.

The highest recorded in Britain is bracken *Pteridium aquilinum* over 16 ft *4,8 m* in Ruislip, Middlesex in 1970.

Smallest
The world's smallest ferns are *Hecistopteris pumila,* found in Central America, and *Azolla caroliniana,* which is native to the United States and has fronds down to ½ in *12 mm*.

GRASSES

Commonest
The world's commonest grass is *Cynodon dactylon* or Bermuda grass. The 'Callie' hybrid, selected in 1966, grows as much as 6 in *15,2 cm* a day and stolons reach 18 ft *5,5 m* in length.

Fastest growing
Some species of the 45 genera of bamboo have been measured to grow at up to 36 in *91 cm* per day (0.00002 mph *0,00003 km/h*).

Tallest
A Thorney bamboo culm (*Bambusa arundinacea*) felled at Pattazhi, Travancore, India in November 1904 measured 121½ ft *37,0 m*. The tallest of the 160 grasses found in Great Britain is the common reed (*Phragmites communis*), which reaches a height of 9 ft 9 in *2,97 m*.

Shortest
The shortest grass native to Great Britain is the very rare sand bent (*Mibora minima*) from Anglesey, Gwynedd which has a maximum growing height of under 6 in *15 cm*.

LEAVES

Largest *World*
The largest leaves of any plant belong to the Raffia palm (*Raphia raffia*) of the Mascarene Islands, in the Indian Ocean and the Amazonian bamboo palm (*R. toedigera*) of South America, whose leaf blades may measure up to 65 ft *19,81 m* in length with petioles up to 13 ft *3,96 m*.

The largest undivided leaf is that of *Alocasia macrorrhiza*, found in Sabah, East Malaysia. One found in 1966 was 9 ft 11 in *3,02 m* long and 6 ft 3½ in *1,92 m* wide, with a unilateral area of 34.2 ft² *3,17 m²*.

Largest *Great Britain*
The largest leaves to be found in outdoor plants in Great Britain are those of *Gunnera manicata* from Brazil with leaves 6–10 ft *1,82–3,04 m* across on prickly stems 5–8 ft *1,52–2,43 m* long.

Fourteen-leafed clover
A fourteen-leafed white clover (*Trifolium repens*) was found by Randy Farland near Sioux Falls, South Dakota, USA on 16 June 1975.

SEEDS

Largest
The largest seed in the world is that of the double coconut or Coco de Mer (*Lodoicea seychellarum*), the single-seeded fruit of which may weigh 40 lb *18 kg*. This grows only in the Seychelles, in the Indian Ocean.

Smallest
The smallest seeds are those of *Epiphytic* orchids, at 35,000,000 to the oz (*cf.* grass pollens at up to 6,000,000,000 grains/oz). A single plant of the American ragweed can generate 8,000,000,000 pollen grains in five hours.

Most viable
The most protracted claim for the viability of seeds is that made for the Arctic lupin (*Lupinus arcticus*) found in frozen silt at Miller Creek in the Yukon, Canada in July 1954 by Harold Schmidt. The seeds were germinated in 1966 and were dated by the radiocarbon method of associated material to at least 8000 BC and more probably to 13,000 BC.

Most conquering conker
The highest recorded battle honours for an untreated conker (fruit of the Common horse-chestnut or *Aesculus hippocastanum*) is a 'five thousander plus', which won the BBC Conker Conquest in 1954. A professor of botany has however opined that this heroic specimen might

Master McLean, the farmer's son from Hertfordshire alongside Britain's monster 30 lb 10 oz *13,9 kg* sugar beet (see Table page 50).

RECORD DIMENSIONS AND WEIGHTS FOR FRUIT VEGETABLES AND FLOWERS GROWN IN THE UNITED KINGDOM

Many data subsequent to 1958 come from the annual *Garden News* and Phostrogen Ltd. Giant Vegetable and Fruit Contest and the Super Sunflower Contest.

APPLE	3 lb 1 oz	*1,357 kg*	V. Loveridge	Ross-on-Wye, Hereford & Worcester	1965
ARTICHOKE	8 lb	*3,625 kg*	A. R. Lawson	Tollerton, North Yorkshire	1964
BEETROOT	29 lb	*13,154 kg*	F. A. Pulley	Maidstone, Kent	1964
BROAD BEAN	23⅜ in	*59,3 cm*	T. Currie	Jedburgh, Borders	1963
	23⅜ in	*59,3 cm*	Mrs M. Adrian	Irvine, Strathclyde	1982
BROCCOLI	28 lb 14¾ oz	*13,100 kg*	J. T. Cooke	Funtington, W. Sussex	1964
BRUSSELS SPROUT[1]	16 lb 1 oz	*7,285 kg*	E. E. Jenkins	Shipston-on-Stour, Warwickshire	1974
CABBAGE[2]	114 lb 3 oz	*51,8 kg*	P. G. Barton	Cleckheaton, W. Yorkshire	1977
CARROT[3]	10 lb 4 oz	*4,649 kg*	E. Stone	East Woodyates, Wiltshire	1984
CAULIFLOWER	52 lb 11½ oz	*23,900 kg*	J. T. Cooke	Funtington, W. Sussex	1966
CELERY	35 lb	*15,875 kg*	C. Bowcock	Willaston, Merseyside	1973
CUCUMBER[4]	13 lb 10¾ oz (indoor)	*6,201 kg*	A. Emery	Rochester, Kent	1984
	8 lb 4 oz (outdoor)	*3,740 kg*	C. Bowcock	Willaston, Merseyside	1973
	43½ in	*110 cm*	A. C. Rayment	Chelmsford, Essex	1984
DAHLIA[5]	10 ft 5 in	*3,17 m*	R. Lond	Diss, Norfolk	1985
DWARF BEAN	17½ in	*43,4 cm*	C. Bowcock	Willaston, Merseyside	1973
GLADIOLUS	8 ft 4½ in	*2,55 m*	A. Breed	Melrose, Roxburgh, Borders	1981
GOOSEBERRY	2.06 oz	*58,5 g*	A. Dingle	Macclesfield, Cheshire	1978
GOURD	196 lb	*88,900 kg*	J. Leathes	Herringfleet Hall, Suffolk	1846
GRAPEFRUIT*[6]	3 lb 8 oz	*1,585 kg*	A. J. Frost	Willington, Bedfordshire	1977
HOLLYHOCK	24 ft 3 in	*7,39 m*	W. P. Walshe	Eastbourne, E. Sussex	1961
KALE[7]	12 ft tall	*3,65 m*	B. T. Newton	Mullion, Cornwall	1950
LEEK	9 lb 5½ oz	*4,235 kg*	C. Bowcock	Willaston, Merseyside	1973
LEEK, POT	117.82 in^3	*1930* cm^3	G. Brownlees	Brandon, Durham	1984
LEMON[8]	4 lb	*1,81 kg*	V. Waldron	Didcot, Oxfordshire	1982
LETTUCE	25 lb	*11,335 kg*	C. Bowcock	Willaston, Merseyside	1974
LUPIN*	6 ft 0½ in	*1,84 m*	J. Lawlor	New Malden, Surrey	1971
MANGOLD	54½ lb	*24,720 kg*	P. F. Scott	Sutton, Humberside	1971
MARROW	105 lb 8 oz	*47,85 kg*	D. C. Payne	Tewkesbury, Glos.	1982
MUSHROOM[9]	54 in circum.	*1,37 m*	—	Hasketon, Suffolk	1957
ONION[10]	7 lb 11¾ oz	*3,508 kg*	W. Rodger	Crail, Fife	1984
PARSNIP[11]	10 lb 8½ oz	*4,776 kg*	C. Moore	Peacehaven, E. Sussex	1980
PEAPOD	10⅛ in	*25,7 cm*	T. Currie	Jedburgh, Borders	1964
PEAR[12]	2 lb 10½ oz	*1,200 kg*	Mrs. K. Loines	Hythe, Hampshire	1973
PETUNIA*	8 ft 4 in	*2,53 m*	G. A. Warner	Dunfermline, Fife	1978
POTATO[13]	7 lb 1 oz	*3,200 kg*	J. H. East	Spalding, Lincolnshire	1963
	7 lb 1 oz	*3,200 kg*	J. P. Busby	Atherstone, Warwickshire	1982
PUMPKIN[14]	440 lb	*199,5 kg*	R. A. Butcher	Stockbridge, Hampshire	1984
RADISH[15]	17 lb	*7,711 kg*	K. Ayliffe	Brecon, Powys	1976
RED CABBAGE	42 lb	*19,05 kg*	R. Straw	Staveley, Derbyshire	1925
RHUBARB	5 lb 11 oz	*2,579 kg*	A. C. Setterfield	Englefield, Berkshire	1978
	5 lb 11 oz	*2,579 kg*	E. Stone	East Woolgates, Wiltshire	1984
RUNNER BEAN	39 in long	*99 cm*	Mrs. E. Huxley	Churton, Cheshire	1976
SAVOY CABBAGE	38 lb 8 oz	*17,450 kg*	W. H. Neil	Retford, Nottinghamshire	1966
SHALLOT*	2 lb 12 oz (47 bulbs)	*1,245 kg*	M. Silverstoff	Falmouth, Cornwall	1977
STRAWBERRY	8.17 oz	*231 g*	G. Anderson	Folkestone, Kent	1983
SUGAR BEET[16]	30 lb 10 oz	*13,9 kg*	K. McLean	Meldreth, Hertfordshire	1984
SUNFLOWER[17]	23 ft 6½ in tall	*7,17 m*	F. Kelland	Exeter, Devon	1976
SWEDE	48 lb 12 oz	*22,11 kg*	A. Foster	Alnwick, Northumberland	1980
TOMATO[18]	4 lb 5 oz	*1,956 kg*	R. A. Butcher	Stockbridge, Hants	1983
TOMATO PLANT[19]	45 ft 9½ in (length)	*13,96 m*	Chosen Hill School	Gloucester, Glos.	1981
TOMATO TRUSS	20 lb 4 oz	*9,175 kg*	C. Bowcock	Willaston, Merseyside	1973
TURNIP[20]	35 lb 4 oz	*15,975 kg*	C. W. Butler	Nafferton, Humberside	1972

1 *A Brussels Sprout plant measuring 11 ft 8 in* 3,55 m *was grown by Ralph G. Sadler of Watchbury Farm, Barford, Warwickshire on 6 July 1978.*

2 *The Swalwell, County Durham Red Cabbage of 1865 grown by William Collingwood (d. 8 Oct 1867) reputedly weighed 123 lb* 55,7 kg *and was 259 in* 6,57 m *in circumference.*

3 *A specimen of 7 kg* 15 lb 7 oz *was grown by Miss I. G. Scott of Nelson, New Zealand in October 1978.*

4 *A 17 lb 4 oz* 7,82 kg *example was grown by Nadine Williams of Knott, Texas, USA in 1982. A Vietnamese variety 6 ft* 1,83 m *long was reported by L. Szabo of Debrecen, Hungary in September 1976.*

5 *A 16 ft 5 in* 5,0 m *dahlia was grown by Sam and Pat Barnes of Chattahoochee, Florida, USA in 1982.*

6 *A 6 lb 8½ oz* 2,966 kg *specimen was weighed for Joshua and Allison Sosnow in Tucson, Arizona, USA on 21 Dec 1984.*

7 *F. Doven of Mt Lawley, Australia grew a kale measuring 4,16 m* 13 ft 7½ in *in 1982.*

8 *An 8 lb 8 oz* 3,88 kg *lemon with a 29½ in* 74,9 cm *girth was grown by Charlotte and Donald Knutzen of Whittier, California, USA in August 1983.*

9 *Same size reported by J. Coombes at Mark, Somerset on 28 July 1965. In September 1968 one weighing 18 lb 10 oz* 8,425 kg *was reported from Whidbey I. Washington, USA. A specimen of the edible* Termitomyces titanicus *found near Kitwe, Zambia on 18 Dec 1978 measured 26 in* 63 cm *in diameter and weighed 5.5 lb* 2,5 kg.

10 *An onion of 7½ lb* 3,4 kg *was grown by Nelson W. Hope of Cardiff, California in 1965 with a girth of 26 in* 66 cm. *Its original gross weight was reputedly 8 lb* 3,62 kg.

11 *One 60 in* 152 cm *long was reported by M. Zaninovich of Waneroo W. Australia.*

12 *A specimen weighing 1,405 kg* 3.09 lb *was harvested on 10 May 1979 at Messrs K. & R. Yeomans, Arding, Armidale, NSW, Australia.*

13 *One weighing 18 lb 4 oz* 8,275 kg *reported dug up by Thomas Siddal in his garden in Chester on 17 Feb 1795. A yield of 515 lb* 233,5 kg *from a 2½ lb parent seed by Bowcock planted in April 1977. Six tubers weighing 54 lb 8 oz* 24,72 kg *by Alan Nunn of Rhodes, Greater Manchester were reported on 18 Sept 1949.*

14 *A squash (Cucurbita moschata) of 513 lb* 232,69 kg *was grown by Harold Fulp, Jr., at Nineveh, Indiana, USA in 1977. A pumpkin (*C. maxima*) of 612 lb* 277,6 kg *won the Half Moon Bay Pumpkin Festival, California prize in 1984.*

15 *A radish of 25 lb* 11,34 kg *was grown by Glen Tucker of Stanbury, South Australia in August 1974 and by Herbert Breslow of Ruskin, Florida, USA in 1977.*

16 *One weighing 45½ lb* 20,63 kg *was grown by R. Meyer of Brawley, California in 1974.*

17 *A sunflower of 7,38 m* 24 ft 2½ in *was grown by Martien Heijms of Oirschot, The Netherlands in 1983.*

18 *Grace's Gardens reported a 6 lb 8 oz* 2,94 kg *tomato grown by Clarence Daily of Monona, Wisconsin in 1977.*

19 *Gordon Graham of Edmond, Oklahoma, has grown a tomato plant of 52 ft* 15,85 m *in April 1985.*

20 *A 73 lb* 33,1 kg *turnip was reported in Dec. 1768 and one of 51 lb* 23,1 kg *from Alaska in 1981.*

* *Not in official contest.*

The heaviest orange ever reported is one weighing 5 lb 8 oz 2,50 kg *exhibited in Nelspruit, South Africa on 19 June 1981. It was the size of a human head but was stolen.*

well have been a 'ringer', probably an ivory or tagua nut (*Phytelephas macrocarpa*). The *Guinness Book of Records* will not publish any category for the largest collection of conkers for fear that trees might suffer wholesale damage

TREES AND WOOD

Most massive tree

The most massive living thing on Earth is the biggest known Giant Sequoia (*Sequoiadendron giganteum*) named the 'General Sherman', standing 267 ft tall, in the Sequoia National Park, California, USA. It has a true girth of 79.8 ft *24,32 m* (1980) (at 5 ft *1,52 m* above the ground). The 'General Sherman' has been estimated to contain the equivalent of 600,120 board feet of timber, sufficient to make 5,000,000,000 matches. The foliage is blue-green, and the red-brown tan bark may be up to 24 in *61 cm* thick in parts. Estimates (1981) place its weight, including its root system, at 6000 long tons *6100 tonnes*. The largest known petrified tree is one of this species with a 295 ft *89,9 m* trunk near Coaldale, Nevada, USA.

The seed of a 'big tree' weighs only 1/6000th of an oz *4,7 mg*. Its growth at maturity may therefore represent an increase in weight of 1,300,000 million-fold.

The tree canopy covering the greatest area is the great Banyan *Ficus benghalensis* in the Indian Botanical Garden, Calcutta with 1775 prop or supporting roots and a circumference of 1350 ft *412 m*. It covers overall some 3 acres *1,2 ha* and dates from *ante* 1787.

Greatest girth *World*

El Arbol del Tule, in the state of Oaxaca, in Mexico is a 135 ft *41 m* tall Montezuma cypress (*Taxodium mucronatum*) with a girth of 117.6 ft *35,8 m* at a height of 5 ft *1,52 m* above the ground in 1982. A figure of 167 ft *51 m* in circumference was reported for the pollarded European chestnut (*Castanea sativa*) known as the 'Tree of the 100 Horses' (Castagno di Cento Cavalli) on Mount Etna, Sicily, Italy in 1972 and measurements up to 180 ft *54,5 m* have been attributed to Baobab trees (*Adansonia digilata*).

Greatest girth *Britain*

The tree of greatest girth in Britain is a sweet ('Spanish') chestnut (*Castanea sativa*) in the grounds of Canford School, Nr. Wimborne, Dorset, with a bole 43 ft 9 in *13,33 m* in circumference. The largest-girthed living British oak is one at Bowthorpe Farm near Bourne, south Lincolnshire, measured in September 1973 to be 39 ft 1 in *11,91 m*. The largest 'maiden' (i.e. not pollarded) oak is the Majesty Oak at Fredville Park, near Nonington, Kent, with a girth of 38 ft 1 in *11,60 m* (1973).

Fastest growing

Discounting bamboo, which is not botanically classified as a tree, but as a woody grass, the fastest rate of growth recorded is 35 ft 3 in *10,74 m* in 13 months by an *Albizzia falcata* planted on 17 June 1974 in Sabah, Malaysia. The youngest recorded age for a tree to reach 100 ft *30,48 m* is 64 months for one of the species planted on 24 Feb 1975, also in Sabah.

Slowest growing

The speed of growth of trees depends largely upon conditions, although some species, such as box and yew, are always slow-growing. The extreme is represented by a specimen of Sitka spruce which required 98 years to grow to 11 in *28 cm* tall with a diameter of less than 1 in *2,5 cm* on the Arctic tree-line. The growing of miniature trees or *bonsai* is an oriental cult mentioned as early as *c.* 1320.

Tallest *World all-time and currently*

The tallest tree ever measured by any governmental forester was recently re-discovered in a report by William Ferguson, Inspector of Victoria State Forests. He reported in February 1872 a fallen Mountain ash (*Eucalyptus regnans*) 18 ft *5,48 m* in diameter at 5 ft *1,52 m* above ground level and 435 ft *132,5 m* in length. According to the researches of Dr A. C. Carder (Canada) the closest measured rivals to this champion have been:

ft	m	
415	*126,5*	Lynn Valley Douglas fir *Pseudotsuga menziesii*, British Columbia, Canada, 1902
393	*119,7*	The Mineral Douglas fir *Pseudotsuga menziesii*, Washington State, USA, 1905
380	*115,8*	Nisqually fir *Pseudotsuga menziesii*, Nisqually River, Washington State, 1899
375	*114,3*	Cornthwaite Mountain ash *Eucalyptus regnans*, Thorpdale, Victoria, Australia, 1880
*367.8	*112,1*	'Tallest Tree', Redwood Creek *Sequoia sempervirens*, Humboldt County, California, USA, 1963
367.6	*112*	Coast redwood *Sequoia sempervirens*, Guerneville, California, USA, 1873

* Tallest standing tree in the world. Crown dying back. Height last re-estimated at 362 ft *110,3 m* in 1972.

Currently the tallest standing broadleaf tree is a Mountain ash in the Styx Valley, Tasmania at 325 ft *99 m*.

Research into a Douglas Fir with a claimed height of 417 ft *127,1 m* and with a butt diameter of 25 ft *7,62 m* supposedly felled by George Cary in Lynn Valley (see above) has been shown by Dr Carder to have been without foundation.

Tallest *Great Britain*

The tallest trees in Great Britain are a Grand fir (*Abies grandis*) at Strone, Cairndow, Strathclyde, and Douglas firs at The Hermitage, Perth, at Moniac Glen, Inverness. All were 197 ft *60 m* in 1983 but one or more of the latter are expected to reach 200 ft *61 m* by June 1985. The tallest in England is a Douglas fir (*Pseudotsuga taxifolia*) measured at 174 ft *53,0 m* at Broadwood, Dunster, Somerset. The tallest measured in Northern Ireland is a Giant Sequoia (*Sequoiadendron giganteum*), measured in 1983 to be 164 ft *50 m* tall at Caledon Castle, County Tyrone. The tallest in Wales is a Grand Fir (*Abies grandis*) at Leighton Park, Powys (pl. 1886) measured in 1982 to be 190 ft *58 m*.

Tallest *Ireland*

The tallest tree in Ireland is a Sitka spruce (*Picea sitchensis*) 166 ft *50,59 m* tall at Curraghmore, Waterford, measured in March 1974.

Tallest Christmas tree

The world's tallest cut Christmas tree was a 221 ft *67,36 m* tall Douglas fir (*Pseudotsuga taxifolia*) erected at Northgate Shopping Center, Seattle, Washington in December 1950. The tallest Christmas tree erected in Britain was the 85 ft 3¼ in *25,98 m* long spruce from Norway erected for the Canterbury Cathedral appeal on the South Bank, London on 20 Nov 1975.

Oldest tree *World*

The oldest recorded tree was a Bristlecone pine (*Pinus longaeva*) designated WPN-114, which grew at 10,750 ft *3275 m* above sea-level on the north-east face of the Wheeler Ridge on the Sierra Nevada, California, USA. During studies in 1963 and 1964 it was found to be about 4900 years old but was cut down with a chain saw. The oldest known *living* tree is the Bristlecone pine named *Methuselah* at 10,000 ft *3050 m* in the California side of the White Mountains confirmed as 4600 years old. In March 1974 it was reported that this tree had produced 48 live seedlings. Dendrochronologists estimate the *potential* life-span of a bristlecone pine at nearly 5500 years, but that of a California Big Tree

(*Sequoia giganteum*) at perhaps 6000 years. No single cell lives more than 30 years. A report in March 1976 stated that some enormous specimens of Japanese cedar (*Cryptomeria japonica*) had been dated by carbon-14 to 5200 BC.

Mexico's Montezuma cypress in Oaxaca needs a class of 30 children to encircle its base (see page 50).

Oldest tree *Great Britain*

Of all British trees that with the longest life is the yew (*Taxus baccata*), for which a maximum age well in excess of 1000 years is usually conceded. The oldest known is the Fortingall Yew near Aberfeldy, Tayside, part of which still grows. In 1777 this tree was over 50 ft *15,24 m* in girth and it cannot be much less than 2500

TALLEST TREES IN THE BRITISH ISLES
By species

		ft	m
ALDER (Italian)	Westonbirt, Gloucester	98	30
ALDER (Common)	Ashburnham Park, East Sussex	105	32
ASH	Old Roar Ghyll, St. Leonards, East Sussex	135	41
BEECH	Beaufront Castle, Northumberland	144	44
BEECH (Copper)	Chart Park Golf Course, Dorking, Surrey	124	38
BIRCH (Swedish)	Taymouth Castle	110	29
CEDAR (Blue Atlas)	Brockhampton Pk, Hereford & Worcs	125	38
CEDAR (of Lebanon)	Leaton Knolls, Shropshire	140	42
CHESTNUT (Horse)	Ashford Chase, Hampshire	130	39
CHESTNUT (Sweet)	Godinton Park, Kent	122	37
CYPRESS (Lawson)	Endsleigh, Devon	133	40
CYPRESS (Leyland)	Bicton, Devon	118	36
CYPRESS (Monterey)	Bicton, Devon	124	38
DOUGLAS FIR	The Hermitage, Perth, Tayside	197	60
ELM (Wych)[1] (Huntingdon)	Howlett's Park Zoo, Kent	132	40
ELM (Wych)[1] (Smooth Leaf)	North Inch, Perth, Tayside	132	40
EUCALYPTUS (Blue Gum)	Glencormack, Co. Wicklow	144	44
GRAND FIR	Strone, Cairndow, Strathclyde	197	60
GINKGO	Linton Park (Maidstone), Kent	98	30
HEMLOCK (Western)	Murthly Castle, Tayside	170	52
HOLLY	Ashburnham Park, East Sussex	80	24
HORNBEAM	Wrest Park, Bedfordshire	105	32
LARCH (European)	Glenlee, Dumfries & Galloway	150	46
LARCH (Japanese)	Blair Castle, Tayside	123	37
LIME	Duncombe Park, North Yorkshire	150	45
METASEQUOIA	Savill Garden, Berkshire	88	27
MONKEY PUZZLE	Lochnaw, Dumfries & Galloway	95	29
OAK (Common)	Leeds Castle, Kent	135	41
OAK (Sessile)	Whitfield Ho., Hereford & Worcs	140	42
OAK (Red)	Cowdray Park, West Sussex	115	35
OAK (Turkey)	Knightshayes, Devon	138	42
PEAR	Borde Hill, West Sussex	64	19
PINE (Corsican)	Adhurst, St. Mary, Hampshire	150	46
PLANE	Bryanston, Dorset	156	48
POPLAR (Black Italian)	Fairlawne, Kent	150	46
POPLAR (Black, native)	Longnor Hall, Shropshire	124	37
POPLAR (Lombardy)	Marble Hill, Twickenham, G. London	130	39
REDWOOD (Coast)	Bodnant, Gwynedd	148	45
SILVER FIR	Raehills, Dumfries	164	50
SPRUCE (Sitka)	River Findhorn, Nairn	195	59
SYCAMORE	Drumlanrig Castle, Dumfries & Galloway	112	34
TULIP-TREE	Taplow House, Buckinghamshire	120	36
WALNUT	Gayhurst, Newport Pagnell, Buckinghamshire	80	24
WALNUT (Black)	Bisham Abbey, Buckinghamshire	118	36
WELLINGTONIA	Castle Leod, Easter Ross, Highland	167	51
WILD SERVICE	Gatton Manor, Surrey	87	26
WILLOW (Weeping)	Ashford Chase, Hampshire	79	24
WINGNUT (Caucasian)	Abbotsbury, Dorset	115	35
YEW	Close Walks, Midhurst, West Sussex	95	29

[1] It was estimated in 1980 that more than 17 million of the 23 million elms in southern England had since 1968 been killed by the fungus that causes Dutch elm disease Ceratocystis ulmi.

years old today. The 1500 years attributed by the Royal Archeological Society to the Eastham yew in Wirral is possible but many are very much bigger and older.

Earliest species
The earliest species of tree still surviving is the Maiden-hair tree (*Ginkgo biloba*) of Chekiang, China, which first appeared about 160,000,000 years ago, during the Jurassic era. It was 'rediscovered' by Kaempfer (Netherlands) in 1690 and reached England *c.* 1754. It has been grown in Japan since *c.* 1100 where it was known as *ginkyō* ('silver apricot') and is now known as *icho*.

Most leaves
Little work has been done on the laborious task of establishing which species has most leaves. A large oak has perhaps 250,000 but a Cypress may have some 45–50 million leaf scales.

Remotest
The tree remotest from any other tree is believed to be one at an oasis in the Ténéré Desert, Niger Republic. In February 1960 it survived being rammed by a lorry driven by a Frenchman. There were no other trees within 50 km *31 miles*. The tree was transplanted and it is now in the Museum at Niamey, Niger.

Most expensive
The highest price ever paid for a tree is $51,000 (*then £18,214*) for a single Starkspur Golden Delicious apple tree from near Yakima, Washington, USA, bought by a nursery in Missouri in 1959.

Largest forest *World*
The largest afforested areas in the world are the vast coniferous forests of the northern USSR, lying mainly between latitude 55° N, and the Arctic Circle. The total wooded area amounts to 2,700,000,000 acres *1100 million ha* (25 per cent of the world's forests), of which 38 per cent is Siberian larch. The USSR is 34 per cent afforested.

Largest forest *Great Britain*
The largest forest in England is Kielder Forest (72,336 acres *29 273 ha*), in Northumberland. The largest forest in Wales is the Coed Morgannwg (Forest of Glamorgan) (42,555 acres *17 221 ha*). Scotland's most extensive forest is the Glen Trool Forest (51,376 acres *20 791 ha*) in Kirkcudbright, Dumfries & Galloway. The United Kingdom is 7 per cent afforested.

Longest avenue of trees
The longest avenue of trees has been the now partly felled private avenue of 1750 beeches in Savernake Forest near Marlborough, Wiltshire. It measured 3.25 miles *5,23 km*.

Wood *Heaviest*
The heaviest of all woods is Black ironwood (*Olea laurifolia*), also called South African ironwood, with a specific gravity of up to 1.49, and weighing up to 93 lb/ft³ *1490 kg/m³*. The heaviest British wood is boxwood (*Buxus sempervirens*) with an extreme of 64 lb/ft³ *1025 kg/m³*.

Wood *Lightest*
The lightest wood is *Aeschynomene hispida*, found in Cuba, which has a specific gravity of 0.044 and a weight of only 2¾ lb/ft³ *44 kg/m³*. The wood of the Balsa tree (*Ochroma pyramidale*) is of very variable density—between 2½ and 24 lb/ft³ *40* and *384 kg/m³*. The density of cork is 15 lb/ft³ *240 kg/m³*.

Champion plant collector
Dr Julian A. Steyermark of the Herbario Nacional, Caracas, Venezuela had by March 1984 made an unrivalled total of 130,450 collections.

KINGDOM PROTISTA

PROTISTA

Protista were first discovered in 1676 by Antonie van Leeuwenhoek of Delft (1632–1723), a Dutch microscopist. Among Protista are characteristics common to both plants and animals. The more plant-like are termed Protophyta (protophytes), including unicellular algae, and the more animal-like are placed in the phylum Protozoa (protozoans), including amoeba and flagellates.

Largest
The largest protozoans in terms of volume, which are known to have existed were calcareous foraminifera (Foraminiferida) belonging to the genus *Nummulites*, a species of which, in the Middle Eocene rocks of Turkey, attained 22 cm *8.6 in* in diameter. The largest existing protozoan, a species of the fan-shaped *Stannophyllum* (Xenophyophorida), can exceed this in length (25 cm *9.8 in* has been recorded) but not in volume.

Smallest
The smallest of all protophytes is the marine

A small part of Calcutta's famous 200 year old Banyan tree which covers 3 acres *1,2 ha* (see page 50).

microflagellate alga *Micromonas pusilla*, with a diameter of less than 2 microns or micrometres $(2 \times 10^{-6}$ m) or *0.00008 in*.

Fastest moving
The protozoan *Monas stigmatica* has been measured to move a distance equivalent to 40 times its own length in a second. No human can cover even seven times his own length in a second.

Fastest reproduction
The protozoan *Glaucoma*, which reproduces by binary fission, divides as frequently as every three hours. Thus in the course of a day it could become a 'six greats grandparent' and the progenitor of 510 descendants.

KINGDOM FUNGI

Largest
Alan Medd of Teesdale Comprehensive School, Barnard Castle, Co. Durham found a puff ball (*Lycoperdon gigantea*) 76 in *193 cm* in circumference in October 1984. A 72 lb *32,6 kg* example of the edible mushroom (*Polyporus frondosus*) was reported by Joseph Opple near Solon, Ohio in September 1976.

The largest officially recorded tree fungus was a specimen of *Oxyporus* (*Fomes*) *nobilissimus*, measuring 56 in *142 cm* by 37 in *94 cm* and weighing at least 300 lb *136 kg* found by J. Hisey in Washington State, USA, in 1946. The largest recorded in the United Kingdom is an ash fungus (*Fomes fraxineus*) measuring 50 in by 15 in *127 cm* by *38 cm* wide, found by the forester A. D. C. LeSueur on a tree at Waddesdon, Buckinghamshire, in 1954.

Most poisonous toadstool
The yellowish-olive death cap (*Amanita phalloides*) is regarded as the world's most poisonous fungus. It is found in England. From six to fifteen hours after tasting, the effects are vomiting, delirium, collapse and death. Among its victims was Cardinal Giulio de' Medici, Pope Clement VII (b. 1478) on 25 Sept 1534.

The Registrar General's Report states that between 1920 and 1950 there were 39 fatalities from fungus poisoning in the United Kingdom. As the poisonous types are mostly *Amanita* varieties, it is reasonable to assume that the deaths were predominantly due to *Amanita phalloides*. The most recent fatality was probably in 1960.

Aeroflora
Fungi were once classified in the subkingdom Protophyta of the Kingdom Protista. The highest total fungal spore count was 161,037 per m³ near Cardiff on 21 July 1971. A plant tree pollen count of 2160 per m³ was recorded near London on 9 May 1971. The lowest counts of airborne allergens are nil. The highest recorded grass pollen count in Britain was one of 2824 per m³ recorded at Aberystwyth on 29 June 1961.

KINGDOM PROCARYOTA

Earliest life form
In June 1980 Prof J. William Schopf announced the discovery of thread-like cellular remnants built by blue-green algae or bacteria-like organisms in calcareous stromatolites dated to 3500 million years old in the 'North Pole' region of northern Western Australia.

The earliest life-form reported from Britain is

The biggest puff ball ever found—one over 6 feet in circumference culled from a wood in County Durham (see page 52).

Kakabekia barghoorniana, a microorganism similar in form to an orange slice, found near Harlech, Gwynedd, Wales in 1964 and dated to 2000 million years ago.

BACTERIA

Antonie van Leeuwenhoek (1632–1723) was the first to observe bacteria in 1675. The largest of the bacteria is the sulphur bacterium *Beggiatoa mirabilis*, which is from 16 to 45 microns in width and which may form filaments several millimetres long.

The bacteria *Thermoactinomyces vulgaris* have been found alive in cores of mud taken from the bottom of Windermere, Cumbria, England which have been dated to 1500 years before the present.

Smallest free-living entity

The smallest of all free-living organisms are pleuro-pneumonia-like organisms (PPLO) of the *Mycoplasma*. One of these, *Mycoplasma laidlawii*, first discovered in sewage in 1936, has a diameter during its early existence of only 100 millimicrons, or 0.000004 in. Examples of the strain known as H.39 have a maximum diameter of 300 millimicrons and weigh an estimated 1.0×10^{-16} gramme. Thus a 190 tonne Blue whale would weigh 1.9×10^{24} or 1.9 quadrillion times as much.

Highest

In April 1967 the US National Aeronautics and Space Administration reported that bacteria had been discovered at an altitude of 135,000 ft (25.56 miles) *41 100 m*.

Longest lived

The oldest deposits from which living bacteria are claimed to have been extracted are salt layers near Irkutsk, USSR, dating from about 600,000,000 years ago. The discovery was not accepted internationally. The US Dry Valley Drilling Project in Antarctica claimed resuscitated rod-shaped bacteria from caves up to a million years old.

Fastest

The rod-shaped bacillus *Bdellovibrio bacteriovorus*, by means of a polar flagellum rotating 100 times/sec, can move 50 times its own length of 2 µm per second. This would be the equivalent of a human sprinter reaching 200 mph *320 km/h* or swimmer crossing the Channel in 6 min.

Toughest

The bacterium *Micrococcus radiodurans* can withstand atomic radiation of 6.5 million röntgens or 10,000 times that fatal to the average man. In March 1983 John Barras (University of Oregon, USA) reported bacteria from sulfurous sea bed vents thriving at 306°C *583°F* in the East Pacific Rise at Lat. 21°N.

VIRUSES

Largest

Dmitriy Ivanovsky (1864–1920) first reported filterable objects in 1892 but Martinus Willem Beijerink (1851–1931) first confirmed the nature of viruses in 1898. These are now defined as aggregates of two or more types of chemical (including either DNA or RNA) which are infectious and potentially pathogenic. The longest known is the rod-shaped *Citrus tristeza* virus with particles measuring 200×10 nm (1 nanometer $= 1 \times 10^{-9}$ m).

Smallest

The smallest known viruses are the nucleoprotein plant viruses such as the satellite of tobacco *necrosis virus* with spherical particles 17 nm in diameter. A putative new infectious submicroscopic organism but without nucleic acid, named a 'prion', was announced from the University of California in February 1982. Viroids (RNA cores without protein coating) are much smaller than viruses. They were discovered by Theodor O. Diener (USA) in February 1972.

PARKS, ZOOS, OCEANARIA AND AQUARIA

PARKS

Largest *World*

The world's largest park is the Wood Buffalo National Park in Alberta, Canada (established 1922), which has an area of 11,172,000 acres (17,560 miles² *45 480 km²*).

Largest *Britain*

The largest National Park in Great Britain is the Lake District National Park which has an area of 866 miles² *2240 km²*. The largest private park in the United Kingdom is Woburn Park (3000 acres *1200 ha*), near Woburn Abbey, the seat of the Dukes of Bedford.

ZOOS

Largest game reserve

It has been estimated that throughout the world there are some 500 zoos with an estimated annual attendance of 330,000,000. The largest zoological reserve in the world has been the Etosha Reserve, Namibia established in 1907 with an area which grew to 38,427 miles² *99 525 km²*.

Oldest

The earliest known collection of animals was that set up by Shulgi, a 3rd dynasty ruler of Ur in 2094–2097 BC at Puzurish in south-east Iraq. The oldest known zoo is that at Schönbrunn, Vienna, Austria, built in 1752 by the Holy Roman Emperor Franz I for his wife Maria Theresa. The oldest existing privately owned zoo in the world is that of the Zoological Society of London, founded in 1826. Its collection, housed partly in Regent's Park, London (36 acres *14,5 ha*) and partly at Whipsnade Park, Bedfordshire (541 acres *219 ha*) (opened 23 May 1931), is the most comprehensive in the United Kingdom. The stocktaking on 1 Jan 1985 accounted for a total of 9044 specimens. These comprised 2636 mammals, 2034 birds, 574 reptiles and amphibians, an estimated total of 1950 fish and an estimated total of 1850 invertebrates. Locusts, ants and bees are excluded from these figures. The record annual attendances are 3,031,571 in 1950 for Regent's Park and 756,758 in 1961 for Whipsnade.

OCEANARIA

Earliest and largest

The world's first oceanarium is Marineland of Florida, opened in 1938 at a site 18 miles *29 km* south of St Augustine, Florida, USA. Up to 5,800,000 gal *26,3 million litres* of sea-water are pumped daily through two major tanks, one rectangular (100 ft *30,48 m* long by 40 ft *12,19 m* wide by 18 ft *5,48 m* deep) containing 375,000 gal *1,7 million litres*, and one circular (233 ft *71 m* in circumference and 12 ft *3,65 m* deep) containing 330,000 gal *1,5 million litres*. The tanks are seascaped, including coral reefs and even a shipwreck. The salt water tank at Hanna-Barbera's Marineland, located at Palos Verdes, California, USA is 251½ ft *76,65 m* in circumference and 22 ft *6,7 m* deep, with a capacity of 530,000 gal *2,4 million litres*. The total capacity of this whole oceanarium is 2,080,000 gal *9,4 million litres*. Their killer whale 'Orky' at 14,000 lb *6350 kg* is the largest in captivity.

AQUARIA

Largest aquarium

The world's largest aquarium, as opposed to fish farm, is the John G. Shedd Aquarium at 12th Street and Lake Shore Drive, Chicago, Illinois, USA, completed in November 1929 at a cost of $3,250,000 (then £668,725). The total capacity of its display tanks is 375,000 gal *1,7 million litres* with reservoir tanks holding 1,665,000 gal *7,5 million litres*. Exhibited are 5500 specimens from 350 species. Most of these specimens are collected by the Aquarium collecting boat based in Miami, Florida, and are shipped by air to Chicago. The record attendances are 78,658 in a day on 21 May 1931, and 4,689,730 visitors in the single year of 1931.

CHAPTER THREE

The Natural World

THE EARTH

The Earth is not a true sphere, but flattened at the poles and hence an oblate spheroid. The polar diameter of the Earth (7899.806 miles *12 713,505 km*) is 26.575 miles *42,769 km* less than the equatorial diameter (7926.381 miles *12 756,274 km*). The Earth has a pear shaped asymmetry with the north polar radius being 148 ft *45 m* longer than the south polar radius. There is also a slight ellipticity of the equator since its long axis (about longitude 37° W) is 522 ft *159 m* greater than the short axis. The greatest departures from the reference ellipsoid are a protuberance of 240 ft *73 m* in the area of Papua New Guinea and a depression of 344 ft *105 m* south of Sri Lanka, in the Indian Ocean.

The greatest circumference of the Earth, at the equator, is 24,901.46 miles *40 075,02 km*, compared with 24,859.73 miles *40 007,86 km* at the meridian. The area of the surface is estimated to be 196,937,400 miles^2 *510 065 600 km^2*. The period of axial rotation, *i.e.* the true sidereal day, is 23 hr 56 min 4.0996 sec, mean time.

The mass of the Earth was first assessed by Dr Nevil Maskelyne (1732–1811) in Perthshire, Scotland in 1774. The modern value is 5,880,000,000,000,000,000,000 tons *5,974 × 10^{21} tonnes* and its density is 5.515 times that of

water. The volume is an estimated 259,875,300,000 miles^3 *1 083 207 000 000 km^3*. The Earth picks up cosmic dust but estimates vary widely with 30,000 tons/*tonnes* a year being the upper limit. Modern theory is that the Earth has an outer shell or lithosphere 50 miles *80 km* thick, then an outer and inner rock layer or mantle extending 1745 miles *2809 km* deep, beneath which there is an iron rich core of radius 2164 miles *3482 km*. If the iron rich core theory is correct, iron would be the most abundant element in the Earth. At the centre of the core the estimated density is 13.09 g/cm^3; the temperature 4500°C and the pressure 23,600 tons f/in^2 or 364 GPa.

Central Australia's renowned Ayer's Rock, named after South Australian former premier Sir Henry Ayers. It often glows red in the twilight (see page 60). *(Denise and Graham Ling)*

---

1. NATURAL PHENOMENA

EARTHQUAKES

(Note: Seismologists record all dates with the year *first*, based not on local time but on Greenwich Mean Time).

Greatest *World*

It is estimated that each year there are some 500,000 detectable seismic or micro-seismic disturbances of which 100,000 can be felt and 1000 cause damage. The deepest recorded hypocentres are of 720 km *447 miles* in Indonesia in 1933, 1934 and 1943.

An inherent limitation in the widely used Gutenberg–Richter scale (published in 1954) precludes its usefulness when extended to the relative strengths of the strongest earthquakes ever recorded. Its use of surface-wave magni-

tudes, based on amplitudes of waves of a period of 20 sec, results in the 'damping' of any increase in amplitude where fault ruptures break over a length much above 60 km *37 miles*. These however provenly may reach a length of 800 to 1000 km *500–620 miles*. This 'overload' or 'saturation effect' has resulted in the adoption since 1977 of the Kanamori scale for comparing the most massive earthquakes. Magnitudes are there defined in terms of energy release using the concept of the seismic moment, devised by K-Aki in 1966. Thus the most massive instrumentally recorded earthquake has been the cataclysmic Lebu shock south of Concepción, Chile on 1960 May 22 estimated at 10^{26} ergs. While this uniquely rates a magnitude of 9.5 on the Kanamori scale, it ranks in only equal 4th place (with the 1922 Chilean earthquake) at Magnitude 8.3 on the Gutenberg–Richter scale. For the removal of doubt the progressive records on the two scales are shown in the table below.

Worst death roll *World*

The greatest loss of life occurred in the earthquake (*ti chen*) in the Shensi, Shansi and Honan provinces of China, of 1556 Feb 2, (new style) (Jan 23 os) when an estimated 830,000 people were killed. The highest death roll in modern times has been in the Tangshan 'quake (Mag. 8.2) in Eastern China on 1976 July 27 (local time was 3 a.m. July 28). A first figure published on 4 Jan 1977 revealed 655,237 killed, later adjusted to 750,000. On 22 Nov 1979 the New China News Agency unaccountably reduced the death toll to 242,000. As late as Jan 1982 the site of the city was still a prohibited area. The greatest material damage was in the 'quake on the Kwanto plain, Japan, of 1923 Sept 1 (Mag. 8.2, epicentre in Lat. 35° 15′ N, Long. 139° 30′ E). In Sagami Bay the sea-bottom in one area sank 400 m *1310 ft*. The official total of persons killed and missing in the *Shinsai* or great 'quake and the resultant fires was 142,807. In Tōkyō and Yokohama 575,000 dwellings were destroyed. The cost of the damage was estimated at £1000 million (now more than £4000 million). It has however been estimated that a 7.5 magnitude shock (G-R scale) 30 miles *48 km* north of Los Angeles would result in damage estimated at $70,000 million.

Worst death roll *Great Britain and Ireland*

The total of the undisputed death roll for Great Britain is two—an apprentice, Thomas Grey, struck by falling masonry from Christ's Hospital Church, near Newgate, London at 6 p.m. on 6 Apr 1580. Mabel Everet of about the same age died of injuries 4 days later.

The East Anglian or Colchester earthquake of 1884 Apr 22 (9.18 a.m.) (epicentres Lat. 51° 48′ N, Long. 0° 53′ E, and Lat. 51° 51′ N, Long. 0° 55′ E) caused damage estimated at more than £12,000 to 1250 buildings. Langenhoe Church was wrecked. Windows and doors were rattled over an area of 53,000 miles² *137 250 km²* and the shock was felt in Exeter and Ostend, Belgium. It has been estimated to have been of magnitude 5.2 on the Richter scale. Researches by Andrew Phillips of the Colchester Institute

in 1984 have dispelled every indication that *any* fatalities or even serious injury can be attributed to this shock.

The highest instrumentally measured magnitude is 6.0 for the Dogger Bank event of 7 June 1931. The strongest Scottish tremor occurred at Inverness at 10.45 p.m. on 1816 Aug 13, and was felt over an area of 50,000 miles² *130 000 km²*. The strongest Welsh tremor occurred in Swansea at 9.45 a.m. on 1906 June 27 (epicentre Lat. 51° 38′ N, Long. 4° W). It was felt over an area of 37,800 miles² *97 900 km²*.

No earthquake with its epicentre in Ireland has ever been instrumentally measured, though the effects of the North Wales shock of 19 July 1984 (mag. 5 to 5.5) dislocated traffic lights in Dublin. However, there was a shock in August 1734 which damaged 100 dwellings and five churches.

VOLCANOES

The total number of known active volcanoes in the world is 850 of which many are submarine. The greatest active concentration is in Indonesia, where 77 of its 167 volcanoes have erupted within historic times. The name volcano derives from the now dormant Vulcano Island (from the God of fire Vulcanus) in the Mediterranean.

Greatest eruption

The total volume of matter discharged in the eruption of Tambora, a volcano on the island of Sumbawa, in Indonesia, 5–7 Apr 1815, was 150–180 km³. The energy of this 1395 mph *2245 km/h* eruption, which lowered the height of the island by 4100 ft *1250 m* from 13,450 ft *4100 m* to 9350 ft *2850 m*, was 8.4×10^{19} joules. A crater seven miles *11 km* in diameter was formed. Some 90,000 were killed or died of famine. This compares with a probable 60–65 km³ ejected by Santoríni and 20 km³ ejected by Krakatoa (see below). The internal pressure at Tambora has been estimated at 3270 kg/cm² or 20.76 tons/in².

The ejecta in the Taupo eruption in New Zealand *c.* AD 130 has been estimated at 30,000 million tonnes/*tons* of pumice moving at one time at 400 mph *700 km/h*. It flattened 16 000 km² *6180 miles²* (over 26 times the devastated area of Mt. St. Helens). Less than 20 per cent of the 14×10^9 tonnes of pumice ejected in this most violent of all documented volcanic events fell within 200 km *125 miles* of the vent.

Longest lava flow

The longest lava flow in historic times, known as *pahoehoe* (twisted cord-like solidifications), is that from the eruption of Laki in 1783 in southeast Iceland which flowed 65–70 km *40.5–43.5 miles*. The largest known pre-historic flow is the Roza basalt flow in North America *c.* 15 million years ago, which had an unsurpassed length (480 km *300 miles*), area (40 000 km² *15,400 miles²*) and volume (1250 km³ *300 miles³*).

Greatest explosion

The greatest explosion (possibly since Santoríni in the Aegean Sea 1626 ± 1 BC) occurred at *c.* 10 a.m. (local time), or 3.00 a.m. GMT, on 27

Aug 1883, with an eruption of Krakatoa, an island (then 18 miles² *47 km²*) in the Sunda Strait, between Sumatra and Java, in Indonesia. A total of 163 villages were wiped out, and 36,380 people killed by the wave it caused. Rocks were thrown 34 miles *55 km* high and dust fell 3313 miles *5330 km* away 10 days later. The explosion was recorded four hours later on the island of Rodrigues, 2968 miles *4776 km* away, as 'the roar of heavy guns' and was heard over 1/13th part of the surface of the globe. This explosion estimated to have had about 26 times the power of the greatest H-bomb test was still only a fifth part of the Santoríni cataclysm.

Highest *Extinct*

The highest extinct volcano in the world is Cerro Aconcagua (stone sentinel) (22,834 ft *6960 m*) on the Argentine side of the Andes. It was first climbed on 14 Jan 1897 by Mathias Zurbriggen; the highest summit climbed until 12 June 1907.

Highest *Dormant*

The highest dormant volcano is Volcán Llullaillaco (22,057 ft *6723 m*), on the frontier between Chile and Argentina.

Largest and highest *Active*

The highest volcano regarded as active is Volcán Antofalla (6450 m *21,162 ft*), in Argentina, though a more definite claim is made for Volcán Guayatiri or Guallatiri (19,882 ft *6060 m*), in Chile, which erupted in 1959. The world's largest active volcano is Mauna Loa (13,677 ft *4168 m*), Hawaii which erupted in 1975 and in April 1984.

Northernmost and southernmost

The northernmost volcano is Beeren Berg (7470 ft *2276 m*) on the island of Jan Mayen (71° 05′ N) in the Greenland Sea. It erupted on 20 Sept 1970 and the island's 39 inhabitants (all male) had to be evacuated. It was possibly discovered by Henry Hudson in 1607 or 1608, but definitely visited by Jan Jacobsz May (Netherlands) in 1614. It was annexed by Norway on 8 May 1929. The Ostenso seamount (5825 ft *1775 m*) 346 miles *556 km* from the North Pole in Lat. 85° 10′ N, Long. 133° W was volcanic. The most souther[l]y active volcano is Mount Erebus (12,450 ft *3795 m*) on Ross Island (77° 35′ S), in Antarctica. It was discovered on 28 Jan 1841 by the expedition of Captain (later Rear-Admiral Sir) James Clark Ross, RN (1800–62), and first climbed at 10 a.m. on 10 Mar 1908 by a British party of five, led by Professor (later Lieut.-Col. Sir) Tannatt William Edgeworth David (1858–1934).

Largest crater

The world's largest *caldera* or volcano crater is that of Toba, north central Sumatra, Indonesia covering 685 miles² *1775 km²*.

GEYSERS

Tallest *World*

The Waimangu (Maori, *black water*) geyser, in New Zealand, erupted to a height in excess of 1500 ft *457 m* in 1904, but has not been active since it erupted violently at 6.20 a.m. on 1 Apr 1917 and killed 4 people. Currently the world's tallest active geyser is the US National Parks' Service Steamboat Geyser, in Yellowstone National Park, which from 1962 to 1969 erupted with intervals ranging from 5 days to 10 months to a height of 250–380 ft *76–115 m*. The greatest measured water discharge has been 825,000 gal *37 850 hl* by the Giant Geyser, also in Yellowstone National Park, Wyoming, which has been dormant since 1955. The *Geysir* ('gusher') near Mount Hekla in south-central Iceland, from which all others have been named, spurts, on occasions, to 180 ft *55 m*, while the adjacent Strokkur, reactivated by drilling in 1963, spurts at 10–15 min intervals.

PROGRESSIVE LIST OF THE WORLD'S STRONGEST INSTRUMENTALLY RECORDED EARTHQUAKES			
Kanamori Scale Magnitudes M_s	Gutenberg–Richter Scale Magnitude M_w	Where $M_s = \frac{2}{3}(\log_{10}E - 11.8)$ and $M_w = \frac{2}{3}[\log_{10}(2E \times 10^4) - 10.7]$ Where E = energy released in dyne/cm	
8.8	8.6	Colombia coast	1906 Jan 31
(8.6)	8.6	Assam, India	1950 Aug 15
9.0	(8½)	Kamchatka, USSR	1952 Nov 4
9.1	(8.3)	Andreanof, Aleutian Is., USA	1957 Mar 9
9.5	(8.3)	Lebu, Chile	1960 May 22

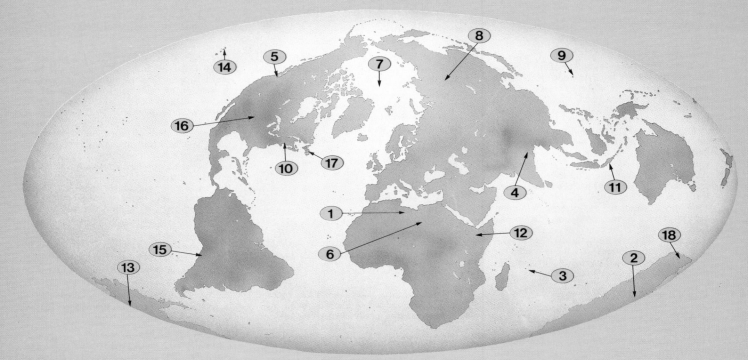

WEATHER RECORDS

1. HIGHEST SHADE TEMPERATURE: *World*
136.4° F *58° C* al'Azīzīyah, Libya, (alt. 367 ft *111 m*)
13.9.1922 *UK & Ireland* 98.2° F *36,77° C* Raunds,
Northants; Epsom, Surrey and Canterbury, Kent
9.8.1911 **(a)**

2. LOWEST SCREEN TEMPERATURE: *World*
−128.6° F −*89,2° C* Vostok, Antarctica, 21.7.1983 **(b)**.
UK & Ireland −17° F −*27,2° C* 11.2.1895 and −27,2° C
−*17° F* 10.1.1982 both Braemar, Grampian, Scotland **(c)**

3. GREATEST RAINFALL (24 hours): *World* 73.62 in
1870 mm, Cilaos, La Réunion, Indian Ocean,
15–16.3.1952 **(d)** *UK & Ireland* 11.00 in
279 mm, Martinstown, Dorset, 18–19.7.1955

4. GREATEST RAINFALL (Calendar Month): *World*
366.14 in *9299 mm*, Cherrapunji, Meghalaya, India, July
1861 *UK & Ireland* 56.54 in *1436 mm*, Llyn Llydau,
Snowdon, Gwynedd, October 1909

4. GREATEST RAINFALL (12 months): *World*
1041.78 in *26 461 mm*, Cherrapunji, Meghalaya,
1.8.1860–31.7.1861 *UK & Ireland* 257.0 in *6527 mm*,
Sprinkling Tarn, Cumbria, in 1954 **(e)**

4. WETTEST PLACE (Annual mean): *World*
Tutunendo, Colombia annual av. 11770 mm *463.4 in.*
UK & Ireland Styhead Tarn (1600 ft *487 m*), Cumbria,
172.9 in *4391 mm*

5. GREATEST SNOWFALL (f) (12 months): *World*
1224.5 in *31 102 mm*, Paradise, Mt Rainier, Washington,
USA 19.2.1971 to 18.2.1972 *UK & Ireland* 60 in *1524 mm*
Upper Teesdale and Denbighshire Hills, Clwyd, Wales, 1947

6. MAXIMUM SUNSHINE: (g) *World* >97 per cent
(over 4300 hours), eastern Sahara, annual average *UK &*
Ireland 78.3 per cent (382 hours) Pendennis Castle,
Falmouth, Cornwall, June 1925

7. MINIMUM SUNSHINE: *World* Nil at North Pole—
for winter stretches of 186 days *UK & Ireland* Nil in a
month at Westminster, London, in December 1890 **(h)**

8. BAROMETRIC PRESSURE (Highest): *World*
1083.8 mb. (*32.00 in*), Agata, Siberia, USSR (alt. 862 ft
262 m), 31.12.1968. *UK & Ireland* 1054.7 mb.
(*31.15 in*), Aberdeen, 31.1.1902

9. BAROMETRIC PRESSURE (Lowest): **(j)** *World*
870 mb (*25.69 in*), 300 miles *482 km* west of Guam,

Pacific Ocean, in Lat. 16°44′ N, Long. 137°46′ E.
12.10.1979 *UK & Ireland* 925.5 mb (*27.33 in*),
Ochtertyre, near Crieff, Tayside, 26.1.1884

10. HIGHEST SURFACE WIND-SPEED: (k) *World*
231 mph *371 km/h*, Mt. Washington (6288 ft *1916 m*),
New Hampshire, USA 12.4.1934 *UK & Ireland* 144 mph
231 km/h (125 knots), Coire Cas ski lift (3525 ft
1074 m), Cairn Gorm, Highland, 6.3.1967 **(l)**

11. THUNDER-DAYS (Year): **(m)** *World* 322 days,
Bogor (formerly Buitenzorg), Java, Indonesia (average,
1916–19) *UK & Ireland* 38 days, Stonyhurst, Lancashire,
1912 and Huddersfield, West Yorkshire, 1967

12. HOTTEST PLACE (Annual mean): **(n)** *World*
Dallol, Ethiopia, 94° F *34,4° C* (1960–66) *UK &*
Ireland Penzance, Cornwall, and Isles of Scilly,
both 52.7° F *11,5° C*, average 1931–60

13. COLDEST PLACE (Extrapolated annual mean):
World Polus Nedostupnosti, Pole of Cold (78° S., 96° E.),
Antarctica, −72° F −*57,8° C* Coldest measured mean:
−70° F −*56,6° C* Plateau Station, Antarctica *UK &*
Ireland Braemar, Grampian 6,34° C *43.41° F*
(1952–81)

14. MOST RAINY DAYS (Year): *World* Mt. Wai-'ale-
'ale (5148 ft *1569 m*), Kauai, Hawaii, up to 350 per
annum *UK & Ireland* Ballynahinch, Galway, 309 days in
1923

15. DRIEST PLACE (Annual mean): *World* Nil—in the
Desierto de Atacama, near Calama, Chile *UK & Ireland*
St Osyth, Lee Wick Farm, Essex, 20.2 in *513 mm*
(1964–82) **(o)**

15. LONGEST DROUGHT: *World* c. 400 years to
1971 Desierto de Atacama, Chile *UK & Ireland* 73 days
Mile End, Greater London, 4.3 to 15.5.1893 **(p)**

16. HEAVIEST HAILSTONES: (q) *World* 1.67 lb
750 g (7½ in *19 cm* diameter, 17⅓ in *44,45 cm*
circumference), Coffeyville, Kansas, USA 3.9.1970 *UK*
and Ireland 5 oz *141 g*, Horsham, West Sussex, 5.9.1958

17. LONGEST SEA LEVEL FOGS (Visibility less than
1000 yd *914,4 m*): *World* Fogs persist for weeks on the
Grand Banks, Newfoundland, Canada, and the average
is more than 120 days per year **(r)** *UK & Ireland*
London duration record was 26.11 to 1.12.1948 and
5.12 to 9.12.1952 (both 4 days 18 hours)

18. WINDIEST PLACE: *World* The Commonwealth
Bay, George V Coast, Antarctica, where gales reach
200 mph *320 km/h UK & Ireland* Tiree, Strathclyde
(89 ft *27 m*); annual average 17.4 mph *28 km/h*. Fair
Isle (1974–78) returned 20.6 mph *33,1 km/h*

Footnotes
(a) The 100.5° F *38,6° C* reported from Tonbridge, Kent was
a non-standard exposure and is estimated to be equivalent
of 97–98° F *36–36,7° C*
(b) Vostok is 11,220 ft *3419 m* above sea-level. The coldest
permanently inhabited place is the Siberian village of
Oymyakon (pop. 600) (63° 16′ N., 143° 15′ E.), (2300 ft
700 m) in the USSR where the temperature reached −96° F
−*71,1° C* in 1964.
(c) The −23° F −*30,5° C* at Blackadder, Borders, on 4 Dec
1879, and the −20° F −*28,9° C* at Grantown-on-Spey
on 24 Feb 1955, were not standard exposures.
The lowest official temperature in England is −15° F
−*26,1° C* at Newport, Shropshire on 10 Jan 1982.
The lowest maximum temperature for a day was −19,1° C
−*2,3° F* at Braemar on 10 Jan 1982.
(d) This is equal to 7435 tons *7554 tonnes* of rain per acre.
Elevation 1200 m *3937 ft.*
(e) The record for Ireland is 145.4 in *3921 mm* near Derriana
Lough, County Kerry in 1948.
(f) The record for a single snow storm is 189 in *4800 mm* at
Mt. Shasta, Ski Bowl, California, and for 24 hr, 76 in *1930 mm*
at Silver Lake, Colorado, USA on 14–15 April 1921.
The greatest depth of snow on the ground was 27 ft 7 in
8407 mm at Helen Lake, Mount Lassen in April 1983. London's
earliest recorded snow was on 25 Sept 1885, and the latest on
27 May 1821. Less reliable reports suggest snow on 12 Sept
1658 (Old Style) and on 12 June 1791.
(g) St Petersburg, Florida, USA, recorded 768 consecutive
sunny days from 9 Feb 1967 to 17 March 1969.
(h) The south-eastern end of the village of Lochranza, Isle
of Arran, Strathclyde is in shadow of mountains from
18 Nov to 8 Feb each winter.
(j) The USS *Repose*, a hospital ship, recorded 25.55 in
856 mb in the eye of a typhoon in 25° 35′ N 128° 20′ E
off Okinawa on 16 Sept 1945.
(k) The highest speed yet measured in a tornado is 280 mph
450 km/h at Wichita Falls, Texas, USA on 2 Apr 1958.
(l) The figure of 177.2 mph *285,2 km/h* at RAF Saxa Vord,
Unst, in the Shetlands, Scotland, on 16 Feb 1962, was not
recorded with standard equipment. There were gales of
great severity on 15 Jan 1362 and 26 Nov 1703.
(m) Between Lat. 35° N and 35° S. there are some 3200
thunderstorms each 12 night-time hours, some of which
can be heard at a range of 18 miles *29 km*.
(n) In Death Valley, California, USA, maximum temperatures
of over 120° F *48,9° C* were recorded on 43 consecutive
days—6 July to 17 Aug 1917. At Marble Bar, Western
Australia (maximum 121° F *49,4° C*) 160 consecutive
days with maximum temperatures of over 100° F *37,8° C* were
recorded—31 Oct 1923 to 7 Apr 1924. At Wyndham,
Western Australia, the temperature reached 90° F *32,2° C*
or more on 333 days in 1946.
(o) The lowest rainfall recorded in a single year was 9.29 in
23,6 cm at one station in Margate, Kent in 1921.
(p) The longest drought in Scotland was one of 38 days at
Port William, Dumfries & Galloway on 3 Apr to 10 May 1938.
(q) Much heavier hailstones are sometimes reported. These
are usually not single but coalesced stones. An ice block of
1–2 kg *35–70 oz*. was reputed to fall at Withington, Manchester
on 2 Apr 1973. The *Canton Evening News* reported on
14 Apr 1981 5 killed and 225 injured by a hailstorm
with stones weighing up to 30 lb *13,6 kg* (sic).
(r) Lower visibilities occur at higher altitudes. Ben Nevis is
reputedly in cloud 300 days per year.

2. WEATHER

Guinness Superlatives Ltd. have published a more specialist volume entitled the *Guinness Book of Weather Facts and Feats* (2nd Edition) by Ingrid Holford (Price £8.95).

The meteorological records given below necessarily relate largely to the last 140–160 years, since data before that time are both sparse and often unreliable. Reliable registering thermometers were introduced as recently as *c.* 1820. The longest continuous observations have been maintained at the Radcliffe Observatory, Oxford since 1815 though discontinuous records have enabled the Chinese to assert that 903 BC was a very bad winter.

Palaeo-entomological evidence is that there was a southern European climate in England *c.* 90,000 BC, while in *c.* 6000 BC the mean summer temperature reached 67° F *19,4° C*, or 6 deg F *3,3 deg C* higher than the present. It is believed that 1.2 million years ago the world's air temperature averaged 95° F *35° C*. The earliest authentic recording of British weather relates to the period 26 Aug–17 Sept 55 BC. The earliest reliably known hot summer was in AD 664 during our driest-ever century and the earliest known severe winter was that of AD 763–4. In 1683–4 there was frost in London from November to April. Frosts were recorded during August in the period 1668–89.

Most equable temperature
The location with the most equable recorded temperature over a short period is Garapan, on Saipan, in the Mariana Islands, Pacific Ocean. During the nine years from 1927 to 1935, inclusive, the lowest temperature recorded was 19,6° C *67.3° F* on 30 Jan 1934 and the highest was 31,4° C *88.5° F* on 9 Sept 1931, giving an extreme range of 11,8 deg C *21.2 deg F*. Between 1911 and 1966 the Brazilian off-shore island of Fernando de Noronha had a minimum temperature of 18,6° C *65.5° F* on 17 Nov 1913 and a maximum of 32,0° C *89.6° F* on 2 Mar 1965, an extreme range of 13,4 deg C *24.1 deg F*.

Greatest temperature ranges
The greatest recorded temperature ranges in the world are around the Siberian 'cold pole' in the eastern USSR. Temperatures in Verkhoyansk (67° 33′ N, 133° 23′ E) have ranged 192 deg F *106,7 deg C* from −94° F *−70° C* (unofficial) to 98° F *36,7° C*. The greatest temperature variation recorded in a day is 100 deg F *55,5 deg C* (a fall from 44° F *6,7° C* to −56° F *−48,8° C*) at Browning, Montana, USA, on 23–24 Jan 1916. The most freakish rise was 49 deg F *27,2 deg C* in 2 min at Spearfish, South Dakota, from −4° F *−20° C* at 7.30 a.m. to 45° F *7,2° C* at 7.32 a.m. on 22 Jan 1943. The British record is 29 deg C *52.2 deg F* (−7° C *19.4° F* to 22° C *71.6° F*) at Tummel Bridge, Tayside on 9 May 1978.

Longest freeze
The longest recorded unremitting freeze in the British Isles was one of 34 days at Moor House, Cumbria, from 23 Dec 1962 to 25 Jan 1963. This was almost certainly exceeded at the neighbouring Great Dun Fell, where the screen temperature never rose above freezing during the whole of January 1963. Less rigorous early data includes a frost from 5 Dec 1607 to 14 Feb 1608 and a 91-day frost on Dartmoor, Devon in 1854–5. No temperature lower than 34° F *1° C* has ever been recorded on Bishop Rock, Isles of Scilly.

Upper atmosphere
The lowest temperature ever recorded in the atmosphere is −143° C *−225.4° F* at an altitude of about 50–60 miles *80,5–96,5 km*, during noctilucent cloud research above Kronogård, Sweden, from 27 July to 7 Aug 1963. A jet stream moving at 408 mph *656 km/h* at 154,200 ft *47 000 m* (29.2 miles *46 km*) was recorded by Skua rocket above South Uist, Outer Hebrides, Scotland on 13 Dec 1967.

Thickest ice
The greatest recorded thickness of ice is 2.97 miles (15,670 ft) *4776 m* measured by radio echo soundings from a U.S. Antarctic Research aircraft at 69° 9′ 38″ S 135° 20′ 25″ E 400 km *250 miles* from the coast in Wilkes Land on 4 Jan 1975.

Deepest permafrost
The deepest recorded permafrost is more than 4500 ft *1370 m* reported from the upper reaches of the Viluy River, Siberia, USSR in February 1982.

Most recent White Christmas and Frost Fair
London has experienced seven 'White' or snowing Christmas Days since 1900. These have been 1906, 1917 (slight), 1923 (slight), 1927, 1938, 1956 (slight) and 1970. These were more frequent in the 19th century and even more so before the change of the calendar, which, by removing 3–13 Sept brought forward all dates subsequent to 2 Sept 1752 by 11 days. The last of the nine recorded Frost Fairs held on the Thames since 1564/65 was from December 1813 to 26 Jan 1814.

Most intense rainfall
Difficulties attend rainfall readings for very short periods but the figure of 1.50 in *38,1 mm* in 1 min at Barst, Guadeloupe on 26 Nov 1970, is regarded as the most intense recorded in modern times. The cloudburst of 'near 2 ft *609 mm* in less than a quarter of half an hour' at Oxford on the afternoon of 31 May (Old Style) 1682 is regarded as unacademically recorded. The most intense rainfall in Britain recorded to modern standards has been 2.0 in *51 mm* in 12 min at Wisbech, Cambridgeshire on 27 June 1970.

Falsest St. Swithin's Days
The legend that the weather on St. Swithin's Day, celebrated on 15 July (Old and New Style) since AD 912, determines the rainfall for the next 40 days is one which has long persisted. There was a brilliant 13½ hr sunshine in London on 15 July 1924, but 30 of the next 40 days were wet. On 15 July 1913 there was a 15-hr downpour, yet it rained on only 9 of the subsequent 40 days in London.

Best and worst British summers
According to Prof. Gordon Manley's survey over the period 1728–1978 the best (*i.e.* driest and hottest) British summer was that of 1976 and the worst (*i.e.* wettest and coldest) that of 1879. Temperatures of >32° C (89.8° F) were recorded on 13 consecutive days (25 June–7 July 1976) within Great Britain including 7 such consecutive days in Cheltenham (1–7 July), where 35,9° C *96.6° F* was reached on 3 July. In 1983 there were 40 days >26,6° C in Britain between 3 July–31 Aug including 17 consecutively (3–19 July). London experienced its hottest month (July) since records began in 1840.

Humidity and discomfort
Human comfort or discomfort depends not merely on temperature but on the combination of temperature, humidity, radiation and windspeed. The United States Weather Bureau uses a Temperature-Humidity Index, which equals two-fifths of the sum of the dry and wet bulb thermometer readings plus 15. A THI of 98.2 has been twice recorded in Death Valley, California—on 27 July 1966 (119° F and 31 per cent) and on 12 Aug 1970 (117° F and 37 per cent). A person driving at 45 mph *72 km/h* in a car without a windscreen in a temperature of −45° F *−42,7° C* would, by the chill factor, experience the equivalent of −125° F *−87,2° C*, *i.e.* within 3.5 deg F *2,0 deg C* of the world record.

Largest mirage
The largest mirage on record was that sighted in the Arctic at 83° N 103° W by Donald B. MacMillan in 1913. This type of mirage known as the Fata Morgana appeared as the same 'Hills, valleys, snow-capped peaks extending through at least 120 degrees of the horizon' that Peary had misidentified as Crocker Land 6 years earlier. On 17 July 1939 a mirage of Snaefells Jokull (4715 ft *1437 m*) on Iceland was seen from the sea at a distance of 335–350 miles *539–563 km*.

Longest lasting rainbow
A rainbow lasting over 3 hours was reported

PROGRESSIVE RECORDINGS OF EXTREME HIGH TEMPERATURES WORLD WIDE

127.4° F	53,0° C	Ouargla, Algeria	27 Aug	1884
130° F	54,4° C	Amos, California, USA	17 Aug	1885
130° F	54,4° C	Mammoth Tank, California, USA	17 Aug	1885
134° F	56,7° C	Death Valley, California, USA	10 July	1913
136.4° F	58,0° C	Al'Aziziyah (el-Azizia), Libya*	13 Sept	1922

* *Obtained by the US National Geographical Society but not officially recognised by the Libyan Ministry of Communications.*

A reading of 140° F 60° C at Delta, Mexico, in August 1953 is not now accepted because of over-exposure to roof radiation. The official Mexican record of 136.4° F 58,0° C at San Luis, Sonora on 11 Aug 1933 is not internationally accepted.

A freak heat flash reported from Coimbra, Portugal, in September 1933 said to have caused the temperature to rise to 70° C 158° F for 120 sec is apocryphal.

PROGRESSIVE RECORDINGS OF EXTREME LOW TEMPERATURES WORLD WIDE

−73° F	−58,3° C	Floeberg Bay, Ellesmere I., Canada		1852[1]
−90.4° F	−68° C	Verkhoyansk, Siberia, USSR	3 Jan	1885
−90.4° F	−68° C	Verkhoyansk, Siberia, USSR	5 & 7 Feb	1892
−90.4° F	−68° C	Oymyakon, Siberia, USSR	6 Feb	1933
−100.4° F	−73,5° C	South Pole, Antarctica	11 May	1957
−102.1° F	−74,5° C	South Pole, Antarctica	17 Sept	1957
−109.1° F	−78,34° C	Sovietskaya, Antarctica	2 May	1958
−113.3° F	−80,7° C	Vostok, Antarctica	15 June	1958
−114.1° F	−81,2° C	Sovietskaya, Antarctica	19 June	1958
−117.4° F	−83,0° C	Sovietskaya, Antarctica	25 June	1958
−122.4° F	−85,7° C	Vostok, Antarctica	7–8 Aug	1958
−124.1° F	−86,7° C	Sovietskaya, Antarctica	9 Aug	1958
−125.3° F	−87,4° C	Vostok, Antarctica	25 Aug	1958
−126.9° F	−88,3° C	Vostok, Antarctica	24 Aug	1960
−128.6° F	−89,2° C	Vostok, Antactica	21 July	1983

[1] *The earliest recorded occasion that mercury froze (at −40° F or −40° C) was by M. V. Lomonosov, near Moscow c. 1750.*

from the coastal border of Gwynedd and Clwyd, North Wales on 14 Aug 1979.

Lightning

The visible length of lightning strokes varies greatly. In mountainous regions, when clouds are very low, the flash may be less than 300 ft *91 m* long. In flat country with very high clouds, a cloud-to-earth flash may measure 4 miles *6 km* though in the most extreme cases such flashes have been measured at 20 miles *32 km*. The intensely bright central core of the lightning channel is extremely narrow. Some authorities suggest that its diameter is as little as half an inch *1,27 cm*. This core is surrounded by a 'corona envelope' (glow discharge) which may measure 10–20 ft *3–6 m* in diameter.

The speed of a lightning discharge varies from 100 to 1000 miles/sec *160–1600 km/sec* for the downward leader track, and reaches up to 87,000 miles/sec *140 000 km/sec* (nearly half the speed of light) for the powerful return stroke. In Britain there is an average of 6 strikes/mile² per annum or 3,7 per km² and an average of 4200 per annum over Greater London alone. Every few million strokes there is a giant discharge, in which the cloud-to-earth and the return lightning strokes flash from and to the top of the thunder clouds. In these 'positive giants' energy of up to 3000 million joules (3×10^{16} ergs) is sometimes recorded. The temperature reaches about 30,000° C, which is more than five times greater than that of the surface of the Sun.

Highest waterspout

The highest waterspout of which there is a reliable record was one observed on 16 May 1898 off Eden, New South Wales, Australia. A theodolite reading from the shore gave its height as 5014 ft *1528 m*. It was about 10 ft *3 m* in diameter. The Spithead waterspout off Ryde, Isle of Wight on 21 Aug 1878 was measured by sextant to be 'about a mile' or *600 m* in height. A waterspout moved around Tor Bay, Devon on 17 Sept 1969 which, according to press estimates, was 1000 ft *300 m* in height.

Cloud extremes

The highest standard cloud form is cirrus, averaging 27,000 ft *8250 m* and above, but the rare nacreous or mother-of-pearl formation sometimes reaches nearly 80,000 ft *24 000 m* (see also Noctilucent clouds, Chapter 4). The lowest is stratus, below 3500 ft *1066 m*. The cloud form with the greatest vertical range is cumulo-nimbus, which has been observed to reach a height of nearly 68,000 ft *20 000 m* in the tropics.

Tornadoes (see also Accidents and Disasters Chap 11)

Britain's strongest tornado was at Southsea, Portsmouth on 14 Dec 1810 (Force 8 on the Meaden-TORRO scale). The Newmarket tornado (Force 6) of 3 Jan 1978 caused property damage estimated at up to £1,000,000. On 23 Nov 1981, 58 tornadoes were reported in one day from Anglesey to Eastern England.

3. STRUCTURE AND DIMENSIONS

OCEANS

Largest

The area of the Earth covered by sea is estimated to be 139,670,000 miles² *361 740 000 km²* or 70.92 per cent of the total surface. The mean depth of the hydrosphere was once estimated to be 12,450 ft *3795 m*, but recent surveys suggest a lower estimate, of 11,660 ft *3554 m*. The total weight of the water is estimated to be 1.3×10^{18} tons, or 0.022 per cent of the Earth's total weight. The volume of the oceans is estimated to be 308,400,000 miles³ *1 285 600 000 km³* compared to 8,400,000 miles³ *35 000 000 km³* of fresh water.

The largest ocean in the world is the Pacific. Excluding adjacent seas, it represents 45.8 per cent of the world's oceans and covers 64,186,300 miles² *166 240 000 km²* in area. The average depth is 12,925 ft *3939 m*. The shortest navigable trans-Pacific distance from Guayaquil, Ecuador to Bangkok, Thailand is 10,905 miles *17 550 km*.

Deepest *World*

The deepest part of the ocean was first pinpointed in 1951 by HM Survey Ship *Challenger* in the Marianas Trench in the Pacific Ocean. The depth was measured by sounding and by echo-sounder and published as 5960 fathoms (35,760 ft *10 900 m*). Subsequent visits (1959–1980) to this same Challenger Deep have resulted in slightly deeper measurements, now refined to 10 915 m (5968 fathoms, *35,810 ft*) or 6.78 miles *10,91 km* published by the US Defense Mapping Agency in 1983. On 23 Jan 1960 the US Navy bathyscaphe *Trieste* descended to the bottom there but the depth calibrations (made for fresh rather than salt water) yielded a figure within one fathom or 6 ft *1,8 m* of the above figure. A metal object, say a pound ball of steel, dropped into water above this trench would take nearly 64 min to fall to the sea-bed 6.78 miles *10,91 km* below, where hydrostatic pressure is over 18,000 lb/in² *1250 bars*.

Deepest *British waters*

The deepest point in the territorial waters of the United Kingdom is an areas 6 cables (*1100 m*) off the island of Raasay, Highland, in the Inner Sound at Lat. 57° 30′ 33″ N, Long. 5° 57′ 27″ W. A depth of 1038 ft (173 fathoms, *316 m*) was found in December 1959 by HMS *Yarnton* (Lt-Cdr A. C. F. David, RN.)

Largest sea

The largest of the world's seas is the South China Sea, with an area of 1,148,500 miles² *2 974 600 km²*. The Malayan Sea, comprising the waters between the Indian Ocean and the South Pacific, south of the Chinese mainland covering 3,144,000 miles² *8 142 900 km²* is not now an entity accepted by the International Hydrographic Bureau.

Largest gulf

The largest gulf in the world is the Gulf of Mexico, with an area of 580,000 miles² *1 500 000 km²* and a shoreline of 3100 miles *4990 km* from Cape Sable, Florida, USA, to Cabo Catoche, Mexico.

Largest bay

The largest bay in the world measured by shoreline length is Hudson Bay, northern Canada, with a shoreline of 7623 miles *12 268 km* and with an area of 317,500 miles² *822 300 km²*. The area of the Bay of Bengal is however 839,000 miles² *2 172 000 km²*. Great Britain's largest bay is Cardigan Bay which has a 140 mile *225 km* long shoreline and measures 72 miles *116 km* across from the Lleyn Peninsula, Gwynedd to St David's Head, Dyfed in Wales.

Longest fjords and sea lochs *World*

The world's longest fjord is the Nordvest Fjord arm of the Scoresby Sund in eastern Greenland, which extends inland 195 miles *313 km* from the sea. The longest of Norwegian fjords is the Sogne Fjord, which extends 183 km *113.7 miles* inland from Sygnefest to the head of the Lusterfjord arm at Skjolden. It averages barely 4,75 km *3 miles* in width and has a deepest point of 1245 m *4085 ft*. If measured from Huglo along the Bømlafjord to the head of the Sørfjord arm at Odda, Hardangerfjorden can also be said to extend 183 km *113.7 miles*. The longest Danish fjord is Limfjorden (100 miles *160 km* long).

Longest sea loch *Great Britain*

Scotland's longest sea loch is Loch Fyne, which extends 42 miles *67,5 km* inland into Strathclyde (formerly Argyllshire.)

Highest seamount

The highest known submarine mountain, or seamount, is one discovered in 1953 near the Tonga Trench, between Samoa and New Zealand. It rises 28,500 ft *8690 m* from the sea bed, with its summit 1200 ft *365 m* below the surface.

Remotest spot from land

The world's most distant point from land is a spot in the South Pacific, approximately 48° 30′ S, 125° 30′ W, which is about 1660 miles *2670 km* from the nearest points of land, namely Pitcairn Island, Ducie Island and Cape Dart, Antarctica. Centred on this spot, therefore, is a circle of water with an area of about 8,657,000 miles² *22 421 500 km²*—about 7000 miles² *18 000 km²* larger than the USSR, the world's largest country (see Chapter 11).

Most southerly

The most southerly part of the oceans is 85° 34′ S, 154° W, at the snout of the Robert Scott Glacier, 305 miles *490 km* from the South Pole.

Longest voyage

The longest possible great circle sea voyage is one of 19,860 miles *31 960 km* from a point 150 miles *240 km* west of Karachi, Pakistan to a point 200 miles *320 km* north of Uka' Kamchatka *via* the Mozambique Channel, Drake Passage and Bering Sea.

Sea temperature

The temperature of the water at the surface of the sea varies from −2° C *28.5° F* in the White Sea to 35,6° C *96° F* in the shallow areas of the Persian Gulf in summer. Ice-focused solar rays have been known to heat lake water to nearly 80° F *26,8° C*. The normal Red Sea temperature is 22° C *71.6° F*. The highest temperature recorded in the ocean is 662° F *350° C*, measured by the research submersible *Alvin* at Lat. 21° N on the East Pacific Rise in November 1979, emanating from a sea-floor geothermal spring at a depth of 2600 m *8530 ft*.

STRAITS

Longest

The longest straits in the world are the Tatarskiy Proliv or Tartar Straits between Sakhalin Island and the USSR mainland running from the Sea of Japan to Sakhalinsky Zaliv : 800 km *497 miles*, thus marginally longer than the Malacca Straits.

Broadest

The broadest named straits in the world are the Davis Straits between Greenland and Baffin Island with a minimum width of 210 miles *338 km*. The Drake Passage between the Diego Ramirez Islands, Chile and the South Shetland Islands is 710 miles *1140 km* across.

Narrowest

The narrowest navigable straits are those between the Aegean island of Euboea and the mainland of Greece. The gap is only 45 yd *40 m* wide at Khalkis. The Seil Sound, Strathclyde, Scotland, narrows to a point only 20 ft *6 m* wide where the Clachan bridge joins the island of Seil to the mainland and said to span the Atlantic.

WAVES
Highest

The highest officially recorded sea wave was

measured by Lt Frederic Margraff USN from the USS *Ramapo* proceeding from Manila, Philippines, to San Diego, California, USA, on the night of 6–7 Feb 1933, during a 68-knot (78.3 mph *126 km/h*) hurricane. The wave was calculated to be 112 ft *34 m* from trough to crest. The highest instrumentally measured wave was one 86 ft *26,2 m* high, recorded by the British ship *Weather Reporter*, in the North Atlantic on 30 Dec 1972 in Lat. 59° N, Long. 19° W. It has been calculated on the statistics of the Stationary Random Theory that one wave in more than 300,000 may exceed the average by a factor of 4.

On 9 July 1958 a landslip caused a 100 mph *160 km/h* wave to wash 1740 ft *530 m* high along the fjord-like Lituya Bay, Alaska, USA.

Highest seismic wave

The highest estimated height of a *tsunami* (often wrongly called a tidal wave) was one of 85 m *278 ft*, which appeared off Ishigaki Island, Ryukyu Chain on 24 Apr 1971. It tossed a 750 ton block of coral more than 2,5 km *1.3 miles*. *Tsunami* (a Japanese word meaning *nami*, a wave; *tsu*, overflowing) have been observed to travel at 490 mph *790 km/h*.

Evidence for a 1000 ft *300 m* ocean wave breaking on the southern shore of Lanai, Hawaiian Islands was reported on 4 Dec 1984. This occurred about 100 000 years ago due to a meteorite, a volcanic eruption or a submarine landslide.

CURRENTS

Greatest

The greatest current in the oceans of the world is the Antarctic Circumpolar Current or West Wind Drift Current which was measured in 1969 in the Drake Passage between South America and Antarctica to be flowing at a rate of 9500 million ft³ *270 000 000 m³* per sec— nearly treble that of the Gulf Stream. Its width ranges from 185 to 1240 miles *300–2000 km* and has a proven surface flow rate of $\frac{4}{10}$ of a knot *0,75 km/h*.

Strongest

The world's strongest currents are the Nakwakto

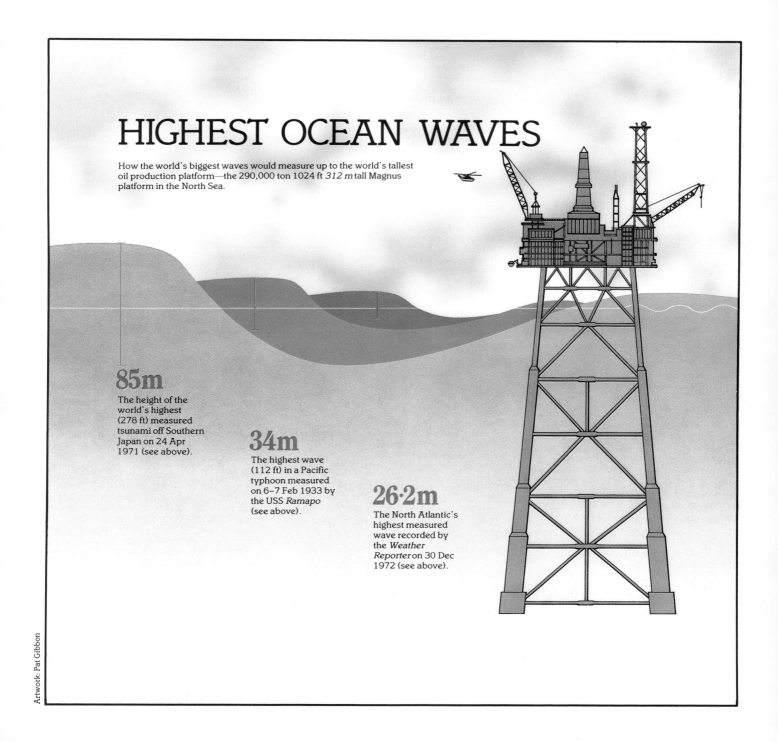

HIGHEST OCEAN WAVES

How the world's biggest waves would measure up to the world's tallest oil production platform—the 290,000 ton 1024 ft *312 m* tall Magnus platform in the North Sea.

85m
The height of the world's highest (278 ft) measured tsunami off Southern Japan on 24 Apr 1971 (see above).

34m
The highest wave (112 ft) in a Pacific typhoon measured on 6–7 Feb 1933 by the USS *Ramapo* (see above).

26·2m
The North Atlantic's highest measured wave recorded by the *Weather Reporter* on 30 Dec 1972 (see above).

Artwork: Pat Gibbon

Rapids, Slingsby Channel, British Columbia, Canada (Lat. 51° 05′ N, Long. 127° 30′ W) where the flow rate may reach 16.0 knots *29,6 km/h*. The fastest current in British territorial waters is 10.7 knots *19,8 km/h* in the Pentland Firth between the Orkney Islands and Caithness.

GREATEST TIDES

Extreme tides are due to lunar and solar gravitational forces affected by their perigee, perihelion and syzygies. Barometric and wind effects can superimpose an added 'surge' element. Coastal and sea-floor configurations can accentuate these forces. The normal interval between tides is 12 hr 25 min.

World

The greatest tides in the world occur in the Bay of Fundy, which divides the peninsula of Nova Scotia, Canada, from the United States' north-easternmost state of Maine and the Canadian province of New Brunswick. Burncoat Head in the Minas Basin, Nova Scotia, has the greatest mean spring range with 47.5 ft *14,50 m*. A range of 54½ ft *16,6 m* was recorded at springs in Leaf Basin in 1953. Tahiti experiences virtually no tide.

Great Britain

The place with the greatest mean spring range in Great Britain is Beachley, on the Severn, with a range of 40.7 ft *12,40 m*, compared with the British Isles' average of 15 ft *4,57 m*. Prior to 1933 tides as high as 28.9 ft *8,80 m* above and 22.3 ft *6.80 m* below datum (total range 51.2 ft *15,60 m*) were recorded at Avonmouth though an extreme range of 52.2 ft *15,90 m* for Beachley was officially accepted. In 1883 a freak tide of greater range was reported from Chepstow, Gwent.

ICEBERGS

Largest and tallest

The largest iceberg on record was an Antarctic tabular 'berg of over 12,000 miles² *31 000 km²* (208 miles *335 km* long and 60 miles *97 km* wide and thus larger than Belgium) sighted 150 miles *240 km* west of Scott Island, in the South Pacific Ocean, by the USS *Glacier* on 12 Nov 1956. The 200 ft *61 m* thick Arctic ice island T.1 (140 miles² *360 km²*) (discovered in 1946) was tracked for 17 years. The tallest iceberg measured was one of 550 ft *167 m* reported off western Greenland by the US icebreaker *East Wind* in 1958.

Most southerly Arctic

The most southerly Arctic iceberg was sighted in the Atlantic by a USN weather patrol in Lat. 28° 44′ N, Long. 48° 42′ W in April 1935. The southernmost iceberg reported in British home waters was one sighted 60 miles *96 km* from Smith's Knoll, on the Dogger Bank, in the North Sea.

Most northerly Antarctic

The most northerly Antarctic iceberg was a remnant sighted in the Atlantic by the ship *Dochra* in Lat. 26° 30′ S, Long. 25° 40′ W, on 30 Apr 1894.

LAND

There is satisfactory evidence that at one time the Earth's land surface comprised a single primeval continent of 80 million miles² *2 × 10⁸ km²*, now termed Pangaea, and that this split about 190 million years ago, during the Jurassic period, into two super-continents, termed Laurasia (Eurasia, Greenland and Northern America) and Gondwanaland (Africa, Arabia, India, South America, Oceania and Antarctica) and named after Gondwana, India,

which itself split 120 million years ago. The South Pole was apparently in the area of the Sahara as recently as the Ordovician period of *c.* 450 million years ago.

ROCKS

The age of the Earth is generally considered to be within the range of 4450 ± 50 million years, by analogy with directly measured ages of meteorites and of the moon. However, no rocks of this great age have yet been found on the Earth since geological processes have presumably destroyed them.

Oldest *World*

The greatest reported age for any scientifically dated rock is 3800 ± 100 million years for granite gneiss rock found near Granite Falls in the Minnesota river valley, USA as measured by the lead-isotope and rubidium-uranium methods by the US Geological Survey and announced on 26 Jan 1975. These metamorphic samples compare with the Amîtsoq gneiss from Godthaab, Greenland unreservedly accepted to be between 3700 and 3750 million years. Zirconium silicate crystals from Mt Narrayer, Australia were dated to 4200 million years (1983).

Oldest *Great Britain*

The original volcanic products from which were formed the gneiss and granulite rocks of the Scourian complex in the north west Highlands and the Western Isles were crystallized 2800 million years ago.

Largest

The largest isolated monolith in the world is the 1237 ft *377 m* high Mount Augustus (3627 ft *1105 m* above sea-level), discovered on 3 June 1858, 200 miles *320 km* east of Carnarvon, Western Australia. It is an upfaulted monoclinal gritty conglomerate 5 miles *8 km* long and 2 miles *3 km* across and thus twice the size of the celebrated monolithic arkose Ayer's Rock (1100 ft *335 m*), 250 miles *400 km* south-west of Alice Springs, in Northern Territory, Australia. It was estimated in 1940 that La Gran Piedra, a volcanic plug in the Sierra Maestra, Cuba weighs 61,355 tons/*tonnes*.

CONTINENTS

Largest

Of the Earth's surface 41.25% or 81,200,000 miles² *210 400 000 km²* is covered by continental masses of which only about two-thirds of 29.08% of the Earth's surface (57,270,000 miles² *148 328 000 km²*) is land above water, with a mean height of 2480 ft *756 m* above sea-level. The Eurasian land mass is the largest, with an area (including islands) of 20,733,000 miles² *53 698 000 km²*. The Afro-Eurasian land mass, separated artificially only by the Suez Canal covers an area of 32,233,000 miles² *83 483 000 km²* or 56.2% of the Earth's land-mass.

Smallest

The smallest is the Australian mainland, with an area of 2,941,526 miles² *7 618 493 km²*, which, together with Tasmania, New Zealand, New Guinea and the Pacific Islands, is described sometimes as Oceania.

Land remotest from the sea *World*

There is an as yet unpinpointed spot in the Dzoosotoyn Elisen (desert), northern Xinjiang Uygur Zizhiqu (Sin Kiang), China's most north westerly province, that is more than 1500 miles *2400 km* from the open sea in any direction. The nearest large city to this point is Urümqi (Urümchi) to its south.

Land remotest from the sea *Great Britain*

The point furthest from the sea in Great Britain is a point near Meriden, West Midlands, England, which is 72½ miles *117 km* equidistant from the Severn Bridge, the Dee and Mersey estuaries and the Welland estuary in the Wash. The equivalent point in Scotland is in the Forest of Atholl, north-west Tayside 40½ miles *65 km* equidistant from the head of Loch Leven, Inverness Firth and the Firth of Tay.

Peninsula

The world's largest peninsula is Arabia, with an area of about 1,250,000 miles² *3 250 000 km²*.

ISLANDS

Largest *World*

Discounting Australia, which is usually regarded as a continental land mass, the largest island in the world is Greenland (renamed Kalaatdlit Nunaat 1 May 1979), with an area of about 840,000 miles² *2 175 000 km²*. There is evidence that Greenland is in fact several islands overlaid by an ice cap without which it would have an area of 650,000 miles² *1 680 000 km²*.

Largest *Great Britain*

The mainland of Great Britain (Scotland, England and Wales) is the eighth largest in the world, with an area of 84,186 miles² *218 024 km²*. It stretches 603½ miles *971 km* from Dunnet Head in the north to Lizard Point in the south and 287½ miles *463 km* across from Porthaflod, Dyfed to Lowestoft, Suffolk. The island of Ireland (32,594 miles² *84 418 km²*) is the 20th largest in the world.

Freshwater

The largest island surrounded by fresh water is the Ilha de Marajó (18,500 miles² *48 000 km²*), in the mouth of the River Amazon, Brazil. The world's largest inland island (*i.e.* land surrounded by rivers) is Ilha do Bananal, Brazil (7000 miles² *18 130 km²*). The largest island in a lake is Manitoulin Island (1068 miles² *2766 km²*) in the Canadian (Ontario) section of Lake Huron. The largest lake island in Great Britain is Inchmurrin in Loch Lomond, Strathclyde/Central, Scotland with an area of 284 acres *115 ha*.

Remotest *World uninhabited*

The remotest island in the world is Bouvet Øya (formerly Liverpool Island), discovered in the South Atlantic by J. B. C. Bouvet de Lozier on 1 Jan 1739, and first landed on by Capt. George Norris on 16 Dec 1825. Its position is 54° 26′ S, 3° 24′ E. This uninhabited Norwegian dependency is about 1050 miles *1700 km* from the nearest land—the uninhabited Queen Maud Land coast of eastern Antarctica.

Remotest *World inhabited*

The remotest inhabited island in the world is Tristan da Cunha, discovered in the South Atlantic by Tristao da Cunha, a Portuguese admiral, in March 1506. It has an area of 38 miles² *98 km²* (habitable area 12 miles² *31 km²*) and was annexed by the United Kingdom on 14 Aug 1816. After evacuation in 1961 (due to volcanic activity) 198 islanders returned in November 1963. The nearest inhabited land is the island of St Helena, 1320 miles *2120 km* to the north-east. The nearest continent, Africa is 1700 miles *2735 km* away.

Remotest *Great Britain*

The remotest of the British islets is Rockall 191 miles *307 km* west of St Kilda, Western Isles. This 70 ft *21 m* high rock measuring 83 ft *25 m* across was not formally annexed until 18 Sept 1955. The remotest British island which has ever been inhabited is North Rona which is 44 miles *70,8 km* from the next nearest land at Cape

Angmaggalik, an Eskimo settlement on the eastern coast of the world's largest island Kalaatdlit Nunaat (formerly Greenland). *(Alex Hansen)*

Wrath and the Butt of Lewis. It was evacuated *c.* 1844. Muckle Flugga, off Unst, in the Shetlands, is the northernmost inhabited with a population of 3 (1971) and is in a latitude north of southern Greenland. Just to the north of it is the rock of Out Stack in Lat. 60° 51′ 35.7″ N.

Highest rock pinnacle

The world's highest rock pinnacle is Ball's Pyramid near Lord Howe Island, Pacific which is 1843 ft *561 m* high, but has a base axis of only 200 m *220 yd.* It was first scaled in 1965.

Northernmost land

On 26 July 1978 Uffe Petersen of the Danish Geodetic Institute observed the islet of OOdaq Ø 30 m *100 ft* across, 1,36 km *1478 yd* north of Kaffeklubben Ø off Pearyland, Greenland in Lat. 83° 40′ 32.5″ N, Long. 30° 40′ 10.1″ W. The island is 706,4 km *438.9 miles* from the North Pole.

Southernmost land

The South Pole, unlike the North Pole, is on land. The Scott-Amundsen South Polar station was built there at an altitude of 9370 ft *2855 m* in 1957. It is drifting bodily with the ice cap 27–30 ft *8–9 m* per annum in the direction 43° W and was replaced by a new structure in 1975.

Greatest archipelago

The world's greatest archipelago is the 3500 mile *5600 km* long crescent of more than 13,000 islands which forms Indonesia.

Newest

The world's newest island, Lateiki Island which appeared after a volcanic eruption was annexed by Tonga in June 1979.

Largest atoll

The largest atoll in the world is Kwajalein in the Marshall Islands, in the central Pacific Ocean. Its slender 176 mile *283 km* long coral reef encloses a lagoon of 1100 miles² *2850 km²*. The atoll with the largest land area is Christmas Atoll, in the Line Islands, in the central Pacific Ocean. It has an area of 248 miles² *642 km²* of which 125 miles² *323 km²* is land. Its principal settlement, London, is only 2½ miles *4,0 km* distant from Paris.

Longest reef

The longest reef is the Great Barrier Reef off Queensland, north-eastern Australia, which is 1260 statute miles *2027 km* in length. Between 1959 and 1971 a large section between Cooktown and Townsville was destroyed by the proliferation of the Crown of Thorns starfish (*Acanthaster planci*).

DEPRESSIONS

Deepest *World*

The deepest depression so far discovered is the bed rock in the Bentley sub-glacial trench, Antarctica at 2538 m *8326 ft* below sea level. The greatest submarine depression is a large area of the floor of the north-west Pacific which has an average depth of 15,000 ft *4570 m*. The deepest exposed depression on land is the shore surrounding the Dead Sea, now 400 m *1312 ft* below sea-level. The deepest point on the bed of this saltiest of all lakes is 728 m *2388 ft* below sea level. The deepest part of the bed of Lake Baykal in Siberia, USSR, is 4872 ft *1485 m* below sea-level.

Deepest *Great Britain*

The lowest lying area in Great Britain is in the Holme Fen area of the Great Ouse, in Cambridgeshire, at 9 ft *2,75 m* below sea-level. The deepest depression in England is the bed of part of Windermere, 94 ft *28,65 m* below sea-level, and in Scotland the bed of Loch Morar, Highland 987 ft *300,8 m* below sea-level.

Largest

The largest exposed depression in the world is the Caspian Sea basin in the Azerbaydzhani, Russian, Kazakh and Turkmen Republics of the USSR and northern Iran (Persia). It is more than 200,000 miles² *518 000 km²* of which 143,550 miles² *371 800 km²* is lake area. The preponderant land area of the depression is the Prikaspiyskaya Nizmennost', lying around the northern third of the lake and stretching inland for a distance of up to 280 miles *450 km*.

CAVES

Longest

The most extensive cave system in the world is that under the Mammoth Cave National Park, Kentucky, USA first discovered in 1799. On 9 Sept 1972 an exploration group led by Dr John P. Wilcox completed a connection, pioneered by Mrs Patricia Crowther on 30 Aug between the Flint Ridge Cave system and the Mammoth Cave system, so making a combined system with a total mapped passageway length which is now over 484 km *301 miles*. The longest cave system in Great Britain is the Ease Gill system which now has 52.4 km *32.5 miles* of explored passage.

Largest cavern

The world's largest cave chamber is the Sarawak Chamber, Lubang Nasib Bagus, in the Gunung Mulu National Park, Sarawak discovered and surveyed by the 1980 British–Malaysian Mulu Expedition. Its length is 700 m *2300 ft*; and its average width is 300 m *980 ft* and it is nowhere less than 70 m *230 ft* high. It would be large enough to garage 7500 buses.

Longest stalactite

The longest known stalactite in the world is a wall-supported column extending 195 ft *59 m* from roof to floor in the Cueva de Nerja, near Málaga, Spain. Probably the longest free-hanging stalactite is one of 7 m *23 ft* in the Poll an Ionain cave in County Clare, Ireland. The tallest cave column is the 106 ft *32,3 m* tall Bicentennial Column in Ogle Cave in Carlsbad Caverns National Park, New Mexico, USA.

Tallest stalagmite

The tallest known stalagmite in the world is La Grande Stalagmite in the Aven Armand cave,

DEEPEST CAVES BY COUNTRIES		
These depths are subject to continuous revisions.		

Depth		
m	Ft	
1535	5036	Rèseau de Foillis (Gouffre Jean Bernard) …France
1470	4824	Snieznaja Piezcziera ………USSR
1338	4390	Puerta de Illamina……………Spain
1246	4088	Sistema Huautla ……………Mexico
1219	3999	Schwersystem ………………Austria
1208	3964	Complesso Fighiera Carchia Italy
975	3199	Anou Ifflis …………………Algeria
878	2880	Holloch …………………Switzerland
876	2875	Brezno pri Gamsovo Glavici Yugoslavia
768	2520	Jaskinia Sniezna ……………Poland
751	2464	Ghar Parau, Zagros …………Iran
308	1010	Ogof Ffynnon Ddu …………Wales
214	702	Giant's Hole System ………England
179	587	Reyfad Pot………………………N Ireland
140	459	Carrowmore Cavern…………Rep. of Ireland

Lozère, France, which has attained a height of 98 ft *29 m* from the cave floor. It was found in September 1897.

MOUNTAINS

The *Guinness Book of Mountains and Mountaineering Facts and Feats* by Edward Pyatt (£8.95) was published in May 1980.

Highest *World*

An eastern Himalayan peak of 29,028 ft *8848 m* above sea-level on the Tibet–Nepal border (in an area first designated Chu-mu-lang-ma on a map of 1717) was discovered to be the world's highest mountain in 1852 by the Survey Department of the Government of India, from theodolite readings taken in 1849 and 1850. In 1860 its height was computed to be 29,002 ft *8840 m*. On 25 July 1973 the Chinese announced a height of 8848,1 m or *29,029 ft 3 in*. In practice the altitude can only be justified as 29,028 ft ± 25 feet or a mean *8848 m*. The 5½ mile *8,85 km* high peak was named Mount Everest after Col. Sir George Everest, CB. (1790–1866), formerly Surveyor-General of India. Other names for Everest are: Sagarmatha (Nepalese), Qomolongma (Chinese) and Mi-ti Gu-ti Cha-pu Long-na (Tibetan). After a total loss of 11 lives since the first reconnaissance in 1921, Everest was finally conquered at 11.30 a.m. on 29 May 1953. (For details of ascents, see under Mountaineering in Chapter 12.) The mountain whose summit is farthest from the Earth's centre is the Andean peak of Chimborazo (20,561 ft *6267 m*), 98 miles *158 km* south of the equator in Ecuador, South America. Its summit is 7057 ft *2150 m* further from the Earth's centre than the summit of Mt Everest. The highest mountain on the equator is Volcán Cayambe (19,285 ft *5878 m*), Ecuador, in Long. 77° 58′ W. A mountaineer atop the summit would be moving at 1671 km/h *1038 mph* relative to the Earth's centre due to the Earth's rotation.

Highest *Insular*

The highest insular mountain in the world is Puncak Jayakusumu (formerly Puncak Sukarno, formerly Carstensz Pyramide) in Irian Jaya, Indonesia, once Netherlands New Guinea. A survey by the Australian Universities' Expedition in 1973 yielded a height of 4884 m *16,023 ft*. Ngga Pula now 4861 m *15,950 ft* was in 1936 possibly *c.* 4910 m *c. 16,110 ft* before the melting of its snow cap.

Sir George Everest, India's Surveyor-General who died in 1866 but whose name has lived on after the renaming of the world's highest mountain (see above). *(Mansell Collection)*

Greatest mountain wall

Mount Rakaposhi (25,498 ft *7772 m*) rises 5,99 vertical kilometers *19,652 ft* from the Hunza Valley, Pakistan in 10 horizontal kilometres *32,808 ft* with an overall gradient of 31°.

Highest *UK and Ireland*

A list of the highest points in the 72 geographical divisions of the United Kingdom and the 26 counties of the Republic of Ireland was given on page 63 of the 23rd (1977) Edition.

The highest mountain in the United Kingdom is Ben Nevis (4406 ft *1343 m* excluding the 12 ft *3,65 m* cairn), 4¼ miles *6,85 km* south-east of Fort William, Highland, Scotland. It was climbed before 1720 but though acclaimed the highest in 1790 was not confirmed to be higher than Ben Macdhui (4300 ft *1310 m*) until 1847. In 1834 Ben Macdhui and Ben Nevis (Gaelic, *Beinn Nibheis*) (first reference, 1778) were respectively quoted as 4570 ft *1393 m* and 4370 ft *1332 m*. The highest mountain in England is Scafell Pike (3210 ft *978 m*) in Cumbria; in Wales is Snowdon (*Yr Wyddfa*) (3560 ft *1085 m*) in Gwynedd; and in the island of Ireland is Carrauntual (3414 ft *1041 m*) in County Kerry.

There is some evidence that, before being ground down by the ice-cap, mountains in the Loch Bà area of the Isle of Mull, Strathclyde were 15,000 ft *4575 m* above sea-level.

Highest *Peaks over 3000 ft 915 m*

There are 577 peaks and tops over 3000 ft *915 m* in the whole British Isles and 165 peaks and 136 tops in Scotland higher than England's highest point, Scafell Pike. The highest mountain off the mainland is Sgùrr Alasdair (3309 ft *1008 m*) on Skye named after Alexander (Gaelic, *Alasdair*) Nicolson, who made the first ascent in 1873.

Highest unclimbed

The highest unclimbed mountain is now only the 31st highest—Zemu Gap Peak (25,526 ft *7780 m*) in the Sikkim Himalaya.

Largest

The world's tallest mountain measured from its submarine base (3280 fathoms *6000 m*) in the Hawaiian Trough to peak is Mauna Kea (Mountain White) on the island of Hawaii, with a combined height of 33,476 ft *10 203 m* of which 13,796 ft *4205 m* are above sea-level. Another mountain whose dimensions, but not height, exceed those of Mount Everest is the volcanic Hawaiian peak of Mauna Loa (Mountain Long) at 13,680 ft *4170 m*. The axes of its elliptical base, 16,322 ft *4975 m* below sea-level, have been estimated at 74 miles *119 m* and 53 miles *85 km*. It should be noted that Cerro Aconcagua (22,834 ft *6960 m*) is more than 38,800 ft *11 826 m* above the 16,000 ft *4875 m* deep Pacific abyssal plain or 42,834 ft *13 055 m* above the Peru-Chile Trench which is 180 miles *290 km* distant in the South Pacific.

Greatest ranges

The world's greatest land mountain range is the Himalaya-Karakoram, which contains 96 of the world's 109 peaks of over 24,000 ft *7315 m*. Himalaya derives from the sanskrit *him*, snow; *alaya*, home. The greatest of all mountain ranges is, however, the submarine Indian/East Pacific Oceans Cordillera extending 19,200 miles *30 900 km* from the Gulf of Aden to the Gulf of California by way of the seabed between Australia and Antarctica with an average height of 8000 ft *2430 km* above the base ocean depth.

Longest lines of sight

Vatnajökull (6952 ft *2118 m*), Iceland has been seen by refracted light from the Faeroe Islands 340 miles *550 km* distant. In Alaska Mt Mc-Kinley (20,320 ft *6193 m*) has been sighted from Mt Sanford (16,237 ft *4949 m*) from a distance of 230 miles *370 km*. McKinley, so named in 1896, was called Denali (Great One) in the Athabascan language.

Greatest plateau

The most extensive high plateau in the world is the Tibetan Plateau in Central Asia. The average altitude is 16,000 ft *4875 m* and the area is 77,000 miles² *200 000 km²*.

Sheerest wall

The 3200 ft *975 m* wide northwest face of Half Dome, Yosemite, California, USA is 2200 ft *670 m* high but nowhere departs more than 7 degrees from the vertical. It was first climbed (Class VI) in 5 days in July 1957 by Royal Robbins, Jerry Gallwas and Mike Sherrick.

Highest halites

Along the northern shores of the Gulf of Mexico for 725 miles *1160 km* there exists 330 subterranean 'mountains' of salt, some of which rise more than 60,000 ft *18 300 m* from bed rock and appear as the low salt domes first discovered in 1862.

Lowest hill

The official map of Seria, Brunei shows an artificial hillock named Bukit Thompson by the 13th hole on the Panaga Golf Course at 15 ft *4,5 m*.

WATERFALLS

Highest

The highest waterfall (as opposed to vaporized 'Bridal Veil') in the world is the Salto Angel in Venezuela, on a branch of the River Carrao, an upper tributary of the Caroni with a total drop of 3212 ft *979 m*—the longest single drop is 2648 ft *807 m*. They were named for the United States pilot James (Jimmy) Angel (died 8 Dec 1956), who had crashed nearby on 9 Oct 1937. The falls, known by the Indians as Cherun-Meru, were first reported by Ernesto Sanchez La Cruz in 1910.

Highest *United Kingdom*

The tallest waterfall in the United Kingdom is Eas a'Chùal Aluinn, from Glas Bheinn (2541 ft *774 m*), Highland, Scotland, with a drop of 658 ft *200 m*. England's highest fall above ground is Caldron (or Cauldron) Snout, on the Tees, with a fall of 200 ft *60 m* in 450 ft *135 m* of cataracts, but no sheer leap. It is on the border of Durham and Cumbria. The cascade in the Gaping Gill Cave descends 365 ft *111 m*. The highest Welsh waterfall is the Pistyll-y-Llyn on the Powys-Dyfed border which exceeds 300 ft *90 m* in descent.

Highest *Ireland*

The highest falls in Ireland are the Powerscourt Falls (350 ft *106 m*), on the River Dargle, County Wicklow.

Greatest

On the basis of the average annual flow, the greatest waterfalls in the world are the Boyoma (formerly Stanley) Falls in Zaïre with 600,000 cusec *17 000 m³/sec*. The peak flow of the Guaíra (Salto das Sete Quedas) on the Alto Paraná river between Brazil and Paraguay at times attained a peak flow rate of 1,750,000 cusec *50 000 m³/sec*. The completion of the Itaipu dam in 1982 ended this claim to fame.

It has been calculated that, when some 5,500,000 years ago the Mediterranean basins began to be filled from the Atlantic through the Straits of Gibraltar, a waterfall 26 times greater than the Guaíra and perhaps 800 m *2625 ft* high was formed.

Widest

The widest waterfalls in the world are the Khône Falls (50–70 ft *15–21 m* high) in Laos, with a width of 6.7 miles *10,8 km* and a flood flow of 1,500,000 cusec *42 500 m³/sec.*

RIVERS

Longest *World*

The two longest rivers in the world are the Amazon (*Amazonas*), flowing into the South Atlantic, and the Nile (*Bahr-el-Nil*) flowing into the Mediterranean. Which is the longer is more a matter of definition than simple measurement.

The true source of the Amazon was discovered in 1953 to be a stream named Huarco, rising near the summit of Cerro Huagra (17,188 ft *5238 m*) in Peru. This stream progressively becomes the Toro then the Santiago then the Apurimac, which in turn is known as the Ene and then the Tambo before its confluence with the Amazon prime tributary the Ucayali. The length of the Amazon from this source to the South Atlantic *via* the Canal do Norte was measured in 1969 to be 4007 miles *6448 km* (usually quoted to the rounded off figure of 4000 miles *6437 km*).

If, however, a vessel navigating down the river turns to the south of Ilha de Marajó through the straits of Breves and Boiuci into the Pará, the total length of the water-course becomes 4195 miles 6750 km. The Pará is not however a tributary of the Amazon, being hydrologically part of the basin of the Tocantins.

The length of the Nile watercourse, as surveyed by M. Devroey (Belgium) before the loss of a few miles of meanders due to the formation of Lake Nasser, behind the Aswan High Dam, was 4145 miles *6670 km*. This course is the hydrologically acceptable one from the source in Burundi of the Luvironza branch of the Kagera feeder of the Victoria Nyanza *via* the White Nile (*Bahrel-Jebel*) to the delta.

Longest *Great Britain*

The longest river in Great Britain is the Severn, which empties into the Bristol Channel and is 220 miles *354 km* long. Its basin extends over 4409 miles² *11 419 km²*. It rises in north-western Powys and flows through Shropshire, Hereford & Worcester, Gloucestershire and Avon and has a record 17 tributaries. The longest river *wholly* in England is the Thames, which is 215 miles, *346 km* long to the Nore. Its remotest source is at Seven Springs, Gloucestershire, whence the River Churn joins the other head waters. The source of the Thames proper is Trewsbury Mead, Coates, Cirencester, Gloucestershire. The basin measures 3841 miles² *9948 km²*. The Yorkshire Ouse's 11 tributaries aggregate 629 miles *1012 km*.

The longest river wholly in Wales is the Usk, with a length of 65 miles *104,5 km*. It rises on the border of Dyfed and Powys and flows out via Gwent into the Severn Estuary. The longest river in Scotland is the Tay, with Dundee, Tayside, on the shore of the estuary. It is 117 miles *188 km* long from the source of its remotest head-stream, the River Tummel, Tayside and has the greatest volume of any river in Great Britain, with a flow of up to 49,000 cusecs *1387 m³* per sec. Of Scottish rivers the Tweed and the Clyde have most tributaries with 11 each.

Longest *Ireland*

The longest river in Ireland is the Shannon, which is longer than any river in Great Britain. It rises 258 ft *78,6 m* above sea-level, in County Cavan, and flows through a series of loughs to Limerick. It is 240 miles *386 km* long, including

the 56 mile *90 km* long estuary to Loop Head. The basin area is 6060 miles² *15 695 km²*.

Shortest river

The world's shortest named river is the D River, Lincoln City, Oregon, USA which connects Devil's Lake to the Pacific Ocean and is 440 ft *134 m* long at low tide.

Largest basin and longest tributary

The largest river basin in the world is that drained by the Amazon (4007 miles *6448 km*). It covers about 2,720,000 miles² *7 045 000 km²*. It has about 15,000 tributaries and subtributaries, of which four are more than 1000 miles *1609 km* long. These include the Madeira, the longest of all tributaries, with a length of 2100 miles *3380 km*, which is surpassed by only 14 rivers in the whole world.

Longest sub-tributary

The longest sub-tributary is the Pilcomayo (1000 miles *1609 km* long) in South America. It is a tributary of the Paraguay (1500 miles *2415 km* long), which is itself a tributary of the Paraña (2500 miles *4025 km*).

Longest estuary

The world's longest estuary is that of the often frozen Ob', in the northern USSR, at 550 miles *885 km*. It is up to 50 miles *80 km* wide.

Largest delta

The world's largest delta is that created by the Ganga (Ganges) and Brahmaputra in Bangla Desh (formerly East Pakistan) and West Bengal, India. It covers an area of 30,000 miles² *75 000 km²*.

Greatest flow

The greatest flow of any river in the world is that of the Amazon, which discharges an average of 4,200,000 cusec *120 000 m³/sec* into the Atlantic Ocean, rising to more than 7,000,000 cusec *200 000 m³/sec* in full flood. The lowest 900 miles *1450 km* of the Amazon average 300 ft *90 m* in depth.

Submarine river

In 1952 a submarine river 250 miles *400 km* wide, known as the Cromwell current, was discovered flowing eastward 300 ft *90 m* below the surface of the Pacific for 3500 miles *5625 km* along the equator. Its volume is 1000 times that of the Mississippi.

Subterranean river

In August 1958 a crypto-river was tracked by radio isotopes flowing under the Nile with 6 times its mean annual flow or 500,000 million m³ *20 million million ft³.*

Largest swamp

The world's largest tract of swamp is in the basin of the Pripet or Pripyat River—a tributary of the Dnieper in the USSR. These swamps cover an estimated area of 18,125 miles² *46 950 km².*

RIVER BORES

World

The bore on the Ch'ient'ang'kian (Hang-choufe) in eastern China is the most remarkable of the 60 in the world. At spring tides the wave attains a height of up to 25 ft *7,5 m* and a speed of 13–15 knots *24–27 km/h.* It is heard advancing at a range of 14 miles *22 km.* The annual downstream flood wave on the Mekong sometimes reaches a height of 46 ft *14 m.* The greatest volume of any tidal bore is that of the Canal do Norte (10 miles *16 km* wide) in the mouth of the Amazon.

Great Britain

The most notable of the 8 river bores in the

United Kingdom is that on the Severn, which attained a measured height of 9¼ ft *2,8 m* on 15 Oct 1966 downstream of Stonebench, and a speed of 13 mph *20 km/h.* It travels from Framilode towards Gloucester.

LAKES AND INLAND SEAS

Largest *World*

The largest inland sea or lake in the world is the Kaspiskoye More (Caspian Sea) in the southern USSR and Iran (Persia). It is 760 miles *1225 km* long and its total area is 139,000 miles² *360 700 km².* Of the total area some 55,280 miles² *143 200 km²* (38.6 per cent) is in Iran, where it is named the Darya-ye-Khazar. Its maximum depth is 1025 m *3360 ft* and its surface is 28,5 m *93 ft* below sea-level. Its estimated volume is 21,500 miles³ *89 600 km³* of saline water. Its surface has varied between 32 m *105 ft* (11th century) and 22 m *72 ft* (early 19th century) below sea level. The USSR Government plan to reverse the flow of the upper Pechora River from flowing north to the Barents Sea by blasting a 70 mile *112 km* long canal with nuclear explosives into the south-flowing Kolva river so that *via* the Kama and Volga rivers the Caspian will be replenished.

Lake in a lake

The largest lake in a lake is Manitou Lake (41.09 miles² *106,42 km²*) on the world's largest lake island Manitoulin Island (1068 miles² *2766 km²*) in the Canadian part of Lake Huron. It contains itself a number of islands.

Underground lake

Reputedly the world's largest underground lake is the Lost Sea 300 ft *91 m* subterranean in the Craighead Caverns, Sweetwater, Tennessee, USA measuring 4½ acres *1,8 ha* and discovered in 1905.

Freshwater lake *World*

The freshwater lake with the greatest surface area is Lake Superior, one of the Great Lakes of North America. The total area is 31,800 miles² *82 350 km²*, of which 20,700 miles² *53 600 km²* are in Minnesota, Wisconsin and Michigan, USA and 11,100 miles² *27 750 km²* in Ontario, Canada. It is 600 ft *182 m* above sea-level. The freshwater lake with the greatest volume is Baykal (see p. 61 and p. 64) with an estimated volume of 5520 miles³ *23 000 km³.*

Freshwater lake *United Kingdom*

The largest lake in the United Kingdom is Lough Neagh (48 ft *14,60 m* above sea-level) in Northern Ireland. It is 18 miles *28,9 km* long and 11 miles *17,7 km* wide and has an area of 147.39 miles² *381,73 km².* Its extreme depth is 102 ft *31 m.*

Freshwater lakes or lochs *Great Britain*

The largest lake in Great Britain, and the largest inland loch in Scotland is Loch Lomond (23 ft *7,0 m* above sea-level), which is 22.64 miles *36,44 km* long and has a surface area of 27.45 miles² *70,04 km².* It is situated in the Strathclyde and Central regions and its greatest depth is 623 ft *190 m.* The lake or loch with the greatest volume is however Loch Ness with 262,845,000,000 ft³ *7 443 000 000 m³.* The longest lake or loch is Loch Ness which measures 24.23 miles *38,99 km.* The three arms of the Y-shaped Loch Awe aggregate, however, 25.47 miles *40,99 km.* The largest lake in England is Windermere, in the county of Cumbria. It is 10½ miles *17 km* long and has a surface area of 5.69 miles² *14,74 km².* Its greatest depth is 219 ft *66,75 m* in the northern half. The largest *natural* lake in Wales is Llyn Tegid, with an area of 1.69 miles² *4,38 km²*, although it should be noted that the largest lake in Wales is that formed by the reservoir at Lake Vyrnwy, where the total surface area is 1120 acres *453,25 ha*.

Freshwater lakes or loughs *Republic of Ireland*
The largest lough in the Republic of Ireland is Lough Corrib in the counties of Mayo and Galway. It measures 27 miles *43,5 km* in length and is 7 miles *11,25 km* across at its widest point with a total surface area of 41,616 acres (65.0 miles² *168 km²*).

Largest lagoon
The largest lagoon in the world is Lagoa dos Patos in southernmost Brazil. It is 158 miles *254 km* long and extends over 4110 miles² *10 645 km²*.

Deepest *World*
The deepest lake in the world is Ozero (Lake) Baykal in central Siberia, USSR. It is 385 miles *620 km* long and between 20 and 46 miles *32–74 km* wide. In 1957 the lake's Olkhon Crevice was measured to be 1940 m *6365 ft* deep and hence 1485 m *4872 ft* below sea-level (see p. 61 and p. 63).

Deepest *Great Britain*
The deepest lake in Great Britain is the 10.30 mile *16,57 km* long Loch Morar, in Highland. Its surface is 30 ft *9 m* above sea-level and its extreme depth 1017 ft *310 m*. England's deepest lake is Wast Water (258 ft *78 m*), in Cumbria. The lake with the greatest mean depth is Loch Ness with *c.* 426 ft *130 m*.

Highest *World*
The highest steam-navigated lake in the world is Lago Titicaca (maximum depth 1214 ft *370 m*), with an area of about 3200 miles² *8285 km²* (1850 miles² *4790 km²* in Peru, 1350 miles² *3495 km²* in Bolivia), in South America. It is 130 miles *209 km* long and is situated at 12,506 ft *3811 m* above sea-level. There is an unnamed glacial lake near Everest at 19,300 ft *5880 m*. Tibet's largest lake Nam Tso of 722 miles² *1956 km²* is at 15,060 ft *4578 m*.

Highest *United Kingdom*
The highest lake in the United Kingdom is the 1.9 acre *0,76 ha* Lochan Buidhe at 3600 ft *1097 m* above sea-level in the Cairngorm Mountains, Scotland. England's highest is Broad Crag Tarn (2746 ft *837 m* above sea-level) on Scafell Pike, Cumbria and the highest named freshwater in Wales is The Frogs Pool, a tarn near the summit of Carnedd Llywelyn, Gwynedd at *c.* 2725 ft *830 m*.

OTHER FEATURES

Desert *Largest*
Nearly an eighth of the world's land surface is arid with a rainfall of less than 25 cm *9.8 in* per annum. The Sahara in N. Africa is the largest in the world. At its greatest length it is 3200 miles *5150 km* from east to west. From north to south it is between 800 and 1400 miles *1275 and 2250 km*. The area covered by the desert is about 3,250,000 miles² *8 400 000 km²*. The land level varies from 436 ft *132 m* below sea-level in the Qattâra Depression, Egypt, to the mountain Emi Koussi (11,204 ft *3415 m*) in Chad. The diurnal temperature range in the western Sahara may be more than 80° F or *45° C*.

Sand dunes
The world's highest measured sand dunes are those in the Saharan sand sea of Isaouane-n-Tifernine of east central Algeria in Lat. 26° 42′ N, Long. 6° 43′ E. They have a wavelength of near 3 miles *5 km* and attain a height of 1410 ft *430 m*.

Gorge *Largest*
The largest land gorge in the world is the Grand Canyon on the Colorado River in north-central Arizona, USA. It extends from Marble Gorge to the Grand Wash Cliffs, over a distance of 217 miles *349 km*. It varies in width from 4 to 13 miles *6–20 km* and is some 5300 ft *1615 m* deep. The submarine Labrador Basin canyon is *c.* 2150 miles *3440 km* long.

The world's only 2 mile deep gorge reported from Peru was unknown to the rest of the world until 1929 (see column 3, this page). (Zbigniew Bzdak/ Canoandes)

Gorge *Deepest*
The deepest canyon is El Cañón de Colca, Peru reported in 1929 which is 3223 m *10,574 ft* deep. It was first traversed by the Polish Expedition CANOANDES '79 kayak team on 12 May–14 June 1981. A stretch of the Kali River in central Nepal flows 18,000 ft *5485 m* below its flanking summits of the Dhaulagiri and Annapurna groups. The deepest submarine canyon yet discovered is one 25 miles *40 km* south of Esperance, Western Australia, which is 6000 ft *1800 m* deep and 20 miles *32 km* wide.

Cliffs *Highest*
The highest sea cliffs yet pinpointed anywhere in the world are those on the north coast of east Moloka'i, Hawaii near Umilehi Point, which descend 3300 ft *1005 m* to the sea at an average gradient of >55°. The west face of Thor Peak, Baffin Island, Canada allowed an abseiling or rappelling record of 3250 ft *990 m* by Steve Holmes (USA) in July 1982. The highest cliffs in North West Europe are those on the north coast of Achill Island, in County Mayo, Ireland, which are 2192 ft *668 m* sheer above the sea at Croaghan. The highest cliffs in the United Kingdom are the 1300 ft *396 m* Conachair cliffs on St Kilda, Western Isles (1397 ft *425 m*). The highest sheer sea cliffs on the mainland of Great Britain are at Clo Mor, 3 miles *4,8 km* south-east of Cape Wrath, Highland, Scotland which drop 921 ft *280,7 m*. England's highest cliff (gradient >45°) is Great Hangman Hill, near Combe Martin, in North Devon, which descends from 1043 ft *318 m* to the sea in 984 ft *300 m*, the last 700 ft *213 m* of which is sheer.

Natural arch *Longest*
The longest natural arch in the world is the Landscape Arch in the Arches National Park, 25 miles *40 km* north of Moab, Utah, USA. This natural sandstone arch spans 291 ft *88 m* and is set about 100 ft *30 m* above the canyon floor. In one place erosion has narrowed its section to 6 ft *1,82 m*. Larger, however, is the Rainbow Bridge, Utah discovered on 14 Aug 1909 with a span of 278 ft *84,7 m* but more than 22 ft *6,7 m* wide.

Natural bridge *Highest*
The highest natural arch is the sandstone arch 25 miles *40 km* WNW of K'ashih, Sinkiang, China, estimated in 1947 to be nearly 1000 ft *312 m* tall with a span of about 150 ft *45 m*.

Longest glaciers
It is estimated that 6,020,000 miles² *15 600 000 km²*, or 10½ per cent of the Earth's land surface, is permanently glaciated. The world's longest known glacier is the Lambert Glacier, discovered by an Australian aircraft crew in Australian Antarctic Territory in 1956–7. It is up to 40 miles *64 km* wide and, with its upper section, known as the Mellor Glacier, it measures at least 250 miles *402 km* in length. With the Fisher Glacier limb, the Lambert forms a continuous ice passage about 320 miles *514 km* long. The longest Himalayan glacier is the Siachen (47 miles *75,6 km*) in the Karakoram range, though the Hispar and Biafo combine to form an ice passage 76 miles *122 km* long. The fastest moving major glacier is the Quarayaq in Greenland flowing 20–24 m *65–80 ft* per day.

Greatest avalanches
The greatest natural avalanches, though rarely observed, occur in the Himalaya but no estimates of their volume had been published. It was estimated that 3,500,000 m³ *120 000 000 ft³* of snow fell in an avalanche in the Italian Alps in 1885. The 250 mph *400 km/h* avalanche triggered by the Mount St. Helens eruption in Washington, USA on 18 May 1979 was estimated to measure 2800 million m³ *96,000 million ft³* (see Disasters, Chapter 11).

CHAPTER FOUR

The Universe & Space

The universe is the entirety of space, matter and anti-matter. An appreciation of its magnitude is best grasped by working outward from the Earth, through the Solar System and our own Milky Way Galaxy, to the remotest extra-galactic nebulae and quasars.

Space floating—the manned maneuvring unit in operation. *(NASA)* (See Astronauts page 71)

The Guinness Book of Astronomy Facts and Feats (2nd Edition) by Patrick Moore was published in June 1983 price £9.95.

LIGHT-YEAR—that distance travelled by light (speed 186,282.397 miles/sec *299 792,458 km/s⁻¹* or 670,616,629.2 mph *1 079 258 848,8 km/h⁻¹ in vacuo*) in one tropical year (365.24219878 mean solar days at January 0,12 hours Ephemeris time in AD 1900) and is 5,878,499,814,000 miles *9 460 528 405 000 km*. The unit was first used in March 1888 and fixed at this constant in October 1983.

MAGNITUDE—a measure of stellar brightness such that the light of a star of any magnitude bears a ratio of 2.511886 to that of a star of the next magnitude. Thus a fifth magnitude star is 2.511886 times as bright, while one of the first magnitude is exactly 100 (or 2.511886⁵) times as bright, as a sixth magnitude star. In the case of such exceptionally bright bodies as Sirius, Venus, the Moon (magnitude – 12.71) or the Sun (magnitude – 26.78), the magnitude is expressed as a minus quantity.

PROPER MOTION—that component of a star's motion in space which, at right angles to the line of sight, constitutes an apparent change of position of the star in the celestial sphere.

METEOROIDS

Meteor shower

Meteoroids are of cometary or asteroidal origin. A meteor is the light phenomenon caused by the entry of a meteoroid into the Earth's atmosphere. The greatest meteor 'shower' on record occurred on the night of 16–17 Nov 1966, when the Leonid meteors (which recur every 33¼ years) were visible between western North America and eastern USSR. It was calculated that meteors passed over Arizona, USA, at a rate of 2300 per min for a period of 20 min from 5 a.m. on 17 Nov 1966.

METEORITES

Oldest

It was reported in August 1978 that dust grains in the Murchison meteorite which fell in Australia in September 1969 pre-date the formation of the Solar System 4600 million years ago.

Largest *World*

When a meteoroid penetrates to the Earth's surface, the remnant is described as a meteorite. This occurs about 150 times per year over the whole land surface of the Earth. Although the chances of being struck are deemed negligible, the most anxious time of day for meteorophobes is 3 p.m. The largest known meteorite is one found in 1920 at Hoba West, near Grootfontein in south-west Africa. This is a block 9 ft *2,75 m* long by 8 ft *2,43 m* broad, estimated to be

132,000 lb (59 tons/*tonnes*). The largest meteorite exhibited by any museum is the 'Tent' meteorite, weighing 68,085 lb (30.39 tons *30 883 kg*) found in 1897 near Cape York, on the west coast of Greenland, by the expedition of Commander (later Rear-Admiral) Robert Edwin Peary (1856–1920). It was known to the Eskimos as the Abnighito and is now exhibited in the Hayden Planetarium in New York City, NY, USA. The largest piece of stony meteorite recovered is a piece of 1770 kg *3902 lb* part of a 4 tonne shower which struck Jilin (formerly Kirin), China on 8 Mar 1976. The oldest dated meteorites are from the Allende fall in Chihuahua, Mexico on 8 Feb 1969 dating back to 4610 million years.

There was a mysterious explosion of $12\frac{1}{2}$ megatons in Lat. 60° 55′ N, Long. 101° 57′ E, in the basin of the Podkamennaya Tunguska river, 40 miles north of Vanavar, in Siberia, USSR, at 00 hrs 17 min 11 sec UT on 30 June 1908. The cause was variously attributed to a meteorite (1927), a comet (1930), a nuclear explosion (1961) and to anti-matter (1965). This devastated an area of about 1500 miles² *3885 km²* and the shock was felt as far as 1000 km (more than *600 miles*) away. The theory is now favoured that this was the terminal flare of stony debris from a comet, possibly Encke's comet, at altitude of only 6 km *or less than 20,000 ft*. A similar event may have occurred over the Isle of Axeholm, Lincolnshire a few thousand years before. A stony meteorite with a diameter of 10 km *6.2 miles* striking the Earth at 25 km/sec *55,925 mph* would generate an explosive energy equivalent to 100 million megatons. Such events should not be expected to recur more than once in 75 million years.

Largest *United Kingdom and Ireland*
The heaviest of the 22 meteorites known to have fallen on the British Isles since 1623 was one weighing at least 102 lb *46,25 kg* (largest piece 17 lb 6 oz *7,88 kg*), which fell at 4.12 p.m. on 24 Dec 1965 at Barwell, Leicestershire. Scotland's largest recorded meteorite fell in Strathmore, Tayside on 3 Dec 1917. It weighed $22\frac{1}{4}$ lb *10,09 kg* and was the largest of four stones totalling 29 lb 6 oz *13,324 kg*. The largest recorded meteorite to fall in Ireland was the Limerick Stone of 65 lb *29,5 kg*, part of a shower weighing more than 106 lb *48 kg* which fell near Adare County Limerick, on 10 Sept 1813. The larger of the two recorded meteorites to land in Wales was one weighing 28 oz *794 g* of which a piece weighing $25\frac{1}{2}$ oz *723 g* went through the roof of the Prince Llewellyn Hotel in Beddgelert, Gwynedd, shortly before 3.15 a.m. on 21 Sept 1949. Debris from the Bovedy Fall in N. Ireland in 1969 spread over 50 miles *80 km*.

Largest craters
It has been estimated that some 2000 asteroid-Earth collisions have occurred in the last 600 million years. A total of 102 collision sites or astroblemes have been recognised. A crater 150 miles *241 km* in diameter and $\frac{1}{2}$ mile *805 m* deep has been postulated in Wilkes Land, Antarctica since 1962. It would be caused by a 13,000 million ton meteorite striking at 44,000 mph *70 811 km/h*. USSR scientists reported in December 1970 an astrobleme with a 60 mile *95 km* diameter and a maximum depth of 1300 ft *400 m* in the basin of the River Popigai. There is a possible crater-like formation or astrobleme 275 miles *442,5 km* in diameter on the eastern shore of the Hudson Bay, Canada, where the Nastapoka Islands are just off the coast.

The largest proven crater is the Coon Butte or Barringer crater, discovered in 1891 near Canyon Diablo, Winslow, northern Arizona, USA. It is 4150 ft *1265 m* in diameter and now about 575 ft *175 m* deep, with a parapet rising 130–155 ft *40–48 m* above the surrounding plain. It has been estimated that an iron-nickel mass with a diameter of 200–260 ft *61–79 m* and weighing about 2,000,000 tons/*tonnes* gouged this crater in *c.* 25,000 BC. Evidence was published in 1963 discounting a meteoric origin for the crypto-volcanic Vredefort Ring (diameter 26 miles *41,8 km*), to the south-west of Johannesburg, South Africa, but this has now been re-asserted. The New Quebec (formerly the Chubb) 'Crater', first sighted on 20 June 1943 in northern Ungava, Canada, is 1325 ft *404 m* deep and measures 6.8 miles *10,9 km* round its rim.

Fireball *Brightest*
The brightest fireball ever photographically recorded was by Dr Zdenek Ceplecha over Sumava, Czechoslovakia on 4 Dec 1974 with a momentary magnitude of −22 or 10,000 times brighter than a full Moon.

Tektites
The largest tektite of which details have been published has been of 3,2 kg *7.04 lb* found in 1932 at Muong Nong, Saravane Province, Laos and now in the Paris Museum.

AURORAE

Most frequent
Polar lights, known since 1560 as Aurora Borealis or Northern Lights in the northern hemisphere and since 1773 as Aurora Australis in the southern hemisphere, are caused by electrical solar discharges in the upper atmosphere and occur most frequently in high latitudes. Aurorae are visible at some time on *every* clear dark night in the polar areas within 20 degrees of the magnetic poles. The extreme height of aurorae has been measured at 1000 km *620 miles*, while the lowest may descend to 45 miles *72,5 km*. Reliable figures exist only from 1952, since when the record high and low number of nights of auroral displays in Shetland (geomagnetic Lat. 63°) has been 203 (1957) and 58 (1965). The most recent great display in north-west Europe was that of 4–5 Sept 1958.

Lowest latitudes
Extreme cases of displays in very low latitudes are Cuzco, Peru (2 Aug 1744); Honolulu, Hawaii (1 Sept 1859) and questionably Singapore (25 Sept 1909).

Noctilucent clouds
Regular observations in Western Europe date only from 1964, since when the record high and low number of nights on which these phenomena (at heights of *c.* 52 miles *85 km*) have been observed have been 41 (1974) and 15 (1970).

THE MOON

The Earth's closest neighbour in space and only natural satellite is the Moon, at a mean distance of 238,855 statute miles *384 400 km* centre-to-centre or 233,812 miles *376 284 km* surface-to-surface. In the present century the closest approach (smallest perigee) was 216,398 miles *348 259 km* surface-to-surface or 221,441 miles *356 375 km* centre-to-centre on 4 January 1912, and the farthest distance (largest apogee) was 247,675 miles *398 598 km* surface-to-surface or 252,718 miles *406 711 km* centre-to-centre on 2 March 1984. The Moon was only a few Earth radii distant during the 'Gerstenkorn period' 3900 million years ago. It has a diameter of 2159.3 miles *3475,0 km* and has a mass of 7.23×10^{19} tons *$7,35 \times 10^{19}$ tonnes* with a mean density of 3.342. The average orbital speed is 2287 mph *3680 km/h*. The first direct hit on the Moon was achieved at 2 min 24 sec after midnight (Moscow time) on 14 Sept 1959, by the Soviet space probe *Luna II* near the *Mare Serenitatis*. The first photographic images of the hidden side were collected by the USSR's *Luna III* from 6.30 a.m. on 7 Oct 1959, from a range of up to 43,750 miles *70 400 km* and transmitted to the Earth from a distance of 470 000 km *292,000 miles*. The oldest of the Moon material brought back to Earth by the *Apollo* programme crews has been soil dated to 4720 million years.

'Blue moon'
Owing to sulphur particles in the upper atmosphere from a forest fire covering 250,000 acres *100 000 ha* between Mile 103 and Mile 119 on the Alaska Highway in northern British Columbia, Canada, the Moon took on a bluish colour, as seen from Great Britain, on the night of 26 Sept 1950. The Moon also appeared green after the Krakatoa eruption of 27 Aug 1883 (see p. 55) and in Stockholm for 3 min on 17 Jan 1884.

Crater *Largest and deepest*
Only 59 per cent of the Moon's surface is directly visible from the Earth because it is in 'captured rotation', *i.e.* the period of rotation is equal to the period of orbit. The largest wholly visible crater is the walled plain Bailly, towards the Moon's South Pole, which is 183 miles *295 km* across, with walls rising to 14,000 ft *4250 m*. The Orientale Basin, partly on the averted side, measures more than 600 miles *965 km* in diameter. The deepest crater is the Newton crater, with a floor estimated to be between 23,000 and 29,000 ft *7000–8850 m* below its rim and 14,000 ft *2250 m* below the level of the plain outside. The brightest directly visible spot on the Moon is *Aristarchus*.

Highest mountains
In the absence of a sea level, lunar altitudes are measured relative to an adopted reference sphere of radius 1738,000 km or *1079.943 miles*. Thus the greatest elevation attained on this basis by any of the 12 US astronauts has been 7830 m *25,688 ft* on the Descartes Highlands by Capt. John Watts Young USN and Major Charles M. Duke Jr on 27 Apr 1972.

Temperature extremes
When the Sun is overhead the temperature on the lunar equator reaches 243°F *117,2°C* (31 deg F *17,2 deg C* above the boiling point of water). By sunset the temperature is 58°F *14,4°C* but after nightfall it sinks to −261°F *−162,7°C*.

THE SUN

Distance extremes
The Earth's 66,620 mph *107 210 km/h* orbit of 584,017,800 miles *939 885 500 km* around the Sun is elliptical, hence our distance from the Sun varies. The orbital speed varies between 65,520 mph *105 450 km/h* (minimum) and 67,750 mph *109 030 km/h*. The average distance of the Sun is 1.000 000 230 astronomical units or 92,955,829 miles *149 597 906 km*.

The closest approach (perihelion) is 91,402,000 miles *147 097 000 km* and the farthest departure (aphelion) is 94,510,000 miles *152 099 000 km*. The Solar System is revolving around the centre of the Milky Way once in each 225,000,000 years, at a speed of 481,000 mph *774 000 km/h* and has a velocity of 42,500 mph *68 400 km/h* relative to stars in our immediate region such as Vega, towards which it is moving.

Temperature and dimensions
The Sun has an internal temperature of about 16 000 000 K, a core pressure of 500,000,000 tons/in² *7,7 PPa* and uses up 4,000,000 tons/

tonnes of hydrogen per sec, thus providing a luminosity of 3×10^{27} candlepower, with an intensity of 1,500,000 candles/in² *1 530 000 candelas*. The Sun has the stellar classification of a 'yellow dwarf' and, although its density is only 1.407 times that of water, its mass is 332,946 times as much as that of the Earth. It has a mean diameter of 865,270 miles *1 392 520 km*. The Sun with a mass of 1.958×10^{27} tons *$1,989 \times 10^{27}$ tonnes* represents more than 99 per cent of the total mass of the Solar System but will exhaust its energy in 10,000 million years.

Sunspots *Largest*

To be visible to the *protected* naked eye, a sunspot must cover about one two-thousandth part of the Sun's disc and thus have an area of about 500,000,000 miles² *1300 million km²*. The largest sunspot occurred in the Sun's southern hemisphere on 8 Apr 1947. Its area was about 7000 million miles² *18 000 million km²* with an extreme longitude of 187,000 miles *300 000 km* and an extreme latitude of 90,000 miles *145 000 km*. Sunspots appear darker because they are more than 1500 deg C cooler than the rest of the Sun's surface temperature of 5525° C. The largest observed solar prominence was one protruding 365,000 miles *588 000 km*, photographed on 19 Dec 1973 during the 3rd and final manned Skylab mission.

Most frequent

In October 1957 a smoothed sunspot count showed 263, the highest recorded index since records started in 1755 (*cf.* previous record of 239 in May 1778). In 1943 one sunspot lasted for 200 days from June to December.

ECLIPSES

Earliest recorded

For the Middle East, lunar eclipses have been extrapolated to 3450 BC and solar ones to 4200 BC. No centre of the path of totality for a solar eclipse crossed London for the 575 years from 20 Mar 1140 to 3 May 1715. On 14 June 2151 at 18.25 GMT the eclipse will be 99 per cent total in central London but total in Sheffield and Norfolk. The most recent occasion when a line of totality of a solar eclipse crossed Great Britain was on 29 June 1927 for 24.5 sec at 6.23 a.m. at West Hartlepool, Cleveland and the next instance will clip the coast at St Just, Cornwall at 10.10 a.m. on Wednesday 11 Aug 1999. On 30 June 1954 a total eclipse was witnessed from Unst, Shetland Islands but the centre of the path of totality was to the north.

A still-surviving old Automobile Association sign showing the line of totality of the last total eclipse in Great Britain at West Hartlepool, Cleveland. The next will be in Cornwall in 1999.

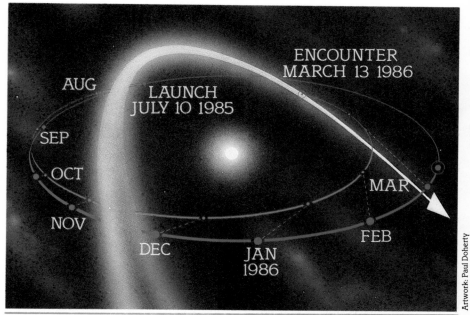

Close encounter of a cometary kind. The space probe Giotto is due to approach within 500 km *310 miles* of Halley's comet on 13 Mar 1986 as the diagram, *above* shows. *Below:* Stephen J. O'Meara who made the first, and faintest ever, *visual* sighting of the present return of Halley's comet with the 24 in Mauna Kea telescope. (*Dennis Millon, Sky and Telescope*)

Longest duration

The maximum *possible* duration of an eclipse of the Sun is 7 min 31 sec. The longest actually *measured* was on 20 June 1955 (7 min 8 sec), seen from the Philippines. One of 7 min 29 sec should occur in mid-Atlantic on 16 July 2186, which will then be the longest for 1469 years. The longest possible in the British Isles is 5½ min. That of 15 June 885 lasted nearly 5 min, as will that of 20 July 2381 in the Borders area. Durations can be extended by observers being airborne as on 30 June 1973 when an eclipse was 'extended' to 72 min aboard *Concorde*. An annular eclipse may last for 12 min 24 sec. The longest totality of any lunar eclipse is 104 min. This has occurred many times.

Most and least frequent

The highest number of eclipses possible in a year is seven, as in 1935, when there were five solar and two lunar eclipses; or four solar and three lunar eclipses, as occurred in 1982. The lowest possible number in a year is two, both of which must be solar, as in 1944 and 1969.

COMETS

Earliest recorded

The earliest records of comets date from the 7th century BC. The speeds of the estimated 2,000,000 comets vary from 700 mph *1125 km/h* in outer space to 1,250,000 mph *2 000 000 km/h* when near the Sun. The successive appearances of Halley's Comet have been traced back to 467 BC. It was first depicted in the Nuremberg Chronicle of AD 684. The first prediction of its return by Edmund Halley (1656–1742) proved true on Christmas Day 1758, 16 years after his death. Its next perihelion should be at 9.3 (*viz.* at 7 a.m. on the 9th) February 1986, 75.81 years after the last, which was on 19 Apr 1910. The 33rd sighting occurred on 16 Oct 1982 at a magnitude of 24.2 by David C. Jewitt and G. Edmond Danielson using the 200 inch *508 cm* Hale telescope at Palomar Observatory, California.

Closest approach

On 1 July 1770, Lexell's Comet, travelling at a speed of 23.9 miles/sec *38,5 km/sec* (relative to the Sun), came within 745,000 miles *1 200 000 km* of the Earth. However, the Earth is believed to have passed through the tail of Halley's Comet, most recently on 19 May 1910.

Largest

Comets are so tenuous that it has been estimated that even the head of one rarely contains solid matter much more than *c.* 1 km *0.6 miles* in diameter. Tails, as in the case of the brightest of all, the Great Comet of 1843, may trail for 205,000,000 miles *330 million km*. The head of Holmes Comet of 1892 once measured 1,500,000 miles *2 400 000 km* in diameter. Comet Bennett which appeared in January 1970 was found to be enveloped in a hydrogen cloud measuring some 8,000,000 miles *12 750 000 km* in length.

Shortest period

Of all the recorded periodic comets (these are members of the Solar System), the one which most frequently returns is Encke's Comet, first identified in 1786. Its period of 1206 days (3.3 years) is the shortest established. Not one of its 51 returns (including 1977) has been missed by astronomers. Now increasingly faint, it is

Artwork: Paul Doherty

expected to 'die' by February 1994. The most frequently observed comets are Schwassmann–Wachmann I, Kopff and Oterma which can be observed every year between Mars and Jupiter.

Longest period

At the other extreme is Delavan's Comet of 1914, whose path was not accurately determined. It is not expected to return for perhaps 24 million years.

PLANETS

Largest

The nine major planets (including the Earth) are bodies within the Solar System and which revolve round the Sun in definite orbits. The search for Planet X continues. Jupiter, with an equatorial diameter of 88,846 miles *142 984 km* and a polar diameter of 83,082 miles *133 708 km* is the largest of the nine major planets, with a mass 317.83 times, and a volume 1321.4 times that of the Earth. It also has the shortest period of rotation resulting in a Jovian day of only 9 hr 50 min 30.003 sec in the equatorial zone.

Smallest and coldest

The smallest and coldest planet is Pluto, with its partner Charon, announced on 22 June 1978 which have an estimated surface temperature of −360° F −220° C (100 deg F 53 deg C above absolute zero). Their mean distance from the Sun is 3,674,488,000 miles *5 913 514 000 km* and their period of revolution is 248.54 years. The diameter is *c*. 3000 km *1860 miles* and the mass is about 1/400th of that of the Earth. Pluto was first recorded by Clyde William Tombaugh (b. 4 Feb 1906) at Lowell Observatory, Flagstaff, Arizona, USA, on 18 Feb 1930 from photographs taken on 23 and 29 Jan and announced on 13 Mar. Because of its orbital eccentricity Pluto moved closer to the Sun than Neptune between 23 Jan 1979 and 15 Mar 1999.

Fastest

Mercury, which orbits the Sun at an average distance of 35,983,100 miles *57 909 200 km*, has a period of revolution of 87.9686 days, so giving the highest average speed in orbit of 107,030 mph *172 248 km/h*.

Sir John Herschel (1792–1871) was the first astronomer to comprehend the Universe's massive dimensions. (see page 69) (*National Portrait Gallery*)

Hottest

For Venus a surface temperature of 462° C *864° F* has been estimated from measurements made from the USSR *Venera* and US Pioneer Cytherean surface probes. Venus has a canyon 4 miles *6,4 km* deep and 250 miles *402 km* long 1000 miles *1609 km* south of Venusian equator.

Nearest

The fellow planet closest to the Earth is Venus, which is, at times, about 25,700,000 miles *41 360 000 km* inside the Earth's orbit, compared with Mars's closest approach of 34,600,000 miles *55 680 000 km* outside the Earth's orbit. Mars, known since 1965 to be cratered, has temperatures ranging from 85° F *29,4° C* to − 190° F − *123° C*.

Surface features

By far the highest and most spectacular is Olympus Mons (formerly Nix Olympica) in the Tharsis region of Mars with a diameter of 500–600 km *310–370 miles* and a height of 26 ± 3 km *75,450–95,150 ft* above the surrounding plain.

Brightest and faintest

Viewed from the Earth, by far the brightest of the five planets visible to the naked eye (Uranus at magnitude 5.5 is only marginally visible) is Venus, with a maximum magnitude of − 4.4. The faintest is Pluto, with magnitude of 15.0.

Densest and least dense

Earth is the densest planet with an average figure of 5.515 times that of water, whilst Saturn has an average density only about one-eighth of this value or 0.687 times that of water.

Conjunctions

The most dramatic recorded conjunction (coming together) of the other seven principal members of the Solar System (Sun, Moon, Mercury, Venus, Mars, Jupiter and Saturn) occurred on 5 Feb 1962, when 16° covered all seven during an eclipse in the Pacific area. It is possible that the seven-fold conjunction of September 1186 spanned only 12°. The next notable conjunction will take place on 5 May 2000.

SATELLITES

Most

Of the nine major planets, all but Venus and Mercury have satellites. The planet with the most is Saturn with 17 certainly established satellites and possibly up to 4 others. The Earth and Pluto are the only planets with a single satellite. The distance from their parent planets varies from the 5827 miles *9377 km* of *Phobos* from the centre of Mars to the 14,700,000 miles *23 700 000 km* of Jupiter's outer satellite *Sinope* (Jupiter IX). The Solar System has a total of 44 established satellites.

Largest and smallest

The largest and heaviest satellite is *Ganymede* (Jupiter III), which is 2.017 times heavier than our own Moon and has a diameter of 3270 miles *5262 km*. The smallest satellite is *Leda* (Jupiter XIII) with a diameter of less than 15 km *9,3 miles*.

Largest asteroids

In the belt which lies between Mars and Jupiter, there are some 45,000 (3226 numbered to March 1985) minor planets or asteroids which are, for the most part, too small to yield to diameter measurement. The largest and first discovered (by G. Piazzi at Palermo, Sicily on 1 Jan 1801) of these is *Ceres*, with a diameter of 637 miles *1025 km*. The only one visible to the naked eye is asteroid 4 *Vesta* (diameter 345 miles *555 km*) discovered on 29 Mar 1807 by Dr Heinrich

Wilhelm Olbers (1758–1840), a German amateur astronomer. The closest measured approach to the Earth by an asteroid was 485,000 miles *780 000 km* in the case of *Hermes* on 30 Oct 1937 (asteroid now lost). The most distant detected is 2060 *Chiron*, found between Saturn and Uranus on 18–19 Oct 1977, by Charles T. Kowal from the Hale Observatory, California, USA.

STARS

Largest and most massive

The most massive known star is the faint-blue R 136a, 179,000 light years distant in the Tarantula Nebula (or 30 Doradus), an appendage of the Large Magellanic Cloud and assessed in February 1983 to have a mass 2100 times greater than our own Sun and a diameter 50 times greater. However, Betelgeux (top left star of Orion) has a diameter of 700 million km *400 million miles* or about 500 times greater than the Sun. In 1978 it was found to be surrounded by a tenuous 'shell' of potassium 1,6 × 10¹² km or 11 000 astronomical units in diameter. The light left Betelgeux in AD 1680.

Smallest and lightest

A mass of 0.014 that of the Sun is estimated for the very faint star RG 0058.8-2807 which was discovered by I. Neill Reid and Gerard Gilmore using the U.K. Schmidt telescope and was announced in April 1983. The white dwarf star L362-81 has an estimated diameter of 3500 miles *5600 km* or only 0.0040 that of the Sun.

Brightest

Sirius A (*Alpha Canis Majoris*), also known as the Dog Star, is apparently the brightest star of the 5776 stars of naked eye visibility in the heavens, with an apparent magnitude of − 1.46. It is in the constellation *Canis Major* and is visible in the winter months of the northern hemisphere, being due south at midnight on the last day of the year. The Sirius system is 8.64 light-years distant and has a luminosity 26 times as much as that of the Sun. It has a diameter of 1,450,000 miles *2,33 million km* and a mass of 4.20 × 10²⁷ tons *4,26 × 10²⁷ tonnes*. The faint white dwarf companion Sirius B has a diameter of only 6000 miles *10 000 km* but is 350,000 times heavier than the Earth. Sirius will reach a maximum of − 1.67 in *c*. AD 61,000.

Farthest

The Solar System, with its Sun's nine principal planets, 48 satellites, asteroids and comets was estimated in 1982 to be 28,000 light-years from the centre of the lens-shaped Milky Way galaxy (diameter 70,000 light-years) so that the most distant stars in our galaxy are estimated to be 63,000 light-years distant.

Nearest

Excepting the special case of our own Sun (*q.v.* above) the nearest star is the very faint *Proxima Centauri*, discovered in 1915, which is 4.22 light-years (24,800,000,000,000 miles *4,00 × 10¹³ km*) away. The nearest 'star' visible to the naked eye is the southern hemisphere binary *Alpha Centauri*, or *Rigel Kentaurus* (4.35 light-years distant), with an apparant magnitude of − 0.29. It was discovered by Nicolas L. da Lacaille (1713–62) in *c*. 1752. In AD 29,700 this binary will reach a minimum distance of 2.84 light years and will appear as the second brightest 'star' with an apparent mag. of − 1.20.

Most and least luminous

If all the stars could be viewed at the same distance the most luminous would be R136a (see Most Massive Star) which has a total luminosity 60 million times greater than that of the Sun and an absolute visual magnitude of about −9.0 so that this star is visually 320,000 times brighter than the Sun. The variable η Carinae in c. 1840 was perhaps visually 4 million times more luminous than the Sun. The faintest star detected is the recently discovered RG 0058.8–2807 (see Lightest Star) which has a total luminosity only 0.00021 that of the Sun and an absolute visual magnitude of 20.2 so that the visual brightness is less than one millionth that of the Sun.

Brightest supernova

Supernovae, or temporary 'stars' which flare and then fade, occur perhaps five times in 1000 years in our galaxy. The brightest 'star' ever seen by historic man is believed to be the supernova SN 1006 in April 1006 near *Beta Lupi* which flared for 2 years and attained a magnitude of −9 to −10. It is now believed to be the radio source G.327.6 + 14.5 nearly 3000 light-years distant.

Constellations

The largest of the 89 constellations is *Hydra* (the Sea Serpent), which covers 1,302.844 deg^2 or 6.3 per cent of the hemisphere and contains at least 68 stars visible to the naked eye (to 5.5 mag.). The constellation *Centaurus* (Centaur), ranking ninth in area embraces however at least 94 such stars. The smallest constellation is *Crux Australis* (Southern Cross) with an area of 68.477 deg^2 compared with the 41,252.96 deg^2 of the whole sky.

Stellar planets

The first direct evidence of a planet-like companion was announced in Jan 1985 by D. McCarthy Jr, F. J. Law and R. G. Probst (US). It is an object in orbit 1000 million km *600 million miles* from the very faint red dwarf star Van Biesbroeck 8 (VB8), 21 light-years distant in Ophiuchus.

Longest name

The longest name for any star is *Shurnarkabtishashutu*, the Arabic for 'under the southern horn of the bull'.

Black Holes

This term for a star that has undergone complete gravitational collapse was first used by Prof John Archibald Wheeler at an Institute for Space Studies meeting in New York City on 29 Dec 1967.

The first tentative identification of a Black Hole was announced in December 1972 in the binary-star X-ray source Cygnus X-1. The best candidate is now LMC X-3 of 10 solar masses and 180,000 light-years distant reported in Jan 1983. The critical size has been estimated to be as low as a diameter of 3.67 miles *5,90 km*. In early 1978 supermassive Black Holes were suggested with a mass of 100 million suns or 2×10^{35} tonnes. One at the centre of the Seyfert galaxy, NGC 4151 in Canes Venatici, was estimated by Michael Preston (GB) in Oct 1983 to be of between 50–100 million solar masses.

THE UNIVERSE

Outside the Milky Way galaxy, which is part of the so-called Local Group of galaxies moving toward the Virgo cluster 50 million light-years distant, at a speed estimated to be between 200 and 500 km/sec *450,000 and 1,100,000 mph*, there exist 10,000 million other galaxies. The largest discrete object in the Universe is a bent filament of galaxies in the constellations Pisces and Cetus, announced by Jack O. Burns and David Batuski of the University of New Mexico, Albuquerque, in May 1984 measuring 730 million light years.

Farthest visible object

The remotest heavenly body visible with the *naked eye* is the Great Galaxy in *Andromeda* (Mag. 3.47), known as Messier 31. This is a rotating nebula in spiral form, and its distance from the Earth is about 2,120,000 light-years, or c 12,500,000,000,000,000,000,000 miles *20 × 10^{18} km* and is moving towards us. It is just possible however that, under ideal seeing conditions, Messier 33, the Spiral in Triangulum (Mag.

5.79), can be glimpsed by the naked eye of keen-sighted people at a distance of 2,360,000 light years.

Quasars

An occultation of 3C-273, observed from Australia on 5 Aug 1962, enabled the existence of quasi-stellar radio sources ('quasars' or QSO's) to be announced by Maarten Schmidt (b. Netherlands 1929). The red shift proved to be z = 0.158. Quasars have immensely high luminosity for bodies so distant and of such small diameter. It was announced in May 1983 that the quasar S5 0014 + 81 had a visual luminosity 1.1×10^{15} times greater than that of the Sun. The first double quasar (0957 + 56) among 1500 known quasars, was announced in May 1980.

Pulsars

The earliest observation of a pulsating radio source or 'pulsar' CP 1919 (now PSR 1919 + 21) by Dr Jocelyn Bell Burnell was announced from the Mullard Radio Astronomy Observatory, Cambridgeshire, England, on 24 Feb 1968. It had been detected on 28 Nov 1967. The fastest spinning, and most accurate stellar clock, is pulsar 1937 + 214 which is in the region of the minor constellation Vulpecula (The Fox) 16,000 light years distant. It has a pulse period of 1.557806449 milli-sec and the amazingly slow spin-down rate of only 1×10^{-19} sec/sec.

Remotest object

Both the interpretation of the very large redshifts exhibited by quasars and the estimation of equivalent distances remain controversial. The record redshift of z = 3.78 for quasar PKS 2000 − 330 (see Table this page) has been interpreted as indicating proximity to the 'observable horizon' at 16,300 million light years, which is 96,000,000,000,000,000,000,000 miles *1,54 × 10^{23} km*. It was announced in April 1983 that the most distant known galaxy, which is associated with the radio source 3C 324, has a redshift of 1.21. The 3 K background radiation or primordial hiss discovered in 1965 by Arno Penzias and Robert Wilson of Bell Laboratories

PROGRESSIVE RECORDS OF THE MOST DISTANT MEASURED HEAVENLY BODIES

The possible existence of galaxies external to our own Milky Way system was mooted in 1789 by Sir William Herschel (1738–1822). These extra-galactic nebulae were first termed 'island universes'. Sir John Herschel (1792–1871) opined as early as 1835 that some might be more than 250,000,000,000 million miles distant. The first direct measurement of any body outside our Solar System was in 1838. Distances in the table below are based on a Hubble ratio of 80 km s^{-1} Mpc^{-1} and assume that the edge of the observable Universe is at a distance of 15 ± 3 thousand million light years. A value of 16,300 million light years has been adopted for this table. The launch of the Space Telescope is expected to produce a new champion with an even higher speed of recession and z value.

Estimated Distance in Light Years[1]	Object	Method	Astronomers	Observatory	Date
about 6 (now 11.08)	61 Cygni	Parallax	F. Bessel	Konigsberg, Germany	1838
> 20 (now 26)	Vega	Parallax	F. G. W. Struve	Dorpat (now Tartu), Estonia	1840
c. 200	Limit	Parallax			by 1900
750,000 (now 2.12 m)[2]	Galaxy M31	Cepheid variable	E. P. Hubble (1889–1953)	Mt. Wilson, Cal., USA	1923
900,000 (now 2.12 m)[2]	Galaxy M31	Cepheid variable	E. P. Hubble	Mt. Wilson, Cal., USA	1924

Millions of Light Years	Recession Speed % of c	Object	Red shift[3]	Astronomers	Observatory	Date
c. 200	1.3	NGC 7619		M. L. Humason	Mt. Wilson, Cal., USA	early 1928
> 2100	13.3	Ursa Major No. 2		Humason & E. P. Hubble	Mt. Wilson, Cal., USA	by 1936[2]
5300	32.6	Cluster 1448	0.403		Palomar, Cal., USA	1956
5900	36.2	3C 295 in Boötes	0.461	R. Minkowski	Palomar, Cal., USA	June 1960
6700	41.0	QSO 3C 147	0.545	M. Schmidt & T. A. Matthews	Palomar, Cal., USA	Feb 1964[5]
13,100	80.1	QSO 3C 9	2.01	M. Schmidt	Palomar, Cal., USA	April 1965
c. 13,200	81.3	QSO 0106 × 01	2.11	E. M. Burbridge *et al.*	Palomar, Cal., USA	Dec 1965
13,300	81.4	QSO 1116 + 12	2.12	C. R. Lynds & A. N. Stockton	Steward, Ariz., USA	March 1966
				M. Schmidt	Palomar, Cal., USA	March 1966
13,400	82.4	QSO Pks 0237 − 23	2.22	H. C. Arp *et al.*	Palomar, Cal., USA	Dec 1966
13,600	83.7	QSO 4C 25.05	2.36	E. T. Olsen & M. Schmidt	Palomar, Cal., USA	Dec 1967[6]
14,300	87.5	QSO 4C 05.34	2.88	R. Lynds & D. Wills	Kitt Peak, Arizona, USA	March 1970
14,700	90.2	QSO OH 471	3.40	R. F. Carswell & P. A. Strittmatter	Steward, Ariz., USA	March 1973
14,800	90.7	QSO OQ 172	3.53	E. J. Wampler *et al.*	Lick, Cal., USA	May 1973
14,900	91.6	QSO Pks 2000 − 330	3.78	B. A. Peterson *et al.*	Siding Spring, NSW, Australia	April 1982

Note: c is the notation for the speed of light. (see p. 65). [1] Term first utilised in March 1888. [2] Re-estimate by G. de Vancouleurs in May 1977. [3] Discovered by Vesto Slipher (1875–1969) from Flagstaff, Arizona, USA 1920. Redshift, denoted by z, is the measure of the speed of recession indicated by the ratio resulting from the subtraction of the rest wavelength of an emission line from the observed wavelength divided by the rest wavelength. [4] In 1934 Hubble opined that the observable horizon would be 3000 m light-years. [5] In Dec 1963 Dr I. S. Shklovsky's (USSR) suggestion that QSO 3C2 was more distant was subsequently confirmed with a value of 0.612 c. [6] In Oct 1968 Dr Margaret Burbidge (GB) published a tentative redshift of 2.38 for QSO 5C 2.56.

appears to be moving at a velocity of 99.9998 per cent *c*.

Age of the Universe
For the age of the Universe a value of 15 ± 3 aeons or gigayears (an aeon or gigayear being 1000 million years) is obtained from cosmochronology and nucleochronology. Based on the presently accepted Friedman models of the Universe with zero cosmological constant then the equivalent Hubble ratio is about 60 km/s/Mpc which compares to the most likely experimental value of 80 km s^{-1} Mpc^{-1}. In 1973 an *ex nihilo* creation was postulated by Edward P. Tryon (US). Modified versions of the Inflationary Model, originally introduced by Alan Guth (US) in 1981, now rival the 'Big Bang' theory of creation.

ROCKETRY AND MISSILES

Earliest uses
War rockets, propelled by a charcoal-saltpetre-sulphur gun-powder, were described by Tseng Kung Liang of China in 1042. These early rockets became known in Europe by 1258. The pioneer of military rocketry in Britain was Col. Sir William Congreve, Bt., MP (1772–1828), Comptroller of the Royal Laboratory, Woolwich, Greater London and Inspector of Military Machines, whose 'six-pound *2,72 kg* rocket' was developed to a range of 2000 yd *1825m* by 1805 and first used by the Royal Navy against Boulogne, France on 8 Oct 1806.

The first launching of a liquid-fuelled rocket (patented 14 July 1914) was by Dr Robert Hutchings Goddard (1882–1945) of the United States, at Auburn, Massachusetts, USA, on 16 Mar 1926, when his rocket reached an altitude of 41 ft *12,5 m* and travelled a distance of 184 ft *56 m*. The USSR's earliest rocket was the semi-liquid fuelled GIRD-IX tested on 17 Aug 1933.

Longest ranges
On 16 Mar 1962, Nikita Khrushchyov, then Prime Minister of the USSR, claimed in Moscow that the USSR possessed a 'global rocket' with a range of 30 000 km (*about 19,000 miles*) *i.e.* more than the Earth's semi-circumference and therefore capable of hitting any target from either direction.

Most powerful *World*
It has been suggested that the USSR lunar booster which blew up at Tyuratam in the summer (? July) of 1969 had a thrust of 10–14

million lb *4,5–6,35 million kg*. There is some evidence of the launch of a USSR 'G' class lunar booster, larger than the US Saturn V, on 11 May 1973.

The most powerful rocket that has been publicised is the Saturn V, used for the Project Apollo and Skylab programmes on which development began in January 1962, at the John F. Kennedy Space Center, Merritt Island, Florida, USA. The rocket is 363 ft 8 in *110,85 m* tall, with a payload of 74 783 kg *73.60 tons* in the case of *Skylab I*, and gulps 13.4 tons *13,6 tonnes* of propellant per sec for 2½ min (2010 tons *2042 tonnes*). Stage I (S-IC) is 138 ft *42,06 m* tall and is powered by five Rocketdyne F-1 engines, using liquid oxygen (LOX) and kerosene, each delivering 1,514,000 lb *686 680 kg* thrust. Stage II (S-II) is powered by five LOX and liquid hydrogen Rocketdyne J-2 engines with a total thrust of 1,141,453 lb *517 759 kg* while Stage III (designated S-IVB) is powered by a single 228,290 lb *103 550 kg* thrust J-2 engine. The whole assembly generates 175,600,000 hp and weighs up to 7,600,000 lb (3393 tons *3447 tonnes*) fully loaded in the case of *Apollo 17*. It was first launched on 9 Nov 1967, from Cape Canaveral (then Kennedy), Florida.

Highest pay load
Skylab I, (launched on 14 May 1973) fell to Earth on its 34,981 st orbit over the Western Australian coast at 16.32 GMT on 11 July 1979. Large pieces of *Skylab I* were found 12 km *7.45 miles* south of Rawlinna and sold to a Hong Kong syndicate. The piece which most worried keraunothnetophobes was a 5175 lb *2347 kg* airlock shroud.

Highest velocity
The first space vehicle to achieve the Third Cosmic velocity sufficient to break out of the Solar System was *Pioneeer 10* (see table p. 70).The Atlas SLV-3C launcher with a modified Centaur D second stage and a Thiokol Te-364-4 third stage left the Earth at an unprecedented 32,114 mph *51 682 km/h* on 2 Mar 1972. The highest recorded velocity of any space vehicle has been 240 000 km/h *149,125 mph* in the case of the US-German solar probe *Helios B* launched on 15 Jan 1976.

Ion rockets
Speeds of up to 100,000 mph *160 000 km/h* are envisaged for rockets powered by an ion discharge. An ion thruster has been maintained for

9715 hours (404 days 19 hrs) at the Lewis Research Center in Cleveland, Ohio, USA. Ion rockets were first used in flight by NASA's SERT I rocket launched on 20 July 1964.

SPACE FLIGHT

The physical laws controlling the flight of artificial satellites were first propounded by Sir Isaac Newton (1642–1727) in his *Philosophiae Naturalis Principia Mathematica* ('Mathematical Principles of Natural Philosophy'), begun in March 1686 and first published in the summer of 1687. The first artificial satellite was successfully put into orbit at an altitude of 142/588 miles *228,5/946 km* and a velocity of more than 17,750 mph *28 565 km/h* from Tyuratam, a site located 170 miles *275 km* east of the Aral Sea on the night of 4 Oct 1957. This spherical satellite *Sputnik* ('Fellow Traveller') *1*, officially designated 'Satellite 1957 Alpha 2', weighed 83,6 kg *184.3 lb*, with a diameter of 58 cm *22.8 in*, and its lifetime is believed to have been 92 days, ending on 4 Jan 1958. It was designed under the direction of Dr Sergey Pavlovich Korolyov (1907–66).

Earliest successful manned satellite
The first successful manned space flight began at 9.07 a.m. (Moscow time), or 6.07 a.m. GMT, on 12 Apr 1961. Cosmonaut Flight Major (later Colonel) Yuriy Alekseyevich Gagarin (born 9 Mar 1934) completed a single orbit of the Earth in 89.34 min in the 4.65 ton *4,72 tonnes* space vehicle *Vostok* ('East') 1. The take-off was from Tyuratam in Kazakhstan, and the landing was 108 min later near the village of Smelovka, near Engels, in the Saratov region of the USSR. The maximum speed was 17,560 mph *28 260 km/h* and the maximum altitude 327 km *203.2 miles* in a flight of 40 868,6 km *25,394.5 miles*. Major Gagarin, invested a Hero of the Soviet Union and awarded the Order of Lenin and the Gold Star Medal, was killed in a jet plane crash near Moscow on 27 Mar 1968.

First extra-terrestrial vehicle
The first wheeled vehicle landed on the Moon was *Lunakhod I* which began its Earth-controlled travels on 17 Nov 1970. It moved a total of 10,54 km *6.54 miles* on gradients up to 30° in the Mare Imbrium and did not become non-functioning until 4 Oct 1971. The lunar speed and distance record was set by the *Apollo 16* Rover with 11.2 mph *18km/h* downhill and 22.4 miles *33,8 km*.

PROGRESSIVE ROCKET ALTITUDE RECORDS

Height in miles	Height in km	Rocket	Place	Launch	Date
0.71	1,14	A 3 in 7,62 cm rocket	near London, England	April	1750
1.24	2	Reinhold Tiling[1] (Germany) solid fuel rocket	Osnabruck, Germany	April	1931
3.1	5	GIRD-X liquid fuel (USSR)	USSR	25 Nov	1933
8.1	13	USSR 'Stratosphere' rocket	USSR		1935
52.46	84,42	A.4 rocket (Germany)[2]	Peenemünde, Germany	3 Oct	1942
c. 85	c. 136	A.4 rocket (Germany)[2]	Heidelager, Poland	early	1944
118	190	A.4 rocket (Germany)[2]	Heidelager, Poland	mid	1944
244	392.6	V-2/W.A.C. Corporal (2-stage) Bumper No. 5 (USA)	White Sands, NM, USA	24 Feb	1949
318	512	Geophysical rocket V-5-V (USSR)	Tyuratam, USSR		1950–52
682	1097	Jupiter C (USA)	Cape Canaveral, Florida, USA	20 Sept	1956
>800	>1300	ICBM test flight R-7 (USSR)	Tyuratam, USSR	Aug	1957
>2700	>4345	Farside No. 5 (4-stage) (USA)	Eniwetok Atoll	20 Oct	1957
70,700	113 770	Pioneer 1-B Lunar Probe (USA)	Cape Canaveral, Florida, USA	11 Oct	1958
215,300,000*	346 480 000	Luna 1 or Mechta (USSR)	Tyuratam, USSR	2 Jan	1959
242,000,000*	389 450 000	Mars 1 (USSR)	USSR	1 Nov	1962
2,845,000,000[3]	4 580 000 000	Pioneer 10 (USA) (see page 70)	Kennedy Space Center, Cape Canaveral, Florida, USA	2 Mar	1972

* Apogee in solar orbit. [1] There is some evidence that Tiling may latterly after have reached 9500 m (5.90 miles) with a solid fuel rocket at Wangerooge, East Friesian Islands, W.31/84 Germany.
[2] The A4 was latterly referred to as the V2 rocket, a code for second revenge weapon (vergeltungswaffe) following upon the V1 'flying bomb'. [3] This distance was attained at 1.30 a.m. on 13 June 1983 when Pioneer 10 crossed the orbit of Neptune. In Oct 1986 it will cross Pluto's mean orbit so leaving the Solar System. It will be more distant than the furthest extension of Pluto's orbit in April 1989 and will continue at 49 000 km/h 30,450 mph towards the edge of the heliosphere (solar magetosphere) and the heliopause (zone of 'solar wind'). In AD 34 593 it will make its nearest approach to the 12th nearest star Ross 248, 10.3 light-years distant. However before AD 1991 Voyager I, travelling faster, will surpass Pioneer 10 in remoteness from Earth.

Closest approach to the Sun by a rocket

The research spacecraft *Helios B* approached within 27 million miles *43,4 million km* of the Sun, carrying both US and West German instrumentation on 16 Apr 1976.

Largest space object

The heaviest object orbited is the Saturn V third stage with *Apollo 15* (space craft) which, prior to trans-lunar injection in parking orbit weighed 140 512 kg *138.29 tons*. The 442 lb *200 kg* US RAE (radio astronomy explorer) B or *Explorer 49* launched on 10 June 1973 has, however, antennae, 1500 ft *415 m* from tip to tip.

Most expensive project

The total cost of the US manned space pro- gramme up to and including the lunar mission of *Apollo 17* has been estimated to be $25,541,400,000 (then £9,823,150,000). The first 15 years of the USSR space programme from 1958 to September 1973 has been estimated to have cost $45,000 million. The cost of the NASA Shuttle programme was $9.9 billion (*£4350 million*) to the launch of *Columbia* on 12 Apr 1981.

ASTRONAUTS

First Undisputed Fatality
Col Vladimir Komarov
(b. 16 Mar 1927) (USSR)
Soyuz 1 24 Apr 1967

Oldest
Dr William Thornton
(54 years 4 months)
ST5 8 Aug–Sept 1983

First Untethered 'Float' in Space
(wearing a Manned Maneuvring Unit)
Man: Capt Bruce McCandless (USN)
(b. 1938)
Challenger 7 Feb 1984
Woman: Dr Kathryn Sullivan
(b. 1952)
Challenger 11 Oct 1984

First Feminine Space Walk
Mde Svetlana Savitskaya-Khatkovsky
Salyut 7 25 July 1984

Longest Manned Flight
237 days Dr Oleg Y. Atkov, 35;
Leonid D. Kizim, 43, and Vladimir A. Solovyev
158 million km *98,1 million miles*
Soyuz T-11 8 Feb–20 Oct 1984
Valeriy Ryumin holds the aggregate duration record at 362 days in 3 flights.

Most on One Mission
5 men and 2 women
13th Shuttle mission from
Cape Canaveral, Florida, USA
Challenger 5 Oct 1984
6 men and 1 woman
16th Shuttle mission from
Cape Canaveral, Florida, USA
Discovery 12 Apr 1985
7 men, 2 monkeys, 24 rats
17th Shuttle mission from
Cape Canaveral. Florida, USA
Challenger 24 April 1985

Youngest
Col Gherman S. Titov
(25 yrs 329 days)
Vostok 2 6 Aug 1961

Earliest
Col Yuriy Gagarin
(b. 9 Nov 1939) (USSR)
Vostok 1 12 Apr 1961

First on Moon
Neil A. Armstrong
(b. 5 Aug 1930) (USA)
Apollo 11 21 July 1969

First Woman
Lt-Col Valentina Tereshkova-Nikolayev
(48 orbits)
(b. 6 Mar 1937) (USSR)
Vostok 6 16 June 1963

First Space Walk
Lt-Col Aleksey A. Leonov
(b. 30 May 1934) (USSR)
Voskhod 2 18 Mar 1965

Longest on Moon
Capt Eugene A. Cernan (USN)
(b. 14 Mar 1934) (USA)
Dr Harrison H. Schmitt
(b. 3 July 1935) (USA)
74 hr 59½ min
Apollo 17 7–19 Dec 1972

PHOTOGRAPHS: NOVOSTI/NASA

The Scientific World

1. ELEMENTS

All known matter in, on and beyond the Earth is made up of chemical elements. It is estimated that there are 10^{87} electrons in the known universe. The total of naturally-occurring elements so far detected is 94, comprising, at ordinary temperatures, two liquids, 11 gases and 81 solids. The so-called 'fourth state' of matter is plasma, when negatively charged electrons and positively-charged ions are in flux.

Lightest and heaviest sub-nuclear particles

By April 1984 the existence of 30 'stable' particles, 53 meson resonance multiplets and 48 baryon resonance multiplets was accepted, representing the eventual discovery of 242 particles and an equal number of anti-particles. The heaviest 'stable' particle fully accepted is the neutral weak gauge boson, the Z°, of mass 92.9 ± 1.6 GeV which was first detected in May 1983 by the UA1 Collaboration, CERN, Geneva, Switzerland using the 540 GeV Super Proton Synchrotron proton-antiproton beam collider. The heaviest particle known is the upsilon triple prime meson, symbol Y''', of mass 10570 MeV and lifetime 5×10^{-23} sec, which consists of a bottom or beauty quark and its anti-quark, and which was first identified in April 1980 by two groups using the Cornell electron storage ring facilities at Cornell University, Ithaca, New York, USA. Sub-atomic concepts require that the masses of the graviton, photon, and neutrino should all be zero. Based on the sensitivities of various cosmological theories, upper limits for the masses of these particles are $7,6 \times 10^{-67}$ g for the graviton; $3,0 \times 10^{-53}$ g for the photon and $1,4 \times 10^{-32}$ g for the neutrino (*cf*. $9,10953 \times 10^{-28}$ g for the mass of an electron.)

Newest particles

It was announced in July 1984 that the UA1 Collaboration, CERN, Geneva, Switzerland had obtained tentative evidence for the existence of the sixth flavour of quark, the top or truth quark, of mass about 40 GeV. In October 1984 two groups using the Cornell University electron storage ring facilities identified two higher mass states of a combination of a bottom or beauty quark and its anti-quark, known as the upsilon (5S) and (6S) meson resonances of mass 10.86 GeV and 11.02 GeV and lifetimes 6×10^{-24} sec and 9×10^{-24} sec respectively.

The discovery in July 1984 by the Crystal Ball Collaboration, Hamburg, West Germany, of a particle of mass 8.32 GeV known as the 'zeta', and which was associated with the existence of the important theoretical particle known as the Higgs boson, has not been confirmed.

Most and least stable

Experiments in 1982 to 1984 have confirmed that the proton definitely has a lifetime in excess of 1×10^{30} years compared to theoretical predictions based on the 'grand unified theory' which suggests that the lifetime may be less than 1×10^{34} years. The least stable or shortest lived particles are the two baryon resonances N(2220) and N(2600), both 1.6×10^{-24} sec.

Substance smelliest

The most evil smelling substance, of the 17,000 smells so far classified, must be a matter of opinion but ethyl mercaptan (C_2H_5SH) and butyl seleno-mercaptan (C_4H_9SeH), are powerful claimants, each with a smell reminiscent of a combination of rotting cabbage, garlic, onions and sewer gas.

Most expensive perfume

The retail prices of the most expensive perfumes tend to be fixed at public relations rather than economic levels. The most expensive fragrant ingredient in perfume is pure French middle note jasmine essence at £2900 per kg or £82.20p per oz. The Chicago-based firm Jōvan marketed from March 1984 a cologne called Andron which

Upper Dr R. S. W. Braithwaite who established the identity of the worlds rarest mineral. *Lower* The Yellowish crystals of scotlandite ($PbSO_3$) see page 78.

contains a trace of the attractant pheromone androstenol which has a cost of $2750 per oz $97 £84 *per gramme*.

Most potent poison

The rickettsial disease, Q-fever can be instituted by a *single* organism but is only fatal in 1 in 1000 cases. About 10 organisms of *Francisella tularenesis* (formerly *Pasteurella tularenesis*) can institute tularaemia variously called alkali disease, Francis disease or deerfly fever, and this is fatal in upwards of 10 cases in 1000.

Most powerful nerve gas

VX, 300 times more toxic than phosgene ($COCl_2$) used in World War I, was developed at the Chemical Defence Experimental Establishment, Porton Down, Wiltshire in 1952. Patents were applied for in 1962 and published in February 1974 showing it to be Ethyl S-2-diisopropylaminoethylmethylphosphonothiolate. The lethal dosage is 10 mg-minute/m^3 airborne or 0,3 mg orally.

Most absorbent substance

The US Department of Agriculture Research Service announced on 18 Aug 1974 that 'H-span' or Super Slurper composed of one half starch derivative and one fourth each of acrylamide and acrylic acid can, when treated with iron, retain water 1300 times its own weight.

Finest powder

The ultimate in fine powder is solid helium which was first postulated to be a monatomic powder as early as 1964.

2. DRINK AND DRUGS

As from 1 Jan 1981 the strength of spirits has been expressed only in terms of percentage volume of alcohol at 20° C. Absolute or '100% vol' alcohol was formerly expressed to be 75.35 degrees over proof or 75.35°OP. In the USA proof is double the actual percentage of alcohol by volume at 60° F *15,6° C* such that absolute alcohol is 200 per cent proof spirit. 'Hangovers' are said to be aggravated by the presence of such toxic congenerics as amyl alcohol ($C_5H_{11}OH$).

Most alcoholic

During independence (1918–40) the Estonian Liquor Monopoly marketed 98 per cent potato alcohol (196 proof US). In 31 US states *Everclear* 190 proof or 95% vol alcohol, is marketed by the American Distilling Co 'primarily as a base for home-made cordials'. Royal Navy rum, introduced in 1655, was 40° OP (79% vol) before 1948, but was reduced to 4.5° UP (under proof) or 46% vol, before its abolition on 31 July 1970. Full strength Pusser's naval rum was again sold by E. D. & F. Man from 1984.

Oldest wine

The oldest datable wine has been an amphora salvaged and drunk by Capt. Jacques Cousteau from the wreck of a Greek trader sunk in the Mediterranean *c* 230 BC. A wine jar recovered in Rome has been found to bear the label 'Q. Lutatio C. Mario Cos' meaning that it was produced in the consulship of Q. Lutatius and C. Marius *i.e.* in 102 BC. A bottle of 1748 Rudesheimer Rosewein was auctioned at Christie's, London for £260 on 6 Dec 1979.

Beer *Strongest world*

The strongest beer as measured by original gravity is the German EKU Kulminatur Urtyp hell 28 with 1131.7° and 13.52% alcohol by volume. The world's most alcoholic beer is Samichlaus Bier brewed by Brauerai Hürlimann of Zürich, Switzerland. It is 13.70 per cent alcohol by volume at 20° C with an original gravity of 1117.8°.

Beer *Strongest Great Britain*

The strongest regularly brewed beer in Britain is Thomas Hardy's brewed by Eldridge Pope & Co at their Dorchester Brewery, Dorset. It has an alcoholic content of 12.48 per cent by volume at 60° F and an original gravity of 1125.8°.

Beer *Weakest*

The weakest liquid ever marketed as beer was a sweet Ersatz beer which was brewed in Germany by Sunner, Colne-Kalk, in 1918. It had an original gravity of 1000.96° and a strength 1/30th that of the weakest beer now obtainable in the U.K.

Most expensive wine

Record prices paid for single bottles *usually* arise when two or more self-promoters are seeking

Beer's closest approach to sherry—a label from a bottle of 12½ per cent alcohol beer from England's West Country.

THOMAS HARDY'S ALE

In 'The Trumpet-Major' Hardy wrote of Dorchester's strong beer "It was of the most beautiful colour that the eye of an artist in beer could desire; full in body, yet brisk as a volcano; piquant, yet without a twang; luminous as an autumn sunset; free from streakiness of taste but finally, rather heady."

BOTTLE Nº **A** 18009   1985

Brewed and Bottled by/Bière de Luxe brassée et mise en bouteilles par
ELDRIDGE, POPE & CO. plc · DORCHESTER · DORSET · ENGLAND

33 cl 'e'

THE 109 ELEMENTS

There are 94 naturally-occurring elements comprising, at ordinary temperatures, two liquids, 11 gases, 72 metals and nine other solids. To date the discovery of a further 15 transuranic elements (Elements 95 to 109) has been claimed of which 10 are undisputed.

Category	Name	Symbol	Discovery of Element	Record
Commonest (lithosphere)	Oxygen	O	1771 Scheele (Germany-Sweden)	46.60% by weight
Commonest (atmosphere)	Nitrogen	N	1772 Rutherford (GB)	78.09% by volume
Commonest (extra-terrestrial)	Hydrogen	H	1776 Cavendish (GB)	90% of all matter
Rarest (of the 94)	Astatine	At	1940 Corson (US) *et al.*	1/100th oz *0,35 g* in Earth's crust
Lightest	Hydrogen	H	1776 Cavendish (GB)	0.005612 lb/ft³ *0,00008989 g/cm³*
Lightest (Metal)	Lithium	Li	1817 Arfwedson (Sweden)	33.30 lb/ft³ *0.5334 g/cm³*
Densest	Osmium	Os	1804 Tennant (GB)	1410 lb/ft³ *22,59 g/cm³*
Heaviest (Gas)	Radon	Rn	1900 Dorn (Germany)	*0.6274 lb/ft³ 0.01005 g/cm³* at 0° C
Newest[1]	Unniloctium	Uno	1984 G. Munzenberg *et al.* (W. Germany) and at Dubna Research Institute, Moscow, USSR	Element 108
Purest	Helium	^{4}He	1868 Lockyer (GB) and Jannsen (France)	2 parts in 10¹⁵ (1978)
Hardest	Carbon	C	— prehistoric	Diamond allotrope, Knoop value 8400
Most Expensive	Californium	Cf	1950 Seaborg (US) *et al.*	Sold in 1970 for $10 per μg
Most Stable[2]	Tellurium	^{128}Te	1782 von Reichenstein (Austria)	Half-life of 1.5 × 10²⁴ years
Least Stable	Lithium (isotope 5)	Li 5	1817 Arfwedson (Sweden)	Lifetime of 4.4 × 10⁻²² sec.
Most Isotopes	Xenon	Xe	1898 Ramsay and Travers (GB)	36
Least Isotopes	Hydrogen	H	1776 Cavendish (GB)	3 (confirmed)
Most Ductile	Gold	Au	*ante* 3000 BC	1 oz drawn to 43 miles *1 g/2,4 km*
Highest Tensile Strength	Boron	B	1808 Gay-Lussac and Thenard (France)	3.9 × 10⁶ lb f/in² *26,8 GPa*
Lowest Melting/Boiling Point (non-metallic)[3]	Helium	^{4}He	1895 Ramsay (GB)	−272,375° C under pressure (2532 kPa) −268,928° C
Lowest Melting/Boiling Point (metallic)	Mercury	Hg	— protohistoric	−38.836° C/356.661° C
Highest Melting/Boiling Point (non-metallic)	Carbon (carbyne 6)	C	prehistoric[4]	3530° C/3870° C
Highest Melting/Boiling Point (metallic)[4]	Tungsten	W	1783 J. J. & F. d'Elhuyar (Spain)	3420° C and 5730° C
Largest Expansion (negative)	Plutonium	Pu	1940 Seaborg (US) *et al.*	−5.8 × 10⁻⁵ cm/cm/deg C between 450–480° C (Delta prime allotrope disc. 1953)
Lowest Expansion (positive)	Carbon (diamond)	C	— prehistoric	1.0 × 10⁻⁶ cm/cm/deg C (at 20° C)
Highest Expansion (metal)	Caesium	Cs	1860 Bunsen & Kirchoff (Germ.)	9.7 × 10⁻⁵ cm/cm/deg C (at 20° C)
Highest Expansion (solid)	Neon	Ne	1898 Ramsay and Travers (GB)	1.94 × 10⁻³ cm/cm/deg C at −248.59° C
Most Toxic	Radium	^{224}Ra	1898 The Curies and Bemont (France)	Naturally occurring isotope 17,000 × more toxic than plutonium 239

[1] *Provisional IUPAC name. A single atom of Une (Element 109) was created by bombardment of bismuth by iron ions at the GSI laboratory, Dormstadt, W. Germany on 29 Aug 1982. It had the highest atomic number (element 109) and the highest atomic mass (266).*
[2] *Double beta decay estimate. Alpha particle record is Samarium 148 at 8 × 10¹⁵ years and Beta particle record is Cadmium 113 at 9 × 10¹⁵ years.*
[3] *Monatomic hydrogen H is expected to be a non-liquifiable superfluid gas.*
[4] *The carbyne forms of carbon were discovered by A. E. Goresy and G. Donnay (USA) and A. M. Sladkov and Yu. P. Koudrayatsev (USSR) in 1968.*

CHEMICAL COMPOUNDS

It has been estimated that there are 6,845,000 described chemical compounds of which some 65,000 are (1984) in common use.

Most Refractory	Tantalum Carbide TaC$_{0.88}$	Melts at 3990 deg C
Most Refractory (plastics)	Modified polymides	900° F *482° C* for short periods
Lowest Expansion	Invar metal (Ni-Fe alloy with C and Mn)	1,3 × 10⁻⁷ cm/cm/deg C at 20° C
Highest Tensile Strength	Sapphire whisker Al_2O_3	6 × 10⁶ lb/in² *42,7 GPa*
Highest Tensile Strength (plastics)	Polyvinyl alcoholic fibres	1.4 × 10⁵ lbf/in² 1,03 GPa
Most Magnetic	Cobalt-copper-samarium Co_5Cu_2Sm	10,500 oersted coercive force
Least Magnetic alloy	Copper nickel alloy CuNi	963 parts Cu to 37 parts Ni
Most Pungent	Vanillaldehyde	Detectable at 2 × 10⁻⁸ mg/litre
Sweetest[1]	Talin from arils of katemfe (Thaumatococcus daniellii) discovered in W. Africa	6150 × as sweet as 1% sucrose
Bitterest	Bitrex (Denatonium benzoate; $C_{28}H_{34}N_2O_3.H_2O$)	3000 × as bitter as quinine sulphate
Most Acidic[2]	Perchloric acid (HClO$_4$)	pH value of normal solution tends to 0.
Most Alkaline	Caustic soda (NaOH) and potash (KOH) and tetramethylammonium hydroxide (N(CH$_3$)$_4$OH)	pH value of normal solution is 14.
Highest Specific Impulse	Hydrogen with liquid fluorine	447 lb f/sec/lb *4382 N/sec/kg*
Most Poisonous	Thiopentone (a barbiturate)	Intracardiac injection will kill in 1 to 2 sec
Highest Ductility in tension (max. superplasticity)	Pb38 Sn62	49½ times pre-stressed length by Ahmed and Langdon, Univ. of S. California, 1977

[1] *Found in 1839, reported in 1852 but the protein thaumatin not isolated until 1972.*
[2] *The most powerful acid, assessed on its power as a hydrogen-ion donor, is a solution of antimony pentafluoride in fluorosulphonic acid—$SbF_5 + FSO_3H$. Concentrated hydrochloric acid HCl, an aqueous solution has a pH value tending to −1.*

publicity. They bear little relation to the market value among vintners. The highest price paid for any bottle (meaning a container as opposed to a measure) is £26,500 for a Jeroboam (equivalent to 6 bottles of Bordeaux) Mouton Rothschild 1870. It was bought for resale by Bill Burford of Dallas, Texas, USA from Whetwham Wines, Altrincham, Greater Manchester on 16 July 1984.

Greatest wine auction and wine tasting
The largest single sale of wine was conducted by Christie's of King Street, St James's, London on 10–11 July 1974 at Quaglino's Ballroom, London when 2325 lots comprising 432,000 bottles realised £962,190. The largest ever reported wine-tasting was that staged by the Wine Institute at St Francis Hotel, San Francisco, California on 17 July 1980 with 125 pourers, 90 openers and a consumption of 3000 bottles.

Most expensive liqueurs
The most expensive liqueur in France is *Eau de vie de pêche* at 190 F (*now £17.00*) for a 75 cl bottle at Fauchon in Paris. Remy Martin's Louis XIII cognac retails at £380 a bottle.

Most expensive spirits
The most expensive bottle of spirits at auction is £780 for a magnum of *Grande Armée Fine Champagne Cognac, 1811* at Christie's Geneva on 13 Nov 1978. *Cognac Chatereau la faut* (1865) retails for 2800 F (*now £255*) a bottle at Fauchon. In Britain *Hennessy Private Reserve Grande Champagne* retails for £120 (including VAT) for a standard bottle.

Largest bottles
The largest bottle normally used in the wine and spirit trade is the Jeroboam (equal to 4 bottles of champagne or, rarely, of brandy and from 5 to 6½ bottles of claret according to whether blown or moulded) and the Double Magnum (equal, since *c.* 1934 to 4 bottles of claret or, more rarely, red Burgundy). A complete set of Champagne bottles would consist of a ¼ bottle, through the ½ bottle, bottle, magnum, Jeroboam, Rehoboam, Methuselah, Salmanazer and Balthazar, to the Nebuchadnezzar, which has a capacity of 16 litres *28.14 pt*, and is equivalent to 20 bottles. In May 1958 a 5 ft *152 cm* tall sherry bottle with a capacity of 20½ Imperial gal *93,19 litres* was blown in Stoke-on-Trent, Staffordshire. This bottle, with the capacity of 131 normal bottles, was named an 'Adelaide'.

Smallest bottles
The smallest and meanest bottles of liquor now sold are White Horse bottles of Scotch whisky containing 1,3 millilitres or *22 minims* at 33p a bottle or £2.16 per 'case' of 12.

Champagne cork flight
The longest distance for a champagne cork to fly from an untreated and unheated bottle 4 ft *1,22 m* from level ground is 105 ft 9 in *32,23 m* by Peter Kirby at Idlewild Park, Reno, Nevada, USA on 4 July 1981.

Most powerful drugs
The most powerful commonly available drug is d-Lysergic Acid Diethylamide tartrate (LSD-25, $C_{20}H_{25}N_3O$) first produced in 1938 for common cold research and as a hallucinogen by Dr Albert Hoffman (Swiss) on 16–19 Apr 1943. The most potent analgesic drug is the morphine-like R33799 confirmed in 1978 to have almost 12,000 times the potency of morphine. Interferon was reported available for $10 US per millionth of a microgramme.

Most lethal man-made chemical
TCDD (2,3,7,8-tetrachlorodibenzo-p-dioxin),

Largest bottle collections
The largest reported collection of unduplicated miniature bottles is one of 26,794 (*see above*) by April 1985 owned by David L. Maund of Upham, Hampshire.

The largest reported collection of distilled spirits or liqueurs in any bar is 1507 unduplicated labels (*see below*) collected by Ian Boasman at Bistro French, Avenham Street, Preston, Lancashire audited in May 1985.

The world's greatest collection of whisky bottles is one of 3100 unduplicated labels assembled by Sig Edward Giaccone at his Whiskyteca, Salo, Lake Garda, Italy (*see right*).

discovered in 1872, is admitted to be 150,000 times more deadly than cyanide at 3.1×10^{-9} moles/kg.

Most prescribed drug

The top-selling prescription drug in the world is the anti-ulcer drug Tagamet marketed by Smithkline-Beckman of Philadelphia, USA. The sales in 1981 were estimated at $800 million. The most prescribed drug in the United Kingdom is the tranquilliser Valium with over 1 million users.

3. PHOTOGRAPHY

CAMERAS

Earliest

The earliest veiled reference to a photograph on glass taken in a camera was in a letter from Joseph Nicéphore Niepce (1765–1833), a French physician and scientist dated 19 July 1822. It was a photograph of a copper engraving of Pope Pius VII taken at Gras, near Chalon-sur-Saône. The earliest photograph taken in England was one of a diamond-paned window in Laycock (or Lacock) Abbey, Wiltshire, taken in August 1835 by William Henry Fox Talbot, MP (1800–77), the inventor of the negative-positive process. The negative of this was donated to the Science Museum, London in 1937 by his granddaughter Matilda. The world's earliest aerial photograph was taken in 1858 by Gaspard Félix Tournachon (1820–1910), alias Nadar, from a balloon near Villacoublay, on the outskirts of Paris, France.

Largest

The largest and most expensive industrial camera ever built is the 27 ton/tonne Rolls Royce camera now owned by BPCC Graphics Ltd of Derby, England completed in 1959. It measures 8 ft 10 in 2,69 m high, 8 ft 3 in 2,51 m wide and 35 ft 10,66 m in length. The lens is a 63″ f 15 Cooke Apochromatic. In 1985 it was still in full use.

Smallest

Apart from cameras built for intra-cardiac surgery and espionage, the smallest camera that has been marketed is the circular Japanese 'Petal' camera with a diameter of 1.14 in 2,9 cm and a thickness of 0.65 in 1,65 cm. It has a focal length of 12 mm 0.47 in. The BBC TV programme Record Breakers showed prints from this camera on 3 Dec 1974.

Fastest

A camera for fusion research built by the Rutherford-Appleton Laboratory at Essex University, Colchester, England and designed by Dr Tom Hall can register images at a rate of 3000 million per sec.

Most expensive camera

The most expensive complete range of camera equipment in the world is that of Nikon of Tokyo, Japan, who marketed in April 1985 their complete range of 21 cameras with 83 lenses and 515 accessories. Fox Talbot of London quoted £90,461 excluding VAT. The highest auction price for an antique camera is £21,000 for a J. B. Dancer stereo camera, patented in 1856 and sold at Christie's, South Kensington on 12 Oct 1977.

4. TELESCOPES

Earliest

Although there is evidence that early Arabian scientists understood something of the magnifying power of lenses, their first use to form a telescope has been attributed to Roger Bacon (c. 1214–92) in England. The prototype of modern refracting telescopes was that completed by Johannes Lippershey for the Netherlands government on 2 Oct 1608.

Largest Reflector World

The largest telescope in the world is the alt-azimuth mounted 6 m 236.2 in telescope sited on Mount Semirodriki, near Zelenchukskaya in the Caucasus Mountains, USSR, at an altitude of 6830 ft 2080 m. Work on the mirror, weighing 70 tons/tonnes was not completed until the summer of 1974. Regular observations were begun on 7 Feb 1976 after 16 years work. The weight of the 42 m 138 ft high assembly is 840 tonnes 827 tons. Being the most powerful of all telescopes its range, which includes the location of objects down to the 25th magnitude, represents the limits of the observable Universe. Its light-gathering power would enable it to detect the light from a candle at a distance of 15,000 miles 24 000 km.

Work is due to start in 1986 on the $70 million Keck 10 metre 393.7 inch reflector comprising 36 independently controlled fitting hexagonal mirrors for Caltech and the University of California. It is to be sited on Mauna Kea, Hawaii and due to be completed by 1989.

Note: The attachment of an electronic charge-coupled device (CCD) increases the 'light-grasp' of a telescope by a factor up to 100 fold. Thus a 200 in 508 cm telescope achieves the light gathering capacity of a 1000 inch 25,4 m telescope.

Largest Reflector Great Britain

The largest British (and European) reflector is the Isaac Newton 100 in 254 cm reflector formerly installed (1969–78) at the Royal Greenwich Observatory, Herstmonceux Castle, East Sussex. It was built in Newcastle upon Tyne, Tyne and Wear, weighs 92 tons 93,5 tonnes, cost £641,000 and was inaugurated on 1 Dec 1967. It has been dismantled and re-erected on the 2423 m 7949 ft high Roque de los Muchachos, La Palma, Canary Islands and became operational in February 1984. It is hoped that the William Herschel 4,2 m 167.3 in reflector will also become operational at this new Northern Hemisphere Observatory in 1988.

Largest Refractor

The largest refracting (i.e. magnification by lenses) telescope in the world is the 62 ft 18,90 m long 40 in 101,6 cm telescope completed in 1897 at the Yerkes Observatory, Williams Bay, Wisconsin, and belonging to the University of Chicago, Illinois, USA. In 1900 a 125 cm 49.2 in refractor 54,85 m 180 ft in length was built for the Paris Exposition but its optical performance was too poor to justify attempts to use it. The largest in the British Isles is the 28 in 71,1 cm at the Royal Greenwich Observatory (then in London) completed in 1894.

Radio Largest steerable dish

Radio waves of extra-terrestrial origin were first detected by Karl Jansky of Bell Telephone Laboratories, Holmdel, New Jersey, USA using a 100 ft 30,48 m long shortwave rotatable antenna in 1932. The world's largest trainable dish-type radio telescope is the 100 m 328 ft diameter, 3000 ton 3048 tonnes assembly at the Max Planck Institute for Radio Astronomy of Bonn in the Effelsberger Valley, W. Germany; it became operative in May 1971. The cost of the installation begun in November 1967 was 36,920,000 DM (then £6,150,000).

Radio Largest dish

The world's largest dish radio telescope is the partially-steerable ionospheric assembly built over a natural bowl at Arecibo, Puerto Rico, completed in November 1963 at a cost of about $9,000,000 (then £3.75 million). The dish has a diameter of 1000 ft 304,8 m and covers 18½ acres 7,82 ha. Its sensitivity was raised by a factor of 1000 and its range to the edge of the observable Universe at some 15,000 million light-years by the fitting of new aluminium plates at a cost of $8.8 million. Rededication was on 16 Nov 1974. The RATAN-600 radio telescope completed in the Northern Caucasus, USSR in 1976 has 895 metal mirror panels mounted in a circle 576 m 1890 ft across.

Radio Largest World

The world's largest radio telescopic installation is the US National Science Foundation VLA (Very Large Array). It is Y-shaped with each arm 13 miles 20,9 km long with 27 mobile antennae (each of 25 m 82 ft diameter) on rails. It is 50 miles 80 km west of Socorro in the Plains of San Augustin, New Mexico, and was dedicated on 10 Oct 1980 at a cost of $78 million (now £41 million).

A computer-linked very long base-line array of 25 m 82 ft radio telescopes stretched over 4200 km 2600 miles on Latitude 49.3° N has been planned by the Canadian Astronomical Society.

Radio Largest Great Britain

The British Science Research Council 5 km radio telescope at Lord's Bridge, Cambridgeshire operated by the Mullard Radio Astronomy Observatory of Cambridge University utilises eight mobile 42 ft 12,80 m rail-borne computer-controlled dish aerials, equivalent to a single steerable dish 5 km 3 miles 188 yd in diameter. The project cost more than £2,100,000 and was completed in 1973.

Solar

The world's largest solar telescope is the 480 ft 146,30 m long McMath telescope at Kitt Peak National Observatory near Tucson, Arizona, USA. It has a focal length of 300 ft 91,44 m and an 80 in 2,03 m heliostat mirror. It was completed in 1962 and produces an image measuring 33 in 83,8 cm in diameter.

Observatory Highest

The highest altitude observatory in the world is the University of Denver's High Altitude Observatory at an altitude of 14,100 ft 4297 m, opened in 1973. The principal instrument is a 24 in 60,48 cm Ealing Beck reflecting telescope.

Observatory Oldest

The oldest astronomical observatory building extant in the world is 'Tower of the Winds' used by Andronichus of Cyrrhos in Athens, Greece c. 70 BC, and equipped with sundials and clepsydra.

Planetaria World

The ancestor of the planetarium is the rotatable Gottorp Globe, built by Andreas Busch in Denmark between 1654 and 1664 to the orders of Olearius, court mathematician to Duke Frederick III of Holstein. It is 34.6 ft 10,54 m in circumference, weighs nearly 3½ tons/tonnes and is now preserved in Leningrad, USSR. The stars were painted on the inside. The earliest optical installation was not until 1923 in the Deutsches Museum, Munich, by Zeiss of Jena, Germany. The world's largest planetarium is in Moscow, USSR, and has a diameter of 82½ ft 25,15 m.

Planetaria Great Britain

The United Kingdom's first planetarium was opened at Madame Tussaud's, Marylebone Road, London, on 19 Mar 1958. Accurate images of 8900 stars (some below naked eye magnitude) are able to be projected on the 70 ft 21,33 m high copper dome.

Space Telescope

The first space observatory was the Orbiting Solar observatory 0504 launched on 18 Oct 1967. The largest will be the $1.2 billion NASA Space Telescope of 10,9 tonnes *10.7 tons* and 13 m *42 ft 7 in* in overall length with a 94 inch *240 cm* reflector to be placed in orbit at *c.* 480 km *300 miles* altitude aboard the US Space Shuttle *Atlantis* in August 1986.

5. NUMEROLOGY

In dealing with large numbers, scientists use the notation of 10 raised to various powers to eliminate a profusion of noughts. For example, 19,160,000,000,000 miles would be written 1.916×10^{13} miles. Similarly, a very small number, for example 0,0000154324 of a gram, would be written $1,54324 \times 10^{-5}$. Of the prefixes used before numbers the smallest is 'tredo' from the Danish tredyvo for 30, indicating 10^{-30} of a unit, and the highest is 'dea' (Greek, deca, ten), symbol D, indicating ten groups of 3 zeros 10^{30} or a quintillion (UK) or a nonillion (US).

Highest numbers

The highest lexicographically accepted named number in the system of successive powers of ten is the centillion, first recorded in 1852. It is the hundredth power of a million, or one followed by 600 noughts. The highest named number outside the decimal notation is the Buddhist *asankhyeya*, which is equal to 10^{140}.

The number 10^{100} is designated a Googol. The term was devised by Dr Edward Kasner (US) (d. 1955). Ten raised to the power of a Googol is described as a Googolplex. Some conception of the magnitude of such numbers can be gained when it is said that the number of electrons in some models of the observable Universe does not exceed 10^{87}.

The highest number ever used in a mathematical proof is a bounding value published in 1977 and known as Graham's number. It concerns bichromatic hypercubes and is inexpressible without the special 'arrow' notation, devised by Knuth in 1976, extended to 64 layers. Mr Candelaria ('the only man infinity fears') of Loma Linda, California has devised a Large Number Denomination System concluding with a milli-decilli-fiveillionillion.

Prime numbers

A prime number is any positive integer (excluding 1) having no integral factors other than itself and unity, *e.g.* 2, 3, 5, 7 or 11. The lowest prime number is thus 2. The highest known prime number is $2^{132,049} - 1$ discovered on 23 Sept 1983 on a Cray One computer, at the University of California's Lawrence Livermore Laboratory, by David Slowinski. The number contains 39,751 digits. The lowest non-prime or composite (excluding 1) number is 4.

Perfect numbers

A number is said to be perfect if it is equal to the sum of its divisors other than itself, *e.g.* $1 + 2 + 4 + 7 + 14 = 28$. The lowest perfect number is $6 (= 1 + 2 + 3)$. The highest known and the 29th so far discovered, is $(2^{132,049} - 1) \times 2^{132,048}$. It is a consequence of the highest known prime (see above).

Most innumerate

The most innumerate people are the Nambiquara of the north west Matto Grosso of Brazil who lack any system of numbers. They do however have a verb which means 'they are two alike'.

Most accurate and most inaccurate version of 'pi'

The greatest number of decimal places to which *pi* (π) has been calculated is 10,013,395 by Yasumasu Kanada (Japan), achieved in November 1983. The published value to two million places, in what has been described as the world's most boring 800 page publication, was 3.141592653589793 . . . (omitting the next 1,999,975 places) . . . 1457297909. In 1897 the General Assembly of Indiana enacted in House Bill No. 246 that *pi* was *de jure* 4.

Earliest measures

The earliest known measure of weight is the *beqa* of the Amratian period of Egyptian civilisation *c.* 3800 BC found at Naqada, Egypt. The weights are cylindrical with rounded ends from 188,7 to 211,2 g *6.65–7.45 oz*. The unit of length used by the megalithic tomb-builders in Britain *c.* 3500 BC appears to have been 2.72 ± 0.003 ft *82,90 cm $\pm$ 0.09 cm*. This was deduced by Prof. Alexander Thom (b. 1894) in 1966.

Time measure *Longest*

The longest measure of time is the *kalpa* in Hindu chronology. It is equivalent to 4320 million years. In astronomy a cosmic year is the period of rotation of the sun around the centre of the Milky Way galaxy, *i.e.* 225 million years. In the Late Cretaceous Period of *c.* 85 million years ago the Earth rotated faster so resulting in 370.3 days per year while in Cambrian times some 600 million years ago there is evidence that the year contained 425 days.

Time measure *Shortest*

Owing to variations in the length of a day, which is estimated to be increasing irregularly at the average rate of about a milli-second per century due to the Moon's tidal drag, the second has been redefined. Instead of being 1/86,400th part of a mean solar day, it has, since 1960, been reckoned as 1/31,556,925,9747th part of the solar (or tropical) year at AD 1900, January 0. 12 hr, Ephemeris time. In 1958 the second of Ephemeris time was computed to be equivalent to $9,192,631,770 \pm 20$ cycles of the radiation corresponding to the transition of a caesium 133 atom when unperturbed by exterior fields. The greatest diurnal change recorded has been 10 milliseconds on 8 Aug 1972 due to the most violent solar storm recorded in 370 years of observations.

The accuracy of the caesium beam frequency standard approaches 8 parts in 10^{14} compared to 2 parts in 10^{13} for the methane-stabilised helium-neon laser and 6 parts in 10^{13} for the hydrogen maser.

Cubism

Minh Thai, 16, a Vietnamese refugee won the World Rubik Cube Championship held in Budapest, Hungary on 5 June 1982. His winning time after standardised dislocations was 22.95 sec. Ernö Rubik (Hungary) patented the device in 1977 with 43,252,003,274,489,856,856,000 possible combinations. Litigation by CBS Inc has averred that the device was invented by Larry D. Nichols (US) in 1972.

6. PHYSICAL EXTREMES *(Terrestrial)*

Temperature *Highest*

The highest man-made temperatures yet attained are those produced in the centre of a thermonuclear fusion bomb, which are of the order of 300,000,000 – 400,000,000° C. Of controllable temperatures, the highest effective laboratory figure reported is 82 million degrees C at the Princeton Plasma Physics Laboratory, USA in the fusion research PLT (Princeton Large Torus) in May 1980. A figure of 3000 million °C was reportedly achieved in the USSR with Ogra injection-mirror equipment in *c.* 1962.

Temperature *Lowest*

The lowest temperature reached is 3×10^{-8} Kelvin above absolute zero in a two stage nuclear demagnetisation cryostat at Espoo, Finland by the team led by Prof. Olli V. Loúnasmaa (b. 1930) and announced in June 1984. Absolute or thermodynamic temperatures are defined in terms of ratios rather than as differences reckoned from the unattainable absolute zero, which on the Kelvin scale is $-273,15°$ C or $-459.67°$ F. Thus the lowest temperature ever attained is 1 in 9.1×10^{9} of the melting point of ice (0° C or 273.15 K or 32° F). Tokyo University's Institute of Solid State Physics announced on 15 Feb 1983 that a team led by Prof. Kazuo Ono had attained a temperature within 0.00003 of a degree of absolute zero at which molecular motion ceases.

Highest pressures

The highest sustained laboratory pressures yet reported are of 1.72 megabars (11,000 tons force/in² *160 GPa*) achieved in the giant hydraulic diamond-faced press at the Carnegie Institution's Geophysical Laboratory, Washington DC reported in June 1978. This laboratory announced solid hydrogen achieved at 57 kilobars pressure on 2 Mar 1979. If created, metallic hydrogen is expected to be silvery white but soft with a density of 1.1 g/cm³. The pressure required for the transition is estimated by H. K. Mao and P. M. Bell to be 1 megabar at 25°C. Using dynamic methods and impact speeds of up to 18,000 mph *29 000 km/h*, momentary pressures of 75,000,000 atmospheres (490,000 tons/in² *7000 GPa*) were reported from the United States in 1958.

Highest velocity

The highest velocity at which any solid visible object has been projected is 150 km/sec *335,000 mph* in the case of a plastic disc at the Naval Research Laboratory, Washington DC, reported in August 1980.

Finest balance

The most accurate balance in the world is the Sartorius Model 4108 manufactured in Göttingen, W. Germany, which can weigh objects of up to 0,5 g to an accuracy of 0,01 μg or 0,00000001 g which is equivalent to little more than one sixtieth of the weight of the ink on this full stop .

Largest bubble chamber

The largest bubble chamber in the world is the $7 million (*then £2.5 million*) installation completed in October 1973 at Weston, Illinois. It is 15 ft *4,57 m* in diameter and contains 7259 gal *33 000 litres* of liquid hydrogen at a temperature of $-247°$C with a super conducting magnet of 3 tesla.

Fastest centrifuge

Ultra-centrifuges were invented by Theodor Svedberg (b. 30 Aug 1884) (Sweden) in 1923. The highest man-made rotary speed ever achieved and the fastest speed of any earthbound object is 4500 mph *7250 km/h* by a swirling tapered 6 in *15,2 cm* carbon fibre rod in a vacuum at Birmingham University, England reported on 24 Jan 1975.

Finest cut

The $13 million Large Optics Diamond Turning Machine at the Lawrence Livermore National Laboratory, California was reported in June

1983 to be able to sever a human hair 3000 times lengthwise.

Longest echo

The longest recorded echo in any building in Great Britain is one of 15 sec following the closing of the door of the Chapel of the Mausoleum, Hamilton, Strathclyde built in 1840–55.

Most powerful electric current

The most powerful electric current generated is that from the Zeus capacitor at the Los Alamos Scientific Laboratory, New Mexico, USA. If fired simultaneously the 4032 capacitors would produce for a few microseconds twice as much current as that generated elsewhere on Earth.

Hottest flame

The hottest flame that can be produced is from carbon subnitride (C_4N_2) which at one atmosphere pressure is calculated to reach 5261 K.

Highest measured frequency

The highest *directly* measured frequency is a visible yellow-green light at 520.2068085 terahertz (a terahertz being a million million hertz or cycles per second) for the o-component of the 17–1 P(62) transition line of iodine 127. The highest measured frequency determined by precision metrology is a green light at 582.491703 terahertz for the b_{21} component of the R(15) 43–0 transition line of iodine 127. However with the decision on the 20 October 1983 by the Conférence Générale des Poids et Mesures (CGPM) to exactly define the metre (m) in terms of the velocity of light (c) such that 'the metre is the length of the path travelled by light in vacuum during a time interval of 1/299,792,458 of a second' then frequency (f) and wavelength (λ) are exactly interchangeable through the relationship $f\lambda = c$.

Lowest friction

The lowest coefficient of static and dynamic friction of any solid is 0.02, in the case of polytetrafluoroethylene ($[C_2F_4]_n$), called PTFE—equivalent to wet ice on wet ice. It was first manufactured in quantity by E. I. du Pont de Nemours & Co Inc in 1943, and is marketed from the USA as Teflon. In the United Kingdom it is marketed by ICI as Fluon. In the centrifuge at the University of Virginia a 30 lb *13,60 kg* rotor magnetically supported has been spun at 1000 rev/sec in a vacuum of 10^{-6} mm of mercury pressure. It loses only one revolution per second per day, thus spinning for years.

Smallest hole

A hole of 40 Å (4×10^{-6} mm) was shown visually using a JEM 100C electron microscope and Quantel Electronics devices at the Dept. of Metallurgy, Oxford on 28 Oct. 1979. To find such a hole is equivalent to finding a pinhead in a haystack with sides of 1.2 miles *1,93 km*. An electron microscope beam on a sample of sodium beta-alumina at the University of Illinois, USA, in May 1983 accidentally bored a hole 2×10^{-9} mm in diameter.

Most powerful laser beams

The first illumination of another celestial body was achieved on 9 May 1962, when a beam of light was successfully reflected from the Moon by the use of a laser (light amplification by stimulated emission of radiation) attached to a 48 in *121,9 cm* telescope at Massachusetts Institute of Technology, Cambridge, Massachusetts, USA. The spot was estimated to be 4 miles *6,4 km* in diameter on the Moon. The device was propounded in 1958 by Dr Charles Hard Townes (born 1915) of the USA. Such a flash for 1/5000th of a second can bore a hole through a diamond by vaporisation at 10,000°C, produced

by 2×10^{23} photons. The 'Shiva' laser was reported at the Lawrence Livermore Laboratory, California to be concentrating 2.6×10^{13} watts into a pinhead-sized target for 9.5×10^{-11} sec in a test on 18 May 1978.

Brightest light

The brightest steady artificial light sources are 'laser' beams with an intensity exceeding the Sun's 1,500,000 candles/in² *232 500 candelas/cm²* by a factor of well in excess of 1000. In May 1969 the USSR Academy of Sciences announced blast waves travelling through a luminous plasma of inert gases heated to 90,000 K. The flare-up for up to 3 micro-seconds shone at 50,000 times the brightness of the Sun *viz.* 75,000 million candles/in² *11 625 million candelas/cm²*. Of continuously burning sources, the most powerful is a 313 kW high-pressure argon arc lamp of 1,200,000 candle-power, completed by Vortek Industries Ltd of Vancouver, BC, Canada in March 1984.

The synchrotron radiation from a 4×0.5 in *100 × 2,5 mm* slit in the SPEAR high energy physics plant at the end of the 2 mile *3,2 km* long Stanford Linear Accelerator, California, USA has been described as the world's most powerful light beam.

The most powerful searchlight ever developed was one produced during the 1939–45 war by the General Electric Company Ltd at the Hirst Research Centre in Wembley, Greater London. It had a consumption of 600 kW and gave an arc luminance of 300,000 candles/in² *46 500 candelas/cm²* and a maximum beam intensity of 2,700,000,000 candles from its parabolic mirror (diameter 10 ft *3,04 m*).

Shortest light pulse

Charles Z. Shank and colleagues of the AT & T Laboratories in New Jersey, USA achieved a light pulse of 8 femtoseconds (8×10^{-15} sec) announced in April 1985. The pulse comprised only 4 or 5 wavelengths of visible light or 2.4 micrometres long.

Most durable light

The average bulb lasts for 750–1000 hr. There is some evidence that a 5 watt carbide filament bulb made by the Shelby Electric Co and presented by Mr Bernell in the Fire Department, Livermore, south Alameda County, California was first shedding light in 1901.

Heaviest magnet

The heaviest magnet in the world is one measuring 60 m *196 ft* in diameter, with a weight of 36,000 tons/*tonnes* for the 10 GeV synchrophasotron in the Joint Institute for Nuclear Research at Dubna, near Moscow, USSR.

Magnetic fields *Strongest and weakest*

The strongest magnetic field strength achieved has been one of 30,1 teslas at the Francis Bitter National Magnet Laboratory at Massachusetts Institute of Technology, by Mathias J. Leupold and Robert J. Weggel, announced in July 1977. The outer magnet is of super-conducting niobium-titanium.

The weakest magnetic field measured is one of 8×10^{-15} tesla in the heavily shielded room at the Francis Bitter National Magnet Laboratory, Cambridge, Massachusetts, USA. It is used for research by Dr David Cohen into the very weak magnetic field generated in the heart and brain.

Most powerful microscope

The world's most powerful electron microscope was announced by Hitachi of Tokyo, Japan on 27 June 1984. It is capable of resolving a single hydrogen atom 1×10^{-8} cm in diameter. The Philips EM 430 transmission electron micro-

scope routinely obtains point resolutions of 0.17 of a nanometre (1.7×10^{-8} cm). The lightest high power microscope in the world is the 1200× McArthur Microscope made in Cambridge, England and weighing 9 oz *255 g*.

Dr. Albert Crewe (b. 1927 in U.K.) of the University of Chicago is projecting a scanning electron microscope by 1986 capable of seeing between atoms.

Loudest noise

The loudest noise created in a laboratory is 210 decibels or 400,000 acoustic watts reported by NASA from a 48 ft *14,63 m* steel and concrete horn at Huntsville, Alabama, USA in October 1965. Holes can be bored in solid material by this means.

Highest note

The highest note yet attained is one of 60,000 megahertz (60 GHz) (60,000 million vibrations/sec), generated by a 'laser' beam striking a sapphire crystal at the Massachusetts Institute of Technology in Cambridge, Massachusetts, USA, in September 1964.

Most powerful particle accelerator

The 2 kilometre *6562 ft* diameter proton synchrotron at the Fermi National Accelerator Laboratory east of Batavia, Illinois, USA is the highest energy 'atom-smasher' in the world. On 14 May 1976 an energy of 500 billion (5×10^{11}) electron volts was attained. Work on doubling the energy to nearly 1 Tera electron volts or 1000 GeV by 1985 was begun in July 1979. On 15 Aug 1983 0.7 TeV was achieved. This involves 1000 super-conducting magnets maintained at a temperature of $-452°$ F $-268,8°$ C by means of the world's largest 4500 litre *990 gal* per hour helium liquefying plant which began operating on 18 Apr 1980.

The aim of CERN (*Conseil Européan pour la Recherche*) to collide beams of protons and antiprotons in their Super Proton Synchroton (SPS) near Geneva, Switzerland at 270 GeV × 2 = 540 GeV was achieved at 4.55 a.m. on 10 July 1981. This was the equivalent of striking a fixed target with protons at 150 TeV or 150 000 GeV.

The US Department of Energy set up a study for a $5 billion Super Superconductivity Collider (SSC) 1995 with two 20 TeV proton and antiproton colliding beams on 16 Aug 1983. If 8 tesla magnets were used the diameter would be 19,6 km *12.1 miles* but with 3 tesla magnets this would be 52,3 km *32.5 miles*.

Quietest place

The 'dead room', measuring 35 ft by 28 ft *10,67 × 8,50 m* in the Bell Telephone System laboratory at Murray Hill, New Jersey, USA, is the most anechoic room in the world, eliminating 99.98 per cent of reflected sound.

Sharpest objects and smallest tubes

The sharpest objects yet made are glass micropipette tubes used in intracellular work on living cells. Techniques developed and applied by Prof Kenneth T. Brown and Dale G. Flaming of the Department of Physiology, University of California, San Francisco achieved by 1977 bevelled tips with an outer diameter of 0.02 μm and 0.01 μm inner diameter. The latter is smaller than the smallest known nickel tubing by a factor of 340 and is 6500 times thinner than human hair.

Highest vacuum

The highest (or 'hardest') vacuums obtained in scientific research are of the order of 10^{-14} torr at the IBM Thomas J. Watson Research Center, Yorktown Heights, New York, USA in October

1976 in a cryogenic system with temperatures down to $-269°C$ $-452°F$. This is equivalent to depopulating (baseball-sized) molecules from 1 metre apart to 80 km apart or from 1 yard to 50 miles.

Lowest viscosity
The California Institute of Technology, USA announced on 1 Dec 1957 that there was no measurable viscosity, *i.e.* perfect flow, in liquid helium II, which exists only at temperatures close to absolute zero $(-273.15°C$ or $-459.67°F)$.

Highest voltage
The highest potential difference ever obtained in a laboratory has been 32 ± 1.5 million volts by the National Electrostatics Corporation at Oak Ridge, Tennessee, USA on 17 May 1979.

Largest wind tunnel *World*
The world's largest wind tunnel is a low-speed tunnel with a 40×80 ft *12,19 × 24,38 m* test section built in 1944 at the Ames Research Center, Moffett Field, California, USA. The tunnel encloses 800 tons/*tonnes* of air and cost approximately $7,000,000 (*then £1,735,000*). The maximum volume of air that can be moved is 60,000,000 ft³ *1 700 000 m³* per min. On 30 July 1974 NASA announced an intention to increase it in size to 80×120 ft *24,38 × 36,57 m* for 345 mph speeds with a 135,000 hp *136 900 cv* system. The most powerful is the 216,000 hp *219000 cv* installation at the Arnold Engineering Test Center at Tullahoma, Tennessee, USA opened in September 1956. The highest Mach number attained with air is Mach 27 at the works of the Boeing Company in Seattle, Washington State, USA. For periods of micro-seconds, shock Mach numbers of the order of 30 (22,830 mph *36 735 km/h*) have been attained in impulse tubes at Cornell University, Ithaca, New York State, USA.

Largest wind tunnel *Great Britain*
The most powerful wind tunnel in the United Kingdom is the intermittent compressed air type installation at the BAC plant at Warton, Lancashire which can be run at Mach 4, which is equivalent to 3044 mph *4898 km/h* at sea level.

7. GEMS AND OTHER PRECIOUS MATERIALS

PRECIOUS STONE RECORDS

Note: The carat was standardised at 205 mg in 1877. The metric carat of 200 mg was introduced in 1914.

DIAMOND (*first recorded in India c. 300 BC recognized as pure crystallised carbon in 1796*)
Largest 3106 metric carats (over 1¼ lb)—*The Cullinan*, found by Mr Gray on 25 Jan 1905 in the Premier Mine, Pretoria, South Africa.
The first synthetic diamonds were produced by Prof H. T. Hall at the General Electric Research Laboratories, USA on 16 Dec 1954. In Feb 1984 a Tass report from Leningrad, USSR announced that the Institute of High Frequency Currents had produced an artificial diamond weighing 4½ lb *2,04 kg*.
Largest Cut Stone 530.2 metric carats of 74 facets. Cleaved from *The Cullinan* in 1908, by Jak Asscher of Amsterdam and polished by Henri Koe known as *The Star of Africa* or Cullinan I and now in the Royal Sceptre. The Cullinan II is of 317.40 carats. Third on the list of the 55 diamonds of more than 100 ct is the Great Mogul of 280 old carats lost in the sack of Delhi in 1739 and arguably the most valuable object ever lost. In Nov 1984 the Zale Corporation of New York announced that it may be feasible to cut their pale yellow 890 ct uncut stone from Africa into a 550–600 ct cut stone.
Other Records Diamond is the *hardest* known naturally-occurring substance, with 5 times the indentation hardness of the next hardest mineral, corundum (Al_2O_3). The peak hardness value on the Knoop scale is 8400 compared with an average diamond of 7000. The rarest colour for diamond is blood red. The largest example is a flawless 5.05 ct stone found in Lichtenburg, S. Africa in 1927 and now in a private collection in the U.S. The diamond per carat record price of $113,000 was set by the 41.3 ct 'Polar Star' bought in Geneva for £2,100,000 on 21 Nov 1980 by Mr Razeen Salih. The 42.92 ct Terestchenko blue diamond was auctioned at Christie's, Geneva on 14 Nov 1984 for $4,580,000. The largest blue diamond is the 45.85 ct Copenhagen Blue.

EMERALD (*green beryl*) $[Be_3Al_2(SiO_3)_6]$
Largest Cut Stone 86,136 carat natural beryl Gleim emerald. Found in Carnaiba, Brazil, Aug 1974. Carved by Richard Chan (Hong Kong). Appraised at $1,292,000 (*£718,000*) in 1982.
Other Records $520,000 (then £305,000) paid for an 18.35 ct gem emerald ring sold at Sotheby Parke Bernet, New York, in Apr 1977.

SAPPHIRE (*corundum any colour but red*) (Al_2O_3)
Largest 2302 carat stone found at Anakie, Queensland, Australia, in *c.* 1935, now a 1318 carat head of President Abraham Lincoln (1809–65).
Largest Cut Stone 1444 carat black star stone carved from 2097 carats in 1953–5 into a bust of General Dwight David Eisenhower (1890–1969).
Note: both the sapphire busts are in the custody of the Kazanjian Foundation of Los Angeles, California, USA. Auction record for a single stone was set by a step-cut sapphire of 66.03 carats at £579,300 from the Rockefeller collection at Sotheby's Zurich on 8 May 1980.

RUBY (*red corundum*) (Al_2O_3)
Largest 3421 carat broken stone reported found in July 1961 (largest piece 750 carats).
Largest Cut Stone 1184 carat natural gem stone of Burmese origin. The largest star ruby is the 650 carat Vidyaraj ruby in Bangalore, India.
Other Records Since 1955 rubies have been the world's most precious gem attaining a record carat price of $100,639 (*then £46,600*) at Christie's sale in Geneva in November 1979 in the case of a 4.12 carat caspian-shaped ruby.

The ability to make corundum prisms for laser technology up to over 12 in *30 cm* in length seems to have little bearing on the market for natural gems.

The world's most expensive gem—the 42.92 carat Terestchenko blue diamond auctioned for $4,580,000 (*now £3.8 million*). (See above)

RECORDS FOR OTHER PRECIOUS MATERIALS

Largest
PEARL
(*Molluscan consecretion*)
14 lb 1 oz *6,37 kg* 9½ in *24 cm* long by 5½ in *14 cm* in diameter—*Pearl of Laotze*
Found: At Palawan, Philippines, 7 May 1934 in shell of giant clam.
Present location: The property of Wilburn Dowell Cobb from 1936 until his death, it was valued at $4,080,000 in July 1971. On 15 May 1980 it was bought at auction in San Francisco by Peter Hoffman, a jeweller of Beverely Hills, California for $200,000 (*then £85,000*). An appraisal for the owners (Peter Hoffman and Victor Barbish) in May 1982 by the San Francisco Gem Laboratory suggested a value of $32,640,000.

The largest black pearl 18,1 mm *0.7 in* in diameter was found in Namarai Bay, Fuji Island on 26 Jan 1984 by Yasuhiro Tokito.

OPAL
(SiO_2nH_2O)
220 troy oz (yellow-orange).
Found: Coober Pedy, South Australia.
Present location: The Olympic Australis (17,700 carats) found in Aug 1956 owned by Altmann & Cherny Pty Ltd is on public display in Melbourne and is valued at $1.8 million (US). An opal containing much 'potch' (colourless material) named the Desert Flame was found at Andamooka, South Australia. The 34,215 carat mass first reported in Sept 1969 was broken up and auctioned off on 29 Aug 1978.

ROCK CRYSTAL (QUARTZ)
SiO_2
Ball: 106¾ lb *40,48 kg* 12⅞ in *32,7 cm* diameter, the *Warner* sphere
Found: Burma, (originally a 1000 lb *450 kg* piece).
Present location: US National Museum, in Washington, DC.

TOPAZ
$Al_2SiO_4(F,OH)_2$
'Brazilian Princess' 21,325 carat 221 facets.
Found: Light blue: from Brazil.
Present location: Exhibited by Smithsonian Institution, November 1978. Valued at $1,066,350 or $50 per carat. Cut from a 79 lb *35,8 kg* crystal. World's largest facetted stone.

AMBER
(*Coniferous fossil resin*)
33 lb 10 oz *15,25 kg*.
Found: Reputedly from Burma acquired in 1860.
Present location: Bought by John Charles Bowing (d. 1893) for £300 in Canton, China. Natural History Museum, London, since 1940.

NEPHRITE JADE
$Ca_2(Mg, Fe)_5(Si_4O_{11})_2(OH)_2$
Boulder of 143 tons/*tonnes* and 21,300 ft³ *603 m³*
Found: In China. Reported 17 Sept 1978.
Present location: Jadeite $Na_2O.Al_2O_34SiO_2$ can be almost any colour excepting red or blue. The largest known example has been a block weighing 33 tons from Burma.

MARBLE
(*Metamorphosed* $CaCO_3$)
90 tons/*tonnes* (single slab)
Found: Quarried at Yule, Colorado, USA.
Present location: A piece of over 45 tons/*tonnes* was dressed from this slab for the coping stone of the Tomb of the Unknown Soldier in Arlington National Cemetery, Virginia, USA.

NUGGETS—GOLD (Au)
7560 oz (472½ lb *214,32 kg*) (reef gold) *Holtermann Nugget*
Found: Beyers & Holtermann Star of Hope Gold Mining Co., Hill End, NSW, Australia, 19 Oct 1872.
Present location: The Holtermann nugget contained some 220 lb *99,8 kg* of gold in a 630 lb *285,7 kg* slab of slate. The purest large nugget was the *Welcome Stranger*, found at Moliagul, Victoria, Australia, which yielded 2248 troy oz *69,92 kg* of pure gold from 2280¼ oz *70,92 kg*.

SILVER (AG)
2750 lb troy *Found:* Sonora, Mexico.
Present location: Appropriated by the Spanish Government before 1821.

OTHER GEM RECORDS:
Largest Crystal of Gem Quality
A 520,000 carat (2 cwt 5 lb *103,8 kg*) aquamarine, $[Be_3Al_2(SiO_3)_6]$ found near Marambaia, Brazil in 1910. Yielded over 200,000 carats of gem quality cut stones.

Rarest and commonest mineral
The world's rarest mineral cannot be certainly established. The total known amount of scotlandite ($PbSO_3$) comprises only a few tens of milligrams. Though probably found in the 19th century in Leadhills, Strathclyde, this first naturally occurring yellowish sulphite was only certainly identified in 1978 by Dr R. S. W. Braithwaite.

The world's commonest mineral is silicate of calcium, iron magnesium and manganese collectively known as olivine.

Densest Gem Mineral
Stibiotantalite $[(SbO)_2(Ta,Nb)_2O_6]$ a rare brownish-yellow mineral found in San Diego County, California, has a density of 7.46. The alloy platiniridium has a density of 22.0.

Smallest Brilliant Cut Diamond
A 57 facet diamond of 0.0012 of a carat (0.24 milligrams) by A. Van Moppes & Zoon (Diamant) BV of Amsterdam certified on 26 Jan 1949.

Largest Crystal
A 380 000 kg *187 tons* beryl ($Be_3Al_2Si_6O_{18}$) measuring 18 m *59 ft* long and 3,5 m *11½ ft* in diameter was recorded at Malakialina, Malagasy in 1976.

Newest Gemstones
Tanzanite was discovered in Tanzania in 1969. It reached $1200 (*then £670*) per carat in 1977. The deep purple Royal Lavalite found in Hotazel, South Africa by Randy Polk of Phoenix, Arizona reached $1300 (*then £840*) per carat in 1982.

CHAPTER SIX

Arts & Entertainments

1. PAINTING

Guinness Superlatives has published a more specialist book *The Guinness Book of Art Facts and Feats* (£6.95) by John FitzMaurice Mills.

Earliest *World*

Evidence of Palaeolithic art was first found in 1834 in the cave of Chaffaud near Sévigné, Vienne, France by Abbé Brouillet with an engraving of two deer on a piece of flat bone from the cave, now dated to *c* 20,000 BC. It was not published until 1861 by Edouard Lartet (1801–71). The oldest known dated examples come from La Ferrassie, near Les Eyzies in the Périgord, France, in layers dated to *c* 25,000 BC. Blocks of stone were found with engraved animals and female symbols; some of the blocks also had symbols painted in red ochre. Pieces of Lake Mungo, NSW, Australia, in a context *ante* 30,000 BC but there is no evidence whether these were used for body-painting or art.

Largest World *All time*

Panorama of the Mississippi, completed by John Banvard (1815–91) in 1846, showing the river for 1200 miles *1930 km* in a strip probably 5000 ft *1525 m* long and 12 ft *3,65 m* wide, was the largest painting in the world, with an area of more than 1.3 acres *0,52 ha*. The painting is believed to have been destroyed when the rolls of canvas, stored in a barn at Cold Spring Harbor, Long Island, New York State, USA, caught fire shortly before Banvard's death on 16 May 1891.

Existing

A larger painting, now only partially in existence, is *The Battle of Gettysburg*, completed in 1883, after 2½ years of work, by Paul Philippoteaux (France) and 16 assistants. The painting was 410 ft *125 m* long, 70 ft *21,3 m* high and weighed 5.36 tons *5,45 tonnes*. It depicts the climax of the Battle of Gettysburg, in southern Pennsylvania, USA, on 3 July 1863. In 1964 the painting was bought by Joe King of Winston-Salem, North Carolina, USA after being stored by E. W. McConnell in a Chicago warehouse since 1933. In 1964, owing to deterioration, the sky was trimmed down so decreasing the area. Jackson Bailey's *Life of Christ* exhibited by Religious Art Institute of America Inc. of Atlanta, Georgia comprises 50 panels 11 × 20 ft *3,35 × 6,09 m* and was completed in 1968–70 with an area of 11,000 ft² *1022 m²*.

'Old Master'

The largest 'Old Master' is *Il Paradiso*, painted on canvas between 1587 and 1590 by Jacopo

The world's most decorative prison walls—Pudu Prison, Kuala Lumpur whose 865 ft *262,6 m* mural set a world record in June 1984.

Robusti, *alias* Tintoretto (1518–94), and his son Domenico (1565–1637) on the east wall of the Sala del Maggior Consiglio in the Palazzo Ducale (Doge's Palace) in Venice, Italy. The work is 22 m *72 ft 2 in* long and 7 m *22 ft 11¼ in* high and contains some 350 human figures.

Largest *Great Britain*

The largest painting in Great Britain is the giant oval *Triumph of Peace and Liberty* by Sir James Thornhill (1676–1734), on the ceiling of the Painted Hall in the Royal Naval College, Greenwich. It measures 106 ft *32,3 m* by 51 ft *15,4 m* and took 20 years (1707–1727) to complete.

A painting 6050 ft² *562 m²* in area and weighing more than a ton was painted for the 4th European Youth Games under the direction of David A. Judge and to the design of Norman G. Warner in Colchester, Essex between 29 Oct 1975 and 24 May 1976 by 365 people.

World's largest Poster

The largest recorded poster was one measuring 200 ft by 100 ft *60,9 × 30,4* erected on the

Thames Embankment, London on 26 Sept 1983 by the Huttan Company for 'Reader's Digest'. The record price for a poster is £62,000 for an advertisement for the 1902 Vienna Exhibition by Koloman Moser (b. Vienna 30 Mar 1868—d. 18 Oct 1918) sold at Christie's, South Kensington, London on 1 April 1985.

Most valuable

The 'Mona Lisa' (*La Gioconda*) by Leonardo da Vinci (1452–1519) in the Louvre, Paris, was assessed for insurance purposes at the highest ever figure of $100,000,000 (*then £35.7 million*) for its move for exhibition in Washington, DC, and New York City, NY, USA, from 14 Dec 1962 to 12 Mar 1963. However, insurance was not concluded because the cost of the closest security precautions was less than that of the premiums. It was painted in *c.* 1503–7 and measures 77 × 53 cm *30.5 × 20.9 in.* It is believed to portray either Mona (short for Ma-

This Koloman Moser advertisement for the 1902 Vienna Exhibition made a record price of £62,000 for a poster. *(Christie's South Kensington)*

donna) Lisa Gherardini, the wife of Francesco del Giocondo of Florence, or Constanza d'Avalos, coincidentally nicknamed La Gioconda, mistress of Guiliano de Medici. Francis I, King of France, bought the painting for his bathroom in 1517 for 4000 gold florins or 92 oz *15,30 kg* of gold worth some £220,000 (mid-1984). Dr Pulitzer claims the Louvre have a painting of Constanza by Leonardo while his Swiss syndicate have the Mona Lisa proper in London first bought from Florence by William Blaker.

HIGHEST PRICE

Auction price *World*

The highest price ever bid at a public auction for any painting is £7,500,000 for *The Adoration of the Magi* by Andrea Mantegna (1431–1506), sold for the Marquess of Northampton at Christie's, London on 18 April 1985 and bought by the J. Paul Getty Museum of Malibu, California. With an 8 per cent buyer's premium, this amounts to £8,100,000.

By A Woman Artist

The highest price ever paid for a painting by a female artist is $1,100,000 (*then £705,000*), at Christie's, New York on 17 May 1983, for *Reading Le Figaro* by Mary Cassatt (b. Pennsylvania, USA, 1844–d. 1926). She worked mainly from Paris.

Abstract

The auction record for an abstract painting is £1,512,000 for *Composition with Red, Blue and Yellow* painted in 1930 by Piet Mondrian (1872–1944) at Christies, London on 27 June 1983. The purchaser was Shigeki Kameyama.

Miniature portrait

The highest price ever paid for a portrait miniature is the £75,000 given by an anonymous buyer at a sale held by Sotheby's, London on 24 Mar 1980 for a miniature of Jane Broughton, aged 21, painted on vellum by Nicholas Hilliard (1547–1619) in 1574. The painted surface measures 1.65 in *42 mm* in diameter.

Modern painting

The record bid at auction for an impressionist painting is $9,900,000 (£7.9 million) for *Landscape with Rising Sun* by Van Gogh (1853–1890) from the estate of the late Mrs Florence J. Gould (d. 1983) by an anonymous private collector at Sotheby Park Bernet, New York City on 25 Apr 1985. The hammer price was $9 million and the buyer's premium was 10 per cent of that.

Living artist *World*

The highest price at auction for a work by a living artist is £1,451,612 (*then $1,819,596*) for 'Two Women' (22 × 28 in *56 × 71 cm*) by Willem de Kooning (b. 24 April 1904) the Dutch-born American at Christie's, New York on 2 Nov 1984. The $1,950,000 paid for the two canvasses *Two Brothers* (1905) and *Seated Harlequin* (1922) by Pablo Diego José Francisco de Paula Juan Nepomuceno Crispín Crispiano de la Santisima Trinidad Ruiz y Picasso (1881–1973) of Spain, bought by the Basle City Government from the Staechelin Foundation in Dec 1967 were even more expensive if inflation is allowed for.

British and Irish

The highest price for any painting by a living United Kingdom born artist is $350,000 (*then £167,000*) for the painting *Triptych* (in memory of George Dyer) by Francis Bacon (b. Dublin, Ireland, 1909, then part of the United Kingdom) sold on 18 May 1981 at Christie's, New York City, USA.

Drawing

The highest price ever paid for any drawing is

£3,546,000 for a study of an apostle's head and hand for the Transfiguration in the Vatican by Raphael (Raffaello Santi 1483–1520) and sold for the 11th Duke of Devonshire (b. 1920) at Christie's, London on 3 July 1984.

MOST PROLIFIC

Painter

Picasso was the most prolific of all painters in a career which lasted 78 years. It has been estimated that Picasso produced about 13,500 paintings or designs, 100,000 prints or engravings, 34,000 book illustrations and 300 sculptures or ceramics. His life-time *oeuvre* has been valued at £500 million. Morris Katz (b. 1932) of Greenwich Village, New York City is the most prolific painter of saleable portraits in the world. His sales total as of 21 April 1982 was 110,600. Described as the 'King of Schlock Art', he sells his paintings 'cheap and often'.

Most repetitious painter

Antonio Bin of Paris has painted the *Mona Lisa* on some 300 occasions. These sell for up to £1000 apiece.

Oldest and youngest RA

The oldest ever Royal Academician has been (Thomas) Sidney Cooper CVO, who died on 8 Feb 1902 aged 98 yr 136 days, having exhibited 266 paintings over the record span of 69 consecutive years (1833–1902). The youngest ever RA has been Mary Moser (1744–1819) (later Mrs Hugh Lloyd), who was elected on the foundation of the Royal Academy in 1768 when aged 24.

Youngest exhibitor

The youngest ever exhibitor at the Royal Academy of Arts Annual Summer Exhibition has been Lewis Melville 'Gino' Lyons (b. 30 Apr 1962). His *Trees and Monkeys* was painted on 4 June 1965, submitted on 17 Mar 1967 and exhibited to the public on 29 Apr 1967.

Largest galleries

The world's largest art gallery is the Winter Palace and the neighbouring Hermitage in Leningrad, USSR. One has to walk 15 miles *24 km* to visit each of the 322 galleries, which house nearly 3,000,000 works of art and objects of archaeological interest. The world's largest modern art museum is the Georges Pompidou National Centre for Art and Culture, Beauborg, opened in Paris in 1977 with 17 700 m² *183,000 ft²* of floor space. The most heavily endowed is the J. Paul Getty Museum, Malibu, California with an initial £700,000,000 in Jan 1974 and now £104 million p.a. for acquisitions. It has 38 galleries.

Finest brush

The finest standard brush sold is the 000 in Series 7 by Winsor and Newton known as a 'triple goose'. It is made of 150–200 Kolinsky sable hairs weighing 15 mg *0.000529 oz.*

MURALS

Earliest

The earliest known murals on man-made walls are the clay relief leopards at Çatal Hüyük in southern Anatolia, Turkey, discovered by James Malaart at level VII in 1961 and dating from *c.* 6200 BC.

Largest

The world's largest 'mural' was unveiled in 44 colours on the 30 storey Villa Regina condominium, Biscayne Bay, Miami, Florida on 14 Mar 1984 covering 300,000 ft² *27 870 m².* The longest recorded continuous mural was one stretching 990 ft *302 m* on the History of Nechells, completed by 6 artists in Birmingham, England on 5 Dec 1984. *Future entries for this category will be assessed on overall area only.*

Largest mosaic

The world's largest mosaic is on the walls of the central library of the Universidad Nacional Autónoma de Mexico, Mexico City. There are four walls, the two largest measuring 12,949 ft² *1203 m²* each representing the pre-Hispanic past. The largest Roman mosaic in Britain is the Woodchester Pavement, Gloucestershire of *c.* AD 325, excavated in 1793, now re-covered with protective earth. It measures 47 ft *14,3 m* square comprising 1½ million tesserae. A brilliant total reconstruction was carried out by Robert and John Woodward in 1973–1982.

MUSEUMS

Oldest

The oldest museum in the world is the Ashmolean Museum in Oxford built in 1679–83. Since 1924 it has housed an exhibition of historic scientific instruments.

Largest

The largest museum in the world is the American Museum of Natural History on 77th to 81st Streets and Central Park West, New York City, NY, USA. Founded in 1874, it comprises 19 interconnected buildings with 23 acres *9 ha* of floor space. The largest museum in the United Kingdom is the British Museum (founded in 1753), which was opened to the public in 1759. The main building in Bloomsbury, London, was built in 1823 and has a total floor area of 17.57 acres *7,11 ha*. Britain's most visited museum is The Science Museum, South Kensington with 3,019,892 attendances in 1984. The world's largest complex of museums is the Smithsonian Institution comprising 13 museums with 5600 employees and 24 million visitors per annum.

'WORK OF ART'

Largest

The largest work of art ever perpetrated was the wrapping in 1983 of 11 islands in Biscayne Bay, Florida, USA in flamingo pink plastic tutus by Christo's 6,500,000 ft² *603 000 m²* work entitled 'Surrounded Islands'.

2. SCULPTURE

Earliest *World*

A piece of ox rib found in 1973 at Pech de l'Aze, Dordogne, France in an early Middle Palaeolithic layer of the Riss glaciation *c.* 105,000 BC has several engraved lines on one side, thought to be possibly intentional. A churingo or curved ivory plaque rubbed with red ochre from the

Patrick Lindsay of Christie's selling Mantegna's *The Adoration of the Magi* for £7,500,000 (exclusive of buyer's premium) on 18 April 1985, a record auction price for a painting. (See page 80)

Middle Palaeolithic Mousterian site at Tata, Hungary has been dated to 100,000 BC by the thorium/uranium method. The earliest known example of sculpture is a 2½ in *6,3 cm* long figure of a horse carved from mammoth ivory dated to *c.* 28,000 BC and found in the Vogelherd cave in south-west Germany.

Great Britain

The earliest example of an engraving found in Britain is of a horse's head on a piece of ribbone from Robin Hood Cave, Creswell Crag, Derbyshire. It dates from the Upper Palaeolithic period (*c.* 15,000 to 10,000 BC). The earliest Scottish rock carving from Lagalochan, Strathclyde dates from *c.* 3000 BC.

Most expensive *World and Ancient*

The highest price ever paid for a sculpture is $3,900,000 (*then £2,400,000*) paid by private treaty in London in early 1977 by The J. Paul Getty Museum, Malibu, California for a 4th century BC bronze statue of a youth attributed to the school of Lysippus. It was found by fishermen on the seabed off Faro, Italy in 1963.

Living sculptor

The highest price paid for the work of a living sculptor is the $1,265,000 (*then £702,780*) given at Sotheby Parke Bernet, New York on 21 May 1982 for the 75 in *190,5 cm* long elmwood *Reclining figure* by Henry Moore, OM, CH, (b. Castleford, West Yorkshire, 30 July 1898).

Largest

The world's largest sculptures are the mounted figures of Jefferson Davis (1808–89), Gen Robert Edward Lee (1807–70) and Gen Thomas Jonathan ('Stonewall') Jackson (1824–63), covering 1.33 acres *0,5 ha* on the face of Stone Mountain, near Atlanta, Georgia. They are 90 ft *27,4 m* high. Roy Faulkner was on the mountain face for 8 years 174 days with a thermo-jet torch working with the sculptor Walker Kirtland Hancock and other helpers from 12 Sept 1963 to 3 Mar 1972. If completed the world's largest sculpture will be that of the Indian chief Tashunca-Uitco (*c.* 1849–77), known as Crazy Horse, of the Oglala tribe of the Dakota or Nadowessioux (Sioux) group. The sculpture was begun on 3 June 1948 near Mount Rushmore, South Dakota, USA. A projected 563 ft *171,6 m* high and 641 ft *195 m* long, it was the uncompleted life work of one man, Korczak Ziółkowski (1908–82). The horse's nostril is 50 ft *15,2 m*

HIGHEST PRICE PAINTINGS—Progressive Records

Price	Equivalent 1985 Value	Painter, title, sold by and sold to	Date
£6500	£253,020	Antonio Correggio's *The Magdalen Reading* (in fact spurious) to Elector Friedrich Augustus II of Saxony.	1746
£8500	£303,850	Raphael's *The Sistine Madonna* (1513–14) from Piacenza to Elector Friedrich Augustus II of Saxony.	1759
£16,000	£344,750	Van Eycks' *Adoration of the Lamb*, 6 outer panels of Ghent altarpiece by Edward Solby to the Government of Prussia.	1821
£24,600*	£777,190	Murillo's *The Immaculate Conception* by estate of Marshal Soult to the Louvre (against Czar Nicholas I) in Paris.	1852
£70,000	£3,423,800	Raphael's *Ansidei Madonna* (1506) from Perugia by the 8th Duke of Marlborough to the National Gallery.	1885
£100,000	£4,960,800	Raphael's *The Colonna Altarpiece* (1503–05) from Perugia by Seldemeyer to J. Pierpont Morgan.	1901
£102,880	£3,895,500	Van Dyck's *Elena Grimaldi-Cattaneo* (portrait) by Knoedler to Peter Widener (1834–1915).	1906
£102,880	£2,921,890	Rembrandt's *The Mill* by 6th Marquess of Lansdowne to Peter Widener.	1911
£116,500	£3,693,040	Raphael's smaller *Panshanger Madonna* by Joseph (later Baron) Duveen (1869–1939) to Peter Widener.	1913
£310,400	£9,778,500	Leonardo da Vinci's *Benois Madonna* (*c.* 1477) to Czar Nicholas II in Paris.	1914
£821,429*	£6,344,100	Rembrandt's *Aristotle Contemplating the Bust of Homer* by estate of Mr and Mrs Alfred W. Erickson to New York Metropolitan Museum of Art.	1961
£1,785,714	£10,268,750	Leonardo da Vinci's *Ginerva de' Benci* (*c.* 1475) by Prince Franz Josef II of Liechtenstein to National Gallery of Art, Washington DC, USA.	1967
£2,310,000*	£11,074,350	Velázquez's *Portrait of Juan de Pareja* by the Earl of Radnor to the Wildenstein Gallery, New York.	1970
£2,729,000*	£3,985,600	Turner's *Juliet and Her Nurse* by Trustees of Whitney Museum, New York to undisclosed bidder at Sotheby Park Bernet, New York.	1980
£7,470,500*	£7,918,730	Turner's *Seascape: Folkestone* from estate of Lord Clark (1903–83) to Leggatt's of London for an unknown buyer.	1984
£8,100,000*		Montegna's *The Adoration of the Magi* by the Marquess of Northampton to the J. Paul Getty Museum, Malibu, California.	1985

* Indicates price at auction, otherwise prices were by private treaty.

deep and 35 ft *10,7 m* in diameter. In 1984 another 200,000 tons of granite blasted off the mountain face brought the total to 7.8 million tons.

Ground figures

In the Nazca Desert, 300 km *185 miles* south of Lima, Peru there are straight lines (one more than 7 miles *11.2 km* long), geometric shapes and shapes of plants and animals drawn on the ground sometime between 100 BC and AD 600 for an uncertain but probably religious, astronomical, or even economic, purpose by a not precisely identified civilization. They were first detected from the air in *c.* 1928 and have also been described as the world's longest works of art.

Hill figures

In August 1968, a 330 ft *100 m* tall figure was found on a hill above Tarapacá, Chile.

The largest human hill carving in Britain is the 'Long Man' of Wilmington, East Sussex, 226 ft *68 m* in length. The oldest of all White Horses in Britain is the Uffington White Horse in Oxfordshire, dating from the late Iron Age (*c.* 150 BC) and measuring 374 ft *114 m* from nose to tail and 120 ft *36 m* high.

Most massive mobile

The most massive mobile is *White Cascade* weighing 8 tons/*tonnes* and measuring 100 ft *30,48 m* from top to bottom installed on 24–25 May 1976 at the Federal Reserve Bank of Philadelphia, Pennsylvania, USA. It was designed by Alexander Calder (1898–1976), whose first mobiles were exhibited in Paris in 1932 and whose *Big Crinkley* sold for a record £555,572 at Sotheby's, New York on 10 May 1984.

3. LANGUAGE & LITERATURE

Earliest

A linguistic mutation is believed to have been the social tool which enabled hunters to become the earliest fast-learning and talkative modern humans *c.* 45,000 BC emerging from the area of Iran. The earliest written language discovered has been on Yangshao culture pottery from Paa-t'o, near Xi'an (Sian) in the Shanxi (Shensi) province of China found in 1962. This bears proto-characters for the numbers 5, 7 and 8 and has been dated to 5000–4000 BC. The earliest dated pictographs are on clay tablets from Nippur, southern Iraq from a level equivalent to Uruk V/VI and dated in 1979 to *c.* 3400 BC. Tokens or tallies from Tepe Asiab and Ganji-I-Dareh Tepe in Iran have however been dated to 8500 BC.

The oldest surviving printed work—the Dharani Scroll from Korea dating from no later than AD 704. (See page 86). *(Sherwood Press, London)*

Oldest

The written language with the longest continuous history is Chinese extending over more than 6000 years from the Yangshao culture (see above) to the present day.

Oldest words in English

It was first suggested in 1979 that languages ancestral to English and to Latvian (both Indo-European) split *c.* 3500 BC. Research shortly to be published will indicate some words of a pre-Indo-European substrate survive in English— apple (apal), bad (bad), gold (gol) and tin (tin).

Commonest language

Today's world total of languages and dialects still spoken is about 5000 of which some 845 come from India. The language spoken by more people than any other is Northern Chinese, or Mandarin, by an estimated 68 per cent of the population, hence 695 million people in 1983. The so-called national language (*Guóyŭ*) is a standardised form of Northern Chinese (*Běifanghuà*) as spoken in the Peking area. This was alphabetised into *zhùyīn fùhào* of 37 letters in 1913 by Wa Chih-hui (1865–1953). In 1958 the *pinyin* system, which is a phonetic pronunciation guide, was introduced. The next most commonly spoken language and the most widespread is English, by an estimated 400,000,000 in mid-1981. English is spoken by 10 per cent or more of the population in 45 sovereign countries.

In Great Britain and Ireland there are six indigenous tongues: English, Cornish, Scots Gaelic, Welsh, Irish Gaelic, and Romany (Gipsy). Of these English is, of course, predominant. Mr Edward (Ned) Maddrell (1877–1974) of Glen Chass, Port St Mary, Isle of Man, died as the last islander whose professed tongue was Manx. Cornish, of which there are now some 300 students, came within an ace of extinction. A dictionary was published in 1887, four years before the death of the then last fluent speaker John Davey. A novel by Melville and Kitty Bennetto 'An Gurun Wosek a Geltya' was published in Nov 1984. In the Channel Islands, apart from Jersey and Guernsey *normand*, there survive words of Sarkese or *Sèrtchais* in which the Parable of the Sower, as recited by some fishermen, was noted and published by Prince Louis Lucien Bonaparte (1813–91) in 1862.

Most complex

The following extremes of complexity have been noted: Chippewa, the North American Indian language of Minnesota, USA, has the most verb forms with up to 6000; Tillamook, the North American Indian language of Oregon, USA, has the most prefixes with 30; Tabassaran, a language in Daghestan, USSR, uses the most noun cases with 35, while Eskimaux use 63 forms of the present tense and simple nouns have as many as 252 inflections. In Chinese the 40 volume *Chung-wén Tà Tz'u-tien* dictionary lists 49,905 characters. The fourth tone of 'i' has 84 meanings, varying as widely as 'dress', 'hiccough' and 'licentious'. The written language

provides 92 different characters of 'i⁴'. The most complex written character in Chinese is that representing *xiè* consisting of 64 strokes meaning 'talkative'. The most complex in current use is *yù* with 32 strokes meaning to urge or implore.

Most and least irregular verbs

Esperanto was first published by its inventor Dr Ludwig Zamenhof (1859–1917) of Warsaw in 1887 without irregular verbs and is now estimated (by text book sales) to have a million speakers. The even earlier interlanguage Volapük, invented by Johann Martin Schleyer (1831–1912), also has absolutely regular configuration. The Turkish language has a single irregular verb—*imek*, to be. According to *The Morphology and Syntax of Present-day English* by Prof. Olu Tomori, English has 283 irregular verbs of which 30 are merely formed with prefixes.

Rarest and commonest sounds

The rarest speech sound is probably the sound written ř in Czech which occurs in very few languages and is the last sound mastered by Czech children. In the southern Bushman language !xo there is a click articulated with both lips, which is written⊙. The *l* sound in the Arabic word *Allah*, in some contexts, is pronounced uniquely in that language. The commonest sound is the vowel *a* (as in the English father); no language is known to be without it.

Literature, smallest

The *Great Soviet Encyclopaedia* states that only one word of Khazar survives—*oqurüm*, meaning 'I have read'.

Vocabulary

The English language contains about 490,000 words plus another 300,000 technical terms, the most in any language, but it is doubtful if any individual uses more than 60,000. Those in Great Britain who have undergone a full 16 years of education use perhaps 5000 words in speech and up to 10,000 words in written communications. The membership of the International Society for Philosophical Enquiry (no admission for IQ's below 148) have an average vocabulary of 36,250 words.

Greatest linguist

If the yardstick of ability to speak with fluency and reasonable accuracy is adhered to, it is doubtful whether any human could maintain fluency in more than 20–25 languages concurrently or achieve fluency in more than 40 in a lifetime.

The most multi-lingual living person in the world is Georges Henri Schmidt (b. Strasbourg, France, 28 Dec 1914), the Chief of the UN Terminology Section in 1965–71. The 1975 edition of *Who's Who in the United Nations*, listed 'only' 19 languages because he was then unable to find time to 'revive' his former fluency in 12 others. Powell Alexander Janulus (b. 1939) has worked with 41 languages in the Provincial Court of British Columbia, Vancouver, Canada. Britain's greatest linguist is George Campbell (b. 9 Aug 1912), who is retired from the BBC Overseas Service where he *worked* with 54 languages.

Historically the greatest linguists have been proclaimed as Cardinal Mezzofanti (1774–1849) (fluent in 26 or 27), Professor Rask (1787–1832), Sir John Bowring (1792–1872) and Dr Harold Williams of New Zealand (1876–1928), who had been fluent in 28 languages.

ALPHABET

Earliest

The development of the use of an alphabet in

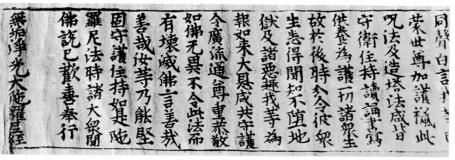

place of pictograms occurred in the Sinaitic world between 1700 and 1500 BC. This western Semitic language developed the consonantal system based on phonetic and syllabic principles. The oldest letter is 'O', unchanged in shape since its adoption in the Phoenician alphabet *c.* 1300 BC. The newest letters added to the English alphabet, are 'j' and 'v' which are of post-Shakespearean use *c.* 1630. Formerly they were used only as variants of 'i' and 'u'. There are 65 alphabets now in use.

Longest and shortest
The language with most letters is Cambodian with 72 (including useless ones) and Rotokas in central Bougainville Island has least with 11 (just a, b, e, g, i, k, o, p, ř, t and u).

Most and least consonants and vowels
The language with most distinct consonantal sounds is that of the Ubykhs in the Caucasus, with 80–85, and that with least is Rotokas, which has only 6 consonants. The language with the most vowels is Sedang, a central Vietnamese language with 55 distinguishable vowel sounds and that with the least is the Caucasian language Abkhazian with two such. The record in written English for consecutive vowels is 6 in the musical term *euouae*. The Estonian word jäääärne, meaning the edge of the ice, has the same 4 consecutively. Uoiauai, is the name of a language in Pará State, Brazil consisting solely of 7 vowels. The English word 'latchstring' has 6 consecutive letters which are consonants, but the Georgian word gvprtskvnis (he is feeling us) has 8 separately pronounced consonants.

Largest letters
The largest permanent letters in the world are the giant 600 ft *183 m* letters spelling READYMIX on the ground in the Nullarbor near East Balladonia, Western Australia. This was constructed in December 1971.

Smallest Letters
The 16 letters MOLECULAR DEVICES have been etched into a salt crystal by an electron beam so that the strokes were only 2 to 3 nm (10^{-9}) wide—the width of 20 hydrogen atoms. This was done by Michael Isaacson at Cornell University, Ithaca, NY, USA in February 1982.

WORDS

Longest words *World*
Lengthy concatenations and some compound or agglutinative words or nonce words are or have been written in the closed up style of a single word e.g. the 182 letter fricassee of 17 sweet and sour ingredients in Aristophanes' comedy *The Ecclesiazusae* in the 4th century BC. A compound 'word' of 195 sanskrit characters (which transliterates into 428 letters in the Roman alphabet) describing the region near Kanci, Tamil Nadu, India appears in a 16th century work by Tirumalāmbā, Queen of Vijayanagara.

English
The longest word in the Oxford English Dictionary is floccipaucinihilipilification (alternatively spelt in hyphenated form with 'n' in seventh place), with 29 letters, meaning 'the action of estimating as worthless', first used in 1741, and later by Sir Walter Scott (1771–1832). Webster's Third International Dictionary lists among its 450,000 entries: pneumonoultramicroscopic-silicovolcanoconiosis (47 letters) the plural of a lung disease contracted by some miners.

The longest regularly formed English word is praetertranssubstantiationalistically (37 letters), used by Mark McShane in his 1963 novel *Untimely Ripped*. The medical term hepaticocholangiocholecystenterostomies (39

letters) refers to the surgical creations of new communications between gallbladders and hepatic ducts and between intestines and gallbladders. The longest words in common use are disproportionableness and incomprehensibilities (21 letters). Interdenominationalism (22 letters) is found in Webster's Dictionary and hence perhaps interdenominationalistically (28 letters) is permissible. H W Jones of Altrincham, Cheshire has compiled 8700 lesser words from its 28 letters.

Longest palindromes
The longest known palindromic word is *saippu-akivikauppias* (19 letters), the Finnish word for a dealer in lye (*i.e.* caustic soda). The longest in the English language is *redivider* (9 letters). The nine-letter word, *Malayalam*, is a proper noun given to the language of the Malayali people in Kerala, southern India while *Kanakanak* near Dillingham, Alaska is a 9 lettered palindromic place-name. The contrived chemical term *detartrated* has 11 letters. Some baptismal fonts in Greece and Turkey bear the circular 25 letter inscription ΝΙΨΟΝ ΑΝΟΜΗΜΑΤΑ ΜΗ ΜΟΝΑΝ ΟΨΙΝ meaning 'wash (my) sins not only (my) face'. This appears at St Mary's Church, Nottingham, St Paul's, Woldingham, Surrey and other churches. The longest palindromic composition devised is one of 65,000 words completed by Edward Benbow of Bewdley, Hereford & Worcs. in Jan 1983. It begins 'Rae hits Eb, sire. Eb . . .' and hence predictably ends '. . . . Beer is best, I hear'

Longest scientific name
The systematic name for deoxyribonucleicacid of the human mitochondria, contains 16,569 nucleotide residues and is thus *c.* 207,000 letters long. It was published in key form in *Nature* on 9 Apr 1981.

Longest anagrams
The longest non-scientific English words which can form anagrams are the 18-letter transpositions 'conservationalists' and 'conversationalists'. The longest scientific transposals are cholecystoduodenostomy/duodenocholecystostomy and hydropneumopericardium/pneumohydropericardium each of 22 letters.

A. J. Capper has found only one 4 letter word with 13 and one 5 letter word with 28 anagrams—these are 'aber' and 'aster'.

Longest abbreviation
The longest known abbreviation is S.K.O.M.K.H.P.K.J.C.D.P.W.B., the initials of the Syarikat Kerjasama Orang-orang Melayu Kerajaan Hilir Perak Kerana Jimat Cermat Dan Pinjam-meminjam Wang Berhad. This is the Malay name for The Cooperative Company of the Lower State of Perak Government's Malay People for Money Savings and Loans Ltd., in Teluk Anson, Perak, West Malaysia (formerly Malaya). The abbreviation for this abbreviation is Skomk. The 55-letter full name of Los Angeles (El Pueblo de Nuestra Señora la Reina de los Angeles de Porciuncula) is abbreviated to LA or 3.63 per cent of its length.

Longest Acronym
The longest acronym is NIIOMTPLABOPARM-BETZHELBETRABSBOMONIMONKONOTDTEKHSTRO-MONT with 56 letters (54 in cirillic) in the *Concise Dictionary of Soviet Terminology* meaning: The laboratory for shuttering, reinforcement, concrete and ferroconcrete operations for composite-monolithic and monolithic constructions of the Department of the Technology of Building—assembly operations the Scientific Research Institute of the Organisation for building mechanisation and technical aid of the Academy of Building and Architecture of the USSR.

WORLD'S LONGEST WORDS

JAPANESE[1]
Chi-n-chi-ku-ri-n (12 letters)
—a very short person (slang)

SPANISH
Superextraordinarisimo (22 letters)
—extraordinary

FRENCH[2]
Anticonstitutionnellement (25 letters)
—anticonstitutionally.
Anthropoclimatologiquement[2] (26 letters)
—anthropoclimatologically

CROATIAN
Prijestolonasljednikovica (25 letters)
—wife of an heir apparent.

ITALIAN
Precipitevolissimevolmente (26 letters)
—as fast as possible.

PORTUGUESE
inconstitucionalissimamente (27 letters)
—with the highest degree of unconstitutionality.

ICELANDIC
Hæstaréttarmálaflutningsmaður (29 letters)
—supreme court barrister

RUSSIAN
ryentgyenoelyektrokardiografichyeskogo (33 Cyrillic letters, transliterating as 38)
—of the radioelectrocardiographic.

HUNGARIAN
Megszentségtelenithetetlenségeskedéseitekért (44 letters)
—for your unprofaneable actions.

TURKISH[5]
Cekoslovakyalılastıramadıklarımızdanmıymıssınız (47 letters)
—'are you not of that group of persons that we were said to be unable to Czechoslovakianise?'

DUTCH[5]
Kindercarnavalsoptochtvoorberei-dingswerkzaamheden (49 letters)
—preparation activities for a children's carnival procession

MOHAWK[3]
tkanuhstasrihsranuhwe'tsraaksahsrakaratattsrayeri' (50 letters)
—the praising of the evil of the liking of the finding of the house is right.

GERMAN[4,5]
Donaudampfschiffahrtselectrizitaetenhaupt betriebswerkbauunterbeamtengesellschaft (80 letters)
—The club for subordinate officials of the head office management of the Danube steamboat electrical services (Name of a pre-war club in Vienna).

SWEDISH[5]
Spårvagnsaktiebolags skensmutsskjutarefack föreningspersonal beklädnadsmagasins förråds-förvaltaren (94 letters)
—Manager of the depot for the supply of uniforms to the personnel of the track cleaners' union of the tramway company.

[1] Patent applications sometimes harbour long compound 'words'. An extreme example is one of 13 kana which transliterates to the 40 letter Kyūkitsūrohekimen-fuchakunenryōsekisanryō meaning 'the accumulated amount of fuel condensed on the wall face of the air intake passage'.
[2] Not accepted by *savants* to be an acceptable French word.
[3] Lengthy concatenations are a feature of Mohawk. Above is an example.
[4] The longest dictionary word in every day usage is Kraftfahrzeugreparaturwerkstätten (33 letters or 34 if the ä is written as ae) meaning motor vehicle repair shops (or service garages).
[5] Agglutinative words are only limited by imagination and are not found in standard dictionaries. The first 100 letter such word was published in 1975 by the late Eric Rosenthal in Afrikaans.

SUPERLATIVE PLACE NAMES IN THE BRITISH ISLES

Artwork: Eddie Botchway

The map should be read in conjunction with the text entries on pp 85–86.

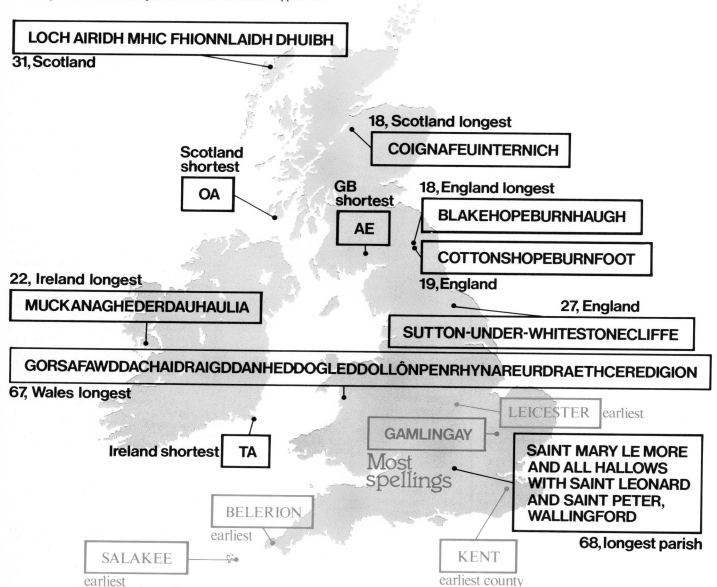

LOCH AIRIDH MHIC FHIONNLAIDH DHUIBH
31, Scotland

18, Scotland longest
COIGNAFEUINTERNICH

Scotland shortest
OA

GB shortest
AE

18, England longest
BLAKEHOPEBURNHAUGH

COTTONSHOPEBURNFOOT
19, England

22, Ireland longest
MUCKANAGHEDERDAUHAULIA

27, England
SUTTON-UNDER-WHITESTONECLIFFE

GORSAFAWDDACHAIDRAIGDDANHEDDOGLEDDOLLÔNPENRHYNAREURDRAETHCEREDIGION
67, Wales longest

Ireland shortest **TA**

LEICESTER earliest

GAMLINGAY
Most spellings

SAINT MARY LE MORE AND ALL HALLOWS WITH SAINT LEONARD AND SAINT PETER, WALLINGFORD
68, longest parish

BELERION
earliest

SALAKEE
earliest

KENT
earliest county

Commonest words and letters

In written English the most frequently used words are in order: the, of, and, to, a, in, that, is, I, it, for *and* as. The most used in conversation is I. The commonest letter is 'e' and the commonest initial letter is 'T'.

Most meanings

The most over-worked word in English is the word *set* which has 58 noun uses, 126 verbal uses and 10 as a participial adjective.

Most succinct word

The most challenging word for any lexicographer to define briefly is the Fuegian (southernmost Argentina and Chile) word 'mamihlapinatapai' meaning 'looking at each other hoping that either will offer to do something which both parties desire but are unwilling to do'.

Most synonyms

The condition of being inebriated has more synonyms than any other condition or object. Delacourt Press of New York City, USA has published a selection of 1224 from 2241 compiled by Paul Dickson of Garrett Park, Maryland, USA.

Most homophones

The most homophonous sounds in English are *air* and *sol* which, according to the researches of Dora Newhouse of Los Angeles, both have 38 homophones. The homonym with most variant spellings is *Air* with Aire, are, Ayer, Ayr, Ayre, err, e'er, ere, eyre and heir.

Most accents

Accents were introduced in French in the reign of Louis XIII (1601–43). The word with most accents is *hétérogénéité*, meaning heterogeneity. An atoll in the Pacific Ocean 320 miles *516 km* east-south-east of Tahiti is named Héréhérétué. An example of a Hungarian word with 6 accents is *újjáépítésére* meaning 'for its reconstruction'.

Shortest pangram (holoalphabetic sentence)

Pangrammists who endeavour to produce meaningful sentences of minimal length utilizing all the letters in the alphabet have now attained the ultimate of 26 letter brevity. Michael Jones of Chicago, Illinois, compiled in 1984 the sentence to describe the situation in which a wryneck woodpecker from the grasslands of Africa climbed up the side of a male bovid which is grazing on sacred Muslim-owned land. viz: 'Veldt jynx grimps waqf zho buck'.

PERSONAL NAMES

Earliest

The earliest personal name which has survived is seemingly that of a predynastic king of Upper Egypt *ante* 3050 BC, who is indicated by the hieroglyphic sign for a scorpion. It has been suggested that the name should be read as

Sekhen. The earliest known name of any resident of Britain is Divitiacus, King of the Suessiones, the Gaulish ruler of the Kent area c. 100 BC under the name Prydhain. Scotland, unlike England, was never fully conquered by the Roman occupiers (AD 43–410). Calgācus (b. c. AD 40), who led the final resistance in Scotland was the earliest native whose name has been recorded.

Longest pedigree

The only non-Royal English pedigree that can with certainty show a clear pre-Conquest descent is that of the Arden family. Shakespeare's mother was a Mary Arden. It is claimed on behalf of the Clan Mackay that their clan can be traced to Loarn, the Irish invader of south west Pictland, now Argyll, c. AD 501.

Longest single name

The longest Christian or given name on record is one of 622 letters given by Mr Scott Roaul Sör-Lökken of Missoula, Montana, USA to his daughter Miss S. Ellen Georgianna Sör Lökken (b. 1979). The 'S' stands for a 598 letter name designed to throw a monkey wrench into the computers of federal bureaucracy. She is known as 'Snow Owl' for short or 'Oli' for shorter.

Longest personal name *World*

The longest name appearing on a birth certificate is that of Rhoshandiatellyneshiaunneveshenk Koyaanfsquatsiuty Williams born to Mr and Mrs James L. Williams in Beaumont, Texas, USA on 12 Sept 1984. On 5 Oct 1984 the father filed an amendment which expanded his daughter's first name to 1,019 letters and the middle name to 36 letters.

United Kingdom

The longest surname in the United Kingdom was the six-barrelled one borne by the late Major L.S.D.O.F. (Leone Sextus Denys Oswolf Fraudatifilius) Tollemache-Tollemache-de Orellana-Plantagenet-Tollemache-Tollemache, who was born on 12 June 1884 and died of pneumonia in France on 20 Feb 1917. Of non-repetitious surnames, the last example of a five-barrelled one was that of the Lady Caroline Jemima Temple-Nugent-Chandos-Brydges-Grenville (1858–1946). The longest single English surname is Featherstonehaugh (17 letters), correctly pronounced on occasions (but improbably on the correct occasion) Featherstonehaw or Feston-haw or Fessonhay or Freestonhugh or Feerston-haw or Fanshaw.

Scotland

In Scotland the surname nin (feminine of mac) Achinmacdholicachinskerray (29 letters) was recorded in an 18th century parish register.

Most Christian names

The great-great-grandson of Carlos III of Spain, Don Alfonso de Borbón y Borbón (1866–1934) had 94 Christian names of which several were lengthened by hyphenation.

Shortest

The commonest single-letter surname is O, prevalent in Korea, but with 52 examples in US phone books (1973–81) and 12 in Belgium. This name causes most distress to those concerned with the prevention of cruelty to computers. Every other letter, except Q, has been traced in US phone books (used as a surname) by A. Ross Eckler. There are two one-lettered Burmese names E (calm), pronounced aye and U (egg), pronounced Oo. U *before* the name means 'uncle'. There exist among the 47,000,000 names on the Dept. of Health & Social Security index 6 examples of a one-lettered surname. Their identity has not been disclosed, but they are 'A', 'B', 'J', 'N', 'O' and 'X'. Two-letter British surnames include By and On and have recently been joined by Oy, Za and others. The Christian name 'A' has been used for 5 generations in the Lincoln Taber family of Fingringhoe, Essex.

Commonest family name *World*

The commonest family name in the world is the Chinese name Chang which is borne, according to estimates, by between 9.7 and 12.1 per cent of the Chinese population, so indicating even on the lower estimate that there are at least some 104 million Changs—more than the entire population of all but 7 of the 170 other sovereign countries of the world.

English

The commonest surname in the English-speaking world is Smith. The most recent published count showed 659,050 nationally insured Smiths in Great Britain, of whom 10,102 were plain John Smith and another 19,502 were John (plus one or more given names) Smith. Including uninsured persons there were over 800,000 Smiths in England and Wales alone, of whom 81,493 were called A. Smith. There were an estimated 2,382,509 Smiths in the USA in 1973. It is no secret that by 1984 there were some 90,000 Singhs in Britain—the name means 'in secret'.

'Macs'

There are, however, estimated to be 1,600,000 persons in Britain with M', Mc or Mac (Gaelic genitive of 'son') as part of their surnames. The commonest of these is Macdonald which accounts for about 55,000 of the Scottish population.

Commonest first names

From the latest available full year (1983) birth registrations for England and Wales at the General Register Office at St Catherine's House, Kingsway, London, the most favoured first forename choice of parents from the classless samples of the 9035 entries bearing the (easily) commonest surname of Smith are (with phonetic variations allowed): boys Christopher, well ahead of Matthew, David, James and Daniel. For girls Sarah, just ahead of Claire, then Emma, Laura and Rebecca (also Rebekah). This survey was carried out by C. V. Appleton. From 1196 to at least 1925 William and John were first and second.

Most versions

Mr Edward A. Nedelcov of Regina, Saskatchewan, Canada has collected 990 versions of the spelling of his family name since January 1960. Mzilikazi of Zululand (b. c. 1795) had his name chronicled in 325 spellings, according to researches by Dr R. Kent Rasmussen.

Most Changed

Excluding members of the royal family the living monogamous woman who has most times changed her name is Lady Home of the Hirsel formerly Lady Douglass-Home; Countess of Home; Lady Dunglass and originally Miss Elizabeth Alington.

Most contrived name

In the United States the determination to derive commercial or other benefit from being the last listing in the local telephone book has resulted in self-given names, starting with up to 9 z's—an extreme example being Zachary Zzzzzzzzzra in the San Francisco book. The U.K. record for terminality at Zz demonstrates admirable British restraint. The alpha and omega of Britain's 82 directories are Mrs Maude E. Aab of Hull, Humberside and Mr P. B. Zzytt of Wells, Somerset. In 1929 the Registrar-General recorded the death of a Jokine Zzuppichine of Liverpool aged 68.

PLACE-NAMES

Earliest

The world's earliest place names are pre-Sumerian e.g. Kish, Ur and Attara. The earliest recorded British place-name is Belerion, the Penwith peninsula of Cornwall, referred to as such by Pytheas of Massilia in c. 308 BC. The name Salakee on St Mary's, Isles of Scilly is however arguably of a pre Indo-European substrate meaning *tin island*. There are reasons to contend that Leicester (Roman, Ligora Castrum) contains an element reflecting its founding by the Western Mediterranean navigators, the Ligurians, as early as c. 1200 BC. The earliest distinctive name for what is now Great Britain was Albion by Himilco c. 500 BC. The oldest name among England's 46 counties is Kent, first mentioned in its Roman form of Cantium (from the Celtic *canto*, meaning a rim, *i.e.* a coastal district) from the same circumnavigation by Pytheas. The earliest mention of England is the form *Angelcymn*, which appeared in the Anglo-Saxon Chronicle in AD. 880.

Longest *World*

The official name for Bangkok, the capital city of Thailand, is Krungtep Mahanakhon. The full name is however: Krungthep Mahanakhon Bovorn Ratanakosin Mahintharayutthaya Mahadilokpop Noparatratchathani Burirom Udomratchanivetmahasathan Amornpiman Avatarnsathit Sakkathattiyavisnukarmprasit (167 letters) which in its most scholarly transliteration emerges with 175 letters. The longest place-name now in use in the world is Taumatawhakatangihangakoauauotamatea-(turipukakapikimaungahoronuku)pokaiwhen-uakitanatahu, the unofficial 85-letter version of the name of a hill (1002 ft *305 m* above sea-level) in the Southern Hawke's Bay district of North Island, New Zealand. This Maori name means 'the hill whereon was played the flute of Tamatea, circumnavigator of lands, for his lady love'. The official version has 57 letters (1 to 36 and 65 to 85). Ijouaououene, a mountain in Morocco, has 8 consecutive vowel letters as rendered by the French.

Great Britain

The longest place-name in the United Kingdom is the concocted 58-letter name Llanfair-pwllgwyngyllgogerychwyrndrobwllllantysilio-gogogoch, which is translated: 'St Mary's Church by the pool of the white hazel trees, near the rapid whirlpool, by the red cave of the Church of St Tysilio'. This is the name used for the reopened (April 1973) village railway station in Anglesey, Gwynedd, Wales, but the *official* name consists of only the first 20 letters of what the Welsh would regard as a 51 letter word since 'll' and 'ch' may be regarded as one. The longest Welsh place-names listed in the Ordnance Survey Gazetteer are Lower Llanfihangel-y-Creuddyn (26 letters), a village near Aberystwyth, Dyfed, and Llansantffraid Cwmdeuddwr (24 letters), Powys. For commercial rather than toponymic reasons the proprietors of the Fairbourne Steam Railway, near Barmouth, North Wales have posted a 67 letter long name on a station board 64 ft *19,5 m* long (see p. 84).

England

The longest single-word (unhyphenated) place-name in England is Blakehopeburnhaugh, a hamlet between Byrness and Rochester in Northumberland, of 18 letters. The nearby Cottonshopeburnfoot (19 letters) is locally rendered as one word though not by the Ordnance Survey. The hyphenated Sutton-under-Whitestonecliffe, North Yorkshire has 27 letters on the Ordnance Survey but with the insertion of 'the' and the dropping of the final 'e' 29 letters in the

Post Office List. The longest parish name is Saint Mary le More and All Hallows with Saint Leonard and Saint Peter, Wallingford (68 letters) in Oxfordshire formed on 5 Apr 1971.

Scotland

The longest single-word place-name in Scotland is Coignafeuinternich in Inverness-shire. Kirkcudbrightshire (also 18 letters) became merged into Dumfries and Galloway on 16 May 1975. A 12-acre *5 ha* loch 9 miles *14 km* west of Stornoway on Lewis, Western Isles is named Loch Airidh Mhic Fhionnlaidh Dhuibh (31 letters).

Ireland

The longest place-name in Ireland is Muckanaghederdauhaulia (22 letters), 4 miles *6 km* from Costello in Camus Bay, County Galway. The name means 'soft place between two seas'.

Shortest

The shortest place names in the world are the French village of Y (population 143), so named since 1241, the Danish village Å on the island Fyn, the Norwegian village of Å (pronounced 'Aw'), the Swedish place Å in Vikholandet, U in the Caroline Islands, Pacific Ocean; and the Japanese town of Sosei which is alternatively called Aioi or O. There was once a '6' in West Virginia, USA. The shortest place-names in Great Britain are the two-lettered places of Ae (population 199 in 1961) Dumfries and Galloway; Oa on the island of Islay, Strathclyde and Bu on Wyre, Orkney Islands. In the Shetland Islands there are skerries called Ve and two stacks called Aa. The island of Iona was originally I. The River E flows into the southern end of Loch Mhór, Invernessshire, and O Brook flows on Dartmoor, Devon. The shortest place-name in Ireland is Ta (or Lady's Island) Lough, a sea-inlet on the coast of County Wexford. Tievelough, in County Donegal, is also called Ea.

Most spellings

The spelling of the Dutch town of Leeuwarden has been recorded in 225 versions since AD 1046. The Cambridgeshire village of Gamlingay is recorded in 110 other spellings since the Gamelinge or Gamlingei of the Doomsday Book in 1086.

PRINTED TEXTS AND BOOKS

Oldest printed

The oldest surviving printed work is the Dharani scroll or *sutra* from wooden printing blocks found in the foundations of the Pulguk Sa pagoda, Kyŏngju, South Korea, on 14 Oct 1966. It has been dated no later than AD 704. It was claimed in November 1973 that a 28-page book of Tang dynasty poems at Yonsei University, Korea was printed from metal type c. 1160.

Oldest mechanically printed

It is widely accepted that the earliest mechanically printed full length book was the 42-line Gutenberg Bible, printed in Mainz, West Germany, in c. 1454 by Johann Henne zum Gensfleisch zur Laden, called 'zu Gutenberg' (c. 1398–c. 1468). Work on water marks published in 1967 indicates a copy of a surviving printed 'Donatus' Latin grammar was made from paper in c. 1450. The earliest exactly dated printed work is the Psalter completed on 14 Aug 1457 by Johann Fust (c. 1400–66) and Peter Schöffer (1425–1502), who had been Gutenberg's chief assistant. The earliest printing by William Caxton (c. 1422–1491) though undated would appear to be *The Recuyel of the Historyes of Troye* in late 1473 to spring 1474.

Largest *Book*

The largest book in the world is the *Super Book* measuring 9 ft × 10 ft 2⅛ in *2,74 × 3,07 m* weighing 557 lb *252,6 kg* consisting of 300 pages published in Denver, Colorado, USA in 1976.

Publication

The largest publication in the world is the 1112 volume set of *British Parliamentary Papers* published by the Irish University Press in 1968–72. A complete set weighs 3¼ tons *3,3 tonnes*, costs £32,804 and would take 6 years to read at 10 hours per day. The production involved the death of 34,000 Indian goats, and the use of £15,000 worth of gold ingots. The total print is 500 sets and the price per set in 1984 was £42,000.

Dictionary

Deutches Wörterbuch started by Jacob and Wilhelm Grimm in 1854 was completed in 34,519 pages and 33 volumes in 1971. Today's price is DM5456.97 (now *£1428*). The largest English language dictionary is the 12-volume Royal quarto *The Oxford English Dictionary* of 15,487 pages published between 1884 and 1928 with a first supplement of 963 pages in 1933. Of the 4-volume supplement, edited by R. W. Burchfield, the final (Se-Z) volume and the Bibliography are due to appear in 1985. The work contains 414,825 words, 1,827,306 illustrative quotations and reputedly 227,779,589 letters and figures, 63.8 times more than the Bible. The greatest outside contributor has been Marghanita Laski with 175,000 quotations since 1958.

The New Grove Dictionary of Music and Musicians (Editor: Stanley Sadie) published in 20 volumes by Macmillan's in February 1981 contains over 22 million words and 4500 illustrations and is the largest specialist dictionary yet published. The price in 1985 is £1100.

Smallest book

The smallest marketed bound printed book with cursive material is one printed on 22 gsm paper measuring 1 mm × 1 mm $\frac{1}{25} \times \frac{1}{25}$ *in*, comprising the children's story *Old King Cole!* and published in 85 copies in March 1985 by The Gleniffer Press of Paisley, Scotland. The pages can only be turned (with care) by the use of a needle.

Longest novel

The longest important novel ever published is *Les hommes de bonne volonté* by Louis Henri Jean Farigoule (b. 26 Aug 1885), *alias* Jules Romains, of France, in 27 volumes in 1932–46. The English version *Men of Good Will* was published in 14 volumes in 1933–46 as a 'novel-cycle'. The 4959 page edition published by Peter Davies Ltd has an estimated 2,070,000 words excluding a 100 page index. The novel *Tokuga-Wa Ieyasu* by Sohachi Yamaoka has been serialised in Japanese daily newspapers since 1951. Now completed it will require nearly 40 volumes in book form.

Encyclopaedias *Earliest*

The earliest known encyclopaedia was compiled by Speusippus (*post* 408–c. 338 BC) a nephew of Plato, in Athens c. 370 BC. The earliest encyclopaedia compiled by a Briton was *Liber exerptionum* by the Scottish monk Richard (d. 1173) at St Victor's Abbey, Paris c. 1140.

Largest

The largest encyclopaedia is *La Enciclopedia Universal Ilustrada Europeo-Americana* (J. Espasa & Sons, Madrid and Barcelona) totalling 105,000 pages and an annual supplement since 1935 comprising 165,200,000 words. The number of volumes in the set in August 1983 was 104, and the price is $2325 (*£1660*).

Most comprehensive (English language)

The most comprehensive English language encyclopaedia is the *Encyclopaedia Britannica*, first published in Edinburgh, Scotland, in December 1768–1771. A group of booksellers in the United States acquired reprint rights in 1898 and completed ownership in 1899. In 1943 the *Britannica* was given to the University of Chicago, Illinois, USA. The current 30-volume 15th edition contains 33,141 pages and 43,000,000 words from 4277 contributors. It is now edited in Chicago and in London.

Longest index

The Tenth Collective Index of *Chemical Abstracts* completed in June 1983 contains 23,948,253 entries in 131,445 pages and 75 volumes, and weighs 380 lb *172,3 kg*.

Maps

The oldest known map of any kind is a clay tablet depicting the river Euphrates flowing through northern Mesopotamia, Iraq, dated *c.* 3800 BC. The earliest surviving product of English map-making is the Anglo Saxon *mappa mundi*, known as the Cottonian manuscript from the late 10th century. The earliest printed map in the world is one of western China dated to 1115. The earliest printed map of Britain was Ptolemy's outline printed in Bologna, Italy in 1477.

A *Giant Relief Map of California*, weighing 38.4 tons *39 tonnes*, was displayed in the Ferry Building, San Francisco from 1924 until 1962. Now in storage, it measures 450 × 18 ft *137,1 × 5,48 m*.

Most expensive work of art

The highest price paid for any book or any work of art was £8,140,000 for the 226 leaf *The Gospel Book of Henry the Lion, Duke of Saxony* at Sotheby's, London on 6 Dec. 1983. The book, 13½ × 10 in *34,3 × 25,4 cm*, was illuminated by the monk Herimann in *c.* 1170 at Helmershansen Abbey with 41 full page illustrations, and was bought by Hans Kraus for the Hermann Abs consortium.

Printed Book

The highest price ever paid for a printed book is $2,400,000 (*then £1,265,000*) for one of the only 21 complete known copies of the Gutenberg Bible, printed in Mainz, W. Germany in *c.* 1454. It was bought from the Carl and Lily Pforzheimer Foundation by Texas University in a sale arranged by Quaritch of London in New York on 9 June 1978.

Broadsheet

The highest price ever paid for a broadsheet has been $412,500 (*then £264,500*) for one of the 22 known copies of *The Declaration of Independence*, printed in Philadelphia in 1776 by Samuel T. Freeman & Co, and sold to the Chapin Library, Williams College, Williamstown, Massachusetts, USA at Christie's, New York City on 22 Apr 1983.

Manuscripts

The highest price ever paid for a complete manuscript is £2.2 million by Armand Hammer at Christie's, London on 12 Dec 1980 for Leonardo da Vinci's 36-page Codex Leicester illustrated manuscript on cosmology compiled in *c.* 1507. It was sold by the trustees of the Holkham estate.

The auction record for a musical manuscript is £330,000 for *The Rite of Spring* by Igor F. Stravinsky (1882–1971), by Otto Haas for the Paul Sacher Collection in Basel, Switzerland at Sotheby's, London on 11 Nov 1982.

Atlas

The highest price paid for an atlas is £340,000 for a Gerardus Mercator atlas of *c.* 1571 of Europe, sold at Sotheby's, London, on 13 Mar 1979.

BIBLE

Oldest

The oldest leather and papyrus Dead Sea Scrolls were discovered in Cave 4 near Qumran in 1952. They comprise fragments of Exodus and Samuel I dating to *c.* 225–200 BC. The oldest known bible is the *Codex Vaticanus* written in Greek *ante* AD 350 and preserved in the Vatican Museum, Rome. The earliest complete Bible *printed* in English was one edited by Miles Coverdale, Bishop of Exeter (*c.* 1488–1569), while living in Antwerp, and printed in 1535. William Tyndale's New Testament in English had, however, been printed in Cologne and in Worms, Germany in 1525 while John Wycliffe's first manuscript translation dates from 1382.

Longest and shortest books

The longest book in the Authorized version of the Bible is the Book of Psalms, while the longest book including prose is the Book of the Prophet Isaiah, with 66 chapters. The shortest is the Third Epistle of John, with 294 words in 14 verses. The Second Epistle of John has only 13 verses but 298 words.

Longest and shortest psalm and verse

Of the 150 Psalms, the longest is the 119th, with 176 verses, and the shortest is the 117th, with two verses. The shortest verse in the Authorised Version (King James) of the Bible is verse 35 of Chapter XI of the Gospel according to St. John, consisting of the two words 'Jesus wept'. The longest is verse 9 of Chapter VIII of the Book of Esther, which extends to a 90-word description of the Persian empire.

Total letters and words, longest name

The total number of letters in the Bible is 3,566,480. The total number of words depends on the method of counting hyphenated words, but is usually given as between 773,692 and 773,746. The word 'and' according to Colin McKay Wilson of the Salvation Army appears 46,227 times. The longest personal name in the Bible is the 18 letter Maher-shalal-hash-baz, the symbolic name of the second son of Isaiah (Isaiah, Chapter VIII, verses 1 and 3). The caption of Psalm 22, however, contains a Hebrew title sometimes rendered Al-'Ayyeleth Hash-Shahar (20 letters).

DIARIES AND LETTERS

Longest diary

The diary of Edward Robb Ellis (b. 1911) of New York City begun in 1927 is estimated after 55 years to run to 15 million words. The diary of T. C. Baskerville of Chorlton-cum-Hardy, Manchester, maintained since 1939 comprises an estimated 5,000,000 words in 140 volumes. Col Ernest Loftus CBE of Harare, Zimbabwe began his daily diary on 4 May 1896 at the age of 12 and has thus completed 89 years.

Letters Longest

The longest personal letter based on a word count is one of 1,402,344 words started on 3 Jan 1982 by Alan Foreman of Erith, Kent, England and posted to his wife Janet on 25 Jan 1984.

To an editor *Longest*

The Upper Dauphin Sentinel of Pennsylvania, USA published a letter of 25,513 words over 8 issues from August to November 1979, written by John Sultzbaugh of Lykens, Pennsylvania.

Most

David Green, a solicitor, of Castle Morris, Dyfed had 106 letters published in the main correspondence columns of *The Times* by 1 May 1985. His record year was 1972 with 12.

Shortest

The shortest correspondence on record was that between Victor Marie Hugo (1802–85) and his publisher Hurst and Blackett in 1862. The author was on holiday and anxious to know how his new novel *Les Misérables* was selling. He wrote '?'. The reply was '!'.

The shortest letter to *The Times* was a letter comprising the single abbreviated symbol 'Dr² ?' in the interrogative from R. S. Cookson of London NW11, on 30 July 1984, in a correspondence on the correct form of recording a plurality of academic doctorates.

Most personal mail

The highest confirmed mail received by any private citizen in a year is 900,000 letters by the baseball star Hank Aaron reported by the US Postal Department in June 1974. About a third were letters of hate engendered by his bettering of 'Babe' Ruth's career record for 'home runs' set in 1927. (See Chap. 12.)

Pen pals most durable

The longest sustained correspondence on record is one of 75 years from 11 Nov 1904 between Mrs Ida McDougall of Tasmania, Australia and Miss R. Norton of Sevenoaks, Kent until Mrs McDougall's death on 24 Dec 1979.

Birthday card—most parsimonious

Mrs Amelia Finch (b. 18 Apr 1912) of Lakehurst, New Jersey, USA and Mr Paul E. Warburgh (b. 1 Feb 1902) of Huntington, New York have been exchanging the same card since 1 Feb 1927.

Christmas cards

The greatest number of personal Christmas cards sent out is believed to be 62,824 by Mrs Werner Erhard of San Francisco, California in December 1975. Many must have been to unilateral acquaintances. The earliest known Christmas card was sent out by Sir Henry Cole (1808–82) in 1843 but did not become an annual ritual until 1862.

AUTOGRAPHS AND SIGNATURES

Earliest

The earliest surviving examples of an autograph are those made by scribes on cuneiform clay tablets from Tell Abu Ṣalābīkh, Iraq dated to the early Dynastic III A *c.* 2600 BC. A scribe named 'a-du' has added 'dub-sar' after his name thus translating to 'Adu, scribe'. The earliest surviving signature on a papyrus is that of the scribe Amen-'aa dated to the Egyptian middle kingdom which began in *c.* 2130 BC and which is in the Leningrad Museum, USSR. A signum exists for William I (the Conqueror) *c.* 1070. The earliest English sovereign whose handwriting is known to have survived is Edward III (1327–77). The earliest full signature extant is that of Richard II (dated 26 July 1386). The Magna Carta does not bear even the mark of King John (reigned 1199–1216), but carries only his seal affixed on 19 June 1215.

Most expensive

The highest price ever paid on the open market for a single autograph letter signed is $100,000 (*then £45,500*), paid on 18 Oct 1979 at a Charles Hamilton auction in New York City for a brief receipt signed by the Gloucestershire-born Button Gwinnett (1732–77), one of the 56 signatories of the United States' Declaration of Independence of 1776.

The highest price paid for a signed autograph letter of a living person is $12,500 (*then £5430*) at the Hamilton Galleries on 22 Jan 1981 for a letter from President Ronald Reagan praising Frank Sinatra.

Generalissimo Stalin (1879–1953) whose written works were distributed and sold in numbers greater than Barbara Cartland and Agatha Christie combined. (see page 88) *(Popperfoto)*

A record $4250 (*then £2500*) was paid at a Hamilton sale on 12 Aug 1982 by Barry D Hoffman for the signed portrait of Al Capone (1899–1947).

Most valuable

Only one example of the signature of Christopher Marlowe (1564–93) is known. It is in the Kent County Archives on a Will of 1583. It is estimated that a seventh Shakespearean signature, should it ever come to light, might realise at least £1 million at auction.

AUTHORS

Most prolific

The champion of the goose quill era was Józef Ignacy Kraszewski (1812–87) of Poland who produced more than 600 volumes of novels and historical works. Until recently very high productivity had been attributed to Charles Hamilton, alias Frank Richards, (1875–1961) with up to 80,000 words a week in 1913 including the whole of the periodicals *Gem* (founded 1907) and *Magnet* (1908–40). In 1984 George Samways (b. 1894) asserted that Hamilton used him and others as 'ghost-writers'.

Soho Tokutomi (1863–1957) wrote the history *Kinsei Nippon Kokuminshi* in 100 volumes of 429,425 pages and 19,452,952 letters in 35 years.

Most novels

The greatest number of novels published by an authoress is 904 by Kathleen Lindsay (Mrs Mary Faulkner) (1903–73) of Somerset West, Cape Province, South Africa. She wrote under two other married names and 8 pen names. Baboorao Arnalkar (b. 9 June 1907) of Maharashtra State, India between 1936 and 1984 has published 1092 short mystery stories in book form and several non-fiction books.

After receiving a probable record 743 rejection slips the British novelist John Creasey MBE (1908–73), under his own name and 25 *noms de plume* had 564 books totalling more than 40,000,000 words published from 1932 to his death on 9 June 1973. The British authoress with the greatest total of full-length titles was Ursula Harvey Bloom (Mrs A. C. G. Robinson, formerly Mrs Denham-Cookes 1892–1984), who reached 560 in 1976, starting in 1924 with *The Great Beginning* and including the best sellers *The Ring Tree* (novel) and *The Rose of Norfolk* (non-fiction). Enid Mary Blyton (1898–1968) (Mrs Darrell Waters) completed 600 titles of children's stories, many of them brief, with 59 in the single year 1955. She was translated into a record 128 languages.

Most text books

Britain's most successful writer of text books is the ex-schoolmaster Ronald Ridout (b. 23 July 1916) who between 1948 and April 1985 had 480 titles published with sales of 83,400,000. His *The First English Workbook* has sold 5,090,000.

The annual aggregate sales of all titles by Louis Alexander of Haslemere, Surrey, reached 4,573,000 in the year 1977.

Highest paid

In 1958 Mrs Deborah Schneider of Minneapolis, Minnesota, USA, wrote 25 words to complete a sentence in a competition for the best blurb for Plymouth cars. She won from about 1,400,000 entrants the prize of $500 (*then £178*) every month for life. On normal life expectations she would have collected $12,000 (*£4285*) per word. No known anthology includes Mrs Schneider's deathless prose but it is in her deed box at her bank 'Only to be opened after death'. She passed $6000 a word by 1983.

Greatest Advance

The greatest advances paid for any book is an amount in excess of £3 million for Frederick Forsyth's seventh novel *The Fourth Protocol*.

Top selling

It was announced on 13 Mar 1953 that 672,058,000 copies of the works of Generalissimo Stalin (born Yózef Vissarionovich Dzhugashvili) (1879–1953), had been sold or distributed in 101 languages.

Currently the top-selling authoress is Barbara Cartland with global sales of 390,000,000 for 390 titles in 17 languages. In 1977, 1980 and 1981 she published 24 titles in the calendar year and 25 in 1982.

The all-time estimate of book sales by Erle Stanley Gardner (1889–1970) (US) to 1 Jan 1985 is 318,165,511 copies in 37 languages. The top selling lady crime writer has been Dame Agatha Christie (*née* Miller) (later Lady Mallowan) (1890–1976) whose 87 crime novels sold an estimated 300,000,000 in 103 languages. *Sleeping Murder* was published posthumously in 1977.

Longest Biography

The longest biography in publishing history is that of Sir Winston Churchill by his son Randolph (4832 pages) and Martin Gilbert (12,480 pages) to date comprising some 7,620,000 words.

Most rejections

The greatest recorded number of publishers' rejections for a manuscript is 204 for his 130,000

The late Agatha Christie (1890–1976) the unrivalled First Lady of Crime Writers. *(Popperfoto)*

word manuscript *World Government Crusade* written in 1966 by Gilbert Young (b. 1906) of Bath, England. The record for rejections before publication (and wide acclaim) is 69 from 55 publishers in the case of Prof. Steven Goldberg's *The Inevitability of Patriarchy*.

Oldest authoress

The oldest authoress in the world was Mrs Alice Pollock (*née* Wykeham-Martin) (1868–1971), of Haslemere, Surrey, whose book *Portrait of My Victorian Youth* (Johnson Publications) was published in March 1971 when she was aged 102 years 8 months.

Literary luncheons

Literary luncheons were inaugurated by Christina Foyle (Mrs Ronald Batty) in October 1930 at the Old Holborn Restaurant, London. Attendances reached over 1500 at the Grosvenor House, Park Lane, London at lunches for Mistinguett (1873–1956) and Dr Edvard Benes (1884–1948) in 1938.

Longest literary gestation

The standard German dictionary *Deutsches Wörterbuch*, begun by the brothers Grimm in 1854, was finished in 1971. *Acta Sanctorum* begun by Jean Bolland in 1643, arranged according to saints' days, reached the month of November in 1925 and an introduction for December was published in 1940. Oxford University Press received back their proofs of *Constable's Presentments* from the Dugdale Society in Dec 1984. They had been sent out for correction 35 years earlier in Dec 1949.

Poet Laureate *Youngest and oldest*

The youngest Poet Laureate was Laurence Eusden (1688–1730), who received the bays on 24 Dec 1718 at the age of 30 years and 3 months. The greatest age at which a poet has succeeded is 73 in the case of William Wordsworth (1770–1850) on 6 Apr 1843. The longest lived Laureate was John Masefield, OM, who died on 12 May 1967, aged 88 years 345 days. The longest which any poet has worn the laurel is 41 years 322 days, in the case of Alfred (later the 1st Lord) Tennyson (1809–92), who was appointed on 19 Nov 1850 and died in office on 6 Oct 1892.

Longest poem

The lengthiest poem ever published has been the Kirghiz folk epic *Manas*, which appeared in printed form in 1958 but which has never been translated into English. It runs to 'more than 500,000 lines'. Short translated passages appear in *The Elek Book of Oriental Verse*.

The longest poem ever written in the English language is one on the life of King Alfred by John Fitchett (1766–1838) of Liverpool which ran to 129,807 lines and took 40 years to write. His editor Robert Riscoe added the concluding 2585 lines.

Roger Brien's (b. Montreal, 1910) *Prométhée—dialogue des vivants et des morts* runs to 456,047 lines written in 1964–81. Brien has written another 497,000 lines of French poetry in over 90 published works.

Most successful

The most translated poem is believed to be *If* by Joseph Rudyard Kipling (1865–1936), first published in 1910. It was put into 27 languages and according to Kipling 'anthologized to weariness'.

HIGHEST PRINTINGS

World

The world's most widely distributed book is the Bible, which has been translated into 286 languages and portions of it into a further 1522 languages. This compares with 222 languages for Lenin. It has been estimated that between 1815 and 1975 some 2,500,000,000 copies were printed of which 1,500,000,000 were handled by Bible Societies. *The English Good News Bible*, translation of the New Testament (which is copyright of The Bible Society), sold 80,000,000 copies in the period 1976–80.

The King James version is not copyright but at least 14 copyrights exist on other versions. The oldest publisher of Bibles is the Cambridge University Press which began with the Geneva version in 1591.

It has been reported that 800,000,000 copies of the red-covered booklet *Quotations from the Works of Mao Tse-tung* were sold or distributed between June 1966, when possession became virtually mandatory in China, and September 1971 when their promoter Marshal Lin Piao died in an air crash.

It is believed that in the USA Van Antwerp Bragg and Co. printed some 60 million copies of the 1879 edition of *The McGuffey Reader*, compiled by Henry Vail in the pre-copyright era for distribution to public schools.

The total disposal through non-commercial channels by Jehovah's Witnesses of *The Truth That Leads to Eternal Life* published by the Watchtower Bible and Tract Society of Brooklyn, New York, on 8 May 1968, reached 105,250,000 in 115 languages by May 1984.

BEST SELLERS

Excluding versions of the Bible, the world's all-time best selling copyright book is the *Guinness Book of Records* first published from 107 Fleet Street, London EC4 in September 1955 by the Guinness Brewery to settle arguments in Britain's 81,400 pubs and edited by Norris Dewar McWhirter (b. 12 Aug 1925) and his twin brother Alan Ross McWhirter (k. 27 Nov 1975). Its cumulative sale in 25 languages to mid-1985 was in excess of 51 million copies and increasing by some 50,000 per week.

Best Seller Lists

The *Sunday Times* best seller list (which excludes books published annually) was first published on 14 Apr 1974. *The Country Diary of an Edwardian Lady* (Michael Joseph, Webb & Bower) held No 1 position for 64 weeks up to the paper's 10 month closure which started on 30 Nov 1978. Its global sales in 13 languages reached 2,613,276 copies by April 1985. The longest duration on the *New York Times* best sellers' list (founded 1935) is 'A Light in the Attic' by Shelby Silverstein (b. 1932) which on 10 Jan 1985 had its 112th week on the lists.

Fiction

The novel with the highest sales has been *Valley of the Dolls* (first published March 1966) by Jacqueline Susann (Mrs Irving Mansfield) (1921–74) with a world-wide total of 27,465,000 to 1 May 1985. In the first 6 months Bantam sold 6.8 million. In the United Kingdom the highest print order has been 3,000,000 by Penguin Books Ltd. for their paperback edition of *Lady Chatterley's Lover*, by D. H. (David Herbert) Lawrence (1885–1930). The total sales to May 1985 were 4,640,000. Alistair Stuart MacLean (b. Scotland, April 1922) between 1955 and 1982 wrote 26 books of which the sales of 18 have exceeded a million copies and 13 have been filmed. *The Cruel Sea* by Nicholas Monsarrat (1910–79) published in 1951 by Cassell, reached sales of 1,200,000 in its *original* edition.

Fastest Publisher

The fastest time in which a book has been published is less than 24 hours by Corgi Books from receipt of final manuscript to finished copies, in the case of John Lisners' *The House of Horrors* a 223 page paperback on the mass murderer in North London Dennis Nilsen sentenced to life imprisonment at 4.23 pm on 4 Nov 1983. (See Crime, Chapter 11.)

Slowest seller

The accolade for the world's slowest selling book (known in US publishing as slooow-sellers) probably belongs to David Wilkins's Translation of the New Testament from Coptic into Latin published by Oxford University Press in 1716 in 500 copies. Selling an average of one each 139 days, it remained in print for 191 years.

PUBLISHERS AND PRINTERS

Oldest Publisher

Cambridge University Press has a continuous history of printing and publishing since 1584. The University received Royal Letters Patent to print and sell all manner of books on 20 July 1534.

In 1978 the Oxford University Press celebrated the 500th anniversary of the printing of the first book in the City of Oxford in 1478. This was before OUP was itself in existence.

Prolific Publisher

In terms of new titles per annum Britain's most prolific publisher in 1984 was Cambridge University Press with 833. The UK published a record 51,155 book titles in 1984 of which a record 11,309 were reprints.

Largest Printer *World*

The largest printers in the world are R. R. Donnelley & Sons Co. of Chicago, Illinois, USA. The company, founded in 1864, has plants in 15 main centres, turning out $1,814,000,000 (*£1500 million*) worth of work per year. More than 133,000 tons of inks and 1,645,000 tons of paper and board are consumed every year.

The largest printer under one roof is the United States Government Printing Office (founded 1860) in Washington, DC, USA. The Superintendent of Documents sold in 1984 almost $60 million (*£50 million*) worth of US governmental publications every year and maintains an inventory of over 17,200 titles in print.

Shown here is one of 7 floors of Glasgow's Mitchell Library—Europe's largest public reference library. *(Alex Hansen)*

Print order

The initial print order for the 53rd Automobile Association Members' Handbook (1984–5) was 4,800,000 copies. The total print since 1908 has been 86,700,000. It is currently printed by web offset by Petty & Sons of Leeds.

The aggregate print of The Highway Code (instituted 1931) reached 90,000,000 after 50 years in mid-1981.

LIBRARIES

Largest *World*

The largest library in the world is the United States Library of Congress (founded on 24 Apr 1800), on Capitol Hill, Washington, DC. By 1984 it contained 80 million items, including 20 million volumes and pamphlets. The buildings contain 64.6 acres *26.14 ha* of floor space and contain 532 miles *856 km* of shelving. The James Madison Memorial Extension was dedicated in April 1980 and has 34.5 acres *14 ha* of floor space.

The largest non-statutory library in the world is the New York Public Library (founded 1895) on Fifth Avenue with a floor space of 525,276 ft² *48 800 m²* and 88 miles *141,6 km* of shelving. Its collection including 81 branch libraries embraces 8,993,227 volumes, 13,387,793 manuscripts and 358,534 maps.

The greatest personal library ever amassed was that of Sir Thomas Phillipps. Dispersal began in 1886. The residue was bought largely unseen by the brothers Lionel Robinson CBE MC and Philip Robinson for £100,000. Sales began on 1 July 1946.

Great Britain

The largest library in the United Kingdom is the British Library, dispersed among more than 20 buildings in London and a 60 acre *24,3 ha* site at Boston Spa, West Yorkshire, with a total staff of over 2500. The British Library Reference Division contains over 11,330,000 volumes. Stock increases involve over 4 miles *6,43 km* of added material annually. The British Library's Newspaper Library at Colindale, North London, opened in 1932, has 556,700 volumes and parcels and 191,600 reels of microfilm comprising 70,000 different titles on 22 miles *35,4 km* of shelving. The British Library Lending Division in West Yorkshire (shelf capacity 96 miles *154,5 km*) runs the largest library inter-lending operation in the world; it handles annually nearly 3 million requests from other libraries (UK and overseas) for items they do not hold in stock. The British Library National Sound Archive holds 500,000 discs and 35,000 hours of recorded tape. The largest public library in the United Kingdom is the extended Mitchell Library, North Street, Glasgow with a floor area of 538,200 ft² *50 000 m²* or 12.3 acres *4,9 ha* and an ultimate capacity for 4,000,000 volumes. The Mitchell also houses Europe's largest public reference library.

Overdue books
The most overdue book taken out by a known borrower was one reported on 7 Dec 1968, checked out in 1823 from the University of Cincinnati Medical Library on Febrile Diseases (London, 1805 by Dr J. Currie). This was returned by the borrower's great-grandson Richard Dodd. The fine calculated to be $2264 (*then £1102 10s*) was waived.

NEWSPAPERS

Oldest *World*
A copy has survived of a news pamphlet published in Cologne, West Germany in 1470. The oldest existing newspaper in the world is the Swedish official journal *Post och Inrikes Tidningar*, founded in 1645. It is published by the Royal Swedish Academy of Letters. The oldest existing commercial newspaper is the *Haarlems Dagblad/Oprechte Haarlemsche Courant*, published in Haarlem, in the Netherlands. The *Courant* was first issued as the *Weeckelycke Courante van Europa* on 8 Jan 1656 and a copy of issue No. 1 survives.

United Kingdom
The newspaper with the earliest origins in the United Kingdom is *Berrow's Worcester Journal* (originally the *Worcester Post Man*), published in Worcester. It was traditionally founded in 1690 and has appeared weekly since June 1709. No complete file exists. The earliest date of foundation for any British newspaper published under the same title is the *Stamford Mercury*, printed since 1712 and traditionally even 1695. The *London Gazette* (originally the *Oxford Gazette*) was first published on 16 Nov 1665. The oldest Sunday newspaper is *The Observer*, first issued on 4 Dec 1791.

Largest and smallest
The most massive single issue of a newspaper was the 7½ lb *3,40 kg* New York Times of Sunday 17 Oct 1965. It comprised 15 sections with a total of 946 pages, including about 1,200,000 lines of advertising and had a cover price in May 1985 of $1.25 (then £1.07) for the Sunday edition. The largest page size ever used has been 51 in × 35 in *130 cm × 89 cm* for *The Constellation*, printed in 1859 by George Roberts as part of the Fourth of July celebrations in New York City, NY, USA. The *Worcestershire Chronicle* was the largest British newspaper. A surviving issue of 16 Feb 1859 measures 32¼ in × 22½ in *82 cm × 57 cm*. The smallest original page size has been 3 × 3¾ in *7,6 × 9,5 cm* of the *Daily Banner* (25 cents per month) of Roseberg, Oregon, USA, issues of which, dated 1 and 2 Feb 1876, survive. The *Answers to Correspondents* published by Messrs Carr & Co, Paternoster Square, London in 1888 was 3½ × 4½ in *9 × 11 cm*. The British Library Newspaper Library has a copy of the *Watford News and Advertiser* of 1 Apr 1899 measuring 2.9 × 3.9 in *7,5 × 10 cm*.

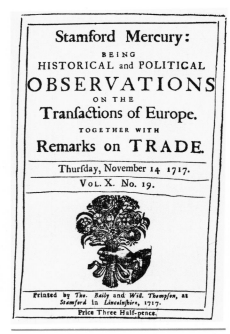

Stamford Mercury:
BEING
HISTORICAL and POLITICAL
OBSERVATIONS
ON THE
Tranſactions of Europe.
TOGETHER WITH
Remarks on TRADE.
Thurſday, November 14 1717.
VOL. X. No. 19.

Printed by Tho. Baily and Will. Thompſon, at
Stamford in Lincolnſhire, 1717.
Price Three Half-pence.

An early edition of the Stamford Mercury, the most durable British newspaper to appear continuously under its own name.

Most expensive
Britain's most expensive paper is *The Sunday Times* at 50p (or 10s 0d in the money prior to 15 Feb 1971), or double the price of the original 1955 fully bound edition.

Most
The United States has 1692 English-language daily newspapers at 1 May 1985 with a combined net paid circulation of 62,000,000 copies per day. The peak year for US newspapers was 1910, when there were 2202. The leading newspaper readers in the world are the people of Sweden, where 554 newspapers are sold for each 1000 compared with the UK figure of 410.

Longest editorship
Sir Etienne Dupuch OBE of Nassau, Bahamas, editor of the *Tribune* since 1 Apr 1919 entered his 66th year in the chair on 1 Apr 1984. The longest editorship of any United Kingdom national newspaper has been more than 59 years by C. P. Scott (1846–1932) of the (then *Manchester*) *Guardian*, who was appointed aged 25 in 1877 and died on 1 Jan 1932.

Most durable feature
The longest lasting feature in the British national press from one pen was *Your Stars* by Edward Lyndoe. It ran from Oct 1933 to 1982 in *The Sunday People*. Frank Lowe has contributed a weekly natural history column to the *Bolton Evening News* every week since 4 Feb 1926. Albert E. Pool (b. 1909) has been a part-time journalist for the *Lincolnshire and South Humberside* (formerly *The Hull*) *Times* since March 1923.

Biggest headline
Tovells School, Grays, Essex reproduced the front page of their local newspaper, the *Thurrock Gazette*, in a blown up edition comprising 11,664 sheets of A1 paper measuring 180 × 270 ft *54,86 × 82,29 m* staked out on 4 July 1984. The headline was 3 ft *91,4 cm* deep.

Most syndicated cartoonist
Ranan R. Lurie (b. 26 May 1932) of the Asahi Shimbun is the most widely syndicated political cartoonist in the world. His work is published in 51 countries in 400 newspapers with a combined circulation of 62 million copies.

Longest lived strip
The most durable newspaper comic strip has been the Katzenjammer Kids (Hans and Fritz) created by Rudolph Dirks and first published in the *New York Journal* on 12 Dec 1897 and perpetuated by his son John. The earliest strip was The Yellow Kid, which first appeared in the New York *Journal* on 18 Oct 1896. The most widely syndicated is *Peanuts* appearing in 2,033 newspapers and *Blondie* which also appears in more than 2,000 papers.

Most misprints
The record for misprints in *The Times* was set on 22 Aug 1978 when on page 19 there were 97 in 5½ single column inches. The passage concerned 'Pop' (Pope) Paul VI.

Most durable advertiser
The Jos Neel Co, a clothing store in Macon, Georgia, USA (founded 1880) has run an 'ad' in the *Macon Telegraph* every day in the upper left corner of page 2 since 22 Feb 1889 or 35,063 times to Feb 1985.

CIRCULATION
Earliest 1,000,000
The first newspaper to achieve a circulation of 1,000,000 was *Le Petit Journal*, published in Paris, France, which reached this figure in 1886, when selling at 5 centimes. The *Daily Mail* first reached a million on 2 Mar 1900.

Highest *World*
The highest circulation for any newspaper in the world is that for the *Yomiuri Shimbun* (founded 1874) of Japan which attained a figure of 13,968,082 copies on 1 April 1985. This is achieved by totalling the figures for editions published in various centres with a morning figure of 9,053,196 and an evening figure of 4,914,886. It reaches 38 per cent of Japan's 34 million households. It has a staff of 3060 and 436 bureaux. *Trud*, the Soviet trade union daily, is printed in 53 cities in 15.4 million copies of which only 70,000 are bought at newsstands.

Great Britain
The highest circulation of any single newspaper in Britain is that of the Sunday newspaper *The News of the World*, printed at 30 Bouverie Street, London EC4. Single issues have attained a sale of 9,000,000 copies with an estimated readership of more than 19,000,000. The paper first appeared on 1 Oct 1843, and surpassed the million mark in 1905. The latest sales figure is 4,698,341 copies per issue (average for 1 July to 31 Dec 1984), with an estimated readership of 10,939,000.

The highest net sale of any daily newspaper in the United Kingdom is that of *The Sun*, founded in London in 1964. The latest sales figure is 4,083,573 (1 July to 31 Dec 1984), with an estimated readership of 12,410,000.

Most read
The national newspaper which achieves the closest to a saturation circulation is *The Sunday Post*, established in Glasgow in 1914. In 1984 its estimated readership in Scotland of 2,653,000 represented 65 per cent of the entire population aged 15 and over. The *Arran Banner* (founded March 1974) has a readership of 97+ per cent on Britain's seventh largest off-shore island.

PERIODICALS
Oldest *World*
The oldest continuing periodical in the world is

Philosophical Transactions of the Royal Society, published in London, which first appeared on 6 Mar 1665.

Great Britain

The bi-monthly *The Gospel Magazine* has been published since 1766. Curtis's *Botanical Magazine* has been in continuous publication since 1 Feb 1787, as several 'parts' a year forming a series of continuously numbered volumes. Britain's oldest weekly periodical is *Lancet* first published in 1823. The *Scots Magazine* began publication in 1739 and ran till 1826, and with three breaks has been produced continuously since 1924.

Largest circulations *World*

The largest circulation of any weekly periodical is that of *TV Guide* (USA) which in 1974 became the first magazine in history to sell a billion (1000 million) copies in a year. The weekly average for July–December 1983 was 17,115,233. In its 40 basic international editions *The Reader's Digest* (established February 1922) circulates 30,141,000 copies monthly in 17 languages, including a United States edition of more than 17,750,000 copies and a United Kingdom edition (established 1939) of 1,536,676 copies (av. January–December 1984).

Parade, the syndicated Sunday newspaper colour magazine, is distributed with 135 newspapers every Sunday. The current circulation is 25,153,000 (April 1985). Britain's highest circulation Sunday colour supplement is the *News of the World's SunDay* at 4,698,341 (1984). (See also p. 90).

Great Britain

The highest circulation of any periodical in Great Britain is that of the *Radio Times* (instituted on 28 Sept 1923). The average weekly sale for July–December 1984 was 3,296,866 copies with a readership of 9,037,000. The highest sale of any issue was 9,778,062 copies for the Christmas issue of 1955. *TV Times* averaged sales of 3,220,401 in the period July–Dec 1984 with an estimated readership of 10,340,000 (July–Dec 1984).

Annual

Old Moore's Almanack has been published annually since 1697, when it first appeared as a broadsheet, by Dr Francis Moore (1657–1715) of Southwark, London to advertise his 'physiks'. The annual sale certified by its publishers W. Foulsham & Co. Ltd of Slough, England is 1 million copies and its aggregate sale is estimat· to be in excess of 108 million.

CROSSWORDS

First

The earliest known crossword was a 9 by 9 Double Diamond published in *St Nicholas* for September 1875 in New York City, USA. This was discovered by Dr Kenneth Miller of Newcastle upon Tyne, England inventor of the colour crossword in 1983. The first crossword published in a British newspaper was one furnished by C. W. Shepherd in the *Sunday Express* of 2 Nov 1924. However a 25 letter acrostic of Roman provenance was discovered on a wall in Cirencester, England in 1868.

Largest

The world's largest published crossword has been one compiled by Robert Trucot of Québec, Canada. It contained 12,489 clues across and 13,125 down and covered 38.28 ft² *3,55 m²*.

Fastest and slowest solution

The fastest recorded time for completing *The Times* crossword under test conditions is 3 min 45.0 sec by Roy Dean, 43 of Bromley, Greater

Sun vans loading midway through the paper's 8 hour print run of over 4 million—the highest of any daily paper in Britain.

London in the BBC 'Today' radio studio on 19 Dec 1970. Dr John Sykes won the *Times* championship 4 times (1972–5). In May 1966 *The Times* of London received an announcement from a Fijian woman that she had just succeeded in completing their crossword No. 673 in the issue of 4 Apr 1932.

Most durable compilers

Adrian Bell (1901–1980) of Barsham, Suffolk contributed a record 4520 crosswords to *The Times* from 2 Jan 1930 until his death. R. J. Baddock of Plymouth (b. 30 Oct 1894) has been a regular contributor to national newspapers since 13 Aug 1926. The most prolific compiler is Roger F. Squires of Ironbridge, Shropshire, who compiles 35 published puzzles single-handedly each week. His total output to August 1985 was over 25,000.

A front page of the Sunday colour supplement 'Parade' with a circulation of nearly 25,000,000— the highest in the world.

ADVERTISING RATES

The highest ever price for a single page has been $327,230 (*£272,691*) for a four-colour back cover in *Parade* (circulation 25.2 million per week) in April 1985 (see above). The record for a four colour inside page is $284,560 (*£182,430*) in *Parade* (in April 1985). The advertising revenue from the November 1982 US edition of *The Reader's Digest* was a peak $14,716,551 (*then £9,495,000*).

The highest expenditure ever incurred on a single advertisement in a periodical is $3,200,000 (*£1,600,000*) by Gulf and Western Industries on 5 Feb 1979 for insertions in *Time* Magazine (US and selected overseas editions). The British record is some £100,000 for a 20-page colour supplement by Woolworths in the *Radio Times* of 16 Nov 1972. The rate for a single page in *Sunday* magazine is £25,000, and £41,000 for a centre spread (April 1985). The world's highest newspaper advertising rate is 37,350,000 Yen (*£117,823*) for a full page in the morning edition and 30,825,000 Yen (*£97,240*) for the evening edition of the *Yomiuri Shimbun* of Tokyo (April 1984). The highest rate in Britain is a full page in *The Sunday Express* at £33,600 (May 1985).

4. MUSIC

The Guinness Book of Music (2nd edition) (price £8.95), by Robert and Celia Dearling with Brian Rust was published in Spring 1981 and contains more detailed treatment of musical facts and superlatives.

Origins

Whistles and flutes made from perforated phalange bones have been found at Upper Palaeolithic sites of the Aurignacian period (*c.* 25,000–22,000 BC) *e.g.* at Istallóskö, Hungary and in Molodova, USSR. The world's earliest surviving musical notation dates from *c.* 1800 BC. A heptatonic scale deciphered from a clay tablet by Dr Duchesne-Guillemin in 1966–7 was found at a site in Nippur, Sumer, now Iraq. An Assyrian love song also *c.* 1800 BC to an Ugaritic god from a tablet of notation and lyric was reconstructed for an 11 string lyre at the University of California, Berkeley on 6 Mar 1974. Musical history is, however, able to be traced back to the 3rd millennium BC, when the yellow bell (*huang chung*) had a recognised standard musical tone in Chinese temple music.

INSTRUMENTS

Piano *Earliest*

The earliest pianoforte in existence is one built in Florence, Italy, in 1720 by Bartolommeo Cristofori (1655–1731) of Padua, and now preserved in the Metropolitan Museum of Art, New York City.

Piano *Grandest*

The grandest grand piano built was one of 1¼ tons/*tonnes* 11 ft 8 in *3,55 m* in length made by Chas. H. Challen & Son Ltd of London in 1935. The longest bass string measured 9 ft 11 in *3,02 m* with a tensile of 30 tons/*tonnes*.

Piano *Most Expensive*

The highest price ever paid for a piano is $390,000 (*then £177,273*) at Sotheby Parke Bernet, New York City on 26 Mar 1980 for a Steinway grand of *c.* 1888 sold by the Martin Beck Theatre and bought by a non-pianist.

Organ largest *World*

The largest and loudest musical instrument ever constructed is the now only partially functional Auditorium Organ in Atlantic City, New Jersey, USA. Completed in 1930, this heroic instrument had two consoles (one with seven manuals and another movable one with five), 1477 stop controls and 33,112 pipes ranging in tone from $\frac{3}{16}$ of an inch *4,7 mm* to the 64 ft *19,5 m* tone. It had the volume of 25 brass bands, with a range of seven octaves. The world's largest fully functional organ is the six manual 30,067 pipe Grand Court Organ installed in the Wanamaker Store, Philadelphia, Pennsylvania, USA in 1911 and enlarged between then and 1930. It has a 64 ft *19,5 m* tone gravissima pipe. The world's largest church organ is that in Passau Cathedral, Germany. It was completed in 1928 by D. F. Steinmeyer & Co. It was built with 16,000 pipes and five manuals. The world's most powerful electronic organ is the 5000 watt Royal V. Rogers organ, designed by Virgil Fox with 465 speakers installed by Orient Shoji Co in Chuo-ku, Tokyo, Japan in June 1983. The chapel organ at West Point US Military Academy, NY has, since 1911, been expanded from 2406 to 18,200 pipes.

Great Britain

The largest organ in Great Britain is that completed in Liverpool Anglican Cathedral on 18 Oct 1926, with two five-manual consoles of which only one is now in use, and 9704 speaking pipes (originally 10,936) ranging from tones ¾ in to 32 ft *1,9 cm to 9,75 m*.

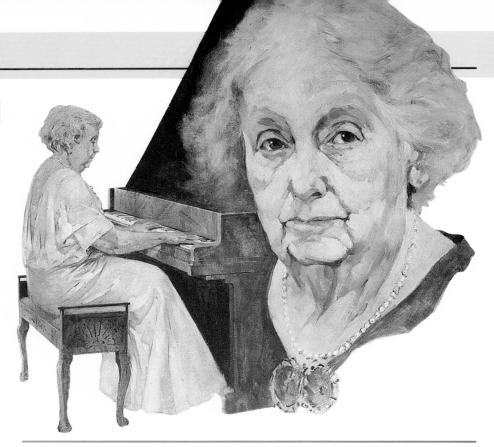

The world's most durable concert pianist, Elsie Hall, who performed publicly for 90 years between 1884 and 1974. *(Reader's Digest)*

Musicians *Most Durable*

Elsie Maude Stanley Hall (1877–1976) gave piano recitals for 90 years giving her final concert in Rustenburg. Transvaal, South Africa aged 97. Charles Bridgeman (1779–1873) of All Saints Parish Church, Hertford, England, who was appointed organist in 1792, was still playing 81 years later in 1873. Norwegian pianist Reidar Thommesen (b. 7 June 1889) played over 30 hours a week in theatre cafés when a nonagenarian.

Loudest organ stop

The loudest organ stop in the world is the Ophicleide stop of the Grand Great in the Solo Organ in the Atlantic City Auditorium (see above). It is operated by a pressure of 100 in *254 cm* of water (3½ lb/in² *24 kPa*) and has a pure trumpet note of ear-splitting volume, more than six times the volume of the loudest locomotive whistles.

Brass instrument *Largest*

The largest recorded brass instrument is a tuba standing 7½ ft *2,28 m* tall, with 39 ft *11,8 m* of tubing and a bell 3 ft 4 in *1 m* across. This contrabass tuba was constructed for a world tour by the band of John Philip Sousa (1854–1932), the United States composer, in *c.* 1896–8, and is still in use. This instrument is now owned by a circus promoter in South Africa.

Horns *Longest Alphorn*

The longest alphorn is one of 17,98 m *59 ft* built from a spruce log by Herr Stocker in Switzerland in 1976. It was demonstrated by Herr Lamy for David Frost on 28 June 1981.

Stringed instrument *Largest*

The largest movable stringed instrument ever constructed was a pantaleon with 270 strings stretched over 50 ft² *4,6 m²* used by George Noel in 1767. The greatest number of musicians required to operate a single instrument was the six required to play the gigantic orchestrion, known as the Apollonican, built in 1816 and played until 1840.

Guitar *Largest and Most Expensive*

The largest and presumably also the loudest playable guitar in the world is one 10 ft 1 in *3,07 m* tall, and in excess of 300 lb *136 kg* in weight, built by Sparkling Ragtime Productions of San Francisco, and the Guild of American Luthiers, Tacoma, Washington, USA in December 1980. The most expensive standard sized guitar is the German chittara battente by Jacob Stadler, dated 1624, which was sold for £10,500 at Christie's, London on 12 June 1974.

'Bass Ten' from Bournemouth who have now succeeded in outnumbering the double bass eleven to one (see page 93).

Double bass *Largest and Most players*

The largest double bass ever constructed was one 14 ft *4,26 m* tall, built in 1924 in Ironia, New Jersey, USA by Arthur K. Ferris, allegedly on orders from the Archangel Gabriel. It weighed 11.6 cwt. *590 kg* with a sound box 8 ft *2,43 m* across, and had leathern strings totalling 104 ft *31,7 m*. Its low notes could be felt rather than heard. On 27 June 1984 5 members of 'Bass Ten' from Bournemouth, Dorset bowed and six fingered a double bass simultaneously in a rendition of Monti's *Czardas* at Hever Castle, Kent.

'Cello *Most valuable*

The highest ever auction price for a violoncello is £145,000 at Sotheby's, London on 8 Nov 1978 for a Stradivari made in Cremona, Italy in 1710.

Violin *Most valuable*

The highest ever price paid at auction for a violin or any musical instrument is £396,000 for La Cathédrale Stradivari dated 1707 at Sotheby's, London on 22 Nov 1984. Some 700 of the 1116 violins by Stradivarius (1644–1737) have survived. His Alarol violin was confirmed by Jacques Francais to have been sold by private treaty by W. E. Hill for $1.2 million (*then £600,000*) to a Singaporean.

Violinist *Underwater*

The pioneer violinist to surmount the problems of playing the violin underwater was Mark Gottlieb. Submerged in Evergreen State College swimming bath in Olympia, Washington, USA in March 1975 he gave a submarine rendition of Handel's Water Music. His most intractable problem was his underwater *détaché*. On 7 Oct 1979 the first underwater quartet performed in the *Challenge the Guinness* TV show on Channel 7 in Tokyo, Japan.

Most durable fiddlers

Rolland S. Tapley retired as a violinist from the Boston Symphony Orchestra after playing for a reputedly unrivalled 58 years from February 1920 to 27 Aug 1978. Otto E. Funk, 62, walked 4165 miles *6702 km* from New York City to San Francisco, California playing his Hopf violin every step of the way westward. He arrived on 16 June 1929 after 183 days on the road.

Drum *Largest*

The largest drum ever constructed was one 12 ft *3,65 m* in diameter weighing 600 lb *272 kg* for the Boston World Peace Jubilee of 1872.

Highest and lowest notes

The extremes of orchestral instruments (excluding the organ) range between a handbell tuned to g^v (6272 cycles/sec) and the sub-contrabass clarinet, which can reach C_{11} or 16.4 cycles/sec. The highest note on a standard pianoforte is c^v (4186 cycles/sec), which is also the violinist's limit. In 1873 a sub double bassoon able to reach $B_{111}\#$ or 14.6 cycles/sec was constructed but no surviving specimen is known. The extremes for the organ are g^{vi} (the sixth G above middle C) (12,544 cycles/sec) and C_{111} (8.12 cycles/sec) obtainable from ¾ in *1,9 cm* and 64 ft *19,5 m* pipes respectively.

Easiest and most difficult instruments

The American Music Conference announced in September 1977 that the easiest instrument is the ukulele, and the most difficult are the French horn and the oboe, which latter has been described as 'the ill woodwind that no-one blows good'.

ORCHESTRAS

Largest *Orchestra*

The most massive orchestra ever assembled was one of 20,100 at the Ullevaal Stadium, Oslo, of

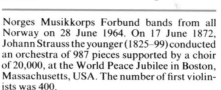

Known as 'La Cathédrale', this 1707 Stradivari violin made £396,000 at auction— the highest price ever for a musical instrument. *(Sotheby's, London)*

Norges Musikkorps Forbund bands from all Norway on 28 June 1964. On 17 June 1872, Johann Strauss the younger (1825–99) conducted an orchestra of 987 pieces supported by a choir of 20,000, at the World Peace Jubilee in Boston, Massachusetts, USA. The number of first violinists was 400.

Marching band

The largest marching band on record was one of 4524 including 1342 majorettes under direction of Danny Kaye at Dodger stadium, Los Angeles on 15 Apr 1985. The longest recorded musical march is one of 61 km *37.9 miles* from Lillehammer to Hamar, Norway in 15 hours when, on 10 May 1980, 26 of 35 members of the Trondheim Brass Band survived the playing of 135 marches.

Most Durable

The Cork Symphony Orchestra has performed under the baton of Dr Aloys Fleischmann for 50 seasons (1935–84).

Most successful bands

Most British Open Brass band Championship titles (inst. 1853) have been won by the Black Dyke Mills Band which has won 22 times from 1862 to 1974 including three consecutive wins in 1972–4. The most successful pipe band is the Shotts & Dykehead Caledonian Pipe Band with their 10th world title in August 1980.

Greatest attendance *Classical*

The greatest attendance at any classical concert has been 400,000 for the Boston Pops Orchestra, conducted by Arthur Fiedler (1895–1979) at the Hatch Memorial Shell, Boston, Massachusetts, USA on 4 July 1976. At the 1978 concert the 83-year-old conductor was presented with a testimonial bearing a record 500,000 signatures.

Pop Festival

The greatest claimed attendance at a Pop Festival has been 600,000

for the 'Summer Jam' at Watkins Glen, New York, USA, on Sunday 29 July 1973 of whom about 150,000 actually paid. There were 12 'sound towers'. The attendance at the third Pop Festival at East Afton Farm, Freshwater, Isle of Wight, England on 30 Aug 1970 was claimed by its promoters, Fiery Creations, to be 400,000.

Single Performer

The largest paying audience ever attracted by a solo performer is an estimated 175,000 in the Maracaña Stadium, Rio de Janeiro, Brazil to hear Frank Sinatra (b. 1915) on 26 Jan 1980. Elton John entertained an estimated 400,000 in

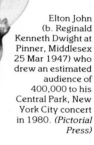

Elton John (b. Reginald Kenneth Dwight at Pinner, Middlesex 25 Mar 1947) who drew an estimated audience of 400,000 to his Central Park, New York City concert in 1980. *(Pictorial Press)*

Central Park, New York City, USA at a free concert in the summer of 1980.

Greatest Choir

Excluding 'sing alongs' by stadium crowds, the greatest choir is one of 60,000 which sang in unison as a finale of a choral contest among 160,000 participants in Breslau, Germany on 2 Aug 1937.

COMPOSERS

Most prolific

The most prolific composer of all time was probably Georg Philipp Telemann (1681–1767) of Germany. He composed 12 complete sets of services (one cantata every Sunday) for a year, 78 services for special occasions, 40-operas, 600 to 700 orchestral suites, 44 Passions, plus concertos and chamber music. The most prolific symphonist was Johann Melchior Molter (c. 1695–1765) of Germany who wrote 169. Joseph Haydn (1732–1809) of Austria wrote 108 numbered symphonies many of which are regularly played today.

Most rapid

Among composers of the classical period the most prolific was Wolfgang Amadeus Mozart (1756–91) of Austria, who wrote c. 1000 operas, operettas, symphonies, violin sonatas, divertimenti, serenades, motets, concertos for piano and many other instruments, string quartets, other chamber music, masses and litanies, of which only 70 were published before he died aged 35. His opera *The Clemency of Titus* (1791) was written in 18 days and three symphonic masterpieces, *Symphony No. 39 in E flat major*, *Symphony in G minor* and the *Jupiter Symphony in C*, were reputedly written in the space of 42 days in 1788. His overture *Don Giovanni* was written in full score at one sitting in Prague in 1787 and finished on the day of its opening performance.

Longest symphony

The longest of all single classical symphonies is the orchestral symphony No. 3 in D minor by Gustav Mahler (1860–1911) of Austria. This work, composed in 1896, requires a contralto, a women's and boys' choir in addition to a full orchestra. A full performance requires 1 hr 40 min, of which the first movement alone takes between 30 and 36 min. The Symphony No. 2 (the Gothic, or No. 1), composed in 1919–22 by Havergal Brian (1876–1972) was played by over 800 performers (4 brass bands) in the Victoria Hall, Hanley, Staffordshire on 21 May 1978 (conductor Trevor Stokes). A recent broadcast required 1 hr 45½ min. Brian wrote an even vaster work based on Shelley's 'Prometheus Unbound' lasting 4 hr 11 min but the full score has been missing since 1961. The symphony *Victory at Sea* written by Richard Rodgers and arranged by Robert Russell Bennett for NBC TV in 1952 lasted for 13 hr.

Longest piano composition

The longest continuous non-repetitious piano piece ever published has been 'The Well-Tuned Piano' by La Monte Young first presented by the Dia Art Foundation at the Concert Hall, Harrison St, New York City on 28 Feb 1980. The piece lasted 4 hr 12 min 10 sec. *Symphonic Variations*, composed by Kaikhosru Shapurji Sorabji (b. 1892) into 500 pages of close manuscript in 3 volumes in the 1930's, would last for 6 hours at the prescribed tempo.

Longest silence

The longest interval between the known composition of a major composer, and its performance in the manner intended, is from 3 Mar 1791 until 9 Oct 1982 (over 191 years), in the

At first destined for a military career, composer-pianist Sergei Rachmaninov monopolized his own compositions some of which were uniquely scored for 12 note chords.

case of Mozart's *Organ Piece for a Clock*, a fugue fantasy in F minor (K 608), arranged by the organ builders Wm Hill & Son and Norman & Beard Ltd at Glyndebourne, East Sussex.

HIGHEST PAID MUSICIANS

Pianist

Wladziu Valentino Liberace (b. West Allis, Wisconsin, USA, 16 May 1917) has earned more than $2 million each 26 week season with a peak of $138,000 (*then £49,285*) for a single night's performance at Madison Square Garden, New York City, USA in 1954. The highest paid classical concert pianist was Ignace Jan Paderewski (1860–1941), Prime Minister of Poland (1919–20), who accumulated a fortune estimated at $5,000,000, of which $500,000 (*then £110,000*) was earned in a single season in 1922–23. The *nouveau riche* wife of a US industrialist once required him to play in her house behind a curtain. For concerts Artur Rubinstein (1887–1982), between 1937 and 1976, commanded 70 per cent of the gross.

Greatest Span

Sergei Vassilievitch Rachmaninov (1873–1943) had a span of 12 white notes and could play a left hand chord of C, E♭, G, C, G.

Singer *Most Successful*

Of great fortunes earned by singers, the highest on record are those of Enrico Caruso (1873–1921), the Italian tenor, whose estate was about $9,000,000 (*then £1,875,000*) and the Italian-Spanish coloratura soprano Amelita Galli-Curci (1889–1963), who received about $3,000,000 (*£750,000*). In 1850, up to $653 was paid for a single seat at the concerts given in the United States by Johanna ('Jenny') Maria Lind, later Mrs Otto Goldschmidt (1820–87), the 'Swedish Nightingale'.

She had a range from g to e[III] of which the middle register is still regarded as unrivalled. The tenor Count John Francis McCormack (1884–1945) of Ireland gave up to 10 concerts to capacity audiences in a single season in New York City.

David Bowie drew a fee of $1.5 million (*then £960,000*) for a single show at the US Festival in Glen Helen Regional Park, San Bernardino County, California on 26 May 1983. The 4 man Van Halen rock band attracted a matching fee.

Worst

While no agreement exists as to the identity of history's greatest singer, there is unanimity on the worst. The excursions of the soprano Florence Foster Jenkins (1868–1944) into lieder and even high coloratura culminated on 25 Oct

Artwork: Pat Gibbon

1944 in her sell-out concert at the Carnegie Hall, New York, USA. The diva's (already high) high F was said to have been made higher in 1943 by a crash in a taxi. It is one of the tragedies of musicology that Madame Jenkins' *Clavelitos*, accompanied by Cosme McMoon, was never recorded for posterity. Her latter day amateur rival has been Mrs Hazel Saunders of Clent, Hereford & Worcester.

OPERA

Longest
The longest of commonly performed operas is *Die Meistersinger von Nürnberg* by Wilhelm Richard Wagner (1813–83) of Germany. A normal uncut performance of this opera as performed by the Sadler's Wells company between 24 Aug and 19 Sept 1968 entailed 5 hr 15 min of music. *The Heretics* by Gabriel von Waydtich (1888–1969) a Hungarian-American, is orchestrated for 110 pieces and lasts 8½ hr.

Shortest
The shortest opera published was *The Deliverance of Theseus* by Darius Milhaud (b. 4 Sept 1892) first performed in 1928 which lasts for 7 min 27 sec.

Aria
The longest single aria, in the sense of an operatic solo, is Brünnhilde's immolation scene in Wagner's *Gotterdammerung*. A well-known recording of this has been precisely timed at 14 min 46 sec.

Opera houses *Largest*
The largest opera house in the world is the Metropolitan Opera House, Lincoln Center, New York City, NY, USA, completed in September 1966 at a cost of $45,700,000. (*then £16,320,000*). It has a capacity of 3800 seats in an auditorium 451 ft *137 m* deep. The stage is 234 ft *71 m* wide and 146 ft *44,5 m* deep. The tallest opera house is one housed in a 42-storey building on Wacker Drive in Chicago, Illinois, USA.

Most tiers
The Teatro della Scala (La Scala) in Milan, Italy, shares with the Bolshoi Theatre in Moscow, USSR, the distinction of having the greatest number of tiers. Each has six, with the topmost being nicknamed the *Galiorka* by Russians.

Opera singers *Youngest and Oldest*
The youngest opera singer in the world has been Jeanette Gloria La Bianca, born in Buffalo, New York on 12 May 1934, who sang Rosina in *The Barber of Seville* at the Teatro dell'Opera, Rome, on 8 May 1950 aged 15 years 361 days, having appeared as Gilda in *Rigoletto* at Velletri 45 days earlier. Ginetta La Bianca was taught by Lucia Carlino and managed by Angelo Carlino. The tenor Giovanni Martinelli sang Emperor Altoum in *Turandot* in Seattle, Washington, USA on 4 Feb 1967 when aged 81.

Danshi Toyotake (b. 1 Aug 1891) has been singing *Gidayu* for 84 years.

Longest encore
The longest operatic encore, listed in the *Concise Oxford Dictionary of Opera*, was of the entire opera Cimarosa's' *Il Matrimonio Segreto* at its première in 1792. This was at the command of the Austro-Hungarian Emperor Leopold II (1790–92).

It was reported on 5 July 1983 that Placido Domingo received 83 curtain calls and was applauded for 1 hr 30 min after singing the lead in Puccini's *La Boheme* at the State Opera House in Vienna, Austria.

SONG

Oldest
The oldest known song is the *shaduf* chant, which has been sung since time immemorial by irrigation workers on the man-powered pivoted-rod bucket raisers of the Nile water mills (or *saqiyas*) in Egypt. The oldest known harmonized music performed today is the English song *Sumer is icumen in* which dates from *c.* 1240.

National anthems
The oldest national anthem is the *Kimigayo* of Japan, in which the words date from the 9th century. The anthem of Greece constitutes the first four verses of the Solomos poem, which has 158 stanzas. The shortest anthems are those of Japan, Jordan and San Marino, each with only four lines. Of the 23 wordless national anthems the oldest is that of Spain dating from 1770.

Longest rendering
'God Save the King' was played non-stop 16 or 17 times by a German military band on the platform of Rathenau Railway Station, Brandenburg, on the morning of 9 Feb 1909. The reason was that King Edward VII was struggling inside the train with the uniform of a German Field-Marshal before he could emerge.

Top songs of all time
The most frequently sung songs in English are *Happy Birthday to You* (based on the original *Good morning to all*), by Mildred and Patty S. Hill of New York (published in 1935 and in copyright until 2010); *For He's a Jolly Good Fellow* (originally the French *Malbrouk*), known at least as early as 1781, and *Auld Lang Syne* (originally the Strathspey *I fee'd a Lad at Michaelmass*), some words of which were written by Robert Burns (1759–96). *Happy Birthday* was sung in space by the Apollo IX astronauts on 8 Mar 1969.

Top selling sheet music
Sales of three non-copyright pieces are known to have exceeded 20,000,000 namely *The Old Folks at Home* by Stephen Foster (1855), *Listen to the Mocking Bird* (1855) and *The Blue Danube* (1867). Of copyright material the two topsellers are *Let Me Call You Sweetheart* (1910, by Whitson and Friedman) and *Till We Meet Again* (1918, by Egan and Whiting) each with some 6,000,000 by 1967. Other huge sellers have been *St Louis Blues*, *Stardust* and *Tea for Two*.

Most successful songwriter
In terms of sales of single records, the most successful of all song writers has been Paul McCartney (see also Gramophone, p. 105) formerly of the Beatles and now of Wings. Between 1962 and 1 Jan 1978 he wrote jointly or solo 43 songs which sold a million or more.

Eurovision Contest
In the 29 contests since 1956 Luxembourg has won outright 5 times (1961–65–72–73–83). France has won 4 outright (1958–60–62–77) and shared 1 (1969). The UK won in 1967 (Sandie Shaw, *Puppet On A String*), 1976 (Brotherhood of Man, *Save Your Kisses For Me*), 1981 (Bucks Fizz, *Making Your Mind Up*) and shared in 1969 (Lulu, *Boom, Bang-a-Bang*). Norway twice scored zero with Jahn Teigen and *Mil etter mil* (1980) and Finn Kalvik and *Aldri i livet* (1981).

HYMNS

Earliest
There are more than 950,000 Christian hymns in existence. The music and parts of the text of a hymn in the *Oxyrhynchus Papyri* from the 2nd century are the earliest known hymnody. The earliest exactly datable hymn is the *Heyr Himna*

Luxembourg's Corinne Hermes, 1983 winner of the Eurovision Song Contest. This annual competition has been won by Luxembourg on a record 5 occasions. (*Rex Features*)

Smiôur (*Hear, the maker of heaven*) from 1208 by the Icelandic bard and chieftain Kolbeinn Tumason (1173–1208).

Longest and shortest
The longest hymn is *Hora novissima tempora pessima sunt; vigilemus* by Bernard of Cluny (12th century), which runs to 2966 lines. In English the longest is *The Sands of Time are sinking* by Mrs Anne Ross Cousin, *née* Cundell (1824–1906), which is in full 152 lines, though only 32 lines in the Methodist Hymn Book. The shortest hymn is the single verse in Long Metre *Be Present at our Table Lord*, anon., but attributed to 'J. Leland'.

Most prolific hymnists
Mrs Frances (Fanny) Jane Van Alstyne *née* Crosby (1820–1915) (USA) wrote 8500 hymns although she had been blinded at the age of 6 weeks. She is reputed to have knocked off one hymn in 15 min. Charles Wesley (1707–88) wrote about 6000 hymns. In the seventh (1950) edition of *Hymns Ancient and Modern* the works of John Mason Neale (1818–66) appear 56 times.

BELLS

Oldest *World*
The oldest bell in the world is the tintinnabulum found in the Babylonian Palace of Nimrod in 1849 by Mr (later Sir) Austen Henry Layard (1817–94) dating from *c.* 1100 BC. The oldest known tower bell is one in Pisa, Italy dated MCVI (1106).

Great Britain
The fragile hand bell known as the Black or Iron Bell of St. Patrick is dated *c.* AD 450. The oldest tower bell in Great Britain is one of 1 cwt *50 kg* at St Botolph, Hardham, Sussex still in use but dated *ante* 1100. The oldest inscribed bell is the Gargate bell at Caversfield church, Oxfordshire and is dated *c.* 1200–1210. The oldest *dated* bell in England is one hanging in Lissett church, near Bridlington, Humberside discovered in October 1972 to bear the date MCCLIIII (1254).

Heaviest *World*
The heaviest bell in the world is the Tsar Kolokol, cast on 25 Nov 1735 in Moscow, USSR. It weighs 193 tons *196 tonnes*, measures 5,9 m *19 ft 4¼ in* diameter and 5,87 m *19 ft 3 in* high, and its greatest thickness is 24 in *60 cm*. The bell

The heaviest bell in the world at 193 tons *196 tonnes*, the Tsar Kolokol in Moscow was cast in 1735. *(Alex Hansen)*

is cracked, and a fragment, weighing about 11 tons/*tonnes* was broken from it. The bell has stood, unrung, on a platform in the Kremlin, in Moscow, since 1836.

The heaviest bell in use is the Mingun bell, weighing 55,555 viss or *90.52 tons* with a diameter of 16 ft 8½ in *5,09 m* at the lip, in Mandalay, Burma, which is struck by a teak boom from the outside. It was cast at Mingun late in the reign of King Bodawpaya (1782–1819). The heaviest swinging bell in the world is the Petersglocke in the South-West tower of Cologne Cathedral, Germany, cast in 1923 with a diameter of 3,40 m *11 ft 1¾ in* weighing 25,4 tonnes *25.0 tons*.

Great Britain

The heaviest bell hung in Great Britain is 'Great Paul' in the south-west tower of St Paul's Cathedral, London, cast in 1881. It weighs 16 tons 14 cwt 2 qrs 19 lb net *17 002 kg* and has a diameter of 9 ft 6½ in *2,90 m* and sounds note E-flat. 'Big Ben', the hour bell in the clock tower of the House of Commons, was cast in 1858 and weighs 13 tons 10 cwt 3 qrs 15 lb *13 761 kg*. It is the most broadcast bell in the world and is note E.

Ringing Peals

A ringing peal is defined as a diatonic 'ring' of five or more bells hung for full-circle change ringing. Of 5500 rings so hung only 70 are outside the United Kingdom and Ireland. The heaviest ring in the world is that of 13 bells cast in 1938–39 for the Anglican Cathedral, Liverpool. The total bell weight is 16½ tons *16,76 tonnes* of which Emmanuel, the tenor bell note A, weighs 82 cwt 11 lb *4170,8 kg*.

Carillon *Largest*

The largest carillon (minimum of 23 bells) in the world is the Laura Spelman Rockefeller Memorial carillon in Riverside Church, New York City, USA with 74 bells weighing 102 tons. The bourdon, giving the note lower C, weighs 40,926 lb *18 563 kg*. This 18.27 ton bell, cast in England, with a diameter of 10 ft 2 in *3,09 cm* is the largest *tuned* bell in the world.

Heaviest

The heaviest carillon in Great Britain is in St Nicholas Church, Aberdeen, Scotland. It consists of 48 bells, the total weight of which is 25 tons 8 cwt 2 qrs 13 lb *25 838 kg*. The bourdon bell weighs 4 tons 9 cwt 3 qrs 26 lb *4571 kg* and is the note G-sharp.

Bell ringing

Eight bells have been rung to their full 'extent' (40,320 unrepeated changes of Plain Bob Major) only once without relays. This took place in a bell foundry at Loughborough, Leicestershire, beginning at 6.52 a.m. on 27 July 1963 and ending at 12.50 a.m. on 28 July, after 17 hr 58 min. The peal was composed by Kenneth Lewis of Altrincham, Greater Manchester, and the eight ringers were conducted by Robert B. Smith, aged 25, of Marple, Greater Manchester. Theoretically it would take 37 years 355 days to ring 12 bells (maximus) to their full extent of 479,001,600 changes. The greatest number of peals (minimum of 5040 changes, all in tower bells) rung in a year is 209 by Mark William Marshall of Ashford, Kent in 1973. The late George E. Fearn rang 2666 peals from 1928 to May 1974. Matthew Lakin (1801–1899) was a regular bell-ringer at Tetney Church near Grimsby for 84 years.

5. THEATRE

Guinness Superlatives has published a more specialist book *The Guinness Book of Theatre Facts and Feats* by Michael Billington, priced £8.95.

Origins

Theatre in Europe has its origins in Greek drama performed in honour of a god, usually Dionysus. The earliest amphitheatres date from the 5th century BC and the largest of all known is one at Megalopolis in central Greece, where the auditorium reached a height of 75 ft *23 m* and had a capacity of 17,000. The first stone-built theatre in Rome erected in 55 BC could accommodate 40,000 spectators.

Oldest *World*

The oldest indoor theatre in the world is the Teatro Olimpico in Vicenza, Italy. Designed in the Roman style by Andrea di Pietro, *alias* Palladio (1508–80), it was begun three months before his death and finished by his pupil Vicenzo Scamozzi (1552–1616) in 1583. It is preserved today in its original form.

Great Britain

The earliest London theatre was James Burbage's 'The Theatre', built in 1576 near Finsbury Fields, London. The oldest theatre still in use in Great Britain is The Royal, Bristol. The foundation stone was laid on 30 Nov 1764, and the theatre was opened on 30 May 1766 with a 'Concert of Music and a Specimen of Rhetorick'. The City Varieties Music Hall, Leeds was a singing room in 1762 and so claims to outdate the Theatre Royal. Actors were legally rogues and vagabonds until the passing of the Vagrancy Act in 1824. The oldest amateur dramatic society is the Old Stagers inaugurated in Canterbury, Kent in 1841. They have performed in every year except the years of World War I and II.

Largest *World*

The world's largest building used for theatre is the National People's Congress Building (*Ren min da hui tang*) on the west side of Tian an men Square, Peking, China. It was completed in 1959 and covers an area of 12.9 acres *5,2 ha*. The theatre seats 10,000 and is occasionally used as such as in 1964 for the play 'The East is Red'. The highest capacity purpose-built theatre is the Perth Entertainment Centre, Western Australia

completed at a cost of \$A 8.3 million (*then £4.2 million*) in November 1976 with 8003 seats. The stage area is 12,000 ft² *1148 m²*.

Great Britain

The highest capacity theatre is the Odeon, Hammersmith, Greater London, with 3483 seats. The largest theatre stage in Great Britain is the Opera House in Blackpool, Lancashire. It was re-built in July 1939 and has seats for 2975 people. Behind the 45 ft *14 m* wide proscenium arch, the stage is 110 ft *33 m* high, 60 ft *18 m* deep and 100 ft *30 m* wide, and there is dressing room accommodation for 200 artistes.

Britain's largest open air theatre is at Scarborough, North Yorkshire opened in 1932 with a seating capacity of 7000 plus standing room for 9000 and a 182 ft *55 m* long stage.

Smallest

The smallest regularly operated professional theatre in the world is the Piccolo in Juliusstrasse, Hamburg, West Germany. It was founded in 1970 and has a maximum capacity of 30 seats.

Largest amphitheatre

The largest amphitheatre ever built is the Flavian amphitheatre or Colosseum of Rome, Italy, completed in AD 80. Covering 5 acres *2 ha* and with a capacity of 87,000, it has a maximum length of 612 ft *187 m* and maximum width of 515 ft *175 m*.

Largest stage

The largest stage in the world is in the Ziegfeld Room Reno, Nevada with 176 ft *53,6 m* passerelle, three main lifts each capable of raising 1200 show girls (64½ tons *65,3 tonnes*), two 62½ ft *19,1 m* circumference turntables and 800 spotlights.

Longest runs

The longest continuous run of any show in the world is *The Mousetrap* by Dame Agatha Mary Clarissa Christie, DBE (*née* Miller, later Lady Mallowan) (1890–1976). This thriller opened on

25 Nov 1952, at the Ambassadors Theatre (capacity 453) and moved after 8862 performances 'down the road' to St Martin's Theatre on 25 Mar 1974. The 30th Anniversary performance on 25 Nov 1982 was the 12,481st. The Vicksburg Theatre Guild of Vicksburg, Mississippi, USA have been playing the melodrama *Gold in the Hills*, by J. Frank Davis discontinuously but every season since 1936.

Revue

The greatest number of performances of any theatrical presentation is 42,921 (to January 1984) in the case of *The Golden Horseshoe Revue*—a show staged at Disneyland Park, Anaheim, California, USA. The show was first put on on 16 July 1955 and has been seen by 16 million people. The three main performers Fulton Burley, Dick Hardwick and Betty Taylor play as many as five houses a day in a routine lasting 45 min.

Broadway

The long-run record for any Broadway show was set on 29 Sept 1983 with the 3389th performance of *Chorus Line*. It opened on 25 July 1975 and had been seen by an estimated 22,300,000 people with a box office receipt of \$260 million. The off-

Broadway musical show *The Fantasticks* by Tom Jones and Harvey Schmidt achieved its 10,500th performance at the Sullivan Street Playhouse, Greenwich Village, New York City on 30 July 1985. It has been played in a record 8681 productions in 67 countries.

Musical shows

The longest-running musical show ever performed in Britain was *The Black and White Minstrel Show* later *Magic of the Minstrels*. The aggregate but discontinuous number of performances was 6464 with a total attendance of 7,794,552. The show opened at the Victoria Palace, London on 25 May 1962 and closed on 4 Nov 1972. It re-opened for a season in June 1973 at the New Victoria and finally closed on 8 Dec 1973.

Jesus Christ Superstar, which opened at Palace Theatre, London on 8 Aug 1972, closed on 23 Aug 1980 after 3357 performances having played to 2 million people with box office receipts of £7 million. By 1984 it had been produced in 37 other countries.

Comedy

The British record for long running comedy is set by *No Sex Please We're British* which reaches its 6000th performance in its 15th year in 1986, having opened at The Strand Theatre on 3 June 1971 and transferred to the Garrick Theatre on 18 Jan 1982. Its director Allan Davis has had his name in lights from the start.

Shortest runs *World*

The shortest run on record was that of *The Intimate Revue* at the Duchess Theatre, London, on 11 Mar 1930. Anything which could go wrong did. With scene changes taking up to 20 min apiece, the management scrapped seven scenes to get the finale on before midnight. The run was described as 'half a performance'.

Broadway

The opening and closing nights of many Broadway shows have coincided. Spectacular failures are known as 'turkeys' of which there were 11 in 1978–79. *Frankenstein*, which opened and closed on Broadway on 4 Jan 1981, lost an estimated $2 million but *A Doll's Life* (23–26 Sept 1982) lost close to $4 million.

Concert

The fastest sell-out in Broadway history occurred when seats for 'Barry Manilow In Concert' for 12 nights (21 Feb–5 Mar 1983) were sold out for $782,160 (*then £500,000*) in 4 hours at the 1983 seat Uris Theatre.

Lowest attendance

The ultimate in low attendances was recorded in December 1983 when the comedy *Bag* in Grantham, Lincolnshire opened to a nil attendance.

Youngest Broadway producer

Margo Feiden (Margo Eden) (b. New York, 2 Dec 1944) produced the musical *Peter Pan*, which opened on 3 Apr 1961 when she was 16 years 5 months old. She wrote *Out Brief Candle*, which opened on 18 Aug 1962. She is now a leading art dealer.

One-man shows

The longest run of one-man shows is 849 by Victor Borge (b. Copenhagen, 3 Jan 1909) in his *Comedy in Music* from 2 Oct 1953 to 21 Jan 1956 at the Golden Theater, Broadway, New York City. The world aggregate record for one-man shows is 1700 performances of *Brief Lives* by Roy Dotrice (b. Guernsey, 26 May 1923) including 400 straight at the Mayfair Theatre, London ending on 20 July 1974. He was on stage

Michael Crawford and Evelyn Laye playing in the longest ever running comedy on the London stage. (See column 1) *(Reg Wilson)*

for more than 2½ hr per performance of this 17th century monologue and required 3 hr for make up and 1 hr for removal of make-up so aggregating 40 weeks in the chair.

Most durable actors and actresses

Kanmi Fujiyama (b. 1929) played the lead role in 10,288 performances by the comedy company Sochiku Shikigeki from Nov 1966 to June 1983. Dame Anna Neagle, DBE (b. 20 Oct 1904) played the lead role in *Charlie Girl* at the Adelphi Theatre, London for 2062 of 2202 performances between 15 Dec 1965 and 27 Mar 1971. She played the role a further 327 times in 327 performances in Australasia. Frances Etheridge has played Lizzie, the housekeeper, in *Gold in the Hills* (see Longest Runs) more than 660 times over a span of 47 years since 1936. Jack Howarth MBE (1896–1984) was an actor on the stage and in television for 76 years from 1907 until his last appearance after 23 years as Albert Tatlock in *Coronation Street* on 25 Jan 1984.

Most roles

The greatest recorded number of theatrical, film and television roles is 2357 from 1951 to May 1984 by Jan Leighton (US).

Longest play

The longest recorded theatrical production has been 'The Acting Life' staged in the Tom Mann Theatre, Sydney, Australia on 17–18 Mar 1984 with a cast of 10. The production required 19¼ hours or 21 hours with intervals.

Shakespeare

The first all-amateur company to have staged all 37 of Shakespeare's plays was The Southsea Shakespeare Actors, Hampshire, England (founded 1947) in October 1966 when, under their amateur director, K. Edmonds Gateley MBE, they presented *Cymbeline*. The longest is *Hamlet* with 4042 lines and 29,551 words. Of Shakespeare's 1277 speaking parts the longest is Hamlet with 11,610 words.

Longest chorus line

The longest chorus line in performing history were up to 120 in some of the early Ziegfeld's Follies. In the finale of *Chorus Line* on the night of 29 Sept 1983 when it broke the record as the longest-running Broadway show ever, 332 top-hatted 'strutters' performed on stage.

Cabaret

The highest paid entertainer is Dolly Parton with up to $400,000 (£333,000) per live concert. Johnny Carson's fee for the non-televised Sears Roebuck Centenary Gala in Oct 1984 was set at 1 million dollars (£833,000).

Ice shows

Holiday on Ice Production Inc, founded by Morris Chalfen in 1945, stages the world's most costly live entertainment with up to seven productions playing simultaneously in several of 75 countries drawing 20,000,000 spectators paying $40 million (*£33.3 million*) in a year. The total skating and other staff exceeds 900. The most prolific producer of Ice Shows was Gerald Palmer (1908–83) with 137 since 1945 including 34 consecutive shows at Empire Pool, Wembley, London with attendances up to 850,000. Hazel Wendy Jolly (b. 1933) has appeared in the Wembley Winter Pantomime for 27 years.

Most ardent theatregoers

Dr H. Howard Hughes (b. 1902) Professor Emeritus of Texas Wesleyan College, Fort Worth, Texas, has attended 5512 shows in the period 1956–83. Britain's leading 'first nighter' Edward Sutro MC (1900–78) saw 3000 first night productions in 1916–56 and possibly more than 5000 in his 60 years of theatre-going. The highest precisely recorded number of theatre attendances in Britain is 3596 shows in 31 years from 28 Mar 1953 to 28 Mar 1985 by John Iles of Salisbury, Wiltshire. He estimates he has travelled 145,024 miles *233 393 km* and seen 180,346 performers in 9,495 hours (over 56 weeks) inside theatres.

Arts Festival

The world's largest arts festival is the annual Edinburgh Festival Fringe (instituted in 1959). In 1983, 454 groups gave 6886 performances of 875 shows between 21 Aug and 10 Sept. Prof. Gerald Berkowitz of Northern Illinois University, USA attended a record 145 separate performances at the 1979 Festival from 15 Aug–8 Sept.

Fashion shows

The most prolific producer and most durable commentator of fashion shows is Adalene Ross of San Francisco, California with totals over 4698 in both categories to mid-1984.

Professional wrestling

The professional wrestler who has received most for a single bout has been Kanii Antonio Inoki of Japan on 26 Jun 1976. He received $2 million for the drawn wrestler v boxer bout against Muhammad Ali in the Budokan Arena, Tokyo. Lou Thesz has won 7 of the world's many 'world' titles. 'Fabulous' Moolah won major US women's alliance titles over the longest span starting in 1956. The heaviest ever wrestler has been William J. Cobb of Macon, Georgia, USA (b. 1926), who was billed in 1962 as the 802 lb *363 kg* (57 st 4 lb) 'Happy' Humphrey. Ed 'Strangler' Lewis (1890–1966) *né* Robert H. Friedrich, fought 6200 bouts in 44 years losing only 33 matches. He won world titles in 1921, 1922, 1928 and 1931–32. See also Ch 12 Heaviest Sportsmen.

6. RECORDED SOUND

Guinness Superlatives has published more specialist books: *The Guinness Book of British Hit Singles (4th edition)* (£5.95 paperback), *The Guinness Book of 500 Number One Hits* (£5.95 paperback), *The Guinness Book of British Hit Albums* (£5.95 paperback), *Hits of the 70's* (£6.50 hardback), *Hits of the 60's* (£5.95 paperback) and *The Guinness Hits Challenge* (£3.95 paperback) all by Tim & Jo Rice, Paul Gambaccini and Mike Read. *The Billboard Book of US Top 40 Hits* by Joel Whitburn is priced £8.95 (paperback), and *The Guinness Book of Recorded Sound* by Robert and Celia Dearling with Brian Rust is priced £9.95 (hardback).

Origins

The gramophone (phonograph) was first *conceived* by Charles Cros (1842–88) a French poet and scientist, who described his idea in sealed papers deposited in the French Academy of Sciences on 30 Apr 1877. However the realisation of a practical device was first *achieved* by Thomas Alva Edison (1847–1931) of the USA.

BBC Hulton

Thomas Edison, the most prolific of all inventors. He first achieved the reproduction of sound in 1877.

The first successful wax cylinder machine was constructed by his mechanic, John Kruesi on 4–6 Dec 1877, demonstrated on 7 Dec and patented on 19 Feb 1878. The horizontal disc was introduced by Emile Berliner (1851–1929).

Earliest Recordings

The earliest birthdate of anyone whose voice is recorded is Alfred, first Baron Tennyson (born 6 Aug 1809). The earliest born singer was Peter Schram, the Danish baritone of whom a cylinder was made in the role of Don Giovanni on his 70th birthday on 5 Sept 1889.

Tape Recording

Magnetic recording was invented by Valdemar Poulsen (1869–1942) of Denmark with his steel wire Telegraphone in 1898. Fritz Pfleumer (German patent 500900) introduced tape in 1928. Tapes were first used at the Blattner Studios, Elstree, Hertfordshire in 1929. Plastic tapes were devised by BASF of Germany in 1932–35, but were not marketed until 1950 by Recording Associates of New York. In April 1983 Olympic Optical Industry Co. of Japan marketed a micro-cassette recorder 10,7 × 5,1 × 1,4 cm *4.2 × 2 × 0.55 in* weighing 125 g *4.4 oz.*

Oldest records

The BBC record library contains over 1,000,000 records, including 5250 with no known matrix. The oldest records in the library are white wax cylinders dating from 1888. The earliest commercial disc recording was manufactured in 1895.

Smallest record

The smallest functional gramophone record is one 1⅜ in *3,5 cm* in diameter of 'God Save the King' of which 250 were made by HMV Record Co in 1924.

Phonographic Identification

Dr Arthur B. Lintgen (b. 1932) of Rydal, Pennsylvania, USA has an as yet unique and proven ability to identify the music on phonograph records purely by visual inspection without hearing a note.

Earliest jazz records

The earliest jazz record made was *Indiana* and *The Dark Town Strutters Ball*, recorded for the Columbia label in New York City, NY, USA, on or about 30 Jan 1917, by the Original Dixieland Jazz Band, led by Dominick (Nick) James La Rocca (1889–1961). This was released on 31 May 1917. The first jazz record to be released was the ODJB's *Livery Stable Blues* (recorded 24 Feb), backed by *The Dixie Jass Band One-Step* (recorded 26 Feb), released by Victor on 7 Mar 1917.

Most successful solo recording artist

No independently audited figures have ever been published for Elvis Aron Presley (1935–77). In view of Presley's worldwide tally of over 170 major hits on singles and over 80 top-selling albums from 1956 continuing after his death, it may be assumed that it was he who must have succeeded Crosby as the top-selling solo artist of all-time. CBS Records reported in August 1983 that sales of albums by Julio Iglesias (b. 1943) in 6 languages had surpassed 100,000,000.

On 9 June 1960 the Hollywood Chamber of Commerce presented Harry Lillis (*alias* Bing) Crosby, Jr (1904–77) with a platinum disc to commemorate the alleged sale of 200,000,000 records from the 2600 singles and 125 albums he had recorded. On 15 Sept 1970 he received a second platinum disc when Decca claimed a sale of 300,650,000 discs. No independently audited figures of his global life-time sales from his royalty reports have ever been published and experts regard figures so high as this before the industry became highly developed as exaggerated.

Most successful group

The singers with the greatest sales of any group have been the Beatles. This group from Liverpool, Merseyside, comprised George Harrison, MBE (b. 25 Feb 1943), John Ono (formerly John Winston) Lennon, MBE (b. 9 Oct 1940–k. 8 Dec 1980), James Paul McCartney, MBE (b. 18 June 1942) and Richard Starkey, MBE *alias* Ringo Starr (b. 7 July 1940). The all-time Beatles sales by May 1985 have been estimated by EMI at over 1000 million discs and tapes.

All 4 ex-Beatles sold many million further records as solo artists. Since their break-up in 1970, it is estimated that the most successful group in the world in terms of record sales is the Swedish foursome ABBA (Agnetha Faltskog, Anni-Frid Lyngstad, Bjorn Ulvaeus and Benny Andersson) with a total of 215 million discs and tapes by May 1985.

Golden discs *Earliest*

The earliest recorded piece eventually to aggregate a total sale of a million copies were performances by Enrico Caruso (b. Naples, Italy, 1873, and d. 2 Aug 1921) of the aria *Vesti la giubba* (*On with the Motley*) from the opera *I Pagliacci* by Ruggiero Leoncavallo (1858–1919), the earliest version of which was recorded with piano on 12 Nov 1902. The first single recording to surpass the million mark was Alma Gluck's *Carry me back to old Virginny* on the Red Seal Victor label on the 12-inch *30,48 cm* single faced (later backed) record 74420. The first actual golden disc was one sprayed by RCA Victor for the US trombonist and band-leader Alton 'Glenn' Miller (1904–44) for his *Chattanooga Choo Choo* on 10 Feb 1942.

Most

The only *audited* measure of gold, platinum and multiplatinum singles and albums within the United States, is certification by the Recording Industry Association of America introduced 14 Mar 1958. Out of the 2,582 RIAA awards made to 1 Jan 1985, The Beatles with 44 (plus one with Billy Preston) have most for a group. McCartney has 23 more awards outside the group and with Wings (including one with Stevie Wonder and one with Michael Jackson). The most awards to an individual is 45 to Elvis Presley (1935–77) spanning 1958 to 1 Jan 1985. Globally however Presley's total of million-selling singles has been authoritatively put at 'approaching 80'.

Most recorded song

Three songs have each been recorded over 1000 times—*Yesterday* written by Paul McCartney and John Lennon (see above) with 1186 versions between 1965 and 1 Jan 1973; *Tie A Yellow Ribbon Round the old Oak Tree* written by Irwin Levine and L. Russell Brown with more than 1200 from 1973 to 1 Apr 1985; and *My Way*, music by Jacques Revaux and the late Claude François and the English lyrics by Paul Anka (b. Ottawa, 30 July 1941).

Most recordings

Miss Lata Mangeshker (b. 1928) between 1948 and 1985 has reportedly recorded not less than 30,000 solo, duet and chorus backed songs in 20 Indian languages. She frequently had 5 sessions in a day and has 'backed' more than 2000 films.

Biggest sellers *Singles*

The greatest seller of any gramophone record to date is *White Christmas* by Irving Berlin (b. Israel Bailin, at Tyumen, Russia, 11 May 1888) with 25,000,000 for the Crosby single (recorded 29 May 1942) and more than 100,000,000 in other versions. The highest claim for any 'pop' record is an unaudited 25,000,000 for *Rock Around the Clock*, copyrighted in 1953 by James E. Myers under the name Jimmy DeKnight and the late Max C. Freedmann and recorded on 12 Apr 1954 by Bill Haley (1927–1981) and the Comets. The top-selling British record of all-time is *I Want to Hold Your Hand* by the Beatles, released in 1963, with world sales of over 13,000,000. The top selling single of all time in the United Kingdom is *Feed the World—Do They Know It's Christmas* written and produced by Bob Geldof and Midge Ure with 3¼ million by May 1985 with a further 3¾ million world wide. The profits were in aid of the Ethiopian Famine Relief Fund.

Albums

The best selling album of all time is *Thriller* by Michael Joseph Jackson (b. Gary, Indiana, 29 Aug 1958) with global sales in excess of 35 million copies by May 1985. The best selling album by British performers is considered to be *Dark Side Of The Moon* recorded by Pink Floyd (Dave Gilmour, Nick Mason, Roger Waters, and Rick Wright), in June 1972–January 1973 in London, with sales of over 17 million by May 1985.

The charts—US Singles

Singles record charts were first published by *Billboard* on 20 July 1940 when the No. 1 was *I'll Never Smile Again* by Tommy Dorsey (b. 19 Nov 1905, d. 26 Nov 1956). Three discs have stayed top for a record 13 consecutive weeks—*Frenesi* by Artie Shaw from December 1940; *I've Heard*

The Band Aid group led by Midge Ure and Bob Geldorf whose 'Feed The World—Do They Know It's Christmas' in aid of Ethiopian Famine Relief set a world record for singles sales—7 million worldwide including 3¼ million in the United Kingdom.
(Duncan Paul Associates/Brian Aris)

Michael Jackson and Guinness Book Editor Norris McWhirter at the Columbia Recording 1984 award ceremony for *Thriller* in New York City.

that Song Before by Harry James from February 1943 and *Goodnight Irene* by Gordon Jenkins and the Weavers from August 1950. *Tainted Love* by Soft Cell stayed on the chart for 43 consecutive weeks from January 1982. The Beatles have had most No. 1 records (21) and Elvis Presley has had most hit singles on Billboard's Hot 100—107 from 1956 to May 1985.

US Albums

Billboard first published an album chart on 15 Mar 1945 when the No. 1 was *King Cole Trio* featuring Nat 'King' Cole (b. 17 Mar 1919, d. 15 Feb 1965). *South Pacific* was No. 1 for 69 weeks (non-consecutive) from May 1949. *Dark Side of The Moon* by Pink Floyd (see above) enjoyed its 571st week on the *Billboard* charts in May 1985.

The Beatles had most No. 1's (15) and Presley most hit albums (83 from 1956 to May 1985).

UK Singles

Singles record charts were first published in Britain on 14 Nov 1952 by *New Musical Express*. *I Believe* by Frankie Laine (b. 30 Mar 1913) held No. 1 position for 18 weeks (non-consecutive) from April 1953, with *Rose Marie* by Slim Whitman (b. 20 Jan 1924) the consecutive record holder with 11 weeks from July 1955. The longest stay has been the 163 weeks of *My Way* by Francis Albert Sinatra (b. 12 Dec 1917) in 10 separate runs from 2 Apr 1969 into 1984. The record for an uninterrupted stay is 56 weeks for Engelbert Humperdinck's *Release Me* from 26 Jan 1967. The Beatles and Presley hold the record for most No. 1 hits with 17 each, with Presley having an overall record of 106 hits in the UK singles chart from 1956 to May 1985.

UK Albums

The first British album chart was published on 8 Nov 1958 by *Melody Maker*. The first No. 1 LP was the film soundtrack *South Pacific* which held the position for a record 70 consecutive weeks and eventually accumulated a record 115 weeks at No. 1. The album with the most total weeks on chart was the soundtrack to *The Sound of Music* with 381 weeks. The Beatles have had most No. 1 albums—12; and Elvis Presley the most hit albums—86.

Fastest selling LPs

The fastest selling record of all time is *John Fitzgerald Kennedy—A Memorial Album* (Premium Albums), recorded on 22 Nov 1963, the day of Mr Kennedy's assassination, which sold 4,000,000 copies at 99 cents (*then 35 p*) in six days (7–12 Dec 1963), thus ironically beating the previous speed record set by the satirical LP *The First Family* in 1962–3. The fastest selling British record is the Beatles' double album *The Beatles*

(Apple) with 'nearly 2 million' in its first week in November 1968.

Richard Clayderman (b. Philippe Pages, 1954) of France is reputed to have sold 25 million LP's in the 3 years to Jan 1983 for which he collected 127 gold and 23 platinum records.

Advance sales

The greatest advance sale was 2,100,000 for *Can't Buy Me Love* by the Beatles, released in the United States on 16 Mar 1964. The Beatles also equalled their British record of 1,000,000 advance sales, set by *I Want to Hold Your Hand* (Parlophone transferred to Apple, Aug 1968) on 29 Nov 1963, with this same record on 20 Mar 1964. The UK record for advance sales of an LP is 1,000,000 for the Epic album *Super Trouper* by ABBA released in November 1980.

Loudest *Pop Group*

The amplification at *The Who* concert at Charlton Athletic Football Ground, London on 31 May 1976 provided by a Tasco PA System had a total power of 76,000 watts from eighty 800 W Crown DC 300 A Amplifiers and twenty 600 W Phase Linear 200's. The readings at 50 m *164 ft* from the front of the sound system were 120 db. Sound engineer Rob Cowlyn with Duran Duran claimed that the audience's level of anticipatory screaming in Australia in November 1983 exceeded 120 dB *before* the group came on stage. The US group Manowar, a heavy metal rock band, claim to have measured a reading of 160 dB in October 1984 is unsupportable. *Exposure to high noise levels is known to cause PSH—Permanent Shift of Hearing or partial up to total instant deafness.*

Grammy Awards

The record number of Grammy awards in a year is 8 by Michael Joseph Jackson in 1984 (see also *US Albums*). The all-time record is 24 by Sir Georg Solti KBE (b. Budapest, 21 Oct 1912).

7. CINEMA

Guinness Superlatives has published a more specialist book *Guinness Book of Film Facts and Feats* by Patrick Robertson, priced £8.95.

FILMS

Origins

The earliest motion pictures ever taken were by Louis Aimé Augustin Le Prince (1842–1890). He was attested to have achieved dim moving outlines on a whitewashed wall at the Institute for the Deaf, Washington Heights, New York, USA as early as 1885–87. The earliest surviving film (sensitized 2⅛ in *53,9 mm* wide paper roll) is from his camera, patented in Britain on 16 Nov 1888, taken in early October 1888 of the garden of his father-in-law, Joseph Whitley in Roundhay, Leeds, West Yorkshire at 10 to 12 frames per second. The first commercial presentation of *motion pictures* was at Holland Bros' Kinetoscope Parlour at 1155 Broadway, New York City on 14 April 1894. Viewers could see 5 films for 25 cents or 10 for 50 cents from a double row of Kinetoscopes developed by William Kennedy Laurie Dickson (1860–1935) assistant to Thomas Alva Edison (1847–1931) in 1889–91. The earliest publicly presented film on a *screen* was *La Sortie de Ouvriers de l'Usine Lumière* probably shot in August or September 1894 in Lyon, France. It was exhibited at 44 Rue de Rennes, Paris on 22 Mar 1895 by the Lumière Brothers, Auguste Marie Louis Nicholas (1862–1954) and Louis Jean (1864–1948).

Earliest 'Talkie'

The earliest sound-on-film motion picture was achieved by Eugene Augustin Lauste (b. Paris 17 Jan 1857) who patented his process on 11 Aug 1906 and produced a workable system using a string galvanometer in 1910 at Benedict Road, Stockwell, London. The earliest public presentation of sound on film was by the Tri-ergon process at the Alhambra cinema, Berlin, Germany on 17 Sept 1922.

Most expensive film

The highest ever budgeted film has been *Star Trek* which received its world première in Washington D.C. on 6 Dec 1979. Paramount Studios stated that the cost of this space epic directed by Robert Wise and produced by Gene Roddenbury, was $46 million (*then £21 million*). A figure of $60 million has been attributed to *Superman II* but never substantiated.

Least expensive film

Cecil Hepworth's highly successful release of 1905 *Rescued by Rover* cost £7 13s 9d (*then $37.40*).

Most expensive film rights

The highest price ever paid for film rights is $9,500,000 (*then £4,950,000*) announced on 20 Jan 1978 by Columbia for *Annie*, the Broadway Musical by Charles Strouse starring Andrea McCardle, Dorothy Loudon and Reid Shelton.

Longest film

The longest film ever premièred was the 48 hr long *The Longest Most Meaningless Movie in the World* in 1970. It was British made and later heavily cut to 90 min.

Highest box office gross

The box office gross championship for films is highly vulnerable to inflated ticket prices. Calculations based on the 1983 value of the dollar shows that *Gone With the Wind* with Clark Gable (1901–1960) and Vivien Leigh (1913–1967) released in 1939 is unsurpassed at $312 million. The highest numerical (as opposed to value) dollar champion is Steven Spielberg's

ET: The Extra-Terrestrial, released on 11 June 1982, and which by 2 Jan 1983 had grossed $322 million (*then £208 million*). On 29 May 1983 *The Return of the Jedi* (20th Century Fox) grossed $8,440,105 (*£5,445,200*) for a single day record, and a record $6,219,929 (*£4,013,000*) for its opening day on 25 May.

Largest loss

It was reported on 20 Nov 1980 that United Artists had withdrawn *Heaven's Gate* because its total cost including distribution and studio overheads had reached $57,000,000.

Most violent

A study on the portrayal of violence showed the worst film on record was *Red Dawn*, released in the US in 1984, with acts of violence occurring at the rate of 134 per hour (2.23 per min).

Highest earnings *By an actor*

The highest rate of pay in cinema history was set by Marlon Brando (b. 3 Apr 1924) for his brief part in *Superman*. He reportedly received $3,700,000 (*then £1,850,000*) and a further $15 million (*then £7.5 million*) after suing for a contracted share of box office royalties. In July 1980 it was reported that Burt Reynolds (b. 11 Feb 1936) received $238,095 per day from 20th Century-Fox for his part in *Cannonball Run*. The highest straight payment for a role has been $12 million (*£7,742,000*) by Sylvester Stallone in *Over the Top* reported in September 1983.

By a Stuntman

Dar Robinson was paid $100,000 (*then £45,500*) for the 1100 ft *335 m* leap from the CN Tower, Toronto in Nov 1979 for *High Point*. His parachute opened at only 300 ft *91 m* above the ground.

Longest Series

Japan's *Tora-San* films have now stretched from *Tora-San I* in August 1968 to *Tora-San XXXII* in 1983 with Kiyoshi Atsumi (b. 1929) starring in each for Shochiku Co.

Character most portrayed

The character most frequently recurring on the screen is Sherlock Holmes, created by Sir Arthur Conan Doyle (1859–1930). Sixty-seven actors portrayed him in 186 films between 1900 and 1984.

Largest studios

The largest complex of film studios in the world are those at Universal City, L.A., California. The Back Lot contains 561 buildings and there are 34 sound stages on the 420 acre *170 ha* site.

Most Prolific Director

Allan Dwan (1885–1981) the Canadian born pioneer directed, from 1909 to the early 'sixties, more than 400 films.

Oscars *Most*

Walter (Walt) Elias Disney (1901–66) won more 'Oscars'—the awards of the United States Academy of Motion Picture Arts and Sciences, instituted on 16 May 1929 for 1927–8—than any other person. The physical count comprises 20 statuettes, and 12 other plaques and certificates including posthumous awards. The only person to win four Oscars in a starring rôle has been Miss Katharine Hepburn, formerly Mrs Ludlow Ogden Smith (b. Hartford, Conn., 9 Nov 1909) in *Morning Glory* (1932–3), *Guess Who's Coming to Dinner* (1967), *The Lion in Winter* (1968) and *On Golden Pond* (1981). She was 12 times nominated. Only 4 actors have won two Oscars in starring rôles—Frederic March (1897–1975) in 1931/32 and 1946, Spencer Tracy in 1937 and 1938, Gary Cooper in 1941 and 1952, and Marlon Brando in 1954 and 1972. Edith Head (Mrs Wiard B. Ihnen) (d. 1981) won 8 individual

awards for costume design. Oscars are named after Mr Oscar Pierce of Texas, USA. The films with most awards have been *Ben Hur* (1959) with 11, followed by *Gone With the Wind* (1939) with 10 and *West Side Story* (1961) with 10. The film with the highest number of nominations was *All About Eve* (1950) with 14. It won six. The youngest ever winner was Shirley Temple (b. 24 Apr 1928) aged 5 with her honorary Oscar, and the oldest George Burns, (b. 20 Jan 1896) aged 80 for *The Sunshine Boys* in 1976.

Versatility showbusiness awards

The only 3 performers to have won Oscars, Emmy, Tony and Grammy awards have been Helen Hayes (b. 1900) in 1932–1976; Richard Rodgers (1902–1979), composer of musicals and Rita Moreno (b. 1931) in 1961–1977. Barbra Streisand (b. 24 Apr 1942 in Brooklyn, NY) received Oscar, Grammy and Emmy awards in addition to a special 'Star of the Decade' Tony award.

CINEMAS

Earliest

The earliest structure designed and exclusively used for exhibiting projected films is believed to be one erected at the Atlanta Show, Georgia USA in October 1895 to exhibit C. F. Jenkins' phantoscope. The earliest cinema constructed in Great Britain was built without permission at Olympia, London, to house the 'Theatregraph' promoted by Robert William Paul (1869–1943). This was completed by 16 Apr 1896.

Largest *World*

The largest cinema in the world is the Radio City Music Hall, New York City, opened on 27 Dec 1932 with 5945 (now 5882) seats. The Roxy, opened in New York City on 11 March 1927 had 6214 (later 5869) seats but was closed on 29 Mar 1960. Cineplex, opened at the Toronto Eaton Centre, Canada on 19 Apr 1979 has 18 separate theatres with an aggregate capacity of 1700.

Great Britain

Great Britain's largest cinema is the Odeon Theatre, Hammersmith, Greater London, with 3483 seats. The Playhouse, Glasgow had 4235 seats.

Drive-In

The world's largest drive-in cinema is Loew's Open Air at Lynn, Mass., USA with a capacity of 5000 cars. The earliest, at Wilson Boulevard, Camden, New Jersey opened on 6 June 1933.

Most cinemas

San Marino has more cinemas per total population than any other country in the world, with 1 cinema for every 1512 inhabitants. Saudi Arabia (population 8.4 million) has no cinemas. Ascension Island has a record 733 cinema seats for a population of 971 (31 Dec 1981).

Highest cinema going

The Chinese ministry of culture reported in September 1984 that there were 27,000 million cinema attendances in 1983—or nearly 27 per person per annum. The Soviet Union claims to have most cinemas in the world, with 163,400 in 1974, but this includes buildings merely equipped with even 16 mm projectors. The USA has 16,965 actual cinemas (1979). The number of cinemas in the UK reached a peak 4714 in 1944 declining to 695 with 1301 screens by 1 Apr 1984. The average weekly admissions has declined from 33,420,000 in 1944 to 1,376,470 by September 1983.

Biggest screen

The permanently installed cinema screen with the largest area is one of 92 ft 9 in × 70 ft 6 in

Above The biggest Big Screen in the world and the Imax Theatre in the Indonesian capital. (See below)

28,28 × 21,48 m installed in the Imax Theatre, Taman Mini Park, Jakarta, Indonesia opened in March 1984. It was made by Harkness Screens Ltd at Boreham Wood, Herts. A temporary screen 297 ft × 33 ft *90,5 × 10 m* was used at the 1937 Paris Exposition.

Most films seen

Albert E. Van Schmus (b. 1921) saw 16,945 films in 32 years (1949–1982) as a rater for Motion Picture Association of America Inc.

8. RADIO BROADCASTING

Origins

The earliest description of a radio transmission system was written by Dr Mahlon Loomis (USA) (b. Fulton County, NY, 21 July 1826) on 21 July 1864 and demonstrated between two kites more than 14 miles *22 km* apart at Bear's Den, Loudoun County, Virginia in October 1866. He received US patent No. 129,971 entitled Improvement in Telegraphing on 20 July 1872. He died in 1886.

Earliest patent

The first patent for a system of communication by means of electro-magnetic waves, numbered No. 12039, was granted on 2 June 1896 to the Italian-Irish Marchese Guglielmo Marconi, GCVO (Hon) (1874–1937). A public demonstration of wireless transmission of speech was, however, given in the town square of Murray, Kentucky, USA in 1892 by Nathan B. Stubblefield. He died destitute on 28 March 1928. The

© Walt Disney Productions

first permanent wireless installation was at The Needles on the Isle of Wight, by Marconi's Wireless Telegraph Co., Ltd., in November 1896.

Earliest broadcast *World*

The world's first advertised broadcast was made on 24 Dec 1906 by the Canadian born Prof Reginald Aubrey Fessenden (1868–1932) from the 420 ft *128 m* mast of the National Electric Signalling Company at Brant Rock, Massachusetts, USA. The transmission included Handel's *Largo*. Fessenden had achieved the broadcast of speech as early as November 1900 but this was highly distorted.

Great Britain

The first experimental broadcasting transmitter in Great Britain was set up at the Marconi Works in Chelmsford, Essex, in December 1919, and broadcast a news service in February 1920. The earliest regular broadcast was made from the Marconi transmitter '2MT' at Writtle, Essex, on 14 Feb 1922.

Transatlantic transmissions

The earliest transatlantic wireless signals (the letter S in Morse Code) were received by Marconi, George Stephen Kemp and Percy Paget from a 10 kW station at Poldhu, Cornwall, at Signal Hill, St John's, Newfoundland, Canada, at 12.30 p.m. on 12 Dec 1901. Human speech was first heard across the Atlantic in November 1915 when a transmission from the US Navy station at Arlington, Virginia was received by US radio-telephone engineers on the Eiffel Tower.

Earliest radio-microphones

The radio-microphone, which was in essence also the first 'bug', was devised by Reg Moores (GB) in 1947 and first used on 76 MHz in the ice show *Aladdin* at Brighton Sports Stadium, East Sussex in September 1949.

Longest BBC national broadcast

The longest BBC national broadcast was the reporting of the Coronation of Queen Elizabeth II on 2 June 1953. It began at 10.15 a.m. and finished at 5.30 p.m., after 7 hr 15 min.

Longest continuous broadcast *World*

The longest continuous broadcast (excluding disc-jockeying) has been one of 484 hr (20 days 4 hr) by Larry Norton of WGRQ FM Buffalo, New York, USA on 19 Mar–8 Apr 1981. *No further claims for the above category will*

The late Walt Disney (1901–66) who amassed a record 32 Oscar awards with his greatest cartoon creation Mickey Mouse. (See page 100 column 2)

be entertained. Radio Telefís Éireann transmitted an unedited reading of *Ulysses* by James Joyce (1882–1941) for 29 hr 38 min 47 sec on 16–17 July 1982.

Local and Hospital radio

The longest local radio transmission has been 84 hr by Robert W. Morgan of Community Radio Station WKRC, Co. Kildare, Ireland on 8–11 Jan 1982. Brian Sheard completed 208 hr 15 min of broadcasting on Manchester Hospital Radio on 15–23 Feb 1980.

Topmost Prize

Mary Buchanan, 15, on WKRQ, Cincinnati, USA won a prize of $25,000 for 40 years (viz $1 million) on 21 Nov 1980.

Brain of Britain Quiz

The youngest person to become 'Brain of Britain' on BBC radio was Anthony Carr, 16, of Anglesey in 1956. The oldest contestant has been the author and translator Hugh Merrick (d. 1981) in his 80th year in August 1977. The record score is 35 by the 1981 winner Peter Barlow of Richmond, Surrey.

Most durable programmes *BBC*

The longest running BBC radio series is *The Week's Good Cause* beginning on 24 Jan 1926. The St Francis Leprosy Guild appeal by Cardinal Basil Hume of 27 Jan 1980 raised a record £89,221. The longest running record programme is *Desert Island Discs* which began on 29 Jan 1942 and on which programme only one guest, Arthur Askey CBE, (1900–82) had been stranded a fourth time (on the 1572nd show on 20 Dec 1980). The programme was presented since its inception by Roy Plomley, OBE who died on 28 May 1985 having presented 1791 editions. The longest running solo radio feature is *Letter from America* by (Alfred) Alistair Cooke, Hon KBE (b. Salford 20 Nov 1908), first broadcast on 24 Mar 1946. The longest running radio serial is *The Archers* which was created by Godfrey Baseley and was first broadcast on 29 May 1950. Up to May 1984 the signature tune *Barwick Green* had been played over 35,390 times. The only one of 367 roles which has been played without interruption from the start has been that of Philip Archer by Norman Painting OBE (b. Leamington Spa, 23 Apr 1924).

Most Heard Broadcaster

Larry King has broadcast on network for 27½ hours a week since 30 Jan 1978 from Washington DC on Mutual Broadcasting Systems to all 50 States (now on 272 Stations).

Earliest antipodal reception

Frank Henry Alfred Walker (b. 11 Nov 1904) on the night of 12 Nov 1924 received on his home-made 2 valve receiver on 75 metres, signals from Marconi's yacht *Electra* (call sign ICCM) in Australian waters at Crown Farm, Cuttimore Lane, Walton-on-Thames, Surrey, England.

Most assiduous Radio Ham

Richard C. Spenceley (d. 30 July 1982) of KV4AA at St Thomas, Virgin Islands built his contacts (QSO's) to a record level of 48,100 in 365 days in 1978.

Most stations

The country with the greatest number of radio broadcasting stations is the United States, where there were 9512 authorised broadcast stations as at Apr 1985 made up of both AM (Amplitude modulation) and FM (Frequency modulation).

Highest listening

The peak recorded listenership on BBC Radio was 30,000,000 adults on 6 June 1950 for the boxing fight between Lee Savold (US) and Bruce Woodcock (GB) (b. Doncaster, S. Yorks, 1921).

Highest response

The highest recorded response from a radio show occurred on 27 Nov 1974 when on a 5 hr talk show on WCAU, Philadelphia, USA, Howard Sheldon, the astrologist registered a call count of 388,299 calls on the 'Bill Corsair Show'.

Smallest Set

The Toshiba AM-FM 302 launched in January 1983 measures 4.9 × 3.5 × 2.2 in *12,4 × 8,9 × 5,6 cm* and weighs 3 oz *85 g*.

9. TELEVISION

Guinness Superlatives have published *The Guinness Book of TV Facts and Feats* by Kenneth Passingham (price £9.95).

Invention

The invention of television, the instantaneous viewing of distant objects by electrical transmissions, was not an act but a process of successive and inter-dependent discoveries. The first commercial cathode ray tube was introduced in 1897 by Karl Ferdinand Braun (1850–1918), but was not linked to 'electric vision' until 1907 by Prof. Boris Rosing (disappeared 1918) of Russia in St Petersburg (now Leningrad). A. A. Campbell Swinton FRS (1863–1930) published the fundamentals of television transmission on 18 June 1908 in a brief letter to *Nature* entitled 'Distant Electric Vision'. The earliest public demonstration of television was given on 27 Jan 1926 by John Logie Baird (1888–1946) of Scotland, using a development of the mechanical scanning system patented by Paul Gottlieb Nipkow (1860–1940) on 6 Jan 1884. He had achieved the transmission of a Maltese Cross over 10 ft *3,05 m* at 8, Queen's Arcade, Hastings, East Sussex by February 1924 and the first facial image (of William Taynton, 15) at 23, Frith Street on 30 Oct 1925. Taynton had to be bribed with 2s 6d. A patent application for the Iconoscope had been filed on 29 Dec 1923 by Dr Vladimir Kosma Zworykin (1889–1982). It was not issued until 20 Dec 1938. Kenjiro Takayanagi (b. 20 Jan. 1899) succeeded in transmitting a 40-line electronic picture on 25 Dec 1926 with a Braun cathode-ray tube and a Nipkow disc at Hamamatsu Technical College, Japan. Baird launched his first television 'service' via a BBC transmitter on 30 Sept 1929 and marketed the first sets, The Baird Televisions, at £26.25 in May 1930. Public transmissions on 30 lines were made from 22 Aug 1932 until 11 Sept 1935.

Earliest service

The world's first high definition (*i.e.* 405 lines) television broadcasting service was opened from Alexandra Palace, Haringey, Greater London, on 2 Nov 1936, when there were about 100 sets in the United Kingdom. The Chief Engineer was Mr Douglas Birkinshaw. A television station in Berlin, Germany, made a low definition (180 line) transmission from 22 Mar 1935. The transmitter burnt out in Aug 1935.

Transatlantic transmission

The earliest transatlantic transmission by satellite was achieved at 1 a.m. on 11 July 1962, *via* the active satellite *Telstar 1* from Andover, Maine, USA, to Pleumeur Bodou, France. The picture was of Mr Frederick R. Kappell, chairman of the American Telephone and Telegraph Company, which owned the satellite. The first 'live' broadcast was made on 23 July 1962 and the first woman to appear was the *haute couturière*, Ginette Spanier, directrice of Balmain, the next day. On 9 Feb 1928 the image of J. L. Baird and of a Mrs Howe was transmitted from Station 2 K Z at Coulsdon, Surrey, England to Station 2 CVJ, Hartsdale, NY, USA.

Longest telecast

The longest pre-scheduled telecast on record was a continuous transmission for 163 hr 18 min by GTV 9 of Melbourne, Australia covering the Apollo XI moon mission on 19–26 July 1969. The longest continuous TV transmission under a single director was the Avro Television Production *Open het Dorp* transmitted in the Netherlands on 26–27 Nov 1962 for 23 hr 20 min under the direction of Theo Ordeman.

Video-tape recording *Earliest*

Alexander M. Poniatoff first demonstrated video-tape recording known as Ampex (his initials plus 'ex' for excellence) in 1956. The earliest demonstration of a home video recorder was on 24 June 1963 at the BBC News Studio at Alexandra Palace, London of the Telcan developed by Norman Rutherford and Michael Turner of the Nottingham Electronic Valve Co.

Most durable shows *World*

The world's most durable TV show is NBC's *Meet the Press* first transmitted on 6 Nov 1947 and weekly since 12 Sept 1948, originated by Lawrence E. Spivak, who appeared weekly as either moderator or panel member until 1975. On 11 Dec 1980 Mike Douglas presented the 4754th version of his show started in 1960.

Great Britain

Andy Pandy was first transmitted on 11 July 1950 but consisted of repeats of a cycle of 26 shows until 1970. *Come Dancing* was first transmitted on 29 Sept 1950 but is seasonal. *Sooty* was first presented on BBC by its devisor Harry Corbett (born 1918) from 1952 to 1967 and is continued by his son Matthew on ITV. *The Good Old Days* light entertainment ran from 20 July 1953 to 31 Dec 1983. Barney Colehan, MBE, produced all 244 programmes. The *BBC News* was inaugurated in vision on 5 July 1954. Richard Baker OBE read the news from 1954 to Christmas 1982. Of current affairs programmes the weekly BBC *Panorama* was first transmitted on 11 Nov 1953 but has summer breaks, whereas Granada's *What The Papers Say* has been transmitted weekly since 5 Nov 1956. The monthly *Sky at Night* has been presented by Patrick Moore OBE without a break or a miss since 26 Apr 1957. The longest serving TV quizmaster is Bamber Gascoigne of Granada's *University Challenge* which has run since 21 Sept 1962. The longest running domestic drama serial is Granada's *Coronation Street* which has run twice weekly since 9 Dec 1960. William Roache has played Ken Barlow without a break since the outset.

Most sets

The US had, by January 1984, 84.8 million TV households, with 32.2 million on Cable TV, 17.8 million on Pay TV and 25 million on Subscription satellite TV, with 3.4 million having video disc or video cassette. The number of homes with colour sets was 71,400,000 (88%) by January 1982. The average number of sets per household surpassed 2.0 in 1982. The number of licences current in the United Kingdom was 18,700,000 on 1 Apr 1985 of which 15,700,000 (84 per cent) were for colour sets. Black and white licences became less commonplace than colour in 1976.

TV Watching

In July 1978 it was estimated that the *average* American child by his or her 18th birthday has watched 710 solid days (17,040 hours) of TV, seen more than 350,600 commercials and more than 15,000 TV murders. In 1983 it was estimated that the US national average watching per household reached a record 7 hr 2 min per day in 83.3 million TV households. There are 571 TV sets per 1000 people in the USA compared with 348 in Sweden and 330 in Britain.

Greatest audience

The greatest projected number of viewers worldwide for a televised event is 2500 million for the live and recorded transmissions of the XXIIIrd Olympic Games in Los Angeles, California from 27 July to 13 Aug 1984. The American Broadcasting Co airing schedule comprised 187½ hours of coverage on 56 cameras.

The programme which attracted the highest ever viewership was the *Goodbye, Farewell and Amen* final episode of M*A*S*H (the acronym for Mobile Army Surgical Hospital 4077) transmitted by CBS on 28 Feb 1983 to 60.3 per cent of all households in the United States. It was estimated that some 125 million people tuned in, taking a 77 per cent share of all viewing. The UK record is 39 million for the wedding of TRH the Prince and Princess of Wales in London on 29 July 1981.

Violet Carson (1903–83) whose role as Ena Sharples loomed so large in the first 25 years of *Coronation Street. (Granada)*

Most expensive production

The Winds of War, a seven part Paramount World War II saga, aired by ABC was the most expensive ever TV production costing $42 million over 14 months shooting. The final episode on 13 Feb 1983 attracted a rating of 41.0 per cent (% of total number of viewers), and a share of 56 per cent (% of total sets turned on that were tuned in).

Largest contracts *World*

The highest rate for any TV contract ever signed was one for $7 million (*then £3,100,000*) for 7 hours of transmission by Marie Osmond by NBC announced on 9 Mar 1981. The figure includes talent and production costs.

Currently television's highest-paid performer is John William Carson (b. 23 Oct 1925), the host of *The Tonight Show*. His current NBC contract reportedly calls for annual payment of $5,000,000 (*now £2,275,000*) for his one hour evening show aired four times weekly. The highest-paid current affairs or news performer is Dan Rather of CBS who reportedly signed an $8 million (*then £4.7 million*) contract for five years from 1982.

Great Britain

The largest contract in British television was one of a reported £9,000,000, inclusive of production expenses, signed by Tom Jones (b. Thomas Jones Woodward, 7 June 1940) of Treforest, Mid Glamorgan, Wales in June 1968 with ABC-TV of the United States and ATV in London for 17 one-hour shows per annum from January 1969 to January 1974.

Highest paid TV Performer

Carroll O'Connor, star of *Archie Bunker's Place*, receives $275,000 (*£182,500*) for each of 22 episodes in the 1982/83 season totalling $6,050,000 (*£4 million*). Peter Falk (b. 16 Sept 1927), the disarmingly persistent detective *Columbo*, was paid from $300,000 to $350,000 for a single episode of his series of six. Singer Kenny Rogers was reported in February 1983 to have been paid $2 million (*then £1,280,000*) for a single taping of a concert for HBO (Home Box Office) TV Channel.

Largest TV prizes *World*

On 24 July 1975 WABC-TV, New York City transmitted the first televised Grand Tier draw of the State Lottery in which the winner took the grand prize of $1,000,000 (*now £454,545*). This was however taxable.

Most successful appeals

The Jerry Lewis Labor Day Telethon on 2 Sept 1984 raised $32,074,566 (*then £26,700,000*) in pledges for the Muscular Dystrophy Association. The Victims of Famine in East Africa and the Sahel appeal raised a record £9,518,736 from 17 July 1984 to 6 Feb 1985 on TV, radio and national press.

Biggest sale

The greatest number of episodes of any TV programme ever sold has been 1144 episodes of 'Coronation Street' by Granada Television to CBKST Saskatoon, Saskatchewan, Canada, on 31 May 1971. This constituted 20 days 15 hr 44 min continuous viewing. A further 728 episodes (Jan 1974–Jan 1981) were sold to CBC in August 1982.

Most prolific scriptwriter

The most prolific television writer in the world is the Rt Hon Lord Willis known as Ted Willis (b. 13 Jan 1918), who in the period 1949–85 has created 30 series, including the first seven years and 2,250,000 words of *Dixon of Dock Green* which ran from 1955 to 1976, 28 stage plays and

One of the world's two earliest Outside Broadcast Scanners was used in the BBC TV coverage of the Coronation of King George VI in May 1937. *(Thorn EMI)*

30 feature films. He had 23 plays produced. His total output since 1942 can be estimated at 18,000,000 words.

'Mastermind' Records

The BBC TV series began on 11 Sept 1972 producing a record 38 points by Miss Margaret Harris (on 'The life and work of Cecil Rhodes') in the 1984 final. Sir David Hunt KCMG, OBE won the 'Mastermind Champions' contest on 3 May 1982.

TV Producer

The most prolific TV producer in the world is Aaron Spelling (b. 1928) who, in 25 years from 1956 to 1981, produced 1435 TV episodes totalling 1457½ hours of air time. His output included *Starsky and Hutch* (89 episodes) and *Charlie's Angels* (109 episodes).

Highest TV advertising rates

The highest TV advertising rate has been $550,000 per ½ min (*then £9,166 per sec*) for ABC network prime time during the transmission of Super Bowl XIX on 19 Jan 1985. In Great Britain the peak time weekday 60 sec spot rate (5.40–10.40 p.m.) for Thames Television is £43,400 + VAT (April 1985). The longest run was 7 min 10 sec by Great Universal Stores on Good Morning Britain for £100,000 on 20 Jan 85.

Most takes

The highest number of 'takes' for a TV commercial is 28 in 1973 by Pat Coombs, the comedienne, who has supported Dick Emery on BBC TV. Her explanation was 'Everytime we came to the punch line I just could not remember the name of the product'.

Commercial records

In 1977 James Coburn of Beverly Hills, California was reputed to have been paid $500,000 (*then £250,000*) for uttering two words on a series of Schlitz beer commercials. The words 'Schlitz Light' were thus at a quarter of a million dollars per syllable. Brooke Shields (b. 31 May 1965) was reportedly paid $250,000 (*then £125,000*) for one minute of film by a Japanese TV commercial film maker in 1979. Faye Dunaway was reported in May 1979 to have been paid $900,000 (*then £450,000*) for uttering 6 words for a Japanese department store TV Commercial. Britain's most durable TV Commercial has been the Brooke Bond chimpanzee commercial first transmitted on 21 Nov 1971 and 1687 more times to October 1979.

World's Smallest Sets

The Seiko TV-Wrist Watch launched on 23 Dec 1982 in Japan has a 1.2 in *30,5 mm* screen and weighs only 80 g *2.8 oz*. Together with the receiver unit and the headphone set the entire black and white system, costing 108,000 Yen (*then £260*), weighs only 320 g *11,3 oz*. The smallest single-piece TV set is the Casio-Keisanki TV-10 weighing 338 g *11.9 oz* with a 2.7 in *6,85 cm* screen launched in Tokyo in July 1983. The smallest colour TV set is the Matsushita Electric Industry Co 1.34 lb *607 g* 'Color-Solo' television with dimensions of 11 × 3,8 × 18 cm *4.3 × 1.5 × 7.0 in* and a 1.5 in *381 mm* screen which can also serve as a portable video monitor. It was displayed in Chicago in June 1983.

Highest Definition

A TV system with a 1125 line definition was demonstrated by NHK (Nippon Hoso Kyokai) built by Hitachi and Sony at Brighton, Sussex on 19 Sept 1982.

CHAPTER SEVEN

The Worlds Structures

The largest scientific building in the world with the base of the 5 engined Stage I end of the Saturn V launcher. The Vehicle Assembly Building at the John F. Kennedy Space Center, Cape Canaveral, USA and the rocket which gulps 13.6 tonnes of liquid oxygen and kerosine per second. *(Kenneth A. Brookes)*

1. BUILDINGS FOR WORKING

LARGEST BUILDINGS

Industrial
The largest industrial plant in the world is the Nizhniy Tagil Railroad Car and Tank Plant, 85 miles *136 km* northwest of Sverdlovsk, USSR which has 827 000 m² or 204.3 acres of floor space. It has an annual capacity to produce 2500 T-72 tanks.

Commercial *World*
The greatest ground area covered by any building in the world under one roof is the auction building of the Co-operative VBA (Verenigde Bloemenveilingen Aalsmeer), which measures 808,75 × 375 m *884.4 × 410.1 yds* with a floor surface of 303,282 m² *74.94 acres.* The first section of this site of the world's largest flower auction at Aalsmeer, Netherlands was completed in February 1972. The building with the largest cubic capacity in the world is the Boeing Company's main assembly plant at Everett, Washington State, USA completed in 1968 with a capacity of 200 million ft³ *5.6 million m³.*

Great Britain

The largest building in Britain is the Ford Parts Center at Daventry, Northamptonshire, which measures 1,978 × 780 ft *602 × 237 m* and 1.6 million ft² or 36.7 acres *14,86 ha*. It was opened on 6 Sept 1972 at a cost of nearly £8 million. It employs 1600 people and is fitted with 14,000 fluorescent lights.

Largest Construction Project

The Madinat Al-Jubail Al-Sinaiyah project in Saudi Arabia (1976–1996) covering 230,412.8

The interior of the Vehicle Assembly Building opposite with a re-usable space shuttle being serviced. (Kenneth A. Brookes)

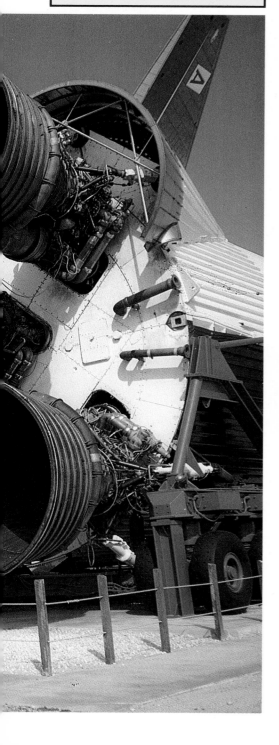

acres *932,43 km²* is the largest in history. The work force on the city and industrial port complex is increasing to a peak of 33,187 from the mid-1982 figure of 17,200. The total earth moving and dredging volume will reach 345 million m³ or *0.82 of a cubic mile*.

Scientific

The most capacious scientific building in the world is the Vehicle Assembly Building (VAB) at Complex 39, the selected site for the final assembly and launching of the Apollo moon spacecraft on the Saturn V rocket, at the John F. Kennedy Space Center (KSC) on Merritt Island, Cape Canaveral, Florida, USA. It is a steel-framed building measuring 716 ft *218 m* in length, 518 ft *158 m* in width and 525 ft *160 m* high. The building contains four bays, each with its own door 460 ft *140 m* high. Construction began in April 1963 by the Ursum Consortium. Its floor area is 343,500 ft² (7.87 acres *3,18 ha*) and its capacity is 129,482,000 ft³ *3 666 500 m³*. The building was 'topped out' on 14 Apr 1965 at a cost of $108,700,000 (*then £38.8 million*).

Administrative

The largest ground area covered by any office building is that of the Pentagon, in Arlington, Virginia, USA. Built to house the US Defense Department's offices it was completed on 15 Jan 1943 and cost an estimated $83,000,000 (*then £20,595,000*). Each of the outermost sides of the Pentagon is 921 ft *281 m* long and the perimeter of the building is about 1500 yd *1370 m*. The five storeys of the building enclose a floor area of 6,500,000 ft² *604 000 m²* (149.2 acres *60,3 ha*). During the day 29,000 people work in the building. The telephone system of the building has over 44,000 telephones connected by 160,000 miles *257 500 km* of cable and its 220 staff handle 280,000 calls a day. Two restaurants, six cafeterias and ten snack bars and a staff of 675 form the catering department of the building. The corridors measure 17 miles *27 km* in length and there are 7748 windows to be cleaned.

Office

The largest office buildings with the largest rentable space in the world are The World Trade

Center in New York City, USA with a total of 4,370,000 ft² *406 000 m²* (100.32 acres *40,6 ha*) in each of the twin towers of which the taller Tower Two (formerly B) is 1362 ft 3¼ in *415,22 m*. The tip of the TV antenna on Tower One is 1710 ft *521,2 m* above street level.

Single office *Great Britain*
The largest single office in the United Kingdom is that of West Midlands Gas at Solihull, West Midlands, built by Spooners (Hull) Ltd in 1962. It now measures 753 by 160 ft *230 by 49 m* (2.77 acres *1,12 ha*) in one open plan room accommodating 2170 clerical and managerial workers.

TALLEST BUILDINGS

World
The tallest office building in the world is the Sears Tower, the national headquarters of Sears, Roebuck & Co. in Wacker Drive, Chicago, Illinois with 110 storeys rising to 1454 ft *443 m* and begun in August 1970. Its gross area is 4,400,000 ft² (101.0 acres *40,8 ha*). It was 'topped out' on 4 May 1973. It surpassed the World Trade Center in New York City in height at 2.35 p.m. on 6 Mar 1973 with the first steel column reaching to the 104th storey. The addition of two TV antennae brought the total height to 1559 ft *475,18 m*. The building's population is 16,700 served by 103 elevators and 18 escalators. It has 16,000 windows. Tentative plans for a 169 storey 2300 ft *701 m* tall building, projected to cost $1250 million, for the Chicago Loop, Illinois, USA were published on 27 Oct 1981.

Great Britain
The tallest office block in Britain and the tallest cantilevered building in the world is the £72 million National Westminster tower block in Bishopsgate, City of London completed in 1979. It has 49 storeys and 3 basement levels, serviced by 21 lifts, and is 600 ft 4 in *183 m* tall. The gross floor area is 636,373 ft² *59,121 m²* (14.6 acres *5,9 ha*).

HABITATIONS

Greatest altitude
The highest inhabited buildings in the world are those in the Indian–Tibet border fort of Bāsisi at *c.* 19,700 ft *5988 m*. In April 1961, however, a 3-room dwelling was discovered at 21,650 ft *6600 m* on Cerro Llullaillaco (22,058 ft *6723 m*), on the Argentine–Chile border, believed to date from the late pre-Columbian period *c.* 1480. A settlement on the T'e-li-mo trail in southern Tibet is at an apparent altitude of 19,800 ft *6019 m*.

Northernmost
The most northerly habitation in the world is the Danish Scientific station set up in 1952 in Pearyland, northern Greenland (Kalaalit Nunaat), over 900 miles *1450 km* north of the Arctic Circle. Eskimo hearths dated to before 1000 BC were discovered in Pearyland in 1969. Polar Eskimos were discovered in Inglefield Land, NW Greenland in 1818. The USSR's drifting research station 'North Pole 15', passed within 1¼ miles *2,8 km* of the North Pole in December 1967. The most northerly continuously inhabited place is the Canadian Department of National Defence outpost at Alert on Ellesmere Island, Northwest Territories in Lat. 82° 30′ N, Long. 62° W, set up in 1950.

Southernmost
The most southerly permanent human habitation is the United States' Scott–Amundsen South Polar Station (see Chapter 10) completed in 1957 and replaced in 1975.

EMBASSIES AND CIVIC BUILDINGS

Largest
The largest embassy in the world is the USSR embassy on Bei Xiao Jie, Peking, China, in the north-eastern corner of the Northern walled city. The whole 45 acre *18,2 ha* area of the old Orthodox Church mission (established 1728), now known as the *Bei guan*, was handed over to the USSR in 1949. The largest in Great Britain is the United States of America Embassy in Grosvenor Square, London. The Chancery Building, completed in 1960, alone has 600 rooms for a staff of 700 on seven floors with a usable floor area of 255,000 ft² (5.85 acres *2,37 ha*).

Great Britain
The oldest municipal building in Britain is the Exeter Guildhall first referred to in a deed of 1160. The Tudor front was added in 1593.

EXHIBITION CENTRES

Largest *Great Britain*
Britain's largest exhibition centre is the National Exhibition Centre, Birmingham opened in February 1976. Five halls which inter-connect cover 87 180 m² *938,397 ft²* or 21.54 acres with a volume of 1 168 466 m³ or *41.26 million ft³*.

INDUSTRIAL STRUCTURES

Tallest chimneys *World*
The world's tallest chimney is the $5.5 million International Nickel Company's stack 1245 ft 8 in *379,6 m* tall at Copper Cliff, Sudbury, Ontario, Canada, completed in 1970. It was built by Canadian Kellogg Ltd., in 60 days and the diameter tapers from 116.4 ft *35,4 m* at the base to 51.8 ft *15,8 m* at the top. It weighs 38,390 tons *39 006 tonnes* and became operational in 1971. The world's most massive chimney is one of 1148 ft *350 m* at Puentes, Spain, built by M. W. Kellogg Co. It contains 20,600 yd³ *15 750 m³* of concrete and 2.9 million lb *1315 tonnes* of steel and has an internal volume of 6.7 million ft³ *189 720 m³*. Europe's tallest chimney serves the Zasavje thermo-power plant in Trboulje, Yugoslavia completed to 350 metres *1181 ft* on 1 June 1976.

Great Britain
The tallest chimney in Great Britain is one of 850 ft *259 m* at Drax Power Station, North Yorkshire, begun in 1966 and topped out on 16 May 1969. It has an untapered diameter of 87 ft 9 in *26 m* and has the greatest capacity of any chimney. The architects were Clifford Tee & Gale of London. The oldest known industrial chimney in Britain is the Stone Edge Chimney, near Chesterfield, Derbyshire built to a height of 55 ft *16,76 m* ante 1771.

Cooling towers
The largest cooling tower in the world is that adjacent to the nuclear power plant at Uentrop, W. Germany which is 590 ft *179,8 m* tall. It was completed in 1976. The largest in the United Kingdom of the Ferrybridge and Didcot type measure 375 ft *114 m* tall and 300 ft *91 m* across the base.

HANGARS

Largest *World*
Hangar 375 ('Big Texas') at Kelly Air Force Base, San Antonio, Texas, USA completed on 15 Feb 1956. It has 4 doors each 250 ft *76,2 m* wide and 60 ft *18,28 m* high weighing 598 tons/ *608 tonnes*. The high bay area measures 2000 × 300 × 90 ft *609,6 × 91,4 × 27,4 m* and is surrounded by a 44 acre *17,8 ha* concrete apron. Delta Air Lines' jet base on a 140 acre *56,6 ha* site at Hartsfield International Airport, Atlanta, Georgia, has 36 acres *14,5 ha* under roof.

Great Britain
The largest hangar building in the United Kingdom is the Britannia Assembly Hall at the former Bristol Aeroplane Company's works at Filton, Avon, now part of British Aerospace. The overall width of the Hall is 1054 ft *321 m*

EARLIEST STRUCTURES

World
The earliest known human structure is a rough circle of loosely piled lava blocks found on the lowest cultural level at the Lower Palaeolithic site at Olduvai Gorge in Tanzania excavated by the Leakeys' in 1960. The structure was associated with artifacts and bones and may represent a work-floor, dating to *c.* 1,700,000 BC. The earliest evidence of *buildings* yet discovered is that of 21 huts with hearths or pebble-lined pits and delimited by stake holes found in October 1965 at the Terra Amata site in Nice, France thought to belong to the Acheulian culture of *c.* 400,000 years ago. Excavation carried out between 28 June and 5 July 1966 revealed one hut with palisaded walls with axes of 49 ft *15 m* and 20 ft *6 m*. The oldest free standing structures in the world are now believed to be the megalithic temples at Mgarr and Skorba in Malta and Ggantija in Gozo dating from *c.* 3250 BC. The remains of a stone tower 20 ft *6,1 m* high originally built into the walls of Jericho has been excavated and is dated to 5000 BC. The foundations of the walls have been dated to as early as 8350 BC.

Great Britain
Twelve small stone clusters, associated with broken bones and charcoal in stratum C of the early palaeolithic site at Hoxne, Suffolk may be regarded as Britain's earliest structures dated *c.* 250,000 BC. Remains of the earliest dated stone shelter and cooking pit were discovered in 1967 at Culver Well, Isle of Portland, Dorset (Mesolithic, 5200 BC ± 135). On the Isle of Jura, Strathclyde, Scotland a hearth consisting of three linked stone circles has been dated to the Mesolithic period 6013 ± 200 BC. The only original piece of Roman building from the 1st century AD surviving is the bottom 14 ft *4,25 m* of the Dover beacon.

Ireland
The earliest known evidence of human occupation in Ireland dates from the Mesolithic period *c.* 7500 at the Carrowmore site in County Sligo. Ireland became enisled or separated from Great Britain *c.* 9050 BC. Nearby megalithic burials dated to 3800 ± 80 BC are the earliest in Europe.

and the overall depth of the centre bay is 420 ft *128 m*. It encloses a floor area of 7½ acres *3,0 ha*. The cubic capacity of the Hall is 33,000,000 ft³ *934 000 m³*. The building was begun in April 1946 and completed by September 1949.

GARAGES

Largest *World*

The world's largest car park is for 20,000 cars at the West Edmonton Mall, Edmonton, Alberta, Canada. There are overflow facilities with an adjoining lot for 10,000 more cars (see below).

Great Britain

Great Britain's highest capacity underground car park is that under the Victoria Centre, Nottingham with a capacity of 1650 cars, opened in June 1972.

Private

The largest private garage ever built was one for 100 cars at the Long Island, New York mansion of William Kissam Vanderbilt (1849–1920).

Parking lot

The parking lots were invented in Los Angeles, California in 1917. The world's most capacious parking is at the West Edmonton Mall, Edmonton, Alberta, Canada, with 30,000 slots (see above and Chapter 9). The largest parking area in Great Britain is that for 15,000 cars and 200 coaches at the National Exhibition Centre, Birmingham (see p. 106).

Filling stations

Little America, west of Cheyenne, Wyoming, USA, at the junction of Interstate Routes 80 and 25 claims to be the world's biggest gas station with 52 diesel and gas pumps—none self-service. The highest in the world is at Leh, Ladakh, India at 3658 m *12,001 ft* operated by Indiaoil. The largest filling station of the 36,000 in the United Kingdom is the Esso service area on the M4 at Leigh Delamere, Wiltshire, opened on 3 Jan 1972. It has 48 petrol and diesel pumps and extends over 43 acres *17,4 ha*.

GLASSHOUSE

Largest *Great Britain*

The largest glasshouse in the United Kingdom is one covering 22.5 acres *9,10 ha* owned by Van Heyningen Bros. at Waterham, Herne Bay, Kent completed in October 1982. The crop of 160,000 tomato plants is under 1155 tons of glass.

Above The world's tallest office block, the Sears Tower in Chicago, Illinois. It has 16 000 windows—almost one for each of its inhabitants. *(Kenneth A. Brookes). Below* The American Embassy—the largest of all those in London with almost 6 acres of floor space. *(Colin Smith)*

GRAIN ELEVATOR

Largest

The world's largest single-unit grain elevator is that operated by the C-G-F-Grain Company at Wichita, Kansas, USA. Consisting of a triple row of storage tanks, 123 on each side of the central loading tower or 'head house', the unit is 2,717 ft *828 m* long and 100 ft *30 m* wide. Each tank is 120 ft *37 m* high, with an inside diameter of 30 ft *9 m* giving a total storage capacity of 20,000,000 bushels *7,3 million hl* of wheat. The largest collection of elevators in the world are the 23 at City of Thunder Bay, Ontario, Canada, on Lake Superior with a total capacity of 103.9 million bushels *37,4 million hl*.

SEWAGE WORKS

Largest *World*

The largest single full treatment sewage works in the world is the West-Southwest Treatment Plant, opened in 1940 on a site of 501 acres *203 ha* in Chicago, Illinois, USA. It serves an area containing 2,940,000 people. It treated an average of 835,000,000 US gal *3160 million litres* of wastes per day in 1973. The capacity of its sedimentation and aeration tanks is 1 280 000 m³ *1.6 million yd³*.

Great Britain

The largest full treatment works in Britain and probably in Europe is the GLC Beckton Works which serves a 2,966,000 population and handles a daily flow of 207 million gal *941 million litres* in a tank capacity of 757,000 ft³ *21 400 m³*.

WOODEN BUILDING

Largest

The world's largest buildings in timber are the two US Navy airship hangers built in 1942–3 at Tillamook, Oregon. Now used by the Louisiana-Pacific Corporation as a saw mill they measure 1000 ft long, 170 ft high at the crown and 296 ft wide at the base (*304,8 m × 51,8 m × 90,22 m*) and are worth $6 million (now £2.7 million).

AIR-SUPPORTED BUILDING

Largest

The world's largest air-supported roof has been that of the 80,600 capacity octagonal Pontiac Silverdome Stadium, Michigan, USA measuring 522 ft *159 m* in width and 722 ft *220 m* in length. The air pressure was 5 lb/in² *34,4 kPa* supporting the 10 acre *4 ha* translucent 'Fiberglas' roofing. The structural engineers were Geiger-Berger Associates of New York City. The largest standard size air hall was one 860 ft *262 m* long, 140 ft *42,6 m* wide and 65 ft *19,8 m* high. One was first sited at Lima, Ohio, USA, made by Irvin Industries of Stamford, Connecticut, USA.

2. BUILDINGS FOR LIVING

WOODEN BUILDINGS

Oldest

The oldest extant wooden buildings in the world are those comprising the Pagoda, Chumanar gate and the Temple of Horyu (Horyu-ji), at Nara, Japan, dating from *c.* AD 670 and com-

The 44 storey 419 ft *127 m* tall Shakespeare Tower in the Barbican in the City of London—the highest residential block of flats in Great Britain. (*Colin Smith*)

pleted in 715. The nearby Daibutsuden, built in 1704–11, once measured 285.4 ft long, 167.3 ft wide and 153.3 ft tall *87 × 51 × 46,75 m*. The present dimensions are 188 × 165.3 × 159.4 ft *57,3 × 50,4 × 48,6 m*.

CASTLES

Earliest *World*

The oldest castle in the world is that at Gomdan, in the Yemen, which originally had 20 storeys and dates from before AD 100.

Great Britain

The oldest stone castle extant in Great Britain is Richmond Castle, Yorkshire, built in *c.* 1075. Iron Age relics from the first century BC or AD have been found in the lower levels of the Dover Castle site.

Ireland

The oldest Irish castle is Ferrycarrig near Wexford dating from *c.* 1180. The oldest castle in Northern Ireland is Carrickfergus Castle, County Antrim, Northern Ireland, which dates from before 1210.

Largest *World, UK and Ireland*

The largest inhabited castle in the world is the Royal residence of Windsor Castle at New Windsor, Berkshire. It is primarily of 12th century construction and is in the form of a waisted parallelogram 1890 ft by 540 ft *576 by 164 m*. The total area of Dover Castle however covers 34 acres *13,75 ha* with a width of 1100 ft *335,2 m* and a curtain wall of 1800 ft *550 m* or if underground works are taken in, 2300 ft *700 m*. The overall dimensions of Carisbrooke Castle (450 ft by 360 ft *110 by 137 m*), Isle of Wight, if its earthworks are included, are 1350 ft by 825 ft *411 m by 251 m*. The largest castle in Scotland is Edinburgh Castle with a major axis of 1320 ft *402 m* and measuring 3360 ft *1025 m* along its perimeter wall including the Esplanade. The most capacious of all Irish castles is Carrickfergus (see above) but that with the most extensive fortifications is Trim Castle, County Meath, built in *c.* 1205 with a curtain wall 1455 ft *443 m* long.

Forts *Largest*

The largest ancient castle in the world is Hradčany Castle, Prague, Czechoslovakia originating in the 9th century. It is a very oblong irregular polygon with an axis of 570 m *1870 ft* and an average traverse diameter of 128 m *420 ft* with a surface area of 7,28 ha *18 acres*. Fort George, Ardersier, Scotland built in 1748–69 measures 2100 ft *640 m* in length and has an average width of 620 ft *189 m*. The total site covers 42½ acres *17,2 ha*.

Thickest walls

Urnammu's city walls at Ur (now Muqayyar), destroyed by the Elamites in 2006 BC were 27 m *88⅓ ft* thick. The walls of the Great Tower or Donjon of Flint Castle, built in 1277–80 are 23 ft *7,01 m* thick. The largest Norman keep in Britain is that of Colchester Castle measuring 152½ ft *46 m* by 111½ ft *34 m*.

PALACES

Largest *World*

The largest palace in the world is the Imperial Palace (*Gu gong*) in the centre of Peking (*Bei jing*, the northern capital), China, which covers a rectangle 1050 yd by 820 yd *960 by 750 m*, an area of 177.9 acres *72 ha*. The outline survives from the construction of the third Ming Emperor, Yung lo of 1402–24, but due to constant re-arrangements most of the intra-mural buildings are 18th century. These consist of 5 halls and 17 palaces of which the last occupied by the

last Empress was the Palace of Accumulated Elegance (*Chu xia gong*) until 1924.

The Palace of Versailles, 23 km *14 miles* southwest of Paris has a facade with 375 windows, 634 yards *580 m* in length. The building, completed in 1682 for Louis XIV occupied over 30,000 workmen under Jules Hardouin-Mansert.

Currently residential

The palace (Istana Nurul Iman) of H.M. the Sultan of Brunei in the capital Bandar Seri Begawan completed in January 1984 at a reported cost of £300 million is the largest in the world with 1788 rooms. The underground garage has to accommodate the Sultan's 110 cars.

Great Britain

The largest palace in the United Kingdom in Royal use is Buckingham Palace, London, so named after its site, bought in 1703 by John Sheffield, the 1st Duke of Buckingham and Normanby (1648–1721). Buckingham House was reconstructed in the Palladian style between 1835 and 1836, following the design of John Nash (1752–1835). The 610 ft *186 m* long East Front was built in 1846 and refaced in 1912. The Palace, which stands in 39 acres *15,8 ha* of garden, has 600 rooms including a ballroom 111 ft *34 m* long.

The largest ever Royal palace has been Hampton Court Palace, Greater London, acquired by Henry VIII from Cardinal Wolsey in 1525 and greatly enlarged by the King and later by William III, Anne and George I, whose son George II was its last resident monarch. It covers 4 acres *1,6 ha* of a 669 acre *270,7 ha* site.

Largest moat

The world's largest moats are those which surround the Imperial Palace in Peking (see above). From plans drawn by French sources it appears to measure 54 yd *49 m* wide and have a total length of 3600 yd *3290 m*. The city's moats total in all 23½ miles *38 km*.

FLATS

Largest

The largest blocks of private flats in Britain are the Barbican Estate, London, EC2 with 2011 flats on a 40 acre *16 ha* site with covered parking space for 2000 cars. The architects were Chamberlain, Powell and Bon.

Tallest *World*

The tallest block of flats in the world are Lake Point Towers of 70 storeys, and 645 ft *197 m* in Chicago, Illinois, USA.

Great Britain

The tallest residential block in Great Britain is the Shakespeare Tower in the Barbican in the City of London, which has 116 flats on 44 storeys and rises to a height of 419 ft 2½ in *127,77 m* above the street. The first of the three Barbican towers was 'topped out' in May 1971.

Most Expensive

The highest price quoted for any apartment is the penthouse of Trump Tower at 5th Avenue and 56th Street, New York City quoted in April 1983 at $10 million (£7,150,000).

A flat with 5 bedrooms and 5 bathrooms in Grosvenor Square, Mayfair, London W1 with south-facing roof garden was reported in April 1985 to be on the market for £3 million for a lease of less than 50 years by the agents Lassman's.

HOTELS

Largest *World*

The hotel with most rooms in the world is the 12

storey Hotel Rossiya in Moscow, USSR, with 3200 rooms providing accomodation for 6,000 guests, opened in 1967. It would thus require more than 8½ years to spend one night in each room. In addition there is a 21 storey 'Presidential' tower in the central courtyard. The hotel employs about 3000 people, and has 93 lifts. The ballroom is reputed to be the world's largest. Muscovites are not permitted as residents while foreigners are charged 16 times more than the very low rate charged to USSR officials. The Izmailovo Hotel complex, opened in July 1980 for the XXIInd Olympic Games in Moscow, was designed to accommodate 9500 people.

The Las Vegas Hilton, Nevada, USA built in 1974–81 has 3174 rooms, 12 international restaurants and a staff of 3600. It has a 10 acre *2,47 ha* rooftop recreation deck and 125,000 ft² *11 600 m²* of convention space.

Great Britain
The greatest sleeping capacity of any hotel in Great Britain is 1859 in the London Forum Hotel, Cromwell Road, London SW7 with a staff of 419. It was opened in 1973. The Regent Palace Hotel, Piccadilly Circus, London, opened 20 May 1915, has however 225 more rooms totalling 1140. The largest hotel is the Grosvenor House Hotel, Park Lane, London, which was opened in 1929. It is of 8 storeys covering 2½ acres *1 ha* and caters for more than 100,000 visitors per year in 470 rooms. The Great Room is the largest hotel room measuring 181 ft by 131 ft *55 by 40 m* with a height of 23 ft *7 m*. Banquets for 1500 are frequently handled. The Regent Hotel, Royal Leamington Spa, Warwickshire was claimed to be the largest in the world when first opened in 1819 with 100 bedrooms and one bathroom.

Tallest
The tallest hotel in the world, measured from the street level of its main entrance to the top, is the 741.9 ft *226,1 m* tall 73 storey Westin Stamford in Raffles City, Singapore topped out in March 1985. The £100 million hotel is operated by Western International Hotels and owned by Portman Properties. Their Detroit Plaza measuring from the rear entrance level is however 748 ft *227,9 m* tall. Britain's tallest hotel is the 27 storey 380 ft *132,24 m* tall London Forum Hotel (see above).

Largest lobby
The world's largest hotel lobby is that of The Grand Hotel, Taipei, Taiwan completed on 10 Oct 1973. It measures 47 × 35 m *154 × 114 ft* and is 9,6 m *31½ ft* high.

Most expensive
The world's costliest hotel accommodation was the Royale Suite in the Nova Park Elysées, Rue François, Paris at $5500 (£3525) per day. It has 8 rooms, 7 bathrooms, 3 terraces and a conference room covering 431,5 m² *4644 ft²*.

The most expensive hotel suite in Britain is the Royal Suite on the 8th floor of the Hotel Inter-Continental, London W1, at £632.50 (incl. VAT) (May 1984).

Spas
The largest spa in the world measured by number of available hotel rooms is Vichy, Allier, France, with 14,000 rooms. Spas are named after the watering place in the Liège province of Belgium where hydropathy was developed from 1626. The highest French spa is Baréges, Hautes-Pyrénées, at 4068 ft *1240 m* above sea level.

HOUSING

Largest estate
The largest housing estate in the United King-

dom is the 1670-acre *675 ha* Becontree Estate, on a site of 3000 acres *1214 ha* in Barking and Redbridge, Greater London, built between 1921 and 1929. The total number of homes is 26,822, with an estimated population of nearly 90,000.

New towns
Of the 23 new towns being built in Great Britain that with the largest eventual planned population is Milton Keynes, Buckinghamshire, with a projected 250,000 for 1992.

Largest house *World*
The largest private house in the world is the 250-room Biltmore House in Asheville, North Carolina, USA. It is owned by George and William Cecil, grandsons of George Washington Vanderbilt II (1862–1914). The house was built between 1890 and 1895 in an estate of 119,000 acres *48 160 ha*, at a cost of $4,100,000 (now £1,708,333) and now valued at $55,000,000 with 12,000 acres *4856 ha*. The most expensive private house ever built is The Hearst Ranch at San Simeon, California, USA. It was built in 1922–39 for William Randolph Hearst (1863–1951), at a total cost of more than $30,000,000 (*then £6,120,000*). It has more than 100 rooms, a 104 ft *32 m* long heated swimming pool, an 83 ft *25 m* long assembly hall and a garage for 25 limousines. The house required 60 servants to maintain it.

Great Britain
The largest house in Great Britain was Wentworth Woodhouse, near Rotherham, South Yorkshire, formerly the seat of the Earls Fitzwilliam and now a teachers' training college. The main part of the house, built over 300 years ago, has more than 240 rooms with over 1000 windows, and its principal façade is 600 ft *183 m* long. The Royal residence, Sandringham House, Norfolk, has been reported to have had 365 rooms before the demolition of 73 surplus rooms in 1975. The largest house in Ireland is Castletown in County Kildare, owned by the Hon. Desmond Guinness and is the headquarters of the Irish Georgian Society. Scotland's largest house is Hopetoun House, West Lothian, built between 1696 and 1756 with a west façade 675 ft *206 m* long.

Smallest
The smallest house in Britain is the 19th century fisherman's cottage at 22 High Street, Conwy, Gwynedd. It has a 72 in *182 cm* frontage, is 122 in *309 cm* high and has two tiny rooms and a staircase. The house with the narrowest known frontage is the 58 inches *1,47 m* of 21, Manor Road, Kingston, Portsmouth. It was built over a footpath.

The naval veteran of the Battle of Jutland (1916) Alexander Wortley (1900–80) lived his last 20 years in a green painted box in the garden of David Moreau in Langley Park, Buckinghamshire. It measured 5 × 4 × 3 ft *1,5 × 1,2 × 0,91 m* with an extension for his feet—small enough as he said to 'keep women out'. He paid no rent, rates or taxes and did not believe in insurance, pensions or governments.

Most expensive *Houses*
The most expensive private house is The Kenstead Hall with the adjoining Beechwood property in The Bishop's Avenue, Hampstead, London, residence of the late king of Saudi Arabia. It was put on the market for £16 million in August 1982.

Oldest
The oldest house in Britain is Eastry Court near Sandwich, Kent dating from AD 603. Some of the original timbers and stone infill still survives behind its present Georgian façade.

Above The hotel with most bedrooms in Great Britain is the Regent Palace, Piccadilly Circus, London. *(Colin Smith) Below* An artist's impression of the world's tallest hotel—the 73 storey Westin Stamford in Singapore.

Stately home most visited

The most visited stately home in the United Kingdom in 1984 was Warwick Castle, near Stratford-on-Avon with 560,000 visitors.

Barracks

The oldest purpose built barracks in the world are believed to be Collins Barracks, formerly the Royal Barracks, Dublin, Ireland, completed in 1704 and still in use.

3. BUILDINGS FOR ENTERTAINMENT

STADIUM

Largest *World*

The world's largest stadium is the open Strahov Stadium in Praha (Prague), Czechoslovakia. It was completed in 1934 and can accommodate 240,000 spectators for mass displays of up to 40,000 Sokol gymnasts.

Football

The largest football stadium in the world is the Maracaña Municipal Stadium in Rio de Janeiro, Brazil, where the football ground has a normal capacity of 205,000, of whom 155,000 may be seated. A crowd of 199,854 was accommodated for the World Cup final between Brazil and Uruguay on 16 July 1950. A dry moat, 7ft *2,13 m* wide and more than 5 ft *1,5 m* deep, protects players from spectators and *vice versa*. Britain's most capacious football stadium is Hampden Park, Glasgow opened on 31 Oct 1903 and once surveyed to accommodate 184,000 compared with an attendance of 149,547 on 17 Apr 1937 and the present licensed limit of 74,400.

Covered

The Azteca Stadium, Mexico City, Mexico, opened in 1968, has a capacity of 107,000 of whom nearly all are under cover. The world's largest retractable roof is being constructed to cover the 60,000 capacity Toronto Blue Jays new stadium near the CN Tower for completion by Aug 1988. The diameter will be 207 m *679 ft*.

The largest covered stadium in Britain is the Empire Stadium Wembley, Brent, Greater London, opened in April 1923. It was the scene of the 1948 Olympic Games and the final of the 1966 World Cup. In 1962–3 the capacity under cover was increased to 100,000 of whom 45,000 may be seated. The original cost was £1,250,000.

Largest roof

The transparent acryl glass 'tent' roof over the Munich Olympic Stadium, W. Germany measures 914,940 ft² (21.0 acres *8,5 ha*) in area resting on a steel net supported by masts. The roof of longest span in the world is the 680 ft *207,2 m* diameter of the Louisiana Superdome (see below). The major axis of the elliptical Texas Stadium completed in 1971 at Irving, Texas is however 240 m *787 ft 4 in*.

Indoor

The world's largest indoor stadium is the 13 acre *5,26 ha* \$173 million (*then £75 million*) 273 ft *83,2 m* tall Superdome in New Orleans, Louisiana, USA, completed in May 1975. Its maximum seating capacity for conventions is 97,365 or 76,791 for football. Box suites rent for \$35,000 excluding the price of admission. A gondola with six 312 in *7,92 m* TV screens produces instant replay.

Ballroom

The dance floor used for championships at Earl's Court Exhibition Hall, Kensington, London extends 256 ft *78 m* in length.

Amusement resort

The world's largest amusement resort is Disney World in 27,443 acres *11 105 ha* of Orange and Osceola counties, 20 miles *32 km* south west of Orlando in central Florida, USA. It was opened on 1 Oct 1971. This \$400 million investment attracted a peak 13,221,000 visitors in 1981. The most attended resort in the world is Disneyland, Anaheim, California (opened 1955) where the total number of visitors reached 233,949,291 to 21 Apr 1984. The greatest attendance in a day was 82,516 on 16 Aug 1969 and the annual peak 11,522,000 in 1980/81.

The \$900 million Epcot Center (Experimental Prototype Community of Tomorrow) near Orlando, Florida, was opened in Oct 1982.

Largest pleasure beach

The largest pleasure beach in the world is Virginia Beach, Virginia, USA. It has 28 miles *45 km* of beach front on the Atlantic and 10 miles *16 km* of estuary frontage. The area embraces 255 miles² *600 km²* and 134 hotels and motels.

Piers *Earliest longest and most*

A pleasure pier was completed at Great Yarmouth, Norfolk in 1808 but was washed away in 1953. The Old Pier, Weymouth, Dorset dates back to 1812. The longest pleasure pier in the world is Southend Pier at Southend-on-Sea in Essex. It is 1.34 miles *2,15 km* in length. It was first opened in August 1889 with final extensions made in 1929. In 1949–50 the pier had 5,750,000 visitors. The pier railway was closed in October 1978.

The resort with most piers is Atlantic City, New Jersey, USA with 6 pre-war and 5 currently. In Britain only Blackpool has three—North, Central and South.

Earliest fair

The earliest major international fair was the Great Exhibition of 1851 in the Crystal Palace, Hyde Park, City of Westminster, Greater London which in 141 days attracted 6,039,195 admissions.

Largest fair

The largest ever International Fair site was that for the St Louis, Missouri, Louisiana Purchase Exposition which covered 1271.76 acres *514,66 ha*. It also staged the 1904 Olympic Games and drew an attendance of 19,694,855.

Record fair attendance

The record attendance for any fair was 64,218,770 for Expo 70 held on an 815 acre *330 ha* site at Osaka, Japan from March to 13 Sept 1970. It made a profit of 19,439,402,017 yen (*then £22.6 million*).

Big wheel

The original Ferris Wheel, named after its constructor, George W. Ferris (1859–96), was erected in 1893 at the Midway, Chicago, Illinois, at a cost of \$385,000 (*then £79,218*). It was 250 ft *76 m* in diameter, 790 ft *240 m* in circumference, weighed 1070 tons *1087 tonnes* and carried 36 cars each seating 60 people, making a total of 2160 passengers. The structure was removed in 1904 to St Louis, Missouri and was eventually sold as scrap for \$1800 (*then £370*). In 1897 a Ferris Wheel with a diameter of 300 ft *91 m* was erected for the Earl's Court Exhibition, London. It had ten 1st-class and 30 2nd-class cars. The largest wheel now operating is 'The Giant Peter' at Himeji Central Park, Himeji City, Hyogo, Japan with a height of 85 m *278 ft 10 in*. It has 46 cars and was completed on 4 May 1984.

Fastest and longest switchbacks

The maximum speeds claimed for switchbacks, scenic railways or roller coasters have in the past been exaggerated for commercial reasons. The twin track triple helix American Eagle at Marriott's Great America, Gurnee, Illinois opened on 23 May 1981 has a vertical drop of 147.4 ft *44,92 m* on which a speed of 66.31 mph *106,73 km/h* is reached. The longest roller coaster in the world is *The Beast* at Kings Island near Cincinnati, Ohio, USA. Scientific tests at the base of its 141 ft *42,98 m* high drop returned a speed of 64.77 mph *104,23 km/h* on 5 Apr 1980. The run of 7400 ft or 1.40 miles *2,25 km* incorporates 800 ft *243,8 m* of tunnels and a 540 degree banked helix. The tallest is the Moonsault Scramble at the Fujikyu Highland Park, nr. Kawaguchi Lake, Japan opened on 24 June 1983. It is 75 m *246 ft* tall (with a speed of 105 km/h *65.2 mph*).

Longest slide

The longest slide in the world is at the Bromley Alpine Slide on Route 11 in Peru, Vermont, USA. This has a length of 4600 ft *1402 m* (0.87 mile) and a vertical drop of 820 ft *250 m*.

Restaurants

The earliest restaurant, so described, was opened by M. Boulanger in Rue des Paulies, Paris in 1765. The Paris restaurant now serving most 'covers' per day is La Cupole with 2,000. The highest restaurant in the world is at the Chacaltaya ski resort, Bolivia at 5340 m *17,519 ft*. The highest in Great Britain is the Ptarmigan Observation Restaurant at 3650 ft *1112 m* above sea-level on Cairngorm (4084 ft *1244 m*) near Aviemore, Highland, Scotland.

Harem largest

The world's most capacious harem is the Winter Harem of the Grand Seraglio at Topaki, Istanbul, Turkey completed in 1589 with 400 rooms. By the time of the deposing of Abdul Hamid II in 1909 the number of *carge* (those who serve) had dwindled from 1200 to 370 odalisques with 127 eunuchs.

Night club *Oldest*

The earliest night club (*boite de nuit*) was 'Le Bal des Anglais' at 6 Rue des Anglais, Paris, 5e France. It was founded in 1843 but closed *c.* 1960.

Largest

The largest night club in the world is Gilley's Club (formerly Shelly's) built in 1955 and extended in 1971 on Spencer Highway, Houston, Texas, USA with a seating capacity of 6000 under one roof covering 4 acres *1,6 ha*. In the more classical sense the largest night club in the world is 'The Mikado' in the Akasaka district of Tōkyō, Japan, with a seating capacity of 2000. It is 'manned' by 1250 hostesses. Binoculars are essential to an appreciation of the floor show.

Lowest

The lowest night club is the 'Minus 206' in Tiberias, Israel on the shores of the Sea of Galilee. It is 206 m *676 ft* below sea-level. An alternative candidate is 'Outer Limits', opposite the Cow Palace, San Francisco, California which was raided for the 151st time on 1 Aug 1971. It has been called 'The Most Busted Joint' and 'The Slowest to Get the Message'.

4. TOWERS AND MASTS

TALLEST STRUCTURES

World

The tallest structure in the world is the guyed Warszawa Radio mast at Konstantynow near Gabin and Płock 60 miles *96 km* north-west of

PUBLIC HOUSES

Oldest
There are various claimants to the title of the United Kingdom's oldest inn. A foremost claimant is 'The Fighting Cocks', St Albans, Hertfordshire (an 11th century structure on an 8th century site). The timber frame of The Royalist Hotel, Digbeth Street, Stow-on-the-Wold, Gloucestershire has been dated to 1000 years before the present. It was the inn 'The Eagle and the Child' in the 13th century and known to exist in AD 947. An origin as early as AD 560 has been claimed for 'Ye Olde Ferry Boat Inn' at Holywell, Cambridgeshire. There is some evidence that it antedates the local church, built in 980, but the earliest documents are not dated earlier than 1100. There is evidence that the 'Bingley Arms', Bardsey, near Leeds, West Yorkshire, restored and extended in 1738, existed as the 'Priest's Inn' according to Bardsey Church records dated 905.

The oldest pub in Ireland is Grace Neill's Bar, Donaghadee, County Down built in 1611. An inn stood on the site of the Brazen Head Inn, Lower Bridge Street, Dublin since the late 12th century. The present structure dates from 1668.

Largest *World*
The largest beer-selling establishment in the world is the Mathäser, Bayerstrasse 5, München (Munich), West Germany, where the daily sale reaches 84,470 pts *48 000 litres*. It was established in 1829, was demolished in World War II and re-built by 1955 and now seats 5500 people. The through-put at the Dube beer halls in the Bantu township of Soweto, Johannesburg, South Africa may, however, be higher on some Saturdays when the average consumption of 6000 gal (48,000 pts *27 280 litres*) is far exceeded.

Great Britain
The largest public house in Great Britain is the Courage House, Downham Tavern, Downham Way, Bromley, Kent built in 1930. Two large bars (counter length 45 ft *13,7 m*) accommodate 1000 customers with 18–20 staff.

Smallest
The smallest pub in Great Britain is the 17th century 'The Nutshell', Bury St Edmunds, Suffolk with maximum dimensions of 15 ft 10 in by 7 ft 6 in *4,82 × 2,28 m* or 118.74 ft² *11,03 m²*. The bar room in the Earl Grey, Quenington, Gloucestershire measures 116.37 ft² *10,81 m²*.

Longest bars *World*
The world's longest permanent bar is the 340 ft *103,6 m* long bar in Lulu's Roadhouse, Kitchener, Ontario, Canada opened on 3 Apr 1984. The famous Working Men's Club bar at Mildura, Victoria, Australia has a counter 298 ft *90,8 m* in length, served by 27 pumps. Temporary bars have been erected of greater length. The Bar at Erickson's on Burnside Street, Portland, Oregon, in its heyday (1883–1920) possessed a bar which ran continuously around and across the main saloon measuring 684 ft *208,48 m*. The chief bouncer Edward 'Spider' Johnson had a chief assistant named 'Jumbo' Reilly who weighed 23 stone and was said to resemble 'an ill-natured orang-utan'. Beer was 5 cents for 16 fluid ounces.

United Kingdom and Ireland
The longest bar in the United Kingdom with beer pumps is the Long Bar at The Cornwall Coliseum Auditorium at Carlyon Bay, St. Austell, Cornwall measuring 104 ft 4 in *31,8 m* and having 34 dispensers (beer and lager). The longest bar in a pub is of 104 ft 3 in *31,77 m* in The Horse Shoe, Drury Street, Glasgow. The Grand Stand Bar at Galway Racecourse, Ireland completed in 1955, measures 210 ft *64 m*.

Longest tenure
There are no collated records on licensees but the 'Glan-y-Afon Inn', Milwr near Holywell, North Wales had a 418 year long (1559–1977) run within a family which ended with the retirement of Mrs Mary Evans.

Longest name
The pub with the longest name is the 49 letter 'Henry J. Bean's But His Friends All Call Him Hank Bar and Grill', Raphael Street, London SW7.

Shortest name
The public house in the United Kingdom with the shortest name was the 'X' at Westcott, Cullompton, Devon but in October 1983 the name was changed to the 'Merry Harriers'.

Commonest name
The commonest pub name in Britain is 'Red Lion' of which there are probably about 630. John A. Blackwell of Poole, Dorset has spotted over 5000 different pub names. Gordon Wright of Wollaton, Nottingham has recorded 16,840 differently-named pubs in a continued recording of 'Inn-Signia' begun in 1914 by his friend the late John W. Leaver of Ruislip, Middlesex.

Highest
The highest public house in the United Kingdom is the 'Tan Hill Inn' in North Yorkshire. It is 1732 ft *528 m* above sea-level, on the moorland road between Reeth, North Yorkshire and Brough, Cumbria. The highest pub open the year round is the 'Cat and Fiddle' in Cheshire, near Buxton, Derbyshire at 1690 ft *515 m*. The White Lady Restaurant, 2550 ft *777 m* up on Cairngorm (4084 ft *1244 m*) near Aviemore, Highland, Scotland is the highest licensed restaurant.

Most visits
Stanley House of Totterdown, Bristol has visited 3303 differently named pubs in Britain by way of public transport only to 1 May 1985. Jimmy Young GM BEM, of Better Pubs Ltd claims to have visited 23,338 different pubs.

'The Ferret & Firkin in the Balloon up the Creek' which with a mere 39 letters has now been dethroned as the longest-named pub by a 49 letter contender. (See Longest name below) *(David L. Roberts)*

---

the capital of Poland. It is 646,38 m *2120 ft 8 in* tall or more than four tenths of a mile. The mast was completed on 18 July 1974 and put into operation on 22 July 1974. It was designed by Jan Polak and weighs 550 tons/*tonnes*. The mast is so high that anyone falling off the top would reach their terminal velocity and hence cease to be accelerating before hitting the ground. Work was begun in July 1970 on this tubular steel construction, with its 15 steel guy ropes. It recaptured for Europe a record held in the USA since the Chrysler Building surpassed the Eiffel Tower in 1929.

Great Britain
The tallest structure in the United Kingdom is the Independent Broadcasting Authority's mast north of Horncastle, Lincolnshire completed in 1965 to a height of 1265 ft *385 m* with 7 ft *2,13 m* added by meteorological equipment installed in September 1967. It serves Yorkshire TV and weighs 210 tons.

TALLEST TOWERS

World
The tallest self-supporting tower (as opposed to a guyed mast) in the world is the $44 million CN Tower in Metro Centre, Toronto, Canada, which rises to 1822 ft 1 in *555,33 m*. Excavation began on 12 Feb 1973 for the 130,000 ton/*tonne* structure of reinforced, post-tensioned concrete topped out on 2 Apr 1975. The 416-seat

PROGRESSIVE LIST OF HIGHEST STRUCTURES IN GREAT BRITAIN

Feet	Metres		
404	*123*	Salisbury Cathedral Spire	*c.* 1305–
525	*160*	Lincoln Cathedral	1307–1548
489	*149*	St Paul's Cathedral, London	1315–1561
518.7	*158,1*	Blackpool Tower, Lancashire	1894–
562	*171,29*	New Brighton Tower, Merseyside	1898–1919
820	*250*	GPO Radio Masts, Rugby	1925–
1000*	*304,8*	ITA Mast, Mendlesham, Suffolk	July 1959
1265	*385*	IBA Mast, Emley Moor, Yorkshire	1965–1969†
1265	*385*	IBA Mast, Belmont	1965–
1272	*387,1*	IBA Mast, Belmont	Sept. 1967

* ITA masts of the same height followed at Lichfield, Staffordshire; Black Hill, Strathclyde; Caldbeck, Cumbria; and Durris, Grampian.
† Severely damaged by icing and replaced.

A PROGRESSIVE RECORD OF THE WORLD'S TALLEST STRUCTURES

Height in ft	m	Structure	Location	Material	Building or Completion Dates
204	*62*	Djoser step pyramid (earliest Pyramid)	Saqqâra, Egypt	Tura limestone casing	*c.* 2650 BC
300.8	*91,7*	Pyramid of Meidum	Meidum, Egypt	Tura limestone casing	*c.* 2600 BC
331.6	*101,1*	Snefru Bent pyramid	Dahshûr, Egypt	Tura limestone casing	*c.* 2600 BC
342	*104*	Snefru North Stone pyramid	Dahshûr, Egypt	Tura limestone casing	*c.* 2600 BC
480.9[1]	*146,5*	Great Pyramid of Cheops (Khufu)	El Gizeh, Egypt	Tura limestone casing	*c.* 2580 BC
525[2]	*160*	Lincoln Cathedral, Central Tower	Lincoln, England	lead sheathed wood	*c.* 1307–1548
489[3]	*149*	St Paul's Cathedral spire	City of London, England	lead sheathed wood	1315–1561
465	*141*	Minster of Notre Dame	Strasbourg, France	Vosges sandstone	1420–1439
502[4]	*153*	St Pierre de Beauvais spire	Beauvais, France	lead sheathed wood	–1568
475	*144*	St Nicholas Church	Hamburg, Germany	stone and iron	1846–1847
485	*147*	Rouen Cathedral spire	Rouen, France	cast iron	1823–1876
513	*156*	Köln Cathedral spires	Cologne, W. Germany	stone	–1880
555[5]	*169*	Washington Monument	Washington, DC, USA	stone	1848–1884
985.9[6]	*300,5*	Eiffel Tower	Paris, France	iron	1887–1889
1046	*318*	Chrysler Building	New York City, USA	steel and concrete	1929–1930
1250[7]	*381*	Empire State Building	New York City, USA	steel and concrete	1929–1930
1572	*479*	KWTV Television Mast	Oklahoma City, USA	steel	Nov 1954
1610[8]	*490*	KSWS Television Mast	Roswell, New Mexico, USA	steel	Dec 1956
1619	*493*	WGAN Television Mast	Portland, Maine, USA	steel	Sept 1959
1676	*510*	KFVS Television Mast	Cape Girardeau, Missouri, USA	steel	June 1960
1749	*533*	WTVM & WRBL Television Mast	Columbus, Georgia, USA	steel	May 1962
1749	*533*	WBIR-TV Mast	Knoxville, Tennessee, USA	steel	Sept 1963
2063	*628*	KTHI-TV Mast	Fargo, North Dakota, USA	steel	Nov 1963
2120.6	*646,38*	Warszawa Radio Mast (see p. 119)	Płock, Poland	galvanised steel	22 July 1974

[1] *Original height. With loss of pyramidion (topmost stone) height now 449 ft 6 in* 137 m
[2] *Fell in a storm.*
[3] *Struck by lightning and destroyed 4 June 1561.*
[4] *Fell April 1573, shortly after completion.*
[5] *Sinking at a rate of 0.0047 ft per annum or* 5 in 12,7 cm *since 1884.*
[6] *Original height. With addition of TV antenna in 1957, now 1052 ft* 320,75 m.
[7] *Original height. With addition of TV tower on 1 May 1951, now 1472 ft* 449 m.
Exterior is clad in limestone from the Empire Quarry, Indiana.
[8] *Fell in gale in 1960.*

restaurant revolves in the Sky Pod at 1140 ft *347,5 m* from which the visibility extends to hills 74½ miles *120 km* distant. Lightning strikes the top about 200 times (30 storms) per annum.

The tallest tower built before the era of television masts is the Eiffel Tower, in Paris, France, designed by Alexandre Gustav Eiffel (1832–1923) for the Paris exhibition and completed on 31 Mar 1889. It was 300,51 m *985 ft 11 in* tall, now extended by a TV antenna to 320,75 m *1052 ft 4 in* and weighs 7340 tonnes *7224 tons*. The maximum sway in high winds is 12,7 cm *5 in*. The whole iron edifice which has 1792 steps, took 2 years, 2 months and 2 days to build and cost 7,799,401 francs 31 centimes.

Great Britain

The tallest self-supported tower in Great Britain is the 1080 ft *329,18 m* tall Independent Broadcasting Authority transmitter at Emley Moor, West Yorkshire, completed in September 1971. The structure, which cost £900,000, has an enclosed room at the 865 ft *263,65 m* level and weighs with its foundations more than 15,000 tons/*tonnes*. The tallest tower of the pre-television era was the New Brighton Tower of 562 ft *171,29 m* built on Merseyside in 1897–1900 and dismantled in 1919–21.

5. BRIDGES

Oldest *World*

Arch construction was understood by the Sumerians as early as 3200 BC and a reference exists to a Nile bridge in 2650 BC. The oldest surviving datable bridge in the world is the slab stone single arch bridge over the River Meles in Smyrna (now Izmir), Turkey, which dates from *c.* 850 BC.

Great Britain

The clapper bridges of Dartmoor and Exmoor (*e.g.* the Tarr Steps over the River Barle, Exmoor, Somerset) are thought to be of prehistoric types although none of the existing examples can be certainly dated. They are made of large slabs of stone placed over boulders. The Romans built stone bridges in England and remains of these have been found at Corbridge (Roman, Corstopitum), Northumberland dating to the 2nd century AD; Chesters, Northumberland and Willowford, Cumbria. Remains of a very early wooden bridge have been found at Aldwinkle, Northamptonshire.

LONGEST

Cable suspension *World*

The world's longest bridge span is the main span of the Humber Estuary Bridge, England at 4626 ft *1410 m*. Work began on 27 July 1972, after a decision announced on 22 Jan 1966. The towers are 162,5 m *533 ft 1⅝ in* tall from datum and are 1⅜ in *36 mm* out of parallel, to allow for the curvature of the Earth. Including the Hessle and the Barton side spans, the bridge stretches 2220 m or 1.37 miles. The bridge was structurally completed on 18 July 1980 at a cost of £96 million and was opened by HM the Queen on 17 July 1981. Tolls, ranging between £1 for cars and £7.50 for heavy vehicles, operative from 4 May 1981, are the highest in Britain. By 1995 the debt is expected to grow to £300 million.

The Mackinac Straits Bridge between Mackinaw City and St Ignace, Michigan, USA, is the longest suspension bridge in the world measured between anchorages (1.58 miles *2543 m*) and has an overall length, including viaducts of the bridge proper measured between abutment bearings, of 3.63 miles *5853,79 m*. It was opened in November 1957 (dedicated 28 June 1958) at a cost of $100 million (*then £35,700,000*) and has a main span of 3800 ft *1158 m*.

The double-deck road-rail Akashi-Kaikyo bridge linking Honshū and Shikoku, Japan is planned to be completed in 1988. The main span will be 5840 ft *1780 m* in length with an overall suspended length with side spans totalling 11,680 ft *3560 m*. Work began on the approaches in October 1978 and the eventual cost is expected to exceed 1000 billion (10^{12}) yen.

Plans for a Messina Bridge linking Sicily with the Italian mainland are dependent upon EEC budgets. One preliminary study calls for towers 1000 ft *304,8 m* tall and a span of 3000 m *9842 ft* or 1.86 miles. The escalating cost of such a project was estimated by 1983 already to have passed the £2000 million mark.

Cantilever *World*

The Quebec Bridge (Pont de Québec) over the St Lawrence River in Canada has the longest cantilever truss span of any in the world—1800 ft *549 m* between the piers and 3239 ft *987 m* overall. It carries a railway track and 2 carriageways. Begun in 1899, it was finally opened to traffic on 3 Dec 1917 at a cost of 87 lives, and $Can.22,500,000 (*then £4,623,000*).

Great Britain

The longest cantilever bridge in Great Britain is the Forth Bridge. Its two main spans are 1710 ft *521 m* long. It carries a double railway track over the Firth of Forth 156 ft *47,5 m* above the water level. Work commenced in November 1882 and the first test trains crossed on 22 Jan 1890 after an expenditure of £3 million. It was officially opened on 4 Mar 1890. Of the 4500 workers who built it, 57 were killed in various accidents.

Steel arch *World*

The longest steel arch bridge in the world is the New River Gorge bridge, near Fayetteville, West Virginia, USA, completed in 1977 with a span of 1700 ft *518,2 m*.

Great Britain

The longest steel arch bridge in Great Britain is the Runcorn–Widnes bridge, Cheshire opened on 21 July 1961. It has a span of 1082 ft *329,8 m*.

Floating bridge

The longest floating bridge in the world is the Second Lake Washington Bridge, Seattle, Washington State, USA. Its total length is 12,596 ft *3839 m* and its floating section measures 7518 ft *2291 m* (1.42 miles *2,29 km*). It was built at a total cost of $15,000,000 (*then £5,357,000*) and completed in August 1963.

Covered bridge

The longest covered bridge in the world is that at Hartland, New Brunswick, Canada measuring 1282 ft *390,8 m* overall, completed in 1899.

Railway bridge

The longest railway bridge in the world is the Huey P. Long Bridge, Metairie, Louisiana, USA with a railway section 22,996 ft *7009 m* (4.35 miles *7 km*) long. It was completed on 16 Dec 1935 with a longest span of 790 ft *241 m*. The Yangtse River Bridge, completed in 1968 in Nanking, China is the world's longest combined highway and railway bridge. The rail deck is 6772 m *4.20 miles* and the road deck is 4589 m *2.85 miles*.

Great Britain

The longest railway bridge in Britain is the second Tay Bridge (11,653 ft *3552 m*), Tayside, Scotland opened on 20 June 1887. Of the 85 spans, 74 (length 10,289 ft *3136 m*) are over the waterway. The 878 brick arches of the London Bridge to Deptford Creek viaduct built in 1836 extend for 3¾ miles *6,0 km*.

Longest bridging

The world's longest bridging is the Second Lake Pontchartrain Causeway, completed on 23 Mar 1969, joining Lewisburg and Metairie, Louisiana, USA. It has a length of 126,055 ft *38 422 m*

(23.87 miles). It cost $29,900,000 (then £12.45 million) and is 228 ft 69 m longer than the adjoining First Causeway completed in 1956. The longest railway viaduct in the world is the rockfilled Great Salt Lake Railroad Trestle, carrying the Southern Pacific Railroad 11.85 miles 19 km across the Great Salt Lake, Utah, USA. It was opened as a pile and trestle bridge on 8 Mar 1904, but converted to rock fill in 1955–60.

The longest stone arch bridging in the world is the 3810 ft 1161 m long Rockville Bridge north of Harrisburg, Pennsylvania, USA, with 48 spans containing 196,000 tons/tonnes of stone and completed in 1901.

Widest bridge

The world's widest long-span bridge is the 1650 ft 502,9 m span Sydney Harbour Bridge, Australia (160 ft 48,8 m wide). It carries two electric overhead railway tracks, 8 lanes of roadway and a cycle and footway. It was officially opened on 19 Mar 1932. The Crawford Street Bridge in Providence, Rhode Island, USA, has a width of 1147 ft 350 m. The River Roch is bridged for a distance of 1460 ft 445 m where the culvert passes through the centre of Rochdale, Greater Manchester and this is sometimes claimed to be a breadth.

HIGHEST

World

The highest bridge in the world is the bridge over the Royal Gorge of the Arkansas River in Colorado, USA. It is 1053 ft 321 m above the water level. It is a suspension bridge with a main span of 880 ft 268 m and was constructed in 6 months, ending on 6 Dec 1929. The highest railway bridge in the world is the single track span at Fades, outside Clermont-Ferrand, France. It was built in 1901–9 with a span of 472 ft 144 m and is 435 ft 132,5 m above the River Sioule. The road bridge at the highest altitude in the world is the 30 m 98.4 ft long Bailey bridge built by Indian Army in Aug 1982 near Khardung La, in Ladakh, India.

Great Britain

The highest railway bridge in Great Britain is the Ballochmyle viaduct over the River Ayr, Strathclyde built 169 ft 51,5 m over the river bed in 1846–8 with the then world's longest masonry arch span of 181 ft 55,16 m.

AQUEDUCTS

World longest Ancient

The greatest of ancient aqueducts was the Aqueduct of Carthage in Tunisia, which ran 87.6 miles 141 km from the springs of Zaghouan to Djebel Djougar. It was built by the Romans during the reign of Publius Aelius Hadrianus (AD 117–38). By 1895, 344 arches still survived. Its original capacity has been calculated at 7,000,000 gal 31,8 million litres per day. The triple-tiered aqueduct Pont du Gard, built in AD 19 near Nîmes, France, is 160 ft 48 m high. The tallest of the 14 arches of Aguas Livres Aqueduct, built in Lisbon, Portugal, in 1784 is 213 ft 3 in 65 m.

World longest Modern

The world's longest aqueduct, in the modern sense of a water conduit, as opposed to an irrigation canal, is the California State Water Project aqueduct, completed in 1974, to a length of 826 miles 1329 km of which 385 miles 619 km is canalised.

Longest Great Britain

The longest bridged aqueduct in Britain is the Pont Cysylltau in Clwyd on the Frankton to Llantisilio branch of the Shropshire Union Canal. It is 1007 ft 307 m long, has 19 arches up to 121 ft 36 m high above low water on the Dee. It was designed by Thomas Telford (1757–1834) of Scotland, and was opened for use in 1805. The oldest is the Dundas aqueduct on the Avon and Kennet canal near Bath. It was built in 1810 and restored in 1984.

6. CANALS

Earliest World

Relics of the oldest canals in the world, dated by archaeologists c. 4000 BC, were discovered near Mandali, Iraq early in 1968.

Earliest Great Britain

The earliest canals in Britain were first cut by the Romans. In the Midlands the 11 mile 17 km long Fossdyke Canal between Lincoln and the River Trent at Torksey was built in about AD 65 and was scoured in 1122. Part of it is still in use today. Though the Exeter canal was cut as early as 1564–6, the first wholly artificial major navigation canal in the United Kingdom was the 18½ mile 29,7 km long canal with 14 locks from Whitecoat Point to Newry, Northern Ireland opened on 28 Mar 1742. In Great Britain the Sankey Navigation Canal in Lancashire, 8 miles 12,8 km in length, with 10 locks, was opened in November 1757.

Longest World

The longest canalised system in the world is the Volga–Baltic Canal opened in April 1965. It runs 1850 miles 2300 km from Astrakhan up the Volga, via Kuybyshev, Gor'kiy and Lake Ladoga, to Leningrad, USSR. The longest canal of the ancient world has been the Grand Canal of China from Peking to Hangchou. It was begun in 540 BC and not completed until 1327 by which time it extended (including canalised river sections) for 1107 miles 1781 km. The estimated work force c. AD 600 reached 5,000,000 on the Pien section. Having been allowed by 1950 to silt up to the point that it was, in no place, more than 6 ft 1,8 m deep, it is now, however, plied by ships of up to 2000 tons/tonnes.

The Beloye More (White Sea) Baltic Canal from Belomorsk to Povenets, in the USSR, is 141 miles 227 km long with 19 locks. It was completed with the use of forced labour in 1933. It cannot accommodate ships of more than 16 ft 5 m in draught.

The world's longest big ship canal is the Suez Canal linking the Red and Mediterranean Seas, opened on 16 Nov 1869 but inoperative from June 1967 to June 1975. The canal was planned by the French diplomatist Count Ferdinand de Lesseps (1805–94) and work began on 25 Apr 1859. It is 100.6 miles 161,9 km in length from Port Said lighthouse to Suez Roads and 197 ft 60 m wide. The construction work force was 8213 men and 368 camels. The largest vessel to transit has been SS British Progress a VLCC (Very Large Crude Carrier) of 228 589 tonnes dwt (length 329,66 m 1081.5 ft; beam 48,68 m 159.7 ft at a maximum draft of 25,60 m 84 ft). This was southbound in ballast on 5 July 1976. USS Shreveport transited southbound on 15–16 Aug 1984 in a record 7 hr 45 min.

Busiest

The busiest big ship canal is the Panama, first transitted on 15 Aug 1914. In 1974 there were a record 14,304 ocean-going transits. The largest liner to transit has been Queen Elizabeth 2 (66,851 gross tons) on 25 Jan 1980 for a toll of $89,154.62 (then £38,760). The ships with the greatest beam to transit have been the Acadia Forest and the Atlantic Forest of 106.9 ft 32,58 m. The lowest toll was 36 US cents by the swimmer Richard

Halliburton in 1928. The fastest transit has been 2 hr 41 min by the US Navy hydrofoil Pegasus on 20 June 1979.

Longest Great Britain

Inland Waterways in Great Britain, normally defined as non-tidal (except for a few tidal 'links' on the Thames, Trent and Yorkshire Ouse) rivers and canals, consist of 2394 miles 3852 km with 110 miles 177 km being restored. Of this total 2125 miles 3420 km are inter-linked.

The longest possible journey on the system would be one of 415¾ miles 669 km and 157 locks from Bedford, on the Great Ouse to near Ripon, North Yorkshire.

Largest seaway

The world's longest artificial seaway is the St Lawrence Seaway (189 miles 304 km long) along the New York State–Ontario border from Montreal to Lake Ontario, which enables ships up to 222 m 728 ft long and 8 m 26.2 ft draught some of which are of 26,000 tons 26 400 tonnes to sail 2342 miles 3769 km from the North Atlantic, up the St Lawrence estuary and across the Great Lakes to Duluth, Minnesota, USA, on Lake Superior (602 ft 183 m above sea level). The project begun in 1954 cost $470,000,000 (then £168 million) and was opened on 25 Apr 1959.

Irrigation canal

The longest irrigation canal in the world is the Karakumskiy Kanal, stretching 528 miles 850 km from Haun-Khan to Ashkhabad, Turkmenistan, USSR. In September 1971 the 'navigable' length reached 280 miles 450 km. The length of the £370 million project will reach 930 miles 1300 km.

LOCKS

Largest World

The world's largest single lock is the sea lock at Zeebrugge, Belgium measuring 500 × 57 × 23 m 1640 × 187 × 75.4 ft giving a volume of 655 300 m³ 857,066 yd³. The Berendrecht Lock, Antwerp planned for completion in 1986 will have the same length but a width of 68 m 223 ft at a depth of 21,5 m 70.5 ft giving a volume of 731 000 m³ 956,000 yd³.

Largest Great Britain

The largest and deepest lock in the United Kingdom is the Royal Portbury Entrance Lock, Bristol which measures 1200 × 140 ft 366 × 42,7 m and has a depth of 66 ft 20,2 m. It was opened in August 1977.

Deepest World

The world's deepest lock is the John Day dam lock on the Columbia river, Oregon and Washington, USA completed in 1963. It can raise or lower barges 113 ft 34,4 m and is served by a 982 ton 998 tonne gate.

Longest flight

The world's highest lock elevator overcomes a head of 68,58 m 225 ft at Ronquières on the Charleroi-Brussels Canal, Belgium. The two 236 wheeled caissons each able to carry 1350 tons take 22 min to cover the 1432 m 4698 ft long ramp. The highest rise of any boat-carrying plane in Britain was the 225 ft 68,6 m of the 935 ft 285 m long Hobbacott Down plane on the Bude Canal, Cornwall.

The longest flight of locks in the United Kingdom is on the Worcester and Birmingham Canal at Tardebigge, Hereford and Worcester, where in a 2½ mile 4 km stretch there are the Tardebigge (30 locks) and Stoke (6 locks) flights which together drop the canal 259 ft 78,9 m. The flight of locks on the Huddersfield Canal, closed in 1944, on the 7¼ mile *11,6 km* stretch to Marsden numbered 42.

Largest cut

The Gaillard Cut (known as 'the Ditch') on the Panama Canal is 270 ft *82 m* deep between Gold Hill and Contractor's Hill with a bottom width of 500 ft *152 m*. In one day in 1911 as many as 333 dirt trains each carrying 357 tons *363 tonnes* left this site. The total amount of earth excavated for the whole Panama Canal as of 1 Oct 1979 was 666,194,450 yd³ *509 338 960 m³* which total will be raised by the further widening of the Gaillard Cut.

7. DAMS

Earliest

The earliest known dams were those uncovered by the British School of Archaeology in Jerusalem in 1974 at Jawa in Jordan. These stone-faced earth dams are dated to *c.* 3200 BC.

Most massive

Measured by volume, the largest dam in the world is the 98 ft *29,8 m* high New Cornelia Tailings earth-fill dam, on the Ten Mile Wash, Arizona, USA with a volume of 274,015,735 yd³ *209 501 000 m³* completed in 1973 to a length of 6.74 miles *10,85 km*.

Largest concrete

The world's largest concrete dam, and the largest concrete structure in the world, is the Grand Coulee Dam on the Columbia River, Washington State, USA. Work on the dam was begun in 1933, it began working on 22 Mar 1941 and was completed in 1942 at a cost of $56 million. It has a crest length of 4173 ft *1272 m* and is 550 ft *167 m* high. It contains 10,585,000 yd³ *8 092 000 m³* of concrete and weighs about 19,285,000 tons *19 595 000 tonnes*. The hydro-electric power plant (now being extended) will have a capacity of 9,780,000 kW.

Highest

The highest dam in the world is the Grande Dixence in Switzerland, completed in September 1961 at a cost of 1600 million Swiss francs (*then £151,000,000*). It is 935 ft *285 m* from base to rim, 2280 ft *695 m* long and the total volume of concrete in the dam is 7,792,000 yd³ *5 957 000 m³*. The Rogunsky earth-fill dam will have a final height of 1066 ft *325 m* across the Vakhsh river, Tadzhikistan, USSR with a crest length of only 2165 ft *660 m*. Building since 1973, completion date is still unconfirmed.

Longest

The 41 m *134.5 ft* high Yacyreta–Apipe dam across the Paraná on the Paraguay–Argentina borders extends for 72 km *44.7 miles*. In the early 17th century an impounding dam of moderate height was built in Lake Hungtze, Kiangsu, China, to a reputed length of 100 km *62 miles*.

The longest sea dam in the world is the Afsluitdijk stretching 20.195 miles *32,5 km* across the mouth of the Zuider Zee in two sections of 1.553 miles *2,499 km* (mainland of North Holland to the Isle of Wieringen) and 18.641 miles *30 km* from Wieringen to Friesland. It has a sea-level width of 293 ft *89 m* and a height of 24 ft 7 in *7,5 m*.

Strongest

The world's strongest structure will be the 242 m *793 ft* high Sayano-Shusenskaya dam on the River Yenisey, USSR which is under construction and designed to bear a load of 18 000 000 tonnes/*tons* from a fully-filled reservoir of 31,300 million m³ *41,000 million yd³* capacity.

United Kingdom

The most massive dam in Britain is the Northumbrian Water Authority's Kielder Dam, 52 m *170 ft* high earth embankment measuring 1140 m *3740 ft* in length and 5 300 000 m³ *6,932,000 yd³*. There are longer low dams or barrages of the valley cut-off type, notably the Hanningfield Dam, Essex, built from July 1952 to August 1956 to a length of 6850 ft *2088 m* and a height of 64.5 ft *19,7 m*. The rock-fill Llyn Brianne Dam, Dyfed is Britain's highest dam reaching 298½ ft *91 m* in Nov 1971 and becoming operational on 20 July 1972.

Largest reservoir *World*

The most voluminous man-made reservoir is at Bratsk (River Angara) USSR, with a volume of 137,214,000 acre-ft *169,25 km³*. The dam was completed in 1964. The world's largest artificial lake measured by surface area is Lake Volta, Ghana, formed by the Akosombo dam completed in 1965. By 1969 the lake had filled to an area of 3275 miles² *8482 km²* with a shoreline 4500 miles *7250 km* in length.

The completion in 1954 of the Owen Falls Dam near Jinja, Uganda, across the northern exit of the White Nile from the Victoria Nyanza marginally raised the level of that *natural* lake by adding 166,000,000 acre-ft *204,75 km³*, and technically turned it into a reservoir with a surface area of 17,169,920 acres *6,9 million ha* (26,828 miles² *69 484 km²*).

The $4 billion Tucurui Dam will, by 1984, convert the Tocantins river into a 1900 km *1180 mile* long chain of lakes.

Largest reservoir *Great Britain*

The most capacious reservoir in Britain is Kielder Water in the North Tyne valley, Northumberland, which filled to 44,000 million gallons *2000 million hl* from 15 Dec 1980 to mid-1982, and which acquired a surface area of 2684 acres *1086 ha* and a perimeter of 27 miles *43,4 km* to become England's second largest lake. Rutland Water has a lesser capacity (27,300 million gallons *124 106 million l*) and a lesser perimeter (24 miles *38,6 km*) but a greater surface area of 3100 acres *1254 ha*. The deepest reservoir in Europe is Loch Morar, Highland, Scotland, with a maximum depth of 1017 ft *310 m* (see also page 64).

The largest wholly artificial reservoir in Great Britain is the Queen Mary Reservoir, built from August 1914 to June 1925, at Littleton, near Staines, Surrey, with an available storage capacity of 8130 million gal *369,6 million hl* and a water area of 707 acres *286 ha*. The length of the perimeter embankment is 20,766 ft *6329 m* (3.93 miles *6,32 km*).

Largest polder

The largest of the five great polders in the old Zuider Zee, Netherlands, will be the 149,000 acre *60 300 ha* (232.8 miles² *602,9 km²*) Markerwaard. Work on the 66 mile *106 km* long surrounding dyke was begun in 1957. The water area remaining after the erection of the 1927–32 dam (20 miles *32 km* in length) is called IJssel Meer, which will have a final area of 487.5 miles² *1262,6 km²*.

Largest levees

The most massive levees ever built are the Mississippi levees begun in 1717 but vastly augmented by the US Federal Government after the disastrous floods of 1927. These extend for 1732 miles *2787 km* along the main river from Cape Girardeau, Missouri, to the Gulf of Mexico and comprise more than 1000 million yd³ *765 million m³* of earthworks. Levees on the tributaries comprise an additional 2000 miles *3200 km*. The Pine Bluff, Arkansas to Venice, Louisiana segment of 650 miles *1046 km* is continuous.

---

8. TUNNELS

LONGEST

Water supply *World*

The world's longest tunnel of any kind is the New York City West Delaware water supply tunnel, begun in 1937 and completed in 1944. It has a diameter of 13 ft 6 in *4,1 m* and runs for 105 miles *168,9 km* from the Rondout Reservoir into the Hillview Reservoir, on the border of Yonkers and New York City, NY, USA.

Water supply *Great Britain*

The longest water supply tunnel in the United Kingdom is the Kielder Water tunnel system. These tunnels have been driven through the rock to link the Tyne Valley with the Wear Valley. A pipe then passes under the river Wear and the tunnel then proceeds to link up with the Tees Valley. The system is 20.2 miles *32,18 km* in length.

Railway *World*

The world's longest main-line rail tunnel is the 22,2 km (*13 miles 1397 yd*) long Oshimizu Tunnel (Daishimizu) on the Tōkyō–Niigata Joetsu line in central Honshū under the Tanigawa mountain which was holed through on 25 Jan 1979. The cost of the whole project will by March 1981 reach £3150 million. Fatalities in 7 years have been 13.

Railway *Great Britain*

Great Britain's longest main-line railway tunnel is the Severn Tunnel (4 miles 628 yd *6 km*), linking Avon and Gwent completed with 76,400,000 bricks between 1873 and 1886.

Sub-aqueous

The 33.46 mile *53,85 km* long Seikan Rail Tunnel has been bored 240 m *787 ft* beneath sea level and 100 m *328 ft* below the sea bed of the Tsugaru Strait between Tappi Saki, Honshū, and Fukushima, Hokkaidō, Japan. Tests started on the sub-aqueous section (14.5 miles *23,3 km*) in 1964 and construction in June 1972. It was holed through on 27 Jan 1983 after a loss of 34 lives. The cost by the finish of tunnelling after 20 years 10 months in March 1985 was 600,000 million yen (about £2500 million).

Subway

The world's longest continuous vehicular tunnel is the Moscow Metro underground railway line from Belyaevo to Medvedkovo. It is *c.* 30,7 km *19.07 miles* long and was completed in 1978/9.

Road *World*

The longest road tunnel is the 10.14 mile *16,32 km* long two-lane St Gotthard Road Tunnel from Göschenen to Airolo, Switzerland, opened to traffic on 5 Sept 1980. Nineteen lives were lost during the construction which cost Sw Fr 686 million (*then £173.6 million*) since autumn 1969.

Great Britain

The longest road tunnel in the United Kingdom is the Mersey Tunnel, joining Liverpool and Birkenhead, Merseyside. It is 2.13 miles *3,43 km* long, or 2.87 miles *4,62 km* including branch tunnels. Work was begun in December 1925 and it was opened by HM King George V on 18 July 1934. The total cost was £7¾ million. The 36 ft *11 m* wide 4-lane roadway carries nearly 7½ million vehicles a year. The first tube of the second Mersey Tunnel was opened on 24 June 1971.

Largest

The largest diameter road tunnel in the world is that blasted through Yerba Buena Island, San Francisco, California, USA. It is 76 ft *23 m* wide, 58 ft *17 m* high and 540 ft *165 m* long. More than 35,000,000 vehicles pass through on its two decks every year.

Hydro-electric, irrigation or sewerage
World

The longest irrigation tunnel in the world is the 51.5 mile *82,9 km* long Orange-Fish Rivers Tunnel, South Africa, begun in 1967 at an estimated cost of £60 million. The boring was completed in April 1973. The lining to a minimum thickness of 9 inches *23 cm* will give a completed diameter of 17 ft 6 in *5,33 m*. The Majes project in Peru involves 98 km *60.9 miles* of tunnels for hydro-electric and water supply purposes. The dam is at 4200 m *13,780 ft* altitude. The Chicago TARP (Tunnels and Reservoir Plan) in Illinois, USA involves 120 miles *193 km* of sewerage tunnelling.

Bridge-Tunnel

The world's longest bridge-tunnel system is the Chesapeake Bay Bridge-Tunnel, extending 17.65 miles *28,40 km* from Eastern Shore, Virginia Peninsula to Virginia Beach, Virginia, USA. It cost $200,000,000 (*then £71,4 million*) and was completed after 42 months and opened to traffic on 15 Apr 1964. The longest bridged section is Trestle C (4.56 miles *7,34 km* long) and the longest tunnel is the Thimble Shoal Channel Tunnel (1.09 miles *1,75 km*).

Canal tunnels *World*

The world's longest canal tunnel is that on the Rove canal between the port of Marseilles, France and the river Rhône, built in 1912–27. It is 4.53 miles *7,29 km* long, 72 ft *22 m* wide and 50 ft *15 m* high, involving 2¼ million yd³ *1,7 million m³* of excavation.

Great Britain

The longest canal tunnel in Great Britain is the Standedge (more properly Stanedge) Tunnel in West Yorkshire on the Huddersfield Narrow Canal built from 1794 to 4 Apr 1811. It measures 3 miles 418 yd *5,21 km* in length and was closed on 21 Dec 1944. The British canal system has contained 84 tunnels exceeding 30 yd *27,4 m* of which 48 are still open. The longest of these is the 3056 yd *2,79 km* long Blisworth Tunnel on the Grand Union in Northamptonshire. The now closed Huddersfield Narrow Canal is the highest in the United Kingdom, at 638 ft *194 m* above sea-level.

Tunnelling records

The longest unsupported example of a machine-bored tunnel is the Three Rivers Water Tunnel driven 30,769 linear feet *9,37 km* with a 10.5 ft *3,2 m* diameter for the City of Atlanta, Georgia, USA from April 1980 to February 1982. S & M Constructors Inc of Cleveland, Ohio achieved 179 ft *54,5 m* in a day through the granite, schist and gneiss.

The NCB record of 251,4 m *824.8 ft* for a 3,80 m *12½ ft* wide, 2 m *6⅓ ft* high roadway by a team of 35 pitmen in 5 days was set at West Cannock No 5 Colliery on 30 Mar–3 Apr 1981.

9. SPECIALISED STRUCTURES

Advertising sign Highest *World*

The highest advertising signs in the world are the four Bank of Montreal logos atop the 72 storey 935 ft *285 m* tall First Canadian Place, Toronto. Each sign, built by Claude Neon Industries Ltd, measures 20 × 22 ft *6,09 × 6,70 m* and was lifted by helicopter.

The mouth of the longest irrigation tunnel in the world—the 51½ mile *89.2 km* long Orange-Fish Rivers Tunnel, South Africa. (See column 1) (*South African Embassy*)

Advertising sign Largest

The most conspicuous sign ever erected was the electric Citroën sign on the Eiffel Tower, Paris. It was switched on on 4 July 1925, and could be seen 24 miles *38 km* away. It was in six colours with 250,000 lamps and 56 miles *90 km* of electric cables. The letter 'N' which terminated the name 'Citroën' between the second and third levels measured 68 ft 5 in *20,8 m* in height. The whole apparatus was taken down after 11 years in 1936. For the largest ground sign see Chapter 6, page 83—Largest letter.

The world's largest neon sign was that owned by the Atlantic Coast Line Railroad Company at Port Tampa, Florida, USA. It measured 387 ft 6 in *118 m* long and 76 ft *23 m* high, weighed 175 tons *178 tonnes* and contained about 4200 ft *1280 m* of red neon tubing. It was demolished on 19 Feb 1970. The world's largest reported hoarding is one 44,5 m *146 ft* long and 17,5 m *57 ft 5 in* tall erected by Propaganda Campanella on Route N9, Buenos Aires, Argentina. Britain's largest illuminated sign is the word PLAYHOUSE extending 90 ft *27 m* across the frontage of the new theatre in Leeds, West Yorkshire opened in 1970.

An interior lit fascia advertising sign in Clearwater, Florida, USA completed by Adco Sign Corp in April 1983 measures 1168 ft 6½ in *356,17 m* in length.

The world's most massive animated sign is reputed to be that outside the Circus Circus Hotel, Reno, Nevada named Topsy, the Clown. It is 127 ft *38,7 m* tall and weighs over 40 tons *40,8 tonnes* with 1.4 miles *2,25 km* of neon tubing. His smile measures 14 ft *4,26 m* across.

Barn Largest

The largest barn in Britain is one at Frindsbury, Kent. Its length is 219 ft *66,7 m* and is still wholly roofed. The Ipsden Barn, Oxfordshire, is 385½ ft *117 m* long but 30 ft *9 m* wide (11,565 ft² *1074 m²*). The longest tithe barn in Britain is one measuring 268 ft *81 m* long at Wyke Farm, near Sherborne, Dorset.

Bonfire Largest

The largest recorded bonfire constructed in Britain was the Coronation bonfire using 800 tons *812 tonnes* of timber, 1000 gal *4546 litres* each of petroleum and tar. It was octagonal in shape and built to a height of 120 ft *36,67 m* with a base circumference of 155 ft *47,2 m* tapering to 20 ft *6,1 m* at the summit, on Arrowthwaite Brows at Whitehaven, Cumbria in 1902.

Breakwater Longest *World and Great Britain*

The world's longest breakwater is that which protects the Port of Galveston, Texas, USA. The granite South Breakwater is 6.74 miles *10,85 km* in length.

The longest breakwater in Great Britain is the North Breakwater at Holyhead, Anglesey, Gwynedd which is 9860 ft (1.86 miles *3005 m*) in length and was completed in 1873.

Buildings demolished by Explosives *Largest*

The largest building demolished by explosives has been the 21 storey Traymore Hotel, Atlantic City, New Jersey, USA, on 26 May 1972 by Controlled Demolition Inc of Towson, Maryland. This 600 room hotel had a cubic capacity of 6,495,500 ft³ *181 340 m³*. The tallest chimney ever demolished by explosives was the Matla Power Station chimney, Kriel, South Africa on 19 July 1981. It stood 275 m *902 ft* and was brought down by The Santon (Steeplejack) Co. Ltd of Manchester, England.

The greatest recorded simultaneous smokestack demolition was when 18 were felled at the London Brick Co Coronation Works at Kempston Hardwick, Bedfordshire on 30 Nov 1980 when Mrs Wyn Witherall fired the 100 lb *45,3 kg* of explosives laid by T. W. Robinson & Co.

Cemetery Largest
The world's largest cemetery is that in Leningrad, USSR, which contains over 500,000 of the 1,300,000 victims of the German army's siege of 1941–3. The largest cemetery in the United Kingdom is Brookwood Cemetery, Brookwood, Surrey. It is owned by the London Necropolis Co. and is 500 acres *200 ha* in extent with more than 225,000 interments.

The Emperor Fountain at Chatsworth, Derbyshire is the tallest in Great Britain and reached a height of 260 ft *79 m*. (The Duchess of Devonshire)

Column Tallest
The tallest columns (as opposed to obelisks) in the world are the 36 fluted pillars 90 ft *27,43 m* tall, of Vermont marble in the colonnade of the Education Building, Albany, New York. Their base diameter is 6½ ft *1,98 m*. The tallest load-bearing stone columns in the world are those measuring 69 ft *21 m* in the Hall of Columns of the Temple of Amun at Karnak, opposite Thebes on the Nile, the ancient capital of Upper Egypt. They were built in the 19th dynasty in the reign of Rameses II in *c*. 1270 BC.

Crematorium Earliest
The oldest crematorium in Britain is one built in 1879 at Woking, Surrey. The first cremation took place there on 26 Mar 1885, the practice having been found legal after the cremation of Iesu Grist Price on Caerlan fields on 13 Jan 1884. The total number of people cremated in Britain since, has been 10,297,829 (to 31 Dec 1984), and the percentage (now 67.44%). The percentage in Japan is 93.4%.

Crematorium Largest
The largest crematorium in the world is at the Nikolo-Arkhangelskoye Cemetery, East Moscow, with 7 twin cremators of British design, completed in March 1972. It has several Halls of Farewell for atheists. Currently, Britain's largest is the City of London Crematorium, E.12, which performed 5395 cremations in 1979. The all-time total of 260,969 at Golders Green Crematorium (since 1902) remains unsurpassed, as does its record 7509 cremations in 1957.

Dock Gate
The world's largest dock gate is that at Nigg Bay, Cromarty Firth, Highlands, Scotland, first operated in March 1974. It measures 408 ft *124 m* long, 50 ft *15,2 m* high with a 4 ft *1,21 m* thick base, is made of reinforced concrete and weighs 16,000 tons *16 257 tonnes* with its sill, quoins and roundheads. The builders were Brown and Root-Wimpey Highland Fabricators.

Dome Largest *World and Great Britain*
The world's largest dome is the Louisiana Superdome, New Orleans, USA. It has a diameter of 680 ft *207,26 m* (See page 110 for further details.) The largest dome of ancient architecture is that of the Pantheon, built in Rome in AD 112, with a diameter of 142½ ft *43 m*.

The largest dome in Britain is that of the Bell Sports Centre, Perth, Scotland, with a diameter of 222 ft *67 m* designed by D. B. Cockburn and constructed in Baltic whitewood by Muirhead & Sons Ltd of Grangemouth, Central, Scotland.

Door Largest *World*
The largest doors in the world are the four in the Vehicle Assembly Building near Cape Canaveral, Florida, with a height of 460 ft *140 m* (see pages 104–5). The world's heaviest door is that leading to the laser target room at Lawrence Livermore National Laboratory, California. It weighs 321.4 tons *326,5 tonnes*, is up to 8 ft *2,43 m* thick and was installed by Overly.

Door Largest *Great Britain*
The largest doors in Great Britain are those to the Britannia Assembly Hall, at Filton airfield, Avon. The doors are 1035 ft *315 m* in length and 67 ft *20 m* high, divided into three bays each 345 ft *105 m* across. The largest simple hinged door in Britain is that of Ye Old Bull's Head, Beaumaris, Anglesey, Gwynedd, which is 11 ft *3,35 m* wide and 13 ft *3,96 m* high.

Door Oldest
The oldest doors in Britain are those of Hadstock Church, Essex, which date from *c*. 1040 AD and exhibit evidence of Danish workmanship.

Dry dock Largest *World*
The largest dry dock in the world is that at Koyagi, Nagasaki, Japan completed in 1972. It measures 990 m *3248 ft* long; 100 m *328 ft* in width and has a maximum shipbuilding capacity of 1,000,000 tons deadweight.

The largest shipbuilding dry dock in the UK is the Belfast Harbour Commission and Harland and Wolff building dock at Belfast, Northern Ireland. It was excavated by Wimpey's to a length of 1825 ft *556 m* and a width of 305 ft *93 m* and could accommodate tankers of 1,000,000 tons deadweight. Work was begun on 26 Jan 1968 and completed on 30 Nov 1969 and involved the excavation of 400,000 yd³ *306 000 m³*. The dry dock under construction at Port Rashid, Dubai, Persian Gulf, opened in March 1979 measures 1722 × 328 ft *525 × 100 m*.

Earthworks Largest *World*

The largest earthworks in the world carried out prior to the mechanical era were the Linear Earth Boundaries of the Benin Empire in the Bendel state of Nigeria. These were first reported in 1900 and partially surveyed in 1967. In April 1973 it was estimated by Mr Patrick Darling that the total length of the earthworks was probably between 4000 and 8000 miles *6400–12 800 km* with the total amount of earth moved estimated at from 500 to 600 million yd³ *380–460 million m³*.

Earthworks Largest *Great Britain*

The greatest prehistoric earthwork in Britain is Wansdyke, originally Woden's Dyke, which ran 86 miles *138 km* from Portishead, Avon to Inkpen Beacon and Ludgershall, south of Hungerford, Berkshire. It is believed to have been built by the pre-Roman Wessex culture. The most extensive single site earthwork is the Dorset Cursus near Gussage St. Michael, dating from *c.* 1900 BC. The workings are 6 miles *9,7 km* in length, involving an estimated 250,000 yd³ *191 000 m³* of excavations. The largest of the Celtic hill-forts is that known as Mew Dun, or Maiden Castle, 2 miles *3 km* SW of Dorchester, Dorset. It covers 115 acres *46,5 ha* and was abandoned shortly after AD 43.

Fence Longest and Highest

The longest fence in the world was the dingo-proof fence enclosing the main sheep areas of Australia. The wire fence is 6 ft *1,8 m* high, 1 ft *30 cm* underground and stretches for 3437 miles *5531 km*. The Queensland State Government discontinued full maintenance in 1982 but 500 km *310 miles* is now being repaired. The world's tallest fences are security screens 20 m *65.6 ft* high erected by Harrop-Allin of Pretoria in November 1981 to keep out Soviet RP67 rocket sabotage missiles from fuel depots and refineries at Sasolburg, South Africa.

Flagstaff Tallest *World*

The tallest flagstaff ever erected was that outside the Oregon Building at the 1915 Panama-Pacific International Exposition in San Francisco, California, USA. Trimmed from a Douglas fir, it stood 299 ft 7 in *91 m* in height and weighed 45 tons *47 tonnes*. The tallest unsupported flag pole in the world is a 190 ft *57,9 m* tall (plus 12½ ft *3,81 m* below ground) metal pole weighing 20,000 lb *9070 kg* erected on 27 June 1981 at Chula Vista, California, USA. The concept was carried through by Jerry Leaf Sales Inc.

Flagstaff Tallest *Great Britain*

The tallest flagstaff in Great Britain is a 225 ft *68 m* tall Douglas fir staff at Kew, Richmond upon Thames, Greater London. Cut in Canada, it was shipped across the Atlantic and towed up the River Thames on 7 May 1958, to replace the old 214 ft *65 m* tall staff of 1919.

Fountain Tallest *World and Great Britain*

The world's tallest fountain is the Fountain at Fountain Hills, Arizona built at a cost of $1,500,000 for McCulloch Properties Inc. At full pressure of 375 lb/in² *26,3 kg/cm²* and at a rate of 5828 Imp. gal/min *26 500 litres/min* the 560 ft *170 m* tall column of water weighs more than 8 tons/*tonnes*. The nozzle speed achieved by the three 600 hp pumps is 146.7 mph *236 km/h*.

The tallest fountain in Great Britain is the Emperor Fountain at Chatsworth, Bakewell, Derbyshire. When first tested on 1 June 1844, it attained the then unprecedented height of 260 ft *79 m*. Since the war it has not been played to more than 250 ft *76 m* and rarely beyond 180 ft *55 m*.

Garbage dump Biggest

Reclamation Plant No. 1, Fresh Kills, Staten Island, opened in March 1974, is the world's largest sanitary landfill. In its first 4 months 450,000 tons *457 000 tonnes* of refuse from New York City was dumped on the site by 700 barges.

Gasholder Largest *World*

The world's largest gasholder is that at Fontaine l'Eveque, Belgium, where disused mines have been adapted to store up to 500 million m³ *17,650 million ft³* of gas at ordinary pressure. Probably the largest conventional gasholder is that at Wien-Simmering, Vienna, Austria, completed in 1968, with a height of 274 ft 8 in *84 m* and a capacity of 10.59 million ft³ *300 000 m³*.

Gasholder Largest *Great Britain*

The largest gasholder ever constructed in Great Britain is the East Greenwich Gas Works No. 2 Holder built in 1891 with an original capacity for 12,200,000 ft³ *346 000 m³*. As constructed its capacity is 8.9 million ft³ *252 000 m³* with a water tank 303 ft *92 m* in diameter and a full inflated height of 148 ft *45 m*. The No. 1 holder (capacity 8.6 million ft³ *243 500 m³*) has a height of 200 ft *61 m*. The River Tees Northern Gas Board's 1186 ft *361 m* deep underground storage in use since January 1959 has a capacity of 330,000 ft³ *9300 m³*.

Globe Largest revolving

The world's largest revolving globe is the 21½ ton/*tonnes* 27 ft 11 in *8,50 m* diameter sphere in Babson College Wellesley, Massachusetts, USA completed at a cost of $200,000 (*then £71,425*) in 1956.

Jetty Longest

The longest deep water jetty in the world is the Quai Hermann du Pasquier at Le Havre, France, with a length of 5000 ft *1524 m*. Part of an enclosed basin, it has a constant depth of water of 32 ft *9,8 m* on both sides.

Kitchen *Largest*

The largest kitchen ever set up has been the Indian Government field kitchen set up in April 1973 at Ahmadnagar, Maharashtra in the famine area which daily provided 1.2 million subsistence meals.

Lamp Post *Tallest*

The tallest lighting columns ever erected are four of 63,5 m *208 ft 4 in* made by Petitjean & Cie of Troyes, France and installed by Taylor Woodrow at Sultan Qaboos Sports Complex, Muscat, Oman.

Lighthouse Brightest and Earliest *World*

The £18½ million 100 m *328 ft* tall rock lighthouse built in 1983–85 40 km *24.8 miles* SW of l'Ile d'Ouessant is visible at 40 nautical miles *74 km*. With reflective clouds at optimal altitude the loom is detectable in Isles of Scilly 105 miles *169 km* distant. The lights with the greatest range are those 1092 ft *332 m* above the ground on the Empire State Building, New York City, NY, USA. Each of the four-arc mercury bulbs has a rated candlepower of 450,000,000, visible 80 miles *130 km* away on the ground and 300 miles *490 km* away from aircraft. They were switched on on 31 Mar 1956.

Lighthouse Brightest *Great Britain*

The lighthouse in Great Britain with the most powerful light is the shorelight at Strumble Head, near Fishguard, Dyfed. It has an intensity of 6,000,000 candelas. The Irish light with the greatest intensity is Aranmore on Rinrawros Point, County Donegal.

Lighthouse Remotest *Great Britain*

The most remote Trinity House lighthouse is The Smalls, about 16 sea miles (18.4 statute miles *29,6 km*) off the Dyfed coast. The most remote Scottish lighthouse is Sule Skerry, 35 miles *56 km* off shore and 45 miles *72 km* northwest of Dunnet Head, Highland. The most remote Irish light is Blackrock, 9 miles *14 km* off the Mayo coast.

Lighthouse Tallest

The world's tallest lighthouse is the steel tower 348 ft *106 m* tall near Yamashita Park in Yokohama, Japan. It has a power of 600,000 candles and a visibility range of 20 miles *32 km*.

Bishop Rock, Isles of Scilly measures 47,8 m *156.8 ft* high to its helipad. The tallest Scottish lighthouse is the 139 ft *42,3 m* tall North Ronaldsay lighthouse, Orkney Islands.

Marquee Largest *World and Great Britain*

The largest tent ever erected was one covering an area of 188,368 ft² *17 500 m²* (4.32 acres *1,7 ha*) put up by the firm of Deuter from Augsburg, W. Germany, for the 1958 'Welcome Expo' in Brussels, Belgium.

The largest marquee in Britain is one made by Piggot Brothers in 1951 and used by the Royal Horticultural Society at their annual show (first held in 1913) in the grounds of the Royal Hospital, Kensington and Chelsea, Greater London. The marquee is 310 ft *94 m* long by 480 ft *146 m* wide and consists of 18¾ miles *30 km* of 36 in *91 cm* wide canvas covering a ground area of 148,800 ft² *13 820 m²*. A tent 435 ft *132,5 m* long was erected in one lift by thirty-five men of the Military Corrective Training Centre, Colchester on 23 July 1980.

The Offshore Europe 1983 exhibition at the Bridge of Don, Showground, Aberdeen, Scotland was housed in 15 contiguous air tents covering 28 400 m² *6.91 acres*.

Maypole

The tallest reported Maypole erected in England was one of Sitka spruce 105 ft 7 in *32,12 m* tall put up in Pelynt, Cornwall on 1 May 1974. The permanent pole at Paganhill, near Stroud, Gloucestershire is 90 ft *27,43 m* tall.

Maze Largest

The oldest dateable representation of a labyrinth is that on a clay tablet from Pylos, Greece from *c.* 1200 BC.

The world's largest hedge maze is that at Longleat, nr Warminster, Wilts, with 1.61 miles *2,59 km* of paths flanked by 16,180 yew trees. It was opened on 6 June 1978 and measures 380 × 175 ft *115,8 × 53,34 m*. 'Il Labirinto' at Villa Pisani, Stra, Italy in which Napoleon was 'lost' in 1807 had 4 miles *6,4 km* of pathways.

Menhir *tallest*

The tallest menhir found is the 380 ton Grand Menhir Brisé, now in 4 pieces, which originally stood 69 ft *22 m* high at Locmariaquer, Britanny, France. Britain's tallest is one of 25 ft *7,6 m* at Rudston, Humberside.

Monument Prehistoric *Largest*

Britain's largest megalithic prehistoric monument and largest existing henge are the 28½ acre *11,5 ha* earthworks and stone circles of Avebury, Wiltshire, 'rediscovered' in 1646. The earliest calibrated date in the area of this neolithic site is *c.* 4200 BC. The whole work is 1200 ft *365 m* in diameter with a 40 ft *12 m* ditch around the perimeter and required an estimated 15 million man-hours of work. The henge of Durrington Walls, Wiltshire, obliterated by road building, had a diameter of 1550 ft *472 m*. It was built from *c.* 2500 BC and required some 900,000 man hours.

The largest trilithons exist at Stonehenge, to the south of Salisbury Plain, Wiltshire, with single sarsen blocks weighing over 45 tons/*tonnes* and requiring over 550 men to drag them up a 9°

gradient. The earliest stage of the construction of the ditch has been dated to 2800 BC. Whether Stonehenge, which required some 30 million man-years, was a lunar calendar, a temple or an eclipse-predictor is still debated.

Monument Tallest

The world's tallest monument is the stainless steel Gateway to the West Arch in St Louis, Missouri, USA, completed on 28 Oct 1965 to commemorate the westward expansion after the Louisiana Purchase of 1803. It is a sweeping arch spanning 630 ft *192 m* and rising to the same height of 630 ft *192 m* and costing $29,000,000 (*then £10.35 million*). It was designed in 1947 by Eero Saarinen (d. 1961).

The tallest monumental column in the world is that commemorating the battle of San Jacinto (21 Apr 1836), on the bank of the San Jacinto river near Houston, Texas, USA. General Sam Houston (1793–1863) and his force of 743 Texan troops killed 630 Mexicans (out of a total force of 1600) and captured 700 others, for the loss of nine men killed and 30 wounded. Constructed in 1936–9, at a cost of $1,500,000 (*then £372,000*), the tapering column is 570 ft *173 m* tall, 47 ft *14 m* square at the base, and 30 ft *9 m* square at the observation tower, which is surmounted by a star weighing 196.4 tons *199,6 tonnes*. It is built of concrete, faced with buff limestone, and weighs 31,384 tons *31 888 tonnes*.

Monument, Youngest ancient

The newest scheduled ancient monuments are a hexagonal pill box and 48 concrete tank traps south of Christchurch, Dorset built in World War II and protected since 1973.

Mound Largest *World*

The gravel mound built as a memorial to the Seleucid King Antiochus I (reigned 69–34 BC) on the summit of Nemrud Dagi (8205 ft *2494 m*) south east of Malatya, Eastern Turkey measures 197 ft *59,8 m* tall and covers 7.5 acres *3 ha*.

Mound Largest *United Kingdom*

The largest artificial mound in Europe is Silbury Hill, 6 miles *9,7 km* west of Marlborough, Wiltshire, which involved the moving of an estimated 670,000 tons *681,000 tonnes* of chalk, at a cost of 18 million man-hours to make a cone 130 ft *39 m* high with a base of 5½ acres *2 ha*. Prof. Richard Atkinson in charge of the 1968 excavations showed that it is based on an innermost central mound, similar to contemporary round barrows, and is now dated to 2745 ± 185 BC. The largest long barrow in England is that inside the hillfort at Maiden Castle (see Earthworks largest GB). It originally had a length of 1800 ft *548 m* and had several enigmatic features such as a ritual pit with pottery, limpet shells, and animal bones, but the date of these is not certain. The longest long barrow containing a megalithic chamber is that at West Kennet (*c.* 2200 BC), near Silbury, measuring 385 ft *117 m* in length.

Naturist resorts

The oldest resort is Der Freilichtpark, Klingberg, W. Germany established in 1903. The largest in the world is the Beau Valley Country Club, Warmbaths, South Africa extending over 4 million m² *988 acres* with up to 20,000 visitors a year. However, 100,000 people visit the smaller centre Helio-Marin at Cap d'Agde, southern France, which covers 90 ha *222 acres*. The term 'nudist camp' is deplored by naturists.

Obelisk (Monolithic) Largest and Oldest

The largest standing obelisk (from the Gk *obeliskos*, skewer or spit) in the world is the Egyptian obelisk brought from Egypt to the hippodrome of Constantinople in Istanbul, Turkey in AD 390. It stands 58 m *190.2 ft* tall.

The unfinished obelisk, probably commissioned by Queen Hatshepsut *c.* 1490 BC, at Aswan is 41,75 m *136.8 ft* in length and weighs 1168 tonnes/tons. The largest obelisk in the United Kingdom is Cleopatra's Needle on the Embankment, London, which is 68 ft 5½ in *20 m* tall and weighs 186.3 tons *189,35 tonnes*. It was towed up the Thames from Egypt on 21 Jan 1878 and positioned on 13 Sept. The longest an obelisk has remained *in situ* is that still at Heliopolis, near Cairo, Egypt, erected by Senusret I *c.* 1750 BC.

Pier Longest *World*

The world's longest pier was the Dammam Pier,

SEVEN WONDERS OF THE WORLD

The Seven Wonders of the World were first designated by Antipater of Sidon in the 2nd century BC. They included the Pyramids of Giza, built by three Fourth Dynasty Egyptian Pharaohs, Khwfw (Khufu or Cheops), Kha-f-Ra (Khafre, Khefren or Chepren) and Menkaure (Mycerinus) near El Giza (El Gizeh), south-west of El Qâhira (Cairo) in Egypt. The Great Pyramid ('Horizon of Khufu') was finished under Rededef *c.* 2580 BC. Its original height was 480 ft 11 in *146,5 m* (now, since the loss of its topmost stones and the pyramidion, reduced to 449 ft 6 in *137 m*) with a base line of 756 ft *230 m* and thus covering slightly more than 13 acres *5 ha*. It has been estimated that a permanent work force of 4000 required 30 years to manoeuvre into position the 2,300,000 limestone blocks averaging 2½ tons/tonnes each, totalling about 5,750,000 tons *5 840 000 tonnes* and a volume of 90,700,000 ft³ *2 568 000 m³*. Some blocks are of 15 tons. A costing exercise published in December 1974, indicated that it would require 405 men 6 years at a cost of $1.13 billion (*then £500 million*).

Of the other six wonders only fragments remain of the Temple of Artemis (Diana) of the Ephesians, built in *c.* 350 BC. at Ephesus, Turkey (destroyed by the Goths in AD 262), and of the Tomb of King Mausolus of Caria, built at Halicarnassus, now Bodrum, Turkey, in *c.* 325 BC. No trace remains of the Hanging Gardens of Semiramis, at Babylon, Iraq *c.* 600 BC; the 40 ft *12 m* tall marble, gold and ivory statue of Zeus (Jupiter), by Phidias (5th century BC) at Olympia, Greece (lost in a fire at Istanbul); the 117 ft *35 m* tall statue by Chares of Lindus of the figure of the god Helios (Apollo) called the Colossus of Rhodes (sculptured 292–280 BC, destroyed by an earthquake in 224 BC); or the 400 ft *122 m* tall world's earliest lighthouse, built by Sostratus of Cnidus (*c.* 270 BC) as a pyramidically shaped tower of white marble, (destroyed by earthquake in AD 1375), on the island of Pharos (Greek, *pharos* = lighthouse), off the coast of El Iskandariya (Alexandria), Egypt.

Saudi Arabia, on the Persian Gulf with an overall length of 6.79 miles *10,93 km*. The work was begun in July 1948 and completed on 15 Mar 1950. The area was subsequently developed by 1980 into the King Abdul Aziz Port with 39 deep water berths.

Pier Longest *Great Britain*

The longest pier in Great Britain is the Bee Ness Jetty, completed in 1930, which stretches 8200 ft *2500 m* along the west bank of the River Medway, 5 to 6 miles *8 to 9,6 km* below Rochester, at Kingsnorth, Kent.

Pyramid Largest

The largest pyramid, and the largest monument ever constructed, is the Quetzacóatl at Cholula de Rivadabia, 63 miles *101 km* south-east of Mexico City, Mexico. It is 177 ft *54 m* tall and its base covers an area of nearly 45 acres *18,2 ha*. Its total volume has been estimated at 4,300,000 yd³ *3 300 000 m³* compared with 3,360,000 yd³ *2,5 million m³* for the Pyramid of Cheops (*see* Seven Wonders of the World). The pyramid-building era here was between the 2nd and 6th centuries AD.

Pyramid Oldest

The oldest known pyramid is the Djoser step pyramid at Saqqâra, Egypt constructed by Imhotep to a height of 204 ft *62 m* originally with a Tura limestone casing in *c.* 2650 BC. The largest known single block comes from the Third Pyramid (the pyramid of Mycerinus) and weighs 290 tonnes *285 tons*. The oldest New World pyramid is that on the island of La Venta in south-eastern Mexico built by the Olmec people *c.* 800 BC. It stands 100 ft *30 m* tall with a base dimension of 420 ft *128 m*.

Scarecrow

The world's largest scarecrow was built by Wayne and Jacqueline Kunkelman to a height of 20 ft *6,09 m* with a spread of 19 ft *5,79 m* at Snipes Farm and Nursery, Morrisville, Pennsylvania, USA in October 1983.

Snow Construction *Largest*

The world's largest snow construction is the Ice Palace built in the winter of 1980–81 using 1600 tons/tonnes of snow, at Tokamachi City, Niigata prefecture, Japan. The overall height was 23 m *75 ft 5 in* and a total of 800 people and 50 bulldozers were used in the construction.

Stairs Longest *World*

The world's longest stairway is the service staircase for the Niesenbahn funicular which rises to 2365 m *7759 ft* near Spiez, Switzerland. It has 11,674 steps and a bannister. The stone cut T'ai Chan temple stairs of 6600 steps in the Shantung Mountains, China ascend 4700 feet in 5 miles *1428 m* in *8 km*. The longest spiral staircase is one 1103 ft *336,2 m* deep with 1520 steps installed in the Mapco–White County Coal Mine, Carmi, Illinois, USA by Systems Control Inc in May 1981.

Stairs Longest *Great Britain*

The longest stairs in Britain are those from the transformer gallery to the surface 1065 ft *324 m* in the Cruachan Power Station, Argyll, Scotland. They have 1420 steps and the Work Study Dept. allows 27 min 41.4 sec for the ascent.

Statue Longest

Near Bamiyan, Afghanistan there are the remains of the recumbent Sakya Buddha, built of plastered rubble, which was 'about 1000 ft *305 m*' long and is believed to date from the 3rd or 4th century AD.

Statue Tallest

The tallest full-figure statue in the world is that of 'Motherland', an enormous pre-stressed concrete female figure on Mamayev Hill, outside Volgograd, USSR, designed in 1967 by Yevgenyi Vuchetich, to commemorate victory in the Battle of Stalingrad (1942–3). The statue from its base to the tip of the sword clenched in her right hand measures 270 ft *82,30 m*. *The Indian Rope Trick* statue by Calle Örnemark near Jönköping, Sweden measures 103 m *337 ft* from the feet of the *fakir* to the top of the rope 25 cm *9.8 in* in diameter. Its total weight is 144 tonnes *141.6 tons*.

Tidal river barrier

The largest tidal river barrier in the world is the Thames Barrier at Woolwich, London with 9 piers and 10 gates. There are 6 rising sector gates 61 m *200 ft 1¼ in* wide and 4 falling radial gates 31,5 m *103 ft 4 in* wide. The site was chosen in 1971. Costs to the end of 1982 were £400 million.

Tomb Largest

The largest tomb yet discovered is that of Emperor Nintoku (died *c*. AD 428) south of Osaka, Japan. It measures 1594 ft *485 m* long by 1000 ft *305 m* wide by 150 ft *45 m* high.

Totem pole Tallest

A totem pole 173 ft *52,73 m* tall was raised on 6 June 1973 at Alert Bay, British Columbia, Canada. It tells the story of the Kwakiutl and took 36 man-weeks to carve.

Vats Largest

The largest vat in the world is named 'Strongbow', used by H.P. Bulmer Ltd., the cider makers of Hereford, England. It measures 64½ ft *19,65 m* in height and 75½ ft *23,0 m* in diameter with a capacity of 1,630,000 gallons *74 099 hectolitres*.

The largest wooden wine cask in the world is the Heidelberg Tun completed in 1751 in the cellar of the Friedrichsbau Heidelberg, West Germany. Its capacity is 1855 hectolitres *40,790 gal*. The world's oldest is that in use since 1715 at Hugelet Fils (founded 1639) Riquewihr, Haut-Rhin by the most recent of the 12 generations of the family.

Wall Longest *World*

The Great Wall of China, completed during the reign of Chhin Shih Huang-ti (246–210 BC), has a main line length of 2150 miles *3460 km* with a further 1780 miles *2860 km* of branches and spurs, with a height of from 15 to 39 ft *4,5 to 12 m* and up to 32 ft *9,8 m* thick. It runs from Shanhaikuan, on the Gulf of Pohai, to Yümênkuan and Yang-kuan and was kept in repair up to the 16th century. Some 32 miles *51,5 km* of the Wall have been destroyed since 1966. Part of the wall was blown up to make way for a dam in July 1979. On 6 Mar 1985 a report from China stated that a 5 year long survey proved that the total length had been 9980 km *6200 miles*.

Wall Longest *Great Britain*

The longest of the Roman Walls built in Britain was the 15–20 ft *4,5–6 m* tall Hadrian's Wall, built AD 122–126. It crossed the Tyne-Solway isthmus for 73¼ miles *118 km* from Bowness-on-Solway, Cumbria, to Wallsend-on-Tyne, Tyne and Wear, being abandoned in AD 383.

The oldest known pyramid in the world—the 4,635 year old memorial to the world's first great architect Imhotep at Saqqâra, Egypt. *(David Cadish)*

Above The world's oldest wine cask has been in regular use since 1715. *(Hoerdt Ribeauville) Below* Part of the Great Wall of China—now believed to have extended much further than the 3930 miles *6325 km* visible *(Vernon E. Craig)*

Water tower

The world's tallest water tower is that at Elizabethtown, New York State, USA built in 1965 to a height of 210 ft *64 m* with a capacity of 250,000 gallons *9462 hl*

Waterwheel Largest *World and Great Britain*

The largest waterwheel in the world is the Mohammadieh Noria wheel at Hama, Syria with a diameter of 131 ft *40 m* dating from Roman times. The Lady Isabella wheel at Laxey, Isle of Man is the largest in the British Isles and was built for draining a lead mine and completed on 27 Sept 1854, and disused since 1929. It has a circumference of 228 ft *69 m*, a diameter of 72½ ft *22 m* and an axle weighing 9 tons/*tonnes*. The largest waterwheel in Britain is the 50 ft 5 in *15,36 m* diameter wheel built in 1870 at the Welsh Industrial and Maritime Museum, Cardiff. It worked until 1925 at Dinorwic, Gwynedd and is 5 ft *1,52 m* in width.

Window Largest

The largest sheet of glass ever manufactured was one of 50 m² *538.2 ft²*, or 20 m *65 ft 7 in* by 2,5 m *8 ft 2½ in*, exhibited by the Saint Gobian Company in France at the *Journées Internationales de Miroiterie* in March 1958. The largest single windows in the world are those in the Palace of Industry and Technology at Rondpoint de la Défense, Paris, with an extreme width of 218 m *715.2 ft* and a maximum height of 50 m *164 ft*.

The record for Pilkington of St Helens, Merseyside is a sheet of 2,5 × 15,2 m *8 ft 2¼ × 49 ft 10½ in* made for the Festival of Britain in 1951.

Wine cellar

The largest wine cellars in the world are at Paarl, those of the Ko-operative Wijnbouwers Vereeniging, known as KWV, near Cape Town, in the centre of the wine-growing district of South Africa. They cover an area of 25 acres *10 ha* and have a capacity of 30 million gal *136 million litres*. The Cienega Winery of the Almaden Vineyards in Hollister, California, USA covers 4 acres *1,6 ha* and can house 37,300 oak barrels containing 1.83 million gallons of wine.

Ziggurat Largest

The largest ziggurat ever built was by the Elamite King Untash *c*. 1250 BC known as the Ziggurat of Choga Zanbil, 30 km *18.6 miles* from Haft Tepe, Iran. The outer base was 105 × 105 m *344 ft* and the fifth 'box' 28 × 28 m *91.8 ft* nearly 50 m *164 ft* above. The largest surviving ziggurat (from the verb *zaqaru*, to build high) or stage-tower is the Ziggurat of Ur (now Mu-quyyar, Iraq) with a base 61 × 45,7 m *200 × 150 ft* built to three storeys surmounted by a summit temple. The first and part of the second storeys now survive to a height of 60 ft *18 m*. It was built in the reign of Ur-nammu (*c.* 2113–2096 BC).

10. BORINGS AND MINES

Deepest *World*
Man's deepest penetration into the Earth's crust is a geological exploratory drilling near Zapolarny, Kola peninsula USSR begun in 1970. On 28 Dec 1983 12 000 m *39,370 ft* or *7.45 miles* was reached. Progress has understandably greatly slowed to 500 m *1640 ft* per annum as the eventual target of 15 000 m *49,212 ft*, in 1989–90 is neared. The drill bit is mounted on a turbine driven by a mud pump. The temperature at 11 km *6.83 miles* was already 200° C *392° F*.

Deepest *Ocean Drilling*
The deepest recorded drilling into the sea bed by the *Glomar Challenger* of the US Deep Sea Drilling Project is one of 5709 ft *1740 m* off N.W. Spain in 1976. The deepest site is now 7034 m *23,077 ft* below the surface on the western wall of the Marianas Trench (see page 58) in May 1978.

Oil fields
The largest oil field in the world is the Ghawar field, Saudi Arabia developed by ARAMCO which measures 150 miles by 22 miles *240 km by 35 km*.

The area of the designated parts of the UK Continental shelf as at 1 Apr 1975 was 223,550 miles² *579 000 km²* with total recoverable reserves of 3200 million tonnes of oil and 51,000,000 million ft³ *1 443 000 million m³* of gas. Gas was first discovered in the West Sole Field in October 1965 and oil in the Forties Field (Block 22/17) at 11,000 ft *3352 m* from the drilling barge *Sea Quest* on 18 Sept 1970, though a small gasfield was detected near Whitby, N. Yorkshire in 1937. The most productive oil field is expected to be Brent (found in July 1971) where the B platform was installed in August 1976. Production in 1979 reached 350,000 barrels a day and peaked at 850,000 bbd in 1983. The whole UK production in 1979 was 76,415,581 tonnes or 19,558 million Imperial gal. The deepest drilling in British waters is 2400 ft *731 m* in Block 206, west of Shetland by Shell using the drill ship *Petrel* in April 1980.

Gas Deposits
The largest gas deposit in the world is at Urengoi, USSR with an eventual production of 180,000 million m³ per year through 6 pipelines from a total estimated to be 7,000,000 million m³.

Oil platforms *Largest*
The world's most massive oil platform is the *Statfjord B* Concrete Gravity-base platform built at Stavanger, Norway and operated by Mobil Exploration Norway Inc. Tow-out to its permanent field began on 1 Aug 1981 and it was the heaviest object ever moved—816,000 tonnes or 803,000 long tons ballasted weight. The £1.1 billion structure was towed by 8 tugs with a combined power of 115,000 hp. The height of the concrete structure is 204 m *670 ft* and the

The head-gear above the world's deepest mine—Western Deep Levels, Carletonville, South Africa. It is now more than 2½ miles deep. (See Table below)

overall height 271 m *890 ft*. It thus weighs almost three times the weight of each of the towers of the World Trade Centre (290,000 long tons). The world's tallest production platform is the £1300 million 1024 ft *312 m* tall BP Magnus platform in the North Sea. Production started in July 1983. The 70 000 tonnes structure was built to withstand 100 ft *30,4 m* waves and deliver 120,000 barrels a day to the Sullom Voe Terminal, Shetland.

Gusher Greatest
The greatest wildcat ever recorded blew at Alborz No 5 well, near Qum, Iran on 26 Aug 1956. The uncontrolled oil gushed to a height of 170 ft *52 m* at 120,000 barrels per day at a pressure of 9000 lb/in² *62 055 kPa*. It was closed after 90 days work by B. Mostofi and Myron Kinley of Texas, USA. The Lake View No. 1 gusher in California, USA on 15 Mar 1910 may have yielded 125,000 barrels in its first 24 hours.

Oil Spills Greatest
The slick from the Mexican marine blow-out beneath the drilling rig *Ixtoc I* in the Gulf of Campeche, Gulf of Mexico, on 3 June 1979 reached 400 miles *640 km* by 5 Aug 1979. It eventually was capped on 24 Mar 1980 after a loss of 3,000,000 barrels (535,000 tons).

The worst oil spill in history was of 236,000 tons/ *tonnes* of oil from the super-tankers *Atlantic Empress* and *Aegean Captain* when they collided off Tobago on 19 July 1979. The worst oil spill in British waters was from the 118,285 dwt *Torrey Canyon* which struck the Pollard Rock off Land's End on 18 Mar 1967 resulting in a loss of 106,000 tons of oil.

Flare Greatest
The greatest gas fire was that which burnt at Gassi Touil in the Algerian Sahara from noon on 13 Nov 1961 to 9.30 a.m. on 28 Apr 1962. The pillar of flame rose 450 ft *137 m* and the smoke 600 ft *182 m*. It was eventually extinguished by Paul Neal ('Red') Adair (b. 1932), of Houston, Texas, USA, using 550 lb *245 kg* of dynamite. His fee was understood to be about $1,000,000 (*then £357,000*).

Water well Deepest *World*
The world's deepest water bore is the Stensvad Water Well 11-W1 of 7320 ft *2231 m* drilled by the Great Northern Drilling Co. Inc. in Rosebud County, Montana, USA in October–November 1961. The Thermal Power Co. geothermal steam well begun in Sonoma County, California in 1955 is now down to 9029 ft *2752 m*.

Water well Deepest *Great Britain*
The deepest well in Great Britain is a water table well 2842 ft *866 m* deep in the Staffordshire coal measures at Smestow. The deepest artesian well in Britain is that at the White Heather Laundry, Stonebridge Park, Brent, Greater London, bored in 1911 to a depth of 2225 ft *678 m*. The deepest known hand dug well is one dug to 1285 ft *391,6 m* in 1858 to March 1862 on the site of Fitzherbert School, Woodingdean, Brighton, East Sussex.

MINES

Earliest *(World)*		41,250 BC ± 1600	Lion Cavern, Haematite (red iron ore)	Ngwenya, Hhohho, Swaziland
Earliest *(GB)*		3390 BC ± 150	Flint	Church Hill, Findon, W. Sussex
Deepest *(World)*[1]		12,391 ft *3777 m* (2.34 miles)	Gold, Western Deep Levels (temp 131°F 55°C)	Carletonville, South Africa
Deepest *(GB, all-time)*		4132 ft *1259 m*	Coal, Arley Seam, Parsonage Colliery (Feb 1949)	Leigh, Greater Manchester
(GB, current)		3690 ft *1127 m*	Coal, Bickershaw Colliery	Bickershaw, Greater Manchester
(Cornwall)		3600 ft *1097 m*	Tin, Williams Shaft, Dolcoath (1910)	Near Camborne, Cornwall
Copper *(deepest, open cast)*		2590 ft *789 m*	Bingham Canyon (began 1904) diameter 2.3 miles *3,7 km*	Utah, USA
Copper *(largest underground)*		356 miles *573 km* tunnels	San Manuel Mine, Magma Copper Co	Arizona, USA
Lead *(largest)*		> 10 per cent of world output	Viburnum Trend	Southeast Missouri, USA
Goldmining *(area)*		> 51 per cent of world output	38 mines of the Witwatersrand Discovery in 1886	South Africa
Gold Mine *(largest world)*[2]		12,100 acres *4900 ha*	East Rand Proprietary Mines Ltd	Boksburg, Transvaal, South Africa
Gold Mine *(largest, GB)*		120,000 fine oz (1854–1914)	Clogau, St David's (disc. 1836)	Gwynedd, Wales
Gold Mine *(richest)*		49.4 million fine oz	Crown Mines (all-time yield)	Transvaal, South Africa
Iron Mine *(largest)*		20 300 million tonnes rich ore	Lebedinsky (45–65% ore)	Kursk region, USSR
Platinum *(largest)*		1,000,000 oz *28 tonnes per annum*	Rustenberg Group, Impala plant	Springs, South Africa
Tungsten Mine *(largest)*		2000 tonnes per day	Union Carbide Mount Morgan mine	Near Bishop, California, USA
Uranium *(largest)*		5000 tons of uranium oxide	Rio Tinto Zinc open cast pit	Rössing, Namibia, SW Africa
Spoil Dump *(largest, world)*		275 million yd³ *210 million m³*	New Cornelia Tailings	Ten Mile Wash, Arizona, USA
Spoil Dump *(largest, GB)*[3]		114 acre *46 ha* 130 ft *40 m* high	Cutacre Clough Colliery tip (18 million tonnes)	Lancashire
Quarry *(largest, world)*		2.81 miles² *7,21 km²*. 2540 ft *774 m* deep. 3700 million short tons *3355 million tonnes*	Bingham Canyon Copper Mine	Nr. Salt Lake City, Utah, USA
Quarry *(largest, GB)*		500 ft *150 m* deep, 1.6 mile *2,6 km* circumference	Old Delabole Slate Quarry (since c. 1570)	Cornwall
Open Cast Coal Mine		1130 ft *325 m* deep 21 m² *8 mile²* area	Fortuna-Garsdorf (lignite) (began 1955)	Nr. Bergheim, W. Germany
Coal Mine *(oldest, U.K.)*		c. 1822	founded by William Stobart	Wearmouth, near Sunderland, Durham

[1] Sinking began in June 1957. Scheduled to reach 3880 m *12 730 ft* by 1992 with 14 000 ft or 2.65 miles regarded as the limit. No 3 vertical ventilation shaft is the world's deepest shaft at 2948,9 m *9675 ft*. This mine requires 130,000 tons of air per day and refrigeration which uses the energy it would take to make 37,000 short tons of ice. An underground shift comprises 11,150 men. The deepest exploratory coal mining shaft is one reaching 6700 ft *2042 m* near Thorez in the Ukranian Donbas field, USSR in 1983.
[2] The world's most productive gold mine may be Muruntau, Kyzyl Kum, Uzbekistan, USSR. According to one western estimate it produces 80 tonnes of gold in a year. It has been estimated that South Africa has produced in 96 years (1886–1982) 36,400 tons or more than 31 per cent of all gold mined since 3900 BC.
[3] Reclamation plan announced 13 Sept 1982 for 1983–1996.

The Mechanical World

Kenneth Eriksson of Äppelbo, Sweden exhibiting a fine sense of economy in his Opel Kadett which used only two tyres for nearly 12½ miles *20 km*. (See page 128.)

1. SHIPS

The Guinness Book of Ships and Shipping Facts and Feats by Tom Hartman was published in August 1983 priced £9.95

EARLIEST SEA-GOING BOATS

Aborigines are thought to have been able to cross the Torres Strait from New Guinea to Australia, then at least 70 km *43½ miles* across, as early as 40,000 BC. They are believed to have used double canoes. The earliest surviving 'vessel' is a pinewood dug-out found in Pesse, Netherlands and dated to *c.* 6315 ± 275 BC and now in the Provincial Museum, Assen. The earliest representation of a boat is disputed between possible rock art outlines of mesolithic skin-boats in Høgnipen, Norway (10,000–7750 BC); Minateda, Spain (12,000–3000 BC) and Kobystan, USSR (8000–6000 BC). An 18 in

45 cm long paddle was found at the Star Carr, North Yorkshire site, described in 1948. It has been dated to *c.* 7600 BC and is now in the Cambridge Museum of Archaeology.

The oldest surviving boat is the 142 ft *43,4 m* long 40 ton Nile boat or Royal Ship of King Cheops buried near the Great Pyramid of Khufu, Egypt *c.* 2515 BC. Its discovery was announced in May 1954 and it has been reassembled in Cairo.

The oldest shipwreck ever found is one of a Cycladic trading vessel located off the islet of Dhókós, near the Greek island of Hydra reported in May 1975 and dated to 2450 BC ± 250.

Earliest power

Propulsion by steam engine was first achieved when in 1783 the Marquis Jouffroy d'Abbans (1751–1832) ascended a reach of the river Saône

near Lyon, France, in the 180 ton *182 tonnes* paddle steamer *Pyroscaphe*.

The tug *Charlotte Dundas* was the first successful power-driven vessel. She was a stern paddle-wheel steamer built for the Forth and Clyde Canal, Scotland in 1801–2 by William Symington (1763–1831), using a double-acting condensing engine constructed by James Watt (1736–1819). The screw propeller was invented and patented by the Kent farmer Sir Francis Pettit Smith (1808–71) in 1836.

Oldest vessels

The oldest mechanically propelled boat in the world of certain date is the 48 ton Bristol steam driven dredger or drag-boat *Bertha* of 50 ft *15,42 m*, designed by I. K. Brunel (1806–59) in 1844 and afloat in the custody of the Exeter Maritime Museum, Devon, England. Mr G. H.

Pattinson's 40 ft *12,20 m* steam launch *Dolly*, which was raised after 67 years from Ullswater, Cumbria, in 1962 and now on Lake Windermere, also probably dates from the 1840s. The world's oldest active steam ship is the *Skibladner*, which has plied Lake Mjøsa, Norway since 1856. She has had two major refits and was built in Motala, Sweden. The oldest motor vessel afloat in British waters is the *Proven* on the run from the Clyde to the Inner Hebrides. She was built in Norway in 1866. The oldest vessel on *Lloyd's Yacht Register* is the twin screw steam yacht *Esperance* built on the Clyde in 1869 and salvaged from Windermere in 1941.

The oldest square-rigged sailing vessel in the world is the restored SV *Ciudad de Inca*, built near Barcelona, Spain in 1858. She is 125 ft *38,1 m* overall with a grt of 127 tons. She was restored in 1981–82 for operation by the China Clipper Society of Maidstone, Kent.

Earliest turbine

The first turbine ship was the *Turbinia*, built in 1894 at Wallsend-on-Tyne, Tyne and Wear, to the design of the Hon. Sir Charles Parsons, OM, KCB (1854–1931). The *Turbinia* was 100 ft *30,48 m* long and of 44½ tons *45,2 tonnes* displacement with machinery consisting of three steam turbines totalling about 2000 shaft horsepower. At her first public demonstration in 1897 she reached a speed of 34.5 knots (39.7 mph *63,9 km/h*).

PASSENGER LINERS

Largest active

The world's largest and the world's longest ever liner is the *Norway* of 70,202.19 grt and 315,66 m *1035 ft 7¼ in* in overall length with a capacity of 2400 passengers. She was built as the *France* in 1961 and renamed after purchase in June 1979 by Knut Kloster of Norway. Her second maiden voyage was from Southampton on 7 May 1980. Britain's largest liner is RMS *Queen Elizabeth 2* of 67,140 gross tons and with an overall length of 963 ft *293 m* completed for the Cunard Line Ltd. in 1969. She set a 'turn round' record of 5 hr 47 min at New York on 21 Nov 1983. In her 1985 World Cruise, the price of the Penthouse suite was set at $309,000 (£216,000).

RMS Queen Elizabeth 2—Britain's largest passenger liner. (See below)

Largest ever

The RMS *Queen Elizabeth* (finally 82,998 but formerly 83,673 gross tons), of the Cunard fleet, was the largest passenger vessel ever built and had the largest displacement of any liner in the world. She had an overall length of 1031 ft *314 m* and was 118 ft 7 in *36 m* in breadth and was powered by steam turbines which developed 168,000 hp. Her last passenger voyage ended on 15 Nov 1968. In 1970 she was removed to Hong Kong to serve as a floating marine university and renamed *Seawise University*. On 9 Jan 1972 she was fired by 3 simultaneous outbreaks. The gutted hull had been cut up and removed by 1978. *Seawise* was a pun on the owner's initials—C. Y. Tung (1911–1982).

WARSHIPS

Battleships *Largest World*

The largest battleship in service in the world is the 887 ft 9 in *270,6 m* long USS *New Jersey* with a full load displacement of 58,000 tons

The Japanese *Yamato*—history's largest ever battleship. (See below)

58 000 tonnes. She was the last fire support ship on active service off the Lebanon coast with her nine 16 in guns from 14 Dec 1983 to 26 Feb 1984. The $405 million refit of USS *Iowa* was completed in May 1984. USS *Missouri* and USS *Wisconsin* have also been re-activated. The 16 inch projectiles of 2700 lb *1225 kg* can be fired 23 miles *39 km*.

Largest all-time

The Japanese battleship *Yamato* (completed on 16 Dec 1941 and sunk south-west of Kyūshū, Japan, by US planes on 7 Apr 1945) and *Musashi* (sunk in the Philippine Sea by 11 bombs and 16 torpedoes on 24 Oct 1944) were the largest battleships ever commissioned, each with a full load displacement of 72,809 tons *73 977 tonnes*. With an overall length of 863 ft *263 m*, a beam of 127 ft *38,7 m* and a full load draught of 35½ ft *10,8 m* they mounted nine 460 mm *18.1 in* guns in three triple turrets. Each gun weighed 162 tons *164,6 tonnes* and was 75 ft *22,8 m* in length firing a 3200 lb *1451 kg* projectile.

Largest Great Britain

Britain's largest ever and last battleship was HMS *Vanguard* (1944–1960) with a full load displacement of 51,420 tons *52 245 tonnes* and an overall length of 814 ft *248,1 m*. She mounted eight 15 in *38 cm* guns.

Guns and Armour

The largest guns ever mounted in any of HM ships were the 18 in *45 cm* pieces in the light battle cruiser (later aircraft carrier) HMS *Furious* in 1917. In 1918 they were transferred to the monitors HMS *Lord Clive* and *General Wolfe*. The thickest armour ever carried was in HMS *Inflexible* (completed 1881), measuring 24 in *60 cm* backed by teak up to a maximum thickness of 42 in *106,6 cm*.

Fastest destroyer

The highest speed attained by a destroyer was 45.25 knots (51.84 mph *83,42 km/h*) by the 2830 ton/*tonne* French destroyer *Le Terrible* in 1935. She was built in Blainville and powered by four Yarrow small tube boilers and two Rateau geared turbines giving 100,000 shaft horse-power. She was removed from the active list at the end of 1957.

The French *Le Terrible*—the fastest ever destroyer. (See above)

AIRCRAFT CARRIERS

Largest *World*

The warships with the largest full load displacement in the world are the Nimitz class US Navy aircraft carriers USS *Dwight D. Eisenhower, Carl Vinson* and *Theodore Roosevelt* at 91,487 tons.

They are 1092 ft *322,9 m* in length overall with 4½ acres *1,82 ha* of flight deck and have a speed well in excess of 30 knots *56 km/h* from their 4 nuclear-powered 260,000 shp geared steam turbines. They have to be refuelled after about 900,000 miles *1 450 000 km* steaming. Their complement is 6300. The total cost of the *Abraham Lincoln*, laid down at Newport News in December 1984 will exceed $3½ billion (£2.6 billion), excluding the 90-plus aircraft carried. USS *Enterprise* is, however, 1102 ft *335,8 m* long and thus still the longest warship ever built.

The Royal Navy's newest aircraft carrier is HMS *Ark Royal*, commissioned in Nov 1984. She has a 550 ft *167,6 m* long flight deck and is 677 ft *206,3 m* long overall, and has a top speed of 28 knots being powered by 4 Rolls Royce Olympus TM3B gas turbines.

SUBMARINES

Largest *World*

The world's largest submarines are of the USSR Typhoon class code named Oscar. The launch of the first at the secret covered shipyard at Severodvinsk in the White Sea was announced by NATO on 23 Sept 1980. It is believed to have a dived displacement of 30,000 tonnes, measure 170 m *557.6 ft* overall and be armed with twenty SS NX 20 missiles with a 5000 nautical mile *9260 km* range, each with 7 warheads. By 1987 two others building in Leningrad will also be operational, each deploying 140 warheads.

Great Britain

The largest submarines ever built for the Royal Navy are the four atomic-powered nuclear missile R class boats with a surface displacement of 7500 tons *7620 tonnes* and 8400 tons *8534 tonnes* submerged, a length of 425 ft *129,5 m*, a beam of 33 ft *10 m* and a draught of 30 ft *9,1 m*. The longest submarine patrol ever spent dived and unsupported is 111 days by H.M. Submarine *Warspite* (Cdr. J. G. F. Cooke RN) in the South Atlantic from 25 Nov 1982 to 15 Mar 1983. She sailed 30,804 nautical miles *57 085 km*.

Fastest

The Russian Alfa-Class nuclear-powered submarines have a reported maximum speed of 42 knots *77,8 km/h* plus. With use of titanium steel they are believed to be able to dive to 2500 ft *762 m*. A US spy satelite over Leningrad's naval yard on 8 June 1983 showed they were being lengthened and are now 79.3 m *260.1 ft* long.

Deepest

The two USN vessels able to descend 12,000 ft *3650 m* are the 3-man *Trieste II* (DSV I) of 303 tons dived recommissioned in November 1973 and the DSV 2 (deep submergence vessel) USS *Alvin*. The *Trieste II* was reconstructed from the record-breaking bathyscaphe *Trieste* but without the Krupp-built sphere, which enabled it to descend to 35,820 ft *10 917 m*. (See Chapter 10 Greatest ocean descent).

TANKERS

Largest

The world's largest tanker and ship of any kind is the 564,739 tonnes deadweight *Seawise Giant*

The illustrations on these pages are all to scale.
Artwork: Pat Gibbon

Ships 123

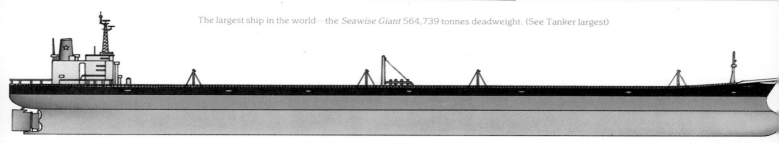

The largest ship in the world—the *Seawise Giant* 564,739 tonnes deadweight. (See Tanker largest)

completed for C. Y. Tung in 1979. She is 458,45 m *1504 ft* long with a beam of 68,86 m *225 ft 11 in* and has a draught of 24,61 m *80 ft 9 in*. She was lengthened by Nippon Kokan in 1980 by adding an 81 m *265 ft 8 in* midship section.

CARGO VESSELS

Largest
The largest vessel in the world capable of carrying dry cargo is the Liberian ore/oil carrier *World Gala* of 133,748 GT *282,462 dwt* with a length of 1109 ft *338 m* and a beam of 179 ft *54,5 m* owned by Liberian Trident Transports Inc. completed in 1973. The largest British ore/oil carrier is Lombard North Central Leasing's *Rimula* built in Sweden in 1974 of 121,165 GT, *227,412 dwt* with a length of 332,77 m *1091 ft 9 in*.

Largest whale factory
The largest whale factory ship is the USSR's *Sovietskaya Ukraina* (32,034 gross tons), with a summer deadweight of 46,000 tons *46 738 tonnes* completed in October 1959. She is 217,8 m *714 ft 6 in* in length and 25,8 m *84 ft 7 in* in the beam.

Largest barges
The world's largest RoRo (Roll-on, Roll-off) ships are the four *El Rey* class barges of 16,700 tons and 580 ft *176,78 m* in length. They were built by the FMC Corp of Portland, Oregon, USA, and are operated by Crowley Maritime Corp of San Francisco between Florida and Puerto Rico with tri-level lodging of up to 376 truck-trailers.

Container ship
Shipborne containerisation began when in 1957 the *Gateway City* was converted by Malcolm MacLean (US).

The world's largest container ship is the *Senshu Maru* (Japan) of 106,500 dwt 928 ft *282,85 m* in length with a beam of 147 ft *44,80 m*.

Most powerful tugs
The world's largest and most powerful tugs are the *Wolraad Waltemade* and her sister ship *John Ross* of 2822 grt rated at 19,200 shaft horse-power and with a bollard pull of 172.7 tons (90% of full power). They have an overall length of 94,623 m *310 ft 5 in* and a beam of 49 ft 10 in *15,2 m*. They were built to handle the largest tankers and were completed in April 1976 (Leith, Scotland) and in October 1976 (Durban, South Africa).

Largest car ferry
The world's largest car and passenger ferry is the 30.5 knot 24,600 grt GTS *Finnjet* which entered service across the Baltic between Helsinki and Travemünde, West Germany on 13 May 1977. She can carry 350 cars and 1532 passengers. On 30 Sept 1984, Slite of Sweden ordered a 36,000 ton car ferry for the Baltic from Wartsila of Finland for 500 cars and 2500 passengers.

The 9700 dwt 21 knot *Railship II* went into service on the Baltic run in Nov 1984. She can carry 88 20 m *65 ft 7 in* long rail cars, is 186,5 m *611 ft 10 in* overall and was built for HM Gehrckens of Hamburg.

Largest propeller
The world's largest ship propeller is the triple bladed screw of 11,0 m *36 ft 1 in* diameter made by Kawasaki Heavy Industries Ltd on 17 Mar 1982 for the 208,000 ton bulk-ore tanker *Hoei Maru*.

Largest hydrofoil
The world's largest naval hydrofoil is the 212 ft *64,6 m* long *Plainview* (310 tons *314 tonnes* full load), launched by the Lockheed Shipbuilding and Construction Co. at Seattle, Washington, USA on 28 June 1965. She has a service speed of 50 knots (57 mph *92 km/h*). Three 165 ton Supramar PTS 150 Mk III hydrofoils carrying 250 passengers at 40 knots *74 km/h* ply the Malmö-Copenhagen crossing. They were built by Westermoen Hydrofoil Ltd. at Mandal, Norway. A 500 ton wing ground effect vehicle capable of carrying 900 tons has been reported in the USSR.

Largest river boat
The world's largest inland river-boat is the 378 ft *115,2 m* long SS *Admiral* now undergoing a 6 year $26.7 million renovation at St Louis, Missouri as a Mississippi river floating 'entertainment center'.

Fastest building
The fastest-ever building time for a major ship was 4 days 15 hrs in the in the case of the 10,920 ton displacement *Robert E. Peory* at Kaiser's Yard, Portland, Oregon, USA on 8 Nov (keel laid) to launch on 12 Nov 1942. She was operational on 15 Nov and was No 440 of the fleet of 2742 11.6 knot such liberty ships built in 18 US shipyards from 27 Sept 1941.

Most powerful icebreaker
A 61,000 ton/*tonne* nuclear powered barge-carrying merchantman designed for work along the USSR's Arctic coast was completed in early 1982 and is known to be designed to break ice. The longest purpose-built icebreaker is the 25 000 ton 460 ft *140 m* long *Rossiya*, powered by 75,000 h.p. nuclear engines launched at Leningrad in November 1983.

The largest *converted* icebreaker has been the 1007 ft *306,9 m* long SS *Manhattan* (43,000 shp), which was converted by the Humble Oil Co. into a 150,000 ton *152 407 tonnes* icebreaker with an armoured prow 69 ft 2 in long. She made a double voyage through the North-West Passage in arctic Canada from 24 Aug to 12 Nov 1969. The North-West Passage was first navigated by Roald Amundsen (Norway) in the sealing sloop *Gjöa* on 11 July 1906.

Yacht most expensive
The refit of the £20 million 470 foot *143,2 m* the Saudi Arabian Royal yacht *Abdul Aziz* was completed on 22 June 1984 at Vospers Yard, Southampton at a cost of £9 million.

Largest dredger
The world's most powerful dredger is the 468.4 ft *142,7 m* long *Prins der Nederlanden* of 10,586 grt. She can dredge 20,000 tonnes/*tons* of sand from a depth of 35 m *115 ft via* two suction tubes in less than an hour.

Wooden ship
The heaviest wooden ship ever built was the *Richelieu*, 333 ft 8 in *101,70 m* long and of 8534 tons launched in Toulon, France on 3 Dec 1873. HM Battleship *Lord Warden*, completed in 1869, displaced 7940 tons *8060 tonnes*. The longest modern wooden ship ever built was the New York built *Rochambeau* (1867–72) formerly *Dunderberg*. She measured 377 ft 4 in *115 m* overall. It should be noted that the biblical length of Noah's Ark was 300 cubits or, at 18 in *45,7 cm* to a cubit, 450 ft *137 m* (see Junks p. 124).

Largest human powered
The largest human powered ship was the giant Tessarakonteres 3-banked catamaran galley with 4000 rowers built for Ptolemy IV *c.* 210 BC in Alexandria, Egypt. It measured 128 m *420 ft* with up to 8 men to an oar of 38 cubits (17,5 m *57 ft*) in length. The world's longest canoe is the 117 ft *35,7 m* long 20 ton Kauri wood Maori war canoe Nga Toki Matawhaorua built by adzes at Kerikeri Inlet, New Zealand in 1940 for a crew of 70 or more. The 'Snake Boat' Nadubhagóm 135 ft *41,1 m* long from Kerala, Southern India has a crew of 109 rowers and 9 'encouragers'.

Light vessels
The earliest station still marked by a light vessel is the Newarp in the North Sea, off Great Yarmouth in 1791. A Nore Lightvessel was first placed in the Thames estuary in 1732.

SAILING SHIPS

Largest
The largest sailing vessel ever built was the *France II* (5806 gross tons), launched at Bordeaux in 1911. The *France II* was a steel-hulled, five-masted barque (square-rigged on four masts and fore and aft rigged on the aftermost mast). Her hull measured 418 ft *127,4 m* overall. Although principally designed as a sailing vessel with a stump topgallant rig, she was also fitted with two steam engines. She was wrecked off New Caledonia on 13 July 1922. The only seven-masted sailing schooner ever built was the 375.6 ft *114,4 m* long *Thomas W. Lawson* (5218 gross tons) built at Quincy, Massachusetts, USA in 1902 and lost in the English Channel on 15 Dec 1907.

France II—the largest sailing ship ever built. (See above)

The world's only surviving First Rate Ship-of-the-Line is the Royal Navy's 104-gun battleship HMS *Victory* laid down at Chatham, Kent on 23 July 1759 constructed from the wood of some 2200 oak trees. She bore the body of Admiral Nelson from Gibraltar to Portsmouth arriving 44 days after serving as his victorious flagship at the Battle of Trafalgar on 21 Oct 1805. In 1922 she was moved to No. 2 dock, Portsmouth—site of the world's oldest graving dock. The length of her cordage (both standing and running rigging) is 100,962 ft (19.12 miles *30,77 km*.)

The world's largest sailing vessel in service is the 342 ft *104 m* 4 masted barque *Kruzenshtern* built in *c.* 1933 and used by USSR marine schools of Kaliningrad and Murmansk.

Largest junks
The largest junk on record was the sea-going *Cheng Ho*, flagship of Admiral Cheng Ho's 62 treasure ships, of *c.* 1420, with a displacement of 3100 tons *3150 tonnes* and a length variously estimated up to 538 ft *164 m* and believed to have had 9 masts. A river junk 361 ft *110 m* long, with treadmill-operated paddle-wheels, was recorded in AD 1161. In *c.* AD 280 a floating fortress 600 ft *182,8 m* square, built by Wang Chün on the Yangtze, took part in the Chin-Wu river war. Present-day junks do not, even in the case of the Chiangsu traders, exceed 170 ft *51,8 m* in length.

Longest day's run under sail
The longest day's run calculated for any commercial vessel was one of 462 nautical miles (532.0 statute miles *856,16 km*) by the clipper *Champion of the Seas* (2722 registered tons) of the Liverpool Black Ball Line running before a north-westerly gale in the south Indian Ocean under the command of Capt. Alex. Newlands in 1854. The elapsed time between the fixes was 23 hr 17 min giving an average of 19.97 knots *37,00 km/h* (see Chapter 11 Yachting for sporting record).

Largest sails
Sails are known to have been used for marine propulsion since 3500 BC. The largest spars ever carried were those in HM Battleship *Temeraire*, completed at Chatham, Kent, on 31 Aug 1877. She was broken up in 1921. The fore and main yards measured 115 ft *35 m* in length. The foresail contained 5100 ft *1555 m* of canvas, weighing 2 tons *2,03 tonnes* and the total sail area was 25,000 ft² *2322 m²*. HM Battleship *Sultan* was ship-rigged when completed at Chatham, Kent on 10 Oct 1871 and carried 34,100 ft² *3168 m²* of sails plus 15,300 ft² *1421 m²* of stunsails. She was not finally broken up until 1946.

Largest wreck
The largest ship ever wrecked has been the 312,186 dwt VLCC (Very Large Crude Carrier) *Energy Determination* which blew up and broke in two in the Straits of Hormuz on 12 Dec 1979. Her full value was $58 million (*then £26.3 million*).

Most massive collision
The closest approach to an irresistible force striking an immovable object occurred on 16 Dec 1977, 22 miles *35 km* off the coast of Southern Africa when the tanker *Venoil* (330,954 dwt) struck her sister ship *Venpet* (330,869 dwt).

OCEAN CROSSINGS

Atlantic *Earliest*
The earliest crossing of the Atlantic by a power vessel, as opposed to an auxiliary engined sailing ship, was a 22-day voyage begun in April 1827, from Rotterdam, Netherlands, to the West Indies by the *Curaçao*. She was a 127 ft *38,7 m* wooden paddle boat of 438 tons, built as the *Calpe* in Dover in 1826 and purchased by the Dutch Government for the West Indian mail service. The earliest Atlantic crossing entirely under steam (with intervals for desalting the boilers) was by HMS *Rhadamanthus* from Plymouth to Barbados in 1832. The earliest crossing of the Atlantic under continuous steam power was by the condenser-fitted packet ship *Sirius* (703 tons *714 tonnes*) from Queenstown (now Cóbh), Ireland, to Sandy Hook, New Jersey, USA, in 18 days 10 hr on 4–22 Apr 1838.

Atlantic *Fastest World*
The fastest Atlantic crossing was made by the *United States* (then 51,988, now 38,216 gross tons), former flagship of the United States Lines. On her maiden voyage between 3 and 7 July 1952 from New York City, to Le Havre, France, and Southampton, England, she averaged 35.59 knots, or 40.98 mph *65,95 km/h* for 3 days 10 hr 40 min (6.36 p.m. GMT, 3 July to 5.16 a.m., 7 July) on a route of 2949 nautical miles *5465 km* from the Ambrose Light Vessel to the Bishop Rock Light, Isles of Scilly, Cornwall. During this run, on 6–7 July 1952, she steamed the greatest distance ever covered by any ship in a day's run (24 hr)—868 nautical miles *1609 km*, hence averaging 36.17 knots (41.65 mph *67,02 km/h*). The maximum speed attained from her 240,000 shp engines was 38.32 knots (44.12 mph *71,01 km/h*) on trials on 9–10 June 1952.

Pacific *Fastest*
The fastest crossing of the Pacific Ocean from Yokohama to Long Beach, California (4840 nautical miles *8960 km*) was 6 days 1 hr 27 min (30 June–6 July 1973) by the container ship *Sea-Land Commerce* (50,315 tons) at an average of 33.27 knots (38.31 mph *61,65 km/h*).

Channel crossing *Fastest*
The fastest crossing of the English Channel by a commercial ferry is 52 min 49 sec from Dover to Calais by Townsend Thorensen's *Pride of Free Enterprise* in a Force 7 Gale on 9 Feb 1982.

HOVERCRAFT (skirted air cushion vehicles)

Earliest
The ACV (air-cushion vehicle) was first made a practical proposition by Sir Christopher Sydney Cockerell, CBE, FRS (b. 4 June 1910), a British engineer who had the idea in 1954, published his Ripplecraft report 1/55 on 25 Oct 1955 and patented it on 12 Dec 1955. The earliest patent relating to air-cushion craft was applied for in 1877 by John I. Thornycroft (1843–1928) of Chiswick, London and the Finn Toivo Kaario developed the idea in 1935. The first flight by a hovercraft was made by the 4 ton/*tonnes* Saunders-Roe SR-N1 at Cowes on 30 May 1959. With a 1500 lb *680 kg* thrust Viper turbojet engine, this craft reached 68 knots *126 km/h* in June 1961. The first hovercraft public service was run across the Dee Estuary by the 60 knot *111 km/h* 24-passenger Vickers-Armstrong VA-3 between July and September 1962.

Largest
The world's largest civil hovercraft is the 305 ton British-built SRN4 Mk III with a capacity of 418 passengers and 60 cars. It is 185 ft *56,38 m* in length, is powered by 4 Bristol Siddeley Marine Proteus engines giving a maximum speed in excess of the permitted cross Channel operating speed of 65 knots.

Fastest warship
The world's fastest warship is the 78 ft *23,7 m* long 100 ton/*tonne* US Navy test vehicle SES-100B. She attained a world record 91.9 knots *103.9 mph* on 25 Jan 1980 on the Chesapeake Bay Test Range, Maryland, USA. The 3000 ton US Navy Large Surface Effect Ship (LSES) was built by Bell Aerospace under contract from the Department of Defense in 1977–81.

Longest flight
The longest hovercraft journey was one of 5000 miles *8047 km* through eight West African countries between 15 Oct 1969 and 3 Jan 1970 by the British Trans-African Hovercraft Expedition.

Highest
The greatest altitude at which a hovercraft is operating is on Lago Titicaca, Peru, where since 1975 an HM2 Hoverferry has been hovering 12,506 ft *3811 m* above sea level.

2. ROAD VEHICLES

Guinness Superlatives has now published automotive records in greater detail in the more specialist publication *Car Facts and Feats* (3rd edition price £7.95).

COACHING

Before the widespread use of tarred road surfaces from 1845 coaching was slow and hazardous. The zenith was reached on 13 July 1888 when J. Selby, Esq., drove the 'Old Times' coach 108 miles *173 km* from London to Brighton and back with 8 teams and 14 changes in 7 hr 50 min to average 13.79 mph *22,19 km/h*. Four-horse carriages could maintain a speed of 21⅓ mph *34 km/h* for nearly an hour. The *Border Union* stage coach, built *c.* 1825, ran 4 in hand from Edinburgh to London (393 miles *632 km*). When it ceased in 1842, due to competition from railways, the allowed schedule was 42 hr 23 min to average better than 9¼ mph *14,9 km/h*.

John Parker (b. July 1939) drove a mail coach and four 136 miles *218,8 km* from Bristol to London in 17 hr 30 mins on 1–2 Aug 1984. Norwich Union's six teams of greys were changed 11 times. An estimated 1 million people lined the route.

The record for changing a team of four horses by a team of 12 ostlers is 27.69 sec set at Olympia, London on 17 Dec 1984.

MOTOR CARS

Most cars
For 1980 it was estimated that the United States, with 155,890,000 vehicles, passed 37.9 per cent of the total world stock of 411,113,000.

Earliest automobiles *Model*
The earliest automobile of which there is record is a two-foot-long steam-powered model constructed by Ferdinand Verbiest (d. 1687) a Belgian Jesuit priest, and described in his *Astronomia Europaea*. His model of 1668 was possibly inspired either by Giovanni Branca's description of a steam turbine, published in his *La Macchina* in 1629, or by writings on 'fire carts' or *Nan Huai-Jen* in the Chu dynasty (*c.* 800 BC).

Earliest automobiles *Passenger-carrying*
The earliest full scale automobile was the first of two military steam tractors, completed at the Paris Arsenal in 1769 by Nicolas-Joseph Cugnot (1725–1804). This reached 2¼ mph *3,6 km/h*. Cugnot's second, larger tractor, completed in May 1771, today survives in the *Conservatoire nationale des arts et métiers* in Paris. The world's first passenger-carrying automobile was a steam-powered road vehicle carrying eight passengers and built by Richard Trevithick (1771–1833). It first ran on 24 Dec 1801 in Camborne, Cornwall.

Earliest automobiles *Internal combustion*

The Swiss Isaac de Rivaz (d. 1828) built a carriage powered by his 'explosion engine' in 1805. The first practical internal-combustion engined vehicle was that built by the Londoner Samuel Brown (Patent 5350, 25 Apr 1826) whose 4 hp *4,05 cv* two cylinder atmospheric gas 88 litre engined carriage climbed Shooters Hill, Blackheath, Kent in May 1826. Britain's continuous motoring history started in Nov 1894 when Henry Hewetson drove his imported Benz Velo in the south-eastern suburbs of London. The first successful petrol-driven car, the Motorwagen, built by Karl-Friedrich Benz (1844–1929) of Karlsruhe, ran at Mannheim, Germany, in late 1885. It was a 5 cwt *250 kg* 3-wheeler reaching 8–10 mph *13–16 km/h*. Its single cylinder 4-stroke chain-drive engine (bore 91,4 mm, stroke 160 mm) delivered 0.85 hp *0,86 cv* at 200 rpm. It was patented on 29 Jan 1886. Its first 1 km road test was reported in the local newspaper, the *Neue Badische Landeszeitung*, of 4 June 1886, under the news heading 'Miscellaneous'. Two were built in 1885 of which one has been preserved in 'running order' at the Deutsches Museum, Munich.

Registrations *Earliest and Most Expensive*

The world's first plates were probably introduced by the Parisian police in France in 1893. Registration plates were introduced in Britain in 1903. The original A1 plate was secured by the 2nd Earl Russell (1865–1931) for his 12 hp *12,1 cv* Napier. This plate, willed in September 1950 to Mr Trevor T. Laker of Leicester, was sold in August 1959 for £2500 in aid of charity. It was reported in April 1973 that a 'cherished' number plate changed hands for £14,000 in a private deal. Licence plate No 3 was reported in Jan 1984 to have been sold at a Hong Kong Government auction for £94,000.

FASTEST CARS (see also p. 126)

Diesel engined

The prototype 230 hp 3 litre Mercedes C 111/3 attained 327,3 km/h *203.3 mph* in tests on the Nardo Circuit, Southern Italy on 5–15 Oct 1978, and in April 1978 averaged 195.398 mph *314,462 km/h* for 12 hours, so covering a world record 2399.76 miles *3773,55 km*.

Rocket powered sleds

The highest speed recorded on ice is 247.93 mph *399,00 km/h* by *Oxygen* driven by Sammy Miller (b. 15 Apr 1945) on Lake George, NY, USA on 15 Feb 1981 (see also p. 130).

Road cars

Various detuned track cars have been licensed for road use but are not purchasable production models. Manufacturers of very fast and very expensive models understandably limit speed tests to stipulated engine revs. The fastest current manufacturer's *claim* (as opposed to independently road-tested) for any road car is the Vector W2A custom order car from Vector Cars, Venice, California with a 'terminal velocity' in excess of 200 mph *321,8 km/h*. The claimed speed at 7000 rpm by the 1984 Ferrari 308 GTO is 189.5 mph *304,9 km/h*. Aston Martin announced on 1 Mar 1985 the production of 50 Vantage-Zagatos with 432 bhp engines and a speed of 187 mph *300 km/h* costing £87,000. The highest ever *tested* speed is 179.9 mph *289,5 km/h* for the Lamborghini Countach LP 500 S in March 1984. The car was kept out of the 'red sector' i.e. at below 7000 rpm. The highest road-tested acceleration reported is 0–60 mph *0–96,5 km/h* in 4.1 sec for a Volkswagen double engined Scirocco prototype in 1983 but Vector Cars have claimed 3.5 sec for their Vector W2A.

John Parker setting out from Bristol for London. His Royal Mail coach and four averaged 7¾ mph *12,5 km/h* on the 136 miles *218.8 km* route. (See opposite column 3)

LARGEST CARS

World

Of cars produced for private road use, the largest has been the Bugatti 'Royale' type 41, known in Britain as the 'Golden Bugatti', of which only six (not seven) were made at Molsheim, France by the Italian Ettore Bugatti, and all survive. First built in 1927, this machine has an 8-cylinder engine of 12,7 litres capacity, and measures over 22 ft *6,7 m* in length. The bonnet is over 7 ft *2 m* long. Of custom built cars the longest is a 10 wheeled 50 ft *15,24 m* long Lamrooster stretched by Ultra-Limo Inc. of Los Angeles to include a swimming pool. (For cars not intended for private use, see Largest engines).

Largest engines *All-time and current records*

The world's most powerful piston engine car is 'Quad Al.' It was designed and built in 1964 by Jim Lytle and was first shown in May 1965 at the Los Angeles Sports Arena. The car featured four Allison V12 aircraft engines with a total of 6840 in³ *112,087 cc* displacement and 12,000 hp. The car has 4-wheel drive, 8 wheels and tyres, and dual 6-disc clutch assemblies. The wheelbase is 160 in *406,4 cm*, and weighs 5860 lb *2658 kg*. It has 96 spark plugs and 96 exhaust pipes.

The largest car ever used was the 'White Triplex', sponsored by J. H. White of Philadelphia,

FASTEST CARS

CATEGORY	MPH	KM/H	CAR	DRIVER	PLACE	DATE
Jet Engined (*official*)	633.468	*1019,4*	Thrust 2	Richard Noble (GB)	Black Rock Desert Nevada, USA	4 Oct 1983
Rocket Engined (*official*)	622.287	*1001,473*	Blue Flame	Gary Gabelich (US)	Bonneville, Utah, USA	23 Oct 1970
Wheel Driven (*turbine*)	429.311	*690,909*	Bluebird	Donald Campbell (UK)	Lake Eyre, Australia	17 July 1964
Wheel Driven (*multi piston engines*)	418.504	*673,516*	Goldenrod	Robert Summers (US)	Bonneville, Utah, USA	12 Nov 1965
Wheel Driven (*single piston engine*)	357.391	*575,149*	Herda-Knapp-Milodon	Bob Herda	Bonneville, Utah, USA	2 Nov 1967
Rocket Engined (*unofficial*)*	739.666	*1190,377*	Budweiser Rocket	Stan Barrett (US)	Edwards Air Force Base, California, USA	17 Dec 1979

* This published speed of Mach 1.0106 is *not* officially sanctioned by the USAF whose Digital Instrumented Radar was not calibrated or certified. The radar information was *not* generated by the vehicle directly but by an operator aiming the dish by means of a TV screen. To claim a speed to 6 significant figures appears quite unsustainable.

Pennsylvania, USA. Completed early in 1928, after two years work, the car weighed about 4 tons *4,06 tonnes* and was powered by three Liberty V12 aircraft engines with a total capacity of 81,188 cc, developing 1500 bhp at 2000 rpm. It was used to break the world speed record but crashed at Daytona, Florida, USA on 13 Mar 1929.

Currently the most powerful car on the road is the 6-wheeled Jameson-Merlin, powered by a 27,000 cc 1760 hp Rolls Royce V12 Merlin aero-engine, governed down to a maximum speed of 185 mph *298 km/h*. It has a range of 300 miles *480 km* with tanks of 60 gal *272 litres* capacity. The vehicle weighs 2.65 tons *2,69 tonnes* overall.

Largest engines *Production car*

The highest engine capacity of a production car was 13½ litres *824 in³*, in the case of the US Pierce-Arrow 6–66 Raceabout of 1912–18, the US Peerless 6–60 of 1912–14 and the Fageol of 1918. The most powerful production car ever built was the V8 engine of 500.1 in³ *8194 cc*, developing 400 bhp, used in the 1970 Cadillac Fleetwood Eldorado.

Petrol consumption

Ford's 15 cc UFO2 (Ultimate Fuel Optimiser) piloted by Dianne Hurrel recorded 3803 mpg *1346 km/litre* at Silverstone, Northants on 4 July 1984. She used the burn/coast method and drove between 13 and 22 mph *21–35 km/h*. The 3 wheeled vehicle has a drag coefficient of 0.113.

Longest fuel range

The greatest distance driven without refuelling on a tank full of fuel (19.41 galls *88,12 l*) is 1150.3 miles *1851,2 km* by an Audi 100 turbo diesel driven by Stuart Bladon with his son Bruce (navigator) and Bob Proctor (RAC observer)

Diane Hurrel (with helmet) and her back-up crew at Silverstone. The UFO2 has the ability to travel the round trip Land's End to John o'Groats twice on a single gallon. *(Ford Motor Company Limited)*

from Land's End to John o'Groats and back to West Falkirk in 22 hrs 28 min in July 1984. The average speed was 51.17 mph *82,33 km/h* giving 59.27 mpg *4.77 l/100 km.*

Most durable car

The highest recorded mileage for a car was 1,184,880 authenticated miles *1 906 879 km* by August 1978 for a 1957 Mercedes 180 D owned by Robert O'Reilly of Olympia, Washington State, USA. Its subsequent fate is unknown. R. L. Bender of Madison, Wisconsin claimed 1,020,000 miles *1 641 530 km* for his car in December 1983. R. L. Bender's car reached 1,021,041 miles *1 643 206 km* on 9 June 1984. He has been driving it since 1958.

Taxis

The largest taxi fleet is that in Mexico City, Mexico with 60,000 'normal' taxis, pesaros (communal fixed route taxis) and settas (airport taxis) in mid 1984. On 1 May 1984 there were 13,200 cabs and 18,000 drivers in London. The longest fare on record is one of 7533 miles *12 133 km* through 10 countries from Marble Arch, London on 19 Sept–18 Oct 1981. The trip was sponsored for charity. The driver was Stephen Tillyer. Francis Edward Kenyon (b. 1904) was continuously licensed as a cab driver in Manchester for 57 years 36 days in 1924–81.

MOST EXPENSIVE CARS

Special

The most expensive car to build has been the US Presidential 1969 Lincoln Continental Executive delivered to the US Secret Service on 14 Oct 1968. It has an overall length of 21 ft 6.3 in *6,56 m* with a 13 ft 4 in *4,06 m* wheel-base and with the addition of 2 tons *2,03 tonnes* of armour plate, weighs 5.35 tons *5,43 tonnes* (12,000 lb *5443 kg*). The estimated research, development and manufacture cost was $500,000 (*then £208,000*) but it is rented at $5000 (*now £2300*) per annum. Even if all four tyres were shot out it can travel at 50 mph *80 km/h* on inner rubber-edged steel discs. Carriage House Motor Cars Ltd of New York City in March 1978 completed 4 years work on converting a 1973 Rolls Royce including lengthening it by 30 in *76,2 cm*. The price tag was $500,000 (*then £263,157*).

Standard

The most expensive British standard car is the Rolls-Royce 8 cylinder 6750 cc Camargue,

quoted in May 1984 at £83,122 (incl. tax). More expensive are custom built models. Jack Barclay Ltd of Berkeley Square, London W1 quote £300,000 for an armour-plated Rolls-Royce Phantom VI (including tax).

The only owner of 25 new Rolls-Royces is believed to be Bhagwan Shri Rajneesh (b. 1931), the Indian mystic of Rajneeshpuram, Oregon, USA. His disciples have bestowed these upon him.

Used

The greatest price paid for any used car has been £270,600 for a 1930 Bentley Speed Six 2 door coupé at Sotheby's on 10 Dec 1984. An offer of $1,500,000 for one of the six 1927 Buggati Royales to the Henry Ford Museum, Deerborn, Illinois was turned down. A Rolls-Royce Silver Ghost of 1907 exhibited in San Jose, California in August 1982 was insured for $2 million. The greatest collection of vintage cars is the William F. Harrah Collection of 1700, estimated to be worth more than $4 million (*£2.3 million*), at Reno, Nevada, USA. Mr Harrah was still looking for a Chalmer's Detroit 1909 Tourabout, an Owen car of 1910–12 and a Nevada Truck of 1915 at the time of his death in 1978.

Most inexpensive

The cheapest car of all-time was the 1922 Red Bug Buckboard, built by Briggs and Stratton Co of Milwaukee, Wisconsin, USA listed at $150–$125. It had a 62 in *1,57 m* wheel base and weighed 245 lb *111 kg*. The early models of the King Midget cars were sold in kit form for self-assembly for as little as $100 (*then £24 16s*) as late as 1948. By May 1984 the cheapest quoted new car price in Britain was £2098 for a Fiat 126, 652 cc 2 door car.

Longest production

The longest any car has been in mass production is 44 years (1938 to date), including wartime interruptions, in the case of the Volkswagen 'Beetle' series, originally designed by Ferdinand Porsche. The 20 millionth car came off the final production line in Mexico on 15 May 1981. Residual production continues in South America. Britain's all-time champion is the Morgan

series 4/4 from 27 Dec 1935 from the Morgan Motor Car of Malvern (founded 1910). Britain's champion seller has been the Mini which originally sold for £496 19s 2d in August 1959. Sales reached 4,940,000 by May 1984.

LONG DISTANCE DRIVING

Round the world driving

The fastest circumnavigation embracing more than an equator's length of driving (24,901.47 road miles *40 075,0 km*) is one in 74 days 1 hr 11 min by Garry Sowerby (driver) and Ken Langley (navigator) of Canada from 6 Sept to 19 Nov 1980 in a Volvo 245 DL westwards from Toronto, Canada through 4 continents and 23 countries. The distance covered was 43 030 km *26,738 miles* (see below for their Cape to Cape record). Between 30 Mar 1964 and 23 Apr 1984 the folk-singers Manfred Müller and Paul-Ernst Luhrs drove round the world covering 78 countries and 250 000 km *174,000 miles*. They started and finished in Bremerhaven, West Germany.

Cape to Cape

The first traverse of the world's greatest land mass (Afro-Eurasia) was achieved by Richard Pape, who left the North Cape in an Austin A90 on 28 July and arrived in Cape Town on 22 Oct 1955 with the milometer recording 17,500 miles *28 160 km* after 86 days. The speed record was set by Ken Langley and Garry Sowerby of Canada driving north in 28 days 13 hr 10 min for 12,531 miles *20 166 km* on 4 Apr–2 May 1984.

Round Britain driving

Owing to the lack of any standardised route and specifications for tachographs, this category has been put in abeyance until September 1985.

The best recorded time for non-stop driving the 3644.3 miles *5864,7 km* Round Britain course on an Official Certified Trial under the surveillance of a motoring organisation and with Tachograph readings, is 78 hr 31 min to average 46.41 mph *74,68 km/h* in a Triumph Acclaim driven by David Gittins, Robert Morgan and Richard Neale on 10–14 May 1982. This charity trial by Hagley and District Round Table was sponsored by DIY Motor Stores, Austin Rover and Lex Mead (Stourbridge). A Marlow Round Table (No. 575) team of Trevor Bownass, Robert

Clark, Richard Scott, with photographer Richard Thomson, covered 3644 miles *5864 km* in 65 hr 14 min to average 55.86 mph *89,89 km/h* in a Saab 900 on 17–20 May 1984.

Mountain driving

Cars have been driven up Ben Nevis, Highland, Scotland (4406 ft *1343 m*) on five occasions. The record times are 7 hr 23 min (ascent) and 1 hr 55 min (descent) by George F. Simpson in an Austin 7 on 6 Oct 1928. Henry Alexander accomplished the feat twice in May 1911 (Model T Ford) and on 13 Sept 1928 (Model A Ford). The most recent ascent was on 5 June 1984 by a 33 year old Land Rover.

Driving in reverse

Charles Creighton (1908–70) and James Hargis of Maplewood, Missouri, USA, drove their Ford Model A 1929 roadster in reverse from New York City 3340 miles *5375 km* to Los Angeles, California on 26 July–13 Aug 1930 without once stopping the engine. They arrived back in New York in reverse on 5 Sept so completing 7180 miles *11 555 km* in 42 days. The highest average speed attained in any non-stop reverse drive exceeding 500 miles *800 km* was achieved by Gerald Hoagland who drove a 1969 Chevrolet Impala 501 miles *806,2 km* in 17 hr 38 min at Chemung Speed Drome, New York, USA on 9–10 July 1976 to average 28.41 mph *45,72 km/h*.

Brian 'Cub' Keene and James 'Wilbur' Wright drove their Chevrolet Blazer 9,031 miles *14 533 km* in 37 days (1 Aug–6 Sept 1984) through 16 US States and Canada. Though it was prominently named 'Stuck in Reverse' law enforcement in Oklahoma refused to believe it and insisted they drove in reverse reverse, i.e. forwards, out of the State.

Battery powered vehicle

John W. Owen and Roy Harvey travelled 919 miles *1479 km* from John o'Groats to Land's End in a Sinclair C5 in 103 hr 15 min on 30 Apr–4 May 1985.

Two wheel driving

The longest recorded distance for driving on 2 wheels is 209,2 km *129.9 miles* in an Opel Kadett by Michael Signoret at the Paul Ricard circuit in Provence, France on 14 Mar 1985.

Oldest driver

Roy M. Rawlins (b. 10 July 1870) of Stockton, California, USA, was warned for driving at 95 mph *152 km/h* in a 55 mph *88,5 km/h* zone in June 1974. On 25 Aug 1974 he was awarded a California State licence valid till 1978 by Mr John Burrafato, but Mr Rawlins died on 9 July 1975, one day short of his 105th birthday. Mrs Maude Tull of Inglewood, California, who took to driving aged 91 after her husband died, was issued a renewal on 5 Feb 1976 when aged 104. Britain's only recorded centenarian driver was Herbert Warren (1874–1975) of Whatlington, Norfolk, who drove a 1954 Standard 10. Major Geoffrey Chance CBE (b. 16 Dec 1893) of Braydon, Wiltshire who began driving in 1908 successfully took a driving test to re-qualify after a 'minor bump' aged 90 years 90 days at Swindon, Wiltshire on 15 March 1984. The oldest age at which a woman has passed the Department of Transport driving test has been 88 years 5 months by Mrs Harriet Emma Jack (*née* Morse) (b. 9 Dec 1887) on 18 May 1976 in Bognor Regis, West Sussex. She was still driving aged 96.

The holder of the earliest driving licence to be issued in Britain is Mr Gerry Bond (b. July 1889) of Bournemouth, Dorset whose first licence is dated Oct 1907.

Youngest driver

Instances of drivers have been recorded in HM Armed Forces much under 17 years. Mrs P. L. M. Williams (b. 3 Feb 1926), now of Risca, Gwent, as Private Patterson in the ATS drove a 5 ton truck in 1941 aged 15. Steve Brewster of Redcar, Cleveland passed the advanced test, 5 days after his standard test, on 30 July 1984 aged 17 years 10 days. David Paul Barrow (b. 28 Mar 1966) of Ormskirk passed his test aged 16 years 114 days on 20 July 1982.

Most durable

The Goodyear Tire and Rubber Co test driver Weldon C. Kocich drove 3,031,577 miles *4 878 850 km* from 5 Feb 1953 to 20 July 1984 so averaging 96,345 miles *155 052 km* per year.

Driving tests

The record for persistence in taking the Ministry of Transport's Learner's Test is held by Mrs Miriam Hargrave (b. 3 Apr 1908) of Wakefield, West Yorkshire, who failed her 39th driving test in eight years on 29 Apr 1970 after 'crashing' a set of red lights. She triumphed at her 40th attempt after 212 lessons on 3 Aug 1970. The examiner was alleged not to have known about her previous 39 tests. In 1978 she was reported to still disdain right-hand turns. The world's easiest tests have been those in Egypt in which the ability to drive 6 m *19.64 ft* forward and the same in reverse has been deemed sufficient. In 1979 it was reported that accurate reversing had been added between two rubber traffic cones. 'High cone attrition' soon led to the substitution of white lines. Mrs Fannie Turner (b. 1903) of Little Rock, Arkansas, USA passed her *written* test for drivers on her 104th attempt in October 1978.

Buses *Earliest*

The first municipal motor omnibus service in the world was inaugurated on 12 Apr 1903 between Eastbourne railway station and Meads, East Sussex, England. A steam-powered bus named *Royal Patent* ran between Gloucester and Cheltenham for 4 months in 1831.

Largest fleet

In 1983 the world's largest bus fleet is the 6580 single-deck buses in Rio de Janeiro, Brazil. Of London Transport's 5412 fleet, 4853 are double-deckers.

Longest

The longest buses in the world are the 10.72 ton *10 870 kg*, 76 ft *23,16 m* long articulated buses, with 121 passenger seats and room also for 66 'strap-hangers' built by the Wayne Corporation of Richmond, Indiana, USA for use in the Middle East.

Longest route

The longest regularly scheduled bus route is by 'Across Australia Coach Lines', who inaugurated a regular scheduled service between Perth and Brisbane on 9 Apr 1980. The route is 5455 km *3389 miles* taking 75 hr 55 min. The longest bus service in Great Britain is 654 miles *1052 km* between Perth and Eastbourne operated by Midland Scottish.

Trolleybuses

Having been the last local authority in Britain with trolleybuses, the West Yorkshire authority reintroduced some in 1985 in the Bradford-Leeds area with a view to reestablishing a fleet.

Caravans *Longest journey*

The longest continuous motor caravan journey is one of 143,716 miles *231 288 km* by Harry B. Coleman and Peggy Larson in a Volkswagen Camper from 20 Aug 1976 to 20 Apr 1978 through 113 countries. Saburo Ouchi (b. 7 Feb 1942) of Tokyo, Japan drove 270 000 km *167,770 miles* in 91 countries from 2 Dec 1969 to 10 Feb 1978.

Largest

The largest caravans built in Britain are the £300,000 'State Super Caravans', 18 m *59 ft 0½ in* in length and 3,5 m *11 ft 5¾ in* wide built by Coventry Steel Caravans Ltd of Newport Pagnell, Buckinghamshire since 1977.

Fastest

The world speed record for a caravan is 124.91 mph *201,02 km/h* by an Alpha V towed by a Le Mans Aston Martin V8 saloon driven by Robin Hamilton at RAF Elvington, North Yorkshire on 14 Oct 1980.

Vehicles *Most massive*

The most massive vehicle ever constructed is the Marion eight-caterpillar crawler used for conveying *Saturn V* rockets to their launching pads at Cape Canaveral, Florida, USA. (*see* Chapter 4, Most powerful rocket). It measures 131 ft 4 in *40 m* by 114 ft *34,7 m* and the two built cost $12,300,000 (*then £5,125,000*). The loaded train weight is 8036 tons *8165 tonnes*. Its windscreen wipers with 42 in *106 cm* blades are the world's largest.

The most massive automotive land vehicle is 'Big Muskie' the 10,700 ton *10 890 tonnes* mechanical shovel built by Bucyrus Erie for the Musk mine. It is 487 ft *148,43 m* long; 151 ft *46,02 m* wide and 222 ft *67,66 m* high with a grab capacity of 325 tons.

The longest vehicle ever built is the Arctic Snow Train owned by the world famous wire-walker Steve McPeak (US). This 54 wheeled 572 ft *174,3 m* long vehicle was built by R G Le Tourneau Inc of Longview, Texas for the US Army. Its gross train weight is 400 tons with a top speed of 20 mph *32 km/h* and it was driven by a crew of 6 when used as an 'Overland Train' for the military. McPeak repaired it and every punctured wheel lonehanded in often sub-zero temperatures in Alaska. It generates 4680 shp and has a capacity of 6522 Imperial gallons *29 648 litres*.

Wrecker *Most powerful*

The world's most powerful wrecker is the Vance Corporation 25 ton *25,4 tonne* 30 ft *9,14 m* long Monster No. 2 stationed at Hammond, Indiana, USA. It can lift in excess of 160 tons *163 tonnes* on its short boom.

Earth mover *Largest*

The world's largest earth mover is the 100 tonne T-800 built at the Lenin Tractor Works in Chelyabinsk, USSR, announced in Sept 1984.

Dumper truck *Largest*

The world's largest dump truck is the Terex Titan 33–19 manufactured by the Terex Division of General Motors Corporation. It has a loaded weight of 539.9 tons *548,6 tonnes* and a capacity of 312½ tons *317,5 tonnes*. When tipping its height is 56 ft *17,06 m*. The 16 cylinder engine delivers 3300 hp. The fuel tank holds 1300 Imperial gallons *5904,6 litres*. It went into service in November 1974.

Tractor *Largest and most powerful*

The world's largest tractor is the $459,000 (*then £285,000*) US Department of Agriculture Wide Tractive Frame Vehicle completed by Ag West of Sacramento, California in June 1982. It measures 33 ft *10,05 m* between its wheels which are designed to run on permanent paths and weighs 21.87 tons *22,22 tonnes*.

The sport of tractor-pulling was put on a national US championship basis in 1967 at Bowling Green, Ohio where the winner was 'The Purple Monster' built and driven by Roger E. Varns. Today there are 12 classes ranging up to '12,200 lb unlimited'.

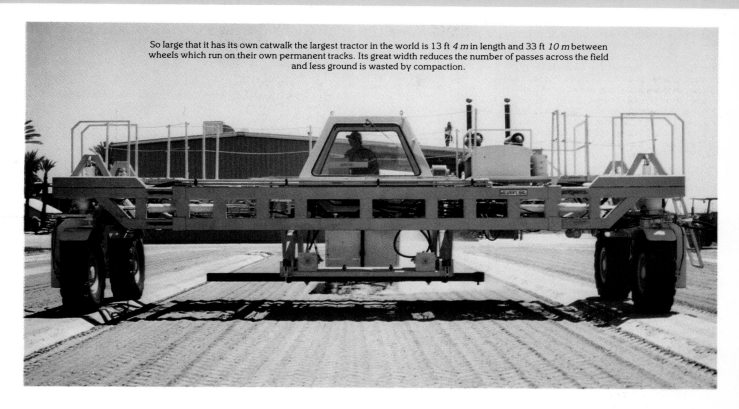

So large that it has its own catwalk the largest tractor in the world is 13 ft *4 m* in length and 33 ft *10 m* between wheels which run on their own permanent tracks. Its great width reduces the number of passes across the field and less ground is wasted by compaction.

Fire engine *Most powerful*

The world's most powerful fire appliance is the 860 hp 8-wheel Oshkosh firetruck used for aircraft fires. It can discharge 41,600 gal *190 000 l* of foam through two turrets in just 150 sec. It weighs 59.0 tons *60 tonnes*. The fastest on record is the Jaguar XJ12 – 'Chubb Firefighter', which, in Nov 1982, attained a speed of 130.57 mph *210,13 km/h* in tests when servicing the *Thrust 2* land speed record trials (see pp. 126 & 162–3).

Ambulance *Largest*

The world's largest ambulances are the 18 m *59 ft 0½ in* long articulated Alligator Jumbulances Mark VI, VII and VIII, operated by The Across Trust to convey the sick and handicapped on holidays and pilgrimages to the Continent. They are built by Van Hool of Belgium with Fiat engines, cost £176,000 and convey 44 patients and staff.

ROAD LOADS

Load heaviest *World*

On 14–15 July 1984 John Brown Engineers & Contractors BV moved the Conoco Kotter Field production deck with a roll out weight of 3805 tonnes for the Continental Netherlands Oil Company of Leidsenhage, Netherlands.

Great Britain

The heaviest road load moved in the United Kingdom has been a 476 tonnes *468,4 tons* 194 ft *59,13 m* long Vacuum Distillation Column from Fawley Power Station to the Esso Refinery at Fawley by Mammoet-Econofreight on 24 July 1981. The gross weight of the load plus bogies (excluding tractors) was 696 tonnes *685 tons* and the overall train length was 336 ft 3½ in *102,50 m*. The longest item moved on British roads has been a 221 ft *67,36 m* long 270 tonne nitric acid column transported by Sunter Bros. from Head Wrightson Teesdale Ltd. factory at Stockton-on-Tees to the I.C.I. complex at Billingham on 25 Mar 1984 (overall train length 96.58 m *316 ft 10 in*).

Tyres *Largest*

The world's largest tyres are manufactured in Topeka, Kansas by the Goodyear Co for giant dumper trucks. They measure 12 ft *3,65 m* in diameter, weigh 12,500 lb *5670 kg* and cost $74,000 (*£49,000*). A tyre 17 ft *5,18 m* in diameter is believed to be the limitation of what is practical.

Skid marks *Longest*

The longest recorded skid marks on a public road have been those 950 ft *290 m* long left by a Jaguar car involved in an accident on the M1 near Luton, Bedfordshire, on 30 June 1960. Evidence given in the High Court case *Hurlock v. Inglis and others* indicated a speed 'in excess of 100 mph *160 km/h* before the application of the brakes. The skid marks made by the jet-powered *Spirit of America*, driven by Norman Craig Breedlove, after the car went out of control at Bonneville Salt Flats, Utah, USA, on 15 Oct 1964, were nearly 6 miles *9,6 km* long.

Amphibious vehicle circumnavigation

The only circumnavigation by an amphibious vehicle was achieved by Ben Carlin (Australia) (d. 7 Mar 1981) in an amphibious jeep 'Half-Safe'. He completed the last leg of the Atlantic crossing (the English Channel) on 24 Aug 1951. He arrived back in Montreal, Canada on 8 May 1958 having completed a circumnavigation of 39,000 miles *62 765 km* over land and 9600 miles *15 450 km* by sea and river. He was accompanied on the trans Atlantic stage by his ex-wife Elinore (US) and on the long trans Pacific stage (Tokyo to Anchorage) by Broye Lafayette De-Mente (b. Missouri, 1928).

Snowmobiles

Richard and Raymond Moore and Loren Matthews drove their snowmobile 5876 miles *9456 km* from Fairbanks, Alaska to Fenton, Michigan, USA, in 39 days from 3 Feb–13 Mar 1980.

Solar Powered Vehicle

The highest speed attained under IHPVA (International Human Powered Vehicle Association) rules by a solely solar powered vehicle is 24.74 mph *39,81 km/h* at Bellflower, California on 1 July 1984 by *Sunrunner*, designed by Joel Davidson and Greg Johanson of Photovoltaic Power Systems.

Tow *Longest*

The longest tow on record was one of 4759 miles *7658 km* from Halifax, Nova Scotia to Canada's Pacific Coast, when Frank J. Elliott and George A. Scott of Amherst, Massachusetts, persuaded 168 passing motorists in 89 days to tow their Model T Ford (in fact engineless) to win a $1000 bet on 15 Oct 1927.

Lawn mowers

The widest gang mower in the world is the 5 ton 60 ft *18,28 m* wide 27 unit Big Green Machine used by the sod farmer Jay Edgar Frick of Monroe, Ohio. It mows an acre in 60 sec. The greatest distance covered in the annual 12 hour Lawn Mower Race (under the rules of the BLMRA, the British Lawn Mower Racing Association) is 276 miles *444,1 km* by Tony Hazelwood, Derek Bell, Tony Smith and Ray Kilminster at Wisborough Green, W. Sussex on 21–22 June 1980. A 12-hour run behind record of 101.15 miles *162,7 km* was set at Wisborough Green on 8–9 July 1984 by the 'Super Gnome' team.

Go-Karting

The highest mileage recorded in 24 hours on a closed twisting circuit for go-karts driven by a 4 man team is 1018 laps of a mile *1638,3 km* at Erbsville Kartway, Waterloo, Ontario, Canada. The 5 h.p. 140 cc Honda engined kart was driven by Owen Nimmo, Gary Ruddock, Jim Timmins and Danny Upshaw on 4–5 Sept 1983.

MOTORCYCLES

Guinness Superlatives Ltd have published more specialist volumes entitled *The Guinness Book of Motorcycling Facts and Feats* by LJK Setright (£7.95).

Earliest (see also Chapter 12)

The earliest internal combustion-engined motorised bicycle was a wooden-framed machine built at Bad Cannstatt in Oct–Nov 1885 by Gottlieb Daimler (1834–1900) of Germany and first ridden by Wilhelm Maybach (1846–1929). It had a top speed of 12 mph *19 km/h* and developed one-half of one horsepower from its single-cylinder 264 cc four-stroke engine at 700 rpm. Known as the 'Einspur', it was lost in a fire in 1903. The first motorcycles of entirely British production were the 1046 cc Holden flat-four and the 2¾ hp Clyde single both produced in 1898. The earliest factory which made motorcycles in quantity was opened in 1894 by Heinrich and Wilhelm Hildebrand and Alois Wolfmüller at Munich, West Germany. In its first two years this factory produced over 1000 machines, each having a water-cooled 1488 cc twin-cylinder four-stroke engine developing about 2.5 bhp at 600 rpm—the highest capacity motor cycle engine ever put into production.

Fastest road machine

The 115 bhp Japanese Honda V65 Magna with a liquid-cooled, in line V-4, 16 valve DoHC engine of 1098 cc capacity has a design speed of 173 mph *278,4 km/h*.

Fastest racing machine

There is no satisfactory answer to the identity of the fastest track machine other than to say that the current Kawasaki, Suzuki and Yamaha machines have all been geared to attain speeds marginally in excess of 300 km/h *186.4 mph* under race conditions.

Duration record

The longest time a solo motorcycle has been kept in nonstop motion is 500 hr by Owen Fitzgerald, Richard Kennett and Don Mitchell who covered 8432 miles *13 570 km* in Western Australia on 10–31 July 1977.

Most on One Machine

The record for most people on a single machine is 35 members of the Brisbane Police Traffic Branch who travelled 506 metres *553 yards* at 25 km/h *15,5 mph* at Surfer's Paradise, Queensland, Australia, on a Yamaha 1100 cc on 22 June 1984.

'Wheelie'

Doug Domokos on the Alabama International Speedway, Talladega, USA on 27 June 1984 covered 145 miles *233,34 km* non-stop on the rear wheel of his Honda XR 500. He stopped only when the gas ran out. The first recorded case of bettering 100 mph *160,9 km/h* on one wheel was by Ottis Lance at Penwell Raceway Park, Texas, USA on 21 May 1983 with 112 mph *180,2 km/h* over 440 yds *402 m* on a Suzuki GS-1000.

Terry McGauran motor-cycled up the 1760 steps of the CN Tower, Toronto, Canada, on 26 June 1984.

Most expensive

The most expensive road motorcycle available in Britain is the Bimota 5B4, powered by a Suzuki GSX 1100 engine, priced at £7999. In June 1980 a 1912 Henderson Model A was auctioned in the US for $18,000 (*then £7825*).

Coast to Coast USA

Dwight B. Mitchell and Steve Kirkpatrick drove 2945 miles *4739 km* from New York City to San Francisco in 74 hr 37 min (av. 39.46 mph *63,5 km/h*) on Honda 400 cc motorcycles on 11–15 June 1983.

Round Britain

Richard Parkhouse of Gwynedd covered all 62 mainland counties of Great Britain by motor cycle (Suzuki 6SX 750 EFE) on a 1634 mile *2629 km* route on 11–12 June 1984 in 28 hours 52 min, averaging 56.6 mph *91,0 km/h*.

BICYCLES

Earliest

The first design for a machine propelled by cranks and pedals, with connecting rods has been attributed to Leonardo da Vinci (1452–1519), or one of his pupils, dated *c.* 1493. The earliest such design actually built was in 1839–40 by Kirkpatrick Macmillan (1810–78) of Dumfries, Scotland. It is now in the Science Museum, Kensington and Chelsea, Greater London. The first practical bicycle was the *vélocipède* built in March 1861 by Pierre and his son Ernest Michaux of Rue de Verneuil, Paris. In 1870, James Starley, in Coventry, constructed the first 'penny farthing' or Ordinary bicycle. It had wire-spoked wheels for lightness and was available with an optional speed gear.

Longest

The longest true tandem bicycle ever built (i.e. without a third stabilizing wheel) is one of 20,40 m *66 ft 11 in* for 35 riders built by the Pedaalstompers Westmalle of Belgium. They rode *c.* 60 m *195 ft* in practice on 20 Apr 1979. The machine weighs 1100 kg *2425 lb*.

Smallest

The world's smallest wheeled rideable bicycle is one with 3,5 cm *1.37 in* wheels weighing 700 g *24.6 oz* built and ridden by Jacques Puyoou of Pau, Pyrénées-Atlantiques, France in 1983. He has also built a tandem 36 cm *14.1 in* long to accommodate Madame Puyoou.

Largest

A classic Ordinary bicycle with wheels of 64 in *162,5 cm* diameter front and 20 in *50,8 cm* back was built *c.* 1886 by the Pope Manufacturing Co of Massachusetts, USA. It is now owned by Paul Niquette of Connecticut.

A bicycle with an 8 ft 2½ in *2,50 m* front wheel with pedal extenders was built in 1878 for circus demonstrations.

Fastest *World and British*

The world speed records for human powered vehicles (HPV's) are 58.64 mph *94,37 km/h* (single rider) by Dave Grylls at the Ontario Speedway, California on 27 Oct 1980; and 62.92 mph *101,25 km/h* (multiple riders) by Dave Grylls and Leigh Barczewski at the Ontario Speedway on 4 May 1980. A British 200 m record was set by S. Poulter in 'Poppy Flyer', in 9.10 sec at Greenham Common, Berkshire on 2 Aug 1981.

Endurance

On 10–21 July 1983, 24 City and Guilds College, London students drove an HPV round Great Britain on a 3675 mile *5914 km* route to average 14.41 mph *23,19 km/h*.

Unicycle records

The tallest unicycle ever mastered is one 101 ft 9 in *31,01 m* tall ridden by Steve McPeak (with a safety wire or mechanic suspended on an overhead crane) for a distance of 376 ft *114,6 m* in Las Vegas in October 1980. The freestyle riding of ever taller unicycles (that is without any safety harness) must inevitably lead to serious injury or fatality. Brock Allison of Red Deer, Alberta, Canada unicycled 5982,3 km *3717.3 miles* from Vancouver to Halifax in 56 days 10¾ hr on 1 May–26 June 1982. Brian Davis, 33 of Tillicoultry, Clackmannan, Scotland rode 901 miles *1450 km* from Land's End to John O'Groats on 16 May to 4 June 1980 in 19 days 1 hr 45 min. Johnnie Severin of At-water, California, USA set a record for 100 miles *160,9 km* in 9 hr 20 min 53 sec on 10 Jan 1981. The sprint record from a standing start over 100 metres is 14.89 sec by Floyd Grandall

of Pontiac, Michigan, USA, in Tokyo, Japan on 24 Mar 1980.

'Wheelie'

A world record duration record of 1 hr 16 min 54 sec was set by Craig Strong (GB) at Picketts Lock, Edmonton, north London on 7 Jan 1983.

Penny-farthing record

The record for riding from Land's End to John O'Groats on Ordinary bicycles, more commonly known in the 1870s as Penny-farthings, is 10 days 7 hr 12 min by James Richard Moir, 37 of St Leonards-on-Sea, East Sussex on 5–15 June 1977. G. P. Mills (Anfield BC) rode this course in 5 days 1 hr 45 min on a 53 inch Humber on 4–10 July 1886.

Underwater cycling

Thirty-two certified Scuba divers in 60 hours on 27–29 Nov 1981 rode a submarine tricycle 64.96 miles *104,54 km* on the bottom of Amphi High School pool, Tucson, Arizona, USA, in a scheme devised by Lucian Spataro to raise money for the Casa De Los Ninos Nursery.

A team of 32 in 72 underwater hours achieved 87.81 miles *141,322 km* in Norvik, Norway on 28–31 Mar 1984.

3. RAILWAYS

The Guinness Rail Factbook by John Marshall was published in May 1985 priced £3.95 and *Guiness Rail—The Records* was published in September 1985 priced £6.95.

TRAINS

Earliest

Wagons running on wooden rails were used for mining as early as 1550 at Leberthal, Alsace, and in Britain for conveying coal at Wollaton near Nottingham from 1603–15 and at Broseley colliery, Shropshire, in October 1605. The earliest commercially successful steam locomotives worked on the Middleton Colliery Railway to Leeds, Yorkshire, authorised by Britain's first Railway Act on 9 June 1758. Richard Trevithick (1771–1883) built his first steam locomotive for the 3 ft *914 mm* gauge iron plateway at Coalbrookdale, Shropshire, in 1803, but there is no evidence that it ran. His second locomotive drew wagons in which men rode on a demonstration run at Penydarren, Mid Glamorgan, Wales, on 22 Feb 1804, but it broke the plate rails. The first permanent public railway to use steam traction was the Stockton & Darlington, from its opening on 27 Sept 1825 from Shildon to Stockton via Darlington, in Cleveland. The 7 ton/*tonne Locomotion* could pull 48 tons/*tonnes* at a speed of 15 mph *24 km/h*. It was designed and driven by George Stephenson (1781–1848). The first regular steam passenger service was inaugurated over a one mile section (between Bogshole Farm and South Street in Whitstable) on the 6¼ mile *10,05 km* Canterbury & Whitstable Railway in Kent on 3 May 1830, hauled by the engine *Invicta*. The first practical electric railway was Werner von Siemens' oval metre-gauge demonstration track about 300 m *328 yd* long at the Berlin Trades Exhibition on 31 May 1879.

Fastest

The highest speed attained by a railed vehicle is 6121 mph *9851 km/h* or Mach 8 by an unmanned rocket sled over the 9½ mile *15,2 km* long rail track at White Sands Missile Range, New Mexico, USA on 5 Oct 1982. The world's fastest rail speed with passengers is 517 km/h *321.2 mph* by the Maglev (magnetic levitation) ML-500 test train over the 7 km *4.3 mile* long JNR experimental track at Miyazaki, Japan in December 1979. The highest speed recorded on any national rail system is 236 mph *380 km/h* by the French SNCF high speed train TGV-PSE on trial near Tonnerre on 26 Feb 1981. The TGV (Train à Grande Vitesse) inaugurated on 27 Sept 1981 by Sept 1983 reduced its scheduled time for the Paris–Lyon run of 425 km *264 miles* to 2 hr exactly, so averaging 212,5 km/h *132 mph*. The peak speed attained is 270 km/h *168 mph*.

A progressive table of railway speed records since 1892 was published in the 23rd edition on page 141.

Steam
The highest speed ever ratified (over 440 yards) for a steam locomotive was 125 mph *201 km/h* over 440 yd *402 m* by the LNER 4–6–2 No. 4468 *Mallard* (later numbered 60022), which hauled seven coaches weighing 240 tons *243 tonnes* gross, down Stoke Bank, near Essendine, between Grantham, Lincolnshire, and Peterborough, Cambridgeshire, on 3 July 1938. Driver Joseph Duddington was at the controls with Fireman Thomas Bray. The engine suffered some damage. On 12 June 1905 a speed of 127.06 mph *204,48 km/h* was claimed for the 'Pennsylvania Special' near Elida, Ohio, USA. This claim has never been accepted by leading railway experts.

Great Britain
British Rail inaugurated their HST (High Speed Train) daily services between London–Bristol and South Wales on 4 Oct 1976. The electric British Rail APT-P (Advanced Passenger Train-Prototype) attained 162 mph *261 km/h*, between Glasgow and Carlisle on its first revenue-earning run on 7 Dec 1981. It covered the 400 miles *644 km* from Glasgow to London in 4¼ hr.

WORLD & UK UNDERGROUND & SUBWAY RECORDS

Epping was linked to West Ruislip on 25 September 1949 making the longest uninterrupted journey on the London Underground— 34.1 of the Central Line's 52 miles *54,8 of 83,6 km.*

Artwork: Robert Burns. Photos: Colin Smith

UNDERGROUND RAILWAYS

Most extensive
The earliest (first section between Faringdon St. and Edgware Road, opened 10 Jan 1863) and one of the most extensive underground or rapid transit railway systems of the 67 in the world is that of the London Underground with 251 miles *404 km* of route, of which 82 miles *131 km* is bored tunnel and 20 miles *32 km* is 'cut and cover'. This whole system is operated by a staff of 11,000 serving 272 stations. The 450 trains comprising 3875 cars carried 563,000,000 passengers in 1983. The greatest depth is 221 ft *67,3 m* near Hampstead on the Northern Line. The longest journey without a change is Epping to West Ruislip—34.1 miles *54,8 km*. The record for touring the then 277 stations is 17 hr 37 min by Colin M. Mulvany of London on 3 Dec 1981.

The subway with most stations in the world is the New York City Transport Authority (first section opened on 27 Oct 1904) with a total of 231.73 route miles *372,93 km* and 1,096,006,529 passengers in 1979. The 458 stations are closer set than London's. The record for travelling the whole system was 21 hr 8½ min by Mayer Wiesen and Charles Emerson on 8 Oct 1973.

Busiest
The world's busiest metro system is that in Greater Moscow with as many as 6½ million passengers per day. To mid-1985 it had 123 stations and 198 km *123 miles* of track. The record transit (with 18 changes) in 1982 (115 stations) was 8 hr 10 min 22 sec by Eric Rudkin of Chaddesden, Derbyshire.

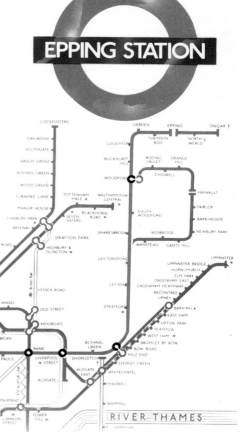

EPPING STATION

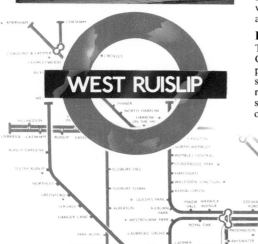

WEST RUISLIP

Colin Mulvany visited every one of the 277 stations then open on London Underground in December 1981. (See previous page. See also this page, column three for his record further afield.)

The fastest point-to-point schedule in Britain is that from Paddington to Bristol Parkway on British Rail's Western Region HST Service at 103.15 mph *166 km/h* in 65 min over 111.75 miles *179,8 km*. On 31 Aug 1984 the HST *Top of the Pops* (drivers Harry Rail and Peter Etheridge) averaged 112.9 mph *181,6 km/h* by covering the distance in 62 mins 33 secs. The peak speed during the run was 129 mph *207,6 km/h*.

Longest non-stop
The longest run on British Rail without any advertised stop is the Night Motorail Service from Inverness to Euston. The distance is 567.75 miles *913,7 km* and the time taken is 11 hr 4 min. The longest passenger journey without a stop is the re-inaugurated Flying Scotsman's 268.5 mile *432,1 km* run from Kings Cross to Newcastle en route to Edinburgh.

Most powerful *World*
The world's most powerful steam locomotive, measured by tractive effort, was No. 700, a triple articulated or triplex 2-8-8-8-4, 6-cylinder engine built by the Baldwin Locomotive Co in 1916 for the Virginian Railroad. It had a tractive force of 166,300 lb *75 434 kg* working compound and 199,560 lb *90 520 kg* working simple.

Probably the heaviest train ever hauled by a single engine was one of 15,300 tons *15 545 tonnes* made up of 250 freight cars stretching 1.6 miles *2,5 km* by the *Matt H. Shay* (No. 5014), a 2-8-8-8-2 engine which ran on the Erie Railroad from May 1914 until 1929.

Longest freight train
The longest and heaviest freight train on record was about 4 miles *6 km* in length consisting of 500 coal cars with three 3600 hp diesels pulling and three more in the middle, on the Iaeger, West Virginia, to Portsmouth, Ohio, USA stretch of 157 miles *252 km* on the Norfolk and Western Railway on 15 Nov 1967. The total weight was nearly 42,000 tons *42 674 tonnes*.

British Rail's heaviest freight train began its regular run on 16 Sept 1983 from Merehead Quarry, Somerset to Acton, West London with 3300 tonnes of limestone in 43 wagons and 2 engines stretching nearly ½ mile *800 m*.

Greatest load
The heaviest single pieces of freight ever conveyed by rail are limited by the capacity of the rolling stock. The world's strongest rail carrier with a capacity of 807 tonnes is the 336 tonne 36 axle 92 m *301 ft 10 in* long 'Schnabel' built for a US railway by Krupp, W. Germany, in March 1981.

The heaviest load carried by British Rail was a 122 ft *37,1 m* long boiler drum, weighing 275 tons *279 tonnes* which was carried from Immingham Dock to Killingholme, Humberside, in September 1968.

The heaviest load ever moved on rails is the 10,700 ton Church of the Virgin Mary built in 1548 in the village of Most, Czechoslovakia, in October–November 1975 because it was in the way of coal workings. It was moved 800 yd *730 m* at 0.0013 mph *0,002 km/h* over 4 weeks at a cost of £9 million.

TRACKS

Longest line
The world's longest run is one of 9438 km *5864½ miles* on the Trans-Siberian line from Moscow to Nakhodka, USSR, in the Soviet Far East. There are 97 stops in the journey which takes 8 days 4 hr 25 min. The 3102 km *1927 miles* Baykal-Amur northern main line (BAM), begun with forced labour in 1938, was restarted in 1974 and put into service on 27 Oct 1984. A total of 10,000 million ft³ *283 million m³* of earth had to be moved and 1,987 bridges built in this £8000 million project.

Longest straight
The longest straight in the world is on the Commonwealth Railways Trans-Australian line over the Nullarbor Plain from Mile 496 between Nurina and Loongana, Western Australia, to Mile 793 between Ooldea and Watson, South Australia, 297 miles *478 km* dead straight although not level. The longest straight on British Rail is the 18 miles *29 km* between Barlby Junction and Brough on the 'down' line on the Selby, North Yorkshire, to Kingston-upon-Hull, Humberside, line.

Widest and narrowest
The widest gauge in standard use is 5 ft 6 in *1,676 m*. This width is used in Spain, Portugal, India, Pakistan, Bangladesh, Sri Lanka, Argentina and Chile. In 1885 there was a lumber railway in Oregon, USA with a gauge of 8 ft *2,4 m*. The narrowest gauge on which public services are operated is 10¼ in *260 mm* on the Wells Harbour (0.7 mile *1,12 km*) and the Wells–Walsingham Railways (4 miles *6,5 km*) in Norfolk, England.

Highest *World*
The world's highest standard gauge (4 ft 8½ in *1,43 m*) track is on the Peruvian State Railways at La Cima, on the Morococha Branch at 15,806 ft *4817 m* above sea-level. The highest point on the main line is 15,688 ft *4781 m* in the Galera tunnel.

Great Britain
The highest point of the British Rail system is at the pass of Drumochter on the former Perth–Inverness border, where the track reaches an altitude of 1484 ft *452 m* above sea-level. The highest railway in Britain is the Snowdon Mountain Railway, which rises from Llanberis, Gwynedd to 3493 ft *1064 m* above sea-level, just below the summit of Snowdon (*Yr Wyddfa*). It has a gauge of 2 ft 7½ in *800 mm*.

Lowest
The lowest point on British Rail is in the Severn Tunnel—144 ft *43,8 m* below sea-level.

Steepest gradient *World*
The world's steepest standard gauge gradient by adhesion is 1:11 between Chedde and Servoz on the metre gauge SNCF Chamonix line, France.

Great Britain
The steepest sustained adhesion-worked gradient on main line in the United Kingdom is the 2 mile *3,2 km* Lickey incline of 1:37.7 just south west of Birmingham. From the tunnel bottom to James Street, Liverpool, on the former Mersey Railway, there is a stretch of 1:27; and between Folkestone Junction and Harbour a mile *1,6 km* of 1:30.

Slightest gradient
The slightest gradient posted on the British Rail system is one indicated as 1 in 14,400 between Pirbright Junction and Farnborough, Hampshire. This could be described alternatively as England's most obtuse summit.

Busiest rail system
The world's most crowded rail system is the Japanese National Railways, which by 1984 carried 18,622,000 passengers daily. Professional pushers are employed in Tōkyō to squeeze in passengers before the doors can be closed. Among articles lost in 1983 were 539,718 umbrellas, 322,176 clothing items, 193,496 spectacles and 182,831 purses.

RAIL TRAVEL

Calling All Stations
Alan M. Witton (b. 1943) of Chorlton, Manchester visited every open British Rail station (2362) in a continuous tour for charity of 16,592¾ miles *26 703 km* in 27,136 minutes on 13 July–28 Aug 1980.

Colin M. Mulvany and Seth N. Vafiadis of London W12, visited every British Rail station (2,378) embracing also the Tyne and Wear, Strathclyde and London Underground systems (333 stations) for charity in 31 days 5 hr 8 min 58 sec over 15,527¾ miles *24 989 km* to average 38.05 mph *61,2 km/h* on 4 June–5 July 1984.

John E. Ballenger of Dunedin, Florida, USA has logged 76,485 miles *123 090 km* of unduplicated rail routes in North and South America.

Paul Marshall of Aberdeen traversed the extreme points of the compass for stations in Great Britain—Thurso (north), Lowestoft (east), Penzance (south) and Arisaig (west) in 58 hrs 14 mins on 29–31 Oct 1984.

Using Amtrak's All Aboard America $299 ticket, valid for a month, James J. Brady of Wilmington, Ohio travelled through 442 (out of 498) stations over 21,485 unduplicated miles of track (out of 23,000) on 11 Feb–11 Mar 1984.

Most Countries in 24 hours
The record number of countries travelled through entirely by train in 24 hours is 10 by W. M. Elbers and R. G. Scholten on 29–30 July 1981. They started in West Germany *via* Netherlands, Belgium, Luxembourg, France, Switzerland, Liechtenstein, Austria, Italy arriving in Yugoslavia 23 hr 34 min later.

Handpumped railcars
A speed of 20 mph was first surpassed at Port Moody, British Columbia, Canada over 300 m *985 ft* by the 5 man team (1 pusher, 4 pumpers) from Port Moody Motors with 33.54 sec on 27 June 1982.

Longest Journey
The longest journey on the British Rail system

is from Penzance, Cornwall to Wick, Caithness, Scotland, *via* London, Glasgow, Aberdeen and Inverness, a round trip of 2229¼ miles *3587,6 km*. It was travelled by John Shaw of Huddersfield for charity on 22–24 Sept 1983 in 50 hr 20 mins.

The highest mileage on British Rail within 24 hours is 1387 miles *2232 km* on 2–3 Oct 1984 by Michael H. Wilcock of Cardiff.

STATIONS

Largest *World*
The world's largest railway station is Grand Central Terminal, Park Avenue and 43rd Street, New York City, NY, USA, built 1903–13. It covers 48 acres *19 ha* on two levels with 41 tracks on the upper level and 26 on the lower. On average more than 550 trains and 180,000 people per day use it, with a peak of 252,288 on 3 July 1947.

Great Britain
The largest railway station in extent on the British Rail system is the 17-platform Clapham Junction, London, covering 27¾ acres *11,22 ha* with a total face of 11,185 ft *3409 m*. The station with the largest number of platforms is Waterloo, London (24½ acres *9,9 ha*), with 21 main and two Waterloo and City Line platforms, with a total face of 15,352 ft *4679 m*. Victoria Station (21¾ acres *8,80 ha*) with 17 platforms has, however, a total face length of 18,412 ft *5611 m*.

Oldest
The oldest station in the world is Liverpool Road Station, Manchester, England first used on 15 Sept 1830. It is now part of a museum.

Busiest
The busiest railway junction in Great Britain is Clapham Junction, Wandsworth, Greater London, on the Southern Region of British Rail, with an average of 2200 trains passing through each 24 hr (May 1984).

Highest
The highest station in the world is Condor, Bolivia at 15,705 ft *4786 m* on the metre gauge Rio Mulato to Potosi line. The highest passenger station on British Rail is Corrour, Highland, at an altitude of 1347 ft *410,5 m* above sea-level.

Waiting rooms
The world's largest waiting rooms are the four in Peking Station, Chang'an Boulevard, Peking,

China, opened in September 1959, with a total standing capacity of 14,000.

Longest platform
The longest railway platform in the world is the Khargpur platform, West Bengal, India, which measures 2733 ft *833 m* in length. The State Street Center subway platform staging on 'The Loop' in Chicago, Illinois, USA, measures 3500 ft *1066 m* in length.

The longest platform in the British Rail system is the 1977 ft 4 in *602,69 m* long platform at Gloucester.

MODEL RAILWAYS

The non-stop duration record for a model train (loco plus 6 coaches) is 864 hr 30 min from 1 June–7 July 1978, covering 678 miles *1091 km*, organised by Roy Catton at 'Pastimes' Toy Store, Mexborough, S. Yorkshire. The longest recorded run by a model *steam* locomotive is 144 miles *231,7 km* in 27 hr 18 min by the 7¼ inch *18,4 cm* gauge 'Winifred' built in 1974 by Wilf Grove at Thames Ditton, Surrey on 8–9 Sept 1979. 'Winifred' works on 80 lb/in² *5,6 kg/cm²* pressure and is coal-fired with cylinders 2⅛ in *54 mm* in diameter and 3⅛ in *79 mm* stroke. The most miniature model railway ever built is one of 1:1000 scale by Jean Damery (b. 1923) of Paris. The engine ran on a 4½ volt battery and measures 5/16 in *7,9 mm* overall.

TRAMS

Longest tram journey
The longest tramway journey now possible is from Krefeld St Tönis to Witten Annen Nord, W. Germany. With luck at the 8 inter-connections the 105,5 km *65.5 mile* trip can be achieved in 5½ hr. By late 1977 there were still some 315 tramway systems surviving of which the longest is that of Leningrad, USSR with 2500 cars on 53 routes. The last in Britain is at Blackpool, Lancashire.

Oldest
The oldest trams in revenue service in the world are Motor cars 1 and 2 of the Manx Electric Railway dating from 1893.

One of four identical waiting rooms at Peking Station, China, which together comprise the largest station passenger waiting area in the world. (*John Marshall*)

4. AIRCRAFT

Guinness Superlatives has published aircraft records in much greater detail in the specialist publication *Guinness Book of Aircraft Facts and Feats* by Michael Taylor and David Mondey (4th edition) (price £8.95).

Note—The use of the Mach scale for aircraft speeds was introduced by Prof. Ackeret of Zürich, Switzerland. The Mach number is the ratio of the velocity of a moving body to the local velocity of sound. This ratio was first employed by Dr Ernst Mach (1838–1916) of Vienna, Austria in 1887. Thus Mach 1.0 equals 760.98 mph *1224,67 km/h* at sea-level at 15°C, and is assumed, for convenience, to fall to a constant 659.78 mph *1061,81 km/h* in the stratosphere, *i.e.* above 11 000 m *36,089 ft*.

EARLIEST FLIGHTS

World
The first controlled and sustained power-driven flight occurred near the Kill Devil Hill, Kitty Hawk, North Carolina, USA, at 10.35 a.m. on 17 Dec 1903, when Orville Wright (1871–1948) flew the 12 hp chain-driven *Flyer I* for a distance of 120 ft *36,5 m* at an airspeed of 30 mph *48 km/h*, a ground speed of 6.8 mph *10,9 km/h* and an altitude of 8–12 ft *2,5–3,5 m* for about 12 sec watched by his brother Wilbur (1867–1912) 4 men and a boy. Both brothers, from Dayton, Ohio, were bachelors because, as Orville put it, they had not the means to 'support a wife as well as an aeroplane'. The *Flyer* is now in the National Air and Space Museum at the Smithsonian Institution, Washington DC.

The first hop by a man-carrying aeroplane entirely under its own power was made when Clément Ader (1841–1925) of France flew in his *Eole* for about 50 m *164 ft* at Armainvilliers, France, on 9 Oct 1890. It was powered by a lightweight steam engine of his own design which developed about 20 hp (15 kW). The earliest 'rational design' for a flying machine, according to the Royal Aeronautical Society, was that published by Emanuel Swedenborg (1688–1772) in Sweden in 1717.

Great Britain
The first officially recognised flight in the British Isles was made by the US citizen Samuel Franklin Cody (1861–1913) who flew 1390 ft *423 m* in his own biplane at Farnborough, Hampshire, on 16 Oct 1908. Horatio Frederick Phillips (1845–1924) almost certainly covered 500 ft *152 m* in his Phillips II '*Venetian blind*' aeroplane at Streatham, in 1907. The first Briton to fly was George Pearson Dickin (1881–1909), a journalist from Southport, Lancashire as a passenger to Wilbur Wright at Auvóur, France on 3 Oct 1908. The first resident British citizen to fly in Britain was J. T. C. Moore-Brabazon (later Lord Brabazon of Tara PC, GBE, MC) (1884–1964) with 3 short but sustained flights on 30 Apr–2 May 1909.

Cross-Channel
The earliest cross-Channel flight by an aeroplane was made on Sunday, 25 July 1909 when Louis Blériot (1872–1936) of France flew his *Blériot XI* monoplane, powered by a 23 hp Anzani engine, 26 miles *41,8 km* from Les Baraques, France, to Northfall Meadow near Dover Castle, England, in 36½ min, after taking off at 4.41 a.m.

Jet-engined *World*
Proposals for jet propulsion date back to Captain Marconnet (1909) of France, and Henri Coanda (1886–1972) of Romania, and to the turbojet proposals of Maxime Guillaume in 1921. The earliest tested run was that of the British Power Jets Ltd's experimental WU (Whittle Unit) on 12 Apr 1937, invented by Flying Officer (now Air Commodore Sir) Frank Whittle (b. Coventry, 1 June 1907), who had applied for a patent on jet propulsion in 1930. The first flight by an aeroplane powered by a turbojet engine was made by the Heinkel He 178, piloted by Flug

Kapitan Erich Warsitz, at Marienehe, Germany, on 27 Aug 1939. It was powered by a Heinkel He S3b engine (834 lb *378 kg* as installed with long tailpipe) designed by Dr Hans 'Pabst' von Ohain and first tested in August 1937.

Great Britain

The first British jet flight occurred when Fl Lt P. E. G. 'Jerry' Sayer, OBE (k. 1942) flew the Gloster-Whittle E.28/39 (wing span 29 ft *8,84 m*, length 25 ft 3 in *7,70 m*) fitted with an 860 lb *390 kg* s. t. Whittle W-1 engine for 17 min at Cranwell, Lincolnshire, on 15 May 1941. The maximum speed was c. 350 mph *560 km/h*.

Supersonic flight

The first supersonic flight was achieved on 14 Oct 1947 by Capt. (later Brig.-Gen) Charles ('Chuck') Elwood Yeager, USAF retd (b. 13 Feb 1923), over Edwards Air Force Base, Muroc, California, USA, in a Bell XS-1 rocket plane ('Glamorous Glennis') with Mach 1.015 (670 mph *1078 km/h*) at an altitude of 42,000 ft *12 800 m*. The first British aircraft to attain Mach 1 in a dive was the de Havilland D. H. 108 tailless research aircraft on 6 Sept 1948, piloted by John Derry.

Trans-Atlantic

The first crossing of the North Atlantic by air was made by Lt-Cdr (later Rear Admiral) Albert Cushion Read (1887–1967) and his crew (Stone, Hinton, Rodd, Rhoads and Breese) in the 84 knot *155 km/h* US Navy/Curtiss flying-boat NC-4 from Trepassey Harbour, Newfoundland, *via* the Azores, to Lisbon, Portugal, on 16–27 May 1919. The whole flight of 4717 miles *7591 km* originating from Rockaway Air Station, Long Island, NY on 8 May, required 53 hr 58 min, terminating at Plymouth, England, on 31 May.

The Newfoundland–Azores flight of 1200 miles *1930 km* took 15 hr 18 min at 81.7 knots *151,4 km/h*.

Non-stop

The first non-stop trans-Atlantic flight was achieved 18 days later from 4.13 p.m. GMT on 14 June 1919, from Lester's Field, St John's, Newfoundland, 1960 miles *3154 km* to Derrygimla bog near Clifden, County Galway, Ireland, at 8.40 a.m. GMT, 15 June, when the pilot, Capt John William Alcock, DSC (1892–1919), and the navigator Lt Arthur Whitten Brown (1886–1948) flew across in a Vickers *Vimy*, powered by two 360 hp Rolls-Royce *Eagle VIII* engines. Both men were created civil KBE's on 21 June 1919 when Alcock was aged 26 years 227 days, and shared a *Daily Mail* prize of £10,000.

Solo

The 79th man to achieve a trans-Atlantic flight but the first to do so solo was Capt (later Brig) Charles Augustus Lindbergh (Hon AFC) (1902–74) who took off in his 220 hp Ryan monoplane *Spirit of St. Louis* at 12.52 p.m. GMT on 20 May 1927 from Roosevelt Field, Long Island, NY, USA. He landed at 10.21 p.m. GMT on 21 May 1927 at Le Bourget airfield, Paris, France. His flight of 3610 miles *5810 km* lasted 33 hr 29½ min and he won a prize of $25,000 (*then £5300*).

Most Flights

Between March 1948 and his retirement on 1 Sept 1984 TWA Captain Charles M. Schimpf logged a total of 2,880 Atlantic crossings—at the rate of 6.4 per month.

Trans-Pacific

The first non-stop Pacific flight was by Major Clyde Pangborn and Hugh Herndon in the Bellanca cabin 'plane *Miss Veedol* from Sabishiro Beach, Japan 4558 miles *7335 km* to Wenatchee, Washington, USA in 41 hr 13 min on 3–5 Oct 1931. (For earliest crossing see 1924 flight below).

Circumnavigational flights

Strict circumnavigation requires passing through two antipodal points thus with a minimum distance of 24,859.75 miles *40 007,89 km*. The FAI permits flights which exceed the length of the Tropic of Cancer or Capricorn viz 22,858.754 miles *36 787,599 km*.

The earliest such flight of 26,345 miles *42 398 km* was by two US Army Douglas DWC amphibians in 57 'hops'. The *Chicago* was piloted by Lt Lowell H. Smith and Lt Leslie P. Arnold and the *New Orleans* was piloted by Lt Erik H. Nelson and Lt John Harding between 6 Apr and 28 Sept 1924 beginning and ending at Seattle, Washington, USA.

The earliest solo claim was by Wiley Hardemann Post (1898–1935) (US) in the Lockheed Vega 'Winnie Mae' starting and finishing at Floyd Bennett Field, New York City on 15–22 July 1933 in 10 'hops'. The distance of 15,596 miles *25 099 km* with a flying time of 115 hr 36 min was however at too high a latitude to qualify.

The first non-stop round-the-world flight completed on 2 Mar 1949 was made by the USAF's Boeing B-50 Superfortress *Lucky Lady II* piloted by Capt James Gallagher from Carswell AFB, Texas in 94 hr 1 min. The aircraft was refuelled 4 times on its 23,452 mile *37 742 km* flight.

The fastest flight has been the non-stop eastabout flight of 45 hr 19 min by three flight-refuelled USAF B-52's led by Maj-Gen Archie J. Old Jr. They covered 24,325 miles *39 147 km* on 16–18 Jan 1957 finishing at March Air Force Base, Riverside, California, having averaged 525 mph *845 km/h* with four in-flight refuellings by KC-97 aerial tankers.

The first circum-polar flight was solo by Capt Elgen M. Long, 44, in a Piper Navajo on 5 Nov–3 Dec 1971. He covered 38,896 miles *62 597 km* in 215 flying hours. The cabin temperature sank to −40°C −40°F over Antarctica.

Circumnavigation *Smallest aircraft*

The smallest aircraft to complete a circumnavigation is the 20 ft 11 in *6,38 m* single-engined 180 hp Thorp T-18 built in his garage by its pilot Donald P. Taylor of Sage, California. His 26,190 mile *42 148 km* flight in 37 stages took 176 flying hours ending at Oshkosh, Wisconsin on 30 Sept 1976.

Largest wing span

The aircraft with the largest wing span ever constructed is the $40 million Hughes H.4 Hercules flying-boat ('Spruce Goose'), which was raised 70 ft *21,3 m* into the air in a test run of 1000 yd *914 m*, piloted by Howard Hughes (1905–76), off Long Beach California, USA, on 2 Nov 1947. The eight-engined 190 ton *193 tonnes* aircraft had a wing span of 319 ft 11 in *97,51 m* and a length of 218 ft 8 in *66,64 m* and never flew again. In a brilliant engineering feat she was moved bodily by Goldcoast Corp aided by the US Navy barge crane YD-171 on 22 Feb 1982 to her final resting place 6 miles *9,6 km* across the harbour under a 700 ft *213,4 m* diameter dome.

Heaviest

The highest recorded gross take off weight of any aircraft has been 379.9 tons *386,0 tonnes* in the case of a Boeing 747-200B 'Jumbo' jet during certification tests of its Pratt & Whitney JT9D-7Q engines on 23 May 1979. Some versions are certified for standard airline operation at a maximum take-off weight of 371.9 tons *377,9 tonnes*.

A Boeing 747 (Capt. Eric Moody) became the 'worlds heaviest glider' when all 4 engines stopped at 37,000 ft *11 275 m* due to volcanic ash from Mt. Galunggung, Indonesia on 24 June 1982 on Flight BA.009 with 263 aboard. The crew got the engines restarted after 13 min and landed the plane at Djakarta.

The $40 million Piasecki Heli-Stat, comprising a framework of light-alloy and composite materials to mount four Sikorsky SH-34J helicopters and the envelope of a Goodyear ZPG-2 patrol airship, was exhibited on 26 Jan 1984 at Lakehurst, New Jersey, USA. Designed for use by the US Forest Service and designated Model 94-37J Logger, it has an overall length of 343 ft *104,55 m* and is intended to carry a payload of 21.4 tons.

Solar powered

The solar-powered *Solar Challenger*, designed by a team led by Dr Paul MacCready, was flown for the first time entirely under solar power on 20 Nov 1980. On 7 July 1981, piloted by Steve Ptacek (USA), the *Solar Challenger* became the first aircraft of this category to achieve a crossing of the English Channel. Taking off from Pontois-Cormeilles, Paris, the 163 mile *262,3 km* journey to Manston, Kent was completed in 5 hr 23 min at a maximum altitude of 3353 m *11,000 ft*. The aircraft has a wingspan of 47 ft *14,3 m*.

Smallest

The smallest aeroplane ever flown is the 'Bumble Bee', designed and built by Robert H. Starr. It is 9 ft 4 in *2,84 m* long, with a wing span of 6 ft 6 in *1,98 m*, and weighs 756 lb *342 kg* empty. It is powered by an 85 hp Continental C85 engine, giving a top speed of 180 mph *290 km/h*. It was first flown on 28 Jan 1984 over Arizona. The smallest jet is the 280 mph *450 km/h* Silver Bullet weighing 432 lb *196 kg* with a 17 ft 5 *,18 m* wing span built by Bob Bishop (USA).

Bombers *Heaviest*

The world's heaviest bomber is the eight-jet swept-wing Boeing B-52H Stratofortress, which has a maximum take-off weight of 488,000 lb (217.86 tons *221,35 tonnes*). It has a wing span of 185 ft *56,38 m* and is 157 ft 6¾ in *48,02 m* in length, with a speed of over 650 mph *1046 km/h*. The B-52 can carry twelve SRAM thermonuclear short range attack missiles or twenty-four 750 lb *340 kg* bombs under its wings and eight more SRAM's or eighty-four 500 lb *226 kg* bombs in the fuselage. The ten-engined Convair B-36J, weighing 183 tons *185 tonnes*, had a greater wing span, at 230 ft *70,10 m* but it is no longer

Dr Paul MacCready (right), designer of the first pure (i.e. non-battery) solar powered aircraft Solar Challenger in discussion with its pilot, Steve Ptacek, who flew it across the English Channel. (See above) (K. J. A. Brookes)

in service. It had a top speed of 435 mph *700 km/h.*

Fastest

The world's fastest operational bombers are the French Dassault Mirage IV, which can fly at Mach 2.2 (1450 mph *2333 km/h*) at 36,000 ft *11 000 m*; the American General Dynamics FB-111A, with a maximum speed of Mach 2.5; and the Soviet swing-wing Tupolev Tu-22M known to NATO as 'Backfire', which has an estimated over-target speed of Mach 2.0 but which may be as fast as Mach 2.5 and a combat radius of up to 3570 miles *5745 km.*

Airliner largest *World*

The highest capacity jet airliner is the Boeing 747 'Jumbo Jet', first flown on 9 Feb 1969 (see Heaviest aircraft) and has a capacity of from 385 to more than 500 passengers with a maximum speed of 602 mph *969 km/h*. Its wing span is 195.7 ft *59,64 m* and its length 231.8 ft *70,7 m*. It entered service on 22 Jan 1970. The Boeing 747-300 with lengthened upper deck allowing extra 37 passengers, entered service in March 1983.

The greatest passenger load recorded was one which carried 306 adults, 328 children and 40 babies (total 674) from the cyclone-devastated Darwin to Sydney, New South Wales, Australia on 29 Dec 1974.

Great Britain

The largest ever British aircraft was the experimental Bristol Type 167 Brabazon, which had a maximum take-off weight of 129.4 tons *131,4 tonnes*, a wing span of 230 ft *70,10 m* and a length of 177 ft *53,94 m*. This eight-engined aircraft first flew on 4 Sept 1949. The Concorde (see below) has a maximum take-off weight of 408,000 lb *185 065 kg* (182.14 tons).

Airliner fastest

The supersonic BAC/Aérospatiale Concorde, first flown on 2 Mar 1969, with a capacity of 128 passengers, cruises at up to Mach 2.2 (1450 mph *2333 km/h*). It flew at Mach 1.05 on 10 Oct 1969, exceeded Mach 2 for the first time on 4 Nov 1970 and became the first supersonic airliner used on passenger services on 21 Jan 1976 when Air France and British Airways opened services simultaneously between, respectively, Paris–Rio de Janeiro and London–Bahrain. Services between London–New York and Paris–New York began on 22 Nov 1977. The New York–London record is 2 hr 56 min 35 sec set on 1 Jan 1983.

Most capacious

The Aero Spacelines Guppy-201 has a cargo hold with a usable volume of 39,000 ft³ *1104,4 m³* and a maximum take-off weight of 75.9 tons *77,1 tonnes*. Wing span is 156.2 ft *47,63 m*, length 143.8 ft *43,84 m* and overall height 48.5 ft *14,78 m*. The giant Lockheed C-5A Galaxy military transport has a main cargo hold with a usable volume of 34,795 ft³ *985,3 m³*, and a maximum take-off weight of 343.3 tons *348,8 tonnes*. Its wing span is 222.7 ft *67,88 m*, length 247.8 ft *75,54 m* and overall height 65.1 ft *19,85 m*. It has in addition forward and rear upper decks with a combined volume of 8030 ft³ *227,4 m³*, which accommodates the flight crew, and provides seating for a relief crew and others, totalling 15 forward and 75 troops on the rear deck. When full details become available it is almost certain that the Galaxy will be superseded by the Soviet Antonov An-400 (NATO name *Condor*) which is estimated to have a wing span of 243.5 ft *74,2 m*.

Largest propeller

The largest aircraft propeller ever used was the 22 ft 7½ in *6,9 m* diameter Garuda propeller, fitted to the Linke-Hofmann R II built in

The largest landplane ever to fly, the Lockheed C-5A Galaxy has a take-off weight of over 340 tons. (See below) *(K. J. A. Brookes)*

Breslau, Germany (now Wroclaw, Poland), which flew in 1919. It was driven by four 260 hp Mercedes engines and turned at only 545 rpm.

Scheduled flights *Longest*

The longest distance scheduled non-stop flight is the weekly Pan-Am Sydney–San Francisco non-stop 13 hr 25 min Flight 816, in a Boeing 747 SP, opened in December 1976, over 7475 statute miles *12 030 km*. The longest delivery flight by a commercial jet is 8936 nautical miles or 10,290 statute miles *16 560 km* from Seattle, Washington, USA to Cape Town, South Africa by the South African Airway's Boeing 747 SP (Special performance) 'Matroosberg' with 178 400 kg *175.5 tons* of pre-cooled fuel in 17 hr 22½ min on 23–24 Mar 1976.

Shortest

The shortest scheduled flight in the world is that by Loganair between the Orkney Islands of Westray and Papa Westray which has been flown with Britten-Norman Islander twin-engined 10-seat transports since September 1967. Though scheduled for 2 min, in favourable wind conditions it has been accomplished in 58 sec by Capt Andrew D. Alsop.

Gary W. Rovetto of Island Air on 21 Mar 1980 flew on the scheduled flight from Center Island to Decatur Island, Washington, USA in 41 sec.

Paris–London

The fastest time to travel the 214 miles *344 km* from central Paris to central London (BBC TV centre) is 38 min 58 sec by David Boyce of Stewart Wrightson (Aviation) Ltd on 24 Sept 1983 by motorcycle–helicopter to Le Bourget; Hawker Hunter jet (pilot Michael Carlton) to Biggin Hill, Kent; helicopter to the TV centre car park.

London–New York

The record for central London to downtown New York City by helicopter and Concorde is 3 hr 59 min 44 sec and the return in 3 hr 40 min 40 sec both by David J. Springbett, 1981 Salesman of the Year, and David Boyce (see above) on 8 and 9 Feb 1982.

HIGHEST SPEED

Official record

The official air speed record is 2193.167 mph *3529,56 km/h* by Capt Eldon W. Joersz and Maj George T. Morgan, Jr, in a Lockheed SR-71A

near Beale Air Force Base, California, USA over a 15 to 25 km course on 28 July 1976.

Air-launched record

The fastest fixed-wing aircraft in the world was the US North American Aviation X-15A-2, which flew for the first time (after modification from X-15A) on 28 June 1964 powered by a liquid oxygen and ammonia rocket propulsion system. Ablative materials on the airframe once enabled a temperature of 3000°F to be withstood. The landing speed was 210 knots (242 mph *389,1 km/h*) momentarily. The highest speed attained was 4534 mph *7297 km/h* (Mach 6.72) when piloted by Maj William J. Knight, USAF (b. 1930), on 3 Oct 1967. An earlier version piloted by Joseph A. Walker (1920–66), reached 354,200 ft *107 960 m* (67.08 miles) also over Edwards Air Force Base, California, USA, on 22 Aug 1963. The programme was suspended after the final flight of 24 Oct 1968.

The US NASA Rockwell International Space Shuttle Orbiter *Columbia* was launched from the Kennedy Space Center, Cape Canaveral, Florida commanded by Cdr John W. Young USN and piloted by Robert L. Crippen on 12 Apr 1981 at the expenditure of $9900 million since 1972. *Columbia* broke all records for space by a fixed wing craft with 16,600 mph *26 715 km/h* at main engine cut-off. After re-entry from 400,000 ft *122 km*, experiencing temperatures of 2160°C *3920°F*, she glided home weighing 97 tonnes/tons with the highest ever landing speed of 216 mph *347 km/h* on Rogers Dry Lake, California on 14 Apr 1981. Under a new FAI Category P for Aerospacecraft, the *Columbia* is holder of the current absolute world record for duration of 8 days 00 hr 04 min 45 sec, with two astronauts, but *Challenger* (launched 18 June 1983) has since set a duration record of 6 days 02 hr 23 min 59 sec with five astronauts including Sally K. Ride, the first female Space Shuttle astronaut, and on a previous mission set a new record altitude of 206.36 miles *332,1 km*. *Columbia* also holds the current absolute world record for the greatest mass lifted to altitude, a figure of 235,634 lb *106 882 kg* or 105.2 tons.

Fastest jet

The world's fastest jet aircraft is the USAF Lockheed SR-71 reconnaissance aircraft (see Official record) which was first flown on 22 Dec 1964 and is reportedly capable of attaining an altitude ceiling of close to 100,000 ft *30 480 m*.

The SR-71 has a wing span of 55.6 ft *16,94 m* and a length of 107.4 ft *32,73 m* and weighs 170,000 lb (75.9 tons *77,1 tonnes*) at take-off. Its reported range is 2982 miles *4800 km* at Mach 3 at 78,750 ft *24 000 m*. At least 30 are believed to have been built. The fastest combat aircraft in the world is the USSR Mikoyan MiG-25 fighter (code name 'Foxbat'). The reconnaissance 'Foxbat-B' has been tracked by radar at about Mach 3.2 (2110 mph *3395 km/h*). When armed with four large underwing air-to-air missiles known to NATO as 'Acrid', the fighter 'Foxbat-A' is limited to Mach 2.8 (1845 mph *2969 km/h*). The single-seat 'Foxbat-A' spans 45 ft 9 in *13,95 m*, is 78 ft 2 in *23,82 m* long and has an estimated maximum take-off weight of 82,500 lb *37 421 kg*.

Fastest biplane
The fastest recorded biplane was the Italian Fiat C.R.42B, with a 1010 hp Daimler-Benz DB601A engine, which attained 323 mph *520 km/h* in 1941. Only one was built.

Fastest piston-engined aircraft
The fastest speed at which a piston-engined aeroplane has ever been measured was for a cut-down privately owned Hawker Sea Fury which attained 520 mph *836 km/h* in level flight over Texas, USA, in August 1966 piloted by Mike Carroll (k. 1969) of Los Angeles. The FAI accredited record for a piston-engined aircraft is 517.055 mph *832,12 km/h* over Mojave, California by Frank Taylor (US) in a modified North American P-51D Mustang powered by a 3000 hp Packard Merlin, over a 15 to 25 km course, on 30 July 1983.

Fastest propeller-driven aircraft
The Soviet Tu-114 turboprop transport is the world's fastest propeller-driven aeroplane. It achieved a recorded speed 545.076 mph *877,212 km/h* carrying heavy payloads over measured circuits. It is developed from the Tupolev Tu-95 bomber, known in the West as the 'Bear', and has four 14,795 hp engines. The turboprop-powered Republic XF-84H prototype US Navy fighter which flew on 22 July 1955 had a top *design* speed of 670 mph *1078 km/h* but was abandoned.

Fastest trans-Atlantic flight
The trans-Atlantic flight record is 1 hr 54 min 56.4 sec by Maj James V. Sullivan, 37, and Maj Noel F. Widdifield, 33 flying a Lockheed SR-71A eastwards on 1 Sept 1974. The average speed, slowed by refuelling by a KC-135 tanker aircraft, for the New York–London stage of 3461.53 miles *5570,80 km* was 1806.963 mph *2908,026 km/h*. The solo record (Gander to Gatwick) is 8 hr 47 min 32 sec by Capt John J. A. Smith in a Rockwell 685 on 12 Mar 1978.

Altitude *Official record*
The official world altitude record by an aircraft taking off from the ground under its own power is 123,524 ft (23.39 miles *37 650 m*) by Aleksandr Fedotov (USSR) in a Mikoyan E.266M, (MiG-25) aircraft, powered by two 30,865 lb *14 000 kg* thrust turbojet engines, on 31 Aug 1977.

Duration
The flight duration record is 64 days 22 hr 19 min and 5 sec, set up by Robert Timm and John Cook in a Cessna 172 'Hacienda'. They took off from McCarran Airfield, Las Vegas, Nevada, USA, just before 3.53 p.m. local time on 4 Dec 1958, and landed at the same airfield just before 2.12 p.m. on 7 Feb 1959. They covered a distance equivalent to six times round the world with continued refuellings, without landing.

The record for duration without refuelling is 84 hr 32 min, set by Walter E. Lees and Frederic A. Brossy in a Bellanca monoplane with a 225 hp Packard Diesel engine, at Jacksonville, Florida, USA on 25–28 May 1931. The longest non-stop flight without refuelling was a 12,532 mile *20 169 km* flight from Okinawa to Madrid, Spain by a USAF B-52H on 10–11 Jan 1962.

AIRPORTS

Largest *World*
The world's largest airport is the £2100 million King Khalid International Airport outside Riyadh, Saudi Arabia covering an area of 86 miles[2] *221 km[2]*, opened on 14 Nov 1983. It has the world's largest control tower 243 ft *74 m* in height. The Hajj Terminal at the £2800 million King Abdul-Aziz airport near Jeddah is the world's largest roofed structure covering 1,5 km[2] *370 acres*. The present 6 runways and 5 terminal buildings of the Dallas/Fort Worth Airport, Texas, USA are planned to be extended to 9 runways and 13 terminals with 260 gates with an ultimate capacity for 150 million passengers. The world's largest airport terminal is Hartsfield Atlanta International Airport opened on 21 Sept 1980 with floor space covering 50.50 acres *20,43 ha*. It has 138 gates handling nearly 50 million passengers a year but has a capacity for 75 million.

Great Britain
Seventy-four airline companies from 68 countries operate scheduled services into Heathrow Airport—London (2958 acres *1197 ha*), and during 1984 there was a total of 272,900 air transport movements handled by a staff of 45,000 employed by the various companies and the British Airports Authority. The total number of passengers, both incoming and outgoing, was 29,147,200. The most flights yet handled by Heathrow in a day was 986 on 19 July 1974 and the largest number of passengers yet handled in a day was 115,570 on 2 Sep 1984. Aircraft fly to more than 90 countries.

The Soviet Union's Mil Mi-12 helicopter is the world's largest. Weighing over 100 tons it has lifted a payload of over 39½ tons to a height of almost 8000 ft *2400 m*. (See opposite page) *(K. J. A. Brookes)*

Busiest

The world's busiest airport is the Chicago International Airport, O'Hare Field, Illinois, USA with a total of 731,742 movements and 45,725,939 passengers in the year 1984. This represents a take-off or landing every 43.1 sec round the clock. Heathrow Airport, London handles more *international* traffic than any other. The busiest landing area ever has been Bien Hoa Air Base, south Vietnam, which handled more than 1,000,000 take-offs and landings in 1970. The world's largest 'helipad' was An Khe, south Vietnam.

Highest and lowest

The highest airport in the world is La Sa (Lhasa) Airport, Tibet at 14,315 ft *4363 m*.

The highest landing ever made by a fixed-wing 'plane is 19,947 ft *6080 m* on Dhaulagiri, Himalaya by a Pilatus Porter, named 'Yeti', supplying the 1960 Swiss Expedition. The lowest landing field is El Lisan on the east shore of the Dead Sea, 1180 ft *360 m* below sea-level, but during World War II BOAC Short C-class flying boats operated from the surface of the Dead Sea 1292 ft *394 m* below sea level. The lowest international airport is Schiphol, Amsterdam, at 13 ft *3,9 m* below sea-level. Rotterdam's airport is fractionally lower at 15 ft *4,5 m*.

Farthest and nearest to city or capital centres

The airport farthest from the city centre it allegedly serves is Viracopos, Brazil, which is 60 miles *96 km* from São Paulo. The Gibraltar airport is 880 yd *800 m* from the centre.

Longest runway *World*

The longest runway in the world is one of 7 miles *11 km* in length (of which 15,000 ft *4572 m* is concreted) at Edwards Air Force Base on the bed of Rogers Dry Lake at Muroc, California, USA. The whole test centre airfield extends over 65 miles² *168 km²*. In an emergency an auxiliary 12 mile *19 km* strip is available along the bed of the Dry Lake. The world's longest civil airport runway is one of 16,076 ft (3.04 miles *4,89 km*) at Pierre van Ryneveld Airport Upington, South Africa constructed in five months from August 1975 to January 1976. A paved runway 20,500 ft (3.88 miles *6,24 km*) long appears on maps of Jordan at Abu Husayn. The longest runway available normally to civil aircraft in the United Kingdom is No. 1 at Heathrow Airport—London, measuring 12,800 ft (2.42 miles *3,90 km*). The most southerly major runway (1.6 miles *2,57 km*) in the world is at Mount Pleasant, East Falkland (Lat 51° 50'S) built in 16 months to May 1985.

HELICOPTERS

Fastest

The official world speed record for a pure helicopter is 228.9 mph *368,4 km/h* set by Gourguen Karapetyan in a Mil A-10 on a 15 to 25 km course near Moscow, USSR on 21 Sept 1978.

Largest

The world's largest helicopter is the Soviet Mil Mi-12 ('Homer'), also known as the V-12. It is powered by four 6500 hp turboshaft engines and has a span of 219 ft 10 in *67 m* over its rotor tips with a length of 121 ft 4½ in *37,00 m* and weighs 103.3 tons *105 tonnes*.

Greatest Load

On 3 Feb 1982 at Podmoscovnoé in the Soviet Union, a Mil Mi-26 heavy-lift helicopter, crewed by G. V. Alfeurov and L. A. Indeev (co-pilot), lifted a total mass of 125,153.8 lb *56 768,8 kg* (55.87 tons *56,77 tonnes*) to 2000 m *6560 ft*.

Smallest

The Aerospace General Co one-man rocket

assisted minicopter weighs about 160 lb *72,5 kg* cruising 250 miles *400 km* at 85 mph *137 km/h*.

Highest

The altitude record for helicopters is 40,820 ft *12 442 m* by an Aérospatiale SA315B *Lama*, over France on 21 June 1972. The highest recorded landing has been at 23,000 ft *7000 m* below the South-East face of Everest in a rescue sortie in May 1971. The World Trade Center helipad is 1385 ft *422 m* above street level in New York City on the South Tower.

Circumnavigation

H. Ross Perot, 23 and Jay Coburn both of Dallas, Texas made the first helicopter circumnavigation in 'Spirit of Texas' on 1–30 Sept 1982. The first solo round-the-world flight in a helicopter was completed by Dick Smith (Australia) on 22 July 1983. Flown from and to the Bell Helicopter facility at Fort Worth, Texas, in a Bell Model 206L Long Ranger III, his unhurried flight began on 5 Aug 1982 and covered a distance of 35,258 miles *56 742 km*.

AUTOGYROS

Earliest

The autogyro or gyroplane, a rotorcraft with an unpowered rotor turned by the airflow in flight, preceded the practical helicopter with engine-driven rotor. Juan de la Cierva (Spain), made the first successful autogyro flight with his model C.4 (commercially named an *Autogiro*) at Getafe, Spain, on 9 Jan 1923.

Speed, altitude and distance records

Wing Cdr Kenneth H. Wallis (GB) holds the straight-line distance record of 543.27 miles *874,32 km* set in his WA-116F autogyro on 28 Sept 1975 non-stop from Lydd, Kent to Wick, Highland. Wg Cdr Wallis flew his WA-116, with 72 hp McCulloch engine, to a record speed

of 111.2 mph *179 km/h* over a 3 km *1.86 mile* straight course on 12 May 1969. On 20 July 1982, flying from Boscombe Down, Wiltshire, he established a new autogyro altitude record of 18,516 ft *5643,7 m* in his WA-121/Mc. This, the smallest and lightest Wallis autogyro to date, is powered by a 100 hp Wallis/McCulloch engine.

FLYING-BOAT

Fastest

The fastest flying-boat ever built has been the Martin XP6M-1 Seamaster, the US Navy 4-jet engined minelayer flown in 1955–9 with a top speed of 646 mph *1040 km/h*. In September 1946 the Martin JRM-2 Mars flying-boat set a payload record of 68,327 lb *30 992 kg*. The official flying-boat speed record is 566.69 mph *912 km/h*, set up by Nikolai Andrievsky and crew of two in a Soviet Beriev M-10, powered by two AL-7 turbojets, over a 15 to 25 km course on 7 Aug 1961. The M-10 holds all 12 records listed for jet-powered flying-boats, including an altitude of 49,088 ft *14 962 m* set by Georgiy Buryanov and crew over the Sea of Azov on 9 Sept 1961.

AIRSHIPS

Earliest

The earliest flight in an airship was by Henri Giffard from Paris in his steam-powered coal-gas 88,300 ft³ *2500 m³* 144 ft *43,8 m* long airship on 24 Sept 1852. The earliest British airship was a 20,000 ft³ *566 m³* 75 ft *22,8 m* long craft built by Stanley Spencer whose maiden flight was from Crystal Palace, Bromley, Greater London on 22 Sept 1902. The latest airship to be built in Britain is the 235,400 ft³ *6666 m³* 193.6 ft *59 m* long Skyship 600 designed and built by Airship Industries. This 20 passenger dirigible (G-SKSC) was flown for the first time at RAE Cardington, Bedfordshire on 6 Mar 1984.

Wing Commander Kenneth H. Wallis in the WA-116F autogyro of his own design in which he broke the straight-line distance record of 543.27 miles *874,32 km*.
(K. J. A. Brookes)

Largest Rigid

The largest rigid airship ever built was the 210.5 ton *213,9 tonne* German *Graf Zeppelin II* (LZ 130), with a length of 245 m *803.8 ft* and a capacity of 7,062,100 ft³ *199 981 m³*. She made her maiden flight on 14 Sept 1938 and in May and August 1939 made radar spying missions in British air space. She was dismantled in April 1940. Her sister ship *Hindenburg* was 5.6 ft *1,70 m* longer.

British

The largest British airship was the R101 built by the Royal Airship Works, Cardington, Bedfordshire, which first flew on 14 Oct 1929. She was 777 ft *236,8 m* in length and had a capacity of 5,508,800 ft³ *155 995 m³*. She crashed near Beauvais, France, killing 48 aboard on 5 Oct 1930.

Non-Rigid

The largest non-rigid airship ever constructed was the US Navy ZPG 3-W which had a capacity of 1,516,300 ft³ *42 937 m³*, was 403.4 ft *122,9 m* long and 85.1 ft *25,93 m* in diameter, with a crew of 21. She first flew on 21 July 1958, but crashed into the sea in June 1960.

Hot-Air

The world altitude, duration and distance records, of 10,365 ft *3159 m*, 1 hr 26 min 52 sec, and 23.03 miles *37,07 km* respectively, are held by the Cameron D-38 hot-air airship flown at Cunderdin, W. Australia on 27 Aug 1982 by R. W. Taaffe (Australia).

Greatest passenger load

The most people ever carried in an airship was 207 in the US Navy *Akron* in 1931. The trans-Atlantic record is 117 by the German *Hindenburg* in 1937.

Distance records

The FAI accredited straight line distance record for airships is 3967.1 miles *6384,5 km*, set up by the German *Graf Zeppelin*, captained by Dr Hugo Eckener, between 29 Oct and 1 Nov 1928. The German Zeppelin L59 flew from Yambol, Bulgaria to south of Khartoum, Sudan and returned on 21–25 Nov 1917 to cover a minimum of 4500 miles *7250 km*.

Duration record

The longest recorded flight by a non-rigid airship (without refuelling) is 264 hr 12 min by a US Navy Goodyear-built ZPG-2 class ship (Cdr J. R. Hunt USN) from South Weymouth NAS, Massachusetts, USA on 4–15 Mar 1957 landing back at Key West, Florida, USA having flown 9448 miles *15 205 km*.

BALLOONING

Earliest

I. William Deiches (b. 1934) of Brentwood, Essex, has adduced that the 'mace-head' of the Scorpion King *c.* 3100 BC found at Hierakonpolis, Egypt is in reality a depiction of a pannelled hot-air balloon of papyrus construction. The earliest recorded ascent was by a model hot-air balloon invented by Father Bartolomeu de Gusmão (*né* Lourenço) (b. Santos, Brazil, 1685), which was flown indoors at the Casa da India, Terreiro do Paço, Portugal on 8 Aug 1709 (for earliest flights see Chapter 10).

Distance record (*Great-circle distance between take-off and first landing point*)

The record distance travelled by a balloon is 5208.68 miles *8382,54 km* by the Raven experimental helium-filled balloon *Double Eagle V* (capacity 11 300 m³ *399,053 ft³*) on 9–12 Nov 1981, from Nagashima, Japan to Covello, California. The crew for this first manned balloon crossing of the Pacific Ocean was Ben

L. Abruzzo, 51, Rocky Aoki, 43 (Japan), Ron Clark, 41 and Larry M. Newman, 34.

Ex-USAF Colonel Joe Kittinger (see Parachuting Chapter 10) became the first man to complete a solo trans-Atlantic crossing by balloon. Accomplished in the helium-filled balloon *Rosie O'Grady* between 14–18 Sept 1984, Kittinger lifted-off from Caribou, Maine and completed a distance of approximately 3534 miles *5688 km* before landing at Savona in northern Italy. The first balloon crossing of the North Atlantic had been made during 12–17 Aug 1978 in the gas balloon *Double Eagle II* crewed by Ben L. Abruzzo, Maxie L. Anderson and Larry M. Newman.

The first crossing of the United States was by the helium-filled balloon *Super Chicken III* (pilots Fred Gorell and John Shoecraft) from Costa Mesa, California, 2515 miles *4047 km* to Blackbeard's Island, Georgia on 9–12 Oct 1981.

Highest Unmanned

The highest altitude attained by an unmanned balloon was 170,000 ft *51 815 m* by a Winzen balloon of 47.8 million ft³ *1,35 million m³* launched at Chico, California in October 1972.

James Stoodley, who in 1942 at just under 14½ and with no previous flying experience, took his 13-year-old brother for a 29 minute joyride in a Piper Cub trainer aircraft. (See column 3)

Manned

The greatest altitude reached in a manned balloon is the unofficial 123,800 ft (23.45 miles *37 735 m*) by Nicholas Piantanida (1933–66) of Bricktown, New Jersey, USA, from Sioux Falls, South Dakota, USA, on 1 Feb 1966. He landed in a cornfield in Iowa but did not survive. The official record is 113,740 ft *34 668 m* by Cdr Malcolm D. Ross, USNR and the late Lt-Cdr Victor A. Prother, USN in an ascent from the deck of USS *Antietam* on 4 May 1961, over the Gulf of Mexico.

Largest

The largest balloon built is one with an inflatable volume of 70 million ft³ *2 million m³* by Winzen Research Inc, Minnesota, USA.

Ballooning (*Hot-air*)

(Modern revival began in USA in 1961. First World Championships 10–17 Feb 1973 at Albuquerque, New Mexico, USA.)

The world's distance record for hot-air balloons is 717.52 miles *1154,74 km*, set by French balloonists Michel Arnould and Hélène Dorigny on 25–26 Nov 1981 in the Cameron Type A-530 *Semiramis* from Ballina, County Mayo, Eire to St Christophe-en-Boucherie, France. This flight

has also been homologated by the FAI as a new world duration record for hot-air balloons of 29 hr 5 min 48 sec, and in addition the *Semiramis* is now the largest hot-air balloon ever built with a volume of 530,000 ft³ *15 008 m³*. On 31 Oct 1980 Julian Nott (GB) attained an altitude, which has been ratified by the FAI, of 55,137 ft *16 805 m*, taking off from Longmont, near Denver, Colorado, USA, in the Cameron-built ICI balloon *Innovation*. The FAI endurance and distance record for a gas and hot-air balloon is 96 hr 24 min and 2074.817 miles *3339,086 km* by *Zanussi* crewed by Donald Allan Cameron (GB) and Major Christopher Davey which failed by only 103 miles *166 km* to achieve the first balloon crossing of the Atlantic on 30 July 1978.

The record altitude in an open basket is 53,000 ft *16 154,4 m* by Chauncey M. Dunn (US) on 1 Aug 1979. He wore a pressure suit.

PERSONAL AVIATION RECORDS

Oldest and youngest passengers

Airborne births are reported every year. The oldest person to fly has been Mrs Jessica S. Swift (b. Anna Stewart 17 Sept 1871) aged 110 yrs 3 months, from Vermont to Florida, USA in Dec 1981. The oldest Briton to fly was probably Mrs Julia Caroline Black (b. 24 Feb 1874 d. 12 May 1980) on a British Caledonian flight from Abbotsinch to Gatwick on 17 Nov 1978 when aged 104 years 8 months.

Youngest and oldest pilots

The youngest age at which anyone has ever qualified as a military pilot is 15 yr 5 months in the case of Sgt Thomas Dobney (b. 6 May 1926) of the RAF. He had overstated his age (14 yr) on entry. The youngest solo pilot has been Cody A. Locke in a Cessna 150 aircraft near Mexicali, Mexico on 24 Feb 1983, when aged 9 years 316 days. The wholly untutored James A. Stoodley aged 14 years 5 months took his 13 year old brother John on a 29 minute joy ride in an unattended US Piper Cub trainer aircraft near Ludgershall, Wiltshire in December 1942.

The world's oldest pilot is Ed McCarty (b. 18 Sept 1885) of Kimberly, Idaho, USA, who in 1979 was flying his rebuilt 30-year-old Ercoupe aged 94. The oldest British pilot is Air Commodore Harold 'Daddy' Probyn CB, CBE, DSO (b. 8 Dec 1891), who first flew with the RFC in 1916 and was flying in Kenya on his 92nd birthday 67 years later in 1983.

Most flying hours

Max Conrad (1903–79) (USA) between 1928 and mid-1974 totalled 52,929 hr 40 min logged flight—more than 6 years airborne. He completed 150 trans-Atlantic crossings in light aircraft. The record as a supersonic passenger is by Mr Fred Finn who made his 476th Concorde crossing in June 1984.

Most take-offs and landings from airports

Al Yates and Bob Phoenix of Texas, USA made 193 take-offs and daylight landings at unduplicated airfields in 14 hr 57 min in a Piper Seminole, on 15 June 1979.

E. K. Coventry (pilot) and D. Bullen (navigator) made full stop landings in a Piper Arrow in all England's 45 counties between dawn and dusk on 24 July 1984.

Human-powered flight

The world distance record for human powered flight was set on 12 June 1979 by Dr Paul MacCready's man powered aircraft *Gossamer Albatross*, piloted and pedalled by Bryan Allen. The *Albatross* took off from Folkestone at 05.51 hrs and landed 22.26 miles *35,82 km* distant at Cap Gris Nez, France at 08.40 hrs. The duration was 2 hr 49 min, and this achievement won the £100,000 prize offered by Henry Kremer for the first man-powered crossing of the English Channel. The 70 lb *31,75 kg* Gossamer Condor (96 ft *29,26 m* wing-span) designed by Dr Paul MacCready, flew the figure-of-8 course between pylons 880 yd *804,6 m* apart, powered by the 9¾ stone *61,2 kg* Bryan Allen at Shafter Airport, California on 23 Aug 1977 to win the £50,000 Kremer prize. The flight lasted 7 min 27.5 sec.

MODEL AIRCRAFT

Altitude, speed and duration

Maynard L. Hill (US) flying radio-controlled models established the World record for altitude of 26,929 ft *8208 m* on 6 Sept 1970 and on 4 July 1983 set a closed circuit distance record of 1231 miles *765 km*. The free flight speed record is 213.70 mph *343,92 km/h* by V. Goukoune and V. Myakinin (both USSR) with a radio-controlled model at Klementyeva, USSR, on 21 Sept 1971. The record duration flight is one of 32 hr 7 min 40 sec by Eduard Svoboda (Czechoslovakia), flying a radio controlled glider on 23–24 Aug 1980. An indoor model powered by a rubber motor designed by J. Richmond (USA) set a duration record of 52 min 14 sec on 31 Aug 1979.

Cross-channel

The first cross-channel model helicopter flight was achieved by an 11 lb *5,00 kg* model Bell 212 radio-controlled by Dieter Zeigler for 32 miles *52 km* between Ashford, Kent and Ambleteuse, France on 17 July 1974.

Smallest

The smallest model aircraft to fly is one weighing 0.004 oz *0,1 g* powered by attaching a horsefly and designed by the insectonaut Don Emmick of Seattle, Washington, USA on 24 July 1979. One flew for 5 minutes at Kirkland, Washington, USA.

Paper aircraft

The flight duration record for a paper aircraft is 16.89 sec by Ken Blackburn in the Reynolds Coliseum, North Carolina State University, USA on 29 Nov 1983. The indoor record with a 12 ft *3,65 m* ceiling is 1 min 33 sec set in the Fuji TV studios, Tōkyō, Japan on 21 Sept 1980. A paper plane was reported and witnessed to have flown 1¼ miles *2,0 km* by 'Chick' C. O. Reinhart from a 10th storey office window at 60 Beaver Street, New York City across the East River to Brooklyn in August 1933, helped by a thermal from a coffee-roasting plant. An indoor distance of 166 ft 4 in *50,09 m* was recorded by James D. Zongker at the Kansas Coliseum, Kansas, USA, on 28 Mar 1985.

5. POWER PRODUCERS

Steam engines

The oldest steam engine in working order is the 1812 Boulton & Watt 26 hp 42 in *1066 mm* bore beam engine on the Kennet & Avon Canal at Great Bedwyn, Wiltshire. It was restored by the Crofton Society in 1971 and still runs periodically.

The largest single cylinder steam engine ever built was that designed by Matthew Loam of Cornwall and made by the Hayle Foundry Co in 1849 for installation for land draining at Haarlem Netherlands. The cylinder was 12 ft *3,65 m* in diameter such that each stroke also of 12 ft *3,65 m* lifted 13,440 gallons *61 096 l* or 60 tons of water.

The most efficient steam engine recorded was Taylor's engine built by Michael Loam for the United Mines, Gwennap, Cornwall in 1840. It registered only 1.7 lb of coal per horsepower per hour.

Earliest atomic pile

The world's first atomic pile was built in a disused squash court at Stagg Field, University of Chicago, Illinois, USA. It went 'critical' at 3.25 pm on 2 Dec 1942.

Power plant Largest *World*

Currently, the world's most powerful installed power station is the Grand Coulee, Washington State, USA with 9.7 million kilowatt hours (ultimately 10,080 MW) which began operating in 1942.

The $11 billion Itaipu power station on the Paranā river by the Brazil-Paraguay border began generating power formally on 25 Oct 1984 and will by 1988/89 attain 12,600,000 kW from 18 turbines. Construction began in 1975 with a force reaching 28,000 workers. A 20,000 MW power station project on the Tunguska River, USSR was announced in February 1982.

The world's largest coal-fired power complex at Ekibastuz, Kazakhstan, USSR began generating in May 1982.

Great Britain

The power station with the greatest installed capacity in Great Britain is Drax, North Yorkshire, with 5 of its 6 660 MW sets yielding 3300 MW in mid 1985. The sixth set will be operational in early 1986. A 3300 MW oil-fired installation is under construction on the Isle of Grain, Kent.

The largest hydroelectric plant in the UK is the North of Scotland Hydroelectricity Board's Power Station at Loch Sloy, Strathclyde. The installed capacity of this station is 130 MW. The Ben Cruachan Pumped Storage scheme was opened on 15 Oct 1965 at Loch Awe, Strathclyde, Scotland. It has a capacity of 400 MW and cost £24,000,000. The 1880 MW underground pumped storage scheme at Dinorwig, Gwynedd is the largest built in Europe with a head of 1739 ft *530 m* and a capacity of 13,770 ft³/sec *390 m³/sec*. The £425 million plant was completed in 1984 and the capacity is 1681 MW.

Nuclear power station *Largest*

The world's largest atomic power station with 4 × 950 MW reactors giving 3800 MW is the station in Leningrad, USSR. Work began in 1974 and it attained full operation in October 1982.

Nuclear reactor *Largest*

The largest single nuclear reactor in the world is the 1500 MW reactor at the Ignalina station, Lithuania, USSR, put on full power in Jan 1984. The largest in the US is the 1255 MW reactor installed at Grand Gulf I, Port Gibson, Mississippi in 1983.

Fusion power

Tokamak-7, the prototype thermonuclear reactor was declared in January 1982 by USSR academician Velikhov to be operating 'reliably for months on end'. The world's largest experimental station is the Joint European Torus at Culham, Oxfordshire built in 1979–84.

Solar power plant

The largest solar furnace in the world is the $141 million 10 megawatt 'Solar I', 12 miles *19,3 km* southeast of Barstow, California first tested in April 1982. It comprises 1818 mirrors in concentric circles focused on a boiler atop a 255 ft *77,7 m* high tower. Sunlight from 222 heliostats is concentrated on a target 114 ft *34,7 m* up in

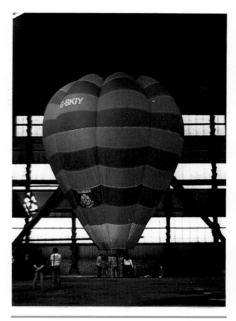

Above and below In March 1985, at Chatham Dockyard, publican Brian Horton of Rochester, lifted and kept aloft this hot air balloon for almost exactly a minute by blowing flame from his mouth.

the power tower. The $30 million thermal solar energy system at Pakerland Packing Co, Bellevue Plant, Green Bay, Wisconsin, USA completed in Jan 1984 comprises 9750 4 × 8 ft *1,21 × 2,43 m* collectors covering 7.16 acres *or 28 985 m²*. It will yield up to 8000 million BTU's a month.

Tidal power station

The world's first major tidal power station is the *Usine marèmotrice de la Rance*, officially opened on 26 Nov 1966 at the Rance estuary in the Golfe de St Malo, Brittany, France. It was built in five years at a cost of 420,000,000 francs (*£34,685,000*), and has a net annual output of 544,000,000 kWh. The 880 yd *804 m* barrage contains 24 turbo alternators. The $1000 million (*£540 million*) Passamaquoddy project for the Bay of Fundy in Maine, USA, and New Brunswick, Canada, remains a project. A $46 million (then £25.5 million) pilot Annapolis River project for the Bay of Fundy was begun in 1981.

Boiler Largest
The largest boilers ever designed are those ordered in the United States from the Babcock & Wilcox Company (USA) with a capacity of 1330 MW so involving the evaporation of 9,330,000 lb *4 232 000 kg* of steam per hour. The largest boilers now being installed in the United Kingdom are the five 660 MW units for the Drax Power Station (see p. 139) designed and constructed by Babcock & Wilcox Ltd.

Generator Largest
Generators in the 2,000,000 kW (or 2000 MW) range are now in the planning stages both in the UK and the USA. The largest now operational is a turbo-generator of 1500 MW being installed at the Ignalina Atomic Power Station in Lithuania (see above).

Turbines Largest
The largest hydraulic turbines are those rated at 815,000 kW (equivalent to 1.1 million hp), 32 ft *9,7 m* in diameter with a 401 ton *407 tonnes* runner and a 312½ ton *317,5 tonnes* shaft installed by Allis-Chalmers at the Grand Coulee 'Third Powerplant', Washington, USA.

Pump
The world's largest reversible pump-turbine is that made by Allis-Chalmers for the Bath County project, Virginia, USA. It has a maximum rating of 457 MW as a turbine and maximum operating head of 393 m *1289 ft*. The impeller/runner diameter is 6349 mm *20 ft 9 in* with a synchronous speed of 257.1 rpm.

Longest Lasting Battery
The zinc foil and sulfur dry pile batteries made by Watlin and Hill of London in 1840 have powered ceaseless tintinnabulation inside a bell jar at the Clarendon Laboratory, Oxford since 1840.

Gasworks Largest
The flow of natural gas from the North Sea is diminishing the manufacture of gas by the carbonisation of coal and the reforming process using petroleum derivatives. Britain's largest ever gasworks, 300 acres *120 ha*, were at Beckton, Newham, Greater London. Currently, the largest gasworks in the UK are the Breakwater Works at Oreston, Plymouth, Devon which opened in 1966–7 and cover an area of 19 acres *7,6 ha*. They convert complex hydrocarbons into methane and produce 50 million ft³ *1 415 850 m³* per day.

Biggest black-out
The greatest power failure in history struck seven north-eastern US States and Ontario, Canada, on 9–10 Nov 1965. About 30,000,000 people in 80,000 miles² *207 200 km²* were plunged into darkness. Only two were killed. In New York City the power failed at 5.27 pm and was not fully restored for 13½ hr. The total consequential losses in the 52 min New York City power failure of 13 July 1977 including looting was put at $1 billion (then £580 million).

Windmill Earliest
The earliest recorded windmills are those used for grinding corn in Iran (Persia) in the 7th century AD.

The earliest date attributed to a windmill in England is 1185 for one at Weedley, near Hull, Humberside. The oldest Dutch mill is the towermill at Zeddam, Gelderland built in c. 1450. The oldest working mill in England is the post-mill at Outwood, Surrey, built in 1665, though the Ivinghoe Mill in Pitstone Green Farm, Buckinghamshire, dating from 1627, has

been restored. The postmill in North Ronaldsay, Orkney Islands operated until 1905.

Windmill *Largest conventional*
The largest Dutch windmill is the Dijkpolder in Maasland built in 1718. The sails measure 95¾ ft *29 m* from tip to tip. The tallest windmill in the Netherlands is De Walvisch in Schiedam built to a height of 108 ft *33 m* in 1794. The tallest windmill still standing in Britain is the 9 storey Sutton mill, Norfolk built in 1853 which before being struck by lightning in 1941 had sails 73 ft *22,2 m* in diameter with 216 shutters.

Windmill Largest
The world's most powerful wind generator is the 3000 kW 150 m *492 ft* tall turbine, built by Grosse Wind energie–Anlage which was set up in 1982 on the Friesian coast of West Germany. A £5.6 million 3000 kW aerogenerator with 60 m *196 ft 10 in* blades on Burgar Hill, Evie, Orkney is planned for completion by Taylor Woodrow in 1985. It should yield 9 million kW/hours per annum. The $14.2 million GEC MOD-5A installation on the North shore of Oahu, Hawaii, USA will produce 7300 kW when the wind reaches 32 mph *51,5 km/h* with 400 ft *122 m* rotors. Installation started in March 1984.

Water Mills
There has been a water-powered corn-mill at Priston Mill near Bath, Avon since pre-Norman times. The earliest record is dated AD 931.

The tallest windmill in Great Britain, the nine-storey Sutton Mill in Norfolk. It had sails 73 ft *22.2 m* in diameter before being struck by lightning in 1941. (Dr Alan Beaumont)

Blast furnace Largest
The world's largest blast furnace is one with an inner volume of 5070 m³ *179,040 ft³* and a 14,8 m *48 ft 6¼ in* diameter hearth at the Oita Works, Kyūshū, Japan completed in October 1976 with an annual capacity of 4,380,000 tons *4 451 500 tonnes*.

Cat cracker Largest
The world's largest catalyst cracker is the Exxon Co's Bayway Refinery plant at Linden, New Jersey, USA with a fresh feed rate of 5,040,000 US gal *19 077 000 litres* per day.

Conveyor belt Longest
The world's longest single flight conveyor belt is one of 18 miles *29 km* in Western Australia by Cable Belt Ltd of Camberley, Surrey. The longest installation in Great Britain is also by Cable Belt and of 5½ miles *8,9 km* underground at Longannet Power Station, Fife, Scotland. The world's longest multi-flight conveyor is one of 100 km *62 miles* between the phosphate mine near Bucraa and the port of El Aaiun, Morocco, built by Krupps and completed in 1972. It has 11 flights of between 9 and 11 km *5.6–6.8 miles* and was driven at 4,5 m/sec *10.06 mph* but has been closed down due to Polisario Front guerrilla activity.

The longest conveyor belt in the world is the Compagnie Minière de l'Ogooué or COMILOG installation built in 1959–62 for the Moanda manganese mine in Gabon which extends 76 km *47.2 miles*. It has 858 towers and 2800 buckets with 155 km *96.3 miles* of wire rope running over 6000 idler pulleys.

Crane Most Powerful *World*
The world's most powerful cranes are those aboard the semi-submersible vessel *Balder* (105,000 tonnes displacement) operated by Heerema Marine Contractors, Switzerland. Each has one 3000 and one 2000 tonne capacity crane which, working in tandem, could raise a 4000 tonne piece. The *Balder* set a record with a 3412 tonne lift in Aug 1983 and in March 1984 was refitted to raise her capacity to close to 6000 tonnes. The American company Brown & Root announced the building of a 140 000 tonne crane-ship with lifting capacity of 6500 tonnes in December 1983.

Gantry crane Most powerful
The 92.3 ft *28,14 m* wide Rahco (R. A. Hanson Disc. Ltd) gantry crane at the Grand Coulee Dam Third Powerplant was tested to lift a load of 2232 long tons *2268 tonnes* in 1975. It lowered a 3,944,000 lb *1789 tonne* generator rotor with an accuracy of $\frac{1}{32}$ in *0,8 mm*.

Crane Tallest mobile
The tallest mobile crane in the world is the 810 tonnes Rosenkranz K10001 with a lifting capacity of 1000 tonnes *984 tons*, a combined boom and jib height of 202 m *663 ft*. It is carried on 10 trucks each limited to 75 ft 8 in *23,06 m* and an axle weight of 118 tonnes *116 tons*. It can lift 30 tonnes *29.5 tons* to a height of 160 m *525 ft*.

Dragline Largest *World*
The Ural Engineering Works at Ordzhonikidze, USSR, completed in March 1962, has a dragline known as the ES-25(100) with a boom of 100 m *328 ft* and a bucket with a capacity of 31.5 yd³ *24 m³*. The world's largest walking dragline is the Bucyrus-Erie 4250W with an all-up weight of 12,000 tons *12 192 tonnes* and a bucket capacity of 220 yd³ *168 m³* on a 310 ft *94,4 m* boom. This machine, the world's largest mobile land

Island, New York in 1896. The first installation in Britain was at Harrods, Knightsbridge, London in November 1898. The escalators on the Leningrad Underground, USSR at Lenin Square have 729 steps and a vertical rise of 59,68 m *195 ft 9½ in.* The longest escalators in Britain are the four in the Tyne Tunnel, Tyne and Wear installed in 1951. They measure 192 ft 8 in *58,7 m* between combs with a vertical lift of 85 ft *25,9 m* and a step speed of up to 1.7 mph *2,7 km/h.* The world's longest 'moving sidewalks' are those installed in 1970 in the Neue Messe Centre, Dusseldorf, W. Germany which measure 225 m *738 ft* between comb plates. The longest in Great Britain is the 375 ft *114,3 m* long Dunlop Starglide at London Airport Terminal 3 installed in March-May 1970.

Excavator Largest

The world's largest excavator is the 13,000 tonne bucket wheel excavator being assembled at the open cast lignite-mine of Hambach, W. Germany with a rating of 200 000 m³ *260,000 yd³* per 20 hr working day. It is 210 m *690 ft* in length and 82 m *269 ft* tall. The wheel is 67,88 m *222 ft* in circumference with 5 m³ *6.5 yd³* buckets.

Forging Largest

The largest forging on record is one of a 450,600 lb *204,4 tonnes* 55 ft *16,76 m* long gen-

The greatest lift on any construction site was achieved by Fluor Corporation at Cilacap, Java, Indonesia in February 1982 when a 270 ft *82,3 m* high crude column 31 ft *9,44 m* in diameter weighing 1,169 short tons *1060 tonnes* was erected. The lift required twin 600 ton guy derrick cranes assisted by a tailing crane. (See opposite, column 3)

machine, is now operating on the Central Ohio Coal Company's Muskingum site in Ohio, USA.

Great Britain

The largest dragline excavator in Britain is 'Big Geordie', the Bucyrus-Erie 1550W 6250 gross hp, weighing 3000 tons *3048 tonnes* with a forward mast 160 ft *48,7 m* high. On open-cast coal workings at Butterwell, Northumberland in September 1975, it proved able to strip 100 tons *101 tonnes* of overburden in 65 sec with its 65 yd³ *49,7 m³* bucket on a 265 ft *80,7 m* boom. It is owned by Derek Crouch (Contractors) Ltd of Peterborough, Cambridgeshire.

Escalator Longest

The term was registered in the US on 28 May 1900 but the earliest 'Inclined Escalator' was installed by Jesse W. Reno on the pier at Coney

Above and left The outdoor escalator at the Ocean Park, Hong Kong has an overall length of 745 ft *227 m* and a total vertical rise of 377 ft *115 m* above sea level. Built by Otis, the escalator can carry 4000 people in either direction.

erator shaft for Japan, forged by the Bethlehem Steel Corp, Pennsylvania in October 1973.

Fork lift truck *Largest World*
Kalmar LMV of Sweden manufactured in 1985 ten counterbalanced fork lift trucks capable of lifting loads up to 80 tonnes *78.7 tons* at a load centre of 2300 mm *90.5 in*. They were built to handle the large diameter pipeline in the Libyan Great Man-made River Project.

Lathe *Largest*
The world's largest lathe is the 126 ft *38,4 m* long 416,2 tonne giant lathe built by Waldrich Siegen of Germany in 1973 for the South African Electricity Supply Commission at Rosherville. It has a capacity for 300 tonne work pieces and a swing-over bed of 5 m *16 ft 5 in* in diameter.

Greatest lift
The heaviest lifting operation in engineering history was the 41,000 short ton (36,607 long tons *37 194 tonnes*) roof of the Velodrome in Montreal, Canada in 1975. It was raised by jacks some 4 in *10 cm* to strike its centering.

Oldest machinery *World*
The earliest machinery still in use is the *dâlu*—a water-raising instrument known to have been in use in the Sumerian civilization which originated *c.* 3500 BC in Lower Iraq thus even earlier than the *Saqiyas* on the Nile.

Great Britain
The oldest piece of machinery (excluding clocks) operating in the United Kingdom is the snuff mill driven by a water wheel at Messrs Wilson & Co's Sharrow Mill in Sheffield, South Yorkshire. It is known to have been operating in 1797 and more probably since 1730.

Nut *Largest*
The largest nuts ever made weigh 5,3 tonnes *104.3 cwt* each and have an outside diameter of 52 in *132 cm* and a 25 in *63,5 cm* thread. Known as 'Pilgrim Nuts', they are manufactured by Doncasters Moorside Ltd of Oldham, Lancashire for use on the columns of a large forging press.

Oil tank *Largest*
The largest oil tanks ever constructed are the five Aramco 1½ million barrel storage tanks at Ju'aymah, Saudi Arabia. The tanks are 72 ft *21,94 m* tall with a diameter of 386 ft *117,6 m* and were completed in March 1980.

Passenger lift *Fastest World*
The fastest domestic passenger lifts in the world are the express lifts to the 60th floor of the 240 m *787.4 ft* tall 'Sunshine 60' building, Ikebukuro, Tōkyō, Japan completed 5 Apr 1978. They were built by Mitsubishi Corp and operate at a speed of 2000 ft/min *609,6 m/min* or 22.72 mph *36,56 km/h*. Much higher speeds are achieved in the winding cages of mine shafts. A hoisting shaft 6800 ft *2072 m* deep, owned by Western Deep Levels Ltd in South Africa, winds at speeds of up to 40.9 mph *65,8 km/h* (3595 ft *1095 m* per min). Otitis-media (popping of the

One of the fork lift trucks, the largest in the world, manufactured by Kalmar LMV of Sweden showing its paces and lifting the 80 tonne proof load. (See left, column 1)

ears) presents problems much above even 10 mph *16 km/h*.

Great Britain
The longest lift in the United Kingdom is one 930 ft long inside the B.B.C. T.V. tower at Bilsdale, West Moor, North Yorkshire, built by J. L. Eve Construction Co Ltd. It runs at 130 ft/min *39,6 m/min*. The longest fast lifts are the two 15-passenger cars in the Post Office Tower, Maple Street, London W1 which travel 540 ft *164 m* at up to 1000 ft/min *304 m/min*.

Michael Bracey established an involuntary duration record when trapped in a lift for 59 hr 55 min in Newcastle-upon-Tyne, England on 29 Feb 1980.

Pipelines *Oil*
The world's earliest pipeline of 2 in *5 cm* cast iron laid at Oil Creek, Pennsylvania, USA in 1863 was torn up by trade unionists.

The longest crude oil pipeline in the world is the Interprovincial Pipe Line Company's installation from Edmonton, Alberta, Canada to Buffalo, New York State, USA, a distance of 1775 miles *2856 km*. Along the length of the pipe 13 pumping stations maintain a flow of 6,900,000 gal *31 367 145 litres* of oil per day. The eventual length of the Trans-Siberian Pipeline will be 2319 miles *3732 km*, running from Tuimazy through Omsk and Novosibirsk to Irkutsk. The first 30 mile *48 km* section was opened in July 1957.

Submarine pipelines

The world's longest submarine pipeline is that of 425 km *264 miles* for natural gas from the Union Oil Platform to Rayong, Thailand opened on 12 Sept 1981. The longest North Sea pipeline is the Ekofisk–Emden line stretching 260 miles *418 km* and completed in July 1975. The deepest North Sea pipeline is that from the Cormorant Field to Firths Voe, Shetland at 530 ft *162 m*.

Natural gas

The longest natural gas pipeline in the world is the Trans-Canada Pipeline which by 1974 had 5654 miles *9099 km* of pipe up to 42 in *106,6 cm* in diameter. The Tyumen–Chelyabinsk–Moscow–Brandenburg gasline stretches 4330 km *2690 miles*.

The large calibre Urengoi-Uzhgorod line to Western Europe began in November 1982 stretches 4451 km *2765 miles* and was completed on 25 July 1983. It has a capacity of 32,000 million m³ *42,000 million yd³* per annum.

Water

The world's longest water pipeline runs a distance of 350 miles *563 km* to the Kalgoorlie gold fields from near Perth in Western Australia. Engineered in 1903, the system has since been extended five-fold by branches.

Pipeline Most expensive

The world's most expensive pipeline is the Alaska pipeline running 798 miles *1284 km* from Prudhoe Bay to Valdez. By completion of the first phase in 1977 it had cost at least $6000 million (£3250 million). The pipe is 48 in *1,21 m* diameter and will eventually carry up to 2 million barrels of crude oil per day.

Press Largest

The world's two most powerful production machines are forging presses in the USA. The Loewy closed-die forging press, in a plant leased from the US Air Force by the Wyman-Gordon Company at North Grafton, Massachusetts, USA weighs 9469 tons *9620 tonnes* and stands 114 ft 2 in *34,79 m* high, of which 66 ft *20,1 m* is sunk below the operating floor. It has a rated capacity of 44,600 tons *45 315 tonnes*, and went into operation in October 1955. The other similar press is at the plant of the Aluminium Company of America at Cleveland, Ohio. There has been a report of a press in the USSR with a capacity of 75 000 tonnes *73,800 tons* at Novo Kramatorsk. The Béché and Grohs counter-blow forging hammer, manufactured in W. Germany are rated at 60,000 tonnes/*tons*. The most powerful press in Great Britain is the closed-die forging and extruding press installed in 1967 at the Cameron Iron Works, Livingston, Lothian. The press is 92 ft *28 m* tall (27 ft *8,2 m* below ground) and exerts a force of 30,000 tons *30 481 tonnes*.

Printer Fastest

The world's fastest printer is the Radiation Inc electro-sensitive system at the Lawrence Radiation Laboratory, Livermore, California. High speed recording of up to 30,000 lines each containing 120 alphanumeric characters per minute is attained by controlling electronic pulses through chemically impregnated recording paper which is rapidly moving under closely spaced fixed styli. It can thus print the wordage of the whole Bible (773,692 words) in 65 sec—3333 times as fast as the world's fastest typist.

Radar installation *Largest*

The largest of the three installations in the US Ballistic Missile Early Warning System (BMEWS) is that near Thule, in Kalaatdlit Nunaat, 931 miles *1498 km* from the North Pole, completed in 1960 at a cost of $500,000,000 (*then £178.5 million*). Its sister stations are one at Cape Clear, Alaska, USA, completed in 1961, and a $115,000,000 (*then £41.07 million*) installation at Fylingdales Moor, North Yorkshire, completed in June 1963. The largest scientific radar installation is the 21 acre *84 000 m²* ground array at Jicamarca, Peru.

Ropeway or telepherique Highest *World*

The highest and longest aerial ropeway in the world is the Teleférico Mérida (Mérida téléphérique) in Venezuela, from Mérida City (5379 ft *1639,5 m*) to the summit of Pico Espejo (15,629 ft *4763,7 m*), a rise of 10,250 ft *3124 m*. The ropeway is in four sections, involving 3 car changes in the 8 mile ascent in 1 hr. The fourth span is 10,070 ft *3069 m* in length. The two cars work on the pendulum system—the carrier rope is locked and the cars are hauled by means of three pull ropes powered by a 230 hp *233 cv* motor. They have a maximum capacity of 45 persons and travel at 32 ft *9,7 m* per sec (21.8 mph *35,08 km/h*). The longest single span ropeway is the 13,500 ft *4114 m* span from the Coachella Valley to Mt San Jacinto (10,821 ft *3298 m*), California, USA, inaugurated on 12 Sept 1963.

Great Britain

Britain's longest cabin lift is that at Llandudno, Gwynedd, opened in June 1969. It has 42 cabins with a capacity of 1000 people per hour and is 5320 ft *1621 m* in length.

Transformer Largest

The world's largest single phase transformers are rated at 1,500,000 kVA of which eight are in service with the American Electric Power Service Corporation. Of these five stepdown from 765 to 345 kV. Britain's largest transformers are those rated at 1,000,000 kVA 400/275 kV built by Hackbridge & Hewittic Co Ltd, Walton-on-Thames, Surrey first commissioned for the CEGB in October 1968.

Transmission lines *Longest*

The longest span between pylons of any power line in the world is that across the Sogne Fjord, Norway, between Rabnaberg and Fatlaberg. Supplied in 1955 by the Whitecross Co Ltd of Warrington, Cheshire, and projected and erected by A. S. Betonmast of Oslo as part of the high-tension power cable from Refsdal power station at Vik, it has a span of 16,040 ft *4888 m* and a weight of 12 tons/*tonnes*. In 1967 two further high tensile steel/aluminium lines 16,006 ft *4878 m* long, and weighing 33 tons *33,5 tonnes*, manufactured by Whitecross and BICC were erected here. The longest in Britain are the 5310 ft *1618 m* lines built by J. L. Eve Co across the Severn with main towers each 488 ft *148 m* high.

Highest

The world's highest are those across the Straits of Messina, with towers of 675 ft *205 m* (Sicily side) and 735 ft *224 m* (Calabria) and 11,900 ft *3627 m* apart. The highest lines in Britain are those made by BICC at West Thurrock, Essex, which cross the Thames estuary suspended from 630 ft *192 m* tall towers at a minimum height of 250 ft *76 m*, with a 130 ton *132 tonnes* breaking load. They are 4500 ft *1371 m* in length.

Highest voltages

The highest voltages now carried are 1,330,000 volts 1224 miles *1970 km* on the DC Pacific Inter-tie in the United States. The Ekibastuz DC transmission lines in Kazakhstan, USSR are planned to be 2400 km *1490 miles* long with 1,500,000 volt capacity.

Valve Largest

The world's largest valve is the 32 ft *9,75 m* diameter, 170 ton/*tonne* butterfly valve designed by Boving & Co Ltd of London for use at the Arnold Airforce Base engine test facility in Tennessee, USA.

Wire ropes *Longest, Strongest and Heaviest*

The longest wire ropes in the world are the 4 made at British Ropes Ltd, Wallsend, Tyneside each measuring 24 000 m *14.9 miles*. The ropes are 35 mm *1.3 in* in diameter, weigh 108,5 tonnes *106.8 tons* each and were ordered by the CEGB for use in the construction of the 2000 MW cross-Channel power cable. The thickest ever made are spliced crane strops from wire ropes 28,2 cm *11¼ in* thick made of 2392 individual wires in March 1979 by British Ropes Ltd of Doncaster at Willington Quay, Tyneside, designed to lift loads of up to 3000 tons/*tonnes*. The heaviest ever wire ropes (4 in number) are each of 130 tonnes/*tons*, made for the twin shaft system of Western Deep Levels Gold Mine, South Africa, by Haggie Rand Ltd of Johannesburg.

TIME PIECES

Clock *Oldest*

The earliest mechanical clock, that is one with an escapement, was completed in China in AD 725 by I Hsing and Liang Lingtsan.

The oldest surviving working clock in the world is the faceless clock dating from 1386, or possibly earlier, at Salisbury Cathedral, Wiltshire, which was restored in 1956 having struck the hours for 498 years and ticked more than 500 million times. Earlier dates, ranging back to c. 1335, have been attributed to the weight-driven clock in Wells Cathedral, Somerset, but only the iron frame is original. A model of Giovanni de Dondi's heptagonal astronomical clock of 1348–64 was completed in 1962.

Clock Largest *World*

The world's most massive clock is the Astronomical Clock in the Cathedral of St Pierre, Beauvais, France, constructed between 1865 and 1868. It contains 90,000 parts and measures 40 ft *12,1 m* high, 20 ft *6,09 m* wide and 9 ft *2,7 m* deep. The Su Sung clock, built in China at K'aifeng in 1088–92, had a 20 ton *20,3 tonnes* bronze armillary sphere for 1½ tons, *1,52 tonnes* of water. It was removed to Peking in 1126 and was last known to be working in its 40 ft *12,1 m* high tower in 1136.

The world's largest clock face is that of the floral clock at Tokachigaoka Park, Otofuke, Hokkaido, Japan, completed on 1 Aug 1982 with a diameter of 18 m *59 ft 0⅝ in*.

Public

The largest four-faced clock in the world is that on the building of the Allen-Bradley Company of Milwaukee, Wisconsin, USA. Each face has a diameter of 40 ft 3½ in *12,28 m* with a minute hand 20 ft *6,09 m* in overall length. The tallest four-faced clock in the world is that of the Williamsburgh Savings Bank in Brooklyn, New York City, NY, USA. It is 430 ft *131 m* above street level.

Great Britain

The largest clock in the United Kingdom is that on the Royal Liver Building (built 1908–11) with dials 25 ft *7,62 m* in diameter and the 4 minute hands each 14 ft *4,26 m* long. The mechanism and dials weigh 22 tons and are 220 ft *67 m* above street level.

Longest stoppage 'Big Ben'

The longest stoppage of the clock in the House of Commons clock tower, London since the first tick on 31 May 1859 has been 13 days from noon 4 Apr to noon 17 Apr 1977. In 1945 a host of starlings slowed the minute hand by 5 min.

Clock Most accurate

The most accurate and complicated clockwork in the world is the Olsen clock, installed in the Copenhagen Town Hall, Denmark. The clock, which has more than 14,000 units, took 10 years to make and the mechanism of the clock functions in 570,000 different ways. The celestial pole motion of the clock will take 25,753 years to complete a full circle and is the slowest moving designed mechanism in the world. The clock is accurate to 0.5 sec in 300 years—50 times more accurate than the previous record.

Clock Most expensive

The highest price paid for any English-made clock is £500,000 for a Thomas Tompion (1639–1713) bracket clock bought by the British Museum by private treaty on 15 July 1982.

Pendulum longest

The longest pendulum in the world is 22,5 m *73 ft 9¾ in* on the water-mill clock installed by Hattori Tokeiten Co. in the Shinjuku NS Building, Tokyo, Japan in 1983.

Watch Oldest

The oldest watch (portable clockwork timekeeper) is one made of iron by Peter Henlein in Nürnberg (Nüremberg), Bavaria, Germany, in *c.* 1504. The earliest wrist watches were those of Jacquet-Droz and Leschot of Geneva, Switzerland, dating from 1790.

Watch Smallest

The smallest watches in the world are produced by Jaeger Le Coultre of Switzerland. Equipped with a 15-jewelled movement they measure just over ½ in *1,2 cm* long and 1/16 in *0,476 cm* in width. The movement, with its case, weighs under 0,25 oz *7 g*.

Watch Thinnest

The world's thinnest wrist watch is the Swiss Concord Delirium IV. It measures 0,98 mm *0.0385 in* thick and retailed for $16,000 *£6800* (including 18 carat gold strap) in June 1980.

Watch Most expensive

Excluding watches with jewelled cases, the most expensive standard men's pocket watch is the Swiss *Grande Complication* by Audemars-Piguet which retailed for £72,000 in January 1985. The *Kallista* watch with 130 carats of precious stones by Vacheron et Constantin of Geneva was valued in Apr 1981 at $5 million (*then £2,272,000*). The record price for an antique watch is $166,300 (*then £75,600*) paid to Capt. Peter Belin USN by L. C. Mannheimer of Zurich at Sotheby Parke Bernet, New York on 29 Nov 1979 for a gold studded case watch of *c.* 1810 by William Anthony of London.

Time measurer Most accurate *World*

The most accurate time-keeping devices are the twin atomic hydrogen masers installed in 1964 in the US Naval Research Laboratory, Washington, DC. They are based on the frequency of the hydrogen atom's transition period of 1,420,450,751,694 cycles/sec. This enables an accuracy to within 1 sec in 1,700,000 years.

Sundial Largest

The world's largest sundial is one with a 25 ft *7,62 m* gnomon and a readable shadow of 125 ft *38,1 m* installed by Walter R. T. Witschey at the Science Museum of Virginia at Richmond, Va on 12 Mar–3 May 1981. The sun's shadow travels 7 in *17,7 cm* per minute at the equinox.

A sundial with a diameter of 26 ft *7,92 m* was built at Hilton Head Island, South Carolina, USA in Aug 1983.

COMPUTERS

A geared calculator date *c.* 80 BC was found in the sea by Antikythera Island off northwest Crete.

The earliest programmable electronic computer was the 1500 valve Colossus formulated by Prof Max H. A. Newman FRS (b. 1897) and built by T. H. Flowers MBE. It was run in December 1943 at Bletchley Park, Buckinghamshire to break the German coding machine Enigma. It arose from the concept published in 1936 by Dr Alan Mathison Turing OBE, FRS (1912–54) in his paper *On Computable Numbers with an Application to the Entscheidungsproblem.* Colossus was declassified on 25 Oct 1975. The world's first stored-programme computer was the Manchester University Mark I which incorporated the Williams storage cathode ray tube (pat. 11 Dec 1946). It ran its first programme, written by Prof Tom Kilburn CBE FRS (b. 1921) for 52 min on 21 June 1948.

Computers were greatly advanced by the invention of the point-contact transistor by John Bardeen and Walter Brattain announced in July 1948, and the junction transistor by R. L. Wallace, Morgan Sparks and Dr William Bradford Shockley (b. 1910) in early 1951. The concept of the integrated circuit, which has enabled micro-miniaturization, was first published on 7 May 1952 by Geoffrey W. A. Dummer MBE (b. 1909) in Washington DC. The Microcomputer was achieved in 1969–73 by M. E. Hoff Jr of Intel Corporation with the production of the microprocessor silicon chip '4004'.

The computer planned to be the world's biggest by a factor of 40 is the $50 million NASF (Numerical Aerodynamic Simulation Facility) at NASA's Ames Research Center, Palo Alto, California. The tenders from CDC and Burroughs called for a capacity of 12.8 giga-flops (12,800 million complex calculations per second).

Most powerful and Fastest *World*

The world's most powerful and fastest computer is the CRAY-1, designed by Seymour R. Cray of Cray Research, Inc, Minneapolis, Minnesota USA. The clock period is 12.5 nanoseconds and memory ranges up to 1,048,576 64-bit words, resulting in a capacity of 8,388,608 bytes of main memory. (N.B. a 'byte' is a unit of storage compressing 8 'bits' collectively equivalent to one alphabetic symbol or two numericals.) It attains speeds of 200 million floating point operations per second. With 32 CRAY DD-19 disk storage units, it has a storage capacity of 7.7568×10^{10} bits. The cost of a mid-range system was quoted in mid-1979 as about $8.8 million (*then £4 million*). The most powerful British computer is the International Computer's Distribution Array Processor—the ICL DAP.

Control Data Corporation announced the CYBER Model 205-444 system from Arden Hills, Minnesota, USA on 2 June 1980 which has a memory of 4 million 64-Bit words and cost $16.5 million (*£7 million*) at delivery in January 1981. In a test on 19 Nov 1982 the CYBER model 205-424 achieved 791,860,000 calculations in a second.

The CRAY-1/S system, introduced in 1981, has an additional 8 million words of buffer memory and a storage capacity of 19 gigabytes or 1.55136×10^{11} bits with a system cost of up to $17 million for the maximum configuration.

Megabits

The megabit barrier was broken in February 1984, with the manufacture of a 1024K bit integrated circuit, the size of a drawing pin head and as thin as a human hair, by 4 Japanese companies, Hitachi, NEC, NTT Atsugi Electrical Communications and Toshiba. Toshiba announced that manufacture of an 80 picosecond LSI (large scale integration) chip of gallium arsenide would start in 1985–86.

IBM had announced the first 512K bit 120 nanosecond dynamic access memory chip ⅜ in *9,5 mm* square from Essex Junction, Vermont, USA, on 15 Sept 1983.

The Olsen clock in Copenhagen Town Hall, Denmark is the most accurate clockwork clock in the world—accurate to ½ sec in 3 centuries. *(Alex Hansen)*

CHAPTER NINE

The Business World

1. COMMERCE

The $(US) has in this chapter been converted generally at a fixed mean rate of $1.20 to the £ Sterling for mid-1985 and at the rates relevant to other years.

Oldest industry

The oldest known industry is flint knapping, involving the production of chopping tools and hand axes, dating from 2.4 million years ago. The earliest evidence of trading dates from 28000 BC in Central Europe. Agriculture is often described as 'the oldest industry in the world', whereas in fact there is no evidence yet that it was practised before *c.* 11,000 BC. Horse-trading may, however, date from as early as 30,000 BC.

Oldest company *World*

The oldest company in the world is the Faversham Oyster Fishery Co, referred to in the Faversham Oyster Fishing Act 1930, as existing 'from time immemorial', *i.e.* in English law from before 1189.

Great Britain

The Royal Mint has origins going back to AD 287. The Oxford University Press celebrated a 500th anniversary in 1978 not of itself but of the earliest origin of printing in Oxford in 1478. The Shore Porters' Society of Aberdeen, a haulier, shipping and warehouse partnership, is known to have been established before 4 June 1498. The Whitechapel Bell Foundry of Whitechapel Road, London, E1, has been in business since *c.* 1570. It has through Master Founder Thomas Mears II indirect successions, since 1810, *via* Rudhalls of Gloucester back to 1270. The retail business in Britain with the oldest history is the Oxford ironmonger Gill & Co. of 127–8, High Street founded by Abel Smythe *c.* 1530. R. Durtnell & Sons, builders, of Brasted, Kent, has been run by the same family since 1591. Mr Richard Durtnell is of the 12th generation. The first bill of adventure signed by the English East India Co, was dated 21 Mar 1601.

Greatest assets *World all-time*

The business with the greatest amount in physical assets has been the Bell System, which comprised the American Telephone and Telegraph Company, and its subsidiaries. The Bell System's total assets on the consolidated balance

The Shield of Achilles which made a record price at auction for English silver when sold by the 10th Duke of Northumberland for £484,000 in 1984.

(See page 155) (*Sotheby's, London*)

sheet at the time of its divestiture and break-up into 8 companies on 31 Dec 1983 reached $149,529 million *£106,800 m*. The plant involved included more than 142 million telephones. The number of employees was 1,036,000. The company's market value of $47,989 million (*then £30,960 million*) was held among 3,055,000 share-holders. A total of 20,109 shareholders had attended the Annual Meeting in April 1961, thereby setting a world record.

Currently the largest assets of any corporation are the $63,278,000,000 (*£52 731 million*) of Exxon Corporation, the world's largest oil company, on 1 Jan 1985. They have 150,000 employees. The first company to have assets in excess of $1 billion was the United States Steel Corporation with $1400 million (*then £287.73 million*) at the time of its creation by merger in 1917.

Great Britain

The biggest British manufacturing company is Imperial Chemical Industries plc with assets employed of £8924 million as at 1 Jan 1985. Its staff and payroll averaged 115,600 during the year. The company, which has more than 300 UK and overseas subsidiaries, was formed on 7 Dec 1926 by the merger of four concerns— British Dyestuffs Corporation Ltd; Brunner, Mond & Co Ltd; Nobel Industries Ltd and United Alkali Co Ltd. The first chairman was Sir Alfred Moritz Mond (1868–1930), later the 1st Lord Melchett.

The net assets of The 'Shell' Transport and Trading Company, plc, at 31 Dec 1983 were £7,855,200,000, comprising mainly its 40 per cent share in the net assets of the Royal Dutch/Shell Group of Companies which stood at £19,566 million. Group companies employ 156,000. 'Shell' Transport was formed in 1897 by Marcus Samuel (1853–1927), later the 1st Viscount Bearsted.

Greatest profit and loss

The greatest net profit ever made by any corporation in 12 months is $7647 million (*£4933 million*) by American Telephone and Telegraph Co from 1 Oct 1981 to 30 Sept 1982.

The Argentine petroleum company YPF (Yacimientos Petrolíferos) (Government owned) lost a trading record US $4,643,995,000 in 1983. The greatest loss ever recorded by private enterprise has been $4900 million (*£3500 million*) for the 4th quarter of 1983 by American Telephone & Telegraph Co due to extraordinary charges relating to its divestiture (see above). The projected loss for the National Coal Board in the tax year ending on 31 Mar 1985 was in excess of £2000 million.

Largest employer

The world's largest employer is Indian Railways with 1,600,000 staff in 1984. Europe's largest employer is Britain's National Health Service with 1,011,872 staff in 1983. The increase since 1970 was declared by Ralph Howell MP to be greater than the increase in the whole population.

Greatest sales

The first company to surpass the $1 billion (US) mark in annual sales was the United States Steel Corporation in 1917. Now there are 570 corporations with sales exceeding £1000 million including 272 from the United States. The *Fortune 500 List* of April 1985 is headed by the Exxon Corporation of New York with $90,854,000,000 (*£75,712 million*) for 1984.

The top gross profits in the United Kingdom in *The Times 1000 1982–83* was British Petroleum with £6586 million. The biggest loss maker was Vauxhall Motors with £53,542,000.

Above: The premises in London's Whitechapel Road of the Whitechapel Bell Foundry which has been in business since *c.* 1570. (See page 145) (*Colin Smith*) *Below:* Rajendra Sethia the Indian-born British businessman with personal debts estimated at £140 million. (*A. P. Wire*)

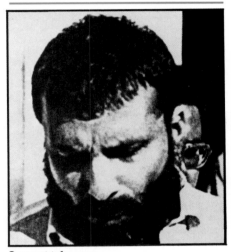

Largest take-over

The largest corporate take-over agreement in commercial history is by Chevron (formerly Standard Oil Co. of California) which on 15 June 1984 bought Gulf Oil Corporation for $13,231,253,000 million (*then £9450 million*). The fees of the financial intermediaries were estimated by *Fortune* to be $63.9 million.

The biggest takeover in Britain took place when BAT Industries won control of Eagle Star Insurance on 18 Jan 1984 with a record bid of £968 million.

Biggest write off

The largest reduction of assets in the history of private enterprise was the $800 million (*£347 million*) write-off of Tristar aircraft development costs announced on 23 Nov 1974.

Greatest Bankruptcy

Rajendra Sethia (b. 1950) was arrested in New Dehli on 2 Mar 1985 on charges including criminal conspiracy and forgery. He had been declared bankrupt by the High Court in London on 18 Jan 1985 when Esal Commodities was stated to be in debt for a record £170 million. His personal debts were estimated at £140 million.

William G. Stern (b. Hungary, 1936) of Golders Green, north London, a US citizen since 1957, who set up Wilstar Group Holding Co in the London property market in 1971 was declared bankrupt for £104,390,248 in February 1979. This figure rose to £142,978,413 by Feb 1983. He was discharged for £500,000 suspended for 2½ years on 28 Mar 1983.

Companies

The number of companies on the register in Great Britain at 31 Dec 1984 was 1,000,791 of which 6589 were public and the balance private companies.

Most directorships

The record for directorships was set in 1961 by Hugh T. Nicholson (1914–1985), formerly senior partner of Harmood Banner & Sons, London who, as a liquidating chartered accountant, became director of all 451 companies of the Jasper group in 1961 and had 7 other directorships.

Accountancy firms *Largest*

The largest firm of accountants worldwide is Arthur Andersen & Co. with 1983 revenues of $1238 million, of which $909 million was in the US. The largest in the UK is Peat Marwick Mitchell & Co. with $1230 million world wide of which £74,300,000 is in the UK.

Advertising agency

The largest advertising agency in 1984, as listed in *Advertising Age*, is Dentsu Incorporated of Japan with estimated billings of $3478.8 million (*£2899 million*). *Advertising Age* ranks Saatchi and Saatchi Compton Ltd No 1 in Britain with 1984 billings of $550,960,000 (*£459,130,000*).

Biggest advertiser

The world's biggest advertiser is Sears, Roebuck and Co, with $925,100,000 (*£771 million*) in 1984 excluding its catalogue.

Aerospace company

The world's largest aerospace company is United Technologies of Hartford, Connecticut with 1984 sales of $16,331,757,000 (*£13,609 million*) and assets of $9,904 million (*£8,253 million*). They have a work force of 205,000. Cessna Aircraft Company of Wichita, Kansas, USA, in the year 1984, had a total sales of $693,586,000 (*then £578 million*). The company has produced more than 175,300 aircraft since Clyde Cessna's first was built in 1911.

Airline *Largest*

The largest airline in the world is the USSR State airline 'Aeroflot', so named since 1932. This was instituted on 9 Feb 1923, with the title of Civil Air Fleet of the Council of Ministers of the USSR, abbreviated to 'Dobrolet'. It operates 1300 aircraft over about 620,000 miles *1,000,000 km* of routes, employs 500,000 people and carried 112 million passengers to 104 countries in 1984. Most luggage is 'self-handled'. Smoking is allowed only after 4 hours flying. The commercial airline carrying the greatest number of passengers (Dec 1984) was United Airlines Inc. of Illinois, USA with 41,273,000 passengers. The company had 47,900 employees and a fleet of 319 jet planes. On 1 Apr 1985 British Airways were operating a fleet of 160 aircraft (including 31 helicopters). Staff employed on airline activities totalled 37,500 and 16 million passengers were carried in 1984/5 on 337,404 miles *543,000 km* of unduplicated routes.

Oldest

The oldest existing national airline is Koninklijke-Luchtvaart-Maatschappij NV (KLM) of the Netherlands, which opened its first scheduled service (Amsterdam–London) on 17 May 1920, having been established on 7 Oct 1919. One of the original constituents of BOAC, Handley-Page Transport Ltd, was founded in May 1919 and merged into Imperial Airways in 1924. Delag (Deutsche Luftschiffahrt AG) was founded at Frankfurt am Main on 16 Nov 1909 and started a scheduled airship service in June

1910. Chalk's International Airline has been flying amphibians between Miami, Florida and the Bahamas since July 1919. Albert 'Pappy' Chalk flew from 1911 to 1975.

Aluminium producer

The world's largest producer of primary aluminium is the Aluminum Company of America (Alcoa) of Pittsburgh, USA with its affiliated companies. The company had an output of 1 919 000 tonnes *1 888 692 tons* in 1983. The Aluminum Company of Canada Ltd owns the largest aluminium smelter in the western world, at Arvida, Quebec, with a capacity of 475,000 short tons *431 000 tonnes* per annum. The parent company Alcan's total sales for the year 1984 were $5467 million (*then £4693 million*).

Art auctioneering

The largest and oldest firm of art auctioneers in the world is the Sotheby Parke Bernet Group of London and New York, founded in 1744. The turnover in 1983–84 was $548 million (*£401 million*). The highest total for any house sale auction was theirs on 18–27 May 1977 at the 6th Earl of Rosebery's home at Mentmore, Buckinghamshire which reached £6,389,933 or *$10.9 million*. The total realized at the art sale at Sotheby Parke, Bernet, New York on 14 May 1985 was $39,286,500 (*then £28,100,000*). This sale of impressionist and modern paintings saw eleven works selling for over $1 million each.

Bank

The International Bank for Reconstruction and Development (founded 27 Dec 1945), the 'World Bank', a United Nations specialised agency, at 1818 H Street NW, Washington, DC, USA, has an authorized share capital of $85 billion (*£70,833 million*). There were 146 members with a subscribed capital of $65,000 million (*£54,167 million*) at 30 June 1984. The International Monetary Fund in Washington, DC, USA has 146 members with total quotas of SDR 89,301.8 million (*$85,677.9 million* or *£81,928.2 million*) at 28 Feb 1985.

The USSR State Bank was claimed by Tass to be the world's largest on 15 Jan 1983 incorporating 'nearly 4500 banking institutions within its single system'. No asset figures were disclosed. The commercial bank with the greatest assets is Citicorp of New York with $129,900 million (*£83,800 million*) at 31 Dec 1982. Its operating income was $747 million (*£482 million*). The Barclays Group had some 5500 branches and offices in over 80 countries (some 3100 in the United Kingdom) in December 1984. Deposits totalled £63,767 million and assets £73,623 million. The bank with the largest network in the United Kingdom is the National Westminster with consolidated total assets of £71,517,000,000 and 3801 branches (3400 in UK) as at 31 Dec 1984. The bank with most branches is The State Bank of India with 10,182 on 1 Jan 1984 with assets of £21,068 million.

Bank building

The world's tallest bank building is the Bank of Montreal's First Bank Tower, Toronto, Canada which has 72 storeys and stands 935 ft *284,98 m*. The largest bank vault in the world, measuring 350 × 100 × 8 ft *106,7 × 30,4 × 2,4 m* and weighing 879 tons *893 tonnes* is in the Chase Manhattan Building, New York City, completed in May 1961. Its six doors weigh up to 40 tons *40,6 tonnes* apiece but each can be closed by the pressure of a forefinger.

Bank bail out *Biggest*

On 26 July 1984 the Federal Deposit Insurance Corp bought $4.5 billion in bad loans from the Continental Illinois National Bank for $3.5 billion and also 'gave' $1 billion cash in return for preferred stock.

Banquet Greatest *Outdoors*

It was estimated that some 30,000 attended a military feast at Radewitz, Poland on 25 June 1730 thrown by King August II (1709–33).

Indoors

The greatest number of people served indoors at a single sitting was 18,000 municipal leaders at the Palais de l'Industrie, Paris on 18 Aug 1889. At the wedding of cousins Menachem Teitelbaum, 18, and Brucha Sima Melsels, 18, conducted by their grandfather Grand Rabbi Moses at Uniondale, Long Island, New York on 5 Dec 1984 the attendance of the Satmar sect of Hasidic Jews was estimated at 17,000 to 20,000. Meal Mart of Brooklyn, a kosher caterer, provided the food including 2 tons of gefilte fish.

Most expensive

The menu for the main 5½ hr banquet at the Imperial Iranian 2500th Anniversary gathering at Persepolis in October 1971 was probably the most expensive ever compiled. It comprised quail eggs stuffed with Iranian caviar, a mousse of crayfish tails in Nantua sauce, stuffed rack of roast lamb, with a main course of roast peacock stuffed with *foie gras*, fig rings and raspberry sweet champagne sherbet, with wines including *Château Lafite-Rothschild* 1945 at £40 (now £215) per bottle from Maxime's, Paris.

Book shop

The book shop with most titles and the longest shelving (30 miles *48 km*) in the world is W. & G. Foyle Ltd, City of Westminster, Greater London. First established in 1904 in a small shop in Islington, the company is now at 113–119 Charing Cross Road. The area on one site is 75,825 ft² *7044 m²*. The most capacious individual bookstore in the world measured by square footage is Barnes & Noble Bookstore of Fifth Ave at 18th Street, New York City, USA with 154,250 ft² *14 330 m²* and with 12.87 miles *20,71 km* of shelving.

Brewer *Oldest*

The oldest brewery in the world is the Weihenstephan Brewery, Freising, near Munich, W. Germany, founded in AD 1040.

Largest World

The largest single brewing organisation in the world is Anheuser-Busch, Inc based in St Louis, Missouri, USA, with 11 breweries in the US. In 1984 the company sold 64,000,000 US barrels, equivalent to *13,215 million Imp. pints*, the greatest annual volume ever produced by a brewing company. The company's St Louis plant covers 100 acres *40,5 ha* and after completion of current modernization projects will have an annual capacity in excess of 13,000,000 US barrels *2684 million Imp. pints*. The largest brewery on a single site is Adolph Coors Co of Golden, Colorado, USA where 13,187,000 barrels *2723 million Imp. pints* were sold in 1984.

Great Britain

The largest brewing company in the United Kingdom based on its 7520 public houses, 963 off-licences and over 100 hotels, is Bass plc. The company has net assets of £1,542,100,000, controls 13 breweries and has 69,192 employees. Its sales figure for the year ending 30 Sept 1984 was £2,252,300,000. The company also has substantial leisure and betting interests.

Brickworks

The largest brickworks in the world is the London Brick Company Limited plant at Stewartby, Bedfordshire. The works, established in 1898, now cover 221 acres *90 ha* and have a production capacity of 13,000,000 bricks and brick equivalent each week.

Building contractors

The largest construction company in the United Kingdom is George Wimpey plc (founded 1880), of London, which undertakes building, civil, offshore, process and marine engineering work worldwide employing 23,000 staff. The turnover of work was £1518 million in over 30 countries in 1984.

Building societies

The biggest building society in the world is the Halifax Building Society of Halifax, West Yorkshire. It was established in 1853 and has total assets exceeding £20,492,000,000. It has 11,648 employees and over 3000 offices. The world's biggest lender is the Japanese Government-controlled House Loan Corporation.

Chemist shop chain

The largest chain of chemist shops in the world is Boots The Chemists, which has 1024 retail branches. The firm was founded by Jesse Boot (b. Nottingham, 1850), later the 1st Baron Trent, who died in 1931.

Chocolate factory

The largest chocolate and confectionery factory is that built by Hershey Chocolate Company in Hershey, Pennsylvania, USA in 1903–5. It has 2,000,000 ft² *185,800 m²* of floor space.

Clothiers

The largest clothiers are the Brenninkmeyer family whose business was founded in the Netherlands in 1841 and whose annual sales are now estimated to be some $6000 million *£4285 million*.

Computer company

The world's largest computer firm is International Business Machines (IBM) Corporation of New York. In Dec 1984 assets were $42,808,000 (*£35,673,333*) and gross income was $45,937,000 (*£38,280,833*). In Oct 1979 it made the largest borrowing in corporate history with $1 billion. Its worldwide employees numbered 394,930 and there are 792,506 stockholders.

Department stores *World*

F. W. Woolworth, who celebrated their centenary year in 1979, now operate a total of 5555 stores world wide. Frank W. Woolworth opened his first Five and Ten Cent Store in Utica, New York State on 22 Feb 1879. The 1984 income from continuing operations was $141 million (*£117,500,000*).

Great Britain

The largest department store in the United Kingdom is Harrods Ltd of Knightsbridge, Royal Borough of Kensington and Chelsea, Greater London named after Henry Charles Harrod (1800–85), who opened a grocery in Knightsbridge Village in 1849. It has a total selling floor space of 15 acres *60 729 m²*, employs 4000 people and achieved record sales of £270 million for the year ending 29 Jan 1985. The record for a day is £5.5 million.

Highest sales per unit area

The department store with the fastest-moving stock in the world is the Marks & Spencer premier branch, known as 'Marble Arch' at 458 Oxford Street, City of Westminster, Greater London. The figure of £1400 worth of goods per square foot of selling space per year is believed to be an understatement. The selling area is 92,400 ft² *8584 m²*. The company has 264 branches in the UK and operates on over 6 million ft² *558 000 m²* of selling space and now has stores on the Continent and in Canada.

Longest wait for a sale

Tony Sprackling, 24, queued for 412 hours (17 days 4 hr) outside Keddies, Queen St., Colchester from 10–27 Dec 1984. His sofa bed was reduced from £399 to £50 and then donated by the store manager.

Distillery

The world's largest distilling company is The Seagram Company Ltd, of Canada. Its sales in the year ending 31 Jan 1985 totalled US $2,821,245,000 (*£2350 million*). The group employs about 14,200 people, including about 6000 in the United States.

The largest establishment for blending and bottling Scotch whisky is owned by John Walker & Sons Limited at Kilmarnock, Strathclyde, where there is a capacity to fill over 3 million bottles each week. 'Johnnie Walker' is the world's largest-selling brand of Scotch whisky. The world's largest-selling brand of gin is Gordon's. Old Bushmills Distillery, County Antrim, Northern Ireland licensed in 1608 claims to have been in production in 1276.

Fisheries

The greatest catch ever recorded with a single throw is 2471 tonnes by the purse seine-net boat M/S 'Flømann' from Hareide, Norway in the Barents Sea on 28 Aug 1983. It was estimated that more than 120 million fish were caught in this shoal.

Grocery stores

The largest grocery chain in the world is Safeway Stores, Incorporated of Oakland, California, USA with sales in 1984 of $19,642,201,000 (*£16,368 million*) and total current assets valued at $1,861,389,000 (*£1,551 million*) as at 29 Dec 1984. The company has 2571 stores totalling 73,284,000 ft² *6 808 303 m²*. The total number of employees is 168,590.

Hotelier

The top revenue-earning hotel business is the Holiday Inn hotel system, with a 1984 total revenue of $3444 million (*£2870 million*), from 1695 hotels (314,998 rooms) at 31 Dec 1984 in 53 countries. The business was founded by Charles Kemmons Wilson with his first Holiday Inn hotel on Summer Avenue, Memphis, Tennessee, USA in 1952.

Insurance

It was estimated in 1978 that the total premiums paid in the United States first surpassed $100 billion (*then £52,600 million*) or $1400 *£736* per household. The company with the highest volume of insurance in force in the world is the Prudential Insurance Company of America of Newark, New Jersey with $532,990 million at 31 Dec 1984, which is more than 2½ times the UK National Debt figure. The admitted assets are $78,924 million.

Great Britain

The largest life assurance group in the United Kingdom is the Prudential Corporation plc. At 1 Jan 1985 the tangible assets were £18,967,100,000 and the total amount assured was £83,454,100,000.

Life policies Largest

The largest life assurance policy ever written was one for $44 million (*£24.4 million*) for a Calgary land developer Victor T. Uy in February 1982 by Transamerica Occidental Life Assurance Co. The salesman was local manager Lorenzo F. Reyes. The highest pay-out on a single life has been some $18 million (*then £7.5 million*) to Mrs Linda Mullendore, wife of an Oklahoma rancher, reported on 14 Nov 1970. Her murdered husband had paid $300,000 in premiums in 1969.

Marine

The largest ever marine insurance loss was £46 million for the self-propelled semi-submersible drilling platform Ocean Ranger (14,914 tons gross) built for Ocean Drilling & Exploration Co of New Orleans in 1976. On 15 Feb 1982 she was lost with 84 lives in the Hibernia Field, off Newfoundland. One of the most expensive vessels afloat is the British passenger ship "Royal Princess", 44,348 tons gross, built in 1984, quoted at $140,800,000.

The largest sum claimed for consequential losses is $1700 million (*£890 million*) against owning, operating and building corporations, and Claude Phillips resulting from the 66 million gallon oil spill from M. T. *Amoco Cadiz* on the Brittany Coast on 16 Mar 1978.

The Holborn, London headquarters of Britain's largest insurance company the Prudential Corporation. *(Colin Smith)*

Land *Owner*

The world's largest landowner is the United States Government, with a holding of 729,800,000 acres (1,140,000 miles² *2 953 000 km²*) which is more than the area of the world's 8th largest country Argentina and 12.8 times larger than the United Kingdom. The world's largest *private* landowner is reputed to be International Paper Co with 9 million acres *3,64 million ha*. The United Kingdom's greatest ever private landowner was the 3rd Duke of Sutherland, George Granville Sutherland-Leveson-Gower, KG (1828–92), who owned 1,358,000 acres *549 560 ha* in 1883. Currently the largest landholder in Great Britain is the Forestry Commission (instituted 1919) with 2,987,933 acres *1 209 200 ha*. The landowner with the largest known acreage is the 9th Duke of Buccleuch (b. 1923) with 336,000 acres *136,035 ha*. The longest tenure is that by St Paul's Cathedral of land at Tillingham, Essex, given by King Ethelbert before AD 616.

Value Highest

The world's most expensive land is in central Hong Kong. In May 1982 freehold land for highrise building reportedly realized up to £11,000 per square foot. The freehold price for a grave site with excellent *Fung Shui* in Hong Kong may cost HK$200,000 for 4 ft × 10 ft *1,21 × 3,04 m* or *£19,400 per ft²*. The real estate value per square metre of the two topmost French vineyards, Grande and Petite Cognac vineyards in Bordeaux, has not been recently estimated. The China Square Inch Land Ltd at a charity auction on 2 Dec 1977 sold 1 cm² *0.155 in²* of land at Sha Tau Kok for HK$2000 (the equivalent of US$17,405,833,737 per acre). The purchasers were Stephen and Tony Nicholson. The most expensive land in Britain is that in the City of London. The freehold price on small prime sites reached £1950/ft² (*£21,230/m²*) in mid 1973.

Highest price

The record price per acre for 'bare' agricultural land (without 'hope' value) in Great Britain is £10,089 at Wrangle, Lincolnshire. It was sold by Richard Parkinson of auctioneers William H. Brown on 9 May 1984. In Jersey a record of £10,454 per acre (where 2¼ vergées equal 1 acre) was paid at Les Landes, St. Martin on 5 July 1984.

Highest rent

The highest rentals in the world in Nov 1984 for prime sites, according to *World Rental Levels* by Richard Ellis of London, are on Manhattan, New York at £42.41 and London (City) £32 per square foot. With added service charges and rates London is top at £54.72.

Greatest auction

The greatest auction was of the Hughes Aircraft Co for $5,000 million (*£4,166 million*) by General Motors of Detroit, Michigan on 5 June 1985.

Greatest barter deal

The biggest barter in trading history was 36 million barrels of oil valued at £900 million exchanged for 10 Boeing 747's for the Royal Saudi Airline in July 1984.

Mineral water

The world's largest mineral water firm is Source Perrier, near Nîmes, France with an annual production of more than 2,100,000,000 bottles, of which 1,200,000,000 now come from Perrier and Contrexeville. The French drink about 60 litres *105½ pt* of mineral water per person per year.

Motor car manufacturer *Largest World*

In 1980 Japan with 11,043,000 vehicles overtook

the USA as the world's No 1 motor manufacturer. The largest manufacturing company in the world is General Motors Corporation of Detroit, Michigan, USA. During 1984 worldwide sales totalled $83,889,900,000 (*£69,908 million*). Its assets at 31 Dec 1984 were valued at $24,214,300,000 (*£20,178 million*). Its total 1984 payroll was $22,505,400,000 (*£18,754 million*) to an average of 748,000 employees. Dividends paid in 1984 were $1,523,700,000 (*£1,269,750,000*).

Great Britain
The largest British manufacturer was BL plc with 490,000 vehicles produced and a sales turnover of £3402 million of which £1415 million was overseas sales in 1984. Direct exports were £827 million.

Largest plant
The largest single automobile plant in the world is the Volkswagenwerk, Wolfsburg, West Germany, with 58,000 employees and a capacity for 4056 vehicles daily. The surface area of the factory buildings is 371 acres *150 ha* and that of the whole plant 4892 acres *1980 ha* with 43.5 miles *70 km* of rail sidings.

Salesmanship
The all-time record for automobile salesmanship in units sold individually is 1425 in 1973 by Joe Girard of Michigan, USA, author of *How to Sell Anything to Anybody*, winner of the No. 1 Car Salesman title each year in 1966–77. His lifetime total of one-at-a-time 'belly to belly' selling was 13,001 sales, all retail with a record 174 in a month. He retired on 1 Jan 1978 to teach others his art and has published also *How to Sell Yourself*.

Oil refineries *Largest*
The world's largest refinery has been the Amerada Hess refinery in St Croix, Virgin Islands with an annual capacity of 28 million tonnes *27.55 million tons*. The largest oil refinery in the United Kingdom is the Esso Refinery at Fawley, Hampshire. Opened in 1921 and much expanded in 1951, it has a capacity of *15,6 million tonnes* per year. The total investment together with the associated chemical plant, on the 1300 acre *526 ha* site is in excess of one billion pounds. The area occupied by the Shell Stanlow Refinery at Ellesmere Port, Cheshire, founded in 1922, and now with a capacity of 18 million tonnes per year, is 2000 acres *810 ha*.

Paper company
The world's largest company in paper, fibre and wood products is Georgia-Pacific of Atlanta, Georgia with sales in 1984 of $7,128 million (*£5,940 million*) and 40,000 workers. The largest paper mill in the United Kingdom is the Bowaters Kemsley Mill near Sittingbourne, Kent with a complex covering an area of 260 acres *105 ha* and a capacity in excess of 300,000 tons/*tonnes* a year.

Pharmaceuticals
The world's largest pharmaceutical company is Johnson & Johnson of New Brunswick, New Jersey with sales of $6,124,500,000 (*£5103 million*) in 1984. Britain's largest drug *and* food turnover in 1983–84 was by Glaxo with £1,200 million.

Photographic store
The photographic store with the largest selling area is Jessop of Leicester Ltd's Photo Centre, Hinckley Road, Leicester opened in June 1979 with an area now of 27,000 ft² *2508 m²*.

Public relations
The world's largest public relations firm is Bursan Marsteller with headquarters in New York and a 1984 net fee income of $84,258,000 (*£70,215,000*). Hill and Knowlton Inc. have most offices worldwide with 56 including one in Beijing, China.

The world's pioneer public relations publication is *Public Relations News,* founded by Mrs Denny Griswold in 1944 and which now circulates in 97 countries.

Publishing
The publishing company generating most net revenue is Time Inc of New York City with $3067 million (*£2556 million*) in 1984. The largest educational book publishing concern in the world is the Book Division of McGraw-Hill Inc of New York with sales of $438,100,000 (*£365.1 million*) in 1984 with 1813 new books and educational products.

Restaurateurs
The largest restaurant chain in the world is that operated by McDonald's Corporation of Oak Brook, Illinois, USA, founded on 15 April 1955 in Des Plaines, Chicago by Ray A. Kroc BH (Bachelor of Hamburgerology). By 31 December 1984 the number of McDonald's restaurants licensed and owned in 35 countries and territories around the world reached 8304, with an aggregate throughput of 50 billion 100 per cent pure beef hamburgers under the motto 'Q.S.C. & V.'—for quality, (fast) service, cleanliness and value. Sales systemwide in 1984 surpassed 10 billion (*£8634 million*). Britain's largest hotel and catering group is Trusthouse Forte which employs up to 47,000 full and part-time staff in the UK, 13,000 overseas, and which had a turnover of £1,148,600,000 in 1983–84. It has 800 hotels world-wide.

San Francisco had, in 1983, 4293 dining establishments or 92.6 per square mile.

Fish and chip restaurant
The world's largest fish and chip shop is Harry Ramsden's, White Cross, Guiseley, West Yorkshire with 180 staff serving 1,600,000 customers per annum, who consumed 290 tons of fish and 450 tons of potatoes. Britain's oldest fryer, Jack Simpson (b. 1885) of Axminster, Devon recalls that a portion with peas plus tea in 1927 was 2p.

Retailer
The largest retailing firm in the world is Sears, Roebuck and Co (founded by Richard Warren Sears in North Redwood railway station, Minnesota in 1886) of Chicago, Illinois, USA. World-wide revenues were $26,500,000,000 (*£22.08 billion*) in the year ending 31 Dec 1984 when Sears Merchandise Group had 796 retail stores, 1119 sales offices and 1700 independent catalogue merchants in the USA and total assets valued at $38,800,000,000 (*£32.33 billion*).

Ship-building
In 1984 there was 18,334,061 gross tonnage of ships, excluding sailing ships, non-propelled vessels and vessels of less than 100 gross tonnage, completed throughout the world. The figures for Romania and People's Republic of China are incomplete. Japan completed 9,711,381 gross tonnage (52.97 per cent of the world total). The United Kingdom ranked sixth with 444,743 gross tonnage. The world's leading shipbuilding firm in 1984 was Hyundai of Korea (South), which completed 45 vessels of 1,252,609 gross tonnage. Physically the largest ship yard in the United Kingdom is Harland and Wolff Ltd of Queen's Island, Belfast, which covers some 300 acres *120 ha*.

Shipping line
The largest shipping owners and operators are Exxon Corporation (see p. 146) whose fleets of owned/managed and chartered tankers in 1984 totalled a daily average of 13,500,000 deadweight tons.

Shopping centre
The world's largest shopping centre is the $900 million West Edmonton Mall, Alberta, Canada first opened on 15 Sept 1981 and completed four years later which covers 5.5 million ft² *510 900 m²* on a 110 acre *44,5 ha* site. It encompasses 700 stores and services as well as 6 major department stores. Parking is provided for 30,000 vehicles for more than 500,000 shoppers per week. The world's first shopping centre was Roland Park Shopping Center, Baltimore, Maryland, USA built in 1896. The world's largest wholesale merchandise mart is the Dallas Market Center, located on Stemmons Freeway, Dallas, Texas, USA with nearly 9.3 million ft² *864 000 m²* in 8 buildings. The complex covers 150 acres *60 ha* with some 3400 permanent showrooms displaying merchandise of more than 26,000 manufacturers. The Center attracts 600,000 buyers each year to its 38 annual markets and trade shows. The largest covered shopping centre in Britain is the Manchester Arndale Centre which has a floor area of

At £10,454 per acre this property at Wrangle, Lincolnshire made a record for agricultural land sold at auction. (See page 148)

2,246,200 ft² *208 672 m²* including the 481,300 ft² *44 713 m²* car park for 1800 cars. It was built in 1976–79 and has a gross shopping area of 1,187,000 ft² *110 270 m²*. The £40 million centre at Milton Keynes, Buckinghamshire, opened in August 1979 has the longest mall in the world—650 m *2132 ft*.

Soft drinks

The world's most popular soft drink is Coca-Cola with over 301,000,000 drinks sold per day by early 1985 in more than 155 countries. Coke was launched as a tonic by Dr John S. Pemberton of Atlanta, Georgia in 1886. The Coca-Cola Company was formed in 1892. The secret '7X' formula was unchanged until 1985 when Coca-Cola had 21.7% of the $28 billion market to Pepsi's 18.8%. Pepsi Co's overall 1984 sales of $8.42 billion were $1.06 billion higher than Coca-Cola.

Steel company *World*

The non-communist world's largest producer of steel has been Nippon Steel of Tōkyō, Japan which produced 29,42 million tonnes *28.96 million tons* of crude steel in 1984. The Fukuyama Works of Nippon Kokan has a capacity of more than 16 000 000 tonnes/*tons* per annum. Its work force is 76,000.

STOCK EXCHANGES

The oldest Stock Exchange of the 138 listed throughout the world is that of Amsterdam, in the Netherlands, founded in 1602.

Most bargains

The highest number of bargains in one day on the London Stock Exchange was 44,106 on 12 Dec 1984 following the offer for sale of British Telecommunications shares. The record for a year is 4,848,671 bargains in the year ending 31 Dec 1984. There were 7060 securities (*cf.* 9749 peak in June 1973) listed at 31 Dec 1984. Their total nominal value was £268,121 million (gilt-edged £114,357 million) and their market value was £1,089,849 million (gilt-edged £114,434 million).

The highest closing figure of *The Financial Times* Industrial Ordinary share index (1 July 1935 = 100) was 1024.5 on 22 Jan 1985. The lowest figure was 49.4 on 26 June 1940. The greatest rise in a day has been 23.7 points to 315.5 on 1 July 1975 in anticipation of anti-inflationary measures, and the greatest fall in a day was 24.0 to 318.8 on 1 Mar 1974 on the realization of the fourth post-war Labour Government.

Most highly valued UK Co

The stock valuation of British Telecom in June 1985 was £14,200 million at 236 pence (40 pence uncalled) per share.

Highest par value

The highest denomination of any share quoted in the world is a single share in F. Hoffmann-La Roche of Basel worth Sw. Fr 101,000 (*£21,992*) on 23 Apr 1976.

U.S. records

The highest index figure on the Dow Jones average (instituted 8 Oct 1896) of selected industrial stocks at the close of a day's trading was 1327.28 on 6 June 1985. The record day's trading was 236,565,110 shares on 3 Aug 1984. The old, record trading volume in a day on the New York Stock Exchange of 16,410,030 shares on 29 Oct 1929, the 'Black Tuesday' of the famous 'crash' was unsurpassed until April 1968. The Dow Jones industrial average, which reached 381.71 on 3 Sept 1929, plunged 30.57 points on 29 Oct 1929, on its way to the Depression's lowest point of 41.22 on 8 July 1932. The largest decline in a day, 38.33 points,

occurred on 28 Oct 1929. The total lost in security values from 1 Sept 1929 to 30 June 1932 was $74,000 million (*then £23,000 million*). The greatest paper loss in a year was $209,957 million (*then £87,500 million*) in 1974. The record daily increase of 28.40 on 30 Oct 1929 was most recently bettered on 3 Nov 1982 with 43.41 points to 1065.49. The percentage record was 15.34% between 3 Mar (53.84) and the next opening on 15 Mar 1933 (62.10). The largest transaction on record 'share-wise' was on 21 June 1984 for 10,000,000 shares of Superior Oil Co. The largest stock trade in the history of the New York Exchange was a 10,000,000 share block of Superior Oil Co. stock at $42⅜ in a $423,750,000 (*then £316,231,343*) transaction on 21 June 1984. The highest price paid for a seat on the NY Stock Exchange was $515,000 (*then £214,580*) in 1969. The lowest 20th century price was $17,000 in 1942. The market value of stocks listed on the New York Stock Exchange reached an all-time high at the end of February 1985—$11,721,905,855,761.

Largest and smallest equity

The greatest aggregate market value of any corporation at year end was $74.0 billion (*then £52,860 million*) for IBM on 31 Dec 1983.

Britain's smallest public listed company is Dura Mill Ltd of Whitworth, Lancashire, producers of very high quality yarn with a capitalization of £85,000 in 30 p shares.

Greatest personal loss

The highest recorded personal paper losses on stock values have been those of Ray A. Kroc, Chairman of McDonald's Corporation with $64,901,718 (*then £27 million*) on 8 July 1974 and Edwin H. Land, President of Polaroid Corporation with $59,397,355 on 28–29 May 1974, when Polaroid stock closed $12.12 down at 43¼ on that day.

Largest new issue

The American Telegraph & Telephone Company offered $1375 million's worth of shares in a rights offer on 27,500,000 shares of convertible preferred stock on the New York market on 2 June 1971. The largest offering on the London Stock Exchange by a United Kingdom company was the £624 million rights offer of British Petroleum Co plc on 23 June 1981.

Greatest flotation

The largest equity offering in history was £3,915,600,000 or 50.2 per cent of British Telecom on behalf of H.M. Government by Kleinwort, Benson Ltd in Nov 1984. It is mooted that with the privatizing of British Gas an offering of £8,000 million may be made in 1987–88.

Largest investment house

The largest securities company in the US, and once the world's largest partnership with 124 partners, before becoming a corporation in 1959, is Merrill, Lynch, Pierce, Fenner & Smith Inc (founded 6 Jan 1914) of New York City, USA. Its parent, Merrill, Lynch and Co, has assets of $30.8 billion, 42,000 employees, 1000 offices and 4.8 million customer accounts. The firm is referred to in the United States stock exchange circles as a 'Breed Apart'.

Largest store

The world's largest store is R. H. Macy & Co Inc at Broadway and 34th Street, New York City, NY, USA. It covers 50.5 acres *20,3 ha* and employs 13,600 who handle 400,000 items. The sales of the company and its subsidiaries in 1983/84 were $4,065,139,000 (*£3387 million*). Mr Rowland Hussey Macy's sales on his first day at his fancy goods store on 6th Avenue, on 27 Oct 1858, were recorded as $11,06 (*then £2.20*).

LONDON STOCK EXCHANGE 1935–1985

The highest number of markings received in one day on the London Stock Exchange was 44,106 on 12 Dec 1984. The record for a year is 4,848,671 bargains in the year ending 31 Dec 1984. There were 7,060 securities (*cf.* 9749 peak in June 1973) listed at 31 Dec 1984. Their total nominal value was £268,121 million (gilt-edged £114,357 million) and their market value was £1,089,849 million (gilt-edged £114,934 million).

Lowest closing figure
49.4 on 26 June 1940 (hostilities in France ended the day before).

Highest ever closing figure on FT Index—1024.5 on 22 Jan 1985.

Greatest fall
Greatest fall in a day 27.9 points to 838.7 on 17 Oct 1984.

Greatest rise
Greatest rise in a day 27.6 points to 824.5 on 1 June 1984.

Sugar Mill

The highest recorded output for any sugar mill was set in 1966–67 by Ingenio de San Cristobal y Anexas, S.A., Veracruz, Mexico with 247,900 tonnes refined from 2,886,074 tonnes of cane ground. The world's largest cane sugar plant is the California & Hawaii Sugar Co plant founded in 1906 at Crokett, California with an output of 8 million lb per day.

Largest supermarket

The world's largest supermarkets (self-service with check-outs) were the Piggly Wiggly chain started in 1916 by Clarence Saunders (1881–1953) in Memphis, Tennessee, USA. Above 25,000 ft² or *2500 m²* net shopping area, stores are usually termed superstores and above 50,000 ft² or *5000 m²*—hypermarkets. The largest such in Britain is the 104,500 ft² *9660 m²* Tesco hypermarket at Weston Favell, Northampton opened in Nov 1978 with a parking capacity for 1300 cars.

Tobacco company

Subsidiary and affiliates of B.A.T. Industries (founded in London in 1902 as British-American Tobacco Co.) comprise the world's largest tobacco concern. They operate 116 tobacco factories in 52 countries: consolidated turnover in 1984 was £14,426 million and total assets were £10,064 million at 31 Dec 1984. The Group's sales in 1984 topped 549,000 million cigarettes.

The world's largest cigarette plant is the $300 million Philip Morris plant at Richmond, Virginia, USA opened in October 1974. Employing 5500 people the factory produces more than 530 million cigarettes a day.

Toy manufacturer

The world's largest single manufacturer of toys is Mattel Inc of Hawthorne, California, USA founded in 1945. Its total net sales for the year ending 29 Dec 1984 were $880,850,000 (*£734 million*).

Toy shop
The world's biggest toy shop is Hamleys of Regent Street Ltd, founded in 1760 in Holborn and removed to Regent Street, London, W1 in 1901. It has selling space of 45,000 ft² *4180 m²* on 6 floors with over 300 employees during the Christmas season. It was taken over by Debenhams on 12 May 1976.

Undertaker (or Mortician)
The world's largest undertaking business is the SCI (Service Corporation International) with 279 funeral homes and 40 flower shops with associated limousine fleets and cemeteries. Their annual revenue in the most recession-proof of industries in the year ending 30 Apr 1983 was $208,536,000 (*£1,345,400*).

Vintners
The oldest champagne firm is Ruinart Père et Fils founded in 1729. The oldest cognac firm is Augier Frères & Co, established in 1643.

2. MANUFACTURED ARTICLES

Antique *Largest*
The largest antique ever sold has been London Bridge in March 1968. The sale was made by Mr Ivan F. Luckin of the Court of Common Council of the Corporation of London to the McCulloch Oil Corporation of Los Angeles, California, USA for $2,460,000 (*then £1,029,000*). The 10,000 tons/*tonnes* of façade stonework were re-assembled at a cost of £3 million, at Lake Havasu City, Arizona and 're-dedicated' on 10 Oct 1971.

Armour *Most Expensive*
The highest auction price paid for a suit of armour is £1,925,000 by B. H. Trupin (US) on 5 May 1983 at Sotheby's, London for the suit made in Milan by Giovanni Negroli in 1545 for Henri II, King of France from the Hever Castle Collection in Kent, England.

Heaviest
The armour of William Somerset, 3rd Earl of Worcester made at the Royal Workshop, Greenwich *c.* 1570 weighed 81 lb 9 oz *37,0 kg*. If his five bullet-proof exchange elements were substituted the total weight reaches 133 lb 13 oz *60,7 kg*.

Beds *Largest functional*
In Bruges, Belgium, Philip, Duke of Burgundy had a bed 12½ ft wide and 19 ft long *3,81 × 5,79 m* erected for the perfunctory *coucher officiel* ceremony with Princess Isabella of Portugal in 1430. The largest bed in Great Britain is the Great Bed of Ware, dating from *c.* 1580, from the Crown Inn, Ware, Hertfordshire, now preserved in the Victoria and Albert Museum, London. It is 10 ft 8½ in wide, 11 ft 1 in long and 8 ft 9 in tall *3,26 × 3,37 × 2,66 m*. The largest bed currently marketed in the United Kingdom is a Super Size Diplomat bed, 9 ft wide by 9 ft long, *2,74 m²* from The London Bedding Centre, Sloane Street, SW1 which would cost more than £4000.

Heaviest
The heaviest bed is a water bed 9 ft 7 in × 9 ft 10 in *2,92 × 2,99 m* owned by Milan Vacek of Canyon County, California since 1977. The thermostatically heated water alone weighs 4205 lb *1907 kg*.

Beer cans
Beer cans date from a test marketing by Krueger Beer of Newark, New Jersey at Richmond, Virginia in 1935. The largest collection has been made by John F. Ahrens of Mount Laurel, New Jersey, USA with nearly 15,000 different cans. A Rosalie Pilsner can sold for $6000 (*then £2700*) in the US in April 1981.

Beer mat collections (*Tegestology*)
The world's largest collection of beer mats is owned by Leo Pisker of Vienna, who had collected over 108,500 different mats from 148 countries by April 1985. The largest collection of purely British mats is 30,400 by Tim J. Stannard of Birmingham.

Blanket
The largest blanket ever made measured 68 × 100 ft *20,7 × 30,48 m* weighing 600 lb *272 kg*. It was knitted in 20,160 squares in 10 months (October 1977–July 1978) by *Woman's Weekly* readers for Action Research for The Crippled Child. It was shown on BBC TV *Record Breakers* in October 1978. The most expensive was a Churro hand-spun serape sold for $115,500 (*then* £79,000) at Sotheby's, New York on 22 Oct 1983.

Bottle caps
Since 1950 Helge Friholm (b. 1910) of Søborg, Denmark has amassed 34,306 different bottle caps (to June 1985) from 145 countries.

Candle
A candle 80 ft *24,38 m* high and 8½ ft *2,59 m* in diameter was exhibited at the 1897 Stockholm Exhibition by the firm of Lindahls. The overall height was 127 ft *38,70 m*. Currently the largest is that made from 1967 to 1985 by Jean-Paul Schwob of Wesserling, Alsace, France, standing 10½ ft *3,20 m* and weighing 1372 lb *622 kg*.

Carpets and rugs *Earliest*
The earliest carpet known is a woollen pile-knotted carpet, red on white ground excavated at Pazyryk, USSR in 1947, dated to the 5th century BC and now preserved in Leningrad.

Largest
Of ancient carpets the largest on record was the gold-enriched silk carpet of Hashim (dated AD 743) of the Abbasid caliphate in Baghdad, Iraq. It is reputed to have measured 180 by 300 ft *54,86 × 91,44 m*. A 52,225 ft² *4851 m²* or 1.23 acre 28 ton red carpet was laid on 13 Feb 1982, by the Allied Corporation, from Radio City Music Hall to the New York Hilton along the Avenue of the Americas.

Most finely woven
The most finely woven old carpet known is one with more than 2490 knots per in² *980 per cm²* from a fragment of an Imperial Mughal prayer carpet of the 17th century now in the Altman collections in the Metropolitan Museum of Art, New York City, NY, USA. The Bikaner Woollen Mills, India announced in March 1985 that they had achieved 260 knots per in² *1023 per cm²*. The most magnificent carpet ever made was the Spring carpet of Khusraw made for the audience hall of the Sassanian palace at Ctesiphon, Iraq. It was about 7000 ft² *650 m²* of silk, gold thread and encrusted with emeralds. It was cut up as booty by military looters in AD 635 and from the known realization value of the pieces must have had an original value of some £100,000,000.

Chair *Largest*
The world's largest chair is the 2000 lb *907 kg* 33 ft 1 in *10,08 m* tall, 19 ft 7 in *5,96 m* wide chair constructed by Anniston Steel & Plumbing Co. Inc for Miller Office Furniture in Anniston, Alabama, USA and completed in May 1981.

Chamber pot
The 33 oz *935 g* silver pot, made by David Willaume and engraved for the 2nd Earl of Warrington made £9,500 at Sotheby's, London on 14 June 1984.

Chandelier *Largest*
The world's largest set of chandeliers (ten) were built for the palace of H.M. Sir Muda Hassanal Bolkiah of Brunei in 1983. His palace or Istana Nurul Iman is in the capital Bandar Seri Begawan. Britain's largest is in the Chinese Room at the Pavilion, Brighton.

Chocolates
The most expensive chocolates are by Charbonel et Walker of Old Bond Street, London at £10.00 per pound *453 g* box.

Christmas cracker
The largest functional cracker ever constructed was one 56 ft 7 in *17,24 m* in length and 9½ ft *2,9 m* in diameter built for British Rail Hull Paragon Station and pulled on 21 Nov 1980.

Cigars *largest*
The largest cigar ever made measures 5,095 m *16 ft 8½ in* in length and weighs 262 kg *577 lb 9 oz* (over ¼ ton) taking 243 hours and using 3330 full tobacco leaves. It was made by Tinus Vinke and Jan Weijmer in Feb 1983 and is in the Tobacco Museum in Kampen, Holland. The largest marketed cigar in the world is the 14 in *35,5 cm* Valdez Emperado by San Andres Cigars.

Most expensive
The most expensive standard cigar in the world is the 11½ in *29,2 cm* long Don Miguel 'Cervantes', which retails in Britain at £15.00.

Cigar bands
Joseph Hruby of Lyndhurst, Ohio has the largest known collection of cigar bands with 175,391 different examples dating from *c.* 1895.

Most voracious smokers
Jim Purol and Mike Papa each smoked 135 cigarettes simultaneously for 5 min on 5 Oct 1978 at Rameys Lounge, Detroit, Michigan, USA. On 3 Sept 1979 at the same venue, they each smoked 27 cigars simultaneously for 5 min and in 1983 Purol smoked 38 pipes. Simon Argevitch of Oakland, California, USA raised his old record to 17 standard size cigars, whilst simultaneously emitting bird calls or singing, on Fishermans Wharf, San Francisco on 3 July 1982. George Anastassopoulos (b. Patras, Greece 20 Aug 1911 kept account of smoking 40,730 cigars from Jan 1950 to June 1984—a rate of 3¼ every day.

Cigarettes *Consumption*
The heaviest smokers in the world are the people of the United States, where 640,000 million cigarettes (an average of 3750 per adult) were consumed at a cost of some $21,200 million (*£11,700 million*) in 1981. The people of China, however, were estimated to consume 725,000 million in 1977. In Senegal 80% of urban males smoke. The peak consumption in the United Kingdom was 3230 cigarettes per adult in 1973. The peak volume was 243,100,000 lb *110,2 million kg* in 1961, compared with 81.6 million kg *180 million lb* in 1983 when 99,000 million cigarettes were sold.

In the United Kingdom 47 per cent of adult men and 35 per cent of adult women smoked in 1984.

Tar/Nicotine content
Of the 141 brands most recently analysed for the Dept of Health and Social Security, the one with highest tar/nicotine content is *Capstan Full Strength* with 25/2.5 mg per cigarette. *Silk Cut Ultra Low King Size*, *Embassy Ultra Mild King Size* and *John Player King Size Ultra Mild* with <4/0.3 are at the lower risk end of the league table. In the Philippines there is a brand with 71 mg nicotine per cigarette.

Most popular

The world's most popular cigarette is 'Marlboro', a filter cigarette made by Phillip Morris, which sold 237,000 million units in 1982. The largest selling British cigarette in 1983 was *Benson and Hedges Special Filter*. The Wills brand 'The Three Castles' was introduced in 1878.

Longest and shortest

The longest cigarettes ever marketed were 'Head Plays', each 11 in *27,9 cm* long and sold in packets of 5 in the United States in about 1930, to save tax. The shortest were 'Lilliput' cigarettes, each 1¼ in *31,7 mm* long, and ⅛ in *3 mm* in diameter, made in Great Britain in 1956.

Largest collection

The world's largest collection of cigarettes is that of Robert E. Kaufman, MD, of 950 Park Avenue, New York City 10028, NY, USA. In April 1985 he had 7855 different cigarettes made in 172 countries. The oldest brand represented is 'Lone Jack', made in the USA in *c.* 1885. Both the longest and shortest (see above) are represented.

Cigarette cards

The earliest known tobacco card is 'Vanity Fair' dated 1876 issued by Wm S. Kimball & Co., Rochester, New York. The earliest British example appeared *c.* 1883 in the form of a calendar issued by Allen & Ginter of Richmond, Virginia, trading from Holborn Viaduct, City of London. The largest known collection is that of Mr Edward Wharton-Tigar, MBE (b. 1913) of London with a collection of more than 1,000,000 cigarette and trade cards in about 45,000 sets.

Cigarette lighter *Most expensive*

The Dunhill Lighthouse Table Lighter is made in 18 ct gold—designed in the shape of a lighthouse set on an island base of amethyst which alone weighs one cwt *50 kg*. It weighs 51.4 oz troy *1600 g* and the windows on the lighthouse stem are amethyst. It sells for £37,500 at Alfred Dunhill, St. James's, London.

Cigarette packets

The earliest surviving cigarette packet is the Finnish 'Petit Canon' packet for 25, made by Tollander & Klärich in 1860, from the Ventegodt Collection. The rarest is the Latvian 700-year anniversary (1201–1901) Riga packet, believed to be unique, from the same collection. The largest verified private collection is one of 60,955 from over 150 countries owned by Vernon Young of Farnham, England.

Credit card collection

The largest collection of valid credit cards at 22 May 1985 is one of 1173 (all different) by Walter Cavanagh (b. 1943) of Santa Clara, California, USA. The cost of acquisition to 'Mr. Plastic Fantastick' was nil, and he keeps them in the world's longest wallet—250 ft *76,2 m* long weighing 35 lb *15,87 kg* worth more than $1.25 million in credit.

Curtain

The largest curtain ever built has been the bright orange-red 4 ton *4064 kg* 185 ft *56 m* high curtain suspended 1350 ft *411 m* across the Rifle Gap, Grand Hogback, Colorado, USA by the Bulgarian-born sculptor Christo, (*né* Javacheff) on 10 Aug 1971. It blew apart in a 50 mph *80 km/h* gust 27 hr later. The total cost involved in displaying this work of art was $750,000 (*then £312,500*).

The world's largest functional curtain is one 550 ft long × 65 ft high *167,6 × 19,8 m* in the Brabazon hanger at British Aerospace Filton, Bristol used to enclose aircraft in the paint spraying bay. It is electrically drawn.

Dolls *Largest*

The most outsize 'doll' ever paraded was made by the Belgian student body KSA on 15 May 1983 in Ostend. It measured 51,07 m *167 ft 6 in* overall. The most massive 'guy' built was one 62 ft 4 in *19 m* high by the Fermain Youth Club, Macclesfield on 5 Nov 1983.

Dress *Most expensive*

The EVA suits for extra-vehicular activity worn by space shuttle crews from 1982 had a unit cost of $2.3 million (*then £1,437,000*). The dress with the highest price tag ever exhibited by a Paris fashion house was one in the Schiaparelli spring/summer collection on 23 Jan 1977. 'The Birth of Venus' designed by Serge Lepage with 512 diamonds was priced at Fr. 7,500,000 (*then £880,000*).

The coronation robe for Emperor Field Marshall Jean-Bédel Bokassa with a 39 ft *11,8 m* long train was encrusted with 785,000 pearls and 1,220,000 crystal beads by Guiselin of Paris for £77,125. It was used at Bangui, Central African Empire (now Republic) on 4 Dec 1977.

Fabrics *Earliest and Most expensive*

The oldest surviving fabric discovered from Level VI A at Çatal Hüyük, Turkey has been radio-carbon dated to 5900 BC.

The most expensive fabric obtainable is Vicuña cloth manufactured by Fuji Keori Ltd of Osaka, Japan at US$3235 (*£2087*) per metre in July 1983. The most expensive evening wear fabric was that designed by Alan Hershman of Duke Street, London at £580 per metre. Each square metre, despite 155,000 hand sewn sequins, weighs less than 7 oz *198 g*.

Finest cloth

The most expensive cloth, the brown-grey throat hair of Indian goats, is Shatoosh (or Shatusa), finer, and more expensive than Vicuña. It was sold by Neiman-Marcus of Dallas, Texas, USA, at $1000 (*£555*) per yard but supplies have now dried up.

Firework

The largest firework ever produced has been *Universe I* exploded for the Lake Toya Festival, Hokkaido, Japan on 28 Aug 1983. The 421 kg *928 lb* shell was 108 cm *42.5 in* in diameter and burst to a diameter of 860 m *2830 ft*, with a 5 colour display. The longest firework 'waterfall' set off in Britain was one of 313 ft *94,45 m* by Swindon Town F.C. on 5 Nov 1983.

Flags *Oldest*

The oldest known flag is one dating to *c.* 500 BC found in the excavation of the princesses graves in Hunan, Changsha, China. The Friesian flag still flown in the Netherlands dates from the 9th century AD.

Largest

The largest flag in the world, the 'Great American Flag', was displayed at Evansville, Indiana on 22 Mar 1980 measuring 411 ft *125 m* by 210 ft *64 m* with a weight of 7 tons/*tonnes* in readiness for its eventual hoisting on the Verrazano Narrows Bridge, New York, USA on 4 July 1981. It was the brainchild of Len Silverfine. The largest Union Flag (or Union Jack) was one 240 × 108 ft *73,15 × 32,91 m* displayed at the Royal Tournament, Earl's Court, London in July 1976. It weighed more than a ton and was made by Form 4Y at Bradley Rowe School, Exeter, Devon. The largest flag *flown* from a flagstaff is a US flag 50 × 100 ft *15,24 × 30,48 m* first raised on 25 Nov 1983 at Outlet Malls of America, Plano, Texas, USA. The study of flags is known as vexillology.

Float

The largest float is the 150 ft *45,7 m* long, 22 ft 6,7 m wide 'Agree' Float bearing 51 All-American Homecoming 'Queens' used at the Orange Bowl parade, Miami, Florida, USA on 29 Dec 1977.

Furniture *Oldest British*

The oldest surviving piece of British furniture is a three-footed tub with metal bands found at Glastonbury, Somerset, and dating from between 300 and 150 BC.

Largest Piece

The largest item of furniture in the world is the wooden bench in Green Park, Obihiro, Hokkaido, Japan which seats 1282 people and measures 400 m *1312 ft 4 in* long. It was completed by a team of 770 on 19 July 1981.

Garden gnome

The earliest recorded garden gnome was one placed in the rockery at Lamport Hall, Northamptonshire, England by Sir Charles Isham Bt. (1819–1903).

Glass

The most priceless example of the art of glassmaking is usually regarded as the glass Portland Vase which dates from late in the 1st century BC or 1st century AD. It was made in Italy, and was in the possession of the Barberini family in Rome from at least 1642. It was eventually bought by the Duchess of Portland in 1792 but smashed while in the British Museum by William Lloyd on 7 Feb 1845. The thinnest glass made is 0,3 mm *⅛₅th of an inch* thick for digital displays by Nippon Glass Corporation.

The highest price paid for a piece of glass and for any antiquity is £520,000 (hammer price) or £572,000 (with premium) for the Roman cage cup from AD 300 (see Table on p 154).

Gold plate

The gold coffin of the 14th century BC Pharaoh Tutankhamun discovered by Howard Carter on 16 Feb 1923 in the Valley of the Kings, western Thebes, Egypt weighed 110,4 kg *243 lb*. The exhibition at the British Museum attracted 1,656,151 people (of whom 45.7 per cent bought catalogues) from 30 Mar to 30 Dec 1972, resulting in a profit of £657,731.22.

Jig-saw *Earliest and largest*

The earliest jig-saws were made as 'dissected maps' by John Spilsbury (1739–69) in Russell Court off Drury Lane, London *c.* 1762. The largest jig-saw ever made is *Rose-Petal Palace*, sponsored by Hallmark Cards Inc, outside Macey's Store on 34th Street, New York City on 19 Aug 1984. It measured 76 × 48 ft *23,16 × 14,63 m* with 14,000 pieces. Gimbels of New York City sold in 1933 a 110.5 ft² *10,26 m²* puzzle with 50,000 pieces made by Eureka Jig Saw Puzzle Co. of Philadelphia, Pennsylvania, USA. Custom-made Stave puzzles made by Steve Richardson of Vermont, USA of 2300 pieces cost $3700 (*then £2430*) in Jan 1983.

The British record is of the cover of 'BEEB' magazine at 73 ft 2½ in × 45 ft 3 in *22,31 × 13,79 m* with 1500 interlocking wooden pieces assembled by 100 school children in Canterbury, Kent on 2 Feb 1985 for BBC TV's *Saturday Superstore* show.

Matchbox labels

The oldest match label of accepted provenance is that of Samuel Jones *c.* 1830. The finest collection of trade mark labels (excluding any bar or other advertising labels) is some 280,000 pieces collected by the phillumenist Robert Jones of Indianapolis, USA. The greatest British prize is a Lucifer & Congreve label of *c.* 1835.

Needles

The earliest needles were made of bone. The largest recorded needle is one 6 ft 1 in *185,5 cm* long made by George Davies of Thomas Somerfield, Bloxwich for stitching on mattress buttons lengthways. One is preserved in the National Needle Museum, Forge Mill, Redditch, Worcestershire.

Nylon *Sheerest*

The lowest denier nylon yarn ever produced is the 6 denier used for stockings exhibited at the Nylon Fair in London in February 1956. The sheerest stockings normally available are 9 denier. An indication of the thinness is that a hair from the average human head is about 50 denier.

Penknife

The penknife with the greatest number of blades is the Year Knife made by the cutlers, Joseph Rodgers & Sons Ltd, of Sheffield, England, whose trade mark was granted in 1682. The knife was built in 1822 with 1822 blades but had to halt at 1973 because there was no further space. It was acquired by Britain's largest hand tool manufacturers, Stanley Works (Great Britain) Ltd of Sheffield, South Yorkshire in 1970.

Pens *Most expensive*

The most expensive writing pens were the 18 carat pair of pens (one fibre-tipped and one ballpoint) capped by diamonds of 3.88 carats sold by Alfred Dunhill (see Cigarette lighter) for £9943 the pair (incl. VAT). The most expensive fountain pen is the Mont Blanc 18 carat gold and platinum nibbed Meisterstück made by Dunhill in Hamburg, West Germany and retailing in April 1984 for $4250 (*then £3035*).

Pistol

In December 1983 it was reported that Mr Ray Bily (US) owned an initialled gold pistol made for Hitler which was valued for insurance purposes at $375,000 (*£267,850*).

Post cards

Deltiology is claimed to be the third largest collecting hobby next only to stamps and coins. Austria issued the first cards in 1869 followed by Britain in 1872. Values tend to be obscured by the philatelic element.

Pot lid

The highest price at auction for a pot lid is £3300 for a seaweed patterned 'Spanish Lady' lid sold at Philips, London on 19 May 1982.

Quilting

The world's largest quilt, designed by A. Platteau, was made by the people of Kortrijk-Rollegem, Belgium. It comprises 16,240 squares measuring 21,24 × 30,35 m *69.6 × 99.5 ft*. On 28 Aug 1982 it was hoisted by two cranes.

Ropes *Largest and Longest*

The largest rope ever made was a coir fibre launching rope with a circumference of 47 in *119 cm* made in 1858 for the British liner *Great Eastern* by John and Edwin Wright of Birmingham. It consisted of four strands, each of 3780 yarns. The longest fibre rope ever made without a splice was one of 10,000 fathoms or 11.36 miles *18 288 m* of 6½ in *16,5 cm* circumference manila by Frost Brothers (now British Ropes Ltd) in London in 1874.

The strongest cable-laid wire rope strop made is one 282 mm *11.1 in* in diameter with a breaking strain of 3250 tonnes.

Shoes

James Smith, founder of James Southall & Co of Norwich, England introduced sized shoes in 1792. The firm began making 'Start-rite' children's shoes in 1923.

Emperor Bokassa of the Central African Empire (now Republic) commissioned pearl-studded shoes from the House of Berluti, Paris for his self-coronation in Dec 1977 at a cost of $85,000 (*then £38,800*).

The most expensive standard shoes obtainable are mink-lined golf shoes with 18 carat gold embellishments and ruby-tipped spikes made by Stylo Matchmakers International Ltd, of Northampton, England which retail for £7700, or $9625 per pair in the USA.

Largest

Excluding cases of elephantiasis, the largest shoes ever sold are a pair size 42 built for the giant Harley Davidson of Avon Park, Florida, USA. The normal limit is size 14. For advertising and display purposes facsimiles of shoes weighing up to 1,5 tonnes have been constructed.

Silver

The largest single pieces of silver are the pair of water jugs of 10,408 troy oz 4.77 cwt *242,7 kg* made in 1902 for the Maharaja of Jaipur (1861–1922). They are 160 cm *5 ft 3 in* tall, with a circumference of 2,48 m *8 ft 1½ in*, and have a capacity of 1800 gallons *8182 litres*. They are now in the City Palace, Jaipur. The silversmith was Gorind Narain.

Snuff *Most expensive*

The most expensive snuff obtainable in Britain is 'Café Royale' sold by G. Smith and Sons (est. 1869) of 74, Charing Cross Road, City of Westminster, Greater London. It sells at £2.06 per oz. as at 1 May 1985.

Sofa *Longest*

The longest standard sofa manufactured for market is the King Talmage Sofa, 12 ft 2 in *3,7 m* in length made by the Talmageville Furniture Manufacturers, California, USA. Barton Grange Hotel, near Preston, Lancashire bought a 14 ft *4,26 m* long pink leather settee for £3250 on 4 Oct 1984.

Table *Longest*

A buffet table 1007,3 m *3304 ft 10 in* long was set up for the 400th anniversary of Hudiksvall, Sweden on 19 June 1982. Some 4000 people including HM The King of Sweden were seated.

Table cloth

The world's largest table cloth is one 219 yd *200 m* long by 2 yd *1,8 m* wide double damask made by John S. Brown & Sons Ltd of Belfast in 1972 and shipped to a royal palace in the Middle East. There was also an order for matching napkins for 450 places.

Tapestry *Earliest*

The earliest known examples of tapestry woven linen are three pieces from the tomb of Thutmose IV, the Egyptian pharaoh and dated to 1483–1411 BC.

Largest

The largest single piece of tapestry ever woven is 'Christ in His Majesty', measuring 72 ft by 39 ft *21,94 × 11,88 m* designed by Graham Vivian Sutherland OM (1903–80) for an altar hanging in Coventry Cathedral, West Midlands. It cost £10,500, weighs ¾ ton *760 kg* and was delivered from Pinton Frères of Felletin, France, on 1 Mar 1962.

Longest embroidery

The famous Bayeux *Telle du Conquest, dite tapisserie de la reine Mathilde*, a hanging 19½ in *49,5 cm* wide by 231 ft *70,40 m* in length depicts events of the period 1064–6 in 72 scenes and was probably worked in Canterbury, Kent, in *c.* 1086. It was 'lost' for 2½ centuries from 1476 until 1724. The Overlord Embroidery of 34

Some 6 ft 1 in *185 cm* in length, this needle was used for stitching on mattress buttons lengthways. (See Col. 1) (*National Needle Museum*)

panels each 8 × 3 ft *2,43 × 0,91 m*, commissioned by Lord Dulverton CBE, TD (b. 1915) from the Royal School of Needlework, London, was completed in 1979 after 100 man years of work and is 41 ft *12,49 m* longer than the Bayeux and has the largest area of any embroidery with 816 ft² *75,8 m²*. An uncompleted 8 in *20,3 cm* deep 1280 ft *390,14 m* embroidery of scenes from C. S. Lewis's Narnia children's stories has been worked by Mrs Margaret S. Pollard of Truro, Cornwall to the order of Mr Michael Maine.

Tartan *Earliest*

The earliest evidence of tartan is the so-called Falkirk tartan, found stuffed in a jar of coins in Bells Meadow, Falkirk, Scotland. It is of a dark and light brown pattern and dates from *c.* AD 245. The earliest reference to a specific named tartan has been to a Murray tartan in 1618 although Mackay tartan was probably worn earlier. There are 1300 tartans known to the Museums of Scottish Tartans at Cumrie, Perthshire. HRH Prince of Wales is eligible to wear 11 including the Balmoral which has been exclusive to the Royal Family since 1852.

Tea Towels

The largest reported collection of unduplicated tea towels is 5967 by Mr Tony Judkin of Luton,

Bedfordshire. In Sept 1984 he was separated from his exasperated wife and put his collection up for sale.

Time capsule

The world's largest time capsule is the Tropico Time Tunnel of 10,000 ft³ *283 m³* in a cave in Rosamond, California, USA, sealed by the Kern Antelope Historical Society on 20 Nov 1966 and intended for opening in AD 2866.

Typewriters

The first patent for a typewriter was by Henry Mill in 1714 but the earliest known working machine was made by Pellegrine Turri (Italy) in 1808.

Vase *Largest*

The largest vase on record is one 8 ft *2,78 m,* in height, weighing 650 lb *294,8 kg,* thown by Sebastiano Maglio at Haeger Potteries of Dundee, Illinois, USA (founded 1872) during August 1976.

The Chinese ceramic authority Chingwah Lee of San Francisco was reported in Aug 1978 to have appraised a unique 39 in *99 cm* Kang Hsi 4-sided vase then in a bank vault in Phoenix, Arizona, USA at '$60 million' (*then £30 million*).

Wallet

The most expensive wallet ever made is a platinum-cornered, diamond studded crocodile creation made by Louis Quatorze of Paris and Mikimoto of Tokyo selling at £56,000 in Sept 1984.

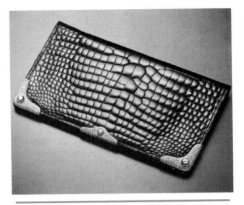

The stealing of empty wallets received a filip with this £56,000 platinum-cornered and diamond studded example.

Wreath *Most expensive*

The most expensive wreath on record was that presented to Sri Chinmoy in New York City, USA on 11 July 1983 by Ashrita Furman and Pahar Meltzer. It was handled by the Garland of Divinity's Love Florist, contained 10,000 flowers, and cost $3500 (*£2260*).

Zip-fastener

The world's longest zip-fastener is 632,45 m *2074 ft* long made for covers of aquatic cables by RIRI of Mendrisio, Italy in Jan 1985. It has 119,007 nylon teeth.

3. AGRICULTURE

Origins

It has been estimated that only 21 per cent of the world's land surface is cultivable and that only 7.6 per cent is actually under cultivation. Evidence adduced in 1971 from Nok Nok Tha and Spirit Cave, Thailand tends to confirm plant cultivation and animal domestication was part of the Hoabinhian culture *c.* 11,000 BC. Reindeer may have been domesticated as early as *c.* 18,000 BC but definite evidence is still lacking. There is also evidence that horses were tethered as early as *c.* 30,000 BC.

Goat was domesticated at Asiab, Iran by *c.* 8050 BC and dog at Star Carr, North Yorkshire by *c.* 7700 BC: the earliest definite date for sheep is *c.* 7200 BC at Argissa-Magula, Thessaly, Greece and for pig and cattle *c.* 7000 BC at the same site. The earliest date for horse is *c.* 4350 BC from Dereivka, Ukraine, USSR. Ancient trackings sighted by a US space shuttle in 1982 indicate perhaps an even earlier domestication of draft animals.

FARMS

Earliest

The earliest dated British farming site is a Neolithic one, enclosed within the Iron Age hillfort at Hembury, Devon, excavated during 1934–5 and now dated to 4210–3990 BC. Pollen analysis from two sites Oakhanger, Hampshire,

RECORDS FOR ANTIQUES

ART NOUVEAU

The highest auction price for any piece of art nouveau is $360,000 (*then £163,600*) for a spiderweb leaded glass mosaic and bronze table lamp by L. C. Tiffany at Christie's, New York on 8 Apr. 1980.

BED

A 1930 black lacquer kingsize bed made by Jean Durand was auctioned at Christie's, New York City on 2 Oct 1983 for £49,668.

BLANKET

The most expensive blanket was a Navajo Churro handspun serape of *c.* 1852 sold for $115,500 (*then £79,500*) with premium at Sotheby's, New York City on 22 Oct 1983.

CARPET

In 1946 the Metropolitan Museum, New York, privately paid $1 million (*then £248,138*) for the 26.5 × 13.6 ft *807 × 414 cm* Anhalt Medallion carpet made in Tabriz or Kashan, Persia *c.* 1590. The highest price ever paid at auction for a carpet is £231,000 for a 17th century 'Polonaise' silk and metal thread carpet at Sotheby's, London on 13 Oct 1982.

CERAMICS

The Greek urn painted by Euphronios and thrown by Euxitheos in *c.* 530 was bought by private treaty by the Metropolitan Museum of Art, New York, for $1.3 million (*then £541,666*) in August 1972.

CHAIR

The highest price ever paid for a single chair is $275,000 (*then £177,500*) with premium on 23 Oct 1982 at Sotheby's in Manhattan, for the Chippendale side chair attributed to Thomas Affleck of Philadelphia, USA and made in *c.* 1770.

CIGARETTE CARD

The most valuable card is one of the 6 known baseball series cards of Honus Wagner, who was a non-smoker, which was sold in New York in December 1981 for $25,000 (*then £13,900*).

DOLLS

The highest price paid at auction for a doll is £16,000 (hammer price) for a William and Mary English wooden doll *c.* 1690 at Sotheby's, London on 29 May 1984.

FURNITURE

The highest price ever paid for a single piece of furniture is £1,300,000 (*FF 15 million*) at Ader Picard Tajan, Monaco on 11 Nov 1984 for a mahogany and ebony collector's chest of drawers thought to have been made for Queen Marie-Antoinette (1755–1793) by G. Benneman.

The English furniture record was set by a black-japanned bureau-bookcase of *c.* 1705. Formerly owned by Queen Mary, it made $860,000 (*then £463,366*) at Christie's, New York on 18 Oct 1981.

GLASS

The auction record is £520,000 for a Roman glass cage-cup of *c.* AD 300 measuring 7 in *17,78 cm* in diameter and 4 in *10,16 cm* in height, sold at Sotheby's, London, on 4 June 1979 to Robin Symes.

GOLD PLATE

The world's highest auction price for a single piece of gold plate is £66,000 (*then $122,000*) for an English George III salver, known as 'The Rutland Salver', made by Paul Storr of London, 1801. The salver, which is 12 in *30,5 cm* in diameter, is engraved with the arms of Manners, Dukes of Rutland and of the 16 towns and cities, the gold Freedom boxes of which were melted down to make the salver. It was sold by Sotheby Parke Bernet, London, on 4 May 1978.

GUNS

The highest price ever paid for a single gun is £125,000 given by the London dealers F. Partridge for a French flintlock fowling piece made for Louis XIII, King of France in *c.* 1615 and attributed to Pierre le Bourgeoys of Lisieux, France (d. 1627). This piece was included in the collection of the late William Goodwin Renwick of the United States sold by Sotheby's, London on 21 Nov 1972 (see

also Pistols). It is now in the Metropolitan Museum, New York, USA.

HAT

The highest price ever paid for a hat is $66,000 (*then £34,750*) by the Alaska State Museum at a New York City auction in Nov 1981 for a Tlingit Kiksadi ceremonial frog helmet from *c.* 1600.

ICON

The record auction price for an icon is $150,000 (*then £67,500*) paid at Christie's, New York on 17 Apr 1980 for the *Last Judgement* (from the George R. Hann collection, Pittsburgh, USA) made in Novgorod in the 16th century.

JADE

The highest price ever paid for an item in jade is $396,000 (£270,307) (with premium) at Sotheby's, New York on 6 Dec 1983 for a mottled brownish-yellow belt-hook and pendant mask of the Warring States Period of Chinese history.

JEWELS

The highest auction price for any jewels is £2,825,000 (or £3.1 million with the buyer's premium) for two pear-shaped diamond drop earings of 58.6 and 61 carats at Sotheby's, Geneva on 14 Nov 1980. Neither the buyer nor seller was disclosed.

MUSICAL BOX

The highest price paid for a musical box is £20,900 (with premium) for a Swiss-made box made for a Persian prince in 1901, sold at Sotheby's, London on 23 Jan 1985.

PAPERWEIGHT

The highest price ever paid for a glass paperweight is $143,000 (£97,278) with premium at Sotheby's, New York City, USA on 2 Dec 1983 for a blue glass weight made at Pantin, Paris *post* 1850.

PISTOL

The highest price paid at auction for a pistol is £110,000 at Christie's London on 8 July 1980 for a Sadeler wheel-lock holster pistol from Munich dated *c.* 1600.

and Winfrith Heath, Dorset (Mesolithic *c.* 5000 BC) indicates that Mesolithic man may have had herds which were fed on ivy during the winter months.

Largest *World*

The largest farms in the world are collective farms (*sovkhozes*) in the USSR. These have been reduced in number from 235,500 in 1940 to only 18,000 in 1980 and have been increased in size so that units of over 60,000 acres *25 000 ha* are not uncommon. The pioneer farm owned by Laucidio Coelho near Campo Grande, Mato Grosso, Brazil in *c.* 1901 was 3358 miles² *8700 km² 2.15 million* acres with 250,000 head of cattle at the time of his death in 1975.

Great Britain

The largest farms in the British Isles are Scottish hill farms in the Grampians. The largest arable farm is that of Elveden, Suffolk, farmed by the Earl of Iveagh. Here 11,246 acres *4553 ha* are farmed on an estate of 22,918 acres *9278 ha*, the greater part of which was formerly derelict land. The 1984 production included 11,799 tonnes *11 580 tons* of grain and 55,910 tonnes *54 904 tons* of sugar beet. The livestock includes 497 beef cattle, 1043 ewes and 5258 pigs.

Cattle station

The world's largest cattle station is the Anna Creek station of 30 113.5 km² *11,626.8 miles²*, South Australia owned by the Kidman family. It is thus 23 per cent the size of England. The biggest component is Strangway at 14 114 km²

5449 miles². Until 1915 the Victoria River Downs Station, Northern Territory had an area of 22,400,000 acres (35,000 miles² *90 650 km²*), the same as England's 20 largest counties put together.

Sheep station

The largest sheep station in the world is Commonwealth Hill, in the north-west of South Australia. It grazes between 60,000 and 70,000 sheep, *c.* 700 cattle and 54,000 uninvited kangaroos in an area of 4080 miles² *10 567 km², i.e.* larger than the combined area of Norfolk and Suffolk. The head count on Sir William Stevenson's 30,000 acre *12 140 ha* Lochinver Station in New Zealand was 117,500 on 1 Jan 1983 on 21,000 acres *8500 ha*. The largest sheep move on record occurred when 27 horsemen moved a mob of 43,000 sheep 40 miles *64 km* from Barcaldine to Beaconsfield Station, Queensland, Australia, in 1886.

Rice Farming

The largest continuous wild rice (*Zizania aquatica*) farm in the world is Clearwater Rice Inc. at Clearbrook, Minnesota, USA with 2000 acres *809 ha*. In 1983 it yielded 386,148 lb.

Turkey farm

The world's largest turkey farm is that of Bernard Matthews plc, centred at Gt Witchingham, Norfolk, with 2300 workers tending 7,900,000 turkeys.

Chicken ranch

The world's largest chicken ranch is the Craton Egg Farm, Ohio, USA which has 4.2 million hens laying some 3.1 million eggs daily.

Piggery

The world's largest piggery is the Sljeme pig unit in Yugoslavia which is able to process 300,000 pigs in a year. Even larger units may exist in Romania but details are at present lacking.

Cow shed

The longest cow shed in Britain is that of the Yorkshire Agricultural Society at Harrogate, North Yorkshire. It is 456 ft *139 m* in length with a capacity of 686 cows. The National Agricultural Centre, Kenilworth, Warwickshire, completed in 1967, has, however, capacity for 782 animals.

Foot-and-mouth disease

The worst outbreak of foot-and-mouth disease in Great Britain was that from Shropshire on 25 Oct 1967 to 25 June 1968 in which there were 2364 outbreaks and 429,632 animals slaughtered at a direct and consequential loss of £150,000,000. The outbreak of 1871, when farms were much smaller, affected 42,531 farms. The disease first appeared in Great Britain at Stratford, East London in August 1839.

Sheep shearing

The highest recorded speed for sheep shearing in a working day was that of John Fagan who

RECORDS FOR ANTIQUES

PLAYING CARDS

The highest price paid for a deck of playing cards is $143,352 (*£98,850*) (with premium) by the New York Metropolitan Museum at Sotheby's, London on 6 Dec 1983.

PORCELAIN AND POTTERY

The highest auction price for any ceramic or any Chinese work of art is £792,000 (with premium) for a blue and white Ming vase of 1426–35 bought by Hirano of Japan at Sotheby's, London on 15 Dec 1981.

POT LID

The highest price paid for a pot lid is £3300 for a seaweed patterned 'Spanish Lady' lid sold at Phillips, London on 19 May 1982.

SILVER

The highest price ever paid for silver is £612,500 for the pair of Duke of Kingston tureens made in 1735 by Meissonnier and sold by Christie's, Geneva on 8 Nov 1977. The English silver record is £484,000 at Sotheby's, London on 3 May 1984 for the Duke of Northumberland's 630 troy oz. Shield of Achilles, made in 1822 by Rundell, Bridge and Rundell. The 100 piece Paul de Lamerie service made for the seventh Earl of Thanet *c.* 1745 was sold by Lord Hothfield at Sotheby's, London on 22 Nov 1984 for £825,000 also with premium.

SNUFF BOX

The highest price ever paid for a snuff box is Sw. Fr. 1,540,000 (*then £435,028*) in a sale at Christie's, Geneva on 11 May 1982 for a gold snuff box dating from 1760–65 and once owned by Frederick the Great of Prussia. It was purchased by S. J. Phillips, the London dealers, for stock.

SPOONS

A Wiener werkstaffe spoon by Josef Hoffmann, Austria *c.* 1905, was sold at Sotheby's, London for £17,600 (with premium) on 28 Apr 1983. A set of 13 Henry VIII Apostle spoons owned by Lord Astor of Hever were sold for £120,000 on 24 June 1981 at Christie's, London.

STUFFED BIRD

The highest price ever paid for a stuffed bird is £9000. This was given on 4 Mar 1971 at Sotheby's, London, by the Iceland Natural History Museum for a specimen of the Great Auk (*Alca impennis*) in summer plumage, which was taken in Iceland *c.* 1821; this particular specimen stood 22½ in *57 cm* high. The Great Auk was a flightless North Atlantic seabird, which was finally exterminated on Eldey, Iceland in 1844, becoming extinct through hunting. The last British sightings were at Co. Waterford in 1834 and St Kilda, Western Isles *c.* 1840.

SWORD

The highest price paid for a sword is the $145,000 (*then £85,800*) paid for the gold sword of honour, presented by the Continental Congress of 1779 to General Marie Jean Joseph Lafayette, at Sotheby Parke Bernet, New York City, USA on 20 Nov 1976.

TAPESTRY

The highest price paid for a tapestry is £550,000 for a Swiss Medieval tapestry frieze in two parts

dated 1468–1476 at Sotheby's, Geneva, on 10 Apr 1981 by the Basle Historische Museum.

THIMBLE

The record auction price for a thimble is £8000 paid by the London dealer Winifred Williams at Christie's, London on 3 Dec 1979 for a Meissen dentil-shaped porcelain piece of *c.* 1740.

TOY

The auction record for a toy is £25,500 for a model train set of Stephenson's *Rocket* made by Marklin of Germany in tin plate in 1909 at Sotheby's, London on 29 May 1984.

TYPEWRITER

The highest price paid for an antique machine is £3000 for an 1886 Daw and Tait machine auctioned at Sotheby's, London on 12 Dec 1980.

WALKING STICK

The highest auction price for a walking stick has been $24,200 (*then £17,285*) at Sotheby Parke Bernet, New York in 1983 for an octagonal whale ivory nobbed stick decorated by Scrimshanders in 1845.

Made for the special envoy to the Shah of Persia, this 1901 cylinder musical box set an auction record of £19,000 in 1985. *(Sotheby's, London)*

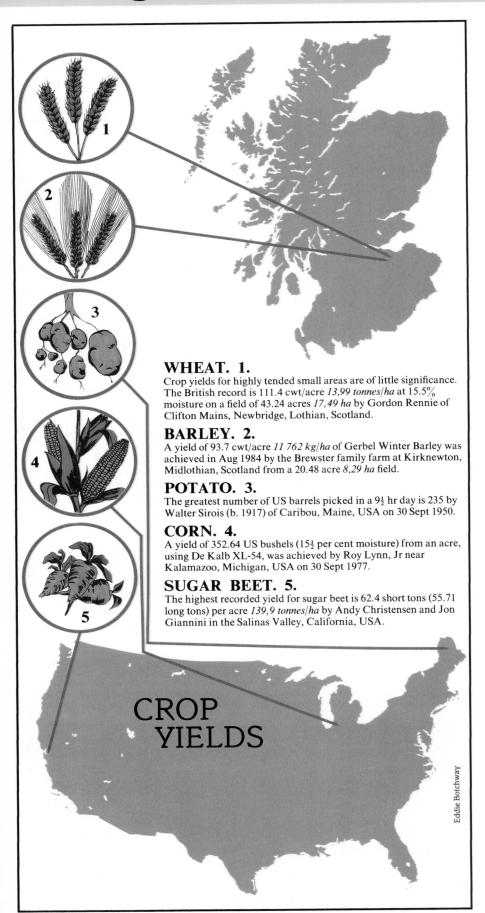

WHEAT. 1.

Crop yields for highly tended small areas are of little significance. The British record is 111.4 cwt/acre *13,99 tonnes/ha* at 15.5% moisture on a field of 43.24 acres *17,49 ha* by Gordon Rennie of Clifton Mains, Newbridge, Lothian, Scotland.

BARLEY. 2.

A yield of 93.7 cwt/acre *11 762 kg/ha* of Gerbel Winter Barley was achieved in Aug 1984 by the Brewster family farm at Kirknewton, Midlothian, Scotland from a 20.48 acre *8,29 ha* field.

POTATO. 3.

The greatest number of US barrels picked in a 9½ hr day is 235 by Walter Sirois (b. 1917) of Caribou, Maine, USA on 30 Sept 1950.

CORN. 4.

A yield of 352.64 US bushels (15½ per cent moisture) from an acre, using De Kalb XL-54, was achieved by Roy Lynn, Jr near Kalamazoo, Michigan, USA on 30 Sept 1977.

SUGAR BEET. 5.

The highest recorded yield for sugar beet is 62.4 short tons (55.71 long tons) per acre *139,9 tonnes/ha* by Andy Christensen and Jon Giannini in the Salinas Valley, California, USA.

CROP YIELDS

Eddie Botchway

machine-sheared 804 lambs (average 89.3 per hour) in 9 hr at Hautora Rd, Pio Pio, New Zealand on 8 Dec 1980. Peter Casserly of Christchurch, New Zealand, achieved a solo blade (i.e. hand-shearing) record of 353 lambs in 9 hours on 13 Feb 1976. In a shearing marathon, four men machine-shore 2519 sheep in 29 hr at Stewarts Trust, Waikia, Southland, New Zealand on 11 Feb 1982.

Mr Lavor Taylor (b. 27 Feb 1896) of Ephraim, Utah claims to have sheared 515,000 sheep to May 1984.

Great Britain
British records for 9 hr have been set at 555 by Roger Poyntz-Roberts (300) and John Savery (255) on 9 June 1971 (sheep caught *by* shearers), and 610 by the same pair (sheep caught *for* shearers) in July 1970.

Sheep *Survival*
The longest recorded survival by a sheep buried in snow is 50 days when Alex Maclennan uncovered 15 dead and 1 live sheep near the River Skinsdale on Mrs Tyser's, Gordonbush Estate, Sutherland, Scotland on 24 Mar 1978 during the great January blizzard.

Mushroom farm
The largest mushroom farm in the world is the Butler County Mushroom Farm, Inc, founded in 1937 in a disused limestone mine near West Winfield, Pennsylvania, USA. It employs over 1000 in a maze of underground galleries 110 miles *177 km* long, producing over 24,000 short tons *21 770 tonnes* of mushrooms per year. The French annual consumption is 7 lb *3,17 kg* per caput.

Largest wheat field
The largest single fenced field sown with wheat was one of 35,000 acres *14 160 ha* sown in 1951 south west of Lethbridge, Alberta, Canada.

Largest vineyard
The world's largest vineyard is that extending over the Mediterranean façade between the Rhône and the Pyrenees in the *départements* Hérault, Gard, Aude, and Pyrenées-Orientales in an area of 840 000 ha *2,075 685 acres* of which 52.3 per cent is *monoculture viticole*.

Largest hop field
The largest hop field in the world is one of 1836 acres *743 ha* near Toppenish, Washington State, USA. It is owned by John I. Haas, Inc, the world's largest hop growers, with hop farms in California, Idaho, Oregon and Washington State, with a total net area of 4560 acres *1845 ha*.

Community garden *Largest*
The largest recorded community garden project is that operated by the City Beautiful Council, and the Benjamin Wegerzyn Garden Center, Dayton. Ohio, USA. It comprises 1173 allotments each of 812¼ ft² *74,45 m²*.

Field to Loaf Record
The fastest time for producing loaves from growing wheat is 40 min 44 sec at O. S. North's Bakery at Heydon, near Royston, Hertfordshire on 10 Sept 1983.

Ploughing
The world championship (instituted 1953) has been staged in 18 countries and won by ploughmen of 11 nationalities of which the United Kingdom has been most successful with 8 championships. The only man to take the title three times has been Hugh B. Barr of Northern Ireland in 1954–5–6. The 1984 champion was Desmond Wright, 48 (Northern Ireland).

The fastest recorded time for ploughing an acre

FIELD TO LOAF

IN 40 MIN 44 SEC

0,404 ha (minimum 32 right-hand turns and depth 9 in *22 cm*) is 11 min 33.5 sec by John Binning using a Fiskars 5 furrow 14 in *35,5 cm* plough towed by a Same Hercules 160 hp tractor on land belonging to Mr E. W. Morgan & Son of Easton Court Farm, Little Hereford, Hereford & Worcester on 24 Sept 1981.

The greatest recorded acreage ploughed with a 6 furrow plough to a depth of 7 in *17,7 cm* in 24 hr is 123.4 acres *49,9 ha* by David Griffiths and Pat Neylan using a Lamborghini R-1056 DT tractor in the Nakuru District, Kenya on 6–7 July 1978. Frank Allinson of Leyburn, N Yorks, ploughed for 250 hr 9 min 50 sec on 14–24 Nov 1981. DMI Inc. of Goodfield, Illinois, USA marketed a 'Hydrawide' plough with 21 furrows in 1978.

Largest rick

A rick of 40,400 bales of straw was completed from 22 July to 3 Sept 1982 by Nick and Tom Parsons with a gang of 8 at Cuckoo-pen Barn Farm, Birdlip, Gloucestershire. It measured 150 × 30 × 60 ft high *45,7 × 9,1 × 18,2 m high* and weighed some 700 tons *711 tonnes*. They baled, hauled and ricked 24,200 bales in 7 consecutive days on 22–29 July.

LIVESTOCK

Highest Priced *Bull*

The highest price ever paid for a bull is $2,500,000 (*then £1,087,000*) for the beefalo (a ⅜ bison, ⅜ charolais, ¼ Hereford) 'Joe's Pride' sold by D. C. Basalo of Burlingame, California to the Beefalo Cattle Co of Canada, of Calgary,

The World's Fastest Loaf

Upper left: Two magistrates investigate the grinding by Ben Palmer, O. S. North and chief chemist Peter Darkes. *Above left:* Peter Bradwell (with cap on) scaling the dough for moulding by Mr North (centre). *Above right:* The team with the baked loaf 40 min 44 sec from reaping.

Below: The previous record-holders from St. Nicholas Mill, Isle of Thanet, Kent at 41 min 13 sec—the Miller, Roy Castle, the Baker's wife, the Baker, the Baker's son-in-law.

Alberta, Canada on 9 Sept 1974. The young 14 month old Canadian Holstein bull 'Pickland Elevation B. ET' was bought by Premier Breeders of Stamfordham, Northumberland for £233,000.

The highest price ever paid for a bull in Britain is 60,000 guineas (£63,000), paid on 5 Feb 1963 at Perth, Scotland, by James R. Dick (1928–74) co-manager of Black Watch Farms, for 'Lindertis Evulse', an Aberdeen-Angus owned by Sir Torquil and Lady Munro of Lindertis, Kirriemuir, Tayside, Scotland. This bull failed a fertility test in August 1963, thus becoming the world's most expensive piece of beef.

Cow

The highest price ever paid for a cow is $1,025,000 (*then £640,625*) for the Holstein Allendairy Glamorous Ivy by Albert Cormier of Georgetown, Ontario, Canada at Doeberiener dispersal sale at Jamestown, Pennsylvania on 20 Nov 1982. The British record is £33,600 for 'Ullswater Beatexus 8th', a British Friesian sold to The British Livestock Embryo Syndicate of Royston, Hertfordshire by Sir Keith and Lady Showering of West Horrington, Wells, Somerset on 9 May 1981 (auctioneers: Hobsons).

Note: Some exceptionally high livestock auction sales are believed to result from collusion between buyer and seller to raise the ostensible price levels of the breed concerned. Others are marketing and publicity exercises with little relation to true market prices.

Above: Depicted in front of the Lamb and Flag, Little Haywood, Staffs (see page 159), Britain's heaviest hog weighed in at 12 cwt 66 lb *639,5 kg.* *Right:* Pigman George Dukes with the hog's dimensions. *(John D. Lacey) Below:* On show at Launceston, Tasmania two Merino sheep (see highest priced wool)..

Sheep

The highest price ever paid for a ram is $A79,000 (*£49,500*) by the Gnowangerup Animal Breeding Centre, Western Australia for a Merino ram from the Colinsvale Stud, South Australia at the Royal Adelaide Show on 10 Sept 1981.

The British auction record is £21,000 paid by Mr W. Sheddon of Brighouse, Balmaclellan, Kirkcudbright, Scotland for A. W. Carswell & Son's Blackface ram on 4 Oct 1978.

The highest price ever paid for wool is $A125 per kg greasy (*£31.50 per lb*) for a bale of extra superfine combing Merino fleece from the Launceston, Tasmania sales on 4 Mar 1982. It was sold by E. J. Dowling & Sons of Ross, Tasmania to Fujii Keori Ltd of Osaka. This Japanese firm has been top bidders each year from 1972 to 1983 inclusive.

Pig

The highest price ever paid for a pig is $56,000 (*then £38,356*) for a cross-bred barrow named 'Bud' owned by Jeffrey Roemisch of Hermleigh, Texas and bought by E. A. 'Bud' Olson and Phil Bonzio on 5 Mar 1983. The UK record is 3300 guineas (£3465), paid by Malvern Farms for the Swedish Landrace gilt 'Bluegate Ally 33rd' owned by Davidson Trust in a draft sale at Reading, Berkshire on 2 Mar 1955.

Horse

The highest price for a draught horse is $47,500 (*£9970*) paid for the 7-year-old Belgian stallion 'Farceur' by E. G. Good at Cedar Falls, Iowa, USA on 16 Oct 1917. A Welsh mountain pony stallion 'Coed Cock Bari' was sold to an Australian builder in Wales in September 1978 for 21,000 guineas (*then £22,050*).

Donkey

Perhaps the lowest ever price for livestock was at a sale at Kuruman, Cape Province, South Africa in 1934 where donkeys were sold for less than 2p each.

Heaviest *Cattle*

Of heavyweight cattle the heaviest on record

was a Holstein-Durham cross named 'Mount Katahdin' exhibited by A. S. Rand of Maine, USA in 1906–10 and frequently weighed at an even 5000 lb *2267 kg*. He was 6 ft 2 in *1,88 m* at the shoulder with a 13 ft *3,96 m* girth and died in a barn fire *c.* 1923. The British record is the 4480 lb *2032 kg* of 'The Bradwell Ox' owned by William Spurgin of Bradwell, Essex. He was 15 ft *4,57 m* from nose to tail and had a girth of 11 ft *3,35 m* when 6 years old in 1830. The largest breed of heavyweight cattle is the Chianini, brought to Italy from the Middle East in pre-Roman times. Mature bulls average 5 ft 8 in *1,73 m* at the forequarters and weigh 2865 lb *1300 kg*. The Airedale Heifer of East Riddlesdon, nr. Keighley, South Yorkshire *c.* 1820 was 11 ft 10.6 in *3,62 m* long and weighed 2640 lb *1197,5 kg*.

The highest recorded birthweight for a calf is 225 lb *102 kg* from a British Friesian cow at Rockhouse Farm, Bishopston, Swansea, West Glamorgan, in 1961.

Pigs

The heaviest hog recorded was the Poland-China hog 'Big Bill' of 2552 lb *22¾ cwt 1157,5 kg* measuring 9 ft *2,75 m* long with a belly on the ground, owned by Burford Butler of Jackson, Tennessee, USA and chloroformed in 1933. Raised by W. J. Chappall he was mounted and displayed in Weekly County, Tennessee until 1946. The British record is held by a Gloucester Old Spot hog of 12 cwt 66 lb *639,5 kg* bred by Joseph Lawton and possibly owned by Joseph Bradbury of Little Haywood, Staffordshire. In 1774 it stood 4 ft 8½ in *1,43 m* in height and was 9 ft 8 in *2,94 m* long. The highest recorded weight for a piglet at weaning (8 weeks) is 81 lb *36,7 kg* for a boar, one of nine piglets farrowed on 6 July 1962 by the Landrace gilt 'Manorport Ballerina 53rd', *alias* 'Mary', and sired by a Large White named 'Johnny' at Kettle Lane Farm, West Ashton, Trowbridge, Wiltshire.

Sheep

The highest recorded birthweight for a lamb in the world is 38 lb *17,2 kg* at Clearwater, Sedgwick County, Kansas, USA in 1975, but neither this lamb nor the ewe survived.

Broiler growth

The record for growth for flocks of at least 2400 at 56 days is 2,901 kg *6.396 lb* with a conversion rate of 2.17 by D. B. Marshall (Newbridge) Ltd of Newbridge, Midlothian, Scotland reported in October 1981.

Above: Being admired is 'Bud', the cross-bred barrow, who was sold at auction in Texas in March 1985 for the record price of $56,000 *(£38,356)*.
Below: Mr W. Lawson of Retford, Notts displaying a 1957 certificate and photograph of 'Wonderful Lady', still the UK record holder for egg-laying. *(Retford Times)*

Prolificacy *Cattle*

On 25 Apr 1964 it was reported that a cow named 'Lyubik' had given birth to seven calves at Mogilev, USSR. Five live and one dead calf were recorded from a Fresian at Te Puke, North Island, New Zealand on 27 July 1980 but none survived. A case of five live calves at one birth was reported in 1928 by T. G. Yarwood of Manchester. The life-time prolificacy record is 30 in the case of a cross-bred cow owned by G. Page of Warren Farm, Wilmington, East Sussex, which died in November 1957, aged 32. A cross-Hereford calved in 1916 and owned by A. J. Thomas of West Hook Farm, Marloes, Dyfed, Wales, produced her 30th calf in May 1955 and died in May 1956, aged 40.

'Soender Jylland's Jens' a Danish black and white bull left 220,000 surviving progeny by artificial insemination when he was put down aged 11 in Copenhagen in September 1978. 'Bendalls Adema', a Friesian bull, died aged 14 at Clondalkin, County Dublin, Ireland on 8 Nov 1978 having sired an estimated 212,000 progeny by artificial insemination.

Pigs

The highest recorded number of piglets in one litter is 34, thrown on 25–26 June 1961 by a sow owned by Aksel Egedee of Denmark. In February 1955 a Wessex sow owned by Mrs E. C. Goodwin of Paul's Farm, Leigh, near Tonbridge, Kent, had a litter of 34, of which 30 were born dead. The highest reported number of live births in Britain is 30 by W. Ives of Dane End Fruit Farm, near Ware, Hertfordshire from a white Welsh sow in September 1979. A sow, 'Gertie' (Large White × Landrace) owned by John Caley of Selby, North Yorkshire farrowed 3 litters of 19, 19 and 23 in under 12 months (18 July 1982–20 May 1983) of which 55 were live born.

Sheep

A case of eight lambs at a birth was reported by D. T. Jones of Priory Farm, Gwent, in June 1956 and by Ken Towse of Buckton near Bridlington in March 1981 but none lived. A case of a sheep living to 26 years was recorded in flock book records by H. Poole, Wexford, Ireland. Many cases of sextuplet lambs have been reported.

Egg-laying

The highest authenticated rate of egg-laying is by a white leghorn chicken hen, no. 2988 at the College of Agriculture, University of Missouri, USA, with 371 eggs in 364 days in an official test conducted by Professor Harold V. Biellier ending on 29 Aug 1979. The UK record is 353 eggs in 365 days in a National Laying Test at Milford, Surrey in 1957 by a Rhode Island Red 'Wonderful Lady' owned by W. Lawson of Welham Grange, Retford, Nottinghamshire.

The heaviest egg reported is one of 16 oz *454 g*, with double yolk and double shell, laid by a white Leghorn at Vineland, New Jersey, USA, on 25 Feb 1956. The largest recorded was one of 'nearly 12 oz' for a 5 yolked egg 12¼ in *31 cm* around the long axis and 9 in *22,8 cm* around the shorter axis laid by a Black Minorca at Mr Stafford's Damsteads Farm, Mellor, Lancashire in 1896.

The highest recorded annual average for a flock is 313 eggs in 52 weeks from a flock of 1000 Warren-Stadler SSL layers (from 21 weeks of age) by Eric Savage, White Lane Farm, Albury, Surrey, England in 1974–5.

Most yolks

The highest claim for the number of yolks in a chicken's egg is 9 reported by Mrs Diane Hainsworth of Hainsworth Poultry Farms, Mount Morris, New York, USA in July 1971 and also from a hen in Kirghizia, USSR in August 1977.

Goose egg

The white goose 'Speckle' owned by Donny Brandenberg, of Goshen, Ohio, USA, on 3 May 1977 laid a 24 oz *680 g* egg measuring 13½ × 9½ in *34 × 24 cm* in circumferences.

Duck

An Indian Runner Duck, owned by Mrs M. Atkinson of Burnham-on-Sea, Somerset, repeatedly laid 362 eggs in 365 days from 1 Aug 1981.

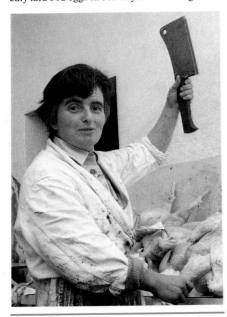

Mrs. Madge Colenso pictured at work. (See under Turkey Plucking) *(Farmers Weekly)*

Milk yields *Cows*

The highest recorded world lifetime yield of milk is 465,224 lb (207.68 tons *211 025 kg*) by the unglamorously named cow No 289 owned by M. G. Maciel & Son of Hanford, California, USA to 1 May 1984. The greatest yield of any British cow was that given by Winton Pel Evo owned by John Waring of Glebe House, Kilnwick near Pocklington with 165 tonnes. The greatest recorded yield for one lactation (maximum 365 days) is 55,661 lb *25 247 kg* by the Holstein 'Beecher Arlinda Ellen' owned by Mr and Mrs Harold L. Beecher of Rochester, Indiana, USA in 1975. The British lactation record (305 days) was set by 'Queenie' (b. 5 May 1974), a Friesian–Ayrshire cross, owned by Peter Healey of Street Farm, Eggington, Bedfordshire at 19 195 kg *42,317 lb* in 1980–81. The highest reported milk yield in a day is 241 lb *109,3 kg* by 'Urbe Blanca' in Cuba on or about 23 June 1982.

Hand milking

Andy Faust at Collinsville, Oklahoma, USA in 1937 achieved 120 US gal *99.92 UK gal* in 12 hr.

Goats

The highest recorded milk yield for any goat is 7714 lb *3499 kg* in 365 days by 'Osory Snow-Goose' owned by Mr and Mrs G. Jameson of Leppington, N.S.W., Australia in 1977. A 15 year old goat owned by Mrs Nanbui Meghani of Bhuj, Gujarat, India was reported in Nov 1984 to have lactated continuously for 12 years.

Butter fat yield

The world record lifetime yield is 16,370 lb 7425 kg by the US Holstein 'Breezewood Patsy Bar Pontiac' in 3979 days (see left also for yield record). Her lactation record for 365 days of 2230 lb *1011 kg* was reported on 8 Oct 1976. The British record butter fat yield in a lifetime is 12,166 lb *5518 kg* by the Ayrshire cow 'Craighead Welma' owned by W. Watson Steele from 273,072 lb at 4.45 per cent. The British record for 365 days is 761 kg *1677.7 lb* by 'Crookgate Aylwinia 7' a Friesian, owned by J. V. Machin of Hill Farm, Penley near Wrexham, Clwyd, set on 5 May 1973. The United Kingdom record for butter fat in one day is 9.30 lb *4,218 kg* (79 lb *35,8 kg* milk at 11.8 per cent) by Queens Letch Farms' Guernsey Cow 'Thisbe's Bronwen of Trewollack'.

Cheese

The most active cheese-eaters are the people of France, with an annual average in 1983 of 19,8 kg *43.6 lb* per person. The world's biggest producer is the United States with a factory production of 4,773,500,000 lbs (2,165,000 tons *2 200 000 tonnes*) in 1980. The UK cheese consumption in 1983 was 6,7 kg *14.8 lb* per head.

Oldest

The oldest and most primitive cheeses are the Arabian *kishk*, made of dried curd of goats' milk. There are today 450 named cheeses in 18 major varieties, but many are merely named after different towns and differ only in shape or the method of packing. France has 240 varieties.

Most expensive

The world's most expensive cheese in its home market is Le Leruns made from Ewes milk at 90 francs per kilo (now *£3.40 per lb*). Cheese made to the Liederkranz formula in Van Wert, Ohio, USA retails for $2.25 per 4 oz; equivalent to $9.00 (*£6.40*) per lb. Britain's most costly traditional cheese is Blue Wensleydale which has no fixed price but is obtainable from some shops for between £2.50 and £3.50 per lb. The rare English Blue Vinney 'changes hands' for *c.* £4.40 per lb.

Largest

The largest cheese ever made was a cheddar of 34,591 lb *15 190 kg* made in 43 hr on 20–22 Jan 1964 by the Wisconsin Cheese Foundation for exhibition at the New York World's Fair, USA. It was transported in a specially designed refrigerated tractor trailer 'Cheese Mobile' 45 ft *13,71 m* long.

CHICKEN PLUCKING

Ernest Hausen (1877–1955) of Fort Atkinson, Wisconsin, USA, died undefeated after 33 years as a champion. On 19 Jan 1939 he was timed at 4.4 sec and reputedly twice did 3.5 sec a few years later.

The record time for plucking 12 chickens clean by a team of 4 women at the annual Chicken Plucking Championship at Masaryktown, Florida, USA is 32.9 sec set on 9 Oct 1976 by Doreena Cary, Diane Grieb, Kathy Roads and Dorothy McCarthy.

TURKEY PLUCKING

Vincent Pilkington of Cootehill, County Cavan, Ireland killed and plucked 100 turkeys in 7 hr 32 min on 15 Dec 1978. His record for a single turkey is 1 min 30 sec on RTE Television in Dublin on 17 Nov 1980.

On 23 May 1983 Joe Glaub (USA) killed 7300 turkeys in a 'working' day. Mrs Madge Colenso gutted 94 turkeys in 60 mins at Rivington Farm, Burstow, Horley, Surrey on 20 Dec 1984.

CHAPTER TEN

Human Achievements

1. ENDURANCE AND ENDEAVOUR

Lunar conquest

Neil Alden Armstrong (b. Wapakoneta, Ohio, USA of Scottish (*via* Ireland) and German ancestry, on 5 Aug 1930), command pilot of the Apollo XI mission, became the first man to set foot on the Moon on the Sea of Tranquility at 02.56 and 15 sec GMT on 21 July 1969. He was followed out of the Lunar Module *Eagle* by Col. Edwin Eugene Aldren, Jr, USAF (b. Glen Ridge, New Jersey, USA of Swedish, Dutch and British ancestry, on 20 Jan 1930), while the Command Module *Columbia* piloted by Lt Col Michael Collins, USAF (b. Rome, Italy, of Irish and pre-Revolutionary American ancestry, on 31 Oct 1930) orbited above.

Eagle landed at 20.17 and 42 sec GMT on 20 July and lifted off at 17.54 GMT on 21 July, after a stay of 21 hr 36 min. The Apollo XI had blasted off from Cape Canaveral, Florida at 13.32 GMT on 16 July and was a culmination of

The world's greatest collection of 3,450 tap dancers assembling at the back of the world's largest department store—Macy's of New York City. (See page 172)

the US space programme which, at its peak, employed 376,600 people and attained in the year 1966–7 a peak budget of $5,900,000,000 (*then £2460 million*).

There is evidence that Pavel Belyayev was the cosmonaut selected by the USSR for a manned circumlunar flight in *Zond 7* on 9 Dec 1968, 12 days before the Apollo VIII flight but no launch took place.

Altitude *Man*

The greatest altitude attained by man was when the crew of the ill-fated Apollo XIII were at apocynthion (*i.e.* their furthest point) 158 miles *254 km* above the lunar surface and 248,655 miles *400 187 km* above the Earth's surface at 1.21 a.m. BST on 15 Apr 1970. The crew were Capt. James Arthur Lovell, Jr USN (b. Cleveland, Ohio, 25 Mar 1928), Fred Wallace

Haise Jr (b. Biloxi, Miss., USA, 14 Nov 1933) and the late John L. Swigert (1931–82).

Altitude *Woman*

The greatest altitude attained by a woman is 340 km *211 miles* by Pilot-Cosmonaut of the USSR Svetlana Savitskaya (b. 1948) during her flight in *Soyuz T7* on 19–27 Aug 1982. The record in an aircraft is 24 336 m *79,842 ft* by Natalia Prokhanova (USSR) (b. 1940) in an E-33 jet, on 22 May 1965.

Speed *Man*

The fastest speed at which humans have travelled is 24,791 mph *39 897 km/h* when the Command Module of Apollo X carrying Col (*now* Brig Gen) Thomas Patten Stafford, USAF (b. Weatherford, Okla. 17 Sept 1930), and Cdr Eugene Andrew Cernan (b. Chicago, 14 Mar 1934) and Cdr (*now* Capt) John Watts Young, USN (b. San Francisco, 24 Sept 1930), reached this maximum value at the 400,000 ft *121,9 km* altitude interface on its trans-Earth return flight on 26 May 1969.

MILESTONES IN ABSOLUTE HUMAN ALTITUDE RECORDS

Altitude Ft	m	Pilot	Vehicle	Place		Date	
80*	24	Jean François Pilâtre de Rozier (1757–1785) (France)	Hot Air Balloon (tethered)	Fauxbourg, Paris	15 & 17	Oct	1783
c.330	c.100	de Rozier and the Marquis d'Arlandes (1742–1809) (France)	Hot Air Balloon (free flight)	LaMuette, Paris[1]	21	Nov	1783
c.3000	c.900	Dr Jacques-Alexander-Cesar Charles (1746–1823) and Ainé Robert (France)	Charliere Hydrogen Balloon	Tuileries, Paris	1	Dec	1783
c.9000	c.2750	Dr J.-A.-C. Charles (France)	Hydrogen Balloon	Nesles, France	1	Dec	1783
c.13,000	c.4000	James Sadler (GB)	Hydrogen Balloon	Manchester		May	1785
25,400[2]	7740	James Glaisher (1809–1903) (UK)	Hydrogen Balloon	Wolverhampton	17	July	1862
31,500	9615	Prof. A. Berson (Germany)	Hydrogen Balloon Phoenix	Strasbourg, France	4	Dec	1894
36,565	11 145	Sadi Lecointe (France)	Nieuport Aircraft	Issy-les-Moulineaux, France	30	Oct	1923
51,961	15 837	Prof. Auguste Piccard and Paul Kipfer (Switzerland)	FNRS 1 Balloon	Augsburg, Germany	27	May	1931
72,395	22 066	Capts Orvill A. Anderson and Albert W. Stevens (US Army Air Corps)	US Explorer II Helium Balloon	Rapid City, South Dakota, USA	11	Nov	1935
79,600	24 262	William Barton Bridgeman (USA)	US Douglas D558–11 Skyrocket	California, USA	15	Aug	1951
126,200	38 465	Capt Iven C. Kincheloe, Jr (USAF)	US Bell X-2 Rocket 'plane	California, USA	7	Sept	1956
169,600	51 694	Joseph A. Walker (USA)	US X-15 Rocket 'plane	California, USA	30	Mar	1961

Statute miles	Km						
203.2	327	Flt-Major Yuriy A. Gagarin (USSR) (1934–68)	USSR Vostok I Capsule	Orbital flight	12	Apr	1961
234,672		Col Frank Borman, USAF, Capt James Arthur Lovell, Jr, USN and Major William A. Anders, USAF	US Apollo VIII Command Module	Circum-lunar flight	25	Dec	1968
248,655	400 171	Capt James Arthur Lovell Jr, USN, Frederick Wallace Haise Jr and John L. Swigert Jr (1931–82)	US Apollo XIII	Abortive lunar landing mission	15	Apr	1970

* There is some evidence that Father Bartolomeu de Gusmo flew in his hot-air balloon in his 4th experiment post August 1709 in Portugal.
[1] Duration c.1.54 to 2.16 pm from Château de LaMuette to Butte aux Cailles, Paris 13°. Volume of the 70 ft 21,3 m high balloon was 60 000 'piedcubes' c.1700 m³.
[2] Glaisher, with Henry Tracey Coxwell (1819–1900) claimed 37,000 ft 11 275 m from Wolverhampton on 5 Sept 1862. Some writers accept 30,000 ft 9145 m.
Note: A complete progressive table comprising entries from 1783 to date was published in the 23rd edition of 1977.

PROGRESSIVE SPEED RECORDS

Speed m.p.h.	Km/h	Person and Vehicle	Place		Date	
25	40	Sledging	Heinola, Finland	c. 6500	BC	
35	55	Horse-riding	Anatolia, Turkey	c. 1400	BC	
45	70	Mountain Sledging	Island of Hawaii (now USA)	ante	AD	1500
50	80	Ice Yachts (earliest patent)	Netherlands		AD	1600
56.75	95	Grand Junction Railway 2–2–2: Lucifer	Madeley Banks, Staffs, England	13	Nov	1830
87.8	141,3	Tommy Todd, downhill skier	La Porte, California, USA		Mar	1873
90.0	144,8	Midland Railway 4–2–2 7 ft 9 in 2,36 m single	Ampthill, Bedford, England		Mar	1897
130.61	210,2	Siemens and Halske electric engine	Marienfeld-Zossen, near Berlin	27	Oct	1903
c.150	c.257,5	Frederick H. Marriott (fl. 1957) Stanley Steamer Wogglebug	Ormond Beach, Florida, USA	26	Jan	1907
210.64	339	Sadi Lecointe (France) Nieuport-Delage 29	Villesauvage, France	25	Sept	1921
415.2	668,2	Flt Lt (Later Wing Cdr) George Hedley Stainforth AFC Supermarine S.6B	Lee-on-Solent, England	29	Sept	1931
623.85	1004	Flugkapitan Heinz Dittmar Me. 163V–1	Peenemunde, Germany	2	Oct	1941
670	1078	Capt Charles Elwood Yeager, USAF Bell XS-1	Muroc Dry Lake, California, USA	14	Oct	1947
967	1556	Capt Charles Elwood Yeager, USAF Bell XS-1	Muroc Dry Lake, California, USA	26	Mar	1948
2905	4675,1	Major Robert M. White, North American X–15	Muroc Dry Lake, California, USA	7	Mar	1961
c.17,560	c.28 260	Flt Maj Yuriy Alekseyevich Gagarin, Vostok 1	Earth orbit	12	Apr	1961
24,226	38 988	Col Frank Borman, USAF, Capt James Arthur Lovell, Jr, USN, Major William A. Anders, USAF Apollo VIII	Trans-lunar injection	21	Dec	1968
24,790.8	39 897,0	Cdrs Eugene Andrew Cernan and John Watts Young, USN and Col Thomas P. Stafford, USAF Apollo X	Re-entry after lunar orbit	26	May	1969

Note: A complete progressive table comprising entries from pre-historic times to date was published in the 23rd edition of 1977.

Speed *Woman*
The highest speed ever attained by a woman is 28 115 km/h *17,470 mph* by Jnr Lt (now Lt Col) Valentina Vladimirovna Tereshkova-Niko-layev (b. 6 Mar 1937) of the USSR in *Vostok 6* on 16 June 1963. The highest speed ever achieved by a woman aircraft pilot is 2687,42 km/h *1669.89 mph* by Svetlana Savitskaya (USSR) reported on 2 June 1975.

Land speed *Man*
The highest reputed land speed is 739.666 mph *1190,377 km/h* or Mach 1.0106 by Stan Barrett (US) in *The Budweiser Rocket*, a rocket engined 3 wheeled car at Edwards Air Force Base, California on 17 Dec 1979 (see also p. 126).

The *official* one mile land speed record is 633.468 mph *1019,467 km/h* set by Richard Noble OBE (b. 1946) on 4 Oct 1983 over the Black

Two of the three humans who have been furthest from Earth Capt James A. Lovell USN and Frederick W. Haise whose abortive lunar mission of 1970 carried them 400,171 km *248,655 miles* from 'home base'. The third man, Lt-Cdr Thomas K. Mattingley was replaced by John L. Swigert just before take-off.

Rock Desert, north Nevada, USA in his 17 000 lb thrust Rolls Royce Avon 302 jet powered *Thrust 2*, designed by John Ackroyd.

The highest land speed attained in Britain is 263.92 mph *424,74 km/h* by Richard Noble in *Thrust 2* at Greenham Common, Berkshire on 25 Sept 1980.

Land speed *Women*

The highest land speed recorded by a woman is 524.016 mph *843,323 km/h* by Mrs Kitty Hambleton *née* O'Neil (US) in the 48,000 hp rocket-powered 3-wheeled S.M.1 *Motivator* over the Alvard Desert, Oregon, USA on 6 Dec 1976. Her official two-way record was 512.710 mph *825,126 km/h* and she probably touched 600 mph *965 km/h* momentarily.

Water speed *Man*

The highest speed ever achieved on water is an estimated 300 knots (345 mph *556 km/h*) by Kenneth Peter Warby, MBE, (b. 9 May 1939) on the Blowering Dam Lake, NSW, Australia on 20 Nov 1977 in his unlimited hydroplane *Spirit of Australia*. The official world water speed record is 514,389 km/h *319.627 mph 277.57 knots* set on 8 Oct 1978 by Warby on Blowering Dam Lake.

Woman

The fastest woman on water is Mary Rife (USA), who has driven her drag boat *Proud Mary* at more than 190 mph *305 km/h.*

Water speed *Propeller driven*

The highest officially recorded speed for propeller-driven craft is 215.33 mph *346,54 km/h* by Eddie Hill in his supercharged hydroplane *The Texan* on Lake Irvine, California on 5 June 1983. On a one-way run *Climax* recorded 205.19 mph *330,22 km/h.*

Most travelled *Man*

The man who had visited more countries than anyone was Jesse Hart Rosdail (1914–77) of Elmhurst, Illinois, USA, a 5th grade teacher. Of all the separately administered countries and territories listed in the *UN Population Report*, he had visited all excepting only North Korea and French Antarctic Territories. He estimated his mileage to visit 215 countries was 1,626,605 statute miles *2 617 766 km.*

Fred Jurgen Specovius (b. 1943) (West Germany) has visited all 170 sovereign countries except the impenetrable North Korea and all the non-sovereign territories except 6. He speaks 6 languages and has used up 14 passports.

The most travelled member of the Travellers Century Club of Los Angeles (limited to those who have visited 100 or more countries) is G. Parke Thompson of Akron, Ohio. His blanket coverage of the world lacks only St Pierre and Miquelon, Pitcairn Is., the four Antarctic territories and the impenetrable North Korea.

Horseback

The most travelled man in the horseback era was probably the Methodist preacher Francis Asbury (b. Birmingham, England), who travelled 264,000 miles *424 850 km* in North America from 1771 to 1815 preaching 16,000 sermons.

Most isolated *Man*

The farthest any human has been removed from his nearest living fellow man is 2233.2 miles *3596,4 km* in the case of the Command Service Module pilot Alfred M. Worden on the US Apollo XV lunar mission of 30 July–1 Aug 1971.

Passport Records

The world's most expensive passports are those from the USSR. In Feb 1982 an emigration permit was 220 roubles (£172) or up to 3500 roubles (over £2700) on the black market. If

The world's most travelled child George Chauncey Clouse (b. 6 Dec 1979) of Indiana, USA who had been to 104 countries before his 5th Birthday.

LONGEST WALKS

The first person reported to have 'walked round the world' is George Matthew Schilling (USA) from 3 Aug 1897 to 1904, but the first verified achievement was by David Kunst (b. 1939) (USA) from 10 June 1970 to 5 Oct 1974. Tomas Carlos Pereira (b. Argentine, 16 Nov 1942) spent ten years, 6 Apr 1968–8 Apr 1978, walking 29,825 miles *48,000 km* around all five continents. George Meegan (b. 2 Oct 1952) from Rainham, Kent, England walked 19,019 miles *30 431 km* from Usuaia, the southern tip of South America to Prudhoe Bay in Northern Alaska, taking 2426 days from 26 Jan 1977 to 18 Sept 1983, and thus completed the first traverse of the Western Hemisphere. Sean Eugene Maguire (b. USA 15 Sept 1956) walked 7327 miles *11791 km* from the Yukon River, north of Livengood, Alaska, to Key West, Florida, USA, in 307 days, 6 June 1978–9 April 1979. The Trans-Canada (Halifax to Vancouver) record walk of 3764 miles *6057 km* is 96 days by Clyde McRae, 23, from 1 May to 4 Aug 1973. John Lees (b. 23 Feb 1945) of Brighton, East Sussex, England between 11 Apr and 3 June 1972, walked 2876 miles *4628 km* across the USA from City Hall, Los Angeles to City Hall, New York City in 53 days 12 hr 15 min (average 53.75 miles *86,49 km* a day). The longest continuous walk in Britain is one of 6824 miles *10 982 km*, around the British coast by John N. Merrill (b. 19 Aug 1943), from 3 Jan to 8 Nov 1978. The feminine record was set over 3524 miles *5671 km* by Mrs Vera Andrews of Clacton-on-Sea, Essex on 31 Mar–8 Nov 1984.

applications involved a whole family or travel to the West, the necessary accompanying visa was refused 996 times in each 1000 applications.

Round the World

The fastest time for a round the world trip on scheduled flights for a circumnavigation is 44 hr 6 min by David J. Springbett (b. 2 May 1938) of Taplow, Buckinghamshire, from Los Angeles eastabout *via* London, Bahrain, Singapore, Bangkok, Manila, Tokyo and Honolulu on 8–10 Jan 1980 over a 23,068 mile *37 124 km* route.

The FAI rates any flight taking off and landing at the same point, which is as long as the Tropic of Cancer (viz 22,858.754 miles 36 787,599 km) as a circumnavigational flight.

North Pole conquest

The claims of neither of the two US Arctic explorers, Dr Frederick Albert Cook (1865–1940) nor Cdr (later Rear Ad.) Robert Edwin Peary (1856–1920), of the US Naval Civil Engineering branch in reaching the North Pole are subject to positive proof. Cook accompanied by the Eskimos, Ah-pellah and Etukishook, two sledges and 26 dogs, struck north from a point 60 miles *96,5 km* north of Svartevoeg, on Axel Heiberg I., Canada, 460 miles *740 km* from the Pole on 21 Mar 1908, allegedly reaching Lat. 89° 31′ N on 19 Apr and the Pole on 21 Apr. Peary, accompanied by his Negro assistant, Matthew Alexander Henson (1866–1955) and the four Eskimos, Ooqueah, Eginwah, Seegloo and Ootah (1875–1955), struck north from his Camp Bartlett (Lat. 87° 44′ N.) at 5 a.m. on 2 Apr 1909. After travelling another 134 miles *215 km*, he allegedly established his final camp, Camp Jessup, in the proximity of the Pole at 10 a.m. on 6 Apr and marched a further 42 miles *67,5 km* quartering the sea-ice before turning south at 4 p.m. on 7 Apr. On excellent pack ice and modern sledges Wally Herbert's 1968–9 Expedition (see below) attained a best day's route mileage of 23 miles *37 km* in 15 hr. Cook claimed 26 miles *41,8 km* twice while Peary claimed a surely unsustainable average of 38 miles *61 km* for 8 consecutive days.

The earliest indisputable attainment of the North Pole over the sea-ice was at 3 p.m. (Central Standard Time) on 19 Apr 1968 by Ralph Plaisted (US) and three companions after a 42-day trek in four Skidoos (snow-mobiles). Their arrival was independently verified 18 hr later by a US Air Force weather aircraft. The sea bed is 13,410 ft *4087 m* below the North Pole.

Naomi Uemura (1941–1984) the Japanese explorer and mountaineer became the first person to reach the North Pole in a solo trek across the Arctic Ice Cap at 4.45 a.m., GMT on 1 May 1978. He had travelled 450 miles *725 km* setting out on 7 Mar from Cape Edward, Ellesmere Island in northern Canada. He averaged nearly 8 miles *13 km* per day with his sled 'Aurora' drawn by 17 huskies.

The first women to set foot on the North Pole was Mrs Fran Phipps, wife of the Canadian bush pilot Weldy Phipps on 5 Apr 1971. Galina Aleksandrovna Lastovskaya (b. 1941) and Lilia Vladislavovna Minina (b. 1959) were crew members of the USSR atomic icebreaker *Arktika* which reached the Pole on 17 Aug 1977.

The soviet scientist Dr Pavel A. Gordienko and 3 companions were arguably the first ever to stand on the exact point Lat. 90° 00′ 00″ N (+ 300 metres) on 23 Apr 1948.

South Pole conquest

The first men to cross the Antarctic circle (Lat. 66° 33′ S.) were the 193 crew of the *Resolution* (462 tons/*tonnes*) (Capt James Cook RN (1728–79) and *Adventure* (336 tons/*tonnes*) (Lt T. Furneaux) on 17 Jan 1773 in 39° E. The first person known to have sighted the Antarctic ice shelf was Capt. F. F. Bellinghausen (Russian) (1778–1852) on 27 Jan 1820 from the vessels *Vostock* and *Mirnyi*. The first known to have sighted the mainland of the continent was Capt William Smith (1790–1847) and Master Edward Bransfield, RN, in the brig *Williams*. They saw the peaks of Trinity Land 3 days later on 30 Jan 1820.

The South Pole (alt. 9186 ft *2779 m* on ice and 336 ft *102 m* bed rock) was first reached at 11 a.m. on 16 Dec 1911 by a Norwegian party led by Capt. Roald Engebereth Gravning Amundsen (1872–1928), after a 53-day march with dog sledges from the Bay of Whales, to which he had penetrated in the *Fram*. Subsequent calculations showed that Olav Olavson Bjaaland (the last survivor, dying in June 1961, aged 88) and Helmer Hanssen probably passed within 400–600 m of the exact pole. The other two members were Sverre H. Hassell (d. 1928) and Oskar Wisting (d. 1936).

Women

The first woman to set foot on Antarctica was Mrs Karoline Mikkelsen on 20 Feb 1935. No woman stood on the South Pole until 11 Nov 1969. On that day Lois Jones, Eileen McSaveney, Jean Pearson, Terry Lee Tickhill (all US), Kay Lindsay (Australia) and Pam Young (NZ) arrived by air.

First on both Poles

Dr Albert P. Crary (USA) reached the North Pole in a Dakota aircraft on 3 May 1952. On 12 Feb 1961 he arrived at the South Pole by Sno Cat on a scientific traverse party from the McMurdo Station. He thus pre-empted David Porter by 18 years.

Arctic crossing

The first crossing of the Arctic sea-ice was achieved by the British Trans-Arctic Expedition which left Point Barrow, Alaska on 21 Feb 1968 and arrived at the Seven Island Archipelago north-east of Spitzbergen 464 days later on 29 May 1969 after a haul of 2920 statute miles *4699 km* and a drift of 700 miles *1126 km* compared with the straight line distance of 1662 miles *2674 km*. The team was Wally Herbert (leader), 34, Major Ken Hedges, 34, RAMC, Allan Gill, 38, and Dr Roy Koerner, 36 (glaciologist), and 40 huskies. The only crossing achieved in a single season was that by Fiennes and Burton (see below) from Alert via the North Pole to the Greenland Sea in open snowmobiles.

Antarctic crossing

The first surface crossing of the Antarctic continent was completed at 1.47 p.m. on 2 Mar 1958, after a trek of 2158 miles *3473 km* lasting 99 days from 24 Nov 1957, from Shackleton Base to Scott Base led by Dr (now Sir) Vivian Ernest Fuchs (born 11 Feb 1908). The 2600 mile *4185 km* trans-Antarctic leg from Sanae to Scott Base of the 1980–82 Trans-Globe Expedition was achieved in 66 days from 26 Oct 1980 to 11 Jan 1981 having passed through the South Pole on 23 Dec 1980. The 3 man party on snowmobiles comprised Sir Ranulph Fiennes (b. 1944), Oliver Shepard and Charles Burton.

Polar Circumnavigation (First)

Sir Ranulph Fiennes, Bt and Charles Burton of the British Trans-Globe Expedition travelled South from Greenwich (2 Sept 1979), via the South Pole (17 Dec 1980) and the North Pole (11 Apr 1982), and back to Greenwich arriving after a 35,000 mile *56 325 km* trek on 29 Aug 1982.

Longest sledge journeys

The longest totally self-supporting Polar sledge journey ever made was one of 1080 miles *1738 km* from West to East across Greenland on 18 June to 5 Sept 1934 by Capt M. Lindsay (1905–1981) (later Sir Martin Lindsay of Dowhill, Bt, CBE, DSO), Lt Arthur S. T. Godfrey, RE, (later Lt Col, k. 1942), Andrew N. C. Croft (later Col, DSO) and 49 dogs. The Ross Sea Party of 10 (3 died) sledged over 2000 miles *3220 km* in the period of 300 days from 6 May 1975.

Greatest ocean descent

The record ocean descent was achieved in the Challenger Deep of the Marianas Trench, 250 miles *400 km* south-west of Guam, in the Pacific Ocean, when the Swiss-built US Navy bathyscaphe *Trieste*, manned by Dr Jacques Piccard (b. 1914) (Switzerland) and Lt Donald Walsh, USN, reached the ocean bed 35,820 ft *(6.78 miles 10 917 m)* down, at 1.10 p.m. on 23 Jan 1960 (see page 58). The pressure of the water was 16,883 lbf/in² *1183 kgf/cm²* and the temperature 37.4° F *3° C*. The descent required 4 hr 48 min and the ascent 3 hr 17 min.

Deep diving records

The record depth for the extremely dangerous activity of breath-held diving is 105 m *344 ft* by Jacques Mayol (France) off Elba, Italy, in December 1983 for men and 147½ ft *45 m* by Giuliana Treleani (Italy) off Cuba in September 1967 for women. Mayol descended on a sled in 104 sec and ascended in 90 sec. The record dive with Scuba (self-contained under-water breathing apparatus) is 437 ft *133 m* by John J. Gruener and R. Neal Watson (USA) off Freeport, Grand Bahama on 14 Oct 1968. The record dive utilizing gas mixtures (nitrogen, oxygen and helium) is a simulated dive of 2250 ft *685,8 m* in a dry chamber by Stephen Porter, Len Whitlock and Erik Kramer at the Duke University Medical Center in Durham, North Carolina on 3 Feb 1981 in a 43 day trial in a sphere of 8 ft *2,43 m*. Patrick Raude and 5 Comex divers left and returned to the bell 'Petrel' at 501 m *1643 ft*, off Cavalaire, France, in 1982.

Deepest underwater escapes

The deepest underwater rescue achieved was of the *Pisces III* in which Roger R. Chapman, 28 and Roger Mallinson, 35 were trapped for 76 hr when it sank to 1575 ft *480 m* 150 miles *240 km* south-east of Cork, Ireland on 29 Aug 1973. She was hauled to the surface by the cable ship *John Cabot* after work by Pisces V, Pisces II and the remote control recovery vessel US CURV on 1 Sept. The greatest depth of an actual escape without any equipment has been from 225 ft *68,58 m* by Richard A. Slater from the rammed submersible *Nekton Beta* off Catalina Island, California, USA on 28 Sept 1970.

Deepest salvage

The greatest depth at which salvage has been achieved is 16,500 ft *5029 m* by the bathyscaphe *Trieste II* (Lt Cdr Mel Bartels, USN) to attach cables to an 'electronic package' on the sea bed 400 miles *645 km* north of Hawaii on 20 May 1972. Project Jennifer by USS *Glomar Explorer* in June/July 1974 to recover a Golf class USSR submarine, 750 miles *1200 km* NW of Hawaii, cost $550 million but was not successful.

Flexible dress divers

The deepest salvage operation ever achieved with divers was on the wreck of HM Cruiser *Edinburgh* sunk on 2 May 1942 in the Barents Sea off Northern Norway inside the Arctic Circle in 803 ft *244,7 m* of water. Twelve divers dived on the wreck in pairs using a bell from the *Stephaniturm* (1423 tons) over 32 days under the direction of former RN officer and project director Michael Stewart from 17 Sept to 7 Oct 1981.

The 431 gold ingots were divided; £14.6 million to the USSR, £7.3 million to HM Government and some £18 million to the salvage contractors, Jessop Marine Recoveries Ltd (10%) and Wharton Williams Ltd (90%). John Rossier, 28 was the first to touch the gold. The longest decompression time was 7 days 10 hr 27 min. The £39.9 million is an all-time record but 34 bars worth £4 million were believed unrecovered.

Greatest penetration into the earth

The deepest penetration made into the ground

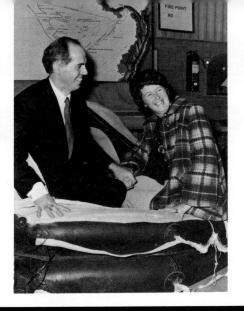

by man is in the Western Deep Levels Mine at Carletonville, Transvaal, South Africa where a record depth of 3777 m *12,500 ft* (2.36 miles) has been attained. The rock temperature at this depth is 131° F *55° C.*

Longest on a raft

The longest recorded survival alone on a raft is 133 days (4½ months) by Second Steward Poon Lim BEM (b. Hong Kong) of the UK Merchant Navy, whose ship, the SS *Ben Lomond,* was torpedoed in the Atlantic 565 miles *910 km* west of St Paul's Rocks in Lat. 00° 30′ N Long.

Maurice and Maralyn Bailey in a reunion with the 4½ ft *1,37 m* rubber dinghy in which they survived 118 days in 1972. (See page 167) *(Avon Inflatables Ltd)*

MARINE CIRCUMNAVIGATION RECORDS
(Compiled by Sq Ldr D. H. Clarke, DFC, AFC)

A true circumnavigation entails passing through two antipodal points (which are at least 12,429 statute miles *20 000 km* apart).

CATEGORY	VESSEL	NAME	START PLACE AND DATE	FINISH DATE AND DURATION
Earliest	*Vittoria* Expedition of Fernão de Magalhães, *c.* 1480–k. 1521	Juan Sebastián de Elcano or del Cano (d. 1526) and 17 crew	Seville, Spain 20 Sept 1519	San Lucar, 6 Sept 1522 30,700 miles *49 400 km*
Earliest British	*Golden Hind* (ex *Pelican*) 100 tons/*tonnes*	Francis Drake (*c.* 1540–96) (Knighted 4 April 1581)	Plymouth, 13 Dec 1577	26 Sept. 1580
Earliest Woman	*Etoile*	Crypto-female valet of M. de Commerson, named Baré	St Malo, 1766	1769
Earliest fore-and-aft rigged vessel	*Union* 98 tons (Sloop)	John Boit Junior, 19–21, (US) and 22 crew	Newport, RI 1794 (via Cape Horn westabout)	Newport, RI 1796
Earliest Yacht	*Sunbeam* 170 ft *51,8 m* 3 Mast Topsail schooner	Lord and Lady Brassey (GB) passengers and crew	Cowes, Isle of Wight 1876	Cowes, Isle of Wight 1877
Earliest Solo	*Spray* 36¾ ft *11,20 m* gaff yawl	Capt Joshua Slocum, 51, (US) (a non-swimmer) (No 1 solo circum)	Newport, RI, *via* Magellan Straits, 24 Apr 1895	3 July 1898 46,000 miles *74 000 km*
Earliest Motor Boat	*Speejacks* 98 ft *29,87 m*	Albert Y. Gowen (US) wife and crew	New York City 1921	New York City 1922
Earliest Motor Boat (Solo)	*Mabel E. Holland* 42 ft *12,8 m* (no sails)	David Scott Cowper (GB)	Plymouth 1984 (via Panama Canal)	Plymouth 170 days 2 hr 15 min (165.7 mpd)
Earliest Woman Solo	*Mazurek* 31 ft 2 in *9,5 m* Bermudan Sloop	Krystyna Chojnowska-Liskiewicz (Poland) (No 58 solo circum)	Las Palmas 28 Mar 1976 westabout *via* Panama	Tied knot 21 Mar 1978
Earliest Woman Solo (*via* Cape Horn)	*Express Crusader* 53 ft *16,15 m* Bermuda Sloop	Naomi James (NZ/GB) (later DBE) (No 59 solo circum)	Dartmouth 9 Sept 1977 (Cape Horn 19 Mar 1978)	Dartmouth 8 June 1978 (266 days 19 hr)
Smallest Boat	*Super Shrimp* 18 ft 4 in *5,58 m* Bermuda Sloop	Shane Acton (GB) Iris Derungs (Swiss)	Cambridge, England August 1972	Cambridge, England August 1980 (E–W *via* Panama Canal)
Earliest Submerged	*US Submarine Triton*	Capt Edward L. Beach USN plus 182 crew	New London, Connecticut 16 Feb 1960	10 May 1960 39,708 miles *49 422 km*
Earliest non-stop Solo (Port to Port)	*Suhaili* 32.4 ft *9,87 m* Bermudan Ketch	Robin Knox Johnston CBE (b. 1939) (No 25 solo circum)	Falmouth, 14 June 1968	22 Apr 1969 (312 days)
Longest non-stop alone at sea	*Dar Przemysla* 46 ft 7 in *14,2 m* Ketch	Henryk Jaskula (Poland) (No 68 solo circum)	Gdynia 1979 (W–E via Cape Horn)	Gdynia 1980 (344 days)
Fastest Solo (speed)	*Manureva* (ex *Pen Duick IV*) 70 ft *21,33 m* Trimaran	Alain Colas (France) (No 40 solo circum)	Saint Malo *via* Sydney	29 Mar 1974 (169 days) (av speed 178.5 mpd)
Earliest solo in both directions	*Solitaire* 34 ft *10,36 m* Bermudan Sloop	Lew Powles (GB) (No 62 & 71 solo circum)	Falmouth 1975 (E–W) Lymington 1980 (W–E)	(*via* Panama) Lymington 1978 (*via* Horn) Lymington 1981
Earliest solo in both directions (*via* Horn)	*Ocean Bound* 41 ft 1 in *12,52 m* Bermudan Sloop	David Scott Cowper (GB) (No 66 & 78 solo circum)	Plymouth 1979 (W–E) Plymouth 1981 (E–W)	Plymouth 1980 Plymouth 1982 (see below)
Fastest Solo (Time)	*Credit Agricole* 56 ft *17,07 m* Bermudan Cutter	Philippe Jeantot (Fr) (No 84 solo circum)	Newport 1982 (W–E *via* Cape Horn)	Newport, 1983 159 days 2 hr 26 min 25,560 miles at av speed 166,94 mpd
Fastest time and fastest speed (yacht)	*Flyer* 76 ft *23,1 m* Bermudan Sloop	Cornelis von Rietschoten (Dutch) (and 15 crew)	Portsmouth 29 Aug 1981 (W–E via Cape Horn)	29 Mar 1982 120 days 6 hr 35 min (220.7 mpd)
Fastest (clipper)	*James Baines* 266 ft *81,07 m*	Capt C. McDonald (GB) and crew	Liverpool to Melbourne (58 days) 1854	Melbourne to Liverpool (69 days) 1855
Fastest Solo Westabout (*via* Cape Horn)	*Ocean Bound* 41 ft 1 in *12,52 m* Bermudan sloop	David Scott Cowper (GB) (No 78 solo circum)	Plymouth 22 Sept 1981 (south of 5 capes)	Plymouth 17 May 1982 (221 sailing days) 31,350 miles *50 451 km* av 141.85 mpd
Fastest-ever time (yacht)	*Awahnee II* 53 ft *16,15 m* Bermuda Cutter	Bob Griffith (US) (5 crew)	Bluff, NZ. 1970 (W–E *via* Horn)	Bluff, NZ, 1971 (88 sailing days plus 23 days stopovers)
Fastest-ever time (clipper)	*Red Jacket* 260 ft *79,24 m*	Capt S. Reid (GB) and crew	From/to Lat 26° 25′ W (*via* Horn)	62 days 22 hr 1854
Earliest Solo Double circumnavigation	*Perie Banou* 33 ft 7 in *10,24 m* Bermudan Sloop	Jon Sanders (Australia) (No 75 & 81 solo circum)	Freemantle 1981 (W–E) (continuously at sea but not non-stop)	(*via* Horn) Freemantle 1982 (*via* Plymouth) 420 days 1982

* Eduard Roditi, author of *Magellan of the Pacific,* advances the view that Magellan's slave, Enrique, was the first circumnavigator. He had been purchased in Malacca and it was shown that he already understood the Filipino dialect Vizayan, when he reached the Philippines from the east. He 'tied the knot' off Limasawa on 28 Mar 1521. The first to circumnavigate in both directions was Capt Tobias Furneaux, RN (1735–81) as second lieutenant aboard the *Dolphin* from/to Plymouth east to west *via* the Magellan Straits in 1766–68 and as captain of the *Adventure* from/to Plymouth west to east *via* Cape Horn in 1772–4.

TRANS-ATLANTIC AND PACIFIC MARINE RECORDS

(Compiled by Sq Ldr D. H. Clarke, DFC, AFC)

TRANS-ATLANTIC MARINE RECORDS

CATEGORY	NAME	VESSEL	START	FINISH	DURATION	DATE
Earliest Canoe	'Finn-Man' (Eskimo)	Kayak 11 ft 10 in *3,6 m*	Greenland	Humber, England	Time not known	1613
Earliest Rowing	John Brown + 5 British deserters from garrison	Ship's boat *c.* 20 ft *6,1 m*	St Helena (10 June)	Belmonte, Brazil (fastest ever row)	28 days (83 mpd)	1799
Earliest Crossing (2 men)	C. R. Webb + 1 crew (US)	*Charter Oak* 43 ft *13,1 m*	New York	Liverpool	35 days 15 hr	1857
Earliest Trimaran (Raft)	John Mikes + 2 crew (US)	*Non Pareil*, 25 ft *7,62 m*	New York	Southampton	51 days	1868
Earliest Solo Sailing (E–W)	Josiah Shackford (US)	15 ton gaff sloop	Bordeaux, France	Surinam (Dutch Guiana)	35 days	1786
Earliest Solo Sailing (W–E)	Alfred Johnson (US)	*Centennial* 20 ft *6,09 m*	Glos., Mass	Wales	46 days	1876
Earliest Woman (with US husband)	Mrs Joanna Crapo (b. Scotland)	*New Bedford* 20 ft *6,09 m* (Bermudan ketch)	Chatham, Mass.	Newlyn, Cornwall	51 days (Earliest with Bermudan rig)	1877
Earliest Single-handed race	J. W. Lawlor (US) (winner)	*Sea Serpent* 15 ft *4,57 m*	Boston (21 June)	Coverack, Cornwall	45 days	1891
Earliest Rowing by 2 men	Georg Harboe and Frank Samuelsen (Nor)	*Fox* $18\frac{1}{3}$ ft *5,58 m*	New York City (6 June)	Isles of Scilly (1 Aug)	55 days (56 mpd)	1897
Fastest Solo Sailing (W–E)	J. V. T. McDonald (GB)	*Inverarity* 38 ft *11,58 m*	Nova Scotia	Ireland	16 days (147 mpd)	1922
Earliest Canoe (with sail)	Franz Romer (Germany)	*Deutscher Sport* $21\frac{1}{2}$ ft *6,55 m*	Las Palmas	St Thomas	58 days (47 mpd)	1928
Earliest Woman Solo (East–West)	Ann Davison (GB)	*Felicity Ann* 23 ft *7,01 m*	Portsmouth Las Palmas	Dominica (20 Nov 1952)	65 days	1952–3
Earliest Woman Solo (W–E)	Gladys Gradley (US)	Lugger 18 ft *5,5 m*	Nova Scotia	Hope Cove, Devon	60 days	1903
Earliest Woman Solo (across 2 oceans)	Anna Woolf (SA)	*Zama Zulu* 43 ft *13,1 m* (Ferroconcrete)	Cape Town	Bowling, Scotland	8920 miles in 109 days	1976
Fastest Woman solo	Naomi James DBE	*Kriter Lady* 53 ft *16,15 m*	Plymouth	Newport, R.I.	25 days 19 hr 12 min	1980
Fastest 2-woman crew	Annick Martin (Fr) Annie Cordelle (Fr)	*Super Marches Bravo* 45 ft *13,7 m*	Plymouth	Newport, R.I.	21 days 4 hr 28 min	1981
Smallest West–East	Wayne Dickinson (US)	*God's Tear* 8 ft 11 in *2,71 m*	Allerton, Mass (30 Oct)	Aranmore Is NW Eire (20 Mar)	142 days	1982–3
Smallest (East–West) (Southern)	Eric Peters (GB)	*Toniky-Nou* 5 ft $10\frac{1}{2}$ in *1,79 m* barrel	Las Palmas (25 Dec)	St Francoise, Guadaloupe (8 Feb)	46 days	1982–3
Fastest Crossing Sailing (multihull) (East–West)	Eric Tabarly (France) + 2 crew	*Pen Duick IV* 67 ft *20,42 m*	Tenerife	Martinique	251.4 miles *404,5 km*/day (10 days 12 hours)	1968
Fastest Crossing Sailing (monohull) (East–West)	Wilhelm Hirte & crew (Ger)	*Kriter II* 80 ft *24,38 m*	Canary Is.	Barbados	13 days 8 hr	1977
Fastest Crossing (multihull) (West–East)	Patrick Morvan (Fr) (3 crew)	*Jet Services II* 60 ft *18,3 m* BM Sloop—Catamaran	Sandy Hook, NJ	Land's End	8 days 16 hr 36 min 375.16 mpd	1984
Fastest Crossing monohull (West–East)	Wilson Marshall (US) & crew	*Atlantic* 185 ft *56,38 m*	Sandy Hook, NJ	Lizard, Cornwall (3054 miles)	12 days 4 hr (fastest noon to noon 341 miles)	1905
Fastest Crossing Sailing Ship (West–East)	A. Eldridge (US) and crew	*Red Jacket* (Clipper) 260 ft *79,24 m*	Sandy Hook, NJ	Liverpool Bar	12 days 00 hr 00 min 277.7 mpd	1854
Fastest Solo East–West (Northern) (monohull)	Kazimierz Jaworski (Poland)	*Spaniel II* 56 ft *17,06 m*	Plymouth	Newport, R.I.	19 days 13 hr 25 min	1980
Fastest East–West (Northern) monohull	Bruno Bacilieri (It) Marc Vallin	*Faram Serenissima* $66\frac{1}{2}$ ft *20,27 m*	Plymouth	Newport, R.I.	16 days 1 hr 25 min	1981
Fastest Solo East–West (Northern) (multihull)	Philip Weld (US)	*Moxie* 51 ft *15,54 m* (Tri)	Plymouth	Newport, R.I.	17 days 23 hr 12 min	1980
Fastest Solo East–West (Southern) (monohull)	Sir Francis Chichester KBE (GB)	*Gipsy Moth V* 57 ft *17,37 m*	Portuguese Guinea	Nicaragua	179.1 miles *288,2 km*/day (22.4 days)	1970
Fastest Ever Yacht Sail (N. route) (East–West)	Chay Blyth (GB) Rob James (GB)	*Brittany Ferries GB* $65\frac{1}{2}$ ft *20 m* (Tri)	Plymouth	Newport, R.I.	14 days 13 hr 54 min 212.1 mpd	1981
Fastest 24 Hour Run	Michael Birch (Can) +8 crew	Formula Tag (BM Sloop—Cat)	Quebec	St Malo	512.3 miles in 23 hr 42 min on 27 Aug	1984
Fastest Solo Rowing East–West	Sidney Genders, (51 years) (GB)	*Khaggavisana* $19\frac{3}{4}$ ft *6,02 m*	Penzance, Cornwall	Miami, Florida *via* Antigua	37.8 miles *60,8 km*/day 160 days 8 hr	1970
Fastest Solo Rowing West–East	Gérard d'Aboville (Fr)	*Capitaine Cook* 5,60 m *18 ft 4 in*	Chatham, Mass 10 July	Ushant, France 20 Sept	71 days 23 hr 72 km *44.8 mpd*	1980
Earliest Solo Rowing East–West	John Fairfax (GB)	*Britannia* 22 ft *6,70 m*	Las Palmas (20 Jan)	Ft Lauderdale, Florida (19 July)	180 days	1969
Earliest Solo Rowing West–East	Tom McClean (Ireland)	*Super Silver* 20 ft *6,90 m*	St John's, Newfoundland (17 May)	Black Sod Bay, Ireland (27 July)	70.7 days	1969
Youngest Solo Sailing	David Sandeman ($17\frac{1}{2}$ years) (GB)	*Sea Raider* 35 ft *10,67 m*	Jersey, C.I.	Newport, R.I.	43 days	1976
Oldest Solo Sailing	Monk Farnham (74 years 276 days)	*Seven Bells* 28 ft *8,53 m*	Shannon, Ireland	Rhode Is.	72 days (3 stops)	1983
Earliest by Sailboard	Christian Marty (Fr) (Escorted by yacht *Assiduous*)	Sodim (type)	Dakar Senegal	Kourou Fr Guiana	37 days 16 hr 4 min (slept on board)	1981–2

TRANS-PACIFIC MARINE RECORDS

CATEGORY	NAME	VESSEL	START	FINISH	DURATION	DATE
Fastest (Trans Pac)	Bob Hanel (US) + 6 crew	*Double Bullet* (BM Sloop—Cat)	Los Angeles	Hawaii	7 days 7 hr 31 min 325.5 mpd	1983
Fastest Yacht (Australia–Horn)	O. K. Pennendreft (Fr) + 13 crew	*Kriter II* 80 ft *24,38 m*	Sydney	Cape Horn	21 days (275 mpd)	1975–6
Fastest Clipper (Australia–Horn)	Capt J. N. Forbes (GB) + crew	*Lightning* 244 ft *74,36 m*	Melbourne	Cape Horn	19 days 1 hr (315 mpd)	1854
Fastest Solo Monohull (Australia–Horn)	Philippe Jeantot (Fr)	*Credit Agricole* 56 ft *17,07 m*	Sydney	Cape Horn	29 days 23 hr (5709 miles, av 190.6 mpd)	1982–3
Fastest seven days solo run	Philippe Jeantot (Fr)	*Credit Agricole* 56 ft *17,07 m*	As above 8 Feb	On passage 15 Feb	Covered 1552 miles	1983
Earliest Solo (Woman)	Sharon Sites Adams (US)	*Sea Sharp II* 31 ft *9,45 m*	Yokohama, Japan	San Diego, Cal	75 days (5911 miles)	1969
Earliest Rowing	John Fairfax (GB) Sylvia Cook (GB)	*Britannia II* 35 ft *10,66 m*	San Francisco, Cal. 26 Apr 1971	Hayman I., Australia 22 Apr 1972	362 days	1971–2
Earliest Rowing Solo	Peter Bird, 36 (GB)	*Hele-on-Britannia* 32 ft *9,75 m*	San Francisco 23 Aug 1982	Gt. Barrier Reef Australia 14 June 1983	294 days 9000 miles *14 480 km*	1982–3
Earliest Solo (Totally Blind)	Hank Dekker (US)	*Dark Star* 25 ft 7 in (BM Sloop)	San Francisco	Honolulu	23 days (Braille charts, Compass and Loran)	1983
Earliest raft (shore to shore)	Vital Alsar (Sp) and 3 crew	*La Balsa* (Balsa logs) 42 ft *12,8 m*	Guayaquil Ecuador	Mooloolaba Australia	160 days	1970

N.B.—The earliest single-handed Pacific crossings were achieved East–West by Bernard Gilboy (US) in 1882 in the 18 ft *5,48 m* double-ender *Pacific* to Australia and West–East by Fred Rebel (Latvia) in the 18 ft *5,48 m Elaine*, (from Australia) and Edward Miles (US) in the $36\frac{3}{4}$ ft *11,2 m Sturdy II* (from Japan) both in 1932, the latter *via* Hawaii.

38° 45′ W at 11.45 a.m. on 23 Nov 1942. He was picked up by a Brazilian fishing boat off Salinópolis, Brazil, on 5 Apr 1943 and was able to walk ashore. In July 1943, he was awarded the BEM and now lives in New York City.

Maurice and Maralyn Bailey survived 118⅓ days in an inflatable dinghy 4½ ft *1,37 m* in diameter in the north-east Pacific from 4 Mar to 30 June 1973.

Shaft sinking record

The one month (31 days) world record is 1251 ft *381,3 m* for a standard shaft 26 ft *7,92 m* in diameter at Buffelsfontein Mine, Transvaal, South Africa, in March 1962. The British record of 131,2 m *430 ft* of 7,92 m *26 ft* diameter shaft was set in No 2 Shaft of the NCB's Whitemoor Mine near Selby, North Yorkshire in 31 days (15 Nov–16 Dec 1982).

Most marriages *World*

The greatest number of marriages accumulated in the monogamous world is 26 by the former Baptist minister Glynn 'Scotty' Wolfe (b. 25 July 1908) of Blythe, California, who first married in 1927. His latest wife was the tattooed Cristine Sue Camacho, 38, married on 28 Jan 1984 but who left on 1 May and was divorced on 8 Nov. His previous oldest wife was 22. His total number of children is, he says, 41. He suffered only 24 mothers-in-law because two of his 24 wives were the subject of re-marriages.

Mrs Beverly Nina Avery, then aged 48, a barmaid from Los Angeles, California, USA, set a monogamous world record in October 1957 by obtaining her sixteenth divorce from her fourteenth husband, Gabriel Avery. She alleged outside the court that five of the 14 had broken her nose.

The record for bigamous marriages is 104 by Giovanni Vigliotto, one of some 50 aliases used by either Fred Jipp (b. New York City, 3 Apr 1936) or Nikolai Peruskov (b. Siracusa, Sicily, 3 Apr 1929) over the span 1949–1981 in 27 US States and 14 other countries. Four victims were aboard one ship in 1968 and two in London. On 28 Mar 1983 in Phoenix, Arizona he was sentenced to 28 years for fraud, 6 years for bigamy and fined $336,000.

Great Britain

The only monogamous citizen married eight times is Olive Joyce Wilson of Marston Green, Birmingham. She has consecutively been Mrs John Bickley; Mrs Don Trethowan; Mrs George Hundley; Mrs Raymond Ward; Mrs Harry Latrobe; Mrs Leslie Harris; Mrs Ray Richards and now Mrs John Grassick. All were divorced except Mr Hundley, who died.

Oldest bride and bridegroom

The oldest recorded bridegroom has been Harry Stevens, 103, married Thelma Lucas, 84, at the Caravilla Retirement Home, Wisconsin on 3 Dec 1984.

The British record was set by Sir Robert Mayer CH, KCVO (1879–1985) who married Jacqueline Noble, 51 in London on 10 Nov 1980 when aged 101 years.

Mrs Winifred Clark (b. 13 Nov 1871) became Britain's oldest recorded bride when she married Albert Smith, 80, at St. Hugh's Church, Cantley, South Yorkshire the day before her 100th birthday.

Longest engagements

The longest engagement on record was between Octavio Guillen, and Adriana Martinez. They finally took the plunge after 67 years in June 1969 in Mexico City, Mexico. Both were then 82.

Longest marriage *World*

The longest recorded marriages are of 86 years between Sir Temulji Bhicaji Nariman and Lady Nariman from 1853 to 1940 resulting from a cousin marriage when both were five. Sir Temulji (b. 3 Sept 1848) died, aged 91 years 11 months, in August 1940 at Bombay. Lazurus Rowe (b. Greenland, New Hampshire, 1725) and Molly Webber were recorded as marrying in 1743. He died first in 1829 after 86 years of marriage.

Great Britain

James Frederick Burgess (born 3 March 1861, died 27 Nov 1966) and his wife Sarah Ann, *née* Gregory (born 11 July 1865, died 22 June 1965) were married on 21 June 1883 at St James's, Bermondsey, London, and celebrated their 82nd anniversary.

Golden Weddings

Despite the advent of the computer, records on golden (or 50 year long) weddings remain still largely uncollated. Unusual cases reported include that of Mrs Agnes Mary Amy Mynott (b. 25 May 1887) who attended the golden wedding of her daughter Mrs Violet Bangs of St Albans on 20 Dec 1980, 23 years after her own. The 3 sons and 4 daughters of Mr and Mrs J. Stredwick of East Sussex *all* celebrated golden weddings between May 1971 and April 1981. Triplets Lucille (Mrs Vogel), Marie (Mrs McNamara) and Alma (Mrs Prom) Pufpaff all celebrated their golden weddings on 12 Apr 1982 having all married in Cleveland, Minnesota in 1932.

Britain's most durable marriage reached an 81st anniversary with Sam Loveridge, 104 (1880–1984) and Annie (*née* Pocock), 100 (b. Taunton, 1884).

Most married

Jack V. and Edna Moran of Seattle, Washington, USA have married each other 40 times since the original and only really necessary occasion on 27 July 1937 in Seaside, Oregon. Subsequent ceremonies have included those at Banff, Canada (1952), Cairo, Egypt (1966) and Westminster Abbey, London (1975).

Mass ceremony

The largest mass wedding ceremony was one of 5837 couples from 83 countries officiated over by Sun Myung Moon (b. 1920) of the Holy Spirit Association for the Unification of World Christianity in the Chamsil Gymnasium, Seoul, South Korea on 14 Oct 1982. The response to the question 'Will you swear to love your spouse for ever?' is 'Ye'.

Most Expensive Wedding

The wedding of Mohammed, son of Shaik Zayid ibn Sa'id al-Makhtum, to Princess Salama in Abu Dhabi in May 1981 lasted 7 days and cost an estimated £22 million in a purpose built stadium for 20,000.

Latest Divorce

In March 1980 a divorce was reported in the Los Angeles Superior Court, California between Bernardine and Leopold Delpes in which both parties were aged 88. The British record age is 101 years by Harry Bidwell at Brighton, Sussex on 21 Nov 1980.

Dining out

The world champion for eating out is Fred E. Magel of Chicago, Illinois, USA who since 1928 has dined out 46,000 times in 60 nations as a restaurant grader (to 21 June 1983). He asserts the one which served largest helpings was Zehnder's Hotel, Frankenmuth, Michigan, USA. Mr Magel's favourite dishes are South African rock lobster and mousse of fresh English strawberries.

World altar champion, Glynn Wolfe of California whose experience of mothers-in-law is unrivalled. (See Most Marriages col. 1)

Party giving

The 'International Year of the Child' children's party in Hyde Park, London was attended by Royal Family and 160,000 children on 30–31 May 1979. The longest street party ever staged was for 5500 children by the Oxford Street Association to celebrate the Royal Wedding of TRH The Prince and Princess of Wales on 25 July 1981 along the entire length from Park Street to St. Giles Circus, London.

The largest Christmas Party ever staged was that thrown by The Boeing Company in the 65,000 seat Kingdome, Seattle, Washington, USA, in two shows totalling 103,152 people on 15 Dec 1979. During St. Patrick's week of 11–17 Mar 1984, Houlihan's Old Place hosted St. Pat's Parties at the 47 Kansas City, Missouri-based Gilbert/Robinson restaurants for a total of 199,189 documented guests.

Toastmasters

The Guild of Professional Toastmasters (founded 1962) has only 12 members. Its founder and President, Ivor Spencer, once had to listen to a speech in excess of 2 hr by the maudlin guest of honour of a retirement luncheon. The Guild also elects the most boring speaker of the year, but for professional reasons, will not publicize the winners' names until a decent interval has elapsed. Red coats were introduced by the pioneer professional, William Knight-Smith (d. 1932) *c.* 1900.

Lecture agency

In 1980 Bob Jones of Wellington, New Zealand addressed a seminar of 1048 people in Auckland on property. He received $NZ200,000 or $NZ16,666 per hour. In March 1981 it was reported that both Johnny Carson and Bob Hope commanded fees of $40,000 (*then £18,000*).

Working week

A case of a working week of 142 hours was recorded in June 1980 by Dr Paul Ashton, 32 the anaesthetics registrar at Birkenhead General Hospital, Merseyside. This left an average each day of 3 hr 42 min 51 sec for sleep. Some non-consultant doctors are actually contracted to work 110 hours a week or be available for 148 hours. Some contracts for fully salaried University lecturers call for a 3 hr week or a 72 hr year spread over 24 weeks.

Working career

The longest working life has been that of 98 years by Mr Izumi (see pp. 13–14), who began work goading draft animals at a sugar mill at Isen, Tokunashima, Japan in 1872. He retired as a sugar cane farmer in 1970 aged 105.

The longest working life recorded in the UK was that of Susan O'Hagan (1802–1909) who was in domestic service with 3 generations of the Hall family of Lisburn, near Belfast, Northern Ireland for 97 years from the age of 10 to light duties at 107.

The longest recorded industrial career in one job in Britain was that of Miss Polly Gadsby who started work with Archibald Turner & Co of Leicester aged 9. In 1932, after 86 years service, she was still at her bench wrapping elastic, at the age of 95. Mr Theodore C. Taylor (1850–1952) served 86 years with J. T. & T. Taylor of Batley, West Yorkshire including 56 years as chairman. Currently the longest serving and the oldest chairman (appointed July 1926) of any board of directors is Mrs Mary Henrietta Anne Moody (b. 7 Apr 1881) of Mark & Moody Ltd, printers and booksellers of Stourbridge, West Midlands. Edward William Beard (1878–1982), a builder of Swindon, Wiltshire retired in October 1981 from the firm he founded in 1896 after 85 years. Commissioner Catherine Bramwell-Booth (b. 1883) has been serving the Salvation Army since 1903. Richard John Knight (b. 2 Apr 1881) was Company Secretary to 7 companies at the time of his death on 12 Nov 1984 aged 103 years.

Most durable coal miner

George Stephenson (b. 21 Apr 1833) worked at William Pit, a Whitehaven Colliery, Cumbria from 1840 (aged 7) for 82 years until his retirement in 1922. He died on 18 Mar 1926 aged 92 years 10 months having received a testimonial of £54 12s.

Longest pension

Miss Millicent Barclay, daughter of Col William Barclay was born posthumously on 10 July 1872 and became eligible for a Madras Military Fund pension to continue until her marriage. She died unmarried on 26 Oct 1969 having drawn the pension for every day of her life of 97 years 3 months.

Medical families

The 4 sons and 5 daughters of Dr Antonio B. Vicencio of Los Angeles all qualified in 1964–82. Eight sons of John Robertson of Benview, Dumbarton, Scotland graduated as medical doctors between 1892 and 1914. Henry Lewis Lutterloh and Elizabeth Grantham of Chatham County, North Carolina, USA were the grandparents of 19 medical doctors. From 1850 to 1962 they practised a total of 704 man-years. The Maurice family of Marlborough, Wiltshire have had the same practice for 6 generations since 1792.

MISCELLANEOUS ENDEAVOURS

ACCORDION PLAYING

Tom Luxton of Oldbury, West Midlands, played an accordion for 84 hr on 4–7 Aug. 1982.

APPLE PEELING

The longest single unbroken apple peel on record is one of 172 ft 4 in *52,51 m* peeled by Kathy Wafler, of Wolcott, NY, USA in 11 hr 30 min at Long Ridge Mall, Rochester, NY on 16 Oct 1976. The apple weighed 20 oz *567 g*.

APPLE PICKING

The greatest recorded performance is 365½ US bushels (354.1 Imperial bushels *128,80 hectolitres*) picked in 8 hr by George Adrian, 32 of Indianapolis, Indiana, USA, on 23 Sept 1980.

AUCTIONEERING

The longest one man auction on record is for 40 hr 7 min by Reg Coates in Gosport, Hampshire on 26–28 Apr 1985.

BAG-CARRYING

The greatest non-stop bag-carrying feat carrying 1 cwt *50,8 kg* of household coal in an open bag is 32 miles *51,5 km* by Brian Newton in 10 hr 18 min from Leicester to the Nottingham border on 27 May 1983.

The record for the 1012,5m *1107.2 yd* course annual Gawthorpe, West Yorkshire race is 4 min 19 sec by Terry Lyons, 36 on 16 Apr 1979.

BAG-PIPES

The longest duration pipe has been one of 100 hr by Neville Workman, Clive Higgins, Patrick Forth and Paul Harris, playing two at a time in shifts, of Churchill School Pipe Band, Harare, Zimbabwe on 9–13 July 1976.

BALANCING ON ONE FOOT

The longest recorded duration for balancing on one foot is 34 hr by Shri N. Ravi in Sathyamangalam City, Tamil Nadu, India on 17–18 Apr 1982. The disengaged foot may not be rested on the standing foot nor may any object be used for support or balance.

BALLOON FLIGHTS

The longest reported toy balloon flight is one of 9000 miles *14 500 km* from Atherton, California, USA, (released by Jane Dorst on 21 May 1972) and found on 10 June at Pietermaritzburg, South Africa. The longest recorded hydrogen-filled balloon flight from the geographical British Isles is one of 5880 miles *9460 km* from Jersey which was returned from Camps Bay, Cape Province, South Africa on 28 Apr 1974, 43 days after release by Gerard Wankling.

BALLOON RELEASE

The largest mass balloon release ever achieved was one of 384,800 balloons by a crew of 420 at Shinjuku, Japan on 3 Nov 1984.

BAND MARATHONS

The longest recorded 'blow-in' is 100 hr 2 min

Marathon one-man band Dave Sheriff in action. He knew that for 70 hours if he lingered the melody stopped.

by the Du Val Senior High School, Lanham, Maryland, USA on 13–17 May 1977. The minimum number of musicians is 10.

BAND ONE-MAN

Rory Blackwell, aided by his left-footed perpendicular percussion-pounder and his right-footed horizontal four pronged differential beater, played 24 (4 melody, 20 percussion) instruments in TV South West Studios, Plymouth, Devon on 2 May 1985. Dave Sheriff of Rugby, Warwickshire played his one-man band (which must include at least 3 instruments played simultaneously) for 70 hr 1 min on 5–8 Mar 1984 at Chappell's Music Store, Milton Keynes, Bucks. The greatest number of instruments played in a single rendition is 314 in 1 min 23.07 sec by Rory Blackwell in Dawlish, Devon on 27 May 1985.

BARREL JUMPING *on Ice Skates*

The official distance record is 29 ft 5 in *8,99 m* over 18 barrels by Yvon Jolin at Terrebonne, Quebec, Canada on 25 Jan 1981. The feminine record is 20 ft 4½ in *6,21 m* over 11 barrels by Janet Hainstock in Michigan, USA, on 15 Mar 1980.

BARREL ROLLING

The record for rolling a full 36 gallon metal beer barrel over a measured mile is 8 min 7.2 sec by Phillip Randle, Steve Hewitt, John Round, Trevor Bradley, Colin Barnes and Ray Glover of Haunchwood Collieries Institute and Social Club, Nuneaton, Warwickshire on 15 Aug 1982. A team of 10 rolled a 63½ kg *140 lb* barrel 240,35 km *150 miles* in 30 hr 31 min in Chlumcany, Czechoslovakia on 27–28 Oct 1982.

BARROW PUSHING

The heaviest loaded one-wheeled barrow pushed for a minimum 200 level feet *60,96 m* is one loaded with bricks weighing a gross 4,788 lb *2,17 tonnes* by Ben Read at Segensworth, Hampshire on 12 Jan 1985.

BARROW RACING

The fastest time attained in a 1 mile *1,609 km* wheelbarrow race is 4 min 50.29 sec by John Coates and Brian Roades of Richmond, BC, Canada on 9 July 1983 at the Ladner Sports Festival, Delta, B.C. Brothers-in-law Malcolm Shipley and Adrian Freeburg pushed each other from John O'Groats to Land's End for charity in 30 days from 28 July–26 Aug 1981.

BATH TUB RACING

The record for the annual international 36 miles *57,9 km* Nanaimo to Vancouver, British Columbia bath tub race is 1 hr 29 min 40 sec by Gary Deathbridge (Australia) on 30 July 1978. Tubs are limited to 75 in *1,90 m* and 6 hp motors. The greatest distance for paddling a hand propelled bath tub in 24 hr is 90.5 miles *145,6 km* by 13 members of Aldington Prison Officers Social Club, nr. Ashford, Kent on 28–29 May 1983.

BATON TWIRLING

The Apple Core Baton Twirling Corps of Bridgeview, Illinois, USA twirled for 92½ hr on 4–8 Apr 1983.

BED MAKING

The record time set under the rigorous rules of the Australian Bedmaking Championships is 28.2 sec solo by Wendy Wall, 34, of Hebersham, Sydney, NSW on 30 Nov 1978. The British pair record with 1 blanket, 2 sheets, an undersheet, an uncased pillow, 1 counterpane and 'hospital' corners is 24.0 sec by Judith Strange and Catheryn Marsden of High Peak College, Buxton, Derbyshire on 11 Mar 1978.

BED OF NAILS

The duration record for lying on a bed of nails (sharp 6-inch *15,2 cm*; 2 in *5 cm* apart) is 273 hr 5 min by Alan Andrews, 26, at Barry, Wales on 5–14 Dec 1983. His fiancée Katherine Weston accompanied him for the last 34 hr. Much longer durations are claimed by uninvigilated *fakirs*— the most extreme case being *Silki* who claimed 111 days in São Paulo, Brazil ending on 24 Aug 1969.

BED PUSHING

The longest recorded push of a normally sessile object is 3233 miles 1150 yd *5204 km* in the case of a wheeled hospital bed by a team of 9 employees of Bruntsfield Bedding centre, Edinburgh on 21 June–26 July 1979.

BED RACE

The record time for the annual Knaresborough Bed Race (established 1966) in North Yorkshire is 12 min 36 sec for the 2 mile 63 yd *3,27 km* course crossing the River Nidd by the Beavers' Team on 9 June 1984. The course record for the 10 mile *16,09 km* Chew Valley Lake race (inst. 1977) in Avon, England is 50 min by the Westbury Harrier 3-man bed team.

BEER LABEL COLLECTING

The greatest collection of different British Beer labels is 27,845 (to 1 Jan 1984) by Keith Osborne, Hon Sec of The Labologists Society (founded by Guinness Exports Ltd in 1958). His oldest is one from D. B. Walker & Co, Warrington of *c.* 1846.

BEER MAT FLIPPING

At the inaugural Ind Coope British Championships Darren Ault, 18, flipped and caught a pile of 67 mats (1.2 mm thick 490 gsm wood pulp board) through 180 degrees in Repton, Derbyshire on 31 May 1985.

BEER STEIN CARRYING

Barmaid Rosie Schedelbauer covered 15 m *49 ft 2¼ in* in 4.0 sec with 5 full steins in each hand in a televised contest at Königssee, West Germany on 29 June 1981.

BEST MAN

The world's champion 'best man' is Mr Wally Gant, a bachelor fishmonger from Wakefield, West Yorkshire, who officiated for the 50th time since 1931 in December 1964.

BICYCLE *Most mounting simultaneously*

On 2 Apr 1984 at Mito, Ibaragi, Japan 16 members of the Mito-Itomi Unicycle Club mounted and rode a single bicycle a distance of 50 m *164 ft*.

BILLIARD TABLE JUMPING

Joe Darby (1861–1937) cleared a full-sized 12 ft *3,65 m* billiard table lengthwise, taking off from a 4 in *10 cm* high solid wooden block, at Wolverhampton, West Midlands on 5 Feb 1892.

BOMB DEFUSING

The highest reported number of unexploded bombs defused by any individual is 8000 by Werner Stephan in West Berlin, Germany, in the 12 years from 1945 to 1957. He was killed by a small grenade on the Grunewald blasting site on 17 Aug 1957. Britain's two most highly decorated bomb disposal officers were the late Cdr H. Syme GC GM* and Lt-Cdr J. Bridge GC GM*.

BREATHING APPARATUS

The continuous duration record for wearing self-contained breathing apparatus is 342 hr 10 min on 4–18 Aug 1984 by a team of 4 firemen from Chertsey, Surrey.

BOOMERANG THROWING

The earliest mention of a word similar to *boomerang* is *wo-murrang* in Collins *Acct. N.S. Wales Vocab.* published in 1798. The earliest certain Australian account of a returning boomerang (term established, 1827) was in 1831 by Major (later Sir Thomas) Mitchell. Curved throwing sticks for wild fowl hunting were found in the tomb of Tutankhamun dating from the mid 14th century BC.

World championships and codified rules were not established until 1970. The Boomerang Association of Australia's championship record for distance reached from the thrower before the boomerang returns is 111 m *364.1 ft* diameter by Bob Burwell in November 1981 at Albury. The longest unofficial out and return record on record is one of 375 ft *114,3 m* by Peter Ruhf (US) at Randwick, Sydney, NSW, Australia on 28 June 1982. The longest flight duration (with self-catch) is one of 28.9 sec by Bob Burwell at Alberg, NSW on 7 Apr 1984. The greatest number of consecutive two handed catches on record is 653 by Bob Croll (Victoria) on the same occasion.

BRICK CARRYING

The greatest distance achieved for carrying a brick 8 lb 15 oz *4,053 kg* in a nominated ungloved hand in an uncradled downward pincher grip is 45 miles *72,4 km* by David and Kym Barger of Lamar, Missouri, USA on 21 May 1977. The British record is 41.1 miles *66,1 km* by Tony Weston near Alton, Hampshire with a 9 lb 3⅝ oz *4,18 kg* brick on 12 May 1984.

The feminine record for a 9 lb 12 oz *4,422 kg* brick is 19.2 miles *30,89 km* by Cynthia Ann Smolko of Denville, New Jersey, USA on 14

Ben Read, who in breaking the 2 ton barrier in barrow-pushing confirmed the truth of Archimedes' 22 century old remarks on long levers.

May 1977. The British feminine record for a 6 lb 9 oz *2,97 kg* smooth-sided brick is 6 miles *9,6 km* by Karen Stevenson of Wallasey, Merseyside on 17 Aug 1984.

BRICKLAYING

Ralph Charnock of Benfleet, Essex set The Brick Development Association Bricklaying Championship record at Colindale, north-west London on 30 Sept 1981. He laid 711 bricks in 60 minutes, according to the strict rules of the Guild of Bricklayers. He broke his record with 725 in 60 min on 17 June 1983 at Wiggins Construct, Thundersley, Essex.

BRICKLIFTING

Alan Keates of Cheadle, Staffordshire lifted 26 8½ in *21,6 cm* bricks of 5 lb *2,26 kg* weight horizontally in Cheadle on 15 May 1984. The span was 66½ in *168,9 cm* and 130 lb *59 kg*.

BRICK RACING

The record times recorded at the Annual NFBTE Young Builders Dry-brick championship in Leicester are 100 metres: 1 min 7.0 sec + 11 penalty points giving a gross 1 min 18.0 sec by Ian Jones on 3 June 1979, and 1 mile (team): 21 min 25 sec + 118 penalties giving an overall time of 23 min 23 sec by William Davis & Company (Leicester) Ltd, on 15 June 1980.

BRICK THROWING

The greatest reported distance for throwing a standard 5 lb *2,268 kg* building brick is 44,54 m *146 ft 1 in* by Geoff Capes at Braybrook School, Orton Goldhay, Cambridgeshire on 19 July 1978.

BUBBLE GUM BLOWING

The greatest reported diameter for a bubble gum bubble is 19¼ in *48,9 cm* by Susan Montgomery, 18 of Fresno, Calif, USA in April 1979. The British record also using 'Bubble Yum' is 16½ in *42 cm* by Nigel Fell, 13 from Derriaghy, N. Ireland in November 1979. This was equalled by John Smith of Willingham, Cambridgeshire on 25 Sept 1983.

BURIAL ALIVE

Voluntary burial alive (for which claims up to 217 days have been published) are inadmissible unless the depth of the coffin is a minimum 2 m *6 ft 6¾ in* below ground; the coffin has a maximum cubic capacity of 1,5 million cc or *54 ft³* and the single aperture for communication and feeding has a maximum dimension of 10 cm or *4 inches*. 'Country' Bill White, 50, was so buried from 31 July to 19 Dec 1981 (141 days) in Killeen, Texas, USA.

CAMPING OUT

The silent Indian *fakir* Mastram Bapu 'contented father' has remained on the same spot by the roadside in the village of Chitra for 22 years 1960–82.

CANAL JUMPING

In the sport of Fierljeppen at Winsam, Friesland, Netherlands, the record is 18.61 m *61 ft 0¾ in* across the water with a 40 ft *12,2 m* aluminium pole set by Aarth de Wit in Aug 1983.

CAN TOP COLLECTING

The longest recorded one-man chain of can tops is one of 11.2 miles *18,02 km* collected since 4 July 1969 by Arthur J. Jordan Sr of Yorkstown, Virginia, USA to the estimated number of 710,000 as of 14 May 1979.

CARD THROWING

Kevin St Onge threw a standard playing card 185 ft 1 in *56,41 m* at the Henry Ford Community College Campus, Dearborn, Michigan, USA on 12 June 1979.

CARRIAGE DRIVING

The only man to drive 48 horses in a single hitch is Dick Sparrow of Zearing, Iowa, USA in 1972–77. The lead horses were on reins 135 ft *41 m* long.

CAR WRECKING

The greatest number of cars wrecked in a stunting career is 1847 to 1 June 1985 by Dick Sheppard of Gloucester, England.

CATAPULTING

The greatest recorded distance for a catapult shot is 1362 ft *415 m* by James M. Pfotenhauer using a patented 16½ ft *5,02 m* 'Monarch IV Supershot' and a 53 calibre lead musket ball on Ski Hill Road, Escanaba, Michigan, USA on 10 Sept 1977.

CHAMPAGNE FOUNTAIN

The greatest number of stories achieved in a champagne fountain, successfully filled from the top and using 10,404 traditional long-stem glasses, is 44 (height 24.7 ft *7,52 m*) achieved by Pascal Leclerc at the Biltmore Hotel, Los Angeles, USA on 18 June 1984.

CLAPPING

The duration record for continuous clapping (sustaining an average of 140 claps per min audible at 100 yd *91 m*) is 50 hr 17 min by Ashrita Furman of Jamaica, New York, USA on 10–12 Aug 1981.

CLUB SWINGING

Albert Rayner set a world record of 17,512 revolutions (4.9 per sec) in 60 min at Wakefield, W Yorkshire on 27 July 1981. M. Dobrilla swung continuously for 144 hr at Cobar, NSW finishing on 15 Sept 1913.

COAL CUTTING

The most productive coal mine in Britain has been Bagworth Colliery, Leicestershire with 5.8

tonnes per man shift in the 41 weeks from April to 31 Dec 1980. The colliery dates from 1829. The individual record for filling is 218 tons in a week of 5 shifts by Jim Marley (b. 1914) at East Walbottle Colliery, Tyne and Wear, England in 1949. This included 47½ tons in 6 hr. The NCB record for a week's production by a 48 man team is 32,333 tonnes at their biggest pit at Kellingley Colliery, Knottingley, West Yorkshire in the pre-Christmas 'Bull Week' in December 1982.

COAL SHOVELLING

The record for filling a ½-ton *508 kg* hopper with coal is 29.4 sec by Piet Groot at the Inangahua A. and P. Show, New Zealand on 1 Jan 1985.

COIN BALANCING

The tallest column of coins ever stacked on the edge of a coin is 205 Canadian 25 cent pieces on top of a Canadian Olympic commemorative coin which was freestanding vertically on the base of a coin flat on the surface by Bruce

McConachy (b. 1963) of West Vancouver, BC, for Fuji-TV in Tōkyō, Japan on 24 Feb 1985. Alex Chervinsky (b. 22 Feb 1908) of Lock Haven, Pennsylvania, USA achieved a pyramid of 390 coins on his 75th birthday.

COIN SNATCHING

The greatest number of 10p pieces clean caught from being flipped from the back of a forearm into the same palm is 70 by Andrew Gleed at the Guinness World of Records, Trocadero, Piccadilly, London on BBC-TV's *Saturday Superstore* on 16 Feb 1985. Claims beyond 100 coins (using US 25 cent pieces) are disproved by the fact that this is beyond the capacity even of the *upturned* human hand.

COMPETITION WINNINGS

The largest individual competition prize win on record is $307,500 (*then £109,821*) by Herbert J. Idle, 55, of Chicago in an encyclopaedia contest run by Unicorn Press Inc on 20 Aug 1953. The

CIRCUS RECORDS

A table of historic circus records from 1859 to date was published in the 26th Edition at p. 233. New records set since 1975 see below

The world's largest permanent circus is Circus Circus, Las Vegas, Nevada, USA opened on 18 Oct 1968 at a cost of $15,000,000 (*then £6,250,000*). It covers an area of 129,000 ft² *11 984 m²* capped by a tent-shaped flexiglass roof 90 ft *27,43 m* high. The largest travelling circus is the Circus Vargas in the USA which can accommodate 5000 people under its Big Top.

Flying Trapeze

Downward circles or 'Muscle grinding'—1350 by Sarah Denu (age 14) (US) Madison, Wisconsin, USA, 21 May 1983. Single heel hang on swinging bar, Angela Revelle (Angelique), Australia, 1977.

Highest Aerial Act

Celeste Starr performed a trapeze act suspended from a cable car on the Teleférico Mérida, Venezuela (15,629 ft *4763 m*) in July 1981.

Triple Twisting Double Somersault

Tom Robin Edelston to catcher John Zimmerman, Circus World, Florida, 20 Jan 1981.

Full Twisting Triple and the Quadruple Somersault

Vasquez Troupe. Miguel Vasquez to catcher Juan Vasquez at Ringling Bros, Amphitheatre, Chicago, USA in Nov 1981.

Triple Back Somersault with 1½ Twists

Terry Cavaretta Lemus (now Mrs. St Jules).

Teeter Board

Six man high perch pyramid, Emilia Ivanova (Bulgaria) of the Kehaiovi Troupe at Inglewood, California, USA, 21 July 1976.

Trampoline

Septuple twisting back somersault to bed and quintuple twisting back somersault to shoulders by Marco Canestrelli to Belmonte Canestrelli at Madison Square, NY, USA on 5 Jan and 28 Mar 1979. Richard Tison (France) performed a triple twisting triple back somersault for television near Berchtesgaden, West Germany on 30 June 1981.

Flexible Pole

Double full twisting somersault to a 2 in *5,08 cm*

diameter pole by Roberto Tabak (aged 11) in Sarasota, Florida, USA in 1977.

Human Pyramid (or Tuckle)

Twelve (3 high) supported by a single understander. Weight 771 kg *1700 lb* or 121.4 stone by Tahar Davis of the Hassani Troupe at BBC TV Pebble Mill Studio, Birmingham, England, on 17 Dec 1979.

9 high by top-mounter Josep-Joan Martínez Lozano, 10, of the Colla Vella dels Xiquets 12 m *39 ft* tall on 25 Oct 1981 in Valls, Spain.

Clown, Oldest

Charlie Revel (b. Andrea Lassere in Spain 24 Apr 1896) performed for 82 years (1899–1981).

JUGGLING RECORDS

7 clubs
Albert Petrovski (USSR), 1963; Sorin Munteanu (Romania), 1975; Jack Bremlov (Czech), currently

8 plates
Enrico Rastelli (Italy), 1896–1931

10 balls
Enrico Rastelli (Italy), 1896–1931

11 rings
Albert Petrovski (USSR), 1963–66; Eugene Belaur (USSR), 1968; Sergei Ignatov (USSR), 1973

Pirouettes with 5 cigar boxes
Kris Kremo (Swiss) (quadruple turn with 3 boxes in mid-air), 1977

Duration 5 clubs
16 min 20 sec, Ignatov in USSR, 1977

3 clubs while running
Brad Heffler (USA) 100 yd *91,44 m* in 13.6 sec (this is termed 'Joggling')

5 Ping-Pong balls with mouth
Gran Picaso (Spain), 1971

5 balls inverted
Bobby May (USA), since 1953

highest value first prize offered in Britain has been a £50,000 new house in a £100,000 competition sponsored by Lever Brothers, British Gas and the New Homes Marketing Board from Mar–Oct 1985.

COW CHIP TOSSING

The record distances in the country sport of throwing dried cow chips depends on whether or not the projectile may or may not be 'moulded into a spherical shape'. The greatest distance achieved under the 'non-sphericalization and 100% organic' rule (established in 1970) is 266 ft

81,07 m by Steve Urner at the Mountain Festival, Tehachapi, California, USA on 14 Aug 1981.

CRAWLING

The longest continuous voluntary crawl (progression with one or other knee in unbroken contact with the ground) on record is 27 miles *43,45 km* by Chris Lock at Durdham Downs, Bristol, England on 18–19 Aug 1984. Over a space of 15 months ending on 9 Mar 1985 Jagdish Chander, 32, crawled 1400 km *870 miles* from Aligarh to Jamma, India to propitiate his favourite Hindu goddess Mata.

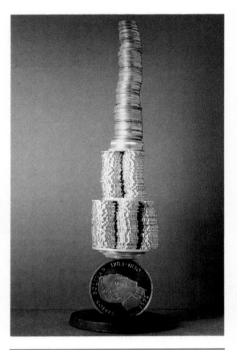

Above Doyen of coin balancers Alex Chervinsky (US) who celebrated his 75th birthday with a pyramid of 390 coins on the edge of one coin (see page 170). *Left* A novel if hazardous and expensive way of launching a new brand of champagne—a 44 storey fountain of 10,404 glasses. (See page 171)

CROCHET

Mrs Barbara Jean Sonntag (b. 1938) of Craig, Colorado, USA crocheted 330 shells plus 5 stitches (equivalent to 4412 stitches) in 30 min at a rate of 147 stitches a minute on 13 Jan 1981. She also set a record for a crochet chain on 31 Oct 1981 with a strand measuring 34.9 miles *56,16 km*. Mrs Sybille Anthony bettered all knitting marathons in a 120 hr crochet marathon at Toombul Shopping-town, Queensland, Australia on 3–7 Oct 1977.

CUBISM

Minh Thai, 16, a Vietnamese refugee won the World Rubik Cube Championship held in Budapest, Hungary on 5 June 1982. His winning time after standardized dislocations was 22.95 sec. Ernö Rubik (Hungary) patented the device in 1975 with 43,252,003,274,489, 856,000 possible combinations.

CUCUMBER SLICING

Norman Johnson of Blackpool College of Art and Technology set a record of 13.4 sec for slicing a 12 in *30,48 cm* cucumber 1½ in *3,81 cm* diameter at 22 slices to the inch (total 244 slices) on West Deutscher Rundfunk in Cologne on 3 Apr 1983.

CUSTARD PIE THROWING

The most times champion in the annual World Custard Pie Championships now at Ditton, Maidstone, Kent (instituted 1968) have been the 'Birds', ('The Bashers') and the 'Coxheath Men' ('Custard Kings') each with 3 wins. The target (face) must be 8 ft 3⅞ in *2,53 m* from the thrower who must throw a pie no more than 10¼ in *26,03 cm* in diameter. Six points are scored for a square hit full in the face.

CHAMPAGNE

Nearing the 27th mile post, Chris Lock struggling successfully to become the world's greatest crawler.

DEBATING *Most protracted*

The Literary and Debating Society of University College, Galway, Ireland, debated the motion 'That Ireland is Green' for 153 hr 20 min on 21–27 Feb 1985. The 188 formal and 120 other participants used words of 17 languages.

DEMOLITION WORK

Fifteen members of the Black Leopard Karate Club demolished a 7-room wooden farmhouse west of Elnora, Alberta, Canada in 3 hr 18 min by foot and empty hand on 13 June 1982.

DOMINO TOPPLING

The greatest number of dominoes (set up singlehanded) toppled is 281,581 out of 320,236 set up, by Klaus Friedrich, 22, in Bayern, West Germany on 27 Jan 1984. The dominoes fell within 12 min 57.3 sec having taken 31 days (10 hours daily) to set up.

The record for a team (maximum 15 people) is 518,242 by Nihon University (leader Takashi Itoh) in Yokohama, Japan on 26 Mar 1985.

DRUMMING

The world's duration drumming record is

DANCING

Largest and longest dances

The largest dance ever staged was that put on by the Houston Livestock show at the Astro Hall, Houston, Texas, USA on 8 Feb 1969. The attendance was more than 16,500 with 4000 turned away. An estimated total of 20,000 dancers took part in the National Square Dance Convention at Louisville, Kentucky, USA on 26 June 1983.

Marathon dancing must be distinguished from dancing mania, or tarantism, which is a pathological condition. The worst outbreak of this was at Aachen, Germany, in July 1374, when hordes of men and women broke into a frenzied and compulsive choreomania in the streets. It lasted for hours till injury or complete exhaustion ensued.

The most severe marathon dance staged as a public spectacle was one by Mike Ritof and Edith Boudreaux who logged 5148 hr 28½ min to win $2000 at Chicago's Merry Garden Ballroom, Belmont and Sheffield, Illinois, USA from 29 Aug 1930 to 1 Apr 1931. Rest periods were progressively cut from 20 to 10 to 5 to nil minutes per hour with 10 inch steps and a maximum of 15 seconds for closure of eyes.

Ballet

In the *entrechat* (a vertical spring from the fifth position with the legs extended criss-crossing at the lower calf), the starting and finishing position each count as one such that in an *entrechat douze* there are *five* crossings and uncrossings. This was performed by Wayne Sleep for the BBC

The world high-kicking champion is a male— Alagarajah Srikandorajah whose ankle surpassed his ear 10,376 times in 6 hrs 6 minutes. (See page 171)

Record Breakers programme on 7 Jan 1973. He was in the air for 0.71 sec.

Most turns

The greatest number of spins called for in classical ballet choreography is the 32 *fouettés rond de jambe en tournant* in 'Swan Lake' by Pyotr Ilyich Chaykovsky (Tschaikovsky) (1840–93). Miss Rowena Jackson (later Chatfield), MBE (b. Invercargill, NZ, 1925) achieved 121 such turns at her class in Melbourne, Victoria, Australia, in 1940.

Most Curtain Calls

The greatest recorded number of curtain calls ever received by ballet dancers is 89 by Dame Margaret Evelyn Arias, DBE *née* Hookham (born Reigate, Surrey, 18 May 1919) *alias* Margot Fonteyn, and Rudolf Hametovich Nureyev (born on a train near Irkutsk, USSR, 17 Mar 1938) after a performance of 'Swan Lake' at the Vienna Staatsoper, Austria, in October 1964.

Largest Cast

The largest number of ballet dancers used in a production in Britain has been 2000 in the London Coster Ballet of 1962, directed by Lillian Rowley, at the Royal Albert Hall, London.

Marathon

The indivual continuous world record for ballroom dancing is 120 hr 30 min by Alain Dumas on 28 June–3 July 1983 at the Disco-Shop, Granby, Quebec, Canada. Nine girls worked shifts as his partner.

Champions

The world's most successful professional ballroom dancing champions have been Bill Irvine, MBE and Bobbie Irvine, MBE, who won 13 world titles between 1960 and 1972. The oldest competitive ballroom dancer is Albert J. Sylvester CBE, JP (b. 24 Nov 1889) of Corsham, Wiltshire. In 1977 he won the topmost amateur Alex Moore award for a 10 dance test with his partner Paula Smith in Bath on 26 Apr 1977. By 1981 he had won nearly 50 medals and trophies since he began dancing in 1964.

Belly dancing

The longest recorded example was one of 106 hr by Eileen Foucher at Rush Green Hospital, Romford, Essex on 30 July–3 Aug 1984.

Charleston

The Charleston duration record is 110 hr 58 min by Sabra Starr of Lansdowne, Pennsylvania, USA on 15–20 Jan 1979.

Conga

The longest recorded conga was one comprising a 'snake' of 8659 people from the South Eastern Region of the Camping and Caravanning Club of Great Britain and Ireland on 4 Sept 1982.

Disco

The longest recorded disco dancing marathon is one of 371 hr by John Sharples of Preston, Lancashire on 18 Jan–3 Feb 1982.

Flamenco

The fastest flamenco dancer ever measured is Solero de Jerez aged 17 who in Brisbane, Australia in September 1967 in an electrifying routine attained 16 heel taps.

High kicking

The world record for high kicks (heel to ear level) is 10,376 in 6 hr 5 min 55 sec by Alagarajah Srikandarajah at Aubigney, France on 22 July 1984. Tara Hobbs, 13, set a speed record of 95 kicks in 1 min on BBC TV's *The Record Breakers* on 2 Sept 1984. Veronica Evans set a speed record for 50 in Manchester on 24 Dec 1931 with 25.0 sec.

Jiving

The duration record for non-stop jiving is 97 hr 42 min by Richard Rimmer (with a relay of partners) of Caterham, Surrey on 11–16 Nov 1979. Under the strict rules of the European Rock n' Roll Association the duration pair record is 22 hr by Mirco and Manuela Catalono in Munich on 6–7 Feb 1981.

Limbo

The lowest height for a bar (flaming) under which a limbo dancer has passed is 6⅛ in *15,5 cm* off the floor by Marlene Raymond, 15 at the Port of Spain Pavilion, Toronto, Canada on 24 June 1973. Strictly no part of the body other than the sole or side of the foot should touch the ground though the brushing of a shoulder blade does not in practice usually result in disqualification. The record on roller skates is 5¼ in *13,33 cm* by Tracey O'Callaghan on June 2 1984 and Sandra Siviour on 30 Mar 1985 both at Bexley North, NSW, Australia to equal Denise Culp of Rock Hill, South Carolina, USA on 22 Jan 1984.

Square dance calling

Alan Covacic called continuously for 24 hr 2 min for the Wheelers and Dealers SDC at St. John's Hospital, Stone, Buckinghamshire on 23–24 Nov 1984.

Tap

The fastest *rate* ever measured for any tap dancer has been 1440 taps per min (24 per sec) by Roy Castle on the BBC TV *Record Breakers* programme on 14 Jan 1973. The greatest ever assemblage of tap dancers in a single routine is 3450 organised outside Macy's Store in New York City, USA on 19 Aug 1984.

42 days 1 hr 6 min 20 sec by Laurent Rebboah of Cupertino, California, USA, on 22 Sept–3 Nov 1983.

DUCKS AND DRAKES

The best accepted ducks and drakes (stone-skipping) record is 24 skips (10 plinkers and 14 pitty-pats) by Warren Klope, 20 of Troy, Michigan being the best score of 6 flat, 4 in *10 cm* limestones, skipped in the annual Mackinac Island, Michigan, USA stone skipping tournament on 5 July 1975. This was equalled by John S. Kolar of Birmingham, Michigan and Glenn Loy Jr of Flint, Michigan on 4 July 1977.

EGG DROPPING

The greatest height from which fresh eggs have been dropped (to earth) and remained intact is 198 m *650 ft* by David S. Donoghue from a helicopter on 2 Oct 1979 on a Tokyo Golf Course.

EGG HUNT

The greatest egg hunt on record involved 72,000 hard-boiled eggs and 40,000 candy eggs at the 26th annual Garrison egg hunt at Homer, Georgia, USA on 7 Apr 1985.

EGG AND SPOON RACING

Chris Riggio of San Francisco, California, USA completed a 28.5 mile *45,86 km* fresh egg and dessert spoon marathon in 4 hr 34 min on 7 Oct 1979.

EGG SHELLING

Two kitchen hands, Harold Witcomb and Gerald Harding, shelled 1050 dozen eggs in a 7¼ hr shift at Bowyers, Trowbridge, Wiltshire on 23 Apr 1971. Both were blind.

EGG THROWING

The longest authenticated distance for throwing a fresh hen's egg without breaking is 96,90 m *317 ft 10 in* by Risto Antikainen to Jyrki Korhonen at Siilinjarvi, Finland on 6 Sept 1982.

ESCAPOLOGY

The most renowned of all escape artists has been Ehrich Weiss *alias* Harry Houdini (1874–1926), who pioneered underwater escapes from locked, roped and weighted containers while handcuffed and shackled with irons.

One of the major manufacturers of strait-jackets acknowledges that an escapologist 'skilled in the art of bone and muscle manipulation' could escape from a standard jacket in seconds. There are however methods by which such circumvention can itself be circumvented. Nick Janson of Benfleet, Essex has demonstrated his ability to escape from handcuffs locked on him by more than 1000 different police officers.

FAMILY TREE *Longest*

The farthest back the lineage of any family has been traced is that of K'ung Ch'iu or Confucius (551–479 BC). His 4 greats grandfather K'ung Chia is known from the eighth century BC. This man's 85th lineal descendants Wei-yi (b. 1939) and Wei-ning (b. 1947) live today in Taiwan (Formosa).

FASHION SHOW *Longest*

The longest distance covered by girl models is 71.1 miles *114,4 km* on 19–21 Sept 1983 by Roberta Brown and Lorraine McCourt at Parke's Hotel, Dublin, Ireland. The male model

Eddie Warke covered a further 11.9 miles *19,1 km* on the catwalk. The compère throughout was Marty Whelan of Radio 2.

FAUX PAS

If measuring by financial consequence, the greatest *faux pas* on record was that of the young multi-millionaire, James Gordon Bennett, committed on 1 Jan 1877 at the family mansion of his demure fiancée one Caroline May, in Fifth Avenue, New York City. Bennett arrived in a two-horse cutter late and obviously in wine. By dint of intricate footwork, he gained the portals to enter the withdrawing room where he was the cynosure of all eyes. He mistook the fireplace for a plumbing fixture more usually reserved for another purpose. The May family broke the engagement and Bennett (1841–1918) was obliged to spend the rest of his foot-loose and fancy-free life based in Paris with the resultant non-collection of millions of tax dollars by the US Treasury.

FEMININE BEAUTY

Female pulchritude being qualitative rather than quantitative does not lend itself to records. It has been suggested that, if the face of Helen of Troy (*c.* 1200 BC) was capable of launching 1000 ships, a unit of beauty sufficient to launch one ship should be a millihelen.

The earliest international beauty contest was that staged by P. T. Barnum (with the people to be the judges) in the United States in June 1855. The Miss America contest was staged at Atlantic City, New Jersey, USA in 1921 and was won by a thin blue-eyed blonde with a 30 in *76,2 cm* chest, Margaret Gorman. The Miss World contest began in London in July 1951. The maximum dimensions of any winner were those of Miss Egypt, Antigone Costanda, in 1954 whose junoesque characteristics were at 40–26–38 in *101–66–96 cm* and thus in advance of the classic Western idea of allure. The United Kingdom is the only country to have produced five winners. They were Rosemarie Frankland (1961); Ann Sidney (1964); Lesley Langley (1965); Helen Morgan (1974), who resigned and Sarah-Jane Hutt (1983). The maximum number of contestants was 68 in November 1975. The shortest reign was that of 18 hours by Miss Germany (Gabriella Brum) in 1980.

The world's largest beauty pageant is the annual Miss Universe contest inaugurated in Long Beach, California, USA, in 1952. The most successful country has been the USA with winners in 1954–56–60–67. The number of countries represented has reached 80 with Miss New Zealand, 19 year-old Lorraine Elizabeth Downes, reigning in 1983–4.

FIRE PUMPING

The greatest gallonage stirrup-pumped by a team of 8 in an 80 hr charity pump is 13,901 gal *63 192 litres* by the White Watch team of the London Salvage Corps in Battersea Park on 2–5 May 1980.

FIRE PUMP MANHANDLING

The longest unaided tow of a fire appliance in excess of 10 cwt *508 kg* in 24 hr on a closed circuit is 211 miles *339,5 km* by a 32 man team of the Dublin Fire Brigade with an 11 cwt *558,8 kg* fire pump on 18–19 June 1983.

FLUTE MARATHON

The longest recorded marathon by a flautist is 48 hr by Joe Silmon in HMS *Grampus* in Gosport, Hampshire on 19–20 Feb 1977.

FLYING DISC THROWING *Formerly Frisbee*

The World Flying Disc Federation indoor records are Men: 121,6 m *399 ft* by Van Miller at Flagstaff, Arizona on 18 Sept 1982; and Women: 229.6 ft *69,9 m* by Suzanne Fields at Cedar Falls, Iowa on 26 Apr 1981. The outdoor records are: Men: 166,42 m *546 ft* by Morten Sandorff, 21 May 1983, Farum, Denmark; and Women: 401.5 ft *122,3 m* by Lizzie Reeve, 14 June 1980, Surrey, England. The throw, run and catch record is 83,10 m *272 ft 7 in* by Steve Bentley on 8 Apr 1982 at Sacramento, California. The group marathon record is 1198 hr by Prince George's Community College Flying High Club on 1 June–22 July 1983 (see Throwing p. 181).

FOOTBAG

The world record for keeping a footbag airborne is 17,872 consecutive kicks or hacks by Andy Linder (US) in Portland, Oregon on 16 Aug 1983 and 6,184 consecutive kicks by Tricia Sullivan, 22, (US) at the BBC TV Centre, London on the *Record-Breakers* on 21 Oct 1984. The sport originated in Oregon, USA in 1972 and was invented by John Stalberger (US).

GIRNING

The only girner to have won 6 national titles is Ron Looney of Egremont, Cumberland in 1979–84.

GLADIATORIAL COMBAT

Emperor Trajan of Rome (AD 98–117) staged a display involving 4941 pairs of gladiators over 117 days. Publius Ostorius, a freed-man, survived 51 combats in Pompeii.

GOLD PANNING

The fastest time recorded for 'panning' 8 planted gold nuggets in a 10 in *25,4 cm* diameter pan is 9.23 sec by Bob Box (*above*) of Ahwahnee, California, and the female record is 10.03 sec by Susan Bryeans (*below*) of Fullerton, California both in the 23rd World Gold Panning Championship on 6 Mar 1983 at Knotts Berry Farm, Buena Park, California, USA.

GOLF BALL BALANCING

Lang Martin balanced 7 golf balls vertically without adhesive at Charlotte, North Carolina, USA on 9 Feb 1980.

GRAPE CATCHING

The greatest distance at which a grape thrown from level ground has been caught in the mouth is 270 ft 4 in *82,4 m* by Paul J. Tavilla at Dedham, Massachusetts on 9 Aug 1979. A claim for 354 ft *107,9 m* by Francis Newman from the 35 storey Brooks Towers in Denver, Colorado on 19 July 1983 is under investigation.

GRAVE DIGGING

It is recorded that Johann Heinrich Karl Thieme, sexton of Aldenburg, Germany, dug 23,311 graves during a 50-year career. In 1826 his understudy dug *his* grave.

GUITAR PLAYING

The longest recorded solo guitar playing marathon is one of 253 hr 20 min by Ray Rogers on 16–27 July 1979 in Mansfield, Ohio, USA in aid of The March of Dimes.

GUM BOOT THROWING

The longest recorded distance for 'Wellie wanging' (a size 8 Challenger Dunlop Boot) is 173 ft *52,73 m* by Tony Rodgers of Warminster, Wilts on 9 Sept 1978. Rosemary Payne established the feminine record at Cannon Hill Park, Birmingham on 21 June 1975 with 129 ft 11 in *39,60 m*.

GUN RUNNING

The record for the Royal Tournament Naval Field Gun competition (instituted 1907, with present rules since 1913) is 2 min 40.6 sec by the Portsmouth Command Field Gun crew at Earl's Court, Kensington & Chelsea, London on 19 July 1984. The barrel alone weighs 8 cwt *406 kg*. The wall is 5 ft *1,52 m* high and the chasm 28 ft *8,53 m* across.

HAGGIS HURLING

The longest recorded distance for throwing a haggis (min. weight 1 lb 8 oz *680 g*) is 180 ft !0 in *55,11 m* by Alan Pettigrew on Inchmoran, Loch Lomond, Scotland on 24 May 1984.

HAIR-DRESSING

Hugo Vanpe cut, set and styled hair continuously for 366 hr on 8–23 June 1984 in Kensington, Johannesburg, South Africa.

HAIR SPLITTING

The greatest reported achievement in hair splitting has been that of the former champion cyclist and craftsman Alfred West (1901–1985) who succeeded in splitting a human hair 17 times into 18 parts on eight occasions.

HANDBELL RINGING

The longest recorded handbell ringing recital has been one of 52 hr 9 min by the 12 Handbell Ringers of Ecclesfield School, Sheffield on 17–19 July 1982.

HANDSHAKING

A world record for handshaking was set up by Theodore Roosevelt (1858–1919), President of the USA, when he shook hands with 8513 people at a New Year's Day, White House Presentation in Washington, DC, USA on 1 Jan 1907. The radio personality Gary Craig reported he had made 15,000 consecutive handshakes among his listeners in Hartford, Connecticut in 1982. Many record claims have been rendered meaningless because aspirants merely tend to arrange circular queues or wittingly or unwittingly shake the same hands repetitively.

HIGH DIVING

The highest regularly performed head first dives are those of professional divers from La Quebrada ('the break in the rocks') at Acapulco, Mexico, a height of 87½ ft *26,7 m*. The leader of the 27 divers in the exclusive Club de Clavadistas is Raul Garcia (b. 1928) with more than 35,000 dives. The first feminine accomplishment was by Mrs Barbara Winters (b. 12 Nov 1953), *née* Mayer, on 7 Dec 1976. The base rocks, 21 ft *6,40 m* out from the take-off, necessitate a leap of 27 ft *8,22 m* out. The water is 12 ft *3,65 m* deep.

The world record high dive is 174 ft 8 in *53,23 m* by Randal Dickison (US) at Ocean Park, Hong Kong on 6 Apr 1985. The feminine record is 120 ft *36,57 m* by Lucy Wardle (US) at the same exhibition. The highest witnessed in Britain is one of 108 ft *32,9 m* into 8 ft *2,43 m* of water at the Aqua show at Earl's Court, London on 22 Feb 1946 by Roy Fransen, 32.

On 8 May 1885, Sarah Ann Henley, aged 24, jumped from the Clifton Suspension Bridge, which crosses the Avon, England. Her 250 ft *76 m* fall was slightly cushioned by her voluminous dress and petticoat acting as a parachute.

She landed, bruised and bedraggled, in the mud on the north bank and was carried to hospital by four policemen. On 11 Feb 1968 Jeffrey Kramer, 24, leapt off the George Washington Bridge 250 ft *76 m* above the Hudson River, New York City, NY and survived. Of the 696 (to 1 Jan 1980) identified people who have made 240 ft *73 m* suicide dives from the Golden Gate Bridge, San Francisco, California, USA since 1937, twelve survived of whom Todd Sharratt, 17, was the only one who managed to swim ashore unaided.

Col Harry A. Froboess (Switzerland) jumped 110 m *360 ft* into the Bodensee from the airship *Graf Hindenburg* on 22 June 1936.

The greatest height reported for a dive into an air bag is 326 ft *99,36 m* by the stuntman Dan Koko from the top of Vegas World Hotel and Casino into a 20 × 40 × 14 ft *6,1 × 12,2 × 4,2 m* target on 13 Aug 1984. His impact speed was 88 mph *141 km/h*. Kitty O'Neill dived 180 ft *54,8 m* from a helicopter over Northridge, California on 9 Sept 1979 onto an air cushion measuring 30 × 60 ft *9,14 × 18,28 m* for a TV film stunt.

HIGHEST SHALLOW DIVE

Henri La Mothe (b. 1904) set a record diving 28 ft *8,53 m* into 12⅜ in *31,43 cm* of water in a child's paddling pool in Northridge, California, on 7 Apr 1979. He struck the water chest first at a speed of 28.4 mph *45,7 km/h*.

HIGH-WIRE ACT

The greatest height above street level of any high wire performance has been from a 140 ft *42,6 m* wire between the 1350 ft *411 m* twin towers of the World Trade Center, New York City by Philippe Petit, 24 of Nemours, France on 7 Aug 1974. He was charged with criminal trespass after a 75 min display of at least 7 crossings. The police psychiatrist opined 'Anyone who does this 110 storeys up can't be entirely right'.

HITCH-HIKING

The title of world champion hitch-hiker is claimed by Raymond L. Anderson (US) who from Nov 1969 to 8 Dec 1984 thumbed lifts totalling 291,001 miles *468 308 km*. It was not till his 6013th 'hitch' that he got a ride in a Rolls-Royce. Stephen Burns, an Australian of Chislehurst, Kent, England hitched round all 48 coterminous states of the USA in 26 days 6 hr in an 11,438 mile *18,407 km* trip in 56 vehicles on 8 Sept–4 Oct 1984. The hitch-hiking record for the 874 miles *1406 km* from Land's End, Cornwall, to John o'Groats, Highland, Scotland, is 17 hr 50 min by Andrew Markham of Brigg, S Humbs. on 3–4 Sept 1979. The time before the first 'hitch' on the first day is excluded. The fastest time recorded for the round trip is 41 hr 42 min by Anthony D. Sproson of Wolverhampton on 17–19 Sept 1984.

HOD CARRYING

Jim Ford of Bury, Lancs carried bricks totalling 355 lb *161 kg* up the minimum 12 foot *3,65 m* ladder (17 rungs) on 28 June 1984 at Hever Castle, Kent on the International Guinness TV Show presented by David Frost. Eric Stenman of Jakobstad, Finland carried 74 bricks of 4 kg *8.8 lb* each so totalling 651 lb *296 kg* in a 4 kg *8.8 lb* hod 5 metres *16.4 ft* on the flat before ascending up a runged ramp to a height of 7 ft *2,13 m* on 25 July 1939.

HOOP ROLLING

In 1968 it was reported that Zolilio Diaz (Spain) had rolled a hoop 600 miles *965 km* from Mieres to Madrid and back in 18 days.

HOP SCOTCH

The longest recorded hop scotch marathon is one of 100 hr by Joellen Glass and Lesa Young of Seattle, Washington, USA on 1–5 Sept 1982.

HOUSE OF CARDS

The greatest number of storeys achieved in building freestanding houses of standard playing cards is 68 to a height of 12 ft 3 in *3,73 m* built by John Sain, 15, of South Bend, Indiana, USA in May 1984.

HULA HOOPING

The highest claim for sustaining gyrating hoops between shoulders and hips is 81 by William Kleeman 'Chico' Johnson (b. 8 July 1939) on BBC TV 'Record Breakers' on 18 Sept 1983. Three complete gyrations are mandatory. The feminine record is 65 by Melody Howe (US) on BBC-TV 'Pebble Mill' in March 1985. The longest recorded marathon for a single hoop is 72 hr by Kym Coberly in Denton, Texas, USA on 17–20 Oct 1984.

HUMAN CANNONBALL

The record distance for firing a human from a cannon is 175 ft *53,3 m* in the case of Emanuel Zacchini, son of the pioneer Hugo Zacchini of 1928 in the Ringling Bros and Barnum & Bailey Circus, Madison Square Gardens, New York City, USA, in 1940. His muzzle velocity has been estimated at 54 mph *86,9 km/h*. On his retirement the management were fortunate in finding that his daughter Florinda was of the same calibre. An experiment on Yorkshire TV on 17 Aug 1978 showed that when Miss Sue Evans, 17 was fired she was ⅜ in *9,5 mm* shorter on landing.

In the Halifax explosion of 6 Dec 1917 (*see* Accidents & Disasters Table, Chap. 11) A. B. William Becker, AM (d. 1969) was blown some 1600 yd *1,46 km* but was found breathing but deaf in a tree.

HUMAN FLY

The longest climb achieved on the vertical face of a building occurred on 25 May 1981 when Daniel Goodwin, 25, scaled the outside of the

Kym Coberly the Texan who raised her hula hoop record from 59 to 72 hours by never letting it drop. (See above) *(D. Kaim)*

1454 ft *443 m* Sears Tower, Chicago in 7 hr 25 min at the rate of 3.2 ft/min *99 cm/min* using 'T' clamps and suction cups. The name of the masked 'human fly', who has ridden at 380 km/h *240 mph* atop a DC-8 jetliner in April 1977 has not been disclosed. It is however believed unlikely that he is a member of the jet set. Lead climber Jean-Claude Droyer (b. 8 May 1946) of Paris and Pierre Puiseux (b. 2 Dec 1953) of Pau, France climbed up the outside of the Eiffel Tower to a height of 300 m *984 ft* with no dynamic mechanical assistance on 21 July 1980. Jean-Claude took 2 hr 18 min 15 sec to complete the climb.

Jaromir Wagner (b. Czechoslovakia 1941) became the first man to fly the Atlantic standing on the wing of an aircraft. He took off from Aberdeen, Scotland on 28 Sept 1980.

JOKE CRACKING

Irishman Steve Emerald at The Duke of Clarence, Southwark, London joked for 42 hr on 23–25 Aug 1984. The duo record is 52 hr by Wayne Malton and Mike Hamilton at the Howard Johnson Motor Hotel, Toronto airport, Ontario, Canada on 13–16 Nov 1975.

JUMBLE SALE

Britain's largest Jumble Sale was 'Jumbly '79' sponsored by *Woman's Own* at Alexandra Palace, London on 5–7 May 1979 in aid of Save The Children Fund. The attendance was 60,000 and the gross takings in excess of £60,000. The Winnetka Congregational Church, Illinois, USA raised $145,161.86 (*then £120,968*) in their 3rd one-day rummage sale on 19 May 1985.

The Cleveland Convention Center, Ohio, White

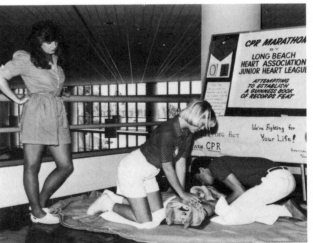

Elephant Sale (inst. 1933) of 28–29 Oct 1981 raised $382,270.19 (*then £212,370*). The 2500 volunteers took $120,000 (*then £66,660*) from more than 10,000 rummagers in the first 2 hours from 208,000 ft² *19 323 m²* of stalls.

KARATE CHOP

Claims for breaking bricks and wooden slats etc. are unsatisfactory because of the lack of any agreed standards upon which comparisons can be made of friability and the spacing of fulcrums.

The 'Never Say Die' team from the Long Beach Junior Heart League of Cardiopulmonary Resuscitators from California who showed they were all heart in setting a record of 5 days 5 hours. (See Kiss of Life below)

KISS OF LIFE

Five members of the St John Ambulance NSW District at Pier One, Sydney maintained a 'Kiss of Life' for 315 hr with 232,150 inflations on 27 Aug–9 Sept 1984. The 'patient' was a dummy. The duration record for continuous CPR (Cardiopulmonary Resuscitation) is 125 hr set at the Hyatt Regency, Long Beach, California by ten teams of two on 1–6 May 1984.

KISSING

The most prolonged osculatory marathon in cinematic history is one of 185 sec by Regis

Toomey and Jane Wyman (later Mrs Ronald Reagan) in *You're In the Army Now* released in 1940. Eddie Leven and Delphine Crha celebrated the breaking of the record for the longest ever kiss of 17 days 9 hr in Chicago, USA on 24 Sept 1985 with a kiss. John McPherson kissed 4444 women in 8 hr in Eldon Square, Newcastle-upon-Tyne on 8 Mar 1985, a rate of 1 each 6.48 sec.

The most protracted kiss underwater was one of 2 min 18 sec by Toshiaki Shirai and Yukiko Nagata on Channel 8, Fuji TV in Tokyo, Japan on 2 Apr 1980.

KITE FLYING *Largest*

The largest kite successfully flown is one of 550 m² *5920 ft²* and 230 kg *507 lb* by 70 Dutchmen for 37 min at Scheveningen, Netherlands on 8 Aug 1981. The longest kite flown is the Thai Snake flown by Herman van den Broek and Jan Pieter Kuil for 22 min 50 sec at Uithuizen, Netherlands on 11 Aug 1984. It was 650 m *2133 ft.*

KITE FLYING *Greatest number*

The most kites flown on a single line is 5,581 by Kazuhiko Asaba, 60 at Kamakura, Japan on 8 Nov 1983.

KITE FLYING *Altitude*

The classic record is 9740 m *31,955 ft* by a chain of 8 kites over Lindenberg, East Germany on 1 Aug 1919. The record for a single kite is 22,500 ft (min)–28,000 ft (max) *6860–8530 m* by Prof. Philip R. and Jay P. Kunz of Laramie, Wyoming, USA on 21 Nov 1967. *Kite Lines* magazine of Baltimore, Maryland, USA does not accept triangulation by line angle and length but only range-finder sightings or radar.

KITE FLYING *Duration*

The longest recorded flight is one of 180 hr 17 min by the Edmonds Community College team at Long Beach, Washington, USA on 21–29 Aug 1982. Managing the flight of the J-25 parafoil was Harry N. Osborne.

Champion thrower Scott Zimmermann (US) demonstrating the throwing of the Aerobie flying disc. Distances 2½ times further than the cricket ball record of 140 yd 2 ft *128,6 m* have been achieved (see page 181).

KNITTING

The world's most prolific hand-knitter of all time has been Mrs Gwen Matthewman of Featherstone, West Yorkshire. She had attained a speed of 111 stitches per min in a test at Phildar's Wool Shop, Central Street, Leeds on 29 Sept 1980. Her technique has been filmed by the world's only Professor of Knitting—a Japanese.

KNOT-TYING

The fastest recorded time for tying the six Boy Scout Handbook Knots (square knot, sheet bend, sheep shank, clove hitch, round turn and two half hitches and bowline) on individual ropes is 8.1 sec by Clinton R. Bailey Sr, 52, of Pacific City, Oregon, USA, on 13 Apr 1977.

LEAP FROGGING

Fourteen members of the Phi Gamma Delta Club at the University of Washington, Seattle, USA, covered 602 miles *968,8 km* in 114 hr 46 min on 20–25 Mar 1983. (Total leaps 108,463—one every 9.77 yd.)

LIFE SAVING

In November 1974 the City of Galveston, Texas and the Noon Optimist Club unveiled a plaque to the deaf-mute lifeguard Leroy Colombo (1905–74) who saved 907 people from drowning in the waters around Galveston Island from 1917 to his death.

LIGHTNING MOST TIMES STRUCK

The only man in the world to be struck by lightning 7 times is ex-Park Ranger Roy C. Sullivan (US) the human lightning conductor of Virginia. His attraction for lightning began in 1942 (lost big toe nail), and was resumed in July 1969 (lost eyebrows), in July 1970 (left shoulder seared), on 16 Apr 1972 (hair set on fire), on 7 Aug 1973 (new hair refired and legs seared), on 5 June 1976 ankle injured, and sent to Waynesboro Hospital with chest and stomach burns on 25 June 1977 after being struck while fishing. In Sept 1983 he died by his own hand reportedly rejected in love.

LION-TAMING

The greatest number of lions mastered and fed in a cage by an unaided lion-tamer was 40, by 'Captain' Alfred Schneider in 1925. Clyde Raymond Beatty handled more than 40 'cats' (mixed lions and tigers) simultaneously. Beatty (b. Bainbridge, Ohio, 10 June 1903, d. Ventura, California, USA, 19 July 1965) was the featured attraction at every show he appeared with for more than 40 years. He insisted upon being called a lion-trainer. More than 20 lion-tamers have died of injuries since 1900.

LOG ROLLING

The record number of International Championships is 10 by Jubiel Wickheim (of Shawnigan Lake, British Columbia, Canada) between 1956 and 1969. At Albany, Oregon on 4 July 1956 Wickheim rolled on a 14 in. *35,5 cm* log against Chuck Harris of Kelso, Washington USA for 2 hr 40 min before losing.

MAGICIAN MOST VERSATILE

Under the surveillance of two officers of the British Magical Society, Paul Scott (b. 1937) performed 49 separate tricks in 4 min at the National Agricultural Centre, Stoneleigh, Warwicks on 9 Sept 1984.

MERRY GO ROUND

The longest merry go round marathon on record is one of 312 hr 43 min by Gary Mandau, Chris Lyons and Dana Dover in Portland, Oregon, USA on 20 Aug–2 Sept 1976.

MESSAGE IN A BOTTLE

The longest recorded interval between drop and pick-up is 72 years in the case of a message thrown from the *SS Arawatta* out of Cairns, Queensland on 9 June 1910 in a lotion bottle and reported to be found on Moreton Island on 6 June 1983.

METEOROLOGICAL BALLOON INFLATION

The inflation of a standardized 1000 gramme meteorological balloon to a diameter of 8 ft *2,43 m* against time was achieved by Nicholas Berkeley Mason in 70 min 2 sec at Heaton Moor RFC, Cheshire on 14 July 1984.

MILK BOTTLE BALANCING

The greatest distance walked by a person continuously balancing a full pint milk bottle on the head is 24 miles *38,6 km* by Ashrita Furman of Jamaica, NY, USA on 10 July 1983.

MORSE

The highest recorded speed at which anyone has received morse code is 75.2 words per minute—over 17 symbols per second. This was achieved by Ted R. McElroy of the United States in a tournament at Asheville, North Carolina, USA on 2 July 1939. The highest speed recorded for hand key transmitting is 475 symbols a minute by Harry A. Turner of the US Army Signal Corps at Camp Crowder, Missouri on 9 Nov 1942. Thomas Morris, a GPO operator, is reputed to have been able to send at 39–40 wpm in c. 1919 but this is not verifiable.

MUSICAL CHAIRS

The largest game on record was one starting with 4514 participants and ending with Scott Ritter, 18, on the last chair at Ohio State University, Ohio, USA on 25 Apr 1982.

NEEDLE THREADING

The record number of times a strand of cotton can be threaded through a number 13 needle (eye ½ in × 1/16 in, *12,7 mm × 1,6 mm*) in 2 hr is 3795 by Miss Brenda Robinson of the College of Further Education, Chippenham, Wiltshire on 20 Mar 1971.

NOODLE MAKING

Mark Pi of the China Gate Restaurant, Columbus, Ohio, USA made 2048 noodle strings (over 5 ft *1,52 m*) in 34.5 sec on 12 Feb 1983.

OMELETTE MAKING

The greatest number of two-egg omelettes made in 30 min is 240 by Royal Navy Cook John E. Bailey (b. 1949) in a trial at HMS Brawdy, Dyfed, Wales on 7 Mar 1970.

ONION PEELING

The record for peeling 50 lb *22,67 kg* of onions is 3 min 18 sec by Alain St. John in Plainfield, Conn., USA, on 6 July 1980. Under revised rules stipulating a minimum of 50 onions, Alfonso Salvo of York, Pennsylvania, USA peeled 50 lb *22,67 kg* of onions (52 onions) in 5 min 23 sec on 28 Oct 1980.

Nicholas Mason, the inflation champion, hits the statutory 8 foot high ceiling in 70 minutes 2 seconds at Heaton Moor RFC. (See page 176)

ORGAN

The longest recorded electric organ marathon is one of 411 hr by Vince Bull at the Comet Hotel, Scunthorpe, South Humberside on 2–19 June 1977. The longest church organ recital ever sustained has been 110 hr by Angie Thompson at St. Stephen's Church, Newport, Brough, Humberside on 16–20 Apr 1985.

PADDLE BOATING

The longest recorded voyage in a paddle boat is 2226 miles *3582 km* in 103 days by the foot power of Mick Sigrist and Brad Rud down the Mississippi River from the headwaters in Minnesota to the Gulf of Mexico on 4 Aug–11 Nov 1979.

PARACHUTING *Longest fall without*

It is estimated that the human body reaches 99 per cent of its low level terminal velocity after falling 1880 ft *573 m* which takes 13–14 secs. This is 117–125 mph *188–201 km/h* at normal atmospheric pressure in a random posture, but up to 185 mph *298 km/h* in a head down position.

Vesna Vulovic, 23, a Jugoslavenski Aerotransport hostess, survived when her DC–9 blew up at 33,330 ft *10 160 m* over the Czechoslovak village of Serbska Kamenice on 26 Jan 1972. She was in hospital for 16 months after emerging from a 27 day coma and having many bones broken. She is now Mrs Breka.

PARACHUTING RECORDS

Category	Name		Place	Date
First from Tower[1]	Louis-Sébastian Lenormand (1757–1839)	quasi-parachute	Montpellier France	1783
First from Balloon	André-Jacques Garnerin (1769–1823)	2230 ft *680 m*	Monceau Park, Paris	22 Oct ... 1797
Earliest Mid-air Rescue	Miss Dolly Shepherd brought down Miss Louie May on her single 'chute	from balloon at 11,000 ft *3350 m*	Longton, Staffordshire	9 June ... 1908
First from Aircraft (man)	'Captain' Albert Berry	Aerial exhibitionist	St. Louis, Missouri	1 Mar ... 1912
(woman)	Mrs Georgina 'Tiny' Broadwick (b. 1893)		Griffith Park, Los Angeles	21 June ... 1913
Lowest Escape	S/Ldr Terence Spencer, DFC, RAF	30–40 ft *9–12 m*	Wismar Bay, Baltic	19 April ... 1945
Longest Duration Fall	Lt Col Wm H. Rankin, USMC	40 min due to thermals	North Carolina	26 July ... 1956
Highest Escape	Flt Lt J. de Salis and Fg Off P. Lowe, RAF	56,000 ft *17 068 m*	Monyash, Derby	9 April ... 1958
Longest Delayed Drop (man)	Capt Joseph W. Kittinger[2]	84,700 ft 16.04 miles *25 816 m* from balloon at 102,800 ft *31 333 m*	Tularosa, New Mexico	16 Aug ... 1960
(woman)	O. Kommissarova (USSR)	14 100 m *46,250 ft*	over USSR	21 Sept ... 1965
(civilian, over UK)	P. Halfacre, R. O'Brien, R. James	27,300 ft *8321 m* from 30,000 ft *9144 m*	Sibson, Peterborough	27 Aug ... 1983
(civilian, world)	R. W. K. Beckett (GB) Harry Ferguson (GB)	30,000 ft *9144 m* from 32,000 ft *9754 m*	D. F. Malan Airport, Capetown	23 Nov ... 1969
(group, U.K.)	S/Ldr J. Thirtle, AFC; Fl Sgt. A. K. Kidd, AFM; Sgts L. Hicks (d. 1971), P. P. Keane, AFM BEM, K. J. Teesdale, AFM	39,183 ft *11 943 m* from 41,383 ft *12 613 m*	Boscombe Down, Wiltshire	16 June ... 1967
Longest Base Jump[3]	Carl Ronald Boenische; Jean K. Campbell Boenische	5784 ft *1763 m*	Trollveggan Spire, Romsdal, Norway	4 July ... 1984
Most Southerly	T/Sgt Richard J. Patton (d. 1973)	Operation Deep Freeze	South Pole	25 Nov ... 1956
Most Northerly	Dr Jack Wheeler (US); pilot Capt. Rocky Parsons	−25° F (−31,6° C)	In Lat. 90° 00' N	15 Apr ... 1981
Cross Channel (Lateral fall)	Sgt. Bob Walters with 3 soldiers and 2 Royal Marines	22 miles *35,4 km* from 25,000 ft *7600 m*	Dover to Sangatte, France	31 Aug ... 1980
Career total (man)	Yuri Baranov and Anatolyi Osipov (USSR)	10,000	over USSR	to Sept ... 1980
(woman)	Valentina Zakoretskaya (USSR)	8000	over USSR	1964–Sept 1980
Highest Landing	Ten USSR parachutists[4]	23,405 ft *7133 m*	Lenina Peak	May ... 1969
Heaviest Load	US Space Shuttle *Columbia* external rocket retrieval	80 ton capacity, triple array, each 120 ft *36,5 m* diameter	Atlantic off Cape Canaveral, Florida	12 Apr ... 1981
Highest from Bridge	Donald R. Boyles	1053 ft *320 m*	Royal Gorge, Colorado	7 Sept ... 1970
Highest Tower Jump	Herbert Leo Schmidtz (US)	KTUL-TV Mast 1984 ft *604 m*	Tulsa, Oklahoma	4 Oct ... 1970
Biggest Star (3.4 sec hold)	72 man team	Formation held 3.4 sec (US Parachuting Assc. rules)	De Land, Florida	3 Apr ... 1983
Highest column (world)	22 Chinese team		China	March ... 1984
(Great Britain)	17 Royal Marine Team		Netheravon, Wilts	18 Apr ... 1984
Lowest Indoor Jump	Andy Smith and Phil Smith	192 ft *58,5 m*	Houston Astrodome, Texas	16–17 Jan 1982
Most travelled	Kevin Seaman from a Cessna Skylane (pilot Charles E. Merritt)	12,186 miles *19 611 km*	Jumps in all 50 US States	26 July–15 Oct ... 1972
Oldest Man	Edwin C. Townsend	85 years 1 day	Riverview, Florida, USA	6 Feb ... 1982
Woman	Mrs. Stella Davenport (GB)	75 years 8 months	Bridlington Aerodrome, Humberside	27 June ... 1981
24 Hr Total	Alan Jones (US)	236	Issaquah, Washington, USA	13–14 July 1984

[1] *The king of Ayutthaya, Siam in 1687 was reported to have been diverted by an ingenious athlete parachuting with two large umbrellas. Faustus Verancsis is reputed to have descended in Hungary with a framed canopy in 1617.*

[2] *Maximum speed in rarefied air was 625.2 mph 1006 km/h. at 90,000 ft 27 430 m—marginally supersonic.*

[3] *'Base' is an acronym for jumping from fixed objects—Building, Antenna, Span and Earth. Carl Boenische was killed on 7 July 1984.*

[4] *Four were killed.*

The British record is 18,000 ft *5485 m* by Flt-Sgt Nicholas Stephen Alkemade, aged 21, who jumped from a blazing RAF *Lancaster* bomber over Germany on 23 Mar 1944. His headlong fall was broken by a fir tree near Oberkürchen and he landed without a broken bone in a snow bank 18 in *45 cm* deep.

PIANO-PLAYING

The longest piano-playing marathon has been one of 1218 hr (50 days 18 hr) playing 22 hr every day (with 5 min intervals each playing hour) from 7 May to 27 June 1982 by David Scott at Wagga Wagga Leagues Football Club, NSW, Australia.

In the now discontinued non-stop category the longest on record was 176¾ hr (7 days 8¾ hr) by Jim Montecino (b. 29 Aug 1903) in the Trocadero Ball Room, Auckland, New Zealand in 1951.

PIANO SMASHING

The record time for demolishing an upright piano and passing the entire wreckage through a circle 9 in *22,8 cm* in diameter is 1 min 37 sec by six members of the Tinwald Rugby Football Club, Ashburton, New Zealand led by David Young on 6 Nov 1977. Messrs Anthony Fukes, Mike Newman and Terry Cullington smashed a piano with bare hands and feet in 2 min 53 sec in Nottingham on 25 Aug 1979. (All wreckage was passed through the circle.)

PIANO TUNING

The record time for pitch raising (one semi-tone or 100 cents) and then returning a piano to a musically acceptable quality is 4 min 20 sec by Steve Fairchild at the Piano Technicians Guild contest at the Dante Piano Co factory, NY, USA on 5 Feb 1980.

PILLAR BOX MOUNTING

The record number of people to pile on top of or hang from a pillar box (oval top of 6 ft² *0,55 m²*) is 32, all students of Wentworth College, York University in Parliament St., York on 27 Feb 1985.

PIPE SMOKING

The duration record for keeping a pipe (3,3 g *0.1 oz* of tobacco) continuously alight with only an initial match under IAPSC (International

Above left Angie Thompson whose first and last chords were separated by 110 hours in her record organ recital. (See page 177) *Above right* 'Two Match Joe' in action at the Iowa State Pipe Smoking Championships. (See page 179) *Below* Dr. Jack Wheeler the Arctic parachutist at the North Pole. A record that cannot be bettered after setting. (See Table page 177)

Association of Pipe Smokers Clubs) rules is 126 min 39 sec by the five-time champion William Vargo of Swartz Creek, Michigan at the 27th World Championships in 1975. The only other 5-time champion is Paul T. Spaniola (USA) (1951–66–70–73–77). On 18 Aug 1984 Joe Oetli achieved 130 min 11 sec at the 15th Iowa State Fair contest using *two* matches. Longer durations have been recorded in less rigorously invigilated contests in which the foul practices of 'tamping' and 'gardening' are not unknown.

PLATE SPINNING

The greatest number of plates spun simultaneously is 72 by Shukuni Sasaki of Takamatsu, Japan at Nio Town Taiyo Exhibition, Kagawa, on 16 July 1981. The British record is 54 set by Holley Gray set during BBC *Record Breakers* on 6 May 1980.

POGO STICK JUMPING

The greatest number of jumps achieved is 130,077 by Guy Stewart in Reading, Ohio, USA on 8–9 Mar 1985.

POLE-SQUATTING

Modern records do not, in fact, compare with that of St Simeon the Younger, (*c.* 521–597 AD) called Stylites (Greek, *stylos* = pillar) a monk who spent his last 45 years up a stone pillar on The Hill of Wonders, near Antioch, Syria. This is probably the longest lasting example of record setting.

There being no international rules, the 'standards of living' atop poles vary widely. The pre-existing record of 440 days was surpassed on 14 May 1985 by Mark Sutton for the Paraplegic Association in Victoria, B.C., Canada.

Robin S. Colley stayed in a barrel (max. capacity 108 gallons) atop a pole (30 ft *9,14 m*) in Plymouth, Devon for 34 days 1 hr on 4 Aug–7 Sept 1982. This authentic achievement was only notified subsequent to the 33 days 1 hr 6 min by Robert 'Rob' C. Roy (b. 1961) outside The Black Horse, Darlaston, Staffordshire on 28 July–30 Aug 1984.

POP GROUP

The duration record for a 4-man pop-playing group is 147 hr by the 'Decorators' at Becketts Bar, Bexhill-on-Sea, East Sussex on 8–14 Jan 1984.

POTATO PEELING

The greatest amount of potatoes peeled by 5 people to an institutional cookery standard with standard kitchen knives in 45 min is 266,5 kg *587 lb 8 oz* by J. Mills, M. McDonald, P. Jennings, E. Gardiner and V. McNulty at Bourke Street Hall, Melbourne, Vic, Australia on 17 Mar 1981.

PRAM PUSHING

The greatest distance covered in pushing a pram in 24 hr is 345.25 miles *555,62 km* by Runner's Factory of Los Gatos, California, USA with an All-Star team of 57 California runners on 23–24 June 1979. A 10 man Royal Marine team from the Commando Training Centre, Lympstone, Devon, with an adult 'Baby', covered 252.65 miles *406.60 km* in 24 hr on 31 Mar–18 Apr 1984.

'PSYCHIATRIST' FASTEST

The world's fastest 'psychiatrist' was Dr Albert L. Weiner of Erlton, New Jersey, USA, who was trained solely in osteopathy but who dealt with up to 50 psychiatric patients a day in four treatment rooms. He relied heavily on narco-analysis, muscle relaxants and electro-shock treatments. In December 1961 he was found guilty on 12 counts of manslaughter from using unsterilized needles.

QUIZZES

The highest number of participants was 80,977 in the All Japan High School Quiz Championship televised by NTV on 31 Dec 1983. The most protracted contest was that lasting 100 hrs 7 min in Shrewsbury, Shropshire on 19–24 Apr 1984. The two teams correctly answered 16,978 of the 25,135 questions.

QUOIT THROWING

The world's record for rope quoit throwing is an unbroken sequence of 4002 pegs by Bill Irby, Snr of Australia in 1968.

RAMP JUMPING

The longest distance ever achieved for motor cycle long jumping is *64,60 m* 212 ft over 16 buses by Alain Jean Prieur (b. 4 July 1939) of France at Montlhéry near Paris on 6 Feb 1977. The pioneer of this form of exhibition—Evel Knievel (b. Robert Craig Knievel, 17 Oct 1938 at Butte, Montana, USA) had suffered 433 bone fractures by his 1975 season. His abortive attempt to cross the 1600 ft *485 m* wide and 600 ft *180 m* deep Snake River Canyon, Idaho on 8 Sept 1974 in a rocket reputedly increased his life-time earnings by $6 million (*then £2¼ million*). The longest jump in Britain is 208 ft *63,30 m* by Chris Bromham at Bromley Common, South London on 29 Aug 1983. The longest ramp jump in a car by a professional stunt driver is 232 ft *70,73 m* by Jacqueline De Creed (*née* Creedy) in a 1967 Ford Mustang at Santa Pod Raceway, Bedfordshire on 3 Apr 1983.

RAPPELING (or Abseiling)

On 26 July 1982 Jim Bridwell and John N. Long (both USA) descended down the face of the precipice adjacent to the Angel Falls in Venezuela on an 1800 ft *548 m* nylon rope. The longest descent down the side of a skyscraper is one of 580 ft *176,7 m* (52 storeys) in Hong Kong by Capt. Martin Fuller (1st Bn Cheshire Regt.) on 1 Sept 1984.

RIDING IN ARMOUR

The longest recorded ride in full armour (8 stone *50,8 kg*) is one of 167 miles *268,7 km* from

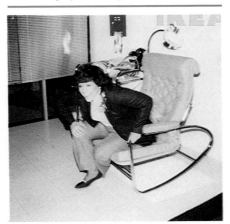

Linda Kennedy (Canada) who provided a moving window display for 18½ days. (See col. 3 above)

Edinburgh to Dumfries in 3 days (riding time 28 hr 30 min) by Dick Brown, 48, on 13–15 June 1979.

RIVETING

The world's record for riveting is 11,209 in 9 hr by J. Moir at the Workman Clark Ltd shipyard, Belfast, Northern Ireland, in June 1918. His peak hour was his seventh with 1409, an average of nearly 23½ per min.

ROCKING CHAIR

The longest recorded 'Rockathon' is 444 hr by Linda Kennedy at the IKEA store, Calgary, Alberta, Canada on 16 Jan–3 Feb 1984.

ROLLING PIN

The record distance for a woman to throw a 2 lb *907 g* rolling pin is 175 ft 5 in *53,4 m* by Lori La Deane Adams, 21 at Iowa State Fair, Iowa, USA, on 21 Aug 1979.

SAND SCULPTURING

The largest sand sculpture on record was an 8498 ft *2590 m* long representation of a 19th century train along Virginia Beach, Virginia, USA on 2 Oct 1983 organized by Louise Lowenthal.

SCOOTER RIDING

The greatest distance covered by a team of 25 in 24 hr is 336.11 miles *540,93 km* by Wimmera Young Farmers, Victoria, Australia on 22–23 Mar 1980.

SEARCH *Longest*

Walter Edwin Percy Zillwood (b. Deptford, London SE8, Dec 1900) traced his missing sister Lena (Mrs Elizabeth Eleanor Allen, b. Nov 1897, d. Jan 1982) after 79 years through the agency of the Salvation Army on 3 May 1980.

SEE-SAW

George Partridge and Tamara Marquez of Auburn High School, Washington, USA on a suspension see-saw completed 1101 hr 40 min (indoor) on 28 Mar–13 May 1977. Georgia Chaffin and Tammy Adams of Goodhope Jr. High School, Cullman, Alabama, USA completed 730 hr 30 min (outdoor) on 25 June–25 July 1975.

SERMON

The longest sermon on record was delivered by the Rev. Ronald Gallagher at the Baptist Temple, Lynchburg, Virginia, USA for 120 hr on 26 June–1 July 1983. From 31 May to 10 June 1969 the 14th Dalai Lama (b. 6 July 1934 as Tenzin Gyalto) the exiled ruler of Tibet, completed a sermon on Tantric Buddhism for 5–7 hr per day to total 60 hr in India.

SHAVING

The fastest demon barber on record is Gerry Harley, who shaved 987 men in 60 min with a safety razor in Gillingham, Kent on 28 Apr 1983 taking a perfunctory 3.64 sec per volunteer. On 13 Aug 1984 he shaved 235 even braver volunteers with a cutthroat razor in a less perfunctory 15.3 sec per face. He drew blood only once.

SHEAF TOSSING

The world's best performance for tossing a 3,63 kg *8 lb* sheaf for height is 19,77 m *64.86 ft* by Trond Ulleberg of Skolleborg, Norway on 11 Nov 1978. Such pitchfork contests date from 1914.

SHOESHINE BOYS

In this category (limited to a team of 4 teenagers; duration of 8 hr; shoes 'on the hoof') the record is 6780 pairs by the Sheffield Citadel Band of Salvation Army, S. Yorkshire, on 27 Feb 1982.

SHORTHAND FASTEST

The highest recorded speeds ever attained under championship conditions are: 300 words per min (99.64 per cent accuracy) for 5 min and 350 wpm (99.72 per cent accuracy, that is, two insignificant errors) for 2 min by Nathan Behrin (USA) in tests in New York in December 1922. Behrin (b. 1887) used the Pitman system invented in 1837. Morris I. Kligman, official court reporter of the US Court House, New York has taken 50,000 words in 5 hr (a sustained rate of 166.6 wpm). Rates are much dependent upon the nature, complexity and syllabic density of the material. Mr. G. W. Bunbury of Dublin, Ireland held the unique distinction of writing at 250 wpm for 10 min on 23 Jan 1894.

Mr Arnold Bradley achieved a speed of 309 words per minute without error using the Sloan-Duployan system with 1545 words in 5 minutes in a test in Walsall, West Midlands on 9 Nov 1920.

SHOUTING

The greatest number of wins in the national town criers' contest is 11 by Ben Johnson of Fowey, Cornwall, who won in 1939, 1949–55, 1966, 1969 and 1973. The first national feminine champion has been Mrs Henrietta Sargent, town-crier, of The Three Horse Shoes, Cricklade, Wiltshire in 1980. On being told she had beaten the other 31 contestants she said 'I'm speechless'. (See also Longest-ranged voice, Chapter 1 page 17.)

SHOWERING

The most prolonged continuous shower bath on record is one of 336 hr by Arron Marshall of Rockingham Park, Western Australia on 29 July–12 Aug 1978. The feminine record is 121 hr 1 min by Lisa D'Amato on 5–10 Nov 1981 at Harper College, Binghamton, New York, USA. Desquamation can be a positive danger.

SINGING

The longest recorded solo singing marathon is one of 180 hr by Robert Sim at The Waterfront Hotel, Kingston-upon-Hull, Humberside on 18–25 Mar 1983. The marathon record for a choir has been 72 hr 2 min by the combined choir of Girls' High School and Prince Edward School, Salisbury (now Harare), Zimbabwe on 7–10 Sept 1979. Acharya Prem Bhikuji started chanting the Akhand Ram Dhum in 1964 and devotees took this up in rotation completing their devotions 13 years later on 31 July 1977 at Jamnagar, India.

SKATE BOARDING

'World' championships have been staged intermittently since 1966. David Frank, 22 covered 238.36 miles *383.6 km* in 31 hr 1 min in Toronto, Canada on 9–10 July 1983.

The highest speed recorded on a skate board under USSA rules is 71.79 mph *115,53 km/h* on a course at Mt Baldy, California in a prone position by Richard K. Brown, 33, on 17 June 1979. The stand-up record is 53.45 mph *86,01 km/h* by John Hutson, 23 at Signal Hill, Long Beach, California on 11 June 1978. The high jump record is 5 ft 5.7 in *1,67 m* by Trevor Baxter (b. 1 Oct 1962) of Burgess Hill, East

Sussex at Grendole, France on 14 Sept 1982. At the 4th US Skateboard Association championship, at Signal Hill on 25 Sept 1977, Tony Alva, 19, jumped 17 barrels (17 ft *5,18m*).

SKIPPING

The longest recorded skipping (5 min/hour breaks) marathon was one of 12 hr 8 min by Frank P. Oliveri (est. 120,744 turns) at Great Lakes Training Center, North Chicago, Illinois, USA on 13 June 1981.

Other records made without a break:

MOST TURNS IN 10 SEC 128 by Albert Rayner, Stanford Sports, Birmingham, 19 Nov 1982

MOST TURNS IN 1 MIN 330 by Brian D. Christensen, Ridgewood Shopping Center, Tennessee, 1 Sept 1979

MOST DOUBLES (WITH CROSS) 1,664 by Sean Birch at Tralee, Co. Kerry, Ireland, 27 Apr 1984

DOUBLE TURNS 10 133 by Katsumi Suzuki, Saitama, Japan, 27 Sept 1979

TREBLE TURNS 381 by Katsumi Suzuki, Saitama, Japan, 29 May 1975

QUADRUPLE TURNS 51 by Katsumi Suzuki, Saitama, Japan, 29 May 1975

QUINTUPLE TURNS 6 by Hideyuki Tateda (b. 1968), Aomori, Japan, 19 June 1982

DURATION 1264 miles *2034 km* by Tom Morris, Brisbane-Cairns, Queensland, 1963

MOST ON SINGLE ROPE (MINIMUM 12 TURNS OBLIGATORY) 160 (50 m rope) by Shimizu Iida Junior High School, Shizuoka-ken, Japan, 10 Dec 1982

MOST TURNS ON SINGLE ROPE (TEAM OF 90) 97 by Erimomisaki School, Hokkaido, Japan, 28 May 1983

ON A TIGHTROPE 58 (consecutive) by Bryan Andro (*né* Dewhurst) TROS TV, Holland, 6 Aug 1981

SLINGING

The greatest distance recorded for a sling-shot is 1434 ft 2 in *437,13 m* using a 51 in *129,5 cm* long sling and a 2 oz *56,5 g* stone by Lawrence L. Bray at Loa, Utah, USA on 21 Aug 1981.

SMOKE RING BLOWING

The highest recorded number of smoke rings formed from the lips from a single pull of a cigarette (cheek-tapping is disallowed) is 355 by Jan van Deurs Formann of Copenhagen achieved in Switzerland in August 1979.

SNAKES AND LADDERS

The longest recorded game of Snakes and Ladders has been one of 260 hr by a team of six (four always in play) from Essex Young Farmers Club, West Mersea, Essex, on 29 Jan to 9 Feb 1982.

SNOW SHOEING

The U.S.S.A. record for covering a mile *1609,34 m* is 7 min 56 sec by Mark Lessard at Corinth, New York, USA in 1979.

SPEAR THROWING

The greatest distance achieved throwing a spear with the aid of a woomera is 326 ft 6 in *99,51 m* (or 9 ft 2 in *2,79 m* beyond the Javelin record) by Bailey Bush on 27 June 1982 at Camden, NSW, Australia.

SPINNING BY HAND

The duration record for spinning a clock balance wheel by unaided hand is 5 min 26.8 sec by Philip Ashley, 16, of Leigh, Lancashire on 20 May 1968. The record using 36 in *91,4 cm* of string with a 7¼ oz *205,5 g* top is 58 min 20 sec by Peter Hodgson at Southend-on-Sea, Essex on 4 Feb 1985.

SPITTING

The greatest distance achieved at the annual tobacco spitting classic (instituted 1955) at Raleigh, Mississippi, USA, is 33 ft 7½ in *10,24 m* by Jeff Barber on 25 July 1981. (In 1980 he reached 45 ft *13,71 m* at Fulton, Miss.). In the 3rd International Spittin', Belchin' and Cussin' Triathlon, Harold Fielden reached 34 ft 0¼ in *10,36 m* at Central City, Colorado, USA, on 13 July 1973. Distance is dependent on the quality of salivation, absence of cross wind, the two finger pucker and coordination of the back arch and neck snap. Sprays or wads smaller than a dime are not measured. Randy Ober of Bentonville, Arkansas, USA spat a tobacco wad 47 ft 7 in *14,50 m* at the Calico 5th Annual Tobacco Chewing and Spitting Championships north of Barstow, California, USA on 4 Apr 1982. The record for projecting a melon seed under WCWSSCA rules is 65 ft 4 in *19,91 m* by John Wilkinson in Luling, Texas, USA, on 28 June 1980. The furthest reported distance for a cherry stone is 65 ft 2 in *19,86 m* by Rick Krause, at Eau Claire, Michigan, USA on 5 July 1980. Spitters who care about their image wear 12 in *30,4 cm* block-ended boots so practice spits can be measured without a tape.

STAIR CLIMBING

The 100 storey record for stair climbing was set by Dennis W. Martz in the Detroit Plaza Hotel, Detroit, Michigan, USA, on 26 June 1978 at 11 min 23.8 sec. Dale Neil, 22, ran a vertical mile on the stairs of the Peachtree Plaza Hotel, Atlanta, Georgia in continuous action of 2 hr 1 min 24 sec on 9 Mar 1984. *These records can only be attempted in buildings with a minimum of 70 storeys.*

The record for the 1760 steps (vertical height 1122 ft *342 m*) in the world's tallest free-standing structure, Toronto's CN Tower, is 10 min 10 sec by Michael Round on 9 Aug 1980. Robert C. Jezequel ran 7 round trips in 6 hr 23 min in 1982 without use of the elevator for a vertical height of 15 708 ft *4787 m*.

Pete Squires raced up the 1575 steps of the Empire State Building, New York City on 12 Feb 1981 in 10 min 59 sec.

In the line of duty Bill Stevenson mounted 334 of the 364 steps of the tower in the Houses of Parliament, 4000 times in the 15 years (1968–83)—equivalent to 24.9 ascents of Everest.

STANDING

The longest period on record that anyone has continuously stood is for more than 17 years in the case of Swami Maujgiri Maharij when performing the *Tapasya* or penance from 1955 to November 1973 in Shahjahanpur, Uttar Pradesh, India. When sleeping he would lean against a plank. He died aged 85 in Sept 1980.

STAMP LICKING

The Post Office staged a contest for tearing from sheets and individually affixing stamps to envelopes in 4 mins. The inaugural winner at St Martin's-le-Grand, City of London on 12 Feb 1984 was the comedian Frankie Howerd with 72.

STILT-WALKING

Hop stringers use stilts up to 15 ft *4.57 m*. In 1892 M. Garisoain of Bayonne stilt-walked 8 km *4.97 miles* into Biarritz in 42 min to average 11,42 km/h *7.10 mph*. In 1891 Sylvain Dornon stilt-walked from Paris to Moscow *via* Vilno in 50 stages for the 1830 miles *2945 km*. Another source gives his time as 58 days. Even with a safety or Kirby wire very high stilts are *extremely* dangerous—25 steps are deemed to constitute 'mastery'. Eddy Wolf (also known as Steady Eddy) of Loyal, Wisconsin, USA mastered stilts measuring 40 ft 2 in *12,24 m* from ground to ankle over a distance of 31 steps without touching his safety handrail wires, in Hollywood, California on 4 Dec 1981. His aluminium stilts weighed 40 lb *18,1 kg* each. Joe Long (b. Kenneth Caesar), who has suffered 5 fractures, mastered 56 lb *25,4 kg* 24 ft *7,31 m* stilts at the BBC TV Centre, London on 8 Dec 1978. The endurance record is 3008 miles *4804 km* from Los Angeles, California to Bowen, Kentucky, USA, from 20 Feb to 26 July 1980 by Joe Bowen. Masaharu Tatsushiro, 28, (Japan) ran 100 m *328 ft* on 1 ft *30,48 cm* high stilts in 14.15 sec in Tōkyō on 30 Mar 1980.

STOWAWAY

The most rugged stowaway was Socarras Ramirez who escaped from Cuba on 4 June 1969 by stowing away in an unpressurized wheel well in the starboard wing of a Douglas DC8 from Havana to Madrid in a 5600 mile *9010 km* Iberian Airlines flight. He survived 8 hr at 30,000 ft *9145 m* where temperatures were $-8°$ F $-22°$ C.

STRETCHER BEARING

The longest recorded carry of a stretcher case with a 10 st *63,5 kg* 'body' is 127 miles *204,34 km* in 45 hr 45 min by two four man teams from the Sri Chinmoy marathon team of Jamaica, NY, USA, on 17–19 Apr 1981.

The record limited to Youth Organizations (under 20 years of age) and 8 hr carrying is 42.02 miles *67,62 km* by 8 members of the Henry Meoles School, Moreton, Wirral, Cheshire on 13 July 1980.

STRING BALL LARGEST

The largest ball of string on record is one of 12 ft 9 in *3,88 m* in diameter, 40 ft *12,19 m* in circumference and weighing 10 tons/*tonnes* amassed by Francis A. Johnson of Darwin, Minnesota, USA, between 1950–78.

SUBMERGENCE

The most protracted underwater endurance record (excluding the use of diving bells) is 147 hr 15 min established by Robert Ingolia in tests in which the US Navy was the beneficiary of all data in 1961.

The *continuous* duration record (i.e. no rest breaks) for 'Scuba' (i.e. self-contained and without surface air hoses) is 105 hr 11 sec by Henk Kuhlmann (b. 16 May 1948) in the Flora Park Swimming Pool, Amsterdam, Netherlands on 21–25 Aug 1984. Measures have to be taken to reduce the risk of severe desquamation in such endurance trials. The pre-existing record was 101 hr 1 min by Michael Stevens at the Holiday Inn, Birmingham on 20–24 Apr 1984.

SUGGESTION BOXES

The most prolific example on record of the use of any suggestion box scheme is that of John Drayton (b. 18 Sept 1907) of Newport, Gwent who has plied British Rail system with a total of 31,028 suggestions from 1924 to 18 Apr 1984 of which one in seven were accepted.

SWINGING

The record duration for continuous swinging in a hammock is 196 hr by Patrick Galvin and Mark Ungar of San Mateo, California on 31 July–8 Aug 1984.

SWITCHBACK RIDING

The endurance record for rides on a roller coaster is 503 hr by M. M. Daniel Glada and Normand St-Pierre at Parc Belmont, Montreal, Canada on 18 July–10 Aug 1983. The minimum qualifying average speed required is 25 mph *40 km/h*.

TAILORING

The highest speed in which the manufacture of a 3 piece suit has been made from sheep to finished article is 1 hr 34 min 33.42 sec by 65 members of the Melbourne College of Textiles, Pascoe Vale, Victoria, Australia on 24 June 1982. The catching and fleecing took 2 min 21 sec, and the carding, spinning, weaving and tailoring occupied the remaining time.

TALKING

The world record for non-stop talking has been 159 hr by Kapila Kumarasinghe, 16 in a lecture on Buddhist culture in Colombo, Sri Lanka on 18–24 June 1981. A feminine non-stop talking record was set by Mrs Mary E. Davis, who on 2–7 Sept 1958 started at a radio station in Buffalo, New York, USA and did not draw breath until 110 hr 30 min 5 sec later in Tulsa, Oklahoma, USA. (See also Filibusters, Chap 11.)

Historically the longest recorded after-dinner speech with unsuspecting victims was one of 3 hr by the Rev. Henry Whitehead (d. March 1896) at the Rainbow Tavern, Fleet Street, London on 16 Jan 1874. At a dinner at St. George's Hotel, Lime Street, Liverpool Paul Osgood (b. 11 Jan 1964) replied to the toast to the guests for 16 hr 6 min on 21–22 Mar 1985.

T-BONE DIVE

The so-called T-bone dives or Dive Bomber crashes by cars off ramps over and on to parked cars are often measured by the number of cars, but owing to their variable size and that their purpose is purely to cushion the shock, distance is more significant.

Jean-Pierre Vignan attained 59,86 m *196 ft 5 in* in a Ford Capri at Montlhéry, Paris on 20 July 1980.

TEETH-PULLING

The man with 'the strongest teeth in the world' is 'Hercules' John Massis (b. Wilfried Oscar Morbée, 4 June 1940) of Oostakker, Belgium, who raised a weight of 233 kg *513⅝ lb* 15 cm *6 in* from the ground with a teeth bit at Evrey, France on 19 Mar 1977. Massis prevented a helicopter from taking off using only a tooth-bit harness in Los Angeles, California, USA on 7 Apr 1979 for a *Guinness Spectacular* TV Show.

THROWING

The greatest distance any inert object heavier than air has been thrown is 1114 ft 6 in *339,69 m*, in the case of the Aerobie flying ring by Tom McRann in Stanford Stadium, Palo Alto, California on 10 May 1985. The plastic 3.95 oz *112 g* projectile was invented by Prof. Alan Adler of Palo Alto, California, USA. (See photograph p. 176).

TIGHTROPE WALKING

The greatest 19th century tightrope walker was Jean François Gravelet, *alias* Charles Blondin (1824–97), of France, who made the earliest crossing of the Niagara Falls on a 3 in *76 mm* rope, 110 ft *335 m* long, 160 ft *48,75 m* above the Falls on 30 June 1859. He also made a crossing with Harry Colcord, pick-a-back on 15 Sept 1860. Though other artists still find it difficult to believe, Colcord was his agent. The oldest wirewalker was 'Professor' William Ivy Baldwin (1866–1953), who crossed the South Boulder Canyon, Colorado, USA on a 320 ft *97,5 m* wire with a 125 ft *38,1 m* drop on his 82nd birthday on 31 July 1948.

TIGHTROPE WALKING *Endurance*

The world tightrope endurance record is 185 days by Henri Rochetain (b. 1926) of France on a wire 394 ft *120 m* long, 82 ft *25 m* above a supermarket in Saint Etienne, France, on 28 Mar–29 Sept 1973. His ability to sleep on the wire has left doctors puzzled. Steven G. Wallenda, 33, walked 2.36 miles *3,81 km* on a wire 250 ft *76,2 m* long 32 ft *9,75 m* high at North Port, Florida, USA on 26 Mar 1983 in 3 hr 31 min.

TIGHTROPE WALKING *Highest and Steepest*

Steve McPeak (b. 21 April 1945) of Las Vegas, Nevada, USA ascended the 46,6 mm *1.83 in* diameter Zugspitzbahn cable for a vertical height of 705 m *2313 ft* in 3 stints aggregating 5 hr 4 min on 24/25/28 June 1981. The maximum gradient over the stretch of 2282 m *7485 ft* was above 30 degrees. Earlier on 28 June 1981 he had walked on a thinner stayed cable 181 steps across a gorge at the top of the 2963 m *9721 ft* mountain with a sheer drop of 960 m *3150 ft* below him.

The first crossing of the River Thames was achieved by Charles Elleano (b. 1911) of Strasbourg, France on a 1050 ft *320 m* wire 60 ft *18,2 m* above the river in 25 min on 22 Sept 1951.

Engineer Peter Hodgson with the silver steel top with which he got within 100 secs of the fast hour long spin. (See page 180) *(Thames TV News)*

Above Queenslander Les Stewart who may celebrate 'Nine hundred and ninety nine thousand nine hundred and ninety nine' some years hence. *Right* The hands of Mary Morel look distinctively blurred as she demonstrated the ability to type numbers at a rate of 7.4 per second.

TREE-CLIMBING

The fastest speed climb up a 100 ft *30,4 m* fir spar pole and return to the ground is one of 27.16 sec by Ed Johnson of Victoria, BC, Canada in July 1982 at the Lumberjack World Championships in Hayward, Wisconsin.

The fastest time up a 9 m *29.5 ft* coconut tree barefoot is 4.88 sec by Fuatai Solo, 17, in Sukuna Park, Fiji on 22 Aug 1980.

TREE-SITTING

The duration record for sitting in a tree is 431 days by Timothy Roy at Golf N'Stuff Amusement Park, Norwalk, Calif., USA from 4 July 1982–8 Sept 1983.

TYPEWRITING *fastest*

The highest recorded speeds attained with a ten-word penalty per error on a manual machine are:

Five Min: 176 wpm net Mrs Carole Forristall Waldschlager Bechen at Dixon, Illinois on 2 Apr 1959. One Hour: 147 words (net rate per min) Albert Tangora (US) (Underwood Standard), 22 Oct 1923.

The official hour record on an electric machine is 9316 words (40 errors) on an IBM machine, giving a net rate of 149 words per min, by Margaret Hamma, now Mrs Dilmore (US), in Brooklyn, New York City, NY, USA on 20 June 1941. Mary Ann Morel (South Africa) set a numerical record at the CABEX '85 Exhibition in Johannesburg, South Africa on 6 Feb 1985 by typing spaced numbers from 1 to 781 in 5 mins. Mrs Barbara Blackburn of Everett, Washington State, can maintain 150 wpm for 50 min (37,500 key strokes) and attain speeds of 170 wpm using the Dvorak Simplified Keyboard (DSK) system.

In an official test in 1946 Stella Pajunas, now Mrs Garnard, attained a rate of 216 words in a minute on an IBM machine.

TYPEWRITING *Longest*

The world duration record for typewriting on an electric machine is 264 hr by Violet Gibson

Burns at The Royal Easter Show, Sydney, Australia on 29 Mar–9 Apr 1985.

The longest duration typing marathon on a manual machine is 120 hr 15 min by Mike Howell, a 23-year-old blind office worker from Greenfield, Oldham, Greater Manchester on 25–30 Nov 1969 on an Olympia manual typewriter in Liverpool. In aggregating 561,006 strokes he performed a weight movement of 2482 tons *2521 tonnes* plus a further 155 tons *157 tonnes* on moving the carriage for line spacing. Les Stewart of Mudjimba Beach, Qld, Australia has typed the numbers 1 to 360,200 in *words* on 7,094 quarto sheets as of 7 Jan 1985. His target is to become a "millionaire".

TYRE SUPPORTING

The greatest number of motor tyres supported in a free-standing 'lift' is 96 by Gary Windebank of Romsey, Hants on Feb 1984. The total weight was 1440 lb *653 kg*. The tyres used were Michelin XZX 155 × 13.

UNSUPPORTED CIRCLE

The highest recorded number of people who have demonstrated the physical paradox of all being seated without a chair is an unsupported circle of 10,323 employees of the Nissan Motor Company at Komazawa Stadium, Tokyo, Japan on 23 Oct 1982.

WAITERS MARATHON

Beverly Hills restaurateur Roger Bourban, Switzerland, *Le garçon rapide*, ran a full mara-

thon in full uniform in London on 9 May 1982 carrying a free standing open bottle of mineral water on a tray in the same hand (gross weight 3 lb 2 oz *1,42 kg*) in 2 hr 47 min.

WALKING ON HANDS

The duration record for walking on hands is 1400 km *871 miles* by Johann Hurlinger, of Austria, who in 55 daily 10 hr stints, averaged 1.58 mph *2,54 km/h* from Vienna to Paris in 1900. Thomas P. Hunt of USAF Academy, Colorado Springs, completed a 50 m *54.68 yd* inverted sprint in 18.4 sec in Tokyo on 22 Sept 1979. Four men (Bob Sutton, Danny Scannell, Phil Johnson and John Hawkins) relayed a mile in Oak Ridge, Tennessee, USA on 13 Mar 1983 in 31 min 15.8 sec.

WALKING ON WATER

Using outsize shoes-cum-floats Fritz Weber walked on the Main from Beyreuth over 300 km *185 miles* to Mainz on 1 Sept to 15 Oct 1983.

WALL OF DEATH

The greatest endurance feat on a wall of death was 6 hr 7 min 38 sec by Hugo Dabbert (b. Hildesheim, 24 Sept 1938) at Rüsselsheim, West Germany on 14 Aug 1980. He rode 6841 laps on the 10 m *32.8 ft* diameter wall on a Honda CM 400T averaging 35,2 km/h *21.8 mph* for the 214,8 km *133.4 miles*.

WHIP CRACKING

The longest stock whip ever 'cracked' (*i.e.* the end made to travel above the speed of sound—760 mph *1223 km/h*) is one of 104 ft 5 in *31,82 m* (excluding the handle) wielded by Noel Harris at Melbourne, Australia on 24 June 1982.

WHISTLING *Loudest and Longest*

Roy Lomas (see above) achieved 122.5 decibels at 2½ metres in the Deadroom at the BBC Manchester Studios on 19 Dec 1983. The whistling marathon record is by David 'Harpo' Hall of Berkeley, California, USA, who completed 25 hr non-stop on the AM San Francisco TV Show on 1 Apr 1983.

WINDOW CLEANING

On 19 Oct 1984 at the Clearview Challenge Cup contest, Sydney, Australia Roy Ridley achieved 18.92 sec without a smear for three standard *40.94 × 45.39 in* 1040 × 1153 mm office windows with a *11.8 in* 300 m long squeegee and *15.83 pts* 9 litres of water.

WIRE SLIDE

The greatest distance recorded in a wire slide is from a height of 175 ft *53,3 m* over a distance of 300 ft *91,44 m* by Grant Page with Bob Woodham over his shoulder across the Australian landmark known as 'The Gap' for the filmed episode in 'The Stunt Men' in 1972.

WOOD-CUTTING

The earliest competitions date from Tasmania in 1874. The records set at the Lumberjack World Championships at Hayward, Wisconsin, USA, (founded 1960) are:

Power Saw	9.74 sec
Sven Johnson (US)	1982
One-Man Bucking	21.70 sec
Merv Jensen (NZ) (d. Apr 1983)	1982
Standing Block Chop	25.38 sec
Mel Lentz (US)	1982
Underhand Block Chop	18.66 sec
Mel Lentz (US)	1982
Two-Man Bucking	9.44 sec
Merv Jensen (NZ) Cliff Hughes (NZ)	1982

Hand Splitting a cord into quarters*

	53 min 40 sec
Richard Sawyer (US)	1982

White pine logs 14 in *35,5 cm* diameter are used for chopping and 20 in *50,8 cm* for sawing.
* Hardwood (white ash) cord of 128 ft³ *3,62 m³* using a quartering wedge at Sag Harbour, NY, on 2 July 1982.

WRITING MINISCULE

In 1926 an account was published of Alfred McEwen's pantograph record in which the 56 word version of the Lord's Prayer was written by diamond point on glass in the space of 0.0016 × 0.0008 in *0,04 × 0,02 mm*. Frank C. Watts of Felmingham, Norfolk demonstrated for photographers on 24 Jan 1968, his ability, without mechanical or optical aid, to write the Lord's Prayer 34 times (9452 letters) within the size of a definitive UK postage stamp (viz.) 0.84 × 0.71 in *21,33 × 18,03 mm*. Tsutomu Ishii of Tokyo demonstrated the ability to write the names of 44 countries (184 letters) on a single grain of rice and TOKYO JAPAN in Japanese on a human hair in April 1983. In Dec 1980 Michael Isaacson, Associate Professor of the School of Applied and Engineering Physics, Cornell University, Ithaca, New York, succeeded in etching the 16 letters in 'molecular devices' on a sodium chloride crystal with a 100,000 volt electron beam. The 'writing' was 2 nanometers wide.

WRITING UNDER HANDICAP

The ultimate feat in 'funny writing' would appear to be the ability to write extemporaneously and decipherably backwards, upside down, laterally inverted (mirror-style) while blindfolded with both hands simultaneously. Three claims to this ability with both hands and feet simultaneously, by Mrs Carolyn Webb of Thirlmere, NSW, Australia, Mrs Judy Hall of Chesterfield, Virginia, USA, and Robert Gray of Toronto, Ontario, Canada are outstanding but have not been witnessed in the act by our staff.

YODELLING

The most protracted yodel on record was that of Errol Bird for 26 hr in Lisburn, Northern Ireland on 27–28 Sept 1984. Yodelling has been defined as 'repeated rapid changes from the chest-voice to falsetto and back again'. The most rapid recorded is 5 tones (3 falsetto) in 1.9 sec by Donn Reynolds of Canada on 25 July 1984.

YO-YO

A Yo-yo was a toy in Grecian times and is depicted on a bowl dated 450 B.C. It was also a Filipino jungle fighting weapon recorded in the 16th century weighing 4 lb *1,81 kg* with a 20 ft *6 m* thong. The word means 'come-come'. Though illustrated in a book in 1891 as a bandalore the craze did not begin until it was started by Donald F. Duncan of Chicago, USA in 1926. The most difficult modern yo-yo trick is the 'Whirlwind' incorporating both inside and outside horizontal loop-the-loops. The individual continuous endurance record is 120 hr by John Winslow of Gloucester, Virginia, USA on 23–28 Nov 1977. Dr Allen Bussey in Waco, Texas, USA on 23 Apr 1977 completed 20,302 loops in 3 hr (including 6886 in a single 60 min period). He used a Duncan Imperial with a 34½ in *87,6 cm* nylon string.

The largest yo-yo ever constructed was one by Dr Tom Kuhn weighing 256 lb *116,11 kg* test launched from a 150 ft *52,2 m* crane in San Francisco, California, USA, on 13 Oct 1979.

High speed yodeller Canadian Donn Reynolds whose leather larynx can emit 157 tone changes for men. (See col. 1 below)

WEALTH AND POVERTY

The comparison and estimations of extreme personal wealth are beset with intractable difficulties. Quite apart from reticence and the element of approximation in the valuation of assets, as Jean Paul Getty (1892–1976) once said 'if you can count your millions you are not a billionaire'. The term millionaire was invented *c.* 1740 and billionaire (in the American sense of one thousand million) in 1861. The earliest dollar centi-millionaire was Cornelius Vanderbilt (1794–1877) who left $100 million in 1877. The earliest billionaires were John Davison Rockefeller (1839–1937); Henry Ford (1863–1947) and Andrew William Mellon (1855–1937). In 1937, the last year in which all 3 were alive, a billion US dollars were worth £205 million but that amount of sterling would today have a purchasing power exceeding £3000 million.

Richest men *World*

Many of the riches of most of the world's 29 remaining monarchs are national rather than personal assets. The least fettered and most monarchical is H.M. Sir Muda Hassanal Bolkiah Mu'izzaddin Waddaulah Hon GCMG (b. 15 July 1946). He appointed himself Prime Minister, Finance and Home Affairs Minister on 1 Jan 1984. Brunei's annual oil revenue is £3,000 million and its foreign reserves are £10,000 million all of which is effactually at his disposal.

The richest man in the United States has been Gordon Peter Getty (b. 1930), fourth son of Jean Paul Getty by his fourth wife Ann Rork, and sole trustee of the Sarah C. Getty Trust valued in Sept 1984 at $4100 million (*£3,400 million*).

Richest man *Great Britain*

The richest man in Great Britain is reputed to be Sir John Moores, CBE the co-founder of Littlewoods football pools in 1924. In 1973 he was estimated to be worth about £400 million (hence £1550 million in 1985). His first job after leaving school at 14 was as a telephone operator. He was born in Eccles, Lancashire on 25 Jan 1896. He reassumed the chairmanship of Littlewoods on 17 Oct 1980 and finally retired in February 1982.

Highest incomes

The greatest incomes derive from the collection of royalties per barrel by rulers of oil-rich sheikhdoms, who have not abrogated personal entitlement. Shaikh Zayid ibn Sultan an-Nuhayan (b. 1918) head of state of the United Arab Emirates arguably has title to some $9000 million of the country's annual gross national product.

The highest gross income ever achieved in a single year by a private citizen is an estimated $105,000,000 (*then £21¼ now £390 million*) in 1927 by the Neopolitan born Chicago gangster Alphonse ('Scarface Al') Capone (1889–1947).

This was derived from illegal liquor trading and alky-cookers (illicit stills), gambling establishments, dog tracks, dance halls, 'protection' rackets and vice in which there were in 1925–27 nil convictions from 915 murders by his 'Italian Mob' in South Chicago. On his business card the former 'bouncer' and brothel-keeper described himself as a 'Second hand Furniture Dealer'. The highest gross earned income in a year by a UK subject is reputedly in excess of £25 million earned by Paul McCartney MBE in the years since 1979.

Proved wills and death duties

Sir John Reeves Ellerman, 2nd Bt, (1909–73) left £53,238,370 on which all-time record death duties were payable. This is the highest value will ever proved in the United Kingdom. On 29 Apr 1985 the estate of Sir Charles Clore (1904–1979) was agreed at £123 million. The Inland Revenue claimed £84 million but settled for £67 million. The greatest will proved in Ireland was that of the 1st Earl of Iveagh (1847–1927), who left £13,486,146. The will of Mrs Gladys Doreen Sprinks of Milford-on-Sea, Hampshire published on 8 Feb 1984 was £7,411,203 (net).

Most millionaires

The United States was estimated to have some 832,500 millionaire families in early 1985 with the million mark expected in mid-1987.

Millionairesses

The world's wealthiest woman was probably Princess Wilhelmina Helena Pauline Maria of Orange-Nassau (1880–1962), formerly Queen of the Netherlands from 1890 to her abdication, 4 Sept 1948, with a fortune which was estimated at over £200 million. The largest amount proved in the will of a woman in the United Kingdom has been the £7,607,168 of the Rt. Hon Countess of Sefton in 1981. Mrs. Anna Dodge (later Mrs. Hugh Dillman) who was born in Dundee, Scotland, died on 3 June 1970 in the United States, aged 103, and left an estate of £40,000,000.

The cosmetician Madame C. J. Walker *née* Sarah Breedlove (b. Delta, Louisiana, USA 23 Dec 1867, d. 1919) is reputed to have become the first self-made millionairess. She was an uneducated Negro orphan scrub-woman whose fortune was founded on a hair straightener.

Millionaire and millionairess *Youngest*

The youngest person ever to accumulate a million dollars was the child film actor Jackie Coogan (b. Los Angeles, 26 Oct 1914) co-star with Sir Charles Chaplin (1889–1977) in 'The Kid' made in 1920. Shirley Temple (b. Santa Monica, California 23 Apr 1928), formerly Mrs John Agar, Jr, now Mrs Charles Black, accumulated wealth exceeding $1,000,000 (*then £209,000*) before she was 10. Her child actress career spanned the years 1934–9.

Richest families

It has been tentatively estimated that the combined value of the assets nominally controlled by the du Pont family of some 1600 members may be of the order of $150,000 million. The family arrived in the USA from France on 1 Jan 1800. Capital from Pierre du Pont (1730–1817) enabled his son Eleuthère Irénée du Pont to start his explosives company in the United States. It was estimated in 1985 that both sons and both daughters of Haroldson Lafayette Hunt were billionaires.

Largest dowry

The largest recorded dowry was that of Elena Patiño, daughter of Don Simón Iturbi Patiño (1861–1947), the Bolivian tin millionaire, who in 1929 bestowed £8,000,000 from a fortune at one time estimated to be worth £125,000,000.

Richard Giordano the £771,600 per year Chairman of BOC whose highest salary in Britain attracts an income tax 'bite' of £453,000.

Greatest miser

If meanness is measurable as a ratio between expendable assets and expenditure then Henrietta (Hetty) Howland Green (née Robinson) (1835–1916), who kept a balance of over $31,400,000 (*then £6.2 million*) in one bank alone, was the all-time world champion. Her son had to have his leg amputated because of her delays in finding a *free* medical clinic. She herself ate cold porridge because she was too thrifty to heat it. Her estate proved to be of $95 million (*then £19 million [and now worth £270 million]*).

Return of cash

The largest amount of *cash* ever found and returned to its owners was $500,000 (US) found by Lowell Elliott, 61 on his farm at Peru, Indiana, USA. It had been dropped in June 1972 by a parachuting hi-jacker.

Jim Priceman, 44, assistant cashier at Doft & Co Inc returned an envelope containing $37.1 million (*then £20.6 million*) in *negotiable* bearer certificates found outside 110 Wall Street to A G Becker Inc of New York City on 6 April 1982. In announcing a reward of $250 (*then £140*) Beckers were acclaimed as 'being all heart'.

Greatest bequests

The greatest bequests in a life-time of a millionaire were those of the late John Davison Rockefeller (1839–1937), who gave away sums totalling $750,000,000 (*now £350 million*). The greatest benefactions of a British millionaire were those of William Richard Morris, later the Viscount Nuffield, GBE, CH (1877–1963), which totalled more than £30,000,000 between 1926 and his death on 22 Aug 1963. The Scottish-born US citizen Andrew Carnegie (1835–1919) is estimated to have made benefactions totalling £70 million during the last 18 years of his life. These included 7689 church organs and 2811 libraries. He had started life in a bobbin factory at $1.20 per week.

The largest bequest made in the history of philanthropy was the $500,000,000 (*then £178,570,000*) gift, announced on 12 Dec 1955, to 4157 educational and other institutions by the Ford Foundation (established 1936) of New York City, NY, USA.

Salary Highest *World*

The highest reported remuneration of any US businessman was $51,544,000 (*£33¼ million*) in salary, bonus and stock options received by Mr Frederick W. Smith, board chairman of Federal Express in 1982. The highest amount in salary and bonuses was $2 million (*£1,290,000*) to George L. Shinn, chairman of First Boston Corporation.

Highest Fees

The highest paid investment consultant in the world is Dr Harry D. Schultz, who operates from Western Europe. His standard consultation fee for 60 minutes is $2000 on weekdays and $3000 at weekends. His quarterly retainer permitting companies to call him on a daily basis is $28,125. He writes and edits an information packed International Newsletter instituted in 1964 now sold at $50 or *£41.66* per copy.

Salary Highest *Great Britain*

The highest salary paid by any public company in 1985 was £771,600 (including fees and taxable benefits) to Mr Richard V. Giordano (b. New York, 1931), Chairman and Chief Executive of BOC (British Oxygen) International.

Share options

The record profit on a share option is £1,010,000 for Sir Francis Tombs (b. 17 May 1924) on 500,000 Turner & Newall shares. He had been appointed chairman in 1982.

Golden handshake

The highest carat handshake reported was one of 'nearly £700,000' attributed to Mr Bill Fieldhouse CBE (b. 1 Jan 1932) from Letraset of which he had been a director since 1969.

Lowest incomes

The poorest people in the world are the Tasaday tribe of cave-dwellers of central Mindanao, Philippines, who were 'discovered' in 1971 without any domesticated animals, agriculture, pottery, wheels or clothes.

Above: Violinist Yehudi Menuhin, a few months before he became, aged 15, the youngest ever non-hereditary entrant into *Who's Who. Below:* The late Sir Alister Hardy (1896–1985), 1985 winner of the annual Templeton prize of £140,000. He died 9 days later. (See page 188)

GLUTTONY RECORDS

Records for eating and drinking by trenchermen do not match those suffering from the rare disease of bulimia (morbid desire to eat) and polydipsia (pathological thirst). Some bulimics exceed 20,000 calories a day and others eat all their waking hours. An extreme consumption of 384 lb 2 oz *174,236 kg* of food in six days by Matthew Daking, aged 12 (known as Mortimer's case) was reported in 1743. Fannie Meyer of Johannesburg, after a skull fracture, was stated in 1974 to be unsatisfied by less than 160 pints of water a day. By October 1978 he was down to 52 pints. Miss Helge Andersson (b. 1908) of Lindesberg, Sweden was reported in January 1971 to have been drinking 40 pints *22,73 litres* of water a day since 1922—a total of 87,600 gal *3982 hectolitres*.

The world's greatest trencherman has been Edward Abraham ('Bozo') Miller (b. 1909) of Oakland, California, USA. He consumes up to 25,000 calories per day or more than 11 times that recommended. He stands 5 ft 7½ in *1,71 m* tall but weighs from 20 to 21½ st *127–139 kg* with a 57 in *144 cm* waist. He had been undefeated in eating contests since 1931 (see below). He ate 27 (2 lb *907 g*) pullets at a sitting in Trader Vic's, San Francisco in 1963. Phillip Yadzik (b. 1912) of Chicago in 1955 ate 77 large hamburgers in 2 hours and in 1957 101 bananas in 15 min. The bargees on the Rhine are reputed to be the world's heaviest eaters with 5200 calories a day. However the New Zealand Sports Federation of Medicine reported in December 1972 that a long-distance road runner consumed 14,321 calories in 24 hr.

While no healthy person has been reported to have succumbed in any contest for eating non-toxic food or drinking non-alcoholic drinks, such attempts, from a medical point of view, must be regarded as *extremely* inadvisable, particularly among young people. Gluttony record attempts should aim at improving the *rate* of consumption rather than the volume. Guinness Superlatives will not list any records involving the consumption of more than 2 litres *3.52 Imperial pints* of beer nor any at all involving spirits. Nor will records for such potentially dangerous categories as live ants, chewing gum, marsh mallow or raw eggs with shells be published. The ultimate in stupidity—the eating of a bicycle—has however been recorded since it is unlikely to attract competition.

Specific records have been claimed as follows:

Liquidising, processing or puréeing foodstuffs is not permitted. However drinking during attempts is permissible.

BAKED BEANS
2780 cold baked beans one by one with a cocktail stick in 30 min by Karen Stevenson, of Wallasey, Merseyside on 4 Apr 1981.

BANANAS
17 (edible weight minimum 4½ oz *128 g* each) in 2 min by Dr Ronald L. Alkana at the University of California, Irvine on 7 Dec 1973.

BEER
Steven Petrosino drank one litre of beer in 1.3 sec on 22 June 1977 at 'The Gingerbreadman', Carlisle, Pennsylvania.

Peter G. Dowdeswell (b. London 29 July 1940) of Earls Barton, Northants holds the following records:
2 pints—2.3 sec Zetters Social Club, Wolverton, Bucks, 11 June 1975.
2 litres—6.0 sec Carriage Horse Hotel, Higham Ferrers, Northants, 7 Feb 1975.

Yards of Ale
2½ pints—5.0 sec RAF Upper Heyford, Oxfordshire, 4 May 1975.
3 pints—5.4 sec Corby Town S.C., Northamptonshire, 23 Jan 1976.
3½ pints—6.0 sec Bier Keller, Leeds, West Yorkshire on 19 Aug 1984.
    6.0 sec Wood Green Shopping Centre, London N22 on 11 Oct 1984.

Upsidedown

2 pints—6.4 sec Top Rank Club, Northants, 25 May 1975.

CHAMPAGNE

1000 bottles per annum by Bobby Acland of the 'Black Raven', Bishopsgate, City of London.

CHEESE

16 oz *453 g* of Cheddar in 1 min 13 sec by Peter Dowdeswell (see above) in Earls Barton, Northants on 14 July 1978.

CHICKEN

1.701 kg *3 lb 12 oz* in 12 min 37 sec by Shaun Barry at the Cardinal Wolsey Hotel, East Molesey, Surrey on 26 Jan 1984.

CLAMS

424 (Littlenecks) in 8 min by Dave Barnes at Port Townsend Bay, Washington, USA on 3 May 1975.

COCKLES

2 pints *113,5 centilitres* in 60.8 sec by Tony Dowdeswell at Kilmarnock, Ayrshire on 1 June 1984.

DOUGHNUTS

12¾ (51 oz *1,445 kg*) in 5 min 46 sec by James Wirth, and 13 (52 oz *1,474 kg*) in 6 min 1.5 sec by John Haight, both at the Sheraton Inn, Canandaigua, New York on 3 Mar 1981.

EELS

1 lb *453 g* of elvers in 13.7 sec by Peter Dowdeswell at Reeves Club, Bristol on 20 Oct 1978.

EGGS

(Hard Boiled) 14 in 58 sec by Peter Dowdeswell (see above) at the Stardust Social Club, Corby, Northants on 18 Feb 1977.

(Soft Boiled) 38 in 75 sec by Peter Dowdeswell in Kilmarnock, Ayrshire on 28 May 1984.

(Raw) 13 in 1.0 sec by Peter Dowdeswell at Kilmarnock, Ayrshire on 16 May 1984.

FRANKFURTERS

23 (2 oz *56,6 g*) in 3 min 10 sec by Lynda Kuerth, 21, at the Veterans Stadium, Philadelphia, on 12 July 1977.

GHERKINS

1 lb *453 g* in 43.6 sec by Rex Barker of Elkhorn, Nebraska, USA on 30 Oct 1975.

1 lb *453 g* (liquidized) in 35.2 sec by Peter L. Citron on TV in San Francisco, USA on 1 Apr 1983. *This category has now been retired.*

GRAPES

3 lb 1 oz of grapes in 34.6 sec by Jim Ellis of Montrose, Michigan, USA on 30 May 1976.

HAGGIS

26 oz *737 g* in 49 sec by Peter Dowdeswell at The Grand Hotel, Hartlepool on 21 Feb 1983.

HAMBURGERS

21 hamburgers (each weighing 3½ oz *100 g* totalling *2,07 kg* of meat) and buns in 9 min 42 sec by Peter Dowdeswell at Cockshut Hill School, Yardley, Birmingham on 30 June 1984.

ICE CREAM

3 lb 6 oz *1,530 kg* in 50.04 sec by Tony Dowdeswell at the Cardinal Wolsey Hotel, East Molesey, Surrey on 26 Jan 1984. The ice cream must be unmelted.

JELLY

20 fl oz *56,8 centilitres* in 13.11 sec by Peter Dowdeswell at Stoke Mandeville, Buckinghamshire on 27 June 1984. The jelly must be gelatinous.

KIPPERS

27 (self-filleted) in 60 min by Karen Stevenson of Wallasey, Merseyside on 5 Mar 1982.

LEMONS

12 quarters (3 lemons) whole (including skin and pips) in 15.3 sec by Bobby Kempf of Roanoke, Virginia, USA on 2 May 1979.

MEAT

One whole roast ox in 42 days by Johann Ketzler of Munich, Germany in 1880.

MEAT PIES

22 (each weighing 5½ oz *156 g*) in 18 min 13 sec by Peter Dowdeswell of Earls Barton, Northants on 5 Oct 1978.

MILK

2 pt (1 Imperial quart or *113,5 centilitres*) in 3.2 sec by Peter Dowdeswell (see above) at Dudley Top Rank Club, West Midlands on 31 May 1975.

OYSTERS (*Eating, Opening*)

4 lb 13 oz *2,18 kg* (edible mass of 250) in 2 min 52.33 sec by Ron Hansen at the Packer's Arms, Queenstown, South Island, New Zealand on 30 June 1982. The record for opening oysters is 100 in 2 min 45.5 sec by W. Heath Jr at Babson Park, Florida, USA on 28 Oct 1983.

PANCAKES

(6 inch *15,2 cm* diameter buttered and with syrup) 62 in 6 min 58.5 sec by Peter Dowdeswell (see above) at The Drapery, Northampton on 9 Feb 1977.

PEANUTS

100 (whole unshelled) singly in 46 sec by Jim Kornitzer, 21 at Brighton, Sussex on 1 Aug 1979.

PEAS

7175 petit pois one by one in 60 mins using chopsticks by Mrs Janet Harris, Seal Hotel, Selsey, West Sussex on 16 Aug 1984.

PICKLED ONIONS

91 pickled onions (total weight 30 oz *850 g*) in 1 min 8 sec by Pat Donahue in Victoria, British Columbia on 9 Mar 1978.

POTATOES

3 lb *1,36 kg* in 1 min 22 sec by Peter Dowdeswell in Earls Barton, Northants on 25 Aug 1978.

POTATO CRISPS

Thirty 2 oz *56,6 g* bags in 24 min 33.6 sec, without a drink, by Paul G. Tully of Brisbane University in May 1969. Charles Chip Inc of Mountville, Pennsylvania produced crisps 4 × 7 in *10 × 17,5 cm* from outsize potatoes in February 1977.

PRUNES

144 in 34 sec by Peter Dowdeswell at Easy Street Nightclub, Nottingham on 26 Apr 1985.

RAVIOLI

5 lb *2,25 kg* (170 squares) in 5 min 34 sec by Peter Dowdeswell at Pleasurewood Hills American Theme Park, Lowestoft, Suffolk on 25 Sept 1983.

SANDWICHES

40 in 17 min 53.9 sec (jam 'butties' 6 × 3¾ × ½ in *15,2 × 9,5 × 1,2 cm*) by Peter Dowdeswell on 17 Oct 1977 at The Donut Shop, Reedley, California, USA.

SAUSAGE MEAT

2630 g *5 lb 12¾ oz* (96 pieces) in 4 min 29 sec by Peter Dowdeswell on Fuji TV, Tōkyō, Japan on 24 Feb 1985. No 'Hot Dog' contest results have been remotely comparable.

SHRIMPS

3 lb *1,36 kg* in 4 min 8 sec by Peter Dowdeswell of Earls Barton, Northants on 25 May 1978.

SNAILS

1 kg *35,27 oz* by Peter Dowdeswell at Hever Castle, Kent in 3 min 45.78 sec on 27 June 1984.

SPAGHETTI

100 yd *91,44 m* in 21.7 sec by Peter Dowdeswell at The Globe Hotel, Weedon, Northants on 25 Feb 1983.

STRAWBERRIES

2 lb 8 oz *1,13 kg* in 27.19 sec by Peter Dowdeswell at the Stardust Centre, Corby, Northamptonshire on 15 Nov 1983.

SUSHI

680 g *1½ lb* of nigiri-zushi in 1 min 13.5 sec in Tōkyō, Japan by Peter Dowdeswell on 22 February 1985.

TORTILLA

74 (total weight 4 lb 1½ oz *1,85 kg*) in 30 min by Tom Nall in the 2nd World Championship at Mariano's Mexican Restaurant, Dallas, Texas, USA on 16 Oct 1973.

TREE

11 ft *3,35 m* Birch (4.7 in *12 cm* diameter trunk) in 89 hrs by Jay Gwaltney, 19 on WKQX's 'Outrageous Contest', Chicago, 11–15 Sept 1980.

WHELKS

100 (unshelled) in 5 min 17 sec by John Fletcher at The Apples and Pears Public House, Liverpool Street Station, London on 18 Aug 1983.

WINKLING

50 shells picked (with a straight pin) in 3 min 15 sec by Mrs B. Charles at Eastbourne, East Sussex on 4 Aug 1982.

GREATEST OMNIVORE

Michel Lotito (b. 15 June 1950) of Grenoble, France, known as Monsieur Mangetout, has been eating metal and glass since 1959. Gastroenterologists have X-rayed his stomach and have described his ability to consume 2 lb *900 g* of metal per day as unique. His diet since 1966 has included 10 bicycles, a supermarket trolley in 4½ days, 7 TV sets, 6 chandeliers and a low calorie Cessna light aircraft which he ate in Caracas, Venezuela. He is said to have provided the only example in history of where a coffin (handles and all) ended up inside a man.

2. HONOURS, DECORATIONS AND AWARDS

Oldest Order

The earliest honour known was the 'Gold of Honour' for extraordinary valour awarded in the 18th dynasty *c.* 1440–1400 BC. A statuette was found at Qan-el-Kebri, Egypt. The order which can trace its origins furthest back is the Military Hospitaller Order of St Lazarus of Jerusalem founded by St Basil the Great in the 4th Century AD. The prototype of the princely Orders of Chivalry is the Most Noble Order of the Garter founded by King Edward III in *c.* 1348. A date as early as AD 809 has been attributed to the Most Ancient Order of the Thistle but is of doubtful provenance.

Eponymous record

The largest object to which a human name is attached is the universe itself—in the case of three different cosmological models devised in 1922 by the Russian mathematician Aleksandr Aleksandrovitch Friedman (1888–1925).

Most titles

The most titled person in the world is the 18th Duchess of Alba (Alba de Tormes), Doña Maria del Rosario Cayetana Fitz-James Stuart y Silva. She is 8 times a duchess, 15 times a marchioness, 21 times a countess and is 19 times a Spanish grandee.

Versatility

The only person to win a Victoria Cross and an Olympic Gold Medal has been Lt Gen Sir Philip Neame, VC, KBE, CB, DSO (1888–1978). He won the VC in 1914 and was an Olympic gold medallist for Britain for rifle shooting in 1924 though under the illusion at the time that he was shooting for the British Empire. The only George Cross holder who was also a Fellow of the Royal Society was Prof Peter Victor Danckwerts, GC, MBE, FRS F Eng (1916–1985) who defused 16 parachute mines in under 48 hr in the London docks during the Battle of Britain as a Sub Lt RNVR in August 1940.

Victoria Cross *Double awards*

The only three men ever to have been awarded a bar to the Victoria Cross (instituted 29 Jan 1856) are:

Surg-Capt (later Lt-Col) Arthur Martin-Leake, VC*, VD, RAMC (1874–1953) (1902 and bar 1915).

Capt Noel Godfrey Chavasse, VC*, MC, RAMC (1884–1917) (1916 and bar posthumously 14 Sept 1917).

Second Lieut (later Capt) Charles Hazlitt Upham, VC*, NZMF (b. 21 Sept 1908) (1941 and bar 1942).

The most VC's awarded in a war were the 634 in World War I (1914–18). The greatest number won in a single action was 11 at Rorke's Drift in the Zulu War on 22–23 Jan 1879. The school with most recipients is Eton College, Col H. H. Jones being the 36th in the Falklands Campaign.

Victoria Cross *Youngest*

The lowest established age for a VC is 15 years 100 days for Hospital Apprentice Andrew (wrongly gazetted as Arthur) Fitzgibbon (born at Peteragurh, northern India, 13 May 1845) of the Indian Medical Services for bravery at the Taku Forts in northern China on 21 Aug 1860. The youngest living VC is Capt Rambahadur Limbu (b. 1 Nov 1939, Chyangthapu, Nepal) of the 10th Princess Mary's Own Gurkha Rifles. The award was for his courage as a L/Cpl while fighting in the Bau district of Sarawak, East Malaysia, on 21 Nov 1965. He retired on 25 Mar 1985.

Victoria Cross *Longest lived*

The longest lived of all the 1351 winners of the Victoria Cross has been Lt Col Harcus Strachan VC. He was born in Bo'ness, Scotland on 7 Nov 1884 and died in Vancouver, Canada on 1 May 1982 aged 97 years 175 days.

Youngest Award

The youngest age at which an official gallantry award has ever been won is 8 years in the case of Anthony Farrer who was given the Albert Medal on 23 Sept 1916 for fighting off a cougar at Cowichan Lake, Vancouver Island, Canada to save Doreen Ashburnham. She was also awarded the AM which in 1971 was exchanged for the George Cross.

Record Price

The highest ever paid for a VC group has been £110,000 for the medals of the Battle of Britain fighter pilot Wing Cdr J. B. Nicholson VC, DFC, AFC (k. 1944), one of the only 3 men ever to win the VC actually defending Britain. The auction was at Christie's, London on 8 May 1983.

The record for a George Cross is £20,250 for that of Sgt Michael Willets (3rd Battalion Parachute Regiment), killed in Ulster in 1971, at Christie's on 14 Mar 1985.

Order of Merit
The Order of Merit (instituted on 23 June 1902) is limited to 24 members. The longest lived holder has been the Rt Hon. Bertrand Arthur William Russell, 3rd Earl Russell, who died on 2 Feb 1970 aged 97 years 260 days. The oldest recipient was Admiral of the Fleet the Hon. Sir Henry Keppel, GCB, OM, (1809–1904), who received the Order aged 93 years 56 days on 9 Aug 1902. The youngest recipient has been HRH the Duke of Edinburgh, KG, KT, OM, GBE, who was appointed on his 47th birthday on 10 June 1968.

Most mentions in despatches
The record number of 'mentions' is 24 by Field Marshal the Rt Hon Sir Frederick Sleigh Roberts Bt, the Earl Roberts, VC, KG, PC, KP, GCB, OM, GCSI, GCIE, VD (1832–1914).

Most post-nominal letters
Lord Roberts, who was also a privy counsellor, was the only non-royal holder of 8 sets of *official* post-nominal letters. Currently the record number is seven by Marshal of the RAF the Rt Hon Lord Elworthy KG, GCB, CBE, DSO, LVO, DFC, AFC (b. 23 Mar 1911) of New Zealand. HRH the Duke of Windsor (1894–1972) when Prince of Wales had 10 sets and was also a privy counsellor *viz.* KG, PC, KT, KP, GCB, GCSI, GCMG, GCIE, GCVO, GBE, MC. He later appended the ISO but never did so in the case of the OM, CH or DSO of which orders he had also been sovereign.

Civilian gallantry
Reginald H. Blanchford of Guernsey, received the MBE for Gallantry in 1950; the Queen's Commendation in 1957; the George Medal in 1958; the OBE for Gallantry in 1961 for saving life from cliff tops. He was also awarded the Life Saving Medal in Gold 1957 with golden bar 1963 and was made a Knight of Grace of the Order of St John in 1970.

USSR
The USSR's highest award for valour is the Gold Star of a Hero of the Soviet Union. Over 10,000 were awarded in World War II. Among the 109 awards of a second star were those to Marshal Iosif Vissarionovich Dzhugashvili, *alias* Stalin (1879–1953) and Lt-General Nikita Sergeyevich Khrushchyov (1894–1971). The only war-time triple awards were to Marshal Georgiy Konstantinovich Zhukov, Hon GCB (1896–1974) (subsequently awarded a fourth Gold Star) and to the leading air aces Guards' Colonel (now Marshal of Aviation Aleksandr Ivanovich Pokryshkin) and Aviation Maj Gen Ivan Nikitovich Kozhedub. Zhukov also uniquely had the Order of Victory, twice, the Order of Lenin (6 times) and the Order of the Red Banner, (thrice). Leonid Brezhnev (1907–1982) was 4 times Hero of the Soviet Union; Hero of Socialist Labour, Order of Victory, Order of Lenin (8 times) and Order of the Red Banner (twice).

Germany
The Knight's Cross of the Iron Cross with swords, diamonds and golden oak-leaves was uniquely awarded to Col Hans Ulrich Rudel (1916–1982) for 2530 operational flying missions on the Eastern Front in 1941–5. He destroyed 519 Soviet armoured vehicles.

USA
The highest US military decoration is the Medal of Honor. Five marines received both the Army and Navy Medals of Honor for the same acts in 1918 and 14 officers and men from 1863 to 1915 have received the medal on two occasions.

A philatelic depiction of the United States foremost gallantry decoration—the Medal of Honor (instituted in 1862) since when only 2,633 have been awarded.

Top jet ace
The greatest number of kills in jet to jet battles is 16 by Capt Joseph Christopher McConnell, Jr, USAF (b. Dover, New Hampshire, 30 Jan 1922) in the Korean war (1950–3). He was killed on 25 Aug 1954. It is possible that an Israeli ace may have surpassed this total in the period 1967–70 but the identity of pilots is subject to strict security.

Top woman ace
The record score for any woman fighter pilot is 12 by Jnr Lt Lydia Litvak (USSR) (b. 1921) on the Eastern Front between 1941 and 1943. She was killed in action on 1 Aug 1943.

Anti-submarine successes
The highest number of U-boat kills attributed to one ship in the 1939–45 war was 15 to HMS *Starling* (Capt Frederic John Walker, CB, DSO***, RN). Captain Walker was in command at the sinking of a total of 25 U-boats between 1941 and the time of his death on 9 July 1944. The US Destroyer Escort *England* sank six Japanese submarines in the Pacific between 18 and 30 May 1944.

Most successful submarine captains
The most successful of all World War II submarine commanders was Leutnant Otto Kretschmer, captain of the U.23 and U.99 who up to March 1940 sank one destroyer and 44 Allied merchantmen totalling 266,629 gross registered tons.

In World War I Kapitän-Leutnant (later Vizeadmiral) Lothar von Arnauld de la Périère, in the U.35 and U.139, sank 195 allied ships totalling 458,856 gross tons. The most successful boats were U.35, which in World War I sank 54 ships of 90,350 grt in a single voyage and 224 ships of 539,711 grt all told, and U.48 which sank 51 ships of 310,007 grt in World War II. The largest target ever sunk by a submarine was the Japanese aircraft carrier *Shinano* (59,000 tons) by *USS Archerfish* (Cdr Joseph F. Enright, USN) on 29 Nov 1944.

Top Scoring Air Aces (World Wars I and II)
The 'scores' of air aces in both wars are *still* hotly disputed. The highest figures officially attributed have been:

World	United Kingdom
World War I	
75[1] Col René Paul Fonck (France) Gr Cordon Ld'H, C de G (26 palms), Méd. Mil., MC*, C de G (Belge) (d. 1953)	73 Major Edward Mannock, VC, DSO**, MC*

World War II

352 Major Erich Hartmann (Germany)	38 Wg Cdr (now AVM) James Edgar Johnson, CB, CBE, DSO**, DFC*[2]

[1] A total of 80 was attributed to Rittmeister Manfred Freiherr (Baron) von Richthofen (Germany) but fewer than 60 of these could subsequently be verified from German records, leaving Col-Gen. Ernst Udet (d. 1941) Ordre pour le Mérite, Iron Cross with the highest number of victories at 62.

[2] The greatest number of successes against flying bombs (V.1's) was by Sqn Ldr Joseph Berry, DFC** (b. Nottingham, 1920, killed 2 Oct 1944) who brought down 60 in 4 months. The most successful fighter pilot in the RAF was Sqn Ldr Marmaduke Thomas St John Pattle, DFC*, of South Africa, with a known total of at least 40. In the Battle of Leyte Gulf, Cdr David McCampbell USN shot down 9 aircraft in one mission on 24 Oct 1944.

The maximum number of bars (repeat awards) ever awarded to the Distinguished Flying Cross (DFC) (instituted 1918) is two. Second bars have been awarded to the following:

 (See also 24th Edition)

Air Cdre A. H. Cobby CBE DSO DFC** GM (Aust.)
Capt Sir Ross McPherson Smith KBE MC* DFC** AFC (Aust.)
Capt W. H. Longton DFC** AFC
Gp Capt R. Halley DFC** AFC
Air Cdre J. W. B. Gregson DSO DFC**
Gp Capt H. A. Whistler DSO DFC**
Sqn Ldr S. B. Harris DFC** AFC
Flt Lt A. L. Taylor DFC**
Wg Cdr R. R. Stanford Tuck DSO DFC**
Wg Cdr B. E. Finucane DSO DFC** (Ireland)
Wg Cdr D. A. P. McMullen DFC**
Gp Capt F. R. Carey DFC** AFC DFM
Sqn Ldr A. Warburton DSO* DFC**
Gp Capt M. M. Stephens DSO DFC**
Gp Capt P. H. Hugo DSO DFC** (S. Africa)
Gp Capt R. W. Oxspring DFC** AFC
Wg Cdr L. C. Wade DSO DFC** (USA)
Gp Capt J. R. D. Braham DSO** DFC** AFC
Sqn Ldr J. A. F. Maclachlan DSO DFC**
Sqn Ldr J. J. LeRoux DFC** (S. Africa)
Sqn Ldr J. E. Walker DFC** (Canada)
Wg Cdr C. M. Miller DFC**
Wg Cdr R. H. Harries DFC* DFC**
Wg Cdr G. U. Hill DFC** (Canada)
AVM F. D. Hughes CB CBE DSO DFC** AFC
Sqn Ldr R. W. McNair DSO DFC** (Canada)
Gp Capt C. F. Gray DSO DFC** (N.Z.)
Wg Cdr S. Skalski DSO DFC** (Poland)
Sqn Ldr J. A. McCairns DFC** MM
Sqn Ldr N. F. Duke DSO DFC** AFC
Sqn Ldr E. R. Butler DFC**
Sqn Ldr R. O. Calvert DFC** (N.Z.)
Flt Lt M. S. Allen DFC**
Air Cdre H. E. White CBE DFC** AFC
Fg Offr A. A. O'Leary DFC** DFM
Flt Lt T. Balluff DFC** AFC
Maj M. Y. Gran DFC** (Norway)
A M Sir Ivor Broom KBE DSO DFC** AFC
Flt Lt K. F. N. Thiele DSO DFC** (N.Z.)
Sqn Ldr F. A. O. Gaze DFC** (Aust.)
Air Cdre E. B. Sismore DSO DFC** AFC (N.Z.)
Flt Lt A. N. Crooks DFC**
Sqn Ldr K. R. Triggs DFC**
Sqn Ldr D. C. Fairbanks DFC** (USA)
Sqn Ldr J. Shepherd DFC**
Flt Ldr J. T. Caine DFC** (Canada)
Sqn Ldr R. Van der Bok DFC** (S. Africa)
Fg Offr C. Brameld DFC**
Sqn Ldr T. J. Broom DFC**
Sqn Ldr K. J. Gurdon DFC**
Sqn Ldr H. V. Peterson DFC** (Canada)
Sqn Ldr J. Berry DFC**
Sqn Ldr D. B. Everett DFC**
Flt Lt M. D. Seale DFC** (Aust.)
Sqn Ldr R. Van Lierde DFC** (Belgium)
Sqn Ldr W. G. G. Duncan Smith DSO* DFC**
Wg Cdr N. T. Quinn DFC**
Wg Cdr C. G. St. D. Jefferies DFC**

Most highly decorated
The six living persons to have been twice decorated with any of the United Kingdom's topmost decorations are Capt C. H. Upham VC and bar; the Viscount De L'Isle VC, KG; HM the Queen Mother CI, GCVO, GBE, who is a Lady of

NOBEL PRIZES

Earliest 1901 for Physics, Chemistry, Medicine and Physiology, Literature and Peace

Oldest Laureate Prof. Francis Peyton Rous (US) (1879–1970) in 1966 shared in Medicine prize aged 87

Youngest Laureates *At time of award:* Prof Sir William Bragg CH OBE MC (1890–1971) 1915 Physics prize at 25 *At time of work:* Bragg and Theodore W Richards (US) (1868–1928) 1914 Chemistry prize at 23 *Literature:* Rudyard Kipling (UK) (1865–1936) 1907 prize at 41 *Peace:* Mrs Mairead Corrigan-Maguire (b. 27 Jan 1944) 1976 Prize (shared) at 32

Most Three Awards: International Committee for Red Cross (founded 1863) (1917, 1944 and 1963 (shared)); Two Awards: Dr Linus Carl Pauling (US) (b. 28 Feb 1901) Chemistry, 1954 and Peace 1962; Mde Marja Sklodowska Curie (Polish-French) (1867–1934) Physics, 1903 (shared) Chemistry 1911 and Prof. Frederick Sanger CBE FRS (b. 13 Aug 1918) Chemistry 1958 and 1980 (shared)

Highest Prize Sw Kr 1,650,000 (for 1984) equivalent to £152,800

Lowest Prize Sw Kr 115,000 (1923) equivalent to £6,620

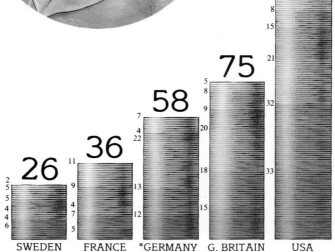

Economics
Literature
Peace
Chemistry
Physics
Physiology or Medicine

SWEDEN 26 — FRANCE 36 — *GERMANY 58 — G. BRITAIN 75 — USA 121

* Germany up to 1948. Federal Republic of Germany after 1948

Left Dr Martin Luther King (US) (1929–1968), youngest male Peace Prize Winner. *(Popperfoto) Right* Mde Marja (Marie) Curie (1867–1934) double winner with Physics 1903 (shared) and Chemistry 1911. *(Popperfoto) Below left to right in two lines* Prof Frederick Sanger CBE FRS (b. 13 Aug 1918) double winner with Chemistry 1958 and 1980 (both shared). *(Popperfoto)* Prof Sir William Bragg CH OBE MC (1890–1971) youngest winner in 1915 with the Physics Prize. *(Mary Evans Picture Library)* Prof Theodore W. Richards (US) (1868–1928) who was only 23 at the time of his work for the 1914 Chemistry Prize awarded when he was 46. *(Mary Evans Picture Library)* Prof Francis Peyton Rous (US) (1879–1970) the oldest laureate who shared in the 1966 Medicine Prize when aged 87. *(Keystone Press)* Dr Linus C. Pauling (US) (b. 28 Feb 1901), the only outright double winner with the Chemistry (1954) and Peace (1962) Prizes. *(Popperfoto)* Rudyard Kipling (GB) (1865–1936) who won the Literature Prize of 1907 aged 41. (*(Popperfoto)*

the Garter and a Lady of the Thistle; HRH the Duke of Edinburgh KG, KT, OM, GBE; HRH Prince Charles KG, KT, GCB and HM King Olaf V of Norway KG, KT, GCB, GCVO. Lord De L'Isle is the only person who has both the highest military and highest civil honour. Britain's most highly decorated woman is the World War II British agent Mrs Odette Hallowes GC, MBE, Légion d'Honneur, Ordre St George (Belge), who survived imprisonment and torture at the hands of the Gestapo in 1943–45. Violette Reine Elizabeth Szabo (*née* Bushnell) GC (1921–45) lost her husband in the French Legion at El Alamein in 1942. He was Etienne Szabo, Médaille Militaire, Legion d'Honneur and Croix de Guerre.

AWARDS

Most Valuable Annual Prize

The Templeton Foundation Prize for Progress in Religion inaugurated in 1972 by Mr John M. Templeton (b. 1912) has at times been more than Nobel Prizes. The awards of £140,000 in 1984 was won by the Rev Michael Bourdeaux (b. 19 Mar 1934) of the Centre for the Study of Religion and Communism, Keston College, Kent and in 1985 by Sir Alister Hardy (b. 10 Feb 1896, d. 23 May 1985).

Most statues

The world record for raising statues to oneself was set by Generalissimo Dr Rafael Leónidas Trujillo y Molina (1891–1961), former President of the Dominican Republic. In March 1960 a count showed that there were 'over 2000'. The country's highest mountain was named Pico Trujillo (now Pico Duarte). One province was called Trujillo and another Trujillo Valdez. The capital was named Ciudad Trujillo (Trujillo City) in 1936, but reverted to its old name of Santo Domingo de Guzmán on 23 Nov 1961. Trujillo was assassinated in a car ambush on 30 May 1961, and 30 May is now celebrated annually as a public holiday. The man to whom most statues have been raised is Buddha. The 20th century champion is Vladimir Ilyich Ulyanov, *alias* Lenin (1870–1924), busts of whom have been mass-produced as also has been the case with Mao Tse-tung (1893–1976) and Ho Chi Minh (1890–1969).

PEERAGE

Most ancient

The oldest extant peerage is the premier Earldom of Scotland, held by the Rt Hon Margaret of Mar, the Countess of Mar and 31st holder of this Earldom (b. 19 Sept 1940), who is the heir-at-law of Roderick or Rothri, 1st Earl (or Mormaer) of Mar, who witnessed a charter in 1114 or 1115 as 'Rothri *comes*'.

Oldest creation

The greatest age at which any person has been raised to the peerage is 93 years 337 days in the case of Sir William Francis Kyffin Taylor, GBE, KC (b. 9 July 1854), created Baron Maenan of Ellesmere, County Shropshire, on 10 June 1948, and died, aged 97, on 22 Sept 1951. The oldest elevation to a Life Peerage has been that of Emmanuel Shinwell PC, CH (b. 18 Oct 1884) on 2 June 1970 when aged 85 years 227 days.

Longest lived peer

The longest lived peer ever recorded was the Rt Hon Frank Douglas-Pennant, the 5th Baron Penrhyn (b. 21 Nov 1865), who died on 3 Feb 1967, aged 101 years 74 days. The oldest peeress recorded was the Countess Desmond, who was alleged to be 140 when she died in 1604. This claim is patently exaggerated but it is accepted that she may have been 104. Currently the oldest holder of a peerage, and the oldest Parliamentarian, is the Rt Hon Lord Shinwell PC, CH (b. 18 Oct 1884), who was first elected to the House of Commons on 15 Nov 1922.

Youngest peers

Twelve Dukes of Cornwall became (in accordance with the grant by the Crown in Parliament) peers at birth as the eldest son of a Sovereign; and the 9th Earl of Chichester posthumously inherited his father's (killed 54 days previously) earldom at his birth on 14 Apr 1944. The youngest age at which a person has had a peerage conferred on him is 7 days old in the case of the Earldom of Chester on HRH the Prince George (later George IV) on 19 Aug 1762.

Longest and shortest peerages

The longest tenure of a peerage has been 87 years 10 days in the case of Charles St Clair, Lord Sinclair, b. 30 July 1768, succeeded 16 Dec 1775 and died aged 94 years 243 days on 30 Mar 1863.

The shortest enjoyment of a peerage was the 'split second' by which the law assumes that the Hon Wilfrid Carlyl Stamp (b. 28 Oct 1904), the 2nd Baron Stamp, survived his father, Sir Josiah Charles Stamp, GCB, GBE, the 1st Baron Stamp, when both were killed as a result of German bombing of London on 16 Apr 1941. Apart from this legal fiction, the shortest recorded peerage was one of 30 min in the case of Sir Charles Brandon, KB, the 3rd Duke of Suffolk, who died, aged 13 or 14, just after succeeding his brother, Henry, when both were suffering a fatal illness, at Buckden, Cambridgeshire, on 14 July 1551.

Highest numbering

The highest succession number borne by any peer is that of the present 35th Baron Kingsale (John de Courcy, b. 27 Jan 1941), who succeeded to the then 746-year-old Barony on 7 Nov 1969. His occupations have included barman, bingo-caller and plumber.

Most creations

The largest number of new hereditary peerages created in any year was the 54 in 1296. The record for all peerages (including 40 life peerages) is 55 in 1964. The greatest number of extinctions in a year was 16 in 1923 and the greatest number of deaths was 44 in 1935.

Most prolific

The most prolific peers of all time are believed to be the 1st Earl Ferrers (1650–1717) and the 3rd Earl of Winchilsea (c. 1620–89) each with 27 legitimate children. In addition, the former reputedly fathered 30 illegitimate children. Currently the peer with the largest family is the Rt Hon Bryan Walter Guinness, 2nd Baron Moyne (b. 27 Oct 1905) with 6 sons and 5 daughters. The most prolific peeress is believed to be Mary Fitzgerald, wife of Patrick, 19th Baron Kingsale who bore 23 children (no twins) who survived to baptism. She died in 1663.

Baronets

The greatest age to which a baronet has lived is 101 years 188 days, in the case of Sir Fitzroy Donald Maclean, 10th Bt., KCB (1835–1936). He was the last survivor of the Crimean campaign of 1853–56. Capt Sir Trevor Wheler, 13th Baronet (b. 20 Sept 1889) entered his 82nd year as a baronet on 11 Aug 1984. The only baronetess is Dame Maureen Dunbar of Hempriggs, who succeeded in her own right as 8th in line of a 1706 baronetcy in 1965.

Knights

The greatest number of knights dubbed in a single day was 432 by James I in the Royal Garden, Whitehall on 23 July 1603. On his coronation day two days later, he appointed 62 Knights of the Garter.

Youngest and oldest

The youngest age for the conferment of a knighthood is 29 days for HRH the Prince George (b. 12 Aug 1762) (later George IV) by virtue of his *ex officio* membership of the Order of the Garter (KG) consequent upon his creation as Prince of Wales on 17 or 19 Aug 1762. The greatest age for the conferment of a knighthood is on a 100th birthday, in the case of the knight bachelor Sir Robert Mayer (1879–1985), additionally made a KCVO by the Queen at the Royal Festival Hall, London on 5 June 1979.

Most brothers

George and Elizabeth Coles of Australia had 5 sons knighted—Sir George, CBE (1885–1977); Sir Arthur (b. 1892); Sir Kenneth (b. 1896); Sir Edgar (b. 1899) and Sir Norman (b. 1907).

Most freedoms

Probably the greatest number of freedoms ever conferred on any man was 57 in the case of Andrew Carnegie (1835–1919), who was born in Dunfermline, Fife but emigrated to the United States in 1848. The most freedoms conferred upon any citizen of the United Kingdom is 42, in the case of Sir Winston Churchill (1874–1965).

Most honorary degrees

The greatest number of honorary degrees awarded to any individual is 96, given to Rev Father Theodore M. Hesburgh (b. 1918), president of the University of Notre Dame, Indiana, USA. These were accumulated from 1954 to May 1984.

Greatest vote

The largest monetary vote made by Parliament to a subject was the £400,000 given to the 1st Duke of Wellington (1769–1852) on 12 Apr 1814. He received in all £864,000. The total received by the 1st, 2nd and 3rd Dukes to January 1900 was £1,052,000.

The Royal Society (founded 1662)

The longest term as an FRS (Fellow of the Royal Society) has been 61 years in the case of Bertrand Russell, 3rd Earl (1872–1970) who was elected in 1908. The longest lived FRS has been Sir Rickard Christophers CIE, OBE (1873–1978) aged 104 years 84 days. John Lubbock (1834–1913), later 1st Baron Avebury, was elected at the age of 23 in 1857.

Erasmus Darwin was elected on 9 Apr 1761 and was followed by his son Robert (1788 to 1848), *his* son Charles (1879 to 1881), his sons Sir George (1879 to 1912), Francis (1882–1925) and Horace (1903 to 1928) and Sir George's son Sir Charles (1922 to 1962) so spanning over 200 years with 5 generations.

Who's Who

The longest entry in *Who's Who* (founded 1848) was that of the Rt Hon Sir Winston Leonard Spencer Churchill, KG, OM, CH, TD (1874–1965), who appeared in 67 editions from 1899 (18 lines) and had 211 lines by the 1965 edition. Currently the longest entry in its wider format is that of Barbara Cartland, the romantic novelist, with 126 lines. Apart from those who qualify for inclusion by hereditary title, the youngest entry has been Sir Yehudi Menuhin, KBE (b. New York City, USA 22 Apr 1916), the concert violinist, who first appeared in the 1932 edition aged 15. The longest entry of the 66,000 entries in *Who's Who in America* is that of Dr Glenn T. Seaborg (b. 19 Apr 1912) whose all-time record of 100 lines compares with the 9 line entry on President Reagan.

Oxford and Cambridge Unions

Four brothers were Presidents of the Union in the case of the sons of the Rt Hon Isaac Foot. Sir Dingle Foot (Balliol, 1927–8); John (Lord Foot) (Balliol, 1930–1) and Rt Hon Michael (Wadham, 1933–4) at Oxford and Hugh (Lord Caradon) (St John's, 1929) at Cambridge. The last named's son Paul was President at Oxford (University College, 1960–1).

CHAPTER ELEVEN

The Human World

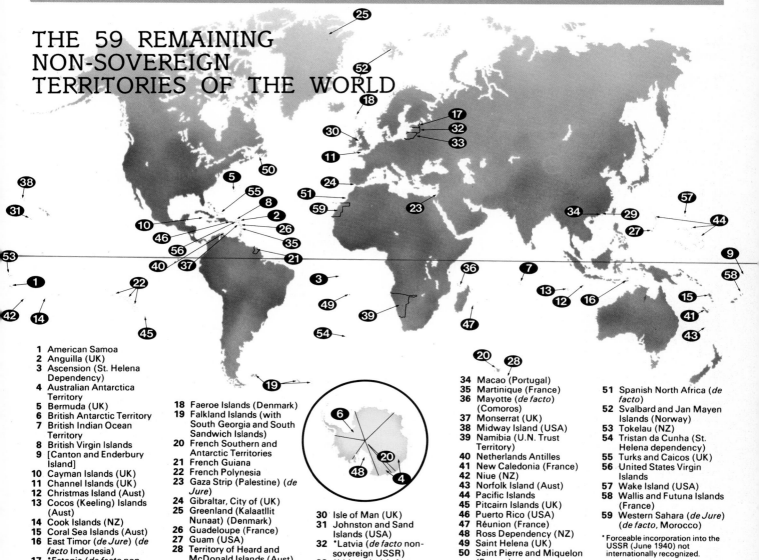

THE 59 REMAINING NON-SOVEREIGN TERRITORIES OF THE WORLD

1 American Samoa
2 Anguilla (UK)
3 Ascension (St. Helena Dependency)
4 Australian Antarctica Territory
5 Bermuda (UK)
6 British Antarctic Territory
7 British Indian Ocean Territory
8 British Virgin Islands
9 [Canton and Enderbury Island]
10 Cayman Islands (UK)
11 Channel Islands (UK)
12 Christmas Island (Aust)
13 Cocos (Keeling) Islands (Aust)
14 Cook Islands (NZ)
15 Coral Sea Islands (Aust)
16 East Timor (de Jure) (de facto Indonesia)
17 *Estonia (de facto non-sovereign USSR)

18 Faeroe Islands (Denmark)
19 Falkland Islands (with South Georgia and South Sandwich Islands)
20 French Southern and Antarctic Territories
21 French Guiana
22 French Polynesia
23 Gaza Strip (Palestine) (de Jure)
24 Gibraltar, City of (UK)
25 Greenland (Kalaatllit Nunaat) (Denmark)
26 Guadeloupe (France)
27 Guam (USA)
28 Territory of Heard and McDonald Islands (Aust)
29 Hong Kong (UK)

30 Isle of Man (UK)
31 Johnston and Sand Islands (USA)
32 *Latvia (de facto non-sovereign USSR)
33 *Lithuania (de facto non-sovereign USSR)

34 Macao (Portugal)
35 Martinique (France)
36 Mayotte (de facto) (Comoros)
37 Monserrat (UK)
38 Midway Island (USA)
39 Namibia (U.N. Trust Territory)
40 Netherlands Antilles
41 New Caledonia (France)
42 Niue (NZ)
43 Norfolk Island (Aust)
44 Pacific Islands
45 Pitcairn Islands (UK)
46 Puerto Rico (USA)
47 Réunion (France)
48 Ross Dependency (NZ)
49 Saint Helena (UK)
50 Saint Pierre and Miquelon (France)

51 Spanish North Africa (de facto)
52 Svalbard and Jan Mayen Islands (Norway)
53 Tokelau (NZ)
54 Tristan da Cunha (St. Helena dependency)
55 Turks and Caicos (UK)
56 United States Virgin Islands
57 Wake Island (USA)
58 Wallis and Futuna Islands (France)
59 Western Sahara (de Jure) (de facto, Morocco)

* Forceable incorporation into the USSR (June 1940) not internationally recognized.

Artwork: Eddie Botchway

1. POLITICAL AND SOCIAL

Detailed information on all the sovereign and non-sovereign countries of the world is contained in *The Guinness Book of Answers* (5th Edition) (Price £7.95).

Largest political division

The British Commonwealth of Nations, a free association of 49 sovereign independent states together with 27 non-sovereign states and dependencies administered by them covers an area of 13,095,000 miles² *33 915 000 km²* with a population which in 1980 surpassed 1,000,000,000. The British Empire began to expand when Henry VII patented trade monopolies to John Cabot in March 1496 and when the East India Co. was incorporated on 31 Dec 1600.

COUNTRIES

The world comprises 170 sovereign countries and 59 separately administered non-sovereign territories making a total of 229. The United Nations still lists the *de jure* territories of East Timor (now incorporated into Indonesia), Western Sahara (now in Morocco) and the uninhabited Canton and Enderbury Islands (now disputed between the US and Kiribati) but does not list the three Baltic States of Estonia, Latvia and Lithuania though their forcible incorporation into the USSR in 1940 has never been internationally recognized. Neither does it list

The map shows the world's 59 remaining *de facto* and *de jure* non-sovereign territories. These added to the 170 sovereign countries bring the world total to 229.

Artwork: Eddie Botchway

the *de facto* territories of Taiwan, Mayotte or Spanish North Africa, the 4 Antarctic Territories or the Australian Territory of Coral Sea Islands and Heard and McDonald Islands.

Largest

The country with the greatest area is the Union of Soviet Socialist Republics (the Soviet Union), comprising 15 Union (constituent) Republics with a total area of 22 402 200 km² *8,648,500 miles²*, or 15.0 per cent of the world's total land area, and a total coastline (including islands) of 106 360 km *66,090 miles*. The country measures 8980 km *5580 miles* from east to west and 4490 km *2790 miles* from north to south and is 91.8 times the size of the United Kingdom. Its population in mid-1983 was 272,500,000 (est.).

The United Kingdom covers 94,221 miles² *244 030 km²* (including 1197 miles² *3100 km²* of inland water), or 0.16 per cent of the total land area of the world. Great Britain is the world's eighth largest island, with an area of 84,186 miles² *218 040 km²* and a coastline 4928 miles *7930 km* long, of which Scotland accounts for 2573 miles *4141 km*, Wales 426 miles *685 km* and England 1929 miles *3104 km*.

Smallest

The smallest independent country in the world is the State of the Vatican City or Holy See (Stato della Città del Vaticano), which was made an enclave within the city of Rome, Italy on 11 Feb 1929. The enclave has an area of 44 hectares *108.7 acres*. The maritime sovereign country with the shortest coastline is Monaco with 3.49 miles *5,61 km* excluding piers and breakwaters. The world's smallest republic is Nauru, less than 1 degree south of the equator in the Western Pacific, which became independent on 31 Jan 1968, has an area of 5263 acres *2129 ha* and a population of 8000 (latest estimate mid-1983).

The smallest colony in the world is Gibraltar (since 1969, the City of Gibraltar) with an area of 2½ miles² *5,8 km²*. However, Pitcairn Island, the only inhabited (47 people, 1985) island of a group of 4 (total area 18½ miles² *48 km²*) has an area of 1½ miles² or 960 acres *388 ha*.

The official residence, since 1834, of the Grand Master of the Order of the Knights of Malta totalling 3 acres *1,2 ha* and comprising the Villa del Priorato di Malta on the lowest of Rome's seven hills, the 151 ft *46 m* Aventine, retains certain diplomatic privileges as does 68 Via Condotti. The Order has accredited representatives to foreign governments and is hence sometimes cited as the smallest 'state' in the world.

Flattest and Most Elevated

The country with the lowest highest point is the Republic of the Maldives which attains 8 ft *2,4 m*. The country with the highest lowest point is Lesotho. The egress of the Senqu (Orange) river-bed is 4530 ft *1381 m* above sea level.

Most impenetrable boundary

The 'Iron Curtain' (858 miles *1380 km*) dividing the Federal Republican (West) and the Democratic Republican (East) parts of Germany, utilizes 2,230,000 land mines and 50,000 miles *80 500 km* of barbed wire, much of it of British manufacture, in addition to many watch-towers containing detection devices. The last of 55,000 SM-70 scatter guns was removed on 30 Nov 1984. The whole strip of 270 yd *246 m* wide occupies 133 miles² *344 km²* of East German territory and cost an estimated $7000 million to build and maintain. It reduced the westward flow from more than 200,000 in 1961 to a trickle including 54 in 1984. The death toll has been 184 since 1962. Construction of the second wall began in East Berlin in March 1984.

Longest and Shortest frontier

The longest *continuous* frontier in the world is that between Canada and the United States, which (including the Great Lakes boundaries) extends for 3987 miles *6416 km* (excluding 1538 miles *2547 km* with Alaska). The frontier which is crossed most frequently is that between the United States and Mexico. It extends for 1933 miles *3110 km* and there are more than 120,000,000 crossings every year. The Sino-Soviet frontier, broken by the Sino-Mongolian border, extends for 4500 miles *7240 km* with no reported figure of crossings. The 'frontier' of the Holy See in Rome measures 2.53 miles *4,07 km*. The land frontier between Gibraltar and Spain at La Linea, closed since 1969, measures 1672 yd *1,53 km*. Zambia, Zimbabwe, Botswana and Namibia (South West Africa) almost merge.

Most frontiers

The country with the most land frontiers is China, with 13—Mongolia, USSR, North Korea, Hong Kong, Macau, Vietnam, Laos, Burma, India, Bhutan, Nepal, Pakistan and Afghanistan. These extend for 24 000 km *14,900 miles*. France, if all her *Départements d'outre-mer* are included, may, on extended territorial waters, have 20 frontiers. The United Kingdom's frontier with the Republic of Ireland measures 223 miles *358 km*.

POPULATIONS

World

The daily increase in the world's population is 213,700, or 148 per minute. For past, present and future estimates (see table).

Most populous country

The largest population of any country is that of China, which in *pinyin* is written Zhongguo (meaning central land). The census of July 1982 was 1,008,175,288. The rate of natural increase in the People's Republic of China is now estimated to be 38,700 a day or 14.1 million per year. The mid-year 1985 estimate would then be close to 1050 million. The census required 5,100,000 enumerators to work for 10 days. India is set to overtake China during the next century.

Least populous

The independent state with the smallest population is the Vatican City or the Holy See (see Smallest country, above), with 1008 inhabitants in 1984 and a nil return for births.

Most densely populated

The most densely populated territory in the world is the Portuguese province of Macau (or Macao), on the southern coast of China. It has an estimated population of 304,000 (mid-1983) in an area of 6.2 miles² *16,05 km²* giving a density of 49,032 per mile² *18 939 per km²*.

The Principality of Monaco, on the south coast of France, has a population of 27,000 (mid-1983) in an area of 473 acres *189 ha* giving a density of 38,179/mile² *14,741/km²*. The above acreage is inclusive of marine infilling which has increased the land area by some 20 per cent. Singapore has 2,517,000 (end-1983) people in an inhabited area of 73 miles² *189 km²*.

Of territories with an area of more than 1000 km² (405 miles² *1049 km²*), Hong Kong contains 5,313,000 (estimated mid-1983), giving the territory a density of 13,117/mile² *5064/km²*. Hong Kong is now the most populous of all colonies. The transcription of the name is from a local pronunciation of the Peking dialect version of Xiang gang (a port for incense). The 1976 by-census showed that the West Area of the urban district of Mong Kok on the Kowloon Peninsula had a density of 252,090/mile² *652,910/mile²*. In 1959, at the peak of the housing crisis, it was reported that in one house designed for 12 people the number of occupants was 459, including 104 in one room and 4 living on the roof.

Of countries over 1000 miles² *2589 km²* the most densely populated is Bangladesh with a population of 94,651,000 (mid-1983 estimate) living in 55,126 miles² *142 775 km²* at a density of 1716/mile² *662/km²*. The Indonesian island of Java (with an area of 48,763 miles² *126 295 km²*) had a population of 94,693,000 (1981 estimate), giving a density of 1941/mile² *750/km²*.

The United Kingdom (94,221 miles² *244 030 km²*) had an estimated population of 56,487,800 at mid-1984, giving a density of 598 persons/mile² *231/km²*. The population density for the Greater London Borough of Kensington and Chelsea is 11,222/km² *29,064/mile²*.

Most sparsely populated

Antarctica became permanently occupied by relays of scientists from October 1956. The population varies seasonally and reaches 2000 at times.

The least populated territory, apart from Antarctica, is Kalaallit Nunaat (formerly Greenland), with a population of 52,000 (estimated mid-1983) in an area of 840,000 miles² *2 175 000 km²* giving a density of one person to every 16.15 miles² *41,83 km²*. Some 84.3 per cent of the island comprises an ice-cap.

The lowest population densities in the United Kingdom are in the Scottish Highlands and Islands with 13,1/km² *33.9/mile²*. The most sparsely populated county in England is Northumberland with 154.15/mile² *59,51/km²*.

WORLD POPULATION *Progressive estimates*

Date	Millions	Date	Millions
10 000 BC	c. 5	1950	2513
AD 1	c. 200	1960	3049
1000	c. 275	1970	3704
1250	375	1975	4033
1500	420	1980	4453
1650	550–600	1981	4530
1700	615	1982	4607
1750	720	1983	4685
1800	900	1984	4763
1900	1625	1985	4845
1920	1862	2000	6100
1930	2070	2025	8200
1940	2295	2100	10,200

† *The UN publication 'State of World Population, 1984' forecast that the world population will not stabilize until 2095 at c. 10,500 million and will reach 6100 million by 31 Dec 2000.*
Note *The all-time peak annual increase of 2.0% c. 1958–1962 had declined to 1.73% by 1975–1980. By 1990 this should decline to 1.5%. This, however, produces an annual increment c. 80 million to even higher figures in the 1990s. The French demographer Biraben has calculated that 60,000 million people died between 40,000 BC and AD 1980. This indicates that there have thus been some 65,000 million specimens of Homo sapiens sapiens who ever lived.*

Emigration

More people emigrate from Mexico than from any other country. An estimated 800,000 emigrated illegally into the USA in 1976 alone. A total of 233,000 emigrated from the UK in 1981. Her largest number of emigrants in any one year was 360,000 in 1852, mainly from Ireland.

Immigration

The country which regularly receives the most legal immigrants is the United States, with an annual limit of 425,000. It has been estimated that in the period 1820–1981, the USA has received 50,252,552 *official* immigrants. One in 24 of the US population is however an *illegal* immigrant to which another 700,000 were added in 1980. The peak year for immigration into the United Kingdom was the 12 months from 1 July 1961 to 30 June 1962, when about 430,000 Commonwealth citizens arrived. The number of new Commonwealth and Pakistani immigrants in 1984 was 24,800 added to an estimated total of 2,200,000 or 4.0% of the population by mid 1984.

Most patient 'Refusenik'

The USSR citizen who has waited longest for an exit visa is Benjamin Bogomolny (b. 7 Apr 1946) who first applied in 1966.

Tourism

In 1984 the United Kingdom received 13,700,000 visitors who spent an estimated £4194 million excluding fares to British carriers.

Birth rate *Highest and Lowest*

The rate for the whole world was 27.5 per 1000 in 1982. The highest estimated by the UN is 54.6 per 1000 for Kenya in 1980. A world wide survey published in 1981 showed only Nepal (48.9) with a still rising birth rate.

Excluding Vatican City, where the rate is negligible, the lowest recorded rate is 9.7 (1983) for the Federal Republic of Germany. The fastest falling is in Thailand where the 3.3 average number of children per family has fallen to 1.8 in 10 years.

The 1984 rate in the United Kingdom was 12.9/1000 (12.8 in England and Wales, 12.5 in Scotland and 17.9 in Northern Ireland), while the 1984 rate for the Republic of Ireland was 18.2 registered births per 1000. The highest number of births in England and Wales (since the first full year of 463,787 in 1838) has been 957,782 in 1920 and the lowest this century 569,259 in 1977. After falling each year since 1964 (875,972) the figure started rising again at the end of 1977 with the 1984 figure being 637,300 or 1741 per day or 1.20 per minute.

Death rate *Highest and Lowest*

The death rate for the whole world was 10.7 per 1000 in 1982. The highest of the latest available estimated death rates is 40.0 deaths per 1000 of the population in Kampuchea in 1975–80.

The lowest of the latest available recorded rates is 3.1 deaths/1000 in Western Samoa in 1980.

The 1984 rate in the United Kingdom was 11.5/1000 (11.5 in England and Wales, 12.1 in Scotland and 10.3 in Northern Ireland). The highest SMI (Standard Mortality Index where the national average is 100) is in Salford, Greater Manchester with a figure of 133. The 1984 rate for the Republic of Ireland was 9.1 registered deaths per 1000.

Natural increase

The rate of natural increase for the whole world is estimated to be 27.5–10.7 = 16.8 per 1000 in 1982 compared with a peak 22 per 1000 in 1965. The highest of the latest available recorded rates is 40.4 (54.6 – 14.2) in Kenya in 1980.

The 1984 rate for the United Kingdom was 1.5 (0.9 in England and Wales, 0.1 in Scotland and 7.2 in Northern Ireland). The rate for the first time in the first quarter of 1975 became one of natural decrease. The figure for the Republic of Ireland was 9.7/1000 in 1983.

The lowest rate of natural increase in any major independent country is in W. Germany with a negative figure of −2.0 per 1000 (9.7 births and 11.7 deaths) for 1983.

Marriage ages

The country with the lowest average ages for marriage is India, with 20.0 years for males and 14.5 years for females. At the other extreme is Ireland, with 26.8 for males and 24.7 for females. In the People's Republic of China the *recommended* age for marriage for men has been 28 and for women 25. In England and Wales the peak ages for marriage are 22.8 years (male) and 19.6 years (female).

Divorces

The country with most divorces is the United States with a total of 1,179,000 in 1983—a rate of 48.13 per cent on the then current annual total of marriages (cf 50.65% in 1979).

Sex ratio

There were estimated to be 1006.7 men in the world for every 1000 women (1981). The country with the largest recorded shortage of males is the USSR, with 1145.9 females to every 1000 males (1981 census). The country with the largest recorded woman shortage is Pakistan, with 906 to every 1000 males in 1981. The figures are, however, probably under-enumerated due to *purdah*. The ratio in the United Kingdom was 1056 females to every 1000 males at mid-1982, and is expected to be 1014.2/1,000 by AD 2000.

Infant mortality

The world rate in 1978 was 91 per 1000 live births. Based on deaths before one year of age, the lowest of the latest available recorded rates is 6.5 in Finland in 1981.

The highest recorded infant mortality rate reported has been 195 to 300 for Burma in 1952 and 259 for Zaïre in 1950. In Ethiopia the infant mortality rate was unofficially estimated to be nearly 550/1000 live births in 1969. Many Third World countries have ceased to make returns.

The United Kingdom figure for 1984 was 9.4/1000 live births (England and Wales 9.2, Scotland 10.1, Northern Ireland 13). The Republic of Ireland figure for 1984 was 10.1.

Life expectation

World expectation of life is rising from 47.4 years (1950–55) towards 64.5 years (1995–2000). There is evidence that life expectation in Britain in the 5th century AD was 33 years for males and 27 years for females. In the decade 1890–1900 the expectation of life among the population of India was 23.7 years.

Based on the latest available data, the highest recorded expectation of life at age 12 months is 73.7 years for males and 79.7 years for females in Iceland (1979–80).

The lowest recorded expectation of life at birth is 27 years for both sexes in the Vallée du Niger area of Mali in 1957 (sample survey, 1957–8). The figure for males in Gabon was 25 years in 1960–1 but 45 for females.

The latest available figures for England and Wales (1981–83) are 71.3 years for males and 77.2 years for females, 69.3 and 75.5 in Scotland, 70 and 76 in Northern Ireland and for the Republic of Ireland (1980) 69.8 years for males and 76.2 for females. The British figure for 1901–10 was 48.53 years for males and 52.83 years for females.

Housing

For comparison, dwelling units are defined as a structurally separated room or rooms occupied by private households of one or more people and having separate access or a common passageway to the street.

The country with the greatest recorded number of private housing units was India, with 100,251,000 occupied in 1972.

Great Britain had a stock of 21,715,000 dwellings as at 1 Jan 1985, of which 60.9% was owner-occupied. The record number of permanent houses built in a year has been 413,715 in 1968.

Physicians

The country with the most physicians is the USSR, with 831,300, or one to every 307 persons. China had an estimated 1.4 million para-medical personnel known as 'bare foot doctors' by 1981. In the United Kingdom there were 158,612 doctors qualified to work as specialists, in general practice or in industry as at 31 Dec 1984.

The country with the lowest recorded proportion is Burkina Faso, with 58 physicians (one for every 92,759 people) in 1970.

Dentists

The country with the most dentists is the United States, where 145,000 were registered members of the American Dental Association in 1984.

Psychiatrists

The country with the most psychiatrists is the United States. The registered membership of the American Psychiatric Association (inst. 1894) was 27,000 in 1984. The membership of the American Psychological Association (inst. 1892) was 65,000 in 1984.

Hospital Largest *World*

The largest mental hospital in the world is the Pilgrim State Hospital, West Brentwood, Long Island, NY, USA, with 3618 beds. It formerly contained 14,200 beds. The largest psychiatric institute is at the University of California, Los Angeles.

The busiest maternity hospital in the world is the Mama Yemo Hospital, Kinshasa, Zaïre with 41,930 deliveries in 1976. The record 'birth-quake' occurred on a day in May 1976 with 175 babies born. It had 599 beds.

Great Britain

The largest hospitals of any kind in Great Britain are Hartwood Hospital near Shotts, Lanarkshire with 1600 staffed beds for mentally ill patients and Winwick Hospital near Warrington, which has 1352 staffed beds.

The largest general hospital in Great Britain is the St James's University Hospital (which is also a teaching hospital), Leeds, West Yorkshire, with 1470 staffed beds.

The largest maternity hospital in Great Britain is the Simpson Memorial Maternity Pavilion, Edinburgh with 225 staffed beds.

The largest children's hospital in Great Britain is Queen Mary's Hospital for Children, at Carshalton, Sutton, Greater London, with 428 staffed beds.

Longest stay in hospital

Miss Martha Nelson was admitted to the Columbus State Institute for the Feeble-Minded in Ohio, USA in 1875. She died in January 1975 aged 103 years 6 months in the Orient State Institution, Ohio after spending more than 99 years in institutions.

CHINA:
Most
Frontiers

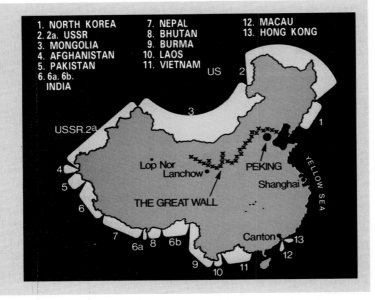

1. NORTH KOREA
2. 2a. USSR
3. MONGOLIA
4. AFGHANISTAN
5. PAKISTAN
6. 6a. 6b. INDIA
7. NEPAL
8. BHUTAN
9. BURMA
10. LAOS
11. VIETNAM
12. MACAU
13. HONG KONG

Artwork:
Eddie Botchway

Most expensive

In mid 1983 the average daily cost of a day's stay in a California hospital was $755 (*then £530*) or $5134 (*£3615*) for average stay. Boston City Hospital, Massachusetts were reported on 1 Dec 1982 to have sent a bill to Michael Saltwick for a 37 day stay and for cancer surgery on his wife for $238,000 (*£153,500*).

CITIES

Oldest *World*

The oldest known walled town in the world is Arīhā (Jericho). The latest radio-carbon dating on specimens from the lowest levels reached by archaeologists indicate habitation there by perhaps 3000 people as early as 7800 BC. The settlement of Dolní Věstonice, Czechoslovakia, has been dated to the Gravettian culture *c.* 27000 BC. The oldest capital city in the world is Dimashq (Damascus), the capital of Syria. It has been continuously inhabited since *c.* 2500 BC.

Great Britain

The oldest town in Great Britain is often cited as Colchester, the old British Camulodunum, headquarters of Belgic chiefs in the 1st century BC. However, the name of the tin trading post Salakee, St Mary's, Isles of Scilly, is derived from pre-Celtic roots and hence *ante* 550 BC. The oldest borough in Britain is reputed to be Barnstaple, Devon whose charter was granted by King Athelstan (927–939) in AD 930.

Most populous *World*

The most populous 'urban agglomeration' in the world is the 'Keihin Metropolitan Area' (Tōkyō-Yokohama Metropolitan Area) of 1081 miles² *2800 km²* containing an estimated 26,343,000 people in 1980. The municipal population of Tōkyō in 1985 was 11,600,069. The population of the metropolitan area of Greater Mexico City in 1979 was published as 13,950,364.

Great Britain

The largest conurbation in Britain is Greater London (established on 1 Apr 1965), with a population of 6,765,100 (1982 estimate). The residential population of the City of London (677.3 acres *274 ha* plus 61.7 acres *24,9 ha* foreshore) is 5200 (1982 estimate) compared with 128,000 in 1801. The peak figure for Greater London was 8,615,050 in 1939.

Largest in area

The world's largest town, in area, is Mount Isa, Queensland, Australia. The area administered by the City Council is 15,822 miles² *40 978 km²*. The largest conurbation in the United Kingdom is the county of Greater London with an area of 609.8 miles² *1579,5 km²*.

Towns, villages and hamlets *Great Britain*

The smallest place with a town council is Llanwrtyd Wells, Powys (pop 614 in 1979). The smallest town with a Royal Charter (granted in 1290) is Caerwys, Clwyd, Wales with a population of 801. The strongest claimant to be Britain's oldest village is Thatcham, Berkshire. The earliest Mesolithic settlement there has been dated to 7720 BC.

Highest *World*

The highest capital in the world, before the domination of Tibet by China, was Lhasa, at an elevation of 12,087 ft *3684 m* above sea-level. La Paz, the administrative and *de facto* capital of Bolivia, stands at an altitude of 11,916 ft *3631 m* above sea-level. El Alto airport is at 4080 m *13,385 ft*. The city was founded in 1548 by Capt Alonso de Mendoza on the site of an Indian village named Chuquiapu. It was originally called Ciudad de Nuestra Señora de La Paz (City of Our Lady of Peace), but in 1825 was renamed La Paz de Ayacucho, its present official name. Sucre, the legal capital of Bolivia, stands

at 9301 ft *2834 m* above sea-level. The new town of Wenchuan, founded in 1955 on the Chinghai-Tibet road, north of the Tangla range, is the highest in the world at 5100 m *16,732 ft* above sea-level.

Great Britain

The highest village in Britain is Flash, in northern Staffordshire, at 1518 ft *462 m* above sea-level. The highest in Scotland is Wanlockhead, in Dumfries and Galloway at 1380 ft *420 m* above sea-level.

Lowest

The settlement of Ein Bokek, which has a synagogue, on the shores of the Dead Sea is the lowest in the world at 1291 ft *393,5 m* below sea-level.

Northernmost

The world's most northerly town with a population of more than 10,000 is the Arctic port of Dikson, USSR in 73° 32′ N. The northernmost village is Ny Ålesund (78° 55′ N.), a coalmining settlement on King's Bay, Vest Spitsbergen, in the Norwegian territory of Svalbard, inhabited only during the winter season. The northernmost capital is Reykjavik, the capital of Iceland, in 64° 08′ N. Its population was estimated to be 80,000 (1985).

Southernmost

The world's southernmost village is Puerto Williams (population about 350), on the north coast of Isla Navarino, in Tierra del Fuego, Chile, 680 miles *1090 km* north of Antarctica. Wellington, the North Island, New Zealand is the southernmost capital city on 41° 17′ S. The world's southernmost administrative centre is Port Stanley (51° 43′ S.), in the Falkland Islands, off South America.

Most remote from the sea

The largest town most remote from the sea is Ürümqi in Xinjiang (formerly Tihwa, Sinkiang), capital of the Uighur Autonomous Region of China, at a distance of about 1400 miles *2250 km* from the nearest coastline. Its population was estimated to be 320,000 in 1974.

2. ROYALTY & HEADS OF STATE

Oldest ruling house and Longest Reign

The Emperor of Japan, Hirohito (born 29 Apr 1901), is the 124th in line from the first Emperor, Jimmu Tenno or Zinmu, whose reign was traditionally from 660 to 581 BC, but more probably from *c.* 40 BC to *c.* 10 BC. The present

WORLD'S MOST POPULOUS *Urban Settlements*
Progressive List

Population	Name		Date
> 100	Dolní Věstonice	Czechoslovakia	c.27000 BC
c. 150	Chemi Shanidar	Iraq	8900 BC
3,000	Jericho (Arīhā)	Occupied Jordan	7800 BC
50,000	Uruk (Erech) (now Warka)	Iraq	3000 BC
250,000	Greater Ur (now Tell Muqayyar)	Iraq	2200 BC
350,000	Babylon (now al-Hillah)	Iraq	600 BC
500,000	Pataliputra (Patna) Bihār	India	400–185 BC
600,000	Seleukia (near Baghdad)	Iraq	300 BC–165 AD
1,100,000	Rome (founded c. 510 BC)	Italy	133 BC
1,500,000	Angkor	Cambodia	900 AD
1.0–1.5 million	Hangchow (now Hangzhou)	China	1279
707,000	Peking (Cambaluc) (now Beijing)	China	1578
1,117,290	Greater London	United Kingdom	1801
8,615,050	Greater London (peak)	United Kingdom	1939
11,600,069	Tokyo	Japan	1985

Note: The UN projections for AD 2000 for Greater Mexico City is 31,616,000.

BRITISH MONARCHY RECORDS

	Kings	Queens Regnant	Queens Consort
LONGEST REIGN OR TENURE	59 years 96 days[1] George III 1760–1820	63 years 216 days Victoria 1837–1901	57 years 70 days Charlotte 1761–1818 (Consort of George III)
SHORTEST REIGN OR TENURE	77 days[2] Edward V 1483	13 days[3] Jane, 6–19 July 1553	154 days Yoleta (1285–6) (second consort of Alexander III)
LONGEST LIVED	81 years 239 days George III (b. 1738–d. 1820)	81 years 243 days Victoria (b. 1819–d. 1901)	85 years 303 days Mary of Teck (b. 1867–d. 1953) (Consort of George V)
MOST CHILDREN (LEGITIMATE)[5]	18 Edward I 1272–1307	9[6] Victoria (b. 1819–d. 1901)	15 Eleanor (c. 1244–90) and Charlotte (b. 1744–d. 1818)
OLDEST TO START REIGN OR CONSORTSHIP	64 years 10 months William IV 1830–7	37 years 5 months Mary I 1553–8	56 years 53 days Alexandra (b. 1844–d. 1925) (Consort of Edward VII)
YOUNGEST TO START REIGN OR CONSORTSHIP	269 days Henry VI in 1422	6 or 7 days Mary, Queen of Scots in 1542	6 years 11 months Isabella (second consort of Richard II in 1396)
MOST MARRIED	6 times Henry VIII 1509–47	3 times Mary, Queen of Scots 1542–67 (executed 1587)	4 times Catherine Parr (b. c. 1512–d. 1548) (sixth consort of Henry VIII)
MOST ALIVE SIMULTANEOUSLY	Between 30 Oct 1683 (birth of George Augustus of Hanover, later George II) and 6 Feb 1685 (death of Charles II) there were 7 monarchs living simultaneously (Charles II, James II, William and Mary, Anne, George I and II) and also Richard Cromwell (d. 1712) the 2nd Lord Protector and *de facto* Head of State in 1658–59.		

Notes (Dates are dates of reigns or tenures unless otherwise indicated).

[1] *James Francis Edward, the Old Pretender, known to his supporters as James III, styled his reign from 16 Sept 1701 until his death 1 Jan 1766 (i.e. 64 years 109 days).*
[2] *There is the probability that in pre-Conquest times Sweyn 'Forkbeard', the Danish King of England, reigned for only 40 days in 1013–14.*
[3] *She accepted the allegiance of the Lords of the Council (9 July) and was proclaimed on 10 July so is often referred to as the '9 (or 10) day Queen'.*
[4] *Richard Cromwell (b. 4 Oct 1626), the 2nd Lord Protector from 3 Sept 1658 until his abdication on 24 May 1659, lived under the alias John Clarke until 12 July 1712 aged 85 years 9 months and was thus the longest lived Head of State.*
[5] *Henry I (b. 1068–d. 1135) in addition to one (possibly two) legitimate sons and a daughter had at least 20 bastard children (9 sons, 11 daughters), and possibly 22, by six mistresses.*
[6] *Queen Anne (b. 1665–d. 1714) had 17 pregnancies, which produced only 5 live births.*

Emperor, who succeeded on 25 Dec 1926 is currently the world's longest reigning monarch.

Her Majesty Queen Elizabeth II (b. 21 Apr 1926) represents dynasties historically traceable at least back until the 4th century AD; in the case Tegid, great grandfather of Cunedda, founder of the House of Gwynedd in Wales; she is 54th in line. If the historicity of some early Scoto-Irish and Pictish kings were acceptable, the lineage could be extended to about 70 generations.

Reigns *Longest All Time*
The longest recorded reign of any monarch is that of Phiops II or Neferkare, a Sixth Dynasty Pharaoh of ancient Egypt. His reign began in *c.* 2281 BC, when he was aged 6, and is believed to have lasted *c.* 94 years. Minhti, King of Arakan (Burma) is reputed to have reigned for 95 years between 1279 and 1374. Musoma Kanijo, chief of the Nzega district of western Tanganyika (now part of Tanzania), reputedly reigned for more than 98 years from 1864, when aged 8, until his death on 2 Feb 1963. The longest reign of any European monarch was that of Afonso I Henrigues of Portugal who ascended the throne on 30 Apr 1112 and died on 6 Dec 1185 after a reign of 73 years 220 days, first as a Count and then as King.

Roman Occupation
During the 369 year long Roman occupation of England, Wales and parts of southern Scotland there were 40 sole and 27 co-Emperors of Rome. Of these the longest reigning was Constantinus I (The Great) from 31 Mar 307 to 22 May 337–30 years 2 months.

Shortest
The Crown Prince Luis Filipe of Portugal was mortally wounded at the time that his father was killed by a bullet, which severed his carotid artery, in the streets of Lisbon on 1 Feb 1908. He was thus technically King of Portugal (Dom Luis III) for about 20 minutes.

Highest post-nominal numbers
The highest post-nominal number ever used to designate a member of a Royal House was 75 briefly enjoyed by Count Heinrich LXXV Reuss (1800–1). All male members of this branch of this German family are called Heinrich and are successively numbered from I upwards *each* century.

British regnal numbers date from the Norman conquest. The highest is 8, used by Henry VIII (1509–1547) and by Edward VIII (1936) who died as HRH the Duke of Windsor, on 28 May 1972. Jacobites liked to style Henry Benedict, Cardinal York (b. 1725), the grandson of James II, as Henry IX in respect of his 'reign' from 1788 to 1807 when he died as last survivor in the male line of the House of Stuart.

Longest lived 'Royals'
The longest life among the Blood Royal of Europe has been that of the late HSH Princess Elizabeth Maria Auguste of Ysenburg and Büdingen, West Germany. She was born on 12 Nov 1883 and died, as Duchess of Vandières, on 10 Oct 1982 aged 98 years 332 days. The greatest age among European Royal Consorts is the 101 years 268 days of HSH Princess Leonilla Bariatinsky (b. Moscow, 9 July 1816), who married HSH Prince Louis of Sayn-Wittgenstein-Sayn and died in Ouchy, Switzerland on 1 Feb 1918. The longest-lived Queen on record has been the Queen Grandmother of Siam, Queen Sawang (b. 10 Sept 1862), 27th daughter of King Mongkut (Rama IV); she died on 17 Dec 1955 aged 93 years 3 months.

HRH Princess Alice Mary, VA, GCVO, GBE, Countess of Athlone (b. 25 Feb 1883) became the longest ever lived British 'royal' on 15 July 1977 and died aged 97 years 313 days on 3 Jan 1981. She fulfilled 20,000 engagements, including the funerals of five British monarchs.

Youngest King and Queen
Forty-five of the world's 169 sovereign states are not republics. They are lead by 1 Emperor, 12 Kings, 4 Queens, 3 princely rulers, 2 Sultans, 3 Amirs, the Pope, a Shaik, a Ruler and one elected monarch. Queen Elizabeth II is Head of

The still exiled 93 year old Empress Zita of Austria who had 23 brothers, sisters, half-brothers and half-sisters. (See Most prolific)

State of 16 other Commonwealth countries. That with the youngest King is Bhutan where King Jigme Singye Wangchuk was born 11 Nov 1955, succeeded on 24 July 1972 when aged 16 years and 8 months. That with youngest Queen is Denmark with Queen Margrethe II (b. 16 Apr 1940).

Heaviest monarch
The world's heaviest monarch is the 6 ft 3 in *1,90 m* tall King Taufa'ahau of Tonga who in Sept 1976 was weighed on the only adequate scales in the country at the airport recording 33 st (462 lb) *209,5 kg*.

Most prolific
The most prolific monogamous 'royals' have

been Prince Hartmann of Liechtenstein (1613–86) who had 24 children, of whom 21 were live born, by Countess Elisabeth zu Salm-Reifferscheidt (1623–88). HRH Duke Roberto I of Parma (1848–1907) also had 24 children but by two wives. One of his daughters HIM Empress Zita of Austria (b. 9 May 1892) was exiled on 23 Mar 1919 but visited Vienna, her titles intact on 17 Nov 1982 reminding republicans that her father succeeded to the throne of Parma in 1854.

Head of State *Oldest and Youngest*
The oldest head of state in the world is the President of Italy, Alessandro Pertini (b. 27 Sept 1896) who resigned on 29 June 1985. Master Sgt Samuel Kanyon Doe, head of state of Liberia was born on 6 May 1952. He became Chairman of the People's Redemption Council in April 1980 aged 27.

Earliest Elected Female
President Vigdis Finnbogadottir (b. 1930) of Iceland became the first democratically elected female head of state on 30 June 1980.

3. LEGISLATURES

PARLIAMENTS—WORLD

Earliest and Oldest
The earliest known legislative assembly or *ukkim* was a bicameral one in Erech, Iraq *c.* 2800 BC. The oldest legislative body is the *Althing* of Iceland founded in AD 930. This body, which originally comprised 39 local chieftains at Thingvellir, was abolished in 1800, but restored by Denmark to a consultative status in 1843 and a legislative status in 1874. The legislative assembly with the oldest continuous history is the Court of Tynwald in the Isle of Man, which celebrated its millenium in 1979.

Largest
The largest legislative assembly in the world is the National People's Congress of the People's Republic of China. The fifth Congress, when convened in 1978, had 3497 members. Its standing committee has 197 members.

Smallest quorum
The House of Lords has the smallest quorum, expressed as a percentage of eligible voters, of any legislative body in the world, namely less than one-third of 1 per cent. To transact business there must be three peers present, including the Lord Chancellor or his deputy. The House of Commons quorum of 40 MPs, including the Speaker or his deputy, is 20 times as exacting.

Highest paid legislators
The most highly paid of all the world's legislators are Members of the US Congress whose basic annual salary was raised on 1 Jan 1985 to $72,600 (*then £60,500*) and limited honoraria to $20,940 (*£17,550*). In addition up to $1,021,167 (*£850,000*) per annum is allowed for office help, with a salary over $50,000 (*now £41,660*) for any one staff member (limited to 16 in number). Senators are allowed up to $143,000 (*£119,200*) per annum for an official office expense account from which official travel, telegram, long distance telephone, air mail, postage, stationery, subscriptions to newspapers, and office expenses in home state are paid. They also command very low rates for filming, speech and radio transcriptions and, in the case of women senators, beauty treatment. When abroad they have access to 'counterpart funds'. A retiring President electing to take also his congressional pension would enjoy an annual pension of $103,500 (*£66,774*).

Longest membership
The longest span as a legislator was 83 years by

József Madarász (1814–1915). He first attended the Hungarian Parliament in 1832–6 as *oblegatus absentium* (*i.e.* on behalf of an absent deputy). He was a full member in 1848–50 and from 1861 until his death on 31 Jan 1915.

UN Speech *Longest*
The longest speech made in the United Nations has been one of 4 hr 29 min by President Dr Fidel Castro Ruz (b. 13 Aug 1927) of Cuba on 26 Sept 1960.

Filibusters
The longest continuous speech in the history of the United States Senate was that of Senator Wayne Morse (1900–74) of Oregon on 24–25 Apr 1953, when he spoke on the Tidelands Oil Bill for 22 hr 26 min without resuming his seat. Interrupted only briefly by the swearing-in of a new senator, Senator Strom Thurmond (b. 1902) (South Carolina, Democrat) spoke against the Civil Rights Bill for 24 hr 19 min on 28–29 Aug 1957. The United States national record duration for a filibuster is 43 hr by Texas State senator Bill Meier against nondisclosure of industrial accidents in May 1977.

Lobbyist *Greatest*
M. C. Ford (1900–1984) of Chicago lobbied the US Congress for 39 years before being invested with the US Marine Corps Medal. He had been tortured by the Japanese in occupied China in 1938–39.

Treaty *Oldest*
The world's oldest treaty is the Anglo-Portuguese Treaty of Alliance signed in London over 600 years ago on 16 June 1373. The text was confirmed 'with my usual flourish' by John de Banketre, Clerk.

Constitutions
The world's oldest constitution is that of the United States of America ratified by the necessary Ninth State (New Hampshire) on 21 June 1788 and declared to be in effect on 4 Mar 1789. The only countries without one document constitutions are Israel, Libya, New Zealand, Oman, and the United Kingdom.

Women's suffrage
The earliest legislature with female voters was the Territory of Wyoming, USA in 1869, followed by the Isle of Man in 1881. The earliest country to have universal suffrage was New Zealand in 1893. The vote of Mrs Lily Maxwell in Manchester on 26 Nov 1867 was declared illegal on 9 Nov 1868.

PARLIAMENTS UNITED KINGDOM

Earliest
The earliest known use of the term 'parliament' is an official English royal document, in the meaning of a summons to the King's (Henry III's) council, dates from 19 Dec 1241.

The Houses of Parliament of the United Kingdom in the Palace of Westminster, London, had 1826 members (House of Lords 1176, House of Commons 650) in June 1985.

Longest
The longest English Parliament was the 'Pensioners' Parliament of Charles II, which lasted from 8 May 1661 to 24 Jan 1679, a period of 17 years 8 months and 16 days. The longest United Kingdom Parliament was that of George V, Edward VIII and George VI, lasting from 26 Nov 1935 to 15 June 1945, a span of 9 years 6 months and 20 days.

Shortest
The parliament of Edward I, summoned to

Westminster for 30 May 1306, lasted only 1 day. The parliament of Charles II at Oxford from 21–28 Mar 1681 lasted 7 days. The shortest United Kingdom Parliament was that of George III, lasting from 15 Dec 1806 to 29 Apr 1807, a period of only 4 months and 14 days.

Sittings *Longest*
The longest sitting in the House of Commons was one of 41½ hr from 4 p.m. on 31 Jan 1881 to 9.30 a.m. on 2 Feb 1881, on the question of better Protection of Person and Property in Ireland. The longest sitting of the Lords has been 19 hr 16 min from 2.30 p.m. on 29 Feb to 9.46 a.m on 1 Mar 1968 on the Commonwealth Immigrants Bill (Committee stage). The longest sitting of a Standing Committee occurred from 10.30 a.m. 11 May to 12.08 p.m. 13 May 1948 when Standing Committee D considered the Gas Bill through two nights for 49 hr 38 min.

Speech *Longest*
The longest recorded continuous speech in the Chamber of the House of Commons was that of Henry Peter Brougham (1778–1868) on 7 Feb 1828, when he spoke for 6 hr on Law Reform. He ended at 10.40 p.m. and the report of this speech occupied 12 columns of the next day's edition of *The Times*. Brougham, created the 1st Lord Brougham and Vaux on 22 Nov 1830, then set the House of Lords record, also with 6 hours on 7 Oct 1831, when speaking on the second reading of the Reform Bill.

The longest back bench speech under present, much stricter, Standing Orders has been one of 4 hr 23 min by Ivan John Lawrence QC MP (b 24 Dec 1936) Conservative member for Burton opposing the Water (Fluoridation) Bill on 6 Mar 1985. John Golding MP (b. 9 Mar 1931) (Labour, Newcastle-under-Lyme) spoke for 11 hr 15 min in committee on small amendments to the British Telecommunications Bill on 8–9 Feb 1983.

The longest speech in Stormont, Northern Ireland was one of 9 hr 26 min by Thomas Gibson Henderson MP (1887–1970) on the Appropriations Bill from 6.32 p.m. on 26th to 3.58 a.m. on 27th May 1936.

Greatest parliamentary petition
The greatest petition has been supposed to be the Great Chartist Petition of 1848 but of the 5,706,000 'signatures' only 1,975,496 were valid. The largest of all time was for the abolition of Entertainment Duty with 3,107,080 signatures presented on 5 June 1951.

Most and least time consuming legislation
The most profligate use of parliamentary time was on the Government of Ireland Bill of 1893–4, which required 82 days in the House of Commons of which 46 days was in Committee. The record for a standing committee is 59 sessions for the Police and Criminal Evidence Bill from 17 Nov 1983 to 29 Mar 1984.

The Abdication Bill (of King Edward VIII) passed all its stages in the Commons (2 hrs) and the Lords (8 mins) on 11–12 Dec 1936 and received the Royal Assent at 1.52 a.m. on the latter date.

Divisions
The record number of divisions in the House of Commons is 64 on 23–24 Mar 1971 including 57 in succession between midnight and noon. The largest division was one of 350–310 on the vote of no confidence on 11 Aug 1892.

ELECTIONS—WORLD

Largest
The largest elections in the world were those beginning on 24 Dec 1984 for the Indian *Lok Sabha* (Lower House) which has 542 elective

seats. The government of Rajiv Gandhi was returned in polls in which 379,000,000 electors were eligible to vote for 5,301 candidates at 480,000 polling stations manned by 2½ million staff. In Maduranthkam (electorate 120,021) there were 90 candidates. R. Esumuthu polled 12.

Closest

The ultimate in close general elections occurred in Zanzibar (now part of Tanzania) on 18 Jan 1961, when the Afro-Shirazi Party won by a single seat, after the seat of Chake-Chake on Pemba Island had been gained by a single vote.

The narrowest recorded percentage win in an election would seem to be for the office of Southern District highway commissioner in Mississippi State, USA on 7 Aug 1979. Robert E. Joiner was declared the winner over W. H. Pyron with 133,587 votes to 133,582. The loser got more than 49.9999 per cent of the votes.

Most decisive

North Korea recorded a 100 per cent turn-out of electors and a 100 per cent vote for the Worker's Party of Korea in the general election of 8 Oct 1962. The next closest approach was in Albania on 14 Nov 1982 when a single voter spoiled national unanimity for the official (and only) Communist candidates, who thus obtained only 99.99993 per cent of the poll in a 100 per cent turn out of 1,627,968.

Most bent

In the Liberian presidential election of 1927 President Charles D. B. King (1875–1961) was returned with a majority over his opponent, Mr Thomas J. R. Faulkner of the People's Party, officially announced as 234,000. President King thus claimed a 'majority' more than 15½ times greater than the entire electorate.

Highest personal majority

The highest ever personal majority by any politician has been 424,545 by Ram Bilas Paswan, 30, the Janata candidate for Hajipur in Bihar, India in March 1977. The electorate was 625,179.

Communist parties

The largest national Communist party outside the Soviet Union (17,000,000 members in 1981) and Communist states has been the Partito Comunista Italiano (Italian Communist Party), with a membership of 2,300,000 in 1946. The total was 1,700,000 in 1976. The membership in mainland China was estimated to be 39,000,000 in 1984.

The Communist Party of Great Britain, formed on 31 July 1920 in Cannon Street Station Hotel, London, attained its peak membership of 56,000 in December 1942, compared with 15,691 in July 1983 of whom 8,270 paid their dues.

Voting age Extremes

The eligibility for voting is 15 years of age in the Philippines and 25 years in Andorra.

Most Coups

Statisticians contend Bolivia, since it became a sovereign country in 1825, had its 190th coup on 30 June 1984 when President Hernan Siles Zuazo, 70 was kidnapped from his official residence by more than 60 armed men.

PRIME MINISTERS AND STATESMEN

Oldest *World*

The longest lived Prime Minister of any country is Christopher Hornsrud, Prime Minister of Norway from 28 Jan to 15 Feb 1928. He was born on 15 Nov 1859 and died on 13 Dec 1960, aged 101 years 28 days. The Hon. Richard Gavin Reid (b. Glasgow 17 Jan 1879), Premier of Alberta, Canada in 1934–35 died on 17 Oct 1980 aged 101 years 274 days.

El Hadji Muhammad el Mokri, Grand Vizier of Morocco, died on 16 Sept 1957, at a reputed age of 116 Muslim (*Hijri*) years, equivalent to 112.5 Gegorian years. The oldest age of first appointment has been 81 years in the case of Morarji Ranchhodji Desai of India (b. 29 Feb 1896) in March 1977.

Longest term of office *World*

Prof. Dr António de Oliveira Salazar, GCMG (Hon.) (1889–1970) was the President of the Council of Ministers (*i.e.* Prime Minister) of Portugal from 5 July 1932 until 27 Sept 1968—36 years 84 days. He was superseded 11 days after going into coma. The longest serving democratically elected premier was Tage Erlander (1901–1985) of Sweden for 22 years 357 days from 10 Oct 1946 to 1 Oct 1969.

Andrei Andreevich Gromyko (b. 6 July 1909) has been Minister of Foreign Affairs of the USSR since 15 Feb 1957 having been Deputy Foreign Minister since 1946. He was elected President of the USSR on 2 July 1985.

Enver Hoxha (b. 16 Oct 1908), First Secretary of the Central Committee of the Albania Party of Labour, ruled from Oct 1944 to his death on 11 Apr 1985.

EUROPEAN ASSEMBLY ELECTION RECORDS

In the European Assembly elections of 14 June 1984 the highest majority in the 81 U.K. constituencies was 95,557 (L. Smith, Lab) in Wales South-East. Lowest was 2,625 (Sir Peter Vanneck, Con) in Cleveland and Yorkshire North. Largest and smallest electorates were 574,022 in Essex North-East and 307,265 in Highlands and Islands. Highest turnout was 42.4 per cent in Wales North. Lowest was 25.2 per cent in London North-East. Northern Ireland voted by proportional representation.

MAJORITIES—UNITED KINGDOM

Party

The largest party majorities were those of the Liberals, with 307 seats and a record of 66.7% of the vote in 1832. In 1931 the Coalition of Conservatives, Liberals and National Labour candidates had a majority of 491 seats and 60.5% of the vote. The narrowest party majority was that of the Whigs in 1847, with a single seat. The highest popular vote for a single party was 13,948,883 for Labour in 1951.

The largest majority on a division was one of

PRIME MINISTERIAL RECORDS

Though given legal warrant in the instrument of the Congress of Berlin in 1878 and an established place in the orders of Precedence in England and Scotland in 1904, the office of Prime Minister was not statutorily recognised until 1917. All previous acknowledged First Ministers had tenure as First Lords of the Treasury with the exception of No. 12, William Pitt, Earl of Chatham, who controlled his ministers as Secretary of State of the Southern Department or as Lord Privy Seal. The first to preside over his fellow King's ministers was Walpole from 1721.

LONGEST SERVING	20 years 326 days	1st	Sir Robert Walpole KG (1676–1745)	3 Apr 1721–12 Feb 1742
LONGEST SERVING (*20th century*)	8 years 243 days	38th	Earl of Oxford and Asquith, KG (1852–1928)	8 Apr 1908–7 Dec 1916
MOST MINISTERIES	5 times	41st	Earl Baldwin, KG (1867–1947)	22 May 1923–28 May 1937
SHORTEST SERVING IN OFFICE	120 days	22nd	George Canning (1770–1827)	10 Apr–8 Aug 1827
YOUNGEST TO ASSUME OFFICE	24 years 205 days	17th	Hon. William Pitt (1759–1806)	19 Dec 1783 (declined when 23 yr 275 days)
OLDEST TO FIRST ASSUME OFFICE	70 years 109 days	31st	Viscount Palmerston, KG, GCB (1784–1865)	6 Feb 1855
GREATEST AGE IN OFFICE	84 years 64 days	33rd	William Gladstone (1809–1898)	3 Mar 1894 (elected at 82 yr 171 days)
LONGEST LIVED	91+ years	47th	Earl of Stockton, OM (b. 10 Feb 1894)	from 6 Apr 1984 (so surpassing No 44)
LONGEST SURVIVAL AFTER OFFICE	41 years 45 days	13th	Duke of Grafton, KG (1735–1811)	from 28 Jan 1770
SHORTEST LIVED	44 years	7th	Duke of Devonshire (1720–1764)	d. 2 Oct 1764 (exact birth date unknown)
SHORTEST MINISTRY	22 days	24th	Duke of Wellington, KG, GCB, GCH (1769–1852)	17 Nov–9 Dec 1834
SHORTEST POSSESSION OF SEALS	c. 48 hours	4th	Earl of Bath (1684–1764)	10–12 Feb 1746
SHORTEST PRIOR SERVICE AS MP	2 years 11 months	17th	Hon. William Pitt (1759–1806)	–19 Dec 1783
LONGEST PRIOR SERVICE AS MP	47 years	31st	Viscount Palmerston, KG, GCB (1784–1865)	1807–6 Feb 1855
LONGEST SUBSEQUENT SERVICE AS MP	22 years 156 days	39th	Earl Lloyd George, OM (1863–1945)	22 Oct 1922–26 Mar 1945
LONGEST SPAN AS MP	63 years 360 days	44th	Sir Winston Churchill, KG, OM, CH (1874–1965)	1 Oct 1900–25 Sep 1964
RICHEST	£7¼ million (now say £190 million)	29th	Earl of Derby, KG, GCMG (1799–1869)	Annual rent roll in 1869 £170,000
POOREST	£40,000 (now > £1 million) in debt	17th	Hon. William Pitt (1759–1806)	Level of personal debt by 1800
TALLEST	6 ft 1½ in 1,83 m	51st	James Callaghan (b. 27 Mar 1912)	
SHORTEST	5 ft 4¾ in 1,64 m	28th	Lord John Russell, KG, GCMG (1792–1878)	Seven month baby: max. wt. 8 stone 50,7 kg
MOST CHILDREN (*fathered*)	15 or 16	13th	Duke of Grafton, KG (1735–1811)	Twice married
MOST CHILDREN (*uniquely mothered*)	2	52nd	Mrs Margaret Thatcher (b. 13 Oct 1925)	Twins born, 21 Aug 1953
MOST LIVING SIMULTANEOUSLY	18	9th–27th	Peel (b. 5 Feb 1788) to death of 9th Earl of Bute (d. 10 Mar 1792)	1788–1792
MOST LIVING EX PRIME MINISTERS	5	9th, 13–16th	Bute, Grafton, North, Shelburne, Portland (Pitt) till Bute died	19 Dec 1783–10 Mar 1792
	5	46–50th	Eden, Macmillan, Home, Wilson, Heath (Callaghan) till Eden died	5 Apr 1976–14 Jan 1977
	5	47–51st	Macmillan, Home, Wilson, Heath, Callaghan (Mrs Thatcher)	from 4 May 1979

Viscountess Astor (Plymouth, Sutton), who on 1 Dec 1919 became the first woman to take her seat in the House of Commons (see Column 3).

463 (464 votes to 1), on a vote of confidence in the conduct of World War II, on 29 Jan 1942. Since the war the largest has been one of 461 (487 votes to 26) on 10 May 1967, during the debate on the government's application for Britain to join the European Economic Community (the 'Common Market').

HOUSE OF LORDS

Oldest member
The oldest member ever was the Rt Hon the 5th Baron Penrhyn, who was born on 21 Nov 1865 and died on 3 Feb 1967, aged 101 years 74 days. The oldest now is the Rt Hon Lord Shinwell PC CH (b. 18 Oct 1884) who first sat in the Lower House in Nov 1922. The oldest peer to make a maiden speech was Lord Maenan (1854–1951) aged 94 years 123 days (see Oldest creation, p. 188).

Youngest member
The youngest present member of the House of Lords has been HRH the Prince Charles Philip Arthur George, KG, PC, KT, GCB, the Prince of Wales (b. 14 Nov 1948). All Dukes of Cornwall, of whom Prince Charles is the 24th, are technically eligible to sit, regardless of age—in his case from his succession on 6 Feb 1952, aged 3. The 20th and 21st holders, later King George IV (b. 1762) and King Edward VII (b. 1841), were technically entitled to sit from birth. The youngest creation of a life peer or peeress under the Peerage Act 1958 has been that of Lady Masham (b. 14 Apr 1935) who was created Baroness Masham of Ilton at the age of 34 years 262 days.

POLITICAL OFFICE HOLDERS

Chancellorship *Longest and shortest tenures*
The Rt Hon Sir Robert Walpole, KG, later the 1st Earl of Orford (1676–1745), served 22 years 5 months as Chancellor of the Exchequer, holding office continuously from 12 Oct 1715 to 12 Feb 1742, except for the period from 16 Apr 1717 to 2 Apr 1721. The briefest tenure of this office was 26 days in the case of the Baron (later the 1st Earl of) Mansfield (1705–93), from 11 Sept to 6 Oct 1767. The only man with four terms in this office was the Rt Hon William Ewart Gladstone (1809–98).

The longest budget speech was that of Rt Hon David (later Earl) Lloyd George, PC, OM (1863–1945) on 29 Apr 1909 which lasted 4 hr 51 min but was interrupted by a tea break. He announced *inter alia* the introduction of car tax and petroleum duty.

Foreign Secretaryship *Longest tenures*
The longest continuous term of office of any Foreign Secretary has been the 10 years 360 days of Sir Edward Grey, KG, MP (later Viscount Grey of Fallodon) from 10 Dec 1905 to 5 Dec 1916. The Most Hon Robert Arthur Talbot Gascoyne-Cecil, Marquis of Salisbury, KG, GCVO, in two spells in 1887–92 and 1895–1900 aggregated 11 years 87 days in this office.

Colonial Secretaryship *Longest tenures*
The longest term of office has been 19 years 324 days by the Rt Hon Henry Bathurst, Earl Bathurst (1762–1834), who was Secretary of State for the Colonial and War Department from 11 June 1812 to 1 May 1827. The longest tenure this century has been the 5 years 78 days of the Rt Hon Alan Tindal Lennox-Boyd, Viscount Boyd of Merton, PC CH (1904–82) from 28 July 1954 to 13 Oct 1959.

Speakership *Longest*
Arthur Onslow (1691–1768) was elected Mr Speaker on 23 Jan 1728, at the age of 36. He held the position for 33 years 43 days, until 18 Mar 1761 allowing for the 'lost' 11 days (3–13 Sept 1752).

MPs *Youngest (see also p 197)*
The youngest ever woman M.P. has been Josephine Bernadette Devlin now Mrs Michael McAliskey (b. 23 Apr 1947) elected for Mid

Britain's first ever woman Cabinet minister one time draper's assistant Margaret Bondfield, Minister of Labour in 1929–31 from the portrait hanging in the town hall of her birthplace at Chard, Somerset.

Ulster (Ind. Unity) aged 21 yr 359 days on 17 Apr 1969. Henry Long (1420–90) was returned for an Old Sarum seat also at the age of 15. His precise date of birth is unknown. Minors were debarred in law in 1695 and in fact in 1832.

Oldest
The oldest of all members was Samuel Young (b. 14 Feb 1822), Nationalist MP for East Cavan (1892–1918), who died on 18 Apr 1918, aged 96 years 63 days. The oldest 'Father of the House' in Parliamentary history was the Rt Hon Charles Pelham Villiers (b. 3 Jan 1802), who was the member for Wolverhampton South when he died on 16 Jan 1898, aged 96 years 13 days. He was a Member of Parliament for 63 years 6 days, having been returned at 17 elections. The oldest member is Robert Edwards MP (Lab) for Wolverhampton South East (b. 16 Jan 1905).

Longest span
The longest span of service of any MP is 63 years 11 months (1 Oct 1900 to 25 Sept 1964) by the Rt Hon Sir Winston Leonard Spencer-Churchill, KG, OM, CH, TD (1874–1965), with breaks only in 1908 and 1922–24. The longest continuous span was that of C. P. Villiers (see above). The longest span in the Palace of Westminster (both Houses of Parliament) has been 73 years by the 10th Earl of Wemyss and March GCVO, who, as Sir Francis Wemyss-Charteris-Douglas, served as MP for East Gloucestershire (1841–6) and Haddingtonshire (1847–83) and then took his seat in the House of Lords, dying on 30 June 1914, aged 95 years 330 days.

Briefest span
There are two 18th century examples of posthumous elections. Capt the Hon Edward Legge RN (1710–47) was returned unopposed for Portsmouth on 15 Dec 1747. News came later that he had died in the West Indies 87 days before polling. In 1780 John Kirkman standing for the City of London expired before polling had ended but was nonetheless duly returned. A. J. Dobbs (Lab, Smethwick) elected on 5 July 1945 was killed on the way to take his seat at Westminster.

Women MPs *Earliest*
The first woman to be elected to the House of Commons was Mme. Constance Georgine Markievicz (*née* Gore Booth). She was elected as member (Sinn Fein) for St Patrick's Dublin, in December 1918. The first woman to take her seat was the Viscountess Astor, CH (1879–1964) (b. Nancy Witcher Langhorne at Danville, Virginia, USA; formerly Mrs Robert Gould Shaw), who was elected Unionist member for the Sutton Division of Plymouth, Devon, on 28 Nov 1919, and took her seat three days later. The first woman to take her seat from the island of Ireland was Lady Fisher *née* Patricia Smiles as unopposed Ulster Unionist for North Down on 15 Apr 1953 as Mrs Patricia Ford.

The first woman cabinet minister was Rt Hon Margaret Grace Bondfield, PC, CH, appointed Minister of Labour in 1929.

Heaviest and Tallest
The heaviest MP of all-time is believed to have been Cyril Smith MBE, Liberal member for Rochdale since October 1972, when in January 1976 his peak reported weight was 29 st 12 lb *189,60 kg*. Sir Louis Gluckstein GBE, TD, QC (1897–1979), who served for East Nottingham (1931–45), was an unrivalled 6 ft 7½ in *2,02 m*. Currently the tallest is the Hon. Archie Hamilton member for Epsom and Ewell at 6 ft 6 in *1,98 m*.

Mayoralties
The longest recorded mayoralty was that of Edmond Mathis (1852–1953) *maire of* Ehuns,

1 Lowest Electorate 1983 Western Isles: 22,822 (23,076 in 1984)

2 Largest Constituency by Area Ross, Cromarty & Skye 2,359,772 acres *955,000 ha*

2 Youngest Current MP Charles Kennedy (SDP/All) (b. 25 Nov 1959) Ross, Cromarty & Skye

3 Least votes since Universal Franchise 5 Lt Cdr W. Boaks DSC RN (Public Safety Democratic Monarchist White Resident) Glasgow (Hillhead) 25 Mar 1982

3 Lowest Expenses £54 James Maxton Glasgow (Bridgeton) 1935

4 Longest Serving Woman MP Dame Irene Ward 1931–1974 Wallsend-Tynemouth

5 & 21 Narrowest Majority 1 vote by H. E. Duke (Unionist) Dec 1910 Exeter, Devon and 1 vote Matthew Fowler (Lib) 1895 Durham

6 Lowest Vote Nil in 1860 for F. R. Lees (Temperance Chartist) Ripon

7 Heaviest Ever Poll (GB) Darwen (Lancs) 92.7% in 1924

8 Dead-Heat Returning Officer declared dead heat (1886) and gave casting vote to J. E. W. Addison (Con) Ashton-Under-Lyne (now Greater Manchester). Dead heat at Cirencester, Gloucester 13 Oct 1892 by-election. New by-election 23 Feb 1893 won by H. L. W. Lawson (Lib)

9 Narrowest Majority Since Universal Franchise A. J. Flint (National Labour) Ilkeston (Derbyshire) by 2 votes 1931

10 Oldest Father of the House C. P. Villiers (Con) in 1898, 96 years of age, Wolverhampton South

11 Narrowest Majority 1983 7 votes Derek Spencer (Con) Leicester South

12 & 18 Most Recounts 7 Peterborough 1966 and 7 Brighton (Kemptown) 1964

13 Youngest Ever MP Aged 15/16 Edmund Waller (1606–87) in 1621 Amersham (Bucks)

14 Greatest Swing: By-Election 44.4% Bermondsey 24 Feb 1983

14 Largest Ever Electorate 217,900 Hendon (Barnet) 1941

14 Smallest Electorate 10,851 City of London 1945

14 Lowest By-Election Poll 9.3% South Poplar (London) Aug 1942

14 Lowest Ever General Election Poll 29.7% 1918 Kennington (London)

14 Lowest General Election Vote 13 B. C. Wedmore (Belgrano) Finchley 9 June 1983

14 Lowest 1983 Poll City of London and Westminster South: 51.8%

14 Most General Election Candidates 11 Finchley 9 June 1983 in which the total 2579 candidates was a record

15 Fastest ever result 57 min Billericay (Essex) 1959

16 Highest Majority by a Woman 38,823 Countess of Iveagh (Con) 1931 Southend (Essex)

17 Youngest MP for GB seat since 1832 21 years 183 days Hon Esmond Harmsworth Isle of Thanet (Kent)

18 Highest Every Majority 62,253 Sir Cooper Rawson (Con) Brighton (Sussex) 1931 and **Most Votes** 75,205

18 & 12 Most Recounts 7 Peterborough 1966 and 7 Brighton (Kemptown) 1964

19 Highest Electorate 1983 Isle of Wight: 97,608 (97,614 in 1985)

19 Most Votes 1983 38,407 Stephen Ross (Lib/All) Isle of Wight

20 Most Rotten Borough (8 Electors for 2 unopposed members) 1821 Old Sarum (Wiltshire) No elections contested 1295–1831

21 & 5 Narrowest Majority 1 vote H. E. Duke (Unionist) Dec 1910 Exeter, Devon and 1 vote Matthew Fowler (Lib) 1895 Durham

22 Fastest 1983 result 69 min Torbay (Devon)

23 First Woman MP to take seat Nancy Astor 1919 Plymouth

24 Current Father of the House L. J. Callaghan (Lab) Elected 1945 (Cardiff South & Penarth)

25 Largest UK Majority 1983 Michael M. Foot (Lab) Blaenau Gwent 23,705

26 Heaviest Ever Poll (UK) Fermanagh & S Tyrone: 93.42% 1951

26 Heaviest Poll 1983 (UK) Fermanagh & S Tyrone: 88.6%

26 Youngest Member UK (since 1832) James Dickson (Liberal) (1859–1941) returned for Dungannon Tyrone on 25 June 1880 aged 21 years 67 days

27 Highest Poll 1983 (GB) Cornwall North 86.08%

28 Most By-Election Candidates 17 Chesterfield 1 Mar 1984. Rt Hon A. N. Wedgewood-Benn contested for a current record 14th time (12 times returned)

United Kingdom ELECTORAL RECORDS

Haute-Saône, France for 75 years (1878–1953). The mayoralty of the City of London dates from 1192 with the 20 year term of Henry Fitz Ailwyn till 1212. The most elections, since these became annual in 1215, has been 8 by Gregory de Rokesley (1274/5 to 1280/1). The earliest recorded mayor of the City of York, Nigel, dates from 1142. Alderman G. T. Paine served as Mayor of Lydd, Kent for 29 consecutive years in 1931 to 1961. The first recorded all-female mayoral team was the Mayor, Mayoress and Deputy Mayor of Lancaster city council in May 1972. In Hyndburn Borough Council in May 1981 there was a fourth lady with the appointment of a Deputy Mayoress.

Local Government Service Duration Records
The office of reeve was first mentioned in AD 787 and evolved to that of shire reeve hence sheriff.

Major Sir Philip Barber Bt, DSO, TD, DL (1876–1961) served as county councillor for Nottinghamshire for 63 years 41 days from 8 Mar 1898 to 18 Apr 1961. Henry Winn (1816–1914) served as parish clerk for Fulletby near Horncastle, Lincolnshire for 76 years.

Clifford Tasker (1906–1980) of Pontefract, West Yorkshire was appointed as presiding officer for elections in 1921 when aged 15, and served for 59 years until March 1980.

Weight of Legislation
The greatest amount of legislation in a year has been 11,453 pages (83 Public general acts and 2251 Statutory Instruments) in 1975. This compares with 46 Acts and 1130 Instruments of 1998 pages in 1928. Most Acts were 123 in 1939 and fewest 39 in 1929 and 1942. The peak for Statutory Instruments was 2916 in 1947.

ARTWORK: EDDIE BOTCHWAY

4. MILITARY AND DEFENCE

Note Guinness Superlatives Ltd. has published a specialist volume entitled *The Guinness Book of Tank Facts and Feats* (3rd edition) by Kenneth Macksey (£7.95). This work deals with all the aspects of the development and history of the tank and other armoured fighting vehicles in greater detail.

WAR

Earliest Conflict
The oldest known offensive weapon is a broken wooden spear found in April 1911 at Clacton-on-Sea, Essex by S. Hazzledine Warren. This is much beyond the limit of carbon-dating and is estimated to have been fashioned before 200,000 BC.

Longest
The longest of history's countless wars was the 'Hundred Years War' between England and France, which lasted from 1338 to 1453 (115 years), although it may be said that the nine Crusades from the First (1096–1104) to the Ninth (1270–91), extending over 195 years comprised a single Holy War. The Swiss Jean Jacques Babel estimated that since *c.* 3500 BC there have only been 292 years without recorded warfare.

Shortest
The shortest war on record was that between the United Kingdom and Zanzibar (now part of Tanzania) from 9.02 to 9.40 a.m. on 27 Aug 1896. The UK battle fleet under Rear-Admiral (later Admiral Sir) Harry Holdsworth Rawson (1843–1910) delivered an ultimatum to the self-appointed Sultan Sa'īd Khalid to evacuate his palace and surrender. This was not forthcoming until after 38 minutes of bombardment. Admiral Rawson received the Brilliant Star of Zanzibar (first class) from the new Sultan Hamud ibn Muhammad. It was proposed at one time that elements of the local populace should be compelled to defray the cost of the ammunition used.

Bloodiest
By far the most costly war in terms of human life was World War II (1939–45), in which the total number of fatalities, including battle deaths and civilians of all countries, is estimated to have been 54,800,000 assuming 25 million USSR fatalities and 7,800,000 Chinese civilians killed. The country which suffered most was Poland with 6,028,000 or 22.2 per cent of her population of 27,007,000 killed. The total combatant death roll from World War I was 9,700,000 compared with the 15,600,000 of World War II.

In the case of the United Kingdom, however, the heaviest armed forces fatalities occurred in World War I (1914–18), with 765,399 killed out of 5,500,000 engaged (13.9 per cent), compared with 265,000 out of 5,896,000 engaged (4.49 per cent) in World War II.

In the Paraguayan war of 1864–70 against Brazil, Argentina and Uruguay, their population was reduced from 1,400,000 to 220,000 of whom only 30,000 were adult males.

Surgeon Major William Brydon CB (1811–1873) was the sole survivor of the 7 day retreat of 16,000 soldiers and camp followers from Kabul, Afghanistan. His horse died two days after his arrival at Jellalabad, India on 13 Jan 1842.

Bloodiest civil
The bloodiest civil war in history was the T'ai-p'ing ('Great Peace') rebellion, in which peasant sympathizers of the Southern Ming dynasty fought the Manchu Government troops in China from 1851 to 1864. The rebellion was led by the deranged Hung Hsiu-ch'üan (executed) who imagined himself to be a younger brother of Jesus Christ. His force was named *T'ai-p'ing T'ien Kuo* (Heavenly Kingdom of Great Peace). According to the best estimates, the loss of life was between 20,000,000 and 30,000,000 including more than 100,000 killed by Government forces in the sack of Nanking on 19–21 July 1864.

Most costly
The material cost of World War II far transcended that of the rest of history's wars put together and has been estimated at $1.5 million million. The total cost to the Soviet Union was estimated in May 1959 at 2,500,000,000,000 roubles (*£100,000 million*) while a figure of $530,000 million has been estimated for the USA. In the case of the United Kingdom the cost of £34,423 million was over five times as great as that of World War I (£6700 million) and 158.6 times that of the Boer War of 1899–1902 (£217 million).

Last battle on British soil
The last pitched land battle in Britain was at Culloden Field, Drummossie Moor, near Inverness, Highland, on 16 Apr 1746. The last Clan battle in Scotland was between Clan Mackintosh and Clan MacDonald at Mulroy, Highland in 1689. The last battle on English soil was the Battle of Sedgemoor, Somerset, on 6 July 1685, when the forces of James II defeated the supporters of Charles II's illegitimate son, James Scott (formerly called Fitzroy or Crofts), the Duke of Monmouth (1649–85). During the Jacobite rising of 1745–6, there was a skirmish at Clifton Moor, Cumbria, on 18 Dec 1745, when the British forces under Prince William, the Duke of Cumberland (1721–65), brushed with the rebels of Prince Charles Edward Stuart (1720–88) with about 12 killed on the King's side and 5 Highlanders. This was a tactical victory for the Scots under Lord George Murray.

Bloodiest battle *Modern*
The battle with the greatest recorded number of *military* casualties was the First Battle of the Somme, France from 1 July to 19 Nov 1916, with 1,043,896—Allied 623,907 (of which 419,654 were British) and 419,989 German. The published German figure of *c.* 670,000 is not now accepted. The gunfire was heard on Hampstead Heath, London. The greatest death roll in a battle has been estimated at *c.* 2,100,000 in the Battle of Stalingrad ending with the German surrender on 2 Feb 1943 by Field Marshal Friedrich von Paulus (d. 1957). The Soviet garrison commander was Gen Vassilyi Chuikov. Additionally 1,515 civilians from a pre-war population of more than 500,000 were found alive after the battle. The final investment of Berlin by the Red Army on 16 Apr–2 May 1945 involved 3,500,000 men; 52,000 guns and mortars; 7750 tanks and 11,000 aircraft on both sides.

Ancient
Modern historians give no credence, on logistic grounds, to the casualty figures attached to ancient battles, such as the 250,000 reputedly killed at Plataea (Greeks *v* Persians) in 479 BC or the 200,000 allegedly killed in a single day.

British
The bloodiest battle fought on British soil was the Battle of Towton, in North Yorkshire, on 29 Mar 1461, when 36,000 Yorkists defeated 40,000 Lancastrians. The total loss has been estimated at between 28,000 and 38,000 killed. A figure of 80,000 British dead was attributed by Tacitus to the battle of AD 61 between Queen Boudicca (Boadicea) of the Iceni and the Roman Governor of Britain Suetonius Paulinus, for the reputed loss of only 400 Romans in an army of 10,000. The site of the battle is unknown but may have been near Borough Hill, Daventry, Northamptonshire, or more probably near Hampstead Heath, Greater London. Prior to this battle the Romans had lost up to 70,000 in Colchester and London.

Greatest naval battle
The greatest number of ships and aircraft ever involved in a sea–air action was 231 ships and 1996 aircraft in the Battle of Leyte Gulf, in the Philippines. It raged from 22 to 27 Oct 1944, with 166 Allied and 65 Japanese warships engaged, of which 26 Japanese and 6 US ships were sunk. In addition 1280 US and 716 Japanese aircraft were engaged. The greatest purely naval battle of modern times was the Battle of Jutland on 31 May 1916, in which 151 Royal Navy warships were involved against 101 German warships. The Royal Navy lost 14 ships and 6097 men and the German fleet 11 ships and 2545 men. The greatest of ancient naval battles was the Battle of Salamis, Greece on 23 Sept 480 BC. There were an estimated 800 vessels in the defeated Persian fleet and 310 in the victorious Greek fleet with a possible involvement of 190,000 men. The death roll at the Battle of Lepanto on 7 Oct 1571 has been estimated at 33,000.

Invasion Greatest *Seaborne*
The greatest invasion in military history was the Allied land, air and sea operation against the Normandy coasts of France on D-day, 6 June 1944. Thirty-eight convoys of 745 ships moved in on the first three days, supported by 4066 landing craft, carrying 185,000 men and 20,000 vehicles, and 347 minesweepers. The air assault comprised 18,000 paratroopers from 1087 aircraft. The 42 available divisions possessed an air support from 13,175 aircraft. Within a month 1,100,000 troops, 200,000 vehicles and 750,000 tons of stores were landed. The Allied invasion of Sicily on 10–12 July 1943 involved the landing of 181,000 men in 3 days.

Airborne
The largest airborne invasion was the Anglo-American assault of three divisions (34,000 men), with 2800 aircraft and 1600 gliders, near Arnhem, in the Netherlands, on 17 Sept 1944.

Last on the soil of Great Britain
The last invasion of Great Britain occurred on 12 Feb 1797, when the Irish-American adventurer General Tate landed at Carreg Gwastad with 1400 French troops. They surrendered near Fishguard, Dyfed, to Lord Cawdor's force of the Castlemartin Yeomanry and some local inhabitants armed with pitchforks. The UK Crown Dependency of the Falkland Islands were occupied by Argentine troops on 2 Apr 1982. British troops re-landed at San Carlos on 21 May and accepted the surrender of Brig Gen Mario Menéndez on 14 June 1982.

Greatest evacuation
The greatest evacuation in military history was that carried out by 1200 Allied naval and civil craft from the beach-head at Dunkerque (Dunkirk), France, between 27 May and 4 June 1940. A total of 338,226 British and French troops were taken off.

Worst sieges
The worst siege in history was the 880-day siege of Leningrad, USSR by the German Army from 30 Aug 1941 until 27 Jan 1944. The best estimate is that between 1.3 and 1.5 million defenders and citizens died. The longest recorded siege was that of Azotus (now Ashdod), Israel which according to Herodotus was invested by Psamtik I of Egypt for 29 years in the period 664–610 BC.

Longest Range Attack
The longest range attacks in air history were

from Ascension Island to Port Stanley, Falkland Is. by refuelled RAF Vulcan bombers carrying 1000 lb *453,5 kg* bombs in a round trip of more than 8000 miles *12 875 km* in May 1982.

DEFENCE

The estimated level of spending on armaments throughout the world in 1984 was in excess of $700,000 million *£583,000 million*. This represents £107 per person per annum, or 10 per cent of the world's total production of goods and services. Also in 1984 there were 25.7 million full-time armed force regulars or conscripts.

The budgeted expenditure on defence by the US government for the fiscal year 1984 was $249,800 million (*£178,400 million*). The first budget resolution for 1985 was $297,000 million.

The defence burden on the USSR has been variously estimated as a percentage of GNP to be > 15% (by China), and up to 13% by the CIA and thus may be nearly treble that of the US. China's budget in 1977 was 17.67%.

ARMED FORCES

Largest
Numerically the largest regular armed force in the world is that of the USSR with 5,115,000 (1984). China's People's Liberation Army of 4,000,000 will lose 1 million by 1987. Her paramilitary forces of armed and unarmed militias are estimated by the International Institute of Strategic Studies at 12 million. The USA's military manpower is 2,135,900 (1984) and that of the United Kingdom 326,849 (1985).

Navies *Largest*
The largest navy in the world in terms of manpower is the United States Navy, with a manpower of 564,800 and 196,600 Marines in mid-1984. The active strength in 1984 included 4 nuclear powered aircraft carriers, with 10 others, 2 battleships, 94 attack nuclear submarines and 4 diesel attack submarines, 28 cruisers, 68 destroyers, 94 frigates and 61 amphibious warfare ships. The USSR navy has a larger submarine fleet of 278 vessels (124 nuclear, 154 diesel). It has 5 aircraft carriers, 36 cruisers, 45 nuclear armed and 23 gun destroyers.

The strength of the Royal Navy in mid-1984 included 4 nuclear submarines with strategic atomic missiles, 13 other nuclear and 15 diesel attack submarines and 3 anti-submarine commando carriers, a helicopter cruiser, 12 guided weapon destroyers, and 42 frigates. The uniformed strength was 70,616 including Fleet Air Arm and Royal Marines (7,512) on 1 Jan 1985. In 1914 the Royal Navy had 542 warships including 72 capital ships with 16 building thus being the largest navy in the world.

Admiral *Longest serving*
Admiral of the Fleet Sir Provo Wallis GCB (1791–1892) first served on *HMS Cleopatra* in Oct 1804. Because of his service on *HMS Cleopatra* in 1805 against the French he was kept on the active list in 1870 for life. He thus was 87 years 4 months on paid active service though he was earlier on the books as a volunteer from 1795–1804 for a further 9 years—a system by which even infants could gain seniority on joining.

Armies *Oldest*
The oldest army in the world is the 83-strong Swiss Guard in the Vatican City, with a regular foundation dating back to 21 Jan 1506. Its origins, however, extend back before 1400.

Largest
Numerically, the world's largest army is that of the People's Republic of China, with a total strength of some 4,000,000 in mid-1984. The

A normally submerged USSR Typhoon class nuclear-powered submarine caught on the surface from astern. One of three of the world's largest ever class of submarine (30,000 tons) carrying twenty SS NX 20 missiles each with 7 independently targetted nuclear warheads—sufficient to obliterate any country within 5000 miles of her. (See also page 122)

total size of the USSR's army in mid-1984 was estimated by the International Institute of Strategic Studies at 1,850,000 men, believed to be organised into 193 divisions. The strength of the British Army was 163,003 at 1 Jan 1985. The NATO agreement requires not less than 55,000 in West Germany. The basic strength maintained in Northern Ireland is in excess of 10,000. Between 1969 and 1 Jan 1984 2365 people have been killed.

Oldest soldiers
The oldest old soldier of all time was probably John B. Salling of the army of the Confederate States of America and the last accepted survivor of the US Civil War (1861–5). He died in Kingsport, Tennessee, USA on 16 Mar 1959, aged 113 years 1 day. The oldest Chelsea pensioner, based *only* on the evidence of his tombstone, was the 111-year-old William Hiseland (b. 6 Aug 1620, d. 7 Feb 1732). The longest serving British soldier has been Field Marshal Sir William Maynard Gomm GCB (1784–1875), who was an ensign in 1794 and the Constable of the Tower at his death aged 91.

Youngest soldiers
Marshal Duke of Caxias (b. 25 Aug 1803, d. 7 May 1880), Brazilian military hero and statesman, entered his infantry regiment at the age of 5 in 1808.

Dr Kenneth Vernon Bailey MC (b. 14 Dec 1897) served as a 2nd Lieutenant in the 2/8th Btn Manchester Regt. for some 6 weeks before his 17th birthday. Probably the youngest enlistment in the 20th century was of William Frederick Price, (b. 1 June 1891), who was enlisted into the Army at Aldershot on 23 May 1903, aged 11 years 356 days.

Youngest conscripts
President Francisco Macias Nguema of Equatorial Guinea decreed in March 1976 compulsory military service for all boys between 7 and 14. Any parent refusing to hand over his or her son 'will be imprisoned or shot'.

Tallest soldiers
The tallest soldier of all time was Väinö Myllyrinne (1909–63) who was inducted into the Finnish Army when he was 7 ft 3 in *2,21 m* and

later grew to 8 ft 1¼ in *2,47 m*. The British Army's tallest soldier was Benjamin Crow who was signed on at Lichfield in November 1947 when he was 7 ft 1 in *2,15 m* tall. Edward Evans (1924–58), who later grew to 7 ft 8½ in *235 cm*, was in the Army when he was 6 ft 10 in *2,08 m*.

British regimental records
The oldest regular regiment in the British Army is the Royal Scots, raised in French service in 1633, though the Buffs (Royal East Kent Regiment) can trace back their origin to independent companies in Dutch pay as early as 1572. The Coldstream Guards, raised in 1650, were, however, placed on the establishment of the British Army before the Royal Scots and the Buffs. The oldest armed body in the United Kingdom is the Queen's Bodyguard of the Yeomen of the Guard formed in 1485. The Honourable Artillery Company, formed from the Fraternity of St. George, Southwark, received its charter from Henry VIII in 1537 but this lapsed until re-formed in 1610. The infantry regiment with most battle honours is The Queen's Lancashire Regiment with 188.

The most senior regiment of the Reserve Army is The Royal Monmouthshire Royal Engineers (Militia) formed on 21 Mar 1577 and never disbanded, with battle honours at Dunkirk, 1940 and Normandy, 1944.

Greatest mutiny
In the 1914–18 War 56 French divisions comprising some 650,000 men and their officers refused orders on the Western Front sector of General Nivelle in April 1917 after the failure of his offensive.

Longest march
The longest march in military history was the famous Long March by the Chinese Communists in 1934–5. In 368 days, of which 268 days were days of movement, from October to October, their force of 90,000 covered 6000 miles *9650 km* from Kiangsi to Yenan in Shensi *via* Yünnan. They crossed 18 mountain ranges and six major rivers and lost all but 22,000 of their force in continual rear-guard actions against Nationalist Kuo-min-tang (KMT) forces.

On the night of 12–13 Sept 1944 a team of nine

from B Company 4th Infantry Battalion of the Irish Army made a night march of 42 miles *67,59 km* in full battle order carrying 40 lb *18,1 kg* in 11 hr 49 min. The record road march (11 men with 40 lb *18,14 kg* packs) over a marathon (26 miles 385 yds *42 195 m*) in 6 hr 26 min 23.22 sec by Company D, 1st Battn US Army Intelligence School, Fort Devens, Mass. on 30 June 1983.

Air Forces *Oldest*

The earliest autonomous air force is the Royal Air Force whose origin began with the Royal Flying Corps (created 13 May 1912); the Air Battalion of the Royal Engineers (1 Apr 1911) and the Corps of Royal Engineers Balloon Section (1878) which was first operational in Botswana (then Bechuanaland) in 1884. The Prussian Army used a balloon near Strasbourg, France as early as 24 Sept 1870.

Largest

The greatest Air Force of all time was the United States Army Air Corps (now called the US Air Force), which had 79,908 aircraft in July 1944 and 2,411,294 personnel in March 1944. The US Air Force including strategic air forces had 592,000 personnel and 3700 combat aircraft in mid-1983. The USSR Air Force is undergoing massive reorganisation but best estimates indicate 465,000 men in mid-1984. It had 5950 combat aircraft and 2300 armed helicopters. In addition, the USSR's Offensive Strategic Rocket Forces had about 325,000 operational personnel in mid-1983. The strength of the Royal Air Force was 93,230 with 620 combat aircraft on 1 Jan 1985.

BOMBS

Heaviest

The heaviest conventional bomb ever used operationally was the Royal Air Force's 'Grand Slam', weighing 22,000 lb *9975 kg* and measuring 25 ft 5 in *7,74 m* long, dropped on Bielefeld railway viaduct, Germany, on 14 Mar 1945. In 1949 the United States Air Force tested a bomb weighing 42,000 lb *19 050 kg* at Muroc Dry Lake, California, USA. The heaviest known nuclear bomb has been the 4 tonne 9 megatonne carried by US B-52 bombers. These bombs 3,67 m *12 ft 0½ in* in length were phased out by Jan 1984.

Atomic

The first atom bomb dropped on Japan by the United States in 1945 had an explosive power equivalent to that of 12,500 short tons *12.5 kilotons* of trinitrotoluene ($C_7H_5O_6N_3$), called TNT. Code-named 'Little Boy' it was 10 ft *3,04 m* long and weighed 9000 lb *4080 kg* and burst 1670 ft *509 m* above Hiroshima. The most powerful thermo-nuclear device so far tested is one with a power equivalent of 57,000,000 short tons of TNT, or 57 megatons, detonated by the USSR in the Novaya Zemlya area at 8.33 a.m. GMT on 30 Oct 1961. The shock wave was detected to have circled the world three times, taking 36 hr 27 min for the first circuit. Some estimates put the power of this device at between 62 and 90 megatons. The largest US H-Bomb tested was the 18–22 megaton 'Bravo' at Bikini Atoll, Marshall Islands on 1 Mar 1954. On 9 Aug 1961, Nikita Khrushchyov, then the Chairman of the Council of Ministers of the USSR, declared that the Soviet Union was capable of constructing a 100-megaton bomb, and announced the possession of one in East Berlin, Germany, on 16 Jan 1963. Such a device could make a crater in rock 355 ft *107 m* deep and 1.8 miles *2,9 km* wide and a fireball 46,000 ft or 8.7 miles *13,9 km* in diameter.

Atom bomb theory began with Einstein's publication of the $E = mc^2$ formula in *Annalen der Physik* in Leipzig on 14 May 1907. This postulated that the latent energy of 1 gram of matter was 89,875,517,873.781 dynes. It became a practicality with the mesothorium experiments of Otto Hahn (1879–1968), Fritz Strassman (b. 1902) and Lise Meitner (1878–1968) on 17 Dec 1938. Work started in the USSR on atomic bombs in June 1942 although their first chain reaction was not achieved until December 1945 by Dr Igor Vasilyevich Kurchatov (1903–1960). The concept of a thermo-nuclear fusion bomb was that of Edward Teller (b. 1908) in 1942. Development was ordered by President Truman on 30 Jan 1950 and code-named 'Super'. The bomb only became practical as a result of a calculation by Stanislaw Ulam (b. Poland 13 Apr 1909).

Largest nuclear weapons

The most powerful ICBM are the USSR's SS-18s (Model 5) believed to be armed with ten 750 kiloton MIRVs (multiple independently-targetable re-entry vehicles). Models 1 and 3 have a single 20 megaton warhead. The US Minuteman III has 3 MIRVs each of 335 kiloton force.

No official estimate has been published of the potential power of the device known as Doomsday, but this far surpasses any tested weapon. If it were practicable to construct, it is mooted that a 50,000 megaton cobalt-salted device could wipe out the entire human race except people deep underground and who did not emerge for at least five years.

'Star Wars'

The first reported successful 'high frontier' interception test in outer space by the United States Strategic Defence Initiative occurred over the Pacific on 10 June 1984.

Largest 'conventional' explosion

The largest use of conventional explosive was for the demolition of the fortifications and U Boat pens at Heligoland on 18 Apr 1947. A net charge of 3797 tons *4061 tonnes* (7122 tonnes gross) was detonated by Commissioned Gunner E. C. Jellis of the RN team headed by Lt F. T. Woosnam RN aboard *HMS Lasso* lying 9 miles *14,5 km* out to sea.

Most bombed country

The most heavily bombed country in the world has been Laos. It has been estimated that between May 1964 and 26 Feb 1973 some 2½ million tons of bombs of all kinds were dropped along the North to South Ho Chi Minh Trail supply route to South Vietnam.

TANKS

Earliest

The first tank was 'No 1 Lincoln' modified to become '*Little Willie*' built by William Foster & Co Ltd of Lincoln. It first ran on 6 Sept 1915. Tanks were first taken into action by the Heavy Section, Machine-Gun Corps, which later became the Royal Tank Corps, at the battle of Flers-Courcelette in France, on 15 Sept 1916. The Mark I Male tank, armed with a pair of 6-pounder guns and 4 machine-guns, weighed 28 tons *28,4 tonnes* and was driven by a motor developing 105 hp which gave it a maximum road speed of 3 to 4 mph *4,8–6,4 km/h*.

Heaviest and fastest

The heaviest tank ever constructed was the German Panzer Kampfwagen Maus II, which weighed 189 tons *192 tonnes*. By 1945 it had reached only the experimental stage and was not proceeded with.

The heaviest operational tank used by any army was the 74 ton *75,2 tonnes* 13-man French Char de Rupture 2C bis of 1922. It carried a 155 mm howitzer and had two 250 hp engines giving a maximum speed of 8 mph *12 km/h*. The world's most heavily armed tank since 1972 has been the Soviet T-72 with a 125 mm *4.92 in* high velocity gun. The British AVRE 'Centurion' has a 165 mm *6.5 in* low velocity demolition gun. The world's fastest tank is the British Scorpion AFV which can touch 50 mph *80,5 km/h* with 75% payload.

The heaviest British armoured vehicle ever built was the 78-ton *79 tonnes* prototype 'Tortoise'. With a crew of seven and a designed speed of 12 mph *19 km/h*, this tank had a width 2 in *5 cm* less than that of the one-time operational 65-ton *66 tonnes* 'Conqueror'.

GUNS

Earliest

Although it cannot be accepted as proved, the best opinion is that the earliest guns were constructed in North Africa, possibly by Arabs, in *c.* 1250. The earliest representation of an English gun is contained in an illustrated manuscript dated 1326 at Oxford. The earliest anti-aircraft gun was an artillery piece on a high angle mounting used in the Franco-Prussian War of 1870 by the Prussians against French balloons.

Largest

The two most massive guns ever constructed were used by the Germans in the siege of Sevastopol on the Eastern Front. They were of a calibre of 800 mm *31.5 in* with barrels 28,87 m *94 ft 8½ in* long and named *Dore* and *Gustav*. Their remains were discovered, one near Metzenhof, Bavaria in Aug 1945 and the other in the Soviet zone. They were built by Krupp as railway guns carried on 24 cars two of which had 40 wheels each. The whole assembly of the gun was 42,9 m *141 ft* long and weighed 1323 tons *1344 tonnes* with a crew of 1500. The range for an 8¼ ton projectile was 29 miles *46,67 km*.

During the 1914–18 war the British Army used a gun of 18 in *457 mm* calibre. The barrel alone weighed 125 tons *127 tonnes*. In World War II the 'Bochebuster', a train-mounted howitzer with a calibre of 18 in *457 mm* firing a 2500 lb *1133 kg* shell to a maximum range of 22,800 yd *20 850 m*, was used from 1940 onwards as part of the Kent coast defences.

Greatest range

The greatest range ever attained by a gun was achieved by the HARP (High Altitude Research Project) gun consisting of two 16.5 in *419 mm* calibre barrels in tandem 36,4 m *119.4 ft* long weighing 150 tonnes/*tons* at Yuma, Arizona, USA. On 19 Nov 1966 an 84 kg *185 lb* projectile was fired to an altitude of 180 km *111.8 miles* or *590,550 ft*. The static V3 underground firing tubes built in 50 degree shafts near Mimoyecques, near Calais, France to bombard London were never operative.

The famous long range gun, which shelled Paris in World War I, was the *Kaiser Wilhelm geschütz* with a calibre of 220 mm *8.66 in*, a designed range of 79.5 miles *127,9 km* and an achieved range of 76 miles *122 km* from the Forest of Cérpy in March 1918. The Big Berthas were mortars of 420 mm *16.53 in* calibre and with a range of less than 9 miles *14 500 m*.

Mortars

The largest mortars ever constructed were Mallets mortar (Woolwich Arsenal, London, 1857), and the 'Little David' of World War II, made in the USA. Each had a calibre of 36¼ in

920 mm, but neither was ever used in action. The heaviest mortar used was the tracked German 600 mm *23.6 in* siege piece known as 'Karl' before Stalingrad, USSR.

Largest cannon

The highest calibre cannon ever constructed is the *Tsar Puchka* (King of Cannons), now housed in the Kremlin, Moscow, USSR. It was built in the 16th century with a bore of 920 mm *36.2 in* and a barrel 10 ft 5 in *3,18 m* long. It weighs 2400 *pouds* (*sic*) or 40 tonnes. The Turks fired up to seven shots per day from a bombard 26 ft *7,92 m* long, with an internal calibre of 42 in *1066 mm* against the walls of Constantinople (now Istanbul) from 12 Apr to 29 May 1453. It was dragged by 60 oxen and 200 men and fired a 1200 lb *543 kg* stone cannon ball.

Military engines

The largest military catapults, or onagers, could throw a missile weighing 60 lb *27 kg* a distance of 500 yd *457 m*.

Conscientious Objector *Most Obdurate*

The only Conscientious Objector to be 6 times court martialled in World War II was Gilbert Lane of Wallington, Surrey. He served 31 months detention and 183 days imprisonment.

Nuclear Delivery Vehicles

As of 1 Jan 1984 the USSR deployed 2524 strategic nuclear delivery vehicles or 274 above the SALT II contractual ceiling. The USA on the same date deployed 1896 vehicles or 354 below the 2250 SALT II limit.

5. JUDICIAL

LEGISLATION AND LITIGATION

Statutes *Oldest*

The earliest surviving judicial code was that of King Ur-Hammu during the third dynasty of Ur, Iraq, in *c.* 2110 BC. The oldest English statute in the Statute Book is a section of the Statute of Marlborough of 1267, retitled in 1948 'The Distress Act, 1267'. Some statutes enacted by Henry II (d. 1189) and earlier kings are even more durable as they have been assimilated into the Common Law. An extreme example is Ine's Law concerning the administration of shires. Ine reigned 689–726 AD.

Longest in the United Kingdom

Measured in bulk the longest statute of the United Kingdom, is the Income Corporation Taxes Act, 1970, which ran to 540 sections, 15 schedules and 670 pages. It is 1½ in *37 mm* thick and costs £8.00. However, its 540 sections are surpassed in number by the 748 of the Merchant Shipping Act, 1894. Of old statutes, 31 George III XIV, the Land Tax Act of 1791, written on parchment, consists of 780 skins forming a roll 1170 ft *360 m* long.

Shortest

The shortest statute is the Parliament (Qualification of Women) Act, 1918, which runs to 27 operative words—'A woman shall not be disqualified by sex or marriage from being elected to or sitting or voting as a Member of the Commons House of Parliament'. Section 2 contains a further 14 words giving the short title.

Most inexplicable

Certain passages in several Acts have always defied interpretation and the most inexplicable must be a matter of opinion. A Judge of the Court of Session of Scotland once sent the Editor his candidate which reads, 'In the Nuts (unground), (other than ground nuts) Order, the expression nuts shall have reference to such nuts, other than ground nuts, as would but for this amending Order not qualify as nuts (unground) (other than ground nuts) by reason of their being nuts (unground).'

Earliest English patent

The earliest of all known English patents was that granted by Henry VI in 1449 to Flemish-born John of Utyman for making the coloured glass required for the windows of Eton College. The peak number of applications for patents filed in the United Kingdom in any one year was 63,614 in 1969. The shortest, concerning a harrow attachment, of 48 words was filed on 14 May 1956 while the longest, comprising 2318 pages of text and 495 pages of drawings, was filed on 31 Mar 1965 by IBM to cover a computer.

Most protracted litigation

The longest contested law suit ever recorded ended in Poona, India on 28 Apr 1966, when Balasaheb Patloji Thorat received a favourable judgement on a suit filed by his ancestor Maloji Thorat 761 years earlier in 1205. The points at issue were rights of presiding over public functions and precedences at religious festivals.

The dispute over the claim of the Prior and Convent (now the Dean and Chapter) of Durham Cathedral to administer the spiritualities of the diocese during a vacancy in the See grew fierce in 1283. It flared up again in 1672 and 1890; an attempt in November 1975 to settle the issue, then 692 years old, was unsuccessful. Neither side admit the legitimacy of writs of appointment issued by the other even though identical persons are named.

Fastest trial

The law's shortest delay occurred in Duport Steel and Others *v.* Sirs and Others heard in the High Court on 25 Jan 1980; the appeal was heard on 26 Jan and the appeal heard in the House of Lords on 1 Feb (am) with the decision given pm.

Longest trial

The longest trial in criminal history was *People of the State of California v Angelo Buono, Jr.* involving 10 charges of the Hillside murders of young women from 18 Oct 1977 to Feb 1978. The jury trial took 345 trial days over 2 years 2 days (16 Nov 1981–18 Nov 1983) with a 57,079 page transcript, 400 witnesses and 2000 exhibits. Judge Ronald M. George imposed nine sentences of life without parole on 9 Jan 1984.

Longest British trials

The longest trial in the annals of British justice was the Tichborne personation case. The civil trial began on 11 May 1871, lasted 103 days and collapsed on 6 Mar 1872. The criminal trial went on for 188 days, resulting in a sentence on 28 Feb 1874 for two counts of perjury (two 7 year consecutive terms of imprisonment with hard labour) on the London-born Arthur Orton, *alias* Thomas Castro (1834–98), who claimed to be Roger Charles Tichborne (1829–54), the elder brother of Sir Alfred Joseph Doughty-Tichborne, 11th Bt (1839–66). The whole case thus spanned 1025 days. The jury were out for only 30 minutes.

The impeachment of Warren Hastings (1732–1818), which began in 1788, dragged on for seven years until 23 Apr 1795, but the trial lasted only 149 days. He was appointed a member of the Privy Council in 1814.

The fraud case *R v Bouzaglo and others* ended before Judge Brian Gibbens on 1 May 1981 having lasted 274 days. They appealed on 10 Dec 1981. Trial costs were estimated at £2.5 million.

The Scot Jack Malloch, who in 1971 won a case as a litigant in person in the House of Lords. (See below)

The fluoridation case *McColl v Strathclyde Regional Council* before Lord Jauncey lasted 204 days ending on 27 July 1982.

Murder

The longest murder trial in Britain was that at the Old Bailey, London of Reginald Dudley, 51, and Robert Maynard, 46 in the Torso Murder of Billy Moseley and Micky Cornwall which ran before Mr Justice Swanwick from 11 Nov 1976 to 17 June 1977 with 136 trial days. Both men were sentenced to life (minimum 15 years) imprisonment. The costs were estimated to exceed £500,000 and the evidence 3,500,000 words.

Longest Tribunal

Divorce

The longest trial of a divorce case in Britain was *Gibbons v. Gibbons and Roman and Halperin*. On 19 Mar 1962, after 28 days, Mr Alfred George Boyd Gibbons was granted a decree *nisi* against his wife Dorothy for adultery with Mr John Halperin of New York City, NY, USA.

Shortest trials

The shortest recorded British murder hearings were *R. v. Murray* on 28 Feb 1957 and *R. v. Cawley* at Winchester assizes on 14 Dec 1959. The proceedings occupied only 30 sec on each occasion.

Litigants in Person

Since the Union of the Parliaments in 1707 the only Scot to win an appeal in person before the House of Lords has been Mr Jack Malloch, an Aberdeen Schoolmaster. In 1971 he was restored to his employment with costs under the dormant but operative Teachers Act, 1882 securing also a professional status in law for all qualified Scottish teachers.

Dr Mark Feldman, a podiatric surgeon, of Lauderhill, Florida became the first litigant in person to secure 7 figures ($1 million) before a jury in compensatory and punitive damages in Sept 1980. The case concerned conspiracy and fraud alleged against 6 other doctors.

Longest address

The longest address in a British court was in *Globe and Phoenix Gold Mining Co. Ltd. v. Amalgamated Properties of Rhodesia*. Mr William

Henry Upjohn, ᴋᴄ (1853–1941) concluded his speech on 22 Sept 1916, having addressed the court for 45 days.

Highest bail *World*
The highest amount ever demanded as bail was $46,500,000 (*then £16,608,333*) against Antonio De Angelis in a civil damages suit by the Harbor Tank Storage Co. filed in the Superior Court, Jersey City, New Jersey, USA on 16 Jan 1964 in the Salad Oil Swindle. He was released on 4 June 1973. Hassen Ebtehaj, later Chairman of the Iranian Bank in Teheran, was in 1967 granted bail in excess of $50 million.

Great Britain
The highest bail figure in a British court is £325,000 each, granted to Roy Garner and Kenneth Howard of North London by the High Court on 31 Mar 1983. They had been in custody after arrest at Gatwick Airport in connection with trading in Krugerrands.

Longest arbitration
The longest arbitration (under the 1950 Act) on record has been the Royce Arbitration. It lasted 239 days and concerned the Milchell Construction Co. and the East Anglian Regional Hospital Board over the building of Peterborough Hospital.

The longest case before an Industrial Tribunal has been 44 days during more than 13 months (2 May 1977–29 June 1978) when the columnist C. Gordon Tether contested the fairness of his dismissal by *The Financial Times* in person.

Longest Inquiry
The longest and most expensive public inquiry has been that over the projected £1,200 million Sizewell B nuclear power station, Suffolk under Sir Frank Layfield, ǫᴄ. It began on 11 Jan 1983 and finished after 340 days of hearings on 7 Mar 1985 in The Snape Maltings, Aldeburgh. Shorthand writers transcribed 16 million words from 195 witnesses. The cost to public funds was £2,407,000.

Dr Sidney Gee winner of the English defamation record for an individual with £100,007 damages from the BBC. (See Column 2)

Best attended trial
The greatest attendance at any trial was that of Major Jesús Sosa Blanco, aged 51, for an alleged 108 murders. At one point in the 12½ hr trial (5.30 p.m. to 6 a.m., 22–23 Jan 1959), 17,000 people were present in the Havana Sports Palace, Cuba. He was executed on 18 Feb 1959.

Greatest damages *Personal injury World*
The greatest personal injury damages ever awarded were to a male child of undisclosed identity born in 1979 at the US Army's Le Herman General Hospital in a medical malpractice suit. If the child which had 'total cerebral palsy' lives out his expectation of life the potential US federal government payment will reach $70 million. Reports of 30 Sept 1983 did not disclose the name of the US Army doctor.

On 24 Nov 1983 a jury in Corpus Christi, Texas, USA awarded punitive damages of $106 million *£75 million* against the Ford Motor Co for alleged design faults in the Ford Mustang II in which Bevary Durrill, 20, died in 1974. An appeal is pending.

Great Britain
On 28 June 1985 Mrs Angela McCusker, 27, of Co. Fermanagh was awarded £500,000 in damages in Belfast High Court for severe brain damage and other injuries received in a car crash with a lorry. She sued her husband, who was driving and the lorry driver and lorry owners.

Breach of contract
The greatest damages ever awarded for a breach of contract were £610,392, awarded on 16 July 1930 to the Bank of Portugal against the printers Waterlow & Sons Ltd, of London, arising from their unauthorized printing of 580,000 five-hundred escudo notes in 1925. This award was upheld in the House of Lords on 28 Apr 1932. One of the perpetrators, Arthur Virgilio Alves Reis, served 16 years (1930–46) in gaol.

Breach of promise
The largest sum involved in a breach of promise suit in the United Kingdom was £50,000, accepted in 1913 by Miss Daisy Markham, *alias* Mrs Annie Moss (d. 20 Aug 1962, aged 76), in settlement against the 6th Marquess of Northampton ᴅsᴏ (1885–1978).

Defamation *World*
A sum of $16,800,000 (*£6,720,000*) was awarded to Dr John J. Wild, 58, at the Hennepin District Court, Minnesota, USA, on 30 Nov 1972 against The Minnesota Foundation and others for defamation, bad-faith termination of a contract, interference with professional business relationship and $10.8 million in punitive damages. The Supreme Court of Minnesota granted an option of a new trial or a $1.5 million *remittitur* to Dr Wild on 10 Jan 1975. There was a no-disclosure clause in the settlement. The $39.6 million awarded in Columbus, Ohio on 1 Mar 1980 to Robert Guccione, publisher of *Penthouse*, for defamation against Lowry Flynt, publisher of *Hustler* was reduced by Judge Craig Wright to $4 million on 17 Apr 1980. The hearing ended in May 1982 with *Penthouse* being cleared of libel.

The greatest damages for defamation ever awarded in the United Kingdom have been £327,000 in the Courts in Edinburgh in favour of Capital Life Assurance Co against the *Scottish Daily Record* and the *Sunday Mail* for articles published in the latter in 1975.

The most expensive defamation trial in Great Britain has been the 87 day long case of *Gee v British Broadcasting Corporation* which ran before Rt Hon Lord Justice Croom-Johnson, ᴘ.ᴄ. ᴅsᴄ, from 22 Oct 1984 to 2 May 1985. The costs

have been estimated at £1.5 million excluding the BBC's internal costs over the 681 days from the offending transmission of *That's Life* on 26 June 1983. Dr Gee was in the witness stand for 27 days but received a record settlement of £100,007.

A $640 million libel suit was brought by the California resort La Costa against *Penthouse* and its publisher in March 1975. In May 1982 a jury found for the magazine. In July their verdict was set aside by a California judge, who was then removed from the case. Costs exceed $10 million to date.

Greatest compensation for Wrongful Imprisonment
William De Palma (b. 1938) of Whittier, California, agreed to a $750,000 (*then £340,000*) settlement for 16 months wrongful imprisonment in McNeil Island Federal Prison, on 12 Aug 1975 after a 15 year sentence for armed robbery in Buena Park on forged fingerprint evidence in 1968.

The greatest Crown compensation in Britain for wrongful imprisonment has been £17,500 paid to Laszlo Virag, 35, who had been sentenced to 10 years imprisonment at Gloucester assizes in 1969 for theft and shooting and wounding a police officer. His acceptance of this sum was announced on 23 Dec 1974 after his having been released in April 1974 on grounds of mistaken identification.

Greatest Alimony
The highest alimony awarded by a court has been $2,261,000 (*then £983,000*) against George Storer Sr, 74, in favour of his third wife Dorothy, 73, in Miami, Florida on 29 Oct 1974. Mr Storer, a broadcasting executive, was also ordered to pay his ex-wife's attorney $200,000 (*then £86,950*) in fees.

Greatest Alimony Suit
Belgian born Sheika Dena Al-Fassi, 23, filed the highest ever alimony claim of $3000 million (*then £1666 million*) against her former husband Sheik Mohammed Al-Fassi, 28, of the Saudi Arabia royal family in Los Angeles, California in February 1982. Mr Marvin Mitchelson explaining the size of the settlement claim alluded to the Sheik's wealth which included 14 homes in Florida alone and numerous private aircraft. On 14 June 1983 she was awarded $81 million (*then £52 million*) and declared she would be 'very very happy' if she was able to collect.

Greatest divorce settlement
The highest High Court divorce award received was £700,000 on 13 Nov 1980 for 'Mrs P' after 23 years of marriage against her former husband from Jersey from whom she had been receiving £6000 per annum. In *Edgar v Edgar* in 1980, £750,000 was awarded but this was set aside on appeal when Mrs Edgar accepted a much lesser figure.

Patent case
The greatest settlement ever made in a patent infringement suit is $55.8 million (*£37.2 million*) in Pfizer Inc v International Rectifier Corp. and Rochelle Laboratories over the antibiotic dioxycycline on 5 July 1983.

Largest suit
The highest amount of damages ever sought to date is $675,000,000,000,000 (then equivalent to 10 times the US national wealth) in a suit by Mr I. Walton Bader brought in the US District Court, New York City on 14 Apr 1971 against General Motors and others for polluting all 50 states.

Largest Law firm
The world's largest law firm is Baker & Mc-

Kenzie with 600 lawyers in 29 countries. It was founded in Chicago in 1949.

Highest costs
The trial judge in *R* v. *Sinclair and others* (the handless corpse murder) ordered the international drug trafficker Alexander James Sinclair, 36 of N.Z. (sentenced to a minimum term of 20 years for the murder of Marty Johnstone found in a quarry at Chorley, Lancashire) to pay £1 million for the Crown's costs.

The most expensive man-hunt in police history was one costing £4 million terminated on 13 June 1981 with the arrest of Peter William Sutcliffe, known as the Yorkshire Ripper, in Sheffield, South Yorkshire. His trial at the Old Bailey, London, cost £250,000 and resulted in his being sentenced to a minimum of 30 years for 13 murders and 7 attempted murders which orphaned 25 children.

Longest lease
The longest lease on record is one concerning a plot for a sewage tank adjoining Columb Barrcks, Mullinger, County Meath, Ireland signed on 3 Dec 1868 for 10,000,000 years. It is to be assumed that a future civil servant will bring up the matter for review early in AD 10,001,868.

Greatest lien
The greatest lien ever imposed by a court is 40,000 million lire (*then £27 million*) on 9 Apr 1974 upon Vittorio and Ida Riva in Milan for back taxes allegedly due on a chain of cotton mills around Turin, Italy.

Wills *Shortest*
The shortest valid will in the world is 'Vše zene', the Czech for 'All to wife', written and dated 19 Jan 1967 by Herr Karl Tausch of Langen, Hesse, Germany. The shortest will contested but subsequently admitted to probate in English law was the case of *Thorne v. Dickens* in 1906. It consisted of the three words 'All for Mother' in which 'mother' was not his mother but his wife. The smallest will preserved by the Record Keeper is an identity disc 1½ in *3.8 cm* in diameter belonging to A.B. William Skinner killed aboard HMS Indefatigable at Jutland in 1916. It had 40 words engraved on it including the signatures of two witnesses and was proved on 24 June 1922.

Longest
The longest will on record was that of Mrs Frederica Evelyn Stilwell Cook proved at Somerset House, London on 2 Nov 1925. It consisted of four bound volumes containing 95,940 words.

Judges *Most Durable*
The oldest recorded active judge was Judge Albert R. Alexander (1859–1966) of Plattsburg, Missouri, USA. He was the magistrate and probate judge of Clinton County until his retirement aged 105 years 8 months on 9 July 1965.

United Kingdom
The greatest recorded age at which any British judge has sat on a bench was 93 years 9 months in the case of Sir William Francis Kyffin Taylor, GBE, KC (*later* Lord Maenan), who was born on 9 July 1854 and retired as presiding judge of the Liverpool Court of Passage in April 1948, having held that position since 1903. Sir Salathiel Lovell (1619–1713) was, however, still sitting when he died on 3 May 1713 in his 94th or 95th year. The greatest age at which a House of Lords judgement has been given was 92 in the case of the 1st Earl of Halsbury (b. 3 Sept 1823) in 1916. Lord Chief Baron of Exchequer in Ireland, the Rt. Hon. Christopher Palles (1831–1920) served for 42 years from 17 Feb 1874 till 1916.

Sir Ernest Wild KC (b. 1869), who in 1897 became England's youngest ever Judge when aged 28. (See below Column 2)

Master of the Rolls
The longest tenure of the Mastership of the Rolls since the office was inaugurated in 1286 has been 24 years 7 months by David de Wollore from 2 July 1346 to 27 March 1371. The longest tenure since the Supreme Court Judicature Act, 1881 has been that of 20 years by Lord Denning (b. 23 Jan 1899) from 1962 to 30 Sept 1982. He had been first appointed a high court judge in 1944. William Morland held the office for 77 days while in 1629 Sir Humphrey May died 'soon after' his appointment on 10 April.

Judge *Youngest*
No collated records on the ages of judicial appointments exist. However David Elmer Ward had to await the legal age of 21 before taking office after nomination in 1932 as Judge of the County Court at Fort Myers, Florida, USA.

The youngest certain age at which any English judge has been appointed is 28, in the case of Sir Ernest Wild, KC (b. 1 Jan 1869) who was appointed Judge of the Norwich Guildhall Court of Record in 1897 aged 28. The lowest age of appointment this century has been 42 years 2 months of Lord Hodson in 1937.

Most Judges
Lord Balmerino was found guilty of treason by 137 of his peers on 28 July 1746. In *R* v. *Canning* at the Old Bailey in 1754 Elizabeth Canning was deported to Connecticut for wilful perjury by 19 judges voting 10 to 9. In *Young, James and Webster* v. *United Kingdom*, the British Rail 'Closed Shop' case, before the European Court of Human Rights in Strasbourg on 3–4 Mar 1981, Mr David Calcutt QC won a judgement for the railwaymen by 18 to 3.

Youngest English QC
The earliest age at which a barrister has taken silk this century is 33 years 8 months in the case of Mr (later the Rt Hon Sir) Francis Raymond Evershed (1899–1966) in April 1933. He was later Lord Evershed, Master of the Rolls. Buller (see above) was nepotistically given silk aged 31, being a nephew of the then Lord Chancellor, Lord Bathurst.

Multimillionaire Melvin M. Belli (b. 30 July

1907) took display advertisements in the press on his 77th birthday to celebrate his 'unparalleled 50-year career in law defending the injured and the poor'.

Most successful
Sir Lionel Luckhoo KCMG CBE, senior partner of Luckhoo and Luckhoo of Georgetown, Guyana succeeded in getting his 245th successive murder charge acquittal by 1 Jan 1985.

Most Durable Solicitors
William George (1865–1967), brother of David Lloyd George, passed his preliminary law examination in May 1880 and was practising until December 1966 aged 101 years 9 months. The most durable firm is Thomson, Snell & Passmore of Tonbridge, Kent begun by the Rev Nicholas Hooper, a part-time scrivener in 1570.

CRIME

Mass Killings *China*
The greatest massacre ever imputed by the government of one sovereign nation against the government of another is that of 26,300,000 Chinese during the regime of Mao Tse-tung between 1949 and May 1965. This accusation was made by an agency of the USSR Government in a radio broadcast on 7 Apr 1969. The broadcast broke down the figure into four periods:—2.8 million (1949–52); 3.5 million (1953–7); 6.7 million (1958–60); and 13.3 million (1961–May 1965). The highest reported death figures in single monthly announcements on Peking radio were 1,176,000 in the provinces of Anhwei, Chekiang, Kiangsu, and Shantung, and 1,150,000 in the Central South Provinces. Po I-po, Minister of Finance, is alleged to have stated in the organ *For a lasting peace, for a people's democracy* 'in the past three years (1950–2) we have liquidated more than 2 million bandits'. General Jacques Guillermaz, a French diplomat estimated the total executions between February 1951 and May 1952 at between 1 million and 3 million. In April 1971 the Executive cabinet or *Yuan* of the implacably hostile government of The Republic of China in Taipei, Taiwan announced its official estimate of the mainland death roll in the period 1949–69 as 'at least 39,940,000'. This figure, however, excluded 'tens of thousands' killed in the Great Proletarian Cultural Revolution, which began in late 1966. The Walker Report published by the US Senate Committee of the Judiciary in July 1971 placed the parameters of the total death roll within China since 1949 between 32.25 and 61.7 million. An estimate of 63.7 million was published by Jean-Pierre Dujardin in *Figaro* magazine of 19–25 Nov 1978.

USSR
The total death roll in the Great Purge, or *Yezhovshchina*, in the USSR, in 1936–8 has, not surprisingly, never been published. Evidence of its magnitude may be found in population statistics which show a deficiency of males from *before* the outbreak of the 1941–5 war. The reign of terror was administered by the *Narodny Kommissariat Vnutrennykh Del* (NKVD), or People's Commissariat of Internal Affairs, the Soviet security service headed by Nikolay Ivanovich Yezhov (1895–1939), described by Nikita Khrushchev in 1956 as a 'degenerate'. S. V. Utechin, regarded estimates of 8,000,000 or 10,000,000 victims as 'probably not exaggerations'. On 17 Aug 1942 Stalin indicated to Churchill in Moscow that 10 million *kulaks* had been liquidated for resisting the collectivization of their farms. Nobel Prize winner Alexander Solzhenitsyn estimated the loss of life from State repression and terrorism from October 1917 to December 1959 under Lenin, Stalin and Khrushchev at 66,700,000.

Nazi Germany
The best estimate of the number of Jewish victims of the Holocaust or the genocidal 'Final Solution' or *Endlösung* ordered by Adolf Hitler (1889–1945) in April 1941 and continued into May 1945 is 5.8 million. Obersturmbannführer (Lt-Col) Karl Adolf Eichmann (b. Solingen, W. Germany 19 Mar 1906) of the SS was hanged in a small room inside Ramleh Prison, near Tel Aviv, Israel, at just before midnight (local time) on 31 May 1962, for his complicity in the deaths of an indeterminably massive number of Jews.

At the SS (*Schutzstaffel*) extermination camp (*Vernichtungslager*) known as Auschwitz-Birkenau (Oświęcim-Brzezinka), near Oświęcim (Auschwitz), in southern Poland, where a minimum of 920,000 people (Soviet estimate is 4,000,000) were exterminated from 14 June 1940 to 18 Jan 1945, the greatest number killed in a day was 6000. The man who operated the release of the 'Zyklon B' cyanide pellets into the gas chambers there during this time was Sgt Major Moll (variously Mold). The Nazi (*Nationalsozialistische Deutsche Arbeiterpartei*) Commandant during the period 1940–3 was Rudolph Franz Ferdinand Höss who was tried in Warsaw from 11 Mar to 2 Apr 1947 and hanged, aged 47, at Oświęcim on 15 Apr 1947.

Forced labour
No official figures have been published of the death roll in Corrective Labour Camps in the USSR, first established in 1918. The total number of such camps was known to be more than 200 in 1946 but in 1956 many were converted to less severe Corrective Labour Colonies. An estimate published in the Netherlands puts the death roll between 1921 and 1960 at 19,000,000. The camps were administered by the *Cheka* until 1922, the OGPU (1922–34), the NKVD (1934–46), the MVD (1946–53) and the KGB (Komitet Gosudarstvennoi Bezopasnostc) since 1953. A study published in 1985 estimated that there are 289 labour camp zones with a population of 4½ million.

In China there are no published official statistics on the numbers undergoing *Lao Jiao* (Education through Labour) nor *Lao Dong Gai Zao* (Reform through manual labour). An estimate published by Bao Ruo-wang, who were released in 1964 due to his father having been a Corsican, was 16,000,000 which then approached 3 per cent of the population.

Genocide
As a percentage of a nation's total population the worst genocide appears to be that in Kampuchea, formerly Cambodia, according to the Khmer Rouge foreign minister Ieng Sary, more than a third of the 8 million Khmers were killed between 17 Apr 1975 and January 1979. The highest 'class' ideals induced indifference to individual suffering to the point of serving as a warrant for massacre. Under the rule of Saloth Sar *alias* Pol Pot, a founder member of the CPK (Communist Party of Kampuchea, formed in September 1960) towns, money and property were abolished and economical execution by bayonet and club introduced for such offences as falling asleep during the day, asking too many questions, playing non-Communist music, being old and feeble, being the offspring of an 'undesirable' or being too well educated. Deaths at the Tuol Sleng interrogation centre reached 582 in a day.

In Chinese history of the 13th–17th centuries there were three periods of wholesale massacre. The numbers of victims attributed to these events are assertions rather than reliable estimates. The figure put on the Mongolian invasions of northern China in 1210–19 and in 1311–

40 are both of the order of 35 million while the number of victims of the bandit leader Chang Hsien-Chung (*c.* 1605–47), known as the Yellow Tiger, in 1643–47 in the Zechuan province has been put at 40 million.

Saving of Life
The greatest number of people saved from extinction by one man is an estimated 90,000 Jews in Budapest, Hungary from July 1944 to January 1945 by the Swedish diplomat Raoul Wallenberg (b. 4 Aug 1912). After escaping an assassination attempt by the Nazis, he was imprisoned without trial by the Soviet Union. On 6 Feb 1957 Mr Gromyko said Prisoner 'Walenberg' had died in a cell in Lubyanka Jail, Moscow on 16 July 1947. Sighting reports within the Gulag system have persisted for 35 years after his disappearance. He was made an Honorary Citizen of the USA on 5 Oct 1981 and in March 1984 there was an agitation in Hungary to restore his removed statue to St Stephan's Park, in Budapest.

Largest criminal organization
The largest syndicate of organized crime is the Mafia or La Cosa Nostra, which has infiltrated the executive, judiciary and legislature of the United States. It consists of some 3000 to 5000 individuals in 25 'families' federated under 'The Commission', with an annual turnover in vice, gambling, protection rackets, tobacco, bootlegging, hijacking, narcotics, loan-sharking and prostitution estimated in a US News & World Report of Dec 1982 at $200 billion. The origin in the US dates from 1869 in New Orleans. The biggest Mafia (derived from an arabic expression connoting beauty, excellence allied with bravery) killing was on 11–13 Sept 1931 when 40 mafiosi were liquidated following the murder in New York of Salvatore Maranzano, *Il Capo di Tutti Capi*, on 10 Sept. The greatest breaches of *omerta* (the vow of silence) were by Joseph Valachi who 'sang like a canary' in 1963 and by Tommaso Buschetta, 56 in 1984.

Murder rate *Highest*
The country with the highest recorded murder rate is Brazil, with 104 homicides for each 100,000 of the population in 1983, or 370 per day. A total of 592 deaths was attributed to one Colombian bandit leader, Teófilo ('Sparks') Rojas, aged 27, between 1948 and his death in an ambush near Armenia on 22 Jan 1963. Some sources attribute 3500 slayings to him during La Violencia of 1945–62.

The highest homicide rates recorded in New York City have been 58 in a week in July 1972 and 13 in a day in August 1972. In 1973 the total for Detroit, Michigan (pop. then 1.5 million) was 751. The Chicago Crime Commission published in March 1983 a list of 1081 unsolved gang slayings since 1919.

Lowest
The country with the lowest officially recorded rate in the world is The Maldives with a nil rate among its naturals since its independence in July 1965. In the Indian state of Sikkim, in the Himalayas, murder is, however, practically unknown, while in the Hunza area of Kashmir, in the Karakoram, only one definite case by a Hunzarwal has been recorded since 1900.

Great Britain
In Great Britain the total number of homicides and deaths from injuries purposely inflicted by other persons in the year 1981 was 612. This figure compares with a murder total of 124 in 1937 and 125 in 1958.

Terrorist Outrages
The greatest civilian death toll from a terrorist bomb was 85 killed and 200 injured at the central

railway station, Bologna, Italy on 2 Aug 1980. Pierluigi Pagliai, 28, described as a suspect, was arrested in a shoot-out in Bolivia on 10 Oct 1982.

Most prolific murderers *World*

It was established at the trial of Behram, the Indian thug, that he had strangled at least 931 victims with his yellow and white cloth strip or *ruhmal* in the Oudh district between 1790 and 1840. It has been estimated that at least 2,000,000 Indians were strangled by Thugs (*burtotes*) during the reign of the Thugee (pronounced tugee) cult from 1550 until its final suppression by the British *raj* in 1853. The greatest number of victims ascribed to a murderess has been 650 in the case of Countess Erzsebet Bathory (1560–1614) of Hungary. At her trial which began on 2 Jan 1611 a witness testified to seeing a list of her victims in her own handwriting totalling this number. All were alleged to be young girls from the neighbourhood of her castle at Csejthe where she died on 21 Aug 1614. She had been walled up in her room for the 3½ years after being found guilty.

20th century

Pedro Alonso López (b. Columbia, 1949) known as the 'Columbian Monster', was reported captured by the villagers of Ambato, Ecuador in early March 1980. He admitted to more than 300 murders of pre-teen girls in Colombia, Peru and Ecuador since 1973. The remains of 53 victims of the 110 admitted to in Ecuador were rapidly detected after his confession.

In drunken rampage lasting 8 hours on 26–27 Apr 1982 Policeman Wou Bom-Kon, 27, killed 57 people and wounded 35 with 176 rounds of rifle ammunition and hand grenades in the Kyong Sang-Namdo province of South Korea. He blew himself up with a grenade.

United Kingdom

Six men were each charged with 21 murders at Lancaster Crown Court on 9 June 1975 concerning the bombing of the two Birmingham public houses Mulberry Bush and Tavern in the Town on 21 Nov 1974. They were John Walker, Patrick Hill, Robert Hunter, Noel McIlkenny, William Power and Hugh Callaghan. The Home Office began, in February 1981, to investigate the attribution of 26 deaths between 1973 and 1979 to the self-confessed arsonist Bruce Lee. In January 1981 he was sent to a mental hospital by Leeds Crown Court, but on 14 Mar 1982 he retracted his confessions and on 2 Dec 1983 the Court of Appeal quashed charges of causing 11 of the deaths.

Judith Minna Ward, 25, of Stockport, Cheshire was convicted on 11 separate murder charges on 4 Nov 1974 making 12 in all arising from the explosion in an army coach on the M.62 near Drighlington, West Yorkshire on 4 Feb 1974. Mary Ann Cotton (*née* Robson) (b. 1832, East Rainton, County Durham), hanged in Durham Jail on 24 Mar 1873 is believed to have poisoned 14, possibly 20, people.

Dennis Andrew Nilsen, 37 of 23 Cranley Gardens, Muswell Hill, north London admitted to 15 one at a time murders between Dec 1978 and Feb 1983. He was sentenced to life with a 25 year minimum on 4 Nov 1983 at the Old Bailey by Rt Hon Lord Justice Croom-Johnson PC, DSC for 6 murders and 2 attempted murders both there and at Cricklewood.

Dominic McGlinchey was reported in November 1983 to have admitted to 30 killings in Northern Ireland. He was convicted of murder on 24 Dec 1984. On 7 May 1981 John Thompson of Hackney, London was found guilty at the Old Bailey of the 'specimen' murder by arson of Archibald Campbell and jailed for life. There were 36 other victims at the Spanish Club, Denmark St, London.

'Smelling out'

The greatest 'smelling out' recorded in African history occurred before Shaka (1787–1828) and 30,000 Nguni subjects near the River Umhlatuzana, Zululand (now Natal, South Africa) in March 1824. After 9 hr, over 300 were 'smelt out' as guilty of smearing the Royal *Kraal* with blood, by 150 witch-finders led by the hideous female *isangoma* Nobela. The victims were declared innocent when Shaka admitted to having done the smearing himself to expose the falsity of the power of his diviners. Nobela poisoned herself with atropine ($C_{17}H_{23}NO_3$), but the other 149 witch-finders were thereupon skewered or clubbed to death.

Suicide

The estimated daily rate of suicides throughout the world surpassed 1000 in 1965. The country with the highest suicide rate is Hungary, with 42.6 per 100,000 of the population in 1977. The country with the lowest recorded rate is Jordan with a single case in 1970 and hence a rate of 0.04 per 100,000. In England and Wales there were 4419 suicides in 1981, or an average of 12.1 per day. In the northern hemisphere April and May tend to be peak months.

Mass Suicide

The total number of victims of the mass cyanide poisoning of the People's Temple cult near Port Kaituma, Guyana on 18 Nov 1978 was 913. The leader was the paranoid 'Rev.' Jim Jones of San Francisco, who had deposited 'millions of dollars' overseas.

The volcanic crater of Mt Mihara on an island in Sagami Bay, south of Yokohama was the scene of more than 1000 suicides in 1933–36.

Mass Poisonings

On 1 May 1981 the first victim of the Spanish cooking oil scandal fell ill. On 12 June it was discovered that his cause of death was the use of 'denatured' industrial colza from rape seed. By May 1984 the death toll was over 350 dead with thousands maimed. The manufacturers Ramon and Elias Ferrero await trial in Carabanchel Jail, Madrid.

Robbery

The greatest robbery on record was that of the Reichsbank following Germany's collapse in April/May 1945. The Pentagon in Washington described the event first published in the *Guinness* Book in 1957 as 'an unverified allegation'. *Nazi Gold* by Ian Sayer and Douglas Botting published in 1984 revealed full details and estimated the total haul at current values as £2,500 million.

On 26 Nov 1983 six masked men removed 6,800 bars of gold and platinum in 76 boxes together with diamonds and travellers' cheques worth £26,369,778 from the Brinks-Mat Ltd Unit 7 warehouse at the Heathrow Trading Estate. Michael McAvoy, 32 of East Dulwich and Brian Robinson, 41 of Lewisham were each sentenced to 25 years at the Old Bailey on 3 Dec 1984.

Britain's biggest ever cash robbery was on 4 Apr 1983 from the Security Express headquarters in Curtain Road, Shoreditch, East London. Four of the gang were convicted on 7 June 1985 but only £2 million was traced.

Art

The greatest recorded art robbery by market valuation was the removal of 19 paintings, valued at £8,000,000 taken from Russborough House, Blessington, County Wicklow, Ireland, the home of Sir Alfred and Lady Beit by 4 men and a woman on 26 Apr 1974. They included the £3 million Vermeer 'Lady Writing a Letter with her maid'. The paintings were recovered on 4 May near Glandore, County Cork. Dr Rose Bridgit Dugdale (b. 1941) was convicted. It is arguable that the value of the *Mona Lisa* at the time of its theft from The Louvre, Paris on 21 Aug 1911 was greater than this figure. It was recovered in Italy in 1913 when Vincenzo Perruggia was charged with its theft. On 1 Sept 1964 antiquities reputedly worth £10,000,000 were recovered from 3 warehouses near the Pyramids, Egypt.

Bank

During the extreme civil disorder prior to 22 Jan 1976 in Beirut, Lebanon, a guerilla force blasted the vaults of the British Bank of the Middle East in Bab Idriss and cleared out safe deposit boxes with contents valued by former Finance Minister, Lucien Dahadah, at $50 million and by another source as an 'absolute minimum' of $20 million.

Britain's greatest ever robbery was of 9 certificates of deposit worth more than £10 million from the Bank of Sepah-Iran, Eastcheap, London on 4–5 Dec 1982. A thermic lance was used.

Train

The greatest recorded train robbery occurred between about 3.03 a.m. and 3.27 a.m. on 8 Aug 1963, when a General Post Office mail train from Glasgow, Scotland, was ambushed at Sears Crossing and robbed at Bridego Bridge near Mentmore, Buckinghamshire. The gang escaped with about 120 mailbags containing £2,631,784 worth of bank notes being taken to London for destruction. Only £343,448 was recovered.

Jewels

The greatest recorded theft of jewels was from the bedroom of the 'well-guarded' villa of Prince Abdel Aziz Bin Ahmed Al-Thani near Cannes, France on 24 July 1980 valued at $16,000,000 (*then £7¼ million*). The haul from Bond Jewellers, Conduit St, London W1 on 20 June 1983 was estimated to be £6 million.

Greatest kidnapping ransom

Historically the greatest ransom paid was that for Atahualpa by the Incas to Francisco Pizarro in 1532–3 at Cajamarca, Peru which constituted a hall full of gold and silver worth in modern money some $170 million (*£95 million*).

The greatest ransom ever reported is 1500 million pesos (*£25,300,000*) for the release of the brothers Jorge Born, 40 and Juan Born, 39, of Bunge and Born, paid to the left wing urban guerilla group Montoneros in Buenos Aires, Argentina on 20 June 1975.

The youngest person kidnapped has been Carolyn Wharton born at 12.46 p.m. on 19 Mar 1955 in the Baptist Hospital, Texas, USA and kidnapped, by a woman disguised as a nurse, at 1.15 p.m. aged 29 min.

Greatest hijack ransom

The highest amount ever paid to aircraft hijackers has been $6 million (*then £3.42 million*) by the Japanese government in the case of a JAL DC-8 at Dacca Airport on 2 Oct 1977 with 38 hostages. Six convicted criminals were also exchanged. The Bangladesh government had refused to sanction any retaliatory action.

Largest narcotics haul

In Oct 1983 it was estimated that the narcotics crime in the USA was running at $80,000 million per annum with cocaine dealers turning a profit of $35,000 million and illegal domestic 'green collar' marijuana growers netting $13,900 million.

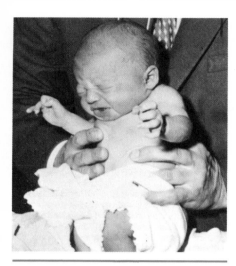

Baby Carolyn the youngest ever victim of a kidnap when aged 29 minutes. (See page 205 column 3)

The greatest drug haul ever achieved was 12,500 kg *12.3 tons* of cocaine with a street value of $1,200 million (£860 million) taken in the Caqueta jungle province of Colombia on 10 Mar 1984 in 10 processing plants protected by the armed wing of the Colombian Communist Party FARC (Fuerzas Armadas Revolucionarias Columbias).

The bulkiest haul was 2850 long tons *2 903 000 kg* of Colombian marijuana in the 14 month long 'Operation Tiburon' concluded by the DEA with the arrest of 495 people and the seizure of 95 vessels announced on 5 Feb 1982.

The Home Office disclosed on 23 Dec 1977 that 13 million LSD tablets with a street value approaching £100 million had been destroyed on the conclusion of 'Operation Julie'.

Greatest banknote forgery
The greatest forgery was the German Third Reich government's forging operation, code name 'Bernhard', engineered by SS Sturmbannfuhrer Alfred Naujocks of the Technical Dept of the German Secret Service Amt VI F in Berlin in 1940–1. It involved £150,000,000 worth of £5 notes.

Biggest bank fraud
The largest amount of money named in a defalcation case has been a gross SwF 222 million then £33,000,000 at the Lugano branch of Lloyd's Bank International Ltd in Switzerland on 2 Sept 1974. Mark Colombo was arrested pending charges including falsification of foreign currency accounts and suppression of evidence.

Computer fraud
Between 1964 and 1973, 64,000 fake insurance policies were created on the computer of the Equity Funding Corporation involving $2000 million.

Stanley Mark Rifkin (b. 1946) was arrested in Carlsbad, California by the FBI on 6 Nov 1978 charged with defrauding a Los Angeles bank of $10.2 million (*then £4.85 million*) by manipulation of a computer system. He was sentenced to 8 years in June 1980.

Theft
It was estimated in Nov 1983 that the greatest theft in the world is running at $160,000 million per annum. This is the value of 'bosses' time' paid for but not worked in the United States in 1983/84.

Welfare swindle
The greatest welfare swindle yet worked was that of the gypsy Anthony Moreno on the French Social Security in Marseille. By forging birth certificates and school registration forms, he invented 197 fictitious families and 3000 children on which he claimed benefits from 1960 to mid-1968. Moreno, nicknamed 'El Chorro' (the fountain), was later reported free of extradition worries and living in luxury in his native Spain having absquatulated with an estimated £2,300,000.

Largest object ever stolen by a single man
On a moonless night at dead calm high water on 5 June 1966 armed with only a sharp axe, N William Kennedy slashed free the mooring lines at Wolfe's Cove, St Lawrence Seaway, Quebec, Canada, of the 10,639 dwt S S *Orient Trader* owned by Steel Factors Ltd of Ontario. The vessel drifted to a waiting blacked out tug thus escaping a ban on any shipping movements during a violent wild-cat waterfront strike. She sailed for Spain.

Maritime fraud
A cargo of 180 000 tonnes of Kuwaiti crude oil on the supertanker *Salem* at Durban was sold without title to the South African government in Dec 1979. The ship mysteriously sank off Senegal on 17 Jan 1980 leaving the government to pay £148 million (*$305 million*) to Shell International who owned the shipment.

CAPITAL PUNISHMENT
Capital punishment is known to have dated at least from neolithic times as evidenced by the finding of Tollsneed man in Denmark. The countries in which capital punishment is still prevalent include China (perhaps 500 shootings per annum); South Africa (about 100 hangings for rape, robbery and murder); Turkey; Iran; USA (re-introduced in 38 States for the most heinous murders); USSR (23 capital offences including profiteering, speculation and currency offences for which some 400 persons have been reportedly shot annually).

Capital punishment was first abolished *de facto* in 1798 in Liechtenstein. The death penalty for murder was formally abolished in Britain on 18 Dec 1969. Between the 5–4 Supreme Court decision against capital punishment in June 1972 and January 1983, 38 of the 50 States of the USA voted to restore it.

Capital punishment in the British Isles dates from AD 450, but was abolished by William I and re-imposed by Henry I, reaching a peak in the reign of Edward VI (1547–53), when an average of 560 persons were executed annually at Tyburn alone. Even into the 19th century, there were 223 capital crimes, though people were, in practice, hanged for not more than 25 of these. Between 1830 and 1964 the most murderers hanged in a year was 27 (24 men, 3 women) in 1903. While in 1956 there were no executions.

Largest hanging
The most people hanged from one gallows was 38 Sioux Indians by William J. Duly outside Mankato, Minnesota, USA for the murder of unarmed citizens on 26 Dec 1862. The Nazi Feldkommandant simultaneously hanged 50 Greek resistance men as a reprisal in Athens on 22 July 1944.

Last hangings
The last public execution in England took place outside Newgate Prison, London at 8 a.m. on 26 May 1868, when Michael Barrett was hanged for his part in the Fenian bomb outrage on 13 Dec 1867, when 12 were killed outside the Clerkenwell House of Detention, London. The earliest non-public execution was of the murderer Thomas Wells on 13 Aug 1868. The last public hanging in Scotland was that of the murderer Robert Smith outside Dumfries Gaol on 12 May 1868 by the hangman Mr Askern. The last in the United States occurred at Owensboro, Kentucky in 1936. The last hangings in the United Kingdom were those of Peter Anthony Allen (b. 4 Apr 1943) hanged at Walton Prison, Liverpool by Mr Leslie Stewart, and John Robson Walby (b. 1 Apr 1940), *alias* Gwynne Owen Evans, at Strangeways Gaol, Manchester both on 13 Aug 1964. They had been found guilty of the capital murder of John Alan West, on 7 Apr 1964. The 15th, youngest and last woman executed this century was Mrs Ruth Ellis (*née* Neilson), 28, for the murder of David Blakely, 25, shot outside the Magdala, Hampstead, on 10 Apr 1955. She was executed on 13 July at Holloway. The last hanging in the Republic of Ireland was in 1954.

Last from yard-arm
The last naval execution at the yard-arm was the hanging of Private John Dalliger, Royal Marines, aboard HMS *Leven* in Victoria Bay near Lu-ta, China, on 13 July 1860. Dalliger had been found guilty of two attempted murders.

Youngest
Although the hanging of persons under 18 was expressly excluded only in the Children's and Young Person's Act, 1933 (Sec. 33), no person under that age was, in fact, executed more recently than 1887. The lowest satisfactorily recorded age was of a boy aged 8 'who had malice, cunning and revenge' in firing two barns and who was hanged at Abingdon, Oxfordshire in the 17th century. The youngest persons hanged since 1900 have been six 18 year olds, the most recent of whom was Francis Robert George ('Flossie') Forsyth on 10 Nov 1960.

Oldest
The oldest person hanged in the United Kingdom since 1900 was a man of 71 named Charles Frembd (*sic*) at Chelmsford Gaol on 4 Nov 1914, for the murder of his wife at Leytonstone, Waltham Forest, Greater London. In 1822 John Smith, said to be 80, of Greenwich, Greater London, was hanged for the murder of a woman.

Last public guillotining
The last person to be publicly guillotined in France was the murderer Eugen Weidmann before a large crowd at Versailles, near Paris, at 4.50 a.m. on 17 June 1939. In January 1978 Marcel Chevalier was nominated to succeed his uncle Andre Obrecht as executioner who in turn succeeded his uncle Henri Desfourneaux. Dr Joseph Ignace Guillotin (1738–1812) died a natural death. He had advocated the use of the machine designed by Dr Antoine Louis in 1789 in the French constituent assembly. The last use before abolition in 1981 was on 10 Sept 1977 at Baumettes Prison, Marseilles for the torturer and murderer Hamida Djandoubi, 28.

Death row
The longest sojourn on Death Row is the 37 years of Sadamichi Hirasawa (b. 18 Feb 1893) in Sendai Jail, northern Japan. He was convicted in 1948 of poisoning 12 bank employees with potassium cyanide to effect a theft of £100. The longest stay in the US is since 1 Mar 1960 by Henry R. Anderson, an attorney, at the Kentucky State Penitentiary in Eddyville. In August 1984 there were 1,351 prisoners (including 18 women) in 38 of the 50 US states on 'Death Row'.

Executioners
The longest period of office of a Public Execu-

tioner was that of William Calcraft (1800–79), who was in action from 1828 to 25 May 1874 and officiated at nearly every hanging outside and later inside Newgate Prison, London. On 2 Apr 1868 he hanged the murderess Mrs Frances Kidder, 25, outside Maidstone Jail, Kent—the last public execution of a woman.

For 56 years from 1900 to the retirement of Albert in February 1956, the Pierrepoint family largely monopolized the task of executing murderers and war criminals. Henry Albert (1876–1922) officiated from 1900–1911 with a record 20 executions in Britain in 1909 and the last double female execution (the baby farmers Mrs Amelia Sachs and Mrs Annie Walters) on 3 Feb 1903. The longest serving executioner has been his eldest brother Thomas Pierrepoint from 1903 to 1948. Albert Pierrepoint, son of Henry Albert, officiated at the hanging of 530 men and 20 women in his career in 9 countries including a record 27 war criminals in a day in Germany. Britain's last hangman was Henry B. Allen who was on call until abolition of hanging for murder in 1969.

Lynching
The worst year in the 20th century for lynchings in the United States has been 1901, with 130 lynchings (105 Negroes, 25 Whites), while the first year with no reported cases was 1952. The last lynching recorded in Britain was that of Panglam Godolan, a suspected murderer, in London on 27 Oct 1958. The last case previous to this was of a kidnapping suspect in Glasgow in 1922.

Corporal punishment
The last use of corporal punishment in one of HM Prisons was on 26 June 1962 and it was abolished in the United Kingdom by the Criminal Justice Act, 1967. The treadmill which 14 prisons operated in 1878 was finally suspended on 1 Apr 1902. Men on the 36-man wheel at Northallerton, Yorkshire raised themselves 9639 ft *2937 m* in an 8-hr day, equivalent to reaching within 111 ft *33,8 m* of the summit of Everest in 3 days.

PRISON SENTENCES

Longest sentences *World*
A 10,000 year sentence was imposed on Deuel Wilhelm Davies, 40 on 4 Dec 1981 in Tuscaloosa, Alabama, USA for a triple murder (including his mother-in-law) in 1976. A sentence of 384,912 years was *demanded* at the prosecution of Gabriel March Grandos, 22, at Palma de Mallorca, Spain on 11 Mar 1972 for failing to deliver 42,768 letters or 9 years per letter.

Juan Corona, a Mexican-American, was sentenced to 25 consecutive life terms, for murdering 25 farm workers in 1970–1 around Feather River, Yuba City, California, at Fairfield on 5 Feb 1973. His 20th century record was surpassed by Dean Corll (27) in 1974 and John Wayne Gacy (33 victims) in 1980.

United Kingdom
Kevin Mulgrew from the Ardoyne district of Belfast was sentenced on 5 Aug 1983 to life imprisonment for the murder of Sergeant Julian Connolley of the UDR, in addition he was given a further 963 years to be served concurrently on 84 other serious charges including 13 conspiracies to murder and 8 attempted murders.

The longest single period served by a reprieved murderer in Great Britain this century was 40 years 11 months by John Watson Laurie, the Goat Fell or Arran murderer, who was reprieved on the grounds of insanity in November 1889 and who died in Perth Penitentiary on 4 Oct 1930.

The longest specific minimum period recom-

mended by a judge under the Murder (Abolition of Death Penalty) Act 1965 has been 35 years in the case of Patrick Armstrong and Michael Hill on 22 Oct 1975 for pub bombings (7 killed, 99 injured) at Guildford and Woolwich in 1974.

The longest prison sentence ever passed under British law was one of three consecutive and two concurrent terms of 14 years, thus totalling 42 years, imposed on 3 May 1961 on George Blake *né* Behar (b. Rotterdam, 11 Nov 1922), for treachery. Blake, formerly UK vice-consul in Seoul, South Korea, had been converted to Communism during 34 months' internment there from 2 July 1950 to April 1953. It had been alleged that his betrayals may have cost the lives of up to 42 British agents. He was 'sprung' from Wormwood Scrubs Prison, Greater London, on 22 Oct 1966.

The longest single sentence passed on a woman under English law was 20 years for Mrs Lona Teresa Cohen *née* Petra (b. 1913) at the Old Bailey, City of London on 2 Mar 1961 for conspiring to commit a breach of the Official Secrets Act, 1911. The sentence of this KGB agent was remitted by the Foreign Secretary on no known lawful authority on 24 July 1969. Ward (see Most Prolific Murderers) was sentenced to 20 years for a single offence and an aggregate 30 years on 4 Nov 1974.

Longest time served
Paul Geidel, (b. 21 Apr 1894) was convicted of second degree murder on 5 Sept 1911 as a 17 year old porter in a New York Hotel. He was released from the Fishkill Correctional Facility, Beacon, New York aged 85 on 7 May 1980 having served 68 years 8 months and 2 days—the longest recorded term in US history. He first refused parole in 1974. Rudolph Hess was captured at Eaglesham on 10 May 1941 and in 1984 entered his 44th year in prison.

The longest serving prisoner in Britain is John Straffen (b. 1930) now in his 31st year behind bars for 3 child murders.

Longest in Broadmoor
The longest period for which any person has been detained in the Broadmoor hospital for the criminally insane, near Crowthorne, Berkshire, is 76 years in the case of William Giles. He was admitted as an insane arsonist at the age of 11 and died there on 10 Mar 1962, at the age of 87.

The first patient from Broadmoor to subsequently hold public office and to be accepted on any party's parliamentary candidates list is Peter Thompson.

Most appearances
A record for arrests was set by Tommy Johns, 60, in Brisbane, Queensland, Australia on 9 Sept 1982 when he faced his 2000th conviction for drunkenness since 1957.

Greatest mass arrests
The greatest mass arrest reported in a democratic country was of more than 13,000 people in an anti-war demonstration designed to block rush-hour traffic in Washington DC, USA on 3–5 May 1971. The largest in the United Kingdom occurred on 17 Sept 1961, when 1314 demonstrators supporting unilateral nuclear disarmament were arrested for obstructing highways leading to Parliament Square, London, by sitting down. As a consequence of the 1926 General Strike there were 3149 prosecutions: incitement (1760) and violence (1389).

FINES

Heaviest *World*
It was reported in January 1979 that Carlo Ponti, husband of Sophia Loren, was to be fined

the equivalent of $26.4 million by the Italian courts in connection with claims for tax alleged to be due but unpaid.

UK
The heaviest fine ever imposed by a United Kingdom Court is £525,000 on the National Graphical Association (NGA) for illegal picketing the *Messenger* newspaper plant, Warrington, Cheshire owned by Mr Eddie Shah on 10 Dec 1983. On 6 Feb 1985 insurers Lloyd's of London fined Peter Dixon £1,000,000 in connection with alleged misappropriation of £38.17 million.

Rarest prosecution
There are a number of crimes in English law for which there have never been prosecutions. Among unique prosecutions are *Rex v. Crook* in 1662 for the praemunire of disputing the King's title and *Rex v. Gregory* for selling honours under the Honours (Prevention of Abuses) Act, 1924, on 18 Feb 1933. John Maundy Gregory (d. 3 Oct 1941 in France as 'Sir' 'Arthur' Gregory) was an honours broker during 6 administrations from 1919 to 1932 and was sentenced to two months in Wormwood Scrubs, London.

PRISONS

Largest *Great Britain*
The most capacious prison in Great Britain is Wormwood Scrubs, West London, with 1208 cells. The highest prison walls in Great Britain are those of Lancaster Prison measuring 36–52 ft *11–15,85 m*. The Maze Prison, opened in 1974, covers 133 acres *53,8 ha* with seven 100 cell blocks surrounded by a 30 ft *9,1 m* wall.

The largest prison in Scotland is Barlinnie, Glasgow, with 753 single cells. Ireland's largest prison is Mountjoy Prison, Dublin, with 808 cells.

Penal camps
The largest penal camp systems in the world have been those near Kolyma, in the USSR, with a population of 500,000 and a death roll in 1932–54 of six fold that figure. The largest labour camp is now said to be the Dubrovlag Complex of 15 camps centred on Pot'ma, Mordovian SSR. The official NATO estimate for all Soviet camps was 'more than one million' in March 1960 compared with a peak of probably 12 million during the Stalinist era.

Devil's Island
The largest French penal settlement was that of St Laurent du Maroni, which comprised the notorious Îles du Diable, Royale and St Joseph (for incorrigibles) off the coast of French Guiana, in South America. It remained in operation for 99 years from 1854 until the last group of repatriated prisoners, including Théodore Rouselle, who had served 50 years, was returned to Bordeaux on 22 Aug 1953. It has been estimated that barely 2000 *bagnards* (ex-convicts) of the 70,000 deportees ever returned. These, however, included the executioner Ladurelle (imprisoned 1921–37), who was murdered in Paris in 1938.

Highest population
The peak prison population, including Borstals and detention centres, for England and Wales was the figure for March 1980 with 44,223. In Scotland the prison population record was 5400 in 1972 and in Northern Ireland 2934 on 16 Nov 1975.

Most secure prison
After it became a maximum security Federal prison in 1934, no convict was known to have lived to tell of a successful escape from the prison of Alcatraz Island in San Francisco Bay, California, USA. A total of 23 men attempted it but 12 were recaptured, 5 shot dead, one drowned and 5 presumed drowned. On 16 Dec 1962, just

before the prison was closed on 21 Mar 1963, one man reached the mainland alive, only to be recaptured on the spot. John Chase held the record with 26 years there.

Most expensive prison
Spandau Prison, Berlin, built 100 years ago for 600 prisoners is now used solely for the person widely and officially purported to be Nazi war criminal Rudolf Hess (b. 26 Apr 1894). The cost of maintenance of the staff of 105 has been estimated at $415,000 (£245,000) per annum.

Longest escape
The longest recorded escape by a recaptured prisoner was that of Leonard T. Fristoe, 77, who escaped from Nevada State Prison, USA, on 15 Dec 1923 and was turned in by his son on 15 Nov 1969 at Compton, California. He had had 46 years of freedom under the name of Claude R. Willis. He had killed two sheriff's deputies in 1920. The longest period of freedom achieved by a British gaol breaker is more than 24 years by Irish-born John Patrick Hannan, who escaped from Verne Open Prison at Portland, Dorset, on 22 Dec 1955 and was still at large in June 1980. He had served only 1 month of a 21-month term for car-stealing and assaulting two policemen.

Greatest gaol break
In February 1979 a retired US Army Colonel Arthur 'Bull' Simons led a band of 14 to break into Gasre prison, Tehran, Iran to rescue two fellow Americans. Some 11,000 other prisoners took advantage of this and the Islamic revolution in what became history's largest ever gaol break.

In July 1971, Raoul Sendic and 105 other Tupamaro guerrillas escaped from a Uruguayan prison through a tunnel 91 m 298 ft long.

The greatest gaol break in the United Kingdom was that from the Maze Prison, on 25 Sept 1983 when 38 IRA prisoners escaped from Block H-7. By June 1985 16 were still at large. The Provisional IRA had been first set up in Ballinamore, County Leitrim, Ireland in 1967.

6. ECONOMIC

MONETARY AND FINANCE
Largest budget World
The greatest governmental expenditure ever made by any country has been $867,660 million (£723,050 million) by the United States government for the fiscal year 1984. The highest ever revenue figure was $683,200 million (£569,300 million) in this same U.S. fiscal year.

The world's greatest fiscal surplus was $8,419,469,844 in the United States in 1947–8. The worst deficit was the $195,355 million in the U.S. fiscal year ending 30 Sept 1983.

Largest budget United Kingdom
The greatest budgeted government expenditure has been £149,273 million for the fiscal year 1985–86. The highest budgeted government receipts have been £139,107 million for the same fiscal year showing a General Government Borrowing Requirement of £10,166 million.

Foreign aid
The total net foreign aid given by the United States government between 1 July 1945 and 1 Jan 1984 was $234,624 million. The country which received most US aid in 1983 was Israel with $2322 million. US foreign aid began with $50,000 to Venezuela for earthquake relief in 1812.

Least taxed
The lowest income-taxed sovereign countries in

the world are Bahrain, Brunei, Kuwait and Qatar where the rate regardless of income is nil. No tax is levied on the Sarkese (inhabitants of Sark) in the Channel Islands or the inhabitants of Tristan da Cunha.

Highest taxation rates
The country with the most confiscatory taxation is Norway where in January 1974 the Labour Party and Socialist Alliance abolished the 80 per cent limit. Some 2000 citizens were then listed in the Lignings Boka as paying more than 100 per cent of their taxable income. The shipping magnate Hilmer Reksten (1898–1980) was assessed at 491 per cent. In the United Kingdom the former top earned and unearned rates of 83 per cent and 98 per cent were reduced to 60 per cent and 75 per cent in the budget on 12 June 1979. The all-time record ruled in 1967–8, when a 'special charge' of up to 9s. (45p) in the £ additional to surtax brought the top rate to 27s. 3d. (or 136%) in the £ on investment income.

Balance of Payments
The record deficit for any country is $107,440 million (then £89,500 million) in 1984 by the USA. The record surplus was 4,587 billion yen (£14,900 million) by Japan in 1984.
The most favourable current balance of payments figure for the United Kingdom has been a surplus of £7,272 million in 1981 (best quarter Jan–Mar £2,698 million). The worst figure was a deficit of £3,591 million in 1974. Monthly figures are regarded as too erratic to be of great significance.

Tax demands highest
The highest recorded personal tax demand is one for $336 million (then £164 million) for 70 per cent of the estate of Howard Hughes. The highest disclosed UK personal income tax demand raised is one for £5,371,220 against the international merchant banker Nicholas Van Hoogstraten, 34, for 1981.

Highest and lowest rates in Great Britain
Income tax was first introduced in Great Britain in 1799 for incomes above £60 per annum. It was discontinued in 1815, only to be re-introduced in 1842 at the rate of 7d. (2.91p) in the £. It was at its lowest at 2d. (0.83p) in the £ in 1875, gradually climbing to 1s. 3d. (6.24p) by 1913. From April 1941 until 1946 the record peak of 10s. (50p) in the £ was maintained to assist in the financing of World War II.

National Debt
The largest national debt of any country in the world is that of the United States, where the gross federal public debt of the Federal Government supassed the 'trillion' (10^{12}) dollar mark on 30 Sept 1981. By January 1985 it had reached $1,667.4 billion. This amount in dollar bills would make a pile 91,103 miles 146 616 km high, weighing 1,267,610 tons.

The National Debt in Great Britain was less than £1 million during the reign of James II in 1687. It was £158,101 million or £2,798 per person at 31 Mar 1985. This amount placed in a pile of brand new £1 notes would be 8685.8 miles 13 978 km in height.

Most Foreign Debt
The first country whose overseas debt surpassed $100 billion was Mexico in 1985. The highest per caput is that of Chile with $17,000 million for a population of 11.5 million in mid-1983 or $1478 per person.

Gross National Product
The country with the largest Gross National Product is the United States reaching $3 trillion

(3×10^{12}) in 1981. By 1 Jan 1985 this was running at $3,819.9 billion. The GNP of the United Kingdom at factor cost was £320,711 million for 1984.

National wealth
The richest nation, measured by average per caput, is the United Arab Emirates with $21,340 in 1982. The USA which had taken the lead in 1910 was 6th behind UAE, Brunei, Qatar, Kuwait and Switzerland. The United Kingdom stood 27th with $9050 (then £5840) per head. It has been estimated that the value of all physical assets in the USA on 1 Jan 1983 was $12.5 trillion ($10^{12}$) or $53,800 per caput. The figure for private wealth in the United Kingdom was £325,000 million (1976) or £5811 per head.

Poorest country
The lowest published annual income per caput of any country in the world is Chad with $80 (then £37) in 1982 but the World Bank has no publishable data for 17 Marxist countries.

Gold reserves World
The country with the greatest monetary gold reserve is the United States, whose Treasury had 262.73 million fine oz of the world's 950 million fine oz on hand in March 1985. Valued at $315 per fine oz, these amounts translate to $82,780 million and $300,000 million respectively. The United States Bullion Depository at Fort Knox, 30 miles 48 km south-west of Louisville, Kentucky, USA has been the principal Federal depository of US gold since Dec 1936. Gold is stored in 446,000 standard mint bars of 400 troy ounces 12,4414 kg measuring $7 \times 3\frac{5}{8} \times 1\frac{5}{8}$ in, $17,7 \times 9,2 \times 4,1$ cm.

Gold and foreign currency reserves Great Britain
The lowest published figure for the sterling area's gold and convertible currency reserves was $298,000,000 (then £74 million) on 31 Dec 1940. The valuation on 1 Apr 1981 was a peak $28,212 million and the peak figure for gold was $7334 million on 31 Dec 1981. The figure for 1 Jan 1984 was $17,817 million of which $5,914 million was in gold.

Minimum Lending Rate
The highest ever figure for the British bank rate (since 13 Oct 1972, the Minimum Lending Rate) has been 17 per cent from 15 Nov 1979 to 3rd July 1980. The longest period without a change was the 12 years 13 days from 26 Oct 1939 to 7 Nov 1951, during which time the rate stayed at 2 per cent. This lowest ever rate had been first attained on 22 Apr 1852.

Worst inflation World
The world's worst inflation occurred in Hungary in June 1946, when the 1931 gold pengö was valued at 130 trillion (1.3×10^{20}) paper pengös. Notes were issued for 'Egymillard billion' (one milliard billion or 10^{21}) pengös on 3 June and withdrawn on 11 July 1946. Vouchers for 1000 billion billion (10^{27}) pengös were issued for taxation payment only. On 6 Nov 1923 the circulation of Reichsbank marks reached 400,338,326,350,700,000,000 and inflation was 755,700 million fold on 1913 levels. The country with the highest current rate of inflation is Argentina with over 1000% in June 1985.

Worst inflation Great Britain
The United Kingdom's worst rate in a year has been for August 1974 to August 1975 when inflation ran at a rate of 26.9 per cent compared with 3.7 per cent for May 1982 to May 1983 and 7.0 per cent for May 1984 to May 1985. The Tax and Price Index (allowing for tax reliefs) was 3.0 per cent in June 1983. The peak TPI extrapolated figure was 31.9 per cent in August 1975.

PAPER MONEY

Earliest

Paper money is an invention of the Chinese first tried in AD 910 and prevalent by AD 970. The world's earliest bank notes (*banco-sedler*) were issued in Stockholm, Sweden, in July 1661. The oldest surviving banknote is one of 5 dalers dated 6 Dec 1662. The oldest surviving printed Bank of England note is one for £555 to bearer, dated 19 Dec 1699 ($4\frac{1}{2} \times 7\frac{1}{2}$ in, *11,4 × 19,6 cm*).

Largest and smallest

The largest paper money ever issued was the one kwan note of the Chinese Ming dynasty issue of 1368–99, which measured 9×13 in *22,8 × 33,0 cm*. In Oct 1983 one sold for £340. The smallest national note ever issued was the 10 bani note of the Ministry of Finance of Romania, in 1917. It measured (printed area) $27,5 \times 38$ mm *1.09 × 1.49 in*. Of German *notgeld* the smallest are the 1–3 pfg of Passau (1920–21) measuring $18 \times 18,5$ mm *0.70 × 0.72 in*.

Highest denominations *World*

The highest denomination notes in circulation are US Federal Reserve Bank notes for $10,000 (£5260). They bear the head of Salmon Portland Chase (1808–73). None has been printed since July 1944 and the US Treasury announced in 1969 that no further notes higher than $100 would be issued. Only 348 $10,000 bills remain in circulation or unretired.

Great Britain

Two Bank of England notes for £1,000,000 still exist, dated before 1812 but these were used only for internal accounting. In November 1977 the existence of a Treasury £1 million note dated 30 Aug 1948 came to light and was sold by private treaty for $A18,500 (*then £11,300*) in Australia.

The highest issued denominations have been £1000 notes, first printed in 1725, discontinued on 22 Apr 1943 and withdrawn on 30 Apr 1945. At least 16 of these notes were still unretired up to Nov 1979 (last data to be published). Of these perhaps 10 are in the hands of collectors or dealers.

Lowest denomination *World*

The lowest denomination legal tender bank note is the 1 sen (or 1/100th of a rupiah) Indonesian note. Its exchange value in mid-1984 was 140 to the new penny.

Great Britain

The lowest denomination Bank of England notes ever printed were the black on pale blue half-crown (now $12\frac{1}{2}$p) notes in 1941, signed by the late Sir Kenneth Peppiatt. Very few examples have survived and they are now valued at from £750.

Highest circulation

The highest ever Bank of England note circulation in the United Kingdom was £12,152,000,000 on 14 Dec 1983—equivalent to a pile of £1 notes 603.95 miles *971,97 km* high.

CHEQUES AND COINS

Largest *World*

The greatest amount paid by a single cheque in the history of banking has been one for Rs. 16,640,000,000 equivalent to £852,791,660 handed over by Hon. Daniel P. Moynihan, US Ambassador to India in New Delhi on 18 Feb 1974. An internal US Treasury cheque for $4,176,969,623.57 was drawn on 30 June 1954.

Largest *Great Britain*

The largest cheque drawn in Britain was one for £604,604,115 drawn on 1 Sept 1982 by British Petroleum Oil Development Ltd, payable to the Inland Revenue against BP's North Sea Oil tax bill. If converted to pound notes this would comprise a stack 36.84 miles *59,28 km* high.

COINS

Oldest

World: *c.* 670 BC electrum staters of King Gyges of Lydia, Turkey[1]

British: *c.* 95 BC Westerham type gold stater (51 known)[2]

Earliest Dated

Samian silver tetradrachm struck in Zankle (now Messina), Sicily dated year 1 *viz* 494 BC—shown as 'A'

Christian Era: MCCXXXIIII (1234) Bishop of Roskilde coins, Denmark (6 known)

British: 1539 James V of Scotland silver 'bonnet piece'

Heaviest

World: 19,71 kg *43 lb 7¼ oz* Swedish 10 daler copper plate 1644[3]

British: 39,94 g *1.4066 oz* Gold £5 piece. The latest mintages are dated 1980, 1981 and 1982. (Legal tender record)[4]

Lightest and Smallest

World: 0.002 g or 14,000 to the oz Nepalese silver ¼ Jawa *c.* 1740

British: 7.27 grains or 61 to the oz Maundy silver one penny piece since 1822

Most Expensive

World: Agrigentum decadrahm sold by private treaty to Nelson Bunker Hunt (US) for $900,000 in Oct 1980

British: £71,500 (including premium) bid for a Henry III gold 20 pence (6 known) at Spink's, London on 13 June 1985 (see below). 20th century record: £40,000 bid for Edward VIII proof sovereign of 1937 at Spink's, London on 7 Dec 1984

Rarest

World: Many 'singletons' known e.g. Only 700 Axumite coins known of which only one of bronze and gold of Kaleb I *c.* AD 500

British: Unique: 1952 George VI half-crown; 1954 Elizabeth II 1d sold in March 1978 for £23,000

[1] Chinese uninscribed 'spade' money of the Chou dynasty has been dated to *c.* 770 BC.
[2] Bellovaci type gold staters circulated as early as *c.* 130 BC but were struck in Northern France and not in Britain.
[3] The largest coin-shaped coin was the 200 Mohur Indian gold coin of 1654 $5\frac{3}{8}$ in *136 mm* in diameter weighing 70 troy oz *2177 g* of which no known example now survives.
[4] The George III 'Cartwheel' Copper 2d coin of 1797 weighed 2.04 oz *58,0 g*. The 5 guinea gold pieces.

Greatest collection

The highest price paid for a coin collection has been $7,300,000 (*then £3,550,000*) for a hoard of 407,000 US silver dollars from the La Vere Redfield estate in a courtroom auction in Reno, Nevada on 27 Jan 1976 by Steven C. Markoff of A-Mark Coin Co. Inc. of Beverley Hills, Cal.

Largest hoards

The largest hoard was one of about 80,000 aurei in Brescello near Modena, Italy in 1814 believed to have been deposited *c.* 37 BC. The numerically largest hoard ever found was the Brussels hoard of 1908 containing *c.* 150,000 coins. A hoard of 56,000 Roman coins was found at Cunetio near Marlborough, Wiltshire on 15 Oct 1978.

The greatest discovery of treasure is the estimated $2000 million of gold coins and platinum ingots from the sunken Tsarist battleship *Admiral Nakhimov* 8524 tons/tonnes 200 ft *60 m* down off the Japanese island of Tsushima. She sank on 27 May 1905. A figure of $2000 million has also been ascribed to the *San Jose* which sank in 700–1200 ft *210–365 m* of water off Colombia in 1708. Diving began in Aug 1984.

Largest mint

The largest mint in the world is the US Treasury's mint built in 1965–9 on Independence Mall, Philadelphia, covering $11\frac{1}{2}$ acres *4,65 ha* with an annual capacity on a 3 shift 7-day week production of 8000 million coins. A single stamping machine can produce coins at a rate of 10,000 per hour.

Charity Fund Raising

The greatest recorded amount raised by a charity walk or run is (Can)$24.7 million by Terry Fox (1958–81) of Canada who ran from St John's, Newfoundland to Thunder Bay, Ontario with an artificial leg in 143 days from 12 Apr–2 Sept 1980. He covered 5373 km *3339 miles*.

Longest and Most Valuable Line of Coins

The most valuable column of coins amassed for charity was worth £13,628 knocked over by Frankie Vaughan at Mecca's Club, Bolton, Lancashire on 18 Aug 1984. The longest and highest value line of coins was 10 miles, 5 feet, 7 inches (*16,12 km*) made-up of 662,353 US quarters to a value of $165,788 (*£138,155*) on 16 Mar at Central City Park, Atlanta, Georgia, USA, sponsored by the National Kidney Foundation of Georgia Inc. The Copper Mountain for the NSPCC at Selfridges, Oxford Street amassed over 3 million coins in 350 days (24 May 1984–7 May 1985) valued at £57,051.34.

LABOUR

Trade union Oldest *Great Britain*

The oldest of the 105 trade unions affiliated to the Trades Union Congress (founded 1868) is the National Society of Brushmakers and General Workers (current membership 725) founded in 1747.

Trade union Largest *World*

The world's largest union has been Solidarność (Solidarity) in Poland which by October 1980 was reported to have 8,000,000 members. The union with the longest name is the International Association of Marble, Slate and Stone Polishers, Rubbers and Sawyers, Tile and Marble Setters' Helpers and Marble Mosaic and Terrazzo Workers Helpers or IAMSSPRSTMSHMMTWH of Washington DC, USA.

Trade union Largest *Great Britain*

The largest union in the United Kingdom is the Transport and General Workers' Union, with 1,473,476 members at April 1985. Their peak membership was 2,086,281 in 1979.

Trade union Smallest

The smallest Trade Union Congress affiliated union is the Society of Shuttlemakers with a membership of just 49. The unaffiliated London Handforged Spoon and Fork Makers' Society instituted in July 1874, has a last reported membership of 6. The Unión de Pilotos de la Autoridad de Energía Eléctrica of Puerto Rico in 1984 boasted 3 members.

Labour dispute *Earliest*

A labour dispute concerning monotony of diet and working conditions was recorded in 1153 BC in Thebes, Egypt. The earliest recorded strike was one by an orchestra leader from Greece named Aristos in Rome *c.* 309 BC. The cause was meal breaks.

Labour dispute *Largest*

The most serious single labour dispute in the United Kingdom was the General Strike of 4–12 May 1926, called by the Trades Union Congress in support of the Miners' Federation. During the nine days of the strike 1,580,000 people were involved and 14,500,000 working days were lost.

During the year 1926 a total of 2,750,000 people were involved in 323 different labour disputes and the working days lost during the year amounted to 162,300,000, the highest figure ever recorded. The figures for 1984 were 26,564,000 working days involving 1154 stoppages with 1,405,000 workers involved.

Britain's most protracted national strike was called by the National Union of Mineworkers from 8 Mar 1984 to 5 Mar 1985. H.M. Treasury estimated the cost to be £2,625 million or £46.50 per head of the population.

Labour dispute *Longest*

The world's longest recorded strike ended on 4 Jan 1961, after 33 years. It concerned the employment of barbers' assistants in Copenhagen, Denmark. The longest recorded major strike was that at the plumbing fixtures factory of the Kohler Co. in Sheboygan, Wisconsin, USA, between April 1954 and October 1962. The strike is alleged to have cost the United Automobile Workers' Union about $12,000,000 (*then £4.8 million*) to sustain.

Unemployment *Highest*

The highest recorded percentage unemployment in Great Britain was on 23 Jan 1933, when the total of unemployed persons on the Employment Exchange registers was 2,903,065, representing 22.8% of the insured working population. The peak figure for the post-war period has been 13.8% (3,225,200) in Jan 1985.

Unemployment *Lowest*

In Switzerland in December 1973 (pop. 6.6 million), the total number of unemployed was reported to be 81. The lowest recorded peacetime level of unemployment in Britain was 0.9 per cent on 11 July 1955, when 184,929 persons were registered. The peak figure for the Employed labour force in the United Kingdom has been 25,520,000 in December 1979.

ASSOCIATION *Largest*

The largest single association in the world is the Blue Cross and Blue Shield Association, the US-based hospital insurance organization with a membership of 79,662,452 on 1 Jan 1984. Benefits paid out in 1983 totalled $34,602,745,060 (*£24,715 million*). The largest association in the United Kingdom is the Automobile Association (formed 1905) with a membership which reached 5,790,792 on 1 Apr 1985.

CONSUMPTIONS

Most Expensive: Truffles at £50.16 per 0.44 oz tin (SR 166.6 per 100 g) in Riyadh, Saudi Arabia in 1985. Strawberries at £17.70 per berry Dublin Fruit Market auction on 5 Apr 1977. Spice—wild gingseng (*Panax quinquefolius*) from Chan Pak Mountain area, China in Nov 1977 at $23,000 (then £10,454) per oz.

HEAVIEST, LONGEST OR TALLEST

Banana Split 2.5 miles *4,02 km* 20,000 bananas Addison County Fair, Vermont 8 Aug 1984

Barbecue 46,386 chicken halves for 15,000 people Honolulu, Hawaii 31 Jan 1981 16,1431 lb *7322 kg* of beef at Sertoma Club, New Port Richey, Florida 24 Mar 1984.

Beefburger 2001 kg *4411 lb* and 36 m² *387.5 ft²* Ukkel, Belgium 26 Mar 1983.

Cake 81,982 lb *37,18 tonnes* by Franz Eichenauer, Atlantic City, New Jersey 4 July 1982 65 tiers 39 ft 11 in *12,17 m* by Elly van Leerdam, Durban, South Africa 1 Apr 1985.

Easter Egg 3430 kg *3,37 tons* by Siegfried Berndt, Leicester, England 7 Apr 1982.

Haggis 541½ lb *245.6 kg* by David A. Hall Ltd of Glasgow, Scotland 25 Jan 1980.

Loaf 2132 ft *649.9 m* rosca de Reyes (twisted form) Acapulco, Mexico 6 Jan 1985 2 cwt *101,6 kg* pan-baked at San Lameer, Natal, South Africa 26 May 1984.

Pie (Fruit) 30,116 lb *13,66 tonnes* 600 bushels of apples at Chelsfield, Kent on 25–27 Aug 1982.

Pie (Meat) 5¾ tons (18 × 6 ft *5,48 × 1,83 m*) at Denby Dale, West Yorkshire 5 Sep 1984.

Pie (Mince) 2260 lb *1025 kg* baked at Ashby-de-la-Zouch, England 15 Oct 1932.

Omelette 35,000 eggs at Cora Hypermarket, Chatelineau, Belgium 7 Oct 1984.

Pastry 489,87 m *1607 ft 2 in* Liseberg Park, Gothenburg, Sweden 15 June 1984.

Pizza 7 tons 26,4 m *86 ft 7 in* in diameter by Marco Cagnazzo, Norwood Hypermarket, Johannesburg, South Africa on 31 Mar 1984.

Potato Mash 18,260 lb *8,26 tonnes* (using a concrete mixer) Grand Forks, North Dakota on 4 Sept 1982.

Sausage A Gran Bottifara feast for 40,000 by Josep Gruguess in Cornella, Barcelona on 9 June 1985 in a paella dish 10 m *32 ft 9 in* in diameter and 45 cm *17¼ in* deep.

Strawberry Bowl 481 lb *218 kg* (18,000 berries) at Great Ormond Street Hospital, London 28 June 1984.

Sundae 27,102 lb *12,29 tonnes* with strawberries, nuts and whipped topping St Albans, Vermont on 15 Apr 1983.

Trifle incl 11 galls *50 litres* of sherry by Mrs Judy Fraser at St Andrew's Hospice, Cleethorpes, England on 19 Aug 1984.

Oldest Club

Britain's oldest gentleman's club is White's, St James', London, opened *c.* 1697 by Francis White (d. 1711), as a Chocolate House, and moved to its present site in 37 St. James's in 1755. This has been described as an 'oasis in a desert of democracy'. Britain's oldest known dining club is the Charterhouse School Founder's Day Dinner held each Twelfth of December. The 1984 dinner to commemorate Old Etonian coal-owner Thomas Sutton (1532–1611) was the 358th.

ENERGY CONSUMPTION

To express the various forms of available energy (coal, liquid fuels and water power, etc., but omitting vegetable fuels and peat), it is the practice to convert them all into terms of coal.

The highest consumption in the world is in the United States, with an average of 13 240 kg *260.1 cwt* per person. With only 5.3 per cent of the world's population the US consumes 28.6 per cent of the world's gasoline and 32.9 per cent of the world's electric power. The United Kingdom average was 5527 kg *108.7 cwt* per person in 1984. The lowest recorded average for 1974 was 13 kg *28.6 lb* per person in Rwanda.

MASS COMMUNICATIONS

Airline

The country with the busiest airlines system is the United States of America where 249,670,706,000 revenue passenger miles were flown on scheduled domestic and local services in 1984. This was equivalent to an annual trip of 1057 miles *1701 km* for every one of the inhabitants of the USA. The United Kingdom airlines flew 603,499,000 km *375,007,146 miles* and carried 40,586,679 passengers on all services excluding Air Taxi operations in 1984.

Merchant shipping

The world total of merchant shipping, excluding vessels of less than 100 tons gross, sailing vessels and barges, was 76,068 vessels of 418,682,442 tons gross on 1 July 1984. The largest merchant fleet in the world as at mid-1984 was that under the flag of Liberia with 1934 ships of 62,024,700 tons gross. The UK figure for mid-1984 was 2468 ships of 15,874,062 tons gross.

Largest and busiest ports

Physically, the largest port in the world is the Port of New York and New Jersey, USA. The port has a navigable waterfront of 755 miles *1215 km* (295 miles *474 km* in New Jersey) stretching over 92 miles² *238 km²*. A total of 261 general cargo berths and 130 other piers give a total berthing capacity of 391 ships at one time. The total warehousing floor space is 422.4 acres *170,9 ha*. The world's busiest port and largest artificial harbour is Rotterdam-Europoort in the Netherlands which covers 38 miles² *100 km²* with 76 miles *122,3 km* of quays. It handled 30,958 sea-going vessels carrying a total of 243 million tonnes of sea-going cargo, and about 182,000 barges in 1984. It is able to handle 310 sea-going vessels simultaneously of up to 318,000 tonnes and 72 ft *21,96 m* draught.

Railways
The country with the greatest length of railway is the United States, with 198,963 miles *320 000 km* of track at 1 Jan 1980. The farthest anyone can get from a railway on the mainland island of Great Britain is 110 miles *177 km* by road in the case of Southend, Mull of Kintyre.

The number of journeys made on British Rail in 12 months to Mar 1985 was 700,700,000 (average 26.4 miles *42,4 km*) compared with the peak year of 1957, when 1101 million journeys (average 20.51 miles *33 km*) were made.

Road *Mileages*
The country with the greatest length of road is the United States (all 50 States), with 3,851,880 miles *6 199 000 km* of graded roads at 1 Jan 1982. Regular driving licences are issuable at 15, without a driver education course only in Hawaii and Mississippi. Thirteen US States issue restricted juvenile licences at 14.

Great Britain has 213,555 miles *343 685 km* of road including 1659 miles *2671 km* of motorway at April 1983 and 20,660,876 vehicles in 1985.

The first sod on Britain's first motorway, the M6 Preston By-Pass, was cut by bulldozer driver Fred Hackett on 12 June 1956 on the section between junctions 29 and 32 opened in December 1958. Britain's longest uninterrupted dual carriageway is from Plymouth to Exeter (A38) and thence by the M5 and M6 for 515 miles *829 km* terminating at Dunblane Fourways Restaurant, Stirling, Scotland.

Traffic volume *Highest*
The highest traffic volume of any point in the world is at the East Los Angeles interchange (Santa Ana, Pomona, Golden State and Santa Monica Freeways), California, USA with a 24-hr average on weekdays of 458,060 vehicles in 1983—318 per minute. The most heavily travelled stretch of road is between 43rd and 47th Street on the Dan Ryan Expressway, Chicago with an average daily volume of 254,700 vehicles.

The territory with the highest traffic density in the world is Hong Kong. By 1 Jan 1984 there were 302,118 motor vehicles on 778.9 miles *1253 km* of serviceable roads giving a density of 4.53 yd *4,14 m* per vehicle. The comparative figure for the United Kingdom in 1984 was 21.44 yd *19,60 m*. The world's busiest bridge is the Howrah Bridge across the river Hooghly in Calcutta. In addition to 57,000 vehicles a day it carries an incalculable number of pedestrians across its 1500 ft *457 m* long 72 ft *21,9 m* wide span.

The greatest traffic density at any one point in Great Britain is at Hyde Park Corner, London. The flow (including the underpass) for 24 hours in 1982 was 214,000 vehicles. The busiest Thames bridge in 1982 was Putney Bridge, with a 24-hr average of 57,700 vehicles compared with 72,500 for the Blackwall Tunnel. Britain's busiest section of motorway is between junctions

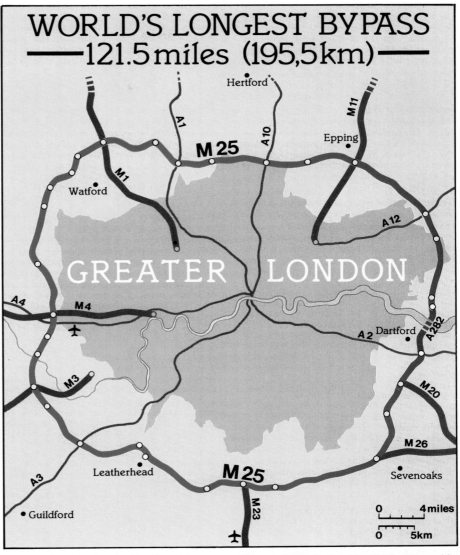

WORLD'S LONGEST BYPASS
—121.5 miles (195,5km)—

3 and 4 of the M4 registering 92,800 vehicles per 24 hours by 1980.

Traffic jams *Largest*
The longest traffic jam ever reported was that of 16 Feb 1980 which stretched northwards from Lyon 176 km *109.3 miles* towards Paris. The longest traffic jam reported in Britain was one of 40 miles *64,3 km* on the M.1 from Junction 13 (Milton Keynes) to Junction 18 (Rugby) on Easter Friday 5 Apr 1985.

Road *Widest*
The widest street in the world is the Monumental Axis running for 1½ miles *2,4 km* from the Municipal Plaza to the Plaza of the Three Powers in Brasilia, the capital of Brazil. The six-lane Boulevard was opened in April 1960 and is 250 m *273.4 yd* wide. The San Francisco–Oakland Bay Bridge Toll Plaza has 23 lanes (17 west bound) serving the Bridge in Oakland, California.

The only instance of 17 carriageway lanes side by side in Britain occurs on the M61 at Linnyshaw Moss, Worsley, Greater Manchester.

Road *Narrowest*
The world's narrowest street is in Port Isaac, Cornwall at the junction of Temple Bar and Dolphin Street. It is popularly known as

'Squeeze-belly alley' and in 19$\frac{5}{16}$ in *49 cm* wide at its narrowest point.

Road *Longest*
The longest motorable road in the world is the Pan-American Highway, from North West Alaska to Santiago, Chile, thence eastward to Buenos Aires, Argentina and terminating in Brasilia, Brazil. There remains a gap known as the Tapon del Darién, in Panama and the Atrato Swamp, Colombia. This was first traversed by the land rover La Cucaracha Cariñosa (The Affectionate Cockroach) of the Trans-Darien Expedition 1959–60 crewed by former SAS man Richard E Bevir (UK) and engineer Terence John Whitfield (Australia). They left Chepo, Panama on 3 Feb 1960 and reached Quibdó, Colombia on 17 June averaging 220 yd *201 m* per hour of indescribable difficulty. The Range Rover VXC 868K of the British Trans-Americas Expedition was the first vehicle to traverse the American continent end-to-end, leaving Alaska on 3 Dec 1971 and arriving in Tierra del Fuego on 9 June 1972 after a journey of 17,018 miles *27 387 km*.

By Pass Longest *World*
The longest by pass in the world is the M.25 6-lane Motorway which orbits London for 121½ miles *195,5 km* begun in 1972 and due for completion in October 1986 at an estimated cost of £909 million.

Most complex interchange

The most complex interchange on the British road system is that at Gravelly Hill, north of Birmingham on the Midland Link Motorway section of the M6 opened on 24 May 1972. There are 18 routes on 6 levels together with a diverted canal and river, which consumed 26,000 tons/*tonnes* of steel, 250,000 tons/*tonnes* of concrete, 300,000 tons/*tonnes* of earth and cost £8,200,000.

Street *Longest World*

The longest designated street in the world is Yonge Street running north and west from Toronto, Canada. The first stretch completed on 16 Feb 1796 ran 34 miles 53 chains *55,783 km.* Its official length now extended to Rainy River at the Ontario–Minnesota border is 1178.3 miles *1896,2 km.*

Longest Great Britain and Commonest Name

The longest designated road in Great Britain is the A1 from London to Edinburgh of 404 miles *650 km.* The longest Roman roads were Watling Street, from Dubrae (Dover) 215 miles *346 km* through Londinium (London) to Viroconium (Wroxeter), and Fosse Way, which ran 218 miles *350 km* from Lindum (Lincoln) through Aquae Sulis (Bath) to Isca Dumnoniorum (Exeter). However, a 10 mile *16 km* section of Fosse Way between Ilchester and Seaton remains indistinct. The commonest street name in Greater London is High Street (122) followed by Station Road (100).

Shortest

The title of 'The Shortest Street in the World' has been claimed since 1907 by McKinley Street in Bellefontaine, Ohio, USA built of 'vitrified brick' and measuring 30 ft *9,14 m* in length. The shortest reported measurement of a street in Britain is the 51 ft 10 in *15,79 m* of Queen Charlotte Street, Windsor, Berkshire. Barnstaple Street in Reading reduced to 5 ft *1,52 m* by re-development ceased to be a designated thoroughfare after 15 Oct 1981.

Steepest

The steepest streets in the world are Filbert Street, Russian Hill and 22nd Street, Dolores Heights, San Francisco with gradients of 31.5 per cent or 1 in 3.17. Lombard Street between Leavenworth and Hyde with 8 consecutive 90 degree turns of 20 ft *6,1 m* radius is described as the 'Crookedest street in the world'. It was so made in 1922 to reduce the gradient to 18.2%. Britain's steepest motorable road is the unclassified Chimney Bank which is signposted '1 in 3' at Rosedale Abbey, North Yorkshire. The County Surveyor states it is 'not quite' a 33 per cent gradient. Of the five unclassified roads with 1 in 3 gradients the most severe is Hard Knott Pass between Boot and Ambleside, Cumbria.

Longest hill

The longest steep hill on any road in the United Kingdom is on the road westwards from Lochcarron towards Applecross in Highland, Scotland. In 6 miles *9,6 km* this road rises from sea-level to 2054 ft *626 m* with an average gradient of 1 in 15.4, the steepest part being 1 in 4.

Road *Highest World*

The highest trail in the world is an 8 mile *13 km* stretch of the Kang-ti-suu between Khaleb and Hsin-chi-fu, Tibet which in two places exceeds 20,000 ft *6080 m.* The highest carriageable road in the world is one 1180 km *733.2 miles* long between Tibet and south western Sinkiang, completed in October 1957, which takes in passes of an altitude up to 18,480 ft *5632 m* above sea-level. Europe's highest pass (excluding the Caucasian passes) is the Col de Restefond (9193 ft *2802 m*) completed in 1962 with 21 hairpins between Jausiers and Saint Etienne-de-Tinée, France. It is usually closed between early October and early June. The highest motor road in Europe is the Pico de Veleta in the Sierra Nevada, southern Spain. The shadeless climb of 36 km *22.4 miles* brings the motorist to 11,384 ft *3469 m* above sea-level and became, on completion of a road on its southern side in Summer 1974, arguably Europe's highest 'pass'.

Highest Great Britain

The highest road in the United Kingdom is the A6293 unclassified tarmac, private extension at Great Dun Fell, Cumbria, (2780 ft *847 m*) leading to a Ministry of Defence and Air Traffic Control installation. A permit is required to use it. The highest public classified road in England is the A689 at Killhope Cross (2056 ft *626 m*) on the Cumbria–Durham border near Nenthead. The highest classified road in Scotland is the A93 road over the Grampians through Cairnwell, a pass between Blairgowrie, Tayside, and Braemar, Grampian, which reaches a height of 2199 ft *670 m.* The highest classified road in Wales is the Rhondda-Afan Inter-Valley road (A4107), which reaches 1750 ft *533 m* 2½ miles *4 km* east of Abergwynfi, Mid Glamorgan. An estate track exists to the summit of Ben a'Bhuird (3860 ft *1176 m*) in Grampian, Scotland. The highest motorway in Great Britain is the trans-Pennine M62, which, at the Windy Hill interchange, reaches an altitude of 1220 ft *371 m.* Its Dean Head cutting is the deepest roadway cutting in Europe at 183 ft *55,7 m.*

Lowest

The lowest road in the world is that along the Israeli shores of the Dead Sea, 1290 ft *393 m* below sea-level. The lowest surface roads in Great Britain are just below sea-level in the Holme Fen area of Cambridgeshire. The world's lowest 'pass' is Rock Reef Pass, Everglades National Park, Florida which is 3 ft *91 cm* above sea-level.

Longest viaduct

The longest elevated road viaduct on the British road system is the 2.97 mile *4779 m* Gravelly Hill to Castle Bromwich section of the M6. It was completed in May 1972.

Biggest square

The Tian an men (Gate of Heavenly Peace) Square in Peking, described as the navel of China, extends over 98 acres *39,6 ha.* The Maiden e Shah in Isfahan, Iran extends over 20.1 acres *8,1 ha.* The oldest London Square is Lincoln's Inn Fields dating to the mid 17th century. The largest is the 6.99 acre *2,82 ha* Ladbroke Square (open to residents only) constructed in 1842–45 while Lincoln's Inn Fields measures 6.84 acres *2,76 ha.*

Traffic lights

Semaphore-type traffic *signals* had been set up in Parliament Square, London in 1868 with red and green gas lamps for night use. It was not an offence to disobey traffic signals until assent was given to the 1930 Road Traffic Bill. Traffic *lights* were introduced in Great Britain with a one-day trial in Wolverhampton on 11 Feb 1928. They were first permanently operated in Leeds, West Yorkshire on 16 Mar and in Edinburgh, Scotland on 19 Mar 1928. The first vehicle-actuated lights were installed by Plessey at the Cornhill–Gracechurch Junction, City of London in April 1932.

Parking meters

The earliest parking meters ever installed were those put in the business district of Oklahoma City, Oklahoma, USA, on 19 July 1935. They were the invention of Carl C. Magee (USA) and reached London in 1958.

Worst driver

It was reported that a 75-year-old *male* driver received 10 traffic tickets, drove on the wrong side of the road four times, committed four hit-and-run offences and caused six accidents, all within 20 minutes, in McKinney, Texas, USA on 15 Oct 1966. The most heavily banned driver in Britain was John Hogg, 28, who, in the High Court, Edinburgh on 27 Nov 1975, received 5¾ years in gaol and his 3rd, 4th and 5th life bans for drunken driving in a stolen car while disqualified. For his previous 40 offences he had received bans of 71½ years plus two life bans.

Milestone

Britain's oldest milestone *in situ* is a Roman stone dating from AD 150 on the Stanegate, at Chesterholme, near Bardon Mill, Northumberland.

Longest ford

The longest ford in any classified road in England is that at Bilbrook, Old Cleeve parish, Somerset which measures 90 yd *82 m* in width.

Inland waterways

The country with the greatest length of inland waterways is Finland. The total length of navigable lakes and rivers is about 50 000 km *31,000 miles.* In the United Kingdom the total length of navigable rivers and canals is 3940 miles *6340 km.*

Longest navigable river

The longest navigable natural waterway in the world is the River Amazon, which sea-going vessels can ascend as far as Iquitos, in Peru, 2236 miles *3598 km* from the Atlantic seaboard. On a National Geographic Society expedition ending on 10 Mar 1969, Helen and Frank Schreider navigated downstream from San Francisco, Peru, a distance of 3845 miles *6187 km* to Bélem.

TELECOMMUNICATIONS

Telephones

The country with the greatest number of telephone lines is the United States, with 108,593,000 lines, equivalent to 468 for every 1000 people. This compares with the United Kingdom figure of 19,550,000 (31 Mar 1983) (sixth largest in the world to the USA, Japan, USSR, West Germany and France), or 348 per 1000 people. The territory with fewest reported telephone lines is Pitcairn Island with 24.

The greatest total of calls made in any country is in the United States, with 380,299 million (1623 calls per person) in 1983. The United Kingdom telephone service connected 22,976,000,000 calls, an average of 408 per person.

The city with most telephones is New York City, NY, USA, with 5,808,145 (821 per 1000 people) at 1 Jan 1981. In 1981 Washington DC reached the level of 1727 telephones per 1000 people.

Telephones *Longest telephone cable*

The world's longest submarine telephone cable is the Commonwealth Pacific Cable (COMPAC), which runs for 9340 miles *15 032 km* from Sydney, Australia, *via* Norfolk Is, Fiji and the Hawaiian Islands to Port Alberni, Canada. It cost about £35,000,000 and was inaugurated on 2 Dec 1963. The final splice was made on 24 Mar 1984.

Telephone Directories

The world's most difficult directory to tear in half is that for Houston, Texas which runs to 2889 pages for 939,640 listings. The easiest would be that for Knippa, Texas—221 listings

POSTAGE STAMPS

EARLIEST	Put on sale at GPO 1 May 1840	1d Black of Great Britain, Queen Victoria, 68,158,080 printed. Available for prepayment of postage on 6 May 1840.
HIGHEST PRICE (TENDER) (WORLD)	$1 million (then £495,000)	5 cent Blue Alexandria USA cover, Nov 25 1846 by George Normann via David Feldmans of Geneva on 9 May 1981.
HIGHEST PRICE (AUCTION) (WORLD)	£615,000	Baden 9 kr black on blue-green, colour error 1851 from the John R. Boker collection sold by Heinrich Köhler in Weisbaden, West Germany on 16 Mar 1985.
HIGHEST PRICE (ERROR)	$500,000 (£227,500)	US 1918 24 cent airmail invert of Jenny biplane 'Princeton' block of 4, by Myron Kaller syndicate on 19 July 1979. A single example reached $180,000 at auction in New York City in May 1982.
HIGHEST PRICE (AUCTION) (UK)	£105,000	Norwegian 4 Skilling Blue, 1855 block of 39 used—found in Trondheim railway station c. 1923 sold by Phillips, New Bond St, London on 5 Mar 1981.
LARGEST PHILATELIC PURCHASE	$11,000,000 (then £4,945,000)	Marc Haas collection of 3000 US postal and pre-postal covers to 1869 by Stanley Gibbons International Ltd of London in August 1979.
LARGEST (SPECIAL PURPOSE)	9¾ × 2¾ in 247,5 × 69,8 mm	Express Delivery of China, 1913.
(STANDARD POSTAGE)	6.3 × 4.33 in 160 × 110 mm	Marshall Islands 75 cents issued 30 Oct 1979.
SMALLEST	0.31 × 0.37 in 8 × 9,5 mm	10 cent and 1 peso Colombian State of Bolivar, 1863–6.
HIGHEST DENOMINATION (WORLD)	£100	Red and black, George V, of Kenya, 1925–7.
(UK)	£5	Orange, Victoria, issued 21 Mar 1882. Pink and Blue Elizabeth II definitive 2 Feb 1977.
LOWEST DENOMINATION	3,000 pengö of Hungary	Issued 1946 when 150 million million pengö = 1p.
RAREST (WORLD)	Unique examples include	British Guiana (now Guyana) 1 cent black on magenta of 1856 (see above); Swedish 3 skilling banco yellow colour error of 1855. Gold Coast provisional of 1885 and the US post-master stamp from Boscowen, New Haven and Lockport, NY.
RAREST (UK) (Issued for postal use)	11 or 12	6d dull purple Inland Revenue Edward VII, issued and withdrawn on 14 May 1904. Only unused specimen in private hands from W. H. Harrison-Cripps sold by Stanley Gibbons for £10,000 on 27 Oct 1972.

Despite a 35-fold inflation since 1882, this Victorian £5 orange is still after 103 years the co-holder of the record for the highest British denomination. (See above)

southerly in the British Isles is at Samarès, Jersey. The oldest is at Sanquhar, Dumfries and Galloway which was first referred to in 1763. In England the Post Office at Shipton-Under-Wychwood, Oxon dates back to April 1845. The highest Post Office in England is at Flash, Staffordshire at 1518 ft 462,6 m.

The longest counter in Britain was one of 185 ft 56,38 m with 33 positions when opened in 1962 at Trafalgar Square, London. The longest in 1985 is at George Square, Glasgow, being 157 ft 47,8 m long with 27 positions.

7. EDUCATION

Compulsory education was first introduced in 1819 in Prussia. It became compulsory in the United Kingdom in 1870.

University Oldest *World*
The Sumerians had scribal schools or É-Dub-ba soon after 3500 BC. The oldest existing educational institution in the world is the University of Karueein, founded in AD 859 in Fez, Morocco. The University of Bologna was founded in 1088.

University Oldest *Great Britain*
The oldest university in the United Kingdom is the University of Oxford, which came into being in c. 1167. The oldest of the existing colleges is probably University College (1249), though its foundation is less well documented than that of Merton College in 1264. The earliest college at Cambridge University is Peterhouse, founded in 1284. The largest college at either university is Trinity College, Cambridge. It was founded in 1546. The oldest university in Scotland is the University of St. Andrews, Fife. It was established as a university in 1411 but theology and medicine may have been taught there since c. 900 AD.

University *Greatest enrolment*
The university with the greatest enrolment in the world is the State University of New York,

on 2 pages. The directory for Anguilla in 1972 was of 26 numbers in typescript.

Switchboard *largest*
The world's biggest switchboard is that in the Pentagon, Washington DC with 25,000 lines and an annual phone bill of $8.7 million.

Optical Fibre Record
The longest distance of which signals have been transmitted without repeaters is 251,6 km 156,3 miles at the British Telecom research laboratory at Martlesham Heath, Suffolk in February 1985. The laser wavelength was 1525 nm and the rate was 35 mega bits/sec.

Postal services
The country with the largest mail in the world is the United States, whose population posted 131 billion letters and packages in 1984 when the US Postal Service employed 702,123 people with the world's largest civilian vehicle fleet of 193,956 cars and trucks. The United Kingdom total was 10,665 million letters and 192 million parcels in the year ending 31 Mar 1984.

The United States also takes first place in the average number of letters which each person posts during one year. The figure was 506 in

1983. The United Kingdom figure was 191 per head in 1983–84.

Postal address *Highest numbering*
The practice of numbering houses began on the Pont Notre Dame, Paris, France in 1463. The highest numbered house in Britain is No 2679 Stratford Road, Hockley Heath, West Midlands, owned since 1964 by Mr and Mrs Howard Hughes. The highest numbered house in Scotland is No 2629 London Road, Mount Vernon, Glasgow, which is part of the local police station.

Pillar-boxes *Oldest*
The oldest pillar-box still in service is one dating from 8 Feb 1853 in Union Street, St Peter Port, Guernsey. It was cast by John Vaudin in Jersey and was restored to its original maroon livery in October 1981. The oldest original box in Great Britain is at Barnes Cross, Holwell (postally in Bishop's Caundle), Dorset, dating from probably later in 1853. The hexagonal roof pillar box in Kent Railway Station, Glanmere, Cork dates from 1857.

Post Offices
The Post Office's northernmost post office is at Haroldswick, Unst, Shetland Islands. The most

USA, with 348,361 students enrolled in 1982. Its oldest college at Potsdam, New York was founded in 1816. Britain's largest university is the University of London with 40,696 internal students and 19,095 external students (in 1982–83) so totalling 59,791. The Open University, first called the University of the Air (Royal Charter 30 May 1969) at Walton Hall near Milton Keynes has 5520 part-time tutors and 76,140 students.

University Largest
Tenders for the $3.4 billion (£1790 million) University of Riyadh, Saudi Arabia closed in June 1978. The University will house 15,000 families and have its own mass transport system.

The largest existing university building in the world is the M. V. Lomonosov State University on the Lenin Hills, south of Moscow, USSR. It stands 240 m *787.4 ft* tall, has 32 storeys and contains 40,000 rooms. It was constructed in 1949–53.

University Most northerly
The world's most northerly university is Inupiat University of the Arctic Barrow, Alaska, USA in *Lat* 71° 16′ N. Eskimo subjects feature in the curricula.

Largest court or quadrangle
The largest College quadrangle at any Oxford or Cambridge college is the Great Court, Trinity College, Cambridge completed in 1605. Its dimensions average 325 ft × 273 ft *99,06 m × 83,2 m.*

Professor Youngest
The youngest at which anybody has been elected to a chair in a university is 19 years in the case of Colin MacLaurin (1698–1746), who was elected to Marischal College, Aberdeen as Professor of Mathematics on 30 Sept 1717. In 1725 he was made Professor of Mathematics at Edinburgh University on the recommendation of Sir Isaac Newton who was a professor at Cambridge aged 26.

Professors Most durable
Dr Joel Hildebrand (1881–1983), Professor Emeritus of Physical Chemistry at the University of California, Berkeley, became first an Assistant Professor in 1913 and published his 275th research paper 68 years later in 1981. The longest period of which any professorship has been held in Britain is 63 years in the case of Thomas Martyn (1735–1825), Professor of Botany at Cambridge University from 1762 until his death. The last professor-for-life was the pathologist Professor Henry Roy Dean (1879–1961) for his last 39 years at Cambridge.

Senior Wranglers
Since 1910 the Wranglers (first class honours students in the Cambridge University mathematical Tripos, part 2) have been placed in alphabetical order only. In 1890 Miss Philippa Garrett Fawcett (d. 1948) in Newnham was placed 'above the Senior Wrangler'.

Youngest undergraduate and graduate
The most extreme recorded case of undergraduate juvenility was that of William Thomson (1824–1907), later Lord Kelvin, OM, GCVO, who entered Glasgow University aged 10 years 4 months in October 1834 and matriculated on 14 Nov 1834. Dr Merrill Kenneth Wolf (b. 28 Aug 1931) of Cleveland, Ohio took his B.A. in music from Yale University in September 1945 in the month of his 14th birthday. Ruth Lawrence (b. 1971) of Huddersfield, West Yorkshire passed Pure Mathematics O level at the age of 9 and Pure Mathematics A level and Grade 1 S level in June 1981 aged 10. She was accepted for entrance to Oxford at the age of 12.

Schools Oldest in Britain
The title of the oldest existing school in Britain is contested. It is claimed that King's School in Canterbury, Kent, was a foundation of Saint Augustine, some time between his arrival in Kent in AD 597 and his death in *c.* 604. Cor Tewdws (College of Theodosius) at Llantwit Major, South Glamorgan, reputedly burnt down in AD 446, was refounded, after an elapse of 62 years, by St Illtyd in 508 and flourished into the 13th century. Winchester College, Hampshire was founded in 1382. The Pedagogue's House, King Edward VI School, Stratford-upon-Avon, Warwickshire was built in 1427.

School Largest World
In 1983/84 South Point High School, Calcutta, India (founded 1954) had an enrolment of 12,350 regular students.

Great Britain
The school with the most pupils in Great Britain was Exmouth Comprehensive, Devon at 2599 (1983–84). The highest enrolment in Scotland has been at Our Lady's Roman Catholic High School, Motherwell, Strathclyde with a peak of 2325 in August 1977. The total in Holy Child School, Belfast, Northern Ireland reached 2752 in 1973 before being split up. The highest enrolment in 1983/84 is 2,329 at the Methodist College, Belfast.

School Most Expensive World
The annual cost of keeping a pupil at Le Rosey, Gstaad, Switzerland in 1983/84 was reputed to be $20,000.

Great Britain
In the academic year 1985–86 St. Andrew's Private Tutorial Centre, Cambridge, England (principal C. T. Easterbrook) charged £11,284 for full-time science students (tuition and accommodation). The most expensive school in Great Britain is Millfield (founded 1935) in Street, Somerset (headmaster C. R. M. Atkinson). The annual fee for boarding entries in 1985–6 is £7,710. The most expensive girls' school in 1985 was Cobham Hall (founded 1960), Kent (headmistress Miss Susan Cameron), with annual fees of £5,121.

Earliest Comprehensive School
Lakes School, Cumbria, formed from an intake from Windermere Grammar School and other Westmorland schools adopted the non-selective comprehensive principle as early as 1945. Calder High School was established after formal rejection of the 11 plus examinations from two West Riding schools in 1950. The earliest purpose-built was Kidbrooke Comprehensive for Girls, London SE opened in 1954.

Oldest old school tie
The practice of wearing distinctive neckties bearing the colours of registered designs of schools, universities, sports clubs, regiments, etc., appears to date from *c.* 1880. The practice originated in Oxford University, where boater bands were converted into use as 'ribbon ties'. The earliest definitive evidence stems from an order from Exeter College for college ties, dated 25 June 1880.

PTA Oldest
The Parent-Teacher Association with the earliest foundation date in Britain is St. Christopher School, Letchworth, Parents' Circle formed in 1919.

Most schools
The greatest documented number of schools attended by a pupil is 265 by Wilma Williams, now Mrs R. J. Horton, from 1933–43 when her parents were in show business in the USA.

Most 'O' and 'A' levels
Dr Francis L. Thomason of London W6 had by January 1984 accumulated 56 O and O/A, 9 A and 1 S levels making a total of 66 of which 30 were in the top grade. A. F. Prime, a prisoner in HM Open Prison Sudbury, accumulated a total of 1 S, 14 A's and 34 O's between 1968 and 1982. Environmental difficulties tend to make study harder in prison than elsewhere.

Stephen Murrell of Crown Woods School, Eltham passed 8 A levels at one sitting in June 1978 achieving 7 at grade A. Robert Pidgeon (b. 7 Feb 1959) of St Peter's School, Bournemouth, secured 13 O level passes at grade A at one sitting in the summer of 1975. Subsequently he passed 3 A levels at grade A and 2 S levels with firsts. Andrew Maclaren (b. 1963) of Chelmsford, Essex passed 14 O levels, 5 A levels all at grade A and 3 S levels at grade one—making 22 top grades. At Queens' College, Cambridge he got first class honours in 1983.

Youngest headmaster
The youngest headmaster of a major public school was Henry Montagu Butler (b. 2 July 1833), appointed Headmaster of Harrow School on 16 Nov 1859, when aged 26 years 137 days. His first term in office began in January 1860.

Most durable don
Dr Martin Joseph Routh (b. Sept 1755) was President of Magdalen College, Oxford, from April 1791 for 63 years 8 months, until his death in his 100th year on 22 Dec 1854. He had previously been a fellow for 16 years and was thus a don for a span of 79 years.

Most durable teachers
David Rhys Davies (1835–1928) taught as a pupil teacher and latterly as teacher and headmaster of Dame Anna Child's School, Whitton, Powys (1879–1928) for a total of 76 years 2 months. Col Ernest Achey Loftus CBE, TD, DL (b. 11 Jan 1884) served as a teacher over a span of 73 years from May 1901 in York, England until 18 Feb 1975 in Zambia retiring as the world's oldest civil servant aged 91 years 38 days. His father William was born in Hull in the reign of William IV in 1832.

Elsie Marguerite Touzel (1889–1984) of Jersey began her teaching career aged 16 in 1905 and was teaching at Les Alpes School, Faldonet until her retirement 75 years later on 30 Sept 1980.

Highest Endowment
The greatest single gift in the history of higher education has been $125 million to Louisiana State University by C. B. Pennington in 1983.

8. RELIGIONS

Oldest
Human burial, which has religious connotations, is known from *c.* 60,000 BC among *Homo sapiens neanderthalensis* in the Shanidar cave, N. Iraq. The earliest named prophet was Zoroaster (Zarathushtra) dated to *c.* 1600 BC.

Largest
Religious statistics are necessarily only approximate. The test of adherence to a religion varies widely in rigour, while many individuals, particularly in the East, belong to two or more religions.

Christianity is the world's prevailing religion, with some 1,070,000,000 adherents in 1983. The Vatican statistics office reported that in 1982 there were 783,660,000 Roman Catholics. The largest non-Christian religion is Islam (Muslim) with some 600,000,000 followers.

ROMAN CATHOLIC RECORDS
Popes & Cardinals

Longest Papal Reign
Pius IX—Giovanni Maria Mastai-Ferretti (1846–1878). 31 years 236 days

Shortest Papal Reign
Stephan II (752). 2 days

Longest Lived Pope
St. Agatho (d. 681) (probably exaggerated). ?106 years
Leo XIII—Gioacchino Pecci (1810–1903). 93 years 140 days

Youngest Elected
Benedict IX—Theophylact (*c.* 1020–1056) in 1032. 11 or 12 years

Last Married
Adrian II (pre-celibacy rule). Elected 867

Last with Children
Alexander VI—Rodrigo Borgia (1431–1503) father of six. Elected 1492

Last non-Cardinal
Urban VI—Bartolomeo Prignano (1318–89), Archbishop of Bari. 8 Apr 1378

Last Briton
Adrian IV—Nicholas Breakspear (*c.* 1100–59), b. Abbots Langley, Hertfordshire. 4 Dec 1154

Last previous non-Italian
Adrian VI—Adrian Florenz Boeyens (Netherlands). Elected 31 Aug 1522

Slowest Election
Gregory X—Teobaldi Visconti, 31 months. Feb 1269–1 Sept 1271

Fastest Election
Julius II—on first ballot. 21 Oct 1503

Slowest Canonization
St. Leo III—over span of 857 years. 816–1673

Oldest Cardinal (*all-time*)
Georgio da Costa (b. Portugal, 1406) d. Rome aged 102 years. 18 Sept 1508

Oldest Cardinal (*current*)
Pietro Parente (b. 16 Feb 1891) 93rd birthday. fl. 16 Feb 1984

Youngest Cardinal (*all-time*)
Luis Antonio de Bourbon (b. 25 July 1727) aged 8 years 147 days. Elected 19 Dec 1735

Youngest Cardinal (*current*)
Alfonso Lopez Trujillo of Columbia (b. 18 Nov 1935). 47 yr 76 days

Longest Serving Cardinal
Cardinal Duke of York, grandson of James VII of Scotland and II of England, 60 years 10 days. 1747–1807

Longest Serving Bishop
Bishop Louis François de la Baume de Suze (1603–1690). 76 yr 273 days from 6 Dec 1613

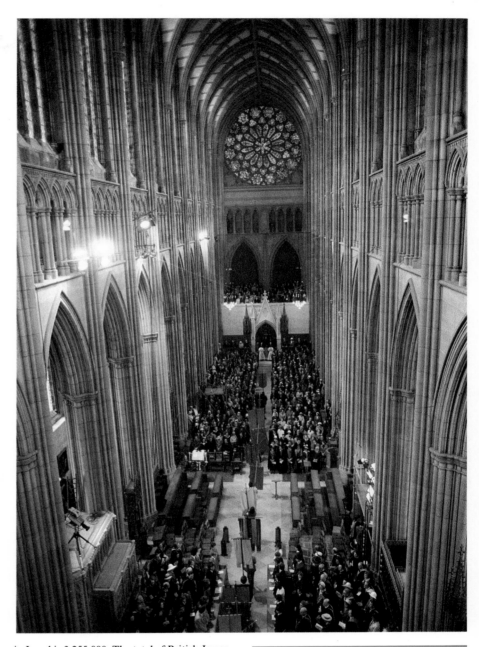

The largest school chapel in England begun in 1868 at Lancing College and now with a capacity of 900.

In the United Kingdom the Anglicans comprise members of the Established Church of England, the Dis-established Church in Wales, the Episcopal Church in Scotland and the Church of Ireland. The Church of England has two provinces (Canterbury and York), 44 dioceses, 10,749 full time diocesan clergymen and 13,395 parishes (1 Jan 1985).

In Scotland the most numerous group is the Church of Scotland (12 Synods, 47 Presbyteries), which had 887,165 members as at 31 Dec 1984.

Largest clergies
The world's largest religious organization is the Roman Catholic Church, with 125 Cardinals, 422 archbishops, 2435 bishops, 408,945 priests and 905,204 nuns in 1984. There are about 420,000 churches.

Jews
The total of world Jewry was estimated to be 16.8 million in 1983. The highest concentration is in North America, with 7.3 million, of whom 2.0 million are in the New York area. The total in Israel is 3,255,000. The total of British Jewry is 410,000 of whom 280,000 are in Greater London, and 13,000 in Glasgow. The total in Tōkyō, Japan, is only 400.

PLACES OF WORSHIP
Earliest *World*
A sculpted stone face, half primate/half feline, discovered by Dr Leslie Freeman of the University of Chicago in the El Juyo cave shrine, Northern Spain, is the oldest known religious shrine and is dated to *c.* 12,000 BC. The oldest surviving Christian church in the world is a converted house in Douro-Europos now Qal'at es Salihiye in eastern Syria, dating from AD 232.

Oldest *Great Britain*
The oldest ecclesiastical building in the United Kingdom is a 6th century cell built by St Brendan in AD 542 on Eileachan Naoimh (pronounced Noo), Garvelloch Islands, Strathclyde. The Church in Great Britain with the oldest origins is St Martin's Church in Canterbury, Kent. It was built in AD 560 on the foundations of a 1st century Roman church. The chapel of St Peter on the Wall, Bradwell-on-Sea, Essex was built in AD 654–660. The oldest church in Ireland is the Gallerus Oratory, built in *c.* 750 at Ballyferriter, near Kilmalkedar, County Kerry. Britain's oldest nunnery is St Peter and Paul Minster, on the Isle of Thanet, Kent. It was founded in *c.* 748 by the Abbess Eadburga of Bugga. The oldest catholic church is St Etheldreda, Ely Place, Holborn, London founded in 1251. The oldest non-conformist chapel is the thatched chapel at Horningsham, Wiltshire dated 1566.

Temple Largest
The largest religious structure ever built is Angkor Wat (City Temple), enclosing 402 acres *162,6 ha* in Kampuchea, south-east Asia. It was built to the Hindu god Vishnu by the Khmer King Suryavarman II in the period 1113–50. Its

curtain wall measures 1400 × 1400 yd *1280 × 1280 m* and its population, before it was abandoned in 1432, was 80,000. The whole complex of 72 major monuments begun *c.* AD 900 extends over 15 × 5 miles *24 × 8 km*. The largest Buddhist temple in the world is Borobudur, near Jogjakarta, Indonesia built in the 8th century. It is 103 ft *31,5 m* tall and 403 ft *123 m* square.

The largest Mormon temple is the Salt Lake Temple, Utah, USA completed in April 1983 and with a floor area of 253,015 ft² or 5.80 acres *23 505 m²*.

Cathedral Largest *World*
The world's largest cathedral is the cathedral church of the Diocese of New York, St John the Divine, with a floor area of 121,000 ft² *11 240 m²* and a volume of 16,822,000 ft³ *476 350 m³*. The cornerstone was laid on 27 Dec 1892, and work on the Gothic building was stopped in 1941. Work re-started in earnest in July 1979. In New York it is referred to as 'Saint John the Unfinished'. The nave is the longest in the world, 601 ft *183,18 m* in length, with a vaulting 124 ft *37,79 m* in height.

The cathedral covering the largest area is that of Santa Mariá de la Sede in Sevilla (Seville), Spain. It was built in Spanish Gothic style between 1402 and 1519 and is 414 ft *126,18 m* long, 271 ft *82,60 m* wide and 100 ft *30,48 m* high to the vault of the nave.

SUPERLATIVE RELIGIOUS BUILDINGS

Top line (left to right): **Largest Mormon Church,** Salt Lake City, Utah, USA (see above). **Earliest known Pagoda Site,** Rangoon, Burma (see page 217). **Most Valuable Sacred Object,** Bangkok, Thailand (see page 217). *Bottom line (left to right):* **World's Largest Church,** The Vatican, Rome (see page 217). **World's tallest Minarets,** Selangor, Malaysia (see page 217). **Tallest Ancient Minaret,** New Delhi, India (see page 217).

Photographs: Popperfoto, Robert Harding, Eric Reeves and Soma Nimit.
Artwork: Eddie Botchway

Cathedral Largest *Great Britain*

The largest cathedral in the British Isles is the Cathedral Church of Christ in Liverpool. Built in modernized Gothic style, work was begun on 18 July 1904, and it was finally consecrated on 25 Oct 1978 after 74 years (*cf.* Exeter 95 years) using ½ million stone blocks and 12 million bricks at an actual cost of some £6 million. The building encloses 104,275 ft² *9687 m²* and has an overall length of 636 ft *193,85 m*. The Vestey Tower is 331 ft *100,88 m* high. It contains the highest vaulting in the world—175 ft *53,34 m* maximum at undertower and the highest Gothic arches ever built being 107 ft *32,61 m* at apices.

Cathedral Smallest

The smallest church in the world designated as a cathedral is that of the Christ Catholic Church, Highlandville, Missouri, USA. Consecrated in July 1983 it measures 14 × 17 ft *4,26 × 5,18 m* and has seating for 18 people. The smallest cathedral in use in the United Kingdom (of old foundation) is St Asaph in Clwyd, Wales, it is 182 ft *55,47 m* long, 68 ft *20,72 m* wide and has a tower 100 ft *30,48 m* high. Oxford Cathedral in Christ Church (College) is 155 ft *47,24 m* long. The nave of the Cathedral of the Isles on the Isle of Cumbrae, Strathclyde measures only 40 × 20 ft *12,19 × 6,09 m*. The total floor area is 2,124 ft² *197,3 m²*.

Church Largest *World*

The largest church in the world is the basilica of St Peter, built between 1492 and 1612 in the Vatican City, Rome. The length of the church, measured from the apse, is 611 ft 4 in *186,33 m*. The area is 162,990 ft² *15 142 m²*. The inner diameter of the famous dome is 137 ft 9 in *41,98 m* and its centre is 119 m *390 ft 5 in* high. The external height is 457 ft 9 in *139,52 m*.

The elliptical Basilique of St Pie X at Lourdes, France, completed in 1957 at a cost of £2,000,000 has a capacity of 20,000 under its giant span arches and a length of 200 m *656 ft*.

The crypt of the underground Civil War Memorial Church in the Guadarrama Mountains, 45 km *28 miles* from Madrid, Spain, is 260 m *853 ft* in length. It took 21 years (1937–58) to build, at a reported cost of £140,000,000, and is surmounted by a cross 150 m *492 ft* tall.

Church Largest *Great Britain*

The largest Church in the United Kingdom is the Collegiate Church of St Peter at Westminster built AD 1050–1745. Its maximum dimensions are overall: length 530 ft *161,5 m*; breadth across transept 203 ft *61,87 m* and internal height 101 ft 8 in *30,98 m*. The largest parish church is the Parish Church of the Most Holy and Undivided Trinity at Kingston-upon-Hull covering 27,235 ft² *2530 m²* and with an external length and width of 288 ft × 124 ft *87,7 × 37,7 m*. It is also believed to be the country's oldest brick building serving its original purpose, dating from *c.* 1285. Both the former Cathedral of St Mungo, Glasgow and Beverley Minster, Humberside are now used as parish churches. The largest school chapel is that of the 150 ft *45,7 m* high Lancing College, West Sussex.

Church Smallest *World*

The world's smallest church is the Union Church at Wiscasset, Maine, USA, with a floor area of 31½ ft² *2,92 m²* (7 × 4½ ft *2,13 × 1,37 m*). St. Gobban's Church, Portbradden, County Antrim, Northern Ireland measures 12 ft 1½ in by 6 ft 6 in *3,7 × 2,0 m*.

Church Smallest *Great Britain*

The smallest church in use in England is Bremilham Church, Cowage Farm, Foxley near Malmesbury, Wiltshire which measures 12 ×

One of the 3 prophets from the world's earliest complete stained glass window in Augsberg Cathedral dating from earlier than AD 1100.

12 ft *3,65 × 3,65 m* and is used for service once a year. The smallest completed medieval English church in regular use is that at Culbone, Somerset, which measures 35 × 12 ft *10,66 × 3,65 m*. The smallest Welsh chapel is St Trillo's Chapel, Rhôs-on-Sea (Llandrillo-yn-Rhos), Clwyd, measuring only 12 × 6 ft *3,65 × 1,83 m*. The smallest chapel in Scotland is St Margaret's, Edinburgh, measuring 16½ × 10½ ft *5,02 × 3,20 m*, giving a floor area of 173¼ ft² *16,09 m²*.

Synagogue Largest *World*

The largest synagogue in the world is the Temple Emanu-El on Fifth Avenue at 65th Street, New York City, NY, USA. The temple, completed in September 1929, has a frontage of 150 ft *45,72 m* on Fifth Avenue and 253 ft *77,11 m* on 65th Street. The Sanctuary proper can accommodate 2500 people, and the adjoining Beth-El Chapel seats 350. When all the facilities are in use, more than 6000 people can be accommodated.

Synagogue Largest *Great Britain*

The largest synagogue in Great Britain is the Edgware Synagogue, Barnet, Greater London, completed in 1959, with a capacity of 1630 seats. That with highest registered membership is Ilford Synagogue with 2492 at 1 Jan 1983.

Mosque Largest

The largest mosque ever built was the now ruinous al-Malawiya mosque of al-Mutawakil in Samarra, Iraq built in AD 842–52 and measuring 9.21 acres *3,72 ha* with dimensions of 784 × 512 ft *238,9 × 156,0 m*. The world's largest mosque in use is the Umayyad Mosque in Damascus, Syria built on a 2000-year-old religious site measuring 157 × 97 m *515 × 318 ft* thus covering an area of 3.76 acres *1,52 ha*. The largest mosque will be the Merdeka Mosque in Djakarta, Indonesia, which was begun in 1962. The cupola will be 45 m *147.6 ft* in diameter and the capacity in excess of 50,000 people.

Minaret *Tallest*

The tallest minarets in the world are the 4 of 105 m *344 ft 5 in* being built for a new mosque in Shah Alam, Selangor, Malaysia. The Qutb Minar, south of New Delhi, India, built in 1194 is 238 ft *72,54 m* tall.

Pagoda *Tallest and Oldest*

The world's tallest pagoda is the Phra Pathom Chedi at Nakhon Pathom, Thailand, which was built for King Mongkut in 1853–70. It rises to 115 m *377 ft*. The oldest pagoda in China is Sung-Yo Ssu in Honan built with 15 12-sided storeys, in AD 523 though the 326 ft *99,3 m* tall Shwedagon Pagoda, Rangoon, Burma is built on the site of a 27 ft *8,2 m* tall pagoda dating to 585 BC.

Sacred Object *Most Valuable*

The sacred object with the highest intrinsic value is the 15th century gold Buddah in Wat Trimitr Temple in Bangkok, Thailand. It is 10 ft *3,04 m* tall and weighs an estimated 5½ tonnes. At $500 per fine ounce its intrinsic worth has been calculated to be £28½ million. The gold under the plaster exterior was only found in 1954.

Nave *Longest*

The longest nave in the United Kingdom is that of St Albans Cathedral, Hertfordshire, which is 285 ft *86,86 m* long. The central tower of Liverpool's Anglican Cathedral (internal overall length 636 ft *193,85 m*) interrupts the nave with an undertower space.

Spire Tallest *World*

The tallest cathedral spire in the world is that of the Protestant Cathedral of Ulm in Germany. The building is early Gothic and was begun in 1377. The tower, in the centre of the west façade, was not finally completed until 1890 and is 160,90 m *528 ft* high. The world's tallest church spire is that of the Chicago Temple of the First Methodist Church on Clark Street, Chicago, Illinois, USA. The building consists of a 22-storey skyscraper (erected in 1924) surmounted by a parsonage at 330 ft *100,5 m*, a 'Sky Chapel' at 400 ft *121,92 m* and a steeple cross at 568 ft *173,12 m* above street level.

Great Britain

The highest spire in Great Britain is that of the church of St Mary, called Salisbury Cathedral, Wiltshire. The Lady Chapel was built in the years 1220–5 and the main fabric of the cathedral was finished and consecrated in 1258. The spire was added later, *ante* 1305, and reaches a height of 404 ft *123,13 m*. The central spire of Lincoln Cathedral completed in *c.* 1307 and which fell in 1548 was 525 ft *160,02 m* tall.

Stained glass *Oldest*

The oldest complete stained glass in the world represents the Prophets in a window of the cathedral of Augsburg, Bavaria, Germany, dating from the second half of the 11th century. The oldest datable stained glass in the United Kingdom has been represented by a figure of St Michael in All Saints Church, Dalbury, Derbyshire of the late 11th century. Pieces of stained glass dated before 850 AD possibly some even to the 7th century excavated nearby by Prof. Rosemary Cramp were placed into a window of that date in St Paul's Church, Jarrow, County Durham.

Stained glass *Largest*

The largest stained glass window is the complete mural of The Resurrection Mausoleum in Justice, Illinois, measuring 22,381 ft^2 *2079 m^2* in 2448 panels completed in 1971. The largest single stained glass window in Great Britain is the East window in Gloucester Cathedral measuring 72 × 38 ft *21,94 × 11,58 m*, set up to commemorate the Battle of Crécy (1346), while the largest area of stained glass is 128 lights, totalling 25,000 ft^2 *2 322 m^2* in York Minster.

Brasses

The world's oldest monumental brass is that commemorating Bishop Yso von Wölpe in Andreaskirche, Verden, near Hanover, W. Germany, dating from 1231. An engraved coffin plate of St Ulrich (d. 973), laid in 1187, was found buried in the Church of SS Ulrich and Afra, Augsburg, W. Germany in 1979. The oldest brass in Great Britain is of Sir John D'Abernon (d. 1277) at Stoke D'Abernon, near Leatherhead, Surrey, dating from *c.* 1320.

A dedication brass dated 24 Apr 1241 in Ashbourne church, Derbyshire has been cited as the earliest arabic writing extant in Britain.

CHURCH PERSONNEL

Saints

There are 1848 'registered' saints (including 60 St Johns) of whom 628 are Italians, 576 French and 271 from the United Kingdom and Ireland. Of these 8 came from Cambridge and 7 from Oxford between 1535 and 1645 but none from the House of Commons. Britain's first Christian martyr was St Alban executed *c.* AD 209. The first US born saint is Mother Elizabeth Ann Bayley Seton (1774–1821) canonized 14 Sept 1975. The total includes 76 Popes.

Most rapidly canonized

The shortest interval that has elapsed between the death of a Saint and his canonization was in the case of St Anthony of Padua, Italy, who died on 13 June 1231 and was canonized 352 days later on 30 May 1232. For the other extreme of 857 years see Papal table.

Bishopric *Longest tenure*

The longest tenure of any Church of England bishopric is 57 years in the case of the Rt Rev. Thomas Wilson, who was consecrated Bishop of Sodar and Man on 16 Jan 1698 and died in office on 7 Mar 1755. Of English bishoprics the longest tenures, if one excludes the unsubstantiated case of Aethelwulf, reputedly Bishop of Hereford from 937 to 1012, are those of 47 years by Jocelin de Bohun (Salisbury) 1142–89 and Nathaniel Crew or Crewe (Durham) 1674–1721.

Bishop *Oldest*

The oldest serving bishop (excluding Suffragans and Assistants) in the Church of England as at mid 1984 was the Right Reverend Douglas Feaver, Bishop of Peterborough, who was born on 22 May 1914.

The oldest Roman Catholic bishop in recent years has been Bishop Angelo Teutonico, formerly Bishop of Aversa (b. 28 Aug 1874), who died aged 103 years 276 days on 31 May 1978. He had celebrated Mass about 24,800 times. Bishop Herbert Welch of the United Methodist Church, who was elected a bishop for Japan and Korea in 1916, died on 4 Apr 1969 aged 106.

Bishop *Youngest*

The youngest bishop of all time was HRH The Duke of York and Albany, KG, GCB, GCH, the second son of George III, who was elected Bishop of Osnabrück, through his father's influence as Elector of Hanover, at the age of 196 days on 27 Feb 1764. He resigned after 39 years' enjoyment. The youngest serving bishop (excluding Suffragans and Assistants) in the Church of England is the Rev Dr David Hope (b. 1940) whose appointment to the See of Wakefield was announced on 2 July 1985.

Oldest parish priest

Father Alvaro Fernandez (b. 8 Dec 1880) served as a parish priest at Santiago de Abres, Spain from 1919 and continued into his 105th year. The oldest Anglican clergyman is the Rev Clement Williams (b. 30 Oct 1879) now of Canterbury, Kent.

Longest incumbency

The longest Church of England incumbency on record is one of 75 years 357 days by the Rev. Bartholomew Edwards, Rector of St Nicholas, Ashill, Norfolk from 1813 to 1889. There appears to be some doubt as to whether the Rev. Richard

9. ACCIDENTS AND DISASTERS

WORST IN THE WORLD

DISASTER	NUMBER KILLED	LOCATION	DATE
Pandemic	75,000,000 ...	Eurasia: The Black Death (bubonic, pneumonic and septicaemic plague)	1347–51
Genocide	c. 35,000,000	Mongol extermination of Chinese Peasantry	1311–40
Influenza	21,640,000	Worldwide: Influenza ....April–Nov	1918
Famine	c. 20,000,000[1]	Northern China (revealed May 1981)	1969–71
Circular Storm[2]	1,000,000	Ganges Delta Islands, Bangladesh ....12–13 Nov	1970
Flood	900,000	Hwang-ho River, China ....Oct	1887
Earthquake	830,000	Shensi Province, China (duration 2 hours) ....23 Jan	1556
Landslide	180,000	Kansu Province, China ......16 Dec	1920
Atomic Bomb	141,000	Hiroshima, Japan ....6 Aug	1945
Conventional Bombing[3]	c. 140,000	Tokyo, Japan ....10 Mar	1945
Volcanic Eruption	92,000	Tambora Sumbawa, Indonesia ....5–7 April	1815
Avalanches	c. 18,000[4]	Yungay, Huascarán, Peru ....31 May	1970
Marine (single ship)	c. 7700	*Wilhelm Gustloff* (25,484 tons) German Liner torpedoed off Danzig by USSR submarine S-13 ....30 Jan	1945
Dam Burst	c. 5000[5]	Manchhu River Dam, Morvi, Gujarat, India ....11 Aug	1979
Panic	c. 4000[6]	Chungking (Zhong qing) China air raid shelter ....c. 8 June	1941
Smog	2,850	London fog, England ....5–13 Dec	1951
Tunnelling (Silicosis)	c. 2500	Hawk's Nest hydroelectric tunnel, W. Virginia, USA	1931–35
Industrial (Chemical)	c. 2500[7]	Union Carbide Methylisocyanate plant, Bhopal, India ....2–3 Dec	1984
Explosion	1963[8]	Halifax, Nova Scotia, Canada ....6 Dec	1917
Fire[9] (single building)	1670	The Theatre, Canton, China ....May	1845
Mining[10]	1572	Hinkeiko Colliery, China (coal dust explosion) ....26 April	1942
Riot	c. 1200	New York anti-conscription riots ....13–16 July	1863
Road[11]	c. 1100	Petrol tanker explosion inside Salang Tunnel, Afghanistan 2 or 3 Nov	1982
Mass Suicide	913	People's Temple cult by cyanide, Jonestown, Guyana ....18 Nov	1978
Crocodiles	c. 900	Japanese soldiers, Ramree I., Burma (disputed) ....19–20 Feb	1945
Railway	>800	Bagmati River, Bihar state, India ....6 June	1981
Fireworks	>800	Daupine's Wedding, Paris ....16 May	1770
Tornado	689	South Central States, USA (3 hours) ....18 Mar	1925
Aircraft (Civil)	583	KLM-Pan Am Boeing 747 ground crash, Tenerife ....27 Mar	1977
Man-eating Animal	436	Champawat district, India, tigress shot by Col. Jim Corbet (d. 1955)	1907
Bacteriological & Chemical Warfare	c. 300	Novosibirsk B & CW plant, USSR ....April–May	1979
Hail	246	Moredabad, Uttar Pradesh, India ....20 April	1888
Terrorism	243	Lorry bomb, US Marine barracks, Beirut, Lebanon ....23 Oct	1983
Off-Shore Oil Plant	123	Alexander L. Kielland 'Flotel' (10,105 tons), North Sea ...27 Mar	1980
Submarine	130	*Le Surcouf* rammed by US merchantman *Thomas Lykes* in Caribbean	1942
		................18 Feb	
Helicopter	54	Israel military 'Sea Stallion', West Bank ....10 May	1977
Ski Lift (Cable car)	42	Cavalese resort, Northern Italy ....9 Mar	1976
Mountaineering	40[12]	USSR Expedition on Mount Everest ....Dec	1952
Elevator (Lift)	23	Vaal Reefs Gold mine lift fell 1.2 miles *1,93 km* ....27 Mar	1980
Lightning	21	Hut in Chinamasa Krael nr. Umtali, Zimbabwe (single bolt) 23 Dec	1975
Yacht Racing	19	28th Fastnet Race—23 boats sank or abandoned in Force 11 gale ....13–15 Aug	1979
Space Exploration	3	Apollo oxygen fire, Cape Kennedy, Fla., USA ....27 Jan	1967
	3	*Soyuz II* re-entry over USSR ....29 June	1971
Nuclear Waste Accident	high but undisclosed[13]	Venting of plutonium extraction wastes, Kyshtym, USSR *c.* Dec	1957

Sherinton was installed at Folkestone from 1524 or 1529 to 1601. If the former is correct it would surpass the Norfolk record. The parish of Farrington, Hampshire had only two incumbents in a 122 year period *viz* Rev. J. Benn (28 Mar 1797 to 1857) and Rev. T. H. Massey (1857 to 5 Apr 1919). From 1675 to 1948 the incumbents of Rose Ash, Devon were from 8 generations of the family of Southcomb.

Longest serving chorister

Harry Phillips (1884–1983) joined the choir of St Michael and All Angels West Felton, Shropshire in 1893 aged 8. He was still serving as a chorister 90 years later in April 1983. Having become a chorister in 1876 at the age of 9, Thomas Rogers was appointed vicar's warden in 1966 at Montacute, Somerset.

Sunday School

Sunday Schools were established by Congregationalists in Neath and Tirdwyncyn, Wales in 1697. Roland E. Daab of St. Paul United Church of Christ, Columbia, Illinois, USA attended for 3,436 consecutive Sunday's without a miss for 66 years to 30 Sept 1984.

Parishes *Largest and Smallest*

The smallest parish in the United Kingdom is The Scares which consists of.rocky islets in Luce Bay with an area of 1.10 acres *0.44 ha* and included in Wigtown, Dumfries and Galloway. In 1982 the parish of Dallinghoo Wield, Suffolk boasted a population of nil and an area of 38 acres *14,6 ha*. The largest parish is Kilmonivaig in Inverness, Highland with an area of 267,233.03 acres *108 145,46 ha*.

Oldest parish register

The oldest part of any parish register surviving in England is a sheet from that of Alfriston, East Sussex recording a marriage on 10 July 1504. Scotland's oldest surviving register is that for Anstruther-Wester, Fife, with burial entries from 1549.

Crowds *Largest*

The greatest recorded number of human beings assembled with a common purpose was an estimated 12,700,000 at the Hindu festival of Kumbh-Mela, which was held at the confluence of the Yamuna (formerly called the Jumna), the Ganges and the invisible 'Sarasvati' at Allaha-

bad, Uttar Pradesh, India, on 19 Jan 1977. The holiest time during this holiest day since 1833 was during the planetary alignment between 9.28 and 9.40 a.m. during which only 200,000 achieved immersion to wash away the sins of a lifetime. The queue at the grave of the chansonier and guitarist Vladimir Visotsky (died 28 July 1980), stretched 10 km *6.2 miles*.

Largest funerals

The funeral of the charismatic C. N. Annadurai (died 3 Feb 1969) Madras Chief Minister was, according to a police estimate attended by 15 million. The longest funeral in Britain was probably that of Vice Admiral Viscount Nelson on 9 Jan 1806. Ticket-holders were seated in St Paul's Cathedral by 8.30 a.m. Many were unable to leave until after 9 p.m.

Biggest demonstrations

A figure of 2.7 million was published from China for the demonstration against the USSR in Shanghai on 3–4 Apr 1969 following the border clashes, and one of 10 million for the May Day celebrations of 1963 in Peking.

WORST IN THE UNITED KINGDOM

DISASTER	NUMBER KILLED	LOCATION	DATE
Pandemic	800,000	The Black Death (bubonic, pneumonic and septicaemic plague)	1347–50
Influenza	225,000	Influenza	Sept–Nov 1918
Famine	1,500,000[1]	Ireland (famine and typhus)	1846–51
Circular Storm	c. 8000	'The Channel Storm'	26 Nov 1703
Flood	c. 2000[2]	Severn Estuary	20 Jan 1606
Earthquake	4	East Anglian Earthquake	22 April 1884
Landslide	144	Pantglas coal tip No 7, Aberfan, Mid Glamorgan	21 Oct 1966
Conventional bombing	1436	London	10–11 May 1941
Avalanches	8	Lewes, East Sussex	27 Dec 1836
Marine (single ship)	c. 800[3]	HMS *Royal George*, off Spithead	29 Aug 1782
Dam Burst	250	Bradfield Reservoir, Dale Dyke, near Sheffield, South Yorkshire (embankment burst)	12 Mar 1864
Panic	183	Victoria Hall, Sunderland, Tyne and Wear	16 June 1883
Smog	2,850	London fog (excess deaths)	5–13 Dec 1951
Explosion	134[4]	Chilwell, Notts. (explosive factory)	1 July 1918
Fire (single building)	188[5]	Theatre Royal, Exeter	5 Sept 1887
Mining	439	Universal Colliery, Senghenydd, Mid Glamorgan	14 Oct 1913
Riot	565 (min)	London anti-Catholic Gordon riots	2–13 June 1780
Road	33	Coach crash, River Dibb, nr Grassington, North Yorks	27 May 1975
Railway	227[6]	Triple collision, Quintins Hill, Dumfries & Galloway	22 May 1915
Tornado	75	Tay Bridge collapsed under impact of two tornadic vortices	28 Dec 1879
Aircraft (Civil)	118[7]	BEA Trident 1C, Staines, Surrey	18 June 1972
Terrorism	21	Birmingham Pub bombs (IRA)	21 Nov 1974
Off-Shore Oil Plant	24	Aboard North Sea pentagonal semi-submersible (see left)	27 Mar 1980
Submarine	99	HMS *Thetis*, during trials, Liverpool Bay	1 June 1939
Mountaineering	6	On Cairngorm, Scotland (4084 ft)	21 Nov 1971
Lightning	31	(Annual total) Worst year on record (annual av. 12)	1914
Yacht Racing	19	28th Fastnet Race—23 boats sank or abandoned in Force 11 gale. Of 316 starters only 128 finished	13–15 Aug 1979

WORST IN WORLD FOOTNOTES

[1] In 1770 the great Indian famine carried away a proportion of the population estimated as high as one-third, hence a figure of tens of millions. The figure for Bengal alone was also probably about 10 million. The loss in the Northern China famine of Feb 1877–Sept 1878 was 9,500,000. It has been estimated that more than 5 million died in the post-World War I famine of 1920–1 in the USSR. The USSR government in July 1923 informed Mr (later President) Herbert Hoover that the ARA (American Relief Administration) had since August 1921 saved 20 million lives from famine and famine diseases.

[2] This figure published in 1972 for the Bangladeshi disaster was from Dr Afzal, Principal Scientific Officer of the Atomic Energy Authority Centre, Dacca. One report asserted that less than half of the population of the 4 islands of Bhola, Charjabbar, Hatia and Ramagati (1961 Census 1.4 million) survived. The most damaging hurricane recorded was Hurricane Frederic in Sept 1979 with an estimated loss of $2,300 billion.

[3] The number of civilians killed by the bombing of Germany has been put variously as 593,000 and 'over 635,000' including 550,000 deaths in the raids of Dresden, Germany on 13–15 Feb 1945. Total Japanese fatalities were 600,000 (conventional) and 220,000 (nuclear).

[4] A total of 18,000 Austrian and Italian troops were reported to have been lost in the Dolomite valleys of Northern Italy on 13 Dec 1916 in more than 100 snow avalanches. Some of the avalanches were triggered by gun-fire.

[5] The dynamiting of a Yangtze Kiang dam at Huayuan Kow by the KMT during the Sino-Japanese war in 1938 is reputed to have resulted in 900,000 deaths.

[6] It was estimated that some 5000 people were trampled to death in the stampede for free beer at the coronation celebration of Czar Nicholas II in Moscow in May 1896.

[7] Final death roll obscured by litigation.

[8] Some sources maintain that the final death roll was over 3000 on 6–7 Dec. Published estimates of the 11,000 killed at the BASF chemical plant explosion at Oppau,

W. Germany on 21 Sept 1921 were exaggerated. The best estimate is 561 killed.

[9] >200,000 killed in the sack of Moscow, freed by the Tartars in May 1571. Worst ever hotel fire 162 killed, Hotel Daeyungak, Seoul, South Korea 25 Dec 1971. Worst Circus fire 168 killed Hartford, Conn. USA 6 July 1944.

[10] The worst gold mining disaster in South Africa was 152 killed due to flooding in the Witwatersrand Gold Mining Co. Gold Mine in 1909.

[11] Some estimates ran as high as 2700 victims from carbon monoxide asphyxiation after Soviet military sealed both ends of the 1.7 mile 2,7 km long tunnel. The worst ever years for road deaths in the USA and the UK have been respectively 1969 (56,400) and 1941 (9169). The global aggregate death roll was put at 25 million by September 1975. The world's highest death rate is 29 per 100,000 in 1978 in Luxembourg and Portugal. The greatest pile-up on British roads was on the M6 near Lymm Interchange, near Thelwell, involving 200 vehicles on 13 Sept 1971 with 11 dead and 60 injured.

[12] According to Polish sources, not confirmed by the USSR. Also 23 died on Mount Fuji, Japan, in blizzard and avalanche on 20 Mar 1972.

[13] More than 30 small communities in a 1200 km² 460 mile² area eliminated from USSR maps since 1958. Possibly an ammonium nitrate-hexone explosion.

WORST IN UK FOOTNOTES

[1] Based on the net rate of natural increase between 1841 and 1851, a supportable case for a loss of population of 3 million can be made out if rates of under-enumeration of 25 per cent (1841) and 10 per cent (1851) are accepted. Potato rot (Phytophthora infestans) was first reported on 13 Sept 1845.

[2] Death rolls of 100,000 were reputed in England and Holland in the floods of 1099, 1421 and 1446.

[3] c. 2800 were lost on HM Troopship Lancastria 16,243 tons off St. Nazaire on 17 June 1940. The Princess Alice collision in the Thames with the Bywell Castle off Woolwich on 3 Sept 1878 killed 786.

[4] HM Armed Cruiser Natal blew up off Invergordon killing 428 on 30 Dec 1915.

[5] In July 1212, 3000 were killed in the crush, burned or drowned when London Bridge caught fire at both ends. The death roll in the Great Fire of London of 1666 was only 8. History's first 'fire storm' occurred in the Quebec Yard, Surrey Docks, Southwark, London during the 300-pump fire in the Blitz on 7–8 Sept 1940. Dockland casualties were 306 killed. Britain's most destructive fire was the £165 million loss at the Army Ordnance depot, Donnington, Shropshire in June 1982.

[6] The 213 yd 194.7 m long troop train was telescoped to 67 yd 61,2 m. Signalmen Meakin and Tinsley were sentenced for manslaughter. Britain's worst underground train disaster was the Moorgate Tube disaster of 28 Feb 1975 when 43 were killed.

[7] The worst crash by a UK operated aircraft was that of the Dan-Air Boeing 727 from Manchester which crashed into a mountain on the Canary Islands on 25 Apr 1980 killing 146 people. There were no survivors.

CHAPTER TWELVE

Sports Games

ALL SPORTS

See also The Guinness Book of Sports Facts by Stan Greenberg, published at £6.95 in 1984.

Earliest

The origins of sport stem from the time when self-preservation ceased to be the all-consuming human preoccupation. Archery was a hunting skill in mesolithic times (by *c.* 8000 BC), but did not become an organised sport until later, certainly *c.* AD 300, among the Genoese and possibly as early as the 12th century BC, as an archery competition is described in Homer's Iliad. The earliest dated evidence for sport is *c.* 2750–2600 BC for wrestling. Ball games by girls depicted on Middle Kingdom murals at Beni Hasan, Egypt have been dated to *c.* 2050 BC.

Fastest

The highest speed reached in a non-mechanical sport is in sky-diving, in which a speed of 185 mph *298 km/h* is attained in a head-down free falling position, even in the lower atmosphere. In delayed drops speeds of 625 mph *1005 km/h* have been recorded at high rarefied altitudes. The highest projectile speed in any moving ball game is *c.* 188 mph *302 km/h* in pelota. This compares with 170 mph *273 km/h* (electronically-timed) for a golf ball driven off a tee.

Slowest

In wrestling, before the rules were modified towards 'brighter wrestling', contestants could be locked in holds for so long that a single bout once lasted for 11 hr 40 min. In the extreme case of the 2 hr 41 min pull in the regimental tug o' war in Jubbulpore, India, on 12 Aug 1889, the winning team moved a net distance of 12 ft *3,6 m* at an average speed of 0.00084 mph *0,00135 km/h*.

Longest

The most protracted sporting contest was an automobile duration test of 222,621 miles *358 273 km* (equivalent to 8.93 times around the equator) by Appaurchaux and others in a Ford Taunus at Miranas, France. This was contested over 142 days in July–Nov 1963.

The most protracted non-mechanical sporting event is the *Tour de France* cycling race. In 1926 this was over 3569 miles *5743 km* lasting 29 days but is now reduced to 23 days.

Largest pitch

The largest pitch of any ball game is that of polo, with 12.4 acres *5,0 ha*, or a maximum length of 300 yd *274 m* and a width, without side boards, of 200 yd *182 m*. With boards the width is 160 yd *146 m*. Twice a year in the Parish of St Columb Major, Cornwall, a game called Hurling (not to be confused with the Irish game) is played on a 'pitch' which consists of the entire Parish, approximately 25 square miles *64,7 km²*.

Youngest and oldest world record breakers

The youngest at which anybody has broken a non-mechanical world record is 12 yr 298 days for Gertrude Caroline Ederle (USA) (b. 23 Oct 1906) with 13 min 19.0 sec for women's 880 yd freestyle swimming at Indianapolis, USA, on 17 Aug 1919. Gerhard Weidner (W. Germany) (b. 15 Mar 1933) set a 20 mile walk record on 25 May 1974, aged 41 yr 71 days.

Youngest and oldest champions

The youngest successful competitor in a world title event was a French boy, whose name is not recorded, who coxed the Netherlands' Olympic pair at Paris on 26 Aug 1900. He was not more than ten and may have been as young as seven. The youngest individual Olympic winner was Marjorie Gestring (USA) (b. 18 Nov 1922), who took the springboard diving title at the age of 13 yr 268 days at the Olympic Games in

Berlin on 12 Aug 1936. Oscar Gomer Swahn (Sweden) (1847–1927) was aged 64 yr 258 days when he won a gold medal in the 1912 Olympic Running Deer team shooting competition.

Youngest and oldest internationals

The youngest age at which any person has won international honours is eight years in the case of Joy Foster, the Jamaican singles and mixed doubles table tennis champion in 1958. The youngest British international has been diver

Swiss skier Erika Hess won a record fourth World Cup slalom title in 1985. *(All-Sport)*

& Pastimes

Beverley Williams (b. 5 Jan 1957), who was 10 yr 268 days old when she competed against the USA at Crystal Palace, London, on 30 Sept 1967. It would appear that the greatest age at which anyone has actively competed for his country was 72 yr 280 days in the case of Oscar Swahn (see above) who won a silver medal for shooting in the Olympic Games at Antwerp on 26 July 1920. He qualified for the 1924 Games but was unable to participate due to illness. Britain's oldest international was Hilda Lorna Johnstone (b. 4 Sept 1902) who was 70 yr 5 days when she was placed twelfth in the Dressage competition at the 1972 Games.

Most versatile
Charlotte 'Lottie' Dod (1871–1960) won the Wimbledon Singles tennis title five times between 1887 and 1893, the British Ladies' Golf Championship in 1904, an Olympic silver medal for archery in 1908, and represented England at hockey in 1899. She also excelled at skating and tobogganing. Mildred 'Babe' Zaharias (née Didrikson) (1914–56) (USA) won two gold medals (80 m hurdles and javelin) and a silver (high jump) at the 1932 Olympic Games. She set world records at those three events in 1930–32. She was an All-American basketball player for three years and set the world record for throwing the baseball 296 ft *90,22 m*. Switching to golf she won the US women's Amateur title in 1946 and the US Women's Open in 1948, 1950 and 1954. She also excelled at several other sports. Charles Burgess Fry (GB) (1872–1956) was probably the most versatile male sportsman at the highest level. On 4 Mar 1893 he equalled the world long jump record of 23 ft 6½ in *7,17 m*. He represented England *r.* Ireland at soccer (1901) and played first-class rugby for the Barbarians. His greatest achievements were at cricket, where he headed the English batting averages in six seasons and captained England in 1912. He was an excellent angler and tennis player.

Most prolific record breaker
Between 24 Jan 1970 and 1 Nov 1977 Vasili Alexeyev (USSR) (b. 7 Jan 1942) broke 80 official world records in weightlifting.

Longest reign
The longest reign as a world champion is 33 years (1829–62) by Jacques Edmond Barre (France)' (1802–73) at real tennis. The longest reign as a British champion is 41 years by the archer

Alice Blanche Legh (1855–1948) who first won the Championship in 1881 and for the 23rd and final time in 1922 aged 67.

Shortest reign
Olga Rukavishnikova (USSR) (b. 13 Mar 1955) held the pentathlon world record for 0.4 sec at Moscow on 24 July 1980. That is the difference between her second place time of 2 min 04.8 sec in the final 800 m event of the Olympic five-event competition, and that of third-placed Nadyezhda Tkachenko (USSR), whose overall points were better, 5083 to 4937.

Heaviest sportsman
The heaviest sportsman of all-time was the professional wrestler William J. Cobb of Macon, Georgia, USA, who in 1962 was billed as the 802 lb (57 st 4 lb *363 kg*) 'Happy Humphrey'. The heaviest player of a ball-game was the 487 lb *221 kg* Bob Pointer, the US Football tackle formerly on the 1967 Santa Barbara High School Team, California, USA.

Greatest earnings
The greatest fortune amassed by an individual in sport is an estimated $69 million by the boxer Muhammad Ali Haj (USA) in 1960–81. The highest paid woman athlete in the world is tennis player Martina Navratilova (b. Prague, Czechoslovakia, 18 Oct 1956) (USA) whose official career earnings were over $9 million by 1985.

Biggest sports contract
In March 1982, the National Football League concluded a deal worth 2,500,000,000 for five years coverage of American Football by the three major TV networks, ABC, CBS and NBC. This represents $14.2 million for each league team.

Largest crowd
The greatest number of live spectators for any sporting spectacle is the estimated 2,500,000 who annually line the route of the New York Marathon. However, spread over 23 days, it is estimated that more than 10,000,000 see the annual *Tour de France* cycling race along the route.

The total attendance at the 1984 summer Olympic Games was given as 5,797,923 for all sports, including 1,421,627 for soccer and 1,129,465 for track and field athletics.

The largest crowd travelling to any single sporting venue is 'more than 400,000' for the annual *Grand Prix d'Endurance* motor race on

Whilst records in mass participation activities continue to fall, the *Round The Bays* race, pictured above, stands out in attracting the most runners. *(All-Sport)*

the Sarthe circuit near Le Mans, France. The record stadium crowd was one of 199,854 for the Brazil *v.* Uruguay soccer match in the Maracaña Municipal Stadium, Rio de Janeiro, Brazil, on 16 July 1950.

Most participants
The *Round the Bays*, 6.5 mile *10,5 km* run in Auckland, New Zealand attracted an estimated 80,000 runners on 27 Mar 1982. The 1983 Women's International Bowling Congress Championship tournament attracted 75,480 bowlers for the 83-day event held 7 Apr—1 July at Showboat Lanes, Las Vegas, Nevada, USA.

Largest television audience
The largest television audience for a single sporting event, excluding Olympic events, was an estimated 1500 million who saw the final of the 1982 soccer World Cup.

Worst disasters

The worst sports disaster in recent history was when an estimated 604 were killed after some stands at the Hong Kong Jockey Club racecourse collapsed and caught fire on 26 Feb 1918. During the reign of Antoninus Pius (AD 138–161) the upper wooden tiers in the Circus Maximus, Rome, collapsed during a gladiatorial combat killing some 1112 spectators. Britain's worst sports disaster was when 66 were killed and 145 injured at the Rangers *v.* Celtic football match at Exit 13 of Ibrox Park stadium, Glasgow on 2 Jan 1971.

COMMONWEALTH GAMES

The Commonwealth Games are multi-sport competitions, held every four years, and contested by sportsmen representing the nations of the British Commonwealth. They were first staged at Hamilton, Canada, opening on 16 August 1930. The eleven nations participating were Australia, Bermuda, British Guiana, Canada, England, Ireland, Newfoundland, New Zealand, Scotland, South Africa and Wales. Six sports were included, but there were women's events only in swimming.

The idea of staging such an event was first put forward by a Yorkshireman, Rev. J. Astley Cooper in the magazine *Greater Britain* in 1891. The first Inter-Empire Sports meeting was held at Crystal Palace, London in 1911, when events were held at four sports—athletics, boxing, swimming and wrestling. This event formed part of the celebrations for the Coronation of King George V.

MEDALS *General*

The most gold medals won is nine by fencer Bill Hoskyns of England and swimmer Michael Wenden of Australia. Hoskyns won three individual épée titles and six team golds between 1958 and 1970. Wenden won the freestyle 100 m in 1966, 1970 and 1974, the 200 m in 1974 and was in the winning Australian freestyle relay

YEAR	VENUE and COUNTRY	No. SPORTS	COUNTRIES	COMPETITORS	
				Men	Women
1930	Hamilton, *Canada*	6	11	—c. 400—	
1934	London, *England*	6	16	—c. 500—	
1938	Sydney, *Australia*	7	15	378	88
1950	Auckland, *New Zealand*	9	12	495	95
1954	Vancouver, *Canada*	9	24	568	94
1958	Cardiff, *Wales*	9	35	967	163
1962	Perth, *Australia*	9	35	727	136
1966	Kingston, *Jamaica*	9	34	854	196
1970	Edinburgh, *Scotland*	9	42	1095	288
1974	Christchurch, *New Zealand*	9	39	977	299
1978	Edmonton, *Canada*	10	46	1149	326
1982	Brisbane, *Australia*	10	46	1179	400
1986	Edinburgh, *Scotland*				

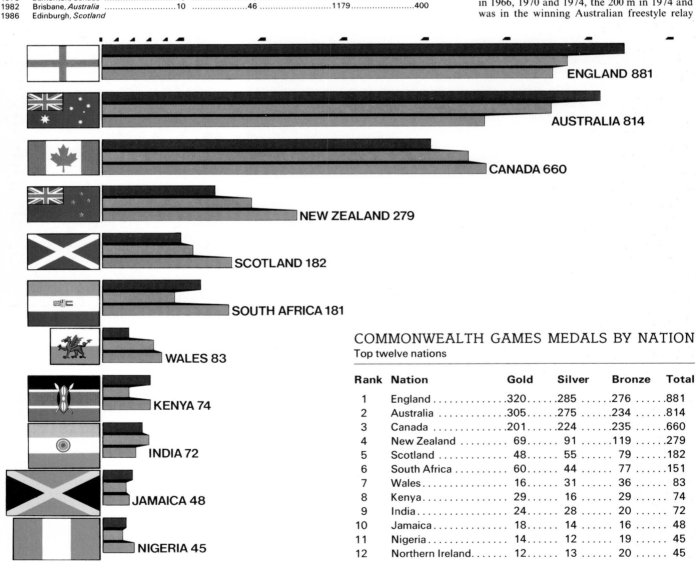

COMMONWEALTH GAMES MEDALS BY NATION
Top twelve nations

Rank	Nation	Gold	Silver	Bronze	Total
1	England	320	285	276	881
2	Australia	305	275	234	814
3	Canada	201	224	235	660
4	New Zealand	69	91	119	279
5	Scotland	48	55	79	182
6	South Africa	60	44	77	151
7	Wales	16	31	36	83
8	Kenya	29	16	29	74
9	India	24	28	20	72
10	Jamaica	18	14	16	48
11	Nigeria	14	12	19	45
12	Northern Ireland	12	13	20	45

ENGLAND 881
AUSTRALIA 814
CANADA 660
NEW ZEALAND 279
SCOTLAND 182
SOUTH AFRICA 181
WALES 83
KENYA 74
INDIA 72
JAMAICA 48
NIGERIA 45
NORTHERN IRELAND 45

50 100 150 200 250 300 350

ATHLETICS Contested at all Games—GAMES BEST PERFORMANCES

MEN

EVENT	min sec		
100 m	10.02w	Allan Wells (Scotland)	1982
200 m	20.12w	Allan Wells (Scotland)	1978
400 m	45.01	Charles Asati (Kenya)	1970
800 m	1:43.95	John Kipkurgat (Kenya)	1974
1500 m	3:32.16	Filbert Bayi (Tanzania)	1974
5000 m	13:14.4	Ben Jipcho (Kenya)	1974
10 000 m	27:46.4	Richard Tayler (New Zealand)	1974
Marathon	2 hr 09:12	Ian Thompson (England)	1974
3000 m steeple	8:20.8	Ben Jipcho (Kenya)	1974
110 m hurdles	13.37	Mark McKoy (Canada)	1982
400 m hurdles	48.83	Alan Pascoe (England)	1974
4 × 100 m relay	39.15	Nigeria	1982
4 × 400 m relay	3:02.8	Trinidad & Tobago	1966
30 km walk	2 hr 10:16	Steve Barry (Wales)	1982
Metres			
High jump	2.31	Milt Ottey (Canada) & Stephen Wray (Bahamas)	1982
Pole vault	5.20	Raymond Boyd (Australia), Jeff Gutteridge (England) and Graham Eggleton (Scotland)	1982
Long jump	8.13	Gary Honey (Australia)	1982
Triple jump	17.81w	Keith Connor (England)	1982
Shot	20.74	Geoff Capes (England)	1978
Discus	64.04	Brad Cooper (Bahamas)	1982
Hammer	75.08	Robert Weir (England)	1982
Javelin	89.48	Michael O'Rourke (New Zealand)	1982
Decathlon	8467 points	Daley Thompson (England)	1978

WOMEN

	min sec		
100 m	10.92w	Angela Taylor (Canada) (& 11.00)	1982
200 m	22.19w	Merlene Ottey (Jamaica)	1982
400 m	51.02	Marilyn Neufville (Jamaica)	1970
800 m	2:01.1	Charlene Rendina (Australia)	1974
1500 m	4:06.34	Mary Stewart (England)	1978
3000 m	8:45.53	Anne Audain (New Zealand)	1982
100 m hurdles	12.78w	Shirley Strong (England)	1982
400 m hurdles	55.89	Debbie Flintoff (Australia)	1982
4 × 100 m relay	43.15	England	1982
4 × 400 m relay	3:27.19	England	1978
Metres			
High jump	1.93	Katrina Gibbs (Australia)	1978
Long jump	6.91w	Shonel Ferguson (Bahamas)	1982
Shot	17.92	Judith Oakes (England)	1982
Discus	62.98	Margaret Ritchie (Scotland)	1982
Javelin	64.46	Suzanne Howland (Australia)	1982
Heptathlon	6282 points	Glynis Nunn (Australia)	1982

w = wind assisted (wind over 2.0 metres per second)

Ben Jipcho established a unique double in 1974, winning and setting records in both the 5000 m and the 3000 m steeplechase. Jenny Turrall (below), the youngest ever gold medallist. (All-Sport/Tony Duffy)

teams at 4 × 100 m in 1966 and 1970 and at 4 × 200 m in all three years. He also won three silver and one bronze medal, and would have won another gold but for the Australian medley relay team being disqualified after finishing first in 1966.

The most medals won of any colour is 13 by Wenden (above) and by fencer Ivan Lund of Australia, three gold, six silver and four bronze, from 1950 to 1962. The women's record is eight by Australian swimmer Dawn Fraser, six gold and two silver, 1958 and 1962.

The most medals won at one Games is six by swimmer Graham Smith of Canada in 1978.

The youngest gold medallist of whom the date of birth is known for certain is Jenny Turrall (Australia) who won the women's 400 m freestyle swimming at 13 years 262 days in 1974. Ved Prakash (India) won the light-flyweight wrestling title in 1970 aged probably 14, although one report gave his age as 12.

SWIMMING & DIVING contested each year—GAMES RECORDS:

MEN

	min sec		
100 m freestyle	51.09	Neil Brooks (Australia) (heat)	1982
200 m freestyle	1:51.52	Andrew Astbury (England)	1982
400 m freestyle	3:53.29	Andrew Astbury (England)	1982
1500 m freestyle	15:23.94	Max Metzker (Australia)	1982
100 m breaststroke	1:02.93	Adrian Moorhouse (England)	1982
200 m breaststroke	2:16.25	Victor Davis (Canada)	1982
100 m butterfly	54.71	Dan Thompson (Canada)	1982
200 m butterfly	2:00.75	Stephen Poulter (England) (heat)	1982
100 m backstroke	57.12	Michael West (Canada)	1982
200 m backstroke	2:02.88	Cameron Henning (Canada)	1982
200 m ind. medley	2:02.25	Alex Baumann (Canada)	1982
400 m ind. medley	4:23.53	Alex Baumann (Canada)	1982
4 × 100 m freestyle	3:24.17	Australia	1982
4 × 200 m freestyle	7:28.81	Australia	1982
4 × 100 m medley	3:47.34	Australia	1982

WOMEN

	min sec		
100 m freestyle	56.97	June Croft (England)	1982
200 m freestyle	1:59.74	June Croft (England)	1982
400 m freestyle	4:08.45	Tracey Wickham (Australia)	1978
800 m freestyle	8:24.62	Tracey Wickham (Australia)	1978
100 m breaststroke	1:11.74	Anne Ottenbrite (Canada) (heat)	1982
200 m breaststroke	2:32.07	Anne Ottenbrite (Canada)	1982
100 m butterfly	1:01.22	Lisa Curry (Australia)	1982
200 m butterfly	2:11.29	Michelle Ford (Australia)	1978
100 m backstroke	1:03.48	Lisa Forrest (Australia)	1982
200 m backstroke	2:13.46	Lisa Forrest (Australia)	1982
200 m ind. medley	2:16.94	Lisa Curry (Australia)	1982
400 m ind. medley	4:51.95	Lisa Curry (Australia)	1982
4 × 100 m freestyle	3:50.28	Canada	1978
4 × 100 m medley	4:14.33	Canada	1982

ARCHERY contested 1982 only, when the winners were:
MEN—2446 Mark Blenkarne (England)
WOMEN—2373 Neroli Fairhall (New Zealand)

BADMINTON contested since 1966.
BOWLS contested each year except 1966.
BOXING contested each year.
CYCLING contested each year since 1934.
FENCING contested 1950–1970.
GYMNASTICS contested 1978.
ROWING contested 1930, 1938–62.
SHOOTING contested 1966, 1974–82.
WATER POLO contested 1950.
WRESTLING contested each year.

WEIGHTLIFTING contested since 1950—GAMES RECORDS for 2-lift totals:

BODYWEIGHT	kg		
52 kg	215	Precious McKenzie (England)	1974
56 kg	235	Geoffrey Laws (England)	1982
60 kg	267.5	Dean Willey (England)	1982
67.5 kg	295	David Morgan (Wales)	1982
75 kg	312.5	Stephen Pinsent (England)	1982
82.5 kg	325	Newton Burrowes (England)	1982
90 kg	337.5	Robert Kabbas (Australia)	1982
100 kg	350	Oliver Orok (Nigeria) & Gary Longford (England)	1982
110 kg	352.5	Russ Prior (Canada)	1974
110 kg+	377.5	Dean Lukin (Australia)	1982

AEROBATICS

Earliest
The first aerobatic 'manoeuvre' is generally considered to be the sustained inverted flight in a Bleriot of Célestin-Adolphe Pégoud (1889–1915), at Buc, France on 21 Sept 1913, but Lieut. Peter Nikolayevich Nesterov (1887–1914), of the Imperial Russian Air Service, performed a loop in a Nieuport Type IV monoplane at Kiev, USSR on 27 Aug 1913.

World Championships
Held biennially since 1960 (excepting 1974), scoring is based on the system devised by Col. José Aresti of Spain. The competition consists of two compulsory and two free programmes. The men's team competition has been won a record five times by the USSR. Igor Egorov (USSR) in 1976 and Petr Jirmus (Czechoslovakia) in 1984 won three out of four programmes. Betty Stewart (USA) won the women's competition in 1980 and 1982. Lidia Leonova (USSR) won a record three medals: first in 1976, second in 1978 and third in 1972. The only medal achieved by Britain has been a bronze in the team event at Kiev, USSR in 1976. The highest individual placing by a Briton is fourth by Neil Williams (1935–77) in 1976.

Inverted flight
The duration record for inverted flight is 4 hr 9 min 5 sec by John 'Hal' McClain in a Swick Taylorcraft on 23 Aug 1980 over Houston International Raceways, Texas, USA.

Loops
On 21 June 1980, R. Steven Powell performed 2315⅝ inside loops in a Bellanca Decathalon over Almont, Michigan, USA. John McClain achieved 180 outside loops in a Bellanca Super Decathalon on 2 Sept 1978 over Houston, Texas, USA.

Ken Ballinger completed 155 consecutive inside loops in a Bellanca Citabria on 6 Aug 1983 over Staverton Airport, Cheltenham, Gloucestershire.

ANGLING

For further information on fishing see The Guinness Guides to Game Fishing *by Dr William Currie, and to* Coarse Fishing *by Michael Prichard and Michael Shepley, published by Guinness Superlatives at £9.95 and £10.95 respectively.*

Oldest existing club
The Ellem fishing club was formed by a number of Edinburgh and Berwickshire gentlemen in 1829. Its first Annual General Meeting was held on 29 April 1830.

Catch *Largest Single*
The largest officially ratified fish ever caught on a rod is a man-eating Great white shark (*Carcharodon carcharias*) weighing 2664 lb *1208 kg* and measuring 16 ft 10 in *5,13 m* long, caught on a 130 lb *58 kg* test line by Alf Dean at Denial Bay, near Ceduna, South Australia, on 21 Apr 1959. A Great white shark weighing 3388 lb *1537 kg* was caught by Clive Green off Albany, Western Australia, on 26 Apr 1976 but will remain unratified as whale meat was used as bait. The biggest ever rod-caught fish by a British angler is a 1260 lb *571,5 kg* Black marlin, by Edward A. Crutch off Cairns, Queensland, Australia on 19 Oct 1973.

In June 1978 a Great white shark measuring 29 ft 6 in *9,00 m* in length and weighing over 10,000 lb *4536 kg* was harpooned and landed by fishermen in the harbour of San Miguel, Azores.

The largest marine animal ever killed by *hand* harpoon was a Blue whale 97 ft *29,56 m* in length, by Archer Davidson in Twofold Bay, New South Wales, Australia, in 1910. Its tail flukes measured 20 ft *6,09 m* across and its jaw bone 23 ft 4 in *7,11 m*.

The largest officially ratified fish ever caught in a British river was a 388 lb *176 kg* sturgeon (9 ft 2 in *2,79 m* long) landed by Alec Allen (1895–1972), helped by David Price, from the River Towy, between Llandilo and Carmarthen, S. Wales, on 25 July 1933.

Catch *Smallest*
The smallest fish to win a competition is a smelt, weighing 1/16 oz *1 dram*, caught by Peter Christian at Buckenham Ferry, Norfolk, England on 9 Jan 1977, in defeating 107 other competitors. For the smallest full-grown fish *see p. 40.*

Spear fishing
The largest fish ever taken underwater was an 804 lb *364 kg* Giant black grouper or jewfish by Don Pinder of the Miami Triton Club, Florida, USA, in 1955. The British spear-fishing record is 89 lb *40,36 kg* for an Angler fish by James Brown (Weymouth Association Divers) in 1969.

Championship records *World freshwater*
The *Confédération Internationale de la Pêche Sportive* championships were inaugurated as European championships in 1953. They were recognised as World Championships in 1957. France won twelve times between 1956 and 1981 and Robert Tesse (France) took the individual title uniquely three times, in 1959–60, 1965. The record weight (team) is 76 lb 8 oz 8 dr *34,71 kg* in 3 hr by West Germany on the Neckar at

Man of many talents; Tony Pawson became the first Briton to win the World Flyfishing Championships, in 1984. As an amateur he also represented Kent at county cricket from 1946 to 1951, and played first division football for Charlton Athletic. (*Basingstoke Gazette*)

Mannheim, West Germany on 21 Sept 1980. The individual record is 37 lb 7 oz 3 dr *16,99 kg* by Wolf-Rüdiger Kremkus (West Germany) at Mannheim on 20 Sept 1980. The most fish caught is 652 by Jacques Isenbaert (Belgium) at Dunajvaros, Yugoslavia on 27 Aug 1967.

World flyfishing
World flyfishing championships were inaugurated by the CIPS in 1981. The first British winner was Henry Anthony 'Tony' Pawson (b. 22 Aug 1921) at Salamanca, Spain in 1984.

Championship records *British*
The National Angling Championship (instituted 1906) has been won seven times by Leeds (1909–10, 1914, 1928, 1948–9, 1952). James H. R. Bazley (Leeds) won the individual title twice (1909, 1927). Since 1972 the event has been split into divisions. Eddie Townsin (Cambridge) won the national title in 1967 and Div. 4 in 1982; Charlie Hibbs (Leigh) won Div. 2 in 1974 and 1984. The record catch is 76 lb 9 oz *34,72 kg* by David Burr (Rugby) in the Huntspill, Somerset in 1965. The largest single fish caught in the Championships is a carp of 14 lb 2 oz *6,41 kg* by John C. Essex on 13 Sept 1975 on the River Nene, Peterborough. The team championship is determined on points earned by team members in each section. The points record in Division 1, where there are 80 teams of 12 anglers, is 883 by Nottingham Federation in 1980 on the lower Trent. The winning team in 1983, Nottingham Federation, produced a team weight of 63,99 kg *141.07 lbs* of fish.

Match fishing
In a sweepstake on the Sillees River, a tributary of the Erne, Co. Fermanagh, Ulster, on 14 May 1981, Peter Burrell weighed in 258 lb 9½ oz *117,29 kg* of fish in the five hour open event.

Casting records
The longest freshwater cast ratified under ICF (International Casting Federation) rules is 175,01 m *574 ft 2 in* by Walter Kummerow (W. Germany), for the Bait Distance Double-Handed 30 g event held at Lenzerheide, Switzerland in the 1968 Championships. The British National record is 148,78 m *488 ft 1 in* by Andy Dickison on the same occasion. The longest Fly Distance Double-Handed cast is 78,38 m *257 ft 2 in* by Sverne Scheen (Norway), also at Lenzerheide in September 1968. Peter Anderson set a British National professional record of 70,50 m *231 ft 3 in* on water at Scarborough on 11 Sept 1977, and Hugh Newton cast 80,47 m *264 ft* on land at Stockholm, Sweden on 20 Sept 1978. The UK Surfcasting Federation record (150 gr 5¼ oz weight) is 815 ft *248 m* by Neil Mackellow on 4 Sept 1983 at Norwich.

IGFA WORLD RECORDS
The International Game Fish Association (IGFA) recognise world records for game fish—both Freshwater and Saltwater—for a large number of species of fish. Their thousands of categories include all-tackle, various line classes and tippet classes for fly fishing.

Freshwater All-Tackle records
The heaviest category recognised by the IGFA is for the sturgeon—468 lb *212,28 kg* by Joey Pallotta on 9 July 1983 off Benicia, California, USA.

An 834 lb *378,30 kg* sturgeon was landed (not by rod) by Garry Oling on 11 Aug 1981 from the Fraser River at Albion, British Columbia, Canada.

Saltwater All-Tackle records
The heaviest category recognised by the IGFA is for the White shark—2664 lb *1208,38 kg* by Alfred Dean on 21 Apr 1959 off Ceduna, Australia.

ARCHERY

Earliest references
Though the earliest evidence of the existence of bows is seen in the Mesolithic cave paintings in Spain, archery as an organized sport appears to have developed in the 3rd century AD. Competitive archery may however date back to the 12th century BC. The oldest archery body in the British Isles is the Royal Company of Archers, the Sovereign's bodyguard for Scotland, dating from 1676, though the Society of Kilwinning Archers, in Scotland, have contested the Papingo Shoot since 1488. The world governing body is the *Fédération Internationale de Tir à l'Arc* (FITA), founded in 1931.

World Records *Single FITA rounds*

Event	Points	Name and Country	Possible	Year
MEN				
FITA	1341	Darrell Pace (USA)	1440	1979
90 m	322	Vladimir Yesheyev (USSR)	360	1980
70 m	339	Tomi Poikolainen (Finland)	360	1983
50 m	345	Richard McKinney (USA)	360	1982
30 m	356	Darrell Pace (USA)	360	1978
Team	3908	USA (Darrell Pace, Richard McKinney, Jerry Pylpchuk)	4320	1983
WOMEN				
FITA	1325	Lyudmila Arshanikova (USSR)	1440	1984
70 m	328	Natalia Butuzova (USSR)	360	1979
60 m	338	Lyudmila Arshanikova (USSR)	360	1984
50 m	331	Paivi Meriluoto (Fin)	360	1982
30 m	353	Valentina Radionova (USSR)	360	1981
Team	3925	USSR (Lyudmila Arshanikova, Natalia Butuzova, Sebinsio Rustamova)	4320	1983

Highest Championship scores
The highest scores achieved in either a world or Olympic championship for Double FITA rounds are: men, 2617 points (possible 2880) by Darrell Pace (b. 23 Oct 1956) (USA) and Richard McKinney (b. 20 Oct 1963) (USA); and women, 2616 points by Kim Jin Ho (S. Korea), both at Long Beach, California, USA on 21–22 Oct 1983.

Kim Jin Ho (S. Korea) set a world record 2616 points at the 1983 World Championships, improving the previous best by a staggering 101 points.

British records
York Round—possible 1296 pts: Single Round, 1160 Steven Hallard at Meriden on 26 June 1983; Double Round, 2240 Steven Hallard at Stoneleigh on 14 Aug 1983.

Hereford (Women)—possible 1296 pts: Single Round, 1182 Elaine Tomkinson at Bingley on 10 Aug 1980; Double Round, 2331 Sue Willcox at Oxford on 27–28 June 1979.

FITA Round (Men): Steven Hallard, 1300 Single Round and 2566 Double Round, both at Castle Ashby, Nottinghamshire on 20 May 1983.

FITA Round (Women's): Single Round, 1273 Pauline Edwards at Worcester on 23 July 1983. Double Round, 2520 Rachel Fenwick at Brussels, Belgium on 12–13 Aug 1978.

Most titles *World*
The greatest number of world titles (instituted 1931) ever won by a man is four by Hans Deutgen (b. 28 Feb 1917) (Sweden) in 1947–50. The greatest number won by a woman is seven by Janina Spychajowa-Kurkowska (b. 8 Feb 1901) (Poland) in 1931–4, 1936, 1939 and 1947. Oscar Kessels (Belgium) (1904–68) participated in 21 world championships.

Most titles *Olympic*
Hubert van Innis (1866–1961) (Belgium) won six gold and three silver medals at the 1900 and 1920 Olympic Games.

Most titles *British*
The greatest number of British Championships is 12 by Horace Alfred Ford (1822–80) in 1849–59 and 1867, and 23 by Alice Blanche Legh (1855–1948) in 1881, 1886–92, 1895, 1898–1900, 1902–9, 1913 and 1921–2. Miss Legh was inhibited from winning from 1882 to 1885—because her mother was champion—and for four further years 1915–8 because there were no Championships owing to the First World War.

Flight shooting
The longest recorded distance ever shot is 1 mile 268 yd *1854,40 m* in the unlimited footbow class by Harry Drake (b. 7 May 1915) (USA) at 3000 ft *915 m* altitude at Ivanpah Dry Lake, California, USA on 24 Oct 1971. The female footbow record is 1113 yd 2 ft 6 in *1018,48 m* by Arlyne Rhode (b. 4 May 1936) at Wendover, Utah, USA on 10 Sept 1978. Alan Webster (England) set the flight record for the handbow with 1231 yd 1 ft 10 in *1126,19 m* on 2 Oct 1982 and April Moon (USA) set a women's record of 1039 yd 1 ft 1 in *950,39 m* on 13 Sept 1981, both at Ivanpah Dry Lake. Drake holds the crossbow flight record with 1359 yd 2 ft 5 in *1243,4 m* on 14 Oct 1967 and the regular footbow record with 1542 yd 2 ft 10 ins *1410,87 m* on 6 Oct 1979 both at Ivanpah Dry Lake.

Greatest draw
Gary Sentman, of Roseberg, Oregon, USA drew a longbow weighing a record 176 lb *79,83 kg* to the maximum draw on the arrow of 28¼ in *72 cm* at Forksville, Penn., on 20 Sept 1975.

24 Hours—target archery
The highest recorded score over 24 hours by a pair of archers is 51,633 during 48 Portsmouth Rounds by Jimmy Watt and Gordon Danby at the Epsom Showgrounds, Auckland NZ, on 18–19 Nov 1977.

24 Hours—field archery
The highest recorded score at field archery is 123,724 by six members of the Holland Moss Field Archery Club at Holland Moss Field, Pimbo, Lancashire on 28–29 Apr 1983. Bill Chambers set an individual record score of 30,506.

BADMINTON

See also The Guinness Book of Badminton *by Pat Davis, published in 1983 at £7.95.*

Origins

A similar game was played in China in the 2nd millennium BC. The modern game may have evolved *c* 1870 at Badminton Hall in Avon, the seat of the Dukes of Beaufort, or from a game played in India. The first modern rules were codified in Poona in 1876. The oldest club is the Newcastle Badminton Club formed as the Armstrong College Club on 24 Jan 1900.

Thomas Cup

The International Championship or Thomas Cup (instituted 1948) has been won eight times by Indonesia in 1958, 1961, 1964, 1970, 1973, 1976, 1979 and 1984.

Uber Cup

The Ladies International Championship or Uber Cup (instituted 1956) has been won five times by Japan (1966, 1969, 1972, 1978 and 1981).

Most titles

The men's singles in the All-England Championships (instituted 1899) have been won a record eight times by Rudy Hartono Kurniawan (Indonesia) (b. 18 Aug 1948) in 1968–74 and 1976. The greatest number of championships won (incl. doubles) is 21 by G. A. Thomas (later Sir George Alan Thomas, Bt.) (1881–1972) between 1903 and 1928. The women's title has been won ten times by Judy Hashman (*née* Devlin) (USA) (b. 22 Oct 1935) in 1954, 1957–8, 1960–4, 1966–7. She also equalled the greatest number of championships won of 17 by Muriel Lucas (later Mrs King Adams) from 1899 to 1910.

Shortest game

In the 1969 Uber Cup in Jakarta, Indonesia,

Gillian Gilks, with over 100 appearances for England dating back to 1966, has also won 11 All England Championship titles, including the singles in 1976 and 1978. (All-Sport)

Noriko Takagi (later Mrs Nakayama) (Japan) beat Poppy Tumengkol (Indonesia) in 9 min.

Longest hit

Frank Rugani drove a shuttlecock 79 ft 8½ in *24,29 m* in indoor tests at San José, California, USA, on 29 Feb 1964.

MOST INTERNATIONAL APPEARANCES

	Times	Men	
England	137	Michael G. Tredgett	1970–85
Scotland	67	Robert S. McCoig	1956–76
Ireland	76	Bill Thompson	1975–85
Wales	51	David Colmer	1964–80

	Times	Women	
England	108	Gillian Gilks (*née* Perrin)	1966–85
Wales	63	Sue Brimble	1969–84
Ireland	68	Barbara Beckett	1971–85
Scotland	58	Pamela Hamilton	1975–85

BASEBALL

Earliest game

The Rev Thomas Wilson, of Maidstone, Kent, England, wrote disapprovingly, in 1700, of baseball being played on Sundays. The earliest baseball game under the Cartwright (Alexander Joy Cartwright Jr 1820–92) rules was at Hoboken, New Jersey, USA, on 19 June 1846, with the New York Nine beating the Knickerbockers 23–1 in four innings.

Home runs *Most*

Henry Louis 'Hank' Aaron (Milwaukee and Atlanta Braves) (b. 5 Feb 1934) holds the major

league career home run record of 755, from 1954 to 1976. Joshua Gibson (1911–47) of Homestead Grays and Pittsburgh Crawfords, Negro League clubs, achieved a career total of nearly 800 homers including an unofficial total of 75 in 1931. The US major league record for home runs in a season is 61 by Roger Eugene Maris (b. 10 Sept 1934) for New York Yankees in 162 games in 1961. George Herman 'Babe' Ruth (1895–1948) hit 60 in 154 games in 1927. The most official home runs in minor leagues is 72 by Joe Bauman of Rosewell, New Mexico in 1954.

Longest home run

The longest home run ever measured was one of 618 ft *188,4 m* by Roy Edward 'Dizzy' Carlyle (1900–56) in a minor league game at Emeryville Ball Park, California, USA, on 4 July 1929. In 1919 Babe Ruth hit a 587 ft *178,9 m* homer in a Boston Red Sox *v.* New York Giants exhibition match at Tampa, Florida.

Longest throw

The longest throw (ball weighs 5–5¼ oz *141–148 g*) is 445 ft 10 in *135,88 m* by Glen Edward Gorbous (b. Canada 8 July 1930) on 1 Aug 1957. The longest throw by a woman is 296 ft *90,2 m* by Mildred Ella 'Babe' Didrikson (later Mrs Zaharias) (US) (1914–56) at Jersey City, New Jersey, USA on 25 July 1931.

Fastest base runner

The fastest time for circling bases is 13.3 sec by Ernest Evar Swanson (1902–73) at Columbus, Ohio, in 1932, at an average speed of 18.45 mph *29,70 km/h*.

Fastest pitcher

The fastest recorded pitcher was Lynn Nolan

US MAJOR LEAGUE RECORDS AL American League, NL National League

BATTING

Batting av., career	.367	Tyrus Raymond Cobb (AL)	1905–28
Batting av., season	.438	Hugh Duffy (Boston, NL)	1894
" "	.422	Napoleon Lajoie (Philadelphia, AL)	1901
Runs, career	2244	Tyrus Raymond Cobb	1905–28
RBIs, career	2297	Henry 'Hank' Aaron	1954–76
" season	190	Lewis Rober 'Hack' Wilson (Chicago, NL)	1930
" game	12	James LeRoy Bottomley (St Louis, NL)	16 Sept 1924
" innings	7	Edward Cartwright (St Louis, AA)	23 Sept 1890
Base hits, career	4191	Tyrus Raymond Cobb	1905–28
" season	257	George Harold Sisler (St Louis, AL)	1920
Hits, consecutive	12	Michael Franklin 'Pinky' Higgins	19–21 June 1938
	12	Walter 'Moose' Dropo	14–15 July 1952
Consecutive games batted safely	56	Joseph Paul DiMaggio (New York, AL)	15 May–16 July 1941
Stolen bases, career	938	Louis Clark Brock	1961–79
" season	130	Rickey Henderson (Oakland, AL)	1982
Consecutive games played	2130	Henry Louis 'Lou' Gehrig	1 June 1925–30 April 1939

PITCHING

Games won, career	511	Denton True 'Cy' Young	1890–1911
" season	60	Charles Gardner Radbourne (Providence, NL)	1884
Consecutive games won	24	Carl Owen Hubbell (New York, NL)	1936–37
Shutouts, career	113	Walter Perry Johnson	1907–27
" season	16	George W. Bradley (St Louis, NL)	1876
"	16	Grover Cleveland Alexander (Philadelphia, NL)	1916
Strikeouts, career	3874*	Lynn Nolan Ryan (New York, NL; California, AL; Houston, NL)	1968–84
" season	383	Lynn Nolan Ryan (California, AL)	1973
No-hit games, career	5	Lynn Nolan Ryan	1966–81
Earned run av., season	0.90	Ferdinand Schupp (140 inn) (New York, NL)	1916
" "	1.01	Hubert 'Dutch' Leonard (222 inn) (Boston, AL)	1914
" "	1.12	Robert Gibson (305 inn) (St Louis, NL)	1968
Complete games, career	751	Denton True 'Cy' Young	1890–1911

*At the start of the 1984 season Ryan had 3874 strikeouts and Steve Carlton (Philadelphia) had 3872.

BASEBALL WORLD SERIES RECORDS AL American League, NL National League

Most wins	22	New York Yankees (AL)	1923–78
Most series played	14	Lawrence P. 'Yogi' Berra (New York, AL) (10 wins)	1947–63
Most home runs in a game	3	George H. 'Babe' Ruth (New York, AL)	6 Oct 1926
	3	Reginald M. Jackson (New York, AL)	18 Oct 1977
Only perfect pitch (in 9 innings)		Donald J. Larson (New York, AL) *v* Brooklyn	8 Oct 1956

JAPANESE LEAGUE RECORDS Superior to those in US major leagues:

Home runs, career	868	Sadaharu Oh (Yomuiri)	1959–80
Stolen bases, career	939	Yutaka Fukumoto (Hankyu)	1969–83

Nolan Ryan, the fastest pitcher of a baseball, has also maintained great accuracy and holds a clutch of pitching records.

Ryan (then of the California Angels) (b. 31 Jan 1947) who, on 20 Aug 1974 at Anaheim Stadium, California, USA, was measured to pitch at 100.9 mph *162,3 km/h.*

Youngest player

The youngest major league player of all time was the Cincinnati pitcher, Joseph Henry Nuxhall (b. 30 July 1928) who started his career in June 1944, aged 15 yr 314 days.

Record attendances and receipts

The World Series record attendance is 420,784 (six games) when the Los Angeles Dodgers beat the Chicago White Sox 4–2 on 1–8 Oct 1959. The single game record is 92,706 for the fifth game at the Memorial Coliseum, Los Angeles, California, on 6 Oct 1959. The highest seating capacity in a baseball stadium is now 74,208 in the Cleveland Municipal Stadium, Ohio, USA. The all-time season record for attendances for both leagues has been 45,557,582 in 1983.

An estimated 114,000 spectators watched a game between Australia and an American Services team in a 'demonstration' event during the Olympic Games at Melbourne, 1 Dec 1956.

BASKETBALL

Origins

The game of 'Pok-ṭa-Pok' was played in the 10th century BC, by the Olmecs in Mexico, and closely resembled basketball in its concept. 'Ollamalitzli' was a variation of this game played by the Aztecs in Mexico as late as the 16th century. If the solid rubber ball was put through a fixed stone ring the player was entitled to the clothing of all the spectators. Modern basketball (which may have been based on the German game *Korbball*) was devised by the Canadian-born Dr James A. Naismith (1861–1939) at the Training School of the International YMCA College at Springfield, Massachusetts, USA, in mid-December 1891. The first game played under modified rules was on 20 Jan 1892. The International Amateur Basketball Federation (FIBA) was founded in 1932, and the English Basketball Association in 1936.

Most titles *Olympic*

The USA have won nine men's Olympic titles. From the time the sport was introduced to the Games in 1936 until 1972 in Munich they won 63 consecutive matches in the Olympic Games until they lost 50–51 to the USSR in the disputed Final match. They won eighth and ninth titles in 1976 and 1984. The women's title was won by the USSR in 1976 and 1980 and by the USA in 1984.

Most titles *World*

The USSR have won most titles at both the men's World Championships (inst. 1950) with three (1967, 1974 and 1982) and women's (inst. 1953) with six (1959, 1964, 1967, 1971, 1975 and 1983).

Most titles *European*

The most European Champions Cup (instituted 1957) wins is seven by Real Madrid, Spain. The women's title has been won 18 times by Daugawa, Riga, Latvia, USSR. The most wins in the European Nations Championships for men is 13 by the USSR, and in the women's event 17 also by the USSR.

Most titles *American Professional*

The most National Basketball Association (NBA) titles (instituted 1947), played for between the leading professional teams in the United States, have been won by the Boston Celtics with 15 victories between 1957 and 1984.

Most titles *English*

The most English National Championship wins (instituted 1936) have been by London Central YMCA, with eight wins in 1957–8, 1960, 1962–4, 1967 and 1969. The English National League title has been won seven times by Crystal Palace 1974, 1976–8, 1980 and 1982–3. Most English Women's Cups (instituted 1965) have been won by Tigers with eight wins, 1972–3, 1976–80 and 1982.

The men's and women's US national sides played All-star opposition in front of the largest indoor crowd to watch a basketball game, for the Indiana Olympic tribute. Both sides went on to win Olympic golds.

Highest score *International*

The highest score recorded in a senior international match is 251 by Iraq against Yemen (33) at New Delhi in November 1982 at the Asian Games. The highest in a British Championship is 125 by England *v.* Wales (54) on 1 Sept 1978. England beat Gibraltar 130–45 on 31 Aug 1978.

Highest score *Match*

The highest aggregate score in an NBA match is 370 when the Detroit Pistons (186) beat the Seattle Nuggets (184) in Denver on 13 Dec 1983. Overtime was played after a 145–145 tie in regulation time.

Highest score *United Kingdom*

The highest score recorded in a match is 250 by the Nottingham YMCA Falcons *v.* Mansfield Pirates at Nottingham, on 18 June 1974. It was a handicap competition and Mansfield received 120 points towards their total of 145. The highest score in a senior National League match is 167 by West Bromwich Kestrels *v.* Milton Keynes (69) on 13 Feb 1983. The highest in the National Cup is 146 by Doncaster *v.* Cleveland (109) on 11 Feb 1976.

Highest score *Individual*

Mats Wermelin, 13, (Sweden) scored all 272 points in a 272–0 win in a regional boys' tournament in Stockholm, Sweden on 5 Feb 1974. The highest single game score in an NBA game is 100 points by Wilton Norman Chamberlain (b. 21 Aug 1936) for Philadelphia *v.* New York on 2 Mar 1962. The most in a college game is 113 points by Clarence 'Bevo' Francis, for Rio Grande College, Ohio *v.* Hillsdale at Jackson, Ohio on 2 Feb 1954. The record score by a woman is 156 points by Marie Boyd (now Eichler) of Central HS, Lonaconing, Maryland, USA in a 163–3 defeat of Ursaline Academy, Cumberland on 25 Feb 1924.

The highest score by a British player is 124 points by Paul Ogden for St Albans School, Oldham (226) *v.* South Chadderton (82) on 9 Mar 1982. The highest individual score in a League match in Britain is 108 by Lewis Young for Forth Steel in his team's 154–74 win over Stirling in the Scottish League Division One at Stirling on 2 Mar 1985. The record in an English National League (Div. One) or Cup match is 73 points by Terry Crosby (USA) for Home Spare Bolton in his team's 120–106 defeat by Cottrills Manchester Giants at Altrincham, Cheshire on 26 Jan 1985.

Most points

Kareem Abdul-Jabbar (formerly Lewis Ferdinand Alcindor) (b. 16 Apr 1947) has scored a career record 33,000 points from 1969 to March 1985 for the Milwaukee Bucks and Los Angeles Lakers. The previous record holder, Wilt Chamberlain had a record average of 30.1 points per game for his total of 31,419. He set a season's record 4029 for Philadelphia in 1962. The record for the most points scored in a college career is (women): 4061, Pearl Moore of Francis Marion College, Florence, S. Carolina, 1975–9, (men): 4045 by Travis Grant for Kentucky State in 1969–72. In the English National League, Ian Day (b. 16 May 1953) has scored 3456 points in 203 games, 1973–84.

Tallest players

The tallest player of all time is reputed to be Suleiman Ali Nashnush (b. 1943) who played for the Libyan team in 1962 when measuring 2,45 m *8 ft.* Aleksandr Sizonenko of Kuibyshev Stroitel and USSR is 2,39 m *7 ft 10 in* tall. The tallest woman player was Iuliana Semenova (USSR) (b. 9 Mar 1952) at a reported 7 ft 2 in *2,18 m* and weighing 281 lb *127,4 kg.* The tallest British player has been the 7 ft 6¼ in *2,29 m* tall

Christopher Greener of London Latvians whose international debut for England was *v.* France on 17 Dec 1969.

Most accurate

The greatest goal shooting demonstration has been by Ted St Martin of Jacksonville, Florida, who, on 25 June 1977, scored 2036 consecutive free throws. In a 24-hr period, 31 May–1 June 1975 Fred L. Newman of San José, California, USA scored 12,874 baskets out of 13,116 throws (98.15 per cent accuracy).

Longest recorded goal

The longest recorded field goal in a match is a measured 92 ft 5¼ in *28,17 m* by Bruce Morris for Marshall University *v.* Appalachian State University at Huntington, West Virginia, USA on 8 Feb 1985. A British record of 75 ft 9½ in *23,10 m* is claimed by David Tarbatt (b. 23 Jan 1949) of Altofts Aces *v.* Harrogate Demons at Featherstone, West Yorkshire on 27 Jan 1980.

Largest ever gate

The Harlem Globetrotters (USA) played an exhibition in front of 75,000 in the Olympic Stadium, West Berlin, Germany, in 1951. The largest indoor basketball attendance was 67,596, including 64,682 tickets sold at the box office, for the Indiana Olympic Basketball Tribute at the Hoosier Dome, Indianapolis, Indiana, USA on 9 July 1984. They saw victories by the US men's and women's Olympic teams over All-Star opposition.

BILLIARDS

Earliest mention

The earliest recorded mention of billiards was in France in 1429, while Louis XI, King of France 1461–83, is reported to have had a billiard table. The first recorded public billiards room in England was the Piazza, Covent Garden, London, in the early part of the 19th century. Rubber cushions were introduced in 1835 and slate beds in 1836.

Keith Sheard scored an average 1,495 points per minute during his record-breaking bar billiards break.

Most titles *Professional*

The greatest number of world championships (instituted 1870) won by one player is eight by John Roberts, Jnr (1847–1919) (England) in 1870 (twice), 1871, 1875 (twice), 1877 and 1885 (twice). The greatest number of United Kingdom titles (instituted 1934) won is seven (1934–39 and 1947) by Joe Davis (1901–78) (England), who also won four world titles (1928–30 and 1932). William F. Hoppe (USA) (1887–1959) won 51 'world' titles in the United States variant of the game between 1906 and 1952.

Most titles *Amateur*

The record for world amateur titles is four by Robert James Percival Marshall (Australia) (b. 10 Apr 1910) in 1936, 1938, 1951 and 1962. The greatest number of English Amateur Championships (instituted 1888) ever won is 15 by Norman Dagley (b. 27 June 1930) in 1965–66, 1970–75, 1978–84. The record number of women's titles is eight by Vera Selby (b. 13 Mar 1930) 1970–8.

Highest breaks

Tom Reece (1873–1953) made an unfinished break of 499,135, including 249,152 cradle cannons (two points each) in 85 hr 49 min against Joe Chapman at Burroughes' Hall, Soho Square, London, between 3 June and 6 July 1907. This was not recognized because press and public were not continuously present. The highest certified break made by the anchor cannon is 42,746 by William Cook (England) from 29 May to 7 June 1907. The official world record under the then baulk-line rule is 1784 by Joe Davis in the United Kingdom Championship on 29 May 1936. Walter Albert Lindrum (Australia) (1898–1960) made an official break of 4137 in 2 hr 55 min against Joe Davis at Thurston's on 19–20 Jan 1932, before the baulk-line rule was in force. Davis has an unofficial personal best of 2502 (mostly pendulum cannons) in a match against Tom Newman (1894–1943) (England) in Manchester in 1930. The highest break recorded in amateur competition is 1149 by Michael Ferreira (India) at Calcutta, India on 15 Dec 1978. On 1 Jan 1983 the more stringent 'two pot' rule under which Robert Marshall (Aus) made a break of 702 at Brisbane on 17 Sept 1953 was restored. No higher break has since been made with this rule in force.

Fastest century

Walter Lindrum made an unofficial 100 break in 27.5 sec in Australia on 10 Oct 1952. His official record is 100 in 46.0 sec set in Sydney in 1941.

3 CUSHION

This pocketless variation dates back to 1878. The world governing body, the *Union Mondiale de Billiard* (UMB) was formed in 1928. The most successful exponent spanning the pre and post international era from 1906 to 1952 was Willie Hoppe who won 51 billiards championships in all forms. Most UMB titles have been won by Raymond Ceulemans (Belgium) (b. 12 July 1935) with 18 (1963–6, 1968–73, 1975–81, 1983).

BAR BILLIARDS

Highest scoring rate

The record scoring rate in a league game has been 28,530 in 19 min 5 sec by Keith Sheard at the Crown and Thistle, Headington, Oxford on 9 July 1984.

24 hours

The highest bar billiards score in 24 hr by a team of five is 1,506,570 by John Burrows, Kent Murray, Ray Hussey, Roy Buckle and Brian Ray of 'The Hour Glass', Sands, High Wycombe, Buckinghamshire on 26–27 Nov 1983.

The longest world championship match was between Karpov (right) and Kasparov (left), lasting a record 159 days from 10 September 1984 to 15 February 1985 before being abandoned with Karpov leading 5–3 in a 'first to six wins' match. 48 games involving 1666 moves were played; 40 games were drawn, including a record 17 consecutive draws.

Г. КАСПАРОВ   А. КАРПОВ

BOARD GAMES

BACKGAMMON

Forerunners of the game have been traced back to a dice and a board game found in excavations at Ur, dated to 3000 BC. Later the Romans played a game remarkably similar to the modern one. The name 'Backgammon' is variously ascribed to Welsh "little battle", or Saxon "back game".

Alan Malcolm Beckerson (b. 21 Feb 1938) devised the shortest game of 16 throws in 1982.

CHESS

Origins

The game originated in ancient India under the name Chaturanga (literally 'four-corps'—an army game). The name chess is derived from the Persian word *shah* (a king or ruler). The earliest reference is from the Middle Persian Karnamak (*c.* AD 590–628), though in December 1972, two ivory chessmen were found in the Uzbek Soviet Republic dateable to AD 200. It reached Britain in *c.* 1255. The *Fédération Internationale des Echecs* was established in 1924.

Most World titles

World champions have been generally recognised since 1886. The longest undisputed tenure was 27 years by Dr Emanuel Lasker (1868–1941) of Germany, from 1894 to 1921. The women's world championship was held by Vera Menchik-Stevenson (1906–44) (USSR, later GB) from 1927 till her death, and was successfully defended a record seven times. Nona Gaprindashvili (USSR) (b. 3 May 1941) held the title from 1962 to 1978 and defended successfully four

times. Robert J. 'Bobby' Fischer (b. Chicago, Illinois, USA, 9 March 1943) is reckoned on the officially adopted Elo System to be the greatest Grand Master of all-time with a 2785 rating. Gary Kasparov (USSR) (b. 13 Apr 1963), at 2715 is currently ranked highest ahead of Anatoliy Yevgenyevitch Karpov (USSR) (b. 23 May 1951), world champion since 1975, at 2705. The highest rated woman player is Susan Polger (Hungary) at 2430. The USSR has won the men's team title a record 15 times and the women's title ten times to 1984.

Youngest and Oldest

The youngest world champion was Mikhail Nekhemevich Tal (USSR) (b. 9 Nov 1936) who won on 7 May 1960 aged 23 yr 180 days. The oldest was Wilhelm Steinitz (1836–1900) who was 58 yr old when he lost his title to Lasker in 1894.

Most British titles

Most British titles have been won by Dr Jonathan Penrose (b. 7 Oct 1933) with ten titles in 1958–63, 1966–9. Rowena Mary Bruce (*née* Dew) (b. 15 May 1919) won 11 women's titles between 1937 and 1969. The first British player to attain official International Grand Master status was Anthony Miles (b. 23 Apr 1955), on 24 Feb 1976. John Nunn (b. 25 Apr 1955) ranks as the top British player at 2615 on the Elo list of 1 Jan 1985.

Least games lost by a world champion

José Raúl Capablanca (Cuba) (1888–1942) lost only 34 games in his adult career, 1909–39. He was unbeaten from 10 Feb 1916 to 21 Mar 1924 and was world champion 1921–7.

Most opponents

Vlastimil Hort (b. 12 Jan 1944) (Czechoslovakia), in Seltjarnes, Iceland on 23–24 Apr 1977,

played 550 opponents including 201 simultaneously; he only lost ten games. Dimitrije Bjelica (Yugoslavia) played a record 301 opponents simultaneously in Sarajevo on 18 Sept 1982. Over a nine-hour period he had 258 wins, 36 draws and 7 losses. The record for most consecutive games played is 663 by Vlastimil Hort over 32½ hours at Porz, W. Germany on 5–6 Oct 1984. He played 60–100 opponents at a time, scoring over 80% wins and averaging 30 moves per game.

Slowest and longest games

The slowest reported moving (before modern rules) in an official event is reputed to have been by Louis Paulsen (Germany) (1833–91) against Paul Charles Morphy (USA) (1837–84) on 29 Oct 1857. The game ended in a draw on move 56 after 15 hours of play of which Paulsen used most of the allotted time. Grandmaster Friedrich Sämisch (1896–1975) (Germany) ran out of the allotted time (2 hr 30 min for 45 moves) after only 12 moves, in Prague, Czechoslovakia, in 1938.

The Master game with most moves on record was when Yedael Stepak (Israel) (b. 21 Aug 1940) beat Yaakov Mashian (Iran, later Israel) (b. 17 Dec 1943) in 193 moves in Tel Aviv, Israel on 23 Mar–16 Apr 1980. The total playing time was a record 24 hr 30 min.

DRAUGHTS

Origins

Draughts, known as checkers in North America, has origins earlier than chess. It was played in Egypt in the second millennium BC. The earliest book on the game was by Antonio Torquemada of Valencia, Spain in 1547. There have been four US v. Great Britain internationals (cross-board) 1905, 1927, 1973 and 1983, three won by the United States and one by Great Britain.

Walter Hellman (USA) (1916–75) won a record six world championships, in 1948–67. Melvin Pomeroy (US) was internationally undefeated from 1914 until his death in 1933.

The British Championship (biennial) was inaugurated in 1886. A record six titles were won by S. Cohen (London), 1924, 1927, 1929, 1933, 1937 and 1939. J. McGill (Kilbride) won six Scottish titles between 1959 and 1974.

Most opponents
Con McCarrick (Ireland) was reported as having played a record 154 games simultaneously, winning 136, drawing 17 and losing one, in 4 hr 30 min at Dundalk, Co. Louth, Ireland on 14 Mar 1982. Newell W. Banks (b. Detroit, USA, 10 Oct 1887) played 140 games simultaneously, winning 133 and drawing seven, in Chicago, Illinois in 1933. His playing time was 145 min, so averaging about one move per sec. In 1947 he played blindfold for 4 hr per day for 45 consecutive days, winning 1331 games, drawing 54 and losing only two, while playing six games at a time.

Longest and shortest games
In competition the prescribed rate of play is not less than 30 moves per hour with the average game lasting about 90 min. In 1958 a match between Dr Marion Tinsley (US) and Derek Oldbury (GB) lasted 7 hr 30 min. The shortest possible game is one of 20 moves composed by Alan Malcolm Beckerson (GB) in 1977.

The Cresta Run, or Grand National as its original planner George Roberts named it, celebrated its centenary in 1985. Briton James Sunley *(below)* holds the record for the Flying Junction section.

SCRABBLE ® Crossword Game

Origins
The crossword game was invented by Alfred M. Butts in 1931 and was developed, refined and trademarked as Scrabble ® Crossword Game by James Brunot in 1948. He sold the North American rights to Selchow & Richter Company, New York, the European rights to J. W. Spear & Sons, London, and the Australian rights to Murfett Pty Ltd, Melbourne.

Highest scores
The highest competitive league game score is 841 by Mark Nyman (GB) in March 1985. His opponent scored 436. The highest competitive single turn score recorded is 392 by Dr Saladin Karl Khoshnaw (of Kurdish origin) in Manchester in April 1982. He laid down "CAZIQUES".

The greatest margin of victory in a league game was achieved by Ron Hendra when he beat Amber Sturdy 730–180 in a London League match in 1983.

Most titles
British National Championships were instituted in 1971. Olive Behan, 1972 and 1975, and Philip Nelkon, 1978 and 1981, have both won twice. The highest score in the Championship has been 1782 (three games total) by Esther Byers in 1985.

BOBSLEIGH AND TOBOGGANING

BOBSLEDDING

Origins
The oldest known sledge is dated *c.* 6500 BC and came from Heinola, Finland. The first known bobsleigh race took place at Davos, Switzerland in 1889. The International Federation of Bobsleigh and Tobogganing was formed in 1923, followed by the International Bobsleigh Federation in 1957.

Most titles *Olympic*
The Olympic four-man bob title (inst. 1924) has been won four times by Switzerland (1924, 1936, 1956 and 1972). The USA (1932, 1936), Switzerland (1948, 1980), Italy (1956, 1968), W. Germany (1952, 1972) and GDR (1976, 1984) have won the Olympic two-man bob (inst. 1932) event twice. The most gold medals won by an individual is three by Meinhard Nehmer (GDR) (b. 13 June 1941) and Bernhard Germeshausen (GDR) (b. 21 Aug 1951) in the 1976 two-man, 1976 and 1980 four-man events. The most medals won is six (two gold, two silver, two bronze) by Eugenio Monti (Italy) (b. 23 Jan 1928), 1956 to 1968. The only British victory was at two-man bob in 1964 by Hon. Robin Thomas Valerian Dixon (b. 21 Apr 1935) and Anthony James Dillon Nash (b. 18 Mar 1936).

Most titles *World*
The world four-man bob title (inst. 1924) has been won 14 times by Switzerland (1924, 1936, 1939, 1947, 1954–7, 1971–3, 1975 and 1982–3). Italy won the two-man title 14 times (1954, 1956–63, 1966, 1968–9, 1971 and 1975). Eugenio Monti was a member of eleven world championship crews, eight two-man and three four-man in 1957–68.

TOBOGGANING

The word toboggan comes from the Micmac American Indian word *tobaakan*. The St Moritz Tobogganing Club, Switzerland, founded in 1887 is the oldest toboggan club in the world. It

is unique in being the home of the Cresta Run, which dates from 1884, and for the introduction of the one-man racing toboggan skeleton. The course is 3977 ft *1212,25 m* long with a drop of 514 ft *157 m* and the record is 51.68 sec (av. 52.48 mph *84,45 km/h*) by Franco Gansser of Switzerland on 23 Feb 1985. On 16 Feb 1985 Gansser set a record from Junction (890,2 m *2920 ft*) of 41.97 sec.

The greatest number of wins in the Grand National (inst. 1885) is eight by the 1948 Olympic champion Nino Bibbia (Italy) (b. 9 Sept 1924) in 1960–4, 1966, 1968 and 1973. The greatest number of wins in the Curzon Cup (inst. 1910) is eight by Bibbia in 1950, 1957–8, 1960, 1962–4, and 1969, who hence won the double in 1960 and 1962–4.

LUGEING

In lugeing the rider adopts a sitting, as opposed to a prone, position. Official international competition began at Klosters, Switzerland, in 1881. The first European championships were at Reichenberg, E. Germany, in 1914 and the first world championships at Oslo, Norway, in 1953. The International Luge Federation was formed in 1957. Lugeing became an Olympic sport in 1964.

Fastest speed
The highest recorded, photo-timed, speed is 137,4 km/h *85.38 mph* by Asle Strand (Norway) at Tandådalens Linbane, Sälen, Sweden on 1 May 1982.

Most titles *World and Olympic*
The most successful rider in the world championships is Thomas Köhler (GDR) (b. 25 June 1940), who won the single-seater title in 1962, 1964 (Olympic), 1966 and 1967 and shared the two-seater title in 1967 and 1968 (Olympic). Margit Schumann (GDR) (b. 14 Sept 1952) has won five women's titles, 1973–5, 1976 (Olympic) and 1977.

BOWLING (TENPIN)

Origins
The ancient German game of nine-pins (*Heidenwerfen*—knock down pagans) was exported to the United States in the early 17th century. In 1841 the Connecticut State Legislature prohibited the game and other states followed. Eventually a tenth pin was added to evade the ban; but there is some evidence of ten pins being used in Suffolk about 300 years ago. The first body to standardise rules was the American Bowling Congress (ABC), established in New York on 9 Sept 1895.

In the United States there were 8351 bowling establishments with 159,877 bowling lanes and 72,000,000 bowlers in 1984. The world's largest bowling centre (now closed) was the Tōkyō World Lanes Centre, Japan with 252 lanes. Currently the largest centre is the Fukuyama Bowl, Osaka, Japan which has 144 lanes. The largest in Europe is the Nottingham Bowl at Nottingham, England, where the game was introduced in 1960, with 48 lanes on two floors.

World championships
The world (Fédération Internationale des Quilleurs) championships were instituted for men in 1954 and for women in 1963. The highest pinfall in the individual men's event is 5963 (in 28 games) by Ed Luther (US) at Milwaukee, Wisconsin, on 28 Aug 1971. For the current schedule of 24 games the men's record is 5242

by Mats Karlsson (Sweden) and the women's is 4806 by Bong Coo (Philippines) both at Caracas, Venezuela in Nov 1983.

Highest scores *World*

The highest individual score for three sanctioned games (possible 900) is 886 by Albert 'Allie' Brandt of Lockport, New York, USA, on 25 Oct 1939. The record by a woman is 853 by Sherrie Langford of Whittier, California at Clearwater, Florida, USA, on 19 Feb 1982. The record for consecutive strikes in sanctioned match play is 33, first achieved by John Pezzin (b. 1930) at Toledo, Ohio, USA on 4 Mar 1976. The highest number of sanctioned 300 games is 27 (to 1985) by Elvin Mesger of Sullivan, Missouri, USA; the women's record is nine by Jeanne Maiden of Solon, Ohio. The maximum 900 for a three-game series was achieved by Glenn Allison (b. 1930) at the La Habra Bowl in Los Angeles, California on 1 July 1982, but this was not recognised by the ABC due to the oiling patterns on the boards. It has been recorded four times in unsanctioned games—by Leon Bentley at Lorain, Ohio, USA, on 26 Mar 1931; by Joe Sargent at Rochester, New York State, USA, in 1934; by Jim Margie in Philadelphia, Pennsylvania, USA, on 4 Feb 1937 and by Bob Brown at Roseville Bowl, California, USA on 12 Apr 1980. Such series must have consisted of 36 consecutive strikes (*i.e.* all pins down with one ball).

The highest average for a season attained in sanctioned competition is 242 by John Rogard of Susquehanna, Pa., USA for 66 games in 1981–82. The women's record is 232 by Patty Ann of New Ulm, Minnesota in 1984–5.

Highest scores *Great Britain*

Army Sergeant Michael Langley set a British record for a three-game series of 835 at S.H.A.P.E., Belgium on 15 Apr 1985. The record score for a single game is 300, first achieved by Albert Kirkham (b. 1931) of Burslem, Staffordshire, on 5 Dec 1965, which has since been equalled on several occasions. The best by a woman is 300 by Georgina Wardle at the Sheffield Bowl, S. Yorkshire on 20 Jan 1985. The three-game series record for a woman player is 740 by Elizabeth Cullen at the Astra Bowl, RAF Brize Norton, Oxfordshire on 15 Mar 1983.

Highest earnings

Earl Anthony (b. 1938) won a record $1,257,021 in Professional Bowlers Association (PBA) competition including a record 41 PBA titles.

SKITTLES

24 Hours

Eight players from the Alkies skittle team knocked down 83,440 West Country skittles on 30–31 Mar 1985 at Torquay, Devon. The highest hood skittle score in 24 hr is 107,487 pins by 12 players from the Plume of Feathers, Daventry, Northamptonshire, on 19–20 Mar 1976. The highest long alley score is 24,909 by the Flintstones Skittles Team (eight players) in Neath, West Glamorgan on 16–17 June 1985. The highest table skittle score in 24 hr is 90,446 skittles by 12 players at the Finney Gardens Hotel, Hanley, Staffs on 27–28 Dec 1980.

BOWLS

OUTDOOR

Origins

Bowls can be traced back to at least the 13th century in England. The Southampton Town Bowling was formed in 1299. A green dating

back to 1294 is claimed by the Chesterfield Bowling Club. After falling into disrepute, the game was rescued by the bowlers of Scotland who, headed by William W. Mitchell (1803–84), framed the modern rules in 1848–9.

Most titles *World*

The only man to win two singles titles is David John Bryant (b. 27 Oct 1931) (England) in 1966 and 1980. Australia won the pairs twice, 1966 and 1980. At Johannesburg, South Africa, in February 1976, the South African team achieved an unprecedented clean sweep of all four titles and the team competition (Leonard Trophy).

Elsie Wilke (New Zealand) won two women's singles titles, 1969 and 1974, and Australia won three of the four women's titles in 1985.

Most titles *International Championship*

In the annual International Championships (inst. 1903) Scotland have won a record 34 times including 11 consecutive wins, 1965 to 1975.

Most titles *English & British*

The record number of English Bowls Association (founded 8 June 1903) championships is 15 won or shared by David Bryant, including six singles (1960, 1966, 1971–3, 1975), three pairs (1965, 1969, 1974), two triples (1966, 1977) and four fours championships (1957, 1968, 1969 and 1971). He has also won six British Isles titles (four singles, one pairs, one fours) in the period 1957–74.

Highest score

The highest score achieved in an international bowls match is the 63–1 victory by Swaziland *v* Japan during the World Championships at Melbourne, Australia on 16 Jan 1980.

Most eights

Freda Ehlers and Linda Bertram uniquely scored three consecutive eights in the Southern Transvaal pairs event at Johannesburg, South Africa on 30 Jan 1978.

Aleta Sill won a record $81,452 on the Ladies Professional Bowlers tour in 1984. She has won a record eight titles in the tour's four-year history.

International appearances

The greatest number of international appearances outdoors by any bowler is 78 reached by Syd Thompson (b. 29 Aug 1912) for Ireland 1947–73. He also has had 50 indoor caps. The youngest bowler to represent England was Gerard Anthony Smyth (b. 29 Dec 1960) at 20 yr 196 days on 13 July 1981. The youngest ever EBA singles champion was David J. Cutler (b. 1 Aug 1954) at 25 yr 16 days in 1979. He had been a member of the winning triples team at 18 yr 18 days in 1972.

INDOOR

The English Indoor Bowling Association became an autonomous body in 1971. Prior to that it was part of the English Bowling Association.

Most titles

The four-corner international championship was first held in 1936. England have won most titles with 20 wins. The National Singles title (inst. 1960) has been won most often by David Bryant with nine wins (1960, 1966, 1971–3, 1975, 1978–9, 1983). David Bryant has won the World Indoor Championship (inst 1979) three times, 1979–81.

The youngest EIBA singles champion, John Dunn (b. 6 Oct 1963) was 17 yr 117 days when he won in 1981.

Highest score

The highest score in a British International match is 52 by Scotland v. Wales (3) at Teeside in March 1972.

C. Hammond and B. Funnell of The Angel, Tonbridge beat A. Wise and C. Lock 55–0 over 21 ends in the second round of the EIBA National Pairs Championships on 17 Oct 1983 at The Angel, Tonbridge, Kent.

BOXING

Earliest references

Boxing with gloves was depicted on a fresco from the Isle of Thera, Greece which has been dated 1520 BC. The earliest prize-ring code of rules was formulated in England on 16 Aug 1743 by the champion pugilist Jack Broughton (1704–89), who reigned from 1734 to 1750. Boxing, which had, in 1867, come under the Queensberry Rules formulated for John Sholto Douglas, 8th Marquess of Queensberry (1844–1900), was not established as a legal sport in Britain until after the ruling, R. *v.* Roberts and Others, of Mr Justice Grantham, following the death of Billy Smith (Murray Livingstone) due to a fight on 24 Apr 1901.

Longest fights

The longest recorded fight with gloves was between Andy Bowen of New Orleans (1867–94) and Jack Burke in New Orleans, Louisiana, USA, on 6–7 Apr 1893. The fight lasted 110 rounds and 7 hr 19 min (9.15 p.m.–4.34 a.m.), and was declared no contest (later changed to a draw). Bowen won an 85 round bout on 31 May 1893. The longest bare knuckle fight was 6 hr 15 min between James Kelly and Jack Smith at Fiery Creek, Dalesford, Victoria, Australia on 3 Dec 1855. The longest bare knuckle fight in Britain was 6 hr 3 min (185 rounds) between Bill Hayes and Mike Madden at Edenbridge, Kent, on 17 July 1849. The greatest number of rounds was 276 in 4 hr 30 min when Jack Jones beat Patsy Tunney in Cheshire in 1825.

Shortest fights

There is a distinction between the quickest knock-out and the shortest fight. A knock-out in $10\frac{1}{2}$ sec (including a 10 sec count) occurred on 23 Sept 1946, when Al Couture struck Ralph Walton while the latter was adjusting a gum shield in his corner at Lewiston, Maine, USA. If the time was accurately taken it is clear that Couture must have been more than half-way across the ring from his own corner at the opening bell. The shortest fight on record appears to be one in a Golden Gloves tournament at Minneapolis, Minnesota, USA, on 4 Nov 1947 when Mike Collins floored Pat Brownson with the first punch and the contest was stopped, without a count, 4 sec after the bell.

The fastest officially timed knock-out in British boxing is 11 sec (including a doubtless fast 10 sec count) when Jack Cain beat Harry Deamer, both of Notting Hill, London at the National Sporting Club on 20 Feb 1922.

The shortest world title fight was the James J. Jeffries (1875–1953)–Jack Finnegan heavyweight bout on 6 Apr 1900, won by Jeffries in 55 sec. The shortest ever British title fight was one of 40 sec (including the count), when Dave Charnley knocked out David 'Darkie' Hughes in a lightweight championship defence in Nottingham on 20 Nov 1961.

Most British titles

The most defences of a British heavyweight title is 14 by 'Bombardier' Billy Wells (1889–1967) from 1911 to 1919. The only British boxer to win three Lonsdale Belts outright was Henry William Cooper (b. 3 May 1934), heavyweight champion (1959–69, 1970–1). He retired after losing to Joe Bugner (b. Hungary, 13 Mar 1950), having held the British heavyweight title from 12 Jan 1959 to 28 May 1969 and from 24 Mar 1970 to 16 Mar 1971.

Tallest

The tallest boxer to fight professionally was Gogea Mitu (b. 1914) of Romania in 1935. He was 7 ft 4 in *233 cm* and weighed 23 st 5 lb (327 lb) *148 kg*. John Rankin, who won a fight in New Orleans, Louisiana, USA, in November 1967, was reputedly also 7 ft 4 in *233 cm*.

Longest career

The heavyweight Jem Mace (GB) (1831–1910), known as 'the gypsy', had a career lasting 35 years from 1855 to 1890, but there were several years in which he had only one fight. Bobby Dobbs (USA) (1858–1930) is reported to have had a 39 year career from 1875 to 1914. Walter Edgerton, the 'Kentucky Rosebud', knocked out John Henry Johnson aged 45 in four rounds at the Broadway AC, New York City, USA, on 4 Feb 1916, when aged 63.

Most fights

The greatest recorded number of fights in a career is 1024 by Bobby Dobbs (USA) (see above). Abraham Hollandersky, *alias* Abe the Newsboy (USA), is reputed to have had up to 1039 fights from 1905 to 1918, but many of them were exhibition bouts.

Most fights without loss

Edward Henry (Harry) Greb (USA) (1894–1926) was unbeaten in 178 bouts, including 117 'No Decision', in 1916–23. Of boxers with complete records Packey McFarland (USA) (1888–1936) had 97 fights (five draws) in 1905–15 without a defeat. Pedro Carrasco (Spain) (b. 7 Nov 1943) won 83 consecutive fights from 22 April 1964 to 3 Sept 1970, drew once and had a further nine wins before his loss to Armando Ramos in a WBC lightweight contest on 18 Feb 1972.

Most knock-outs

The greatest number of finishes classed as 'knock-outs' in a career (1936–63) is 145 by Archie Moore (USA) (b. Archibald Lee Wright, 13 Dec 1913 or 1916). The record for consecutive KO's is 44 by Lamar Clark (b. 1 Dec 1934) (USA) from 1958 to 11 Jan 1960. He knocked out six in one night (five in the first round) at Bingham, Utah, on 1 Dec 1958.

Largest purse

The total purse for the world middleweight fight between 'Marvelous' Marvin Hagler (b. 23 May 1954) and Thomas Hearns (USA) at Las Vegas on 16 Apr 1985, was estimated as $17 million (including a guaranteed $11 million). Hagler won in the third round.

Highest earnings in career

The largest fortune made in a fighting career is an estimated $69 million (including exhibitions) by Muhammad Ali from October 1960 to December 1981 in 61 fights comprising 549 rounds.

Attendances *Highest*

The greatest paid attendance at any boxing fight has been 120,757 (with a ringside price of $27.50) for the Tunney *v.* Dempsey world heavyweight title fight at the Sesquicentennial Stadium, Philadelphia, Pennsylvania, USA, on 23 Sept 1926. The indoor record is 63,350 at the Ali *v.* Leon Spinks fight in the Superdrome, New Orleans, Louisiana, on 15 Sept 1978. Record receipts of $7,293,600 were reported for the WBC world heavyweight title fight at Las Vegas on 11 June 1982 when Larry Holmes (USA) (b. 3 Nov 1949) beat Gerry Cooney (USA) (b. 24 Aug 1956). The British attendance record is 82,000 at the Len Harvey *v.* Jock McAvoy fight at White City, London, on 10 July 1939.

The highest non-paying attendance is 135,132 at the Tony Zale *v.* Billy Pryor fight at Juneau Park, Milwaukee, Wisconsin, USA, on 16 Aug 1941.

Attendances *Lowest*

The smallest attendance at a world heavyweight title fight was 2434 at the Clay *v.* Liston fight at Lewiston, Maine, USA, on 25 May 1965.

WORLD HEAVYWEIGHT CHAMPIONS

Earliest title fight

The first world heavyweight title fight, with gloves and 3 min rounds, was that between John Lawrence Sullivan (1858–1918) and 'Gentleman' James John Corbett (1866–1933) in New Orleans, Louisiana, USA, on 7 Sept 1892. Corbett won in 21 rounds.

Longest and shortest reigns

The longest reign of any world heavyweight champion is 11 years 8 months and 7 days by Joe Louis (USA) (b. Joseph Louis Barrow, 1914–81), from 22 June 1937, when he knocked out James Joseph Braddock in the eighth round at Chicago, Illinois, USA, until announcing his retirement on 1 Mar 1949. During his reign Louis made a record 25 defences of his title. The shortest reign was by Leon Spinks (USA) (b. 11 July 1953) for 212 days from 15 Feb to 15 Sept 1978. Ken Norton (USA) (b. 9 Aug 1945) was recognised by the WBC as champion for 83 days from 18 Mar–9 June 1978. The longest lived world heavyweight champion was Jack Dempsey who died on 31 May 1983 aged 87 yr 341 days.

Most recaptures

Muhammad Ali (b. Cassius Marcellus Clay Jr. 17 Jan 1942) is the only man to regain the heavyweight championship twice. Ali first won the title on 25 Feb 1964 defeating Sonny Liston. He defeated George Foreman on 30 Oct 1974 having been stripped of the title by the world boxing authorities on 28 Apr 1967. He won the WBA title from Leon Spinks on 15 Sept 1978 having previously lost to him on 15 Feb 1978.

Undefeated

Rocky Marciano (b. Rocco Francis Marchegiano) (1923–69) is the only world heavyweight champion to have been undefeated during his entire professional career (1947–56). He won all his 49 fights, 43 by knockouts or stoppages.

Larry Holmes won all 48 of his bouts, including 33 by knockouts and 19 successful heavyweight title defences to May 1985.

Oldest and Youngest

The oldest man to win the heavyweight crown was Jersey Joe Walcott (USA) (b. Arnold Raymond Cream, 31 Jan 1914) who knocked out Ezzard Mack Charles (1921–75) on 18 July 1951 in Pittsburgh, Pennsylvania, when aged 37 yr 168 days. Walcott was the oldest holder at 38 yr 236 days, losing his title to Rocky Marciano (1923–69) on 23 Sept 1952. The youngest age at which the world title has been won is 21 yr 331 days by Floyd Patterson (USA) (b. 4 Jan 1935), when he won the vacant title by beating Archie Moore in Chicago, Illinois, USA, on 30 Nov 1956.

Heaviest and lightest

The heaviest world champion was Primo Carnera (Italy) (1906–67), the 'Ambling Alp', who won the title from Jack Sharkey in six rounds in New York City, NY, USA, on 29 June 1933. He scaled 267 lb *121 kg* for this fight but his peak weight was 270 lb *122 kg*. He had an expanded chest measurement of 53 in *134 cm* and the longest reach at $85\frac{1}{2}$ in *217 cm* (finger tip to finger tip). The lightest champion was Robert James 'Bob' Fitzsimmons (1863–1917), from Helston, Cornwall, who at a weight of 167 lb *75 kg*, won the title by knocking out James Corbett in 14 rounds at Carson City, Nevada, USA, on 17 Mar 1897.

The greatest differential in a world title fight was 86 lb *39 kg* between Carnera (270 lb *122 kg*) and Tommy Loughran (184 lb *83 kg*) of the USA, when the former won on points at Miami, Florida, USA, on 1 Mar 1934.

Tallest and shortest

The tallest world champion according to measurements by the Physical Education Director of the Hemingway Gymnasium, Harvard University, was Carnera at 6 ft 5.4 in *196,6 cm* although he was widely reported and believed to be up to 6 ft 8½ in *204 cm*. Jess Willard (1881–1968), who won the title in 1915, often stated to be 6 ft 6¼ in *199 cm* was in fact 6 ft 5¼ in *196 cm*. The shortest was Tommy Burns, world champion from 23 Feb 1906 to 26 Dec 1908, who stood 5 ft 7 in *170 cm* and weighed between 168 and 180 lb *76–81 kg*.

WORLD CHAMPIONS *Any weight*

Longest reign

Joe Louis's heavyweight duration record of 11 years 252 days stands for all divisions.

Youngest and oldest

The youngest age at which any world championship has been won is 17 yr 176 days by Wilfred Benitez (b. New York, 12 Sept 1958) of Puerto Rico, who won the WBA light welterweight title in San Juan, PR, on 6 Mar 1976. The oldest world champion was Archie Moore who was recognised as a light heavyweight champion up to 10 Feb 1962 when his title was removed. He was then believed to be between 45 and 48. Bob Fitzsimmons had the longest career of any official world titleholder with over 32 years from 1882 to 1914. He won his last world title aged 40 yr 183 days in San Francisco, California on 25 Nov 1903.

Longest fight

The longest world title fight (under Queensberry Rules) was that between the lightweights Joe Gans (1874–1910), of the USA, and Oscar Matthew 'Battling' Nelson (1882–1954), the 'Durable Dane', at Goldfield, Nevada, USA, on 3 Sept 1906. It was terminated in the 42nd round when Gans was declared the winner on a foul.

Most recaptures

The only boxer to win a world title five times at one weight is 'Sugar' Ray Robinson (USA) (b. Walker Smith, Jr, 3 May 1921), who beat Carmen Basilio (USA) in the Chicago Stadium on 25 Mar 1958, to regain the world middleweight title for the fourth time. The record number of title bouts in a career is 33 or 34, at bantam and featherweight, by George Dixon (1870–1909), *alias* 'Little Chocolate', of Canada, between 1890 and 1901.

Greatest weight span

The only man to hold world titles at three weights *simultaneously* was Henry 'Homicide Hank' Armstrong (b. 12 Dec 1912), now the Rev Henry Jackson, of the USA, at featherweight, lightweight and welterweight from August to December 1938.

Greatest 'tonnage'

The greatest 'tonnage' recorded in any fight is 700 lb *317 kg* when Claude 'Humphrey' McBride (Oklahoma) 340 lb *154 kg* knocked out Jimmy Black (Houston), who weighed 360 lb *163 kg* in the third round at Oklahoma City on 1 June 1971. The greatest 'tonnage' in a world title fight was 488¾ lb *221¼ kg*, when Carnera, then 259¼ lb *117¾ kg* fought Paolino Uzcudun 229½ lb *104 kg* of Spain in Rome on 22 Oct 1933.

Marvin Hagler, undisputed middleweight champion since 1980, was guaranteed $5.6 million for his defence against WBC light middleweight champion Thomas Hearns (guaranteed $5.4 million). The total payout following three rounds of undiluted aggression was an estimated $17 million. *(All-Sport)*

Most knock-downs in Title fights

Vic Toweel (South Africa) (b. 12 Jan 1929) knocked down Danny O'Sullivan of London 14 times in ten rounds in their world bantamweight fight at Johannesburg on 2 Dec 1950, before the latter retired.

AMATEUR

Most Olympic titles

Only two boxers have won three Olympic gold medals: southpaw László Papp (b. 25 Mar 1926) (Hungary), middleweight 1948, light-middleweight 1952 and 1956; Teofilo Stevenson (b. 23 Mar 1952) (Cuba), heavyweight 1972, 1976 and 1980. The only man to win two titles in one celebration was Oliver L. Kirk (USA), who won both bantam and featherweight titles in St Louis, Missouri, USA, in 1904, when the US won all the titles. In 1908 Great Britain won all five titles.

Oldest gold medallist

Richard Kenneth Gunn (1871–1961) (GB) won the Olympic featherweight gold medal on 27 Oct 1908 in London aged 37 yr 254 days.

World Championships

Two boxers have won two world championships (inst. 1974): Teofilo Stevenson (Cuba), heavyweight 1974 and 1978, and Angel Herrera (b. 2

Aug 1952) (Cuba), featherweight 1978 and lightweight 1982.

Most titles *Great Britain*

The greatest number of ABA titles won by any boxer is six by Joseph Steers at middleweight and heavyweight between 1890 and 1893. Alex 'Bud' Watson (b. 27 May 1914) of Leith, Scotland won the Scottish heavyweight title in 1938, 1942–3, and the light-heavyweight championship 1937–9, 1943–5 and 1947, making ten in all. He also won the ABA light-heavyweight title in 1945 and 1947.

Longest span

The greatest span of ABA title-winning performances is that of the heavyweight Hugh 'Pat' Floyd (b. 23 Aug 1910), who won in 1929 and gained his fourth title 17 years later in 1946.

CANOEING

Origins

The acknowledged pioneer of canoeing as a modern sport was John Macgregor (1825–92), a British barrister, in 1865. The Canoe Club was formed on 26 July 1866.

Most titles *Olympic*

Gert Fredriksson (b. 21 Nov 1919) of Sweden has won most Olympic gold medals with six in 1948, 1952, 1956 and 1960. The most by a woman is three by Ludmila Pinayeva (*née* Khvedosyuk) (b. 14 Jan 1936) (USSR), in 1964, 1968 and 1972. The most gold medals at one Games is three by Vladimir Parfenovich (b. 2 Dec 1958) (USSR) in 1980 and by Ian Ferguson (b. 20 July 1952) (New Zealand) in 1984.

Most titles *World*

13 titles have been won by Rüdiger Helm (GDR) (b. 6 Oct 1956), ten world and three Olympic between 1976 and 1983. Birgit Fischer (now Schmidt) (GDR) (b. 25 Feb 1962) won all three gold medals in the world championships of 1981–3, one in 1979 and one at the 1980 Olympics for a women's record of eleven. The most individual titles by a British canoeist is three by Alan Emus, canoe sailing 1961, 1965 and 1969.

Most titles *British*

The most British Open titles (instituted 1936) ever won is 32 by John Laurence Oliver (Lincoln Canoe Club) (b. 12 Jan 1943) from 1966 to 1976 including 12 individual events. David Mitchell (Chester S&CC) won eight British slalom titles in 1963–8, 1970–1.

Highest speed

The Olympic 1000 m best performance of 3 min 02.70 sec set in a heat by the USSR K4 at Moscow on 31 July 1980, represents an average speed of 12.24 mph *19,70 km/h*. They achieved 13.14 mph *21,15 km/h* for the first 250 m.

Longest journey

The longest journey ever made by canoe is 12,181 miles *19 603 km* by father and son Dana and Donald Starkell from Winnipeg, Manitoba, Canada by ocean and river to Belem, Brazil from 1 June 1980 to 1 May 1982. All portages were human powered.

The longest journey without portages or aid of any kind is one of 6102 miles *9820 km* by Richard H. Grant and Ernest 'Moose' Lassy circumnavigating the eastern USA via Chicago, New Orleans, Miami, New York and the Great Lakes from 22 Sept 1930 to 15 Aug 1931.

Longest open sea voyage

Beatrice and John Dowd, Ken Beard and Steve Benson (Richard Gillett replaced him mid-journey) paddled 2170 miles *3491 km* (of a total 2192 miles *3527 km*) from Venezuela to Miami, Florida, USA, via the West Indies, 11 Aug 1977–29 Apr 1978 in two Klepper Aerius 20 kayaks.

Cross-Channel

The singles record across the English Channel is 3 hr 33 min 47 sec by Andrew William Dougall Samuel (b. 12 July 1937) of Glasgow, from Shakespeare Bay, Dover, to Wissant, France, on 5 Sept 1976. The doubles record is 2 hr 54 min 54 sec by Andrew Samuel and Sgt John David Anderson (RAF) (b. 18 Mar 1957) in a K2 *Accord*, from Shakespeare Bay, Dover to Cap Gris Nez, France on 22 Aug 1980.

The record for a double crossing is 12 hr 47 min in K1s by nine members of the Canoe Camping Club, GB, on 7 May 1976.

North Sea

On 4–5 June 1976 Derek Hutchison, Tom Caskey and Dave Hellawell paddled K1s from Felixstowe, Suffolk to Ostend, Belgium, over 100 miles *160 km* across open sea, in 31 hr.

Loch Ness

The fastest time for a K1 from Fort Augustus to

Ian Ferguson of New Zealand won three gold medals at the 1984 Olympics, including the individual 500 metres K-1. *(Stewart Kendall)*

DOWNSTREAM CANOEING

River	Miles	Km	Name and Country	Route	Date	Duration
RHINE	708	*1140*	David Montgomery (GB)	Chur, Switzerland to Willemstad, Neth.	1984	12 days 8½ hr
	714	*1149*	Four RAF canoeists (GB)	Chur to Willemstad	28 Apr–7 May 1981	8 days 16 hr
MURRAY-DARLING	1980	*3186*	Six students of St Albert's College, UNE (Australia)	Gunnedah, NSW to Lake Alexandrina, SA	Dec 1975	—
MISSISSIPPI	2552	*4107*	Valerie Fons and Verlen Kruger (USA)	Lake Itasca, Minnesota to Gulf of Mexico	27 Apr–20 May 1984	23 days 10 hr 20 min
ZAIRE (CONGO)	2600	*4185*	John and Julie Batchelor (GB)	Moasampanga to Banana	8 May–12 Sept 1974	128 days
AMAZON	3800	*6115*	Alan Trevor Holman (GB/Aus) (b. 21 Feb 1944)	Quitani, Peru to Cabo Maguavi, Brazil	9 Aug–3 Dec 1982	116 days
MISSISSIPPI–MISSOURI	3810	*6132*	Nicholas Francis (GB)	Three Forks, Montana to New Orleans, La.	13 July–25 Nov 1977	135 days
			Mary Schmidt and Bev Gordon (US)	Three Forks to New Orleans	4 July–13 Oct 1984	98 days (unratified)
NILE	4000	*6500*	John Goddard (US), Jean Laporte and André Davy (France)	Kagera to the Delta	Nov 1953–July 1954	9 months

Lochend (22.7 miles *36,5 km*) is 3 hr 33 min 4 sec by Andrew Samuel (Trossachs Canoe and Boat Club) on 19 Oct 1975.

Highest altitude
In September 1976 Dr Michael Leslie Jones (1951–78) and Michael Hopkinson of the British Everest Canoe Expedition canoed down the River Dudh Kosi, Nepal from an altitude of 17,500 ft *5334 m.*

Longest race
The longest race ever staged was 3283 miles *5283 km* from Rocky Mountain House, Alberta to the Expo 67 site at Montreal, Quebec as the Canadian Government Centennial Voyageur Canoe Pageant and Race. Ten canoes represented Canadian provinces and territories. The winner of the race, which took from 24 May to 4 Sept 1967, was the Province of Manitoba canoe *Radisson.*

24 Hours
The solo 24-hour canoe record is 225,4 km *140.1 miles* by Charles Frederick Elliott (b. 30 Jan 1940) in a WW.K1 in the annual Western Australia Canoe Marathon on the Swan River, on 13–14 Nov 1982. The women's record was set at 156,4 km *97.2 miles* by Lydia Formentin in 1979.

Greatest lifetime distance
Fritz Lindner of Berlin, W. Germany, totalled 91 486 km *56,847 miles* from 1928 to 1983.

Eskimo Rolls
Bruce Jeffery Parry (Australia) (b. 25 Sept 1960) achieved 1000 eskimo rolls in 52 min 37.7 sec at Carrara, Queensland, Australia on 2 Oct 1983. Julian Dean achieved 1555 continuous rolls at Casterton Swimming Pool, Cumbria, taking 1 hr 49 min 45 sec on 6 Dec 1983. A 'hand-rolling' record of 100 rolls in 3 min 23 sec was set by John Bouteloup at Crystal Palace, London on 25 Feb 1980.

CARD GAMES

CONTRACT BRIDGE
Bridge (a corruption of Biritch, a now-obsolete Russian word whose meanings include 'declarer') is thought to be either of Levantine origin, similar games having been played there in the early 1870s, or to have come from India.

Auction Bridge (highest bidder names trump) was invented *c.* 1902. The contract principle, present in several games (notably the French game *Plafond, c.* 1917) was introduced to Bridge by Harold Sterling Vanderbilt (USA) on 1 Nov 1925 during a Caribbean voyage aboard the SS *Finland.* It became a world-wide craze after the USA *v.* Great Britain challenge match between Romanian-born Ely Culbertson (1891–1955) and Lt-Col Walter Thomas More Buller (1887–1938) at Almack's Club, London, in September 1930. The USA won the 200-hand match by 4845 points.

Most World titles
The World Championship (Bermuda Bowl) has been won most often by Italy's Blue Team (*Squadra Azzura*), 1957–9, 1961–3, 1965–7, 1969, 1973–5. Italy also won the Olympiad in 1964, 1968 and 1972. Giorgio Belladonna (b. 7 June 1923) was in all these winning teams.

Most master points
In the latest ranking list based on Master Points awarded by the World Bridge Federation, the leading male player in the world was Giorgio Belladonna (Italy) with 1821¼ points. The lead-ing Briton is Boris Schapiro (b. 22 Aug 1909) in 22nd place with 353 points. The world's leading woman player is Dorothy Hayden Truscott (USA) with 331¼ points. Third ranked Rika 'Rixi' Markus is the leading British woman and was the first woman Grand Master, with 281 points.

Barry Crane of Los Angeles has led the American Contract Bridge League rankings since 1968 and by August 1984 had a record total of 33,008 master points. The most master points scored in a year is 3270 by Grant Baze (USA) in 1984.

The first man to win 10,000 master points was Oswald Jacoby (USA) (1902–84) in October 1967. He had been a member of the winning World Championship team in 1935 and on 4 Dec 1983 became the oldest member of a winning team of a major open team championship in the Curtis Reisinger Trophy.

Youngest Life Master
Dougie Hsieh (b. 23 Nov 1969) of New York City became the world's youngest ever Life Master in 1981 at 11 yr 306 days. The youngest ever female Master is Patricia Thomas (b. 10 Oct 1968) at 14 yr 28 days in 1982.

Perfect deals
The mathematical odds against dealing 13 cards of one suit are 158,753,389,899 to 1, while the odds against receiving a 'perfect hand' consisting of all 13 spades are 635,013,559,596 to 1. The odds against each of the four players receiving a complete suit (a 'perfect deal') are 2,235,197,406,895,366,368,301,559,999 to 1.

CRIBBAGE
The invention of the game (once called Cribbidge) is credited to the English dramatist Sir John Suckling (1609–42).

Rare hands
William E. Johnson of Waltham, Mass., USA had four maximum 29 point hands, 1974–81. Paul Nault of Athol, Mass, USA had two such hands within eight games in a tournament on 19 Mar 1977. At Blackpool, Lancashire, Derek

Rixi Markus, Britain's leading female bridge player, became the first Woman Grand Master in 1973.

Hearne dealt two hands of six clubs with the turn-up the remaining club on 8 Feb 1976. Bill Rogers of Burnaby, BC, Canada scored 29 in the crib in 1975.

WHIST
Whist, first referred to in 1529 (*as trump*), was the world's premier card game until 1930. The rules were standardised in 1742.

Highest score
The highest score claimed for 24 hands is 214 by Mrs Margaret Shipley of Dorset Social Club, South Shields, Tyne & Wear.

CAVING—(see also pp. 61–62)

PROGRESSIVE WORLD DEPTH RECORDS
Compiled by Dr A. C. Waltham, Trent Polytechnic, Nottingham.

ft	m	Cave	Country	Cavers	Date
453	138	Macocha	Czechoslovakia	J. Nagel *et al.*	1748
741	226	Grotta di Padriciano	Italy	A. Lindner *et al.*	1839
1076	328	Grotta di Trebiciano	Italy	A. Lindner *et al.*	1841
1509	460	Geldloch	Austria	—	1923
1574	480	Antro di Corchia	Italy	E. Fiorentino Club.	1934
1978	603	Trou du Glaz	France	P. Chevalier *et al.*	1947
2418	737	Reseau de la Pierre St Martin	France	G. Lepineux *et al.*	July 1953
2962	903	Gouffre Berger	France	F. Petzl *et al.*	Sept 1954
3123	952	Gouffre Berger	France	L. Potié *et al.*	Aug 1955
3681	1122	Gouffre Berger	France	F. Petzl *et al.*	July 1956
3715	1133	Gouffre Berger	France	K. Pearce	Aug 1963
3842	1171	Reseau de la Pierre St Martin	France	A.R.S.I.P.	Aug 1966
4335	1321	Reseau de la Pierre St Martin	France	A.R.S.I.P.	Aug 1975
4457	1358	Gouffre Jean Bernard	France	Groupe Vulcain	July 1979
4600	1402	Gouffre Jean Bernard	France	P. Penez	Mar 1980
4773	1455	Gouffre Jean Bernard	France	P. Penez & F. Vergier	Feb 1981
4888	1490	Gouffre Jean Bernard	France	P. Penez & J. Fantoli	Feb 1982
5035	1535	Gouffre Jean Bernard	France	Groupe Vulcain	Oct 1983

N.B. The Gouffre Jean Bernard and the Reseau de la Pierre St Martin have both been explored via multiple entrances. The Jean Bernard has never been entirely descended, and the Pierre St Martin was only completely descended in one visit in 1978; consequently after August 1963 the 'sporting' records for the greatest descent into a cave should read:

ft	m	Cave	Country	Cavers	Date
3743	1141	Gouffre Berger	France	Spéléo Club de Seine	July 1968
4335	1321	Reseau de la Pierre St Martin	France	P. Courbon *et al.*	Sept 1978
4457	1358	Gouffre Jean Bernard	France	A. Ciezewski *et al.*	Feb 1980
4495	1370	Snezhnaya-Mezhonnogo	USSR	A. Morozov *et al.*	1984

The deepest cave explored through a single entrance is:

ft	m	Cave	Country	Cavers	Date
4391	1338	Sima de la Puerta de Illamina	Spain	F. Vergier	Aug 1981

CRICKET

See also The Guinness Book of Cricket Facts and Feats *by Bill Frindall, published at £8.95 in 1983.*

Origins

The earliest evidence of the game of cricket is from a drawing depicting two men playing with a bat and ball dated *c.* 1250. The game was played in Guildford, Surrey, at least as early as 1550. The earliest major match of which the full score survives was one in which a team representing England (40 and 70) was beaten by Kent (53 and 58 for 9) by one wicket at the Artillery Ground in Finsbury, London, on 18 June 1744. Cricket was played in Australia as early as 1803. The first international match was played between Canada and USA in 1844. Fifteen years later those countries were host to the first English touring team. The first touring team to visit England was an Australian Aborigine XI in 1868.

FIRST-CLASS CRICKET (1815 to 1985)

A substantial reduction in the English first-class cricket programme since 1968 has rendered many of the record aggregates for a season unassailable.

BATTING RECORDS—TEAMS

Highest innings

The highest recorded innings by any team was one of 1107 runs in 10 hr 30 min by Victoria against New South Wales in an Australian Sheffield Shield match at Melbourne on 27–28 Dec 1926.

The highest innings in Test cricket and the highest made in England is 903 runs for 7 wickets declared in 15 hr 17 min, by England against Australia at Kennington Oval, London, on 20, 22 and 23 Aug 1938. The highest innings in a county championship match is 887 in 10 hr 50 min by Yorkshire *v.* Warwickshire at Edgbaston, Birmingham on 7–8 May 1896.

Lowest innings

The lowest recorded innings is 12 made by Oxford University *v.* the Marylebone Cricket Club (MCC) at Cowley Marsh, Oxford on 24 May 1877, and 12 by Northamptonshire *v.* Gloucestershire at Gloucester on 11 June 1907. On the occasion of the Oxford match, however, the University batted a man short. The lowest in modern times is 14 by Surrey *v.* Essex at Chelmsford on 30 May 1983. The lowest score in a Test innings is 26 by New Zealand *v.* England in the second innings at Auckland on 28 Mar 1955.

The lowest aggregate for two innings is 34 (16 in first and 18 in second) by Border *v.* Natal in the South African Currie Cup at East London on 19 and 21 Dec 1959.

Greatest victory

The greatest recorded margin of victory is an innings and 851 runs, when Pakistan Railways (910 for 6 wickets declared) beat Dera Ismail Khan (32 and 27) at Lahore on 2–4 Dec 1964. The largest margin in England is an innings and 579 runs by England over Australia at The Oval on 20–24 Aug 1938 when Australia scored 201 and 123 with two men short in both innings. The most one-sided county match was when Surrey (698) defeated Sussex (114 and 99) by an innings and 485 runs at The Oval on 9–11 Aug 1888.

Against England in India, Mohammed Azharuddin scored centuries in each of his first three Tests, an unprecedented achievement eclipsing the great names in Test history. *(All-Sport/Adrian Murrell)*

INDIVIDUAL CAREER RECORDS—All First-Class Cricket (FC) and Test Cricket (Test)

		Name	Team	Year
BATTING				
Most runs	FC 61,237	Sir John Berry 'Jack' Hobbs (1882–1963) (av 50.65)	Surrey/England	1905–34
	Test 8654	Sunil Manohar Gavaskar (b. 10 July 1949) (av 50.61)	India (106 Tests)	1971–85
Most centuries	FC 197	Sir Jack Hobbs (in 1315 innings)	Surrey/England	1905–34
	Test 30	Sunil Gavaskar	India	1971–85
Highest average	FC 95.14	Sir Donald George Bradman (b. 27 Aug 1908) (28,067 runs in 338 innings)	NSW/South Australia/ Australia	1927–49
	Test 99.94	Sir Don Bradman (6996 runs in 80 innings)	Australia	1928–48
BOWLING				
Most wickets	FC 4187	Wilfred Rhodes (1877–1973) (av 16.70)	Yorkshire/England	1898–1930
	Test 355	Dennis Keith Lillee (b. 18 July 1949) (av 23.92)	Australia (70 Tests)	1971–84
Most hat-tricks	FC 7	Douglas Vivian Parson Wright (b. 21 Aug 1914)	Kent	1932–57
	Test 2	Hugh Trumble (1867–1938)	Australia	1890–1904
	2	Thomas James Matthews (1884–1943) (in same match)	Australia	1912
Lowest average (min 15 wkts)	Test 10.75	George Alfred Lohmann (1865–1901) (112 wkts)	England (18 Tests)	1886–96
WICKET-KEEPING				
Most dismissals	FC 1646	Robert William Taylor (b. 17 July 1941)	Derbyshire/England	1960–84
	Test 355	Rodney William Marsh (b. 11 Nov 1947)	Australia (96 Tests)	1970–84
Most catches	FC 1471	Robert Taylor	Derbyshire/England	1960–84
	Test 343	Rodney Marsh	Australia	1970–84
Most stumpings	FC 415	Leslie Ethelbert George Ames (b. 3 Dec 1905)	Kent/England	1926–51
	Test 52	William Albert Stanley Oldfield (1894–1976)	Australia (54 Tests)	1920–37
FIELDING				
Most catches	FC 1018	Frank Edward Woolley (1887–1978)	Kent/England	1906–38
	Test 122	Gregory Stephen Chappell (b. 7 Aug 1948)	Australia (87 Tests)	1970–84
MOST MATCHES				
First class	1107	Wilfred Rhodes	Yorkshire/England	1898–1930
Test	114	Michael Colin Cowdrey (b. 24 Dec 1932)	England	1954–75

INDIVIDUAL SEASON'S RECORDS—All First-Class Cricket in England

		Name	Team	Year
BATTING				
Most runs	3816	Denis Charles Scott Compton (b. 23 May 1918) (av 90.85)	Middlesex/England	1947
Most centuries	18	Denis Compton (in 50 innings with 8 not outs)	Middlesex/England	1947
Highest average	115.66	Sir Donald Bradman (2429 runs in 26 innings, with 5 not outs)	Australians	1938
BOWLING				
Most wickets	304	Alfred Percy 'Tich' Freeman (1888–1965) (1976.1 overs) (av 18.05)	Kent	1928
Lowest average (min 100 wkts)	8.54	Alfred Shaw (1842–1907) (186 wkts)	Nottinghamshire	1880
WICKET-KEEPING				
Most dismissals	127	Leslie Ames (79 caught, 48 stumped)	Kent	1929
Most catches	96	James Graham Binks (b. 5 Oct 1935)	Yorkshire	1960
Most stumpings	64	Leslie Ames	Kent	1932
FIELDING				
Most catches	78	Walter Reginald Hammond (1903–65)	Gloucestershire	1928

INDIVIDUAL RECORDS IN A TEST SERIES

		Name	Team	Year
BATTING				
Most runs	974	Sir Donald Bradman (av 139.14)	Australia v. England (5 T)	1930
Most centuries	5	Clyde Leopold Walcott (b. 17 Jan 1926)	West Indies v. Australia (5 T)	1954–55
Highest average	563.00	Walter Reginald Hammond (563 runs in 2 innings, 1 not out)	England v. New Zealand (2 T)	1932–33
BOWLING				
Most wickets	49	Sydney Francis Barnes (1873–1967) (av 10.93)	England v. South Africa (4 T)	1913–14
Lowest average (min 20 wkts)	5.80	George Alfred Lohmann (35 wkts)	England v. South Africa (3 T)	1895–96
WICKET-KEEPING				
Most dismissals	28	Rodney Marsh (all caught)	Australia v. England (5 T)	1982–83
Most stumpings	9	Percy William Sherwell (1880–1948)	South Africa v. Australia (5 T)	1910–11
FIELDING				
Most catches	15	Jack Morrison Gregory (1895–1973)	Australia v. England (5 T)	1920–21
ALL-ROUND				
400 runs/ 30 wickets	475/34	George Giffen (1859–1927)	Australia v. England (5 T)	1894–95

Most runs in a day

The greatest number of runs scored in a day is 721 all out (ten wickets) in 5 hr 48 min by the Australians v. Essex at Southchurch Park, Southend-on-Sea on 15 May 1948. The Test record for runs in a day is 588 at Old Trafford, Manchester, on 27 July 1936 when England added 398 and India were 190 for 0 in their second innings by the close.

BATTING RECORDS—INDIVIDUALS

Highest innings

The highest individual innings recorded is 499 in 10 hr 35 min by Hanif Mohammad (b. 21 Dec 1934) for Karachi v. Bahawalpur at Karachi, Pakistan, on 8, 9 and 11 Jan 1959. The highest score in England is 424 in 7 hr 50 min by Archibald Campbell MacLaren (1871–1944) for Lancashire v. Somerset at Taunton on 15–16 July 1895. The record for a Test match is 365 not out in 10 hr 14 min by Sir Garfield St Aubrun Sobers (b. 28 July 1936) playing for West Indies against Pakistan at Sabina Park, Kingston, Jamaica, on 27 Feb–1 Mar 1958. The England Test record is 364 by Sir Leonard Hutton (b. 23 June 1916) v. Australia at The Oval on 20, 22 and 23 Aug 1938.

Longest innings

The longest innings on record is one of 16 hr 10 min for 337 runs by Hanif Mohammad (Pakistan) v. West Indies at Bridgetown, Barbados, on 20–23 Jan 1958. The English record is 13 hr 17 min by Len Hutton in his record Test score of 364.

Most runs *Off an over*

The first batsman to score 36 runs off a six-ball over was Sir Garfield Sobers (Nottinghamshire) off Malcolm Andrew Nash (b. 9 May 1945) (Glamorgan) at Swansea on 31 Aug 1968. His feat was emulated by Ravishankar Jayadritha Shastri (b. 27 May 1962) for Bombay v. Baroda at Bombay, India on 10 Jan 1985 off the bowling of Tilak Raj.

Most runs *Off a ball*

The most runs scored off a single hit is ten by Albert Neilson Hornby (1847–1925) off James Street (1839–1906) for Lancashire v. Surrey at The Oval on 14 July 1873, and ten by Samuel Hill Wood (later Sir Samuel Hill Hill-Wood) (1872–1949) off Cuthbert James Burnup (1875–1960) in the Derbyshire v. MCC match at Lord's, London, on 26 May 1900.

Most sixes *In an innings*

The highest number of sixes hit in an innings is 15 by John Richard Reid (b. 3 June 1928), in an innings of 296, lasting 3 hr 40 min, for Wellington v. Northern Districts in the Plunket Shield Tournament at Wellington, New Zealand, on 14–15 Jan 1963. The Test record is ten by Walter Hammond in an innings of 336 not out for England v. New Zealand at Auckland on 3 Mar and 1 Apr 1933.

Most sixes *In a match*

William James Perver Stewart (b. 31 Oct 1934) hit a record 17 sixes (ten in the first innings and seven in the second) for Warwickshire v. Lancashire at Blackpool on 29–31 July 1959. His two innings were of 155 and 125.

Most boundaries in an innings

The highest number of boundaries was 68 (all in fours) by Percival Albert Perrin (1876–1945) in an innings of 343 not out for Essex v. Derbyshire at Chesterfield on 18–19 July 1904.

Double hundreds

The only batsman to score double hundreds in

The slowest hundred on record is by Mudassar Nazar (b. 6 Apr 1956) of Pakistan v. England at Lahore on 14–15 Dec 1977. He required 9 hr 51 min for 114, reaching the 100 in 9 hr 17 min. The slowest double hundred recorded is one of 10 hr 52 min (426 balls) by Anshuman Dattajirao Gaekwad (b. 23 Sept 1952) during an innings of 201 for India v. Pakistan at Jullundur on 25–29 Sept 1983.

Highest partnership

The record partnership for any wicket is the fourth wicket stand of 577 by Gul Mahomed (b. 15 Oct 1921), who scored 319, and Vijay Samuel Hazare (b. 11 Mar 1915) 288 in the Baroda v. Holkar match at Baroda, India, on 8–10 Mar 1947. The highest stand in English cricket is the first-wicket partnership of 555 by Percy Holmes (1886–1971) (224 not out) and Herbert Sutcliffe (1894–1978) (313) for Yorkshire v. Essex at Leyton on 15–16 June 1932.

The highest Test partnership is 451 for the second wicket by William Harold Ponsford (b. 19 Oct 1900) (266) and Sir Donald Bradman (244) for Australia v. England at the Oval on 18 Aug 1934, and 451 for the third wicket by Mudassar Nazar (231) and Javed Miandad Khan (b. 12 Jun 1957) (280 not out) for Pakistan v. India at Hyderabad, Pakistan on 14–15 Jan 1983.

BOWLING

Most wickets *In an innings*

The taking of all ten wickets by a single bowler has been recorded many times but only one

Ravi Shastri (left) became only the second man to hit six sixes off one over, and during the same innings scored the fastest ever double century, in 113 minutes. A week earlier he took 422 minutes to score a century—one of the slowest in Test cricket. Graeme Fowler (201) and Mike Gatting (207) became the first English batsmen to both score double centuries in the same innings, in Madras in Jan 1985. *(All-Sport/Adrian Murrell)*

both innings is Arthur Edward Fagg (1915–77), who made 244 and 202 not out for Kent v. Essex at Colchester on 13–15 July 1938. Sir Donald Bradman scored a career record 37 double hundreds 1927–49.

'Carrying bat'

Cecil John Burditt Wood (1875–1960), of Leicestershire, is the only batsman to carry his bat through both completed innings of a match, and score a hundred in both innings, (107 not out, 117 not out) on 12–14 June 1911 v Yorkshire at Bradford.

Fastest scoring

The fastest 50 was completed off 13 balls in 8 min (1.22 to 1.30 p.m.) and in 11 scoring strokes by Clive Clay Inman (b. 29 Jan 1936) in an innings of 57 not out for Leicestershire v. Nottinghamshire at Trent Bridge, Nottingham on 20 Aug 1965. Full tosses were bowled to expedite a declaration.

The fastest hundred was completed in 35 min off between 40 and 46 balls by Percy George Herbert Fender (b. 22 Aug 1892), when scoring 113 not out for Surrey v. Northamptonshire at Northampton on 26 Aug 1920. Steven Joseph O'Shaughnessy (b. 9 Sept 1961) also scored a hundred in 35 minutes for Lancashire v. Leicestershire at Old Trafford, Manchester off 54 balls on 13 Sept 1983. In all he scored 105 and with Graeme Fowler (b. 20 Apr 1957) put on 201 runs for the 1st wicket in 45 mins. The match was 'dead' and irregular bowlers were used.

The hundred in fewest recorded deliveries was by David William Hookes (b. 3 May 1955) in 34 balls, in 43 min, for South Australia v. Victoria

at Adelaide on 25 Oct 1982. In all he scored 107 from 40 balls in this the second innings, following 137 in the first innings. The most prolific scorer of hundreds in an hour or less was Gilbert Laird Jessop (1874–1955), with 11 between 1897 and 1913. The fastest Test hundred was one in 70 min off 67 balls by Jack Gregory (1895–1973) for Australia v. South Africa at Johannesburg on 12 Nov 1921. Edwin Boaler Alletson (1884–1963) scored 189 runs in 90 min for Nottinghamshire v. Sussex at Hove on 20 May 1911.

A double hundred in 113 min was scored by Ravi Shastri for Bombay v. Baroda at Bombay on 10 Jan 1985 (see most runs off an over). He received 123 balls. Clive Hubert Lloyd (b. 31 Aug 1944), for West Indians v. Glamorgan at Swansea on 9 Aug 1976, and Gilbert Jessop (286), for Gloucestershire v. Sussex at Hove on 1 June 1903, both scored 200 in 120 min. Lloyd received 121 balls but the figure for Jessop is not known.

The fastest treble hundred was completed in 181 min by Denis Compton, who scored 300 for the MCC v. North-Eastern Transvaal at Benoni on 3–4 Dec 1948.

Slowest scoring

The longest time a batsman has ever taken to score his first run is 1 hr 37 min by Thomas Godfrey Evans (b. 18 Aug 1920), who scored 10 not out for England v. Australia at Adelaide on 5–6 Feb 1947. The longest innings without scoring is 87 minutes by Vincent Richard Hogg (b. 3 July 1952) for Zimbabwe–Rhodesia 'B' v. Natal 'B' at Pietermaritzburg in the South African Castle Bowl competition on 20 Jan 1980.

bowler has achieved this feat on three occasions—Alfred Freeman of Kent, against Lancashire at Maidstone on 24 July 1929, against Essex at Southend on 13–14 Aug 1930 and against Lancashire at Old Trafford on 27 May 1931. The fewest runs scored off a bowler taking all ten wickets is ten, when Hedley Verity (1905–43) of Yorkshire dismissed (eight caught, one lbw, one stumped) Nottinghamshire at Leeds on 12 July 1932. The only bowler to bowl out all ten was John Wisden (1826–84) of Sussex, playing for North v. South at Lord's in 1850.

Most wickets *Match*
James Charles Laker (b. 9 Feb 1922) of Surrey took 19 wickets for 90 runs (9–37 and 10–53) for England v. Australia in the Fourth Test at Old Trafford, on 27–31 July 1956. No other bowler has taken more than 17 wickets in a first-class match.

Most wickets *In a day*
The greatest number of wickets taken in a day's play is 17 (for 48 runs) by Colin Blythe (1879–1917), for Kent v. Northamptonshire at Northampton on 1 June 1907; by Hedley Verity for 91 runs, for Yorkshire v. Essex at Leyton on 14 July 1933; and by Thomas William John Goddard (1900–66) for 106 runs, for Gloucestershire v. Kent at Bristol on 3 July 1939.

Most consecutive wickets
No bowler in first-class cricket has yet achieved five wickets with five consecutive balls. The nearest approach was that of Charles Warrington Leonard Parker (1882–1959) (Gloucestershire) in his own benefit match against Yorkshire at Bristol on 10 Aug 1922, when he struck the stumps with five successive balls but the second was called as a no-ball. The only man to have taken four wickets with consecutive balls more than once is Robert James Crisp (b. 28 May 1911) for Western Province v. Griqualand West at Johannesburg on 24 Dec 1931 and against Natal at Durban on 3 Mar 1934.

Patrick Ian Pocock (b. 24 Sep 1946) took five wickets in six balls, six in nine balls and seven in eleven balls for Surrey v. Sussex at Eastbourne on 15 Aug 1972. In his own benefit match at Lord's on 22 May 1907, Albert Edwin Trott (1873–1914) of Middlesex took four Somerset wickets with four consecutive balls and then later in the same innings achieved a 'hat trick'.

Most consecutive maidens
Hugh Joseph Tayfield (b. 30 Jan 1929) bowled 16 consecutive eight-ball maiden overs (137 balls without conceding a run) for South Africa v. England at Durban on 25–26 Jan 1957. The greatest number of consecutive six-ball maiden overs bowled is 21 (131 balls) by Rameshchandra Gangaram 'Bapu' Nadkarni (b. 4 Apr 1932) for India v. England at Madras on 12 Jan 1964. The English record is 17 overs (105 balls) by Horace Leslie Hazell (b. 30 Sept 1909) for Somerset v. Gloucestershire at Taunton on 4 June 1949. Alfred Shaw (1842–1907) of Nottinghamshire bowled 23 consecutive four-ball maiden overs (92 balls) for North v. South at Trent Bridge on 17 July 1876.

Most balls
The most balls bowled in a match is 917 by Cottari Subbanna Nayudu (b. 18 Apr 1914), 6–153 and 5–275, for Holkar v. Bombay at Bombay on 4–9 Mar 1945. The most balls bowled in a Test match is 774 by Sonny Ramadhin (b. 1 May 1929) for West Indies v. England, 7–49 and 2–179, at Edgbaston on 29 May–4 June 1957. In the second innings he bowled a world record 588 balls (98 overs).

Most expensive bowling
The greatest number of runs hit off one bowler in one innings is 362, scored off Arthur Alfred Mailey (1886–1967) in the New South Wales v. Victoria match at Melbourne on 24–28 Dec 1926. The greatest number of runs ever conceded by a bowler in one match is 428 by Cottari Subbanna Nayudu in the Holkar v. Bombay match above. The most runs conceded in a Test innings is 298 by Leslie O'Brien 'Chuck' Fleetwood-Smith (1910–71) for Australia v. England at the Oval on 20–23 Aug 1938.

Fastest
The highest electronically measured speed for a ball bowled by any bowler is 99.7 mph *160,45 km/h* by Jeffrey Robert Thomson (b. 16 Aug 1950) (Australia) during the Second Test v. the West Indies in December 1975. Albert Cotter (1884–1917) of New South Wales, Australia, is reputed to have broken a stump on more than 20 occasions.

ALL-ROUNDERS

The Double
The 'double' of 1000 runs and 100 wickets in the same season was performed a record number of 16 times by Wilfred Rhodes between 1903 and 1926. The greatest number of consecutive seasons in which a player has performed the 'double' is 11 (1903–13) by George Herbert Hirst (1871–1954), of Yorkshire and England. Hirst is also the only player to score 2000 runs (2385) and take 200 wickets (208) in the same season (1906).

Test Cricket
The best all-round Test career record is that of Ian Terrence Botham (b. 24 Nov 1955) with 4159 runs (av. 36.48), 312 wickets (av. 26.25) and 84 catches in 73 matches to 1 June 1985. Botham is the only player to score a hundred and take eight wickets in a single innings in the same Test, with 108 and eight for 34 for England v. Pakistan at Lord's on 15–19 June 1978. He scored a hundred (114) and took more than ten wickets (6–58 and 7–48) in a Test, for England v. India in the Golden Jubilee Test at Bombay on 15–19 Feb 1980. This feat was emulated by Imran Khan Niazi (b. 25 Nov 1952) with 117, 6–98 and 5–82 for Pakistan v. India at Faisalabad on 3–8 Jan 1983. Botham completed the double of 1000 runs and 100 wickets in the fewest Test matches (21) on 30 Aug 1979. Kapil Dev Nikhanj (b. 6 Jan 1959) of India achieved this double in the shortest time span, 1 year 107 days and at the youngest age, 21 yr 27 days, in his 25th Test. The double of 2000 runs and 200 wickets was achieved in fewest matches (42) by Botham and at the youngest age by Kapil Dev at 24 yr 68 days. Botham completed 3000 runs and 300 wickets in 72 Tests at 28 yr 259 days.

WICKET-KEEPING

Most dismissals *Innings*
The most dismissals by a wicket-keeper in an innings is eight (all caught) by Arthur Theodore Wallace 'Wally' Grout (1927–68) for Queensland against Western Australia at Brisbane on 15 Feb 1960. The most stumpings in an innings is six by Henry 'Hugo' Yarnold (1917–74) for Worcestershire v. Scotland at Broughty Ferry, Tayside, on 2 July 1951. The Test record is seven (all caught) by Wasim Bari (b. 23 Mar 1948) for Pakistan v. New Zealand at Auckland on 23 Feb 1979, and by Robert Taylor for England v. India at Bombay on 15 Feb 1980.

Most dismissals *Match*
The greatest number of dismissals by a wicket-keeper in a match is 12 by Edward Pooley (1838–1907), eight caught, four stumped, for Surrey v. Sussex at The Oval on 6–7 July 1868; nine

The most successful Test captain is Clive Hubert Lloyd (b. 31 Aug 1944), who led the West Indies in a record 74 Test matches from 22 November 1974 to 2 January 1985. Of these 74, 36 were won, 12 lost and 26 were drawn. His team set records for most successive Test wins, 11 in 1984, and most Tests without defeat, 27, between losses to Australia in December 1981 and January 1985 (through injury Lloyd missed one of those matches, when West Indies were captained by Vivian Richards).

In all Lloyd played in 110 Test matches, a total exceeded only by Colin Cowdrey (England). He scored 7515 runs (av. 46.67), including 19 centuries, held 89 catches and took 10 wickets. Prior to his run as Test captain he scored 2282 runs (av. 38.67); since then his batting record and his team's performance was:

Season	Against	Runs	Av.	W	D	L
1974–5	India	636	79.50	3	0	2
1975	Pakistan	164	54.66	0	2	0
1975–6	Australia	469	46.90	1	0	5
1976	India	283	47.16	2	1	1
1976	England	296	32.88	3	2	0
1977	Pakistan	336	42.00	2	2	1
1978	Australia	128	64.00	2	0	0
1979–80	Australia	201	67.00	2	0	0
1979–80	New Zealand	103	16.66	0	2	1
1980	England	169	42.25	1	3	0
1980–1	Pakistan	106	21.20	1	3	0
1981	England	383	76.60	2	2	0
1981–2	Australia	275	55.00	1	1	1
1983	India	407	67.83	2	3	0
1983–4	India	496	82.66	3	3	0
1984	Australia	170	42.50	3	1	0
1984	England	255	51.00	5	0	0
1984–5	Australia	356	50.85	3	1	1
Totals		5233	51.30	36	26	12

Photo: Adrian Murrell/All Sport

caught, three stumped by Donald Tallon (1916–84) of Australia for Queensland v. New South Wales at Sydney on 2–4 Jan 1939; and also nine caught, three stumped by Hedley Brian Taber (b. 29 Apr 1940) for New South Wales v. South Australia at Adelaide 13–17 Dec 1968. The record for catches is 11 by Arnold Long (b. 18 Dec 1940), for Surrey v. Sussex at Hove on 18 and 21 July 1964, by Rodney Marsh for Western Australia v. Victoria at Perth on 15–17 Nov 1975 and by David Leslie Bairstow (b. 1 Sept 1951) for Yorkshire v. Derbyshire at Scarborough on 8–10 Sept 1982. The most stumpings in a match is nine by Frederick Henry Huish (1869–1957) for Kent v. Surrey at The Oval on 21–23 Aug 1911. The Test record for dismissals is ten, all caught, by Robert Taylor for England v. India at Bombay, 15–19 Feb 1980.

FIELDING

Most catches *Innings and Match*
The greatest number of catches in an innings is seven, by Michael James Stewart (b. 16 Sept 1932) for Surrey v. Northamptonshire at Northampton on 7 June 1957, and by Anthony Stephen Brown (b. 24 June 1936) for Gloucestershire v. Nottinghamshire at Trent Bridge on 26 July 1966.

The most catches in a Test match is seven by Greg Chappell for Australia v. England at Perth on 13–17 Dec 1974, and by Yajurvindra Singh (b. 1 Aug 1952) for India v. England at Bangalore on 28 Jan–2 Feb 1977.

Walter Hammond held a match record total of ten catches (four in the first innings, six in the second) for Gloucestershire v. Surrey at Cheltenham on 16–17 Aug 1928. The record for a wicket-keeper is 11 (see wicket-keeping).

Longest throw
A cricket ball (5½ oz *155 g*) was reputedly thrown 140 yd 2 ft *128,6 m* by Robert Percival, a left-hander, on Durham Sands racecourse on Easter Monday, 18 Apr 1881.

OTHER TEST RECORDS

Test appearances
The most appearances as Test Captain is 74 by Clive Lloyd of West Indies from 1974 to 1985. The most innings batted in Test matches is 193 in 108 Tests by Geoffrey Boycott (b. 21 Oct 1940). He scored the English record aggregate of 8114 runs (av. 47.72) between 1964 and 1982. Sunil Gavaskar played in a record 90 consecutive Tests from 1975 to 1985. The English record for consecutive Tests is 65 by Alan Philip Eric Knott (b. 9 Apr 1946), 1971–77 and by Ian Botham, 1978–84.

Longest match
The lengthiest recorded cricket match was the 'timeless' Test between England and South Africa at Durban on 3–14 Mar 1939. It was abandoned after ten days (eighth day rained off) because the boat taking the England team home was due to leave. The total playing time was 43 hr 16 min and a record Test match aggregate of 1981 runs were scored.

Largest crowds
The greatest attendance at a cricket match is about 394,000 for the Test between India and England at Eden Gardens, Calcutta on 1–6 Jan 1982. The record for a Test series is 933,513 for Australia and England (5 matches) in 1936–37. The greatest recorded attendance at a cricket match on one day was 90,800 on the second day

ENGLISH ONE-DAY CRICKET RECORDS

GC/NWT—Gillette Cup (inst. 1963)/Nat West Bank Trophy (from 1981)—60 overs matches
JPL—John Player League (inst. 1969)—40 overs matches   B & H—Benson & Hedges Cup (inst. 1972)—55 overs matches

MOST WINS
GC/NWT—4 Lancashire 1970–2, 1975
JPL—3 Kent 1972–3, 1976
B & H—3 Kent 1973, 1976, 1978

HIGHEST INDIVIDUAL INNINGS
GC/NWT—206 Alvin Isaac Kallicharan (b. 21 Mar 1949) Warwickshire v. Oxfordshire, Edgbaston, 1984
JPL—176 Graham Alan Gooch (b. 23 July 1953) Essex v. Glamorgan, Southend, 1983
B & H—198* Graham Gooch, Essex v. Sussex, Hove, 1982

BEST INDIVIDUAL BOWLING
GC/NWT—7–15 Alan Leonard Dixon (b. 27 Nov 1933) Kent v. Surrey, The Oval, 1967
JPL—8–26 Keith David Boyce (b. 11 Oct 1943) Essex v. Lancashire, Old Trafford, 1971
Alan Ward (b. 10 Aug 1947) took 4 wickets in 4 balls, Derbyshire v. Sussex, Derby, 1970
B & H—7–12 Wayne Wendell Daniel (b. 16 Jan 1956) Middlesex v. Minor Counties (East), Ipswich, 1978

MOST DISMISSALS IN INNINGS
GC/NWT—6 Robert William Taylor (b. 17 July 1941) Derbyshire v. Essex, Derby, 1981
JPL—7 Bob Taylor, Derbyshire v. Lancashire, Old Trafford, 1975
B & H—8 Derek John Somerset Taylor (b. 12 Nov 1942) Somerset v. Cambridge University, Taunton, 1982

HIGHEST INNINGS TOTAL
GC/NWT—392–5 Warwickshire v. Oxfordshire, Edgbaston, 1984
JPL—310–5 Essex v. Glamorgan, Southend, 1983
B & H—350–3 Essex v. Oxford & Cambridge Universities, Chelmsford, 1979

LOWEST COMPLETED INNINGS TOTAL
GC/NWT—41 Cambridgeshire v. Buckinghamshire, Cambridge, 1972; 41 Middlesex v. Essex, Westcliff, 1972; 41 Shropshire v. Essex, Wellington, 1974
JPL—23 Middlesex v. Yorkshire, Headingley, 1974
B & H—56 Leicestershire v. Minor Counties, Wellington, 1982

HIGHEST PARTNERSHIP
GC/NWT—234* 4th wkt David Lloyd (b. 18 Mar 1947) & Clive Lloyd, Lancashire v. Gloucestershire, Old Trafford, 1978
JPL—273 2nd wicket Graham Gooch & Kenneth Scott McEwan (b. 16 July 1952) Essex v. Nottinghamshire, Trent Bridge, 1983
B & H—285* 2nd wicket Cuthbert Gordon Greenidge (b. 1 May 1951) & David Roy Turner (b. 5 Feb 1949) Hampshire v. Minor Counties (South), Amersham, 1973

* Not out

of the Test between Australia and West Indies at Melbourne on 11 Feb 1961. The English record is 159,000 for the Test between England and Australia at Headingley, Leeds, on 22–27 July 1948, and the record for one day probably a capacity of 46,000 for a match between Lancashire and Yorkshire at Old Trafford on 2 Aug 1926. The English record for a Test series is 549,650 for the series against Australia in 1953. The highest attendance for a limited-overs game is 84,153 at the Benson & Hedges World Series Cup match between Australia and England at Melbourne on 23 Jan 1985.

WORLD CUP
The Prudential World Cup has been held at four-yearly intervals from 1975. It was won in 1975 and 1979 by West Indies and in 1983 by India. The highest team score was 338 for 5 by Pakistan v. Sri Lanka at Swansea on 9 June 1983, and the lowest 45 by Canada v. England at Old Trafford on 14 June 1979. A higher team score, 348 for 9, was achieved by Bermuda v. Malaysia, in the preceding ICC Trophy matches, at Wednesbury, W. Midlands on 16 June 1982. The highest individual score was 175 not out by Kapil Dev for India v. Zimbabwe at Tunbridge Wells on 18 June 1983. The best bowling was seven wickets for 51 runs by Winston Walter Davis (b. 18 Sept 1958) for West Indies v. Australia at Headingley on 12 June 1983.

ONE-DAY INTERNATIONALS
The highest individual innings is 189 not out by Isaac Vivian Alexander Richards (b. 7 Mar 1952) for West Indies v. England on 31 May 1984 at Old Trafford in a 55 over match. The best bowling performance is by Winston Davis (as above) in the World Cup competition.

ENGLISH COUNTY CHAMPIONSHIP
The greatest number of victories since 1890, when the championship was officially constituted, has been secured by Yorkshire with 29 outright wins, and one shared with Nottinghamshire and Middlesex in 1949. The most 'wooden spoons' have been won by Northamptonshire, with eleven since 1923. They did not win a single match between May 1935 and May 1939. The record number of consecutive title wins is seven by Surrey from 1952 to 1958. The greatest number of appearances in county championship matches is 763 by Wilfred Rhodes for Yorkshire between 1898 and 1930, and the greatest number of consecutive appearances is 423 by Kenneth George Suttle (b. 25 Aug 1928) of Sussex between 1954 and 1969. James Binks played in every county championship match for Yorkshire between his debut in 1955 and his retirement in 1969—412 matches. The seven sons of the Rev Henry Foster, of Malvern, uniquely all played county cricket for Worcestershire between 1899 and 1934.

OLDEST AND YOUNGEST
The oldest man to play in a Test match was Wilfred Rhodes, aged 52 yr 165 days, when he played for England v. West Indies at Kingston, Jamaica on 12 April 1930. Rhodes made his Test debut in the last Test of William Gilbert Grace (1848–1915), who at 50 yr 320 days at Nottingham on 3 June 1899 was the oldest ever Test Captain. The youngest Test captain was the Nawab of Pataudi (later Mansur Ali Khan) at 21 yr 77 days on 23 Mar 1962 for India v. West Indies at Bridgetown, Barbados. The youngest Test player was Mushtaq Mohammad (b. 22 Nov 1943), aged 15 yr 124 days, when he

played for Pakistan v. West Indies at Lahore on 26 March 1959. England's youngest player was Dennis Brian Close (b. 24 Feb 1931) aged 18 yr 149 days v. New Zealand at Old Trafford on 23 July 1949.

The oldest player in first-class cricket was Col Cottari Kanakaiya Nayudu (1895–1967) (India), aged 68 yr 4 days, when he played for the Maharashtra Governor's XI v. Chief Minister's XI at Nagpur, India on 4 Nov 1963. The youngest is reputed to be Qasim Feroze (Pakistan) (b. 21 Jan 1958) who played for Bahawalpur v. Karachi Whites on 19 Jan 1971 aged 12 yr 363 days. The oldest Englishman was George Robert Canning, the 4th Lord Harris (1851–1932) who played for Kent v. All India at Catford on 4 July 1911 aged 60 yr 151 days. The youngest English first-class player was Charles Robertson Young when he played for Hampshire against Kent at Gravesend on 13 June 1867, aged 15 yr 131 days.

WOMEN'S CRICKET

Earliest

The first recorded women's match took place at Gosden Common, Surrey, England on 26 July 1745. *Circa* 1807 Christina Willes is said to have introduced the roundarm bowling style. The first Test match was Australia v. England at Brisbane on 28–31 Dec 1934. The International Women's Cricket Council was formed in 1958.

Batting *Individual*

The highest individual innings recorded is 224 not out by Mabel Bryant for Visitors v. Residents at Eastbourne, East Sussex, in August 1901. The highest innings in a Test match is 189 by Elizabeth Alexandra 'Betty' Snowball for England v. New Zealand at Christchurch, NZ on 16 Feb 1935. The highest Test innings in England is 179 by Rachel Flint (*née* Heyhoe) (b. 11 June 1939) for England v. Australia at The Oval, London on 27–28 July 1976. Rachel Flint also has scored the most runs in Test cricket with 1594 (av. 63.76) in 25 matches from December 1960 to July 1979.

Batting *Team*

The highest innings score by any team is 567 by Tarana v. Rockley, at Rockley, NSW Australia in 1896. The highest Test innings is 503 for five wickets declared by England v. New Zealand at Christchurch, NZ on 16 and 18 Feb 1935. The most in a Test in England is 379 by Australia v. England at The Oval, London on 26–27 July 1976. The highest innings total by any team in England is 410 for two wickets declared by the South v. East at Oakham, Leicestershire on 29 May 1982.

The lowest innings in a Test is 35 by England v. Australia at St Kilda, Melbourne, Australia on 22 Feb 1958. The lowest in a Test in England is 63 by New Zealand at Worcester on 5 July 1954.

Bowling

The greatest number of wickets taken in Test matches is 77 (av. 13.49) by Mary Beatrice Duggan (England) (1925–73) in 17 Tests from 1949 to 1963. She recorded the best Test analysis with seven wickets for six runs for England v. Australia at St Kilda, Melbourne on 22 Feb 1958.

On 26 June 1931 Rubina Winifred Humphries (b. 19 Aug 1915), for Dalton Ladies v. Woodfield SC, took all ten wickets for no runs. (She also scored all her team's runs.) This bowling feat was equalled by Rosemary White (b. 22 Jan 1938) for Wallington LCC v. Beaconsfield LCC in July 1962.

World Cup

Three women's World Cups have been staged.

Winston Davis (in action here v. India) produced the best bowling performance in one day internationals during the 1983 World Cup, taking 7–51 against Australia. *(All-Sport/Adrian Murrell)*

Australia won in 1978 and 1982 and England in 1973. The highest individual score in this series is 138 not out by Janette Ann Brittin (b. 4 July 1959) for England v. International XI at Hamilton, New Zealand on 14 Jan 1982.

MINOR CRICKET RECORDS
(where excelling those in First Class Cricket)

Highest individual innings

In a Junior House match between Clarke's House (now Poole's) and North Town, at Clifton College, Bristol, 22–23, 26–28 June 1899, Arthur Edward Jeune Collins (1885–1914) scored an unprecedented 628 not out in 6 hr 50 min, over five afternoons' batting, carrying his bat through the innings of 836. The scorer, E. W. Pegler, gave the score as '628—plus or minus 20, shall we say'.

Fastest individual scoring

Stanley Keppel 'Shunter' Coen (South Africa) (1902–67) scored 50 runs (11 fours and one six) in 7 min for Gezira v. the RAF in 1942. The fastest hundred by a prominent player in a minor match was by Vivian Frank Shergold Crawford (1879–1922) in 19 min at Cane Hill, Surrey on 16 Sept 1899. David Michael Roberts Whatmore (b. 6 Apr 1949) scored 210 (including 25 sixes and 12 fours) off 61 balls for Alderney v. Sun Alliance at Alderney on 19 June 1983. His first 100 came off 33 balls and his second off 25 balls.

Successive sixes

Cedric Ivan James Smith (1906–79) hit nine successive sixes for a Middlesex XI v. Harrow and District at Rayner's Lane, Harrow in 1935.

This feat was repeated by Arthur Dudley Nourse (1910–81) in a South African XI v. Military Police match at Cairo, Egypt in 1942–3. Nourse's feat included six sixes in one over.

Fastest and Slowest scoring rates

In the match Royal Naval College, Dartmouth v. Seale Hayne Agricultural College in 1923, Kenneth Anderson Sellar (now Cdr 'Monkey' Sellar, DSO, DSC, RN) (b. 11 Aug 1906) and Leslie Kenneth Allen Block (later Judge Block, DSC) (1906–80) were set to score 174 runs in 105 min but achieved this total in 33 min, so averaging 5.27 runs per min. Playing for Gentlemen of Leicestershire CC v. Free Foresters, at Oakham, Rutland, on 19 Aug 1963, Ian H. S. Balfour batted for 100 min without adding to his score of five. He went on to make 39.

Consecutive not out hundreds

Gerald Vivian William Lukehurst (b. 5 Oct 1917), hit six consecutive not out hundreds for Gore Court and F. Day's XI between 3 July and 20 July 1955.

Most runs off a ball

A scoring stroke of 11 (all run, with no overthrows) was achieved by Lt (later Lt-Col) Philip Mitford (1879–1946), QO Cameron Highlanders, in a Malta Governor's Cup match on 28 May 1903.

Most runs off an over

H. Morely scored 62, nine sixes and two fours, off an eight-ball over from R. Grubb which had four no-balls in a Queensland country match in 1968–9.

Greatest stand

T. Patten and N. Rippon made 641 for the third wicket for Buffalo v. Whorouly at Gapsted, Victoria, Australia, on 19 Mar 1914.

Bowling

Stephen Fleming, bowling for Marlborough College 'A' XI, New Zealand v. Bohally Intermediate at Blenheim, New Zealand in December 1967 took nine wickets in nine consecutive balls. In February 1931 in South Africa, Paul Hugo also took nine wickets with nine consecutive balls for Smithfield School v. Aliwal North. In the Inter-Divisional Ships Shield at Purfleet, Essex, on 17 May 1924, Joseph William Brockley (b. 9 Apr 1907) took all ten wickets, clean bowled, for two runs in 11 balls—including a triple hat trick. Jennings Tune took all ten wickets, all bowled, for 0 runs in five overs for Cliffe v. Eastrington in the Howden and District League at Cliffe, Yorkshire on 6 May 1922.

In 1881 Frederick Robert Spofforth (1835–1926) at Bendigo, NSW, Australia clean bowled all ten wickets in *both* innings. J. Bryant for Erskine v. Deaf Mutes in Melbourne on 15 and 22 Oct 1887, and Albert Rimmer for Linwood School v. Cathedral GS at Canterbury, New Zealand in December 1925 repeated the feat. In 1910, H. Hopkinson, of Mildmay CC London, took 99 wickets for 147 runs.

Maurice Hanes bowled 107 consecutive balls (17 overs and five balls) for Bedworth II v. A P Leamington II at Bedworth, Warwickshire on 16 June 1979, without conceding a run.

Wicket-keeping

In Ceylon, playing for Mahinda College v. Galle CC, at the Galle Esplanade, Welihinda Badalge Bennett (b. 25 Jan 1933) caught four and stumped six batsmen in one innings, on 1 March 1953.

Fielding

In a Wellington, New Zealand secondary schools 11-a-side match on 16 Mar 1974, Stephen Lane, 13, held 14 catches in the field (seven in each innings) for St Patrick's College, Silverstream v. St Bernard's College, Lower Hutt.

CROQUET

Earliest references

Croquet was probably derived from the French game *Jeu de Mail* first mentioned in the 12th century. In its present-day form, it originated as a country-house lawn game in Ireland in the 1830s when it was called 'crokey' and was introduced to Hampshire 20 years later. The first club was formed in the Steyne Gardens, Worthing, West Sussex in 1865.

Most championships

The greatest number of victories in the Open Croquet Championships (instituted at Evesham, Hereford & Worcester, 1867) is ten by John William Solomon (b. 1932) (1953, 1956, 1959, 1961, 1963–8). He also won ten Men's Championships (1951, 1953, 1958–60, 1962, 1964–5, 1971 and 1972), ten Open Doubles (with Edmond Patrick Charles Cotter) (1954–5, 1958–9, 1961–5 and 1969) and one Mixed Doubles (with Freda Oddie) in 1954, making a total of 31 titles. Solomon has also won the President's Silver Cup (inst. 1934) on nine occasions (1955, 1957–9, 1962–4, 1968 and 1971), and was Champion of Champions on all four occasions that this competition has been run (1967–70).

Dorothy Dyne Steel (1884–1965), fifteen times winner of the Women's Championship (1919–39), won the Open Croquet Championship four times (1925, 1933, 1935–36). She had also five Doubles and seven Mixed Doubles for a total of 31 titles.

International trophy

The MacRobertson International Shield (instituted 1925) has been played for eleven times. Great Britain have a record seven wins (in 1925, 1937, 1956, 1963, 1969, 1974 and 1983). Five international appearances were made by J. C. Windsor (Australia) in 1925, 1928, 1930, 1935 and 1937 and John Solomon (GB) in 1951, 1956, 1963, 1969 and 1974.

Lowest handicap

Historically the lowest playing handicap has been that of Humphrey Osmond Hicks (Devon) (b. 1904) with minus 5½. In 1974 the limit was however fixed at minus 5. The player holding the lowest handicap is G. Nigel Aspinall with minus 5.

CROSS-COUNTRY RUNNING

WORLD CHAMPIONSHIPS

The earliest recorded international cross-country race took place over 14,5 km *9 miles 18 yd* from Ville d'Avray, outside Paris, on 20 Mar 1898 between England and France (England won by 21 points to 69). The inaugural International Cross-Country Championships took place at the Hamilton Park Racecourse, Scotland, on 28 Mar 1903. The greatest margin of victory is 56 sec or 390 yd *356 m* by John 'Jack' Thomas Holden (England) (b. 13 Mar 1907) at Ayr Racecourse, Scotland, on 24 Mar 1934. Since 1973 the events have been official world championships under the auspices of the International Amateur Athletic Federation.

The greatest men's team wins have been those of England, with a minimum of 21 points (the first six runners to finish) on two occasions, at Gosforth Park, Newcastle, Tyne and Wear, on 22 Mar 1924, and at the Hippodrome de Stockel, Brussels, Belgium, on 20 Mar 1932.

Most appearances

Marcel Van de Wattyne (Belgium) (b. 7 July 1924) ran in a record 20 races, 1946–65. The

Zola Budd (007) at 18 became the youngest senior champion at the 1985 World Championships in Lisbon, winning the 5000 m course by 23 seconds. *(All-Sport)*

women's record is 16 by Jean Lochhead (Wales) (b. 24 Dec 1946), 1967–79, 1981, 1983–4.

Most wins

The greatest number of team victories have been by England with 45 for men, 11 for junior men and 6 for women. The USA have a record seven women's team victories.

The greatest number of men's individual victories is four by Jack Holden (England) in 1933–5 and 1939, by Alain Mimoun-o-Kacha (France) (b. 1 Jan 1921) in 1949, 1952, 1954 and 1956 and by Gaston Roelants (Belgium) (b. 5 Feb 1937) in 1962, 1967, 1969 and 1972. The women's race has been won five times by Doris Brown-Heritage (USA) (b. 17 Sept 1942) 1967–71, and by Grete Waitz (née Andersen) (Norway) (b. 1 Oct 1953), 1976–81 and 1983.

English championship

The English Cross-Country Championship was inaugurated at Roehampton, Wandsworth, London, in 1877. The most individual titles won is four by Percy H. Stenning (1854–92) (Thames Hare and Hounds) in 1877–80 and Alfred E. Shrubb (1878–1964) (South London Harriers) in 1901–4. The most successful club in the team race has been Birchfield Harriers from Birmingham with 27 wins and one tie between 1880 and 1953. The largest field was the 1907 starters and 1806 finishers in the senior race in 1985 at Milton Keynes, Buckinghamshire.

Largest field

The largest recorded field in any cross-country race was 11,763 starters (10,810 finished) in the 30 km *18.6 miles* Lidingöloppet, near Stockholm, Sweden, on 3 Oct 1982.

CURLING

Origins

Although a 15th century bronze figure in the Florence Museum appears to be holding a curling stone, the earliest illustration of the sport was in one of the Flemish painter Pieter Bruegel's winter scenes *c.* 1560. The game was probably introduced into Scotland by Flemings in the 15th century. The earliest documented club is Muthill, Tayside, Scotland, formed in 1739. Organized administration began in 1838 with the formation in Edinburgh of the Grand (later Royal) Caledonian Curling Club, the international legislative body until the foundation of the International Curling Federation in 1966. The first indoor ice rink to introduce curling was in Montreal, Canada in 1807, and the first in Britain was at Southport, Merseyside in 1878.

The USA won the first Gordon International Medal series of matches, between Canada and the USA, at Montreal in 1884. Curling has been a demonstration sport at the Olympic Games of 1924, 1932 and 1964 and will be again in 1988.

Most titles

The record for World Championships (inst. 1959) for the Air Canada Silver Broom is 16 wins by Canada, in 1959–64, 1966, 1968–72, 1980, 1982–3, 1985. The most Strathcona Cup (inst. 1903) wins is seven by Canada (1903, 1909, 1912, 1923, 1938, 1957, 1965) against Scotland. The most Women's World Championships (inst. 1979) is three titles by Canada (1980, 1984–5).

'Perfect' games

Stu Beagle, of Calgary, Alberta, Canada, played a perfect game (48 points) against Nova Scotia in the Canadian championships (Brier) at Fort William (now Thunder Bay), Ontario, on 8 Mar 1960. Bernice Fekete, of Edmonton, Alberta, Canada, skipped her rink to two consecutive

eight-enders on the same ice at the Derrick Club, Edmonton, on 10 Jan and 6 Feb 1973. Two eight-enders in one bonspiel were scored at the Parry Sound Curling Club, Ontario, Canada on 6–8 Jan 1983. Andrew McQuistin, of Stranraer, skipped a Scotland rink to a 1–0 win over Switzerland, scoring in the tenth end after nine consecutive blank ends, in the Uniroyal World Junior Championships at Kitchener-Waterloo, Ontario, Canada on 16 Mar 1980.

Largest bonspiel

The largest bonspiel in the world is the Manitoba Curling Association Bonspiel held annually in Winnipeg, Canada. In 1985, there were 848 teams of four men, a total of 3392 curlers, using 171 sheets of curling ice.

Largest rink

The world's largest curling rink is the Big Four Curling Rink, Calgary, Alberta, Canada, opened in 1959. 96 teams and 384 players are accommodated on two floors each with 24 sheets of ice.

CYCLING

Earliest race

The earliest recorded bicycle race was a velocipede race over 2 km *1.24 miles* at the Parc de St Cloud, Paris, on 31 May 1868, won by Dr James Moore (GB) (1847–1935) (later Chevalier de la Legion d'Honneur).

Highest speed

The highest speed ever achieved on a bicycle is 140.5 mph *226,1 km/h* by Dr Allan V. Abbott, 29, of San Bernadino, California, USA, behind a wind-shield mounted on a 1955 Chevrolet over ¾ mile *1,2 km* at Bonneville Salt Flats, Utah, USA on 25 Aug 1973. His speed over a mile *1,6 km* was 138.674 mph *223,174 km/h*. It should be noted that considerable help is provided by the slipstreaming effect of the lead vehicle. Fred Markham recorded an official unpaced 8.80 sec for 200 m (50.84 mph *81,81 km/h*) on a streamlined bicycle at Ontario, California, USA, on 6 May 1979.

BRITISH RECORDS

OPEN AIR TRACKS

MEN

Distance	min sec	Name	Place	Date
Professional unpaced standing start:				
5 km	6:20.90	Ian Hallam (b. 24 Nov 1948)	Leicester, Leicestershire	30 July 1979
Amateur unpaced flying start:				
500 m	30.5	Paul McHugh	Leicester, Leicestershire	12 June 1984
Amateur unpaced standing start:				
1 km	1:08.3	Mark Barry (b. 13 May 1964)	Leicester, Leicestershire	10 July 1982
10 km	13:01.08	David Lloyd (b. 12 Oct 1949)	Leicester, Leicestershire	14 July 1981
20 km	26:01.05	David Lloyd	Leicester, Leicestershire	14 July 1981
1 hour	28 miles 513 yd *45,531 km*	David Lloyd	Leicester, Leicestershire	26 July 1981
Amateur motor-paced standing start:				
50 km	41:46.00	Michael Coles	Leicester, Leicestershire	12 Aug 1981
1 hour	43 miles 1426 yd *70,506 km*	Rik Notley	Leicester, Leicestershire	31 July 1976

WOMEN

Distance	min sec	Name	Place	Date
unpaced standing start:				
1 km	1:16.893	Brenda Atkinson	Leicester, Leicestershire	4 Aug 1981
3 km	3:59.10	Amanda Jones (b. 24 Mar 1962)	Leicester, Leicestershire	1 Aug 1981
5 km	6:41.75	Amanda Jones	Leicester, Leicestershire	31 Aug 1982
10 km	14:01.1	Amanda Jones	Leicester, Leicestershire	30 June 1981
20 km	28:31.30	Amanda Jones	Leicester, Leicestershire	30 June 1981
1 hour	25 miles 1190 yd *41,322 km*	Amanda Jones	Leicester, Leicestershire	30 June 1981

ROAD CYCLING RECORDS

(British) as recognised by the Road Time Trials Council (out-and-home records)

MEN

Distance	hr min sec	Name	Course area	Date
10 miles	19 11	David Lloyd	Tonbridge, Kent	5 Sept 1981
25 miles	49 24	Alf Engers (b. 1941)	Kelvedon, Essex	5 Aug 1978
30 miles	1 00 11	Martin Pyne	Kelvedon, Essex	30 May 1981
50 miles	1 39 51	Ian Cammish (b. 1 Oct 1956)	Boroughbridge, North Yorkshire	25 June 1983
100 miles	3 31 53	Ian Cammish	Brentwood, Essex	24 July 1983
12 hours	287.282 miles *462,32 km*	Glenn Longland	Ringwood, Hampshire	14 Aug 1983
24 hours	507.00 miles *815,93 km*	Roy Cromack	Cheshire	26–27 July 1969

WOMEN

Distance	hr min sec	Name	Course area	Date
10 miles	21 25	Beryl Burton (b. 12 May 1937)	Blyth, Nottinghamshire	29 Apr 1973
25 miles	53 21	Beryl Burton	Catterick, North Yorkshire	17 June 1976
30 miles	1 08 36	Beryl Burton	Kelvedon, Essex	3 Oct 1981
50 miles	1 51 30	Beryl Burton	Boroughbridge, North Yorkshire	25 July 1976
100 miles	3 55 05	Beryl Burton	Essex	4 Aug 1968
12 hours	277.25 miles *446,19 km*	Beryl Burton	Wetherby, West Yorkshire	17 Sept 1967
24 hours	438.16 miles *705,15 km*	Anne Mann	Abbess Roding, Essex	25–26 June 1983

ROAD RECORDS ASSOCIATION'S STRAIGHT-OUT DISTANCE RECORDS

	MEN				WOMEN			
Distance	hr min sec	Name	Date		hr min sec	Name	Date
25 miles	42 37	David Lloyd	21 Sept 1982		56 05	Pauline Strong	4 Oct 1981
50 miles	1 35 45	David Lloyd	26 Oct 1974		1 55 00	Eileen Sheridan	10 Oct 1954
100 miles	3 28 40	Ray Booty	28 Sept 1956		4 16 01	Eileen Sheridan	18 June 1952
1000 miles	2 days 10 40 00	Reg Randell	19–21 Aug 1960		3 days 1 00 00	Eileen Sheridan	9–12 July 1954

		MEN					WOMEN			
	hr	min	sec	Name	Date	hr	min	sec	Name	Date
London to Edinburgh (380 miles 610 km)	18	49	42	Cliff Smith	2 Nov 1965	20	11	35	Eileen Sheridan	3–4 June 1954
London to Bath and back (212 miles 341 km)	9	03	07	John Woodburn	13 June 1981	10	41	22	Eileen Sheridan	26 Aug 1952
London to York (197 miles 317 km)	7	41	13	Bob Addy	6 Aug 1972	9	05	20	Eileen Sheridan	15 Aug 1953
London to Birmingham (112.8 miles 181,5 km)	4	19	13	Phil Bayton	7 Nov 1982	5	12	18	Kathy Bellingham	18 Oct 1980
London to Brighton and back (107 miles 172 km)	4	15	8	Phil Griffiths	20 July 1977	4	55	28	Gill Clapton	15 July 1972
Land's End to London (287 miles 461 km)	12	34	0	Robert Maitland	17 Sept 1954	13	43	33	Ann Horswell	8 Sept 1970

The greatest distance ever covered in one hour is 122,771 km *76 miles 504 yd* by Leon Vanderstuyft (Belgium) (1890–1964) on the Montlhery Motor Circuit, France, on 30 Sept 1928, achieved from a standing start paced by a motorcycle. The 24 hr record behind pace is 860 miles 367 yd *1384,367 km* by Hubert Ferdinand Opperman (later Hon Sir) (b. 29 May 1904) in Melbourne, Australia on 23 May 1932.

Most titles *Olympic*

The most gold medals won is three by Paul Masson (France) (1874–1945) in 1896, Francisco Verri (Italy) (1885–1945) in 1906 and Robert Charpentier (France) (1916–66) in 1936. Daniel Morelon (France) won two in 1968, and a third in 1972. He also won a bronze medal in 1964. In the 'unofficial' 1904 cycling programme, Marcus Hurley (USA) (1884–1950) won four events.

Most titles *British*

Beryl Burton (b. 12 May 1937), 25 times British all-round time trial champion (1959–83), has won 70 individual road TT titles, 14 track pursuit titles and 12 road race titles. Mrs Burton's career overshadows all male achievements. Ian Hallam (b. 24 Nov 1948) won a record 25 men's titles, 1969–82.

Tour de France

The greatest number of wins in the Tour de France (inaugurated 1903) is five by Jacques Anquetil (France) (b. 8 Jan 1934), 1957, 1961–4 and by Eddy Merckx (Belgium) (b. 17 June 1945), 1969–72 and 1974. The closest race ever was in 1968 when after 4665 km *2898.7 miles* over 25 days (27 June–21 July) Jan Janssen (Netherlands) (b. 19 May 1940) beat Herman van Springel (Belgium) in Paris by 38 sec. The fastest average speed was 37,84 km/h *23.51 mph* by Bernard Hinault (France) (b. 14 Nov 1954) in 1981. The longest race was 5745 km *3569 miles* in 1926, and most participants were 170 starters in 1982 and 1984. The longest ever stage was the 486 km from Les Sables d'Olonne to Bayonne in 1919. The longest in 1984 was 338 km from Nantes to Bordeaux.

Tour of Britain (Milk Race)

Four riders have won the Tour of Britain twice each—Bill Bradley (1959–60), Les West (1965, 1967), Fedor den Hertog (Netherlands) (1969, 1971) and Yuri Kashurin (USSR) (1979, 1982). The closest race ever was in 1976 when after 1035 miles *1665,67 km* over 14 days (30 May–12 June) Bill Nickson (GB) (b. 30 Jan 1953) beat Joe Waugh (GB) by 5 sec. Den Hertog recorded the fastest average speed of 25.20 mph *40,55 km/h* in the 1971 race (1096 miles *1763,84 km*). Malcolm Elliott (b. 1 July 1961) won a record six stages in 1983. The longest Milk Race was in 1969 (1515 miles *2438,16 km*) although the longest ever Tour of Britain was in 1953 (1631 miles *2624,84 km* starting and finishing in London)

Six-day races

The most wins in 6-day races is 88 out of 233

events by Patrick Sercu (b. 27 June 1944), of Belgium, 1964–83.

Longest one-day race

The longest single-day 'massed start' road race is the 551–620 km *342–385 miles* Bordeaux–Paris, France, event. Paced over all or part of the route, the highest average speed was in 1981 with 47,186 km/h *29.32 mph* by Herman van Springel (Bel) (b. 14 Aug 1943) for 584,5 km in 13 hr 35 min 18 sec.

Land's End to John o' Groats

The 'end to end' record for the 847 miles *1363 km* is 1 day 21 hr 3 min 16 sec (average speed 18.80 mph *30,25 km/h*) by John Woodburn (b. 22 Dec 1936) on 14–15 Aug 1982. The feminine record is 2 days 11 hr 7 min by Eileen Sheridan (b. 18 Oct 1923) on 9–11 July 1954. She completed 1000 miles *1609 km* in 3 days 1 hr.

Endurance

Thomas Edward Godwin (1912–75) (GB) in the 365 days of 1939 covered 75,065 miles *120 805 km* or an average of 205.65 miles *330,96 km* per day. He then completed 100,000 miles *160 934 km* in 500 days to 14 May 1940.

Jay Aldous and Matt DeWaal cycled 14,290 miles *22 997 km* on a round trip from Place Monument, Salt Lake City, Utah, USA in 106 days, 2 Apr–16 July 1984.

Nicholas Mark Sanders (b. 26 Nov 1957) of Glossop, Derbyshire, circumnavigated the world (13,609 road miles *21 901 km*) between 7 Feb and 5 July (138 days) in 1981. He cycled 4802 miles *7728 km* around Britain in 22 days, 10 June–1 July 1984. Len Haldeman was reported to have ridden from Santa Monica, California to New York City, 2976 miles *4789 km* in a record 9 days 20 hr 2 min in 1982. The Trans-Canada record is 14 days 22 hr 47 min by Wayne Phillips of Richmond, BC, 3800 miles *6115 km* from Vancouver, BC to Halifax, Nova Scotia, on 13–28 June 1982.

Carlos Vieira cycled for 191 hr 'non-stop' at Leira, Portugal, on 8–16 June 1983. The distance covered was 2407,64 km *1496.04 miles* and he was moving 98.7% of the time.

Cycle touring

The greatest mileage amassed in a cycle tour was more than 402,000 miles *643 700 km* by the itinerant lecturer Walter Stolle (b. Sudetenland, 1926) from 24 Jan 1959 to 12 Dec 1976. He visited 159 countries starting from Romford,

WORLD RECORDS

(In events contested by professional and amateur riders only the better mark is given)

OPEN AIR TRACKS
MEN

Distance	min sec	Name and Country	Place	Date
Professional unpaced standing start:				
5 km	5:47.163	Francesco Moser (Italy) (b. 19 June 1951)	Mexico City	23 Jan 1984
10 km	11:39.72	Francesco Moser (Italy)	Mexico City	19 Jan 1984
20 km	23:21.592	Francesco Moser (Italy)	Mexico City	23 Jan 1984
100 km	2 hr 14:02.51	Ole Ritter (Denmark) (b. 29 Aug 1941)	Mexico City	18 Nov 1971
1 hour	51,151.35 km *31 miles 1380 yd*	Francesco Moser (Italy)	Mexico City	23 Jan 1984
Amateur unpaced standing start:				
1 km	1:02.547	Marc Malchow (GDR)	Mexico City	14 Oct 1980
Amateur unpaced flying start:				
200 metres	10.322	Lutz Hesslich (GDR)	Tbilisi, USSR	7 May 1985
500 metres	27.31	Gordon Singleton (Canada)	Mexico City	9 Oct 1980
1 km	59.682	Alan Cuff (NZ)	Mexico City	27 July 1980
Professional motor-paced:				
100 km	1 hr 12:04.115	Max Hurzler (Swi)	Zürich, Switzerland	22 Aug 1984
Amateur motor-paced:				
100 km	1 hr 13:31.326	Aleksandr Romanov (USSR)	Tbilisi, USSR	11 May 1983
1 hour	83,261 km *51 miles 1295 yd*	Aleksandr Romanov (USSR)	Tbilisi, USSR	11 May 1983
WOMEN				
Unpaced standing start:				
1 km	1:14.249	Erika Salumyae (USSR)	Tashkent, USSR	1984
5 km	6:41.75	Amanda Jones (GB)	Leicester	31 July 1982
10 km	13:34.39	Keetie Van Oostenhage (Netherlands)	Munich, W. Germany	16 Sept 1978
20 km	27:26.66	Keetie Van Oostenhage (Netherlands)	Munich, W. Germany	16 Sept 1978
100 km	2 hr 41:32.6	Marie Cressari (Italy)	Milan, Italy	17 Oct 1974
1 hour	43,082 km *26 miles 1355 yd*	Keetie Van Oostenhage (Netherlands)	Munich, W. Germany	16 Sept 1978
Unpaced flying start:				
200 metres	11.753	Natalia Krushelnitskaya (USSR)	Tbilisi, USSR	14 Sept 1980
500 metres	31.70	Galina Tsareva (USSR)	Tbilisi, USSR	6 Oct 1978
1 km	1:10.463	Erika Salumyae (USSR)	Tashkent, USSR	1984

WORLD RECORDS

INDOOR TRACKS

MEN
Professional unpaced standing start:

1 hour...... 46 847 km *29 miles 192 yd*	Siegfried Adler (West Germany)	Zürich, Switzerland	2 Aug 1968

Professional unpaced flying start:

500 metres 28:48.6	Urs Freuler (Switzerland)	Vienna, Austria	2 Oct 1981

Amateur unpaced standing start:

1 km 1:02.955	Lothar Thoms (GDR) (b. 18 May 1956)	Moscow, USSR	22 July 1980
5 km 5:48.256	Gintautus Umaras (USSR)..............	Moscow, USSR	Aug 1984
10 km...................... 12:06.29	Hans-Henrik Oersted (Denmark) (b. 13 Dec 1954)	Copenhagen, Denmark ...	28 Nov 1978
20 km.......................... 24:52.83	Mikhail Sveshnikov (USSR)	Moscow, USSR	28 Apr 1983

Amateur unpaced flying start:

200 metres 10.021	Lutz Hesslich (GDR)	Moscow, USSR	22 Aug 1984
500 metres 26.479	Michael Hübner (GDR)	Moscow, USSR	19 Aug 1984
1 km 1:00.279	Sergei Kopylov (USSR)	Moscow, USSR	30 July 1982

Amateur motor-paced:

50 km 33:29.082	Aleksandr Romanov (USSR)	Moscow, USSR	28 Apr 1985
100 km .... 1 hr 08:02.448	Aleksandr Romanov (USSR)	Moscow, USSR	28 Apr 1985
1 hour...... 87,430 km *54 miles 575 yd*	Aleksandr Romanov (USSR)	Moscow, USSR	28 Apr 1984

WOMEN
Unpaced standing start:

1 km 1:13.777	Erika Salumyae (USSR)	Moscow, USSR	21 Sept 1983
5 km 6:39.565	Erika Salumyae (USSR)	Moscow, USSR	8 Jan 1985
10 km........................ 13:41.519	Galina Tsareva (USSR)	Moscow, USSR	18 Jan 1983
20 km.......................... 27:46.73	Galina Tsareva (USSR)	Moscow, USSR	28 Apr 1983
100 km .... 2 hr 31:30.43	Mieke Havik (Netherlands)	Rotterdam, Netherlands ...	19 Sept 1983
1 hour...... 41,087 km *25 miles 934 yd*	O. Sidorenko	....	1982

Unpaced flying start:

200 metres 11.494	Erika Salumyae (USSR)	Moscow, USSR	12 May 1985
500 metres 31.112	Natalia Krushelnitskaya (USSR)	Moscow, USSR	23 Apr 1982
1 km 1:08.24	Erika Salumyae (USSR)	Moscow, USSR	19 Aug 1984

LONG DISTANCE BESTS

24 hr .... 830,1 km *515.8 miles*	Teuvo Louhivouri (Finland)	Tampere to Kolari, Finland	9–10 Sept 1974
1 000 km .... 32 hr 4 min	Herman de Munck (Belgium)	Keerbergen, Belgium 23–24	Sept 1983
1 000 miles ....51 hr 12 min 32 sec	Herman de Munck (Belgium)	Keerbergen, Belgium 23–25	Sept 1983

Nick Sanders, of Derbyshire, specialises in endurance cycling events. He holds the records for circumnavigating the world—13,609 miles—and for cycling around the coastline of Great Britain, 4802 miles averaging 218.3 miles per day. In between he cycled to the source of the Nile.

Essex, England. From 1922 to 25 Dec 1973 Tommy Chambers (1903–84) of Glasgow, rode a verified total of 799,405 miles *1 286 517 km*.

Visiting every continent, John W. Hathaway (b. England, 13 Jan 1925) of Vancouver, Canada covered 50,600 miles *81 300 km* from 10 Nov 1974 to 6 Oct 1976. Veronica and Colin Scargill, of Bedford, travelled 18,020 miles *29 000 km* around the world, on a tandem, 25 Feb 1974–27 Aug 1975.

The most participants in a bicycle tour was 18,362 in the 56 mile *90 km* London to Brighton Bike Ride on 24 June 1984.

Highest
Nicholas and Richard Crane cycled their mountainbikes to the summit of Mount Kilimanjaro, Tanzania 5894 m *19 340 ft* on 31 Dec 1984.

CYCLO-CROSS

The greatest number of world championships (inst. 1950) have been won by Eric de Vlaeminck (Belgium) (b. 23 Aug 1945) with the amateur and Open in 1966 and six professional titles in 1968–73. British titles (inst. 1955) have been won most often by John Atkins (b. 7 Apr 1942) with five amateur (1961–2, 1966–8), seven professional (1969–75) and one Open title in 1977.

Pennine Way
John North (b. 18 Aug 1943) of Rawtenstall, Lancashire, cycled or carried his machine along the 271 miles *436 km* Pennine Way from Edale, Derbyshire to Kirk Yetholm, Borders in 2 days 8 hr 45 min on 9–11 June 1978.

MOST WORLD TITLES

The greatest number of world titles for a particular event won since the institution of the amateur championships in 1893 and the professional championships in 1895 are:

Event		Holder		Years
Amateur Sprint	7	Daniel Morelon (France) (b. 28 July 1944)		1966–7, 1969–71, 1973, 1975
Amateur 100 km Motor Paced	7	Leon Meredith (UK) (1882–1930)		1904–5, 1907–9, 1911, 1913
Amateur 1 km time trial	4	Lothar Thoms (GDR) (b. 18 May 1956)		1977–9, 1981
Amateur Tandem Sprint	4	Vladimir Vackar (b. 6 Feb 1949) and Miroslav Vymazal (Cze)		1973–4, 1977–8
Amateur Road Race	2	Giuseppe Martano (Italy)		1930, 1932
	2	Gustav Adolf Schur (GDR) (b. 23 Feb 1931)		1958–9
Amateur Pursuit	3	Guido Messina (Italy) (b. 5 Jan 1931)		1947–8, 1953
	3	Tiemen Groen (Netherlands)		1964–6
	3	Detlef Macha (GDR) (b. 13 Dec 1958)		1978, 1981–2
Professional Sprint	8	Koichi Nakano (Japan) (b. 14 Nov 1955)		1977–84
Professional Pursuit	4	Hugh Porter (UK) (b. 27 Jan 1940)		1968, 1970, 1972–3
Professional 100 km Motor Paced	6	Guillermo Timoner (Spain) (b. 1928)		1955, 1959–60, 1962, 1964–5
Professional Road Race	3	Alfredo Binda (Italy) (b. 11 Aug 1902)		1927, 1930, 1932
	3	Henri 'Rik' Van Steenbergen (Belgium) (b. 9 Sept 1924)		1949, 1956–7
	3	Eddy Merckx (Belgium) (b. 17 June 1945)		1967, 1971, 1974
Women's titles	7	Beryl Burton (UK) (b. 12 May 1937)		1959–60, 1962–3, 1966 (pursuit) 1960, 1967 (road)
	7	Yvonne Reynders (Belgium)		1961, 1964–5 (pursuit) 1959, 1961, 1963, 1966 (road)

John Woodburn took only one day 21 hours 3 mins to cycle the 847 mile journey from Land's End to John o'Groats.

CYCLE SPEEDWAY

First mention of the sport is at Coventry in 1920 and it was first organised in 1945. The sport's governing body, the Cycle Speedway Council, was formed in 1973. Most British senior team championships (inst. 1950) is six by Wednesfield (1974, 1976–8, 1981 and 1983) and by Offerton, Cheshire (1962, 1964–5, 1969, 1972–3). The most individual titles is four by Derek Garnett (b. 16 July 1937) (1963, 1965, 1968 and 1972).

ROLLER CYCLING

Paul Swinnerton (GB) achieved a record 102 mph *164 km/h* for 200 m on rollers on 12 Feb 1982 at Stoke-on-Trent. The four-man 12 hr record is 717.9 miles *1155,5 km* by a Northampton team at the Guildhall, Northampton, on 28 Jan 1978. The 24 hr solo record is 792.7 miles *1275,7 km* by Bruce W. Hall at San Diego University, Calif., USA on 22–23 Jan 1977.

STATIONARY CYCLING

Rudi Jan Jozef De Greef (b. 28 Dec 1955) stayed stationary without support for 10 hr at Meensel-Kiezegem, Belgium on 19 Nov 1982.

DARTS

Further information can be obtained from the Guinness Book of Darts *by Derek Brown, published by Guinness Superlatives Ltd at £7.50 (hard-back) and £5.95 (paperback, 1982 edition).*

Origins

The origins of darts date from the use by archers of heavily weighted ten-inch throwing arrows for self-defence in close quarters fighting. The 'dartes' were used in Ireland in the 16th century and darts was played on the *Mayflower* by the Plymouth pilgrims in 1620. The modern game dates from at least 1896 when Brian Gamlin of Bury, Lancashire, is credited with inventing the present numbering system on the board. The first recorded score of 180 was by John Reader at the Highbury Tavern in Sussex in 1902. Today there are an estimated 6,000,000 darts players in the British Isles.

Most titles

Eric Bristow (b. 25 Apr 1957) has most wins in the World Masters Championship (inst. 1974) with five, in 1977, 1979, 1981 and 1983–4, and in the World Professional Championship (inst. 1978) with four, in 1980–1 and 1983–4. Bristow

completed a unique treble in 1983 by also winning the World Cup singles. The only men to win the annual *News of the World* individual Championship twice are Tommy Gibbons (Ivanhoe Working Men's Club) of Conisbrough, South Yorkshire, in 1952 and 1958; Tom Reddington (b. 1922) of New Inn, Stonebroom, Derbyshire in 1955 and of George Hotel, Alfreton, Derbyshire 1960; Tom M. Barrett (1909–81) (Odco Sports Club, London) in 1964 and 1965; Stefan Lord (b. 4 Dec 1954) of the Stockholm Super Darts Club, Sweden in 1978 and 1980, and Eric Bristow in 1983 and 1984. John Lowe (b. 21 July 1945) is the only other man to have won each of the four major titles: World Masters, 1976 and 1980; World Professional, 1979; World Cup Singles, 1981; and *News of the World*, 1981.

The National Darts Association of Great Britain individual title was won by Tom O'Regan (b. 28 Feb 1939) of the Northern Star, New Southgate, Greater London in 1970–2. Maureen Flowers (b. 6 Dec 1946), in 1979 and 1980, is the only double winner of the NDA women's individual title.

World Cup

The first World Cup was held at the Wembley Conference Centre, London in 1977. Wales were the inaugural champions and England won in 1979, 1981 and 1983.

Record prize

John Lowe won £102,000 for achieving the first 501 scored with the minimum nine darts in a major event on 13 Oct 1984 at Slough in the quarter-finals of the World Match-play Championships. His darts were six successive treble 20s, treble 17, treble 18 and double 18.

Longest unbeaten run

Mike Bowell (b. 31 May 1947) of Paulton Darts League, Avon, won 152 consecutive competition games from 9 Feb 1971 to 29 Nov 1974. The White Horse Inn, Ashton-under-Lyne, Manchester, were undefeated in a total of 169 matches from 31 May 1979 to 9 Feb 1981.

Fastest match

The fastest time taken for a match of three games of 301 is 1 min 58 sec by Ricky Fusco (GB) at the Perivale Residents Association Club, Middlesex, on 30 Dec 1976.

Fastest 'Round the board'

The record time for going round the board clockwise in 'doubles' at arm's length is 9.2 sec by Dennis Gower at the Millers Arms, Hastings, East Sussex on 12 Oct 1975 and 14.5 sec in numerical order by Jim Pike (1903–60) at the Craven Club, Newmarket in March 1944. The record for this feat at the 9 ft *2,7 m* throwing distance, retrieving own darts, is 2 min 13 sec by Bill Duddy (b. 29 Sept 1932) at The Plough, Haringey, London on 29 Oct 1972.

Least darts
Scores of 201 in four darts, 301 in six darts, 401 in seven darts and 501 in nine darts, have been achieved on various occasions. The lowest number of darts thrown for a score of 1001 is 19 by Cliff Inglis (b. 27 May 1935) (160, 180, 140, 180, 121, 180, 40) at the Bromfield Men's Club, Devon on 11 Nov 1975. A score of 2001 in 52 darts was achieved by Alan Evans (b. 14 June 1949) at Ferndale, Glamorgan on 3 Sept 1976. 3001 in 79 darts was thrown by Charlie Ellix (b. 18 Oct 1941) at The Victoria Hotel, Tottenham, London on 29 April 1977.

Ten hour scores
The record number of trebles scored in 10 hr is 2787 by David Broad (b. 11 Feb 1939) from 9984 darts thrown on 26 Feb 1983 at Blantyre Sports Club, Malawi. David Broad scored a record 3085 doubles (out of 9945 darts) in 10 hr at Blantyre on 17 Mar 1984. The greatest score amassed in 10 hr is 487,588 by Bruce Campbell and Peter Dawson at the Waikiki Hotel, Safety Bay, Western Australia, on 14 Oct 1978.

24 hr scores
Eight players from Paddock Wood and District Lions Club scored 1,585,445 in 24 hr on one board at the John Brunt VC public house, Paddock Wood, Kent on 16–17 Feb 1985.

Million and one up
Eight players from the Captain Webb, Wellington, Telford, Shropshire scored 1,000,001 with 38,481 darts in one session on 6–9 Apr 1985.

EQUESTRIAN SPORTS

See also The Guinness Guide to Equestrianism *by Dorian Williams, published by Guinness Superlatives Ltd. (price £8.95).*

Origins
Evidence of horse-riding dates from a Persian engraving dated *c.* 3,000 BC. Pignatelli's academy of horsemanship at Naples dates from the 16th century. The earliest jumping competition was at the Agricultural Hall, Islington, London, in 1869. Equestrian events have been included in the Olympic Games since 1912.

Most Olympic medals
The greatest number of Olympic gold medals is five by Hans-Günter Winkler (b. 24 July 1926) (W. Germany) who won four team gold medals as captain in 1956, 1960, 1964 and 1972 and won the individual Grand Prix in 1956. The most team wins in the Prix des Nations is five by Germany in 1936, 1956, 1960, 1964 and 1972. The lowest score obtained by a winner is no faults by Frantisek Ventura (1895–1969) (Czechoslovakia) on *Eliot*, 1928 and Alwin Schockemöhle (b. 29 May 1937) (W. Germany) on *Warwick Rex*, 1976. Pierre Jonqueres d'Oriola (b. 1 Feb 1920) (France) uniquely won the individual gold medal twice, 1952 and 1964. Richard John Hannay Meade (b. 4 Dec 1938) (Great Britain) is the only British rider to win three gold medals—as an individual in 1972 and team titles in 1968 and 1972, all in the 3-day event.

Most titles *World*
The men's world championships (inst. 1953) have been won twice by Hans-Günter Winkler (W. Germany) (1954–5) and Raimondo d'Inzeo (Italy) (1956 and 1960). The women's title (1965–74) was won twice by Jane 'Janou' Tissot (*née* Lefebvre) (France) (b. Saigon, 14 May 1945) on *Rocket* (1970 and 1974).

King George V Gold Cup and Queen Elizabeth II Cup
David Broome (b. 1 Mar 1940) has won the King George V Gold Cup (first held 1911) a record five times, 1960 on *Sunsalve*, 1966 on *Mister Softee*, 1972 on *Sportsman*, 1977 on *Philco* and 1981 on *Mr Ross*. The Queen Elizabeth II Cup (first held 1949), for women, has been won four times by Elizabeth Edgar (b. 28 Apr 1943), 1977 on *Everest Wallaby*, 1979 on *Forever*, 1981 and 1982 on *Everest Forever*. The only horse to win both these trophies is *Sunsalve* in 1957 (with Elisabeth Anderson) and 1960.

President's Trophy (World Team Championship)
Instituted in 1965, the Trophy has been won a record ten times by Great Britain, 1965, 1967, 1970, 1972–4, 1977–9 and 1983.

Three-day event
The Badminton Three-Day Event (inst. 1949) has been won six times by Lucinda Green (*née* Prior-Palmer) (b. 7 Nov 1953) in 1973 (on *Be Fair*), 1976 (*Wide Awake*), 1977 (*George*), 1979 (*Killaire*), 1983 (*Regal Realm*) and 1984 (*Beagle Bay*)

Jumping records
The official *Fédération Equestre Internationale* high jump record is 8 ft 1¼ in *2,47 m* by *Huasó*, ridden by Capt Alberto Larraguibel Morales (Chile) at Vina del Mar, Santiago, Chile, on 5 Feb 1949, and 27 ft 6¾ in *8,40 m* for a long jump over water by *Something*, ridden by André Ferreira (S. Africa) at Johannesburg on 26 Apr 1975.

The British record is 7 ft 7⁵⁄₁₆ in *2,32 m* by the 16.2 hands *167 cm* grey gelding *Lastic* ridden by Nick Skelton (b. 30 Dec 1957) at Olympia, London, on 16 Dec 1978. On 25 June 1937, at Olympia, the Lady Wright (*née* Margery Avis Bullows) set the best recorded height for a British equestrienne on her liver chestnut *Jimmy Brown* at 7 ft 4 in *2,23 m*.

The greatest recorded height reached bareback is 7 ft *2,13 m* by Michael Whitaker (b. 17 Mar 1960) on *Red Flight* at Dublin on 14 Nov 1982.

Driving
Great Britain have most wins at the biennial World Driving Championships (inst. 1972) with three, in 1972, 1974 and 1980.

Longest ride
Thomas L. Gaddie (USA) rode 11,217.2 miles *18 052 km* from Dallas, Texas to Fairbanks, Alaska and back in 295 days, 12 Feb to 2 Dec 1980, with seven horses.

FENCING

Origins
'Fencing' (fighting with single sticks) was practised as a sport, or as a part of a religious ceremony, in Egypt as early as *c.* 1360 BC. The first governing body for fencing in Britain was the Corporation of Masters of Defence founded by Henry VIII before 1540 and fencing has been practised as sport, notably in prize fights, since that time. The foil was the practice weapon for the short court sword from the 17th century. The épée was established in the mid-19th century and the light sabre was introduced by the Italians in the late 19th century.

Most titles *World*
The greatest number of individual world titles won is five by Aleksandr Romankov (USSR) (see table), but Christian d'Oriola (France) won four world foil titles, 1947, 1949, 1953–4 as well as two individual Olympic titles. Of the three

MOST OLYMPIC AND WORLD FENCING TITLES

Event		Olympic Gold Medals		World Championships (not held in Olympic years)
Men's Foil, Individual	2	Christian d'Oriola (France) (b. 3 Oct 1928) 1952, 56	5	Aleksandr Romankov (USSR) (b. 7 Nov 1953) 1974, 77, 79, 82, 83
	2	Nedo Nadi (Italy) (1894–1952) 1912, 20		
Men's Foil, Team	6	France 1924, 32, 48, 52, 68, 80	13	USSR 1959, 61–3, 65–6, 69–70, 73–4, 79, 81–2
Men's Epée, Individual	2	Ramón Fonst (Cuba) (1883–1959) 1900, 04	3	Georges Buchard (France) (b. 21 Dec 1893) 1927, 31, 33
			3	Aleksey Nikanchikov (USSR) (1940–72) 1966–7, 70
Men's Epée, Team	6	Italy 1920, 28, 36, 52, 56, 60	10	Italy 1931, 33, 37, 49–50, 53–5, 57–8
Men's Sabre, Individual	2	Dr Jenö Fuchs (Hungary) (b. 29 Oct 1882) 1908, 12	3	Aladár Gerevich (Hungary) (b. 16 Mar 1910) 1935, 51, 55
	2	Rudolf Kárpáti (Hungary) (b. 17 July 1920) 1956, 60	3	Jerzy Pawlowski (Poland) (b. 25 Oct 1932) 1957, 65–6
	2	Jean Georgiadis (Greece) (b. 1874) 1896, 1906	3	Yakov Rylsky (USSR) (b. 25 Oct 1928) 1958, 61, 63
	2	Viktor Krovopouskov (USSR) (b. 29 Sept 1948) 1976, 80		
Men's Sabre, Team	9	Hungary 1908, 12, 28, 32, 36, 48, 52, 56, 60	17	Hungary 1930–1, 33–5, 37, 51, 53–5, 57–8, 66, 73, 78, 81, 82
Women's Foil, Individual	2	Ilona Schacherer-Elek (Hungary) (b. 17 May 1907) 1936, 48	3	Helène Mayer (Germany) (1910–53) 1929, 31, 37
			3	Ilona Schacherer-Elek (Hungary) 1934–5, 51
			3	Ellen Müller-Preis (Austria) (b. 6 May 1912) 1947, 49, 50 (shared)
Women's Foil, Team	4	USSR 1960, 68, 72, 76	14	USSR 1956, 58, 61, 63, 65–6, 70–1, 74–5, 77–9, 82

MOST AMATEUR FENCING ASSOCIATION TITLES

Foil	(Instituted 1898)	7	John Emrys Lloyd (b. 8 Sept 1905)	1928, 1930–3, 1937–8
Epée	(Instituted 1904)	6	Edward O. 'Teddy' Bourne (b. 30 Sept 1948)	1966, 1972, 1974, 1976–8
Sabre	(Instituted 1898)	6	Dr Roger F. Tredgold (1912–75)	1937, 1939, 1947–9, 1955
Foil (Ladies)	(Instituted 1907)	10	Gillian M. Sheen (now Mrs Donaldson)	1949, 1951–8, 1960

women foilists with three world titles, only Ilona Schacherer-Elek won two individual Olympic titles (1936 and 1948).

Most titles *Olympic*

The most individual Olympic gold medals won is three by Ramón Fonst (Cuba) (1883–1959) in 1900 and 1904 (two) and by Nedo Nadi (Italy) (1894–1952) in 1912 and 1920 (two). Nadi also won three team gold medals in 1920 making a then unprecedented total of five gold medals at one celebration. Edoardo Mangiarotti (Italy) (b. 7 Apr 1919) with six gold, five silver and two bronze, holds the record of 13 Olympic medals. He won them for foil and épée from 1936 to 1960. The most gold medals by a woman is four (one individual, three team) by Elena Novikova-Belova (USSR) (b. 28 July 1947) from 1968 to 1976, and the record for all medals is seven (two gold, three silver, two bronze) by Ildikó Sagi-Retjö (formerly Ujlaki-Retjö) (Hungary) (b. 11 May 1937) from 1960 to 1976.

British Olympic records

The only British fencer to win a gold medal is Gillian Mary Sheen (b. 21 Aug 1928) in the 1956 foil. A record three Olympic medals were won by Edgar Seligman (1867–1958) with silver medals in the épée team event in 1906, 1908 and 1912. Henry William Furse Hoskyns (b. 19 Mar 1931) has competed most often for Great Britain with six Olympic appearances, 1956–76.

FIELD SPORTS

FOXHUNTING

Earliest references

Hunting the fox in Britain became popular from the second half of the 18th century though it is mentioned very much earlier. Prior to that time hunting was confined principally to the deer and the hare.

Pack *Oldest*

The Old Charlton Hunt (later the Goodwood) in West Sussex (now extinct), the Duke of Monmouth and Lord Grey of Werke at Charlton, Sussex, and the Duke of Buckingham in north Yorkshire, owned packs which were entered to fox only during the reign (1660–85) of Charles II.

Pack *Largest*

The pack with the greatest number of hounds has been the Duke of Beaufort's hounds maintained at Badminton, Avon, since 1786. At times hunting six days a week, this pack once had 120 couples at hounds. It now meets four days a week.

Longest span

Jean Bethel 'Betty' McKeever (*née* Dawes) (b 26 Feb 1901) has been Master of the Blean Beagles in Kent since 1909. The 10th Duke of Beaufort (1900–84) was Master of Foxhounds from 1924 until his death in 1984 and hunted on 3895 days from 1920–67.

Longest hunt

The longest recorded hunt was one held by Squire Sandys which ran from Holmbank, northern Lancashire to Ulpha, Cumbria, a total of nearly 80 miles *128 km* in reputedly only 6 hr, in January or February 1743. The longest duration hunt was one of 10 hr 5 min by Charlton Hunt of West Sussex, which ran from East Dean Wood at 7.45 am to a kill over 57¼ miles *92 km* away at 5.50 pm on 26 Jan 1738.

Most Days Hunting

Between 1969 and 1985, J. N. P. Watson, Hunting Correspondent to Country Life, hunted with 212 different packs of foxhounds, staghounds and harehounds in Britain, Ireland, USA and Europe.

GAME SHOOTING

Record heads

The world's finest head is the 23-pointer stag in the Maritzburg collection, E. Germany. The outside span is 75½ in *191 cm*, the length 47½ in *120 cm* and the weight 41½ lb *18,824 kg*. The greatest number of points is probably 33 (plus 29) on the stag shot in 1696 by Frederick III (1657–1713), the Elector of Brandenburg, later King Frederick I of Prussia.

Largest tally to a single sportsman

556,813 head of game fell to the guns of the 2nd Marquess of Ripon between 1867 and when he dropped dead on a grouse moor after shooting his 52nd bird on the morning of 22 Sept 1923. This figure included 241,234 pheasants, 124,193 partridge and 31,900 hares. (His game books are held by the gunmakers, James Purdey and Sons.)

FIVES

ETON FIVES

A handball game against the buttress of Eton College Chapel was first recorded in 1825. New courts were built at Eton in 1840, the rules were codified in 1877, rewritten laws were introduced three times and last amended in 1981.

Most titles

One pair has won the Amateur Championship (Kinnaird Cup) eight times—Anthony Hughes and Arthur James Gordon Campbell (1958, 1965–8, 1971, 1973 and 1975). Hughes was also in the winning pair in 1963 and has played in 16 finals. The Clubs' championship (the Alan Barber Cup) has been won a record twelve times by Old Cholmeleians (1969–70, 1975, 1977–85). The Douglas Keeble Cup for the National League has been won a record eight times by Old Edwardians (1975–7, 1981–5).

RUGBY FIVES

As now known, this game dates from *c.* 1850 with the first inter-public school matches recorded in the early 1870s. The Oxford *v.* Cambridge contest was inaugurated in 1925 and the Rugby Fives Association was founded in the home of Dr Edgar Cyriax (1874–1954), in Welbeck Street, London, on 29 Oct 1927. The dimensions of the Standard Rugby Fives court were approved by the Association in 1931.

Most titles

The greatest number of Amateur Singles Championships (instituted 1932) ever won is eleven by Wayne Enstone in 1973–8 and 1980–4. The record for the Amateur Doubles Championship (instituted 1925) is seven shared by John Frederick Pretlove (1952, 1954, 1956–9, 1961) and David E. Gardner (1960, 1965–6, 1970–2, 1974).

The invitation World Championships was first held in 1983. On the first three occasions Wayne Enstone won the singles and Enstone and S. Ashton won the doubles.

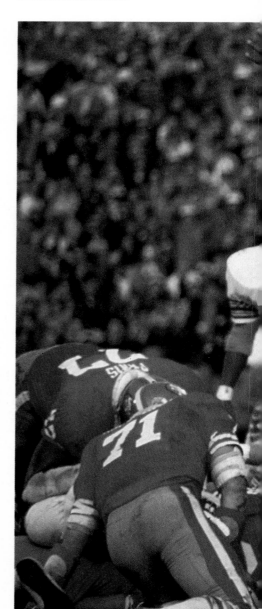

LARGEST BRITISH BAGS

Hare	1,215	*11 guns*	Holkham, Norfolk, 19 Dec 1877
Rabbit	6,943	*5 guns*	Blenheim, Oxfordshire, 17 Oct 1898
Geese (Brent)	704[1]	*32 punt-guns*	Colonel Russell i/c, River Blackwater, Essex, *c.* 1860
Grouse	1,070	*1 gun*	Thomas, 6th Baron Walsingham in Yorkshire, 30 Aug 1888
Grouse	2,929	*8 guns*	Littledale and Abbeystead, Lancashire, 12 Aug 1915
Partridge (Wild)	2,015[2]	*6 guns*	Rothwell, Lincolnshire, 3 Oct 1952
Pheasant	3,937	*7 guns*[3]	Hall Barn, Beaconsfield, Buckinghamshire, 18 Dec 1913
Pigeon	561	*1 gun*	K. Ransford, Salop-Powys, 22 July 1970
Snipe	1,108	*2 guns*	Tiree, Inner Hebrides, 25 Oct–3 Nov 1906
Woodcock	228	*6 guns*	Ashford, County Galway, Ireland, 28 Jan 1910
Woodpigeon	550	*1 gun*	Major A. J. Coates, near Winchester, Hampshire, 10 Jan 1962

[1] *Plus about 250 later picked up.*   [2] *Plus 104 later picked up.*
[3] *Including H.M. King George V.*

FOOTBALL (AMERICAN)

See also American Football—The Records *by Miles Aiken and Peter Rowe, published by Guinness Superlatives Ltd. at £6.95.*

PROFESSIONAL RECORDS—AMERICAN FOOTBALL

Record				Holder	Year
Most points	career	2002		George Blanda	1949–75
	season	176		Paul Hornung (Green Bay)	1960
	game	40		Ernie Nevers (Chicago Cardinals)	1929
Most touchdowns	career	126		Jim Brown (Cleveland)	1957–65
	season	24		John Riggins (Washington Redskins)	1983
	game	6		Ernie Nevers (Chicago Cardinals)	1929
		6		William 'Dub' Jones (Cleveland)	1951
		6		Gale Sayers (Chicago)	1965
Most yards gained rushing	career	13,309		Walter Payton (Chicago Bears)	1975–84
	season	2105		Eric Dickerson (Los Angeles Rams)	1985
	game	275		Walter Payton (Chicago Bears)	1977
Most passes completed	career	3686		Fran Tarkenton (Minnesota, NY Giants)	1961–78
	season	360		Dan Fouts (San Diego)	1981
	game	42		Richard Todd (New York Jets)	1980

Left: The San Francisco 49ers (red shirts) equalled the highest ever score, 38, in the XIX Superbowl against the Miami Dolphins. *Above:* Eric Dickerson set a new season rushing record in 1985. *(All-Sport/Tony Duffy)*

Origins

American Football, a direct descendant of the British games of soccer and rugby, evolved at American Universities in the 19th century. The first match under the Harvard Rules was played by Harvard against McGill University of Montreal at Cambridge, Mass., in 1874. The Intercollegiate Football Association was founded in 1876. The professional game dates from August 1895 when Latrobe played Jeanette at Latrobe, Pennsylvania. The American Professional Football Association was formed in 1919. This became the National Football League (NFL) in

1922 and the American Football League (AFL) in 1960; they merged in 1970. The USFL was formed in 1982.

Super Bowl

First held in 1967 between the winners of the NFL and the AFL. Since 1970 it has been contested by the winners of the National and American Conferences of the NFL. Pittsburgh Steelers have most wins, four, 1975–6 and 1979–80. The highest aggregate score was in 1979 when Pittsburgh beat Dallas Cowboys 35–31. The record victory margin was when the Los Angeles Raiders beat Washington Redskins 38–9 in 1984. The highest team score of 38 was equalled when San Francisco 49ers beat Miami Dolphins 38–16 in 1985. The Green Bay Packers won a record 11 NFL titles between 1929 and 1967.

College Football *Highest team score*

Georgia Tech, Atlanta, Georgia scored 222 points, including a record 32 touchdowns, against Cumberland University, Lebanon, Tennessee (nil) on 7 Oct 1916.

FOOTBALL (ASSOCIATION)

See also Soccer—The Records by Jack Rollin published by Guinness Superlatives Ltd. in 1985, at £9.95 (hardback) and £6.95 (limp).

Origins

A game with some similarities termed *Tsu-chu* was played in China in the 4th and 3rd centuries BC. One of the earliest references to the game in England is a Royal Proclamation by Edward II in 1314 banning the game in the City of London. The earliest clear representation of football is an Edinburgh print dated 1672–3. The game was standardised with the formation of the Football Association in England on 26 Oct 1863. The oldest club is Sheffield FC, formed on 24 Oct 1857. Eleven per side became standard in 1870.

PROFESSIONAL

Longest match

The duration record for first class fixtures was set in the Copa Libertadores in Santos, Brazil, on 2–3 Aug 1962, when Santos drew 3–3 with Penarol FC of Montevideo, Uruguay. The game lasted 3 hr 30 min (with interruptions), from 9.30 pm to 1 am.

The longest British match on record was one of 3 hr 23 min between Stockport County and Doncaster Rovers in the second leg of the Third Division (North) Cup at Edgeley Park, Stockport, Greater Manchester on 30 Mar 1946.

Longest unbeaten streak

Nottingham Forest were undefeated in 42 consecutive Division I matches from 20 Nov 1977 to 9 Dec 1978. In Scottish Football Glasgow Celtic were undefeated in 62 matches (49 won, 13 drawn), 13 Nov 1915–21 April 1917.

Most postponements

The Scottish Cup tie between Inverness Thistle and Falkirk during the winter of 1978–9 was postponed a record 29 times due to weather conditions. Finally Falkirk won the game 4–0.

GOAL SCORING

Teams

The highest score recorded in a first-class match is 36. This occurred in the Scottish Cup match between Arbroath and Bon Accord on 12 Sept

John Petrie's record of 13 goals in a first-class match has stood since 1885. Arbroath beat Bon Accord 36–0, with the referee apparently disallowing other legitimate goals to keep the score reasonable.

1885, when Arbroath won 36–0 on their home ground. But for the lack of nets and the consequent waste of retrieval time the score must have been even higher. Seven further goals were disallowed for offside.

The highest margin recorded in an international match is 17, when England beat Australia 17–0 at Sydney on 30 June 1951. This match is not listed by England as a *full* international. The highest in the British Isles was when England beat Ireland 13–0 at Belfast on 18 Feb 1882.

The highest score between English clubs in any major competition is 26, when Preston North End beat Hyde 26–0 in an FA Cup tie at Deepdale, Lancashire, on 15 Oct 1887. The biggest victory in an FA Cup Final is six when Bury beat Derby County 6–0 at Crystal Palace on 18 Apr 1903, in which year Bury did not concede a single goal in the five Cup matches.

The highest score by one side in a Football League (Division I) match is 12 goals when West Bromwich Albion beat Darwen 12–0 at West Bromwich, West Midlands on 4 Apr 1892; when Nottingham Forest beat Leicester Fosse by the same score at Nottingham on 21 Apr 1909; and when Aston Villa beat Accrington 12–2 at Perry Barr, W. Midlands on 12 Mar 1892.

The highest aggregate in League Football was 17 goals when Tranmere Rovers beat Oldham Athletic 13–4 in a Third Division (North) match at Prenton Park, Merseyside, on Boxing Day,

Jimmy McGrory set several scoring records in Scottish football; his career total of 550 for Celtic is a British record. *(Norman Barrett)*

1935. The record margin in a League match has been 13 in the Newcastle United 13, Newport County 0 (Division II) match on 5 Oct 1946 and in the Stockport County 13, Halifax 0 (Division III (North)) match on 6 Jan 1934.

The highest number of goals by any British team in a professional league in a season is 142 in 34 matches by Raith Rovers (Scottish Division II) in the 1937–8 season. The English League record is 134 in 46 matches by Peterborough United (Division IV) in 1960–1.

Individual

The most scored by one player in a first-class match is 16 by Stephan Stanis (*né* Stanikowski, b. Poland, 15 July 1913) for Racing Club de Lens *v.* Aubry-Asturies, in Lens, France, in a wartime French Cup game on 13 Dec 1942.

The record number of goals scored by one player in an international match is ten by Sofus Nielsen (1888–1963) for Denmark *v.* France (17–1) in the 1908 Olympics and by Gottfried Fuchs (1889–1972) for Germany who beat Russia 16–0 in the 1912 Olympic tournament (consolation event) in Sweden.

Season

The best season League records are 60 goals in 39 League games by William Ralph 'Dixie' Dean (1907–80) for Everton (Division I) in 1927–8 and 66 goals in 38 games by James Smith (1902–76) for Ayr United (Scottish Division II)

BRITISH GOAL SCORING RECORDS		
SCOTTISH CUP		
13	John Petrie for Arbroath v Bon Accord on 5 Sept 1885	
FOOTBALL LEAGUE		
10	Joe Payne (1914–77) for Luton Town v Bristol Rovers (Div 3S) at Luton on 13 Apr 1936	
F. LEAGUE DIV I		
7	Ted Drake (b. 16 Aug 1912) for Arsenal v Aston Villa at Birmingham on 14 Dec 1935 James David Ross for Preston NE v Stoke at Preston on 6 Oct 1888	
FA CUP (PRELIM)		
10	Chris Marron for South Shields v Radcliffe at South Shields on 20 Sept 1947	
FA CUP		
9	Edward 'Ted' McDougall (b. 8 Jan 1947) for Bournemouth v Margate at Bournemouth on 20 Nov 1971	
SCOTTISH DIV I		
8	James Edward McGrory (1904–82) Celtic v Dunfermline at Celtic Park, Glasgow on 14 Jan 1928	
HOME INTERNATIONAL		
6	Joe Bambrick (b. 3 Nov 1905) for Ireland v Wales at Belfast on 1 Feb 1930	
AMATEUR INTERNATIONAL		
6	William Charles Jordan (1885–1949) for England v France at Park Royal, London on 23 Mar 1908; Vivian John Woodward (1879–1954) for England v Holland at Stamford Bridge, London on 11 Dec 1909; Harold A. Walden for Great Britain v Hungary at Stockholm, Sweden on 1 July 1912	

in the same season. With three more in Cup ties and 19 in representative matches Dean's total was 82.

Career

Artur Friedenreich (1892–1969) (Brazil) scored an undocumented 1329 goals in a 43 year first class football career. The most goals scored in a specified period is 1216 by Edson Arantes do Nascimento (Brazil) (b. 23 Oct 1940), known as Pelé, from 7 Sept 1956 to 2 Oct 1974 in 1254 games. His best year was 1959 with 126, and the *milesimo* (1000th) came in a penalty for his club Santos in the Maracaña Stadium, Rio de Janeiro on 19 Nov 1969 when playing his 909th first-class match. He later played for New York Cosmos and on his retirement on 1 Oct 1977 his total had reached 1281, in 1363 games. He added two more goals later in special appearances. Franz 'Bimbo' Binder (b. 1 Dec 1911) scored 1006 goals in 756 games in Austria and Germany between 1930 and 1950.

The international career record for England is 49 goals by Robert 'Bobby' Charlton (b. 11 Oct 1937). His first was *v.* Scotland on 19 Apr 1958 and his last on 20 May 1970 *v.* Colombia.

The greatest number of goals scored in British first-class football is 550 (410 in Scottish League matches) by James McGrory of Glasgow Celtic (1922–38). The most scored in League matches is 434, for West Bromwich Albion, Fulham, Leicester City and Shrewsbury Town, by George Arthur Rowley (b. 21 Apr 1926) between 1946 and April 1965. Rowley also scored 32 goals in the F.A. Cup and one for England 'B'.

Fastest goals

The fastest Football League goals on record were scored in 6 sec by Albert E. Mundy (b. 12 May 1926) (Aldershot) in a Division IV match *v.* Hartlepool United at Victoria Ground, Hartlepool, Cleveland on 25 Oct 1958, by Barrie Jones (b. 31 Oct 1938) (Notts Co) in a Division III match *v.* Torquay United on 31 Mar 1962, by Keith Smith (b. 15 Sept 1940) (Crystal Palace) in a Division II match *v.* Derby County at the Baseball Ground, Derby on 12 Dec 1964 and by Tommy W. Langley (b. 8 Feb 1958) (Queen's Park Rangers) in a Division II match *v.* Bolton Wanderers on 11 Oct 1980.

The fastest confirmed hat-trick is in 2½ minutes by Ephraim 'Jock' Dodds (b. 7 Sept 1915) for Blackpool *v* Tranmere Rovers on 28 Feb 1943, and by Jimmy Scarth (b. 26 Aug 1920) for Gillingham *v* Leyton Orient in Div III (Southern) on 1 Nov 1952. A hat-trick in 1 min 50 sec is claimed for Maglioni of Independiente *v.* Gimnasia y Escrima de la Plata in Argentina on 18 Mar 1973. John McIntyre (Blackburn Rovers) scored four goals in 5 min *v.* Everton at Ewood Park, Blackburn, Lancashire on 16 Sept 1922. William 'Ginger' Richardson (West Bromwich Albion) scored four goals in 5 min from the kick-off against West Ham United at Upton Park on 7 Nov 1931. Frank Keetley scored six goals in 21 min in the 2nd half of the Lincoln City *v.* Halifax Town league match on 16 Jan 1932. The

international record is three goals in 3½ min by Willie Hall (Tottenham Hotspur) for England against Ireland on 16 Nov 1938 at Old Trafford, Greater Manchester.

Fastest own goal

Torquay United's Pat Kruse (b. 30 Nov 1953) equalled the fastest goal on record when he headed the ball into his own net only 6 sec after kick-off *v.* Cambridge United on 3 Jan 1977.

Most experienced youngster? Norman Whiteside, at 17 yr 42 days, was the youngest player to compete in the World Cup finals, for Northern Ireland in 1982. In the following domestic season he became the youngest scorer in an FA Cup final, and the first player to score in both major domestic finals.
(All-Sport/ David Cannon)

GOALKEEPING

Individual record

The longest that any goalkeeper has succeeded in preventing any goals being scored past him in international matches is 1142 min for Dino Zoff (Italy), from September 1972 to June 1974. The Football League record is 1103 min by Steve Death (b. 19 Sept 1949) for Reading in Division IV from 24 March to 18 Aug 1979.

FA CHALLENGE CUP AND SCOTTISH FA CUP

Most wins

The greatest number of FA Cup wins is seven by Aston Villa, 1887, 1895, 1897, 1905, 1913, 1920 and 1957 (nine final appearances) and by Tottenham Hotspur, 1901, 1921, 1961, 1962, 1967, 1981 and 1982 (seven appearances). Newcastle United and Arsenal have been in the final 11 times. The highest aggregate scores have been 6–1 in 1890 and 4–3 in 1953.

The greatest number of Scottish FA Cup wins is 27 by Celtic in 1892, 1899, 1900, 1904, 1907–8, 1911–12, 1914, 1923, 1925, 1927, 1931, 1933, 1937, 1951, 1954, 1965, 1967, 1969, 1971, 1972, 1974, 1975, 1977, 1980 and 1985.

Youngest player

The youngest player in a FA Cup Final was Paul Allen (b. 28 Aug 1962) of West Ham United, who played against Arsenal on 10 May 1980 aged 17 years 256 days. Derek Johnstone (Rangers) (b. 4 Nov 1953) was 16 years 11 months old when he played in the Scottish League Cup Final against Celtic on 24 Oct 1970. The youngest goal scorer in the FA Cup Final was Norman Whiteside (b. 7 May 1965) for Manchester United *v.* Brighton at 18 yr 19 days on 26 May 1983. The youngest player ever in the FA Cup competition was Scott Endersby (b. 20 Feb 1962) who was only 15 years 288 days old when he played in goal for Kettering *v.* Tilbury on 26 Nov. 1977.

Most medals

Three players have won five FA Cup winner's medals: James Forrest (Blackburn Rovers) (1884–6, 1890–1); the Hon Sir Arthur Fitzgerald Kinnaird, KT (Wanderers) (1873, 1877–8) and Old Etonians (1879, 1882); and Charles H. R. Wollaston (Wanderers) (1872–3, 1876–8).

The most Scottish Cup winners' medals won is eight by Charles Campbell (Queen's Park) in 1874–6, 1880–2, 1884 and 1886.

Longest tie

The most protracted FA Cup tie in the competition proper was that between Stoke City and Bury in the third round with Stoke winning 3–2 in the fifth meeting after 9 hr 22 min of play in January 1955. The matches were at Bury (1–1) on 8 Jan; Stoke on Trent on 12 Jan (abandoned after 22 min of extra time with the score 1–1); Goodison Park (3–3) on 17 Jan; Anfield (2–2) on 19 Jan; and finally at Old Trafford on 24 Jan. In the 1972 final qualifying round Alvechurch beat Oxford City after five previous drawn games (total playing time 11 hours).

FOOTBALL LEAGUE CUP
(inst. 1960–1, 1982–5 known as Milk Cup)

The most wins is four by Liverpool, 1981–4.

SCOTTISH LEAGUE CUP
(inst. 1946–7)

The most wins is 12 by Rangers between 1947 and 1984.

LEAGUE CHAMPIONSHIPS

World

The record number of successive national League championships is nine by Celtic (Scotland) 1966–74, CSKA, Sofia (Bulgaria) 1954–62 and MTK Budapest (Hungary) 1917–25. The Sofia club hold a European postwar record of 23 league titles.

Everton completed a unique double by winning the *(top)* League Championship and *(bottom)* the Cup Winners' Cup in the 1984–5 season. They emerged from the shadow of Liverpool to become the most successful team of the year. *(All-Sport/David Cannon)*

English

The greatest number of League Championships (Division I) is 15 by Liverpool in 1901, 1906, 1922, 1923, 1947, 1964, 1966, 1973, 1976–7, 1979–80 and 1982–84. The record number of wins in a season is 33 from 42 matches by Doncaster Rovers in Division III (North) in 1946–7. The Division I record is 31 wins from 42 matches by Tottenham Hotspur in 1960–1. In 1893–4 Liverpool won 22 and drew 6 in 28 Division II games. They also won the promotion match.

'Double'

The only FA Cup and League Championship 'doubles' are those of Preston North End in 1889, Aston Villa in 1897, Tottenham Hotspur in 1961 and Arsenal in 1971. Preston won the League without losing a match and the Cup without having a goal scored against them throughout the whole competition.

Scottish

Glasgow Rangers have won the Scottish League Championship 36 times between 1899 and 1978 and were joint champions on another occasion. Their 76 points in the Scottish Division I in 1920–1 represents a record in any division.

Closest win

In 1923–4 Huddersfield won the Division I championship over Cardiff by 0.02 of a goal with a goal average of 1.81.

TOURNAMENT RECORDS

World Club Championship

This club tournament was started in 1960 between the winners of the European Cup and the Copa Libertadores, the South American equivalent. The most wins is three by Penarol, Uruguay in 1961, 1966 and 1982. Independiente, Argentina won in 1973 and 1984 and reached the final in 1975, but couldn't agree dates for the matches with Bayern Munich.

European Championship (*formerly Nations Cup*)

The European equivalent of the World Cup started in 1958 and is staged every four years. West Germany are the only country to have won twice, in 1972 and 1980. They also lost in the 1976 final, to Czechoslovakia.

European Champion Clubs Cup

The European Cup for the League champions of the respective nations was approved by FIFA on 8 May 1955 and was run by the European governing body UEFA (Union of European Football Associations) which came into being in the previous year. Real Madrid won the first final, and have won a record six times (including five times consecutively) 1956–60, 1966. The highest score in a final was Real Madrid's 7–3 win over Eintracht Frankfurt at Hampden Park, Glasgow on 18 May 1960.

Glasgow Celtic became the first British club to win the Cup beating Inter-Milan 2–1 in Lisbon, Portugal, on 25 May 1967. They also became the first British club to win the European Cup and the two senior domestic tournaments (League and Cup) in the same season. Liverpool, winners in 1977, 1978, 1981 and 1984, have been the most successful British club and in the 1983–4 season emulated Celtic by also winning two domestic competitions—League and Milk Cup.

European Cup Winners Cup

A tournament for the national Cup winners started in 1960–1. Clubs to win twice have been AC Milan 1968 and 1973, Anderlecht 1976 and 1978, and Barcelona 1979 and 1982. Tottenham Hotspur were the first British club to win the trophy, beating Atletico Madrid 5–1 in Rotterdam in 1963.

The 1986 World Cup Competition is to be the 13th tournament, and is being held in Mexico from 31 May–29 June. *The Fédération Internationale de Football Association (FIFA)*, which was founded on 21 May 1904, instituted the first World Cup on 13 July 1930, in Montevideo, Uruguay. Thirteen nations took part then, playing for a trophy named after Jules Rimet, the late Honorary President of FIFA from 1921–1954. The first team to win the competition three times were to keep the trophy, a feat achieved by Brazil in 1970.

A new trophy of solid gold, standing 36 cms high and known as the FIFA World Cup, was designed by an Italian from an entry of 53 submitted for selection and used in 1974 for the first time.

Only six countries have won the World Cup. On only three occasions—Uruguay 1930, Italy 1938 and Brazil 1970— have teams achieved a 100 per cent record in the finals.

Goal scoring and Appearances

Antonio Carbayal (b. 1923) (Mexico) is the only player to have appeared in five World Cup final tournaments, keeping goal for Mexico in 1950, 1954, 1958, 1962 and 1966, playing 11 games in all. Uwe Seeler (b. 5 Nov 1936) (West Germany) holds the record for the most appearances in

The most goals scored in a final is three by Geoff Hurst *(below)* (b. 8 Dec 1941) for England *v.* West Germany on 30 July 1966. Two players, both Brazilian, have scored in two finals, Vava (real name Edwaldo Izito Neto) in 1958 and 1962 and Pelé in 1958 and 1970. The fastest goal in World Cup competition was one in 27 sec by Bryan Robson (b. 11 Jan 1957) for England *v.* France in Bilbao on 16 June 1982.

THE WORLD CUP *Past, Present & Future*

final tournaments, playing as a centre forward in 21 games in the 1958–1970 events, whilst Pelé is the only player to have been with three World Cup winning teams, in 1958, 1962 and 1970. The youngest ever to play in the World Cup is Norman Whiteside who played for Northern Ireland *v.* Yugoslavia aged 17 yr 42 days on 17 June 1982. The record goal scorer is Just Fontaine (b. Marrakesh, Morocco, 18 Aug 1933) of France who scored 13 goals in six matches in the final stages of the 1958 competition in Sweden. Gerd Müller (b. 3 Nov 1945) (West Germany) scored 10 goals in 1970 and four in 1974 for the highest aggregate of 14 goals. Fontaine and Jairzinho (Brazil) are the only two players to have scored in every match in a final series, as Jairzinho scored seven in six games in 1970.

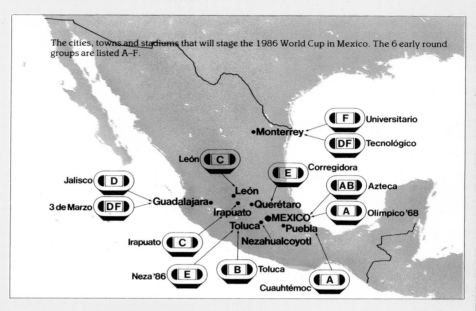

The cities, towns and stadiums that will stage the 1986 World Cup in Mexico. The 6 early round groups are listed A–F.

(*Above*) Record-breaking stars of a record-breaking team, Jairzinho (*l.*) and Pelé (*r.*) in 1970, and (*right*) top goalscorer Gerd Müller of West Germany. (*Syndication International*)

The highest score in a World Cup match occurred in a qualifying match in Auckland on 15 Aug 1981 when New Zealand beat Fiji 13–0. The highest score during the final stages is 10, scored by Hungary in a 10–1 win over El Salvador at Elche, Spain on 15 June 1982.

The highest scoring team in a final tournament has been West Germany who scored 25 in six matches in 1954, for the highest average of 4.17 goals per game.

The best defensive record belongs to England, who in six matches in 1966 conceded only three goals. Curiously, no team has ever failed to score in a World Cup Final.

TOURNAMENT STATISTICS

Year	Venue	Total Attendances	Average	No. of Matches	Goals	Average	Highest Scorer	
1930	Uruguay	434,500	24,139	18	70	3.88	Guillermo Stabile (Arg)	8
1934	Italy	395,000	23,235	17	70	4.11	Angelo Schiano (Ita)	4
							Oldrich Nejedly (Cze)	4
							Edmund Conen (Ger)	4
1938	France	483,000	26,833	18	84	4.66	Leonidas da Silva (Bra)	8
1950	Brazil	1,337,000	60,772	22	88	4.00	Ademir (Bra)	7
1954	Switzerland	943,000	36,270	26	140	5.38	Sandor Kocsis (Hun)	11
1958	Sweden	868,800	24,800	35	126	3.60	Just Fontaine (Fra)	13
1962	Chile	776,000	24,250	32	89	2.78	Drazen Jerkovic (Yug)	5
1966	England	1,614,677	50,458	32	89	2.78	Eusebio (Por)	9
1970	Mexico	1,673,975	52,312	32	95	2.96	Gerd Müller (W. Ger)	10
1974	W. Germany	1,774,022	46,685	38	97	2.55	Grzegorz Lato (Pol)	7
1978	Argentina	1,610,215	42,374	38	102	2.68	Mario Kempes (Arg)	6
1982	Spain	1,766,277	33,967	52	146	2.81	Paola Rossi (Ita)	6

WORLD CUP FINALS

Year	Winners	Host Nation	Runners Up	Score	Venue	Attendance
1930	Uruguay	Uruguay	Argentina	4–2	Montevideo	90,000
1934	Italy	Italy	Czechoslovakia	*2–1	Rome	50,000
1938	Italy	France	Hungary	4–2	Paris	45,000
1950	Uruguay	Brazil	Brazil	†2–1	Rio de Janeiro	199,850
1954	West Germany	Switzerland	Hungary	3–2	Berne	60,000
1958	Brazil	Sweden	Sweden	5–2	Stockholm	49,737
1962	Brazil	Chile	Czechoslovakia	3–1	Santiago	68,679
1966	England	England	West Germany	*4–2	Wembley, London	93,802
1970	Brazil	Mexico	Italy	4–1	Mexico City	107,412
1974	West Germany	West Germany	Holland	2–1	Munich	77,833
1978	Argentine	Argentina	Holland	*3–1	Buenos Aires	77,000
1982	Italy	Spain	West Germany	3–1	Madrid	90,089

† Deciding match (contested on a league basis)
* a.e.t.

UEFA Cup

Originally known as the International Inter-City Industrial Fairs Cup, this club tournament began in 1955. The first competition lasted three years, the second two years. In 1960–1 it became an annual tournament and since 1971–2 has been replaced by the UEFA Cup. The first British club to win the trophy was Leeds United in 1968. The most wins is three by Barcelona in 1958, 1960 and 1966.

PLAYERS

Most durable player

The most durable player in League history has been Terence Lionel Paine (b. 23 Mar 1939) who made 824 league appearances from 1957 to 1977 playing for Southampton and Hereford Utd. Norman John Trollope (b. 14 June 1943) made 770 League appearances for one club, Swindon Town, between 1960 and 1980.

Transfer fees

The greatest transfer fee quoted for a player is 15,895 million lire (£6.9 million) by Napoli in 1984 for Diego Maradona (Argentina) (b. 30 Oct 1960) from Barcelona. This exceeded the c. £5 million that Barcelona paid for Maradona in 1982.

The record fee between British clubs was £1,500,000 (incl VAT and other levies) paid by Manchester United to West Bromwich Albion for Bryan Robson on 3 Oct 1981.

Heaviest goalkeeper

The biggest goalkeeper in representative football was the England international Willie J. 'Fatty' Foulke (1874–1916), who stood 6 ft 3 in *1,90 m* and weighed 22 st 3 lb *141 kg*. His last games were for Bradford City, by which time he was 26 st *165 kg*. He once stopped a game by snapping the cross bar.

Oldest and youngest caps

The oldest cap has been William Henry 'Billy' Meredith (1874–1958) (Manchester City and United) who played outside right for Wales v. England at Highbury, London, on 15 Mar 1920 when aged 45 yr 229 days. He played internationally for a record span of 26 years (1895–1920).

Norman Whiteside played for Northern Ireland v. Yugoslavia, at 17 yr 42 days on 17 June 1982, the youngest ever to play in the World Cup.

The youngest cap in the four home countries internationals has been Norman Kernaghan (Belfast Celtic) who played for Ireland v. Wales in 1936 aged 17 yr 80 days. It is possible, however, that W. K. Gibson (Cliftonville) who played for Ireland v. Wales on 24 Feb 1894 at 17 was slightly younger. England's youngest home international was Duncan Edwards (1936–58), the Manchester United left half, against Scotland at Wembley on 2 Apr 1955, aged 18 yr 183 days. The youngest Welsh cap was John Charles (b. 27 Dec 1931), the Leeds United centre half, against Ireland at Wrexham on 8 Mar 1950, aged 18 yr 71 days. Scotland's youngest international has been Johnny Lambie, Queen's Park inside-forward, at 17 yr 92 days v. Ireland on 20 Mar 1886.

Most international appearances

The greatest number of appearances for a national team is 150 by Hector Chumpitaz (b. 12 Apr 1943) (Peru) from 1963 to 1982. This includes all matches played by the national team. The record for full internationals against other national teams is 115 by Bjorn Nordqvist (Sweden) (b. 6 Oct 1942) from 1963 to 1978.

ATTENDANCES

Greatest crowds

The greatest recorded crowd at any football match was 205,000 (199,854 paid) for the Brazil v. Uruguay World Cup match in the Maracaña Municipal Stadium, Rio de Janeiro, Brazil on 16 July 1950. The record attendance for a European Cup match is 136,505 at the semi-final between Glasgow Celtic and Leeds United at Hampden Park, Glasgow on 15 Apr 1970.

The British record paid attendance is 149,547 at the Scotland v. England international at Hampden Park, Glasgow, on 17 Apr 1937. It is, however, probable that this total was exceeded (estimated 160,000) on the occasion of the FA Cup Final between Bolton Wanderers and West Ham United at Wembley Stadium on 28 Apr 1923, when the crowd broke in on the pitch and the start was delayed 40 min until the pitch was cleared. The counted admissions were 126,047.

The Scottish Cup record attendance is 146,433 when Celtic played Aberdeen at Hampden Park on 24 Apr 1937. The record attendance for a League match in Britain is 118,567 for Rangers v. Celtic at Ibrox Park, Glasgow on 2 Jan 1939.

Carol Thomas, of Rowntree Ladies FC and England, has a record 51 caps and has captained her country on the last 44 occasions, having made her debut in November 1974.

The highest attendance at an amateur match has been 120,000 in Senayan Stadium, Jakarta, Indonesia, on 26 Feb 1976 for the Pre-Olympic Group II final, North Korea v. Indonesia.

Smallest crowd

The smallest crowd at a full home international was 2315 for the Wales v. Northern Ireland match of 27 May 1982 at the Racecourse Ground, Wrexham, Clwyd. The smallest paying attendance at a Football League fixture was for the Stockport County v. Leicester City match at Old Trafford, Greater Manchester, on 7 May 1921. Stockport's own ground was under suspension and the 'crowd' numbered 13 but an estimated 2000 gained free admission. When West Ham beat Castilla of Spain (5–1) in the European Cup Winners Cup at Upton Park, Greater London, on 1 Oct 1980 and when Aston Villa beat Besiktas of Turkey (3–1) in the European Cup at Villa Park on 15 Sept 1982, there were no paying spectators due to disciplinary action by the European Football Union.

OLYMPIC GAMES

The only country to have won the Olympic football title three times is Hungary in 1952, 1964 and 1968. The United Kingdom won the unofficial tournament in 1900 and the official tournaments of 1908 and 1912. The highest Olympic score is Denmark (17) v. France 'A' (1) in 1908.

OTHER MATCHES

Highest scores *Teams*

In a Felixstowe Sunday League match on 11 Mar 1984 Ipswich Exiles beat Seaton Rovers 45–0.

In an under-14 league match between Midas FC and Courage Colts, in Kent, on 11 Apr 1976, the full time score after 70 min play was 59–1. Top scorer for Midas was Kevin Graham with 17 goals. Courage had scored the first goal.

Needing to improve their goal 'difference' to gain promotion in 1979, Ilinden FC of Yugoslavia, with the collusion of the opposition, Mladost, and the referee, won their final game of the season by 134–1. Their rivals in the promotion race won their match, under similar circumstances by 88–0.

Highest scores *Individual*

Linda Curl of Norwich Ladies scored 22 goals in a 40–0 league victory over Milton Keynes Reserves at Norwich on 25 Sept 1983.

Highest scores *Season*

The greatest number of goals in a season reported for an individual player in junior professional league football is 96 by Tom Duffy (b. 7 Jan 1937), who played centre forward for Ardeer Thistle FC, Strathclyde in the 1960–1 season. Paul Anthony Moulden (b. 6 Sept 1967) scored 289 goals in 40 games for Bolton Lads Club in Bolton Boys Federation intermediate league and cup matches in 1981–2. An additional 51 goals scored in other tournaments brought his total to 340, the highest season figure reported in any class of competitive football for an individual.

Fastest goals

Wind-aided goals in 3 sec after kick-off have been scored by a number of players. Tony Bacon, of Schalmont HS scored three goals v. Icabod Crane HS in 63 sec at Schenectady, New York, USA on 8 Oct 1975.

Fastest own goal

The fastest own goal on record was one in 5 sec 'scored' by Peter Johnson of Chesham United in a match against Wycombe Wanderers on 21 Feb 1976.

MOST INTERNATIONAL APPEARANCES *British Isles*

England	108	Robert Frederick 'Bobby' Moore (b. 12 Apr 1941)	West Ham U/Fulham	1962–73
Northern Ireland	110	Patrick A. Jennings (b. 12 June 1945)	Watford/Tottenham H/Arsenal	1964–85
Scotland	97	Kenneth M. Dalglish (b. 4 Mar 1951)	Celtic/Liverpool	1971–85
Wales	68	Ivor Allchurch (b. 29 Dec 1929)	Swansea C/Newcastle/Cardiff C/Worcester C	1950–68
Rep. of Ireland	60	Michael J. 'Johnny' Giles (b. 6 Jan 1940)	Manchester U/Leeds U/West Bromwich A	1960–79

Longest ties

The aggregate duration of ties in amateur soccer have not been collated but it is recorded that in the London FA Intermediate Cup first qualifying round Highfield FC Reserves had to meet Mansfield House FC on 19 and 26 Sept and 3, 10 and 14 Oct 1970 to get a decision after 9 hr 50 min play with scores of 0–0, 1–1, 1–1, 3–3, and 0–2. In the Hertfordshire Intermediate Cup, London Colney beat Leavesden Hospital after 12 hr 41 min play and seven ties from 6 Nov to 17 Dec 1971.

Largest tournament

The Metropolitan Police 5-a-side Youth Competition in 1981 attracted an entry of 7008 teams, a record for an FA sanctioned competition.

Most and Least successful teams

The Home Farm FC, Dublin, Ireland, between 12 Oct 1968 and 10 Oct 1970 won 79 consecutive matches. Winlaton West End FC, Tyne and Wear, completed a run of 95 league games without defeat between 1976 and 1980. In six successive years the Larkswood County Junior School team of 1959–60 was unbeaten, winning 118 games and drawing three. Stockport United FC, of the Stockport Football League, lost 39 consecutive League and Cup matches, September 1976 to 18 Feb 1978.

Most indisciplined

In the local Cup match between Tongham Youth Club, Surrey and Hawley, Hampshire, on 3 Nov 1969 the referee booked all 22 players including one who went to hospital, and one of the linesmen. The match, won by Tongham 2–0, was described by a player as 'A good, hard game'.

In a Gancia Cup match at Waltham Abbey, Essex on 23 Dec 1973, the referee, Michael J. Woodhams, sent off the entire Juventus-Cross team and some club officials. Glencraig United, Faifley, nr Clydebank, had all 11 team members and two substitutes for their match against Goldenhill Boys' Club on 2 Feb 1975 booked in the dressing room before a ball was kicked. The referee, Mr Tarbet of Bearsden, took exception to the chant which greeted his arrival. It was not his first meeting with Glencraig. The teams drew 2–2.

Ball control

Robert Walters juggled a regulation soccer ball for 13 hr 2 min (478,960 repetitions) non-stop with feet, legs and head without the ball ever touching the ground at Corley Service Station, Warwickshire on 23 Nov 1984. Mikael Palmquist (Sweden) headed a regulation football non-stop for 4½ hr at Göteborg, Sweden in 1984.

Radoslav Metodiev Nikolov juggled a ball with his feet for 2 hr 57 min 3 sec while covering a distance of 17,950 m *11.15 miles* around a running track at Plovdiv, Bulgaria on 18 Aug 1984. He kicked the ball 18,110 times.

FOOTBALL (GAELIC)

Earliest references

The game developed from inter-parish 'free for all' with no time-limit, no defined playing area nor specific rules. The earliest reported match was Meath v. Louth, at Slane in 1712. Standardisation came with the formation of the Gaelic Athletic Association in Thurles, Ireland, on 1 Nov 1884.

Most titles

The greatest number of All Ireland Championships won by one team is 28 by Ciarraidhe

Wigan and Hull were involved in the highest scoring Challenge Cup Final in 1985. A memorable final, it was Wigan's eighth victory since the Cup began in 1897. *(All-Sport)*

(Kerry) between 1903 and 1984. The greatest number of successive wins is four by Wexford (1915–18) and Kerry twice (1929–32, 1978–81). Leinster has won most Inter-provincial championships (Railway Cup) with 18 between 1928 and 1974. Sean O'Neill (Down) holds the record of eight medals with Ulster (1960–71).

Highest scores

The highest team score in an All-Ireland final was when Dublin, 27 (5 goals, 12 points) beat Armagh, 15 (3 goals, 6 points) on 25 Sept 1977. The highest combined score was 45 points when Cork (26) beat Galway (19) in 1973. A goal equals three points. The highest individual score in an All-Ireland final has been 2 goals, 6 points by Jimmy Keaveney (Dublin) v. Armagh in 1977, and by Michael Sheehy (Kerry) v. Dublin in 1979.

Lowest scores

In four All-Ireland finals the combined totals have been 7 points; 1893 Wexford (1 goal, till 1894 worth 5 points, 1 point) v. Cork (1 point); 1895 Tipperary (4 points) v. Meath (3 points); 1904 Kerry (5 points) v. Dublin (2 points); 1924 Kerry (4 points) v. Dublin (3 points).

Most appearances

The most All-Ireland finals contested is ten by Dan O'Keeffe (Kerry) of which seven (a record) were on the winning side.

Largest crowd

The record crowd is 90,556 for the Down v. Offaly final at Croke Park, Dublin, in 1961.

FOOTBALL (RUGBY LEAGUE)

There have been four different scoring systems in rugby league football. For the purpose of these records all points totals remain as they were under the system in operation at the time they were made.

Origins

The Rugby League was formed on 29 Aug 1895 at the George Hotel, Huddersfield, W. Yorks. Twenty one clubs from Yorkshire and Lancashire were present and all but one agreed to resign from the Rugby Union and form the 'Northern Rugby Football Union'. Though payment for loss of wages was the major cause of the breakaway the 'Northern Union' did not embrace full professionalism until 1898. A reduction in the number of players per team from 15 to 13 took place in 1906. The present title is 'Rugby Football League'.

Most titles

There have been seven World Cup Competitions. Australia have most wins, with four, 1957, 1968, 1970 and 1977 as well as a win in the International Championship of 1975.

The Northern Rugby League was formed in 1901. The word 'Northern' was dropped in 1980. Wigan have won the League Championship a record nine times (1909, 1922, 1926, 1934, 1946, 1947, 1950, 1952 and 1960).

In the Rugby League Challenge Cup (inaugurated 1896–7 season) Leeds have most wins with ten, 1910, 1923, 1932, 1936, 1941–2 (wartime), 1957, 1968, 1977–8. Oldham is the only club to appear in four consecutive Cup Finals (1924–7).

Since 1974 there have been five major competitions for RL clubs: Challenge Cup, League Championship, Premiership, John Player Trophy and County Cup. Over this period only Widnes have won three in one season (Challenge Cup, John Player Trophy and Lancashire Cup) in 1978–79. Wigan has a record 34 wins in these five competitions.

Three clubs have won all possible major Rugby League trophies in one season: Hunslet, 1907–8 season, Huddersfield, 1914–15 and Swinton, 1927–8, all won the Challenge Cup, League Championship, County Cup and County League (now defunct).

HIGHEST SCORES

Senior match

The highest aggregate score in a game where a senior club has been concerned was 121 points, when Huddersfield beat Swinton Park Rangers by 119 (19 goals, 27 tries) to 2 (one goal) in the first round of the Northern Union Cup on 28 Feb 1914. The highest score in League football is 112 points by Leeds v. Coventry (nil) on 12 Apr 1913.

Challenge Cup Final

The highest score in a Challenge Cup Final is 38 points (8 tries, 7 goals) by Wakefield Trinity v. Hull (5) at Wembley on 14 May 1960. The record aggregate is 52 points when Wigan beat Hull 28–24 at Wembley on 4 May 1985. The greatest winning margin was 34 points when Huddersfield beat St Helens 37–3 at Oldham on 1 May 1915.

International match

The highest score in an international match is Australia's 63–13 defeat of England at Paris, France on 31 Dec 1933. The highest score in a World Cup match is the 53–19 win by Great Britain over New Zealand at Hameau, Paris on 4 Nov 1972.

Touring teams

The record score for a British team touring Australasia is 101 points by England v. South Australia (nil) at Adelaide in May 1914. The record for a touring team in Britain is 92 (10 goals, 24 tries) by Australia against Bramley's 7 (2 goals, 1 try) at the Barley Mow Ground, Bramley, near Leeds, on 9 Nov 1921.

Most points *Season*

St. Helens scored a record 1267 points (215 tries, 195 goals, 17 drop goals) in the 1984–5 season, playing in 42 Cup and League games.

HIGHEST INDIVIDUAL SCORES

Most points, goals and tries in a game

George Henry 'Tich' West (1882–1927) of Hull Kingston Rovers scored 53 points (10 goals and a record 11 tries) in a First Round Challenge Cup-tie v. Brookland Rovers on 4 Mar 1905.

The most goals in a Cup match is 22 kicked by Jim Sullivan (1903–77) for Wigan v. Flimby and Fothergill on 14 Feb 1925. The most goals in a League match is 15 by Mick Stacey for Leigh v. Doncaster on 28 Mar 1976. The most tries in a League match is 10 by Lionel Cooper (b. Australia 1922) for Huddersfield v. Keighley on 17 Nov 1951.

Most points *League*

Jimmy Lomas (Salford) scored a record 39 points (5 tries, 12 goals) against Liverpool City (78–0) on 2 Feb 1907.

Most points *Season*

The most number of points in a season was 496 by Benjamin Lewis Jones (Leeds) (b. 11 Apr 1931) 194 goals, 36 tries, in 1956–7.

Most points *Career*

Neil Fox scored 6220 points (2575 goals, 358 tries, 4 drop goals) in a senior Rugby League career from 10 Apr 1956 to the end of the 1979–80 season.

Most tries *Season*

Albert Aaron Rosenfeld (1885–1970) (Huddersfield), an Australian-born wing-threequarter, scored 80 tries in 42 matches in the 1913–14 season.

Most tries *Career*

Brian Bevan (b. Australia, 24 Apr 1924), a wing-threequarter, scored 796 tries in 18 seasons (16 with Warrington, two with Blackpool Borough) from 1946 to 1964. He scored 740 for Warrington, 17 for Blackpool and 39 in representative matches.

Most goals *Season*

The record number of goals in a season is 221 by David Watkins (b. 5 Mar 1942) (Salford) in the 1972–3 season. His total was made up in League, Cup, other competitions, and a Salford v. New Zealand match.

Most points *Career*

Jim Sullivan (Wigan) kicked 2859 goals in his club and representative career, 1921–46.

Most consecutive scores

David Watkins (Salford) played and scored in every club game during seasons 1972–3 and 1973–4; contributing 41 tries and 403 goals—a total of 929 points, in 92 games.

Individual international records

Jim Sullivan (Wigan) played in most internationals (60 for Wales and Great Britain) kicked most goals (160) and scored most points (329).

Mick Sullivan (no kin) (b. 12 Jan 1934) of Huddersfield, Wigan, St Helens and York played in 51 international games for England and Great Britain and scored a record 45 tries.

Most Challenge Cup Finals

Eric Batten (Leeds, Bradford Northern and Featherstone Rovers) played in a record eight Challenge Cup Finals including war-time guest appearances between 1941 and 1952 and was on four winning sides.

Seven players have been in four Challenge Cup winning sides—Alan Edwards, Eric Batten, Alex Murphy, Brian Lockwood, Mick Adams, Keith Elwell and Eric Hughes. Alan Edwards was the only one to do so with four different clubs, Salford 1938, Leeds 1942, Dewsbury 1943, Bradford Northern 1949.

Youngest player

Harold Wagstaff (1891–1939) played his first League game for Huddersfield at 15 yr 175 days, for Yorkshire at 17 yr 141 days, and for England at 17 yr 228 days.

The youngest player in a Cup Final was Shaun Edwards (b. 17 Oct 1966) at 17 yr 201 days for Wigan when they lost 6–19 to Widnes at Wembley on 5 May 1984. He became the youngest Great Britain international when he played against France at Headingley, Leeds on 1 Mar 1985 at 18 yr 135 days.

Most durable player

The most appearances for one club is 769 by Jim Sullivan for Wigan, 1921–46. He played a record 921 first class games in all. The longest continuous playing career is that of Augustus John 'Gus' Risman (b. Cardiff 21 Mar 1911) who played his first game for Salford on 31 August 1929 and his last for Batley on 27 December 1954.

Keith Elwell (b. 12 Feb 1950) played in 239 consecutive games for Widnes from May 1977 to September 1982. In his career, 1972–85, he received a record 28 winners' or runners-up medals in the major competitions.

Most and least successful teams

Wigan won 31 consecutive league games from February 1970 to February 1971. Hull won all 26 League Division II matches in the 1978–9 season. Doncaster hold the record of losing 40 consecutive League games from 16 Nov 1975 to 21 Apr 1977.

Record transfer fees

The highest RL transfer fee is £72,500 paid to Wigan for fullback George H. Fairbairn (b. 27 July 1954) by Hull Kingston Rovers on 7 June 1981.

Greatest crowds

The greatest attendance at any Rugby League match is 102,569 for the Warrington v. Halifax Challenge Cup Final replay at Odsal Stadium, Bradford, on 5 May 1954.

The record attendance for any international match is 70,204 for the Test between Australia and England on the Sydney Cricket Ground on 6 June 1932. The highest international attendance in Britain is 43,500 for the Test between Great Britain and Australia at Odsal Stadium, Bradford on 29 January 1949.

FOOTBALL (RUGBY UNION)

See also The Guinness Book of Rugby Facts and Feats (*2nd edition*) by Terry Godwin, published in 1983 at £8.95.

Records are determined in terms of present day scoring values, i.e. a try at 4 points; a dropped goal, penalty or goal from a mark at 3 points; and a conversion at 2 points. The actual *score, in accordance with which ever of the eight earlier systems was in force at the time, is also given, in brackets.*

Origins

Though there are records of a game with many similarities to Rugby dating back to the Roman occupation, the game is traditionally said to have originated from a breach of the rules of the football played in November 1823 at Rugby School by William Webb Ellis (later the Rev) (c. 1807–72). This handling code of football evolved gradually and was known to have been played at Cambridge University by 1839. The Rugby Football Union was founded on 26 Jan 1871.

INTERNATIONAL CHAMPIONSHIP

The International Championship was first contested by England, Ireland, Scotland and Wales in 1884. France first played in 1910.

Most wins

Wales have won a record 21 times outright and tied for first a further ten times. Since 1910 Wales have 15 wins and 9 ties and England 15 wins and 7 ties.

Highest team score

The highest score in an International Championship match was set in 1910 when Wales beat France 49–14 or 59–16 on present day scoring values (8 goals, 1 penalty goal, 2 tries to 1 goal, 2 penalty goals, 1 try).

Season's scoring

Jean-Patrick Lescarboura (France) (b. 12 Mar 1961) scored a record 54 points (10 penalty goals, 6 conversions, 4 dropped goals) in 1984.

Individual match records

W. J. Bancroft kicked a record 9 goals (8 conversions and 1 penalty goal) for Wales v. France at Swansea on 1910.

HIGHEST TEAM SCORES

Internationals

The highest score in any full International was when France beat Spain by 92 points (including 19 tries) to nil at Oléron, France on 4 Mar 1979.

The highest aggregate score for any International match between the Four Home Unions is 69 when England beat Wales by 69 points (7 goals, 1 drop goal and 6 tries) to 0 at Blackheath, London in 1881. (Note: there was no point scoring in 1881.)

The highest score by any Overseas side in an International in the British Isles is 53 points (7 goals, 1 drop goal and 2 tries) to 0 when South Africa beat Scotland at Murrayfield, Edinburgh, on 24 Nov 1951 (44–0).

Tour match

The record score for any international tour match is 125–0 (17 goals, 5 tries and 1 penalty goal) (103–0) when New Zealand beat Northern New South Wales at Quirindi, Australia, on 30 May 1962. The highest under scoring in use for the game is 117–6 for New Zealand's defeat of South Australia on 1 May 1974.

Match

In Denmark, Comet beat Lindo by 194–0 on 17 Nov 1973. The highest British score is 174–0 by 7th Signal Regiment v. 4 Armoured Workshop, REME, on 5 Nov 1980 at Herford, W. Germany. Scores of over 200 points have been recorded in school matches, for example Radford School beat Hills Court 214 points (31 goals and 7 tries) to 0 (200–0) on 20 Nov 1886.

Season

The highest number of points accumulated in a season by a rugby club is 1607 points by Pontypool, Gwent in 1983–4. The record number of tries is 269 by Bridgend, Glamorgan, 1983–4.

HIGHEST INDIVIDUAL SCORES

Internationals

Colin Mair scored 30 points (9 conversions, 4 penalty goals) for Scotland v. Japan at Tokyo on 18 Sept 1977. The highest individual points score in any match between members of the International Board is 26 by Alan Hewson (b. 1953) (1 try, 2 conversions, 5 penalty goals and a drop goal) for New Zealand against Australia at Auckland on 11 Sept 1982.

Ian Scott Smith (Scotland) (1903–72) scored a record six consecutive international tries in 1925; comprised of the last three v. France and two weeks later, the first three v. Wales. His 24 tries, 1924–33, is the record for an international career.

The most points scored in an international career is 301 by Andrew Robertson Irvine (Heriots) (b. 16 Sept 1951), 273 for Scotland (including 12 v. Romania) and 28 for the British Lions from 1973 to 1982.

Season

The first class rugby scoring record for a season is 581 points by Samuel Arthur Doble (1944–77) of Moseley, in 52 matches in 1971–2. He also scored 47 points for England in South Africa out of season.

Career

William Henry 'Dusty' Hare (b. 29 Nov 1952) of Leicester, scored 5571 points in first class games from 1971–85, comprising 1800 for Nottingham, 2876 for Leicester, 240 for England, 88 for the British Lions and 567 in other representative matches.

Match

Jannie van der Westhuizen scored 80 points (14 tries, 9 conversions, 1 dropped goal, 1 penalty goal) for Carnarvon (88) v. Williston (12) at North West Cape, S. Africa on 11 March 1972. In a junior house match in February 1967 at William Ellis School, Edgware, Greater London, between Cumberland and Nunn, Thanos Morphitis, 12, contributed 90 points (13 tries and 19 conversions) (77) to Cumberland's winning score.

All-rounder

Canadian international, Barrie Burnham, scored all possible ways—try, conversion, penalty goal, drop goal, goal from mark—for Meralomas v. Georgians (20–11) at Vancouver, BC, on 26 Feb 1966.

Most International Appearances

The following totals are limited to matches between the seven member countries of the 'International Rugby Football Board' and France. Including 12 appearances for the British Lions, Mike Gibson has played in 81 international matches. Willie John McBride (b. Co. Antrim, 6 June 1940) made a record 17 appearances for the British Lions, as well as 63 for Ireland.

Youngest International

Edinburgh Academy pupils Ninian Jamieson Finlay (1858–1936) and Charles Reid (1864–1909) were both 17 yr 36 days old when they played for Scotland v. England in 1875 and 1881 respectively. However, as Finlay had one less leap year in his lifetime up to his first cap, the outright record must be credited to him. Daniel Brendan Carroll (b. 17 Feb 1892) was aged only 16 yr 149 days when he played for Australia in the 1908 Olympic Games Rugby tournament — not considered to be a 'full' international.

County Championships

The County Championships (inst. 1889) have been won most often by Gloucestershire with 15 titles (1910, 1913, 1920–2, 1930–2, 1937, 1972, 1974–6 and 1983–4). The most individual appearances is 104 by Richard Trickey (Sale) (b. 6 Mar 1945) for Lancashire between 1964 and 1978.

Club Championships

The most outright wins in the RFU Club Competition (John Player Cup, inst. 1971–2) is three by Leicester, 1979–81. Gloucester won in 1972 and 1978 and shared the Cup in 1982.

The most wins in the Welsh Rugby Union Challenge Cup (Schweppes Welsh Cup, inst. 1971–2) is five by Llanelli, 1973–6 and 1985. The most wins in the Scottish League Division One (inst. 1973–4) is eight by Hawick, 1973–4 to 1977–8, 1981–2 and 1983–5.

Seven-a-sides *Origins*

Seven-a-side rugby dates from 28 Apr 1883 when Melrose RFC Borders, in order to alleviate the poverty of a club in such a small town, staged a seven-a-side tournament. The idea was that of Ned Haig, the town's butcher.

Middlesex Seven-a-sides

The Middlesex Seven-a-sides were inaugurated in 1926. The most wins is nine by Richmond (inc. once by their second Seven) (1951, 1953, 1955, 1974–5, 1977, 1979–80, 1983).

Greatest crowd

The record paying attendance is 104,000 for Scotland's 12–10 win over Wales at Murrayfield, Edinburgh, on 1 Mar 1975.

Highest posts

The world's highest Rugby Union goal posts are 110 ft ½ in *33,54 m* high at the Roan Antelope Rugby Union Club, Luanshya, Zambia. The posts at Brixham RFC, Devonshire, are 57 ft *17,37 m* high with an additional 1 ft *0,30 m* spike.

Longest kicks

The longest recorded successful drop-goal is 90 yd *82 m* by Gerald Hamilton 'Gerry' Brand (b. 8 Oct 1906) for South Africa v. England at Twickenham, Greater London, on 2 Jan 1932. This was taken 7 yd *6 m* inside the England 'half' 55 yd *50 m* from the posts and dropped over the dead ball line.

The place kick record is reputed to be 100 yd *91 m* at Richmond Athletic Ground, Greater London, by Douglas Francis Theodore Morkel (b. 1886) in an unsuccessful penalty for South Africa v. Surrey on 19 Dec 1906. This was not measured until 1932. In the match Bridlington School 1st XV v. an Army XV at Bridlington, Humberside on 29 Jan 1944, Ernie Cooper (b. 21 May 1926), captaining the school, landed a penalty from a measured 81 yd *74 m* from the post with a kick which carried over the dead ball line.

MOST INTERNATIONAL APPEARANCES

Country	Caps	Name	Years
Ireland	69	Cameron Michael Henderson Gibson (b. 3 Dec 1942)	1964–79
New Zealand	55	Colin Earl Meads (b. 3 June 1936)	1957–71
Wales	55	John Peter Rhys 'JPR' Williams (b. 2 Mar 1949)	1969–81
France	52	Roland Bertranne (b. 6 Dec 1949) (in all—69)	1971–81
Scotland	51	Andrew R. Irvine (b. 16 Sept 1951)	1973–82
	51	James Menzies 'Jim' Renwick (b. 12 Feb 1952)	1972–83
England	43	Anthony Neary (b. 25 Nov 1948)	1971–80
Australia	39	Peter G. Johnson (b. 3 Nov 1938)	1958–72
	39	Gregory Victor Davis (1939–81)	1963–72
South Africa	38	Frederick Christoffel Hendrick Du Preez (b. 28 Nov 1935)	1960–71
	38	Jan Hendrik Ellis (b. 5 Jan 1943)	1965–76

J. P. R. Williams, for 13 years a stalwart for Wales. *(All-Sport)*

Fastest try

The fastest try in an international game was when H. L. 'Bart' Price scored for England *v.* Wales at Twickenham on 20 Jan 1923 less than 10 sec after kick off.

Most tries

Alan Morley (b. 25 June 1950) has scored 447 tries in senior rugby in 1968–85 including 355 for Bristol, a record for one club. John Huins scored 85 tries in 1953–4, 73 for St Luke's College, Exeter and 12 more for Neath and in trial games.

Longest try

The longest 'try' ever executed is by a team of 15, from Power-House RUFC, Victoria, Australia, who ran a try of 1470.6 miles *2366,7 km* on 4–13 Mar 1983 around Albert Park Lake, Victoria. There were no forward passes or knock-ons, and the ball was touched down between the posts in the prescribed manner (Law 12).

Most successful team

The Leamington Spa junior team played 92 successive games without defeat from 6 Oct 1980 to 13 Apr 1984.

GAMBLING

World's biggest win

The world's biggest individual gambling win is $40 million by Mike Wittkowski in the Illinois State Lottery, announced on 3 Sep 1984. From $35 worth of 'Lotto' tickets bought by his family, the winning six numbers will bring him $2 million annually for 20 years.

World's biggest loss

An unnamed Italian industrialist was reported to have lost £800,000 in 5 hr at roulette in Monte Carlo, Monaco on 6 Mar 1974. A Saudi Arabian prince was reported to have lost more than $1 million in a single session at the Metro Club, Las Vegas, USA in December 1974.

*Dennis Turner (*left*) won £937,807, the record pools jackpot, and was presented with his cheque by actor Howard Keel. It was Mr Turner's first time of winning after 25 years of filling in coupons. He had placed a 36p stake.*

Largest casino

The largest casino in the world is the Resorts International Casino, Atlantic City, NJ, USA. It reported a record month in July 1983 with winnings of $29.3 million. The Casino comprises 60,000 ft² *5574 m²*, containing 127 gaming tables and 1640 slot machines. Attendances total over 35,000 daily at peak weekends.

BINGO

Bingo is a lottery game which, as keno, was developed in the 1880s from lotto, whose origin is thought to be the 17th century Italian game *tumbule.* It has long been known in the British Army (called Housey-Housey) and the Royal Navy (called Tombola). The winner was the first to complete a random selection of numbers from 1 to 90. The USA version called Bingo differs in that the selection is from 1 to 75. There are six million players in the United Kingdom.

Largest house

The largest 'house' in Bingo sessions was 15,756 at the Canadian National Exhibition, Toronto on 19 Aug 1983. Staged by the Variety Club of Ontario Tent #28, there was total prize money of $C250,000 with a record one-game payout of $C100,000.

Earliest and latest Full House

A 'Full House' call occurred on the 15th number by Norman A. Wilson at Guide Post Workingmen's Club, Bedlington, Northumberland on 22 June 1978, by Anne Wintle of Brynrethin, Mid Glamorgan, on a coach trip to Bath on 17 Aug 1982 and by Shirley Lord at Kahibah Bowling Club, New South Wales, Australia on 24 Oct 1983. 'House' was not called until the 86th number at the Hillsborough Working Men's Club, Sheffield, S. Yorkshire on 11 Jan 1982. There were 32 winners.

ELECTIONS

The highest ever individual bet was £90,000 to win £20,000 for the Conservative party to return the most MPs in the 1983 General Election, by an unnamed man. A bet of £5000 at 200–1 was placed by Frank Egerton in April 1975 that his political Centre Party would win the next General Election. It didn't.

FOOTBALL POOLS

Two unnamed punters won *c.* £1.5 million each in November 1972 on the state run Italian pools. The winning dividend paid out by Littlewoods Pools in their first week in February 1923 was £2 12s 0d (*£2.60*). In 1983–84 the three British Pools companies which comprise the Pool Promoters Association (Littlewoods, Vernons and Zetters) had a total record turnover of £473,331,500 of which Littlewoods contributed over 70%.

Biggest win

The greatest sum won from the British Pools is £953,874.10 by David Preston, 47, of Burton-on-Trent, Staffs, on 23 Feb 1980. This total comprised £804,573.35 from Littlewoods Pools and £149,300.75 from Vernons Pools. On 13 Apr 1985 Dennis Turner from Burslem, Staffs. won £937,807 for a 36 p stake on Littlewoods Pools for the largest cheque ever paid by one company.

The record payout to two people is £1,561,146.36 by Littlewoods on 1 December 1984—the first time two £¾ million cheques were paid in a single week. The winners were Mr. 'Cec' Carr and 33 workmates from a City of London bank who collected £784,411.26, and park constable Syd Barnard, of Brighton, who won £776,735.10. On 27 March 1985, Littlewoods paid a record treble—the first time three people each won over £½ million each. They were: Mrs. Patricia

Samways, of Dorchester, Dorset, who collected £574,847.55; Kevin Adams and seven friends, of Sunderland, Tyne & Wear, with £513,805.23 and George Pinnock, of Colchester, Essex, who received £512,138.19—a record total of £1,600,790.97. Littlewoods record total payout in one week is £2,345,545 on 2 April 1985.

The odds for selecting 8 draws (if there are only 8 draws) from 55 matches for an all-correct line are 1,217,566.350 to 1 against. (In practice, the approximate odds of winning a dividend of any size on Littlewoods Pools are 80 to 1.)

HORSE RACING

Highest ever odds

The highest secured odds were 1,670,759 to 1 by George Rhodes of Aldershot, Hampshire. For a 5p bet, with a 10% bonus for the 'ITV Seven', less tax, he was paid £86,056.42 by the William Hill Organisation on 30 Sept 1984. Edward Hodson of Wolverhampton landed a 3,956,748 to 1 bet for a 55p stake on 11 Feb 1984, but his bookmaker had a £3000 payout limit. The world record odds on a 'double' are 31,793 to 1 paid by the New Zealand Totalisator Agency Board on a five shilling tote ticket on *Red Emperor* and *Maida Dillon* at Addington, Christchurch, in 1951.

Greatest pay-out

A group of punters won $764,283 for a $1 bet at Sportsman's Park, Chicago in March 1985. The bet involved selecting the first two horses in order in two races and the first three in a third. The largest payout by a British bookmaker is £185,640 by Corals, paid to Ernie Platt for a £10 Ante-Post Accumulator (tax paid) placed on 14 Dec 1984 and collected on 4 May 1985.

Biggest tote win

The best recorded tote win was one of £341 2s 6d to 2s (*£341.12½ to 10p*) representing odds of 3,410½ to 1, by Catharine Unsworth of Blundellsands, Liverpool at Haydock Park on a race won by *Coole* on 30 Nov 1929. The highest odds in Irish tote history were £289.64 for 10p unit on *Gene's Rogue* at Limerick on 28 Dec 1981.

Largest bookmaker

The world's largest bookmaker is Ladbrokes of London with a turnover from gambling in 1984 of £787 million. The largest chain of betting shops is that of Ladbrokes with 1416 shops in the United Kingdom at the end of 1984.

Topmost tipster

The only recorded instance of a racing correspondent forecasting ten out of ten winners on a race card was at Delaware Park, Wilmington, Delaware, USA on 28 July 1974 by Charles Lamb of the *Baltimore News American.*

JAI-ALAI

The highest parimutuel payout in the USA was for a group of punters who won $988,326 (less $197,664 paid to the Internal Revenue) for a $2 ticket naming six consecutive winning Jai-Alai players at Palm Beach, Florida on 1 Mar 1983.

ROULETTE

The longest run on an ungaffed (*i.e.* true) wheel reliably recorded is six successive coups (in No. 10) at El San Juan Hotel, Puerto Rico on 9 July 1959. The odds with a double zero were 1 in 38⁶ or 3,010,936,383 to 1.

SLOT MACHINES

The biggest beating handed to a 'one-armed bandit' was $2,478,716.15 by Rocco Dinubilo from Fresno, California at Harrah's Tahoe Casino, Nevada, USA on 31 Dec 1983.

GLIDING

Origins
Isadore William Deiches has researched evidence of the use of gliders in Ancient Egypt c. 2500–1500 BC. Emanuel Swedenborg (1688–1772) of Sweden made sketches of gliders c. 1714. The earliest man-carrying glider was designed by Sir George Cayley (1773–1857) and carried his coachman (possibly John Appleby) about 500 yd *457 m* across a valley in Brompton Dale, North Yorkshire in the summer of 1853.

Most titles *World*
The most World individual championships (inst. 1948) won is three by Helmut Reichmann (b. 1942) (W. Germany) in 1970 and 1974 (Standard class), 1978 (15 metre class) and by Douglas George Lee (GB) (b. 7 Nov 1945) in 1976, 1978 and 1981 (all Open class).

Most titles *British*
The British national championship (inst. 1939) has been won six times by Ralph Jones (b. 29 Mar 1936). The first woman to win this title was Anne Burns (b. 23 Nov. 1915) of Farnham, Surrey on 30 May 1966.

Altitude Records *Women*
The women's single-seater world record for absolute altitude is 12 637 m *41,449 ft* by Sabrina Jackintell (USA) in an Astir GS on 14 Feb 1979. The British single-seater record is 8701 m *28,539 ft* by Alison Jordan in an Astir CS on 8 Oct 1978.

GLIDING—SELECTED WORLD RECORDS
(*Single-seaters*)

DISTANCE	907.7 miles *1460,8 km*	Hans-Werner Grosse (W. Germany) in an ASW-12 on 25 Apr 1972 from Lübeck to Biarritz
DECLARED GOAL DISTANCE	779.4 miles *1254,26 km*	Bruce Drake, David Speight, S. H. 'Dick' Georgeson (all NZ) all in Nimbus 2s, Te Anau to Te Araroa, 14 Jan 1978
GOAL AND RETURN	1023.2 miles *1646,68 km*	Tom Knauff (USA) in a Nimbus 3 from Williamsport, Pennsylvania to Knoxville, Tennessee on 25 April 1983
ABSOLUTE ALTITUDE	46,266 ft *14 102 m*	Paul F. Bikle, Jr (USA) in a Schweizer SGS 1-23E over Mojave, California on 25 Feb 1961
ALTITUDE GAIN	42,303 ft *12 894 m*	Paul Bikle on 25 Feb 1961 (see above)

SPEED OVER TRIANGULAR COURSE

100 km	121.35 mph *195,30 km/h*	Ingo Renner (Australia) in a Nimbus 3 on 14 Dec 1982
300 km	100.78 mph *162,19 km/h*	Hans-Werner Grosse (W. Germany) in an ASW-22 over Australia on 9 Dec 1984
500 km	99.20 mph *159,64 km/h*	Hans-Werner Grosse (W. Germany) in an ASW-22 on 20 Dec 1983
750 km	98.58 mph *158,65 km/h*	Hans-Werner Grosse (W. Germany) in an ASW-22 over Australia on 8 Jan 1985
1000 km	90.29 mph *145,32 km/h*	Hans-Werner Grosse (W. Germany) in an ASW-17 over Australia on 3 Jan 1979
1250 km	82.79 mph *133,24 km/h*	Hans-Werner Grosse (W. Germany) in an ASW-17 over Australia on 9 Dec 1980

BRITISH NATIONAL RECORDS[1]
(*Single-seaters*)

589.9 miles *949,7 km*		Karla Karel in a LS-3 over Australia on 20 Jan 1980
360 miles *579,36 km*		H. C. N. Goodhart in a Skylark 3, Lasham, Hants, to Portmoak, Scotland on 10 May 1959
621.9 miles *1000,88 km*		William Malpas in a Mini-Nimbus, State College, Pa. to Bluefield, Va., USA on 28 Sept 1981
37,729 ft *11 500 m*		H. C. N. Goodhart in a Schweizer 1-23 over California, USA on 12 May 1955
33,022 ft *10 065 m*		D. Benton in a Nimbus 2 on 18 Apr 1980
88.99 mph *143,3 km/h*		E. Paul Hodge in a Standard Cirrus over Rhodesia on 30 Oct 1976
91.2 mph *146,8 km/h*		Edward Pearson in a Nimbus 2 over S.W. Africa on 30 Nov 1976
87.8 mph *141,3 km/h*		Bradley James Grant Pearson in an ASW-20 over South Africa on 28 Dec 1982
68.2 mph *109,8 km/h*		Michael R. Carlton in a Kestrel 19 over South Africa on 5 Jan 1975

[1] *British National Records may be set up by British pilots in any part of the world.*

HANG GLIDING

Origins
In the eleventh century the monk, Eilmer, is reported to have flown from the 60 ft *18,3 m* tower of Malmesbury Abbey, Wiltshire. The earliest modern pioneer was Otto Lilienthal (1848–96) (Germany) with about 2500 flights in gliders of his own construction between 1891 and 1896. In the 1950s Professor Francis Rogallo of the National Space Agency, USA, developed a flexible 'wing' from his space capsule re-entry researches.

Championships
The World Team Championships have been won most often by Great Britain (1978–9, 1981, 1985).

Greatest distance
The official FAI record is 300,62 kms *186.80 miles* by John Pendry (GB) flying an Airwave Magic 3 from Horseshoe Meadows, Owens Valley, California to Summit Mtn., Monitop Range, Nevada, USA on 13 July 83. The Womens official FAI record is 233,90 km *145.34 miles* by Judy Leden (GB) flying a Wills Wing Duck 160 from Horseshoe Meadows, Owens Valley, California to Luning, Nevada, USA on 13 July 1983. The British best is 209,20 km *130 miles* by John Pendry, flying a Magic 3 from Ditchling, West Sussex to Colyton near Seaton, Devon in April 84.

Greatest ascent
The official FAI height gain record is 4175 m *13,700 ft* by Ian Kibblewhite (New Zealand) in a Lightning 195 at Cerro Gordo, Owens Valley, California, USA on 22 July 1981. The British record is 3230 m *10,600 ft* by John Stirk at Wether Fell, North Yorkshire on 6 July 1984.

A breath-taking view for Judy Leden during her successful attempt on the women's world record for distance travelled in a straight line in a hang glider. The picture was taken at 18,000 ft *5486 m*, and is over Boundary Peak on the California-Nevada border.

The atmosphere of the British Open; Tom Watson, record holder for the 72 hole aggregate, approaches the 72nd during 1983 tournament. *(All-Sport)*

GOLF

See also The Guinness Book of Golf Facts and Feats (2nd edition) *by Donald Steel, published at £8.95.*

Origins
Although a stained glass window in Gloucester Cathedral, dating from 1350, portrays a golfer-like figure, the earliest mention of golf occurs in a prohibiting law passed by the Scottish Parliament in March 1457 under which 'goff be utterly cryit doune and not usit'. The Romans had a cognate game called *paganica* which may have been carried to Britain before AD 400. The Chinese Nationalist Golf Association claim the game is of Chinese origin ('*Ch'ui Wan*—the ball hitting game') in the 3rd or 2nd century BC. There were official ordinances prohibiting a ball game with clubs in Belgium and Holland from 1360. Gutta percha balls succeeded feather balls in 1848 and by 1902 were in turn succeeded by rubber-cored balls, invented in 1899 by Coburn Haskell (USA). Steel shafts were authorised in the USA in 1925 and in Britain in 1929.

Club *Oldest*
The oldest club of which there is written evidence is the Gentlemen Golfers (now the Honourable Company of Edinburgh Golfers) formed in March 1744—ten years prior to the institution of the Royal and Ancient Club of St Andrews, Fife. However the Royal Burgess Golfing Society of Edinburgh claim to have been founded in 1735.

Course *Highest*
The highest golf course in the world is the Tuctu Golf Club in Morococha, Peru, which is 4369 m *14,335 ft* above sea-level at its lowest point. Golf has, however, been played in Tibet at an altitude of over 4875 m *16,000 ft*.

The highest golf course in Great Britain is one of nine holes at Leadhills, Strathclyde, 1500 ft *457 m* above sea-level.

Longest hole
The longest hole in the world is the 7th hole (par-7) of the Sano Course, Satsuki GC, Japan, which measures 831 m *909 yd*. In August 1927 the sixth hole at Prescott Country Club in Arkansas, USA, measured 838 yd *766 m*. The longest hole on a championship course in Great Britain is the sixth at Troon, Strathclyde, which stretches 577 yd *528 m*.

Largest green
Probably the largest green in the world is that of the par-6 695 yd *635 m* fifth hole at International GC, Bolton, Massachusetts, USA, with an area greater than 28,000 ft² *2600 m²*.

Biggest bunker
The world's biggest bunker (called a trap in the USA) is Hell's Half Acre on the 585 yd *535 m* seventh hole of the Pine Valley course, Clementon, New Jersey, USA, built in 1912 and generally regarded as the world's most trying course.

Longest course
The world's longest course is the par-77 8325 yd *7612 m* International GC, (*see also above*), from the 'Tiger' tees, remodelled in 1969 by Robert Trent Jones. Floyd Satterlee Rood used the United States as a course, when he played from the Pacific surf to the Atlantic surf from 14 Sept 1963 to 3 Oct 1964 in 114,737 strokes. He lost 3511 balls on the 3397.7 mile *5468 km* trail.

Longest drives
In long-driving contests 330 yd *300 m* is rarely surpassed at sea-level. In officially regulated long driving contests over level ground the greatest distance recorded is 392 yd *358 m* by William Thomas 'Tommie' Campbell (b. 24 July 1927) (Foxrock Golf Club) at Dun Laoghaire, Co. Dublin, in July 1964.

On an airport runway Liam Higgins (Ireland) drove a Spalding Top Flite ball 579,8 m *634.1 yd* at Baldonnel military airport, Dublin, Ireland on 25 Sept 1984. The greatest recorded drive on an ordinary course is one of 515 yd *471 m* by Michael Hoke Austin (b. 17 Feb 1910) of Los Angeles, California, USA, in the US National Seniors Open Championship at Las Vegas, Nevada, on 25 Sept 1974. Austin, 6 ft 2 in *1,88 m* tall and weighing 210 lb *92 kg* drove the ball to within a yard of the green on the par-4 450 yd *412 m* fifth hole of the Winterwood Course and it rolled 65 yd *59 m* past the flagstick. He was aided by an estimated 35 mph *56 km/h* tailwind.

A drive of 2640 yd (1½ miles) *2414 m* across ice was achieved by an Australian meteorologist named Nils Lied at Mawson Base, Antarctica, in 1962. Arthur Lynskey claimed a drive of 200 yd *182 m* horizontal and 2 miles *3200 m* vertical off Pikes Peak, Colorado (14,110 ft *4300 m*) on 28 June 1968. On the moon the energy expended on a mundane 300 yd *274 m* drive would achieve, craters permitting, a distance of 1 mile *1,6 km*.

Longest putt
The longest recorded holed putt in a major tournament was one of 86 ft *26 m* on the vast 13th green at the Augusta National, Georgia by Cary Middlecoff (b. 6 Jan 1921) (USA) in the 1955 Masters' Tournament. Robert Tyre 'Bobby' Jones Jr (1902–71) was reputed to have holed a putt in excess of 100 ft *30 m* at the fifth green in the first round of the 1927 Open at St. Andrews.

SCORES

Lowest 9 holes and 18 holes *Men*
At least four players are recorded to have played a long course (over 6000 yd *5486 m*) in a score of 58, most recently Monte Carlo Money (USA) (b. 3 Dec 1954) the par-72, 6607 yd *6041 m* Las Vegas Municipal GC, Nevada, USA on 11 Mar 1981. The lowest recorded score on a long course in Britain is 58 by Harry Weetman (1920–72) the British Ryder Cup golfer, for the 6171 yd *5642 m* Croham Hurst Course, Croydon, Surrey, on 30 Jan 1956. Alfred Edward Smith (1903–85) the Woolacombe professional, achieved an 18-hole score of 55 (15 under bogey 70) on his home course on 1 Jan 1936. The course measured 4248 yd *3884 m*. The detail was 4, 2, 3, 4, 2, 4, 3, 4, 3 = 29 out, and 2, 3, 3, 3, 3, 2, 5, 4, 1 = 26 in.

Nine holes in 25 (4, 3, 3, 2, 3, 3, 1, 4, 2) was recorded by A. J. 'Bill' Burke in a round in 57 (32 + 25) on the 6389 yd *5842 m* par-71 Normandie course St Louis, Missouri, USA on 20 May 1970. The tournament record is 27 by Mike Souchak (USA) (b. 10 May 1927) for the second nine (par-35) first round of the 1955 Texas Open (*see 72 holes*), Andy North (USA) (b. 9 Mar 1950) second nine (par-34), first round, 1975 BC Open at En-Joie GC, Endicott, NY, José Maria Canizares (Spain) (b. 18 Feb 1947), first nine, third round, in the 1978 Swiss Open on the 6811 yd *6228 m* Crans-Sur course and by Robert Lee (GB) (b. 12 Oct 1961) first nine, first round, in the Monte Carlo Open on the 5714 m *6249 yd* Mont Agel course on 28 June 1985.

The United States PGA tournament record for 18 holes is 59 (30 + 29) by Al Geiberger (b. 1 Sept 1937) in the second round of the Danny Thomas Classic, on the 72-par 7249 yd *6628 m* Colonial GC course, Memphis, Tennessee on 10 June 1977. Three golfers have recorded 59 over 18 holes in non-PGA tournaments; Samuel Jackson Snead (b. 27 May 1912) in the third round of the Sam Snead Festival at White Sulphur Springs, West Virginia, USA on 16 May 1959; Gary Player (South Africa) (b. 1 Nov 1935) in the second round of the Brazilian Open in Rio de Janeiro on 29 Nov 1974, and David Jagger (GB) (b. 9 June 1949) in a Pro-Am tournament prior to the 1973 Nigerian Open at Ikoyi Golf Club, Lagos.

Lowest 18 holes *Women*
The lowest recorded score on an 18-hole course (over 6000 yd *5486 m*) for a woman is 62 (30 + 32) by Mary 'Mickey' Kathryn Wright (b. 14 Feb 1935) (USA) on the Hogan Park Course (par-71, 6286 yd *5747 m*) at Midland, Texas, USA, in November 1964. Wanda Morgan (b. 22 Mar 1910) recorded a score of 60 (31 + 29) on the Westgate and Birchington Golf Club course, Kent, over 18 holes (5002 yd *4573 m*) on 11 July 1929.

Lowest 18 holes *Great Britain*
The lowest score recorded in a first class professional tournament on a course of more than 6000 yd *5486 m* in Great Britain is 61 (29 + 32), by Thomas Bruce Haliburton (1915–75) of Wentworth GC in the Spalding Tournament at Worthing, West Sussex, in June 1952, and 61 (32 + 29) by Peter J. Butler (b. 25 Mar 1932) in the Bowmaker Tournament on the Old Course at Sunningdale, Berkshire, on 4 July 1967.

Lowest 36 holes
The record for 36 holes is 122 (59 + 63) by Sam Snead in the 1959 Sam Snead Festival on 16–17 May 1959. Horton Smith (1908–1963), twice US Masters Champion, scored 121 (63 + 58) on a short course on 21 Dec 1928 (*see 72 holes*). The lowest score by a British golfer has been 124 (61 + 63) by Alexander Walter Barr 'Sandy'

Golf

Lyle (b. 9 Feb 1958) in the Nigerian Open at the 6024 yd *5508 m* (par-71) Ikoyi Golf Club, Lagos in 1978.

Lowest 72 holes

The lowest recorded score on a first-class course is 255 (29 under par) by Leonard Peter Tupling (b. 6 Apr 1950) (GB) in the Nigerian Open at Ikoyi Golf Club, Lagos in February 1981, made up of 63, 66, 62 and 64 (average 63.75 per round).

The lowest 72 holes in a US professional event is 257 (60, 68, 64, 65) by Mike Souchak in the 1955 Texas Open at San Antonio.

The lowest 72 holes in an Open championship in Europe is 262 (67, 66, 66, 63) by Percy Alliss (GB) (1897–1975) in the 1932 Italian Open at San Remo, and by Lu Liang Huan (Taiwan) (b. 10 Dec 1935) in the 1971 French Open at Biarritz. Kelvin D. G. Nagle (b. 21 Dec 1920) of Australia shot 261 in the Hong Kong Open in 1961. The lowest for four rounds in a British first class tournament is 262 (66, 63, 66 and 67) by Bernard Hunt in the Piccadilly tournament on the par-68 6184 yd *5655 m* Wentworth East Course, Virginia Water, Surrey on 4–5 Oct 1966.

Horton Smith scored 245 (63, 58, 61 and 63) for 72 holes on the 4700 yd *4297 m* course (par-64) at Catalina Country Club, California, USA, to win the Catalina Open on 21–23 Dec 1928.

Highest score

The highest score for a single hole in the British Open is 21 by a player in the inaugural meeting at Prestwick in 1860. Double figures have been recorded on the card of the winner only once, when Willie Fernie (1851–1924) scored a ten at Musselburgh, Lothian, in 1883. Ray Ainsley of Ojai, California, took 19 strokes for the par-4 16th hole during the second round of the US Open at Cherry Hills Country Club, Denver, Colorado, on 10 June 1938. Most of the strokes were used in trying to extricate the ball from a brook. Hans Merell of Mogadore, Ohio, took 19 strokes on the par-3 16th (222 yd *203 m*) during the third round of the Bing Crosby National Tournament at Cypress Point Club, Del Monte, California, USA, on 17 Jan 1959. It is recorded that Chevalier von Cittern went round 18 holes in 316, averaging 17.55 per hole, at Biarritz, France in 1888. Steven Ward took 222 strokes for the 6212 yd *5680 m* Pecos Course, Reeves County, Texas, USA, on 18 June 1976—but he was only aged 3 years 286 days.

Most shots for one hole

A woman player in the qualifying round of the Shawnee Invitational for Ladies at Shawnee-on-Delaware, Pennsylvania, USA, in *c.* 1912, took 166 strokes for the short 130 yd *118 m* 16th hole. Her tee shot went into the Binniekill River and the ball floated. She put out in a boat with her exemplary but statistically minded husband at the oars. She eventually beached the ball 1½ miles *2,4 km* downstream but was not yet out of the wood. She had to play through one on the home run. In a competition at Peacehaven, Sussex, England in 1890, A. J. Lewis had 156 putts on one green without holing out.

Rounds fastest *Individual*

With such variations in lengths of courses, speed records, even for rounds under par, are of little comparative value. Rick Baker completed 18 holes (6142 yd *5616 m*) in 25 min 48.47 sec at Surfer's Paradise, Queensland, Australia on 4 Sept 1982, but this test permitted the striking of the ball whilst still moving. The record for a still ball is 28.09 min by Gary Shane Wright (b. 27 Nov 1946) at Tewantin-Noosa Golf Club, Queensland (18 holes, 6039 yd *5522 m*) on 9 Dec 1980.

Bernhard Langer topped the earnings list of the European Order of Merit circuit in 1984 with a record £139,344. *(All-Sport/David Cannon)*

Rounds fastest *Team*

Seventy-seven players completed the 18-hole 6502 yd *5945 m* Kern City course, California, USA in 10 min 30 sec on 24 Aug 1984 using only one ball. They scored 80!

Rounds slowest

The slowest stroke play tournament round was one of 6 hr 45 min taken by South Africa in the first round of the 1972 World Cup at the Royal Melbourne GC, Australia. This was a four-ball medal round, everything holed out.

Most rounds

The greatest number of rounds played on foot in 24 hr is 22 rounds and five holes (401 holes) by Ian Colston, 35, at Bendigo GC, Victoria (par-73, 6061 yd *5542 m*) on 27–28 Nov 1971. The British record is 360 holes by Antony J. Clark at Childwall GC, Liverpool on 18 July 1983. Gaston Gravelle played 326 holes in 12 hours on the 6,499 yd *5940 m* course at Notre-Dame-de-la-Salette, Quebec, Canada on 2 Sept 1984, being driven between shots in a golf cart. Dr R. C. 'Dick' Hardison, aged 61, played 236 holes under USGA rules in 12 hours at Sea Mountain GC, Punalina, Hawaii on 31 July 1984, maintaining an average score of 76 per round, with an average time per hole of 3.05 min. His best round was a 68, achieved in 49 min 58 sec, including a second nine of 30 in 24 min 28 sec. He used seven fore caddies and 26 electric golf carts, which he drove himself. The most holes played on foot in a week (168 hr) is 1128 by Steve Hylton at the Mason Rudolph Golf Club (6060 yd *5541m*), Clarkesville, Tennessee, USA, from 25–31 Aug 1980.

Throwing the golf ball

The lowest recorded score for throwing a golf ball round 18 holes (over 6000 yd or *5500 m*) is 82 by Joe Flynn (USA), 21, at the 6228 yd *5694 m* Port Royal Course, Bermuda, on 27 Mar 1975.

CHAMPIONSHIP RECORDS

The Open

The Open Championship was inaugurated in 1860 at Prestwick, Strathclyde, Scotland. The lowest score for 9 holes is 28 by Denis Durnian (b. 30 June 1950), at Royal Birkdale, Southport, Lancashire in the second round on 15 July 1983.

The lowest round in The Open is 63 by Mark Hayes (b. 12 July 1949) (USA) at Turnberry, Strathclyde, on 7 July 1977, and Isao Aoki (b. 31 Aug 1942) (Japan) at Muirfield, East Lothian, on 19 July 1980. Thomas Henry Cotton (b. 26 Jan 1907) at Royal St George's, Sandwich, Kent completed the first 36 holes in 132 (67 + 65) on 27 June 1934. The lowest 72-hole aggregate is 268 (68, 70, 65, 65) by Tom Watson (b. 4 Sept 1949) (USA) at Turnberry, ending on 9 July 1977.

US Open

The United States Open Championship was

inaugurated in 1895. The lowest 72-hole aggregate is 272 (63, 71, 70, 68) by Jack Nicklaus (b. 21 Jan 1940) on the Lower Course (7015 yd *6414 m*) at Baltusrol Country Club, Springfield, New Jersey, on 12–15 June 1980. The lowest score for 18 holes is 63 by Johnny Miller (b. 29 Apr 1947) on the 6921 yd *6328 m* par-71 Oakmont Country Club course, Pennsylvania on 17 June 1973; by Jack Nicklaus (*see above*) and by Tom Weiskopf (USA) (b. 9 Nov 1942), both on 12 June 1980.

US Masters'

The lowest score in the US Masters' (instituted on the par-72 6980 yd *6382 m* Augusta National Golf Course, Georgia, in 1934) has been 271 by Jack Nicklaus in 1965 and Raymond Floyd (b. 4 Sept 1942) in 1976. The lowest rounds have been 64 by Lloyd Mangrum (1914–74) (first round, 1940), Jack Nicklaus (third round, 1965), Maurice Bembridge (GB) (b. 21 Feb 1945) (fourth round, 1974), Hale Irwin (b. 3 June 1945) (fourth round, 1975), Gary Player (S. Africa) (fourth round, 1978) and Miller Barber (b. 31 Mar 1931) (second round, 1979).

World Cup (formerly Canada Cup)

The World Cup (instituted as the Canada Cup in 1953) has been won most often by the USA with 16 victories between 1955 and 1983. The only men to have been on six winning teams have been Arnold Palmer (b. 10 Sept 1929) (1960, 1962–4, 1966–7) and Jack Nicklaus (1963–4, 1966–7, 1971 and 1973). Only Nicklaus has taken the individual title three times (1963–4, 1971). The lowest aggregate score for 144 holes is 544 by Australia, Bruce Devlin (b. 10 Oct 1937) and David Graham (b. 23 May 1946), at San Isidro, Buenos Aires, Argentina on 12–15 Nov 1970. The lowest individual score has been 269 by Roberto de Vicenzo (Argentina) (b. 14 Apr 1923), also in 1970.

Ryder Cup

The biennial Ryder Cup professional match between USA and the British Isles or Great Britain (Europe since 1979) was instituted in 1927. The USA have won 21½ to 3½ to date. William Earl 'Billy' Casper (b. San Diego, California, USA, 24 June 1931) has the record of winning most matches in the Trophy with 20 in 1961–75. Christy O'Connor Sr (b. 21 Dec 1924) (GB) played in ten matches up to 1973.

Walker Cup

The USA *v.* GB & Ireland series instituted in 1921 (for the Walker Cup since 1922 and now held biennially) has been won by the USA 25½–2½ to date. Joseph Boynton Carr (GB&I) (b. 18 Feb 1922) played in ten contests (1947–67).

Curtis Cup

The biennial ladies' Curtis Cup match between USA and Great Britain and Ireland was first held in 1932. The USA have won 19, GB&I two and two matches have been tied. Mary McKenna (GB&I) (b. 29 Apr 1949) played in a record eighth match in 1984.

Richest prizes

The greatest first place prize money was $500,000 (total purse $1,100,000) won by Johnny Miller in 1982 and Raymond Floyd in 1985, at Sun City, Bophuthatswana, S. Africa. Both won in play-offs, from Severiano Ballesteros and Craig Stadler respectively.

Highest earnings *US PGA and LPGA circuits*

The all time professional money-winner is Jack Nicklaus, with $4,520,824 to 1 Jan 1985. The record for a year is $530,808 by Tom Watson in 1980. The record career earnings for a woman is $1,789,248 from 1970 to 1 Jan 1985 by JoAnne Carner (*née* Gunderson) (b. 4 April 1939). She won a season's record $310,399 in 1982.

Highest earnings *European circuit*

Bernhard Langer (W. Germany) (b. 27 Aug 1957) won a European record £139,344 in European Order of Merit tournaments (£160,882 in all European events) in 1984.

Most tournament wins

The record for winning tournaments in a single season is 18 (plus one unofficial), including a record 11 consecutively, by John Byron Nelson (b. 4 Feb 1912) (USA), from 8 Mar–4 Aug 1945. Sam Snead won 84 official US PGA Tour events 1936–65, and has been credited with a total 134 tournament victories since 1934. The Ladies PGA record is 85 by Kathy Whitworth (b. 27 Sept 1939) from 1962 to 1984.

Biggest winning margin

The greatest margin of victory in a major tournament is 21 strokes by Jerry Pate (b. 16 Sept 1953) (USA) in the Colombian Open with 262 on 10–13 Dec 1981.

Youngest and oldest champions

The youngest winner of The Open was Tom Morris, Jr. (1851–75) at Prestwick, Strathclyde in 1868 aged 17 yr 249 days. The youngest winners of The Amateur title were John Charles Beharrell (b. 2 May 1938) at Troon, Strathclyde, on 2 June 1956, and Robert 'Bobby' E. Cole (b. 11 May 1948) (South Africa) at Carnoustie, Tayside, on 11 June 1966, both aged 18 yr 1 month. The oldest Open Champion was 'Old Tom' Morris (1821–1908), aged 46 yr 99 days

when he won at Prestwick in 1867. In recent times the 1967 champion, Roberto de Vicenzo was aged 44 yr 93 days. The oldest winner of The Amateur was the Hon Michael Scott (1878–1959) at Hoylake, Merseyside in 1933, when 54 yr 297 days. The oldest United States Amateur Champion was Jack Westland (1904–82) at Seattle, Washington, on 23 Aug 1952, aged 47 yr 253 days.

Longest span

Jacqueline Ann Mercer (*née* Smith) (b. 5 Apr 1929) won her first South African title at Humewood GC, Port Elizabeth in 1948, and her fourth at Port Elizabeth GC on 4 May 1979, 31 years later.

Most club championships

Bernard Charles Cusack (b. 24 Jan 1920) has won a record total of 34 Club championships, including 33 consecutively, at the Narembeen GC, Western Australia, between 1943 and 1982. The women's record is 31 by Molly St John Pratt (b. 19 Oct 1912) at the Stanthorpe GC, Queensland, Australia from 1931 to 1979, and also by 67 year old Helen Gray at Todmorden GC, Lancashire between 1951 and 1979. The record for consecutive wins is 22 (1959–80) by Patricia Mary Shepherd (b. 7 Jan 1940) at Turriff GC, Aberdeenshire, Scotland.

Record tie

The longest delayed result in any National Open Championship occurred in the 1931 US Open at Toledo, Ohio. George von Elm (1901–61) and Billy Burke (1902–72) tied at 292, then tied the first replay at 149. Burke won the second replay by a single stroke after 72 extra holes.

Largest tournament

The Volkswagen Grand Prix Open Amateur Championship in the United Kingdom attracted a record 321,779 (206,820 men and 114,958 women) competitors in 1984.

HOLES IN ONE

Longest

The longest straight hole ever holed in one shot is the tenth (447 yd *408 m*) at Miracle Hills Golf Club, Omaha, USA by Robert Mitera (b. 1944) on 7 Oct 1965. Mitera stood 5 ft 6 in *1,68 m* tall and weighed 165 lb *75 kg* (11 st 11 lb). He was a two handicap player who normally drove 245 yd *224 m*. A 50 mph *80 km/h* gust carried his shot over a 290 yd *265 m* drop-off. The longest 'dog-leg' hole achieved in one is the 480 yd *439 m* fifth at Hope Country Club, Arkansas by L. Bruce on 15 Nov 1962. The feminine record is 393 yd *359 m* by Marie Robie on the first hole of the Furnace Brook Golf Club, Wollaston, Mass., USA, on 4 Sept 1949. The longest hole in one performed in the British Isles is the seventh (par-4, 393 yd *359 m*) at West Lancashire GC by Peter Richard Parkinson (b. 26 Aug 1947) on 6 June 1972.

Most

The greatest number of holes-in-one in a career is 66 by Harry Lee Bonner from 1967 to 1983, most at his home 9-hole course of Las Gallinas, San Rafael, California, USA. The British record is 31 by Charles T. Chevalier (1902–73) of Heaton Moor Golf Club, Stockport, Greater Manchester between 20 June 1918 and 1970.

The most holes-in-one in a year is 28 by Scott Palmer from 5 June 1983 to 31 May 1984, all on par –3 or par –4 holes between 130 yd *119 m* and 260 yd *238 m* in length at Ballboa Park, San Diego, California, USA.

Consecutive

There are at least 16 cases of 'aces' being achieved in two consecutive holes, of which the

MOST TITLES *World's major championships:*

The Open	Harry Vardon (1870–1937)	6	1896, 1898–9, 1903, 11,14
The Amateur	John Ball (1861–1940)	8	1888, 90, 92, 94, 99, 1907, 10, 1912
US Open	Willie Anderson (1880–1910)	4	1901, 03–5
	Robert Tyre Jones, Jr. (1902–71)	4	1923, 26, 29–30
	William Ben Hogan (b. 13 Aug 1912)	4	1948, 50–1, 53
	Jack William Nicklaus (b. 21 Jan 1940)	4	1962, 67, 72, 80
US Amateur	Robert Tyre Jones, Jr. (1902–71)	5	1924–5, 27–8, 30
PGA Championship (USA)	Walter Charles Hagan (1892–1969)	5	1921, 24–7
	Jack William Nicklaus (b. 21 Jan 1940)	5	1963, 71, 73, 75, 80
Masters' Championship (USA)	Jack William Nicklaus (b. 21 Jan 1940)	5	1963, 65–6, 72, 75
US Women's Open	Elizabeth 'Betsy' Earle-Rawls (b. 4 May 1928)	4	1951, 53, 57, 60
	'Mickey' Wright (b. 14 Feb 1935)	4	1958–59, 61, 64
US Women's Amateur	Glenna C. Vare (*née* Collett) (b. 20 June 1903)	6	1922, 25, 28–30, 35
British Women's	Charlotte Cecilia Pitcairn Leitch (1891–1977)	4	1914, 20–1, 26
	Joyce Wethered (b. 17 Nov 1901) (Now Lady Heathcoat-Amory)	4	1922, 24–5, 29

Note: Nicklaus is the only golfer to have won five different major titles (The Open, US Open, Masters, PGA and US Amateur titles) twice and a record 19 all told (1959–80). His remarkable record in The US Open is four firsts, eight seconds and two thirds. In 1930 Bobby Jones achieved a unique 'Grand Slam' of the US and British Open and Amateur titles.

Otto Bucher (*left*), who holed-in-one at the age of 99 years 244 days, pictured with Seve Ballesteros, whose brother runs the club where the feat was achieved.

greatest was Norman L. Manley's unique 'double albatross' on the par-4 330 yd *301 m* seventh and par-4 290 yd *265 m* eighth holes on the Del Valle Country Club Course, Saugus, California, on 2 Sept 1964. The first woman to record consecutive 'aces' was Sue Prell, on the 13th and 14th holes at Chatswood Golf Club, Sydney, Australia on 29 May 1977.

The closest to achieving three consecutive holes in one was the late Dr Joseph Boydstone on the 3rd, 4th and 9th at Bakersfield GC, California, USA, on 10 Oct 1962 and the Rev Harold Snider (b. 4 July 1900) who aced the 8th, 13th and 14th holes of the par-3 Ironwood course, Arizona, USA on 9 June 1976.

Youngest and oldest

The youngest golfer recorded to have shot a hole-in-one was Coby Orr (5 years) of Littleton, Colorado on the 103 yd *94 m* fifth at the Riverside Golf Course, San Antonio, Texas in 1975. The oldest golfers to have performed this feat are: (men) 99 yr 244 days Otto Bucher (Switzerland) (b. 12 May 1885) on the 130 yd *100 m* 12th at La Manga GC, Spain on 13 Jan 1985; (women) 87 yr Ruth Needham on the 91 yd *83 m* 3rd at Escanaba Country Club, Michigan, USA on 11 July 1983. The British record was set by Samuel Richard Walker (b. 6 Jan 1892) at the 156 yd *143 m* 8th at West Hove GC, Sussex at the age of 92 yr 169 days on 23 June 1984.

The oldest player to score his age is C. Arthur Thompson (1869–1975) of Victoria, British Columbia, Canada, who scored 103 on the Uplands course of 6215 yd *5682 m* aged 103 in 1973.

GREYHOUND RACING

Earliest meeting

In September 1876 a greyhound meeting was staged at Hendon, North London with a railed hare operated by a windlass. Modern greyhound racing originated with the perfecting of the mechanical hare by Owen Patrick Smith at Emeryville, California, USA, in 1919. St. Petersburg Kennel Club located in St. Petersburg, Florida, USA which opened on 3 Jan 1925, is the oldest greyhound track in the world still in operation on its original site. The earliest greyhound race behind a mechanical hare in the British Isles was at Belle Vue, Manchester, opened on 24 July 1926.

Derby

The only two greyhounds to have won the English Greyhound Derby twice (instituted 1927, now over 500 m *546 m*) are *Mick the Miller* (whelped in Ireland, June 1926 and died 1939) on 25 July 1929, when owned by Albert H. Williams, and on 28 June 1930 (owned by Mrs Arundel H. Kempton), and *Patricia's Hope* on 24 June 1972 (when owned by Gordon and Basil Marks and Brian Stanley) and 23 June 1973 (when owned by G. & B. Marks and J. O'Connor). The highest prize was £35,000 to *Indian Joe* for the Derby on 28 June 1980. The only greyhounds to win the English, Scottish and Welsh Derby 'triple' are *Trev's Perfection*, owned by Fred Trevillion, in 1947, *Mile Bush Pride*, owned by Noel W. Purvis, in 1959, and *Patricia's Hope* in 1972. The only greyhound to win the American Derby, at Taunton, Mass., twice was *Real Huntsman* in 1950–51.

Grand National

The only greyhound to have won the Grand National (inst. 1927 over 525 yd *480 m*, now 500 m, and five flights) three times is *Sherry's Prince*, a 75 lb *32 kg* dog (whelped in April 1967, died July 1978) owned by Mrs Joyce Mathews of Sanderstead, Surrey, in 1970, 1971 and 1972.

Fastest greyhound

The highest speed at which any greyhound has been timed is 41.72 mph *67,14 km/h* (410 yd *374 m* in 20.1 sec) by *The Shoe* on the then straightaway track at Richmond, NSW, Australia on 25 Apr 1968. It is estimated that he covered the last 100 yd *91,44 m* in 4.5 sec or at 45.45 mph *73,14 km/h*. The highest speed recorded for a greyhound in Great Britain is 39.13 mph *62,97 km/h* by *Beef Cutlet*, when covering a straight course of 500 yd *457 m* in 26.13 sec at Blackpool, Lancashire, on 13 May 1933.

Fastest speeds for four-bend tracks

The fastest automatically timed speed recorded for a full 4-bend race is 38.89 mph *62,59 km/h* at Brighton, E. Sussex by *Glen Miner* on 4 May 1982 with a time of a 29.62 sec for 515 m *563 yd*. The fastest over hurdles is 37.64 mph *60.58 km/h* at Brighton by *Wotchit Buster* on 22 Aug 1978.

Most wins

The most career wins is 137 by the American greyhound, *Indy Ann*, who competed in 1955–56. The world record for consecutive victories is 31 by an American greyhound *Joe Dump* from 18 Nov 1978 to 1 June 1979. *Westpark Mustard*, owned by Mr and Mrs Cyril Scotland, set a British record of 20 consecutive wins between 7 Jan and 28 Oct 1974.

Highest earnings

The career earnings record is held by *Marathon Hound* with over $225,000 in the USA, 1981–4. The richest first prize for a greyhound race is $100,000 won by *DD's Jackie* in the 1982 Greyhound Grand Prix at Hollywood, Florida, USA.

Longest odds

Apollo Prince won at odds of 250–1 at Sandown GRC, Springvale, Queensland, Australia on 14 Nov 1968.

GYMNASTICS

Earliest references

A primitive form of gymnastics was practised in ancient Greece and Rome during the period of the ancient Olympic Games (776 BC to AD 393) but Johann Friedrich Simon was the first teacher of modern gymnastics at Basedow's School, Dessau, Germany in 1776.

Most titles *World*

The greatest number of individual titles won by a man in the World Championships is ten by Boris Shakhlin (b. 27 Jan 1932) (USSR) between 1954 and 1964. He also won three team titles. The female record is ten individual wins and five team titles by Larissa Semyonovna Latynina (b. 27 Dec 1934) of the USSR, between 1956 and 1964. Japan has won the men's team title a record five times (1962, 1966, 1970, 1974, 1978) and the USSR the women's team title on eight occasions (1954, 1958, 1962, 1970, 1974, 1978, 1981 and 1983).

The most overall titles in Modern Rhythmic Gymnastics is three by Maria Gigova (Bulgaria)

Ecaterina Szabo (Romania) won five medals—four gold and a silver—at the 1984 Olympics, more than anyone else at the Games. (*All-Sport/Trevor Jones*)

Gymnastics

Most titles *British*

The British Gymnastic Championship was won ten times by Arthur John Whitford (b. 2 July 1908) in 1928–36 and 1939. He was also in four winning teams. Wray 'Nik' Stuart (b. 20 July 1927) equalled the record of nine successive wins, 1956–64. The women's record is eight by Mary Patricia Hirst (b. 18 Nov 1918) (1947, 1949–50 and 1952–6). The most overall titles in Modern Rhythmic Gymnastics is by Sharon Taylor with five successive, 1977–81.

Most titles *World Cup*

In the first World Cup Competition, in London in 1975, Ludmilla Tourischeva (now Mrs Valeriy Borzov) (b. 7 Oct 1952) (USSR) won all five gold medals available.

Somersaults

Ashrita Furman performed 6,773 forward rolls over 10 miles *16,09 km* in Central Park, New York, USA on 19 Nov 1980. Corporal Wayne Wright of the Royal Engineers made a successful dive and tucked somersault over 37 men at Old Park Barracks, Dover, Kent on 30 July 1980. Shigeru Iwasaki (b. 1960) backwards somersaulted over 50 m *54.68 yd* in 10.8 sec at Tokyo, Japan on 30 Mar 1980.

Largest gymnasium

The world's largest gymnasium is Yale University's nine-storey, Payne Whitney Gymnasium at New Haven, Connecticut, USA, completed in 1932 and valued at $18,000,000 *£10,285,000*.

in 1969, 1971 and 1973 (shared). Galina Shugurova (USSR) (b. 1955) won eight apparatus titles from 1969–77.

Most titles *Olympic*

Japan (1960, 1964, 1968, 1972 and 1976) have won the men's team title most often. The USSR have won the women's title eight times (1952–80). The only men to win six individual gold medals are Boris Shakhlin (USSR), with one in 1956, four (two shared) in 1960 and one in 1964, and Nikolai Andrianov (USSR) (b. 14 Oct 1952), with one in 1972, four in 1976 and one in 1980.

Vera Caslavska-Odlozil (b. 3 May 1942) (Czechoslovakia), has won most individual gold medals with seven, three in 1964 and four (one shared) in 1968. Larissa Latynina won six individual gold medals and was in three winning teams in 1956–64 making nine gold medals. She also won five silver and four bronze making 18 in all—an Olympic record. The most medals for a male gymnast is 15 by Nikolai Andrianov (USSR), 7 gold, 5 silver and 3 bronze in 1972–80. Aleksander Ditiatin (USSR) (b. 7 Aug 1957) is the only man to win a medal in all eight categories in the same Games, with 3 gold, 4 silver and 1 bronze at Moscow in 1980.

Highest score *Olympics*

Nadia Comaneci (Romania) (b. 12 Nov 1961) was the first to achieve a perfect score, with seven of 10.00 at the Montreal Olympics in July 1976.

Youngest International and World Champion

Pasakevi 'Voula' Kouna (b. 6 Dec 1971) was aged 9 yr 299 days at the start of the Balkan Games at Serres, Greece on 1–4 Oct 1981, when she represented Greece. Olga Bicherova (USSR) (b. 26 Oct 1966) won the women's world title at 15 yr 33 days on 28 Nov 1981. The youngest male world champion was Dmitri Belozerchev (USSR) (b. 17 Dec 1966) at 16 years 315 days at Budapest, Hungary on 28 Oct 1983.

In the gymnastics events at the Los Angeles Olympics in 1984, a record 46 'perfect marks' of 10.00 were awarded. Mary Lou Retton (USA) (*above*) won the individual All-Round title. (*All-Sport*)

CONSECUTIVE FEATS

Athletes are permitted to perform these endeavours in sets, but must remain in position throughout the activity.

Chins (from dead hang position) 170 Lee Chin Yong (b. 15 Aug 1925) at Backyon Gymnasium, Seoul, Korea on 10 May 1983.

Chins—One-arm (from a ring) 22 Robert Chisholm (b. 9 Dec 1952) at Queen's University, Kingston, Ontario, Canada on 3 Dec 1982. (Also 18 two-finger chins, 12 one-finger chins.)

Parallel bar dips 718 Roger Perez (b. 11 July 1962) in 30 min 40 sec at Cosumnes River College, Sacramento, California, USA on 14 Dec 1983.

Press-ups (push-ups) 24,300 by Jeffrey L. Warwick (USA) at Humboldt Family Branch YMCA, Buffalo, NY, USA on 16 June 1985 (in 14 hr 41 min).

Push-ups (one arm) 3010 Colin Hewick at the South Holderness Sports Centre, Humberside on 16 May 1985.

Push-ups (finger tip) 3010 Colin Hewick at the South Holderness Sports Centre on 14 Oct 1984 (in 3 hr 12 min).

Push-ups (one finger) 100 Harry Lee Welch Jr. at Durham, N. Carolina, USA on 31 Mar 1985.

Hand-stand push-ups 500 Danny Castoldi at the University of Southern California, Los Angeles, USA on 9 July 1983.

Sit-ups 43,418 Louis Scripa Jr. (USA) at Jack La Lanne's American Health & Fitness Spa, Sacramento, Cal., USA on 6–7 Oct 1984 (in 22 hr 10 min).

Leg raises 21,598 Louis Scripa Jr. in 6 hours at Fairfield, Cal., USA on 8 Dec 1983.

Jumping Jacks 40,014 August Hoffman Jr. at Van Nuys, Cal., USA on 4 Dec 1982.

Pummel Horse double circles 48, done consecutively, by Andrew Morris on BBC television on 9 Sept 1984.

HANDBALL

Origins

Handball, similar to association football with hands substituted for feet, was first played *c.* 1895. It was introduced into the Olympic Games at Berlin in 1936 as an 11-a-side outdoor game with Germany winning, but when re-introduced in 1972 it was an indoor game with seven-a-side, the standard size of team since 1952.

The International Handball Federation was founded in 1946. The first international match was held at Halle/Saale, W. Germany when Austria beat Germany 6–3.

Most Championships

Three Olympic titles have been won by the USSR—men 1976, women 1976 and 1980 and by Yugoslavia—men 1972 and 1984, women 1984. The most victories won in world championship (inst. 1938) competition are by Romania with four men's and three women's titles from 1956 to 1974. The Super Cup is contested by men's Olympic and World Champions. First held in 1979, West Germany and the USSR have each won once.

The most European Cup titles is ten in the women's event by Spartak Kiev, USSR between 1970 and 1985.

Highest score

The highest score in an international match was recorded when the USSR beat Afghanistan 86–2 in the 'Friendly Army Tournament' at Miskolc, Hungary in August 1981.

HARNESS RACING

Origins

Trotting races were held in Valkenburg, Netherlands in 1554. In England the trotting gait (the simultaneous use of the diagonally opposite legs) was known in the 16th century. The sulky first appeared in harness racing in 1829. Pacers thrust out their fore and hind legs simultaneously on one side.

Most successful driver

The most successful sulky driver in North American harness racing history has been Herve Filion (b. 1 Feb 1940) of Quebec, Canada with a record 8998 wins and $45.2 million in purse money to the end of the 1984 season. He won his 13th North American championship in 1982. The most wins in a year is 637 by Herve Filion in 1974. The greatest earnings in a year is $9,059,184 by William O'Donnell (b. 4 May 1948) who won 422 races in 1984.

Highest price

The highest price ever paid for a pacer is $19.2 million for *Nihilator* who was syndicated by Wall Street Stable and Almahurst Stud Farm in 1984. The highest price paid for a trotter is $5.25 million for *Mystic Park* by Lana Lobell Farms from Gerald & Irving Wechter of New York and Robert Lester of Florida, announced on 13 July 1982.

Greatest winnings

The greatest amount won by a trotting horse is $3,041,262 by *Ideal du Gazeau* (France) to July 1983. The record for a harness horse is $2,041,367 by *Cam Fella*, who also had 28 consecutive victories, 19 May–26 Nov 1983. *Niatross* (USA) won $2,019,213 in just two years 1979–80. The single season record is $1,751,695 by *On The Road Again* in 1984.

The largest ever purse was £2,161,000 for the Woodrow Wilson two-year-old race over 1 mile at the Meadowlands, New Jersey on 16 Aug 1984. Of this sum a record $1,080,500 went to the winner *Nihilator*, driven by Bill O'Donnell.

HOCKEY

Origins

A representation of two players with curved snagging sticks apparently in an orthodox 'bully' position was found in Tomb No. 17 at Beni Hasan, Egypt and has been dated to *c.* 2050 BC. There is a British reference to the game in Lincolnshire in 1277. The modern game evolved in South London in the 1870s. The English Hockey Association was founded in 1875, but the current English governing body, the Hockey Association was formed on 18 Jan 1886. The Fédération Internationale de Hockey was formed on 7 Jan 1924.

The first organised club was the Blackheath Rugby and Hockey Club founded in 1861. The oldest club with a continuous history is Teddington HC formed in the autumn of 1871. They played Richmond on 24 Oct 1874 and used the first recorded circle *versus* Surbiton at Bushey Park on 9 Dec 1876. The first international match was the Wales *v.* Ireland match at Rhyl on 26 Jan 1895. Ireland won 3–0.

Most Olympic medals

The Indians were Olympic Champions from the re-inception of Olympic hockey in 1928 until 1960, when Pakistan beat them 1–0 at Rome. They had their eighth win in 1980. Of the seven Indians who have won three Olympic team gold medals two have also won a silver medal—Leslie Walter Claudius (b. 25 Mar 1927) in 1948, 1952, 1956 and 1960 (silver) and Udham Singh (b. 4 Aug 1928) in 1952, 1956, 1964 and 1960 (silver). A women's tournament was added to the Olympic Games in 1980, and the winners have been Zimbabwe in 1980 and the Netherlands in 1984.

HARNESS RACING *Records against time*

TROTTING

World (mile track)	1:53.8	...*Fancy Crown* (driver, William O'Donnell) at Springfield, Illinois, USA	15 Aug 1984
	1:53.8	...*Cornstalk* (driver, Howard Bessinger) (US) at Springfield, Illinois, USA	16 Aug 1984
World race record (mile)	1:54.8	...*Lindy's Crown* (driver, Howard Beissinger) (US) at Du Quoin, Illinois	30 Aug 1960
British record (mile)	2:06.8	...*Ted Trot* (driver, John Blisset) at Chasewater, West Midlands	21 June 1975

PACING

World (mile track)	1:49.2	...*Niatross* (driver, Clint Galbraith) (US) at Lexington, Kentucky, USA	1 Oct 1980
World race record (mile)	1:50.6	...*Colt Fortysix* (driver, Chris Boring) (US) at Springfield, Illinois, USA	16 Aug 1984
British record (mile)	2:02.1	...*Lydia M* (driver, James Pickard) at York	10 July 1982

Little known in Britain, harness racing is big game in America. A record $19.2 million was paid for *Nihilator* (*above*) who won the richest prize for a race, $1,080,500, in New Jersey in 1984.

World Cup

Pakistan have won most men's World Cups (inst. 1971) with three, 1971, 1978 and 1982. The Netherlands have won most women's World Cups (inst. 1974) with three, 1974, 1978 and 1983.

MEN

Highest international score

The highest score in international hockey was when India defeated the United States 24–1 at Los Angeles, California, USA, in the 1932 Olympic Games. The greatest number of goals in a home international match was when England defeated France 16–0 at Beckenham on 25 Mar 1922.

Most international appearances

Michael Peter (b. 7 May 1949) represented West Germany over 250 times between 1969 and 1984, indoors and out. The most by a home countries player is 139 by H. David Judge (b. 19 Jan 1936) with 124 for Ireland and 15 for Great Britain from 1957 to 1978.

Greatest scoring feats

The greatest number of goals scored in international hockey is 150 by Paul Litjens (Netherlands) (b. 9 Nov 1947) in 112 games to April 1979. M. C. Marckx (Bowden 2nd XI) scored 19 goals against Brooklands 2nd XI (score 23–0) on 31 Dec 1910. He was selected for England in March 1912 but declined due to business priorities. Between 1923 and 1958, Fred H. Wagner scored 1832 goals for Beeston HC, Nottingham Casuals and the Nottinghamshire county side. David Ashman has scored 1373 goals for one club, Hamble Old Boys, Southampton, from 1958 to 1984.

The fastest goal in an international was in 7 sec by John French for England *v.* West Germany at Nottingham, on 25 Apr 1971.

Greatest goalkeeping

Richard James Allen (b. 4 June 1902) (India) did not concede a goal during the 1928 Olympic Tournament and only a total of three in the following two Olympics of 1932 and 1936. In these three Games India scored a total of 102 goals.

Longest game

The longest international game on record was one of 145 min (into the sixth period of extra time), when Netherlands beat Spain 1–0 in the Olympic tournament at Mexico City on 25 Oct 1968. Club matches of 205 min have twice been recorded: The Hong Kong Football Club beat Prison Sports Dept as the first to score in 'sudden death' play-off after 2–2 at full time on 11 Mar 1979 and Gore Court beat Hampstead in the

first round of the English Club Championships in 1983.

WOMEN

Origins

The earliest women's club was East Molesey in Surrey, England formed in *c.* 1887. The Wimbledon Ladies Hockey Club, founded one year later, is still in existence. The first national association was the Irish Ladies' Hockey Union founded in 1894. The All England Women's Hockey Association held its first formal meeting in Westminster Town Hall, London, on 23 Nov 1895. The first international match was an England *v.* Ireland game in Dublin in 1896. Ireland won 2–0.

Most international appearances

Valerie Robinson made a record 142 appearances for England in 1963–84.

Highest scores

The highest score in a women's international match was when England beat France 23–0 at Merton, Greater London, on 3 Feb 1923. In club hockey, Ross Ladies beat Wyeside, at Ross-on-Wye, Herefordshire, 40–0 on 24 Jan 1929, when Edna Mary Blakelock (b. 22 Oct 1904) scored a record 21 goals.

Highest attendance

The highest attendance at a women's hockey match was 65,165 for the match between England and the USA at Wembley, London, on 11 Mar 1978.

Michael Peter of West Germany has represented his country more times than any other hockey player. He made his international debut in 1969 and has since made over 250 appearances. *(All-Sport)*

HORSE RACING

Guinness Books has now published international racing information in greater detail in the 1985 specialist publication *Horse Racing—The Records* (price £6.95).

Origins

Horsemanship was an important part of the Hittite culture of Anatolia, Turkey dating from 1400 BC. The 33rd ancient Olympic Games of 648 BC in Greece featured horse racing. The earliest races recorded in England were those held in about AD 200 at Netherby, Cumbria, between Arab horses imported by the Romans.

Racecourse *Largest*

The world's largest racecourse is at Newmarket. It now comprises the Rowley Mile Course and the July Course, whose grandstands are about a mile apart, although a portion of the course is common to both. The Beacon Course of 4 miles 397 yd *6,80 km*, is no longer in use. The course is situated in the middle of Newmarket Heath, *c* 2500 acres, the largest training area in the world.

Largest prizes

The richest day's racing ever was staged at Hollywood Park, Los Angeles, USA on 10 Nov 1984, when the prize money totalled $10 million

Horse Racing

for the seven races. Included was a record $3 million for the Breeders' Cup Classic.

A record $2.6 million was received by *Spend A Buck*, $600,000 for winning the Jersey Derby, Garden State Park, NJ, USA on 27 May 1985, together with a $2 million bonus for also winning the Kentucky Derby and two preparatory races at Garden State Park.

Most runners

The most horses in a race is 66 in the Grand National on 22 Mar 1929. The record for the Flat is 58 in the Lincolnshire Handicap at Lincoln on 13 Mar 1948. The most runners at a Flat meeting was 214 in seven races at Newmarket on 15 June 1915, and National Hunt—229 in eight races at Worcester on 13 Jan 1965.

Dead-heats

There is no recorded case in Turf history of a quintuple dead-heat. The nearest approach was in the Astley Stakes, at Lewes, Sussex, on 6 Aug 1880 when *Mazurka*, *Wandering Nun* and *Scobell* triple dead-heated for first place a head in front of *Cumberland* and *Thora*, who dead-heated for fourth place. Each of the five jockeys thought he had won. The only three known examples of a quadruple dead-heat were between *Honest Harry*, *Miss Decoy*, *Young Daffodil* and *Peteria* at Bogside, on 7 June 1808, between *Defaulter*, *The Squire of Malton*, *Reindeer* and *Pulcherrima* in the Omnibus Stakes at The Hoo, Hertfordshire, on 26 Apr 1851, and between *Overreach*, *Lady Golightly*, *Gamester* and *The Unexpected* at Newmarket on 22 Oct 1855. Since the introduction of the photo-finish, the highest number of horses dead-heating has been three, on several occasions.

Horses *Most successful*

The horse with the best win-loss record was *Kincsem*, a Hungarian mare foaled in 1874, who was unbeaten in 54 races (1876–9) throughout Europe, including the Goodwood Cup of 1878. *Camarero*, foaled in 1951, won his first 56 races in Puerto Rico from 19 Apr 1953 to 17 Aug 1955. (In his career to 1956 he won 73 of 77 races). The most wins in a career is 137 from 159 starts by *Galgo Jr* (foaled 1928) in Puerto Rico between 1930 and 1936; in 1931 he won a record 30 races in one year.

Triple Crown winners

The English Triple Crown (2000 Guineas, Derby, St Leger) has been won 15 times, most recently by *Nijinsky* in 1970. The American Triple Crown (Kentucky Derby, Preakness Stakes, Belmont Stakes) has been achieved 11 times, most recently by *Affirmed* in 1978.

Horse *Highest price*

The most expensive horse ever is *Shareef Dancer* syndicated for $40 million in August 1983 by his owner Sheikh Maktoum al Maktoum. 40 shares were issued at $1 million each. The most paid for a yearling is $10.2 m for *Snaafi Dancer* on 20 July 1983 at Keeneland, Kentucky, by Sheikh Mohammed al Maktoum.

Horses *Greatest winnings*

The career earnings record is $6,597,947 by the gelding *John Henry* (foaled 1975) with 39 wins from 83 races, from 1977 to 1984. The leading money-winning mare is *All Along* (foaled 1979) with $3,018,420 in France and the USA, 1981–4.

Horses *Biggest weight*

The biggest weight ever carried is 30 stone *190 kg* by both Mr Maynard's mare and Mr Baker's horse in a match won by the former over a mile at York on 21 May 1788.

Horses *Oldest winners*

The oldest horses to win on the Flat have been

MAJOR RACE RECORDS

RACE	RECORD TIME / Jockey	MOST WINS		LARGEST FIELD
		Trainer	Owner	
FLAT				
Derby (1780) 1½ miles *2414 m* Epsom	2 min 33.8 sec *Mahmoud 1936*	9—Lester Piggott 1954, 57, 60, 68, 70, 72, 76, 77, 83	7—Robert Robson 1793, 1802, 09, 10, 15, 17, 23 7—John Porter 1868, 82, 83, 86, 90, 91, 99 7—Fred Darling 1922, 25, 26, 31, 38, 40, 41	5—3rd Earl of Egremont 1782, 1804, 05, 07, 26 5—H. H. Aga Khan III 1930, 35, 36, 48, 52	34 (1862)
2000 Guineas (1809) 1 mile *1609 m* Newmarket	1 min 35.8 sec *My Babu 1948*	9—Jem Robinson 1825, 28, 31, 33, 34, 35, 36, 47, 48	7—John Scott 1842, 43, 49, 53, 56, 60, 62	5—4th Duke of Grafton 1820, 21, 22, 26, 27 5—5th Earl of Jersey 1831, 34, 35, 36, 37	28 (1930)
1000 Guineas (1814) 1 mile *1609 m* Newmarket	1 min 36.85 sec *Oh So Sharp 1985*	7—George Fordham 1859, 61, 65, 68, 69, 81, 83	9—Robert Robson 1818, 19, 20, 21, 22, 23, 25, 26, 27	8—4th Duke of Grafton 1819, 20, 21, 22, 23, 25, 26, 27	29 (1926)
Oaks (1779) 1½ miles *2414 m* Epsom	2 min 34.21 sec *Time Charter 1982*	9—Frank Buckle 1797, 98, 99, 1802, 03, 05, 17, 18, 23	12—Robert Robson 1802, 04, 05, 07, 08, 09, 13, 15, 18, 22, 23, 25	6—4th Duke of Grafton 1813, 15, 22, 23, 28, 31	26 (1848)
St Leger (1776) 1 m 6 f 127 yd *2932 m* Doncaster	3 min 01.6 sec *Coronach 1926 Windsor Lad 1934*	9—Bill Scott 1821, 25, 28, 29, 38, 39, 40, 41, 46	16—John Scott 1827, 28, 29, 32, 34, 38, 39, 40, 41, 45, 51, 53, 56, 57, 59, 62	7—9th Duke of Hamilton 1786, 87, 88, 92, 1808, 09, 14	30 (1825)
King George VI and Queen Elizabeth Stakes (1951) 1½ miles *2414 m* Ascot	2 min 26.98 sec *Grundy 1975*	7—Lester Piggott 1965, 66, 69, 70, 74, 77, 84	3—Vincent O'Brien 1958, 70, 77 3—Noel Murless 1966, 67, 68 3—Dick Hern 1972, 79, 80	2—Nelson Bunker Hunt 1973, 74	19 (1951)
Prix de l'Arc de Triomphe (1920) 2400 metres *1 mile 864 yd* Longchamp, France	2 min 28 sec *Detroit 1980*	4—Jacques Doyasbère 1942, 44, 50, 51 4—Frédéric 'Freddy' Head 1966, 72, 76, 79 4—Yves Saint-Martin 1970, 74, 82, 84	4—Charles Semblat 1942, 44, 46, 49 4—François Mathet 1950, 51, 70, 82 4—Alec Head 1952, 59, 76, 81	6—Marcel Boussac 1936, 37, 42, 44, 46, 49	30 (1967)
VRC Melbourne Cup (1861) 3200 metres *1 mile 1739 yd* Flemington, Victoria, Australia	3 min 19.1 sec *Rain Lover 1968*	4—Bobby Lewis 1902, 15, 19, 27 4—Harry White 1974, 75, 78, 79	7—Bart Cummings 1965, 66, 67, 74, 75, 77, 79	4—Etienne de Mestre 1861, 62, 67, 78	39 (1890)
Kentucky Derby (1875) 1¼ miles *2012 m* Churchill Downs, USA	1 min 59.4 sec *Secretariat 1973*	5—Eddie Arcaro 1938, 41, 45, 48, 52 5—Bill Hartack 1957, 60, 62, 64, 69	6—Ben Jones 1938, 41, 44, 48, 49, 52	8—Calumet Farm 1941, 44, 48, 49, 52, 57, 58, 68	23 (1974)
Irish Sweeps Derby (1866) 1½ miles *2414 m* The Curragh	2 min 28.8 sec *Tambourine 1962*	6—Morny Wing 1921, 23, 30, 38, 42, 46	5—Vincent O'Brien 1953, 57, 70, 77, 84	5—H. H. Aga Khan III 1925, 32, 40, 48, 49	24 (1962)
NATIONAL HUNT				
Grand National (1839) 4½ miles *7242 m* Liverpool	9 min 01.9 sec *Red Rum 1973*	5—George Stevens 1856, 63, 64, 69, 70	4—Fred Rimell 1956, 61, 70, 76	3—Capt James Machell 1873, 74, 76 3—Sir Charles Assheton-Smith 1893, 1912, 13 3—Noel Le Mare 1973, 74, 77	66 (1929)
Cheltenham Gold Cup (1924) 3¼ miles *5230 m* Cheltenham	6 min 23.4 sec *Silver Fame 1951*	4—Pat Taaffe 1964, 65, 66, 68	5—Tom Dreaper 1946, 64, 65, 66, 68	7—Dorothy Paget 1932, 33, 34, 35, 36, 40, 52	22 (1982)
Champion Hurdle (1927) 2 miles *3218 m* Cheltenham	3 min 51.7 sec *See You Then 1985*	4—Tim Molony 1951, 52, 53, 54	5—Peter Easterby 1967, 76, 77, 80, 81	4—Dorothy Paget 1932, 33, 40, 46	24 (1964)

the 18-year-olds *Revenge* at Shrewsbury in September 1790, *Marksman* at Ashford, Kent in September 1826 and *Jorrocks* at Bathurst, Australia in February 1851. At the same age *Wild Aster* won three hurdle races in six days in March 1919 and *Sonny Somers* won two steeplechases in February 1980.

Jockeys *Most successful*
The most successful jockey of all time has been William Lee 'Bill' Shoemaker (USA) (b. weighing 2½ lb *1,1 kg*, 19 Aug 1931) now weighing 94 lb *43 kg* and standing 4 ft 11 in *1,50 m*. His career earnings reached $100 million for 8446 winners to 3 Mar 1985. His first race was on 19 Mar 1949 and he rode his first winner on 20 Apr 1949.

The Breeders Cup Classic held in Los Angeles is the richest race in the world with $3 million. (*All-Sport/Alvin Chung*)

The greatest amount ever won by any jockey in a year is $12,045,813 by Chris McCarron (USA) (b. 1955) in the USA in 1984. The most winners ridden in a year is 546, from a record 2199 mounts, by Chris McCarron in 1974.

Jockeys *Wins on one card*

The most winners ridden on one card is eight by Hubert S. Jones, 17, from 13 rides at Caliente, Cal., USA on 11 June 1944, by Oscar Barattuci, at Rosario City, Argentina, on 15 Dec 1957, by Dave Gall, from ten rides at Cahokia Downs, East St Louis, Illinois, USA on 18 Oct 1978 and by Chris Loseth, from ten rides at Exhibition Park, Vancouver, BC, Canada on 9 Apr 1984. The longest winning streak is 12 by Sir Gordon Richards (b. 5 May 1904) (one race at Nottingham on 3 Oct, six out of six at Chepstow on 4 Oct and the first five races next day at Chepstow) in 1933.

The indomitable Lester Piggott has ridden 28 winners in the five English Classics during his career of 38 seasons. A child wonder, he rode his first professional winner in 1948 before he had reached 13 years of age. *(All-Sport/Trevor Jones)*

Jockeys *Youngest and oldest*

The youngest jockey was Australian-born Frank Wootton (1893–1940) (English champion jockey 1909–12), who rode his first winner in South Africa aged 9 years 10 months. The oldest jockey was Harry Beasley, who rode his last race at Baldoyle, Co. Dublin, Ireland on 10 June 1935 aged 83.

Jockey *Lightest*

The lightest recorded jockey was Kitchener (d. 1872), who won the Tradesmen's Plate (Chester Cup) on *Red Deer* in 1844 at 3 st 7 lb *22 kg*. He was said to have weighed only 2 st 7 lb *16 kg* in 1840.

Trainers

Jack Van Berg (USA) has the greatest number of wins in a year, 496 in 1976, and in a career, over 4200 to 1984. The greatest amount won in a year is $5,803,912 by D. Wayne Lukas (USA) in 1984.

Owners

The most lifetime wins by an owner is 4,775 by Marion Van Berg in North America in the 35 years up to his death in 1971. The most winners in a year is 494 by Dan R. Lasater (USA) in 1974 when he also won a record $3,022,960 in prize money.

BRITISH TURF RECORDS

Horses *Most successful*

Eclipse (foaled 1764) still has the best win-loss record, being unbeaten in a career of 18 races between May 1769 and October 1770. The longest winning sequence is 21 races by *Meteor* (foaled 1783) between 1786 and 1788. As the 1000 Guineas and the Oaks are restricted to fillies, only they can possibly win all five Classics. *Sceptre* came closest in 1902 when she won the 2000 Guineas, 1000 Guineas, Oaks and St Leger. In 1868 *Formosa* won the same four but dead-heated in the 2000 Guineas. The biggest winning margin in a Classic is 20 lengths by *Mayonaise* in the 1000 Guineas in 1859. The most races won in a season is 23 by three-year-old *Fisherman* in 1856. *Catherina* (foaled 1830) won a career record 79 out of 176 races, 1832–41. The most successful sire was *Stockwell* (foaled 1849) whose progeny won 1153 races (1858–76) and in 1866 set a record of 132 races won. The greatest amount ever won by an English-trained horse is £526,910 by the mare *Time Charter* (foaled 1979) from 1981 to 1984.

Jockeys *Most successful*

Sir Gordon Richards won 4870 races from 21,834 mounts from his first mount at Lingfield on 16 Oct 1920 to his last at Sandown on 10 July 1954. His first win was on 31 Mar 1921. In 1953, at his 28th and final attempt, he won the Derby, six days after his knighthood. He was champion jockey 26 times between 1925 and 1953 and won a record 269 races in 1947. The most Classic races won by a jockey is 29 by Lester Piggott (b. 5 Nov 1935) from his first on *Never Say Die*, in the 1954 Derby to the 1985 2000 Guineas on *Shadeed*. (Derby—1, St Leger—8, Oaks—6, 2000 Guineas—4, 1000 Guineas—2).

Trainers *Most successful*

The record first-prize money earned in a season is £872,614 by Henry Cecil in 1982. The most Classics won by a trainer is 40 by John Scott (1794–1871) of Malton, Yorkshire between 1827 and 1863. Alec Taylor of Manton, Wiltshire headed the trainers' list for a record 12 seasons between 1907 and 1925. In 1867 John Day Jr. of Danebury, Hampshire won 146 races.

Owners *Most successful*

H H Aga Khan III (1877–1957) was leading owner a record 13 times between 1924 and 1952. The record first-prize money won in a season is £461,488 by Robert Edmund Sangster (b. 23 May 1936) in 1983. The most wins in a season is 115 by David Robinson in 1973. The most Classics won is 20 by the 4th Duke of Grafton (1760–1844) between 1813 and 1831 and by the 17th Earl of Derby (1865–1948) between 1910 and 1945.

THE DERBY

The greatest of England's five Classics is the Derby Stakes, inaugurated on 4 May 1780, and named after the 12th Earl of Derby (1752–1834). The distance was increased in 1784 from a mile to 1½ miles *2414 km*. The race has been run at Epsom Downs, Surrey, except for the two war periods, when it was run at Newmarket, and is for three-year-olds only. Since 1884 the weights have been: colts 9 st *57 kg*, fillies 8 st 9 lb *55 kg*. Geldings were eligible until 1904.

Largest and smallest winning margins

Shergar, ridden by Walter R. Swinburn, won the Derby by a record ten lengths in 1981. There have been two dead-heats: in 1828 when *Cadland* beat *The Colonel* in the run-off, and in 1884 between *St Gatien* and *Harvester* (stakes divided).

Longest and shortest odds

Three winners have been returned at odds of 100–1: *Jeddah* (1898), *Signorinetta* (1908) and *Aboyeur* (1913). The shortest priced winner was *Ladas* (1894) at 2–9 and the hottest losing favourite was *Surefoot*, fourth at 40–95 in 1890.

Largest prize

The richest prize on the British Turf was £227,680 in the 205th Derby on 6 June 1984, won by Luigi Migletti's *Secreto*.

NATIONAL HUNT

For more details see The Guinness Guide to Steeplechasing *by Gerry Cranham, Richard Pitman and John Oaksey, published by Guinness Superlatives Ltd. (price £11.95).*

Horse *Greatest winnings*

The greatest amount earned by a British-trained jumper is £196,053 by the 1982 Cheltenham Gold Cup winner *Silver Buck* (foaled 1972) from 1977 to 1984.

Horses *Most successful*

Triple champion hurdler *Sir Ken* (foaled 1947) won a record 16 hurdle races in succession, April 1951 to March 1953. *Dudley* (foaled 1914) also won 16 races in succession under NH Rules, Jan–Nov 1925.

Jockeys *Most successful*

John Francome (b. 13 Dec 1952) won a career record 1138 winners over jumps (from 5061 mounts, from his first at Worcester on 2 Dec 1970 to his last at Huntingdon on 8 Apr 1985, when he retired.

The record number of wins in a season is 149 by John 'Jonjo' O'Neill (b. 13 Apr 1952) in 1977–8. The most wins in a day is six by amateur Charlie Cunningham at Rugby on 29 Mar 1881. The record number of successive wins is ten by John Alnam 'Johnny' Gilbert (b. 26 July 1920), 8–30 Sept 1959. The record number of championships is seven by Gerald Wilson (1903–68) 1933–1938 and 1941, and by John Francome (one shared) in 1976, 1979, 1981–5.

Trainers *Most successful*

The most first-prize money earned in a season is £358,837 from a record 120 winners by Michael Dickinson in 1982–3. He also achieved the unique feat in a championship race of training the first five horses in the 1983 Cheltenham Gold

WORLD SPEED RECORDS

Distance	Time min sec	mph	km/h	Name	Age	Weight carried lb	kg	Course	Date	
¼ mile	20.8	43.26	69,62	Big Racket (Mexico) 4		114	51,7	Mexico City, Mexico	5 Feb	1945
½ mile	44.4	40.54	65,24	Sonido (Venezuela) 2		111	50,3	‡Caracas, Venezuela	28 June	1970
				Western Romance (Canada) 3		116	52,6	Stampede Park, Calgary, Alberta, Canada	19 April	1980
				Northern Spike (Canada) 5		119	54,0	Winnipeg, Canada	23 Apr	1982
⅝ mile	53.6†	41.98	67,56	Indigenous (GB) 4		131	59,4	‡*Epsom, Surrey	2 June	1960
	53.70††	41.90	67,43	Spark Chief (GB) 4		110	49,8	‡*Epsom, Surrey	30 Aug	1983
	55.2	40.76	65,60	Chinook Pass (USA) 3		113	51,1	Longacres, Seattle, Washington, USA	17 Sept	1982
¾ mile	1:06.2	40.78	65,62	gelding by Blink—Broken ....2 Tendril (GB)		123	55,7	*Brighton, East Sussex	6 Aug	1929
	1:07.2	40.18	64,66	Grey Papa (USA) 6		112	59,8	Longacres, Seattle, Washington, USA	4 Sept	1972
				Petro D. Jay (USA) 6		120	54,4	Turf Paradise, Phoenix, Arizona, USA	9 May	1982
1 mile	1:31.8	39.21	63,10	Soueida (GB) 4		126	57,1	*Brighton, East Sussex	19 Sept	1963
				Loose Cover (GB) 3		110	49,8	*Brighton, East Sussex	9 June	1966
				Traditional Miss (GB) 6		132	59,9	Chepstow, Wales	27 June	1981
				Traditional Miss (GB) 6		132	59,9	Chepstow, Wales	31 Aug	1981
	1:32.0			Royal Heroine (USA) 4		123	55,8	Hollywood Park, Cal.	10 Nov	1984
1¼ miles	1:57.4	38.33	61,68	Double Discount (USA) 4		116	52,6	Santa Anita, Arcadia, California, USA	6 Oct	1977
1½ miles	2:23.0	37.76	60,76	Fiddle Isle (USA) 5		124	56,2	Santa Anita, Arcadia, California, USA	21 Mar	1970
				John Henry (USA) 5		126	57,1	Santa Anita, Arcadia, California, USA	16 Mar	1980
2 miles	3:16.75	36.59	58,89	Il Tempo (NZ) 7		130	59,0	Trentham, New Zealand	17 Jan	1970
2½ miles	4:14.6	35.35	56,90	Miss Grillo (USA) 6		118	53,5	Pimlico, Baltimore, Maryland, USA	12 Nov	1948
3 miles	5:15.0	34.29	55,18	Farragut (Mexico) 5		113	51,2	Agua Caliente, Mexico	9 Mar	1941

† Hand timed. †† Electronically timed. ‡ Straight courses. * Epsom and Brighton courses include a sharp descent of ¼ mile.

Cup, and on 27 Dec 1982 he trained 12 winners (from 21 runners) at six meetings. Fred Winter won a record eight trainers' championships, 1971–5, 1977–8 and 1985.

GRAND NATIONAL

The first Grand National Steeple Chase may be regarded as the Grand Liverpool Steeple Chase of 26 Feb 1839 though the race was not given its present name until 1847. It became a handicap in 1843. Until 1930 five-year-olds were eligible, but since then it has been for six-year-olds and above. Except for 1916–8 and 1941–5 when it was run at Gatwick, the race has been run at Aintree, near Liverpool, over 30 fences.

Most wins

The only horse to win three times is *Red Rum* (foaled 1965) in 1973, 1974 and 1977, from five runs. He came second in 1975 and 1976. *Manifesto* ran a record eight times (1895–1904). He won in 1897 and 1899, came third three times and fourth once.

Highest prize

The highest prize and the richest ever over jumps in Great Britain was £54,769 won by *Hallo Dandy*, ridden by Neale Doughty and trained by Gordon W. Richards on 31 Mar 1984 and by *Last Suspect*, ridden by Hywel Davies and trained by Tim Forster, on 30 Mar 1985.

Highest weight

The highest weight ever carried to victory is 12 st 7 lb *79,4 kg* by *Cloister* (1893), *Manifesto* (1899), *Jerry M.* (1912) and *Poethlyn* (1919).

HURLING

Earliest reference

A game of very ancient origin, hurling was included in the Tailteann Games (inst 1829 BC). It only became standardised with the formation of the Gaelic Athletic Association in Thurles, Ireland, on 1 Nov 1884. The Irish Hurling Union was formed on 24 Jan 1879.

Most titles *All-Ireland*

The greatest number of All-Ireland Championships won by one team is 24 by Cork between 1890 and 1978. The greatest number of successive wins is four by Cork (1941–4).

Most titles *Inter-provincials*

Munster holds the greatest number of inter-provincial (Railway Cup) championships with 34 (1928–77).

Most appearances

The most appearances in All-Ireland finals is ten shared by Christy Ring (Cork and Munster) and John Doyle (Tipperary). They also share the record of All-Ireland medals won with eight each. Ring's appearances on the winning side were in 1941–4, 1946 and 1952–4, while Doyle's were in 1949–51, 1958, 1961–2 and 1964–5. Ring also played in a record 22 inter-provincial finals (1942–63) and was on the winning side 18 times.

Highest and lowest scores

The highest score in an All-Ireland final (60 min) was in 1896 when Tipperary (8 goals, 14 points) beat Dublin (no goals, 4 points). The record aggregate score was when Cork (6 goals, 21 points), defeated Wexford (5 goals, 10 points) in the 80 min final of 1970. A goal equals three points. The highest recorded individual score was by Nick Rackard (Wexford), who scored 7 goals and 7 points against Antrim in the 1954 All-Ireland semi-final. The lowest score in an All-Ireland final was when Tipperary (1 goal, 1 point) beat Galway (nil) in the first championship at Birr in 1887.

Longest stroke

The greatest distance for a 'lift and stroke' is one of 129 yd *117 m* credited to Tom Murphy of Three Castles, Kilkenny, in a 'long puck' contest in 1906. The record for the annual *An Poc Fada* (Long Puck) contest (instituted 1961) in the ravines of the Cooley Hills, north of Dundalk, County Louth, is 65 pucks (drives) plus 87 yd *79 m* over the course of 3 miles 320 yd *5120 km* by Fionnbar O'Neill (Cork) in 1966. This represents an average of 84.8 yd *77,5 m* per drive.

Largest crowd

The largest crowd was 84,865 for the final between Cork and Wexford at Croke Park, Dublin, in 1954.

ICE HOCKEY

Origins

There is pictorial evidence that a hockey-like game (*Kalv*) was played on ice in the early 16th century in The Netherlands. The game was probably first played in North America on 25 Dec 1855 at Kingston, Ontario, Canada, but Halifax also lays claim to priority. The International Ice Hockey Federation was founded in 1908. The National Hockey League (NHL) of North America was inaugurated 1917.

World Championships and Olympic Games

World Championships were first held for amateurs in 1920 in conjunction with the Olympic Games, which were also considered as World Championships up to 1968. From 1977 World Championships have been open to professionals. The USSR have won 19 world titles between 1954 and 1983, including the Olympic titles of 1956, 1964 and 1968. They have won three further Olympic titles in 1972, 1976 and 1984. Canada have also won 19 titles, between 1920 and 1961, including 6 Olympic titles (1920, 1924, 1928, 1932, 1948 and 1952). The longest Olympic career is that of Richard Torriani (b. 1 Oct 1911) (Switzerland) from 1928 to 1948. The most gold medals won by any player is three achieved by USSR players Vitaliy Davidov, Anatoliy Firssov, Viktor Kuzkin and Aleksandr Ragulin in 1964, 1968 and 1972, and by Vladislav Tretyak in 1972, 1976 and 1984.

Stanley Cup

The Stanley Cup, presented by the Governor-General, Lord Stanley (original cost $48.67), became emblematic of National Hockey League supremacy 33 years after the first contest at Montreal in 1893. It has been won most often by the Montreal Canadiens with 22 wins in 1916, 1924, 1930–1, 1944, 1946, 1953, 1956–60, 1965–6, 1968–9, 1971, 1973, 1976–9.

British Competitions

The English National (later British) League championship (inst. 1935) has been won by the Wembley Lions four times in 1936–7, 1952 and 1957 and by Streatham (now Redskins) in 1950, 1953, 1960 and 1982. Murrayfield Racers have won the Northern League (inst. 1966) six times, 1970–2, 1976, 1979 and 1980. The Icy Smith Cup (first held 1966), emblematic of British club supremacy until 1981, was won by Murrayfield Racers nine times, 1966, 1969–72, 1975 and 1979–81. The British club championship (inst. 1982) was won by Dundee Rockets in 1982, 1983 and 1984.

Most goals *Team*

The greatest number of goals recorded in a world championship match was when Canada beat Denmark 47–0 in Stockholm, Sweden on 12 Feb 1949. The NHL record is 21 goals when Montreal

Canadiens beat Toronto St Patrick's, at Montreal, 14–7 on 10 Jan 1920.

Most goals and points *Individual*

The most goals scored in a season in the NHL is 92 in the 1981–2 season by Wayne Gretzky (b. 26 Jan 1961) (Edmonton Oilers). He also scored a record 212 points (including 120 assists). He scored an additional 12 points (5 goals, 7 assists) in the Stanley Cup playoffs and 14 points (6 goals, 8 assists) for Canada in the World Championships in April 1982. He scored a record 125 assists the following season, 1982–83. Gretzky scored his 400th NHL goal on 13 Jan 1985 for an average .915 goals per game. The North American career record for goals is 1071 (801 in the NHL) by Gordie Howe (b. 31 Mar 1928) (Detroit Red Wings, Houston Aeros, New England Whalers and Hartford Whalers) from 16 Oct 1946 in 32 seasons ending in 1979–80. He took 2204 games to achieve the 1000th goal, but Robert Marvin 'Bobby' Hull (b. 3 Jan 1939) (Chicago Black Hawks and Winnipeg Jets) scored his 1000th in 1600 games on 12 Mar 1978.

Most goals and points *British*

The highest score and aggregate in a League match was set when Cleveland Bombers beat Richmond Flyers 41–2 at Billingham Forum on 19 Feb 1983. Ted Phillips (b. 19 Oct 1957) scored a record 20 points (13 goals, 7 assists). The most individual goals scored in a senior game is 14 by Roy Halpin (Canada) (b. 18 Oct 1955) for Dundee Rockets in a 24–1 win over Durham Wasps at Dundee on 4 Apr 1982. Dave Stoyanovich (Canada) (b. 1959) set British senior records of 162 goals and 258 points in 51 games in the 1984–5 season.

Most points one game

The North American major league record for most points scored in one game is ten (3 goals, 7 assists) by Jim Harrison (b. 9 July 1947) (for Alberta, later Edmonton Oilers) in a World Hockey Association match at Edmonton on 30 Jan 1973, and by Darryl Sittler (b. 18 Sept 1950) (6 goals, 4 assists) for Toronto Maple Leafs in a NHL match at Toronto on 7 Feb 1976.

Fastest scoring *World*

In the NHL the fastest goal was after 4 sec in the second period by Joseph Antoine Claude Provost (b. 17 Sept 1933) (Montreal Canadiens) *v.* Boston Bruins at Montreal on 9 Nov 1957. Doug Smail of the Winnipeg Jets scored 5 sec from the opening whistle against St Louis on 20 Dec 1981. Canadian Bill Mosienko (Chicago Black Hawks) (b. 2 Nov 1921) scored three goals in 21 sec *v.* New York Rangers on 23 Mar 1952. Toronto scored eight goals in 4 min 52 sec *v.* New York Americans on 19 Mar 1938.

In minor leagues, Kim D. Miles scored in 3 sec for Univ of Guelph *v.* Univ of W Ontario on 11 Feb 1975. Three goals in 12 sec was achieved by Steve D'Innocenzo for Holliston *v.* Westwood in a high school match in Massachusetts, USA on 9 Jan 1982. The Skara Ishockeyclubb, Sweden, scored three goals in 11 sec against Örebro IK at Skara on 18 Oct 1981. The Vernon Cougars scored five goals in 56 sec against Salmon Arm Aces at Vernon, BC, Canada on 6 Aug 1982. The Kamloops Knights of Columbus scored seven goals in 2 min 22 sec *v.* Prince George Vikings on 25 Jan 1980.

Fastest scoring *Great Britain*

The fastest goal in the Heineken League was scored by Steve Johnson for Durham Wasps after four seconds *v.* Ayr Bruins at Ayr, Scotland on 6 Nov 1983. Kenny Westman (Nottingham Panthers) scored a hat trick in 30 sec *v.* Brighton Tigers on 3 Mar 1955.

In an English Junior League (under-16) game Jonathan Lumbis scored a hat-trick in 13 sec for Nottingham Cougars *v.* Peterborough Jets on 4 Nov 1984.

Most successful goaltending

The most matches played by a goaltender in an NHL career without conceding a goal is 103 by Terrance 'Terry' Gordon Sawchuck (1929–70) of Detroit, Boston, Toronto, Los Angeles and New York Rangers, between 1950 and 1967. Gerry Cheevers (b. 2 Dec 1940), Boston Bruins, went a record 33 successive games without a defeat in 1971–2.

Longest match

The longest match was 2 hr 56 min 30 sec (playing time) when Detroit Red Wings beat Montreal Maroons 1–0 in the sixth period of overtime at the Forum, Montreal, at 2.25 a.m. on 25 Mar 1936. Norm Smith, the Red Wings goaltender, turned aside 92 shots for the NHL's longest single shutout.

ICE SKATING

Origins

The earliest reference to ice skating is in early Scandinavian literature referring to the 2nd century though its origins are believed, on archaeological evidence, to be ten centuries earlier still. The earliest English account of 1180 refers to skates made of bone. The earliest skating club was the Edinburgh Skating Club formed in about 1742. The first recorded race was from Wisbech to Whittlesea, East Anglia, in 1763. The earliest artificial rink in the world was opened at the Baker Street Bazaar, Portman Square, London, on 7 Dec 1842, although the surface was not of ice. The first artificial ice rink was opened in the King's Road, Chelsea, London on 7 Jan 1876. The National Skating Association of Great Britain was founded in 1879. The International Skating Union was founded at Scheveningen, Netherlands in 1892.

FIGURE SKATING

Most titles *Olympic*

The most Olympic gold medals won by a figure skater is three by Gillis Grafström (1893–1938) of Sweden in 1920, 1924, and 1928 (also silver medal in 1932); by Sonja Henie (1912–69) of Norway in 1928, 1932 and 1936; and by Irina Rodnina (b. USSR 12 Sept 1949) with two different partners in the Pairs event in 1972, 1976, and 1980.

Most titles *World*

The greatest number of individual world figure skating titles (instituted 1896) is ten by Ulrich Salchow (1877–1949) of Sweden, in 1901–5 and 1907–11. The women's record (inst. 1906) is also ten individual titles by Sonja Henie between 1927 and 1936. Irina Rodnina has won ten pairs titles (inst. 1908), four with Aleksey Ulanov (b. 4 Nov 1947) 1969–72, and six with her husband Aleksandr Zaitsev (b. 16 June 1952) 1973–8. The most ice dance titles (inst. 1952) won is six by Ludmila Pakhomova (b. 31 Dec 1946) and Aleksandr Gorshkov (b. 8 Oct 1946) (USSR) 1970–4 and 1976.

Most titles *British*

The most individual British titles is 11 by Jack Ferguson Page (1900–47) (Manchester SC) in

Husband and wife Irina Rodnina and Aleksandr Zaitsev dominated the world pairs between 1973 and 1978. Irina Rodnina won the event ten years in a row for a record number of titles. *(All-Sport/ Tony Duffy)*

1922–31 and 1933, and six by Cecilia Colledge (b. 28 Nov 1920) (Park Lane FSC, London) in 1935–7 (two), 1938 and 1946. Page and Ethel M. Muckelt (1885–1953) won nine pairs titles, 1923–31. The most by an ice dance couple is six by Jayne Torvill (b. 7 Oct 1957) and Christopher Dean (b. 27 July 1958), 1978–83.

Triple Crown
The only British skaters to win the 'Grand Slam' of World, Olympic and European titles in the same year are John Anthony Curry (b. 9 Sept 1949) in 1976 and the ice dancers Jayne Torvill and Christopher Dean in 1984. Karl Schäfer (Austria) (1909–76) and Sonja Henie achieved double 'Grand Slams', both in the years 1932 and 1936.

Andrea Schöne (GDR), holder of three of the five recognised speed skating records. In the 1500 m event she averages 45.78 km/h 27.20 mph. (All-Sport)

SPEED SKATING WORLD RECORDS

MEN

Distance	min sec	Name (Country)	Place	Date
500 metres	36.57*	Pavel Pegov (USSR)	Medeo, USSR	26 Mar 1983
1000 metres	1.12.58	Pavel Pegov (USSR)	Medeo, USSR	25 Mar 1983
1500 metres	1.53.26	Oleg Bozhyev (USSR)	Medeo, USSR	24 Mar 1984
3000 metres	4.03.31	André Hoffmann (GDR)	Davos, Switzerland	13 Jan 1985
5000 metres	6.49.15	Viktor Shasherin (USSR)	Medeo, USSR	23 Mar 1984
10,000 metres	14.21.51	Igor Malkov (USSR)	Medeo, USSR	24 Mar 1984

WOMEN

Distance	min sec	Name (Country)	Place	Date
500 metres	39.69	Christa Rothenburger (GDR)	Medeo, USSR	25 Mar 1983
1000 metres	1.19.31	Natalia Petruseva (USSR)	Medeo, USSR	26 Mar 1983
1500 metres	2.03.34	Andrea Schöne (GDR)	Medeo, USSR	24 Mar 1984
3000 metres	4.20.91	Andrea Schöne (GDR)	Medeo, USSR	23 Mar 1984
5000 metres	7.32.82	Andrea Schöne (GDR)	Sarajevo, Yugoslavia	9 Feb 1985

* represents an average speed of 49.22 km/hr *30.58 mph*. Note that Medeo, Alma Ata, USSR is situated at an altitude of 1691 m above sea level.

WORLD SHORT TRACK SPEED SKATING RECORDS

MEN

Distance	min sec	Name (Country)	Place	Date
500 metres	45.08	Louis Grenier (Canada)	Amsterdam, Netherlands	16 Mar 1985
1000 metres	1.36.55	Louis Grenier (Canada)	Amsterdam, Netherlands	17 Mar 1985
1500 metres	2.27.27	Tatsuyoshi Ishihara (Japan)	Dan Haag, Netherlands	28 Mar 1981
3000 metres	5.04.24	Tatsuyoshi Ishihara (Japan)	Amsterdam, Netherlands	17 Mar 1985

WOMEN

Distance	min sec	Name (Country)	Place	Date
500 metres	48.89	Eiko Shishii (Japan)	Amsterdam, Netherlands	16 Mar 1985
1000 metres	1.43.58	Hiromi Takeuchi (Japan)	Amsterdam, Netherlands	16 Mar 1985
		Natalie Lambert (Canada)	Amsterdam, Netherlands	17 Mar 1985
1500 metres	2.41.75	Sylvie Daigle (Canada)	Kobe, Japan	16 Apr 1983
3000 metres	5.32.31	Sylvie Daigle (Canada)	Kobe, Japan	17 Apr 1983

BRITISH SHORT TRACK SPEED SKATING RECORDS

MEN

Distance	min sec	Name	Place	Date
500 metres	45.61	Wilfred O'Reilly	Amsterdam, Netherlands	16 Mar 1985
1000 metres	1.35.97	Wilfred O'Reilly	Moncton, Canada	3 Apr 1982
1500 metres	2.32.84	Wilfred O'Reilly	Amsterdam, Netherlands	15 Mar 1985
3000 metres	5.22.08	Wilfred O'Reilly	Amsterdam, Netherlands	17 Mar 1985

WOMEN

Distance	min sec	Name	Place	Date
500 metres	51.78	Kim Ferran	Brugge, Belgium	18 Mar 1984
1000 metres	1.47.57	Kim Ferran	Brugge, Belgium	18 Mar 1984
1500 metres	2.46.88	Amanda Worth	Tokyo, Japan	8 Apr 1983
3000 metres	5.59.08	Amanda Worth	Richmond, England	1 Mar 1985

BRITISH OUTDOOR RECORDS

MEN

Distance	min sec	Name	Place	Date
500 metres	39.41	Archie Marshall	Davos, Switzerland	20 Jan 1980
1000 metres	1.19.23	Archie Marshall	Davos, Switzerland	20 Jan 1980
1500 metres	2.05.88	Derek Webber	Davos, Switzerland	23 Jan 1983
3000 metres	4.24.71	Derek Webber	Davos, Switzerland	22 Jan 1983
5000 metres	7.32.75	Brian Carvis	Inzell, W. Germany	7 Jan 1984
10,000 metres	15.35.74	Alan Luke	Inzell, W. Germany	7 Mar 1982

WOMEN

Distance	min sec	Name	Place	Date
500 metres	46.53	Kim Ferran	Inzell, W. Germany	5 Jan 1980
1000 metres	1.31.85	Kim Ferran	Madonna di Campiglio, Italy	10 Jan 1979
1500 metres	2.21.86	Amanda Horsepool	Inzell, W. Germany	27 Dec 1980
3000 metres	4.54.74	Kim Ferran	Inzell, W. Germany	6 Jan 1979

Highest marks
The highest tally of maximum six marks awarded in an international championship was 29 to Jayne Torvill and Christopher Dean (GB) in the World ice dance championships at Ottawa, Canada on 22–24 Mar 1984. This comprised seven in the compulsory dances, a perfect set of nine for presentation in the set pattern dance and 13 in the free dance including another perfect set from all nine judges for artistic presentation. They previously gained a perfect set of nine sixes for artistic presentation in the free dance at the 1983 World Championships in Helsinki, Finland and at the 1984 Olympic Games in Sarajevo, Yugoslavia. In their career Torvill and Dean received a record total of 136 sixes.

The most by a soloist was seven to Donald Jackson (b. 2 Apr 1940) (Canada) in the world men's championship at Prague, Czechoslovakia, in 1962.

Distance
Robin Cousins (GB) (b. 17 Mar 1957) achieved 19 ft 1 in *5,81 m* in an Axel jump and 18 ft *5,48 m* with a back flip at Richmond Ice Rink, Surrey on 16 Nov 1983.

Largest rink
The world's largest indoor ice rink is in the Moscow Olympic arena which has an ice area of 8064 m² *86,800 ft²*. The five rinks at Fujikyu Highland Skating Centre, Japan total 26 500 m² *285,243 ft²*.

SPEED SKATING

Most titles *Olympic*
The most Olympic gold medals won in speed skating is six by Lidia Skoblikova (b. 8 Mar 1939) of Chelyabinsk, USSR, in 1960 (two) and 1964 (four). The male record is by Clas Thunberg (1893–1973) (Finland) with five gold (including one tied), and also one silver and one tied bronze in 1924 and 1928. Eric Heiden (USA) (b. 14 June 1958) also won five gold medals, all at Lake Placid, NY, USA, in 1980.

Most titles *World*
The greatest number of world overall titles (inst. 1893) won by any skater is five by Oscar Mathisen (Norway) (1888–1954) in 1908–9 and 1912–14, and Clas Thunberg in 1923, 1925, 1928–9 and 1931. The most titles won in the women's events (inst. 1936) is four by Inga Voronina (*née* Artomonova) (1936–66) (USSR) in 1957, 1958, 1962 and 1964 and Atje Keulen-Deelstra (b. 31 Dec 1938) (Netherlands) 1970, 1972–4.

The record score achieved in the world overall title is 160.807 points by Viktor Shasherin

(USSR) (b. 23 July 1962) at Medeo, USSR, 23–24 Mar 1984. The record women's score is 171.760 points by Andrea Schöne (GDR) (b. 1 Dec 1960) at Medeo, 23–24 Mar 1984.

Longest race

The 'Elfstedentocht' ('Tour of the Eleven Towns') was held in the Netherlands from the 1800s to 1963 and again in 1985, covering 200 km *124 miles 483 yd*. It was transferred first to Lake Vesijärvi, near Lahti, Finland and in 1984 to Canada as the International Race of 11 Cities on the Ottawa River. The record time for 200 km is 6 hr 5 min 12 sec by Jan-Roelof Kruithof (Netherlands) on 25 Feb 1979 at Oulu, Finland. Kruithof won the race eight times, 1974, 1976–7, 1979–83.

24 hours

Ton Smits (Netherlands) skated 506,375 km *314.65 miles* in 24 hours in Eindhoven, Netherlands on 15–16 Dec 1984.

ICE AND SAND YACHTING

Origins

The sport originated in the Low Countries from the year 1600 (earliest patent granted) and along the Baltic coast. The earliest authentic record is Dutch, dating from 1768. Land or sand yachts of Dutch construction were first reported on beaches (now in Belgium) in 1595. The earliest International championship was staged in 1914.

Largest yacht

The largest ice yacht was *Icicle*, built for Commodore John E. Roosevelt for racing on the Hudson River, New York, in 1869. It was 68 ft 11 in *21 m* long and carried 1070 ft² *99 m²* of canvas.

Highest speeds *Ice*

The highest speed officially recorded is 143 mph *230 km/h* by John D. Buckstaff in a Class A stern-steerer on Lake Winnebago, Wisconsin, USA, in 1938. Such a speed is possible in a wind of 72 mph *115 km/h*.

Highest speeds *Sand*

The official world record for a sand yacht is 107 km/h *66.48 mph* set by Christian-Yves Nau (b. 1944) (France) in *Mobil* at Le Touquet, France on 22 Mar 1981, when the wind speed reached 120 km/h *75 mph*. A speed of 88.4 mph *142,26 km/h* was attained by Nord Embroden (USA) in *Midnight at the Oasis* at Superior Dry Lake, California, USA on 15 Apr 1976.

JUDO

Origins

Judo is a modern combat sport which developed out of an amalgam of several old Japanese fighting arts, the most popular of which was ju-jitsu (jiu-jitsu), which is thought to be of Chinese origin. Judo has greatly developed since 1882, when it was first devised by Dr Jigoro Kano (1860–1938). The International Judo Federation was founded in 1951.

Most titles *World and Olympic*

World championships were inaugurated in Tō-kyō in 1956. Women's championships were first held in 1980 in New York. Yashiro Yamashita won nine consecutive Japanese titles 1977–85, four world titles; Heavyweight 1979, 1981 and 1983 and Open 1981, and the Olympic Open category in 1984. He retired undefeated after 203 successive wins, 1977–85. Two other men have won four world titles, Wilhelm Ruska (b. 29 Aug 1940) (Netherlands), 1967, 1971 Heavyweight and the 1972 Olympic Heavyweight and Open titles, and Shozo Fujii (Japan) (b. 12 May 1950), the Middleweight title 1971, 1973, 1975, and 1979. Ingrid Berghmans (Belgium) with six, has won most medals by a woman in world championships, gold (Open) and bronze (72 kg) in 1980, gold (Open) and silver (72 kg) in 1982 and two golds (both 72 kg and Open) in 1984.

Most titles *British*

The greatest number of titles (inst. 1966) won is nine by David Colin Starbrook (b. 9 Aug 1945) (6th dan); Middleweight 1969–70, Light-heavyweight 1971–5 and the Open division 1970–1. A record six titles in the women's events (inst. 1971) were won by Christine Child (now Mrs Gallie) (b. 1946) (6th dan): Heavyweight in 1971–5 and the Open division in 1973. Neil Adams (b. 27 Sept 1958) has the most successful international record of any British player. He won two junior (1974 and 1977) and five senior (1979–80, 1983–5) European titles; four World championships medals (one gold, one silver, two bronze) and two Olympic silver medals. To 1985 he has won eight British senior titles.

Highest grades

The efficiency grades in Judo are divided into

pupil (*kyu*) and master (*dan*) grades. The highest awarded is the extremely rare red belt *Judan* (10th dan), given only to 13 men so far. The Judo protocol provides for an 11th dan (*Juichidan*) who also would wear a red belt, a 12th dan (*Junidan*) who would wear a white belt twice as wide as an ordinary belt and the highest of all, *Shihan*, but these have never been bestowed. The highest British native Judo grade is 8th dan by Charles Stuart Palmer (b. 1930). Christine Gallie (née Child) was awarded her 6th Dan in 1983.

KARATE

Origins

Based on techniques devised from the sixth century Chinese art of Shaolin boxing (Kempo), Karate was developed by an unarmed populace in Okinawa as a weapon against armed Japanese oppressors *c.* 1500. Transmitted to Japan in the 1920s by Funakoshi Gichin, this method of combat was refined into Karate and organised into a sport with competitive rules. The five major styles of Karate in Japan are: *Shotokan, Wado-ryu, Goju-ryu, Shito-ryu* and *Kyokushinkai*, each of which place different emphasis on speed and power, etc. Other styles include *Sankukai, Shotokai* and *Shukokai. Wu shu* is a comprehensive term embracing all Chinese martial arts. *Kung fu* is one aspect of these arts popularised by the cinema. (*See also p. 175*).

The Governing Body for the sport in Britain is the Martial Arts Commission upon which all the martial arts are represented.

World championships

Great Britain have won a record three world titles (inst 1970) at the Kumite team event, 1975, 1982 and 1984.

Top exponents

The leading exponents among karatekas are a number of 10th dans in Japan. The leading exponents in the United Kingdom are Tatsuo Suzuki (8th dan, *Wado-ryu*) (b. 27 Apr 1928) chief instructor to the European Karatedo Wadokai; Keinosuke Enoeda (8th dan, *Shotokan*), resident instructor to the Karate Union of Great Britain and Steve Arneil (7th dan, *Kyokushinkai*), British national born in South Africa.

LACROSSE

MEN'S LACROSSE

The game is of American Indian origin, derived from the inter-tribal game *baggataway*, and was played before 1492 by Iroquois Indians in lower Ontario, Canada and upper New York State, USA. The French named it after their game of *Chouler à la crosse*, known in 1381. It was introduced into Great Britain in 1867. The English Lacrosse Union was formed in 1892. Lacrosse was included in the Olympic Games of 1908 and featured as an exhibition sport in the 1928 and 1948 Games.

Most titles *World*

The United States have won three of the four World Championships, in 1967, 1974 and 1982 and also won the pre-Olympic tournament in 1984. Canada won the other world title in 1978 beating the USA 17–16 after extra time—this was the first drawn international match.

Most titles *English*

The English Club Championship (Iroquois Cup—inst. 1890), has been won most often by

Ingrid Berghmans of Belgium, the leading exponent of women's judo and holder of a record six world championship titles. (*All-Sport/John Gichigi*)

Stockport with 15 wins between 1897 and 1934. The record score in a final was set by Sheffield University, 30–5 v. Hampstead in 1982 and 30–1 v. Kenton in 1983.

Most international appearances

The record number of international representations is 33 for England by James Michael 'Mike' Roberts (Urmston) (b. 22 Feb 1946), to 1982. He is the only man to play in all four World Championships.

Highest scores

The highest score in an international match was the United States' 28–4 win over Canada at Stockport, Greater Manchester on 3 July 1978. England's highest score was their 19–11 win over Canada at Melbourne in 1974.

Fastest scoring

Rod Burns scored only 4 sec into the game for South Manchester and Wythenshawe v. Sheffield Univ. on 6 Dec 1975.

WOMEN'S LACROSSE

The first reported playing of lacrosse by women was in 1886. The All-England Women's Lacrosse Association was formed in 1912. The game has evolved from the men's game so that the rules now differ considerably.

World Championships

The first official championships, held in 1982 at Trent Bridge, Nottingham, England, were won by the USA.

Most international appearances

Caro Macintosh (b. 18 Feb 1932) made a record 52 appearances for Scotland, 1952–9. The record for Great Britain is eight by Celia Brackenridge (b. 22 Aug 1950), 1970–9.

Highest score

The highest score by an international team was by Great Britain and Ireland with their 40–0 defeat of Long Island during their 1967 tour of the USA.

MARBLES

The British Marbles Championships are held annually at Tinsley Green, Sussex on Good Friday. Len Smith, winner of most titles, is a picture of concentration. *(AP)*

Origins

Marbles may have been a children's game in Ancient Egypt, and was introduced into Britain by the Romans in the 1st Century AD. It became a competitive sport under the British Marbles Board of Control at the Greyhound Hotel, Tinsley Green, Crawley, West Sussex in 1926.

Most championships

The British Championship (established 1926) has been won most often by the Toucan Terribles with 20 consecutive titles (1956–75). Three founder members, Len Smith, Jack and Charlie

Dempsey played in every title win. They were finally beaten in 1976 by the Pernod Rams, captained by Len Smith's son, Paul. Len Smith (b. 13 Oct 1917) has won the individual title 15 times (1957–64, 1966, 1968–73) but lost in 1974 to his son Alan.

Speed record

The record for clearing the ring (between 5¾ and 6¼ ft *1,75–1,90 m* in diameter) of 49 marbles is 2 min 57 sec by the Toucan Terribles at Worthing, West Sussex in 1971.

MODERN PENTATHLON & BIATHLON

Points scores in riding, fencing, cross country and hence overall scores have no comparative value between one competition and another. In shooting and swimming (300 m) the scores are of record significance and the best achievements are shown.

The Modern Pentathlon (Riding, Fencing, Swimming, Shooting and Running) was inaugurated into the Olympic Games at Stockholm in 1912. The Modern Pentathlon Association of Great Britain was formed in 1922. L'Union Internationale de Pentathlon Moderne et Biathlon (UIPMB) was founded in 1948. Originally the UIPM, the administration of Biathlon (cross-country skiing and shooting) was added in 1957, and the name modified accordingly.

MODERN PENTATHLON

Most titles *World* (Inst. 1949)

András Balczó (Hungary) (b. 16 Aug 1938) won the record number of world titles, six individual and seven team. He won the world individual title in 1963, 1965–7 and 1969 and the Olympic title in 1972. His seven team titles (1960–70) comprised five world and two Olympic.

Women's world championships were first held in 1981. Great Britain won the three team titles 1981–83, with Sarah Parker (b. 16 July 1956) a member of each of those teams. Wendy Johana Norman (b. 20 Feb 1965) won the individual title in 1982 and team golds in 1981–2. She also won the individual world cup title in 1980 and Great Britain won each of the three world cup team titles, 1978–80.

Most titles *Olympic*

The greatest number of Olympic gold medals won is three by András Balczó, a member of the winning team in 1960 and 1968 and the 1972 individual champion. Lars Hall (b. 30 Apr 1927) (Sweden) has uniquely won two individual Championships (1952 and 1956). Pavel Lednev (USSR) (b. 25 Mar 1943) won a record seven medals (two gold, two silver, three bronze),

1968–80. The best British performance is the team gold medal at Montreal, Canada 18–22 July 1976 by Jim Fox, Adrian Philip Parker and Daniel Nightingale. The best individual placing is fourth by Jeremy Robert 'Jim' Fox (b. 19 Sept 1941) at Munich in 1972.

Probably the greatest margin of victory was by William Oscar Guernsey Grut (b. 17 Sept 1914) (Sweden) in the 1948 Games in London, when he won three events and was placed fifth and eighth in the other two events.

Most titles *British*

The pentathlete with most British titles is Jim Fox, with ten (1963, 1965–8, 1970–4). Wendy Norman has won a record four women's titles, 1978–80 and 1982.

BIATHLON

The biathlon, which combines cross-country skiing and rifle shooting was first included in the Olympic Games in 1960, and world championships were first held in 1958.

Most titles *Olympic Games*

Magnar Solberg (Norway) (b. 4 Feb 1937), in 1968 and 1972, is the only man to have won two Olympic individual titles. The USSR have won all five 4 × 7,5 km relay titles, 1968–84. Aleksandr Tikhonov (b. 2 Jan 1947) who was a member of the first four teams also won a silver in the 1968 20 km.

Most titles *World Championship*

Frank Ullrich (GDR) (b. 24 Jan 1958) has won a record six individual world titles, four at 10 km, 1978–81, including the 1980 Olympics, and two at 20 km 1982–3. Aleksandr Tikhonov was in ten winning USSR relay teams, 1968–80 and won four individual titles.

The biathlon world cup (inst 1979) was won three times by Frank Ullrich, 1980–2. He was 2nd in 1979 and 3rd in 1983.

MOTORCYCLE RACING

See also The Guinness Book of Motorcycling Facts and Feats by L. J. K. Setright (price £7.95) and The Guinness Guide to Motorcycling by Peter Carrick (price £10.95).

Earliest race

The first motorcycle race was held over a mile *1,6 km* on an oval track at Sheen House, Richmond, Surrey, on 29 Nov 1897, won by Charles Jarrott (1877–1944) on a Fournier. The oldest motorcycle races in the world are the Auto-Cycle Union Tourist Trophy (TT) series, first held on the 15.81 mile *25,44 km* 'Peel' ('St John's') course in the Isle of Man on 28 May 1907, and still run in the island on the 'Mountain' circuit.

Modern Pentathlon HIGHEST SCORES (In major competition)

	Performance	Points	Name and Place	Date and Venue
WORLD				
Shooting	200/200	—[1]	Charles Leonard (USA) (b. 23 Feb 1913)	3 Aug 1936, Berlin, Germany
	200/200	1132	Daniele Masala (Italy) (b. 12 Feb 1955)	21 Aug 1978, Jönkoping, Sweden
	200/200	1132	George Horvath (Sweden) (b. 14 Mar 1960)	22 July 1980, Moscow, USSR
Swimming	3 min 08.22 sec	1368	John Scott (USA) (b. 14 Apr 1962)	27 Aug 1982, London, England
BRITISH				
Shooting	198/200	1088	Timothy Kenealy (b. 3 Mar 1950)	Helsinki, Finland, 4 June 1979
Swimming	3 min 16.224 sec	1304	Richard Lawson Phelps (b. 19 Apr 1961)	31 July 1984, Los Angeles, USA

[1] *points not given in 1936 Olympic Games.*

Fastest circuits *World*

The highest average lap speed attained on any closed circuit is 160.288 mph *257,958 km/h* by Yvon du Hamel (Canada) (b. 1941) on a modified 903 cc four-cylinder Kawasaki Z1 at the 31 degree banked 2.5 mile *4,02 km* Daytona International Speedway, Florida, USA, in March 1973. His lap time was 56.149 sec.

The fastest road circuit is the Francorchamps circuit near Spa, Belgium. It is 8.74 miles *14,12 km* in length and was lapped in 3 min 50.3 sec (average speed 137.150 mph *220,721 km/h*) by Barry Stephen Frank Sheene (GB) (b. 11 Sept 1950) on a 495 cc four-cylinder Suzuki during the Belgian Grand Prix on 3 July 1977.

Fastest circuits *United Kingdom*

The fastest circuit in the United Kingdom is the Portstewart-Coleraine-Portrush circuit in Londonderry, N. Ireland. The lap record (10.1 mile *16,26 km* lap) is 4 min 53.2 sec (average speed 124.060 mph *199,655 km/h*) by John Glyn Williams (1946–78) on a 747 cc four-cylinder Yamaha on lap five of the 750cc event of the North West 200, on 21 May 1977.

The lap record for the outer circuit (2.767 miles *4,453 km*) at the Brooklands Motor Course, near Weybridge, Surrey (open between 1907 and 1939) was 80.0 sec (average speed 124.51 mph *200,37 km/h*) by Noel Baddow 'Bill' Pope (later Major) (1909–71) of the United Kingdom on a Brough Superior powered by a supercharged 996 cc V-twin '8-80' JAP engine developing 110 bhp, on 4 July 1939.

Fastest race *World*

The fastest road race is the 500 cc Belgian Grand Prix held on the Francorchamps circuit (*see above*). The record time for this ten lap (87.74 mile *141,20 km*) race is 38 min 58.5 sec (average speed 135.068 mph *217,370 km/h*) by Barry Sheene, on a 495 cc four-cylinder Suzuki, on 3 July 1977.

Fastest race *United Kingdom*

The fastest race in the United Kingdom is the 750 cc event of the North-West 200 held on the Londonderry circuit (*see above*). The record lap speed is 127.63 mph *205,395 km/h* by Tom Herron (1949–79) on a 747 cc Yamaha in 1978.

Longest race

The longest race is the Liège 24 hr. The greatest distance ever covered is 2761.9 miles *4444,8 km* (average speed 115.08 mph *185,20 km/h*) by Jean-Claude Chemarin and Christian Leon, both of France, on a 941 cc four-cylinder Honda on the Francorchamps circuit on 14–15 Aug 1976.

Longest circuit

The 37.73 mile *60,72 km* 'Mountain' circuit, over which the principal TT races have been run since 1911 (with minor amendments in 1920), has 264 curves and corners and is the longest used for any motorcycle race.

Most successful riders *Tourist Trophy*

The record number of victories in the Isle of Man TT races is 14 by Stanley Michael Bailey Hailwood (1940–81) between 1961 and 1979. The first man to win three consecutive TT titles in two events was James A. Redman (Rhodesia) (b. 8 Nov 1931). He won the 250 cc and 350 cc events in 1963–5. Mike Hailwood won three events in one year, in 1961 and 1967 and this feat was emulated by Joey Dunlop in 1985.

The TT circuit speed record is 118.47 mph *190,66 km/h* by Joey Dunlop on a Honda on 4 June 1984.

Most successful riders

World championships

The most world championship titles (instituted by the *Fédération Internationale Motocycliste* in 1949) won are 15 by Giacomo Agostini (Italy) (b. 16 June 1942), the 350 cc in 1968–74, and 500 cc in 1966–72, 1975. He is the only man to win two world championships in five consecutive years (350 and 500 cc titles 1968–72).

Agostini won 122 races in the world championship series between 24 Apr 1965 and 29 Aug 1976, including a record 19 in 1970, also achieved by Mike Hailwood in 1966. Klaus Enders (W. Germany) (b. 1937) won six world side-car titles, 1967, 1969–70, 1972–4.

Trials

Yrjo Vesterinen (Finland) won a record three World trials championships, 1976–8.

Moto-cross

Joël Robert (Belgium) (b. 11 Nov 1943) won six 250 cc moto-cross world championships (1964, 1968–72). Between 25 Apr 1964 and 18 June 1972 he won a record fifty 250 cc Grands Prix. He became the youngest moto-cross world champion on 12 July 1964 when he won the 250 cc title aged 20 yr 244 days.

Most successful machines

Itālian MV-Agusta machines won 37 world championships between 1952 and 1973, and 276 world championship races between 1952 and 1976. Japanese Honda machines won 29 world championship races and five world championships in 1966. In the seven years they contested

A superb competitor, Mike Hailwood holds records for the Isle of Man TT races and the World Championships. In 1963 he broke every lap and race record but one in the entire World Championship series. *(All-Sport)*

the championship (1961–7) their annual average was 20 race wins.

Youngest and oldest world champions

Alberto 'Johnny' Cecotto (Venezuela) (b. 25 Jan 1956) is the youngest to win a world championship. He was 19 yr 211 days when he won the 350 cc title on 24 Aug 1975. The oldest was Hermann-Peter Müller (1909–76) of W. Germany, who won the 250 cc title in 1955 aged 46.

Highest speeds

Official world speed records must be set with two runs over a measured distance made in opposite directions within a time limit—1 hr for FIM records and 2 hr for AMA records.

Donald A. Vesco (USA) (b. 8 Apr 1939) riding his 21 ft *6,4 m* long *Lightning Bolt* streamliner, powered by two 1016 cc Kawasaki engines on Bonneville Salt Flats, Utah, USA on 28 Aug 1978 set AMA and FIM absolute records with an overall average of 318.598 mph *512,733 km/h* and had a fastest run at an average of 318.66 mph *513,165 km/h*.

The highest speed achieved over two runs in the UK is 191.897 mph *308.82 km/h* by Roy Francis Daniel (b. 7 Dec 1938) on his 998 cc supercharged twin-engined RDS Triumph at Elvington, N. Yorks on 29 July 1978. His average time for the flying 440 yd *402 m* was 4.69 sec.

The world record for 1 km *1,093.6 yd* from a standing start is 16.68 sec by Henk Vink (b. 24 July 1939) (Netherlands) on his supercharged 984 cc four-cylinder Kawasaki, at Elvington Airfield, North Yorkshire on 24 July 1977. The faster run was made in 16.09 sec.

The world record for 440 yd *402 m* from a standing start is 8.805 sec by Henk Vink on his supercharged 1132 cc four-cylinder Kawasaki at Elvington Airfield, North Yorkshire on 23 July 1977. The faster run was made in 8.55 sec.

The fastest time for a single run over 440 yd *402 m* from a standing start is 7.08 sec by Bo O'Brechta (USA) riding a supercharged 1200 cc Kawasaki-based machine at Ontario, California, in 1980. The highest terminal velocity recorded at the end of a 440 yd *402 m* run from a standing start is 199.55 mph *321,14 km/h* by Russ Collins (USA) at Ontario on 7 Oct 1978.

MOTOR RACING

See also The Guinness Guide to Grand Prix Motor Racing by Eric Dymock; revised edition published in 1983 at £11.95.

Earliest races

There are various conflicting claims, but the first automobile race was the 201 mile *323 km* Green Bay to Madison, Wisconsin, USA run in 1878 won by an Oshkosh steamer. In 1887 Count Jules Felix Philippe Albert de Dion de Malfiance (1856–1946) won the *La Velocipede* 19.3 miles *31 km* race in Paris in a De Dion steam quadricycle in which he is reputed to have exceeded 37 mph *59 km/h*. The first 'real' race was from Paris to Bordeaux and back (732 miles *1178 km*) on 11–13 June 1895. The first to finish was Emile Levassor (1844–97) of France, in a Panhard-Levassor two-seater, with a 1.2 litre Daimler engine developing 3½ hp. His time was 48 hr 47 min (average speed 15.01 mph *24,15 km/h*). The first closed circuit race was held over five laps of a mile *1,6 km* dirt track at Narragansett Park, Cranston, Rhode Island, USA, on 7 Sept 1896, won by A. H. Whiting, driving a Riker electric.

The oldest race in the world, still regularly run, is the RAC Tourist Trophy, first staged on 14 Sept 1905, in the Isle of Man. The oldest continental race is the French Grand Prix first held on 26–27 June 1906. The Coppa Florio, in Sicily, has been irregularly held since 1900.

Fastest circuits

The highest average lap speed attained on any closed circuit is 250.958 mph *403,878 km/h* in a trial by Dr Hans Liebold (b. 12 Oct 1926) (Germany) who lapped the 7.85 mile *12,64 km* high-speed track at Nardo, Italy in 1 min 52.67 sec in a Mercedes-Benz C111-IV experimental coupé on 5 May 1979. It was powered by a V8 engine with two KKK turbochargers with an output of 500 hp at 6,200 rpm.

The highest average race lap speed for a closed circuit is 214.158 mph *344,654 km/h* by Mario Gabriele Andretti (USA) (b. Trieste, Italy, 28 Feb 1940) driving a 2.6 litre turbocharged Viceroy Parnelli-Offenhauser on the 2 mile *3,2 km*, 22 degree banked oval at Texas World Speedway, College Station, Texas, USA on 6 Oct 1973.

The fastest road circuit was the Francorchamps circuit near Spa, Belgium, then 8.761 miles *14,10 km* in length which was lapped in 3 min 13.4 sec (average speed 163.086 mph *262,461 km/h*) on 6 May 1973, by Henri Pescarolo (France) (b. 25 Sept 1942) driving a 2993 cc V12 Matra-Simca MS670 Group 5 sports car. The race lap average speed record at Berlin's AVUS track was 171.75 mph *276,38 km/h* by Bernd Rosemeyer (Germany) (1909–38) in a 6-litre V16 Auto Union in 1937.

The General Motors' High Speed Circuit (2.03 mile *3,27 km* with a 21.4 degree banking all round), at Millbrook, Bedfordshire, was lapped in 41.48 secs (average speed 176.16 mph *283,49 kph*) by Tom Walkinshaw (b. 1947) and partnered by Michael Scarlett, Technical Editor 'Autocar', driving a 5343 cc V12 Jaguar XJS Group A racing saloon in June 1985.

Fastest pit stop

Robert William 'Bobby' Unser (USA) (b. 20 Feb 1934) took 4 sec to take on fuel on lap 10 of the Indianapolis 500 on 30 May 1976.

Fastest race

The fastest race is the Busch Clash at Daytona, Florida over 125 miles *201 km* on a 2½ miles 31 degree banked track. In 1979 Elzie Wylie

'Buddy' Baker (b. 25 Jan 1941) averaged 194.384 mph *312,831 km/h* in an Oldsmobile. Bill Elliott set the world record for a 500 mile *805 km* race in 1985 when he won at Talladega, Alabama at an average speed of 186.288 mph *299,793 km/h*. The NASCAR qualifying record is 205.109 mph *330,082 km/h* by Bill Elliott in a Ford Thunderbird at Daytona on 12 Feb 1985.

Most race wins by driver

Richard Lee Petty (USA) (b. 2 July 1937) won 200 NASCAR Grand National races in 947 starts, 1958–84. His best season was 1967 with 27 wins. His total earnings reached a record $5,504,877 on 29 July 1984. Geoff Bodine (b. 18 Apr 1949) won 55 races in 1978.

WORLD CHAMPIONSHIP GRAND PRIX MOTOR RACING

Drivers *Most successful*

The World Drivers' Championship, inaugurated in 1950, has been won a record five times by Juan-Manuel Fangio (Argentina) (b. 24 June 1911) in 1951, 1954–7. He retired in 1958, after having won 24 Grand Prix races (two shared).

The most Grand Prix victories is 27 by John Young 'Jackie' Stewart (GB) (b. 11 June 1939) between 12 Sept 1965 and 5 Aug 1973. The most Grand Prix points is 404½ by Niki Lauda (Austria) (b. 22 Feb 1949) in 157 Grands Prix, with 24 wins from 1971 to 1984. The most Grand Prix victories in a year is seven by James 'Jim' Clark (GB) (1936–68) in 1963 and by Alain Prost (France) (b. 24 Feb 1955) in 1984. The most Grand Prix starts is 176 (out of a possible

Niki Lauda of Austria has scored more Grand Prix points than anyone else, and has won the Drivers Championship three times—in 1975 and 1977 with Ferrari and in 1984 with McLaren. *(All-Sport)*

Nelson Piquet, pictured at the Austrian Grand Prix where he set a speed record of 248,235 km/h *154.250 mph* during qualifying. *(All-Sport/ Vandystadt)*

184) between 18 May 1958 and 26 Jan 1975 by Norman Graham Hill (GB) (1929–75). Between 20 Nov 1960 and 5 Oct 1969 he took part in 90 consecutive Grands Prix.

Oldest and youngest

The youngest world champion was Emerson Fittipaldi (Brazil) (b. 12 Dec 1946) who won his first world championship on 10 Sept 1972 aged 25 yr 273 days. The oldest world champion was Juan-Manuel Fangio who won his last world championship on 18 Aug 1957 aged 46 yr 55 days.

The youngest Grand Prix winner was Bruce Leslie McLaren (1937–70) of New Zealand, who won the United States Grand Prix at Sebring, Florida, on 12 Dec 1959 aged 22 yr 104 days. The oldest Grand Prix winner (in pre-World Championship days) was Tazio Giorgio Nuvolari (Italy) (1892–1953), who won the Albi Grand Prix at Albi, France on 14 July 1946 aged 53 yr 240 days. The oldest Grand Prix driver was Louis Alexandre Chiron (Monaco) (1899–1979), who finished 6th in the Monaco Grand Prix on 22 May 1955 aged 55 yr 292 days. The youngest Grand Prix driver was Michael Christopher Thackwell (New Zealand) (b. 30 Mar 1961) who took part in the Canadian GP on 28 Sept 1980, aged 19 yr 182 days.

Manufacturers

Ferrari have won a record eight manufacturers' world championships, 1961, 1964, 1975–7, 1979, 1982–3. Ferrari have 89 race wins in 374 Grands Prix, 1950–84.

Fastest race

The fastest overall average speed for a Grand Prix race on a circuit in current use is 224,050 km/h *139.218 mph* in the 1983 British Grand Prix (*see below*). The fastest qualifying speed was set in the Austrian Grand Prix at Zeltweg on 18 Aug 1984 at 248,235 km/h *154.250 mph* by Nelson Piquet in a Brabham BMW. The race itself, on 19 Aug 1984, was won by Niki Lauda in a McLaren TAG at an average 223,883 km/h, including a race lap record of 230,305 km/h *143.109 mph*.

Closest finish

The closest finish to a World Championship race was in the Italian Grand Prix at Monza on 5 Sept 1971. Just 0.61 sec separated winner Peter Gethin (GB) from the fifth placer.

BRITISH GRAND PRIX

First held in 1926 as the RAC Grand Prix, and held annually with the above name since 1949, the venue alternates between Brands Hatch, Kent and Silverstone, Northants.

Fastest speed

The fastest race time is 1 hr 24 min 39.78 sec, average speed 224,050 km/h *139.218 mph* by Alain Prost (France) in a Renault Elf Turbo RE30 on 16 July 1983 over 67 laps (316,14 km *196.44 miles*). The race lap record is 1 min 14.21 sec (av. speed 228,996 km/h *142.291 mph* also by Alain Prost in 1983. The practice lap record is 1 min 09.462 sec (244,549 km/h *151.956 mph*) by René Arnoux in a Ferrari 126C3 on 15 July 1983, all set at Silverstone.

Most wins

The most wins by a driver is five by Jim Clark, 1962–65 and 1967, all in Lotus cars. Ferrari have most wins with ten, 1951–4, 1956, 1958, 1961, 1976, 1978 and 1983.

LE MANS

The greatest distance ever covered in the 24 hour *Grand Prix d'Endurance* (first held on 26–27 May 1923) on the old Sarthe circuit at Le Mans, France is 5333,724 km *3314.222 miles* by Dr Helmut Marko (Austria) (b. 27 Apr 1943) and Jonkheer Gijs van Lennep (Netherlands) (b. 16 Mar 1942) in a 4907 cc flat-12 Porsche 917K Group 5 sports car, on 12–13 June 1971. The record for the current circuit is 5088,507 km *3161.938 miles* (av. speed 212,021 km/h *131.747 mph*) by Klaus Ludwig (W. Germany), Paulo Barillo (Italy) and John Winter (W. Germany) in a Porsche 956 on 15–16 June 1985. The race lap record (8.475 mile *13,64 km* lap) is 3 min 25.1 sec (average speed 148.61 mph *239,16 km/h* by Jochen Mass (W. Germany) in a Porsche 962C in 1985. The practice lap record is 3 min 14.8 sec (av. speed 156.62 mph *252,05 km/h*) by Hans Stuck (W. Germany) in a Porsche 962C on 14 June 1985.

Most wins

The race has been won by Ferrari cars nine times, in 1949, 1954, 1958 and 1960–5. The most wins by one man is six by Jacques Bernard 'Jacky' Ickx (Belgium) (b. 1 Jan 1945), 1969, 1975–7 and 1981–2.

The race has been won 13 times by British cars: Bentley in 1924 and 1927–30, Lagonda in 1935, Jaguar in 1951, 1953 and 1955–7, Aston Martin in 1959 and a Gulf-Ford in 1975.

INDIANAPOLIS 500

The Indianapolis 500 mile *804 km* race (200 laps) was inaugurated in the USA on 30 May 1911. The most successful driver has been Anthony Joseph 'A.J.' Foyt, Jr (USA) (b. 16 Jan 1935) who won in 1961, 1964, 1967 and 1977. The record time is 3 hr 3 min 21.06 sec (average speed 163.612 mph *263,308 km/h*) by Rick Mears (USA) driving a Penske March-Cosworth on 26 May 1984. The qualifying four-lap record average speed is 212.583 mph *342,11 km/h* by Poncho Carter in a March-Buick on 24 May 1985. The single lap qualifying record was set that day by Scott Brayton at 214.199 mph *344,710 km/h*.

The record prize fund was nearly $2,800,000 in 1984. The individual prize record is $434,060 by Rick Mears in 1984.

RALLIES

Earliest

The earliest long rally was promoted by the Parisian daily *Le Matin* in 1907 from Peking, China to Paris over about 7500 miles *12 000 km* on 10 June. The winner, Prince Scipione Borghese (1872–1927) of Italy, arrived in Paris on 10 Aug 1907 in his 40 hp Itala accompanied by his chauffeur, Ettore, and Luigi Barzini.

Longest

The longest ever rally was the *Singapore Airlines* London–Sydney Rally over 19,329 miles *31 107 km* from Covent Garden, London on 14 Aug 1977 to Sydney Opera House, won on 28 Sept 1977 by Andrew Cowan, Colin Malkin and Michael Broad in a Mercedes 280E. The longest held annually is the Safari Rally (first run 1953 through Kenya, Tanzania and Uganda) which is up to 3874 miles *6234 km* long, as in the 17th Safari held between 8 and 12 Apr 1971. It has been won a record five times by Shekhar Mehta (b. Uganda 1945) in 1973, 1979–82.

Monte Carlo

The Monte Carlo Rally (first run 1911) has been won a record four times by Sandro Munari (b. 1940) (Italy) in 1972, 1975, 1976 and 1977 and by Walter Röhrl (b. 7 Mar 1947) (with co-driver Christian Geistdorfer) in 1980, 1982–84, each time in a different car. The smallest car to win was an 851 cc Saab driven by Erik Carlsson (Sweden) (b. 5 Mar 1929) and Gunnar Häggbom (Sweden) on 25 Jan 1962, and by Carlsson and Gunnar Palm on 24 Jan 1963.

Britain

The RAC Rally (first held 1932) has been

recognised by the FIA since 1957. Hannu Mikkola (Finland) (b. 24 May 1942) (with co-driver Arne Hertz) has a record four wins in a Ford Escort, 1978–9 and an Audi Quatro, 1981–2.

World Championship

Walter Röhrl is the only man to win two drivers' world championships (inst. 1979), 1980 and 1982.

DRAGGING

Piston engined

The lowest elapsed time recorded by a piston-engined dragster is 5.484 sec by Gary Beck (USA) at the 28th annual US Nationals at Indianapolis in 1982. The highest terminal velocity recorded is 257.14 mph *413,83 km/h* by Rocky Epperly (USA) at Irvine, California on 15 Oct 1983. Not accepted by the National Hot Rod Association, Donald Glenn Garlits (USA) (b. 1932) set an American Hot Rod Association record of 260.49 mph *419,21 km/h* on 11 July 1982 at Gary, Indiana in an AHRA approved top fuel dragster powered by a 480 cubic inch, supercharged, fuel injected Dodge V8 engine.

The world record for two runs in opposite directions over 440 yd *402 m* from a standing start is 6.70 sec by Dennis Victor Priddle (b. 1945) of Yeovil, Somerset, driving his 6424 cc supercharged Chrysler dragster developing 1700 bhp using nitromethane and methanol, at Elvington Airfield, North Yorkshire on 7 Oct 1972. The faster run was made in 6.65 sec.

Rocket or jet-engined

The highest terminal velocity recorded by any dragster is 392.54 mph *631,732 km/h* by Kitty O'Neil (USA) at El Mirage Dry Lake, California, USA on 7 July 1977. The lowest elapsed time was 3.72 sec also by Kitty O'Neil on the same occasion.

Terminal velocity is the speed attained at the end of a 440 yd 402 m *run made from a standing start and elapsed time is the time taken for the run.*

Highest speeds *See also pp. 126 and 162*

The world speed record for compression ignition engined cars is 190.344 mph *306,328 km/h* (average of two runs in opposite directions over a measured mile *1,6 km*) by Robert Havemann driving his *Corsair* streamliner, powered by a turbocharged 6981 cc 6-cylinder GMC 6–71 diesel engine developing 746 bhp, at Bonneville Salt Flats, Utah, USA, in August 1971. The faster run was made at 210 mph *337 km/h*.

The most successful land speed record breaker was Major Sir Malcolm Campbell (1885–1948) of the United Kingdom. He broke the official record nine times between 25 Sept 1924, with 146.157 mph *235,216 km/h* in a Sunbeam, and 3 Sept 1935, when he achieved 301.129 mph *480,620 km/h* in the Rolls-Royce engined *Bluebird*.

Duration record

The greatest distance ever covered in one year is 400 000 km *248,548.5 miles* by François Lecot (1879–1949), an innkeeper from Rochetaillée, near Lyon, France, in a 1900 cc 66 bhp Citroën 11 sedan, mainly between Paris and Monte Carlo, from 22 July 1935 to 26 July 1936. He drove on 363 of the 370 days allowed.

MOUNTAINEERING

See also The Guinness Book of Mountains and Mountaineering Facts and Feats *by Edward Pyatt published at £8.95*

Origins

Although bronze-age artifacts have been found on the summit of the Riffelhorn, Switzerland (9605 ft *2927 m*), mountaineering, as a sport, has a continuous history dating back only to 1854. Isolated instances of climbing for its own sake exist back to the 13th century. The Atacamenans built sacrificial platforms near the summit of Llullaillaco (22,058 ft *6723 m*) in late pre-Columbian times *c*. 1490. The earliest recorded rock climb in the British Isles was of Stac na Biorrach, St Kilda (236 ft *71,9 m*) by Sir Robert Moray in 1698.

Mount Everest

Mount Everest (29,028 ft *8848 m*) was first climbed at 11.30 a.m. on 29 May 1953, when the summit was reached by Edmund Percival Hillary (b. 20 July 1919), created KBE, of New Zealand, and the Sherpa, Tenzing Norgay (b., as Namgyal Wangdi, in 1914, formerly called Tenzing Khumjung Bhutia), who was awarded the GM. The successful expedition was led by Col (later Hon Brigadier) Henry Cecil John Hunt, CBE, DSO (b. 22 June 1910), who was created a Knight Bachelor in 1953, a life Baron on 11 June 1966 and KG on 23 Apr 1979.

The Sherpa, Sundare (or Sungdare) has climbed Everest a record four times in 1979, 1981, 1982 and 1985. Ang Rita Sherpa, with ascents in 1983, 1984 and 1985, is the first person to scale Everest three times without the use of bottled oxygen. Reinhold Messner (Italy) was the first to make the entire climb solo on 20 Aug 1980. Messner and Peter Habeler (b. 22 July 1942) (Austria) made the first entirely oxygen-less ascent on 8 May 1978. The first Britons to reach the summit were Douglas Scott (b. 29 May 1941) and Dougal Haston (1940–77) on 24 Sept 1975. Five women have reached the summit, the first being Junko Tabei (b. 22 Sept 1939) (Japan) on 16 May 1975. The oldest person was Richard Daniel Bass (b. 21 Dec 1929) aged 55 yr 130 days on 30 Apr 1985.

Reinhold Messner (b. 17 Sept 1944), with his ascent of Kangchenjunga in 1982, became the first person to climb the world's three highest mountains, having earlier reached the summits of Everest and K2. He has successfully scaled a record 12 of the world's 14 mountains of over 8 000 m *26,250 ft.*

Greatest walls

The highest final stage in any wall climb is that on the south face of Annapurna I (26,545 ft *8091 m*). It was climbed by the British expedition led by Christian John Storey Bonington (b. 6 Aug 1934) when from 2 Apr to 27 May 1970, using 18,000 ft *5500 m* of rope, Donald Whillans (b. 9 Aug 1933) and Dougal Haston scaled to the summit. The longest wall climb is on the Rupal-Flank from the base camp at 3560 m *11,680 ft* to the South Point 8042 m *26,384 ft* of Nanga Parbat—a vertical ascent of 4482 m *14,704 ft.* This was scaled by the Austro-German-Italian Expedition led by Dr Karl Maria Herrligkoffer in April 1970.

Europe's greatest wall is the 6,600 ft *2000 m* north face of the Eigerwand (Ogre wall) first climbed by Heinrich Harrer and Fritz Kasparek of Austria and Anderl Heckmair and Wiggerl Vörg of Germany on 21–24 July 1938. The north-east face of the Eiger had been climbed on 20 Aug 1932 by Hans Lauper, Alfred Zürcher, Alexander Graven and Josef Knubel. The greatest alpine solo climb was that of Walter Bonatti (b. Bergamo, Italy, 22 June 1930) of the South West Pillar of the Dru, Montenvers now called the Bonatti Pillar, with five bivouacs in 126 hr 7 min on 17–22 Aug 1955.

The most demanding free climbs in the world are those rated at 5.13, the premier location for these being in the Yosemite Valley, California, USA. The top routes in Britain are graded E7.7b, which relates closely to 5.13.

Highest bivouac

Two Japanese, Hironobu Kamuro (1951–83) and Hiroshi Yoshino (1950–83), bivouacked at 8800 m *28,870 ft* on Everest on the night of 8/9 Oct 1983. Yoshino died on 9 Oct while Kamuro died either during the bivouac night or also next day.

MOUNTAIN RACING

Mount Cameroun

Timothy Leku Lekunze (Cameroun) descended from the summit 13,353 ft *4070 m* to Buea at 3000 ft *914 m* in 1 hr 11 min 49 sec on 28 Jan 1985, achieving a vertical rate of 144 ft *44 m* per min. He finished second overall behind Michael Short (GB) who ran to the summit and back in a record 3 hr 56 min 17 sec, including a record 2 hr 34 min 27 sec ascent.

Ben Nevis

The record time for the race from Fort William Town Park to the Cairn on the summit of Ben Nevis (4418 ft *1346,6 m*) and return is 1 hr 25 min 34 sec by Kenneth Stuart (b. 25 Feb 1957) and the feminine record is 1 hr 43 min 25 sec by Pauline Haworth (b. 1 Aug 1956), both on 1 Sept 1984. The full course by the bridle path is about 14 miles *22 km* but distance is saved by crossing the open hillside. The mountain was first climbed *c.* 1720 and the earliest run, by William Swan in 2 hr 41 min, was in 1895.

Snowdon

The Snowdon Race (Ras Yr Wyddfa) has been run annually since 1976 from Llanberis to the summit of Snowdon and back. The fastest time is 1 hr 3 min 46 sec by Fausto Bonzi (Italy) on 21 July 1984. On the same date Pauline Haworth set a ladies record of 1 hr 24 min 3 sec.

FELL RUNNING

In the 1972 Skiddaw Fell Race (3053 ft to 250 ft *930 to 107m*) a vertical descent rate of 128 ft *39m* per min was achieved by George Jeffrey Norman (b. 6 Feb 1945) (Altrincham AC).

Joss Naylor (b. 10 Feb 1936) won the Ennerdale mountain race (23 miles *37 km*) nine times, 1968–1977. The fastest time is 3 hr 21 min 4 sec by Billy Bland (Keswick AC) in 1980.

The Yorkshire three peak record for the current 24 mile course is 2 hr 50 min 34 sec by Hugh Symonds of Kendal AC on 29 Apr 1984. The record for the former 23 mile course was 2 hr 37 min 30 sec by John Wild on 25 Apr 1982.

The Lakeland 24-hr record is 72 peaks achieved by Joss Naylor, on 22–23 June 1975. He covered 105 miles *168 km* with 37,000 ft *11 227 m* of ascents and descents in 23 hr 11 min.

The record for traversing the 85 mile *136.79 km* cross-country route of the nine 4000 ft *1219,2 m* Scottish peaks is 22 hr 33 min by J. S. 'Stan' Bradshaw (Clayton-le-Moors Harriers) on 30 May 1982.

The 'Three Thousander' record over the 14 Welsh peaks of over 3000 ft *914 m* is 4 hr 46 min 22 sec, by Joss Naylor on 17 June 1973.

The Ten Peaks run is from Burnthwaite Farm, Wasdale Head, Cumbria to the top of Skiddaw *via* England's nine other highest mountains and tops. The record time is 6 hr 56 min by Joss Naylor, wholly on foot, in May 1975.

The record for the Bob Graham Round of 42 Lakeland Peaks covering a total distance of 72 miles *116 km* and 27,000 ft *8230 m* of ascent and descent, is 13 hr 54 min by Billy Bland, 34, on 19 June 1982. Ernest Roger Baumeister (Dark Peak Fell Runners Club) (b. 17 Dec 1941) ran the double Bob Graham Round in 46 hr 34½ min on 30 June–1 July 1979.

Three Peaks record
The Three Peaks route from sea level at Fort William, Inverness-shire, to sea level at Caernarvon, *via* the summits of Ben Nevis, Scafell Pike and Snowdon, was walked by Arthur Eddleston (1939–84) (Cambridge H) in 5 days 23 hr 37 min on 11–17 May 1980. Peter and David Ford, David Robinson, Kevin Duggan and John O'Callaghan, of Luton and Dunstable, ran the distance in relay in 54 hr 39 min 14 sec on 7–9 Aug 1981. The fastest individual total time for climbing the three mountains is 4 hr 16 min by Joss Naylor on 8–9 July 1971.

On 23 June 1984 a team of 3 from the Greater Manchester Police Tactical Aid Group covered the distance in 8 hrs 22 min, being transported between the peaks by helicopter. Their running time was 5 hr 4 min.

A total climbing time of 7 hr 47 min was achieved by Brian Stadden on 13–15 Aug 1982 for Five Peaks, adding the highest points in Northern Ireland—Slieve Donard (2796 ft *852 m*) and in the Republic of Ireland—Carrauntaul (3414 ft *1041 m*) to the Three Peaks.

Pennine Way
The record for traversing the 271 mile *436 km* long Pennine Way is 2 days 21 hr 55 min by Michael Cudahy, 43, on 1–3 June 1984.

NETBALL

Origins
The game was invented in the USA in 1891 and introduced into England in 1895 by Dr Toles. The All England Women's Netball Association

England's captain Jillean Hipsey—their most capped player with over 70 appearances since her debut in 1978. *(Eileen Langsley)*

was formed in 1926. The oldest club in continuous existence is the Polytechnic Netball Club of London founded in 1907.

Most titles *World*
Australia have won the World Championships (inst. 1963) a record five times, 1963, 1971, 1975, 1979 and 1983.

Most titles *English*
The National Club's Championships (inst. 1966) have been won seven times by Sudbury Netball Club (1968–69, 1970–1 (both shared), 1973, 1983–4).

Surrey have won the County Championships (inst. 1932) a record 18 times (1949–64, 1966, 1969 (shared) and 1981).

Christchurch Ladies Club won the Ipswich and District Summer Netball league for 25 successive years, 1959–83.

Most international appearances
The record number of internationals is 80 by June Wightman (b. 28 June 1946) for Northern Ireland, 1964–84. Lesley Owen (b. 16 Oct 1942) played 73 times for Wales 1968–80. The record for England is 71 by Jillean Hipsey, 1978–85.

Highest scores
The World Tournament record score was in Auckland, New Zealand in 1975 when England beat Papua New Guinea 114 goals to 16. The record number of goals in the World Tournament is 402 by Judith Heath (England) (b. 1942) in 1971.

OLYMPIC GAMES

See also The Guinness Book of Olympic Facts and Feats *by Stan Greenberg published in 1983 at £8.95.*

Note: These records include the Games held at Athens in 1906.

Origins
The earliest celebration of the ancient Olympic Games of which there is a certain record is that of July 776 BC, when Coroibos, a cook from Elis, won the foot race, though their origin dates from perhaps as early as *c.* 1370 BC. The ancient Games were terminated by an order issued in Milan in AD 393 by Theodosius I, 'the Great' (*c.* 346–95), Emperor of Rome. At the instigation of Pierre de Fredi, Baron de Coubertin (1863–1937), the Olympic Games of the modern era were inaugurated in Athens on 6 Apr 1896.

The Coliseum Stadium, setting of the 1984 Olympics at Los Angeles. In all, 13 world records were broken or equalled (of which 10 were in men's swimming events), and 47 Olympic marks. *(Steve Hale)*

Ever present
Four countries have never failed to be represented at the 21 celebrations of the Summer Games: Australia, Greece, Great Britain and Switzerland. Of these only Great Britain has been present at all Winter celebrations as well.

Largest crowd
The largest crowd at any Olympic site was 150,000 at the 1952 ski-jumping at the Holmenkøllen, outside Oslo, Norway. Estimates of the number of spectators of the marathon race through Tōkyō, Japan on 21 Oct 1964 were 500,000 to 1,500,000. The total spectator attendance at Los Angeles in 1984 was given as 5,797,923 (see All Sports).

Most medals *Individual gold*
In the ancient Olympic Games victors were given a chaplet of wild olive leaves. Leonidas of Rhodos won 12 running titles 164–152 BC. The most individual gold medals won by a male competitor in the modern Games is ten by Raymond Clarence Ewry (USA) (1874–1937) (see Track and Field Athletics). The female record is seven by Vera Caslavska-Odlozil (Czechoslovakia) (see Gymnastics). The most gold medals won by a British competitor is four by Paul Radmilovic (1886–1968) in water polo, 1908, 1912 and 1920 and the 4 × 200 m freestyle relay in 1908, and swimmer Henry Taylor (1885–1951) in 1906 and 1908. The Australian swimmer Iain Murray Rose, who won four gold medals, was born in Birmingham, England on 6 Jan 1939. The only Olympian to win four consecutive individual titles in the same event has been Alfred A. Oerter (b. 19 Sept 1936) of the USA, who won the discus in 1956–68.

Swimmer Mark Andrew Spitz (USA) (b. 10 Feb 1950) won a record seven golds at one celebration, at Munich in 1972, including three in relays. The most won in individual events at one celebration is five by speed skater Eric Heiden (USA) (b. 14 June 1958) at Lake Placid, USA, in 1980.

The only man to win a gold medal in both the Summer and Winter Games is Edward F. Eagan (USA) (1898–1967) who won the 1920 Light-Heavyweight boxing title and was a member of the winning four-man bob in 1932.

Most medals *National*

The total figures for medals for all Olympic events (including those now discontinued) for the Summer (1896–1984) and Winter Games (1924–84):

	Gold	Silver	Bronze	Total
1. USA	750	575	478	1803
2. USSR (formerly Russia)	408	340	303	1051
3. GB (including Ireland to 1920)	175	216	207	598
4. Germany (Germany 1896–1964, West Germany from 1968)	170	215	213	598

Excludes medals won in Official Art competitions in 1912–48.

Most medals *Individual*

Gymnast Larissa Latynina (USSR) (b. 27 Dec 1934) won a record 18 medals (see Gymnastics). The record at one celebration is eight by gymnast Aleksandr Ditiatin (USSR) (b. 7 Aug 1957) in 1980.

Youngest and oldest gold medallists

The youngest ever winner was a French boy (whose name is not recorded) who coxed the Netherlands pair in 1900. He was 7–10 years old and he substituted for Dr Hermanus Brockmann, who coxed in the heats but proved too heavy. The youngest ever female champion is Marjorie Gestring (USA) (b. 18 Nov 1922, now Mrs Bowman), aged 13 yr 267 days, in the 1936 women's springboard event. Oscar Swahn (*see p. 220*) was in the winning Running Deer shooting team in 1912 aged 64 yr 258 days.

Youngest and oldest *Great Britain*

The youngest competitor to represent Britain in the Olympic Games was Magdalena Cecilia Colledge (b. 28 Nov 1920) aged 11 yr 73 days when she skated in the 1932 Games. The oldest was Hilda Lorna Johnstone (b. 4 Sept 1902) aged 70 yr 5 days in the Equestrian Dressage in the 1972 Games.

Longest span

The longest span of an Olympic competitor is 40 years by Dr Ivan Osiier (Denmark) (1888–1965) in fencing, 1908–32 and 1948, and Magnus Konow (Norway) (1887–1972) in yachting, 1908–20, and 1936–48. The longest feminine span is 24 years (1932–56) by the Austrian fencer Ellen Müller-Preis (b. 6 May 1912). Raimondo d'Inzeo (b. 8 Feb 1925) competed for Italy in equestrian events at a record eight celebrations from 1948 to 1976, gaining one gold, two silver and three bronze medals. Janice Lee York Romary (b. 6 Aug 1928) the US fencer, competed in all six Games from 1948 to 1968, and Lia Manoliu (Romania) (b. 25 Apr 1932) competed from 1952 to 1972 winning the discus in 1968.

The longest span of any British competitor is 28 years by Enoch Jenkins (b. 6 Nov 1892) who appeared in the 1924 and the 1952 Games in the clay pigeon shooting event, and the longest feminine span by Dorothy Jennifer Beatrice Tyler (*née* Odam) (b. 14 Mar 1920) who high-jumped from 1936 to 1956. The record number of appearances for Great Britain is six by fencer Bill Hoskyns from 1956 to 1976. Durward Randolph Knowles (b. 2 Nov 1917) competed in yachting for Britain in 1948 and in the following six Games for the Bahamas.

ORIENTEERING

Origins

Orienteering as now known was invented by Major Ernst Killander in Sweden in 1918. It was based on military exercises of the 1890s. The term was first used for an event at Oslo, Norway on 7 Oct 1900. World championships were instituted in 1966. Annual British championships were instituted in 1967 following the formation of the British Orienteering Federation.

Most titles *World*

Sweden has won the men's relay six times between 1966 and 1979 and the women's relay six times, 1966, 1970, 1974–6, 1981 and 1983. Two women's individual titles have been won by Ulla Lindkvist (Sweden) (b. 3 Aug 1939), 1966 and 1968 and Annichen Kringstad-Svensson (Sweden) (b. 15 July 1960), 1981 and 1983. The men's title has been won twice by Åge Hadler (Norway) (b. 14 Aug 1944) in 1966 and 1972, Egil Johansen (Norway) (b. 18 Aug 1954) 1976 and 1978, and Ogvin Thon (Norway) (b. 25 Mar 1958) in 1979 and 1981.

Most titles *British*

The men's relay has been won twice by Oxford University, 1975, 1979, and the women's relay three times by Derwent Valley Orienteers, 1975, 1979 and 1980. Geoffrey Peck (b. 27 Sept 1949) has won the men's individual title a record five times, 1971, 1973, 1976–7 and 1979 as well as the over-35s title in 1985. Carol McNeill (b. 20 Feb 1944) has won the women's title six times, 1967, 1969, 1972–76. She also won the over-35s title in 1984 and 1985.

Most competitors

The most competitors at an event in one day is 22,510 on the first day of the Swedish O-Ringen at Småland on 18 July 1983.

PARACHUTING

(See also p. 177)

Origins

Parachuting became a regulated sport with the institution of world championships in 1951. A team title was introduced in 1954 and women's events were included in 1956.

Most titles *World*

The USSR won the men's team titles in 1954, 1958, 1960, 1966, 1972, 1976, and 1980, and the women's team title in 1956, 1958, 1966, 1968, 1972, and 1976. Nikolai Ushamyev (USSR) has won the individual title twice, 1974 and 1980.

Most titles *British*

Sgt Ronald Alan 'Scotty' Milne (b. 5 Mar 1952) of the Parachute Regiment has won the British title five times in 1976–7, 1979–81. Rob Colpus and Geoff Sanders have each shared ten British titles for Relative Work parachuting, the 4 Way and 8 Way titles won by their team 'Symbiosis' in 1976–7, 1979, 1981–2.

Greatest accuracy

Jacqueline Smith (GB) (b. 29 Mar 1951) scored ten consecutive dead centre strikes (10 cm *4 in* disc) in the World Championships at Zagreb, Yugoslavia, 1 Sept 1978. At Yuma, Arizona, USA, in March 1978, Dwight Reynolds scored a record 105 daytime dead centres, and Bill Wenger and Phil Munden tied with 43 nighttime DCs, competing as members of the US Army team, the Golden Knights. With electronic measuring the official FAI record is 50 DCs by Alexander Aasmiae (USSR) at Ferghana, USSR, Oct 1979.

The Men's Night Accuracy Landing Record on an electronic score pad is 27 consecutive dead centres by Cliff Jones (USA) in 1981.

Parascending

Distance: Paul Truelove flew a measured distance in free flight, after release, of 4500 m *2.8 miles* in a downwind dash at Driffield, Humberside on 30 Mar 1985.
Duration: Lee Clements sustained free flight for 16 min 1 sec on a Harley Paramount 11 at RAF Elvington, England on 17 June 1984.
Accuracy: Nigel Horder scored four successive dead centres at the Dutch Open, Flevhof, Netherlands on 22 May 1983.

PELOTA VASCA
(Jaï Alaï)

Origins

The game, which originated in Italy as *longue paume* and was introduced into France in the 13th century, is said to be the fastest of all ball games. The glove or *gant* was introduced c. 1840 and the *chistera* was invented by Jean 'Gantchiki' Dithurbide of Ste Pée, France. The *grand chistera* was invented by Melchior Curuchague of Buenos Aires, Argentina in 1888.

The world's largest *frontón* (enclosed stadium) is the World Jaï Alaï at Miami, Florida, USA, which had a record attendance of 15,052 on 27 Dec 1975.

World Championships

The Federacion Internacional de Pelota Vasca stage world championships every four years (first in 1952). The most successful pair have been Roberto Elias and Juan Labat (Argentina), who won the *Trinquete Share* four times, 1952, 1958, 1962 and 1966. Labat won a record seven world titles in all. The most wins in the long court game *Cesta Punta* is three by Hamuy of Mexico, with two different partners, 1958, 1962 and 1966.

Highest speed

An electronically measured ball velocity of 188 mph *302 km/h* was recorded by José Ramon Areitio at the Newport Jai Alai, Rhode Island, USA on 3 Aug 1979.

Longest domination

The longest domination as the world's No. 1 player was enjoyed by Chiquito de Cambo (*né* Joseph Apesteguy) (France), (1881–1955) from the beginning of the century until succeeded in 1938 by Jean Urruty (France) (b. 19 Oct 1913).

PÉTANQUE

Origins

The origins of pétanque or boules can be traced back over 2000 years, but it was not until 1945 that the Fédération Français de Pétanque et Jeu

Provençal was formed, and subsequently the Fédération Internationale (FIPJP). The first recognised British club was formed on 30 Mar 1966 as the Chingford Club de Pétanque and the British Pétanque Association was founded in 1974.

World Championships

Winner of the most world championships (inst. 1959) has been France with seven titles.

PIGEON RACING

Earliest references

Pigeon racing developed from the use of homing pigeons for carrying messages. The sport originated in Belgium from commercial services and the earliest long-distance race was from London to Antwerp in 1819, involving 36 pigeons.

Longest flights

The greatest recorded homing flight by a pigeon was made by one owned by the 1st Duke of Wellington (1769–1852). Released from a sailing ship off the Ichabo Islands, West Africa, on 8 April, it dropped dead a mile from its loft at Nine Elms, Wandsworth, London on 1 June 1845, 55 days later, having flown an airline route of 5400 miles *8700 km*, but an actual distance of possibly 7000 miles *11 250 km* to avoid the Sahara Desert. The official British duration record (into Great Britain) is 1173 miles *1887 km* in 15 days by C.S.O. (owned by Rosie and Bruce of Wick) in the 1976 Palamos Race. In the 1975 Palamos Race, *The Conqueror*, owned by Alan Raeside, homed to Irvine, Strathclyde, 1010 miles *1625 km*, in 43 hr 56 min. The greatest number of flights over 1000 miles flown by one pigeon is that of *Dunning Independence* owned by D. Smith which annually flew from Palamos to Dunning, Perthshire, Scotland 1039 miles *1662 km* between 1978 and 1981.

Highest speeds

In level flight in windless conditions it is very doubtful if any pigeon can exceed 60 mph *96 km/h*. The highest race speed recorded is one of 3229 yd *2952 m* per min (110.07 mph *177,14 km/h*) in the East Anglian Federation race from East Croydon on 8 May 1965 when the 1428 birds were backed by a powerful south south-west wind. The winner was owned by A. Vigeon & Son, Wickford, Essex.

The highest race speed recorded over a distance of more than 1000 km *621.37 miles* is 2432.7 yd *2224,5 m* per min (82.93 mph *133,46 km/h*) by a hen in the Central Cumberland Combine race over 683 miles 147 yd *1099,316 km* from Murray Bridge, South Australia to North Ryde, Sydney on 2 Oct 1971.

24 hr records

The world's longest reputed distance in 24 hr is 803 miles *1292 km* (velocity 1525 yd *1394 m* per min) by E. S. Petersen's winner of the 1941 San Antonio R.C. event in Texas, USA.

The best 24 hr performance into the United Kingdom is 724 miles 219 yd *1165,3 km* by E. Cardno's *Mormond Lad*, on 2 July 1977, from Nantes, France to Fraserburgh, Grampian. Average speed was 1648 yd *1507 m* per min (56.18 mph *90,41 km/h*).

Most first prizes

Owned by R. Green, of Walsall Wood, West Midlands, *Champion Breakaway* won 59 first prizes from 1972 to May 1979.

Highest priced bird

The highest recorded price paid for a pigeon is approximately £25,000 by a Japanese fancier for *De Wittslager* to Georges Desender (Belgium) in October 1978.

POLO

Earliest games

Polo is usually regarded as being of Persian origin having been played as *Pulu c.* 525 BC. Other claims have come from Tibet and the Tang Dynasty of China AD 250. The earliest polo club of modern times was the Kachar Club (founded in 1859) in Assam, India. The oldest still existing club is the Calcutta Polo Club (1862). The game was introduced into England from India in 1869 by the 10th Hussars at Aldershot, Hampshire and the earliest match was one between the 9th Lancers and the 10th Hussars on Hounslow Heath, Greater London, in July 1871. The earliest international match between England and the USA was in 1886.

Most titles

The British Open Championship for the Cowdray Park Gold Cup was first held in 1956. The most wins is five by Stowell Park, 1973–4, 1976, 1978 and 1980.

Highest handicap

The highest handicap based on eight 7½-min 'chukkas' is ten goals introduced in the USA in 1891 and in the United Kingdom and in Argentina in 1910. The latest of the 41 players ever to receive ten-goal handicaps are Thomas Wayman (USA), Guillermo Gracida Jr (Mexico) and in 1984 the Argentinians Gonzalo Pierez, Alfonso Pierez and Alfredo Harriott. The last (of six) ten-goal handicap players from Great Britain was Gerald Balding in 1939. A match of two 40-goal teams was staged for the only time, at Palermo, Buenos Aires, Argentina, in 1975.

The highest handicaps of current United Kingdom players are nine by Julian Hipwood (b. 23 June 1946) and by Howard Hipwood (b. 24 Mar 1950). Claire J. Tomlinson of Gloucestershire has a handicap of four, the highest ever attained by a woman.

Highest score

The highest aggregate number of goals scored in an international match is 30, when Argentina beat the USA 21–9 at Meadow Brook, Long Island, New York, USA, in Sept 1936.

POWERBOAT RACING

Origins

A petrol engine was first installed in a boat by Jean Joseph Etienne Lenoir (1822–1900) on the River Seine, Paris in 1865. Actual powerboat racing started in about 1900, the first prominent race being from Calais to Dover in 1903. International racing was largely established by the presentation of a Challenge Trophy by Sir Alfred Harmsworth in 1903. Thereafter racing developed mainly as a 'circuit' or short, sheltered course type competition. Offshore or sea passage races also developed, initially for displacement (non-planing) cruisers. Offshore events for fast (planing) cruisers began in 1958 with a 170 mile *273 km* passage race from Miami, USA to Nassau, Bahamas. Outboard motor, i.e. the combined motor/transmission detachable propulsion unit type racing began in the USA in about 1920. Both inboard and outboard motor boat engines are mainly petrol fuelled, but since 1950 diesel (compression ignition) engines have appeared and are widely used in offshore sport.

Highest Speeds (*For the world water speed record see page 163.*)

The highest speed recorded by a propeller-driven boat is 229.00 mph *368,54 km/h* by *The Texan*, a Kurtis Top Fuel Hydro Drag Boat, driven by Eddie Hill on 5 Sept 1982 at Chowchilla, California, USA. He also set a 440 yd *402 m* elapsed time record of 5.16 seconds in this boat at Firebird Lake, Arizona, USA on 13 Nov 1983. The official American Drag Boat Association record is 223.88 mph *360,29 km/h* by *Final Effort* a Blown Fuel Hydro boat driven by Bob Burns at Creve Coeur Lake, St Louis, Missouri, USA on 15 July 1985 over a ¼ mile *402 m* course.

The fastest speed recognised by the Union Internationale Motonautique for an outboard powered boat is in the Class OZ unlimited, circuit boat: 157.424 mph *253,342 km/h* by the late George Andrew Jr (USA) in a Karelsen three-point hydroplane powered by a 200 hp 2.4 litre V-6 Mercury engine at Moore Haven, Florida, USA in April 1984. This was the average speed for two runs, the faster being at 158.199 mph *254.590 km/h*.

The fastest speed recognised for an offshore boat was set by *Innovation*, a 35 ft *10,7 m* Maelstrom boat powered by three Johnson Evinrude outboard engines each of 214 cu in *3507 cc*, driven by Mike Drury at a mean speed for two runs of 131.088 mph *210,966 km/h* at New Orleans, Louisiana, USA on 31 March 1984.

The fastest speed recorded for a diesel (compression ignition) boat is 213,08 km/h *132.40 mph* by the 24 ft *7,3 m* BU221 *Rothman's World Leader*, driven by Carlo Bonomi at Venice, Italy on 5 Dec 1982.

Highest race speeds

The highest speeds recorded in races are:
Offshore: 103.29 mph *166,22 km/h* by Tony Garcia (USDA) in a Class I powerboat at Key West, Florida, USA in November 1983.
Circuit: 131.12 mph *211,02 km/h* by F. Foresti (Italy) in the R4 category.

Longest races

The longest offshore race has been the Port Richborough London to Monte Carlo Marathon Offshore International event. The race extended over 2947 miles *4742 km* in 14 stages on 10–25 June 1972. It was won by *H.T.S.* (*GB*) driven by Mike Bellamy, Eddie Chater and Jim Brooker in 71 hr 35 min 56 sec for an average of

'The Flying Fish', the fastest non-mechanical craft on water, is ridden by Steve Hegg, Olympic cycling gold medallist in the 4000 m pursuit. Behind the project were Dr Alec Brooks and Dr Allan Abbott—the latter also holds the absolute speed record on a bicycle.

41.15 mph *66,24 km/h*. The longest circuit race is the 24 hour race held annually since 1962 on the River Seine at Rouen, France. The 1983 winners Francois Greens, Jan van Brockels and Roger Robin of Belgium drove a Johnson outboard engined Piranha boat at an average speed of 75,02 km/h *46.63 mph*.

Longest Jetboat Jumps

The longest ramp jump achieved by a jetboat has been 120 ft *36,57 m* by Peter Horak (USA) in a Glastron Carlson CVX 20 Jet Deluxe with a 460 Ford V8 engine (take-off speed 55 mph *88 km/h*) for a documentary TV film, at Salton Sea, California, USA on 26 Apr 1980. The longest leap on to land is 172 ft *38,7 m* by Norm Bagrie (NZ) from the Shotover River on 1 July 1982 in the 1½ ton jetboat *Valvolene*.

RACKETS

Origins

There is record of the sale of a racket court at Southernhay, Exeter, Devon dated 12 Jan 1798. The game which is of 17th century origin was played by debtors in the Fleet Prison, London in the middle of the 18th century, and an inmate, Robert Mackay, claimed the first 'world' title in 1820. The first closed court champion was Francis Erwood at Woolwich in 1860. A new court was constructed at the Seacourt Club, Hayling Island, Hampshire in 1979.

Longest reign

Of the 22 world champions since 1820 the longest reign is by Geoffrey Willoughby Thomas Atkins (b. 20 Jan 1927) who held the title after beating the professional James Dear (1910–81) in 1954 and retired, after defending it four times, in April 1972.

Most Amateur titles

Since the Amateur singles championship was instituted in 1888 the most titles won by an individual is nine by Edgar Maximilian Baerlein (1879–1971) between 1903 and 1923. Since the institution of the Amateur doubles championship in 1890 the most shares in titles has been eleven by David Sumner Milford (1905–84), between 1938 and 1959 and John Ross Thompson (b. 10 May 1918) between 1948 and 1966. Milford also won seven Amateur singles titles (1930–51), an Open title (1936) and held the World title from 1937 to 1946. Thompson has additionally won an Open singles title and five Amateur singles titles.

RACQUETBALL

Racquetball using a 40 ft by 20 ft court was invented in 1950 by Joe Sobek at the Greenwich YMCA, Connecticut, USA, originally as Paddle Rackets. The International Racquetball Association was founded in 1968 by Bob Kendler (USA). John Treharne won three British titles, 1981–83.

Racketball using a 32 ft by 21 ft course (as for squash) was introduced to Britain by Ian Wright in 1976. The British Racketball Association was formed and staged inaugural British National Championships in 1984. Men's and women's champions were Denis Secher and Greer Batty respectively.

RODEO

Origins

Rodeo which developed from 18th century *fiestas* came into being in the early days of the North American cattle industry. The sport originated in Mexico and spread from there into the cattle regions of the USA. Steer wrestling came in with Bill Pickett (1870–1932) of Texas, in 1900.

The largest rodeo in the world is the Calgary Exhibition and Stampede at Calgary, Alberta, Canada. In 1981 the total paid attendance for the rodeo events over ten days was 122,268. The National Finals Rodeo is organised annually by the Professional Rodeo Cowboys Association (PRCA). In 1985 a record of over $1.5 million prize money was offered for the event, staged in Las Vegas, Nevada, USA.

Most world titles

The record number of all-around titles in the PRCA world championships is six by Larry Mahan (USA) (b. 21 Nov 1943) in 1966–70 and 1973 and, consecutively, 1974–9 by Tom Ferguson (b. 20 Dec 1950). Tom Ferguson had record career earnings of $956,737 to 31 May 1985. Jim Shoulders (b. 1928) of Henryetta, Oklahoma, USA has won a record 16 world championships between 1949 and 1959. The record figure for prize money in a single season is $153,391 by Roy Cooper (b. 13 Nov 1955) of Durant, Oklahoma, USA in 1983. The record for one rodeo is $30,677 by Dee Pickett at the National Finals Rodeo, Oklahoma City in December 1984.

Youngest champion

The youngest winner of a world title is Metha Brorsen, of Oklahoma, USA, who won the International Rodeo Association Cowgirls barrel-racing event in 1975 at 11 years old. The youngest champion in Professional Rodeo Cowboys Association/Women's Professional Rodeo Association competition is Jackie Jo Perrin of Antlers, Oklahoma, USA, who won the barrel-racing title in 1977 at age 13.

Time records

Records for PRCA timed events, such as calf-roping and steer-wrestling, are not always comparable, because of the widely varying conditions due to the size of arenas and amount of start given the stock. The fastest time recorded for roping a calf is 5.7 sec by Lee Phillips at Assiniboia, Saskatchewan, Canada in 1978, and the fastest time for overcoming a steer is 2.4 sec by James Bynum, at Marietta, Oklahoma, USA, in 1955, by Carl Deaton at Tulsa, Oklahoma, USA in 1976 and by Gene Melton at Pecatonica, Illinois, USA, in 1976.

The highest score in bull riding was 98 points out of a possible 100 by Denny Flynn on *Red Lightning* at Palestine, Illinois, USA in 1979.

Champion bull

The top bucking bull was probably *Tornado*, who bucked out of the chute 220 times before Freckles Brown, in 1967, became the first cowboy to ride him to the eight-second bell. *Tornado* retired a year later after a 14-year career.

Champion bronc

Traditionally a bronc called *Midnight* owned by Jim McNab of Alberta, Canada was never ridden in 12 appearances at the Calgary Stampede.

ROLLER SKATING

Origins

The first roller skate was devised by Jean Joseph Merlin (1735–1803) of Huy, Belgium, in 1760 and demonstrated by him in London but with disastrous results. James L. Plimpton of New York produced the present four-wheeled type and patented it in January 1863. The first indoor rink was opened in the Haymarket, London, in about 1824.

Most titles *Speed*

Most world speed titles have been won by Alberta Vianello (Italy) with 16 between 1953 and 1965. Most British national individual men's titles have been won by Michael Colin McGeogh (b. 30 Mar 1946) with 15 in 1966–83. Chloe Ronaldson (b. 30 Nov 1939) has won 40 individual and 13 team ladies' senior titles from 1958 to 1983.

Most titles *Figure*

The records for figure titles are five by Karl Heinz Losch in 1958–9, 1961–2 and 1966, and four by Astrid Bader, both of W. Germany, in 1965–8. Most world pair titles have been taken by Dieter Fingerle (W. Germany) with four in 1959, 1965–7 with two different partners.

Speed skating

The fastest speed put up in an official world record is 25.78 mph *41,48 km/h* when Giuseppe Cantarella (Italy) (b. 13 Aug 1944) recorded 34.9 sec for 440 yd *402 m* on a road at Catania, Sicily on 28 Sept 1963. The world mile record on a rink is 2 min 25.1 sec by Gianni Ferretti (Italy) (b. 11 May 1948) at Inzell, W. Germany on 28 Sept 1968. The greatest distance skated in 1 hr on a rink by a woman is 35,399 km *21.995 miles* by Marisa Anna Danesi (Italy) (b. 25 Nov 1935) at Inzell, W. Germany on 28 Sept 1968. The men's record on a track is 37,230 km *23.133 miles* by Alberto Civolani (Italy) (b. 16 Mar 1933) at Inzell, W. Germany on 28 Sept 1968. He went on to skate 50 miles *80,46 km* in 2 hr 20 min 33.1 sec.

Largest rink

The greatest indoor rink ever to operate was located in the Grand Hall, Olympia, London. Opened 1890 and closed in 1912 it had an actual skating area of 68,000 ft² *6 300 m²*. The current largest is the Fireside Roll-Arena, Hoffman Estates, Illinois, USA with a total skating surface of 29,859 ft² *2774 m²*.

Endurance

Theodore James Coombs (b. 1954) of Hermosa Beach, California, skated 5193 miles *8357 km* from Los Angeles to New York and back to Yates Center, Kansas from 30 May to 14 Sept 1979.

Land's End to John o'Groats

Steve Fagan, 20, roller skated the distance, 925 miles *1488 km*, in 9 days 10 hr 25 min on 1–10 May 1984.

ROLLER HOCKEY

Roller hockey (previously known as Rink Hockey in Europe) was introduced to Britain as Rink Polo, at the old Lava rink, Denmark Hill, London in the late 1870s. The Amateur Rink Hockey Association was formed in 1908, and in 1913 became the National Rink Hockey (now Roller Hockey) Association. Britain won the inaugural World Championship in 1936 since when Portugal has won most titles with 12 between 1947 and 1982. The European Championship (inst. 1926) was won by Portugal a record 15 times between 1947 and 1977.

ROWING

Oldest race

The Sphinx stela of Amenhotep II (1450–1425 BC) records that he *stroked* a boat for some

The colourful International Dragon Boat Races are now in their eleventh year, drawing teams from all over the world, including Britain. The competitors' delight is evident in the Chinese team pictured above.

three miles. The earliest established sculling race is the Doggett's Coat and Badge, which was first rowed on 1 Aug 1716 from London Bridge to Chelsea and is still contested annually. Although rowing regattas were held in Venice in 1300 the first English regatta probably took place on the Thames by the Ranelagh Gardens, near Putney in 1775.

Most Olympic medals

Six oarsmen have won three gold medals: John B. Kelly (USA) (1889–1960), father of the late HSH Princess Grace of Monaco, in the sculls (1920) and double sculls (1920 and 1924); his cousin Paul Vincent Costello (USA) (b. 27 Dec 1899) in the double sculls (1920, 1924 and 1928); Jack Beresford, Jr (GB) (1899–1977) in the sculls (1924), coxless fours (1932) and double sculls (1936), Vyacheslav Ivanov (USSR) (b. 30 July 1938) in the sculls (1956, 1960 and 1964) and Siegfried Brietzke (GDR) (b. 12 June 1952) in the coxless pairs (1972) and coxless fours (1976, 1980) and Pertti Karpinen (Finland) (b. 17 Feb 1953) in the sculls 1976, 1980 and 1984.

World Championships

World rowing championships distinct from the Olympic Games were first held in 1962, at first four-yearly, but from 1974 annually, except in Olympic years.

The most gold medals won is five by Ulrich Diessner (GDR) (b. 27 Dec 1954), four at coxed fours 1977–9 and 1982 and one at coxed pairs in 1983. He also won an Olympic gold medal at

coxed fours in 1980. Four single sculls titles have been won by Peter-Michael Kolbe (W. Germany) (b. 2 Aug 1953), 1975, 1978, 1981 and 1983 and in the women's events by Christine Hahn (née Schieblich) (GDR) (b. 31 Dec 1954), 1974–5, 1977–8 (as well as the 1976 Olympic title). Crews to win four gold medals have been the twins Bernd and Jörg Landvoigt (GDR) (b. 23 Mar 1951), coxless pairs 1974–5, 1978–9 (and the Olympic titles of 1976 and 1980), and Siegfried Brietzke, Andreas Decker, Stefan Sempler and Wolfgang Mager (GDR), coxless fours 1974–5, 1977, 1979 (and the 1976 Olympic title).

Boat Race

The earliest University Boat Race, which Oxford won, was from Hambledon Lock to Henley Bridge on 10 June 1829. Outrigged eights were first used in 1846. In the 131 races to 1985, Cambridge won 68 times, Oxford 62 times and there was a dead heat on 24 Mar 1877.

The race record time for the course of 4 miles 374 yd *6779 km* (Putney to Mortlake) is 16 min 45 sec by Oxford on 18 Mar 1984. This represents an average speed of 15.09 mph *24,28 km/h*. The smallest winning margin has been by a canvas by Oxford in 1952 and 1980. The greatest margin (apart from sinking) was Cambridge's win by 20 lengths in 1900.

Boris Rankov (Oxford, 1978–83) rowed in a record six winning boats. Susan Brown (b. 29 June 1958), the first woman to take part, coxed the winning Oxford boats in 1981 and 1982.

Daniel Topolski coached Oxford to ten successive victories 1976–85.

The heaviest man ever to row in a University boat has been Stephen G. H. Plunkett (Queen's) the No. 5 in the 1976 Oxford boat at 229 lb *104 kg*. The 1983 Oxford crew averaged a record 204.3 lb *92,5 kg*. The lightest oarsman was the 1882 Oxford Stroke, Alfred Herbert Higgins, at 9 st 6½ lb *60 kg*. The lightest coxes, Francis Henry Archer (Cambridge) (1843–89) in 1862 and Hart Parker Vincent Massey (Oxford) (b. Canada, 30 Mar 1918) in 1939, were both 5 st 2 lb *32,6 kg*.

Head of the River

A processional race for eights instituted in 1926, the Head has an entry limit of 420 crews (3780 competitors). The record for the course Mortlake–Putney (the reverse of the Boat race) is 17 min 10.42 sec by the ARA National Squad in 1982.

Henley Royal Regatta

The annual regatta at Henley-on-Thames, Oxfordshire, was inaugurated on 26 Mar 1839. Since then the course, except in 1923, has been about 1 mile 550 yd *2112 m* varying slightly according to the length of boat. In 1967 the shorter craft were 'drawn up' so all bows start level.

The most wins in the Diamond Challenge Sculls (inst. 1844) is six consecutively by Stuart A. Mackenzie (b. 5 Apr 1937) (Australia and GB)

MEN—Fastest times over 2 000 m course (still water)

	min sec	Country	Place	Date	
Single Sculls	6:49.68	Nikolai Dovgan, USSR	Amsterdam, Netherlands	26 Aug	1978
Double Sculls	6:12.48	Norway	Montreal, Canada	23 July	1976
Coxed Pairs	6:49.75	GDR	Duisberg, W Germany	4 Sept	1983
Coxless Pairs	6:32.63	GDR	Lucerne, Switzerland	23 Aug	1982
Coxed Fours	6:05.21	GDR	Lucerne, Switzerland	17 June	1984
Coxless Fours	5:53.65	GDR	Montreal, Canada	23 July	1976
Quadruple Sculls	5:45.97	GDR	Duisberg, W. Germany	4 Sept	1983
Eights	5:27.14	USA	Lucerne, Switzerland	17 June	1984

WOMEN—Fastest times over 1 000 m course (still water)

	min sec	Country	Place	Date	
Single Sculls	3:30.74	Cornelia Linse, GDR	Lucerne, Switzerland	18 June	1984
Double Sculls	3:09.97	GDR	Lucerne, Switzerland	18 June	1984
Coxless Pairs	3:26.32	GDR	Amsterdam, Netherlands	21 Aug	1977
Coxed Fours	3:11.18	GDR	Duisberg, W. Germany	4 Sept	1983
Quadruple Sculls	3:02.48	GDR	Duisberg, W. Germany	4 Sept	1983
Eights	2:54.05	USA	Lucerne, Switzerland	16 June	1984

Cross Channel
Ivor Lloyd sculled across the English Channel in a record 3 hr 35 min 1 sec on 4 May 1983.

River Thames
A crew of five from Poplar Fire Station, London Fire Brigade rowed the navigable length of the Thames, 185.88 miles *299,14 km*, from Lechlade Bridge, Gloucestershire to Southend Pier, Essex in 45 hr 32 min in a 22 ft 10 in *6,96 m* skiff on 16–18 Apr 1984.

Longest race
The longest annual rowing race is the annual Tour du Lac Leman, Geneva, Switzerland for coxed fours (the five man crew taking turns as cox) over 160 km *99 miles*. The record winning time is 12 hr 52 min by LAGA Delft, Netherlands on 3 Oct 1982.

Finland's Pertti Karppinen won the single sculls for the third successive Olympics to equal the record of three gold medals. *(Sporting Pictures)*

1957–62. The record time is 7 min 40 sec by Sean Drea (Neptune RC, Ireland) on 5 July 1975. The Grand Challenge Cup (inst. 1839) for eights, has been won 27 times by Leander crews between 1840 and 1953. The record time for the event is 6 min 13 sec by Harvard Univ, USA, and a combined Leander/Thames Tradesmen crew, both on 5 July 1975.

Sculling
The record number of wins in the Wingfield Sculls (Putney to Mortlake) (instituted 1830) is seven by Jack Beresford, Jr. from 1920 to 1926. The fastest time for the course has been 21 min 11 sec by Leslie Frank 'Dick' Southwood (b. 18 Jan 1906) in winning the Wingfield Sculls on 12 Aug 1933. The most world professional sculling titles (instituted 1831) won is seven by William Beach (Australia) (1850–1935), 1884–87.

Highest speed
The highest recorded speed on non-tidal water for 2000 m *2187 yd* is by an American eight in 5 min 27.14 sec (22,01 km/h *13.68 mph*) at Lucerne, Switzerland on 17 June 1984. A crew from Penn AC, USA, was timed in 5 min 18.8 sec (14.03 mph *22,58 km/h*) in the FISA Championships on the River Meuse, Liege, Belgium, on 17 Aug 1930.

24 hours
The greatest distance rowed in 24 hrs (upstream and downstream) by a crew of eight is 130 miles *209 kms* by members of the Renmark Rowing Club, South Australia, on 20–1 Apr 1984.

SHINTY

Origins
Shinty (from the Gaelic *sinteag*, a bound) has roots reaching back more than 2000 years to the ancient game of *camanachd*, the sport of the curved stick, the diversion of the heroes of Celtic history and legend. It was effective battle training, exercising speed and co-ordination of eye and arm along with aggression and cool self-control. In spite of the break up of the clan system in the Highlands of Scotland, the "ball plays", involving whole parishes, without limit in number or time except the fall of night, continued in areas such as Lochaber, Badenoch and Strathglass. Whisky and the inspiration of the bagpipes were important ingredients of these occasions. The ruling body of this apparently ungovernable game was established in 1893 when the Camanachd Association was set up at Kingussie, Highland.

Most titles
Newtonmore, Highland has won the Camanachd Association Challenge Cup (instituted 1896) a record 27 times (1896–1985). Johnnie Campbell, David Ritchie and Hugh Chisholm, all of Newtonmore have won a record 11 winners' medals. In 1923 the Furnace Club, Argyll won the cup without conceding a goal throughout the competition.

In 1984 Kingussie Camanachd Club won all five senior competitions, including the Camanachd Cup final. This feat was equalled by Newtonmore in 1985.

Highest scores
The highest Scottish Cup Final score was in 1909 when Newtonmore beat Furnace 11–3 at Glasgow, Dr Johnnie Cattanach scoring eight hails or goals. In 1938 John Macmillan Mactaggart scored ten hails for Mid-Argyll in a Camanachd Cup match.

SHOOTING

Earliest club
The Lucerne Shooting Guild (Switzerland) was formed c.1466 and the first recorded shooting match was at Zurich in 1472.

Most Olympic medals
The record number of medals won is 11 by Carl Townsend Osburn (USA) (1884–1966) in 1912, 1920 and 1924, consisting of five gold, four silver and two bronze. Six other marksmen have won five gold medals. The only marksman to win three individual gold medals has been Gudbrand Gudbrandsönn Skatteboe (Norway) (1875–1965), in 1906. Separate events for women were first held in 1984.

Bisley
The National Rifle Association was instituted in 1859. The Queen's (King's) Prize has been shot since 1860 and has only once been won by a woman—Marjorie Elaine Foster (1894–1974) (score 280) on 19 July 1930. Arthur George Fulton (1887–1972) won a record three times (1912, 1926, 1931). Both his father and his son also won the Prize.

SHOOTING—INDIVIDUAL WORLD RECORDS

World records are accepted only when set at major international championships.

Malcolm Cooper of Great Britain broke three world records in two days in June 1985, to add to his existing one set whilst winning the gold medal at the Los Angeles Olympics. *(All-Sport)*

MEN

FREE RIFLE Three positions 3 × 40 shots at 300 m

1164/1200	Malcolm Cooper (GB)	Zürich, Switzerland	10 June 1985
	Prone 60 shots at 300 m		
595/600	Kalle Leskinen (Finland)	Olso, Norway	June 1983
595/600	Toni Müller (Switzerland)	Oslo, Norway	June 1983
595/600	Malcolm Cooper (GB)	Zürich, Switzerland	10 June 1985

STANDARD RIFLE Three positions 3 × 20 shots at 300 m

583/600	Malcolm Cooper (GB)	Zürich, Switzerland	8 June 1985

SMALL·BORE RIFLE Three positions 3 × 40 shots at 50 m

1173/1200	Viktor Vlasov (USSR)	Moscow, USSR	23 July 1980
1173/1200	Vladimir Lvov (USSR)	Bucharest, Romania	Sept 1983
1173/1200	Malcolm Cooper (GB)	Los Angeles, USA	1 Aug 1984
	Prone 60 shots at 50 m		
600/600	Alistair Allan (GB)	Titograd, Yugoslavia	21 Sept 1981
600/600	Ernest van de Zande (USA)	Rio de Janeiro, Brazil	1 Nov 1981

FREE PISTOL 60 shots at 50 m

581/600	Aleksandr Melentev (USSR)	Moscow, USSR	20 July 1980

RAPID FIRE PISTOL 60 shots at 25 m

599/600	Igor Puzryev (USSR)	Titograd, Yugoslavia	21 Sept 1981

CENTRE FIRE PISTOL 60 shots at 25 m

597/600	Thomas D. Smith (USA)	Sao Paulo, Brazil	1963

STANDARD PISTOL 60 shots at 25 m

584/600	Eric Buljong (USA)	Caracas, Venezuela	20 Aug 1983

RUNNING GAME TARGET 60 shots at 50 m with small-bore rifle

595/600	Igor Sokolov (USSR)	Miskulc, Hungary	9 Aug 1981

OLYMPIC TRAP 200 birds

200/200	Danny Carlisle (USA)	Caracas, Venezuela	20 Aug 1983

OLYMPIC SKEET 200 birds

200/200	Matthew Dryke (USA)	Sao Paulo, Brazil	4 Nov 1981

AIR RIFLE 60 shots at 10 m

590/600	Harald Stenvaag (Norway)	The Hague, Netherlands	19 Mar 1982
590/600	Philippe Héberlé (France)	St. Etienne, France	7 Feb 1985

AIR PISTOL 60 shots at 10 m

591/600	Vladas Tourla	Caracas, Venezuela	20 Aug 1983

WOMEN

STANDARD RIFLE Three positions 3 × 20 shots at 50 m

592/600	Marlies Helbig (GDR)	Titograd, Yugoslavia	Sept 1981
	Prone 60 shots at 50 m		
598/600	E. Rolinska (Poland)	Suhl, GDR	1971

SMALLBORE SPORT PISTOL 60 shots at 25 m

593/600	Li Yingzi (China)	Fuzhou, China	8 Dec 1984

OLYMPIC TRAP 200 birds

195/200	Susan Nattrass (Canada)	Seoul, S. Korea	1978

OLYMPIC SKEET 200 birds

194/200	Svetlana Yakimova (USSR)	Caracas, Venezuela	Nov 1982
194/200	Meimei Feng (China)	Caracas, Venezuela	Nov 1982

AIR RIFLE 40 shots at 10 m

395/400	Anna Malekhova (USSR)	The Hague, Netherlands	19 Mar 1982
395/400	Marlies Helbig (GDR)	Innsbruck, Austria	Sept 1983

AIR PISTOL 40 shots at 10 m

389/400	Liu Haiying (China)	Fuzhou, China	8 Dec 1984

The highest score (possible 300) for the final of the Queen's Prize is 295 by Lindsay Peden (Scotland) on 24 July 1982. The record for the Silver Medals is 150 (possible 150) by Martin John Brister (City Rifle Club) (b. 1951) and the Lord Swansea on 24 July 1971. This was equalled by John Henry Carmichael (WRA Bromsgrave RC) on 28 July 1979 and Robert Stafford on 26 July 1980, with the size of the bullseyes reduced.

Small-Bore

The National Small-Bore Rifle Association, of Britain, was formed in 1901. The British team record (1966 target) is 1988 × 2000 by Lancashire in 1968–9 and London in 1980–1. The British individual small-bore rifle record for 60 shots prone is 600 × 600, first achieved by John Palin (b. 16 July 1934) in Switzerland in 1972. Richard Hansen shot 5000 bullseyes in 24 hr at Fresno, Cal, USA on 13 June 1929.

Clay Pigeon

Most world titles have been won by Susan Nattrass (Canada) (b. 5 Nov 1950) with six in 1974–5, 1977–9, 1981. The record number of clay birds shot in an hour is 2215 by Joseph Kreckman at the Paradise Shooting Centre, Cresco, Pennsylvania, USA on 28 Aug 1983 (from 3176 shots from the hip). Graham Douglas Geater (b. 21 July 1947) shot 2264 targets in an hour on a Trapshooting range at the NILO Gun Club, Papamoa, New Zealand on 17 Jan 1981.

The maximum 200/200 was achieved by Ricardo Ruiz Rumoroso at the Spanish clay pigeon championships at Zaragoza on 12 June 1983.

Noel D. Townend achieved the maximum 200 consecutive Down the Line targets at Nottingham on 21 Aug 1983.

Bench rest shooting

The smallest group on record at 1000 yd *914 m* is 5.093 in *12,94 cm* by Rick Taylor with a 300 Weatherby at Williamsport, Penn., USA on 24 Aug 1980.

Highest score in 24 hr

The Easingwold Rifle and Pistol Club team of John Smith, Edward Kendall, Phillip Kendall and Paul Duffield scored 120,242 points (averaging 95.66 per card) on 6–7 Aug 1983.

SKIING

See also The Guinness Book of Skiing by Peter Lunn, published in 1983 at £8.95.

Origins

The most ancient ski in existence was found well preserved in a peat bog at Hoting, Sweden, dating from c. 2500 BC. The earliest recorded military use of skiing was at the Battle of Isen, near Oslo, Norway in 1200. The Trysil Shooting and Skiing Club, founded in Norway in 1861, claims it is the world's oldest. The oldest ski competitions are the Holmenkøllen Nordic events which were first held in 1866. The first downhill races were staged in Australia in the 1850s. The International Ski Federation (FIS) was founded on 2 Feb 1924, succeeding the International Skiing Commission, founded at Christiania (Oslo), Norway on 18 Feb 1910. The Ski Club of Great Britain was founded on 6 May 1903. The National Ski Federation of Great Britain was formed in 1964 and changed its name to the British Ski Federation in 1981.

Most titles *World Championships—Alpine*

The world Alpine championships were inaugurated at Mürren, Switzerland, in 1931. The greatest number of titles won has been by Christel Cranz (b. 1 July 1914) of Germany, with seven individual—four Slalom (1934, 1937–9) and three Downhill (1935, 1937, 1939), and five Combined (1934–5, 1937–9). She also won the gold medal for the Combined in the 1936 Olympics. The most won by a man is seven by Anton 'Toni' Sailer (b. 17 Nov 1935) (Austria) who won all four in 1956 (Giant Slalom, Slalom, Downhill and the non-Olympic Alpine Combination) and the Downhill, Giant Slalom and Combined in 1958.

Most titles *World Championships—Nordic*

The first world Nordic championships were those of the 1924 Winter Olympics in Chamonix, France. The greatest number of titles won is nine by Galina Kulakova (b. 29 Apr 1942) (USSR) in 1968–78. She also won four silver and four bronze medals for a record 17 in total. The most won by a man is eight, including relays, by Sixten Jernberg (b. 6 Feb 1929) (Sweden) in 1956–64. Johan Grøttumsbraaten (1899–1942) of Norway won six individual titles (two 18 km cross-country, four Nordic combined) in 1926–32. The record for a jumper is five by Birger Ruud (b. 23 Aug 1911) of Norway, in 1931–2 and 1935–7. Ruud is the only person to win Olympic events in each of the dissimilar Alpine and Nordic disciplines. In 1936 he won the ski-jumping and the Alpine downhill (which was not then a separate event, but only a segment of the combined event).

WORLD CUP

The World Cup was introduced for Alpine events in 1967 and for Nordic events in 1981. The most individual event wins is 79 by Ingemar Stenmark (Sweden) (b. 18 Mar 1956) in 1974–84, including a record 14 in one season in 1979. Franz Klammer (Austria) (b. 3 Dec 1953) won a record 35 downhill races, 1974–85. Annemarie Moser (née Pröll) (Austria) (b. 27 Mar 1953) won a women's record 62 individual event wins, 1970–9. She had a record 11 consecutive downhill wins from Dec 1972 to Jan 1974.

Most titles *British*

The most British skiing overall titles won is four by Stuart Fitzsimmons (b. 28 Dec 1956) in 1973, 1975–6 and 1979. The most ladies' titles won is four by Isobel M. Roe, 1938–9, 1948–9, Gina Hathorn (b. 6 July 1949) 1966, 1968–70, and Valentina Iliffe (b. 17 Feb 1956) 1975–6, 1979–80.

Ski-jumping

The longest ski-jump ever recorded is one of 186 m *610 ft* by Matti Nykänen (b. 17 July 1963) (Finland) at Planica, Yugoslavia on 17 Mar 1985. The female record is 110 m *361 ft* by Tiina Lehtola (b. 3 Aug 1962) (Finland) at Ruka, Finland on 29 Mar 1981. The longest dry ski-jump is 92 m *302 ft* by Hubert Schwarz (W. Ger) at Berchtesgarten, W. Germany on 30 June 1981.

Highest speed—downhill

The highest speed claimed for a skier is 208,936 km/h *129.827 mph* by Franz Weber (Austria) and the fastest by a woman is 200,780 km/h *124.759 mph* by Melissa Dimino (USA) both at Les Arcs, France on 19 Apr 1984. The highest average speed in the Olympic downhill race was 104,53 km/h *64.95 mph* by William D. Johnson (USA) (b. 30 Mar 1960) at Sarajevo, Yugoslavia on 16 Feb 1984. The fastest in a World Cup downhill is 107,82 km/h *67.00 mph* by Harti Weirather (Austria) (b. 25 Jan 1958) at Kitzbühl, Austria on 15 Jan 1982.

Highest speed—cross country

Bill Koch (USA) (b. 13 Apr 1943) on 26 March 1981 skied ten times round a 5 km *3.11 miles* loop on Marlborough Pond, near Putney, Vermont, USA. He completed the 50 km in 1 hr 59 min 47 sec, an average speed of 25,045 km/h *15.57 mph*. A race includes uphill and downhill sections; the record time for a 50 km race is 2 hr 10 min 49.9 sec by Gunde Svan (Sweden) (b. 12 Jan 1962) in the 1985 World Championships, an average speed of 22,93 km/h *14.25 mph*. The record for a 15 km Olympic or World Championship race is 38 min 52.5 sec by Oddvar Braa (Norway) (b. 16 Mar 1951) at the 1982 World Championships, an average speed of 23,15 km/h *14.38 mph*.

Most World Cup titles: ALPINE

MEN

Overall	4	Gustavo Thoeni (Italy)	1971–3, 1975
Downhill	5	Franz Klammer (Austria)	1975–8, 1983
Slalom	9	Ingemar Stenmark (Sweden)	1975–81, 1983–4
Giant Slalom	7	Ingemar Stenmark	1975–6, 1978–81, 1984

Jean-Claude Killy (France) (b. 30 Aug 1943) is the only person to win all four titles—downhill, slalom, giant slalom and overall. He won them all in 1967.

WOMEN

Overall	6	Annemarie Moser (Austria)	1971–5, 1979
Downhill	7	Annemarie Moser	1971–5, 1978–9
Slalom	4	Erika Hess (Switzerland)	1981–3, 1985
Giant Slalom	3	Annemarie Moser	1971–2, 1975

NORDIC

MEN

Jumping	2	Armin Kogler (Austria)	1981–2
		Matti Nykänen (Finland)	1983, 1985
Cross-country	2	Aleksandr Zavialov (USSR)	1981, 1983
	2	Gunde Svan (Sweden)	1984–5

WOMEN

Cross-country	2	Marja-Liisa Kirvesniemi (née Hämäläinen) (Finland)	1983–4

Franz Klammer of Austria has won more World Cup downhill races than any other man, having re-emerged in 1985 in typically dashing fashion. *(All-Sport)*

MOST OLYMPIC TITLES—SKIING

Men Alpine	3	Anton 'Toni' Sailer (Austria) (b. 17 Nov 1935)	Downhill, slalom, giant slalom, 1956
	3	Jean-Claude Killy (France) (b. 30 Aug 1943)	Downhill, slalom, giant slalom, 1968
Men Nordic	4[1]	Sixten Jernberg (Sweden) (b. 6 Feb 1929)	50 km, 1956; 30 km, 1960; 50 km and 4 × 10 km, 1964
Women Alpine	2	Andrea Mead-Lawrence (USA) (b. 19 Apr 1932)	Slalom, giant slalom, 1952
	2	Marielle Goitschel (France) (b. 28 Sept 1945)	Giant slalom, 1964; slalom, 1968
	2	Marie-Therese Nadig (Switz) (b. 8 Mar 1954)	Downhill, giant slalom, 1972
	2[2]	Rosi Mittermaier (now Neureuther) (W. Germany) (b. 5 Aug 1950)	Downhill, slalom, 1976
	2[3]	Hanni Wenzel (Liechtenstein) (b. 14 Dec 1956)	Giant slalom, slalom 1980
Women Nordic	4[4]	Galina Kulakova (USSR) (b. 29 Apr 1942)	5 km, 10 km and 3 × 5 km relay, 1972; 4 × 5 km relay, 1976
	3 (individual)	Marja-Liisa Hämäläinen (Finland) (b. 10 Aug 1955)	5 km, 10 km and 20 km 1984

[1] Jernberg also won three silver and two bronze for a record nine Olympic medals.
[2] Also won silver medal in Giant Slalom in 1976.
[3] Wenzel won a silver in the 1980 Downhill and a bronze in the 1976 Slalom.
[4] Kulakova also won two silver and two bronze medals in 1968, 1976 and 1980.

Closest Verdict
The narrowest winning margin in a championship ski race was one hundredth of a second by Thomas Wassberg (Sweden) over Juha Mieto (Finland) (b. 20 Nov 1949) in the Olympic 15 km Cross-country race at Lake Placid, USA on 17 Feb 1980. His winning time was 41 min 57.63 sec.

Highest altitude
Jean Atanassilf and Nicolas Jaeger skied from 8200 m *26,900 ft* to 6200 m *20,340 ft* on the 1978 French Expedition on Mt Everest.

Steepest descent
The steepest descents in alpine skiing history have been by Sylvain Saudan. At the start of his descent from Mont Blanc on the north-east side down the Couloir Gervasutti from 4248 m *13,937 ft* on 17 Oct 1967 he skied to gradients of *c.* 60°.

Longest run
The longest all-downhill ski run in the world is the Weissfluhjoch-Küblis Parsenn course, near Davos, Switzerland, which measures 12,23 km *7.6 miles*. The run from the Aiguille du Midi top of the Chamonix lift (vertical lift 2759 m *9052 ft*) across the Vallée Blanche is 20,9 km *13 miles*.

Longest races
The world's longest ski races are the Grenader, run just North of Oslo, Norway and the Konig Ludwig Lauf in Oberammergau, W. Germany. Both are of 90 km *55.9 miles*. The Canadian Ski Marathon at 160 km *99 miles* from Lachute, Quebec to Ottawa, Ontario is longer, but is run in two parts on consecutive days.

The world's greatest Nordic ski race is the Vasaloppet, which commemorates an event of 1521 when Gustav Vasa (1496–1560), later King Gustavus Eriksson, fled 85,8 km *53.3 miles* from Mora to Sälen, Sweden. He was overtaken by loyal, speedy scouts on skis, who persuaded him to return eastwards to Mora to lead a rebellion and become the king of Sweden. The re-enactment of this return journey is now an annual event at 89 km *55.3 miles*, contested by about 12,000 skiers. The fastest time is 3 hr 58 min 8 sec by Konrad Hallenbarter (Switzerland) on 6 Mar 1983. The Vasaloppet is now the longest of ten long distance races in ten countries constituting the World loppet.

The longest downhill race is the *Inferno* in Switzerland, 14 km *8.7 miles* from the top of the Schilthorn to Lauterbrunnen. In 1981 there was a record entry of 1401, with Heinz Fringer (Switzerland) winning in a record 15 min 44.57 sec.

Long Distance Nordic skiing records
In 24 hr Teuvo Rantanen covered 315 km *195 miles* at Jyväskylä, Finland on 24–25 Mar 1984. The women's record is 197,83 km *122.9 miles* by Marlene Severs at East Burke, Vermont, USA on 7–8 Mar 1985.

In 48 hr Bjørn Løkken (Norway) (b. 27 Nov 1937) covered 513,568 km *319 miles 205 yd* on 11–13 Mar 1982.

Ski-Parachuting
The greatest recorded vertical descent in parachute ski-jumping is 3300 ft *1006 m* by Rick Sylvester (b. 3 Apr 1942) (US) who on 28 July 1976 skied off the 6600 ft *2011 m* summit of Mt Asgard in Auyuittuq National Park, Baffin Island, Canada, landing on the Turner Glacier, the jump for a sequence in the James Bond film 'The Spy Who Loved Me'.

Ski-Bob *Origins*
The ski-bob was invented by J. C. Stevenson of Hartford, Connecticut, USA in 1891, and patented (No. 47334) on 19 Apr 1892 as a 'bicycle with ski-runners'. The Fédération Internationale de Skibob was founded on 14 Jan 1961 in Innsbruck, Austria and the first world championships were held at Bad Hofgastein, Austria in 1967. The Ski-Bob Association of Great Britain was registered on 23 Aug 1967. The highest speed attained is 166 km/h *103.4 mph* by Erich Brenter (b. 1940) (Austria) at Cervinia, Italy, in 1964.

Ski-Bob *World Championships*
The only ski-bobbers to retain a world championship are: men—Alois Fischbauer (Austria) (b. 6 Oct 1951), 1973 and 1975, Robert Mühlberger (W. Germany), 1979 and 1981; women—Gerhilde Schiffkorn (Austria) (b. 22 Mar 1950), 1967 and 1969, Gertrude Geberth (Austria) (b. 18 Oct 1951), 1971 and 1973.

Snowmobile
A record speed of 148.6 mph *239,1 km/h* was set by Tom Earhart (USA) in a Budweiser-Polaris snowmobile designed and owned by Bob Gaudreau at Lake Mille Lacs, Minnesota, USA on 25 Feb 1982. (*See also p. 129*).

Longest lift
The longest gondola ski lift is 6239 m *3.88 miles* long at Grindelwald-Männlichen, Switzerland (in two sections, but one gondola). The longest chair lift in the world was the Alpine Way to Kosciusko Châlet lift above Thredbo, near the Snowy Mountains, New South Wales, Australia. It took from 45 to 75 min to ascend the 3.5 miles *5,6 km*, according to the weather. It has now collapsed. The highest is at Chacaltaya, Bolivia, rising to 5029 m *16,500 ft*.

GRASS SKIING

Grass skis were first manufactured by Josef Kaiser (W. Ger) in 1963. World Championships (awarded for giant slalom, slalom and combined) were first held in 1979. The most titles won is five by Ingrid Hirschhofer (Austria). The most by a man is four by Erwin Gansner (Switzerland), two each in 1981 and 1983.

The speed record is 86,88 km/h *53.99 mph* by Erwin Gansner; the British record is 79,11 km/h *49.16 mph* by Nigel Smith, both at Owen, West Germany on 5 Sept 1982.

SNOOKER & POOL

Further information is available in Snooker—The Records *by Clive Everton (£6.95 limp-back) published in 1985 by Guinness Superlatives Ltd.*

Origins
Research shows that snooker was originated by Colonel Sir Neville Francis Fitzgerald Chamberlain (1856–1944) as a hybrid of 'black pool', 'pyramids' and billiards, in Jubbulpore, India in 1875. It did not reach England until 1885, where the modern scoring system was adopted in 1891. Championships were not instituted until 1916. The World Professional Championship was instituted in 1927.

Most titles *World*
The world professional title (inst 1927) was won a record 15 times by Joe Davis, 1927–40 and 1946. The most wins in the amateur championships (inst 1963) have been two by Gary Owen (England) in 1963 and 1966, and Ray Edmonds (England) 1972 and 1974.

Most titles *Women*
Maureen Baynton (*née* Barrett) won a record eight women's amateur championships between 1954 and 1968, as well as seven at billiards.

World Championships *Youngest*
The youngest player to win a world title is Jimmy White (GB) (b. 2 May 1962) who was 18 yr 191 days old when he won the World Amateur Snooker championship in Launceston, Tasmania, Australia on 9 Nov 1980.

Highest breaks
Over 100 players have achieved the 'maximum' break of 147. The first to do so was E. J. 'Murt' O'Donoghue (b. New Zealand 1901) at Griffiths, NSW, Australia on 26 Sept 1934. The first officially ratified 147 was by Joe Davis against Willie Smith at Leicester Square Hall, London on 22 Jan 1955. The first maximum achieved in a major tournament was by John Spencer (b. 18 Sept 1935) at Slough, Berkshire on 13 Jan 1979, but the table had oversized pockets. Steve Davis (b. 22 Aug 1957) had a ratified break of 147 against John Spencer in the Lada Classic at Oldham on 11 Jan 1982. The first 147 scored in the World Championships was by Cliff Thorburn (Canada) (b. 16 Jan 1948) against Terry Griffiths at the Crucible Theatre, Sheffield on 23 April 1983, thereby winning a £10,000 jackpot prize.

The official world amateur record break is 140 set by Joe Johnson (England) (b. 29 July 1952) in the TUC Club, Middlesbrough, Cleveland in 1978. David Taylor (b. 29 July 1943) made three consecutive frame clearances of 130, 140, and 139 (total 409) at Minehead, Somerset, on 1 June 1978. Jim Meadowcroft (b. 15 Dec 1946) made four consecutive frame clearances of 105, 115, 117 and 125 at Connaught Leisure Centre, Worthing on 27 Jan 1982.

The first century break by a woman in competi-

Popular Irishman Dennis Taylor won snooker's richest prize when he beat Steve Davis in the 1985 Embassy World Championships. In a thrilling final, Taylor won on the last black of the last possible frame. *(All-Sport)*

tive play was 114 by Stacey Hillyard in a league match at Bournemouth on 15 Jan 1985.

POOL

Pool or championship pocket billiards with numbered balls began to become standardized *c.* 1890. The greatest exponents were Ralph Greenleaf (USA) (1899–1950) who won the 'world' professional title 19 times (1919–37) and William Mosconi (USA) (b. 27 June 1913) who dominated the game from 1941 to 1957.

The longest consecutive run in an American straight pool match is 625 balls by Michael Eufemia at Logan's Billiard Academy, Brooklyn, NY, on 2 Feb 1960. The greatest number of balls pocketed in 24 hr is 15,780 by Vic Elliott at the Royal George, Lincoln, Lincs. on 2–3 Apr 1985.

The record time for potting all 15 balls in a speed competition is 40.06 sec by Ross McInnes (b. 19 Jan 1955) at Clacton, Essex on 11 Sept 1983.

SOFTBALL

Origins

Softball, the indoor derivative of baseball, was invented by George Hancock at the Farragut Boat Club of Chicago, Illinois in 1887. Rules were first codified in Minneapolis, Minnesota, USA in 1895 as Kitten Ball. The name Softball was introduced by Walter Hakanson at a meeting of the National Recreation Congress in 1926. The name was adopted throughout the USA in 1930. Rules were formalised in 1933 by the International Joint Rules Committee for Softball and adopted by the Amateur Softball Association of America. The International Softball Federation was formed in 1950 as governing body for both fast pitch and slow pitch. It was re-organised in 1965.

Most titles

The USA has won the men's world champion-

ship (inst. 1966) four times, 1966, 1968, 1976 (shared), and 1980. The USA has twice won the women's title (inst. 1965) in 1974 and 1978.

SPEEDWAY

Origins

Motorcycle racing on large dirt track surfaces has been traced back to 1902 in the United States. The first organized 'short track' races were at the West Maitland (New South Wales, Australia) Agricultural Show in November 1923. The sport evolved in Great Britain with small diameter track racing at Droylsden, Greater Manchester on 25 June 1927 and a cinder track event at High Beech, Essex, on 19 Feb 1928.

British championships

The National League was contested from 1932 to 1964. The Wembley Lions who won in 1932, 1946–7, 1949–53, had a record eight victories. In 1965 it was replaced by the British League which Belle Vue have won four times, including three times in succession (1970–2). Wimbledon are the only club to have competed every year in National and British Leagues. Belle Vue (Manchester) had a record nine victories (1933–

7, 1946–7, 1949 and 1958) in the National Trophy Knock-out Competition (held 1931–64). This was replaced in 1965 by the Knock Out Cup, which has been won three times by Cradley Heath, Belle Vue, Ipswich and Wimbledon.

World championships

The World Speedway Championship was inaugurated at Wembley, London in September 1936. The most wins have been six by Ivan Gerald Mauger (New Zealand) (b. 4 Oct 1939) in 1968–70, 1972, 1977 and 1979. He also won four World Team Cup, two World Pairs and two world long track titles. Barry Briggs (New Zealand) (b. 30 Dec 1934) made a record 17 consecutive appearances in the finals (1954–70) and won the world title in 1957–8, 1964 and 1966. He also scored a record 201 points in world championship competition.

England have most wins in the World Team Cup (inst. 1960) with eight, and the World Pairs Championship (inst. 1968) with seven. Poland uniquely competed in 21 successive World Team Cup finals, 1960–80 and in a 22nd in 1984. The maximum 30 points were scored in the World Pairs Championship by Jerzy Szczakiel (b. 28 Jan 1949) and Andrzej Wyglenda (Poland) at Rybnik, Poland in 1971 and by Arthur Dennis Sigalos (b. 16 Aug 1959) and Robert Benjamin 'Bobby' Schwartz (b. 10 Aug 1956) (USA) at Liverpool, New South Wales, Australia on 11 Dec 1982.

Ove Fundin (Sweden) (b. 23 May 1933) also won twelve world titles, five individual, one Pairs, and six World Team Cup medals in 1956–70.

Most points

In League racing the highest score recorded was when Crayford beat Milton Keynes 76–20 in the new 16-heat formula for the National League on 26 Oct 1982. A maximum possible score was achieved by Bristol when they defeated Glasgow (White City) 70–14 on 7 Oct 1949 in the National League Division Two. The highest number of League points scored by an individual in a season was 516 by Stephen Faulder Lawson (b. 11 Dec 1957) for Glasgow in the National League in 1982.

The only rider to have scored maximum points in every match of a Test series was Arthur 'Bluey' Wilkinson (b. 27 Aug 1911) in five matches for Australia *v.* England in Sydney in 1937–8.

WORLD CHAMPIONSHIP RECORDS: SOFTBALL

MEN

Most runs scored	14	Takayuki Ietke (Japan)	1984
Most home runs	4	Robert 'Bob' Burrows (Canada)	1976
Most hits	17	Basil McLean (New Zealand)	1976
RBIs	14	Chuck Teuscher (USA)	1966
	14	Robert 'Bob' Burrows (Canada)	1976
Highest average	.583	Takayuki Ietke (Japan)	1984
Most wins (pitching)	6	Owen Walford (New Zealand)	1976
	6	Owen Walford (USA, formerly NZ)	1980
Most innings pitched	59	Ty Stofflet (USA)	1976
Most strikeouts	98	Ty Stofflet (USA)	1976
Most perfect games	1	By seven men	—

WOMEN

Most runs scored	13	Kathy Elliott (USA)	1974
Most hits	17	Miyoko Naruse (Japan)	1974
Most doubles	4	Vicki Murray (New Zealand)	1982
	4	Suh-Chiung Ju (Taiwan)	1982
Most triples	6	Miyoko Naruse (Japan)	1974
	6	Yug-Feng Yang (Taiwan)	1982
RBIs	11	Miyoko Naruse (Japan); Keiko Usui (Japan); Kathy Elliott (USA)	1974
Highest average	.550	Tamara Bryce (Panama)	1978
Most wins (pitching)	6	Lorraine Wooley (Australia)	1965
	6	Nancy Welborn (USA)	1970
Most innings pitched	50	Nancy Welborn (USA)	1970
Most strikeouts	76	Joan Joyce (USA)	1974
Most perfect games	2	Joan Joyce (USA)	1974

SQUASH RACKETS

See also The Guinness Book of Squash *by Michael Palmer, published in 1984 at £7.95.*

Earliest champion
Although rackets (US spelling racquets) with a soft ball was played in 1817 at Harrow School, Harrow, Greater London, there was no recognised champion of any country until John A. Miskey of Philadelphia won the American Amateur Singles Championship in 1907.

World Championships
Geoffrey B. Hunt (b. 11 Mar 1947) (Australia) won four World Open (inst. 1976) titles, 1976–7 and 1979–80, and three World Amateur (inst. 1967) titles. Jahangir Khan (Pakistan) (b. 10 Dec 1953) has also won four World Open titles, 1981–4 and the ISRF World individual title (formerly World Amateur) in 1979 and 1983. Australia have won a record four men's team titles, 1967, 1969, 1971 and 1973 and three women's team titles, 1976, 1981 and 1983.

Most titles *Open Championship*
The most wins in the Open Championship (amateurs or professionals), held annually in Britain, is eight by Geoffrey Hunt in 1969, 1974, 1976–81. Hashim Khan (Pakistan) (b. 1915) won seven times, 1950–5 and 1957, and also won the Vintage title six times in 1978–83.

The most British open women's titles is 16 by Heather Pamela McKay (*née* Blundell) (Australia) (b. 31 July 1941) from 1961 to 1977. She also won the World Open title in 1976 and 1979. In her career from 1959 to 1980 she only lost two games (one in 1960, one in 1962).

Most titles *Amateur Championship*
The most wins in the Amateur Championship is six by Abdelfattah Amr Bey (Egypt) (b. 14 Feb 1910), who won in 1931–3 and 1935–7. Norman Francis Borrett (b. 1 Oct 1917) of England won in 1946–50.

Longest and shortest championship matches
The longest recorded competitive match was one of 2 hr 45 min when Jahangir Khan beat Gamal Awad (Egypt) (b. 8 Sept 1955) 9–10, 9–5, 9–7, 9–2, the first game lasting a record 1 hr 11 min, in the final of the Patrick International Festival at Chichester, West Sussex, England on 30 Mar 1983. Deanna Murray beat Christine Rees in only 9½ min in a Ladies Welsh title match at Rhos-on-Sea, Clwyd, on 21 Oct 1979.

Most international appearances
The men's record is 106 by Christopher Wilson (b. 1 May 1949) for Scotland, 1969–84. The women's record is 71 by Geraldine Barniville for Ireland, 1973–83.

Largest crowd
The finals of the British Open Squash Championships at Wembley Conference Centre, London had a record attendance for squash of 2,904 on 23 Apr 1985.

SURFING

Origins
The traditional Polynesian sport of surfing in a canoe (*ehorooe*) was first recorded by Captain James Cook, RN, FRS (1728–79) on his first voyage at Tahiti in December 1771. Surfing on a board (*Amo Amo iluna ka lau oka nalu*) was first described 'most perilous and extraordinary . . . altogether astonishing and is scarcely to be credited' by Lt (later Capt) James King, RN, FRS in March 1779 at Kealakekua Bay, Hawaii Island. A surfer was first depicted by this voyage's official artist John Webber. The sport was revived at Waikiki by 1900. Hollow boards were introduced in 1929 and the light plastic foam type in 1956.

Most titles
World Amateur Championships were inaugurated in May 1964 at Sydney, Australia; two titles have been won by Joyce Hoffman (US) in 1965 and 1966 and by Mike Novakov (Australia) who won the Kneeboard event in 1982 and 1984. A World Professional circuit was started in 1975 and Mark Richards (Australia) has won the men's title four times, 1979–82.

Highest waves ridden
Makaha Beach, Hawaii provides the reputedly highest consistently high waves often reaching the rideable limit of 30–35 ft *9–10 m*. The highest wave ever ridden was the *tsunami* of 'perhaps 50 ft *15,24 m*', which struck Minole, Hawaii on 3 Apr 1868, and was ridden to save his life by a Hawaiian named Holua.

Longest ride *Sea wave*
About four to six times each year rideable surfing waves break in Matanchen Bay near San Blas, Nayarit, Mexico which makes rides of *c.* 5700 ft *1700 m* possible.

Longest ride *River bore*
The longest recorded rides on a river bore have been set on the Severn bore, England. The official British Surfing Association record for riding a surfboard in a standing position is 0.8 mile *1,3 km* by Nick Hart (b. 11 Dec 1958) from Lower Rea to Hempsted on 26 Oct 1984. The longest ride on a surfboard standing or lying down is 2.94 miles *4,73 km* by Colin Kerr Wilson (b. 23 June 1954) on 23 May 1982.

SWIMMING

Earliest references
In Japan, swimming in schools was ordered by Imperial edict of Emperor Go-Yozei (1586–1611) in 1603 but competition was known from 36 BC. Sea water bathing was fashionable at Scarborough, North Yorkshire as early as 1660. In Great Britain competitive swimming originated from at least 1791. The earliest pool was Pearless Pool, North London, opened in 1743. Swimming races were particularly popular in the 1820s in Liverpool, where the earliest pool opened at St George's Pier Head, Liverpool in 1828.

Largest pools
The largest swimming pool in the world is the sea-water Orthlieb Pool in Casablanca, Morocco. It is 480 m *1574 ft* long and 75 m *246 ft* wide, and has an area of 3.6 ha *8.9 acres*. The largest land-locked swimming pool with heated water was the Fleishhacker Pool on Sloat Boulevard, near Great Highway, San Francisco, California, USA. It measured 1000 × 150 ft *304,8 × 45,7 m* and up to 14 ft *4,26 m* deep and contained 7,500,000 US gal *28 390 hectolitres* of heated water. It was opened on 2 May 1925 but has now been abandoned. The greatest spectator accommodation is 13,614 at Osaka, Japan. The largest in use in the United Kingdom is the Royal Commonwealth Pool, Edinburgh, completed in 1970 with 2000 permanent seats, but the covered over and unused pool at Earls Court, London (opened 1937) could seat some 12,000 spectators.

Fastest swimmer
The fastest speed measured in a 50 m pool is by the world record holders for 50 metres (see table): men: Robin Leamy 7,98 km/h *4.96 mph* and Dara Torres 7,03 km/h *4.37 mph*.

Most world records
Men: 32, Arne Borg (Sweden) (b. 18 Aug 1901), 1921–9. Women: 42, Ragnhild Hveger (Denmark) (b. 10 Dec 1920), 1936–42. Under modern conditions (only metric distances in 50 m pools) the most is 26 by Mark Andrew Spitz (USA) (b. 10 Feb 1950), 1967–72, and 23 by Kornelia Ender (GDR) (b. 25 Oct 1958), 1973–6.

Most world titles
In the world championships (inst 1973) the most medals won is ten by Kornelia Ender with eight gold and two silver in 1973 and 1975. The most by a man is eight by Ambrose 'Rowdy' Gaines (USA) (b. 17 Feb 1959), five gold and three silver, in 1978 and 1982. The most gold medals is six by James Montgomery (USA) (b. 24 Jan 1955) in 1973 and 1975. The most medals in a single championship is six by Tracy Caulkins (USA) (b. 11 Jan 1963) in 1978 with five golds and a silver.

OLYMPIC RECORDS
Most medals *Men*
The greatest number of Olympic gold medals won is nine by Mark Spitz (USA): 100 m and 200 m freestyle 1972; 100 m and 200 m butterfly 1972; 4 × 100 m freestyle 1968 and 1972; 4 × 200 m freestyle 1968 and 1972; 4 × 100 m medley 1972. *All but one of these performances (the 4 × 200 m freestyle of 1968) were also new world records.* He also won a silver (100 m butterfly) and a bronze (100 m freestyle) in 1968 for a record eleven medals.

Most medals *Women*
The record number of gold medals won by a woman is four shared by Patricia McCormick (*née* Keller) (USA) (b. 12 May 1930), the high and springboard diving double in 1952 and 1956 (also the female record for individual golds), Dawn Fraser (Australia) (b. 4 Sept 1937), the 100 m freestyle (1956, 1960 and 1964) and the 4 × 100 m freestyle (1956) and Kornelia Ender (GDR) the 100 and 200 m freestyle, 100 m butterfly and 4 × 100 m medley in 1976. Dawn Fraser is the only swimmer to win the same event on three successive occasions.

The most medals won by a woman is eight by Dawn Fraser, who in addition to her four golds won four silvers (400 m freestyle 1956, 4 × 100 m freestyle 1960 and 1964, 4 × 100 m medley 1960), Kornelia Ender who in addition to her four golds won four silvers (200 m individual medley 1972, 4 × 100 m medley 1972, 4 × 100 m freestyle 1972 and 1976) and Shirley Babashoff (USA) (b. 3 Jan 1957), who won two golds (4 × 100 m freestyle 1972 and 1976) and six silvers (100 m freestyle 1972, 200 m freestyle 1972 and 1976, 400 m and 800 m freestyle 1976, 4 × 100 m medley 1976).

Most individual gold medals
The record number of individual gold medals won is four by Charles M. Daniels (USA) (1884–1973) (100 m freestyle 1906 and 1908, 220 yd freestyle 1904, 440 yd freestyle 1904); Roland Matthes (GDR) (b. 17 Nov 1950) with 100 m and 200 m backstroke 1968 and 1972; Mark Spitz and Pat McCormick. The most individual golds by a British swimmer is three by Henry Taylor.

Most medals *British*
The record number of gold medals won by a British swimmer (excluding Water Polo, *q.v.*) is four by Henry Taylor (1885–1951) in the mile freestyle (1906), 400 m freestyle (1908), 1500 m freestyle (1908) and 4 × 200 m freestyle (1908).

SWIMMING—WORLD RECORDS (*set in 50 m pools*)

MEN

FREESTYLE

	Min. Sec.	Name, Country and date of birth	Place	Date	
50 metres	22.54	Robin Leamy (USA) (b. 1 Apr 1961)	Milwaukee, Wisconsin, USA	15 Aug	1961
100 metres	49.36	Ambrose 'Rowdy' Gaines (USA) (b. 17 Feb 1959)	Austin, Texas, USA	3 Apr	1981
200 metres	1:47.44	Michael Gross (W. Germany) (b. 17 June 1964)	Los Angeles, USA	29 July	1984
400 metres	3:47.80	Michael Gross (W. Germany)	Remscheid, W. Germany	27 June	1985
800 metres	7:52.33	Vladimir Salnikov (USSR) (b. 21 May 1960)	Los Angeles, USA	14 July	1983
1500 metres	14:54.76	Vladimir Salnikov (USSR)	Moscow, USSR	22 Feb	1983
4 × 100 metres relay	3:19.03	United States (Chris Cavanaugh, Michael Heath, Matthew Biondi, Ambrose 'Rowdy' Gaines)	Los Angeles, USA	2 Aug	1984
4 × 200 metres relay	7:15.69	United States (Michael Heath, David Larson, Jeffery Float, Lawrence Bruce Hayes)	Los Angeles, USA	30 July	1984

BREASTSTROKE

100 metres	1:01.65	Steven Lundquist (USA) (b. 20 Feb 1961)	Los Angeles, USA	29 July	1984
200 metres	2:13.34	Victor Davis (Canada) (b. 19 Feb 1964)	Los Angeles, USA	2 Aug	1984

BUTTERFLY

100 metres	53.08	Michael Gross (W. Germany)	Los Angeles, USA	30 July	1984
200 metres	1:57.01	Michael Gross (W. Germany)	Remscheid, W. Germany	29 June	1985

BACKSTROKE

100 metres	55.19	Richard Carey (USA) (b. 13 Mar 1963)	Caracas, Venezuela	21 Aug	1983
200 metres	1:58.14	Igor Polyanski (USSR) (b. 20 Mar 1967)	Gera, GDR	3 Mar	1985

MEDLEY

200 metres	2:01.42	Alex Baumann (Canada) (b. Prague 21 Apr 1964)	Los Angeles, USA	4 Aug	1984
400 metres	4:17.41	Alex Baumann	Los Angeles, USA	30 July	1984
4 × 100 metres relay	3:39.30	United States (Richard Carey, Steven Lundquist, Pedro Pablo Morales, Ambrose 'Rowdy' Gaines)	Los Angeles, USA	4 Aug	1984

WOMEN

FREESTYLE

50 metres	25.61	Dara Torres (USA) (b. 15 Apr 1967)	Mission Viejo, California, USA	21 July	1984
100 metres	54.79	Barbara Krause (GDR) (b. 7 July 1959)	Moscow, USSR	21 July	1980
200 metres	1:57.75	Kristin Otto (GDR) (b. 7 Feb 1965)	Magdeburg, GDR	23 May	1984
400 metres	4:06.28	Tracey Wickham (Australia) (b. 24 Nov 1962)	West Berlin, W. Germany	24 Aug	1978
800 metres	8:24.62	Tracey Wickham (Australia)	Edmonton, Canada	5 Aug	1978
1500 metres	16:04.49	Kim Lineham (USA) (b. 11 Dec 1962)	Fort Lauderdale, Florida, USA	19 Aug	1979
4 × 100 metres relay	3:42.41	GDR (Kristin Otto, Karin Konig, Heike Friedrich, Birgit Meineke)	Moscow, USSR	21 Aug	1984
4 × 200 metres relay	8:02.27	GDR (Kristin Otto, Astrid Strauss, Cornelia Sirch, Birgit Meineke)	Rome, Italy	23 Aug	1983

BREASTSTROKE

100 metres	1:08.29	Sylvia Gerasch (GDR) (b. 16 Mar 1969)	Moscow, USSR	23 Aug	1984
200 metres	2:28.33	Silke Hörner (GDR)	Leipzig, GDR	5 June	1985

BUTTERFLY

100 metres	57.93	Mary Meagher (USA) (b. 27 Oct 1964)	Milwaukee, Wisconsin, USA	16 Aug	1981
200 metres	2:05.96	Mary Meagher	Milwaukee, Wisconsin, USA	13 Aug	1981

BACKSTROKE

100 metres	1:00.59	Ina Kleber (GDR) (b. 29 Sept 1964)	Moscow, USSR	24 Aug	1984
200 metres	2:09.91	Cornelia Sirch (GDR) (b. 23 Oct 1966)	Guayaquil, Ecuador	8 Aug	1982

MEDLEY

200 metres	2:11.73	Ute Geweniger (GDR) (b. 24 Feb 1964)	East Berlin, GDR	4 July	1981
400 metres	4:36.10	Petra Schneider (GDR) (b. 11 Jan 1963)	Guayaquil, Ecuador	1 Aug	1982
4 × 100 metres relay	4:03.69	GDR (Ina Kleber, Sylvia Gerasch, Ines Geissler, Birgit Meineke)	Moscow, USSR	24 Aug	1984

Steve Lundquist (*below*) setting the 100 m breaststroke world record time at the 1984 Olympics, where out of 15 men's events, ten world records were broken. (*Inset*) John Sieben celebrates his 200 m butterfly Olympic gold and world record; Michael Gross, looking on here, broke Sieben's record in June 1985. (*All-Sport/Tony Duffy*)

Henry Taylor won a record eight medals in all with a silver (400 m freestyle 1906) and three bronzes (4 × 200 m freestyle 1906, 1912, 1920). The most medals by a British woman is four by M. Joyce Cooper (now Badcock) (b. 18 Apr 1909) with one silver (4 × 100 m freestyle 1928) and three bronze (100 m freestyle 1928, 100 m backstroke 1928, 4 × 100 m freestyle 1932).

Closest verdict

The closest recorded win in the Olympic Games was in the Munich 400 m individual medley final of 30 Aug 1972 when Gunnar Larsson (Sweden) (b. 12 May 1951) got the verdict over Tim McKee (USA) (b. 14 Mar 1953) by 2/1000th of a second in 4 min 31.981 sec to 4 min 31.983 sec—a margin of 3 mm or the length grown by a finger nail in three weeks. This led to a change in international rules with timings and places decided only to hundredths.

DIVING

Most Olympic medals *World*

The most medals won by a diver are five (three gold, two silver) by Klaus Dibiasi (b. Austria, 6 Oct 1947) (Italy) in four Games from 1964 to 1976. He is also the only diver to win the same event (highboard) at three successive Games (1968, 1972 and 1976). Pat McCormick (*see above*) won four gold medals.

Most Olympic medals *British*

The highest placing by a Briton has been the silver medal by Beatrice Eileen Armstrong (later Purdy) (1894–1981) in the 1920 highboard event. The best placings by male divers are the bronze medals by Harold Clarke (b. 1888) (plain high diving, 1924) and Brian Phelps (b. 21 Apr 1944) (highboard, 1960).

Most world titles

Phil Boggs (USA) (b. 29 Dec 1949) won three springboard gold medals, in 1973, 1975 and 1978 but Klaus Dibiasi (Italy) won four medals (two gold, two silver) in 1973 and 1975. Irina Kalinina (USSR) (b. 8 Feb 1959) has won five medals (three gold, one silver, one bronze) in 1973, 1975 and 1978. Greg Louganis (USA) (b. 29 Jan 1960), won one world title in 1978 and two in 1982, as well as two Olympic gold medals in 1984.

Highest scores

Greg Louganis achieved record scores at the 1984 Olympic Games in Los Angeles, with 754.41 points for the 11-dive springboard event and 710.91 for the highboard. At the world

championships in Guayaquil, Ecuador in 1984 he was awarded a perfect score of 10.0 by all seven judges for his highboard inward 1.5 somersault in the pike position.

The first diver to be awarded a score of 10.0 by all seven judges was Michael Finneran (b. 21 Sept 1948) in the 1972 US Olympic Trials, in Chicago, Illinois, for a backward 1½ somersault, 2½ twist, from the 10 m board.

CHANNEL SWIMMING

Earliest

The first to swim the English Channel from shore to shore (without a life jacket) was the Merchant Navy captain Matthew Webb (1848–83) who swam breaststroke from Dover, England to Calais Sands, France, in 21 hr 45 min from 12.56 p.m. to 10.41 a.m., 24–25 Aug 1875. He swam an estimated 38 miles *61 km* to make the 21-mile *33 km* crossing. Paul Boyton (USA) had swum from Cap Gris-Nez to the South Foreland in his patent life-saving suit in 23 hr 30 min on 28–29 May 1875. There is good evidence that Jean-Marie Saletti, a French soldier, escaped from a British prison hulk off Dover by swimming to Boulogne in July or August 1815. The first crossing from France to England was made by Enrico Tiraboschi, a wealthy Italian living in Argentina, in 16 hr 33 min on 12 Aug 1923, to win the *Daily Sketch* prize of £1000.

The first woman to succeed was Gertrude Caroline Ederle (b. 23 Oct 1906) (USA) (*see also p. 220*) who swam from Cap Gris-Nez, France to Deal, England on 6 Aug 1926, in the then overall record time of 14 hr 39 min. The first woman to swim from England to France was Florence Chadwick (b. 1918) (USA) in 16 hr 19 min on 11 Sept 1951. The first Englishwoman to succeed was Mercedes Gleitze (later Carey) (1900–81) who swam from France to England in 15 hr 15 min on 7 Oct 1927.

Fastest

The official Channel Swimming Association (founded 1927) record is 7 hr 40 min by Penny Dean (b. 21 Mar 1955) of California, USA, from Shakespeare Beach, Dover to Cap Gris-Nez, France, on 29 July 1978.

The fastest crossing by a relay team is 7 hr 17 min, by six Dover lifeguards, from England to France on 9 Aug 1981.

Earliest and latest

The earliest date in the year on which the

Channel has been swum is 6 June by Dorothy Perkins (England) (b. 1942) in 1961, and the latest is 28 Oct by Michael Peter Read (GB) (b. 9 June 1941) in 1979.

Youngest and oldest

The youngest conqueror is Marcus Hooper (GB) (b. 14 June 1967) who swam from Dover to Sangatte, France in 14 hr 37 min on 5–6 Aug 1979, when he was aged 12 yr 53 days. The youngest girl is Samantha Claire Druce (GB) (b. 21 Apr 1971) who was 12 yr 119 days on 18 Aug 1983 when she swam from Dover to Cap Gris-Nez in 15 hr 27 min.

The oldest has been Ashby Harper (b. 1 Oct 1916) of Albuquerque, USA at 65 years 332 days when he swam from Dover to Cap Blanc Nez in 13 hr 52 min on 28 Aug 1982. The oldest woman was Stella Ada Rosina Taylor (b. 20 Dec 1929) aged 45 yr 350 days when she did the swim in 18 hr 15 min on 26 Aug 1975.

Double crossing

Antonio Abertondo (Argentina) (b. 1919), swam from England to France in 18 hr 50 min (8.35 a.m. on 20 Sept to 3.25 a.m. on 21 Sept) and after about 4 min rest returned to England in 24 hr 16 min, landing at St Margaret's Bay at 3.45 a.m. on 22 Sept 1961, to complete the first 'double crossing' in 43 hr 10 min. Kevin Murphy (b. 1949) completed the first double crossing by a Briton in 35 hr 10 min on 6 Aug 1970. The first swimmer to achieve a crossing both ways was Edward Harry Temme (1904–78) on 5 Aug 1927 and 19 Aug 1934.

The fastest double crossing was in 18 hr 15 min by Irene van der Laan (Netherlands) (b. 27 Dec 1960) on 18 Aug 1983. The first British woman to achieve the double crossing was Alison Streeter (b. 29 Aug 1964) in 21 hr 16 min on 4 Aug 1983. The fastest by a relay team is 16 hr 5½ min (including a 2 min rest) by six Saudi Arabian men on 11 Aug 1977.

Triple crossing

The first triple crossing was by Jon Erikson (USA) (b. 6 Sept 1954) in 38 hr 27 min on 11–12 Aug 1981.

Most conquests

The greatest number of Channel conquests is 31 by Michael Read (GB) from 24 Aug 1969 to 19 Aug 1984, including a record six in one year. Cindy Nicholas made her first crossing on 29 July 1975 and her nineteenth (and fifth two-way) on 14 Sept 1982.

LONG DISTANCE SWIMMING

Longest swims

The greatest recorded distance ever swum is 1826 miles *2938 km* down the Mississippi, USA between Ford Dam near Minneapolis and Carrollton Ave, New Orleans, Louisiana, by Fred P. Newton, (b. 1903) of Clinton, Oklahoma from 6 July to 29 Dec 1930. He was 742 hr in the water.

The greatest distance covered in a continuous swim is 299 miles *481,5 km* by Ricardo Hoffmann (b. 5 Oct 1941) from Corrientes to Santa Elena, Argentina in the River Parana in 84 hr 37 min on 3–6 Mar 1981.

The longest ocean swim is one of 128.8 miles *207,3 km* by Walter Poenisch Snr (USA) (b. 1914) who started from Havana, Cuba, and arrived at Little Duck Key, Florida, USA (in a shark cage and wearing flippers) 34 hr 15 min later on 11–13 July 1978.

In 1966 Mihir Sen of Calcutta, India uniquely swam the Palk Strait from Sri Lanka to India (in 25 hr 36 min on 5–6 Apr); the Straits of

Strokes of genius; Alex Baumann of Canada set world records in both the 200 m and 400 m medley events at Los Angeles. *(All Sport/Tony Duffy)*

Gibraltar (in 8 hr 1 min on 24 Aug); the length of the Dardanelles (in 13 hr 55 min on 12 Sept), the Bosphorus (in 4 hr on 21 Sept) and the length of the Panama Canal (in 34 hr 15 min on 29–31 Oct).

Irish Channel

The swimming of the 23 mile *37 km* wide North Channel from Donaghadee, Northern Ireland to Portpatrick, Scotland was first accomplished by Tom Blower of Nottingham in 15 hr 26 min in 1947. A record time of 11 hr 21 min was set by Kevin Murphy on 11 Sept 1970. The first Irish-born swimmer to achieve the crossing was Ted Keenan on 11 Aug 1973 in 52–56°F *11–13°C* water in 18 hr 27 min.

Bristol Channel

The first person to achieve a crossing of the Bristol Channel was Kathleen Thomas (now Mrs Day) (b. Apr 1906) who swam from Penarth, South Glamorgan to Weston-super-Mare, Avon in 7 hr 20 min on 5 Sept 1927. The record for the longer swim from Glenthorne Cove, Devon to Porthcawl, Mid-Glamorgan is 10 hr 46 min by Jane Luscombe (b. 13 Jan 1961) of Jersey, CI, on 19 Aug 1976.

Lake swims

The fastest time for swimming the 22.7 mile *36,5 km* long Loch Ness, is 9 hr 57 min by David Morgan (b. 25 Sept 1963) on 31 July 1983. The

Sarah Hardcastle (*above*) at 15 won Olympic bronze and set a new British record in the 800 m freestyle. (*Above right*) Adrian Moorhouse, still the best Briton at 100 m breaststroke. (*All Sport/Tony Duffy*)

first successful swim was by Brenda Sherratt (b. 1948) of West Bollington, Cheshire on 26–27 July 1966. David Morgan achieved a unique double crossing of Loch Ness in 23 hr 4 min on 1 Aug 1983. The fastest time for swimming Lake Windermere, 10.5 miles *16,9 km* is 3 hr 49 min 56 sec by Karen Toole, 17, of Darlington on 5 Sept 1981. The fastest time for the Lake Windermere International Championship,

BRITISH NATIONAL *long course* RECORDS

MEN

Event	Time Min. Sec.	Name and date of birth	Place	Date
FREESTYLE				
100 metres	51.32	David Lowe (b. 28 Feb 1960)	Rome, Italy	24 Aug 1983
200 metres	1:51.52	Andrew Astbury (b. 29 Nov 1960)	Brisbane, Australia	2 Oct 1982
400 metres	3:53.29	Andrew Astbury	Brisbane, Australia	4 Oct 1982
800 metres	8:12.39	David Stacey (b. 22 Feb 1965)	Los Angeles, USA	3 Aug 1984
1500 metres	15:30.10	David Stacey (b. 22 Feb 1965)	Los Angeles, USA	3 Aug 1984
4 × 100 metres relay	3:23.61	UK (David Lowe, Roland Lee, Paul Easter, Richard Burrell)	Los Angeles, USA	2 Aug 1984
4 × 200 metres relay	7:24.78	UK (Neil Cochran, Paul Easter, Paul Howe, Andrew Astbury)	Los Angeles, USA	30 July 1984
BREASTSTROKE				
100 metres	1:02.93	Adrian Moorhouse (b. 24 May 1964)	Brisbane, Australia	6 Oct 1982
200 metres	2:15.11	David Andrew Wilkie (b. 8 Mar 1954)	Montreal, Canada	24 July 1976
BUTTERFLY				
100 metres	54.28	Andrew Jameson (b. 19 Feb 1965)	Los Angeles, USA	30 July 1984
200 metres	2:00.21	Philip Hubble (b. 19 July 1960)	Split, Yugoslavia	11 Sept 1981
BACKSTROKE				
100 metres	57.72	Gary Abraham (b. 8 Jan 1959)	Moscow, USSR	24 July 1980
200 metres	2:04.23	Douglas Campbell (b. 30 Sept 1960)	Moscow, USSR	26 July 1980
MEDLEY				
200 metres	2:04.13	Robin Brew (b. 28 June 1962)	Los Angeles, USA	4 Aug 1984
400 metres	4:25.38	Stephen Poulter (b. 18 Feb 1961)	Los Angeles, USA	30 July 1984
4 × 100 metres relay	3:47.39	UK (Neil Harper, Adrian Moorhouse, Andrew Jameson, Richard Burrell)	Los Angeles, USA	4 Aug 1984

WOMEN

Event	Time Min. Sec.	Name and date of birth	Place	Date
FREESTYLE				
100 metres	56.60	June Croft (b. 17 June 1963)	Amersfoort, Netherlands	31 Jan 1982
200 metres	1:59.74	June Croft	Brisbane, Australia	4 Oct 1982
400 metres	4:10.27	Sarah Hardcastle (b. 9 April 1969)	Los Angeles, USA	31 July 1984
800 metres	8:32.60	Sarah Hardcastle	Los Angeles, USA	3 Aug 1984
1500 metres	16:43.95	Sarah Hardcastle	Montreal, Canada	21 Apr 1985
4 × 100 metres relay	3:50.12	UK (June Croft, Nicola Fibbens, Debra Gore, Annabelle Cripps)	Los Angeles, USA	31 July 1984
4 × 200 metres relay	8:15.21	UK (Annabelle Cripps, Sarah Hardcastle, Ruth Gilfillan, June Croft)	Crystal Palace, London	26 Feb 1984
BREASTSTROKE				
100 metres	1.11.05	Susannah 'Suki' Brownsdon (b. 16 Oct 1965)	Split, Yugoslavia	8 Sept 1981
200 metres	2:33.16	Susannah 'Suki' Brownsdon	Cardiff, Wales	4 May 1985
BUTTERFLY				
100 metres	1:01.48	Nicola Fibbens (b. 29 Apr 1964)	Los Angeles, USA	2 Aug 1984
200 metres	2:11.97	Samantha Purvis (b. 24 June 1967)	Los Angeles, USA	4 Aug 1984
BACKSTROKE				
100 metres	1:03.61	Beverley Rose (b. 21 Jan 1964)	Los Angeles, USA	31 July 1984
200 metres	2:16.00	Katharine Read (b. 30 June 1969)	Coventry, England	28 May 1984
MEDLEY				
200 metres	2:17.31	Sharron Davies (b. 1 Nov 1962)	Blackpool, England	20 Apr 1980
400 metres	4:46.83	Sharron Davies	Moscow, USSR	26 July 1980
4 × 100 metres relay	4:12.24	UK (Helen Jameson, Margaret Kelly, Ann Osgerby, June Croft)	Moscow, USSR	20 July 1980

16.5 miles *26,5 km*, is 6 hr 10 min 33 sec by Mary Beth Colpo (USA) (b. 1961) on 5 Aug 1978.

Longest duration

The longest duration swim ever achieved was one of 168 continuous hours, ending on 24 Feb 1941, by the legless Charles Zibbelman, *alias Zimmy* (b. 1894) in a pool in Honolulu, Hawaii, USA. The longest duration swim by a woman was 87 hr 27 min in a salt-water pool by Myrtle Huddleston (USA) at Raven Hall, Coney Island, NY, USA, in 1931.

24 hours

Jon Hestoy (Iceland) swam 89,174 km *55.41 miles* in a 25 m pool at Aarhus, Denmark on 29–30 May 1982. The record in a 50 m pool is 87,528 km *54.39 miles* by Bertrand Malègue at St. Etienne, France on 31 May–1 June 1980.

Greatest lifetime distance

Gustave Brickner (b. 10 Feb 1912) of Charleroi, Pennsylvania, USA in 57 years to November 1984 had recorded 37,802 miles *60 834 km.*

Long distance relays

The New Zealand national relay team of 20 swimmers swam a record 182,807 km *113.59 miles* in Lower Hutt, NZ in 24 hours, passing 160 km *100 miles* in 20 hr 47 min 13 sec on 9–10 Dec 1983. The most participants in a swim relay is 1900, 38 teams of 50, in Sao Paulo, Brazil on 1 Apr 1984. A team of four from Capalaba State Primary School—Kim Wilson, Tanya Obstoj, Paul Giles, Darren Sheldrick—set an endurance record of 168 hr with one of the team in the water at any time, covering 540,8 km *336 miles* on 12–19 Dec 1983 at Sheldon, Queensland, Australia.

Underwater Swimming

Paul Cryne (UK) and Samir Sawan al Awami of Qatar swam 49.04 miles *78,92 km* in a 24 hr period from Doha, Qatar to Umm Said and back on 21–22 Feb 1985 using subaqua equipment. They were swimming underwater for 95.5% of the time.

Tony Boyle, Eddie McGettigan, Laurence Thermes and Gearoid Murphy swam a relay of 332.88 miles *535,71 km* underwater in 168 hr using subaqua equipment at the Mosney Holiday Centre, Co. Meath, Ireland, 22–29 June 1985.

The first underwater cross-Channel swim was achieved by Fred Baldasare (b. 1924) (USA), who completed a 42 mile *67,5 km* distance from France to England with Scuba equipment in 18 hr 1 min on 10–11 July 1962.

Sponsored swimming

The greatest amount of money collected in a charity swim was £50,909.08 by the Lions Club of Jersey, CI with 2268 swimmers in 378 teams on 22–24 Feb 1985, at the Fort Regent Pool, St Helier.

TABLE TENNIS

Origins

The earliest evidence relating to a game resembling table tennis has been found in the catalogues of London sports goods manufacturers in the 1880s. The old Ping Pong Association was formed in 1902 but the game proved only a temporary craze until resuscitated in 1921. The English Table Tennis Association was formed on 24 Apr 1927.

Most English titles

The highest total of English men's titles (instituted 1921) is 20 by G. Viktor Barna (1911–72)

Team and Individual TABLE TENNIS CHAMPIONSHIPS

MOST WINS IN WORLD CHAMPIONSHIPS (Instituted 1926–7)

Event	Name and Nationality	Times	Years
Men's Singles (St Bride's Vase)	G. Viktor Barna (Hungary) (1911–72)	5	1930, 1932–5
Women's Singles (G. Geist Prize)	Angelica Rozeanu (Romania) (b. 15 Oct 1921)	6	1950–5
Men's Doubles	G. Viktor Barna (Hungary)	8	1929–35, 1939
Women's Doubles	Maria Mednyanszky (Hungary) (1901–79)	7	1928, 1930–5
Mixed Doubles (Men)	Ferenc Sido (Hungary) (b. 1923)	4	1949–50, 1952–3
(Women)	Maria Mednyanszky (Hungary)	6	1927–8, 1930–1, 1933–4

G. Viktor Barna gained a personal total of 15 world titles, while 18 have been won by Maria Mednyanszky.
Note: With the staging of championships biennially the breaking of the above records would now be virtually impossible.

MOST TEAM TITLES

Event	Team	Times	Years
Men's Team (Swaythling Cup)	Hungary	12	1927–31, 1933–5, 1938, 1949, 1952, 1979
Women's Team (Marcel Corbillon Cup)	Japan	8	1952, 1954, 1957, 1959, 1961, 1963, 1967, 1971

MOST WINS IN ENGLISH OPEN CHAMPIONSHIPS (Instituted 1921)

Event	Name and Nationality	Times	Years
Men's Singles	Richard Bergmann (Austria, then GB) (1920–70)	6	1939–40, 1948, 1950, 1952, 1954
Women's Singles	Maria Alexandru (Romania) (b. 1941)	6	1963–4, 1970–2, 1974
Men's Doubles	G. Viktor Barna (Hungary, then GB)	7	1931, 1933–5, 1938–9, 1949
Women's Doubles	Diane Rowe (GB) (now Scholer) (b. 14 Apr 1933)	12	1950–6, 1960, 1962–5
Mixed Doubles (Men)	G. Viktor Barna (Hungary, then GB)	8	1933–6, 1938, 1940, 1951, 1953
(Women)	Diane Rowe (GB) (now Scholer)	4	1952, 1954, 1956, 1960

(b. Hungary, Gyözö Braun). The women's record is 17 by Diane Rowe (b. 14 Apr 1933), now Mrs Eberhard Scholer. Her twin Rosalind (now Mrs Cornett) has won nine (two in singles).

The most titles won in the English Closed Championships is 20 by Desmond Douglas (b. 20 July 1955), a record eight men's singles, 1976 and 1979–85, eight men's doubles and four mixed doubles. A record seven women's singles were won by Jill Patricia Hammersley (now Parker *née* Shirley) (b. 6 Dec 1951) in 1973–6, 1978–9, 1981.

Internationals

The youngest ever international was Joy Foster, aged 8, when she represented Jamaica in the West Indies Championships at Port of Spain, Trinidad in Aug 1958. The youngest ever to play for England was Carl Prean (b. 20 Aug 1967), aged 14 yr 191 days, against Portugal at Lisbon on 27 Feb 1982.

Jill Parker played for England on a record 413 occasions, 1967–83.

Counter hitting

The record number of hits in 60 sec is 163 by English Internationals Graham Sandley and Desmond Douglas at Brighton Poly, E. Sussex on 5 Sept 1984, and by sisters Lisa and Jackie Bellinger at Stopsley Sports Centre, Luton, Beds. on 23 June 1985. With a bat in each hand, Gary D. Fisher of Olympia, Wash., USA, completed 5000 consecutive volleys over the net in 44 min 28 sec on 25 June 1979.

Highest speed

No conclusive measurements have been published but in a lecture M. Sklorz (W. Germany) stated that a smashed ball had been measured at speeds up to 170 km/h *105,6 mph.*

TAE KWON-DO

The founder and father of this martial art is General Choi Hong Hi 9th Dan, the highest Dan awarded. Tae Kwon-Do was officially recognised as part of Korean tradition and culture on 11 Apr 1955.

The highest Dan in Britain is Master Rhee Ki Ha 8th Dan, the Chief Instructor of the United Kingdom Tae Kwon-Do Association.

TENNIS (LAWN)

See also The Guinness Book of Tennis Facts and Feats *by Lance Tingay, published in 1983 at £8.95.*

Origins

The modern game is generally agreed to have evolved as an outdoor form of the indoor game of Tennis (see separate entry). 'Field Tennis' is mentioned in an English magazine—*Sporting Magazine*—of 29 Sept 1793. The earliest club for such a game, variously called Pelota or Lawn Rackets, was the Leamington Club founded in 1872 by Major Harry Gem. The earliest attempt to commercialise the game was by Major Walter Clopton Wingfield (1833–1912) who patented a form called 'sphairistike' on 23 Feb 1874. It soon became called Lawn Tennis. Amateur players were permitted to play with and against professionals in 'Open' tournaments in 1968.

Grand Slam

The grand slam is to hold at the same time all four of the world's major championship singles: Wimbledon, the United States, Australian and French championships. The first man to have won all four was Frederick John Perry (GB) (b. 18 May 1909) with the French title in 1935. The first man to hold all four championships simultaneously was John Donald Budge (USA) (b. 13 June 1915) with the French title in 1938. The first man to achieve the grand slam twice was Rodney George Laver (Australia) (b. 9 Aug 1938) having won in 1962 as an amateur and again in 1969 when the titles were 'open' to professionals.

Three women have achieved the grand slam: Maureen Catherine Connolly (USA) (1934–69), later Mrs Norman E. Brinker, in 1953; Margaret Jean Court (*née* Smith) (Australia) (b. 16 July 1942) in 1970 and Martina Navratilova (USA) (b. Prague, Czechoslovakia 18 Oct 1956) in 1983–4. Miss Navratilova won six successive grand slam singles titles in 1983–4 and with Pamela Howard Shriver (USA) (b. 4 July 1962) won eight successive grand slam tournament women's doubles titles and 109 successive matches in all events in April 1983 to July 1985.

The most singles championships in 'grand slam' tournaments is 24 by Margaret Court (eleven Australian, five French, five USA, three Wimbledon), 1960–73. The men's record is 12 by Roy Emerson (Australia) (b. 3 Nov 1936) (six Australian, two each French, USA, Wimbledon), 1961–7.

Fastest service
The fastest service timed with modern equipment is 138 mph *222 km/h* by Steve Denton (USA) (b. 5 Sept 1956) at Beaver Creek, Colorado, USA on 29 July 1984. The fastest *ever* measured was one of 163.6 mph *263 km/h* by William Tatem Tilden (1893–1953) (USA) in 1931.

Longest game
The longest known singles game was one of 37 deuces (80 points) between Anthony Fawcett (Rhodesia) and Keith Glass (GB) in the first round of the Surrey championships at Surbiton, Surrey, on 26 May 1975. It lasted 31 min. Noëlle Van Lottum and Sandra Begijn played a game lasting 52 mins in the semi-finals of the Dutch Indoor Championships at Ede, Gederland on 12 Feb 1984.

The longest rally in tournament play is one of 643 times over the net between Vicky Nelson and Jean Hepner at Richmond, Virginia, USA in October 1984. The 6 hr 22 min match was won by Nelson 6–4, 7–6. It concluded with a 1 hr 47 min tiebreak, 13–11, for which one point took 29 mins.

The longest tiebreaker was 26–24 for the fourth and decisive set of a first round Men's Doubles at the Wimbledon Championships on 1 July 1985. Jan Gunnarsson (Sweden) and Michael Mortensen (Denmark) defeated John Frawley (Australia) and Victor Pecci (Paraguay) 6–3, 6–4, 3–6, 7–6.

Greatest crowd
30,472 people were at the Astrodome, Houston, Texas, on 20 Sept 1973, when Billie-Jean King (*née* Moffitt) (b. 22 Nov 1943) (USA) beat Robert Larimore Riggs (b. 25 Feb 1918) (USA). The record for an orthodox tennis match is 25,578 at Sydney, NSW, Australia on 27 Dec 1954 in the Davis Cup Challenge Round (first day) Australia *v.* USA.

Highest earnings
Ivan Lendl (Czechoslovakia) (b. 7 Mar 1960) won a men's record $2,028,850 in 1982. The record for a woman is $2,173,556 in 1984 (including a $1 million Grand Slam bonus) by Martina Navratilova. Earnings from special restricted events and team tennis are not included. Navratilova's lifetime earnings by 8 July 1985 reached $9,552,224.

The one match record is $500,000 by James Scott Connors (USA) (b. 2 Sept 1952) when he beat John David Newcombe (Australia) (b. 23 May 1944) in a challenge match at Caesar's Palace, Las Vegas, USA on 26 Apr 1975. The highest total prize money is $3,073,500 for the 1985 US Championships.

Longest span as national champion
Walter Westbrook (b. June 1898) won the US National Clay Court men's doubles with Harvey Snodgrass in 1925. 58 years later he won the US National 85-and-over Clay Court men's singles championship. In the final he defeated Kirk Reid, whom he had first defeated to win the Western Clay Court Championships in 1925.

Dorothy May Bundy-Cheney (USA) (b. Sept 1916) won 141 US titles at various age groups from 1941 to 1984.

INTERNATIONAL TEAM COMPETITIONS

Davis Cup (inst. 1900)
The most wins in the Davis Cup, the men's international team championship, have been (to 1983) by the USA with 28. The most appearances for Cup winners is eight by Roy Emerson (Australia), 1959–62, 1964–7. The British Isles/Great Britain have won nine times in 1903–6, 1912, 1933–6.

Nicola Pietrangeli (b. 11 Sept 1933) (Italy) played a record 163 rubbers, 1954 to 1972, winning 120. He played 109 singles (winning 78) and 54 doubles (winning 42). He took part in 66 ties. The record number of rubbers by a British player is 65 (winning 43) by Michael J. Sangster (b. 9 Sept 1940), 1960–8; the most wins is 45 from 52 rubbers by Fred Perry, including 34 of 38 singles, 1931–6.

Wightman Cup (inst. 1923)
The Wightman Cup has been won 46 times by the United States and 10 times by Great Britain. Virginia Wade (GB) (b. 10 July 1945) played in a record 20 ties and 55 rubbers, 1965–84. Christine Marie Lloyd (*née* Evert) (USA) (b. 21 Dec 1954) won all 24 of her singles matches, 1971 to 1984.

Federation Cup (inst. 1963)
The most wins in the Federation Cup, the women's international team championship, is 11 by the USA. Virginia Wade (GB) played each year from 1967 to 1983, in a record 55 ties, playing 100 rubbers, including 56 singles (winning 36) and 44 doubles (winning 30). Chris Lloyd won all her 28 singles matches and 14 of 15 doubles, 1977 to 1982.

WIMBLEDON CHAMPIONSHIPS

Most wins *Women*
Six times singles champion Billie-Jean King has won ten women's doubles and four mixed

(*Left*) Rod Laver uniquely won two Grand Slams, in 1962 and 1969. (*Right*) Aaron Krickstein (USA) became the youngest ever winner of a Grand Prix tournament, aged 16 yr 61 days at Tel Aviv in 1983. (*All-Sport*)

Boris Becker, the youngest ever men's champion at Wimbledon, was also the first unseeded player to win. No unseeded player had ever managed to win a set in the final before. *(Tommy Hindley)*

John McEnroe has dominated the men's Grand Prix circuit in recent years, winning the 1985 Masters for the third in succession and a record fifth time. *(All Sport/Roger Gould)*

Oldest champions

The oldest champion was Margaret Evelyn du Pont (*née* Osborne) (USA) (b. 4 Mar 1918) at 44 yr 125 days when she won the mixed doubles in 1962 with Neale Fraser (Aus). The oldest singles champion was Arthur Gore (GB) in 1909 at 41 yr 182 days.

Greatest crowd

The record crowd for one day is 38,291 on 27 July 1979. The record for the whole championship is 397,983 in 1985.

UNITED STATES CHAMPIONSHIPS

Most wins

Margaret Evelyn du Pont (*née* Osborne) won a record 24 titles between 1941 and 1960. She won a record 13 women's doubles (12 with Althea Louise Brough), eight mixed doubles and three singles. The men's record is 16 by William Tatem Tilden, including seven men's singles, 1920–25, 1929—a record for singles shared with Richard Dudley Sears (1861–1943), 1881–7; William A. Larned (1872–1926), 1901–2, 1907–11, and at women's singles by Molla Mallory (*née* Bjurstedt) (1892–1959), 1915–6, 1918, 1920–2, 1926 and Helen Moody (*née* Wills), 1923–5, 1927–9, 1931.

Youngest and Oldest

The youngest champion was Vincent Richards (1903–59), who was 15 yr 139 days when he won the men's doubles with Bill Tilden in 1918. The youngest singles champion was Tracy Ann Austin (b. 12 Dec 1962) who was 16 yr 271 days when she won the women's singles in 1979. The oldest champion was Margaret du Pont who won the mixed doubles at 42 yr 166 days in 1960. The oldest singles champion was William Larned at 38 yr 242 days in 1911.

FRENCH CHAMPIONSHIPS

Most wins (from International status 1925)

Margaret Court won a record 13 titles, five

doubles during the period 1961 to 1979, to total a record 20 titles. Elizabeth Montague Ryan (USA) (1892–1979) won a record 19 doubles (12 women's, 7 mixed) titles from 1914 to 1934.

Most wins *Men*

The greatest number of wins by a man has been 13 by Hugh Laurence Doherty (GB) (1875–1919) with five singles titles (1902–6) and a record eight men's doubles (1897–1901, 1903–5) partnered by his brother Reginald Frank (1872–1910).

Most wins *Singles*

The greatest number of singles wins was eight by Helen Newington Moody (*née* Wills) (USA) (b. 6 Oct 1905), who won in 1927–30, 1932–3, 1935 and 1938. The most men's singles wins since the Challenge Round was abolished in 1922 is five consecutively, by Bjorn Borg (Sweden) in 1976–80. William Charles Renshaw (GB) (1861–1904) won seven singles in 1881–6 and 1889.

Most wins *Mixed doubles*

The male record is four wins shared by Elias Victor Seixas (USA) (b. 30 Aug 1923) in 1953–6, Kenneth Norman Fletcher (Australia) (b. 15 June 1940) in 1963, 1965–6, 1968 and Owen Keir Davidson (Australia) (b. 4 Oct 1943) in 1967, 1971, 1973–4. The female record is seven by Elizabeth Ryan (USA) from 1919 to 1932.

Most appearances

Arthur William Charles 'Wentworth' Gore (1868–1928) (GB) made a record 36 appearances at Wimbledon between 1888 and 1927. In 1964, Jean Borotra (b. 13 Aug 1898) of France, made his 35th appearance since 1922. In 1977 he appeared in the Veterans' Doubles aged 78.

Youngest champions

The youngest champion was Charlotte 'Lottie' Dod (1871–1960), who was 15 yr 285 days when she won in 1887. The youngest male champion was Boris Becker (W. Germany) (b. 22 Nov 1967) who won the men's singles title in 1985 at 17 yr 227 days. The youngest ever player at Wimbledon is reputedly Mita Klima (Austria) who was 13 yr in the 1907 singles competition. The youngest player to win a match at Wimbledon is Kathy Rinaldi (b. 24 Mar 1967) (USA), at 14 yr 91 days on 23 June 1981.

singles, four women's doubles and four mixed doubles, 1962–73. The men's record is nine by Henri Cochet (France) (b. 14 Dec 1901), four singles, three men's doubles and two mixed doubles, 1926–30. Bjorn Borg won a record six singles, 1974–81.

Youngest and oldest
The youngest male and female championships were the 1981 mixed doubles champions, Andrea Jaeger (b. 4 June 1965) at 15 yr 339 days and Jimmy Arias (b. 16 Aug 1964) at 16 yr 296 days. The youngest singles winner was Mats Wilander (Sweden) (b. 22 Aug 1964) at 17 yr 288 days in 1982.

The oldest champion was Elizabeth Ryan who won the 1934 women's doubles with Simone Mathieu (France) at 42 yr 88 days. The oldest singles champion was Andres Gimeno in 1972 at 34 yr 301 days.

Grand Prix Masters
The first WCT Masters Championships were staged in Dallas, Texas in 1971. Qualification to this annual event is by relative success in the preceding year's Grand Prix tournaments. John Patrick McEnroe (USA) (b. 16 Feb 1959) has won a record five titles, 1979, 1981, 1983–5. James Scott Connors (USA) (b. 7 Sept 1952) uniquely qualified for 13 consecutive years, 1972–84. He chose not to play in 1975 and 1976, and won in 1977 and 1980.

TENNIS (REAL OR ROYAL)

The game originated as *jeu de paume* in French monasteries *c.* 1050. A tennis court is mentioned in the sale of the Hôtel de Nesle, Paris bought by King Philippe IV of France in 1308. The oldest of the surviving active courts in Great Britain is that at Falkland Palace, Fife, Scotland, built by King James V of Scotland in 1539.

Most titles *World*
The first recorded World Tennis Champion was Clerge (France) *c.* 1740. Jacques Edmond Barre (France) (1802–73) held the title for a record 33 yr from 1829 to 1862. Pierre Etchebaster (1893–1980), a Basque, holds the record for the greatest number of successful defences of the title with eight between 1928 and 1952.

The inaugural women's world championship in 1985 was won by Judy Clarke (Australia).

Most titles *British*
The Amateur Championship of the British Isles (instituted 1888) has been won 16 times by Howard Rea Angus (b. 25 June 1944) 1966–80 and 1982. Angus, a left-hander, is also the first British amateur to win a World title, in 1975.

TIDDLYWINKS

National Championships
Alan Dean (Edwinstowe, Notts) (b. 22 July 1949) has won the singles title a record five times, 1971–3, 1976, 1978. He has also won the pairs title five times. Jonathan Mapley (b. 1947) has won the pairs title a record six times, 1972, 1975, 1977, 1980 and 1983–4.

Guinness Trophy
England has been unbeaten against Scotland, Ireland and Wales since the Trophy's inception in 1960. The closest result has been their 59½–52½ win over Wales at Warwick on 7 Apr 1968.

Potting records
The record for potting 24 winks from 18 in *45 cm* is 21.8 sec by Stephen Williams (Altrincham Grammar School) in May 1966. Allen R. Astles (University of Wales) potted 10,000 winks in 3 hr 51 min 46 sec at Aberystwyth, Cardiganshire in February 1966. The greatest number of winks potted in 3 min by a relay of four is 29 by Paul Light, Paul Hoffman, Andrew James and Geoff Thorpe at 'The Castle', Cambridge on 6 Dec 1974.

TRACK AND FIELD ATHLETICS

See also The Guinness Book of Athletics Facts and Feats, by Peter Matthews, published by Guinness Superlatives Ltd at £8.95.

Origins
Track and field athletics date from the ancient Olympic Games. The earliest accurately known Olympiad dates from July 776 BC, at which celebration Coroibos won the foot race. The oldest surviving measurements are a long jump of 7,05 m *23 ft 1¼ in* by Chionis of Sparta in *c.* 656 BC and a discus throw of 100 cubits (about 46.30 m *152 ft*) by Protesilaus.

Bob Mathias is the youngest ever male Olympic champion at athletics—he won the decathlon in 1948 at the age of 17. Four years later he became the first man to retain a decathlon title. *(All Sport)*

PROGRESSIVE POLE VAULT RECORDS 1900–1985

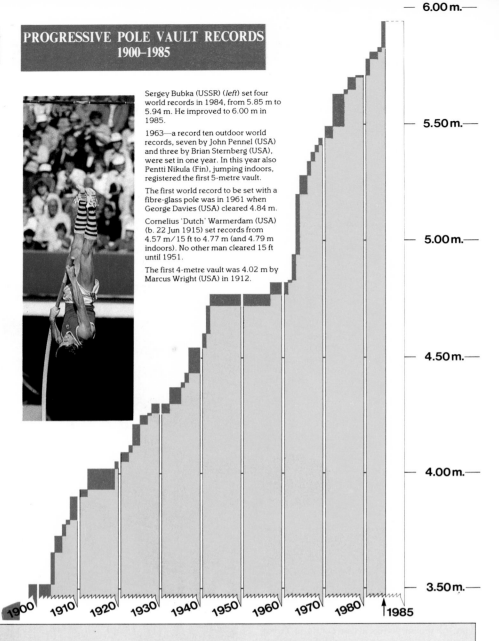

Earliest landmarks

The first time 10 sec ('even time') was bettered for 100 yd under championship conditions was when John Owen, then aged 30, recorded 9⅘ sec in the AAU Championship at Analostan Island, Washington, DC, USA, on 11 Oct 1890. The first recorded instance of 6 ft *1,83 m* being cleared in the high jump was when Marshall Jones Brooks (1855–1944) jumped 6 ft 0⅛ in *1,832 m* at Marston, near Oxford, on 17 Mar 1876. The breaking of the 'four-minute barrier' in the 1 mile *1609,34 m* was first achieved by Dr (now Sir) Roger Gilbert Bannister, CBE (b. Harrow, London, 23 Mar 1929), when he recorded 3 min 59.4 sec on the Iffley Road track, Oxford, at 6.10 p.m. on 6 May 1954.

Fastest speed

The fastest speed recorded in an individual world record is 36,51 km/h *22.69 mph*, but this does not allow for the effects of the delay in reaching peak speed from a standing start. Maximum speeds exceeding 40 km/h *25 mph* for men and 36,5 km/h *22.5 mph* for women have been measured; for instance for Carl Lewis and Evelyn Ashford respectively for their final 100 metres in the 1984 Olympic sprint relays.

Highest jumper above own head

The greatest height cleared above an athlete's own head is 23¼ in *59 cm* by Franklin Jacobs (USA) (b. 31 Dec 1957), who cleared 7 ft 7¼ in *2,32 m* at New York, USA, on 27 Jan 1978. He is only 5 ft 8 in *1,73 m* tall. The greatest height cleared by a woman above her own head is 30,5 cm *12 in* by Cindy John Holmes (USA) (b. 29 Aug 1960), 5 ft *1,525 m* tall, who jumped 6 ft *1,83 m* at Provo, Utah, USA on 1 June 1982.

Most Olympic titles *Men*

The most Olympic gold medals won is ten (an absolute Olympic record) by Ray C. Ewry (USA) (1874–1937) in the Standing High, Long and Triple Jumps in 1900, 1904, 1906 and 1908.

Most Olympic titles *Women*

The most gold medals won by a woman is four shared by Francina 'Fanny' E. Blankers-Koen

Sergey Bubka (USSR) (*left*) set four world records in 1984, from 5.85 m to 5.94 m. He improved to 6.00 m in 1985.

1963—a record ten outdoor world records, seven by John Pennel (USA) and three by Brian Sternberg (USA), were set in one year. In this year also Pentti Nikula (Fin), jumping indoors, registered the first 5-metre vault.

The first world record to be set with a fibre-glass pole was in 1961 when George Davies (USA) cleared 4.84 m.

Cornelius 'Dutch' Warmerdam (USA) (b. 22 Jun 1915) set records from 4.57 m/15 ft to 4.77 m (and 4.79 m indoors). No other man cleared 15 ft until 1951.

The first 4-metre vault was 4.02 m by Marcus Wright (USA) in 1912.

Chart axis labels: 6.00 m., 5.50 m., 5.00 m., 4.50 m., 4.00 m., 3.50 m.
Year labels: 1900, 1910, 1920, 1930, 1940, 1950, 1960, 1970, 1980, 1985

WORLD RECORDS *MEN*

World records for the men's events (excluding the walking records—see under WALKING) scheduled by the International Amateur Athletic Federation. Fully automatic electric timing is mandatory for events up to 400 metres.

RUNNING

	Min Sec	Name and Country	Place	Date
100 metres	9.93A	Calvin Smith (USA) (b. 8 Jan 1961)	Colorado Springs, Colorado, USA	3 July 1983
200 metres	19.72A	Pietro Mennea (Italy) (b. 28 June 1952)	Mexico City, Mexico	12 Sept 1979
400 metres	43.86A	Lee Edward Evans (USA) (b. 25 Feb 1947)	Mexico City, Mexico	18 Oct 1968
800 metres	1:41.73	Sebastian Newbold Coe (GB) (b. 29 Sept 1956)	Florence, Italy	10 June 1981
1000 metres	2:12.18	Sebastian Newbold Coe (GB)	Oslo, Norway	11 July 1981
1500 metres	3:29.67	Steven Cram (GB) (b. 14 Oct 1960)	Nice, France	16 July 1985
1 mile	3:46.31	Steven Cram (GB)	Oslo, Norway	27 July 1985
2000 metres	4:51.4	John George Walker (NZ) (b. 12 Jan 1952)	Oslo, Norway	30 June 1976
3000 metres	7:32.1	Henry Rono (Kenya) (b. 12 Feb 1952)	Oslo, Norway	27 June 1978
5000 metres	13:00.40	Said Aouita (Morocco) (b. 2 Nov 1960)	Oslo, Norway	27 July 1985
10,000 metres	27:13.81	Fernando Mamede (Portugal) (b. 1 Nov 1951)	Stockholm, Sweden	2 July 1984
20,000 metres	57:24.2	Josephus Hermens (Netherlands) (b. 8 Jan 1950)	Papendal, Netherlands	1 May 1976
25,000 metres	1 hr 13:55.8	Toshihiko Seko (Japan) (b. 15 July 1956)	Christchurch, New Zealand	22 Mar 1981
30,000 metres	1 hr 29:18.8	Toshihiko Seko (Japan)	Christchurch, New Zealand	22 Mar 1981
1 hour	20 944 m *13 miles 24 yd 2 ft*	Josephus Hermens (Netherlands)	Papendal, Netherlands	1 May 1976

HURDLING

		Name and Country	Place	Date
110 metres (3' 6" *106 cm*)	12.93	Renaldo Nehemiah (USA) (b. 24 Mar 1959)	Zürich, Switzerland	19 Aug 1981
400 metres (3' 0" *91,4 cm*)	47.02	Edwin Corley Moses (USA) (b. 31 Aug 1955)	Koblenz, W. Germany	31 Aug 1983
3000 metres steeplechase	8:05.4	Henry Rono (Kenya)	Seattle, Washington, USA	13 May 1978

RELAYS

		Name and Country	Place	Date
4 × 100 metres	37.83	United States National Team: Sam Graddy, Ronald James Brown, Calvin Smith, Frederick Carlton Lewis	Los Angeles, USA	11 Aug 1984

A *These records were set at high altitude—Mexico City 2240 m 7349 ft, Colorado Springs 2195 m 7201 ft. Best marks at low altitude have been: 100 m: 9.96 sec, Melvin Bernard Lattany (USA) (b. 10 Aug 1959), Athens, Georgia, USA, 5 May 1984. 200 m: 19.75 sec, Frederick Carlton 'Carl' Lewis (USA) (b. 1 July 1961), Indianapolis, Indiana, USA, 19 June 1983. 400 m: 44.26 sec, Alberto Juantorena (Cuba) (b. 21 Nov 1950), Montreal, Canada, 29 July 1976. Long Jump: 8.79 m 28 ft 10¼ in, Carl Lewis, Indianapolis, Indiana, USA, 19 June 1983. 4 × 400 m relay: USA (Herman Frazier, Benny Brown, Fred Newhouse, Maxie Parks) Montreal, Canada, 31 July 1976.*

4 × 200 metres	1:20.26†	University of Southern California, USA: Joel Andrews, James Sanford, William Mullins, Clancy Edwards	Tempe, Arizona, USA	27 May 1978
4 × 400 metres	2:56.16A	United States National Team: Vincent Edward Matthews, Ronald J. Freeman, George Lawrence James, Lee Edward Evans	Mexico City, Mexico	20 Oct 1968
4 × 800 metres	7:03.89	Great Britain: Peter Elliott, Gary Peter Cook, Steven Cram, Sebastian Newbold Coe	Crystal Palace, London	30 Aug 1982
4 × 1500 metres	14:38.8	West Germany: Thomas Wessinghage, Harald Hudak, Michael Lederer, Karl Fleschen	Cologne, W. Germany	17 Aug 1977

† *The time of 1:20.23 achieved by the Tobias Striders (Guy Abrahams, Mike Simmons, Donald O'Riley Quarrie, James Gilkes) at Tempe, Ariz., USA on 27 May 1978 was not ratified as the team was composed of varied nationalities.*

FIELD EVENTS	ft	in	m			
High Jump	7	10	*2,39*	Zhu Jianhua (China) (b. 29 Mar 1963)	Eberstadt, W. Germany	10 June 1984
Pole Vault	19	8¼	*6,00*	Sergey Bubka (USSR) (b. 4 Dec 1963)	Paris, France	13 July 1985
Long Jump	29	2½	*8,90*A	Robert Beamon (USA) (b. 29 Aug 1946)	Mexico City, Mexico	18 Oct 1968
Triple Jump	58	11½	*17,97*	William Augustus 'Willie' Banks (USA) (b. 11 Mar 1956)	Indianapolis, USA	16 June 1985
Shot 7.26 kg *16 lb*	72	10¾	*22,22*‡	Udo Beyer (GDR) (b. 9 Aug 1955)	Los Angeles, California, USA	25 June 1983
Discus 2 kg *4 lb 6.55 oz*	235	9	*71,86*†	Yuriy Dumchev (USSR) (b. 5 Aug 1958)	Moscow, USSR	29 May 1983
Hammer 7.26 kg *16 lb*	283	3	*86,34*	Yuri Georgiyevich Sedykh (USSR) (b. 11 Jun 1955)	Cork, Ireland	3 July 1984
Javelin 800 g *28.22 oz*	343	10	*104,80*	Uwe Hohn (GDR) (b. 16 July 1962)	East Berlin, GDR	20 July 1984

DECATHLON

8847 points (1985 scoring tables)	Francis Morgan 'Daley' Thompson (GB) (b. 30 July 1958) (1st day: 100 m 10.44 sec, Long Jump 8,01 m *26′ 3¼″*, Shot Put 15,72 m *51′ 7″*, High Jump 2,03 m *6′ 8″*, 400 m 46.97 sec)	Los Angeles, USA (2nd day: 110 m Hurdles 14.33 sec, Discus 46,56 m *152′ 9″*, Pole Vault 5,00 m *16′ 4¾″*, Javelin 65,24 m *214′ 0″*, 1500 m 4:35.00 sec)	8–9 Aug 1984

‡ *Note: One professional performance is superior to the IAAF mark, but the same highly rigorous rules as to measuring and weighing were not necessarily applied.*
75 0 *22,86* *Brian Ray Oldfield (USA) (b. 1 Jan 1945)* *El Paso, Texas, USA* *10 May* *1975*

† *Walter Ben Plucknett (USA) (b. 13 Apr 1954) threw 237 ft 4 in 72,34 m at Stockholm, Sweden on 7 July 1981 but was subsequently disqualified from competition.*

WORLD RECORDS WOMEN

World records for the women's events scheduled by the International Amateur Athletic Federation. The same stipulation about automatically timed events applies in the six events up to 400 metres as in the men's list.

RUNNING	Min sec	Name and Country	Place	Date
100 metres	10.76	Evelyn Ashford (USA) (b. 15 Apr 1957)	Zürich, Switzerland	22 Aug 1984
200 metres	21.71	Marita Koch (GDR) (b. 18 Feb 1957)	Karl Marx Stadt, GDR	10 June 1979
		Marita Koch	Potsdam, GDR	21 July 1984
400 metres	47.99	Jarmila Kratochvilova (Czechoslovakia) (b. 26 Jan 1951)	Helsinki, Finland	10 Aug 1983
800 metres	1:53.28	Jarmila Kratochvilova (Czechoslovakia)	Munich, W. Germany	26 July 1983
1000 metres	2:30.6	Tatyana Providokhina (USSR) (b. 26 Mar 1953)	Podolsk, USSR	20 Aug 1978
1500 metres	3:52.47	Tatyana Kazankina (USSR) (b. 17 Dec 1951)	Zürich, Switzerland	13 Aug 1980
1 mile	4:15.8	Natalya Artyomova (USSR) (b. 5 Jan 1963)	Leningrad, USSR	6 Aug 1984
2000 metres	5:28.72	Tatyana Kazankina (USSR)	Moscow, USSR	4 Aug 1984
3000 metres	8:22.62	Tatyana Kazankina (USSR)	Leningrad, USSR	26 Aug 1984
5000 metres	14:58.89	Ingrid Kristiansen (née Christensen) (Norway) (b. 21 Mar 1956)	Oslo, Norway	28 June 1984
10000 metres	30:59.42	Ingrid Kristiansen (Norway)	Oslo, Norway	27 July 1985

HURDLING				
100 metres (2′ 9″ *84 cm*)	12.36	Grazyna Rabsztyn (Poland) (b. 20 Sept 1952)	Warsaw, Poland	13 June 1980
400 metres (2′ 6″ *76 cm*)	53.58	Margarita Ponomaryova [now Khromova] (USSR) (b. 19 June 1963)	Kiev, USSR	22 June 1984

RELAYS				
4 × 100 metres	41.53	GDR: Silke Gladisch, Marita Koch, Ingrid Auerswald, Marlies Göhr [*née* Oelsner]	E. Berlin, GDR	31 July 1983
4 × 200 metres	1:28.15	GDR: Marlies Göhr [*née* Oelsner], Romy Müller [*née* Schneider], Bärbel Wöckel [*née* Eckert], Marita Koch	Jena, GDR	9 Aug 1980
4 × 400 metres	3:15.92	GDR: Gesine Walther, Sabine Busch, Dagmar Rübsam, Marita Koch	Erfurt, GDR	3 June 1984
4 × 800 metres	7:50.17	USSR: Nadezha Olizarenko, Lyubov Gurina, Lyudmila Borisova, Irina Podyalovskaya	Moscow, USSR	4 Aug 1984

FIELD EVENTS	ft	in	m			
High Jump	6	9½	*2,07*	Lyudmila Andonova (Bulgaria) (b. 12 May 1960)	East Berlin, GDR	20 July 1984
Long Jump	24	4½	*7,43*	Anisoara Cusmir (now Stanciu) (Romania) (b. 28 June 1962)	Bucharest, Romania	4 June 1983
Shot 4 kg *8 lb 13 oz*	73	11	*22,53*	Natalya Lisovskaya (USSR) (b. 16 July 1962)	Sochi, USSR	27 May 1984
Discus 1 kg *2 lb 3.27 oz*	244	7	*74,56*	Zdenka Silhava (Czechoslovakia) (b. 15 June 1954)	Nitra, Czechoslovakia	26 Aug 1984
Javelin 600 g *24.74 oz*	247	4	*75,40*	Petra Felke (GDR) (b. 30 July 1959)	Schwerin, GDR	4 June 1985

HEPTATHLON

6946 points (1985 scoring tables)	Sabine Paetz [*née* Möbius] (GDR) (b. 16 Oct 1957) (100 m hurdles 12.64 sec; High Jump 1,80 m *5 ft 10¾ in*; Shot 15.37 m *50 ft 5¼ in*; 200 m 23.37 sec; Long Jump 6,86 m *22 ft 6¼ in*; Javelin 44,62 m *146 ft 5 in*; 800 m 2 min 08.93sec	Potsdam, GDR	5-6 May 1984

THE MARATHON

The marathon distance of 26 miles 385 yd *42,195 km* was standardised in 1924. There are no official records because of the varying severity of courses. The best recorded times are:

	Hr	min	sec			
MEN	2	7	11	Carlos Alberto Sousa Lopes (Portugal) (b. 18 Feb 1947)	Rotterdam, Netherlands	20 Apr 1985
WOMEN	2	21	00	Ingrid Kristiansen (Norway) (b. 21 Mar 1956)	London	21 Apr 1985

British records are:

	Hr	min	sec			
MEN	2	8	05	Stephen Henry Jones (b. 4 Aug 1955)	Chicago, USA	21 Oct 1984
WOMEN	2	28	06	Sarah L. Rowell (b. 19 Nov 1962)	London	21 Apr 1985

(Netherlands) (b. 26 Apr 1918) with 100 m, 200 m, 80 m hurdles and 4 × 100 m relay, 1948; Betty Cuthbert (Australia) (b. 20 Apr 1938) with 100 m, 200 m, 4 × 100 m relay, 1956 and 400 m, 1964; and Bärbel Wöckel (*née* Eckert) (b. 21 Mar 1955) (GDR) with 200 m and 4 × 100 m relay in 1976 and 1980.

Most wins at one Games

The most gold medals at one celebration is five by Paavo Johannes Nurmi (Finland) (1897–1973) in 1924, and the most individual is four by Alvin C. Kraenzlein (USA) (1876–1928) in 1900, with 60 m, 110 m hurdles, 200 m hurdles and long jump.

Most Olympic medals *Men*

The most medals won is 12 (nine gold and three silver) by Paavo Nurmi (Finland) in the Games of 1920, 1924 and 1928.

Most Olympic medals *Women*

The most medals won by a woman athlete is seven by Shirley de la Hunty (*née* Strickland) (Australia) (b. 18 July 1925) with three gold, one silver and three bronze in the 1948, 1952 and 1956 Games. A recently discovered photo-finish indicates that she finished third, not fourth, in the 1948 200 metres event, thus unofficially increasing her medal haul to eight. Irena Szewinska (*née* Kirszenstein) (Poland) (b. 24 May 1946) won three gold, two silver and two bronze in 1964, 1968, 1972 and 1976, and is the only woman athlete to win a medal in four successive games.

Most Olympic titles *British*

The most gold medals won by a British athlete (excluding Tug of War and Walking, *q.v.*) is two by: Charles Bennett (1871–1949) (1500 m and 5000 m team, 1900); Alfred Tysoe (1874–1901) (800 m and 5000 m team, 1900); John Rimmer (1879–1962) (4000 m steeplechase and 5000 m team, 1900); Albert G. Hill (1889–1969) (800 m and 1500 m, 1920); Douglas Gordon Arthur Lowe (1902–81) (800 m 1924 and 1928) and Sebastian Newbold Coe (b. 9 Oct 1955) (1500 m 1980 and 1984).

Most Olympic medals *British*

The most medals won by a British athlete is four by Guy M. Butler (1899–1981) gold for the 4 × 400 m relay and silver for 400 m in 1920 and bronze for each of these events in 1924 and by Seb Coe, who also won silver medals at 800 m in

LONGEST WINNING SEQUENCE
Iolanda Balas (Romania) (b. 12 Dec 1936) (above) won 140 successive high jump competitions from 1956 to 1967. The record for track races is 109 (including 94 finals) at 400 metres hurdles by Edwin Corley Moses (USA) (b. 31 July 1955) (left) from 1977 to 1984.

UNITED KINGDOM (NATIONAL) RECORDS *MEN*

RUNNING

	min sec	Name	Place	Date
100 metres	10.11	Allan Wipper Wells (b. 3 May 1952)	Moscow, USSR	24 July 1980
200 metres	20.21	Allan Wipper Wells	Moscow, USSR	28 July 1980
400 metres	44.82	Derek Antony Redmond (b. 3 Sept 1965)	Oslo, Norway	27 July 1985
800 metres	1:41.73	Sebastian Newbold Coe (b. 29 Sept 1956)	Florence, Italy	10 June 1981
1000 metres	2:12.18	Sebastian Newbold Coe	Oslo, Norway	11 July 1981
1500 metres	3:29.67	Steven Cram (b. 14 Oct 1960)	Nice, France	16 July 1985
1 mile	3:46.31	Steven Cram	Oslo, Norway	27 July 1985
2000 metres	4:57.71	Steven Michael James Ovett	Oslo, Norway	7 July 1982
3000 metres	7:32.79	David Robert Moorcroft (b. 10 Apr 1953)	London (Crystal Palace)	17 July 1982
5000 metres	13:00.41	David Robert Moorcroft	Oslo, Norway	7 July 1982
10,000 metres	27:30.3†	Brendan Foster (b. 12 Jan 1948)	London (Crystal Palace)	23 June 1978
20,000 metres	58:39.0	Ronald Hill (b. 25 Sept 1938)	Leicester	9 Nov 1968
25,000 metres	1 hr 15:22.6	Ronald Hill	Bolton, Lancashire	21 July 1965
30,000 metres	1 hr 31:30.4	James Noel Carroll Alder (b. 10 June 1940)	London (Crystal Palace)	5 Sept 1970
1 hour	12 miles 1268 yd *20 472m*	Ronald Hill	Leicester	9 Nov 1968

† *Ratified at 27:30.6*

HURDLING

	min sec	Name	Place	Date
110 metres	13.43	James Mark Holtom (b. 6 Feb 1958)	Brisbane, Australia	4 Oct 1982
400 metres	48.12	David Peter Hemery (b. 18 July 1944)	Mexico City, Mexico	15 Oct 1968
3000 metres Steeplechase	8:13.78	Colin Robert Reitz (b. 5 April 1960)	Oslo, Norway	21 July 1984

RELAYS

	min sec	Name	Place	Date
4 × 100 metres	38.62	United Kingdom: Michael Anthony McFarlane, Allan Wipper Wells, Robert Cameron Sharp, Andrew Emlyn McMaster	Moscow, USSR	1 Aug 1980
4 × 200 metres	1:24.1	Great Britain: Brian William Green, Roger Wilfred Walters, Ralph Banthorpe, Martin Edward Reynolds	Paris, France	2 Oct 1971
4 × 400 metres	2:59.13	United Kingdom: Kriss Akabusi, Gary Peter Cook, Todd Bennett, Phil Brown	Los Angeles, USA	11 Aug 1984
4 × 800 metres	7:03.89	United Kingdom: Peter Elliott, Gary Peter Cook, Steven Cram, Sebastian Newbold Coe	London (Crystal Palace)	30 Aug 1982
4 × 1500 metres	14:56.8	United Kingdom: Alan David Mottershead, Geoffrey Michael Cooper, Stephen John Emson, Roy Wood	Bourges, France	24 June 1979

FIELD EVENTS

	ft in	m	Name	Place	Date
High Jump	7 5	2,26	Geoffrey Peter Parsons (b. 14 Aug 1964)	London (Crystal Palace)	13 July 1984
Pole Vault	18 6½	5,65	Keith Frank Stock (b. 18 Mar 1957)	Oslo, Norway	7 July 1981
Long Jump	27 0	8,23	Lynn Davies (b. 20 May 1942)	Bern, Switzerland	30 June 1968
Triple Jump	57 7¾	17,57	Keith Leroy Connor (b. 16 Sept 1957)	Provo, Utah, USA	5 June 1982
Shot 7.26 kg *16 lb*	71 1½	21,68	Geoffrey Lewis Capes (b. 23 Aug 1949)	Cwmbran, Gwent	18 May 1980
Discus 2 kg *4 lb 6.55 oz*	211 0	64,32†	William Raymond Tancred (b. 6 Aug 1942)	Woodford, Essex	10 Aug 1974
Hammer 7.26 kg *16 lb*	254 5	77,54	Martin Girvan (b. 17 Apr 1960)	Wolverhampton, West Midlands	12 May 1984
Javelin 800 g *28.22 oz*	299 10	91,40	Arne-Roald Bradstock (b. 24 Apr 1962)	Arlington, Texas, USA	4 May 1985

† *William Raymond Tancred threw 64.94 m* 213 ft 1in *at Loughborough on 21 July 1974 and Richard Charles Slaney (b. 16 May 1956) threw 64,66 m* 212 ft *at Eugene, Oregon, USA on 6 July 1984 but these were not ratified.*

DECATHLON (1985 Scoring Table)

				Date
8847 points	Francis Morgan 'Daley' Thompson (b. 30 July 1958)		Los Angeles, USA	8–9 Aug 1984

(1st day: 100 m 10.44 sec, Long Jump 8,01 m *26' 3¼"*, Shot Put 15,72m *51' 7"*, High Jump 2,03 m *6' 8"*, 400 m 46.97 sec)

(2nd day: 110 m Hurdles 14.33 sec, Discus 46,56 m *152' 9"*, Pole Vault 5,00 m *16' 4¾"*, Javelin 65,24 m *214' 0"*, 1500 m 4:35.00 sec)

1980 and 1984. Three British women athletes have won three medals: Dorothy Hyman (b. 9 May 1941) with a silver (100 m, 1960) and two bronze (200 m, 1960 and 4 × 100 m relay, 1964), Mary Denise Rand (now Toomey, *née* Bignal), (b. 10 Feb 1940) with a gold (long jump), a silver (pentathlon) and a bronze (4 × 100 m relay), all in 1964 and Kathryn Jane Cook (née Smallwood) (b. 3 May 1960), all bronze—at 4 × 100 m relay 1980 and 1984, and at 400 m in 1984.

Olympic champions *Oldest and youngest*

The oldest athlete to win an Olympic title was Irish-born Patrick J. 'Babe' McDonald (USA) (1878–1954) who was aged 42 yr 26 days when he won the 56 lb *25,4 kg* weight throw at Antwerp, Belgium on 21 Aug 1920. The oldest female champion was Lia Manoliu (Romania) (b. 25 Apr 1932) aged 36 yr 176 days when she won the discus at Mexico City on 18 Oct 1968. The youngest gold medallist was Barbara Pearl Jones (USA) (b. 26 Mar 1937) who was a member of the winning 4 × 100 m relay team, aged 15 yr 123 days, at Helsinki, Finland on 27 July 1952. The youngest male champion was Robert Bruce Mathias (USA) (b. 17 Nov 1930) aged 17 yr 263 days when he won the decathlon at London on 5–6 Aug 1948.

The oldest Olympic medallist was Tebbs Lloyd Johnson (1900–84), aged 48 yr 115 days when he was third in the 1948 50,000 m walk. The oldest women's medallist was Dana Zátopkova aged 37 yr 348 days when she was second in the javelin in 1960.

World record breakers *Oldest and youngest*

For the greatest age at which anyone has broken a world record under IAAF jurisdiction *see p. 220*. The female record is 35 yr 255 days for Dana Zátopkova, *née* Ingrova (b. 19 Sept 1922) of Czechoslovakia, who broke the women's javelin record with 55,73 m *182 ft 10 in* at Prague, Czechoslovakia, on 1 June 1958. The youngest individual record breaker is Carolina Gisolf (b. 13 July 1913) (Netherlands) who set a women's high jump mark with 1.61 m *5 ft 3¾ in* at Maastricht, Netherlands on 18 July 1928, aged 15 yr 5 days. The male record is 17 yr 198 days by Thomas Ray (1862–1904) when he pole-vaulted 3.42 m *11 ft 2¾ in* on 19 Sept 1879 (both pre-IAAF records).

Most records in a day

Jesse Owens (1913–80) (USA) set six world records in 45 min at Ann Arbor, Michigan on 25 May 1935 with a 9.4 sec 100 yd at 3.15 p.m., a 26 ft 8¼ in *8,13 m* long jump at 3.25 p.m., a 20.3 sec *220 yd* (and 200 m) at 3.45 p.m. and a 22.6 sec 220 yd low hurdles (and 200 m) at 4.00 p.m.

Most national titles *Great Britain*

The greatest number of senior AAA titles (excluding those in tug of war events) won by one athlete is 14 individual and one relay title by Emmanuel McDonald Bailey (Trinidad) (b. 8 Dec 1920), between 1946 and 1953. The most won outdoors in a single event is 13 by Denis Horgan (Ireland) (1871–1922) in the shot put between 1893 and 1912. 13 senior titles were also won by Michael Anthony Bull (b. 11 Sept 1946) at pole vault, eight indoor and five out and by Geoffrey Lewis Capes (b. 23 Aug 1949) at shot, six indoor and seven out.

The greatest number of WAAA titles won by one athlete is 14 by Suzanne Allday (*née* Farmer) (b. 26 Nov 1934) with seven each at shot and discus between 1952 and 1962.

Most international appearances

The greatest number of international matches contested for any nation is 89 by Bjørn Bang Andersen (b. 14 Nov 1937) for Norway, 1960–81.

The greatest number of full Great Britain international appearances (outdoors and indoors) is 73 by Verona Marolin Elder (*née* Bernard) (b. 5 Apr 1953) from 1971 to 1983. The men's record is 67 by Geoff Capes, 1969–80. Mike Bull had 66 full internationals or 69 including the European Indoor Games, before these were official internationals. The most outdoors is 61 by Andrew Howard Payne (b. South Africa, 17 Apr 1931) from 1960 to 1974.

Oldest and youngest internationals
The oldest full Great Britain international was Hector Harold Whitlock (b. 16 Dec 1903) at the 1952 Olympic Games, aged 48 yr 218 days. The oldest woman was Christine Rosemary Payne (*née* Charters) (b. 19 May 1933) in the Great Britain *v.* Finland match on 26 Sept 1974, aged 41 yr 130 days. The youngest man was Ross Hepburn (b. 14 Oct 1961) *v.* the USSR on 26 Aug 1977, aged 15 yr 316 days, and the youngest woman was Janis Walsh (b. 28 Mar 1960) *v.* Belgium (indoor) at 60 m and 4 × 200 m relay on 15 Feb 1975, aged 14 yr 324 days.

Longest career
Duncan McLean (1884–1980) of Scotland set a world age (92) record of 100 m in 21.7 sec in August 1977, over 73 years after his best ever sprint of 100 yd in 9.9 sec in South Africa in February 1904. At Athens, Greece, on 10 Oct 1976, Dimitrion Yordanidis, aged 98, completed a marathon race in 7 hr 33 min.

Marathon
The most runners in a marathon were the *c.* 17,500, of whom 15,841 finished, in the London marathon of 21 Apr 1985.

London to Brighton race
Ian Thompson (b. 16 Oct 1949) (Luton United H) won the 54.3 miles *87,4 km* race (inst. 1951) in 5 hr 15 min 15 sec on 28 Sept 1980, averaging 10.33 mph *16,62 km/h*. The most wins is four by Bernard Gomersall (b. 28 Aug 1932) in 1963–6.

'End to end'
The fastest confirmed run from John o'Groats to Land's End is 12 days 1 hr 59 min by Kenneth

British record holder Wendy Sly runs in the 1984 Olympic Games, where she gained the Olympic silver medal at 3000 metres. *(All Sport)*

UNITED KINGDOM (NATIONAL) RECORDS *WOMEN*

RUNNING

	Min sec				
100 metres	11.10	Kathryn Jane Smallwood [now Cook] (b. 3 May 1960)	Rome, Italy	5 Sept	1981
200 metres	22.10	Kathryn Jane Cook [*née* Smallwood]	Los Angeles, USA	9 Aug	1984
400 metres	49.43	Kathryn Jane Cook [*née* Smallwood]	Los Angeles, USA	6 Aug	1984
800 metres	1:57.42	Kirsty Margaret McDermott (b. 6 Aug 1962)	Belfast, N. Ireland	24 June	1985
1000 metres	2:35.62	Christina Tracy Boxer (b. 25 Mar 1957)	London (Crystal Palace)	30 Aug	1982
1500 metres	4:00.57	Christina Tracy Boxer	Gateshead, Tyne and Wear	6 July	1984
1 mile	4:19.41	Kirsty Margaret McDermott	Oslo, Norway	27 July	1985
2000 metres	5:33.15	Zola Budd (b. 26 May 1966)	London (Crystal Palace)	13 July	1984
3000 metres	8:37.06	Wendy Sly [*née* Smith] (b. 5 Nov 1959)	Helsinki, Finland	10 Aug	1983
5000 metres	15:13.07	Zola Budd	Helsinki, Finland	4 July	1985
10000 metres	32:57.17	Kathryn Mary Binns (b. 13 Jan 1958)	Sittard, Netherlands	14 Aug	1980

RELAYS

4 × 100 metres	42.43	United Kingdom: Heather Regina Hunte [now Oakes], Kathryn Jane Smallwood [now Cook], Beverley Lanita Goddard [now Callender], Sonia May Lannaman	Moscow, USSR	1 Aug	1980
4 × 200 metres	1:31.57	United Kingdom: Donna-Marie Louise Hartley [*née* Murray], Verona Marolin Elder [*née* Bernard], Sharon Colyear [now Danville], Sonia May Lannaman	London (Crystal Palace)	20 Aug	1977
4 × 400 metres	3:25.51	United Kingdom: Michelle Scutt, Helen Catherine Barnett, Gladys Taylor, Joslyn Yvonne Hoyte-Smith	Los Angeles, USA	11 Aug	1984
4 × 800 metres	8:23.8	Great Britain: Joan Florence Allison [*née* Page], Sheila Janet Carey [*née* Taylor], Patricia Barbara Lowe [now Cropper], Rosemary Olivia Stirling [now Wright]	Paris, France	2 Oct	1971

HURDLING

100 metres	12.87	Shirley Elaine Strong (b. 18 Nov 1958)	Zürich, Switzerland	24 Aug	1983
400 metres	56.04	Susan Anita Jayne Morley (b. 6 Jan 1960)	Helsinki, Finland	10 Aug	1983

UNITED KINGDOM (NATIONAL) RECORDS *WOMEN*

FIELD EVENTS	ft	in	m			
High Jump	6	4¾	*1,95*	Diana Clare Elliot (now Davies) (b. 7 May 1961)	Oslo, Norway	26 June 1982
Long Jump	22	7¾	*6,90*	Beverley Kinch (b. 14 Jan 1964)	Helsinki, Finland	14 Aug 1983
Shot 4 kg *8 lb 13 oz*	62	3¾	*18,99**	Margaret Elizabeth Ritchie (b. 6 July 1952)	Tucson, Arizona, USA	7 May 1983
Discus 1 kg *2 lb 3.27 oz*	221	5	*67,48*	Margaret Elizabeth Ritchie	Walnut, California, USA	26 April 1981
Javelin 600 g *21.16 oz*	241	5	*73,58*	Theresa Ione Sanderson (b. 14 Mar 1956)	Edinburgh, Scotland	26 June 1983

HEPTATHLON (1984 Tables)

6347 points	Judith Earline Veronica Livermore (b. 14 Nov 1960) (100 m hurdles 13.23 sec; High Jump 1,87 m *6′ 1½″*; Shot 13,54 m *44′ 5¼″*; 200 m 24.75; Long Jump 6,10 m *20′ 0¼″*; Javelin 38,60 m *126′ 8″*; 800 m 2 min 12.50 sec)	Sofia, Bulgaria	10–11 Sept 1983

* Venessa Anne Head (b. 1 Sept 1956) achieved 19,06 m *62 ft 6½ in* indoors at St. Athan, Gwent on 7 Apr 1984.

John Craig (S. Africa) (b. 27 Nov 1935) on 29 Aug–10 Sept 1984. A faster 10 days 3 hr 30 min was claimed by Fred Hicks (GB) for 876 miles *1410 km* on 20–30 May 1977.

Six-day races

The greatest distance covered by a man in six days (*i.e.* the 144 permissible hours between Sundays in Victorian times) is 1023.2 km *635 miles 1385 yards* by Yiannis Kouros (Greece) (b. 13 Feb 1956) at Colac, Australia on 26 Nov–1 Dec 1984. On the same occasion Eleanor Adams (UK) (b. 20 Nov 1947) set the women's record at 806 km *500 miles 1452 yards*.

Longest non-stop run

The greatest non-stop run recorded is 352.9 miles *568 km* in 121 hr 54 min by Bertil Järlåker (Sweden) (b. 1936) at Norrköping, Sweden, 26–31 May 1980. He was moving for 95.04 per cent of the time.

Longest running race

The longest races ever staged were the 1928 (3422 miles *5507 km*) and 1929 (3665 miles *5898 km*) Trans-continental races from New York City, NY, to Los Angeles, California, USA. The Finnish-born Johnny Salo (1893–1931) was the winner in 1929 in 79 days, from 31 Mar to 18 June. His elapsed time of 525 hr 57 min 20 sec (averaging 6.97 mph *11,21 km/h*) left him only 2 min 47 sec ahead of Englishman Pietro 'Peter' Gavuzzi (1905–81).

Longest runs

The longest ever solo run is 10,608 miles *17 072 km* by Robert J. Sweetgall (USA) (b. 8 Dec 1947) around the perimeter of the USA starting and finishing in Washington, DC, 9 Oct 1982–15 July 1983. Ron Grant (Australia) (b. 15 Feb 1943) ran around Australia, 13 383 km *8316 miles* in 217 days 3 hr 45 min, running every day from 28 Mar to 31 Oct 1983. Max Telford (NZ) (b. Hawick, Scotland, 2 Feb 1935) ran 5110 miles *8224 km* from Anchorage, Alaska to Halifax, Nova Scotia, in 106 days 18 hr 45 min from 25 July to 9 Nov 1977. The fastest time reported for the cross-America run is 46 days 8 hr 36 min by Frank Giannino Jr (USA) (b. 1952) for the 3100 miles *4989 km* from San Francisco to New York on 1 Sept–17 Oct 1980.

Greatest mileage

Douglas Alistair Gordon Pirie (b. 10 Feb 1931) (GB), who set five world records in the 1950s, estimated that he had run a total distance of 216,000 miles *347,600 km* in 40 years to 1981.

The greatest distance run in one year is 15,472 miles *24,890 km* by Tina Maria Stone (b. Naples, Italy, 5 Apr 1934) of Irvine, California, USA in 1983.

Jay F. Helgerson (b. 3 Feb 1955) of Foster City, California, ran a certified marathon (26 miles 385 yd) or longer, each week for 52 weeks from 28 Jan 1979 to 19 Jan 1980, totalling 1418 racing miles *2282 km*.

Mass relay records

The record for 100 miles *160,9 km* by 100 runners belonging to one club is 7 hr 53 min 52.1 sec by Baltimore Road Runners Club, Towson, Maryland, USA, on 17 May 1981. The women's record is 10 hr 47 min 9.3 sec on 3 Apr 1977 by the San Francisco Dolphins Southend Running Club, USA. The best club time for a 100 × 400 metres relay is 1 hr 29 min 11.8 sec (average 53.5 sec) by the Physical Training Institute, Leuven, Belgium on 19 Apr 1978. The best women's club time for 100 × 100 metres is 23 min 28 sec by Amsterdamse dames athletiek-vereniging, on 26 Sept 1981 in Amsterdam, Netherlands.

ULTRA LONG DISTANCE TRACK WORLD RECORDS

WORLD BESTS—LONG DISTANCE TRACK EVENTS

	hr:min:sec			
50 km	2:48:06	Jeff Norman (UK)	Timperley, Manchester	7 Jun 1980
50 miles	4:51:49	Don Ritchie (UK)	Hendon, London	12 Mar 1983
100 km	6:10:20	Don Ritchie (UK)	Crystal Palace	28 Oct 1978
100 miles	11:30:51	Don Ritchie (UK)	Crystal Palace	15 Oct 1977
200 km	15:11:10	Yiannis Kouros (Gre)	Montauban, France	15–16 Mar 1985
200 miles	27:48:35	Yiannis Kouros (Gre)	Montauban, France	15–16 Mar 1985
500 km	60:23:00	Yiannis Kouros (Gre)	Colac, Australia	26–29 Nov 1984
500 miles	105:42:09	Yiannis Kouros (Gre)	Colac, Australia	26–30 Nov 1984
1000 km	136:17:00	Yiannis Kouros (Gre)	Colac, Australia	26–31 Nov 1984
	kilometres			
24 hours	283.600	Yiannis Kouros (Gre)	Montauban, France	15–16 Mar 1985
48 hours	452.270	Yiannis Kouros (Gre)	Montauban, France	15–17 Mar 1985
6 days	1023.2	Yiannis Kouros (Gre)	Colac, Australia	26 Nov–1 Dec 1984

LONG DISTANCE ROAD BESTS

Where superior to track bests and run on properly measured road courses.

50 miles	4:50:21	Bruce Fordyce (SAf)	London–Brighton	25 Sept 1983
1000 miles	12d 12:36:20	Siegfried Bauer (NZ)	Melbourne–Colac, Australia	15–28 Nov 1983
	kilometres			
24 hours	284.853	Yiannis Kouros (Gre)	New York	7–8 Nov 1984

WORLD BESTS—WOMEN'S LONG DISTANCE TRACK EVENTS

	hr:min:sec			
15 km	49:44.0	Silvana Cruciata (Ita)	Rome	4 May 1981
20 km	1:06:55.5	Rosa Mota (Por)	Lisbon	14 May 1983
25 km	1:31:04.3	Chantal Langlacé (Fra)	Amiens	3 Sep 1983
30 km	1:49:55.7	Chantal Langlacé (Fra)	Amiens	3 Sep 1983
50 km	3:44:08	Eleanor Adams (UK)	Bingham, Notts	20 Nov 1982
50 miles	6:17:30†	Monika Kuno (W. Germany)	Vogt, W. Germany	8–9 Jul 1983
100 km	8:01:01	Monika Kuno (W. Germany)	Vogt, W. Germany	8–9 Jul 1983
100 miles	15:44:21	Lynn Fitzgerald (UK)	Nottingham	31 Jul–1 Aug 1983
200 km	21:38:40	Lynn Fitzgerald (UK)	Nottingham	31 Jul–1 Aug 1983
200 miles	44:44:08	Eleanor Adams (UK)	Montauban, France	15–17 Mar 1985
500 km	88:48:00	Eleanor Adams (UK)	Colac, Australia	26–30 Nov 1984
500 miles	143:49:00	Eleanor Adams (UK)	Colac, Australia	26 Nov–1 Dec 1984
	kilometres			
1 hour	18.084	Silvana Cruciata (Ita)	Rome	4 May 1981
24 hrs	216.648	Rosalind Paul (now Cox) (UK)	Nottingham	22–23 Aug 1982
48 hrs	334.038	Eleanor Adams (UK)	Montauban, France	15–17 Mar 1985
6 days	806.0	Eleanor Adams (UK)	Colac, Australia	26 Nov–1 Dec 1984

† Timed on one running watch only.

LONG DISTANCE ROAD BESTS

Where superior to track bests and run on properly measured road courses.

50 km	3:13:51	Janis Klecker (USA)	Tallahassee	17 Dec 1983
40 miles	4:43:22	Mrcy Schwam (USA)	Chicago	3 Oct 1982
50 miles	5:59:26	Marcy Schwam (USA)	Chicago	3 Oct 1982
100 km	7:26:01	Chantal Langlacé (Fra)	Migennes, France	17 Jun 1984
100 miles	15:07:45	Christine Barrett (UK)	Forthampton, Gloucestershire	14 Apr 1984
500 km	82:10§	Annie van der Meer (Hol)	Paris–Colmar	8–11 Jun 1983

§ for 518 km.

It should be noted that road times must be assessed with care as course conditions can vary considerably.

The longest relay ever run was 15 059 km *9357 miles* by 20 members of the Melbourne Fire Brigade around Australia on Highway No. 1 in 43 days 23 hr 58 min, 10 July–23 Aug 1983. The most participants is 4800, 192 teams of 25, in the Batavierenrace, 167,2 km *103.89 miles* from Nijmegan to Enschede, Netherlands, won in 9 hr 30 min 44 sec on 23 Apr 1983.

Highland Games
The weight and height of cabers (Gaelic *cabar*) vary considerably. Extreme values are 25 ft *7,62 m* and 280 lb *127 kg*. The Braemar caber (19 ft 3 in *5,86 m* and 120 lb *54,4 kg*) in Grampian, Scotland, was untossed from 1891 until 1951 when it was tossed by George Clark. The best authentic mark recorded for throwing the 56 lb weight for height, using one hand only is 17 ft 2 in *5,23 m* by Geoffrey Lewis Capes (GB) (b. 23 Aug 1949) at Lagos, Nigeria on 5 Dec 1982. The best throw recorded for the Scots hammer is 151 ft 2 in *46,08 m* by William Anderson (b. 6 Oct 1938) at Lochearnhead on 26 July 1969.

Highest one-legged jump
One-legged Arnie Boldt (b. 1958), of Saskatche-

Yiannis Kouros has, since he won the Sparthathlon in 1983, dominated the world of ultra distance running, smashing numerous records including the 6-day record, unbettered since 1888. (Ceri Slade)

The world mile record stands at 6 min 7.1 sec ... Donald Davis (on the left) runs backwards at record speed.

wan, Canada, cleared 2.04 m *6 ft 8¼ in* in Rome, Italy on 3 Apr 1981.

Backwards running
Anthony 'Scott' Weiland, 27, ran the Detroit marathon backwards in 4 hr 7 min 54 sec on 3 Oct 1982. Donald Davis (b. 10 Feb 1960) (USA) ran 1 mile backwards in 6 min 7.1 sec at the University of Hawaii on 21 Feb 1983. Ferdie Adoboe (USA) ran 100 yd backwards in 12.8 sec (100 m in 14.0 sec) at Amherst, Mass. on 28 July 1983.

Fastest blind sprinting
Graham Henry Salmon (GB) (b. 5 Sept 1952) ran 100 m *109 yd* in 11.4 sec at Grangemouth, Scotland on 2 Sept 1978.

Pancake racing
Dale R. Lyons (b. 26 Feb 1937) (GB) has run several marathons during which he tosses a 2 oz *57 g* pancake repeatedly en route in a 1½ lb *0,68 kg* pan. His fastest time is 2 hr 57 min 16 sec at Wolverhampton on 25 Mar 1984.

TRAMPOLINING

Origins
Trampolines were used in show business at least as early as 'The Walloons' of the period 1910–12. The sport of trampolining (from the Spanish word *trampolin*, a springboard) dates from 1936, when the prototype 'T' model trampoline was developed by George Nissen (USA).

Most titles
Four men have won a world title (instituted 1964) twice; Dave Jacobs (USA) in 1967–8, Wayne Miller (b. 1946) (USA), in 1966 and 1970, Richard Tison (b. 17 Aug 1956) (France) in 1974 and 1976 (shared), and Evgeni Janes (USSR), 1976 (shared) and 1978. Judy Wills (b. 1948) (USA) won the first five women's titles (1964–8). Two European titles (1969 and 1971) have been won by Paul Luxon (b. 1952) (GB), the 1972 world champion. A record seven United Kingdom titles have been won by Wendy Wright (1969–70, 1972–5, 1977). The most by a man have been five by Stewart Matthews (b. 19 Feb 1962) (1976–80).

Youngest international *Great Britain*
Andrea Holmes (b. 2 Jan 1970) competed for Britain at 12 yr 131 days in the World Championships at Montana, USA on 13 May 1982.

Somersaults
Richard Cobbing of Gateshead Metro Trampoline Club performed 1610 consecutive somer-saults at Gateshead, Tyne and Wear, on 22 July 1984.

TUG OF WAR

Origins
Though ancient China and Egypt have been suggested as the originators of the sport, it is known that neolithic flint miners in Norfolk, England practised 'rope-pulling'. The first rules were those framed by the New York AC in 1879. Tug of War was an Olympic sport from 1900 until 1920. In 1958 the Tug-of-War Association was formed to administer Britain's 600 clubs.

Most titles
The Wood Treatment team (formerly the Bosley Farmers) of Cheshire have represented England since 1964, winning two World and ten European Championships at 720 kg *1587 lb*. They also won 20 consecutive AAA Catchweight Championships 1959–78. Hilary Brown (b. 13 Apr 1934) was in every team. Trevor Brian Thomas (b. 1943) of British Aircraft Corporation Club is the only holder of three winner's medals in the European Open club competitions.

Longest pulls
The longest recorded pull (prior to the introduction of AAA rules) is one of 2 hr 41 min when 'H' Company beat 'E' Company of the 2nd Battalion of the Sherwood Foresters (Derbyshire Regiment) at Jubbulpore, India, on 12 Aug 1889. The longest recorded pull under AAA Rules (in which lying on the ground or entrenching the feet is not permitted) is one of 11 min 23 sec for the first pull between the Isle of Oxney and St Claret's at Chertsey, Surrey on 26 May 1979. The record time for 'The Pull' (inst. 1898), across the Black River, between freshman and sophomore teams at Hope College, Holland, Mich, USA, is 3 hr 51 min on 23 Sept 1977, but the method of bracing the feet precludes the replacing of the preceding records.

VOLLEYBALL

Origins
The game was invented as *Minnonette* in 1895 by William G. Morgan at the YMCA gymnasium at Holyoke, Massachusetts, USA. The International Volleyball Association was formed in Paris in April 1947. The Amateur (now English) Volleyball Association of Great Britain was formed in May 1955.

Most world titles
World Championships were instituted in 1949 for men and 1952 for women. The USSR has won six men's titles (1949, 1952, 1960, 1962, 1978, 1982) and four women's (1952, 1956, 1960 and 1970).

Most Olympic titles
The sport was introduced to the Olympic Games for both men and women in 1964. The USSR have won a record three men's (1964, 1968 and 1980) and three women's (1968, 1972 and 1980) titles. The only player to win four medals is Inna Ryskal (USSR) (b. 15 June 1944), who won silver medals in 1964 and 1976 and golds in 1968 and 1972. The record for men is held by Yuriy Poyarkov (USSR) (b. 10 Feb 1937) who won gold medals in 1964 and 1968 and a bronze in 1972.

Most internationals *Great Britain*
Ucal Ashman (b. 10 Nov 1957) made a record 144 international appearances for England, 1976–85. The women's record is 150 by Ann Jarvis (b. 3 June 1955) for England, 1974–85.

WALKING

Most Olympic medals
Walking races have been included in the Olympic events since 1906 but walking matches have been known since 1589. The only walker to win three gold medals has been Ugo Frigerio (Italy) (1901–68) with the 3000 m and 10,000 m in 1920 and 1924. He also holds the record of most medals with four (he won the bronze medal at 50,000 m in 1932) a total shared with Vladimir Golubnichiy (USSR) (b. 2 June 1936), who won gold medals for the 20,000 m in 1960 and 1968, the silver in 1972 and the bronze in 1964.

The best British performance has been two gold medals by George Edward Larner (1875–1949) for the 3500 m and the 10 miles in 1908, but Ernest J. Webb (1872–1937) won three medals being twice 'walker up' to Larner and finishing second in the 10,000 m in 1912.

Most titles
Four time Olympian, Ronald Owen Laird (b. 31 May 1938) of the New York AC, USA, won a total of 65 National titles from 1958 to 1976, plus four Canadian championships. The greatest number of UK National titles won by a British walker is 27 by Vincent Paul Nihill (b. 5 Sept 1939) from 1963 to 1975.

Longest race
The Paris–Colmar, until 1980 Strasbourg–Paris, event (inst. 1926 in the reverse direction), now about 518 km *322 miles* is the world's longest annual race walk.

Ronald Weigel of East Germany holds the world record for the 50 km road walk; his pace an average 8.53 mph *13.72 km/h. (Sporting Pictures [UK])*

ROAD WALKING
WORLD BEST PERFORMANCES

It should be noted that severity of road race courses and the accuracy of their measurement may vary, sometimes making comparisons of times unreliable.

MEN
20 km in 1 hr 19 min 29.6 sec, Josef Pribilinec (Czechoslovakia) (b. 6 July 1960) at Bergen, Norway on 24 Sept 1983.
30 km in 2 hr 03 min 06 sec, Daniel Bautista (Mexico) at Cherkassy, USSR on 27 Apr 1980.
50 km in 3 hr 38 min 31 sec, Ronald Weigel (GDR) at East Berlin, GDR on 20 July 1984.

WOMEN
10 km in 44 min 51.6 sec, Olga Krishtop (USSR) at Penza, USSR on 5 Aug 1984.
20 km in 1 hr 36 min 35.7 sec, Susan Cook (Australia) at Melbourne, Australia on 22 Dec 1982.
50 kmin 5 hr 01 min 52 sec, Lillian Millen (GB) (b. 5 Mar 1945) at York, GB on 16 Apr 1983.

BRITISH BEST PERFORMANCES

MEN
20 km in 1 hr 22 min 37 sec, Ian Peter McCombie (b. 11 Jan 1961) at Thamesmead, London on 11 May 1985.
30 km in 2 hr 10 min 16 sec, Steven John Barry at Brisbane, Australia on 7 Oct 1982.
50 km in 4 min 02 min 00 sec, Christopher Lloyd Maddocks (b. 28 Mar 1957) at Vilanova, Spain on 18 Mar 1984.

WOMEN
10 km in 48 min 47 sec, Irene Lillian Bateman (b. 13 Nov 1947) at York on 20 June 1981.
20 km in 1 hr 40 min 45 sec, Irene Lillian Bateman at Basildon, Essex on 9 Apr 1983.

TRACK WALKING—WORLD RECORDS

The International Amateur Athletic Federation recognises men's records at 20 km, 30 km, 50 km and 2 hours, and women's at 5 km and 10 km. This table also includes world bests for other standard distances.

Event	Time			Name, country and date of birth	Place	Date	
	hr	min	sec				
MEN							
3 km		10	54.6	Carlo Mattioli (Italy) (23 Oct 1954)	Milan, Italy (indoors)	6 Feb	1980
10 km		38	31.4	Werner Heyer (GDR) (14 Nov 1956)	East Berlin (indoors)	12 Jan	1980
20 km	1	18	40.0	Ernesto Canto (Mexico) (18 Oct 1959)	Fana, Norway	5 May	1984
30 km	2	06	07.3	Maurizio Damilano (Italy) (6 Apr 1957)	San Donato Milanese	5 May	1985
50 km	3	41	38.4	Raul Gonzalez (Mexico) (29 Feb 1952)	Fana, Norway	25 May	1979
1 hour		15 253 metres		Ernesto Canto (Mexico)	Fana, Norway	5 May	1984
2 hours		28 565 metres		Maurizio Damilano (Italy)	San Donato Milanese	5 May	1985
WOMEN							
3 km		12	31.57	Giulliana Salce (Italy) (b. 6 June 1955)	Florence, Italy (indoors)	6 Feb	1985
5 km		21	36.2	Olga Krishtop (USSR)	Penza, USSR	4 Aug	1984
10 km		44	56.10	Yan Hong (China) (b. 23 Oct 1966)	Shanghai, China	16 Mar	1985

TRACK WALKING—BRITISH RECORDS

				Name	Place	Date	
MEN							
3 km			11	41.73	Ian Peter McCombie (11 Jan 1961)	London (Crystal Palace)	13 July	1985
			11	28.0	Philip John Vesty (unratified) (5 Jan 1863)	Leicester	9 May	1984
10 km			40	53.60	Philip John Vesty	Cwmbran, Gwent	28 May	1984
20 km		1	26	22.0	Steven John Barry	Brighton, W. Sussex	28 June	1981
30 km		2	19	18	Christopher Lloyd Maddocks (28 Mar 1957)	Birmingham	22 Sept	1984
50 km		4	05	47.3	Christopher Lloyd Maddocks	Birmingham	22 Sept	1984
1 hour			13 987 metres		Steven John Barry	Brighton, W. Sussex	28 June	1981
2 hours			26 037 metres		Ronald Edward Wallwork (26 May 1941)	Stretford, Lancashire	31 July	1971
WOMEN							
3 km			13	25.2	Carol Joan Tyson (15 Dec 1957)	Östersund, Sweden	6 July	1979
5 km			23	11.2	Carol Joan Tyson	Östersund, Sweden	30 June	1979
10 km			48	11.4	Marion Fawkes (3 Dec 1948)	Gunnisfalt, Sweden	8 July	1979

The fastest performance is by Robert Pietquin (Belgium) (b. 1938) who walked 507 km *315 miles* in the 1980 race in 60 hr 1 min 10 sec (deducting 4 hr compulsory stops). This represents an average speed of 8.45 km/h *5.25 mph.* Gilbert Roger (France) (b. 1914) won six times (1949, 1953–4, 1956–8). The first woman to complete the race was Annie van der Meer (Netherlands) (b. 24 Feb 1947), who was 10th in 1983 in 82 hr 10 min.

Dumitru Dan (1890–1978) of Romania was the only man of 200 entrants to succeed in a contest in walking 100,000 km *62,137 miles* organised by the Touring Club de France on 1 Apr 1910. He covered 96,000 km *59,651 miles* up to 24 Mar 1916 so averaging 43,85 km *27.24 miles* a day.

'End to end'
The fastest Land's End to John o'Groats walk is 12 days 21 hr 15 min for 851 miles *1370 km* by Norman Fox (b. 29 May 1947) on 1–13 Sept 1983. The women's record is 13 days 17 hr 42 min by Ann Sayer (b. 16 Oct 1936) on 20 Sept–3 Oct 1980. The Irish 'End to End' record over the 400.2 miles *644 km* from Malin Head, Donegal to Mizen Head, Cork is 5 days 22 hr 30 min, set by John 'Paddy' Dowling (b. 15 June 1929) on 18–24 Mar 1982.

London to Brighton
The record time for the 53 miles *85 km* walk is 7 hr 35 min 12 sec by Donald James Thompson (b. 20 Jan 1933) on 14 Sept 1957. Richard Esmond Green (b. 22 Apr 1924) completed the course a record 45 times from 1950 to 1980.

Longest non-stop walk
WO2 Malcolm Barnish of the 19th Regiment, Royal Artillery walked 412.08 miles *663.17 km* in 6 days 10 hr 32 min at Dortmund, W. Germany on 12–18 May 1985. This was 442 laps of a 1640.86 yd *1500,4 m* closed circuit. He was not permitted any stops for rest and was moving 98.74 per cent of the time.

24 hours
The best official performance for distance walked on a track in 24 hr is 133 miles 21 yd *214,06 km* by Huw Nielson (GB) at Walton-on-Thames, Surrey, on 14–15 Oct 1960. The best by a woman is 202,3 km *125.7 miles* by Annie van der Meer at Rouen, France, on 30 Apr–1 May 1984 over a 1,185 km lap road course.

Walking backwards
The greatest ever exponent of reverse pedestrianism has been Plennie L. Wingo (b. 24 Jan 1895) then of Abilene, Texas, who completed his 8000 mile *12 875 km* trans-continental walk from Santa Monica, California to Istanbul, Turkey, from 15 Apr 1931 to 24 Oct 1932. The longest distance recorded for walking backwards in 24 hr is 133,5 km *82.95 miles* by Donald A. Davis in Honolulu, Hawaii, USA on 22–23 Apr 1983.

WATER POLO

Origins
Water polo was developed in England as 'Water Soccer' in 1869 and first included in the Olympic Games in Paris in 1900.

Most Olympic titles
Hungary has won the Olympic tournament most often with six wins in 1932, 1936, 1952, 1956, 1964 and 1976. Great Britain won in 1900, 1908, 1912 and 1920.

Five players share the record of three gold medals; Britons, George Wilkinson (1879–1946) in 1900, 1908, 1912; Paulo 'Paul' Radmilovic (1886–1968), and Charles Sidney Smith (1879–1951) in 1908, 1912, 1920; and Hungarians Deszo Gyarmati (b. 23 Oct 1927) and György Kárpáti (b. 23 June 1935) in 1952, 1956, 1964. Gyarmati's wife (Eva Szekely) and daughter (Andrea) won gold and silver medals respectively in swimming. Paul Radmilovic also won a gold medal for the 4 × 200 m freestyle relay in 1908.

ASA championships
The greatest number of Amateur Swimming Association titles is 14 between 1956 and 1982, by London Polytechnic, who have also won a record ten National League (formed 1963) titles—1964, 1969–70, 1972–7, 1979.

Most goals
The greatest number of goals scored by an individual in an international is 13 by Debbie Handley for Australia (16) *v* Canada (10) at the World Aquatic Games in Guayaquil, Ecuador in 1982.

Most international appearances
The greatest number of international appearances is 412 by Alexei Barkalov (USSR) (b. 18 Feb 1946), 1965–80. The British record is 126 by Martyn Thomas, of Cheltenham, 1964–78.

WATER SKIING

Origins
The origins of water skiing lie in walking on planks and aquaplaning. A 19th century treatise on sorcerers refers to Eliseo of Tarentum who, in the 14th century, 'walks and dances' on the water. The first report of aquaplaning was on America's Pacific coast in the early 1900s. At Scarborough, Yorkshire, on 15 July 1914, a single plank-gliding contest was won by H. Storry.

The 1983 world champion in the women's tricks (freestyle figures) event, Natalia Ponomaryeva. She and Ana Maria Carrasco have battled for the world record (see Stop Press). (All Sport)

The present day sport of water skiing was pioneered by Ralph W. Samuelson (1904–77) on Lake Pepin, Minnesota, USA, on two curved pine boards in the summer of 1922, though claims have been made for the birth of the sport on Lake Annecy (Haute Savoie), France at about the same time. The first world organisation, the United Internationale de Ski Nautique, was formed in Geneva on 27 July 1946. The British Water Ski Federation was founded in London in 1954.

Most titles
World Overall Championships (inst. 1949) have been won twice by Alfredo Mendoza (USA) in 1953 and 1955, Mike Suyerhoud (USA) in 1967 and 1969, George Athans (Canada) in 1971 and 1973 and Sammy Duvall (USA) in 1981 and 1983, and three times by Willa McGuire (*née* Worthington) of the USA in 1949–50 and 1955 and Elizabeth 'Liz' Allan-Shetter (USA) in 1965, 1969 and 1975. Liz Allan-Shetter has won a record eight individual championship events and is the only person to win all four titles—slalom, jumping, tricks and overall in one year, at Copenhagen, Denmark in 1969. The USA has won the team championship on 14 successive occasions 1957–83. The most British Overall titles (instituted 1953) won by a man is seven by Michael Hazelwood (b. 14 Apr 1958) in 1974, 1976–9, 1981, 1983; the most by a woman is nine by Karen Jane Morse (b. 1956) in 1971–6, 1978, 1981, 1984.

Highest speed
The fastest water skiing speed recorded is 230,26 km/h *143.08 mph* by Christopher Michael Massey (Australia) on the Hawkesbury River, Windsor, New South Wales, Australia on 6 Mar 1983. His drag boat driver was Stanley Charles Sainty. Donna Patterson Brice (b. 1953) set a feminine record of 178,81 km/h *111.11 mph* at Long Beach, California on 21 Aug 1977. The fastest recorded speed by a British skier over a measured kilometre is 131,217 km/h *81.535 mph* (average) on Lake Windermere, Cumbria on 18 Oct 1973 by Billy Rixon. The fastest by a British woman is 122,187 km/h *75.92 mph* by Elizabeth Hobbs on Windermere, 14 Oct 1982.

Longest run
The greatest distance travelled is 2099,7 km *1304.6 miles* by Will Coughey on 18–19 Feb 1984 on Lake Tikitapu, New Zealand.

Barefoot
The first person to water ski barefoot is reported to be Dick Pope Jr at Lake Eloise, Florida, on 6 Mar 1947. The barefoot duration record is 2 hr 42 min 39 sec by Billy Nichols (USA) (b. 1964) on Lake Weir, Florida, on 19 Nov 1978. The backward barefoot record is 39 min by Paul McManus (Aust). The British duration record is 67 min 5 sec by John Doherty on 1 Oct 1974. The official barefoot speed record (two runs) is 177,06 km/h *110.02 mph* by Lee Kirk (USA) at Firebird Lake, Phoenix, Ariz, on 11 June 1977. His fastest run was 182,93 km/h *113.67 mph.* The fastest by a woman is 118,56 km/h *73.67 mph* by Karen Toms (Australia) on the Hawkesbury River, Windsor, New South Wales on 31 Mar 1984. The British record is: (men's) 114,86 km/h *71.37 mph* by Richard Mainwaring at Holme Pierrepont, Notts. on 2 Dec 1978; (women's) 70,75 km/h *43.96 mph* by Linda Wright at Holme Pierrepont, Notts. in Sept 1984. The fastest official speed backward barefoot is 100 km/h *62 mph* by Robert Wing (Aus) on 3 Apr 1982.

The barefoot jump record is 18,70 m *61 ft 4 in* by Brett Wing (Australia) at Marine World in 1981. The British record is 15,80 m *51 ft 10 in* by Keith Donnelly in Ireland in 1978.

WATER SKIING RECORDS

WORLD RECORDS MEN

Slalom	5 buoys on a 10,75 m line	Bob LaPoint (USA)	Shreveport, Florida, USA	1984
Tricks	10130 points	Patrice Martin (France)	Martigues, France	28 Oct 1984
Jumping	61,5 m *202 ft*	Glenn Thurlow (Aus)	Moomba, Melbourne, Australia	14 Mar 1983

WORLD RECORDS WOMEN

Slalom	4 buoys on a 11,25 m line	Deena Brush (USA)	Palm Beach, Florida, USA	2 Oct 1983
Tricks	7850 points	Natalia Ponomaryeva (née Rumyantseva) (USSR)	Montbéliard, France	24 June 1984
	7850 points	Natalia Ponomaryeva	Milan	16 Sep 1984
Jumping	45,8 m *150 ft 2 in*	Sue Lipplegoes (Australia)	Kirtons Farm, Reading, Berkshire	31 July 1983

BRITISH RECORDS MEN

Slalom	4 buoys on a 10,75 m line	Andy Mapple (b. 3 Nov 1962)	McCormick Lake, Seffner, Florida USA	29 Apr 1984
Tricks	8650 points	John Battleday (b. 1 Feb 1957)	Lyon, France	5 Aug 1984
Jumping	61,1 m *200 ft 5 in*	Michael Hazelwood (b. 14 Apr 1958)	Melbourne, Australia	9 Mar 1985

BRITISH RECORDS WOMEN

Slalom	4½ buoys at 12 m	Karen Jane Morse (b. 14 Aug 1956)	France	1982
Tricks	6820 points	Nicola Rasey (b. 6 June 1966)	Martigues, France	27 Oct 1984
Jumping	44,9 m *147 ft*	Kathy Hulme (b. 11 Feb 1959)	Kirtons Farm, Reading, Berkshire	1 Aug 1982

WORLD WEIGHTLIFTING RECORDS

Bodyweight class	Lift	kg	lb	Name and Country	Place	Date
52 kg *114½ lb* FLYWEIGHT	Snatch	115,5	254½	Neno Terziyski (Bulgaria)	San Marino	9 May 1983
	Jerk	152,5	336	Neno Terziyski (Bulgaria)	Vittoria, Spain	27 Apr 1984
	Total	262,5	578½	Neno Terziyski (Bulgaria)	Vittoria, Spain	27 Apr 1984
56 kg *123¼ lb* BANTAMWEIGHT	Snatch	133	293	Oksen Mirzoyan (USSR)	Varna, Bulgaria	12 Sept 1984
	Jerk	170,5	375¾	Naim Suleimanov (Bulgaria)	Belgrade	12 Sept 1984
	Total	300	661¼	Naim Suleimanov (Bulgaria)	Varna, Bulgaria	11 May 1984
60 kg *132¼ lb* FEATHERWEIGHT	Snatch	142,5	314	Naim Suleimanov (Bulgaria)	Sarajevo, Yugoslavia	24 Nov 1984
	Jerk	185,5	408¾	Naim Suleimanov (Bulgaria)	Sarajevo, Yugoslavia	24 Nov 1984
	Total	327,5	722	Naim Suleimanov (Bulgaria)	Sarajevo, Yugoslavia	24 Nov 1984
67.5 kg *148¾ lb* WELTERWEIGHT	Snatch	155,5	342¾	Vladimir Grachev (USSR)	Minsk, USSR	15 Mar 1984
	Jerk	200	440¾	Aleksandr Varbanov (Bulgaria)	Varna, Bulgaria	13 Sept 1984
	Total	352,5	777	Andreas Behm (GDR)	Schwedr, GDR	20 July 1984
75 kg *165¼ lb* MIDDLEWEIGHT	Snatch	167,5	369¼	Vladimir Kuznyetsov (USSR)	Moscow, USSR	26 Oct 1983
	Jerk	211	465	Zdravko Stoichkov (Bulgaria)	Varna, Bulgaria	14 Sept 1984
	Total	377,5	832	Zdravko Stoichkov (Bulgaria)	Varna, Bulgaria	14 Sept 1984
82.5 kg *181¼ lb* LIGHT-HEAVYWEIGHT	Snatch	182,5	402¾	Yuri Vardanyan (USSR)	Varna, Bulgaria	14 Sept 1984
	Jerk	224	493¾	Yuri Vardanyan (USSR)	Varna, Bulgaria	14 Sept 1984
	Total	405	892½	Yuri Vardanyan (USSR)	Varna, Bulgaria	14 Sept 1984
90 kg *198¼ lb* MIDDLE-HEAVYWEIGHT	Snatch	195,5	431	Blagoi Blagoyev (Bulgaria)	Varna, Bulgaria	1 May 1983
	Jerk	233	513½	Viktor Solodov (USSR)	Varna, Bulgaria	15 Sept 1984
	Total	422,5	931¼	Viktor Solodov (USSR)	Varna, Bulgaria	15 Sept 1984
100 kg *220½ lb*	Snatch	200	440¼	Yuri Zakharevich (USSR)	Odessa, USSR	4 Mar 1983
	Jerk	241,5	532¼	Pavel Kuznyetsov (USSR)	Varna, Bulgaria	15 Sept 1984
	Total	440	970	Yuri Zakharevich (USSR)	Odessa, USSR	4 Mar 1983
110 kg *242½ lb* HEAVYWEIGHT	Snatch	200,5	442	Yuri Zakharevich (USSR)	Varna, Bulgaria	16 Sept 1984
	Jerk	247,5	545½	Vyacheslav Klokov (USSR)	Moscow, USSR	30 Oct 1983
	Total	442.5	975½	Leonid Taranenko (USSR)	Varna, Bulgaria	16 Sept 1984
Over 110 kg *242½ lb* SUPER-HEAVYWEIGHT	Snatch	211	465	Aleksandr Gunyashev (USSR)	Rheims, France	1 June 1984
	Jerk	265	585	Anatoliy Pisarenko (USSR)	Varna, Bulgaria	16 Sept 1984
	Total	465	1025	Aleksandr Gunyashev (USSR)	Rheims, France	1 June 1984

BRITISH WEIGHTLIFTING RECORDS (in kg)

Class	Snatch		Date	Jerk		Date	Total		Date
52 kg	92,5	Precious McKenzie	25 Jan 1974	122,5	Precious McKenzie	25 Jan 1974	215	Precious McKenzie	25 Jan 1974
56 kg	105	Dean Willey	15 June 1981	132,5	Geoff Laws	1982	235	Geoff Laws	1982
60 kg	122,5	Dean Willey	26 Feb 1983	152,5	Dean Willey	26 Mar 1983	272,5	Dean Willey	26 Feb 1983
67,5 kg	142,5	Dean Willey	30 Mar 1985	170	Dean Willey	1 Aug 1984	312,5	Dean Willey	30 Mar 1985
75 kg	150	David Morgan	28 Jan 1984	185,5	David Morgan	24 Sept 1983	330	David Morgan	24 Sept 1983
82,5 kg	155	Newton Burrowes	3 Apr 1982	185	Newton Burrowes	27 Feb 1982	340	Newton Burrowes	3 Apr 1982
90 kg	160	Gary Langford	13 Apr 1980	201	David Mercer	26 May 1984	352,5	David Mercer	5 Aug 1984
100 kg	160,5	Gary Langford	7 Mar 1982	202,5	Peter Pinsent	17 Sept 1983	362,5	Peter Pinsent	17 Sept 1983
110 kg	180	Gary Taylor	30 Mar 1985	200	Brian Strange	28 Feb 1976	375	Gary Taylor	30 Mar 1985
Super	162,5	John Burns	5 Sept 1982	200	Andrew Kerr	9 Nov 1974	350	Brian Strange	4 Mar 1978

WEIGHTLIFTING

Origins

Competitions for lifting weights of stone were held in the ancient Olympic Games. The first championships entitled 'world' were staged at the Café Monico, Piccadilly, London, on 28 Mar 1891 and then in Vienna, Austria on 19–20 July 1898, subsequently recognised by the IWF. Prior to that time, weightlifting consisted of professional exhibitions in which some of the advertised poundages were open to doubt.

The International Weightlifting Federation (IWF) was established in 1920, and their first official championships were held in Tallinn, Estonia on 29–30 Apr 1922.

Most Olympic Medals

Norbert Schemansky (USA) (b. 30 May 1924) won a record four Olympic medals: Gold, middle-heavyweight 1952; Silver, heavyweight 1948; Bronze, heavyweight 1960 and 1964.

Most titles *World*

The most world title wins, including Olympic Games, is eight by John Davis (USA) (1921–84) in 1938, 1946–52; by Tommy Kono (USA) (b. 27 June 1930) in 1952–9; and by Vasili Alexeyev (USSR) (b. 7 Jan 1942) 1970–7.

Youngest world record holder and champion

Naim Suleimanov (Bulgaria) (b. 23 Nov 1967) set 56 kg world records for clean and jerk (160 kg) and total (285 kg) at 15 yr 123 days at Allentown, New Jersey, USA on 26 Mar 1983. On 23 Oct 1983 in Moscow, USSR he became the youngest world champion at 15 yr 334 days.

Most successful British lifter

The only British lifter to win an Olympic title has been Launceston Elliot (1874–1930), the open one-handed lift champion in 1896 at Athens. Louis George Martin (b. Jamaica, 11

1983 world champion and record holder at 15, Naim Suleimanov broke the world record a further 11 times in 1984. *(Bruce H. Klemens)*

WORLD POWERLIFTING RECORDS (All weights in kilograms)

Class	Squat		Bench Press		Deadlift		Total	
MEN								
52 kg	242,5	Joe Cunha (USA) 1981	146,5	Joe Cunha 1982	233	Hideaki Inaba (Jap) 1983	567,5	Hideaki Inaba (Jap) 1980
56 kg	237,5	Hideaki Inaba (Jap) 1982	152,5	Hiroyaki Isagawa (Jap) 1984	289,5	Lamar Gant (USA) 1982	625	Lamar Gant 1982
60 kg	295	Joe Bradley (USA) 1980	180	Joe Bradley 1980	296,5	Lamar Gant 1983	707,5	Joe Bradley 1982
67,5 kg	297	Robert Wahl (USA) 1982	194	Kristoffer Hulecki (Swe) 1982	312,5	Raimo Valineva (Fin) 1981	732,5	Joe Bradley 1981
75 kg	327,5	Mike Bridges (USA) 1980	217,5	James Rouse (USA) 1980	325,5	Eric Coppin (Bel) 1985	850	Rick Gaugler (USA) 1982
82,5 kg	379,5	Mike Bridges 1982	240	Mike Bridges 1981	357,5	Veli Kumpuniemi (Fin) 1980	952,5	Mike Bridges 1982
90 kg	375	Fred Hatfield (USA) 1980	255	Mike MacDonald (USA) 1980	372,5	Walter Thomas (USA) 1982	937,5	Mike Bridges 1980
100 kg	400	Fred Hatfield 1982	261,5	Mike MacDonald 1977	377,5	James Cash (USA) 1982	952,5	James Cash 1982
110 kg	393,5	Dan Wohleber (USA) 1981	270	Jeffrey Magruder (USA) 1982	395	John Kuc (USA) 1980	1000	John Kuc 1980
125 kg	412,5	David Waddington (USA) 1982	278,5	Tom Hardman (USA) 1982	385	Terry McCormick (USA) 1982	1005	Ernie Hackett (USA) 1980
125 + kg	445	Dwayne Fely (USA) 1982	300	Bill Kazmaier (USA) 1981	402	Bill Kazmaier 1981	1100	Bill Kazmaier 1981
WOMEN								
44 kg	140	Anna-Liisa Prinkkala (Fin) 1983	75	Teri Hoyt (USA) 1982	165	Nancy Belliveau (USA) 1985	350	Cheryl Jones (USA) 1985
48 kg	147	Majik Jones (USA) 1983	82,5	Michelle Evris (USA) 1981	182,5	Majik Jones (USA) 1984	390	Majik Jones 1984
52 kg	177,5	Sisi Dolman (Hol) 1983	95	Mary Ryan (USA) 1984	177,5	Sisi Dolman 1985	405	Sisi Dolman 1985
56 kg	184	Vicki Steenrod (USA) 1984	112	Vicki Steenrod 1984	190	Vicky Steenrod 1984	475	Vicky Steenrod 1984
60 kg	200,5	Ruthi Shafer (USA) 1983	105	Vicki Steenrod 1985	213	Ruthi Shafer 1983	502,5	Vicki Steenrod 1985
67,5 kg	230	Ruthi Shafer 1984	105,5	C. Gerard (Fra) 1984	244	Ruthi Shafer 1984	565	Ruthi Shafer 1984
75 kg	212,5	Beverley Francis (Aus) 1981	140	Beverley Francis 1981	210	Pam Mathews (Aus) 1982	550	Beverley Francis 1983
82,5 kg	227,5	Juanita Trujillo (USA) 1985	150	Beverley Francis 1981	227,5	Vicky Gagne (USA) 1981	577,5	Beverley Francis 1983
90 kg	213	Gael Martin (Aus) 1983	120,5	Gael Martin 1983	210	Rebecca Waibler (GFR) 1982	525	Gael Martin 1982
90 + kg	247,5	Jan Todd (USA) 1981	130	Gael Martin 1982	230	Wanda Sander (USA) 1981	567,5	Gael Martin 1982

BRITISH POWERLIFTING RECORDS All weights in kilograms

Class	Squat		Bench Press		Deadlift		Total	
MEN								
52 kg	217,5	P. Stringer 1980	130	P. Stringer 1981	222,5	P. McKenzie 1975	530	P. Stringer 1982
56 kg	235	P. Stringer 1982	137,5	P. Stringer 1983	229	P. McKenzie 1973	567,5	N. Bhairo 1982
60 kg	247,5	A. Galvez 1981	140,5	P. Stringer 1985	275	E. Pengelly 1977	645	E. Pengelly 1979
67,5 kg	275	E. Pengelly 1981	165	H. Salih 1979	295	E. Pengelly 1982	710	E. Pengelly 1982
75 kg	302,5	J. Howells 1979	185	P. Fiore 1981	310	R. Limerick 1984	760	S. Alexander 1983
82,5 kg	337,5	M. Duffy 1984	210	M. Duffy 1981	355	R. Collins 1980	855	R. Collins 1980
90 kg	347,5	D. Caldwell 1985	222,5	J. Chandler 1983	350,5	R. Collins 1980	870	D. Caldwell 1985
100 kg	380	A. Stevens 1984	222,5	F. Nobile 1982	362,5	A. Stevens 1984	955	A. Stevens 1984
110 kg	372,5	A. Stevens 1984	232,5	J. Neighbour 1985	380	A. White 1982	920	A. White 1982
125 kg	380	S. Zetolofsky 1984	227,5	A. Kerr 1982	365	S. Zetolofsky 1984	957,5	S. Zetolofsky 1984
125 + kg	382,5	S. Zetolofsky 1984	258	T. Purdoe 1971	377,5	A. Kerr 1982	982,5	A. Kerr 1983
WOMEN								
44 kg	105	J. White 1984	57,5	J. White 1983	130	A. Brown 1982	277,5	J. White 1984
48 kg	125	S. Smith 1985	72,5	S. Smith 1983	132,5	M. Green 1984	315	M. Green 1984
52 kg	140	J. Hunter 1984	72,5	S. Smith 1982	162,5	J. Hunter 1984	372,5	J. Hunter 1984
56 kg	140	D. Mears 1983	70	J. Hunter 1985	162,5	J. Hunter 1985	372,5	J. Hunter 1985
60 kg	155	R. Bass 1983	80	R. Bass 1985	177,5	D. Webb 1984	402,5	R. Bass 1984
67,5 kg	165	D. Webb 1982	82,5	R. Bass 1984	175	D. Webb 1983	417,5	R. Bass 1984
75 kg	195	P. Morgan 1984	95	J. Oakes 1981	202,5	J. Oakes 1984	492,5	J. Oakes 1984
82,5 kg	207,5	J. Oakes 1983	112,5	J. Oakes 1983	205	J. Oakes 1984	510	J. Oakes 1984
90 kg	167,5	J. Jackson 1983	100	J. Kerr 1983	187,5	Y. Hanson-Nortey 1984	430	J. Kerr 1982
90 + kg	162,5	J. Kerr 1981	112,5	V. Head 1982	185	J. Kerr 1981	440	J. Kerr 1980

Nov 1936) won four World and European mid-heavyweight titles in 1959, 1962–3, 1965. He won an Olympic silver medal in 1964 and a bronze in 1960 and three Commonwealth gold medals in 1962, 1966, 1970. His total of British titles was 12.

Greatest lift
The greatest weight ever raised by a human being is 6270 lb *2844 kg* (2.80 tons *2,84 tonnes*) in a back lift (weight raised off trestles) by the 26 st *165 kg* Paul Anderson (USA) (b. 17 Oct 1932), the 1956 Olympic heavyweight champion, at Toccoa, Georgia, USA, on 12 June 1957. The greatest lift by a woman is 3564 lb *1616 kg* with a hip and harness lift by Josephine Blatt (*née* Schauer) (1869–1923) at the Bijou Theatre, Hoboken, New Jersey, USA, on 15 Apr 1895.

Greatest overhead lifts
The greatest overhead lifts made from the ground are the clean and jerks achieved by super-heavyweights (see world record table). The greatest overhead lift ever made by a woman is 289 lb *131 kg* by Karyn Tartar in New York in December 1984.

Greatest power lifts
Paul Anderson, as a professional, achieved 1200 lb *544 kg* in a squat so aggregating, with a 627 lb *284 kg* bench press and an 820 lb *371 kg* dead lift, a career total of 2647 lb *1200 kg*.

Yuri Vardanyan in 1984 overcame his own world record that had stood for 4 years—regarded as a stupendous feat in the weightlifting world. *(Bruce H. Klemens)*

Hermann Görner (1891–1956) (Germany) performed a one-handed dead lift of 734½ lb *333,1 kg* in Dresden on 20 July 1920. Görner also raised 24 men weighing 4123 lb *1870 kg* on a plank on the soles of his feet in London on 12 Oct 1927 and carried on his back a 1444 lb *654 kg* piano for 52½ ft *16 m* at Leipzig on 3 June 1921. Willie Whoriskey achieved a British record one-handed deadlift of 670.9 lb *304,3 kg* at Bloxwich, W. Midlands on 26 Nov 1983. Clive Lloyd (b. 23 Aug 1961) achieved a one-handed straddle lift of 669 lb *303,5 kg* at Grosvenor House, London on 12 Aug 1983. This was a record 3.46 times his body weight of 87,8 kg *193.5 lb*.

The greatest power lift by a woman is a squat of 545½ lb *247,5 kg* by Jan Suffolk Todd (b. 22 May 1952) (USA) (weighing 88,5 kg *195 lb*) at Columbus, Georgia, USA in Jan 1981. Cammie Lynn Lusko (b. 5 Apr 1958) (USA) became the first woman to lift more than her body weight with one arm, with 59,5 kg *131 lbs* at a body weight of 58,3 kg *128.5 lb*, at Milwaukee, Wisconsin, USA on 21 May 1983.

John Decker lifted 25 tons *25,4 tonnes* by bench presses (1000 lifts of 56 lb *25,4 kg*) within an hour at Congleton, Cheshire on 16 Aug 1984.

A deadlifting record of 2 378 755 kg *5,244,169 lb* in 24 hr was set by a team of ten from ASC Unterwössen at Kreuzheben, W. Germany on 27–28 Jan 1984.

A team of nine from the David Pinder Appeal lifted 1 316 230 kg *2,901,786 lb* in 24 hr with bench presses at the Pentonville Prison Officers' Club, London on 13–14 July 1985.

Body weight feats

Lamar Gant (USA) was the first man to deadlift five times his own bodyweight, lifting 299,5 kg *661 lb* when 59,5 kg *132 lb* in 1985. Stefan Topurov (Bulgaria) clean and jerked 180 kg *396½ lb*, three times his bodyweight, at Moscow, USSR on 24 Oct 1983.

Strandpulling

The International Steel Strandpullers' Association was founded by Gavin Pearson (Scotland) in 1940. The greatest ratified poundage to date is a super-heavyweight right arm push of 815 lb *369,5 kg* by Malcolm Bartlett (b. 9 June 1955) of Oldham, Lancashire. He has also won a record 19 British Open titles. The record for the Back Press Anyhow is 645 lb *292,5 kg* by Barry Anderson, of Leeds, in 1975.

WRESTLING

Origins

The earliest depictions of wrestling holds and falls on wall plaques indicate that organised wrestling dates from *c.* 2750–2600 BC. It was the most popular sport in the ancient Olympic Games and victors were recorded from 708 BC. The Greco-Roman style is of French origin and arose about 1860. The International Amateur Wrestling Federation (FILA) was founded in 1912.

Most titles *Olympic*

Three Olympic titles have been won by: Carl Westergren (1895–1958) (Sweden) in 1920, 1924, 1932; Ivar Johansson (1903–79) (Sweden) in 1932 (two), 1936; and Aleksandr Medved (b. 16 Sept 1937) (USSR) in 1964, 1968, 1972. Four Olympic medals were won by Eino Leino (b. 7 Apr 1891) at freestyle 1920–32 and by Imre Polyák (Hungary) (b. 16 Apr 1932) at Greco-Roman in 1952–64.

Most titles *World*

The freestyler Aleksandr Medved (USSR) (b. 16 Sept 1937) won a record ten world championships with the light-heavyweight titles in 1962–4 (Olympic) and 1966, heavyweight 1967–8 (Olympic), and super-heavyweight in 1969–72 (Olympic). The only wrestler to win the same title in seven successive years has been Valeriy Rezantsev (b. 2 Feb 1947) (USSR) in the Greco-Roman light-heavyweight class in 1970–6, including the Olympic Games of 1972 and 1976.

Most titles and longest span *British*

The most British titles won is ten by heavyweight Kenneth Alan Richmond (b. 10 July 1926) between 1949 and 1960. The longest span for BAWA titles is 24 years by George Mackenzie (1890–1957) between 1909 and 1933. He represented Great Britain in five successive Olympiads, 1908 to 1928.

Most wins

In international competition, Osamu Watanabe (b. 21 Oct 1940), of Japan, the 1964 Olympic freestyle featherweight champion, was unbeaten and unscored-upon in 187 consecutive matches. Wade Schalles (USA) won 821 bouts from 1964 to 1984, with 530 of these victories by pin.

Longest bout

The longest recorded bout was one of 11 hr 40 min when Martin Klein (1885–1947) (Estonia representing Russia) beat Alpo Asikäinen

(1888–1942) (Finland) for the Greco-Roman middleweight 'A' event silver medal in the 1912 Olympic Games in Stockholm, Sweden.

Heaviest heavyweight

The heaviest wrestler in Olympic history is Chris Taylor (1950–79), bronze medallist in the super-heavyweight class in 1972, who stood 6 ft 5 in *1,96 m* and weighed over 420 lb *190 kg*. FILA introduced an upper weight limit of 130 kg *286 lb* for international competition in 1985.

CUMBERLAND AND WESTMORLAND WRESTLING

J. Baddeley (middleweight in 1905–6, 1908–10, 1912) and Ernest Aubrey Bacon (b. 1893) (lightweight in 1919, 1921–3, 1928–9) both won six titles in the British amateur championships (inst. 1904).

PROFESSIONAL WRESTLING

Professional wrestling dates from 1874 in the USA. Georges Karl Julius Hackenschmidt (USSR) (1877–1968), Estonian-born, was undefeated at Greco-Roman contests from 1900 to his retirement in 1911. (*See also p. 97*).

SUMO WRESTLING

The sport's origins in Japan date from *c.* 23 BC. The heaviest ever *sumotori* is Samoan-American Salevaa Fuali Atisnoe of Hawaii, *alias* Konishiki, who in 1985 had a peak weight of 496 lb *225 kg*. Weight is amassed by over alimentation with a high protein stew called *chankonabe*. The most successful wrestlers have been Sadaji Akiyoshi (b. 1912) *alias* Futabayama, winner of 69 consecutive bouts in the 1930s, Koki Naya (b. 1940) *alias* Taiho ('Great Bird'), who won the Emperor's Cup 32 times up to his retirement in 1971 and the *ozeki* Torokichi *alias* Raiden who in 21 years (1789–1810) won 254 bouts and lost only ten for the highest ever winning percentage of 96.2. Taiho and Futabayama share the record of eight perfect tournaments without a single loss. The youngest of the 59 men to attain the rank of *Yokozuna* (Grand Champion) was Toshimitsu Ogata (b. 16 May 1953) *alias* Kitanoumi, in July 1974 aged 21 years and two months. He set a record in 1978 winning 82 of the 90 bouts that top *rikishi* fight annually and has a career record 951 wins. Hawaiian born Jesse Kuhaulua (b. 16 June 1944), now a Japanese citizen named Daigoro Watanabe, *alias* Takamiyama was the first non-Japanese to win an official tournament in July 1972 and in 1981 set a record of 1231 consecutive top division bouts. He weighed in at 450 lb *204 kg* before his retirement in 1984.

YACHTING

Origins

Yachting in England dates from the £100 stake race between Charles II and his brother James, Duke of York, on the Thames on 1 Sept 1661 over 23 miles from Greenwich to Gravesend. The oldest club in the world is the Royal Cork Yacht Club (formerly the Cork Harbour Water Club), established in Ireland in 1720. The oldest active club in Britain is the Starcross Yacht Club at Powderham Point, Devon. Its first regatta was held in 1772.

Olympic titles *World*

The first sportsman ever to win individual gold medals in four successive Olympic Games was Paul B. Elvström (b. 24 Feb 1928) (Denmark) in the Firefly class in 1948 and the Finn class in 1952, 1956 and 1960. He also won eight other

world titles in a total of six classes. The lowest number of penalty points by the winner of any class in an Olympic regatta is three points (five wins, one disqualified and one second in seven starts) by *Superdocious* of the Flying Dutchman class (Lt. Rodney Stuart Pattisson RN (b. 5 Aug 1943) and Iain Somerled Macdonald-Smith (b. 3 July 1945)) at Acapulco Bay, Mexico in October 1968.

Olympic titles British

The only British yacht to win two titles was *Scotia* in the Open class and Half-One Ton class at the 1900 Regatta with Lorne Campbell Currie (1871–1926), and John H. Gretton (1867–1947). The only British yachtsman to win in two Olympic regattas is Rodney Pattisson in 1968 (*see above*) and again with *Superdoso* crewed by Christopher Davies (b. 29 June 1946) at Kiel, W. Germany in 1972. He gained a silver medal in 1976 with Julian Brooke Houghton (b. 16 Dec 1946).

Admiral's Cup

The ocean racing series with the most participating nations (three boats allowed to each nation) is the Admiral's Cup held by the Royal Ocean Racing Club. A record 19 nations competed in 1975, 1977 and 1979. Britain has a record eight wins.

America's Cup

The America's Cup was originally won as an outright prize by the schooner *America* on 22 Aug 1851 at Cowes and was later offered by the New York Yacht Club as a challenge trophy. On 8 Aug 1870 J. Ashbury's *Cambria* (GB) failed to capture the trophy from the *Magic*, owned by F. Osgood (USA). Since then the Cup has been challenged by Great Britain in 16 contests, in 2 contests by Canada, and by Australia 7 times, but the United States were undefeated winning 77 races and only losing eight until 1983 when *Australia II*, skippered by John Bertrand and owned by a Perth syndicate headed by Alan Bond beat *Liberty* 4–3, the narrowest series victory, at Newport, RI, USA. The closest race ever was the fourth race of the 1962 series, when the 12 metre sloop *Weatherly* beat her Australian challenger *Gretel* by about three and a half lengths, a margin of only 26 sec, on 22 Sept 1962. The fastest time ever recorded by a 12 metre boat for the triangular course of 24.3 sea miles is 2 hr 46 min 58 sec by *Gretel* in 1962.

Longest race

The longest regular sailing race is the quadrennial Whitbread Round the World race (inst. Aug 1973) organized by the Royal Naval Sailing Association. The distance is 26,180 nautical miles from Portsmouth, and return with stops and re-starts at Cape Town, Auckland and Mar del Plata. The record (sailing) time is 120 days 6 hr 35 min by *Flyer* crewed by Cornelis van Rietschoten (Netherlands), finishing on 29 Mar 1982 (*see also p. 165*).

Greatest distance

The greatest distance covered in a day's run under sail was set by the 81 foot *24,6 m* catamaran *Formula Tag* (skipper: Michael Birch). During the 1984 Transat TAG Race between Quebec and St Malo she covered 512.55 nautical miles in 23.70 hours for an average of 21.63 knots. She must have achieved at least 518 nm in the full 24 hours. For one period of 24.6 mins she averaged 31.68 knots.

Highest speeds

The official world sailing speed record is 36.04 knots (41.50 mph *66,78 km/h*) by the 73½ ft *22,40 m* proa *Crossbow II* over a 500 m *547 yd* course in Portland Harbour, Dorset, on 17 Nov 1980. The vessel (sail area 1400 ft² *130,06 m²*) was designed by Rod McAlpine-Downie and owned and steered by Timothy Colman. In an unsuccessful attempt on the record in October 1978, *Crossbow II* is reported to have momentarily attained a speed of 45 knots (51 mph *83 km/h*). The fastest 24 hr single-handed run by a sailing yacht was recorded by Nick Keig (b. 13 June 1936), of the Isle of Man, who covered 340 nautical miles in a 37½ ft *11,43 m* trimaran *Three Legs of Mann I* during the Falmouth to Punta, Azores race on 9–10 June 1975, averaging 14.16 knots (16.30 mph *26,23 km/h*). The fastest bursts of speed reached were about 25 knots (28.78 mph *46,32 km/h*).

Marinas, *Largest*

The largest marina in the world is that of Marina Del Rey, Los Angeles, California, USA, which has 7500 berths. The largest in Britain is the Brighton Marina, East Sussex, with 2313 berths.

Most competitors

The most boats ever to start in a single race was 1947, of which 1767 finished in the Round Zealand (Denmark) race on 17–20 June 1983, over a course of 375 km *233 miles*. The greatest number to start in a race in Britain was 1247 keeled yachts and multihulls on 29 June 1985 from Cowes in the Annual Round-the-Island race. The fastest time achieved in this annual event is 4 hr 40 min 45 sec by the 60 ft *18 m* trimaran *Apricot*, designed by Nigel Irens, and sailed by him and Tony Bullimore on 29 June 1985.

Highest

The greatest altitude at which sailing has taken place is 16,109 ft *4910 m* on Laguna Huallatani, Bolivia, in Mirror Dinghy 55448, variously by Peter Williams, Gordon Siddeley, Keith Robinson and Brian Barrett, on 19 Nov 1977. The highest for boardsailing is 4970 m *16,300 ft* by Juan Felipe Marti, Juan Ojeda, Fermin Tarres and Philippe Levrel on Tilicho's Lake, Nepal on 20 Oct 1983.

Boardsailing or windsurfing was introduced into the Olympics in 1984 with Stephan van den Berg (*above*) taking the title. (*All-Sport*)
John Stephenson (*below*) made the most northerly windsurf attempt at 76°N in the Arctic Circle. He is seen here negotiating a Greenland iceberg.

BOARDSAILING

Origins

The High Court ruled on 7 Apr 1982 that Peter Chilvers (when aged 12) had devised a prototype of a boardsailer in 1958 in England. In 1968 Henry Hoyle Schweitzer and Jim Drake pioneered the sport, often termed windsurfing, in California, USA. World championships were first held in 1973 and the sport was added to the Olympic Games in 1984 when the winner was Stephan van den Berg (Netherlands), who also won five world titles 1979–83.

English Channel

The record time for boardsailing across the English Channel is 1 hr 4 min 33 sec by Baron Arnaud de Rosnay (France) on 4 July 1982 from Cap Gris Nez to Dover at an average speed of 16.9 knots (19.5 mph *31,3 km/h*). After 45 mins rest he returned to Wissant, France in 1 hr 4 min 37 sec.

Highest Speed

The record speed for boardsailing is 32.35 knots *59,91 km/h* by Michael Pucher (Austria) at Port-Saint-Louis, Marseille, France on 17 Apr 1985 in a Force 9 wind. On the same occasion Peter Bridgeman set a British record of 31.89 knots *59,10 km/h* and Patti Wittcomb (USA) set a women's record of 27.28 knots *50,55 km/h*.

Endurance

Stéphane Peyron of France set an endurance record of 70 hr 3 min on 16–19 July 1984.

The longest wind surf ever made was by Timothy John Batstone (b. 22 Apr 1959) in circumnavigating 1794 miles *2887 kms* round Great Britain on 2 May–10 July 1984. He did 70 miles *112,6 kms* in a single stretch, made 40 sail changes and had zero falls on eight days.

Longest 'snake'

The longest 'snake' of boardsails was set by 51 windsurfers in tandem across Pembroke Bay, Guernsey on 22 July 1984.

ACTIVITY	NO. IN TEAM	DURATION	RECORD HOLDERS
Backgammon	Pair	151 hr 11 min	Dick Newcomb and Greg Peterson at Rockford, Illinois, USA, 30 June–6 July 1978
Badminton (*singles*)	Pair	74 hr 41 min	Mike Watts and Bryan Garnham at Swansea, 15–18 Oct 1981.
Badminton (*doubles*)	4	77 hr 1 min	Paul Farmer, Andrew Hood, Ben Smith and Loraine Storey at Chilwell, Nottingham, 29 May–1 June 1984
Basketball	5	102 hr	Sigma Nu Fraternity at Indiana University, Pennsylvania, USA, 13–17 Apr 1983.
Bingo calling	2	285 hr 24 min	Phillip Carter and Mark Kiely at the Top Rank Club, Kingston, Surrey, 8–20 May 1983.
Bowling (*Ten Pin*)	1	195 hr 1 min	Jim Webb at Gosford City Bowl, New South Wales, Australia, 1984.
Bowls (*outdoor*)	4	90 hr 1 min	Two teams from Loyal Order of Moose, Carmarthen Lodge at Carmarthen Bowling Club, Wales, 16–20 Sept 1983.
Bowls (*indoor*)	4	75 hr	Two teams from Elgin Indoor Bowling Club, Morayshire, Scotland, 9–12 Aug 1984.
Bridge (*Contract*)	4	180 hr	Four students at Edinburgh University, 21–28 Apr 1972.
Chess	Pair	200 hr	Roger Long and Graham Croft at Dingles, Bristol, 11–19 May 1984.
Cribbage	4	120 hr	Geoff Lee, Ken Whyatt, Ray Charles and Paul Branson at Mapperley, Nottingham, 16–21 Mar 1982.
Cricket	11	316 hr	Two teams from Belper, Derbyshire, 14–27 Aug 1983.
Croquet	4	113 hr 25 min	Hilary Lund-Yates, Hilary Cuthbert, Simon Clay and Roger Swift at Birmingham University, 18–23 June 1983.
Curling	4	67 hr 55 min	Capital Winter Club, Fredericton, New Brunswick, Canada, 9–12 Apr 1982.
	Pair	38 hr	Jim Paul and Chris McCrady at the Brockville Country Club, Ontario, Canada, 26–28 Mar 1982.
Darts	Pair	133 hr 13 min	Trevor Blair and Keith Palmer at Bingham Leisure Centre, Notts, 2–7 March 1985.
Dominoes	Pair	137 hr 10 min	Sammy Riley and John Ireland at the Longford Hotel, Warrington, Cheshire, 27 May–1 June 1985.
Draughts	Pair	108 hr	Tony Johnston and Steve Abbott at Hatfield Polytechnic, Herts, 28 Jan–1 Feb 1985.
Fives (*Rugby*)	Pair	31 hr	J. S. R. Macdonnell and N. J. Parfit at Sherborne School, Dorset, 25–26 March 1985.
Football (*Soccer*)	11	65 hr 1 min	Callinafercy Soccer Club, Co. Kerry, Ireland, 1–3 Aug 1980.
(*outdoor*)	5	74 hr 30 min	Two teams at Liswerry Leisure Centre, Newport, Gwent, Wales, 23–26 June 1983.
(*indoor*)	5	104 hr 10 min	Two teams from the A.C.E. '83 group, at Summerhill College, Sligo, Ireland, 27–31 Mar 1983.
Handball	11	40 hr	Two teams from Meervogels '60 club, Akersloot, Holland, 15–16 May 1985.
Hockey (*outdoor*)	11	35 hr 23 min	Two teams from Hilson Park Hockey Club in Johannesburg, South Africa, 25–26 June 1983.
Hockey (*indoor*)	6	44 hr 19 min	Cecil Jones High School, Southend, Essex, 15–17 March 1985.
Horsemanship	1	101 hr	Michael Jones at Redruth Plains, Queensland, Australia, 19–23 June 1984.
Ice skating	1	109 hr 5 min	Austin McKinley at Christchurch, New Zealand, 21–25 June 1977.
Judo	Pair	245 hr 30 min	Five of six people at Smithfield RSL Youth Club, New South Wales, Australia, 3–13 Jan 1984.
Monopoly (*Parker Bros.*)	4	660 hr	Caara Fritz, Randy Smith, Phil Bennett and Terry Sweatt at Atlanta, Georgia, USA, 12 July–8 Aug 1981.
Netball	7	38 hr	The 'Pan-Ems' at the Emerton Youth Centre, Mt. Druitt, NSW, Australia, 30 Sept–1 Oct 1984.
Pool	Pair	300 hr 16 min	Barry Wicks and Derek Shaw; also Paul Haslam and Vincent Moore at the New Inn, Galgate, Lancaster, 21 May–2 June 1984. (384 hr 3 min by Christopher Pearman and Mark Lemm in Horbury, West Yorks, 2–18 Aug 1984 but with rest break discrepancy).
Racquetball	Pair	40 hr 22 min	Daryl Houlden and Eddy Oogjes at Rochester, Victoria, Australia, 20–22 July 1984.
Roller Skating	1	344 hr 18 min	Isamu Furugen at Naha Roller Skate Land, Okinawa, Japan, 11–27 Dec 1983.
Scrabble	Pair	153 hr	Peter Finan and Neil Smith at St. Anselm's College, Wirral, Merseyside, 18–25 Aug 1984.
Skiing (*Alpine*)	1	138 hr	Luc Labrie at Daie Comeau, Quebec, Canada, 20–25 Feb 1984.
Skiing (*Alpine*)	Pair	82 hr 9 min	With no waiting for lifts—John Rutter and Andrew Hampel at Silverwood Winter Park, New Brunswick, Canada, 25–28 Jan 1984.
Skittles	6	168 hr	Gloucester & District Irish Society at Gloucester, 15–22 Aug 1981.
Snooker	Pair	300 hr 30 min	Sam Ellis and Glyn Travis at Bridlington Snooker Centre, Humberside, 14–26 May 1985.
Softball (*fast pitch*)	9	57 hr	Two teams from Austin, Minnesota, USA, 24–26 July 1981.
Softball (*slow pitch*)	10	95 hr	Two teams from the crew of USS Willamette (A0180) at US Naval Station, Pearl Harbour, Hawaii, 26–30 April 1984.
Squash	2	121 hr 16 min	Paul Holmes and Andy Head at Hove Squash Club, Hove, Sussex, 18–23 Apr 1984.
Table Football	Pair	57 hr 2 min	Brian Rankin and Trevor Spencer at Sportsshoes Unlimited, Bradford, Yorkshire, 18–20 July 1985.
Table Tennis	Pair	147 hr 47 min	S. Unterslak and J. Boccia at Dewaal Hotel, Cape Town, South Africa, 12–18 Nov 1983.
	Doubles	101 hr 1 min	Lance, Phil and Mark Warren and Bill Weir at Sacramento, Cal., USA, 9–13 Apr 1979.
Tennis (*Lawn*)	Pair	117 hr	Mark and Jim Pinchoff at the Fitness Resort, Lafayette, Louisiana, USA, 14–19 May 1985.
	Doubles	96 hr 25 min	Ann Wilkinson, Peter Allsopp, John Thorpe and David Dicks at Mansfield Lawn Tennis Club, Notts, 17–21 Aug 1983.
Tiddlywinks	6	300 hr	Southampton University Tiddlywinks Club, 20 Feb–5 Mar 1981.
Trampolining	1	266 hr 9 min	Jeff Schwartz at Glenview, Illinois, USA, 14–25 Aug 1981.
Volleyball	6	84 hr	Two teams from Beta Theta Pi fraternity, Bethany College, Bethany, West Virginia, 27–30 Sept 1984.
Water Polo	7	24 hr 50 min	Two teams from Puyallup High School, Washington, USA, 12–13 Oct 1984.

IMPORTANT

Rest breaks of five minutes for each completed hour played (not calculated according to a running total) are permitted in these endurance marathons. Such breaks are aggregable but at no time can the earned rest period be exceeded. The number of participants in team events is shown in the table, all must be in action throughout the attempt, except that a drop out rate of up to 20% of the people is permitted. No substitutes are allowed. Claims for new records must be accompanied by full authentication.

Marathon record holders (*from top to bottom*) in tennis singles, tenpin bowling and lawn bowls: Mark Pinchoff, Jim Webb and Carmarthen Lodge.

STOP PRESS

CHAPTER 1

HUMAN BEING

MOST VARIABLE STATURE (p. 11) Lord Adare (4th Earl of Dunraven and Mount-Earl, b. 12 Feb 1841, d. 14 June 1926) recorded that the Scots-born medium Daniel Home (b. 1833) elongated his body 11 inches *28 cm*.

HEAVYWEIGHTS (p. 11) T. J. Albert Jackson (b. 22 lb *9,97 kg* Kent Nicholson in Mississippi) claimed a weight of 'nearly 900 pounds' *408 kg* in March 1985—so rivalling Albert Pernitsch.

OLDEST TWINS (p. 14) Mildred died on 4 May 1985 44 days short of the twins' would-be 105th birthday. The odds against centenarian twins have now probably shortened to about 500 million to 1.

LARGEST BICEPS (p. 17–18) Gary Aprahamian died on 13 June 1985.

LONGEST MOUSTACHE (p. 19) Birger Pellas's moustache had reached 2,59 m *8 ft 5 in* on 26 Apr 1985.

FAST TALKING (p. 20) John Helm of Yorkshire TV can recite the 92 Football League clubs in 26 sec.

LONGEST COMA (p. 21) It was reported in early Jan 1985 that Alice Collins (b. 1891) of Columbia, South Carolina, USA had revived, having lapsed into a coma 75 years 2 months earlier. She had fallen down two flights of stairs in Oct 1909.

LEADING CAUSE OF DEATH (p. 21) Deaths from diseases of the circulatory system totalled 278,849 in England and Wales in 1984.

HICCOUGHING (p. 22) In Feb 1985 Charles Osborne was reported to be down to 10 hics per minute from his earlier high of 40.

PILL TAKING (p. 23) Mr Kilner's total rose to an estimated 442,700 by 1 Jan 1985.

MOST OPERATIONS (p. 23) Joseph Ascough underwent his 328th operation on 4 July 1985—this time a laser beam was used.

CHAPTER 2

LIVING WORLD

COMMONEST CRUSTACEANS (p. 27) In 1985 the standing stock of krill in the southern ocean was estimated at 650 million tonnes.

OLDEST ELEPHANT (p. 28) Nepal's royal elephant 'Prem Prased' died in Katmandu on 27 Feb 1985 aged 81 years.

TALLEST HORSE (p. 32) For 19 hand read 19.1½ h.h.

DOG FUNERAL (p. 33 in 31st Edition) Researches by Malcolm E. Barker, author of 'Bummer & Lazarus: San Francisco's Famous Dogs', showed the reported funeral in October 1863 to be journalistic invention.

LARGEST CAT (UK) (p. 34) 'Poppa' died on 25 June 1985.

SMALLEST RABBITS (p. 35) The smallest breeds of domestic rabbit are the Netherland dwarf and the Polish, both of which have a weight range of 2–2½ lb *0,9–1,13 kg* when fully grown.

CHAMPION BIRD SPOTTER (p. 37) Mr Chesterfield's total was 6,161 by 1 Apr 1985.

HIGHEST FLYING BIRDS (p. 37) The reported collision of a Ruppell's griffon (Gyps ruepelli) with an aeroplane at 37,000 ft *11,277 m* over Abidjan, Ivory Coast, in 1973 remains unacceptable to some leading experts.

LONGEST FROG JUMP (p. 40) 'Weird Harold, trained by Janet Seiber, achieved 21 ft 1½ in *6,43 m* at Angels Camp, California, USA on 20 May 1985. Caption: for Sabaterpi read Sabater Pi.

MOST VALUABLE FISH (p. 41) The current price of Royal Beluga caviare is £1200.

SMALLEST STARFISH (p. 41) A *Patnella parvivipora* discovered by W. Zeidler on the west side of the Eyre Peninsula, South Australia in 1975 has a maximum radius of 4,7 mm *0.18 in.*

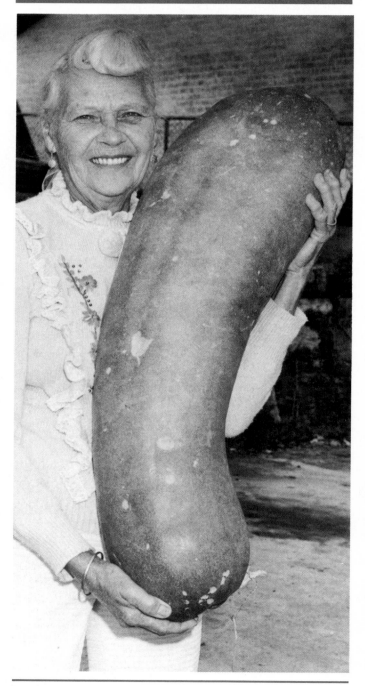

Move over Texas! Mrs Eileen Chappel achieves the rare distinction of doubling a world record (formerly held in Texas) with her monster 17 kg *37¼ lb* cucumber in Queensland, Australia. *(Brisbane Telegraph)*

TOUGHEST INSECT (p. 43) The larva of the chironomid fly *Polypedilum vanderplanki* can tolerate temperatures from 103°C *217°F* to −270°C −*486°F.*

EARLIEST REPTILE (p. 45) 15 inch *38,1 cm* long insectivor from south central Kentucky, USA, discovered in 1972, was confirmed on 22 Oct 1984 as dating from 310 million years ago.

LONGEST DAISY CHAIN (p. 48) 6,980 ft 7 in *2,12 km* by villagers of Good Easter, Chelmsford, Essex on 27 May 1985.

LARGEST CUCUMBER (INDOOR) (p. 50) Mrs Eileen Chappel grew a 17 kg *37 lb 4 oz* monster at Nudgee, Queensland, Australia in the six months before it was weighed on 29 Apr 1985.

LARGEST PUMPKIN (p. 50) Norman Gallagher of Chalen, Washington, USA grew a 612 lb *277,6 kg* monster 135 in *3,42 m* in girth for the 10th annual World Championship in Half Moon Bay, San Francisco, California, USA on 8 Oct 1984. Amend UK record holder to 444 lb *201,4 kg.*

LARGEST AQUARIUM (p. 53) The $40 million Monterey Bay Aquarium, California, USA opened on 2 Oct 1985, is now the largest. The two biggest tanks hold 335,000 and 326,000 US gallons.

SMALLEST VIRUSES (p. 53) Dr Rohwer of Bethesda, Maryland, USA stated in Sept 1984 that scrapie-specific protein was smaller than the concept of yet to be identified 'prion'.

CHAPTER 3

NATURAL WORLD

DEEPEST OCEAN (p. 58) A Japanese survey vessel in Mar 1983 reassessed the Marianas Trench at 10 924 m *35,840 ft.*

CHAPTER 4

UNIVERSE & SPACE

LIGHT YEAR (p. 65) For km/s^{-1} read km s^{-1}.

CHAPTER 5

SCIENTIFIC WORLD

CHEMICAL COMPOUNDS (p. 73) Highest ductility in tension (superplasticity)—aluminium bronze 55 times by Y. Natatani, T. Ohnishi and K. Higashi, University of Osaka 1983.

MOST ACCURATE VERSION OF pi (π) (p. 76) A calculation to 16,777,216 places was announced by Yasumasa Kanada and Y. Tamura after 30 hours on the main frame computer in Tokyo University on 24 July 1985.

DIAMONDS (p. 78) The Argyle field, Western Australia yielded 6.2 million carats in 1983 and 5.7 million in 1984 and is now the most prolific in the world.

RUBY (p. 78) In July 1985 the jeweller James Kazanjian of Beverly Hills, California, displayed a 5½ inch *14 cm* tall 8500 carat ruby carved into the Liberty Bell.

CHAPTER 6

ARTS & ENTERTAINMENTS

MOST EXPENSIVE PAINTING (Australian Supplement p. 318) *Melbourne Burning* by Arthur Boyd (b. Murrumbeena, Victoria 1920) set an auction record for an Australian painting by a living artist when it sold for $A285,000 (*£141,439*) at Sotheby's, Melbourne on 31 July 1985. This is also the highest price for an Australian painting sold in Australia and was bought by the businessman Robert Holmes à Court.

LARGEST POSTER (pp. 79–80) On 7 Oct 1984 students of Osaka Gakun University in Osaka, Japan constructed a poster of 2071 m² (40,24 × 51,47 m) or *3,764 ft² (132 ft × 168 ft 10 in*).

EARLIEST LANGUAGE (p. 82) The earliest known piece of English writing (c. 630 AD) is a fragment of Irish uncial script in an ecclesiastical history sold for £75,000 by the Folger Shakespeare Library, Washington DC to the British Rail Pension Fund at Sotheby's, London on 25 June 1985.

WORDS LONGEST (p. 83) By mid-July 1985 Simon Proctor of Maidstone, Kent raised H. W. Jones's record to 15,592 excluding plurals.

TERMINALITY (p. 85) The 1985 S to Z London Telephone Directory includes the 'Zzzzzz' Coffee Shop in Gray's Inn Road, WC1.

LARGEST PUBLICATION (p. 86) The price rose to £53,500 by mid-July 1985.

MOST PROLIFIC AUTHOR (p. 87) For 429,425 pages read 42,468 pages.

NEWSPAPERS (p. 90) Sweden's consumption had risen to 580 for every 1000 inhabitants by mid-1985.

POP ATTENDANCE (p. 93) The total attendance at Michael Jackson's 'Victory Tour' in the United States, July–Dec 1984, brought in a record tour gross revenue of $81 million (*then £67.5 million*).

LONGEST RUNNING REVIEW (p. 96) The total number of performances of *The Golden Horseshoe Review* had reached 45,051 by 9 Aug 1985.

BEST SELLING ALBUMS (p. 98) Sales of *Thriller* had reached 38.5 million by 1 Aug 1985.

HIGHEST BOX OFFICE GROSS (p. 100) for 25 May read 25 May 1983.

TV WATCHING (p. 102) The National Coalition on TV Violence published an estimate in June 1985 that, by its 16th birthday, the average US child will have seen 50,000 TV murders or attempted murders and 200,000 acts of violence. Between the ages of 2 and 11 the average viewing time is 27.3 hours per week.

TV PRODUCER (p. 103) Aaron Spelling's output by mid 1985 rose to more than 1580 TV episodes totalling 2037 hours of air time, as well as 199½ hours of TV movies and 3 feature films. The total 2237 broadcast hours is equal to 12.1 million feet *3688 km* of film and, projected 24 hours a day, it would take 93.4 days—just over 3 months—to screen it all. The average American TV is turned on 6 hours per day. At that rate, Spelling has produced enough film to last 374 days.

TV SCREEN LARGEST (p. 103) The Sony Jumbo Tron colour TV screen at the Tsukuba International Exposition '85 near Tokyo in March 1985 measured 80 ft × 150 ft *24,3 m × 45,7 m*.

CHAPTER 7

STRUCTURES

AMUSEMENT RESORT (p. 110) Attendance at Disneyland, Anaheim, California reached 248,784,456 by 4 Aug 1985.

BIG WHEEL (p. 110) The 85 m *278 ft 10 in* diameter wheel installed in the City of Tsukuba, Japan by Senyo Kogyo Co has a capacity of 384 persons.

CHAPTER 8

MECHANICAL WORLD

LARGEST CAR FERRY (p. 123) The 36,200 grt *M/S Mariella*, built in Åbo, Finland, went into service on 18 May 1985. She can carry 2500 passengers, 600 cars or trailers and is 177 m *580.7 ft* long and 29 m *95.1 ft* in the beam.

PETROL CONSUMPTION (p. 126) On 9 July 1985 the Mechanical Engineering Department of King's College, London won the Shell-*Motor* magazine prize at Silverstone, Northants with 4,010 miles per gallon *1419 km/litre*.

MOST EXPENSIVE USED CAR (p. 127) At Sotheby's, New York on 29 June 1985 John Lennon's 1965 Phantom V Rolls Royce, painted in a psychedelic floral motif, was sold for $2,299,000 (then £1,768,000) to Jim Pattison, Chairman of the Expo '86 World Fair in Vancouver, Canada.

LONGEST PRODUCTION (p. 127) Mini sales reached 4,980,000 by July 1985. Bernard Ferriman, 83, sold his own preproduction model, the first ever built, for £2,500 on 5 Aug 1985. The off-white vehicle, which he bought for £296 in 1962, went to car distributors Penta of Reading.

OLDEST AND YOUNGEST DRIVERS (p. 128) Mark Collins Hall of Otley, West Yorks, passed his test on 24 July 1985 aged 16 years 103 days. Mark Blackbourn of Lincoln having passed his driving test the day after his 17th birthday went on to pass the advanced test less than 48 hours later on 7 Aug 1985. Mrs Jack was still driving in 1985 aged 97.

CHAPTER 9

BUSINESS WORLD

GREATEST LOSS (p. 146) The NCB loss published on 29 July 1985 proved to be £2,225 million.

STOCK EXCHANGES (p. 150) The Dow Jones hit 1359.54 on 19 July 1985.

GOLD AT AUCTION (p. 154) The highest price for any gold artefact is £950,400 for the 22 carat font made by Paul Storr to the design of Humphrey Repton in 1797. It was sold by Lady Anne Cavendish-Bentinck and bought by Armitage of London at Christie's on 11 July 1985.

FASTEST PLOUGHING (pp. 156–7) On 1 Nov 1984 at Hodstock Priory Farm, Blythe, Nottinghamshire, Robert Dee using a Fiat 180-90 DT tractor ploughed 1.104 acres in 11 min 21.8 sec.

WOOL PRICE (p. 158) Fuji Keori Ltd of Osaka, Japan bought a bale of Saxon Merino wool at Launceston, Tasmania on 28 Feb 1985 for a world record $A168 (*then £111*) per kg greasy.

SEPTUPLET LAMBS (p. 160) A Border Leicester-Merino crossbred ewe owned by Roger Saunders gave birth to 4 ram and 3 ewe live lambs at Strathdownie, Victoria, Australia on 19 June 1984.

CHAPTER 10

HUMAN ACHIEVEMENTS

PARTY GIVING (p. 167) The record was increased to 206,854 at the same venue on 11–17 Mar 1985.

WORKING CAREER (pp. 167–8) Mrs Moody died on 5 Aug 1985.

BUBBLE GUM BLOWING (p. 169) Susan Montgomery Williams of Fresno, California, USA raised her own record to 22 in *55,8 cm* in June 1985. Vasnik Bains of Southall, Middlesex set an inaugural record of 10.1 in *25¾ cm*, using 3 pieces of Bubblicious soft bubble gum, on 22 June 1985 at *The Guinness World of Records* permanent exhibition at the Trocadero, Piccadilly, London.

ONE MAN BAND (p. 168) The duration record was extended to 77 hr 2 min by Sadhak Hurst, 32 in Brisbane, Australia on 5–8 June 1985.

BARROW PUSHING (p. 168) John Sarich of London, Ontario, Canada on 29 June 1985 pushed 5400 lb *2450 kg* of bricks in a 700 lb *317,5 kg* barrow for 56 ft 8 in *17,27 m*.

BED OF NAILS (p. 169) The duration record was improved to 274 hr 2 min by Inge Widar Svinger ending on TV's 'Good Morning Norway' programme on 3 Nov 1984.

BEER LABEL COLLECTING (p. 169) Jan Solberg of Oslo has amassed 218,600 different labels from around the world.

BEER MAT FLIPPING (p. 169) For Repton read Brewery Vaults, Burton-on-Trent, Staffs.

BRICK CARRYING (p. 169) Reg Morris of Walsall covered 61¾ miles *99,37 km* with a 9 lb *4,08 kg* brick in the West Midlands on 16 July 1985.

COIN SNATCHING (p. 170) Dean Gould of Felixstowe, Suffolk on 31 May 1985 snatched 78 coins in the same style as Andrew Gleed. This category is now retired in favour of the international style in which the coins must be caught palm down in a single downward sweep.

DOMINO TOPPLING (p. 172) A further study of the video tape of the event of 26 Mar 1985 has caused a reconsideration of the claim which is thus in abeyance.

GRAPE CATCHING (p. 173) Paul Tavilla (b. 1934) was reported on 9 July 1985 to have caught a grape in his mouth tossed from the 38 storey Shawmut Bank Building, Boston, Mass from a height of 520 ft 5 in *158,62 m*.

HIGH DIVING (p. 174) Roy Fransen (b. 1915) was killed at Cranford, Middlesex on 6 July 1985 while performing his high dive stunt.

HANDBELL RINGING (p. 174) Ecclesfield School extended their record to 56 hr on 21–23 July 1985.

PARACHUTING RECORDS (p. 177) On 16 June 1985 23 parachutists achieved a 'canopy formation' stack over Houston Gulf Airport, Texas, USA having exited at 15,000 ft *4572 m*. David Huber made 250 jumps in 24 hrs over Issaquah, Washington State, USA on 3–4 July 1985.

PLANE PULLING (p. 179) Dave Gauder, 30, frustrated the take-off of two Piper Cherokees by holding two tow ropes despite a pull of 612 kg *1349 lb* at Bobbington, Staffs on 16 July 1985.

POLE-SQUATTING (p. 179) Mark Sutton finally descended on 1 July 1985 after 488 days.

SKIPPING (p. 180) The endurance record was extended to 12 hr 34 min by Randall Schneider on 2 Aug 1985 in Janesville, Wisconsin, USA.

SPITTING (p. 180) Jeff Barber won a record 13th National Spitting title at Raleigh, Miss. on 29 June 1985.

SUGGESTION BOXES (p. 181) Mr Drayton's total rose to 31,253 by 12 June 1985.

SUBMERGENCE (p. 181) The continuous duration record using 'Scuba' was extended to 112 hr 33 min by sub-officer Roger Cragg, 39, of East Sussex Fire Brigade on 2–7 July 1985 in a Royal Navy tank on Hastings seafront.

GLUTTONY (pp. 184–5) Mr Dowdeswell has lowered his own record times thus: **3 pint yard** 5.00 sec, Royal Oak, Bishop's Cleeve, Gloucestershire, 6 July 1985; **3½ pint yard** 5.44 secs Easby Street, Nottingham, 5 July 1985; **Strawberries** 2 lb in 12.95 secs, Easby Street, Nottingham, 5 July 1985. **Shrimps** 3 lb *1,36 kg* in 3 min 10 sec at Weymouth, Dorset on 7 Aug. 1985. **Oysters** 6 lb *2,72 kg* (edible mass of 288) in 1 min 33 sec by Tommy Greene in Annapolis, Maryland on 6 July 1985. **Snails** 1 kg *35.27 oz* in 2 min 43 sec at Hamilton's Brasserie, London by Tommy 'Muskrat' Greene on 14 Aug 1985.

DFC TABLE (p. 186) Add A M Sir Harold Martin KCB DSO* DFC** AFC (1918–1985).

CHAPTER 11

HUMAN WORLD

LIFE EXPECTATION (p. 191) The Japanese male expectation of life was reported to have reached 74 years in July 1985.

CITIES (p. 192) The largest city in the world in AD 790 was between Ch'ang-an, China, Baghdad, Iraq and Constantinople, Turkey (per *Times Atlas of World History*).

HEAVIEST MONARCH (p. 193) The King of Tonga was reported in July 1985 to have succeeded in slimming down to 380 lb *172 kg*.

LONGEST TERM OF OFFICE (p. 195) Pyotr Lomako (b. 1904) has served in the government of the USSR as Minister for Non-Ferrous Metallurgy from 1940. He was still in place in July 1985.

SUICIDE (p. 205) The suicide total for England and Wales in 1984 was 4,315 or 11.7 per day.

BALANCE OF PAYMENTS (p. 208) The US adverse balance was $123 million (then £102.5 billion) in 1984 and forecast to $150 billion (£125 billion) in 1985.

NATIONAL DEBT (p. 208) By 1 Jan 1985 US citizens were in debt for $5.243 trillion compared with the federal debt of $1.902 trillion.

MOST FOREIGN DEBT (p. 208) Brazil's debt had reached $103 billion by mid-1985.

WORST DEFICIT (p. 208) The US deficit was reportedly running at $213 billion in July 1985.

CHARITY FUND RAISING (p. 209) The globally televised 'Live Aid' concerts, organised by Bob Geldof and Bill Graham, with 60 rock acts in Philadelphia and London on 20 July 1985, raised £35 million within two weeks with an estimated further £50 million to come for famine relief. The estimated viewership, via a record 12 satellites, 1.6 billion or one-third of the world's population.

LARGEST HOARDS (p. 209) On 20 July two sons of Mel Fisher found the main cargo of the Spanish *Nuestra Senhora de Atocha* sunk off Key West, Florida in 1622. The value of the cargo already recovered was $80 million but is now expected to attain close to $400 million mainly in silver bars. The EIC Diving Group announced in July 1985 that they have recovered 6 tons or 1,030,000 copper coins from the wreck of the *Admiral Gardner* which sank on the Goodwin Sands, off Kent on 25 Jan 1809.

Roger Cragg signals receipt of the newsflash from the surface that after more than 4 days he has broken the continuous scuba submergence record. (see col. 3)

LARGEST ASSOCIATION (WORLD) (p. 210) Membership at 1 Jan 1985 was 79,500,000 and benefits paid out in 1984 were $35,743,907,000.

BANANA SPLIT (p. 210) 2.88 miles *4,63 km*, including 24,000 bananas at Olympia, Washington, USA on 28 July 1985.

STRAWBERRY BOWL (p. 210) A 'bowl' of 513 lb *232,7 kg* of strawberries was filled at Battle, East Sussex on 4 July 1985.

YORKSHIRE PUDDING (p. 210) The record was one of 105.8 ft² *9,82 m²* made at Scarborough, North Yorks on 1 Aug 1985. The monster pudding of 44 dozen eggs, 87 lb of flour and 29 gal of milk was sliced up to raise £1000 for Ethiopian famine relief.

YOUNGEST UNDERGRADUATE AND GRADUATE (p. 214) Ruth Lawrence (St Hugh's, Oxford) graduated with a first class degree, top of 191 entrants, on 4 July 1985.

MOST SUCCESSFUL TEACHER (p. 214) Cyril Leonard Mapley (b. 22 May 1923), Head of the Drawing Office at Tunbridge Wells Technical High School, Kent, has achieved an 'A' level pass rate unmatched by others. In 1981 49 out of 53 (91%) in his classes in their fifth year gained 'A' levels in one-eighth normal time and thus two years in advance of the entry age.

ACCIDENTS AND DISASTERS (p. 218) The crash of JAL's Boeing 747, flight 123, near Tokyo on 12 Aug 1985, in which 520 passengers and crew perished, was the worst single plane crash in aviation history.

CHAPTER 12

SPORTS, GAMES & PASTIMES

BASEBALL (p. 226)Nolan Ryan achieved his 4000th career strikeout in July 1985.

CHESS (p. 229) The latest ELO ratings rate Karpov first at 2720 from Kasparov 2700; highest ranked British player is John Nunn at 2600.

BOARD GAMES—SCRABBLE (p. 230) A game score of 849 was achieved by Maurice Rocker in the South Yorkshire Open Championships on 6 July 1985.

SKITTLES (p. 231) Long Alley score by Flintstones Skittle team was 29,409.

CANOEING (p. 234) Most world titles by British canoeist—Richard Fox won the world men's K1 slalom title for the third time in 1985.

CANOEING (p. 235) 1000 Eskimo Rolls in 44 min 7 sec by Steve Flint; 100 Hand Rolls in 2 min 55 sec by Michael Wynne; both at Larkfield Leisure Centre, Maidstone, Kent on 18 July 1985.

CARD GAMES—BRIDGE (p. 235) Barry Crane was killed in July 1985; his record total of master points was 35,137.6. The ACBL rankings are now led by Paul Soloway with 23,848.1 points.

CRICKET (p. 239) Wicket-keeping—David Edward East (b. 27 July 1959) equalled the world record by catching eight Somerset batsmen in one innings for Essex at Taunton on 27 July 1985.

CRICKET (p. 240) Lowest completed innings total in Nat West Trophy: 39 Ireland *v.* Sussex at Hove on 3 July 1985.

CYCLING (p. 243) Highest speed ever achieved on a bicycle—152.284 mph *245,077 km/h* by John Howard (USA) at Bonneville Salt Flats, Utah, USA on 20 July 1985.
(p. 244) Tour de France—Bernard Hinault equalled the record with his fifth win, 1978–9, 1981–2, 1985. World outdoor records achieved at Colorado Springs, USA: men—amateur unpaced flying start 200 m: 10.10 Lutz Hesslich (GDR) on 7 July, 1 km: 59.50 Shaun Wallace (GB) (b. 20 Nov 1961) on 5 July; women—unpaced flying start 200 m: 11.398 Connie Paraskevin (USA) on 7 July. World outdoor professional 5 km unpaced standing start: 5:45.646 Hans-Henrik Oersted (Denmark) at Bassano del Grappa, Italy on 19 July 1985. Jonathan Boyer cycled across America in a record 9 days 2 hr 6 min in July 1985.

FENCING (p. 247) Cornelia Hanisch (W. Germany) (b 12 June 1952) won three women's world foil titles, 1979, 1981 and 1985.

FOOTBALL—AMERICAN (p. 249) Herschel Walker set a seasons 'yards gained rushing' record of 2411 yards in the USFL for the New Jersey Generals in 1985.

FOOTBALL—ASSOCIATION (p. 255) Penlake Junior Football Club have remained unbeaten for 131 games (winning 130, drawing one) in the Warrington Hilden Friendly League, 1981–5.

FOOTBALL—RUGBY UNION (p. 257) On 18 Nov 1984 in Group 9 of the French Third Division, Laverdac beat Vergt by 350 points (66 tries, 40 conversions, two drop goals) to nil. Vergt kicked off and then stood still all afternoon in protest against the French Rugby Federation's decision to ban four of their players.

GYMNASTICS (p. 264) 25,753 Press-Ups by Paul Lynch at the Hippodrome Club, London on 18 July 1985.

GYMNASTICS (p. 264) Sit ups: Mark Norman Allan Paul Pfelz did 45,005 at Baltimore, Maryland on 26–28 July 1985 (though in 58 hr 15 min at a much slower rate than Louis Scripa's previous record).

HARNESS RACING (p. 265) Pacing world race record 1 mile—1:50.6 also by *Nihilator* at Meadowlands, New Jersey, USA on 19 July 1985.

HORSE RACING (p. 266) A record $13.1 million for a yearling was paid by a group headed by Robert Sangster for a colt by *Nijinsky* out of *My Charmer* at the Keeneland Sales, Lexington, Kentucky, USA on 23 July 1985.
(p. 267) King George VI & Queen Elizabeth Stakes—Trainer Dick Hern, a record fourth win 1985.
(p. 268) On 1 Aug 1985 Henry Cecil passed his own record for record prize money by a trainer in a season.

KARATE (p. 272) Top exponents: David Donovan, British national coach is 7th Dan *Ishinryu*.

MOTOR CYCLING (p. 274) Freddie Spencer (USA) became, in 1985, the first man ever to win world titles at both 250 cc and 500 cc in the same year.

MOTOR RACING (p. 276) The British Grand Prix at Silverstone on 21 July produced record Grand Prix speeds. The race was won by Alain Prost in a McLaren at an average speed of 146.274 mph *235,405 km/h*. A qualifying lap record was set on 20 July by Keke Rosberg (Finland) in a Williams-Honda of 1 min 05.91 sec, an average speed of 160.925 mph *258,983 km/h*.

PARASCENDING (p. 279) On 1 Aug 1985 at Artesia Airport, New Mexico, USA Andrew Wakelin set records for distance—7300 m, height gain—400 m and duration—19 min 33 sec on a Scorcerer 33 canopy on a 1600 ft line.

ROLLER SKATING (p. 281) Most British titles: Michael McGeogh and John Fry had won 19 titles to 1985. Chloe Ronaldson's total was 40 individual and 14 team titles.

ROLLER SKATING (p. 281) Annie Lambrechts (Belgium) skated the greatest distance in 1 hour, 37,097 km *23.051 miles* at Louvain in July 1985.

SPEEDWAY (p. 287) Erik Gundersen (Denmark) (b. 8 Oct 1959) became in 1985 the first man to hold simultaneously titles at singles, pairs, team and long-track events.

SWIMMING (p. 289) World 50 m best: 22.52 Dano Halsell (Switzerland) (b. 16 Feb 1963) at Bellinzona, Switzerland on 21 July 1985.

SWIMMING (p. 289) World record men's 100 m freestyle: 48.95 Matthew Biondi (USA) at Mission Viejo, Cal., USA on 7 Aug 1985. Men's 200 m butterfly: 1:56.65 Michael Gross at Sofia, Bulgaria on 10 Aug 1985.

TRACK & FIELD ATHLETICS (pp. 296 & 299) World and British record 2000 metres: 4:51.39 Steven Cram, Budapest, Hungary 4 Aug 1985. British record: 3000

In one of the greatest races in athletics history Steve Cram (right) smashed the world record for 1500 metres with 3:29.67, as he and Said Aouita (left), 3:29.71, became the first to run the distance in less than 3½ minutes. Cram went on to set two more world records, at 1 mile and 2000 metres, in just 19 days. Aouita went on to take a hundreth of a second off Dave Moorcroft's 5000 m world record. (*All-Sport/Steve Powell*)

metres steeplechase: 8:13.50 Colin Reitz, Budapest 4 Aug 1985. (p. 296) World record men's high jump: 2·40 m *7 ft 10¼ in* Rudolf Povarnitsin (USSR) at Donetsk, USSR on 11 Aug 1985.

TRACK AND FIELD (p. 299) British men's discus record: 65,16 m *213 ft 10 in* Richard Slaney at Eugene, Oregon, USA on 1 July 1985.
(p. 302) Arvind Pandya of India ran backwards across America, Los Angeles to New York, in 107 days, 18 Aug–3 Dec 1984.

WATERSKIING (pp. 304—5) Women's Tricks, World Record: 8350 by Ana Maria Carrasco (Venezuela) at McCormick Lake, Florida on 14 Sept 1984.

WEIGHTLIFTING (p. 306) A squat record of 2,168,625 kg *4,780,994 lb* in 24 hr was set by a team of ten from Ware Boys' Club, Ware, Herts. on 20–1 July 1985.

POWERLIFTING (p. 306) Women's World records: 52 kg squat 172,5 kg Sisi Dolman 1984. British records men bench press: 60 kg–142,5 kg C. Lewis 1985; 100 kg–225 kg A. Stevens 1985; 125 kg–237,5 kg S. Spillane 1985. British records women: Squat 60 kg–160 kg R. Bass 1985; Bench press 48 kg–75 kg S. Smith 1985; 52 kg–75 kg J. Hunter 1985. Total 48 kg–325 kg S. Smith 1985; 60 kg–415 kg R. Bass 1985.

INDEX

AN ASTERISK INDICATES A FURTHER
REFERENCE IN THE STOP PRESS

Indexing by

Anna Pavord

Acknowledgements

Editorial Staff Colin C. Smith; David L. Roberts; Julian Farino; Alex E. Reid; Tessa Pocock; Muriel Ling.

Bernadette Bidwell, Ann Collins, Barbara Edwards, Sheila Goldsmith, Moira F. Stowe.

Also to D. Richard Bowen, Roger Bowes (Chairman), David Browne, John Catchpole, Amanda Clark, Mlle Béatrice Frei, David F. Hoy (Managing Director), Ben Matsumoto, Michael Stephenson (Publishing Director).

Contributors Peter J. Matthews; Stan Greenberg; C. V. Appleton; John W. Arblaster, AIM; Richard Ayling; Howard Bass; Pat Besford; Henry G. Button; Sq Ldr D. H. Clarke, DFC, AFC; Dr A. C. Corder (Big Tree Search); Eric Dymock; Colin Dyson; Clive Everton; Frank L. Forster; M. H. Ford; Darryl Francis; Bill Frindall; Elizabeth Hawley; A. Herbert (New Zealand); Derek Hurst; International Boxing Research Organization; Sir Peter Johnson, Bt; Prof D. King-Hele, FRS; Michael D. Lampen; John Lees; Littlewoods Pools; John Marshall; K. G. McWhirter, MA, MSC; Peter Lunn, CMG, OBE; Dr G. T. Meaden (Editor *Journal of Meteorology*); Andy Milroy; Alan Mitchell, BA, BAg(For); David Mondey; Patrick Moore, OBE; Tony Needell; Mrs Susann Palmer; John Randall; Chris Rhys; Tim Rice; Jack Rollin; Irvin Saxton; Wm. L. Schultz (*Circus World Museum*, Wisconsin, USA); Bill Smith; Graham Snowdon; Donald Steel; Jack Stephens; Lance Tingay; Juhani Virola; Dr A. C. Waltham; Gerry L. Wood, FZS.

1986 Cover design: David Roberts. Artwork: Rob Burns.

Norris McWhirter and
... look wha

Today, 30 years after its first appearance, the Guinness Book of Records has become a record in itself as the world's best-selling book. Now there is a whole library of Guinness Books covering some 60 titles embracing over 40 subjects. The thoroughness, detail and care which has made the Guinness Book of Records famous goes into all our other titles.

If you have a special interest in say, Soccer—Guinness have several different books about it and new ones come out every year. The same goes for dozens of other subjects, from Rock Music to Rugby.

There are Guinness Books on entertainment and music.

Guinness books for collectors; Guinness sports guides — even a book of wine.

THE GUINNESS GUIDE TO STEEPLECHASING — Cranham Pitman Oaksey

THE BOOK OF ANSWERS

GUINNESS FILM FACTS & FEATS

GUINNESS SNOOKER THE RECORDS

GUINNESS SPACE FLIGHT THE RECORDS

GUINNESS SOCCER THE RECORDS

GUINNESS AMERICAN FOOTBALL THE RECORDS

HORSE RACING THE RECORDS

GUINNESS Book of BADMINTON — Pat Davis

The GUINNESS book of SILVER

GUINNESS BOOK OF TV FACTS AND FEATS

GUINNESS BOOK OF AIRCRAFT FACTS & FEATS

THE GUINNESS BOOK OF MUSIC

THE GUINNESS GUIDE TO GAME FISHING — WILLIAM B. CURRIE

GUINNESS BOOK OF RECORDS 1986

THE GUINNESS GUIDE TO BALLET — OLEG KERENSKY

500 NUMBER ONE HITS

THE GUINNESS BOOK OF GOLF FACTS & FEATS

GUINNESS FACTBOOK RAIL — THE PREHISTORIC AGE

The Billboard book of USA TOP 40 HITS

W9-ARJ-526

PROGRESS IN BRAIN RESEARCH

VOLUME 100

NEUROSCIENCE: FROM THE MOLECULAR TO THE COGNITIVE

PROGRESS IN BRAIN RESEARCH

VOLUME 100

NEUROSCIENCE:
FROM THE MOLECULAR TO THE
COGNITIVE

EDITED BY

FLOYD E. BLOOM

Department of Neuropharmacology, The Scripps Clinic and Research Institute, La Jolla, CA 92307, USA

ELSEVIER
AMSTERDAM – LONDON – NEW YORK – TOKYO
1994

BOWLING GREEN STATE
UNIVERSITY LIBRARIES

© 1994 Elsevier Science B.V. All rights reserved.

No part of this publication may be reproduced, stored in a retrieval system or transmitted in any form or by any means, electronic, mechanical, photocopying, recording or otherwise, without the written permission of the Publisher, Elsevier Science B.V., Copyright & Permissions Department, P.O. Box 521, 1000 AM Amsterdam. The Netherlands.

No responsibility is assumed by the Publisher for any injury and/or damage to persons or property as a matter of products liability, negligence or otherwise, or from any use or operation of any methods, products, instructions or ideas contained in the material herein. Because of the rapid advances in the medical sciences, the publisher recommends that independent verification of diagnoses and drug dosages should be made.

Special regulations for readers in the U.S.A.: This publication has been registered with the Copyright Clearance Center Inc. (CCC) Salem, Massachusetts. Information can be obtained from the CCC about conditions under which photocopies of parts of this publication may be made in the U.S.A. All other copyright questions, including photocopying outside of the USA, should be referred to the Publisher.

ISBN 0-444-81678-x (volume)
ISSN 0-444-80104-9 (series)

Elsevier Science B.V.
P.O. Box 211
1000 AE Amsterdam
The Netherlands

Library of Congress Cataloging-in-Publication Data

Neuroscience : from the molecular to the cognitive / edited by Floyd
E. Bloom.
      p.   cm. -- (Progress in brain research ; v. 100)
   Includes bibliographical references and index.
   ISBN 0-444-81678-X (alk. paper). -- ISBN 0-444-80104-9 (series :
alk. paper)
   1. Neurosciences.   I. Bloom, Floyd E.   II. Series.
   [DNLM: 1. Central Nervous System--physiology.   W1 PR667 v.100
1994 / WL 300 N4939 1994]
QP355.2.N49   1994
612.8'2--dc20
DNLM/DLC
for Library of Congress   94-12298
                                                              CIP

Printed on acid-free paper

Printed in The Netherlands

List of Contributors

H. Akil, Mental Health Research Institute, Department of Psychiatry, University of Michigan Medical School, Ann Arbor, MI 48105, USA

D. Bär, Department of Neurology, Rudolf Magnus Institute for Neurosciences, Utrecht University, Universiteitsweg 100, 3584 CG Utrecht, The Netherlands

F.E. Bloom, Department of Neuropharmacology, The Scripps Research Institute, La Jolla, CA, USA

H. Cameron, Laboratory of Neuroendocrinology, Rockefeller University, 1230 York Avenue, New York, NY 10021, USA

T.J. Carew, Department of Psychology, Yale University, POB 11-A, Yale Station, New Haven, CT 06520, USA

H.M. Chao, Laboratory of Neuroendocrinology, Rockefeller University, 1230 York Avenue, New York, NY 10021, USA

D.W. Choi, Department of Neurology and Center for the Study of Nervous System Injury, Box 8111, Washington University School of Medicine, 660 S. Euclid Avenue, St. Louis, MO 63110, USA

A.C. Cuello, McGill University, Department of Pharmacology and Therapeutics, McIntyre Medical Building, 3655 Drummond Street, Suite 1325, Montreal, Quebec, Canada H3G 1Y6

N.C. Danbolt, Anatomical Institute, University of Oslo, P.O.B. 1105 Blindern, N-0317 Oslo, Norway

I. Divac, Department of Medical Physiology, Panum Institute, University of Copenhagen, Blegdamsvej 3C, DK-2200 Copenhagen, Denmark

N.J. Emptage, Department of Psychology, Yale University, 2 Hillhouse Avenue, Box 11A Yale Station, New Haven, CT 06520, USA

S.Y. Felten, Department of Neurobiology and Anatomy, Box 603, University of Rochester School of Medicine and Dentistry, 601 Elmwood Avenue, Rochester, NY. 14642, USA

D.L. Felten, Department of Neurobiology and Anatomy, Box 603, University of Rochester School of Medicine and Dentistry, 601 Elmwood Avenue, Rochester, NY. 14642, USA

G. Fink, MRC Brain Metabolism Unit, University Department of Pharmacology, 1 George Square, Edinburgh EH8 9JZ, UK

L. Giovannelli, Department of Preclinical and Clinical Pharmacology, University of Florence, Viale Morgagni 65, 50134 Florence, Italy

W.H. Gispen, Department of Medical Pharmacology, Rudolf Magnus Institute for Neurosciences, Utrecht University, Universiteitweg 100, 3584 CG Utrecht, The Netherlands

E. Gould, Laboratory of Neuroendocrinology, Rockefeller University, 1230 York Avenue, New York, NY 10021, USA

W.T. Greenough, Beckman Institute, Department of Psychology, Neuroscience Program and Department of Cell and Structural Biology, University of Illinois, Urbana, IL, USA

M.E.R. Hallonet, Institut d'Embryologie Cellulaire et moléculaire, du CNRS et du Collège de France, 49bis avenue de la belle Gabrielle, 94736 Nogent-sur-Marne Cedex, France

R. Hari, Low Temperature Laboratory, Helsinki University of Technology, 02150 Espoo, Finland

M.A. Hofman, Graduate School of Neurosciences Amsterdam, Netherlands Institute for Brain Research, Meibergdreef 33, 1105 AZ Amsterdam, The Netherlands

B.T. Hyman, Neurology Service, Massachusetts General Hospital and Harvard Medical School, Boston, MA 02114, USA

G. Jaim-Etcheverry, Department of Cell Biology and Histology, School of Medicine, University of Buenos Aires, Paraguay 2155, 1121 Buenos Aires, Argentina

G.A.R. Johnston, Department of Pharmacology, The University of Sydney, NSW, 2006, Australia

J.D. Kocsis, Department of Neurology, Yale University School of Medicine, New Haven, CT 06510; and PVA/EPVA Neuroscience Research Center, VA Hospital, West Haven, CT 06516, USA

S.C. Landis, Department of Neurosciences, Case Western Reserve University, School of Medicine, Cleveland, OH 44106, USA

N.M. Le Douarin, Institut d'Embryologie Cellulaire et moléculaire, du CNRS et du Collège de France, 49bis avenue de la belle Gabrielle, 94736 Nogent-sur-Marne Cedex, France

V. Luine, Department of Psychology, Hunter College, New York 10021, NY, USA

A.M. Magarinos, Laboratory of Neuroendocrinology, Rockefeller University, 1230 York Avenue, New York, NY 10021, USA

P.J. Magistretti, Institut de Physiologie, Faculté de Médecine, Université de Lausanne, CH-1005 Lausanne, Switzerland

E.A. Marcus, Department of Biology, Yale University, 2 Hillhouse Avenue, Box 11A Yale Station, New Haven, CT 06520, USA

R. Marois, Interdepartmental Neuroscience Program, Yale University, 2 Hillhouse Avenue, Box 11A Yale Station, New Haven, CT 06520, USA

B.S. McEwen, Laboratory of Neuroendocrinology, Rockefeller University, 1230 York Avenue, New York, NY 10021, USA

J. Mendlewicz, Department of Psychiatry, Free University Clinics of Brussels, Erasme Hospital, route de Lennik 808, 1070 Brussels, Belgium

P.B. Molinoff, Department of Pharmacology, University of Pennsylvania School of Medicine, Philadelphia, PA 19104-6084, USA

O.P. Ottersen, Anatomical Institute, University of Oslo, P.O.B. 1105 Blindern, N-0317 Oslo, Norway

C. Pavlides, Laboratory of Neuroendocrinology, Rockefeller University, 1230 York Avenue, New York, NY 10021, USA

G. Pepeu, Department of Preclinical and Clinical Pharmacology, University of Florence, Viale Morgagni 65, 50134 Florence, Italy

O. Pompeiano, Dipartimento di Fisiologia e Biochimica, Via S. Zeno 31, 56127 Pisa, Italy

O. Pourquié, Institut d'Embryologie Cellulaire et moléculaire, du CNRS et du Collège de France, 49bis avenue de la belle Gabrielle, 94736 Nogent-sur-Marne Cedex, France

D.B. Pritchett, Department of Pharmacology, University of Pennsylvania School of Medicine, Philadelphia, PA 19104-6084, USA

G. Raisman, Norman and Sadie Lee Research Centre, Laboratory of Neurobiology, National Institute for Medical Research, The Ridgeway, Mill Hill, London NW7 1AA, UK

R. Ranney Mize, Department of Anatomy and the Neuroscience Center, Louisiana State University Medical Center, 1901 Perdido Street, New Orleans, LA 70112, USA

G.W. Rebeck, Neurology Service, Massachusetts General Hospital and Harvard Medical School, Boston, MA 02114, USA

L.P. Renaud, Neurosciences Unit, Loeb Research Institute, Ottawa Civic Hospital and University of Ottawa, Ottawa, Ontario, Canada K1Y 4E9

J.L. Roberts, Dr. Arthur M. Fishberg Research Center for Neurobiology, Mount Sinai School of Medicine, One Gustave Levy Place, New York, NY 10029, USA

P. Rudomin, Department of Physiology, Biophysics and Neurosciences, Centro de Investigación y de Estudios Avanzados, México D.F

M. Schachner, Department of Neurobiology, Swiss Federal Institute of Technology, 8093 Zurich, Switzerland

N.A. Simonian, Neurology Service, Massachusetts General Hospital and Harvard Medical School, Boston, MA 02114, USA

R.L. Spencer, Laboratory of Neuroendocrinology, Rockefeller University, 1230 York Avenue, New York, NY 10021, USA

C.N. Stefanis, Department of Psychiatry, Athens University Medical School, Eginition Hospital, 72–74 Vas Sophias Ave., 115 28 Athens, Greece

D.G. Stein, Institute of Animal Behavior, Rutgers, The State University of New Jersey, Newark, NJ 07102, USA

J. Storm-Mathisen, Anatomical Institute, University of Oslo, P.O.B. 1105 Blindern, N-0317 Oslo, Norway

D.F. Swaab, Graduate School of Neurosciences Amsterdam, Netherlands Institute for Brain Research, Meibergdreef 33, 1105 AZ Amsterdam, The Netherlands

D.A. Utzschneider, Department of Neurology, Yale University School of Medicine, New Haven, CT 06510; and PVA/EPVA Neuroscience Research Center, VA Hospital, West Haven, CT 06516, USA

J. Verhaagen, Department of Medical Pharmacology, Rudolf Magnus Institute for Neurosciences, Utrecht University, Universiteitweg 100, 3584 CG Utrecht, The Netherlands

X. Wang, Neuroscience Program, University of Illinois, Urbana, IL, USA

Y. Watanabe, Laboratory of Neuroendocrinology, Rockefeller University, 1230 York Avenue, New York, NY 10021, USA

S.J. Watson, Mental Health Research Institute, Department of Psychiatry, University of Michigan Medical School, Ann Arbor, MI 48105, USA

S.G. Waxman, Department of Neurology, LCI 708 Yale School of Medicine 333 Cedar Street New Haven, CT 06510, USA

I.J. Weiler, Beckman Institute and Department of Psychology, University of Illinois, Urbana, IL, USA

K. Williams, Department of Pharmacology, University of Pennsylvania School of Medicine, Philadelphia, PA 19104-6084, USA

C. Woolley, Laboratory of Neuroendocrinology, Rockefeller University, 1230 York Avenue, New York, NY 10021, USA

W.G. Young, Department of Neuropharmacology, The Scripps Research Institute, La Jolla, CA, USA

J. Zhong, Department of Pharmacology, University of Pennsylvania School of Medicine, Philadelphia, PA 19104-6084, USA

M.J. Zigmond, Department of Neuroscience, University of Pittsburgh, 570 Crawford Hall, Pittsburgh, PA 15260, USA

Preface

All editors like to regard their volumes as unique. Reflecting back through the series of the prior 99 volumes in this series, that premise is strongly supported. However, in all modesty, we would have to assert that the present volume carries at least two features that distinguish it from its predecessor volumes in the series: (1) it is a commemorative milestone issue; and (2) unlike most of the prior volumes, it does not provide an overview of a specific scientific meeting. Instead, for appropriate and creative reasons on the part of the Publisher, Elsevier Science, Amsterdam, it was determined to have a special number in the series to commemorate the one hundredth volume. The question then evolved as to exactly what form this commemorative effort would take and how it would be organized.

After due consideration of a variety of ideas by the editorial advisory board to the *Progress in Brain Research* series, the idea was put forward that the volume should reflect the views of the international body of active neuroscientists, to report on contemporary topics of their choice. Accordingly, authors were invited to write on any topic, given that their choice represented the topic most near and dear to their own efforts over a significant period of the recent past, and to which they would likely continue to be devoted in the future. The authors were also urged where possible to reflect on the evolution of their selected topics and their likely future course.

In that sense this volume reflects not "just" a single scientific meeting, but rather an overview sample of the problems and methodologies that epitomize brain research broadly at this special moment in the maturation of the field. The editorial advisory board were polled for their recommendations of the scientists to be invited, and the inevitably required selection of countries. The collection of essays in this volume therefore reflect these choices, and in addition, another inevitable reflection of the hectic environment of scientific publications, many of our invitees who accepted, were in the end, simply unable to provide their chapters within the deadline.

Given this background of its origination, it seems remarkable that the chapters comprising this volume assorted themselves so readily into five or six easily established categories of topics: developmental brain research, molecular brain research, integrative brain research, neuroplasticity, and neuro-psychiatric conditions. These topics do indeed seem to reflect well on the major streams of effort of our field when measured against the indices of the leading journals.

We are indebted to the authors for their diligent efforts to provide their chapters rapidly. We offer here a volume which reports on a sample of recognized leaders in the neuroscientific community at a significant instant in the history of this renowned series and in the evolution of the field. It is likely, given the high momentum of progress in this field, that many of these topics, and some wholly unexpected by our authors, will establish new directions for the next one hundred volumes.

F.E. Bloom
The Scripps Research Institute, La Jolla, CA

N. Spiteri
Elsevier Science, Amsterdam

Then and Now

Dominick P. Purpura

President, IBRO

Despite the harsh political climate that characterized the Cold War in 1961, scientists dedicated to the understanding of brain mechanisms overcame communication barriers to attend a "Colloquium on Brain Mechanisms" sponsored by the International Brain Research Organization. The central theme of the Colloquium was "Sensorimotor Integration". The formal papers and extensive discussions appeared as Volume One of *Progress in Brain Research* in 1963. Elsevier's prescience in recognizing the emergence of brain research as a major growth industry in the life sciences may have been as important as the reports of the Colloquium. Not surprisingly, much of what was discussed during the 1961 Pisa meeting was but a prologue to current problems. Alfred Fessard provided the Colloquium's last words: "In conclusion, it seems that in the general case of a multineuronal assembly engaged in a specific sensori-motor operation, the question of a special mechanism destined to confer upon it *in isolation* the quality of an 'entity' does not really exist. It can only be called 'integrated' in relation to all other congruent assemblies, at all levels of the neuraxis, which participate in the particular operation".

Three decades later "integration" remains the central goal of brain research, its Holy Grail – now defined as vertical integration from "the Molecular to Cognition", the theme of the present milestone volume of *Progress in Brain Research*. In the intervening years since the first volume, no aspect of the universe of discourse referred to now as "neuroscience" has escaped close pursuit in the hundred volumes of *Progress*. Examples abound here from considerations of the molecular subunit structure of transmembrane channels to complex cognitive processes. In keeping with the international spirit of the inaugural volume, the Editor has succeeded in encouraging sixty-six neuroscientists from fourteen countries to examine the canon of brain research and this they have accomplished with due respect for the constraints of space. Remarkable is it also that the Editor was able to elicit from many contributors their views and speculations and even some of their most prophetic visions. Milestones give pause for review to examine the present and map the future course of discovery.

It was not intended that this commemorative issue of *Progress in Brain Research* would be a comprehensive repository of the most recent advances in neuroscience. Rather it may be viewed as an affirmation of the coming of age of brain research as a scholarly endeavor that now permits objective inquiry into problems that have perplexed humankind since the dawn of human consciousness. To speak about "brain mechanisms" 30 years ago was to infer causality without process. Today even the most complex brain mechanisms are explicable in terms of cellular, molecular and genetic events: Reductionism as champion not challenger of Integration. None of the participants of the 1961 Colloquium ventured into the forbidden realm of pathobiology, unable as they were to grasp at fundamentals of molecular pathogenesis. Today, as this volume attests, neuroscience is at the threshold of comprehending the essential mechanisms that give rise to Alzheimer's disease, epilepsy, stroke, multiple sclerosis and serious mental disorders. Translating understanding to application, though arduous, augers well for the future of brain research and the human condition.

The Editor is to be further congratulated for alerting us in his own contribution to the ineluctable problem of data overload on the "infobahn". How neuroscience deals with the appalling mass of "facts" being disgorged daily from thousands of laboratories throughout the world will be as critical to the success of the neuroscience enterprise as any number of new conceptual advances. The world community of neuroscientists in IBRO now consists of more than 30 000 neuroscientists in over 70 countries. Considering the intellectual power of this workforce, it will surely not be another 30 years before the appearance of the 200th volume of *Progress in Brain Research*. Surely, the need for rapid communication will only intensify as new technologies drive new advances and vice versa. *Progress in Brain Research* will continue to inform us about the next revolution in neuroscience, the understanding of how the brain works in health and disease. But whether the new canon will be conveyed on paper or via the "infobahn" remains to be seen. Elsevier was midwife to the *Progress* series and hand maiden to brain research. Now we celebrate the marriage of neuroscience and informatics. The offspring of the consummation will further test Elsevier's prescience.

Contents

SECTION I

Developmental Brain Research

F. Bloom (Editor)
Progress in Brain Research, Vol. 100
© 1994 Elsevier Science B.V. All rights reserved

CHAPTER 1

Cell migrations and establishment of neuronal connections in the developing brain: a study using the quail-chick chimera system

Nicole M. Le Douarin, Marc E.R. Hallonet and Olivier Pourquié

Institut d'Embryologie Cellulaire et moléculaire, du CNRS et du Collège de France, 49bis avenue de la belle Gabrielle, 94736 Nogent-sur-Marne Cedex, France

Introduction

In vertebrates, the first morphological sign of emergence of the nervous system is the appearance of the neural plate, the medio-dorsal line of which is in intimate contact with a mesodermal structure, the notochord. Laterally, the neural epithelium is separated from the presumptive superficial ectoderm by a transitional zone, the neural fold. The next important step in neurogenesis is the transformation of the initially flat neural anlage into a tubular structure. The dorsomedial part of the neural plate thus becomes medioventral and its lateral ridges reach the medio-dorsal line where they fuse to form the neural crest and the roof plate. During these morphogenetic events, the floor plate acquires important inductive properties under the influence of the notochord (Yamada et al., 1991) and the neural tube becomes divided into six compartments along the dorsoventral axis: ventrally the floor plate in contact with the notochord, the roof plate dorsally, and laterally the alar and basal plates corresponding respectively to the dorsal and ventral quarters of the neural tube. Although these territories have long been recognized and named, it is only recently that their developmental significance is being really investigated.

One of the characteristics of vertebrates among the chordates is the emergence of the neural crest and the development of the brain at the rostral end of the neural tube (Gans and Northcutt, 1983). The process of cephalization involves the activity of a number of genes (Simeone et al., 1992) as well as an intricate network of intercellular signalling. An important requirement in attempts to decipher how the brain is built is to be able to follow embryonic cells within the neural primordium while the complexity arises, i.e. from the early stages of the neural plate up to completion of neurogenesis. This involves the construction of fate maps and the tracing of neuroepithelial cells along their developmental history. By using the quail-chick chimera system we have undertaken a study in which movements and fate of the neuroepithelial territories were followed in the embryo in ovo during the entire period of development. We have thus been able to sort out what is the respective contribution of the alar and basal plates of the mes- and rhombencephalon to structures like the cerebellum and various brain stem nuclei (Hallonet et al., 1990; Tan and Le Douarin, 1991; Hallonet and Le Douarin, 1993). Moreover, we have isolated an immunoglobulin-like (Ig-like) cell surface glycoprotein (called BEN) whose expression is developmentally regulated in definite subsets of neurons (Pourquié et al., 1990, 1992a,b). On the basis of fate mapping results at the mid- and hindbrain levels and combinations of the quail-chick chimerism with anti-BEN immunoreactivity, we could show that establishment of connections between the inferior olivary nucleus and Purkinje cells of the cerebellar cortex involves BEN expression for the period of time corresponding to the growth of the climbing fibers and the onset of synaptogenesis (Pourquié et al., 1992b). The developmental significance of these results is further discussed.

Following the fate of neuroepithelial territories in embryonic chimeras

The quail-chick marker system was initially based on the nuclear structure of quail cells, characterized by the presence of a large mass of heterochromatin associated with the nucleolus in all embryonic and adult cell types of this species (*Coturnix coturnix japonica*). Thus, quail cells are easy to distinguish from chick cells in which the constitutive heterochromatin is evenly distributed in the nucleus as it is in most animal species (Le Douarin, 1969, 1973, 1982). Since the time this observation was made, other means have been devised to analyze the chimeric tissues in a more refined way. Species-specific and cell type specific antibodies have been produced and as indicated in Table I, some allow neuronal somas or neurites to be selectively labeled in one or the other of the two species. The antibodies that we have produced against the cell surface glycoprotein BEN (for bursal epithelium

TABLE I

Species-specific antibodies recognizing either neurites or neurones of quail and chick

Species-specific antibodies	Quail	Chick
Chick anti-quail serum[a]	All cells	Nothing
Mouse Mabs		
39B11	Nothing	Neurites
37F5[b]	Nothing	Neuronal somas
CN	Nothing	Neurites
QN	Neurites	Nothing
CQN[c]	Neurites	Neurites
BEN1[d]	Peripherally projecting neurones, inferior olivary neurones	

[a]Lance-Jones and Lagenaur (1987); [b]Takagi et al. (1989); [c]Tanaka et al. (1990); [d]Pourquié et al. (1990).

and neurons, Pourquié et al., 1990) have been largely used in the work reviewed in this article. The BEN protein is interesting because it is not only a neuronal marker but it displays developmentally regulated expression in several classes of neurons in both the central nervous system (CNS) and the peripheral nervous system (PNS). The activity of the encoding gene is likely to be related to important steps in neurogenesis. This is why we have particularly investigated the onset of BEN expression in several neuronal systems.

The experimental design used to follow the fate of embryonic cells through the quail-chick marker system consists of substituting definite territories in the chick embryo with their quail counterpart from the same developmental stage. The taxonomic proximity of the two species and the fact that, at least during the first half of the developmental period, the two embryos have about the same size and chronology of development, make it possible to construct viable chimeras in ovo. Neural chimeras, in which parts of either the spinal cord (Kinutani et al., 1986) or the brain (Balaban et al., 1988; Hallonet et al., 1990; Teillet et al., 1991; Guy et al., 1992, 1993) have been implanted, can hatch. Chicken with a chimeric brain remain in a healthy condition for a significant period of time during which they can walk, fly and compete for food with other birds.

In quail to chick combinations, however, an immune rejection of the graft takes place several weeks after the host's immune system has become mature (Kinutani et al., 1986) and this constitutes a limitation to this technique, if the behavior of the chimeras is to be followed during long periods after birth. Interestingly, neural tissue grafts, performed before vascularization of the neuroepithelium, between animals of the same species albeit across major histocompatibility (MHC) barrier do not induce an immune response from the host and yield healthy birds. This was used to define which parts of the brain are responsible for the manifestation of a genetic form of epilepsy depending on an autosomal recessive gene in the chicken Fayoumi (Fepi) strain. Selective substitution of certain areas of encephalic vesicles in E2 (embryonic day 2) normal chicken by their counterpart from a Fepi chicken results in the transfer of the disease which can

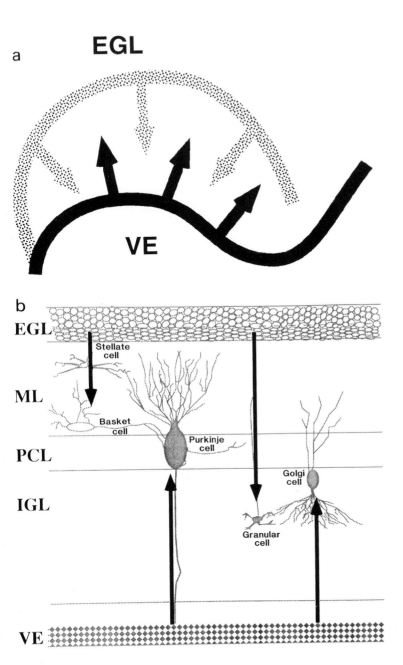

a

EGL

VE

b

EGL

Stellate
cell

ML

Basket
cell

PCL

Purkinje
cell

Golgi
cell

IGL

Granular
cell

VE

Fig. 1. (A) Schematic representation of the two proliferative layers of the cerebellum. The epithelium lining the fourth ventricule (VE) yields cells migrating centrifugally towards the periphery, whereas the external granular layer (EGL) produces cells migrating into the cerebellum. Arrows indicate the direction of these migrations. Rostral is to the right. (B) Summary of classical descriptions concerning the origin and migration of cells of the cerebellar cortex from their two germinative layers. Purkinje and Golgi cells are produced by the ventricular epithelium, whereas granular cells come from the EGL and follow a strictly radial migration along glial fibers. Interneurons of the molecular layer are classically described as deriving from the EGL (see Hallonet et al., 1990 and references therein). EGL, external granular layer; ML, molecular layer; PCL, Purkinje cell layer; IGL, internal granular layer; VE, ventricular epithelium.

be studied in the chimeras for prolonged periods of time (Teillet et al., 1991; Guy et al., 1992, 1993).

Mapping of the mesencephalon and rhombencephalon

When we started our work on the origin of the cerebellar anlage, it was well known that complex cell movements involving radial and tangential cell migrations take place during the ontogeny of this structure. Namely, radial outward migrations are responsible for positioning of Purkinje cells, whereas the cells originating from the so-called rhombic lip, and destined to form the external granular layer (EGL), undergo tangential migrations over the outer surface of the neuroepithelium. Later on, the cells of the EGL migrate radially inward, and it has been classically accepted that they form the molecular layer and the internal granular layer (IGL) (Fig. 1) (see Hallonet et al., 1990 and references therein). The problem we raised concerned (i) the limits of the cerebellar territory within the encephalic vesicles and (i) the origin of each cell type of the cerebellar cortex from one or the other of the two cell proliferative layers of the cerebellar anlage, i.e. the ventricular epithelium and the EGL. It was classically accepted that the cerebellum is derived from the metencephalic vesicle. Exchanges of the metencephalon (corresponding to prospective rhombomeres (r) 1 and 2) were performed between quail and chick at the 10–14 somites stages as represented in Fig. 2A. The results obtained were unexpected: a large part of the cerebellar cortex originated in fact from the mesencephalic vesicle. By doing unilateral grafts of the quail mes- and metencephalic vesicles in chick embryos, Martinez and Alvarado-Mallart (1989) reached a similar conclusion, i.e. that the presumptive cerebellar territory transgresses the primitive mes-metencephalic boundary.

A refined analysis of the contribution of r1 to the cerebellar cortex was done by grafting limited areas of the alar plate between quail and chick embryos over surfaces corresponding to 20° to 120° from the medio-dorsal plan (Hallonet and Le Douarin, 1993) (Fig. 2B). It was found that the roof plate does not contribute to the cerebellum which arises exclusively from the alar plate. Interestingly, the metencephalic alar plate is able to yield all the cell types found in the cerebellar cortex (i.e. granular and Golgi cells as well as Purkinje neurons) including cells of the molecular layer (Fig. 3). In contrast, the mesencephalic contribution to the cerebellum does not concern granular neurons which are all derived from the metencephalon. In other words, the EGL is entirely derived from the anterior half of the metencephalon corresponding to r1. Moreover, the more dorsal the origin of the EGL cells the less rostral was the extent of their migration (see Hallonet and Le Douarin, 1993, for details).

The morphogenetic movements of the neural tube leading to the participation of the mesencephalic alar plate in cerebellar cortex could be visualized by following step by step the relative position of grafted and host's tissues. As represented in Fig. 4, a longitudinal morphogenetic distortion affects the neural tube from E5 onward and leads to the rostral displacement of its ventral aspect associated with the caudal displacement of its dorsal aspect. As a result, a large area of mesencephalic material is carried backward forming the rostromedial intrusion inserted into the metencephalic roof. The EGL, originating from the alar plate of r1, thus covers the whole cerebellar cortex through a movement of cells following a caudorostral and laterodorsal direction. The posterior half of the metencephalon (r2) gives rise to the choroid plexus and participates to the *medulla oblongata* with the myelencephalon.

Fig. 2. (*A*) Isotopic and isochronic graft of the metencephalic vesicle (in black) between quail and chick were performed at the 12-somite stage in ovo. (*B*) Three types of isotopic and isochronic reciprocal exchanges were performed at the 11- to 14-somite stage between quail and chick embryos. Graft types: (*A*) (I) bilateral rostral half of the metencephalic vesicle, (II) bilateral caudal half of the mesencephalic vesicle; (*C*) (III) unilateral caudal mesencephalon and rostral metencephalon. Extension of the grafts: (*B,D*) lateral extensions of bilateral and unilateral grafts, respectively. The lateral extensions of the grafted territories varied from the roof plate of the neural tube (R) to dorsal (d), lateroventral (lv) boundaries, limited at a maximum of 25°, 45°, 90° and 120° respectively from the sagittal plane (from Hallonet and Le Douarin, 1993).

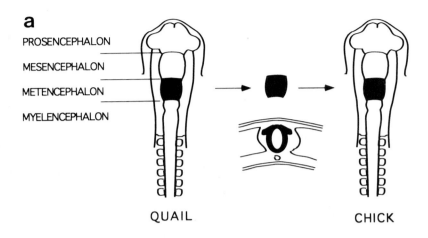

a

PROSENCEPHALON

MESENCEPHALON

METENCEPHALON

MYELENCEPHALON

QUAIL

CHICK

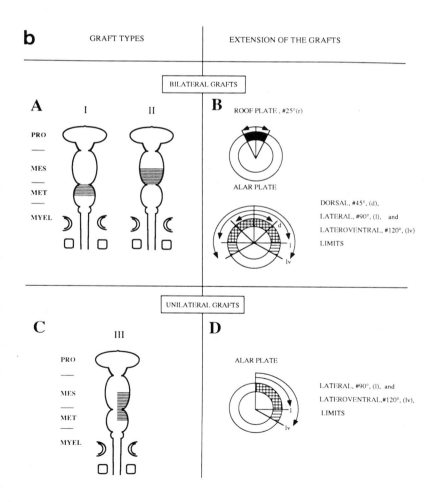

b

GRAFT TYPES

EXTENSION OF THE GRAFTS

BILATERAL GRAFTS

A I II

PRO

MES

MET

MYEL

B

ROOF PLATE , #25°(r)

ALAR PLATE

DORSAL, #45°, (d),

LATERAL, #90°, (l), and

LATEROVENTRAL, #120°, (lv)

LIMITS

UNILATERAL GRAFTS

C III

PRO

MES

MET

MYEL

D

ALAR PLATE

LATERAL, #90°, (l), and

LATEROVENTRAL,#120°, (lv),

LIMITS

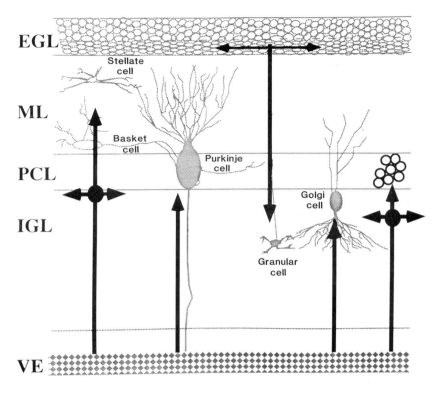

EGL

Stellate cell

ML

Basket cell

Purkinje cell

PCL

Golgi cell

IGL

Granular cell

VE

Fig. 3. Summary of the results of quail-chick chimeras analysis concerning the origin and migrations of cells of the cerebellar cortex from the two germinative layers of the cerebellum. Purkinje and Golgi cells come from the ventricular epithelium. Purkinje cells apparently follow a radial migration from the ventricular epithelium to their peripheral location. Granular cells come from the EGL and follow strictly radial migration along glial fibers but they can accomplish tangential migration in the deep levels of the EGL. The interneurons of the molecular layer do not originate from the EGL but from the ventricular epithelium as do the Purkinje and Golgi neurons. They seem to follow transversal migration. We also observe a population of small cells localized in the Purkinje cell layer. These cells follow radial migrations with a small tangential component.

Fate of the myelencephalon: respective contribution of basal and alar plate to the brain stem nuclei

The myelencephalon lies in a caudal position with respect to the metencephalon and gives rise to the *medulla oblongata*. It extends caudally from r3 to r8. Since its first description by His (1891), the dorso-ventral migration of cells originating from the so-called "rhombic lip" forming the lateral ridges of the 4th ventricle roof has been well documented.

By using the quail-chick chimera system, we could analyze the respective contribution of the basal and alar plate to the nuclei deriving from the myelencepha-

lon down to the level of somite 6 (Tan and Le Douarin, 1991). This was achieved by exchanging dorsal or ventral portions (i.e. halves or even quarters of the neural tube) of the myelencephalic vesicle between chick and quail embryos (Fig. 5). Chimerism analysis in these animals revealed that the motor nuclei of the abducens, facial, glossopharyngeal, vagal and of part of the trigeminal nerves are derived from the basal plate of the myelencephalon. In contrast, nuclei with essentially sensory components such as the *nuclei angularis, laminaris* or *magnocellularis* were shown to arise from the alar plate. Another category of associative nuclei, such as the precerebellar *inferior olivaris nucleus* and the *nuclei pontis lateralis* and

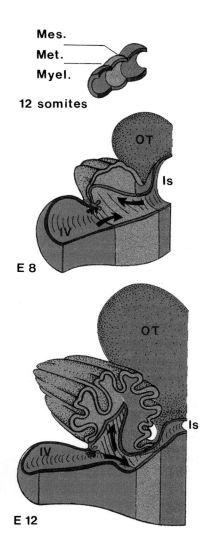

medialis which provide the cerebellum with climbing and mossy fibers inputs respectively, originate from the alar plate. These nuclei undergo an extensive dorso-ventral migration, so that finally they lie ventrally to basal plate derivatives (Fig. 6). Nuclei such as the *reticularis gigantocellularis* or *subtrigeminalis* are of mixed origin, perhaps reflecting their origin from the intermediate zone between alar and basal plate.

Other types of grafts involving the replacement of the entire myelencephalon or of its lateral half allowed the extent of cell migration along the anteroposterior and dorsoventral axis to be evaluated by analyzing the chimerism at the ridges of the graft. It was thus possible to establish the myelencephalic contribution to certain important alar plate derived nuclei. In particular, the inferior olivary nucleus which provides the cerebellar cortex with climbing fibers was found to originate not only from the myelencephalon but also from the spinal cord down to the level of somite 6.

In contrast, the *nuclei pontis lateralis* and *medialis* which yield a contingent of mossy fibers, have a mixed myelencephalic and metencephalic origin. These experiments demonstrated in addition that nu-

Fig. 4. Schematic three-dimensional reconstructions summarizing the morphogenetic movements modelling the mesencephalic, metencephalic and myelencephalic vesicles. During embryogenesis, mesencephalic material intrudes rostromedially into the dorsal extent of the metencephalic vesicle. Ventrally, a longitudinal movement rostrally displaces the floors of the myelencephalic, metencephalic and mesencephalic vesicles. Consequently, when the external granular layer, which is generated in the metencephalic vesicle, spreads over the cerebellar anlage, it covers the rostromedial part of the cerebellum, which is generated in the mesencephalic vesicle. Rostral lies to the right of the diagram. The reconstructions are viewed from the medial aspect (from Le Douarin, 1993). Mes, mesencephalic vesicle; Met, metencephalic vesicle; Myel, myelencephalic vesicle; Is, isthmus; IV, fourth ventricle; OT, optic tectum. Arrows indicate the direction of the morphogenetic movements modelling the neural tube.

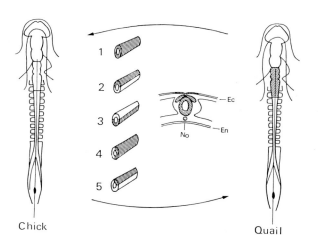

Fig. 5. Schematic representation of the five types of isotopic and isochronic transplantations of the myelencephalon between quail and chick embryos, performed at the 10- to 12- somite stage. 1, whole myelencephalon; 2, dorsal half of myelencephalon; 3, ventral half of myelencephalon; 4, right half of myelencephalon; 5, dorsal quarter of myelencephalon (from Tan and Le Douarin, 1991). Ec, ectoderm; En, endoderm; No, notochord.

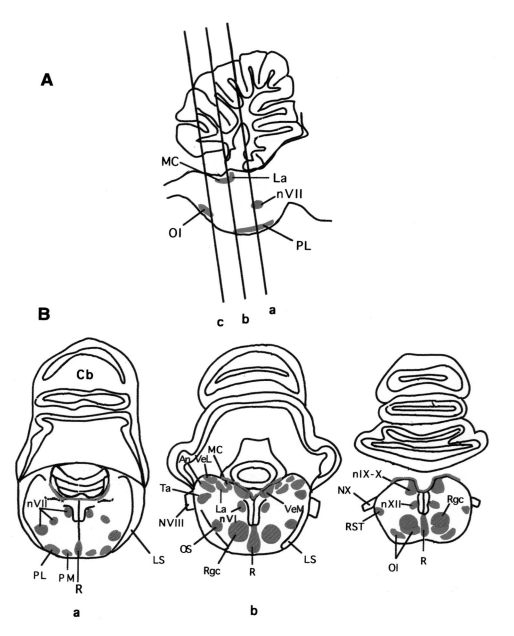

Fig. 6. Summary of the neuronal origin from the alar plate (in blue) and basal plate (in red) of the nuclei of the medulla oblongata. The hatched nuclei have a dual alar and basal plate origin. (A) Parasagittal section of post-hatched chick brain. Oblique lines indicate the positions of transverse sections shown in B. (B) Transverse sections of post-hatched chick hind brain. An, nucleus angularis; Cb, cerebellum; La, nucleus laminaris; LS, lemniscus spinalis; MC, nucleus magnocellularis; nVI, nucleus nervi abducentis; nVII, nucleus nervi facialis; NVIII, nerve VIII; nIX-X, nucleus nervi glossopharyngei and nucleus motorius dorsalis nervi vagi; NX, nervus vagus; nXII, nucleus nervi hypoglossi; OI, nucleus olivaris inferior; PL, nucleus pontis lateralis; PM, nucleus pontis medialis; R, nucleus raphe; Rgc, nucleus reticularis gigantocellularis; RST, nucleus reticularis subtrigeminalis; VeL, nucleus vestibularis lateralis; VeM, nucleus vestibularis medialis.

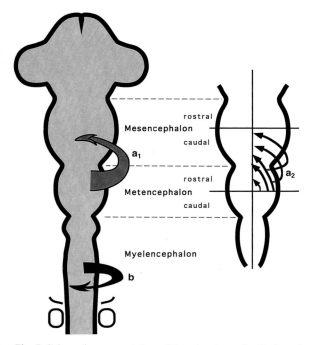

Fig. 7. Schematic representation of the migrations of cells from the anterior metencephalic alar plate leading to the formation of the EGL (top arrow labelled a₁). In a₂, it is shown that cells of the metencephalic wall located between 20° and 120° migrate anteriorly and towards the midline of the encephalic vesicles that they cover up to the mid-mesencephalic level. Cells located the most dorsally are those which undergo the less extended migration. In contrast the cells originating ventrally migrate further rostrally (see text and Hallonet and Le Douarin, 1993, for details). The arrow labelled b represents the dorsoventral migratory stream of the *medulla oblongata* which gives rise to the nuclei endowed of associative functions located ventrally in the brain stem.

clei derived from the alar plate such as the inferior olivary nucleus were made up of cells which accomplish extensive longitudinal as well as dorso-ventral migrations. In contrast, no significant longitudinal movements are detectable in the basal plate derived nuclei. This may be related to the original segmentation of the rhombencephalon into rhombomeres which seem to be separated by barriers to cell migration early in development (Fraser et al., 1990). The patterning of alar plate derivatives in contrast seems largely to escape from the rhombometameric constraints since alar plate derived cells navigate freely across these barriers.

In conclusion, the study of the fate map of the myelencephalon (Tan and Le Douarin, 1991) demonstrated that motor nuclei are derived from cells of basal plate origin migrating essentially along a radial direction; whereas cells forming most nuclei endowed with associative functions (such as the inferior olivary nucleus and most nuclei of the reticular formation) originate from the alar plate. They reach their ventral position after a dorso-ventral migration which could be clearly visualized by the quail-chick marker system.

The particular behavior of cells of the rhombic lip masks the original dorso-ventral polarity of the myelencephalon which is similar to that of the spinal cord, in which the alar plate gives rise to interneurons and the neural crest yields sensory ganglia (Hamburger, 1948; Wenger, 1950; Leber et al., 1990).

It is striking that at the level of the first rhombomere (r1) from which all the EGL of the cerebellum originates, cells of the alar plate migrate along laterodorsal and postero-anterior vectors as indicated in Fig. 7. Cells are endowed with a remarkably high proliferative capacity since they cover the entire cerebellar plate including its rostro-medial component which is derived from the mesencephalon (Fig. 4). These morphogenetic processes are under the control of developmental genes among which the Wnt1 gene has been identified (McMahon and Bradley, 1990; Thomas and Capecchi, 1990).

Cells of the alar plate originating from the myelencephalon are also endowed with a large proliferation potential and exhibit a unique migratory behavior which leads them to lie ventral to the progeny of the basal plate. The opposite movements of the metencephalic and myelencephalic cells are illustrated in Fig. 7.

One can say therefore that the initial dorsoventral polarity of the spinal cord in terms of fate and functions of cells originating from the basal and alar plates is conserved in the mid- and hindbrain.

In the next section, we consider the expression of BEN glycoprotein: its biochemical characteristics and its use to trace the climbing fibers from the inferior olivary nucleus to the Purkinje cells of the cerebellar cortex.

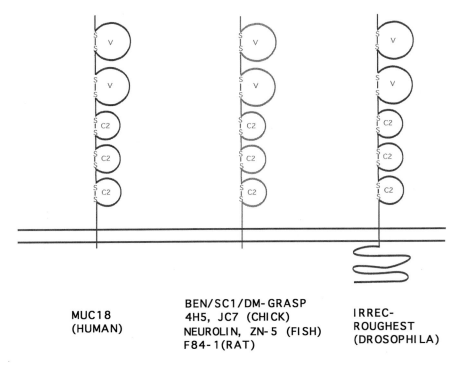

MUC18
(HUMAN)

BEN/SC1/DM-GRASP
4H5, JC7 (CHICK)
NEUROLIN, ZN-5 (FISH)
F84-1(RAT)

IRREC-
ROUGHEST
(DROSOPHILA)

Fig. 8. Schematic representations of BEN, MUC 18 and IrreC molecules. These three molecules show a homology at the amino acid level of around 25% over the length of their extracellular domains. The first two Ig-domains have been classified as V-type for BEN and MUC 18 although this is not as clear for IrreC. The next three domains are of the C2 type.

Expression of BEN during spinal cord and brain stem development

BEN is an avian cell surface molecule of the Ig-superfamily which is widely expressed during chick embryonic development but is restricted to neuronal subsets in the nervous system. We have identified this molecule by means of a monoclonal antibody (Pourquié et al., 1990). SDS-PAGE analysis of the immuno-purification product obtained from the various cell types expressing BEN, i.e. the epithelium of the bursa of Fabricius, hemopoietic cells (thymocytes) and cells of the CNS, yielded molecules with slightly different M_r ranging from 110 000 for the epithelial form of BEN to 100 000 and 95 000 for its hemopoietic and neural forms, respectively.

Variations in N-glycosylation appeared to be mostly responsible for this molecular heterogeneity. This was further confirmed by the presence of the HNK-1 carbohydrate epitope only on the protein extracted from brain and thymus. We have microsequenced parts of the protein and used degenerate oligonucleotides to clone a cDNA encoding this molecule (Pourquié et al., 1992a). Its sequence turned out to be identical to that of the DM-GRASP (Burns et al., 1991) and SC1 (Tanaka et al., 1991) proteins also described in the

Fig. 9. (A) Transverse sections of a chick embryo immunostained with anti-BEN Mab, at E2.5. BEN-reactivity is conspicuous on motoneurons (MN) and in their axons forming the early spinal nerve (SN) and on the floor plate (FP) (Bar: 75 μm). (B) E4.5 embryo. BEN reactivity has appeared on DRG neurons and their axons contributing to the spinal nerve and forming in the spinal cord the dorsal funiculus (Bar: 100 μm). (C) E8 embryo. BEN protein expression is now down-regulated and progressively disappears in both motoneurons and DRG neurons (Bar: 100 μm). (D) Schematic representation of BEN expression during spinal nerve formation. The drawings show transverse sections of the spinal cord and the DRG at increasing stages of development expressed according to the developmental table of Hamburger and Hamilton (1951).

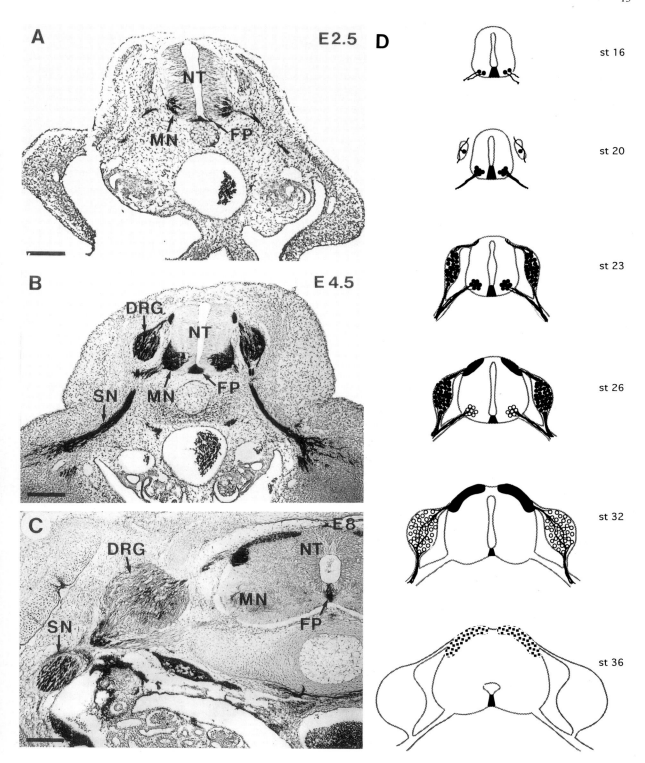

A   E 2.5

NT

MN   FP

B   E 4.5

DRG

NT

SN   MN   FP

C   E 8

DRG

NT

MN

SN   FP

D

st 16

st 20

st 23

st 26

st 32

st 36

chick embryo. BEN/DM-GRASP/SC1 has the typical structure of an integral membrane protein with a large external domain associated with a hydrophobic transmembrane portion and a short intracytoplasmic tail. The extracellular region of the BEN molecule is composed of five Ig-like domains, as in the human melanoma marker MUC18 (Lehmann et al., 1989) and in IrreC, a recently identified *Drosophila* molecule involved in retinal axon guidance (Ramos et al., 1993).

Although the overall homology at the amino acid level between BEN and MUC18 or IrreC is only 25%, the structure of these three molecules is basically similar. They may therefore constitute a new subgroup in the large Ig-superfamily (Fig. 8). Species homologs of BEN protein have now been discovered in other vertebrates such as goldfish, zebrafish and rat (Laessing et al., 1993; Kanki and Kuwada, 1993; Prince et al., 1992). As far as its putative function is concerned, this protein was shown by in vitro assays to mediate homophilic adhesive interactions (Burns et al., 1991; Tanaka et al., 1991; El Deeb et al., 1992).

We have first studied BEN protein expression in the peripheral nervous system. It is present during development on all neural crest derived neurons (Pourquié et al., 1990) soon after they start to extend their processes. In the sympathetic, parasympathetic and enteric nervous systems, the BEN antigen is detectable soon after gangliogenesis and remains present in PNS ganglia until at least hatching.

In the spinal cord, motoneurons start expressing the BEN gene when extending neurites. The floor plate, a specialized population of epithelial cells lying in the midline of the neural tube, is BEN-positive from E2 to E10. In the spinal ganglia, the expression of this protein starts in neurons soon after gangliogenesis and closely parallels its expression in motoneurons (Fig. 9). The immunoreactivity starts in both motor and sensory neurons cell bodies and spreads in the fibers fasciculating to form the spinal nerves. It finally disappears in a centrifugal manner at the time of synaptogenesis. The protein remains however present on the dorsal funiculi formed by the central afferent fibers of the DRG (up to E10) (Fig. 9). At E8, immunoreactivity is no longer detected in cell bodies of either sensory or motor neurons, but remains on their fibers.

Later in development, the protein disappears from the spinal nerve roots. Interestingly, the BEN protein was shown to be expressed at the level of the functional neuromuscular synapse where it co-localizes with the acetycholine receptor (Fournier-Le Ray and Fontaine-Pérus, 1991). Therefore, at the level of the motor and sensory neurons, BEN gene expression is associated with axonal outgrowth and migration and is downregulated from cell body to synapse. These results, together with in vitro data suggesting a role for this molecule in homophilic adhesion, support the contention that it could play a role in nerve fiber fasciculation and synapse formation in the PNS.

Expression of BEN in the rhombencephalon

The earliest expression of the BEN gene was detected on basal plate derivatives of the rhombencephalon, namely the floor plate which becomes immunoreactive first and later in the nuclei formed by cranial nerves motoneurons. The onset of expression of the protein does not strictly follow a craniocaudal gradient in the cephalic region, as it does in the spinal cord. The protein first appears in somas of the facial nerve neurons, and slightly later, in the other motor nuclei (Chang et al., 1992; Guthrie and Lumsden, 1992). Expression was also first detectable on cell bodies and early pioneering axons soon after neurons become postmitotic. A few hours later, the BEN gene product was also detected in the cranial sensory ganglia. As observed for the spinal motoneurons and the DRG neurons, down regulation occurs from the cell body to the synapse around the time of synaptogenesis. Sensory neurons derived from the alar plate such as the *nucleus laminaris* start to express the BEN gene from about E6 (our unpublished observations). From E8 onwards, BEN expression is also detected on other nuclei, and particularly in the inferior olivary nucleus which has been the subject of further investigations.

Association of BEN with climbing fibers axonogenesis and synaptogenesis

The cerebellar cortex is connected to the rest of the brain by two main afferent systems. The mossy fibers

15

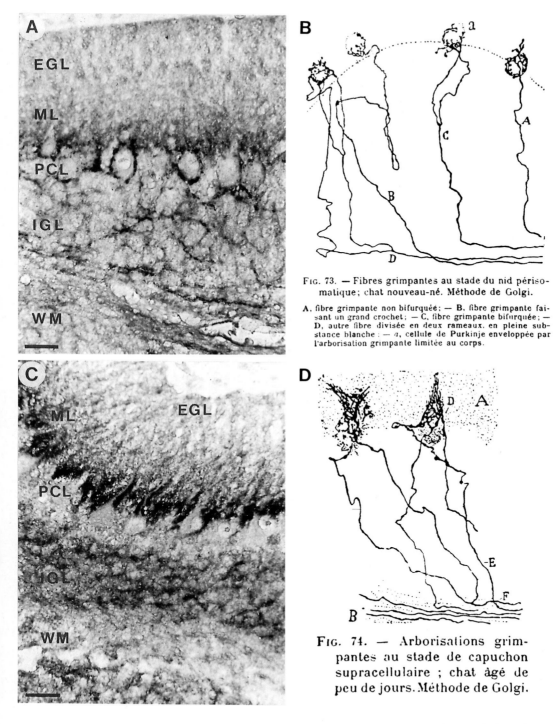

Fig. 73. — Fibres grimpantes au stade du niso-matique; chat nouveau-né. Méthode de Golgi.

A, fibre grimpante non bifurquée; — B, fibre grimpante fai-sant un grand crochet; — C, fibre grimpante bifurquée; — D, autre fibre divisée en deux rameaux, en pleine sub-stance blanche : — a, cellule de Purkinje enveloppée par l'arborisation grimpante limitée au corps.

Fig. 74. — Arborisations grim-pantes au stade de capuchon supracellulaire ; chat âgé de peu de jours. Méthode de Golgi.

Fig. 10. Comparison between BEN protein immunoreactivity in the cerebellar cortex, and the classical descriptions of Ramon y Cajal (1911) of climbing fibers maturation. (*A*) Sagittal section of the cerebellar cortex at E15 showing the reactivity localized in the white matter (WM), the internal granular layer (IGL) and the Purkinje cell layer (PCL) evocating the nest stage described by Cajal illustrated in (*B*) (Bar: 20 μm). (*C*) Sagittal section of the cerebellar cortex a E16 (Bar: 20 μm). The maximal reactivity is now translocated at the bottom of the apical den-drite of Purkinje cells resembling the supracellular stage described by Cajal as shown in (*D*). EGL: external granular layer.

originate from various brain locations and establish synaptic connections with the granular and Golgi neurons known as glomeruli. The second type of afferents corresponds to the climbing fibers. They arise exclusively from the inferior olivary nucleus, which is derived from the myelencephalon as shown by the experiments reported above. Fibers from the inferior olivary nucleus establish connexions with the deep nuclei neurons and project to the cerebellar cortex to synapse on the Purkinje cell dendrites. As previously shown (Tan and Le Douarin, 1991) the inferior olivary nucleus neurons arise from the alar plate of the myelencephalon down to the level of somite 6. The climbing fibers contact the Purkinje cells according to a sequence of maturation stages of which Ramon y Cajal (1911) has provided a classical description (Fig. 10).

BEN expression in the developing cerebellar system turned out to be particularly interesting (Pourquié et al., 1992b). From E8–E9, BEN is strongly expressed by inferior olivary nucleus neurons. From E10 onward, the emergence and growth of climbing fibers arising from the inferior olivary nucleus can be followed. BEN immunoreactivity is successively detected on fibers in the cerebellar peduncles, the white matter and the Purkinje cell layer. The contacts established between the growing climbing fibers and the Purkinje cells in E14 and E18 embryos as revealed by BEN immunocytochemistry are strikingly similar to those seen by Cajal after Golgi staining (Fig. 10). The origin of the BEN positive fibers from the inferior olivary nucleus and thus their identity with the climbing fibers was further assessed by using the quail-chick chimera system.

From the fate mapping experiments of the rhombencephalon described previously, we knew that the presumptive territory of the inferior olivary nucleus is located in the myelencephalon and the rostral part of the spinal cord whereas the cerebellar cortex arises from the mesencephalon and the anterior metencephalon. Therefore chimeras were constructed by substituting the presumptive cerebellar territory (including its mes- and metencephalic components) of a chick by its quail counterpart. In such birds, the inferior olivary nucleus is composed of host cells, whereas the cerebellar cortex is derived from the graft.

We have taken advantage of this system and used species specific antibodies which recognize chick but not quail neuronal fibers. In these cerebellar chimeras, only the fibers afferent to the cerebellar cortex are of chick origin. Double staining experiments using these species specific antibodies together with anti-BEN antibodies showed that the immunoreactive chick fibers were also BEN positive. Together with the histological observation of BEN immunoreactivity during ontogenesis of the cerebellum, we conclude that BEN is expressed on climbing fibers during their axonogenesis and synaptogenesis.

Conclusions and discussion

This series of investigations demonstrates the use that can be made of the combination of two techniques: the quail-chick chimera system to trace morphogenetic movements of epithelia and migrations of embryonic cells and molecular methods to characterize the emergence of various cell types in the nervous system. The particular study carried out on the climbing fibers illustrates that such an approach can also be useful to illustrate and follow the onset of connexions between distant structures within the developing brain.

The investigations performed on the BEN/DM-GRASP/SC1 molecule suggest that its transient expression by definite subsets of neurons during development might be related to its role in axonal guidance and/or fasciculation and likely also to growth cone and target cell recognition during the establishment of certain types of synapses.

One striking fact in the biology of this molecule is that it is not specific for a particular type of neurons but rather of neurons emerging as homogenous groups. Although expression of BEN during development seems a general feature of motoneurons over the whole nervous system, other types of neurons also present this characteristic. Such is the case for virtually all the neurons arising from the neural crest and certain interneurons in the brain. Its distribution suggests that it could play a role in recognition and perhaps adhesion of homologous neurons together with a similar role in the projection of these neurons to restricted sets of targets.

Acknowledgements

We are indebted to Dr Françoise Dieterlen for critical reading of the manuscript. We thank Evelyne Bourson, Michelle Scaglia and Michelle Muesser for secretarial assistance. Our thanks go to Yann Rantier, Thierry Guérot and Sophie Gournet for photography and artwork. Financial support was provided by the Centre National de la Recherche Scientifique (CNRS), the Fondation pour la Recherche Médicale Française, and the Ligue Française pour la Recherche contre le Cancer and the Association Française contre les Myopathies (AFM).

References

Balaban, E., Teillet, M.A. and Le Douarin, N.M. (1988) Application of the quail-chick chimera system to the study of brain development and behavior. *Science*, 241: 1339–1342.

Burns, F.R., Von Kannen, S., Guy, L., Raper, J.A., Kamholz, J. and Chang, S. (1991) DM-GRASP, a novel immunoglobulin superfamily axonal surface protein that supports neurite extension. *Neuron*, 7: 209–220.

Chang, S., Fan, J. and Nayak, J (1992) Pathfinding by cranial nerve VII (facial) motoneurons in the chick hindbrain. *Development*, 114: 815–823.

El-Deeb, S., Thompson, S.C. and Covault, J. (1992) Characterization of a cell surface adhesion molecule expressed by a subset of developing chick neurons. *Dev. Biol.*, 149: 213–227.

Fournier Le Ray, C. and Fontaine-Pérus, J. (1991) Influence of spinal cord stimulation on the innervation pattern of muscle fibers in vivo. *J. Neurosci.*, 11: 3840–3850.

Fraser, S., Keynes, R. and Lumsden, A. (1990) Segmentation in the chick embryo hindbrain is defined by cell lineage restrictions. *Nature*, 344: 431–435.

Gans, C. and Northcutt, R.G. (1983) Neural crest and the origin of vertebrates: a new head. *Science*, 220: 268–274.

Guthrie, S. and Lumsden, A. (1992) Motor neuron pathfinding following rhombomere reversals in the chick embryo hindbrain. *Development*, 114: 663–673.

Guy, N., Teillet, M.A., Schuler, B., Lasalle, G.L., Le Douarin, N.M., Naquet, R. and Batini, C. (1992) Pattern of electroencephalographic activity during light induced seizures in genetic epileptic chicken and brain chimeras. *Neurosci. Lett.*, 145: 55–58.

Guy, N.T.M., Batini, C., Naquet, R. and Teillet, M.A. (1993) Avian photogenic epilepsy and embryonic brain chimeras – neuronal activity of the adult prosencephalon and mesencephalon. *Exp. Brain Res.*, 93: 196–204.

Hallonet, M.E.R. and Le Douarin, N.M. (1993) Tracing neuroepithelial cells of the mesencephalic and metencephalic alar plates during cerebellar ontogeny in quail-chick chimeras. *Eur. J. Neurosci.*, 5: 1145–1155.

Hallonet, M.E.R., Teillet, M.A. and Le Douarin, N.M. (1990) A new approach to the development of the cerebellum provided by the quail-chick marker system. *Development*, 108: 19–31.

Hamburger, V. (1948) The mitotic patterns in the spinal cord of the chick embryo and their relation to histogenetic processes. *J. Comp. Neurol.*, 88: 221–284.

Hamburger, V. and Hamilton, H.L. (1951) A series of normal stages in the development of the chick embryo. *J. Morphol.*, 88: 49–92.

His, W. (1891) Die Entwicklung des menschlichen Rautenhirns vom Ende des ersten bis zum Beginn des dritten Monats. I. Verlängertes Mark. *Abh. Sächs Ges. Wiss., Mat. Phys. K. I.*, 29: 1–74.

Kanki, J.P. and Kuwada, J.Y. (1993) Cloning and characterization of a Zebrafish cDNA similar to chick DM-GRASP, a neural cell surface protein in the immunoglobulin superfamily. *Soc. Neurosci. Abstr.*, 19: 1090.

Kinutani, M., Coltey, M. and Le Douarin, N.M. (1986) Postnatal development of a demyelinating disease in avian spinal cord chimeras. *Cell*, 45: 307–314.

Laessing, U., Giordano, S., Lottspeich, F. and Stuermer, C.A.O. (1993) Molecular cloning of neurolin and its expression in Goldfish and embryonic Zebrafish CNS. *Soc. Neurosci. Abstr.*, 19: 1090.

Lance-Jones, C.C. and Lagenaur, C.F. (1987) A new marker for identifying quail cells in embryonic avian chimeras: a quail-specific antiserum. *J. Histochem. Cytochem.*, 35: 771–780.

Le Douarin, N.M. (1969) Particularités du noyau interphasique chez la Caille japonaise (*Coturnix coturnix japonica*). Utilisation de ces particularités comme 'marquage biologique' dans les recherches sur les interactions tissulaires et les migrations cellulaires au cours de l'ontogenèse. *Bull. Biol. Fr. Belg.*, 103: 435–452.

Le Douarin, N.M. (1973) A Feulgen-positive nucleolus. *Exp. Cell. Res.*, 77: 459–468.

Le Douarin, N.M. (1982) *The Neural Crest*, Cambridge University Press, Cambridge, 259 pp.

Le Douarin, N.M. (1993) Embryonic neural chimaeras in the study of brain development. *Trends Neurosci.*, 16(2): 64–72.

Leber, S.M., Breedlove, S.M. and Sanes, J.R. (1990) Lineage, arrangements and death of clonally related motoneurons in chick spinal cord. *J. Neurosci.*, 10: 2451–2462.

Lehmann, J.M., Riethmuller, G. and Johnson, J.P. (1989) MUC18, a marker of tumor progression in human melanoma, shows sequence similarity to the neural cell adhesion molecules of the immunoglobulin superfamily. *Proc. Natl. Acad. Sci. USA*, 86: 9891–9895.

Martinez, S. and Alvarado-Mallart, R.M. (1989) Rostral cerebellum originates from the caudal portion of the so-called "mesencephalic" vesicle: a study using chick/quail chimeras. *Eur. J. Neurosci.*, 1: 549–560.

McMahon, A.P. and Bradley, A. (1990) The Wnt-1 (int-1) proto-oncogene is required for development of a large region of the mouse brain. *Cell*, 62: 1073–1085.

Pourquié, O., Coltey, M., Thomas, J.L. and Le Douarin, N.M. (1990) A widely distributed antigen developmentally regulated in the nervous system. *Development*, 109: 743–752.

Pourquié, O., Corbel, C., Le Caer, J.P., Rossier, J. and Le Douarin, N.M. (1992a) BEN, a surface glycoprotein of the immuno-

18

globulin superfamily, is expressed in a variety of developing systems. *Proc. Natl. Acad. Sci. USA*, 89: 5261–5265.

Pourquié, O., Hallonet, M.E.R. and Le Douarin, N.M. (1992b) BEN glycoprotein expression is associated with climbing fibers axonogenesis in the avian cerebellum. *J. Neurosci.*, 12: 1548–1557.

Prince, J.T., Nishiyama, A., Healy, P.A., Beasley, L. and Stallcup, W.B. (1992). Expression of the F84-1 glycoprotein in the spinal cord and the cranial nerves of the developing rat. *Dev. Brain Res.*, 68: 193–202.

Ramon Y Cajal, S. (1911) *Histologie du Système Nerveux de l'Homme et des Vertébrés* (reprinted by Consejo Superior de Investigaciones Cientificas, Madrid, 1955), Maloine, Paris.

Ramos, R.G.P., Igloi, G.L., Lichte, B., Baumann, U., Maier, D., Schneider, T., Brandstätter, H.J., Fröhlich, A. and Fischbach, K.-F. (1993) The irregular chiasm C-roughest locus of *Drosophila*, which affects axonal projections and programmed cell death, encodes a novel immunoglobulin-like protein. *Genes Dev.*, 7: 2533–2547.

Simeone, A., Acampora, D., Gulisano, M., Stornaiuolo, A. and Boncinelli, E. (1992). Nested expression of four homeobox genes in developing rostral brain. *Nature*, 358: 687–690.

Takagi, S., Tsuji, T., Kinutani, M. and Fujisawa, H. (1989) Monoclonal antibodies against species-specific antigens in the chick central nervous system: putative application as transplantation markers in the chick-quail chimeras. *J. Histochem. Cytochem.*, 37: 177–184.

Tan, K. and Le Douarin, N.M. (1991) Development of the nuclei and cell migration in the medulla oblongata – application of the quail-chick chimera system. *Anat. Embryol.*, 183: 321–343.

Tanaka, H., Kinutani, M., Agata, A., Takashima, Y. and Obata, K. (1990) Pathfinding during spinal tract formation in Quail-Chick chimera analysed by species specific monoclonal antibodies. *Development*, 110: 565–571.

Tanaka, H., Matsui, T., Agata, A., Tomura, M., Kubota, I., Mcfarland, K.C., Kohr, B., Lee, A., Phillips, H.S. and Shelton, D.L. (1991) Molecular cloning and expression of a novel adhesion molecule, SC1. *Neuron.*, 7: 535–545.

Teillet, M.A., Naquet, R., Lasalle, G.L., Merat, P., Schuler, B. and Le Douarin, N.M. (1991) Transfer of genetic epilepsy by embryonic brain grafts in the chicken. *Proc. Natl. Acad. Sci. USA*, 88: 6966–6970.

Thomas, K.R. and Capecchi, M.R. (1990) Targeted disruption of the murine int-1 proto-oncogene resulting in severe abnormalities in midbrain and cerebellar development. *Nature*, 346: 847–850.

Wenger, C. (1950) An experimental analysis of relations between parts of the brachial spinal cord of the embryonic chick. *J. Exp. Zool.*, 114: 51–91.

Yamada, T., Placzek, M., Tanaka, H., Dodd, J. and Jessell, T.M. (1991) Control of cell pattern in the developing nervous system: polarizing activity of the floor plate and notochord. *Cell*, 64: 635–647.

F. Bloom (Editor)
Progress in Brain Research, Vol. 100
© 1994 Elsevier Science B.V. All rights reserved

CHAPTER 2

Development of sympathetic neurons: neurotransmitter plasticity and differentiation factors

Story C. Landis

Department of Neurosciences, Case Western Reserve University, School of Medicine, Cleveland, OH 44106, USA

Introduction

Almost two decades ago, studies of sympathetic neurons developing in cell culture revealed that postmitotic neurons could alter their neurotransmitter phenotype (Landis and Patterson, 1981). By growing neurons dissociated from the superior cervical ganglia of newborn rats in the presence of non-neuronal cells, such as heart or skeletal muscle, noradrenergic neurons were induced to become functionally cholinergic. The induction of cholinergic properties by co-culture with non-neuronal cells does not require cell contact but occurs through the release of a soluble cholinergic inducing activity into the medium. That the cholinergic factor produced by non-neuronal cells causes individual neurons that express noradrenergic properties to become cholinergic was formally demonstrated in studies of neuron/heart microcultures in which the changing transmitter properties of single neurons were followed over time (Potter et al., 1986). While initial analyses in this system focussed on the classical transmitters, norepinephrine and acetylcholine, subsequent studies indicated neuropeptide expression by sympathetic neurons is also influenced by the same classes of environmental factors (Kessler, 1985; Nawa and Sah, 1990).

It is now clear that neurotransmitter plasticity analogous to that initially uncovered in vitro occurs in vivo, both during development and following injury. Further, significant progress has been made in identifying the differentiation factors that affect sympathetic

neurotransmitter phenotype. Two of these, leukemia inhibitory factor (LIF) and ciliary neurotrophic factor (CNTF), are members of a recently described family of cytokines, and have actions on hematopoietic cells and neurons, including sympathetic, sensory and motor neurons (Patterson, 1992). The present challenge is to define where and how these cytokines and other differentiation factors normally act, not only to influence the properties of sympathetic neurons but also those of the other classes of responsive neurons. The recent generation of transgenic mice deficient in LIF and CNTF will aid in this endeavor (Rao et al., 1993a; Masu et al., 1993).

Transmitter plasticity occurs during development and after injury in vivo

To determine whether the neurotransmitter phenotype of sympathetic neurons is plastic during development in vivo as in vitro, we examined how sympathetic neurons acquire their adult complement of transmitters (Landis, 1990). Mature sympathetic neurons possess an extensive repertoire of neurotransmitter phenotypes: while many are noradrenergic, a minority are cholinergic and most contain one or more neuropeptides selected from the following: neuropeptide Y, enkephalin, vasoactive intestinal peptide (VIP), somatostatin or calcitonin gene-related peptide (CGRP). Initially most, if not all, sympathetic neurons express noradrenergic properties, including those that in the adult will be cholinergic. The best characterized cholinergic sympathetic neurons innervate sweat glands, concentrated in footpads. The properties expressed by the developing sweat gland innervation are strikingly different from those expressed by the mature innervation. When axons contact the developing glands, they exhibit noradrenergic properties and the cholinergic and peptidergic markers that characterize the mature innervation are undetectable. Choline acetyltransferase activity and VIP and CGRP immunoreactivities appear during the second and third postnatal weeks as the expression of noradrenergic properties decreases.

The changes in transmitter properties of sweat gland neurons are retrogradely specified by interactions with the target tissue (Landis, 1990). When sweat gland primordia in early postnatal rats are replaced with parotid gland, a target receiving noradrenergic sympathetic innervation, the sweat gland neurons that innervate the transplanted parotid gland retain catecholamines and fail to develop choline acetyltransferase or VIP. In addition, the terminals of presumptive sweat gland neurons that innervate the footpads of *Tabby* mutant mice that lack sweat glands fail to acquire the normal cholinergic and peptidergic phenotype. Conversely, when sweat gland-containing skin is transplanted to the lateral thorax so that sympathetic neurons that would normally innervate noradrenergic targets in hairy skin innervate sweat glands instead, the innervation of the transplanted glands exhibits properties appropriate for the novel target rather than hairy skin. Although catecholamine containing fibers initially form a plexus in the transplanted glands, by 6 weeks catecholamines have largely disappeared from the sympathetic axons and choline acetyltransferase activity and VIP have been induced.

Striking changes occur in neuropeptide expression in adult sympathetic neurons in vivo after injury. For example, the superior cervical ganglion normally contains little VIP and only an occasional neuron is immunoreactive. If the carotid nerves carrying postganglionic axons of neurons in the superior cervical ganglion are cut, however, there is a dramatic induction of VIP protein and mRNA which is accompanied by a significant increase in the number of intensely VIP immunoreactive neurons (Hyatt-Sachs et al.,

1993). Similarly, little substance P (SP) is present, no immunoreactive cell bodies are detectable and only occasional fibers contain SP. After axotomy, SP content and tachykinin mRNA increase and numerous SP-immunoreactive cell bodies appear (Rao et al., 1993b). The very large increases observed after cutting postganglionic axons contrast with the modest increases seen after section of the superior cervical trunk carrying preganglionic input to the ganglion. Since some neurons in the superior cervical ganglion send axons through the cervical sympathetic trunk, the small increases observed after cutting the cervical sympathetic trunk may arise from axotomy rather than denervation.

Cell culture studies provide evidence that ganglionic non-neuronal cells play a role in mediating neuropeptide induction that occurs in response to axotomy. For example, co-culture with ganglionic non-neuronal cells, fibroblasts, satellite and Schwann cells, increases VIP content in dissociated cell cultures and this effect is mimicked by treatment of neuron-enriched cultures by medium conditioned by ganglionic non-neuronal cells (Sun et al., 1994). VIP is also induced when adult ganglia are placed in explant culture and medium conditioned by explanted ganglia induces VIP in neuron-enriched cultures (Sun et al., 1994). How axotomy causes ganglionic non-neuronal cells to produce peptide-inducing factors is unknown but it seems likely that both a retrograde signal initiated by axon transection and intercellular signalling between axotomized neuron cell bodies and ganglionic non-neuronal cells are involved.

The neurotransmitter plasticity displayed by sympathetic neurons is not unique. Examination of the development of transmitter properties has disclosed a number of examples of altered expression of transmitter synthetic enzymes and neuropeptides and suggests that not only quantitative, but also qualitative, changes in transmitter expression are common (Patterson and Nawa, 1993). The most thoroughly studied example is the transient catecholaminergic cells of the gut which give rise to many if not all the neurons, cholinergic, serotonergic and peptidergic, of the enteric nervous system (Baetge et al., 1990). Gershon and colleagues have put forward the hypothesis that the local environment, rather than the target, provides the instructive cues that result in the acquisition of the adult transmitter phenotype. Increases in neuropeptide expression, both peptide content and its mRNA, are also a common consequence of axotomy in peripheral neurons. As in sympathetic neurons, following nerve section or crush, VIP and galanin are induced in dorsal root ganglion neurons and CGRP and galanin increase in motor neurons.

Cholinergic differentiation factors are members of the neuropoietic cytokine family

Two proteins have been identified that induce cholinergic function in cultured sympathetic neurons. Cholinergic differentiation factor (CDF), an approximately 45 kDa glycoprotein, was purified from heart cell conditioned medium. It has subsequently been found to be identical to leukemia inhibitory factor, a multifunctional cytokine with effects of a variety of non-neuronal cells (Yamamori et al., 1989). The second cholinergic factor, ciliary neurotrophic factor, was purified from sciatic nerve on the basis of its ability to support the survival of chick ciliary neurons and was subsequently shown to induce cholinergic function in cultured sympathetic neurons. Pattern-based sequence comparison and homology modeling of protein fold suggest that CDF/LIF and CNTF are members of a family of hemopoietic cytokines that also includes interleukin-6, granulocyte colony-stimulating factor and oncostatin M (Patterson, 1992). Further evidence that the grouping of at least CDF/LIF, CNTF, interleukin-6 and oncostatin M together based on their predicted structure is correct comes from examination of their candidate receptor molecules (Ip et al., 1992). The evidence at present suggests that the CDF/LIF receptor is comprised of two subunits, gp 130 and LIFRβ, and that this receptor can be converted into a CNTF receptor by the addition of a CNTFRα subunit. At least one of these subunits, gp130, also contributes to the IL-6 and oncostatin M receptors. The development of a rapid reverse transcriptase polymerase chain reaction screen for the effects of candidate molecules on transmitter expression by sympathetic neurons will certainly add new differ-

entiation factors to the present list (Fann and Patterson, 1993).

While the first neuronal action identified for LIF was the induction of cholinergic function in cultured sympathetic neurons, an ever increasing list of actions on neurons in cell cultures is being compiled. Further, to the extent that comparisons have been made, many of these activities are shared with CNTF. LIF and CNTF both alter the expression of neuropeptides in cultured sympathetic neurons, increasing VIP, SP and somatostatin and decreasing NPY. They increase the survival of motor neurons and choline acetyltransferase activity in cultured motor neurons (Arakawa et al., 1990; Martinou et al., 1992) while LIF decreases the expression of tyrosine hydroxylase in cranial sensory neurons (Fan and Katz, 1993). It also increases the production of neurons from spinal cord precursors and sensory neurons from neural crest (Murphy et al., 1991). Both LIF and CNTF support the survival of oligodendrocytes in cell culture (Barres et al., 1993). One interesting exception to the list of common activities is the ability of CNTF but not LIF to support the survival of chick ciliary neurons. In a small number of cases, these analyses of the actions of exogenous CNTF and LIF have been extended to in vivo systems. For example, CNTF has been shown to support the survival of axotomized neonatal motor neurons (Sendtner et al., 1990).

The identification of the cholinergic differentiation factor present in heart cell conditioned medium as LIF as well as other reports on the effects of interleukins on neuron survival and differentiation has resulted in the recognition that cytokines acting on hematopoietic cells may also act in the developing nervous system. Developing a catalogue of candidate effects using reduced culture systems should expedite elucidation of the roles of these factors in vivo.

Do the cholinergic differentiation factors influence sympathetic neurotransmitter phenotype in vivo?

Several lines of evidence suggest that the noradrenergic/cholinergic transmitter switch induced in the sweat gland innervation is not mediated by either LIF or CNTF, but by a novel member of the cytokine family. Extracts of developing and adult rat footpads contain an activity that induces choline acetyltransferase activity and VIP and reduces catecholamines and tyrosine hydroxylase in cultured sympathetic neurons (Rao et al., 1992; Rohrer, 1992). Sweat glands appear to be the source of this activity since significantly less cholinergic inducing activity is extracted from footpads of Tabby mutant mice that lack sweat glands than from footpads of normal mice. The cholinergic inducing activity in the extract is not immunoprecipitated or blocked by LIF antisera (Rao et al., 1992). Consistent with this finding, the neurotransmitter properties of the sweat gland innervation in transgenic mice which are deficient in LIF is indistinguishable from normal (Rao et al., 1993a). While a majority of the cholinergic inducing activity can be immunoprecipitated from footpad extracts with CNTF antisera (Rao et al., 1992; Rohrer, 1992), immunoblot and northern blot analysis did not reveal the presence of authentic CNTF protein or mRNA even though both were detectable in sciatic nerve which approximately equivalent amounts of cholinergic inducing activity as footpads (Rao et al., 1992). Recent data from transgenic mice that lack CNTF indicate, as in the case of the LIF deficient mice, that the neurotransmitter properties of the sweat gland innervation are normal (Masu et al., 1993). Taken together, these observations suggest that the sweat gland differentiation factor is related to, but distinct from, CNTF.

While LIF does not appear to be responsible for the adrenergic/cholinergic switch that takes place in the sweat gland innervation, it does play an important role in the induction of neuropeptides in adult sympathetic neurons after axotomy. LIF induces VIP and SP, peptides induced by axotomy in vivo, in sympathetic neurons in dissociated cell culture (Nawa and Patterson, 1990). LIF mRNA rises within sympathetic ganglia within several hours after axotomy. VIP and SP are induced when sympathetic ganglia are placed in explant culture, presumably because this entails axotomy. This induction is significantly suppressed when function-blocking LIF antibodies are included in the medium (Sun et al., 1994). Finally, the induction of VIP and neurokinin A, which like SP is derived from the β-preprotachykinin mRNA, is largely absent when

superior cervical ganglia of LIF deficient mice are explanted into culture or axotomized in situ (Rao et al., 1993a). It is of interest that the role of LIF revealed in these studies while not that of directing the noradrenergic/cholinergic switch initially predicted by the cell culture studies is nonetheless consistent with them. LIF does mediates a change in neurotransmitter properties, peptide expression, in sympathetic neurons but does so in a different context than anticipated, in response to injury and not during development.

Small molecule transmitters, like the cytokines, function as differentiation factors

Analysis of the developing sweat gland innervation has revealed that establishing a functional synapse requires not only retrograde signalling but also anterograde. First, production of the cholinergic differentiation factor by sweat glands requires noradrenergic innervation (Habecker and Landis, 1993). In culture, sweat gland cells produce cholinergic inducing activity only when they are co-cultured with sympathetic neurons. This effect is blocked by adrenergic antagonists, suggesting that it is mediated by catecholamines. Similarly, the cholinergic inducing activity present in extracts of footpads of rat pups was reduced when the glands were surgically denervated (Rohrer, 1992) and eliminated when the sympathetic innervation was specifically lesioned at birth by treatment with 6-hydroxydopamine (Habecker and Landis, 1993). Second, cholinergic innervation is required for the development of secretory responsiveness (Grant and Landis, 1994). During development, the onset of sweat secretion in response to nerve stimulation or cholinergic agonists occurs after the appearance of cholinergic properties in the innervation and glands respond to agonists only if activated by nerve stimulation. When innervation and the transmitter switch is delayed, the development of physiological responsiveness is also delayed. Finally, adult rats, sympathectomized at birth, do not sweat. These data suggest that a factor(s) associated with the cholinergic innervation is required for gland function and acetylcholine is an excellent candidate. When we disrupted transmission in developing rats with the muscarinic antagonist, atropine, the acquisition of secretory function was prevented. After atropine was withdrawn, responsiveness developed. Thus, activation of muscarinic receptors is responsible for the induction and also maintenance of secretory responsiveness.

Our observations on the development of sympathetic neurons provide evidence that complex reciprocal interactions may be required to establish functional synapses between these neurons and their target tissues. Further, in addition to the instructive role(s) that member of the neuropoietic cytokine family play, we have found that the transmitters, norepinephrine and acetylcholine, act as differentiation signals.

References

Arakawa, Y., Sendtner, M. and Thoenen, H. (1990) Survival effects of ciliary neurotrophic factor (CNTF) on chick embryonic motorneurons in culture: comparison with other neurotrophic factors and cytokines. *J. Neurosci.,* 10: 3507–3515.

Baetge, G., Pintar, J.E. and Gershon, M.D. (1990) Transiently catecholaminergic (TC) cells in the bowel of the fetal rat: precursors of noncatecholaminergic enteric neurons. *Dev. Biol.,* 141: 353–380.

Barres, B., Schmid, R., Sendtner, M. and Raff, M. (1993) Multiple extracellular signals are required for long-term oligodendrocyte survival. *Development,* 118: 283–295.

Fan, G. Katz, D. (1993) Non-neuronal cells inhibit catecholaminergic differentiation of primary sensory neurons: role of leukemia inhibitory factor. *Development,* 118: 83–93.

Fann, M. and Patterson, P.H. (1993) A novel approach to screen for cytokine effects on neuronal gene expression. *J. Neurochem.,* 61: 1359–1355.

Grant, M. and Landis, S. (1994) Induction and maintenance of secretory responsiveness in sweat glands by acetylcholine. *J. Neurosci.,* submitted.

Habecker, B. and Landis, S. (1993) Noradrenergic transmission influences sweat gland cholinergic differentiation factor production. *Soc. Neurosci. Abstr.,* 19: 710.11.

Hyatt-Sachs, H., Schreiber, R., Bennett, T. and Zigmond, R. (1993) Phenotypic plasticity in adult sympathetic ganglia in vivo: effects of deafferentation and axotomy on the expression of vasoactive intestinal peptide. *J. Neurosci.,* 13: 1642–1653.

Ip, Y., Nye, S., Boulton, T., Davis, S., Taga, T., Li, Y., Birren, S., Yasukawa, K., Kishimoto, T., Anderson, D. and Yancopoulos, G. (1992) CNTF and LIF act on neuronal cells via shared signalling pathways that involve the IL-6 signal transducing receptor component gp130. *Cell,* 69: 1121–1132.

Kessler, J.A. (1985) Differential regulation of peptide and catecholamine characters in cultured sympathetic neurons. *Neuroscience,* 15: 827–839.

Landis, S.C. (1990) Target regulation of neurotransmitter phenotype. *Trends Neurosci.,* 13: 344–350.

Landis, S.C. and Patterson, P.H. (1981) Neural crest cell lineages. *Trends Neurosci.,* 4: 1172–175.

Martinou, J., Martinou, I. and Kato, A. (1992) Cholinergic differentiation factor (CDF/LIF) promotes survival of isolated rat embryonic motoneurons in vitro. *Neuron,* 8: 737–744.

Masu, Y., Wolf, E., Holtmann, B., Sendtner, M., Brem, G. and Thoenen, H. (1993) Disruption of the CNTF gene results in motor neuron degeneration. *Nature,* 365: 27–32.

Murphy, M., Reid, K., Hilton, D. and Bartlett, P. (1991) Generation of sensory neurons is stimulated by leukemia inhibitory factor. *Proc. Natl. Acad. Sci. USA,* 88: 3498–3501.

Nawa, H. and Patterson, P. (1990) Separation and partial characterization of neuropeptide-inducing factors in heart cell conditioned medium. *Neuron,* 4: 269–277.

Nawa, H. and Sah, D.W. (1990) Different biological activities in conditioned media control the expression of a variety of neuropeptides in cultured sympathetic neurons. *Neuron,* 4: 279–287.

Patterson, P. (1992) The emerging neuropoietic cytokine family: first CDF/LIF, CNTF and IL-6; next ONC, MGF GCSF? *Curr. Opinions Neurobiol.,* 2: 94–97.

Patterson, P.H. and Nawa, H. (1993) Neuronal differentiation factors/cytokines and synaptic plasticity. *Cell,* 72: 123–137.

Potter, D.D., Landis, S.C., Matsumoto, S.G. and Furshpan, E.J. (1986) Synaptic functions in rat sympathetic neurons in microcultures. II. Adrenergic/cholinergic dual status and plasticity. *J. Neurosci.,* 6: 1080–1096.

Rao, M.S., Patterson, P.H. and Landis, S.C. (1992) Multiple cholinergic differentiation factors are present in footpad extracts: comparison with known cholinergic factors. *Development,* 116: 731–744.

Rao, M.S., Escary, J., Sun, Y., Perreau, J., Patterson, P.H., Zigmond, R.E., Brulet, P. and Landis, S.C. (1993a) Leukemia inhibitory factor mediates an injury response but not a target-mediated developmental transmitter switch in sympathetic neurons. *Neuron,* 11: 1–12.

Rao, M., Sun, Y., Vaidyanathan, U., Landis, S. and Zigmond, R. (1993b) Regulation of substance P is similar to that of vasoactive intestinal peptide after axotomy or explantation of the rat superior cervical ganglion. *J. Neurobiol.,* 24: 571–580.

Rohrer, H. (1992) Cholinergic neuronal differentiation factors: evidence for the presence of both CNTF-like and non-CNTF-like factors in developing footpad. *Development,* 114: 689–698.

Sendtner, M., Kreutzberg, G.W. and Thoenen, H. (1990) Ciliary neurotrophic factor prevents the degeneration of motor neurons after axotomy. *Nature,* 345: 440–441.

Sun, Y., Rao, M.S., Zigmond, R.E. and Landis, S.C. (1994) Regulation of vasoactive intestinal peptide expression in sympathetic neurons in culture and after axotomy: the role of cholinergic differentiation factor/leukemia inhibitory factor. *J. Neurobiol.,* 25: in press.

Yamamori, T., Fukada, K., Aebersold, R., Korsching, S., Fann, M.J. and Patterson, P.H. (1989) The cholinergic neuronal differentiation factor from heart cells is identical to leukemia inhibitory factor. *Science,* 246: 1412–1416.

F. Bloom (Editor)
Progress in Brain Research, Vol. 100
© 1994 Elsevier Science B.V. All rights reserved

CHAPTER 3

Lessons from genetic knockout mice deficient in neural recognition molecules

Melitta Schachner

Department of Neurobiology, Swiss Federal Institute of Technology, 8093 Zurich, Switzerland

Introduction

A variety of cell surface glycoproteins expressed by neurons and glia have been recognized as important mediators of recognition among neural cells, determining the specificity of cell interactions during development and during functional maintenance, regeneration and modification of synaptic activity in the adult. Most of the recognition molecules' functions have been derived from perturbation experiments in vitro using antibodies and the isolated recognition molecules themselves as functional blockers and ligands or competitors, respectively. As the ultimate test for a particular recognition molecule's function, however, its action in the intact organism should be observed. With the advent of recombinant DNA technology and availability of embryonic stem cells, it has been possible to ablate the genes encoding neural recognition molecules in the mouse and to study the nervous system in the molecule's absence, with the hope of eventually identifying its role in a complex cellular environment.

The present review summarizes our experience with genetic knockout mutants of the mouse deficient in three neural recognition molecules: (1) the major peripheral myelin glycoprotein of mammals, the immunoglobulin superfamily derived recognition molecule PO; (2) the adhesion molecule on glia AMOG, a recognition molecule and integral component of the Na,K-ATPase; and (3) the minor glycoprotein of central and peripheral nervous system myelin forming

cells, the myelin-associated glycoprotein MAG. The three molecules are all mostly expressed in the nervous system and therein predominantly produced by glial cells at later stages of their development. It was hoped that this spatial and temporal restriction in expression would be beneficial for the production of a viable mutant animal. Analysis of the three mutants shows the range of phenotypes that can be expected from general considerations on knockout strategies. Our findings carry implications for future strategies intended to elucidate the functional role of a neural recognition molecule by genetic ablation.

All three mutants were generated by using homologous recombination in embryonic stem cells to replace the endogenous genes on the mouse chromosome by an insertionally inactivated gene (see references cited below).

The PO knockout mouse or the expected abnormal phenotype (Giese et al., 1992)

PO is the major protein of peripheral myelin of mammals. It is uniquely expressed by myelinating Schwann cells of the mammalian peripheral nervous system and accounts for 60% of the protein in the myelin sheath. It is also expressed in the compacted myelin throughout adulthood. A member of the immunoglobulin superfamily containing only one immunoglobulin-like domain, PO may engage in homophilic binding within the surface membrane of the same cell (cis-interaction) or between apposing surface membranes (trans-interaction) of myelinating Schwann cells (see Giese et al. (1992) for references).

The behaviour of the PO knockout mice was apparently normal until 2 weeks postnatally when the mice showed weak vibrations when lifted by the tail. Four-week-old mutants showed clasping of hindlimbs when lifted by the tail, uncoordinated swimming performance, slight tremors, and dragging or jerking movements of the hindlimbs. With increasing age, these behavioural traits became more pronounced, with some showing convulsions, and self-mutilation and consistently weak fore- and hindlimbs, but nevertheless without paralysis. Mice survived, with the oldest mouse maintained being now 14 months old. This abnormal mutant phenotype is reminiscent of some genetically transmitted peripheral neuropathies in humans, such as the polyneuropathy of the Charcot-Marie-Tooth or Dejerine-Sottas types. Indeed, mutations in PO have been found in these diseases (Kulkens et al., 1993; Hayasaka et al., 1993a,b; Su et al., 1993).

When peripheral nerves from 9 to 10-week-old mice were inspected for morphological abnormalities, a high degree of hypomyelination of larger calibre axons was conspicuous. Axon-Schwann cell units achieved a normal one-to-one ratio of association, but myelin-like sheaths formed fewer turns around axons with much less membrane compaction than in wild-type mice. Non-myelinating Schwann cells appeared normal. Some axons were only covered by a basal lamina, indicating the earlier presence of a Schwann cell, while still others contained myelin-like figures typically seen in Schwann cells undergoing Wallerian degeneration.

As an important prerequisite to understand the mutant phenotype, we investigated whether other neural recognition molecules known to be expressed during myelination in peripheral nerves are present in the mutant. The neural recognition molecule Ll is normally expressed by all premyelinating Schwann cells and downregulated when myelination starts. This downregulation was also observed in the mutant, in that myelin-like figures were Ll-negative. In contrast to Ll, NCAM, which is normally downregulated at the onset of myelination, remains highly expressed in the mutant in what would normally be myelinating

Schwann cells. Other molecules showing a characteristic developmental regulation of expression in normal myelinating Schwann cells were also abnormally expressed; the low affinity nerve growth factor receptor, MAG and the extracellular matrix glycoprotein tenascin, all of which are downregulated with the onset of normal myelination, were instead highly expressed in the mutant. The proteolipid protein which is normally hardly detectable in the cytoplasm of myelinating Schwann cells is present in the myelin-like figures of the mutant. The myelin basic protein which is highly expressed in the compact myelin of normal mice is downregulated in the mutant. Two carbohydrate structures which are expressed by overlapping sets of neural recognition molecules (see Horstkorte et al. (1993) and Hall et al. (1993) for references) are abnormally absent, in the case of the L2/HNK-l carbohydrate, or normally expressed, in the case of the oligomannosidic L3 carbohydrate.

These results show that the majority of molecules that appear to be functionally involved in myelination and other molecules with as yet unknown functions in peripheral nervous system myelination are severely dysregulated in the mutant.

Insights into the function of PO derived from the PO knockout mutant

Although the histological defects observed in PO knockout mice could be called expected, since they are largely consistent with models of PO functions advanced previously on the basis of in vitro perturbation experiments, the interpretation of the mutant phenotype appears more complex. On the one hand, the erratic pattern of secondary effects on Schwann cell gene expression does not allow the conclusion that all abnormal features of the mutant are directly due to the absence of PO. Of the nine marker molecules investigated, only two, namely Ll and the L3 oligomannosidic carbohydrate, showed the expression expected from the wildtype. Given these multiple examples of abnormal gene expression in the mutant, it is plausible to assume that certain features of the mutant phenotype are not directly due to the absence of PO. For example, the continued expression of NCAM and MAG could be the cause rather than the consequence of one or all aspects of myelin abnormalities. On the other hand, it is also conceivable that the ability of some Schwann cell processes to engage in a limited amount of spiralling may be due to the continued expression of neural recognition molecules, such as NCAM and MAG. Possibly even other dysregulated molecules, such as proteolipid protein could at least partially compensate for the absence of PO. Our observations thus emphasize that it is not sufficient to analyze the behavioural and histological pheno-types of a mutant, but that a detailed analysis of secondary effects on gene expression may be necessary for a complete understanding of the mutant pheno-type.

The adhesion molecule on glia (AMOG) knockout mouse or the interpretable abnormal phenotype (Magyar et al., 1993)

AMOG was first described on the basis of in vitro experiments showing that antibodies against AMOG inhibited the migration of cerebellar granule cells along Bergmann glial processes (see Müller-Husmann et al. (1993) for references). AMOG is hardly detectable outside the central nervous system and is mainly expressed by glial cells, but also by certain types of neurons. Its expression is first detectable in the brain at late embryonic ages, increases during the first 2 weeks after birth along with the general maturation of the brain and reaches highest levels in the adult. Sequence analysis of AMOG revealed it to be a close homologue of the $\beta 1$ subunit of the Na,K-ATPase. The rat and human species homologues of AMOG were identified also as the $\beta 2$ subunit of the enzyme by low stringency hybridization using a $\beta 1$ subunit probe.

AMOG is a recognition molecule by several operational criteria. AMOG is tightly associated with the α subunits of the Na,K-ATPase, which co-purify with AMOG during stringent immunoaffinity chromatography purification procedures. The functional integration of AMOG into an ion pump introduces a new concept in the link between cell recognition and signal transduction: coupling of cell recognition with ion transport implicates cell interactions in the regulation of ionic homeostasis and the cellular parameters dependent on the ionic environment such as voltage-dependent ion channels, size of extracellular space volume and cell volume.

AMOG knockout mutants were behaviourally unremarkable during their first 2 weeks. At 14–15 days, mutant mice showed reduced righting behaviour and orientation when lifted by the tail. Within only 2–3 days, this motor incoordination rapidly worsened and AMOG mutant mice developed paralysis of their forelimbs and were unable to hold their heads upright. The hind limbs started to become tremorous and the animals were no longer able to stand. Shortly before their death at days 17 or 18, mutants were generally very weak and lay on their side but still showed normal grasping reflexes and responded to sound.

The abnormal phenotype was immediately obvious when inspecting the size of the lateral and third ventricles which were considerably enlarged in comparison to wild-type or heterozygous littermates. While the cortices of cerebellum and cerebrum, the hippocampus and optic nerve showed no histological abnormalities, the brain stem, thalamus, striatum and, to a lesser degree, spinal cord were all abnormal: Swollen cellular processes and vacuoles were detectable in frequent association with blood vessels. The most likely interpretation of these observations is that the vacuoles result from swelling and subsequent degeneration of astrocytic processes. In contrast to the PO mutant, other recognition molecules, such as NCAM, Ll or MAG were expressed at similar levels in AMOG mutants and wild-type littermates. Also, the $\beta 1$ subunit of Na,K-ATPase was normally expressed in the mutant. However, some dysregulation in the levels of the α subunits was seen, which were reduced in the mutant.

Insights into the function of AMOG derived from the mutant

The abnormal phenotype of the mutant begs the question as to the relation between cause and consequence of the lack of AMOG expression. Also, the question as to which of the two functional roles indicated for AMOG, namely cell-cell recognition on the one hand and pump activity on the other, needs consideration.

The mutant shows no evidence that AMOG plays a profound morphogenetic role during formation of the hippocampus, optic nerve, and cerebellar and cerebral cortices. Although antibodies against AMOG were initially found to interfere with granule neuron migration along Bergmann glial cells in vitro, this disturbance may be rather the consequence of an abnormal pump activity that can be elicited by the antibodies (Gloor et al., 1990) than caused by a defect in cell recognition between the two interacting partner cell types. It is also conceivable that other recognition molecules known to be involved in the migration process, such as tenascin, thrombospondin or Ll are able to compensate for the defect in AMOG (see Magyar et al. (1993) for references). From these observations it would appear necessary to analyze more systematically at different developmental stages whether AMOG plays a subtle, yet detectable role in morphogenetic cell interactions.

From the observations on the mutant phenotype it is evident that, without prior knowledge of the molecule's function, the mutant abnormalities would have been difficult to interpret on a molecular basis. Since spongiform encephalopathies resulting in neurodegeneration have been observed in many pathological situations, the non-uniform degeneration of certain cell types would have been impossible to rationalize. On the other hand, some of the functions deduced from in vitro perturbation experiments are less prominent in the animal than expected from these experiments, rendering a profound role of AMOG during morphogenesis more unlikely. Rather, it is conceivable that AMOG would be more instrumental in recognition-mediated triggering of pump activity in the adult, when expression of the molecule is highest. Despite these uncertainties in interpretation, the abnormalities of the mutant phenotype have allowed the design of further experiments to probe the complex functional roles of AMOG in the central nervous system.

The myelin-associated glycoprotein (MAG) knockout mouse or the enigmatic normal phenotype (unpublished observations)

MAG is a transmembrane glycoprotein of the immu-noglobulin superfamily which is heavily glycosylated in its extracellular domain (see Schneider-Schaulies et al. (1991) for references). It occurs in developmentally regulated, alternatively spliced forms in the central and peripheral nervous system. MAG is also an adhesion molecule by several criteria. In addition to its adhesive role, MAG can also promote neurite outgrowth, again by a heterophilic mechanism. From these observations and the fact that MAG expresses the functionally important L2/HNK-l carbohydrate (Martini et al., 1992), a neurite outgrowth promoting role of MAG during regeneration in the peripheral nervous system could be envisaged.

No overtly abnormal phenotype of the mutant has been detected so far, through ages of several months. Behaviourally, the mutants show no gross defects. Histologically, myelin in the optic and sciatic nerves of 8-week-old mutants had an overall normal appearance at the light microscopic level.

Insights into the function of MAG derived from the mutant at the present stage of investigations

Although inferences about the function of MAG during the initiation of the myelination process were derived from the precise timing of its expression at the onset of myelination, the MAG mutant does not support the notion that MAG is an essential ingredient in myelin formation. It is at present difficult to reconcile the observations on the mutant with those resulting from in vitro experiments using anti-sense RNA approaches (Owens and Bunge, 1991). It is, however, conceivable that acute ablations in cell culture are less prone to evoke compensatory mechanisms than a chronic ablation as created by the knockout situation. What these compensatory mechanisms might be will need to be determined. Also, a more detailed analysis of myelin morphology in the adult and at early formative stages will need to be performed to be sure that subtle abnormalities may not have escaped detection. Again, knowledge of MAG's discrete temporal and spatial expression pattern and of some of its functions in vivo will make this search a focussed one. On the other hand, MAG may not have an essential function and may be an evolutionary vestige that has been retained during phylogeny for optimization of a function which could be carried out, in the absence of MAG, also by another or several other recognition molecules. However, in the absence of a presently detectable abnormal phenotype, all speculations about the possible causes of the apparent normality remain unfounded.

Conclusions

Ablating molecules that appear to be of significance in development and maintenance of nervous system functions appear to represent an intriguing, but also risky approach. In this short review, three mutants were characterized that cover a broad spectrum of expectations from the knowledge on the structure and in vitro functions of the molecules. On the one hand, the PO mutant presents itself indeed as expected, but with the caveat that other mechanisms related indirectly to the absence of PO may account for the observed abnormalities. Such indirect, either dysregulatory or compensatory effects will have to be taken more into consideration in the interpretation of any mutant phenotype.

The adhesion molecule on glia (AMOG) knockout mutant displays a very complex phenotype that is both expected and unexpected in the sense that the dual function of the molecule does not become apparent. An abnormality in pump activity was expected, but somewhat unexpected was that no morphogenetic aberrations have so far been observed. With the knowledge of the structure and function of the molecule and its spatial and temporal expression in the nervous system, the design of further experiments that could clarify the evolvement of the mutant's abnormal phenotype is now feasible.

The other extreme of the mutant's contribution to an understanding of a molecule's function is represented by the MAG mutant which so far has not yielded any abnormal phenotype. One could argue that, as an evolutionary vestige, MAG is not an essential ingredient in the formation and maintenance of myelin and that compensatory mechanisms could come into play that may attribute to MAG a superfluous or, at the most, an optimization role in the myelination process. On the other hand, it could very well

be that the present level of investigations has not been detailed enough to allow subtle abnormalities to be recognized. Until such possibilities are exhausted, the gene's function in vivo will remain elusive.

Given these three examples of mutant phenotypes, the general usefulness of knockout strategies ablating an entire gene will need to be reconsidered. It seems that in future strategies, more subtle ablation methods should be introduced in order to minimize compensatory mechanisms. One will have to invest heavily into acute knockout possibilities as afforded by recombinant events that are inducible by external stimuli. As complementary experimental strategies, acute manipulations of the animal using blocking antibodies, antisense oligonucleotide and RNA approaches or competing soluble fragments of the recognition molecule under study should be undertaken. Although these methods also have their drawbacks, with these combined possibilities ahead, the analysis of the function of neural recognition molecules in the authentic environment in vivo will hopefully attain its full power.

References

Giese, P., Martini, R., Lemke, G., Soriano, P. and Schachner, M. (1992) Mouse PO gene disruption leads to hypomyelination, abnormal expression of recognition molecules and degeneration of myelin and axons. Cell, 71: 565–576.

Gloor, S., Antonicek, H., Sweadner, K.J., Pagliusi, S., Frank, R., Moos, M. and Schachner, M. (1990) The adhesion molecule on glia (AMOG) is a homologue of the β subunit of the Na,K-ATPase. J. Cell Biol., 110: 165–174.

Hall, H., Liu, L., Schachner, M. and Schmitz, B. (1993) The L2/HNK-1 carbohydrate mediates adhesion of neural cells to laminin. Eur. J. Neurosci., 5: 34–42.

Hayasaka, K., Himoro, M., Sato, W., Takatta, G., Uyemura, K., Shimizu, M., Bird, T.D., Coneally, P.M. and Chance, P.F. (1993a) Charcot-Marie-Tooth neuropathy type IB is associated with mutations of the myelin P0 gene. Nature Genet., 5: 31–34.

Hayasaka, K., Himoro, M., Swaishi, Y., Nanao, K., Takahashi, T., Takada, G., Nicholson, G.A., Ouvrier, R.A. and Tachi, N. (1993b) De novo mutation of the myelin PO gene in Dejerine-Sottas disease (hereditary motor and sensory neuropathy type III). Nature Genet., 5: 266–268.

Horstkorte, R., Schachner, M., Magyar, J.P., Vorherr, T. and Schmitz, B. (1993) The fourth immunoglobulin-like domain of NCAM contains a carbohydrate recognition domain for oligomannosidic glycans implicated in association with L1 and neurite outgrowth. J. Cell Biol., 121: 1409–1421.

Kulkens, T., Bolhuis, P.A., Wolterman, R.A., Kemp, S., te Nijenhuis, S., Valentijn, L.J., Hensels, G.W., Jennekens, F.G.I., de

Visser, M., Hoogendijk, J. and Baas, F. (1993) Deletion of the serine 34 codon from the major peripheral myelin protein P0 gene in Charcot-Marie-Tooth disease type lB. *Nature Genet.*, 5: 35–39.

Magyar, J.P., Bartsch, U., Wang, Z-Q., Howells, N., Aguzzi, A., Wagner, E. and Schachner, M. (1993) Degeneration of neural cells in the central nervous system of mice deficient in the gene for the adhesion molecule on glia (AMOG), the $\beta 2$ subunit of murine Na,K-ATPase. Submitted.

Martini, R., Xin, Y., Schmitz, B. and Schachner, M. (1992) The L2/HNK-1 carbohydrate epitope is involved in the preferential outgrowth of motor neurons on ventral roots and motor nerves. *Eur. J. Neurosci.*, 4: 628–639.

Müller-Husmann, G., Gloor, S. and Schachner, M. (1993) Func-tional characterization of β isoforms of murine Na,K-ATPase: The adhesion molecule on glia (AMOG/$\beta 2$), but not $\beta 1$, pro-motes neurite outgrowth. *J. Biol. Chem,*. 268: 26260–26267.

Owens, G.C. and Bunge, R. (1991) Schwann cells infected with a recombinant retrovirus expressing myelin-associated glycopro-tein antisense RNA do not form myelin. *Neuron*, 7: 565–575.

Schneider-Schaulies, J., Kirchhoff, F., Archelos, J. and Schachner, M. (1991) Down-regulation of myelin-associated glycoprotein on Schwann cells by interferon-gamma and tumor necrosis factor-alpha affects neurite outgrowth. *Neuron*, 7: 995–1005.

Su, Y., Brooks, D.G., Li, L., Lepercq, J., Trofatter, J.A., Ravetch, J.V. and Lebo R.V. (1993) Myelin protein zero gene mutated in Charcot-Marie-Tooth type 1B patients. *Proc. Natl. Acad. Sci. USA*, 90: 10856–10860.

Molecular Brain Research

F. Bloom (Editor)
Progress in Brain Research, Vol. 100
© 1994 Elsevier Science B.V. All rights reserved

CHAPTER 4

Quantitative analysis of neuronal gene expression

James L. Roberts

Dr. Arthur M. Fishberg Research Center for Neurobiology, Mount Sinai School of Medicine, One Gustave Levy Place, New York, NY 10029, USA

Overview

The vast diversity of neuronal and glial cell types derives primarily from the heterogeneity of gene expression in these two types of brain cells. However, a significant proportion of this diversity also resides in the quantitative aspect of the exact level of expression of a specific gene within neuronal or glial cell. For example, a given neuron may express the mRNAs encoding five different subunits for the $GABA_A$ receptor Cl^- channel, but the actual level of expression of each individual subunit mRNA will ultimately determine which types $GABA_A$ Cl^- channels will actually be expressed within that neuron. If four are expressed at 100 copies per cell and the fifth is present at 10 mRNA molecules per cell, then any special properties conferred by the latter subunit to the Cl^- channel function will be under-represented. Thus, the question arises, once a gene has been turned on within the neuron or glia, at what level will it be expressed as cytoplasmic mRNA.

The biosynthesis of a gene product in eukaryotes is a long and complicated process. It begins with the transcription of the gene by RNA polymerase II in the nucleus to form the primary transcript and the subsequent processing of introns from the primary transcript in order to produce a mature mRNA. The mRNA is then transported from the nucleus to the cytoplasm in an energy dependent process where that mRNA can then be translated into its encoded protein. Finally, the mRNA is degraded in the cytoplasm, a process which under certain circumstances can be regulated. Modu-

lation of gene expression can occur at all of these levels. In general, transcriptional control is the major level at which gene expression is regulated, and through the action of various transcription factors upon cis-acting enhancer elements in the promoter region of the gene, the appropriate transcriptional rate is determined. Regulation can also occur at the nuclear RNA processing stage. Indeed, in many neural genes there is a modulation of RNA splicing or termination sites of transcription which can generate different mRNAs from a single gene transcript. This modulation, however, has more to do with the type of mRNA made, rather than the level. Finally, a mRNA is turned over in the cytoplasm at a specific rate, which in conjunction with its synthetic rate, will determine the overall level of that mRNA in the cytoplasm. The rate of cytoplasmic degradation can also be modulated by neuronal activity and other types of information input to the cell.

Not only will the level of expression of a particular gene help to dictate function within the cell, but the level of mRNA will also be able to define how rapidly changes in gene expression can occur. As a consequence of the different biochemical events taking place at different stages of the mRNA biosynthetic pathway there can be quite different response times to change. For example, levels of neuropeptide encoding mRNAs often change quite slowly, because those mRNAs are often present in tens of thousands of copies within individual neurons. On the other hand, one can rapidly observe changes in the mRNA for the transcription factor cFos after depolarization of a neuron with the induction of *cfos* gene transcription. In the basal state, there are only about 20–30 *cfos* mRNA molecules present in the cell, thus the synthesis of 200 new *cfos* mRNA molecules after 10 min of neuronal stimulation would have a major effect on the level of *cfos* gene expression. A similar change of 200 new mRNAs for the neuropeptide described above would not significantly alter the level of that mRNA. The change in new mRNA synthesis would have to persist for many hours to show changes in the cytoplasmic mRNA levels. On the other hand, however, one can rapidly affect the level of a neuropeptide mRNA by enhancing its degradation within the cytoplasm, accomplishing in less than 1 h what might take days to accomplish by lowering the level of transcription. Of course, this mechanism can only work in one direction. Thus, knowledge of the actual level of a specific mRNA provides information both as to the possible function of that gene in the cell as well as the mechanisms by which its change may be useful in modulating the function of that cell.

Methods of quantitative analysis of gene expression

While there are numerous methods of quantitating levels of a specific RNA transcript utilizing blot hybridization technologies, this chapter focuses on the solution hybridization/nuclease protection assay because of its unique properties. These properties give distinct advantages for analyzing gene expression in the brain, foremost being the extreme sensitivity of the assay. Using conventional autoradiography techniques, one can readily quantitate levels as small as 50 fg of a specific RNA transcript, and with the use of phosphoimagery techniques, sensitivity can be taken down at least another order of magnitude. Thus, this technique becomes quite useful for quantitating levels of transcripts which may be present at a very low copy number within the population of neurons under investigation, such as neurotransmitter receptors. This also makes it helpful in identifying the low abundance in nuclear transcripts involved in the biosynthesis of this specific mRNA. Secondly, because one can identify the size of the species being analyzed, numerous different RNAs of different size of protected fragments

can be analyzed in a single sample. We have called this type of assay a "multiplex" solution hybridization assay and have recently reported the details and its application to quantitation of neuroendocrine gene expression (Jakubowski and Roberts, 1992). This also becomes an important issue in looking at multiple transcripts from a single gene. Ultimately, spliced RNAs can be identified based upon which portions of the probe get protected or on the other hand, multiple transcripts in the biosynthetic pathway can also be identified (Levin et al., 1989; Jakubowski and Roberts, 1994). This latter issue becomes quite important in analysis of gene expression in quantitating different nuclear transcripts along the mRNA biosynthetic pathway.

Another useful aspect quantitating levels of the primary transcript of a particular gene using this technique is the ability to determine mRNA turnover rates utilizing transcription inhibitors to block transcription acutely. In classic biochemical studies, the loss of mRNA from the cytoplasm is measured after blockade of new RNA synthesis. However, quite often artifacts are introduced since short-lived transcripts disappear rapidly and their products may affect the half-lives of longer lived transcripts. Utilizing the approach of "decay from steady state" at the primary transcript level, one need only analyze the first 20–30 min after blockade of transcription, avoiding this pitfall. Since the primary transcript turns over much more rapidly with a $t_{1/2}$ in the range of minutes, one can follow the loss of the primary transcript and determine an initial decay rate. Under steady state conditions, two principles apply; the synthetic rate of new primary transcript and the cytoplasmic mRNA turnover rate must be equal and the loss of primary transcript by processing must equal the rate of synthesis of the primary transcript. Hence, the rate of the loss of primary transcript must be equal to the rate of cytoplasmic mRNA turnover. We have verified this technique in a study of the GnRH gene (Yeo et al., 1994b). This becomes extremely useful in either in vivo situations or in in vitro cultures where sufficient amounts of labeled RNA cannot be incorporated into RNA to perform the more classical pulse chase labeling techniques for determining mRNA half-life.

Levels of neuroendocrine gene expression

Very crucial in all these arguments is the concept that, at least to a first approximation, the level of a specific mRNA is to some degree proportional to the level of protein translated from that mRNA. Thus, an mRNA which is present in thousands of copies in the cell will produce more protein within that cell than the mRNA that is present in only a few dozen copies. In general, this concept holds true. Neuropeptide encoding mRNAs, for example, POMC in the arcuate nucleus (16 000 copies) (Fremeau et al., 1989) or vasopressin in the paraventricular nucleus (30 000 copies) (Sherman et al., 1988; Sherman and Watson, 1988) are quite abundant. At the other end of the spectrum, the mRNAs which encode specific neurotransmitter receptors, such as dopamine D2 or $GABA_A$ receptor proteins are significantly less abundant in the range of tens to hundreds of copies of mRNA per cell (Autelitano et al., 1989; Berman et al., 1994). This difference in novel expression generally reflects a fact that you only have 10 000–50 000 molecules of receptor present on the surface of a cell, whereas there will be millions of molecules of a peptide in secretory granules. Thus, the cell needs to be able to synthesize larger amounts of neuropeptide, because it will be released and turned over extracellularly, whereas the receptor will be utilized many times before it is finally turned over.

Gonadotropin releasing hormone gene expression as an example

Utilizing the information obtained from performing quantitative analysis of gene expression, we were able to elucidate an interesting pathway for GnRH gene regulation in the rodent hypothalamus. As discussed above, the GnRH gene is expressed at approximately 12 000 copies of mRNA per GnRH neuron in the hypothalamus (Jakubowski and Roberts, 1994). As such, it falls into that class where one would presume it does not exhibit rapid regulation due to the large mass of the mRNA in the cytoplasm. Utilizing the quantitative assays described above, we had made the interesting observation that in the animal, the levels of

nuclear RNA transcripts for GnRH are far higher than those seen for most genes, comprising approximately 20–40% of the total number of GnRH transcripts in the neuron (Jakubowski and Roberts, 1994). In particular, the primary transcript and its processing intermediates were present in very high levels. Initially we thought that this simply reflected inefficient or slow processing of the RNA, thus the precursor and its intermediates accumulated to a higher level. Another possible explanation was that transcription of the GnRH gene was occurring in an extremely high rate, and the steady state high level of primary transcript and processing intermediates reflected this very high level of synthesis. This would presume, however, that degradation was also at a very high rate.

In a separate set of studies, using an in situ hybridization approach, investigators found a very rapid, almost twofold rise in GnRH mRNA in the hypothalamus after only 60 min of NMDA treatment (Petersen et al., 1991). Because of the rapidity and magnitude of this effect, requiring the synthesis of about 10 000 new GnRH mRNA molecules in less than 1 h, our first reaction was that possibly this was a result of some type of in situ hybridization phenomenon where the NMDA treatment caused an increase in the accessibility of pre-existing GnRH mRNA to the probe, enhancing the observed signal. We subsequently investigated this phenomenon using the solution hybridization/nuclease protection assay and found that indeed there was an increase in the actual numbers of GnRH mRNA molecules present in the hypothalamus, exactly as reported by the in situ hybridization technique (Gore and Roberts, 1994). Interestingly, this dramatic rise in cytoplasmic mRNA was not accompanied by reciprocal changes in the levels of nuclear GnRH primary transcript, processing intermediates or mRNA, suggesting that the change was not due to a dramatic rise in the rate of the transcription of the GnRH gene or translocation of the nuclear transcripts to the cytoplasm. Only one explanation was left to account for the ability of the GnRH neuron to produce such rapid increase in the level of cytoplasmic GnRH mRNA. The GnRH gene would have to be transcribed at a very high rate and then turned over in the cytoplasm at an equivalently high rate, in essence yielding a system that has an extremely rapid "flow-through". By blocking the degradation of GnRH mRNA in the cytoplasm, the rapid flow-through rate then allows the cell to accumulate new GnRH mRNA quickly. This mechanism is also able to account for the high levels of precursor and processing intermediate in the nucleus; with an extremely high rate of synthesis in the nucleus and degradation in the cytoplasm, there are relatively more molecules reflecting the initial states of mRNA biosynthesis in the nucleus.

To test this hypothesis, we utilized an immortalized GnRH neuronal cell line, the GT1 cells, to determine the kinetic parameters of GnRH gene transcription, RNA processing and cytoplasmic GnRH mRNA turnover. Again, utilizing the solution hybridization/ nuclease protection assay, we were able to exactly quantitate levels of primary transcript, processing intermediates as well as nuclear and cytoplasmic GnRH mRNA (Yeo et al., 1994a). Utilizing two different RNA synthesis inhibitors, actinomycin D which inhibits DA polymerase binding to DNA, and DRB, an ATP analog more specific to RNA Pol II activity, we addressed the issue of how rapidly the different GnRH RNA molecules were chased through their biosynthetic pathway when transcription was stopped. From these studies, we found that the primary transcript for GnRH was turned over rapidly, with a half-life of approximately 15 min, while the cytoplasmic mRNA has an extremely long half-life of 60–80 h. Thus, while our studies in the rat hypothalamus discussed above strongly argued that the GnRH mRNA was turning over very rapidly, the observations in the GT1 cultured cell line argued just the opposite, that GnRH mRNA had an extremely long half-life. Either our interpretation of the GnRH mRNA synthetic events in the animal were incorrect or the GT1 cells were not a good model for studying GnRH mRNA biosynthesis.

Shedding light on this quandary, recently Wray et al. (1993) reported experiments where they measured the half-life of GnRH mRNA in embryonic rat hypothalamic explant cultures, utilizing an in situ hybridization technique for quantitating the mRNA. In these cultures, which maintain many of the types of neuronal contacts on the GnRH neuron seen in the intact animal, the GnRH mRNA had a half-life of only 2–4 h

after actinomycin D treatment, in stark contrast to the observations we made in the GT1 cells. However, these observations are in complete agreement with our interpretations based on the NMDA regulation studies discussed above. Thus, it appears that in the in vivo GnRH neuron, the turnover of GnRH mRNA is much more rapid than that seen in the cultured cell line, cells which are essentially devoid of all the normal inputs to the GnRH neuron. It appears that through contacts maintained in vivo, the turnover rate of GnRH mRNA in the cytoplasm is dramatically increased creating a biosynthetic pathway which is capable of sustaining rapid changes in GnRH mRNA to meet the demands of the GnRH neuron for production of its primary neuropeptide. Supporting this conclusion, we have recently discovered that in the GT1 cells, GnRH mRNA degradation is induced by protein kinase C activation, suggesting that in the basal state of GT1 cells, the GnRH mRNA turnover pathway is essentially off, giving the long half-life we observed.

Interestingly, this mechanism of gene regulation can also explain another phenomenon observed in several neuroendocrine systems, including GnRH (reviewed in King and Rubin, 1992); "new" neurons expressing the neuropeptide can be recruited at times of high demand. In the model where GnRH mRNA is rapidly turned over (see Fig. 1), some neurons may degrade the mRNA so quickly that they are in essence "negative" for GnRH. Upon proper stimulation, the GnRH mRNA degradation is suppressed, the neuron accumulates the mRNA and begins expressing GnRH

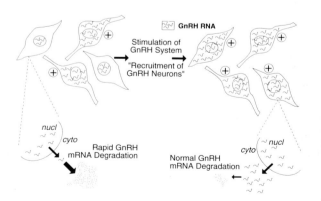

Fig. 1. Model of GnRH gene expression in GnRH neurons.

peptide. Possibly similar mechanisms are involved in other neuroendocrine systems.

Conclusions

Hopefully this chapter has highlighted the value of performing quantitative analysis of gene expression for the insights in elucidating the mechanisms by which neural cells can change the levels of gene expression. The absolute level of expression of a given gene can often yield useful information in determining the function that that gene will have within a neuron. In other cases, the relative levels of different RNA transcripts shed light on the mechanisms responsible for changing the levels and give the investigators clues as to which stages of the regulatory pathway are most likely to be involved in modulating the production of a gene transcript.

References

Autelitano, D.J., Snyder, L., Sealfon, S.C. and Roberts, J.L. (1989) Dopamine D2-receptor mRNA is differentially regulated by dopaminergic agents in rat anterior and neurointermediate pituitary. *Mol. Cell. Endocrinol.*, 67: 101–105.

Berman, J.A., Roberts, J.L. and Pritchett, D.B. (1994) Molecular and pharmacological characterization of GABA$_A$ receptors in the rat pituitary. *J. Neurochem.*, in press.

Fremeau, R.T. Jr., Autelitano, D.J., Blum, M., Wilcox, J. and Roberts, J.L. (1989) Intervening sequence-specific in situ hybridization: detection of the pro-opiomelanocortin gene primary transcript in individual neurons. *Mol. Brain Res.*, 6: 197–202.

Gore, A.C. and Roberts, J.L. (1994) Regulation of gonadotropin-releasing hormone gene expression by the excitatory amino acids kainic acid and *N*-methyl-D,L-aspartate in the male rat. *Endocrinology*, in press.

Jakubowski, M. and Roberts, J.L. (1992) Multiplex solution hybridization-RNase protection assay for quantitation of different RNA transcripts from snap-frozen neuroendocrine tissues of individual animals. *J. Neuroendocrinol.*, 4: 79–89.

Jakubowski, M. and Roberts, J.L. (1994) Processing of gonadotropin-releasing hormone gene transcripts in the rat brain. *J. Biol. Chem.*, 269: 4078–4083.

King, J.C. and Rubin, B.S. (1992) GnRH subgroups: a microarchitecture. In: W.F. Crowley and P.M. Conn (Eds.), *Modes of Action of GnRH and GnRH Analogs,* Springer-Verlag, Berlin, pp. 161–178.

Levin, N.J., Blum, M. and Roberts, J.L. (1989) Modulation of basal and corticotropin-releasing factor stimulated proopiomelanocortin gene expression by vasopressin in rat anterior pituitary. *Endocrinology,* 125: 2957–2966.

Petersen, S.L., McCrone, S., Keller, M. and Gardner, E. (1991) Rapid increases in LHRH mRNA levels following NMDA. *Endocrinology,* 129: 1679–1681.

Sherman, T.G. and Watson, S.J. (1988) Differential expression of vasopressin alleles in brattleboro heterozygote. *J. Neurosci.*, 8: 3797–3811.

Sherman, T.G., Day, R., Civelle, O., Douglass, J., Herbert, E., Akil, H. and Watson, S.L. (1988) Regulation of hypothalamic magnocellular neuropeptides and their mRNAs in the brattleboro rat: coordinate responses to further osmotic challenge. *J. Neurosci.*, 8: 3797–3811.

Wray, S., Key, S., Bachus, S. and Gainer H. (1993) Regulation of LHRH and oxytocin gene expression in CNS slice-explant cultures: effects of second messengers. Abstract 571.4, *23rd Annual Society for Neuroscience Meeting*, Washington, DC.

Yeo, T.S., Dong, K.-W., Zeng, Z., Blum, M. and Roberts, J.L. (1994a) Transcriptional and post-transcriptional regulation of gonadotropin releasing hormone gene expression by protein kinase C pathway in mouse hypothalamic GT1 cells. *Mol. Endocrinol.*, in press.

Yeo, T.S., Jakubowski, M., Dong, K.-W., Blum, M. and Roberts, J.L. (1994b) Characterization of gonadotropin releasing hormone gene transcripts in a mouse hypothalamic neuronal GT1 cell line. *J. Biol. Chem.*, in press.

F. Bloom (Editor)
Progress in Brain Research, Vol. 100
© 1994 Elsevier Science B.V. All rights reserved

CHAPTER 5

Molecular pharmacology of NMDA receptors: modulatory role of NR2 subunits

Perry B. Molinoff, Keith Williams, Dolan B. Pritchett and Jie Zhong

Department of Pharmacology, University of Pennsylvania School of Medicine, Philadelphia, PA 19104-6084, USA

Introduction

Glutamate is the major fast excitatory neurotransmitter in the vertebrate central nervous system (CNS). The last decade has seen an explosion of interest in the pharmacology, physiology and pathophysiology of glutamatergic systems and of the cell surface receptors that mediate the effects of glutamate on CNS neurons. Ligand-gated ion channels that are sensitive to glutamate are classified on the basis of their sensitivity to the selective agonists *N*-methyl-D-aspartate (NMDA), AMPA and kainate (Fig. 1). Glutamate also activates receptors that are coupled to G proteins, the so-called "metabotropic" receptors (Fig. 1). Over the last several years, genes coding for subunits of AMPA/kainate, kainate and NMDA receptors and for a family of metabotropic receptors have been cloned (Fig. 1) (Nakanishi, 1992; Seeburg, 1993). The ion channel receptors are thought to be oligomeric complexes composed of combinations of two or more types of subunits similar to pentameric nicotinic acetylcholine receptors. Metabotropic receptors are composed of a single polypeptide with limited structural similarity to other G protein-linked receptors (Nakanishi, 1992).

NMDA receptors play a pivotal role in the generation of various forms of synaptic plasticity, including some types of associative long-term potentiation and long-term depression, and in defining neuronal architecture and synaptic connectivity including experience-dependent synaptic modifications in the develop-

ing nervous system (Collingridge and Lester, 1989). Excessive or abnormally prolonged activation of NMDA receptors has been implicated in a number of pathological states including ischemic neuronal cell death, epilepsy and chronic neurodegenerative diseases (Choi, 1988). Dysfunction or abnormal regulation of NMDA receptors may also be involved in the etiology of schizophrenia. Activation of NMDA receptors is antagonized by ethanol, and these receptors may mediate some of the acute and/or chronic effects of ethanol in the CNS.

The NMDA receptor contains an integral ion channel that gates Na^+, K^+ and Ca^{2+} and is blocked at resting membrane potentials by physiological concentrations of Mg^{2+}. The Mg^{2+} block of the ion channel is voltage-dependent and is relieved during membrane depolarization, allowing activation of the receptor by NMDA or glutamate. This conditional activation of the receptor, requiring both membrane depolarization and glutamate binding, may underlie the associative nature of induction of long-term potentiation. The NMDA receptor/channel complex contains a number of distinct recognition sites for endogenous and exogenous ligands (Fig. 2). These include binding sites for glutamate (or NMDA), glycine, Mg^{2+}, Zn^{2+}, polyamines and open-channel blockers such as phencyclidine (PCP) and MK-801. The receptor is also modulated by histamine, arachidonic acid, pH and redox reagents. There is an absolute requirement for glycine for the channel to be opened by NMDA or glutamate. Thus, glycine can be con-

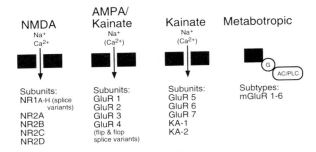

Fig. 1. Classification of mammalian glutamate receptors and corresponding cloned subunits.

sidered a "co-agonist" at the NMDA receptor complex.

Cloned subunits of the NMDA receptor: structure and function

A major advance in our understanding of the structural and functional properties of NMDA receptors has come with the cloning of cDNAs encoding subunits of the receptor. The first clone to be isolated, NMDAR1 (NR1), encodes a polypeptide with a protein molecular weight (105 kDa) and structural to-

pography similar to that of the GluR subunits (Moriyoshi et al., 1991). The proposed topography includes four (or five) transmembrane regions and a large extracellular amino terminal domain (Fig. 3). Many of the properties of native NMDA receptors are seen with homomeric NR1 receptors expressed in *Xenopus* oocytes (Moriyoshi et al., 1991). For example, homomeric NR1 receptors have been shown to require glycine as a co-agonist to gate Ca^{2+}, and they are blocked in a voltage-dependent manner by Mg^{2+}. The receptors are also sensitive to Zn^{2+} and open-channel blockers such as MK-801.

Four related rat brain cDNA clones, designated NR2A, NR2B, NR2C and NR2D, were isolated by homology to NR1 and GluR1-4 (Fig. 3) (Monyer et al., 1992; Ishii et al., 1993). Equivalent cDNAs, termed $\zeta 1$ (NR1) and $\varepsilon 1$–4 (NR2A–D) were cloned from mouse brain (Kutsuwada et al., 1992; Meguro et al., 1992). The NR2 subunits are large polypeptides (≈ 160 kDa) and are 50–70% homologous to each other but only 15–20% identical to NR1. NR2 subunits do not form functional homomeric receptors. However, co-expression of NR1 and NR2 subunits generates channels that produce much larger whole-

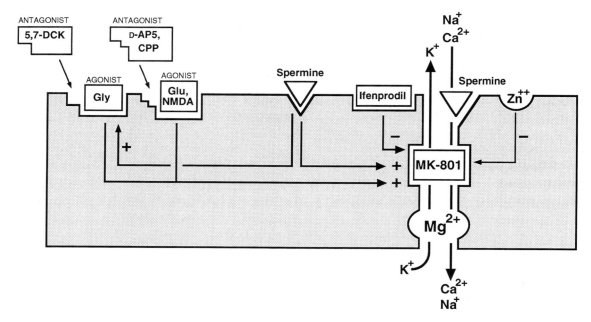

Fig. 2. Schematic model of the NMDA receptor.

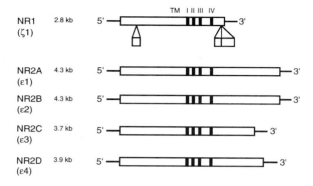

Fig. 3. Schematic of the cDNAs encoding subunits of the NMDA receptor. All subunits contain four putative transmembrane domains (TMI-IV). The NR1 gene is transcribed as eight alternatively spliced mRNAs by the inclusion or deletion of one 5' and/or two 3' exons.

cell currents than are seen with homomeric NR1 receptors. This suggests that the two kinds of subunit form heteromeric multisubunit complexes. Results of in situ hybridization histochemistry have shown that mRNAs encoding each of the NR2 subunits are selectively expressed in particular brain regions and their expression changes during development, whereas NR1 mRNA is expressed throughout the brain (Monyer et al., 1992; Nakanishi, 1992; Watanabe et al., 1992). The subunit composition of native NMDA receptors in identified brain regions has not yet been defined, but the receptors are likely to consist of combinations of NR1 and one or more NR2 subunits.

The TMII regions of NR1 and NR2A-D contain a conserved asparagine residue in a position analogous to the glutamine or arginine (Q/R) residue that controls the permeability of GluR1–4 channels to divalent cations. Mutation of this asparagine in NR1 or in NR2A or NR2C to glutamine or arginine reduces or abolishes Ca^{2+} permeability and voltage-dependent blockade by Mg^{2+} and decreases the affinity for MK-801 (Burnashev et al., 1992; Sakurada et al., 1993). These results suggest that the TMII region of NR1 and NR2 subunits may be involved in forming the ion-channel pore of NMDA receptors and that the conserved asparagine residues are critical for the control of permeability to divalent cations. Mutation of the

asparagine in NR1 has somewhat different effects on Mg^{2+} block and Ca^{2+} permeability than does mutation of the equivalent residue in NR2 subunits (Burnashev et al., 1992). This suggests a non-equivalent or non-symmetrical contribution of TMII regions in NR1 and NR2 subunits to formation of the ion-channel pore.

The diversity of NMDA receptor subunits and potential subunit combinations has been increased by the discovery of splice variants of the original NR1 subunit. Eight variants have been described based on the alternative splicing of a 5' exon and one or two adjacent 3' exons (Fig. 3) (Sugihara et al., 1992; Hollmann et al., 1993). The inclusion of these exons changes the amino acid sequence in the presumed extracellular amino- and carboxy-terminal portions of the protein. The 5' insert contains multiple positively charged residues while the inserts in the 3' end of the molecule contain consensus sequences for phosphorylation catalyzed by protein kinase C (Tingley et al., 1993). The carboxy terminus may thus be located intracellularly and be preceded by five rather than four transmembrane regions (Seeburg, 1993).

Properties of recombinant heteromeric NMDA receptors

Although the NR1 subunit can form functional NMDA receptors when expressed in oocytes, it is likely that native NMDA receptors are heterooligomers composed of combinations of NR1 and NR2 subunits. A number of recent studies have shown that the inclusion of different NR2 subunits in heteromeric NMDA receptors can markedly alter the functional and pharmacological properties of the receptors. Some of these differences are strikingly similar to those seen in studies of native NMDA receptors in different brain regions or during various stages of development.

Receptors containing the NR2C subunit are less sensitive to blockade by Mg^{2+} and MK-801 than are receptors containing NR2A or NR2B subunits (Kutsuwada et al., 1992; Monyer et al., 1992; Ishii et al., 1993). Since the NR2C subunit is expressed predominantly in the cerebellum, this is consistent with the hypothesis that NR2C may be a major determinant of the properties of cerebellar NMDA receptors,

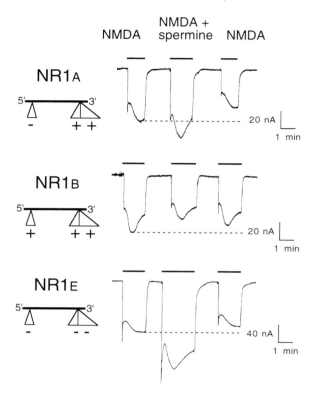

NR1A

5' △ ── △ 3'
  −   + +

NR1B

5' △ ── △ 3'
  +   + +

NR1E

5' △ ── △ 3'
  −   − −

NMDA   NMDA + spermine   NMDA

20 nA | 1 min

20 nA | 1 min

40 nA | 1 min

Fig. 4. Spermine stimulation is seen at NR1A and NR1E but not NR1B receptors. Effects of 100 μM spermine on inward currents induced by NMDA were measured in oocytes expressing homomeric NR1A, NR1B, and NR1E receptors and voltage-clamped at −70 mV. The splicing patterns of the subunit cDNAs are shown.

which have a lower affinity for open-channel blockers, such as MK-801, than do receptors in the cerebral cortex and hippocampus.

The single channel properties of NR1/NR2A and NR1/NR2B receptors are different from those of NR1/NR2C receptors (Stern et al., 1992). Both NR1/NR2A and NR1/NR2B receptors exhibit conductance levels and opening patterns that are very similar to those of native NMDA receptors on hippocampal neurons. In contrast, NR1/NR2C receptors have a lower unitary conductance than NR1/NR2A and NR1/NR2B. The properties of NR1/NR2C receptors resemble those of native NMDA receptors on large cerebellar neurons (Stern et al., 1992).

Differences in sensitivity to glycine and to glutamate-site antagonists have also been reported for re-

ceptors containing different NR2 subunits. For example, NR1/NR2B receptors have a 10-fold higher affinity for glycine than do NR1/NR2A receptors (Kutsuwada et al., 1992). The consequences of a difference in sensitivity to glycine of native receptors are not known, but if the concentration of glycine in the synapse is not saturating, then changes in the concentration of glycine could selectively alter the activity or the activation threshold of some subtypes of NMDA receptor.

Polyamines such as spermine have a variety of effects on native NMDA receptors. These include "glycine-dependent" stimulation, which involves an increase in the affinity of the receptor for glycine, "glycine-independent" stimulation, which is seen in the presence of saturating concentrations of glycine, voltage-dependent inhibition, and a decrease in the affinity of the receptor for NMDA and glutamate. Variability in the effects of spermine on native NMDA receptors studied electrophysiologically has been observed. Results of studies using recombinant NMDA receptors are beginning to explain the inconsistent results observed in studies of native receptors on cultural neurons. Homomeric NR1 receptors expressed from splice variants such as NR1A or NR1E that do not contain a 5' insert exhibit glycine-independent stimu-

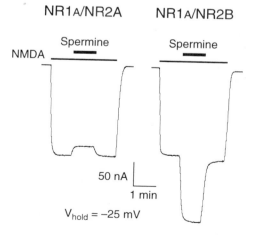

NR1A/NR2A   NR1A/NR2B

          Spermine   Spermine
NMDA _____   _____

50 nA |
      1 min

V$_{hold}$ = −25 mV

Fig. 5. Spermine stimulation occurs at NR1A/NR2B but not NR1A/NR2A receptors. The effects of 100 μM spermine on responses to 100 μM NMDA (with 10 μM glycine) were measured in oocytes expressing NR1A/NR2A and NR1A/NR2B receptors and voltage-clamped at −25 mV.

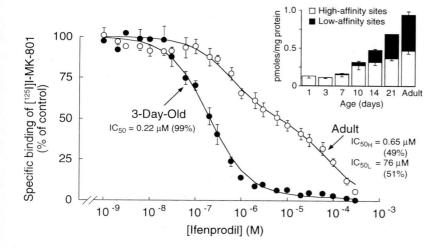

Fig. 6. Inhibitory effects of ifenprodil on NMDA receptors in developing rat brain. The effects of ifenprodil on the binding of $[^{125}I]$I-MK-801 were determined using membranes prepared from 3-day-old and adult rat forebrain. Inset: The number of binding sites having a high or a low affinity for ifenprodil was determined using membranes prepared from rats of different ages. The density of receptors increased by approximately 8-fold between postnatal day 1 and adult. Data are from Williams et al., 1993.

lation by spermine. In contrast, homomeric receptors expressed from variants such as NR1B, containing a 5′ insert, do not show spermine stimulation (Fig. 4) (Durand et al., 1993). Moreover, in studies of heteromeric receptors, it was found that NR1A/NR2B but not NR1A/NR2A receptors show glycine-independent stimulation by spermine (Fig. 5). Voltage-dependent inhibition is seen at both types of receptor (data not shown). Thus, inclusion in a heteromeric receptor of

an NR1 variant such as NR1A is necessary for stimulation by polyamines, but the manifestation of this stimulatory effect is controlled by the type of NR2 subunit present in the receptor complex (Williams et al., 1994).

The atypical antagonist ifenprodil discriminates two subtypes of native NMDA receptors present in equal proportions in adult rat forebrain, one having a high affinity and the other a low affinity for ifenprodil.

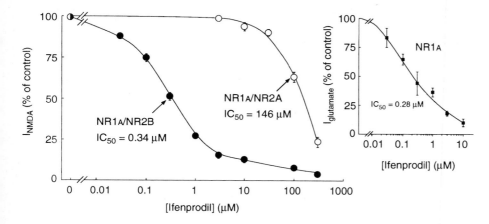

Fig. 7. Effects of ifenprodil on recombinant NMDA receptors. The effects of ifenprodil on responses to NMDA or glutamate were studied in oocytes expressing heteromeric NR1A/NR2B and NR1A/NR2A receptors and (inset) homomeric NR1A receptors. Data are from Williams, (1993) and Williams et al. (1993).

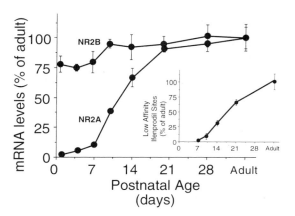

Fig. 8. Expression of receptor subtypes and subunit mRNAs in developing rat brain. Levels of mRNAs encoding NR2A and NR2B were measured by solution hybridization/RNase protection assays in rat cerebral cortex. Inset: The number of receptors having a low affinity for ifenprodil (data from Williams et al., 1993) is expressed as a percentage of the density in adult rat forebrain.

The two subtypes are differentially expressed during postnatal development. In neonatal rats only the form of the receptor with a high affinity for ifenprodil is expressed (Fig. 6) (Williams et al., 1993). Receptors having a low affinity for ifenprodil are expressed after postnatal day 7 (Fig. 6, inset). In studies of recombinant NMDA receptors, ifenprodil has a high affinity at homomeric NR1A receptors (Fig. 7, inset) and at heteromeric NR1A/NR2B receptors but a low affinity at NR1A/NR2A receptors (Fig. 7) (Williams, 1993). The time course of expression of NR2 mRNAs has been defined in the developing brain. NR2B mRNA is expressed at high levels in neonatal and adult rat forebrain. In contrast, NR2A mRNA is found at very low levels in neonates, and expression increases markedly between postnatal days 7 and 21 with a time course that is similar to the expression of receptors having a low affinity for ifenprodil (Fig. 8) (see also Watanabe et al., 1992). Thus, inclusion of NR2A in native NMDA receptors is probably responsible for the delayed development of receptors with a low affinity for ifenprodil.

Future directions

An appreciation of the functional and pharmacologi-

cal diversity of NMDA receptors is leading to an understanding of the structural features of these receptors and the way in which particular features relate to function. There will undoubtedly be rapid progress in the identification of the subunit composition of at least some native NMDA receptors. Furthermore, site-directed mutagenesis and the use of chimeric subunits will allow tentative identification of regions of NR1 and NR2 subunits that control sensitivity to agonists, antagonists, and modulators of these receptors and will reveal more about the gating and permeability properties of the corresponding channels. The regulation of receptor subunit expression in both the developing and mature nervous systems and the effects of post-translational modifications are also areas of considerable interest and potential importance. The expression of different forms of neurotransmitter receptors, regulated ultimately by the expression of the genes coding for the receptors, may control much of the functional diversity and specialization of neurons in the CNS. The potential array of NMDA receptor subtypes, like that of other ligand-gated channels, is experimentally daunting. However, the diversity of genes and splice variants makes it possible to anticipate the development of therapeutic agents directed at particular subtypes of NMDA receptor. This may lead to the development of improved therapeutic approaches for the treatment of epilepsy and/or reduc-tion of excitotoxic cell death in CNS ischemia. Understanding the repertoire and molecular properties of glutamate receptors will also contribute to a better understanding of phenomena such as long-term poten-tiation and long-term depression that may underlie higher brain functions including learning and memory and may lead to the development of agents that facilitate the development and/or retention of higher brain functions.

Acknowledgment

Supported by USPHS grants GM 34781 and NS 30000

References

Burnashev, N., Schoepfer, R., Monyer, H., Ruppersberg, J.P., Günther, W., Seeburg, P.H. and Sakmann, B. (1992) Control by asparagine residues of calcium permeability and magnesium blockade in the NMDA receptor. *Science,* 257: 1415–1419.

Choi, D.W. (1988) Glutamate neurotoxicity and diseases of the nervous system. *Neuron,* 1: 623–634.

Collingridge, G.L. and Lester, R.A.J. (1989) Excitatory amino acid receptors in the vertebrate central nervous system. *Pharmacol. Rev.,* 41: 143–210 .

Durand, G.M., Bennett, M.V.L. and Zukin, R.S. (1993) Splice variants of the *N*-methyl-D-aspartate receptor NR1 identify domains involved in regulation by polyamines and protein kinase C. *Proc. Natl. Acad. Sci. USA,* 90: 6731–6735.

Hollmann, M., Boulter, J., Maron, C., Beasley, L., Sullivan, J., Pecht, G. and Heinemann, S. (1993) Zinc potentiates agonist-induced currents at certain splice variants of the NMDA receptor. *Neuron,* 10: 943–954.

Ishii, T, Moriyoshi, K., Sugihara, H., Sakurada, K., Kadotani, H., Yokoi, M., Akazawa, C., Shigemoto, R., Mizuno, N., Masu, M. and Nakanishi, S. (1993) Molecular characterization of the family of the *N*-methyl-D-aspartate receptor subunits. *J. Biol. Chem.,* 268: 2836–2843.

Kutsuwada, T., Kashiwabuchi, N., Mori, H., Sakimura, K., Kushiya, E., Araki, K., Meguro, H., Masaki, H., Kumanishi, T., Arakawa, M. and Mishina, M. (1992) Molecular diversity of the NMDA receptor channel. *Nature,* 358: 36–41.

Meguro, H., Mori, H., Araki, K., Kushiya, E., Kutsuwada, T., Yamazaki, M., Kumanishi, T., Arakawa, M., Sakimura, K. and Mishina M. (1992) Functional characterization of a heteromeric NMDA receptor channel expressed from cloned cDNAs. *Nature,* 357: 70–74.

Monyer, H., Sprengel, R., Schoepfer, R., Herb, A., Higuchi, M., Lomeli, H., Burnashev, N., Sakmann, B. and Seeburg, P.H. (1992) Heteromeric NMDA receptors: molecular and functional distinction of subtypes. *Science,* 256: 1217–1221.

Moriyoshi, K., Masu, M., Ishii, T., Shigemoto, R., Mizuno, N. and Nakanishi, S. (1991) Molecular cloning and characterization of the rat NMDA receptor. *Nature,* 354: 31–37.

Nakanishi, S. (1992) Molecular diversity of glutamate receptors and implications for brain function. *Science,* 258: 597–603.

Sakurada, K., Masu, M. and Nakanishi, S. (1993) Alteration of Ca^{2+} permeability and sensitivity to Mg^{2+} and channel blockers by a single amino acid substitution in the *N*-methyl-D-aspartate receptor. *J. Biol. Chem.,* 268: 410–415.

Seeburg, P.H. (1993) The molecular biology of mammalian glutamate receptor channels. *Trends Neurosci.,* 16: 359–365.

Stern, P., Béhé, P., Schoepfer, R. and Colquhoun, D. (1992) Single-channel conductances of NMDA receptors expressed from cloned cDNAs: comparison with native receptors. *Proc. R. Soc. London Ser. B,* 250: 271–277.

Sugihara, H., Moriyoshi, K., Ishii, T., Masu, M. and Nakanishi, S. (1992) Structures and properties of seven isoforms of the NMDA receptor generated by alternative splicing. *Biochem. Biophys. Res. Commun.,* 185: 826–832.

Tingley, W.G., Roche, K.W., Thompson, A.K. and Huganir, R.L. (1993) Regulation of NMDA receptor phosphorylation by alternative splicing of the C-terminal domain. *Nature,* 364: 70–73.

Watanabe, M., Inoue, Y., Sakimura, K. and Mishina, M. (1992) Developmental changes in distribution of NMDA receptor channel subunit mRNAs. *NeuroReport,* 3: 1138–1140.

Williams, K. (1993) Ifenprodil discriminates subtypes of the *N*-methyl-D-aspartate receptor: selectivity and mechanisms at recombinant heteromeric receptors. *Mol. Pharmacol.,* 44: 851–859.

Williams, K., Zappia, A.M., Pritchett, D.B., Shen, Y.M. and Molinoff, P.B. (1994) Sensitivity of the *N*-methyl-D-aspartate receptor to polyamines is controlled by NR2 subunits. *Mol. Pharmacol.,* in press.

Williams, K., Russell, S.L., Shen, Y.M. and Molinoff, P.B. (1993) Developmental switch in the expression of NMDA receptors occurs in vivo and in vitro. *Neuron,* 10: 267–278.

F. Bloom (Editor)
Progress in Brain Research, Vol. 100
© 1994 Elsevier Science B.V. All rights reserved

CHAPTER 6

Glutamate receptors and the induction of excitotoxic neuronal death

Dennis W. Choi

Department of Neurology and Center for the Study of Nervous System Injury, Box 8111, Washington University School of Medicine, 660 S. Euclid Avenue, St. Louis, MO 63110, USA

Introduction

Glutamate or related excitatory amino acids probably mediate the death of central neurons in several human pathological conditions, for example after toxic food ingestion, or after acute insults such as hypoxia-ischemia, trauma, or prolonged seizures (Olney, 1986; Choi, 1988). In addition, intriguing clues have emerged suggesting that this glutamate-mediated neuronal death, "excitotoxicity", may contribute to the pathogenesis of certain neurodegenerative disorders, such as Huntington's disease, Alzheimer's disease, or motor neuron disease.

To facilitate consideration of underlying mechanisms, we have proposed that excitotoxic neuronal death might be considered in three stages analogous to the stages of long-term potentiation: induction, amplification and expression (Choi, 1992). In this scheme, induction consists of the initial cellular changes immediately attributable to glutamate exposure. Amplification consists of subsequent modulatory events that amplify these initial derangements, increasing their intensity and promoting the injury of additional neurons. Expression consists of the cytotoxic cascades directly responsible for neuronal disintegration.

The most active area of investigation in the excitatory amino acid field at present is probably the study of glutamate receptors. Glutamate activates three major families of ionophore-linked receptors classified by their preferred agonists: N-methyl-D-aspartate

(NMDA), kainate and α-amino-3-hydroxy-5-methyl-4-isoxazolepropionic acid (AMPA) (Watkins et al., 1990). Multiple functional receptor subunits from each family have been cloned (Hollmann et al., 1989; Nakanishi, 1992; Sommer and Seeburg, 1992). Glutamate also activates a family of metabotropic receptors that activate second messenger systems rather than directly gating ion channels (see below). Historically, NMDA receptors have received the greatest attention with regard to excitotoxicity, but more recently it has become apparent that non-NMDA receptors may play an important role. This brief review presents an overview of the participation of glutamate receptors in excitotoxic induction, with mention of some recent developments with regard to AMPA and metabotropic receptors.

Induction of excitotoxicity: why are NMDA receptors often prominently involved?

The induction of glutamate neurotoxicity consists of the development of an initial set of intracellular derangements, to a great extent resulting directly from glutamate receptor activation. These initial derangements serve as triggers for subsequent amplification and expression events. Although potentially lethal, induction events precede irreversible injury. Neurons can be rescued following full induction by removing extracellular Na^+ and Ca^{2+} for 30 min. Induction is most simply accomplished by receptor overstimulation, but normal physiological levels of receptor activation may become neurotoxic if neuronal energy levels are compromised (Beal et al., 1993).

The channels gated by NMDA, or AMPA/kainate receptors (AMPA and kainate receptors are overlapping populations, and difficult to distinguish pharmacologically) are permeable to both Na^+ and K^+. Channels gated by NMDA receptors, but only a minority subset of channels gated by AMPA/kainate receptors (see below), additionally possess high permeability to Ca^{2+}.

If glutamate exposure is intense, widespread cortical neuronal death can be induced by exposure times as short as 2–3 min, a phenomenon we have termed "rapidly-triggered excitotoxicity". Two components of injury are distinguishable: (1) an acute component, marked by immediate neuronal swelling and dependent on the presence of extracellular Na^+ and Cl^-; and (2) a delayed component marked by neuronal disintegration occurring over a period of hours after exposure, dependent on the presence of extracellular Ca^{2+}. The first component probably reflects the influx of extracellular Na^+, accompanied passively by the influx of Cl^- and water, resulting in cell volume expansion. The second component is likely triggered by excessive Ca^{2+} influx. Although either the acute Na^+-dependent component or the delayed Ca^{2+}-dependent component of glutamate neurotoxicity can alone produce irreversible neuronal injury, the latter component normally predominates.

Experiments with glutamate antagonists suggest that both AMPA/kainate and NMDA type glutamate receptors contribute to acute neuronal swelling, but that most delayed disintegration requires NMDA receptor activation. Death following brief intense glutamate exposure can be almost completely blocked by selective blockade of NMDA receptors, but selective blockade of AMPA/kainate receptors has only a small effect on late neuronal death. Only when both NMDA and AMPA/kainate receptors are blocked is acute glutamate-induced neuronal swelling eliminated. However, selective AMPA/kainate receptor activation can cause the widespread death of cortical neurons if exposure time is extended for several hours. With 24-h exposure, 10 μM of either kainate or AMPA are highly lethal, a phenomenon we have termed "slowly-triggered excitotoxicity" to emphasize the requirement for prolonged receptor activation.

Abnormal entry of extracellular Ca^{2+} may be the primary factor responsible for the induction of both rapidly triggered and slowly triggered excitotoxicity. The dependence of rapidly triggered toxicity upon extracellular Ca^{2+} and NMDA receptor activation is consistent with the idea that it is initiated by excessive Ca^{2+} influx through the Ca^{2+}-permeable NMDA receptor- gated channel. Slowly triggered, AMPA/kainate receptor-mediated excitotoxicity may also be initiated by excessive Ca^{2+} influx. Most channels gated by AMPA or kainate receptors have limited Ca^{2+} permeability (but see below), so Ca^{2+} influx induced by these receptors may occur mainly via indirect routes, such as voltage-gated Ca^{2+} channels, reverse operation of the Na^+-Ca^{2+} exchanger, or membrane stretch-activated conductances.

A key role of Ca^{2+} entry in rapidly triggered excitotoxicity is supported by a quantitative correlation between the extent of cortical neuronal death induced by exposure to glutamate receptor agonists and the amount of extracellular $^{45}Ca^{2+}$ that accumulates in neurons during the exposure period (Hartley et al., 1993). During brief intense glutamate exposure, NMDA receptors mediate neuronal $^{45}Ca^{2+}$ accumulation which is several-fold greater than that induced by comparable exposure to high concentrations of K^+, kainate, or AMPA. The critical reason why NMDA receptor-mediated excitotoxicity is rapidly triggered may be this high rate of Ca^{2+} influx.

Variations in AMPA/kainate receptor behavior may have important implications for excitotoxic death

While as noted above, most AMPA/kainate receptors gate channels permeable only to monovalent cations, it has become recently recognized that a minority subset of these receptors do gate channels permeable to several divalent cations, including Ca^{2+} (Iino et al., 1990). Expression studies with cloned AMPA receptor subunits suggests that expression of an edited form of the GluR2 (alternatively termed GluR-B) subunit dominantly confers Ca^{2+}-impermeability to channels formed by combinations of GluR1/GluR-A, GluR3/ GluR-C, or GluR4/GluR-D subunits (Sommer and Seeburg, 1992). Early studies with high affinity kainate receptors formed from GluR6 subunits suggest that RNA editing may also determine the Ca^{2+} permeability of these receptors (Köhler et al., 1993).

If indeed Ca^{2+} influx triggered by glutamate receptor activation is a critical mediator of excitotoxic injury, the prediction arises that the presence of AMPA/kainate receptors gating Ca^{2+}-permeable channels should confer enhanced vulnerability to death induced by AMPA or kainate. Specifically, neurons bearing substantial numbers of such atypical AMPA/ kainate receptors should be destroyed by exposures to AMPA or kainate too brief to destroy neurons lacking these receptors.

To test this idea, we have utilized kainate-activated Co^{2+} uptake as a histochemical marker for cells bearing Ca^{2+}-permeable AMPA receptors (Pruss et al., 1991). While most cultured cortical neurons exhibit little kainate-activated Co^{2+} uptake, about 15% of the neuronal population showed high levels of uptake. This minority subpopulation was selectively destroyed after AMPA or kainate exposures of only 10–60 min, exposure times too brief to cause much death in the general neuronal population (Turetsky et al., 1992). Studies by Reid et al. (1993) showed that this subpopulation expresses a distinctive profile of AMPA receptor subunits as determined by immunostaining. Neurons exhibiting kainate-activated Co^{2+} uptake were much less likely to express GluR2/GluR3, and much more likely to express GluR1 or GluR4, than the general cortical neuronal population. Thus, expression of AMPA receptors lacking the GluR2 subunit may account for the divalent cation permeability properties of Co^{2+} uptake-positive cells. Of note, most of these cells also stain for glutamic acid decarboxylase, indicating that they are GABAergic (H. Yin, D. Turetsky, J. Weiss and D. Choi, unpublished observations). Our findings fit with another recent study showing that single inhibitory neurons in layer 4 of visual cortex have reduced levels of GluR2/ GluR-B mRNA compared to layer 5 pyramidal neurons (H. Monyer and P. Seeburg, personal communication). It is intriguing to speculate that the preferential loss of cortical

GABAergic neurons may occur in disease states associated with the excitotoxic overstimulation of AMPA receptors, an occurrence that could have important functional implications, for example the development of a seizure focus.

Another feature of AMPA/kainate receptor behavior that may influence participation in excitotoxicity is desensitization. If AMPA receptor desensitization is blocked with cyclothiazides (Yamada and Rothman, 1992), an enhanced contribution to glutamate neurotoxicity results (Bateman et al., 1993). Presumably, desensitization is critical in limiting net influx of Na^+ through AMPA receptor-gated channels; reduction of desensitization presumably permits this influx (and thus resultant secondary Ca^{2+} influx) to reach lethal proportions. While kainate has been considered in the past to be a non-desensitizing agonist on AMPA receptors, more recent work with rapid perfusion techniques suggests that some desensitization still occurs with kainate stimulation (Patneau et al., 1993), and cyclothiazide does potentiate kainate-induced membrane current (Patneau et al., 1993) and toxicity (M. Goldberg and K. Yamada, unpublished observations). The identification of drugs capable of increasing AMPA receptor desensitization may be a useful pathway in the future for the development of new neuroprotective agents based on non-competitive AMPA receptor inhibition.

How does metabotropic receptors activation influence excitotoxicity

The role of metabotropic receptor in excitotoxic injury has been difficult to define because of limitations in available pharmacology. Recently, the cloning of several metabotropic receptor subtypes (and splice variants), and the emergence of partially selective agonists and antagonists has permitted some progress.

Original descriptions of metabotropic receptor focused on the activation of inositol phosphate metabolism, leading to the formation of inositol-1,4,5-trisphosphate and release of Ca^{2+} from intracellular stores (Schoepp and Conn, 1993). Extrapolating from the idea that intracellular Ca^{2+} overload was a key early step in excitotoxic cell death, an injury promoting role of metabotropic receptor activation seemed most likely.

However, studies by Koh et al. (1991) revealed that the broad spectrum selective metabotropic receptor agonist, *trans*-1-aminocyclopentane-1,3-dicarboxylic acid (tACPD), was not intrinsically excitotoxic; rather, it reduced rapidly triggered excitotoxicity in cortical cultures. Subsequent in vivo studies have indicated that the situation is complex. Injection of tACPD into rat hippocampus produced seizures and neuronal loss (Schoepp and Conn, 1993), and injection into striatum potentiated NMDA-induced toxicity (McDonald and Schoepp, 1992).

How can these disparate results be reconciled? The answer likely lies in the multiplicity of cellular actions mediated by various metabotropic receptor subtypes. While some subtypes increase phosphoinositide hydrolysis, others increase or decrease cAMP levels. In addition to releasing intracellular Ca^{2+} stores, metabotropic receptor activation has several actions likely to promote excitotoxic injury, including: (1) increasing NMDA and AMPA/kainate receptor-mediated membrane current; (2) promoting slow onset potentiation or long term potentiation at excitatory synapses; (3) reducing GABAergic inhibition; and (4) reducing inhibitory K^+ currents, I_M and I_{AHP}. On the other hand, metabotropic receptor activation also has several actions that may protect neurons from excitotoxic injury, including (1) reducing synaptic glutamate release; (2) promoting long term depression; and (3) reducing Ca^{2+} influx through voltage-gated Ca^{2+} channels. Thus, the net effect of metabotropic receptor activation on excitotoxic injury may depend critically on the balance between injury promoting, and injury attenuating effects.

One key variable may be the presence of organized excitatory circuits. In intact systems, where these circuits are preserved, pro-excitant effects of metabotropic receptor activation may predominate, leading to increased glutamate release and injury enhancement. In simplified systems such as cell culture, attenuation of circuit inhibition may be less important than attenuation of Ca^{2+} currents entering directly through voltage-gated channels, resulting in a net reduction of excitotoxic injury.

A challenge for the future will be the definition of specific metabotropic receptor subtypes responsible for various actions. It may turn out that certain subtypes predominantly mediated pro-excitant effects (for example, mGluR1 or mGluR5), whereas other subtypes (for example mGluR2, mGluR3, or mGluR4) predominantly mediate pro-inhibitory effects (Nakanishi, 1992). If so, this would represent auspicious circumstances for therapeutic manipulation of the receptor system.

Conclusions

Activation of either NMDA or AMPA/kainate receptors can induce excitotoxic neuronal death. NMDA receptors in particular play a key role in the induction of excitotoxic neuronal death by high concentrations of glutamate, probably reflecting their ability to mediate high levels of Ca^{2+} influx. Recent advances in the pharmacology and molecular biology of AMPA/kainate and glutamate metabotropic receptors have strengthened arguments that these receptors may also contribute importantly to, or influence, the induction of excitotoxicity. Specific manipulation of glutamate receptor subtypes may constitute a useful clinical therapeutic strategy aimed at reducing certain types of pathological neuronal death.

Acknowledgments

Supported in part by NIH grant NS 30337.

References

Bateman, M.C., Bagwe, M.R., Yamada, K.A. and Goldberg, M.P. (1993) Cyclothiazide potentiates AMPA neurotoxicity and oxygen-glucose deprivation injury in cortical culture. *Soc. Neurosci. Abstr.,* 19: 1643.

Beal, M.F., Hyman, B. and Koroshetz, W. (1993) Do defects in mitochondrial energy metabolism underlie the pathology of neurodegenerative diseases? *Trends Neurosci.,* 16: 125–131.

Choi, D.W. (1988) Glutamate neurotoxicity and diseases of the nervous system. *Neuron,* 1: 623–634

Choi, D.W. (1992) Excitotoxic cell death. *J. Neurobiol.,* 23: 1261–1276.

Hartley, D.M., Kurth, M., Bjerkness, L., Weiss, J.H. and Choi, D.W. (1993) Glutamate receptor-induced $^{45}Ca^{2+}$ accumulation in cortical cell culture correlates with subsequent neuronal degeneration. *J. Neurosci.*, 13: 1993–2000

Hollmann, M., O'Shea-Greenfield, A., Rogers, S.W. and Heinemann, S. (1989) Cloning by functional expression of a member of the glutamate receptor family. *Nature*. 342: 643–648.

Iino, M., Ozawa, S. and Tsuzuki, K. (1990) Permeation of calcium through excitatory amino acid receptor channels in cultured rat hippocampal neurones. *J. Physiol.*, 424: 151–165.

Koh, J.Y., Palmer, E. and Cotman, C.W. (1991) Activation of the metabotropic glutamate receptor attenuates *N*-methyl-D-aspartate neurotoxicity in cortical cultures. *Proc. Natl. Acad. Sci. USA,* 88: 9431–9435.

Köhler, M., Burnashev, N., Sakmann, B. and Seeburg, P. (1993) Determinants of Ca^{++} permeability in both TM1 and TM2 of high affinity kainate receptor channels: diversity by RNA editing. *Neuron,* 10: 491–500.

McDonald, J.W. and Schoepp, D.D. (1992) The metabotropic excitatory amino acid receptor agonist 1S,3R-ACPD selectively potentiates *N*-methyl-D-aspartate-induced brain injury. *Eur. J. Pharmacol.*, 215: 353–354.

Nakanishi, S. (1992) Molecular diversity of glutamate receptors and implications for brain function. *Science,* 258: 597–603.

Olney, J.W. (1986) Inciting excitotoxic cytocide among central neurons. *Adv. Exp. Med. Biol.*, 203: 631–645.

Patneau, D.K., Vyklicky Jr., L. and Mayer, M.L. (1993) Hippocampal neurons exhibit cyclothiazide-sensitive rapidly desensitizing responses to kainate. *J. Neurosci.*, 13: 3496–3509

Pruss, R.M., Akeson, R.L., Racke, M.M. and Wilburn, J.L. (1991) Agonist-activated cobalt uptake identifies divalent cation-permeable kainate receptors on neurons and glial cells. *Neuron,* 7: 509–18

Reid, S., Yin, H. and Weiss, J.H. (1993) Cortical neurons subject to kainate triggered Co^{2+} accumulation display differential AMPA/kainate receptor immunoreactivity. *Soc. Neurosci. Abstr.*, 19: 474

Schoepp, D. and Conn, P.J. (1993) Metabotropic glutamate receptors in brain function and pathology. *Trends Pharmacol. Sci.*, 14: 13–20.

Sommer, B. and Seeburg, P.H. (1992) Glutamate receptor channels: novel properties and new clones. *Trends Pharmacol. Sci.*, 13: 291–296.

Turetsky, D.M., Goldberg, M.P. and Choi, D.W. (1992) Kainate-activated cobalt uptake identifies a subpopulation of cultured cortical cells that are preferentially vulnerable to kainate-induced damage. *Soc. Neurosci. Abstr.*, 18: 81.

Watkins, J.C., Krogsgaard-Larsen, P. and Honore, T. (1990) Structure-activity relationships in the development of excitatory amino acid receptor agonists and competitive antagonists. *Trends Pharmacol. Sci.*, 11: 25–33.

Yamada, K.A. and Rothman, S.M. (1992) Diazoxide blocks glutamate desensitization and prolongs excitatory postsynaptic currents in rat hippocampal neurons. *J. Physiol. (London),* 458: 409–423

F. Bloom (Editor)
Progress in Brain Research, Vol. 100
© 1994 Elsevier Science B.V. All rights reserved

CHAPTER 7

Sodium/potassium-coupled glutamate transporters, a "new" family of eukaryotic proteins: do they have "new" physiological roles and could they be new targets for pharmacological intervention?

Niels C. Danbolt, Jon Storm-Mathisen, Ole P. Ottersen

Anatomical Institute, University of Oslo, P.O.B. 1105 Blindern, N-0317 Oslo, Norway

Introduction

Chemical signalling is critically dependent on effective mechanisms for terminating transmitter action and for maintaining an extracellular concentration of transmitter that is low enough to avoid undue activation of the appropriate receptors. In the central nervous system, the major transmitters are removed from the extracellular space by uptake into the presynaptic element or glial cells. This uptake is effected by plasma membrane transporters that are driven by transmembrane ion gradients and that are selective for a single transmitter or a few closely related transmitter species (Amara and Kuhar, 1993). These transporters have attracted much interest since they are in the position to regulate the efficacy of synaptic transmission and thus provide potential targets of pharmacological intervention. Several important drugs in current use are thought to exert their effects through action on transmitter transporters. The tricyclic antidepressants, acting on monoamine transporters, are notable examples (Amara and Kuhar, 1993).

The first neurotransmitter transporter to be cloned was a GABA transporter (Guastella et al., 1990). Glycine transporters and several monoamine transporters were cloned subsequently and it became clear that they all belong to a family of molecules with similar ion dependence (sodium and chloride) and

molecular structure (12 putative transmembrane domains) (Amara and Kuhar, 1993). Only recently did attempts to clone a glutamate transporter meet with success. The breakthrough came with three independent reports, each using a different approach and identifying a separate transporter, that were published almost simultaneously in late autumn 1992 (Kanai and Hediger, 1992; Pines et al., 1992; Storck et al., 1992). The three transporters displayed about 50% sequence identity, but had no significant primary structural homology to the superfamily of Na^+ and Cl^- coupled transporters or to any other known eukaryotic protein. Thus, glutamate transporters represent a "new" family of molecules. The number of transmembrane domains is not known as the hydropathy plots give room for several interpretations (see below).

A perturbed function at glutamate synapses has been implicated in many disease states, including ischemia and epilepsy, and several neurodegenerative disorders such as amyotrophic lateral sclerosis and Huntington's chorea (Whetsell and Shapira, 1993). Given the recent advances in the understanding of the molecular biology and function of the glutamate transporters, it is time to ask whether these have potentials as clinically beneficial targets of pharmacological intervention. For rational drug design it is essential to know: (1) the physiological roles of the glutamate transporters; (2) whether the transporters are subject to regulation; and (3) whether the transporters are heterogeneous in terms of functional properties and cellular and regional distribution. These issues are addressed in the present overview.

Glutamate transporters: physiological roles

It has long been known, primarily through the work of Kanner and collaborators, that glutamate uptake is electrogenic and dependent on external Na^+ and internal K^+ (Kanner and Schuldiner, 1987; Danbolt et al., 1990). Detailed studies on the stoichiometry of glutamate uptake have been carried out on Müller cells, a specialized form of glial cells, isolated from the salamander retina (Attwell et al., 1991; Bouvier et al., 1992). These cells are not equipped with glutamate receptors and the current elicited by glutamate therefore reflects electrogenic uptake. Analyses based on whole cell patching indicate that glutamate (carrying one net negative charge) is transported into the cell together with two sodium ions and that the return of the carrier to the outside of the cell is coupled to an outward transport of one potassium and one hydroxyl ion. This stoichiometry provides glutamate uptake with a substantial driving force which on theoretical grounds would be sufficient to maintain an external glutamate concentration as low as $0.6 \mu M$ (i.e. less than 1:10 000 of the assumed intracellular concentration). This value is in good agreement with microdialysis data from brain.

The maintenance of a low level of external glutamate is one obvious function of the glutamate transporter. This function is crucial as glutamate becomes neurotoxic when its extracellular concentration exceeds a certain level. The magnitude of this level is hard to determine, due to the efficiency of the uptake and the lack of good uptake blockers. It may amount to a few hundred μM (Nicholls and Attwell, 1990) or be as low as $1 \mu M$ (Frandsen and Schousboe, 1990). The importance of glial glutamate transporters for reducing glutamate neurotoxicity is illustrated by experiments showing that neurons are much more sensitive when grown alone than in co-culture with glia (Rosenberg et al., 1992) and that cells on the surface of tissue slices are much more sensitive than cells situated deeper into the slices (Garthwaite et al., 1992). The toxic effects are due to excessive depolarization associated with swelling, and an accumulation of calcium recruited from the extracellular space or from intracellular stores. In conditions such as anoxia and ischemia, the driving force of glutamate uptake collapses due to the breakdown of the electrochemical sodium and potassium gradients, and glutamate transport will be compromised or reversed. In fact, there is increasing evidence to suggest that the extracellular overflow of glutamate in ischemic and anoxic conditions primarily reflects inadequate or reversed glutamate transport and that exocytotic release plays a minor role (Nicholls and Attwell, 1990).

As pointed out in the Introduction, neurotransmitter transporters are generally regarded as instrumental for terminating the synaptic action of the respective transmitters. This view is supported by numerous studies demonstrating a prolonged and enhanced transmitter action after inhibition of uptake (Amara and Kuhar, 1993). Surprisingly, it is still not clear to what extent this holds true in the case of the glutamate transporters. The issue is whether the diffusion of glutamate away from the synaptic cleft is so fast that the decay of the synaptic current is determined simply by the kinetics of the receptor channels. This appears to be the case for the NMDA receptor channels, which have a long activated lifetime compared to the estimated time course of glutamate in the synaptic cleft, and which may be saturated following glutamate release from a single vesicle (Clements et al., 1992). Compared to the NMDA receptors, the AMPA receptor channels have a lower affinity to glutamate and a shorter duration, leading Clements et al. (1992) to predict that the decay of the current through these could in part depend on the rate of transmitter clearance. If so, changes in uptake activity would be expected to alter the synaptic efficacy.

Due to the lack of adequate uptake blockers, this prediction is difficult to verify experimentally. All the known compounds that inhibit glutamate uptake with "high" affinity, are competitive inhibitors which have merely about the same affinity as glutamate, are themselves transported and can exchange with intracellular excitatory amino acids. Because the extracellular space is narrow and the glutamate concentration in the synaptic cleft after a single event may amount to mM levels (Clements et al., 1992), it is not clear whether the inhibitor gets into the synaptic cleft at concentrations sufficient to compete successfully with synaptically released glutamate. Isaacson and Nicoll (1993) recently studied the effects of a new glutamate uptake blocker, L-*trans*-pyrrolidine-2,4-dicarboxylate (L-*trans*-PDC), on the time course and kinetics on NMDA and non-NMDA receptor mediated synaptic currents in the hippocampal slice preparation. They concluded that the decay time course of both types of current could be explained by the kinetics of the receptors and that clearance of glutamate from the synaptic cleft by lateral diffusion was faster. Similar results were obtained by using L-*trans*-PDC at the cerebellar mossy fibre to granular cell synapses (Sarantis et al., 1993) and previously at various sites by use of other less potent glutamate uptake blockers. The implication would be that the role of the glutamate transporters is restricted to that of maintaining a favorable gradient for glutamate diffusion from the synaptic cleft.

However, this conclusion may not be valid for all systems or in all experimental situations. Recently, Kovalchuk and Attwell (1994) and Barbour et al. (1994) have found that L-*trans*-PDC, D-aspartate and other glutamate uptake inhibitors do prolong the decay time of the synaptic currents at the parallel and climbing fibre synapses onto Purkinje cells in the cerebellum. The latter authors provide calculations indicating that the restricted diffusion dictated by the geometry of the cerebellar axo-spinous synapses explains the long normal timecourse of the synaptic current and its prolongation by inhibition of glutamate uptake. The "outlet" of the space lateral of the synaptic cleft in this type of synapse is through the narrow surround of the spine necks and the entering and leaving parallel fibre axons. This space is confined by glial lamellae imbued with glutamate transporters (Fig. 1). Previously, Eliasof and Werblin (1993) have reported that inhibition of glutamate uptake abolished the light response in horizontal cells of the salamander retina, indicating that deficient uptake compromised the rapid decrease in synaptic glutamate concentration that signals light onset through the cone-horizontal

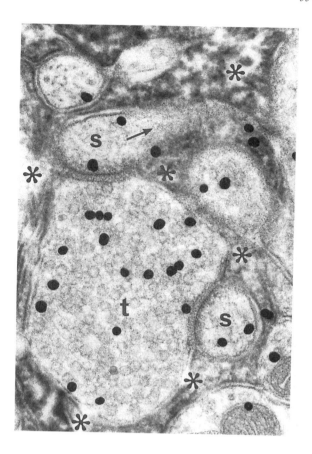

Fig. 1. A parallel fibre bouton (t) in the cerebellar molecular layer forming synapses with asymmetric membrane specializations onto two dendritic spines (s). The arrow points in the direction of the narrow spine neck (tangentially cut). The space surrounding the synapse is completely ensheathed with processes (∗) of Bergmann fibres, a type of astrocyte, immunoperoxidase labelled for an intracellular epitope of the glutamate transporter GLAST. Similar localization is seen for GLT1. The bouton is enriched with glutamate (30 nm particles) as shown by postembedding immunogold labelling with antibody to the glutaraldehyde fixed amino acid (see Zhang et al., 1993). Other neuronal structures contain some "metabolic" glutamate. Quantitation in similar material has shown the particle density in parallel fibre boutons to be about 3.5 times higher than in Purkinje cell dendrites and 4 times higher than in astrocytic processes (Ottersen et al., 1992). Modified from Lehre et al. (1994).

cell synapse. Uptake blockers that bind irreversibly with high affinity will be required to settle the question of whether glutamate uptake affects the timecourse of synaptic events at glutamatergic synapses in general.

Another question that pertains to the physiological roles of glutamate transporters is whether the basal level of glutamate is sufficiently high to exert a background activation of glutamate receptors. This is probably not the case for the AMPA receptors, which have low affinity for glutamate. The NMDA, receptors, on the other hand, exhibit a K_d in the low micromolar range and a proportion of these receptors may well be activated by the basal concentration of glutamate. The same may be true of presynaptic metabotropic glutamate receptors, which also show a high affinity for glutamate. Activation of the latter receptors facilitates glutamate release (Herrero et al., 1992), providing a possible feedback link between glutamate uptake activity and synaptic efficacy.

Regulation of glutamate transport

All glutamate transporters that have been cloned so far are equipped with potential protein kinase C dependent phosphorylation sites. Direct evidence that PKC phosphorylation is involved in the regulation of glutamate transport was recently provided by Casado et al. (1993). Phorbol esters were found to produce an increase in glutamate transport in C6 cells (a cell line of glial origin) and a concomitant increase in the phosphorylation level of the glutamate transporter (isolated by antibodies to GLT1). By site directed mutagenesis of GLT1 and transfection to HeLa cells, it could be shown that the effect of the phorbol ester was dependent on serine 113, which thus appears to be the biologically relevant phosphorylation site. The physiological stimulus for this regulatory mechanism remains to be identified, but alpha$_1$ and beta-adrenergic receptors may be involved, as activation of both types of receptor has been found to modulate glutamate uptake (for review, see: Amara and Kuhar, 1993). Phosphorylation may possibly underlie early observations of an increased glutamate uptake in the striatum after in vivo electrical stimulation of the frontal cortex (Nieoullon et al., 1983).

There is solid evidence that arachidonic acid has an inhibitory effect on glutamate uptake in glial cells and nerve terminals (Barbour et al., 1989) although it is still unclear whether this effect is caused by a direct action on the transporter molecules or, indirectly, through an interaction with their lipidic environment. This effect may be of physiological relevance during the induction of long term potentiation, which is associated with an increased production of arachidonic acid (Bliss and Collingridge, 1993). It has previously been reported (Herrero et al., 1992) that arachidonic acid may increase synaptic strength by stimulating glutamate release, acting presynaptically in concert with metabotropic glutamate receptors. A simultaneous inhibition of glutamate uptake would have a synergistic effect. Interestingly, glutamate uptake has been found to be inhibited also by NO (Pogun and Kuhar, 1993), which, like arachidonic acid, has been proposed to act as a "retrograde messenger" during the induction of LTP.

Another class of endogenous compounds that may influence glutamate uptake is the glucocorticoids. Glucocorticoids have been found to inhibit glutamate uptake in astrocytes (Virgin et al., 1991), apparently by reducing the affinity to glutamate. It is conceivable that this mechanism may contribute to the neurotoxic effects of high glucocorticoid levels.

It was recently shown, by quantitative immunoblotting, that the levels of GLT1 and GLAST in the striatum were decreased after decortication (Levy et al., 1993). This finding raises the possibility that the expression of the glial transporters is regulated by glutamate itself or by another factor that is released from corticostriatal terminals. The finding also casts doubt on the common assumption that the decrease in glutamate uptake after nerve transection is fully explained by a loss of presynaptic uptake sites.

The fact that glutamate transport thus appears to be subject to elaborate regulatory mechanisms strongly suggests an important role for the glutamate transporters in brain function, maybe through mechanisms that yet remain to be discovered. The notion of important regulatory roles is reinforced by the findings of multiple types of glutamate transporters, with different regional and cellular localizations.

Heterogeneity of glutamate transporters

The three first cloned glutamate transporters exhibit an

amino acid sequence identity of about 50% (Kanai et al., 1993b; Danbolt, 1994). The predicted number of membrane spanning domains was different for each transporter, but this may reflect differences in the interpretation of the hydropathy plots which differ only marginally between GLT1, GLAST, and EAAC1. Information is still scarce with regard to possible functional heterogeneities between the three transporters. Estimations of the affinities to glutamate have given lower K_m values for GLT1 than for GLAST and EAAC1 (Kanai et al., 1993b), but a comparison under identical experimental conditions by Fairman et al. (1993) on the human counterparts of GLAST, GLT and EAAC (termed EAAT-1, -2 and -3) expressed in COS-7 cells gave K_m values of 57, 101 and 70 μM, respectively.

Information is more plentiful with regard to the differential localization of the three transporters. The distributions of two of these (GLT1 and GLAST) have been compared in the same material by use of immunocytochemistry (Lehre et al., 1994) and in situ hybridization (Torp et al., 1994). The two techniques have produced consistent results and indicate that there are pronounced regional differences in the expression of the two transporters. The highest concentration of GLAST is found in the cerebellum while GLT1 predominates in telencephalic structures including the hippocampus, neocortex and striatum. However, the cellular distribution is very similar: both GLAST and GLT1 are expressed in glial cells (Fig. 1), but in different proportions depending on the region. Indeed, analyses of consecutive ultrathin sections labelled postembedding with antibodies to the respective transporters have revealed that GLAST and GLT1 are co-localized in the same glial cells in the hippocampus and cerebellum (Chaudhry et al., 1994). One possible interpretation of this finding is that the glial glutamate transporter is a heterooligomer and that the ratio between GLAST and GLT1 (and possibly other) subunits differs among different brain regions. This would further increase the possibilities for functional variation and would be in agreement with the observation that antibodies to GLT1 are capable of immunoprecipitating more than 90% of the glutamate uptake activity in rat brains (Danbolt et al., 1992). In

view of the latter results and the apparent absence of GLT1 and GLAST from nerve terminals, it is interesting that Na$^+$-dependent high affinity excitatory amino acid transport has been demonstrated directly in hippocampal glutamatergic nerve terminals by ultrastructural immunogold localization of exogenous D-aspartate (Gundersen et al., 1993).

The distribution of EAAC1, which was cloned from another species (rabbit), has not been studied under conditions similar to those used for GLAST and GLT1. In their original report, Kanai and Hediger (1992) concluded on the basis of the distribution of hybridizing mRNA that this transporter was primarily neuronal. Recently, the same authors succeeded in cloning a rat homologue of EAAC1 (Kanai et al., 1993a), but as yet no information is available on its distribution. Most likely, several additional excitatory amino acid transporters remain to be identified.

Perturbations of the extracellular glutamate level: pathological consequences

An inappropriate action of glutamate is thought to be a pathogenetic factor in many neurological diseases (Whetsell and Shapira, 1993). Overt neurotoxicity, caused by an extracellular glutamate overflow in the range of 100 μM or more, is implicated in catastrophic events such as anoxia, ischemia and severe brain trauma. It should be emphasized, however, that neurotoxic effects could become apparent at much lower glutamate concentrations if the energy status of the tissue is suboptimal. In such conditions, the efficiency of glutamate transport may decrease, causing an elevation (maybe slight) of the basal glutamate level, which in turn will produce an increased metabolic demand on the neurons. Thus, the stage would be set for a vicious circle that could ultimately lead to cell death. This mechanism could be reinforced by a reduction of glutathione synthesis secondary to a glutamate induced inhibition of the cellular uptake of cysteine through the cysteine-glutamate antiporter (Murphy et al., 1989). A mismatch between the metabolic demand imposed by glutamate and the ability to withstand metabolic stress (Beal et al., 1993) may contribute to cell death, e.g. in Parkinson's disease and amyotrophic lateral sclerosis (ALS). The latter disease (Rothstein et al., 1992), and a mouse counterpart (Battaglioli et al., 1993), are associated with a decreased glutamate uptake, notably in the regions that are commonly affected by this disease. Interestingly, a decreased superoxide dismutase activity has been discovered in a familial form of ALS (Rosen et al., 1993). While these two defects have yet to be identified in the same patients, the findings highlight the possibility that a low level of glutamate excitotoxicity and reduced antioxidative capacity may act in concert to cause neurodegeneration (Coyle and Puttfarcken, 1993).

Although neurodegenerative diseases are bound to have a predominant role in any discussion of glutamate-related pathology, it should be emphasized that an inappropriate action of glutamate is likely to be relevant in other diseases as well. Epilepsy is one important example which is highlighted by the recent findings of During and Spencer (1993). These authors demonstrated by use of microdialysis probes that epileptic seizures in humans were associated with an increase in the extracellular level of glutamate. Interestingly, this increase appeared to precede seizure onset, suggesting that it could be responsible for triggering the attack.

On the other hand, reduced glutamatergic activity has been implicated in the pathogenetic mechanisms of schizophrenia and other psychoses (Riederer et al., 1992). Localized or generalized disturbances in the regulation of glutamate uptake could possibly be involved in such mechanisms.

Glutamate transporters: possible targets of pharmacological intervention?

Since perturbations of the concentration of extracellular glutamate may be involved in many diseases, there is a need for drugs that can counteract such perturbations. As outlined above, the glutamate transporters play a central role in the maintenance of the extracellular glutamate level and would be appropriate targets for such drugs. It is conceivable that a modulation of uptake activity could be effected without undue interference with synaptic transmission through AMPA receptors. The recognition that glutamate transporters

are subject to various forms of regulation (see above) opens possible avenues for therapies aimed at increasing or decreasing the uptake activity. It is also of importance that neuronal and glial uptake are handled by different transporter molecules and that the two glial transporters differ substantially with regard to their regional distribution. These features provide the possibility of designing drugs that are selective for a given cell type or region. The availability of region-selective drugs would be of importance as most neurodegenerative diseases show a predilection for specific brain areas. It even implies the possibility of carefully targeted inhibition of uptake with a view to augment deficient glutamatergic activity. Clearly, the glutamate transporters hold promise as targets of pharmacological intervention.

Future developments

Where is the work on glutamate transporters heading? In the near future, we can foresee the identification of additional members of the excitatory amino acid transporter family, cloned on the basis of homology with GLAST, GLT1 and EAAC1, and new knowledge of the structure and localization of the genes encoding the transporters. Site directed mutagenesis and other methods will uncover the molecular anatomy of the transporting and regulatory sites, and insight will be gained in how the proteins are folded with respect to the phospholipid membrane. Eventually, the production of large amounts and the crystallization of the molecules will allow their three-dimensional structure to be described. The availability of the cloned transporters will aid studies of their function and the development of pharmacological tools (ligands of transport sites, modulators, oligonucleotides) for blockade and regulation of activity. Such tools may prove useful for probing the functional state of the transporters and of glutamatergic synapses, inter alia by imaging techniques. Transgenic animals with selective lack of transporter types or expressing mutated transporters may form models of human disease. The exact localizations of the transporter types and changes in these, depending on functional state and pathology, can now be studied by specific antibodies and nucleotide probes. Based on this work, it will be possible to uncover the functional role(s) of the transporters in the intact organism and their involvement in disease processes. It is likely that this will eventually lead to innovation of therapy and diagnostic procedures for several different neurological and psychiatric disorders, such as stroke, motor neuron disease, dementia and schizophrenia.

Acknowledgements

We are grateful to David Attwell, Boris Barbour and Roger Nicoll for making preprints of unpublished work available to us.

References

Amara, S.G. and Kuhar, M.J. (1993) Neurotransmitter transporters – recent progress. *Annu. Rev. Neurosci.*: 16: 73–93.

Attwell, D., Sarantis, M., Szatkowski, M., Barbour, B. and Brew, H. (1991) Patch-clamp studies of electrogenic glutamate uptake: ionic dependence, modulation and failure in anoxia. In: H. Wheal and A. Thomson (Ed.), *Excitatory Amino Acids and Synaptic Transmission,* Academic Press, London, pp 223–237.

Barbour, B., Szatkowski, M., Ingledew, N. and Attwell, D. (1989) Arachidonic acid induces a prolonged inhibition of glutamate uptake into glial cells. *Nature,* 342: 918–920.

Barbour, B., Keller, B.U., Llano, I. and Marty, A. (1994) Prolonged presence of glutamate during excitatory synaptic transmission to cerebellar Purkinje cells. Submitted.

Battaglioli, G., Martin, D.L., Plummer, J. and Messer, A. (1993) Synaptosomal glutamate uptake declines progressively in the spinal cord of a mutant mouse with motor neuron disease. *J. Neurochem.,* 60: 1567–1569.

Beal, M.F., Hyman, B.T. and Koroshetz, W. (1993) Do defects in mitochondrial energy metabolism underlie the pathology of neurodegenerative diseases? *Trends Neurosci.,* 16: 125–131.

Bliss, T.V. and Collingridge, G.L. (1993) A synaptic model of memory: long-term potentiation in the hippocampus. *Nature,* 361: 31–39.

Bouvier, M., Szatkowski, M., Amato, A. and Attwell, D. (1992) The glial cell glutamate uptake carrier countertransports pH-changing anions. *Nature,* 360: 471–474.

Casado, M., Bendahan, A., Zafra, F., Danbolt, N.C., Aragón, C., Giménez, C. and Kanner, B.I. (1993) Phosphorylation and modulation of brain glutamate transporters by protein kinase C. *J. Biol. Chem.,* 268: 27313–27317.

Chaudhry, F.A., Lehre, K.P., Danbolt, N.C., Ottersen, O.P. and Storm-Mathisen, J. (1994) Localization of glutamate transporters on the plasma membrane of astrocytes: electron microscopic post-embedding immunogold observations on freeze-substituted tissue. In preparation.

Clements, J.D., Lester, R.A.J., Tong, G., Jahr, C.E. and Westbrook, G.L. (1992) The time course of glutamate in the synaptic cleft. *Science,* 258: 1498–1501.

Coyle, J.T. and Puttfarcken, P. (1993) Oxidative stress, glutamate, and neurodegenerative disorders. *Science,* 262: 689–695.

Danbolt, N.C. (1994) The high affinity uptake system for excitatory amino acids in the brain. *Prog. Neurobiol.,* in press.

Danbolt, N.C., Pines, G. and Kanner, B.I. (1990): Purification and reconstitution of the sodium- and potassium-coupled glutamate transport glycoprotein from rat brain. *Biochemistry,* 29: 6734–6740.

Danbolt, N.C., Storm-Mathisen, J. and Kanner, B.I. (1992): A $[Na^+ + K^+]$coupled L-glutamate transporter purified from rat brain is located in glial cell processes. *Neuroscience,* 51: 295–310.

During, M.J. and Spencer, D.D. (1993) Extracellular hippocampal glutamate and spontaneous seizure in the conscious human brain. *Lancet,* 341: 1607–1610.

Eliasof, S. and Werblin, F. (1993) Characterization of the glutamate transporter in retinal cones of the tiger salamander. *J. Neurosci.,* 13: 402–411.

Fairman, W.A., Arriza, J.L. and Amara, S.G. (1993) Pharmacological characterization of cloned human glutamate transporter subtypes. *Soc. Neurosci. Abstr.,* 19: 496.

Frandsen, A. and Schousboe, A. (1990) Development of excitatory amino acid induced cytotoxicity in cultured neurons. *Int. J. Dev. Neurosci.,* 8: 209–216.

Garthwaite, G., Williams, G.D. and Garthwaite, J. (1992) Glutamate toxicity – an experimental and theoretical analysis. *Eur. J. Neurosci.,* 4: 353–360.

Guastella, J., Nelson, N., Nelson, H., Czyzyk, L., Keynan, S., Miedel, M.C., Davidson, N., Lester, H.A. and Kanner, B.I. (1990) Cloning and expression of a rat brain GABA transporter. *Science,* 249: 1303–1306.

Gundersen, V., Danbolt, N.C., Ottersen, O.P. and Storm-Mathisen, J. (1993) Demonstration of glutamate/aspartate uptake activity in nerve endings by use of antibodies recognizing exogenous D-aspartate. *Neuroscience,* 57: 97–111.

Herrero, I., Miras-Portugal, M.T. and Sanchez-Prieto, J. (1992) Positive feedback of glutamate exocytosis by metabotropic presynaptic receptor stimulation. *Nature,* 360: 163–166.

Isaacson, J.S. and Nicoll, R.A. (1993) The uptake inhibitor L-trans-PDC enhances responses to glutamate but fails to alter the kinetics of excitatory synaptic currents in the hippocampus. *J. Neurophysiol.,* 70: 2187–2191.

Kanai, Y. and Hediger, M.A. (1992) Primary structure and functional characterization of a high-affinity glutamate transporter. *Nature,* 360: 467–471.

Kanai, Y., Lee, W.-S., Bhide, P.G. and Hediger, M.A. (1993a) Functional analysis and distribution of expression of the neuronal high affinity glutamate transporter. *Soc. Neurosci. Abstr.,* 19: 496.

Kanai, Y., Smith, C.P. and Hediger, M.A. (1993b) The elusive transporters with a high affinity for glutamate. *Trends Neurosci.,* 16: 365–370.

Kanner, B.I. and Schuldiner, S. (1987) Mechanism of transport and storage of neurotransmitters. *CRC Crit. Rev. Biochem.,* 22: 1–38.

Kovalchuk, Y. and Attwell D. (1994) Effects of adenosine and a glutamate uptake blocker on excitatory synaptic currents at two synapses in isolated rat cerebellar slices. *J. Physiol. (London) Proc.*, 475: 153P–154P.

Lehre, K.P., Levy, L.M., Ottersen, O.P., Storm-Mathisen, J. and Danbolt, N.C. (1994) Differential expression of two glial glutamate transporters in the rat brain: quantitative and immunocytochemical observations. Submitted.

Levy, L.M., Lehre, K.P., Walaas, I., Storm-Mathisen, J. and Danbolt, N.C. (1993) Down regulation of a glial glutamate transporter in striatum after destruction of the glutamatergic corticostriatal projection. *J. Neurochem.*, 61: S208.

Murphy, T.H., Miyamoto, M., Sastre, A., Schnaar, R.L. and Coyle, J.T. (1989) Glutamate toxicity in a neuronal cell line involves inhibition of cystine transport leading to oxidative stress. *Neuron*, 2: 1547–1558.

Nicholls, D. and Attwell, D. (1990) The release and uptake of excitatory amino acids. *Trends Pharmacol. Sci.*, 11: 462–468.

Nieoullon, A., Kerkerian, L. and Dusticier, N. (1983) Presynaptic dopaminergic control of high affinity glutamate uptake in the striatum. *Neurosci. Lett.*, 43: 191–196.

Ottersen, O.P., Zhang, N. and Walberg, F. (1992) Metabolic compartmentation of glutamate and glutamine: morphological evidence obtained by quantitative immunocytochemistry in rat cerebellum. *Neuroscience*, 46: 519–534.

Pines, G., Danbolt, N.C., Bjørås, M., Zhang, Y., Bendahan, A., Eide, L., Koepsell, H., Seeberg, E., Storm-Mathisen, J. and Kanner, B.I. (1992) Cloning and expression of a rat brain L-glutamate transporter. *Nature*, 360, 464–467.

Pogun, S. and Kuhar, M.J. (1993) Glutamic acid (Glu) uptake inhibition by nitric oxide (NO). *Soc. Neurosci. Abstr.*, 19: 1351.

Riederer P., Lange K. W., Kornhuber J. and Danielczyk W. (1992) Glutamatergic-dopaminergic balance in the brain. Its importance in motor disorders and schizophrenia. *Arzneimittelforschung*, 42: 265–268.

Rosen, D.R., Siddique, T., Patterson, D., Figlewicz, D.A., Sapp, P., Hentati, A., Donaldson, D., Goto, J., O'Regan, J.P., Deng, H.X., Rahmani, Z., Krizus, A., McKenna-Yasek, D., Cayabyab, A., Gaston, S.M., Berger, R., Tanzi, R.E., Halperin, J.J., Herzfeldt, B., Van den Bergh, R., Hung, W.Y., Bird, T., Deng, G., Mulder, D.W., Smyth, C., Laing, N.G., Soriano, E., Pericak-Vance, M.A., Haines, J., Rouleau, G.A., Gusella, J.S., Horvitz, H.R. and Brown, R.H. (1993) Mutations in Cu/Zn superoxide dismutase gene are associated with familial amyotrophic lateral sclerosis. *Nature*, 362: 59–62.

Rosenberg, P.A., Amin, S. and Leitner, M. (1992) Glutamate uptake disguises neurotoxic potency of glutamate agonists in cerebral cortex in dissociated cell culture. *J. Neurosci.*, 12: 56–61.

Rothstein, J.D., Martin, L J. and Kuncl, R.W. (1992) Decreased glutamate transport by the brain and spinal cord in amyotrophic lateral sclerosis. *N. Engl. J. Med.*, 326: 1464–1468.

Sarantis, M., Ballerini, L., Miller, B., Silver, R.A., Edwards, M. and Attwell, D. (1993) Glutamate uptake from the synaptic cleft does not shape the decay of the non-NMDA component of the synaptic current. *Neuron*, 11: 541–549.

Storck, T., Schulte, S., Hofmann, K. and Stoffel, W. (1992) Structure, expression, and functional analysis of a Na^+-dependent glutamate/aspartate transporter from rat brain. *Proc. Natl. Acad. Sci. USA*, 89: 10955–10959.

Torp, R., Danbolt, N.C., Babaie, E., Bjørås, M., Seeberg, E., Storm-Mathisen, J. and Ottersen, O.P. (1994) Differential expression of two glial glutamate transporters in the rat brain: an in situ hybridization study. *Eur. J. Neurosci.*, in press.

Virgin, C.E., Ha, T.P., Packan, D.R., Tombaugh, G.C., Yang, S.H., Horner, H.C. and Sapolsky, R.M. (1991) Glucocorticoids inhibit glucose transport and glutamate uptake in hippocampal astrocytes: implications for glucocorticoid neurotoxicity. *J. Neurochem.*, 57: 1422–1428.

Whetsell, W.O. and Shapira, N.A. (1993) Biology of disease – neuroexcitation, excitotoxicity and human neurological disease. *Lab. Invest.*, 68: 372–387.

Zhang, N., Storm-Mathisen, J. and Ottersen, O.P. (1993) A model system for specificity testing and antigen quantitation in single and double labelling postembedding electron microscopic immunocytochemistry. *Neurosci. Protocols*, 93-050-13: 1–20.

F. Bloom (Editor)
Progress in Brain Research, Vol. 100
© 1994 Elsevier Science B.V. All rights reserved.

CHAPTER 8

GABA$_C$ receptors

Graham A.R. Johnston

Department of Pharmacology, The University of Sydney, NSW, 2006, Australia

Introduction

Much progress has been made in recent years in our understanding of the rich variety of receptors for the inhibitory neurotransmitter GABA (γ-aminobutyric acid, 4-aminobutanoic acid). The current classification of GABA receptors was introduced by Hill and Bowery in 1981 and is based on pharmacological characteristics, GABA$_A$ receptors being antagonised by bicuculline, and GABA$_B$ receptors being insensitive to bicuculline antagonism and activated selectively by baclofen (2-p-chlorophenyl-4-aminobutanoic acid). It is becoming increasingly clear, however, that GABA can activate receptors that are insensitive to both bicuculline and baclofen and that the GABA$_A$/GABA$_B$ classification represents an oversimplification of the range of receptors available to this inhibitory neurotransmitter.

GABA receptors insensitive to both bicuculline and baclofen may represent a major class of GABA receptors in the animal kingdom. These receptors have been called GABA$_C$ or GABA$_{NANB}$ ("non-A, non-B") receptors. Such GABA receptors have been described in vertebrate retina, cerebellum, cerebral cortex, optic tectum, spinal cord, many insect species and bacteria. Molecular biological studies have shown that mammalian retinal and insect mRNA injected into *Xenopus* oocytes leads to expression of bicuculline-insensitive, baclofen-insensitive GABA receptors. Cloning of cDNAs indicates that a specific protein subunit, designated ρ_1, may be associated with the retinal receptors.

Early studies

The discovery, in 1970, of the GABA antagonist action of the convulsant alkaloid bicuculline provided vital pharmacological evidence for the role of GABA as an inhibitory neurotransmitter in the CNS. Bicuculline-sensitive synaptic inhibition was observed all over the brain and spinal cord providing a convenient pharmacological means to support other evidence for GABA being the major inhibitory neurotransmitter (Johnston, 1991). By 1981, it was clear that not all GABA receptors could be antagonised by bicuculline, and that a specific class of bicuculline-insensitive GABA receptors were activated by the GABA analogue, baclofen (Hill and Bowery, 1981) leading to the GABA$_A$/GABA$_B$ classification of GABA receptors. GABA$_A$ receptors were insensitive to baclofen, antagonised by bicuculline and gated chloride ion channels in neuronal membranes. GABA$_B$ receptors were insensitive to bicuculline, activated by baclofen and were linked to second messenger systems. By 1984, a range of GABA analogues had been described that could inhibit neuronal activity in a bicuculline-insensitive manner but did not interact with GABA$_B$ receptors as indicated by a lack of effect on [^{3}H]baclofen binding (Drew et al., 1984), giving rise to the possibility of a third class of GABA receptors, tentatively labelled GABA$_C$. The lead compound was *cis*-4-aminocrotonic acid (CACA), an unsaturated analogue of GABA in a partially folded conformation; CACA was approximately one-quarter as potent as GABA in inhibiting the firing of spinal neurones in

62

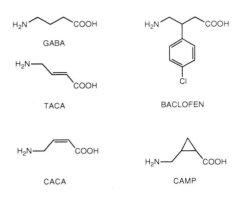

Fig. 1. Structures of GABA, baclofen, TACA (*trans*-4-amino-crotonic acid), CACA (*cis*-4-aminocrotonic acid) and CAMP (*cis*-2-(aminomethyl)-cyclopropane carboxylic acid. CACA and CAMP may be selective ligands for $GABA_C$ receptors.

cats under pentobarbitone anaesthesia, whereas the corresponding *trans*-isomer, TACA, was a bicuculline-sensitive inhibitor equal in potency to GABA (Johnston et al., 1975). The structures of these and some related compounds are shown in Fig. 1. TACA but not CACA inhibited the binding of [³H]baclofen to rat cerebellar membranes (Drew et al., 1984). These studies showed that CACA was a neuronal inhibitor whose action did not appear to be linked to either bicuculline-sensitive ($GABA_A$) or baclofen-sensitive ($GABA_B$) receptors, but only the structural similarity between CACA and GABA linked the inhibitory action of CACA to a possible third class of GABA receptors.

Novel pharmacology of GABA receptors in the optic tectum and retina

Sivilotti and Nistri (1989) found GABA effects in frog optic tectum which exhibited a novel pharmacology. GABA and TACA were equipotent (ED_{50} 110 μM) in enhancing excitatory postsynaptic field potentials in a chloride dependent manner. CACA was some five times less potent (ED_{50} 500 μM). The effects of GABA, TACA and CACA were relatively insensitive to bicuculline (100 μM) but could be blocked by picrotoxin (IC_{50} 78 μM). The benzodiazepine midazolam did not influence this action of GABA. Pento-

barbitone acted as a partial agonist, enhancing the field potentials in a picrotoxin-sensitive manner, and antagonising the GABA effects.

A number of studies on retina, published in 1991, led to further interest in a possible third major class of GABA receptors. Matthews et al. (1991) published an abstract entitled "Inhibition of presynaptic calcium current via $GABA_C$ receptors" describing their work on the large synaptic terminals of bipolar neurones in goldfish retina which receive feedback innervation from GABAergic amacrine cells. They reported that 5 μM CACA, like GABA, suppressed calcium currents in these terminals. Baclofen was ineffective. CACA did not activate $GABA_A$ chloride conductances in bipolar neurones. These results suggested "a physiological role for $GABA_C$ in modulation of presynaptic Ca current".

Polenzani et al. (1991) published an extensive paper suggesting that "mammalian retina contains RNAs encoding GABA receptors with distinct pharmacology". They injected poly(A)$^+$ RNA from bovine retina into *Xenopus* oocytes which resulted in the expression of GABA receptors which were insensitive to bicuculline and baclofen. These receptors could not be modulated by benzodiazepines or barbiturates that modulate classic $GABA_A$ receptors. Activation of the receptors produced a chloride current that could be blocked by picrotoxin.

Cutting et al. (1991) cloned a cDNA for a GABA receptor subunit, ρ_1, the mRNA for which is highly expressed in the retina. On injection into *Xenopus* oocytes, ρ_1 mRNA expressed GABA receptors insensitive to bicuculline. Activation of these receptors produced a picrotoxin-sensitive chloride conductance.

Further studies by this group (Shimada et al., 1992) on the pharmacology of these expressed ρ_1 subunit homooligomeric receptors was considered to provide "substantial evidence for a distinct and unique physiologic and pharmacologic role for this newest member of the GABA receptor gene family". The authors go on to state "if further evidence supports a self-associating role for this subunit, these genetic, pharmacologic and physiologic distinctions may be sufficiently unique to merit naming the receptors formed from these subunits $GABA_C$".

Patch clamp studies

Two papers published in the same issue of *Nature* in January 1993 described patch clamp studies on novel GABA responses in retina. Feigenspan et al. (1993) described GABA gated bicuculline-insensitive chloride channels in cultured rod bipolar cells of rat retina, which were not modulated by flunitrazepam, pentobarbitone and alphaxalone and were only marginally blocked by picrotoxin. CACA ($100\,\mu$M) evoked small but consistent responses, comprising about 10% of the current induced by $20\,\mu$M GABA and TACA. Bicuculline ($100\,\mu$M) reduced the currents induced by GABA and TACA by about 50% without influencing the currents induced by CACA. Feigenspan et al. (1993) concluded "the bicuculline- and baclofen-insensitive GABA receptors were activated selectively by the GABA analogue *cis*-4-aminocrotonic acid (CACA). Hence they may be similar to those receptors termed GABA$_C$ receptors." The accompanying paper of Qian and Dowling (1993) reported similar responses in dissociated rod-driven horizontal cells but not in bipolar cells from white perch retina. GABA responses in the retinal horizontal cells were insensitive to $500\,\mu$M bicuculline, $10\,\mu$M diazepam, $100\,\mu$M pentobarbitone, $500\,\mu$M phaclofen and $500\,\mu$M 2-hydroxysaclofen (the last two compounds being GABA$_B$ antagonists). The responses could be blocked by $500\,\mu$M picrotoxin. CACA produced similar bicuculline-insensitive, picrotoxin-sensitive responses to GABA but was considerably weaker, with EC$_{50}$ values of $48.5\,\mu$M for CACA and $1.87\,\mu$M for GABA. CACA appeared to behave as a partial agonist, its maximal effect being about half that produced by GABA.

Novel pharmacology of receptors expressed in *Xenopus* oocytes

Extensive studies of the pharmacology of GABA ρ_1 receptors expressed in *Xenopus* oocytes have been reported. Woodward et al. (1993) found the following EC$_{50}$ agonist values: TACA $0.6\,\mu$M, GABA $1.3\,\mu$M, and CACA $75\,\mu$M. ZAPA, THIP, 3-aminopropyl-phosphinic acid, 3-aminopropyl(methyl)-phosphinic

acid, and δ-aminovaleric acid acted as antagonists. Bicuculline had some weak antagonist activity but was at least 5000 times less potent than at GABA$_A$ receptors. Kusama et al. (1993) found the following agonist K_d values: TACA $0.6\,\mu$M, GABA $1.7\,\mu$M and CACA $74\,\mu$M in excellent agreement with those of Woodward et al. (1993). Kusama et al. (1993) found, however, that ZAPA, THIP and 3-aminopropyl phosphinic acid were essentially inactive. TACA, CACA and CAMP (*cis*-2-(aminomethyl)-cyclopropanecarboxylic acid, another conformationally restricted GABA analogue) showed the most selectivity between ρ_1 and GABA$_A$ receptors resulting from the expression of $\alpha_s\beta_1$ subunits in *Xenopus* oocytes. CAMP was more than 150 times more potent against ρ_1 than $\alpha_s\beta_1$ receptors. CAMP has been shown to be a bicuculline-insensitive inhibitor of the firing of cat spinal neurones in vivo with a potency varying between one-twentieth and equipotent with GABA (Allan et al., 1980).

Binding studies

Some studies on the binding of [^{3}H]GABA to rat brain membranes reveal binding that is insensitive to bicuculline and to baclofen. Balcar et al. (1986) reported that the binding of [^{3}H]GABA to cerebral cortical membranes prepared from newborn and adult rats could be partially inhibited by $100\,\mu$M CACA and that this inhibition produced by CACA was additive to that produced by $100\,\mu$M bicuculline and $100\,\mu$M baclofen. Drew and Johnston (1992) reported studies on [^{3}H]GABA binding to rat cerebellar membranes and described a calcium-independent [^{3}H]GABA component that was insensitive to bicuculline and baclofen. They termed this binding GABA$_{NANB}$, to indicate that the binding sites involved were different from classically described GABA$_A$ and GABA$_B$ binding sites. Scatchard analysis indicated two components for the GABA$_{NANB}$ binding with K_d values of $42\,$nM and $9\,\mu$M, respectively. Up to 60% of the [^{3}H]GABA bound to rat cerebellar membranes appeared to bind to GABA$_{NANB}$ binding sites. This binding was inhibited by CACA (IC$_{50}$ $2\,\mu$M), TACA (IC$_{50}$ $22\,\mu$M) and CAMP (42% at $1\,\mu$M), and was insensitive to 2-hydroxysaclofen, securinine, gabapentin and 3-

aminopropylphosphonic acid (Drew and Johnston, unpublished). We have begun studying the binding of [^{3}H]CACA to rat cerebellar membranes (Drew, Duke and Johnston, unpublished). Both GABA and TACA are potent inhibitors of [^{3}H]CACA binding ($IC_{50} < 25$ nM) with CACA itself showing moderate potency (IC_{50} 0.5 μM).

Studies on insects and bacteria

The majority of GABA receptors described in insects appear to be insensitive to bicuculline and baclofen (Lummis, 1992). They gate chloride channels that can be weakly antagonised by picrotoxin. The function of these insect GABA receptors can be enhanced by benzodiazepines, although the pharmacology of the benzodiazepine enhancement seems to follow that of the vertebrate peripheral benzodiazepine sites that are not linked to GABA$_A$ receptors more closely than the vertebrate CNS benzodiazepines sites that are linked to such bicuculline-sensitive receptors. Many insecticides act on GABA receptors and part of their selective action between insects and vertebrates may be due to differences in GABA receptors. Recently, a series of insecticidal 1,2,3-triazoles have been described that block bicuculline-insensitive GABA responses in muscle cells of the nematode *Ascaris* which "may also prove to be useful antagonists of the GABA$_C$ receptor subtype" (Holden-Dye et al., 1994)

GABA binds to receptors in bacteria that appear to respond to mammalian GABA$_A$ agonists, such as muscimol, but not to mammalian GABA$_A$ antagonists, such as SR95531 (Balcar, 1990). The benzodiazepine, diazepam, binds to receptors in bacteria that can be modulated by GABA (Lummis et al., 1991). These sites are similar to those found in insects in that they resemble vertebrate peripheral binding sites but, as in insects, these sites can be modulated by GABA.

Conclusions

There is increasing evidence for the existence of classes of GABA receptors that are not covered by GABA$_A$ receptors, pharmacologically defined as bicuculline-sensitive, baclofen-insensitive receptors, and

GABA$_B$ receptors, defined as baclofen-sensitive, bicuculline-insensitive receptors. GABA$_C$ receptors which are bicuculline-insensitive, baclofen-insensitive, linked to chloride channels and selectively activated by CACA and CAMP, may represent just one of such a class of receptors. GABA$_C$ receptors may be more widespread in insects and bacteria than in vertebrates where they may be localised in certain parts of the nervous system such as the retina.

GABA$_C$ receptors may represent receptors that subsequently evolved into GABA$_A$ receptors by gaining bicuculline-sensitivity, together with altered agonist and modulator specificity. The ρ_1 protein, which is highly expressed in retina and has considerable sequence homology with GABA$_A$ sub-unit proteins, yields homooligomeric receptors in *Xenopus* oocytes which have many but not all of the pharmacological properties of GABA$_C$ receptors as deduced from electrophysiological and neurochemical studies on neuronal membranes. A combination of molecular biology, electrophysiology, pharmacology and medicinal chemistry will be needed to provide more comprehensive information on GABA$_C$ and other receptors which do not fit the classic definitions of GABA$_A$ and GABA$_B$ receptors.

Acknowledgements

The author is grateful to the Australian NH&MRC for financial support and to Dr Robin Allan, Ms Muallâ Akinci, Dr Colleen Drew, Dr Rujee Duke, Dr Frances Edwards and Dr Ken Mewett for their collaboration on studies of GABA$_C$ receptors.

References

Allan, R.D., Curtis, D.R., Headley, P.M., Johnston, G.A.R., Lodge, D. and Twitchin, B. (1980) The synthesis and activity of *cis*- and *trans*-2-(aminomethyl)cyclopropanecarboxylic acid as conformationally restricted analogues of GABA. *J. Neurochem.*, 34: 652–654.

Balcar, V.J. (1990) Presence of a highly efficient "binding" to bacterial contamination can distort data from binding studies. *Neurochem Res.*, 15: 1239–1240.

Balcar, V.J., Joó, F., Kása, P., Dammasch, I.E. and Wolff, J.R. (1986) GABA receptor binding in rat cerebral cortex and superior cervical ganglion in the absence of GABAergic synapses. *Neurosci. Lett.*, 66: 269–274.

Cutting, G.R., Lu, L., O'Hara, B., Kasch, L.M., Donovan, D., Shimada, S., Antonarakis, S.E., Guggino, W.B., Uhl, G.R. and Kazazian, H.H. (1991) Cloning of the GABA ρ_1 cDNA: a novel GABA subunit highly expressed in retina. *Proc. Natl. Acad. Sci.*, 88: 2673–2677.

Drew, C.A. and Johnston, G.A.R. (1992) Bicuculline- and baclofen-insensitive γ-aminobutyric acid binding to rat cerebellar membranes. *J. Neurochem.*, 58: 1087–1092.

Drew, C.A., Johnston, G.A.R. and Weatherby, R.P. (1984) Bicuculline-insensitive GABA receptors: studies on the binding of (–)-baclofen to rat cerebellar membranes.

Feigenspan, A., Wössle, H. and Bormann, J. (1993) Pharmacology of GABA receptor Cl⁻ channels in rat retinal bipolar cells. *Nature*, 361: 159–162.

Hill, D.R. and Bowery N.G. (1981) ³H-Baclofen and ³H-GABA bind to bicuculline-insensitive GABA$_B$ sites in rat brain. *Nature*, 290: 149–152.

Holden-Dye, L., Willis, R.J. and Walker, R.J. (1994) Azole compounds antagonise the bicuculline insensitive GABA receptor on the cells of the parasitic nematode *Ascaris suum*. *Br. J. Pharmacol.*, in press.

Johnston, G.A.R. (1991) GABA$_A$ antagonists. *Semin. Neurosci.*, 3: 205–210.

Johnston, G.A.R., Curtis, D.R., Beart, P.M., Game, C.J.A., McCulloch, R.M. and Twitchin, B. (1975) *cis*- and *trans*-4-aminocrotonic acid as GABA analogues of restricted conformation. *J. Neurochem.*, 24: 157–160.

Kusama, T., Spivak, C.E., Whiting, P., Dawson, V.L., Schaeffer, J.C. and Uhl, G.R. (1993) Pharmacology of GABA ρ_1 and GABA α/β receptors expressed in *Xenopus* oocytes and COS cells. *Br. J. Pharmacol.*, 109: 200–206.

Lummis, S.C.R. (1992) Insect GABA receptors: characterization and expression in *Xenopus* oocytes following injection of cockroach CNS mRNA. *Mol. Neuropharmacol.*, 2: 167–172.

Lummis, S.C.R., Nicoletti, G., Johnston, G.A.R. and Holan G. (1991) Gamma-aminobutyric acid-modulated benzodiazepine binding sites in bacteria. *Life Sci.*, 49: 1079–1086.

Matthews, G., Ayoub, G. and Heidelberger, R. (1991) Inhibition of presynaptic calcium current via GABAC receptors. *Soc. Neurosci. Abstr.*, 17: 900.

Polenzani, L., Woodward, R.M. and Miledi R. (1991) Expression of mammalian g-aminobutyric acid receptors with distinct pharmacology in *Xenopus* oocytes. *Proc. Natl. Acad. Sci. USA*, 88: 4318–4322.

Qian, H. and Dowling, J.E. (1993) Novel GABA responses from rod-driven retinal horizontal cells. *Nature*, 361:162–164.

Shimada, S., Cutting, G. and Uhl, G.R. (1992) γ-Aminobutyric acid A or C receptor? γ-Aminobutyric acid ρ_1 receptor RNA induces bicuculline-, barbiturate-, and benzodiazepine-insensitive γ-aminobutyric acid responses in *Xenopus* oocytes. *J. Pharmacol. Exp. Ther.*, 41: 683–687.

Sivilotti, L. and Nistri, A. (1989) Pharmacology of a novel effect of γ-aminobutyric acid on the frog optic tectum in vitro. *Eur. J. Pharmacol.*, 164: 205–212.

Woodward, R.M., Polenzani, L. and Miledi, R. (1993) Characterization of bicuculline/baclofen-insensitive (ρ-like) γ-aminobutyric acid receptors expressed in *Xenopus* oocytes. 2. Pharmacology of γ-aminobutyric acid$_A$ and γ-aminobutyric acid$_B$ receptor agonists and antagonists. *Mol. Pharmacol.*, 43: 609–625.

F. Bloom (Editor)
Progress in Brain Research, Vol. 100
© 1994 Elsevier Science B.V. All rights reserved

CHAPTER 9

The central cholinergic system during aging

Giancarlo Pepeu and Lisa Giovannelli

Department of Preclinical and Clinical Pharmacology, University of Florence, Viale Morgagni 65, 50134 Florence, Italy

Introduction

After the seminal papers of Drachman and Leavitt (1974), suggesting a relationship between impairment of the cholinergic system and memory deficits in aging, and of Davies and Maloney (1976) showing a decrease in cortical choline acetyltransferase (ChAT) activity in the cerebral cortex of patients affected by Alzheimer's disease, Bartus et al. (1982) marshalled the data available at that time and proposed the "cholinergic hypothesis of geriatric memory dysfunction". Discussing the aging of the cholinergic system today means, unavoidably, assessing the impact of this hypothesis on research and clinical practice, and its present importance. The recent admission by the FDA of tacrine, a potent reversible cholinesterase inhibitor (Freeman and Dawson, 1991), for the treatment of senile dementia of Alzheimer's and Alzheimer's type disease (AD) is a consequence of this hypothesis and further reason for its critical appraisal.

The hypothesis proposed by Bartus was mostly based on observation that in patients affected by AD, ChAT activity is strongly reduced in the cerebral cortex and hippocampus as a consequence of the degeneration of forebrain cholinergic nuclei (Bigl et al., 1990). Inconsistent data existed at that time on the extent of cholinergic dysfunction in non-pathological aging. Since much evidence indicates that forebrain cholinergic pathways play a role in cognitive processes (Collerton, 1986), the hypothesis offered a rationale for searching for drugs active on memory impairment, which is a predominant symptom of AD, as well as a frequent cause of complaint in normal aging.

Undoubtedly, the hypothesis exerted an important heuristic effect by stimulating investigations aimed at defining the extent of cholinergic hypofunction, its relationship to cognitive impairment, and the development of therapeutic agents. However, its limits became rapidly evident since it was soon demonstrated that aging and particularly AD affect many neuronal systems besides the cholinergic (Hardy et al., 1985).

In this review, the question of whether the cholinergic hypothesis of memory impairment is still viable will be addressed by examining the recent evidence of cholinergic hypofunction associated with pathological and non-pathological aging, and its behavioral correlates. Furthermore, the possibility of correcting the hypofunction is discussed. For more information on aging and the cholinergic system, see Decker (1987), Sherman and Friedman (1990) and Pepeu et al. (1993a).

Loss and morphological changes of the cholinergic neurons

While the loss of neurons in the forebrain cholinergic nuclei in AD patients has been repeatedly confirmed (Bigl et al., 1990), investigations on their loss and morphological changes in normal aging in man, non-human primates, and rodents have generated controversial results. In aging men, a reduced density of the cortical cholinergic network has been demonstrated (Geula and Mesulam, 1989), and 50% of the total neuronal population of the nucleus basalis, including cholinergic and non-cholinergic neurons, has been found to be lost by 90 years of age, in comparison to the number found between 16 and 29 years (deLacalle et al., 1991). Investigations in old rats have demonstrated either a decrease or no change in the number of cholinergic neurons, a decrease and even an increase in size, a loss of dendritic spines or no morphological changes. Armstrong et al. (1993) point out that the lack of uniformity of the studies, with respect to sex, strain, age and histochemical methods, may explain the differences. Nevertheless, a decrease in the number of ChAT immunopositive cells in discrete forebrain nuclei is found in old behaviorally impaired rats as compared with non-behaviorally impaired animals of the same age. However, the finding that the loss of ChAT immunopositive neurons is not matched, in the same area, by that of neurons immunolabeled with antibodies against p75[NGF] or counterstained for Nissl substance suggests that the cholinergic neurons in aging rats do not actually die but only lose their ChAT immunoreactivity (Armstrong et al., 1993). Information on whether a decrease in ChAT immunopositive neurons also occurs in the striatum and the brainstem ascending cholinergic systems is still scarce.

Age-associated changes in ACh synthesis and release

Here there is a clear difference between the findings in AD and in non-pathological aging. In the first case, a decrease in cortical and hippocampal ChAT activity has been constantly reported (Bartus et al., 1982; Hardy et al., 1985). In the latter, it appears from the reviews of Decker (1987) and Sherman and Friedman (1990) that, in the cerebral cortex and hippocampus of aging humans and rodents, either no or small disparate changes in ChAT activity have generally been found. Moreover, it cannot be excluded that the decrease in ChAT activity, sometimes observed in normal aged humans, might be attributable to undetected AD cases. Since ChAT activity of the cholinergic neurons is normally very high, and ChAT does not catalyze a rate-limiting reaction, it is possible that determination under optimal substrate and co-factor conditions may mask small age-associated decreases in activity.

ACh synthesis also depends on high affinity choline uptake (HACU) whose rate is directly coupled to neuronal activity. Either no change or only a small decrease in HACU has been found in aging rats, with remarkable differences between rat strains and cerebral regions investigated (Decker, 1987; Sherman and Friedman, 1990). Nevertheless, these findings represent uptake under resting conditions. The possibility that a decrease in HACU activity might actually occur during aging is supported by the findings of a marked reduction in old rats in [^{3}H]hemicholinium binding, a marker of HACU sites (Forloni and Angeretti, 1992), and total tritium content, after incubation with [^{3}H]choline of electrically stimulated cortical slices (Vannucchi et al., 1990).

The marked reduction in cortical ChAT activity occurring in AD patients results in a decrease in acetylcholine (ACh) formation and release. This was shown by Sims et al. (1980) in their conclusive study on cortical biopsies. Also in non-pathological aging, most ex vivo and in vivo studies have demonstrated a decrease in ACh release from the brain. This finding is direct evidence of age-associated cholinergic hypofunction. In cortical slices, the basal efflux is not affected, but a marked reduction has been found in the evoked ACh release (Pedata et al., 1983) in rodents and in man (Feuerstein et al., 1992). The decrease usually begins between 11 and 14 months of age (Vannucchi and Pepeu, 1987), long before either morphological changes of the cholinergic neurons or ChAT reduction have ever been detected. In vivo, experiments with the microdialysis technique have confirmed the findings on brain slices. A decrease in ACh release, ranging from 35 to 60% was found in the cortex, hippocampus and striatum of 18–22-month old rats in comparison with that found in 2 to 3-month old rats (see references in Pepeu et al., 1993b). In the striatum, a 30% decrease occurred in 9-month-old rats. Interestingly, a decrease in choline efflux was also reported, suggesting that age-related changes in choline availability may underly the decrease in ACh release. The only discordant finding was obtained by Fischer et al. (1991b) who demonstrated no change in ACh release from the hippocampus of 24-month-old cognitively impaired female rats with a significant decrease in the number of ChAT-positive neurons in the septal-diagonal band.

This result and the finding that the decrease in ACh release may even occur at 9–14 months of age, long before the loss of ChAT immunopositive neurons, suggest that the decrease in ACh release and morphological changes are not directly correlated. The possibility should be considered that the decrease in ACh release may also depend on age related modifications of the choline pools used for ACh synthesis (Vannucchi et al., 1990), and on presynaptic modulation. Giovannelli et al. (1988) demonstrated a decrease of the inhibitory action of adenosine A_1 receptors on ACh release from old rats. Crawley and Wenk (1989) claim that the inhibitory effect of galanine on ACh release also is enhanced in AD.

Age associated changes in cholinergic receptors

Nordberg et al. (1992) demonstrated a significant decrease in the number of cortical M1 and M2 receptors and nicotinic receptors in the human brain during normal aging. In AD there is an increase in M1 and M2 receptors and a decrease in nicotinic receptors which was also observed by positron emission tomography (Nordberg et al., 1990). In aged rats, the reports of either a decrease or no change in the density of muscarinic binding sites were reviewed by Sherman and Friedman (1990). The reasons for the differences are not only the usual lack of uniformity of the studies, but also the presence of five different muscarinic receptor subtypes, and their plasticity. It may be assumed that a loss of presynaptic receptors, resulting from the disappearance of cholinergic nerve endings, induces a compensatory upregulation of postsynaptic receptors. Changes in density and affinity of the binding sites, and dysfunctions of their transducing mechanisms could be responsible for the limited therapeutic usefulness of cholinomimetics.

Relationship between the age-associated cholinergic hypofunction and cognitive impairment

Although much evidence demonstrates a cholinergic modulation of information processing (Warburton and Rusted, 1993), the relationship between cholinergic dysfunction and cognitive impairment in aging and AD is far from clear. An association between cognitive impairment and decrease in ACh release has been shown in aging rats (Vannucchi et al., 1990). However, association does not necessarily indicate causal relationship. Experimental lesions of the forebrain cholinergic nuclei are followed by deficits in the acquisition and performance of learned behaviors (Smith, 1988). However, caution should be exerted in attributing the deficits solely to cholinergic hypofunction since none of the lesion procedures so far used is strictly specific for cholinergic neurons (Fibiger, 1991). The same caution should hold for the aging process. Nevertheless, in animals, the recovery of the cholinergic hypofunction induced by drugs and transplants is always associated with improvement of the cognitive deficit (Fischer et al., 1987, 1991a; Gage et al., 1988; Vannucchi et al., 1990).

Can age-associated cholinergic hypofunction be improved?

Many drugs have been proposed for correcting the cholinergic hypofunction associated with normal aging and AD (Becker and Giacobini, 1991). The main approach has been to inhibit brain cholinesterase in order to increase ACh concentration in the synaptic cleft. This approach has led to the introduction of tacrine in the therapy of AD, after the unsuccessful trials with physostigmine. The true effectiveness and tolerability of tacrine in a long-term treatment, and whether its efficacy depends on cholinesterase inhibition or on other actions such as potassium channel inhibition, or muscarinic agonistic properties (Freeman and Dawson, 1991) will soon be demonstrated by its widespread use, and by comparison with new cholinesterase inhibitors. However, the most promising approach is presented by the trophic factors. It has been shown that nerve growth factor (NGF) promotes maintenance of function and survival of adult cholinergic neurons of the basal forebrain on which its specific receptors are located (for references see Hefti et al., 1991). In aging rats, a relationship exists between hippocampal NGF levels and spatial learning (Henriksson et al.,

1992), and intraventricular administration of NGF for 2 weeks increases the size of ChAT immunopositive forebrain neurons, stimulates ChAT activity in specific cholinergic nuclei, and improves spatial memory (Fischer et al., 1987, 1991a; Williams, 1991). These findings have led Olson et al. (1992) to test NGF on a patient affected by AD. Even if the observed improvement has been limited, the trial is important from a heuristic viewpoint, and the discovery of new trophic factors, along with means to manipulate their expression, may soon offer new possibilities to this therapeutic approach.

In aged rats, correction of age-associated cholinergic hypofunction has also been obtained with short-term intraperitoneal, or long-term oral administration of phosphatidylserine (PtdSer). In clinical trials, PtdSer treatments were beneficial in age-associated memory impairment and AD, even though its effects were not as rapid and clearcut as in rats. The mechanism of action, involving an effect on choline utilization, is still not understood (see references in Pepeu et al., 1993a,b)

Conclusions

The available experimental and clinical data make it possible to conclude that brain cholinergic dysfunction is actually associated with the aging process. This dysfunction may develop at different ages, involve few or several cholinergic nuclei, and vary in severity, being more severe in AD. However, to define the extent to which this cholinergic dysfunction is responsible for cognitive deficits is still a matter of research, and the hypothesis of Bartus et al. (1982) still needs the final demonstration that should come from the therapeutic results obtained with cholinergic agents. Unfortunately, we are all aware that so far the results have been somewhat disappointing (Kumar and Calache, 1991). It will be interesting to see whether the use of tacrine will change the picture. Finally, we would like to close on an optimistic note. As shown by the work with NGF and PtdSer, the aging of the cholinergic neurons appears to be reversible in the rat. Whether this is true in other animal species, including man, needs to be investigated. However, to understand the molecular basis for the recovery of cholinergic dysfunction in the rat may offer new leads for therapeutic intervention.

Acknowledgements

This work was supported by a grant from C.N.R., Target Project on Aging.

References

Armstrong, D.M., Sheffield, R., Buszaki, G., Chen, K.S., Hersh, L.B., Nearing, B. and Gage, F.H. (1993) Morphological alterations of choline acetyltransferase-positive neurons in the basal forebrain of aged behaviorally characterized Fisher 344 rats. *Neurobiol. Aging*, 14: 457–470.

Bartus, R.T., Dean, R.L., Beer, B. and Lippa, A.S. (1982) The cholinergic hypothesis of geriatric memory dysfunction. *Science*, 217: 408–410.

Becker, R.E. and Giacobini E., Eds. (1991) *Cholinergic Basis for Alzheimer Therapy*, Birkhauser, Boston.

Bigl, V., Arendt, T. and Biesold, D. (1990) The nucleus basalis of Meynert during ageing and in dementing neuropsychiatric disorders. In M. Steriade and D. Biesold (Eds.), *Brain Cholinergic System*, Oxford University Press, Oxford, pp. 364–386.

Collerton , D. (1986) Cholinergic function and intellectual decline in Alzheimer's disease. *Neuroscience*, 19: 1–28.

Crawley, J.N. and Wenk, G.L. (1989) Co-existence of galanin and acetylcholine: is galanin involved in memory processes and dementia? *Trends Neurosci.*, 12: 278–281.

Davies, P. and Maloney, A.J.R. (1976) Selective loss of cholinergic neurons in Alzheimer's disease. *Lancet*, 2: 1403.

Decker, M.W. (1987) The effects of aging on hippocampal and cortical projections of the forebrain cholinergic system. *Brain Res. Rev.*, 12: 423–438.

de Lacalle, S., Iraizos, I. and Gonzalo, L.M. (1991) Differential changes in cell size and number in topographic subdivisions of human basal nucleus in normal aging. *Neuroscience*, 43: 445–456.

Drachman, D.A. and Leavitt, J. (1974) Human memory and the cholinergic system: a relationship to ageing? *Arch. Neurol.*, 30: 113–121.

Feuerstein, T.J., Lehman, J., Sauermann, W., Van Velthoven, V. and Jackisch, R. (1992) The autoinhibitory feedback control of acetylcholine release in human neocortex tissue. *Brain Res.*, 572: 64–71.

Fibiger, H. (1991) Cholinergic mechanisms in learning, memory and dementia: a review of recent evidence. *Trends Neurosci.*, 14: 220–223.

Fischer, W., Wictorin, K., Bjorklund, A., Williams, L.R., Varon, S. and Gage, F.H. (1987) Amelioration of cholinergic neurons atrophy and spatial memory impairment in aged rats by nerve growth factor. *Nature*, 329: 65–68.

Fischer, W., Bjorklund, A., Chen, K. and Gage, F.H. (1991a) NGF improves spatial memory in aged rodents as a function of age. *J. Neurosci.*, 11: 1889–1906.

Fischer, W., Nilsson, O.G. and Bjorklund, A. (1991b) *In vivo* acetylcholine release as measured by microdialysis is unaltered in the hippocampus of cognitively impaired aged rats with degenerative changes in the basal forebrain. *Brain Res.*, 556: 44–52.

Forloni, G. and Angeretti , N. (1992) Decreased ^{3}H-hemicholinium binding to high-affinity choline uptake sites in aged rat brain. *Brain Res.*, 570: 354–357.

Freeman, S.E. and Dawson, R.M. (1991) Tacrine: a pharmacological review. *Prog. Neurobiol.*, 36: 257–277.

Gage, F.H., Armstrong, D.M., Williams, L.R. and Varon, S. (1988) Morphologic response of axotomized septal neurons to nerve growth factor. *J. Comp. Neurol.*, 269: 147–155.

Geula, C. and Mesulam, M.M. (1989) Cortical cholinergic fibers in ageing and Alzheimer's disease: a morphometric study. *Neuroscience*, 33: 469–476.

Giovannelli, L., Giovannini, M.G., Pedata, F. and Pepeu, G. (1988) Purinergic modulation of cortical acetylcholine release is decreased in aging rats. *Exp. Gerontol.*, 23: 175–181.

Hardy , J., Adolfsson, R., Alafuzoff, I., Bucht, G., Marcusson, J., Nyberg, P., Perdahl, E., Wester, P. and Winblad, B. (1985) Transmitter deficits in Alzheimer's disease. *Neurochem. Int.*, 7: 345–363.

Hefti, F., Brachet, P., Will, B. and Christen, Y. (1991) *Growth Factors and Alzheimer's Disease.* Springer, Berlin.

Henriksson, B.G., Soderstrom, S., Gower, A.J., Ebendal, T., Winblad, B. and Mohammed, A.H. (1992) Hippocampal nerve growth factor levels are related to spatial learning ability in aged rats. *Behav. Brain Res.*, 48: 15–20.

Kumar, V. and Calache N. (1991) Treatment of Alzheimer's disease with cholinergic drugs. *Int. J. Clin. Ther. Toxicol.*, 29: 23–37

Nordberg, A., Hartvig, P., Lilja A., Viitanen M., Amberla K., Lundqvist, H., Andersson, Y., Ulin, J., Winblad, B. and Langstrom, B. (1990) Decreased uptake and binding of ^{11}C-nicotine in brain of Alzheimer patients as visualized by positron emission tomography. *J. Neural Transmission*, 2: 215–224.

Nordberg, A., Alafuzoff I. and Winblad, B. (1992) Nicotinic and muscarinic subtypes in the human brain: changes with aging and dementia. *J. Neurosci. Res.*, 31: 103–111.

Olson, L., Nordberg, A., Von Holst, H., Backman, L., Ebendahl, T., Alafuzoff, I., Amberla, K., Hartvig, P., Herlitz, A., Lilja, A., Lundqvist, H., Langstrom, B., Meyersson, B., Persson, A., Viitanen, M. and Winblad, B. (1992) Nerve growth factor affects ^{11}C-nicotine binding, blood flow, EEG, and verbal episodic memory in an Alzheimer patient. *J. Neural Transmission*, 4: 79–95.

Pedata, F., Slavikova, J., Kotas, A. and Pepeu, G. (1983) Acetylcholine release from rat cortical slices during postnatal development and aging. *Neurobiol. Aging*, 4: 31–34.

Pepeu, G., Casamenti, F., Marconcini-Pepeu., I. and Scali, C. (1993a) The brain cholinergic system in aging mammals. *J. Reprod. Fertil., Suppl.*, 46: 155–162.

Pepeu, G., Casamenti, F., Scali, C. and Jeglinski, W. (1993b) Effect of serine phospholipids on memory and brain cholinergic mechanisms in aging rats. *Neurosci. Res. Commun.*, 13: S63–S66.

Sherman, K.A. and Friedman, E. (1990) Pre- and post-synaptic cholinergic dysfunction in aged rodent brain regions: new findings and an interpretative review. *Int. J. Dev. Neurosci.*, 8: 689–708.

Sims, N.R., Bowen, D.M., Smith, C.C.T., Flack, R.H.A., Davison, A.N., Snowden, J.S. and Neary, D. (1980) Glucose metabolism and acetylcholine synthesis in relation to neuronal activity in Alzheimer's disease. *Lancet*, 1: 333–335.

Smith, G. (1988) Animal models of Alzheimer's disease: experimental cholinergic denervation. *Brain Res. Rev.*, 13: 103–118.

Vannucchi, M.G. and Pepeu, G. (1987) Effect of phosphatidylserine on acetylcholine release and content in cortical slices from aging rats. *Neurobiol. Aging*, 8: 403–407.

Vannucchi, M.G., Casamenti, F. and Pepeu, G. (1990) Decrease of acetylcholine release from cortical slices in aged rats: investigations into its reversal by phosphatidylserine. *J. Neurochem.*, 55: 819–825.

Warburton, D.M. and Rusted, J.M. (1993) Cholinergic control of cognitive resources. *Neuropsychobiology*, 28: 43–46.

Williams, L.R. (1991) Exogenous nerve growth factor stimulates choline acetyltransferase activity in aging Fischer 344 male rats. *Neurobiol. Aging*, 12: 39–46.

F. Bloom (Editor)
Progress in Brain Research, Vol. 100
© 1994 Elsevier Science B.V. All rights reserved

CHAPTER 10

Co-existence of chemical messengers in neurons

Guillermo Jaim-Etcheverry

Department of Cell Biology and Histology, School of Medicine, University of Buenos Aires, Paraguay 2155, 1121 Buenos Aires, Argentina

Introduction

While three decades ago the idea that a single neuron could store and release more than one active substance seemed farfetched, nowadays the co-existence of chemical messengers in central and peripheral nerve cells appears to be the rule rather than the exception.

During this period, the co-existence of putative transmitters in neurons has received serious consideration and experimental evidence has accumulated to substantiate this possibility. Hundreds of original reports, reviews and commentaries have been published on this topic and the mechanisms of neurotransmitter co-existence have been analyzed in numerous international meetings.

Work done in our laboratory has contributed to the evolution of this concept and is summarized here. Moreover, some general comments on the possible role of the mechanism of co-transmission are made. Detailed data on these problems may be found in the references mentioned in the text.

The co-existence of neurotransmitters in the vesicles of sympathetic fibers

In the late 1960s, at the Institute of Cell Biology directed by Eduardo De Robertis in Buenos Aires, together with Luis Zieher, we were investigating the specificity of a cytochemical reaction that was presumed to identify 5-hydroxytryptamine (serotonin) at the ultrastructural level. These studies were initiated with the idea of exploring the mechanisms of mono-amine storage in sympathetic nerves. Thus, encouraged by the results obtained using rabbit blood platelets as a model (Jaim-Etcheverry and Zieher, 1968a), we rushed to try the reaction on the fibers that innervate the pineal gland of the rat. These nerves, studied in detail by Pellegrino de Iraldi et al. (1963) at the same laboratory some years earlier, have the peculiarity that, in addition to noradrenaline (NA), they physiologically contain serotonin taken up from the pinealocytes that produce the amine in high concentrations. In 1968, we could show that both NA and serotonin are stored in synaptic vesicles of pineal nerve fibers (Fig. 1) and we proposed that putative transmitters could co-exist within the dense-cored vesicles present in the nerve terminals (Jaim-Etcheverry and Zieher, 1968b).

The existence of cells storing more than one active substance was already known. Some endocrine cells, belonging to the APUD system described by Pearse (1969), had been shown to contain both a biogenic amine and a polypeptide hormone. Incidentally, with the cytochemical procedure that we were using, we could demonstrate at that time that serotonin was stored in the same granule that contained the peptide hormone, i.e. insulin in the guinea pig pancreas and calcitonin in the C cells of the sheep thyroid gland (Jaim-Etcheverry and Zieher, 1968c,d).

Our proposal that neurotransmitters could co-exist in the same vesicular storage organelles of neurons was initially received with a great scepticism that continued for many years thereafter. The reaction to these results when they were presented in a series of meetings in Europe during 1969 and in the United States in

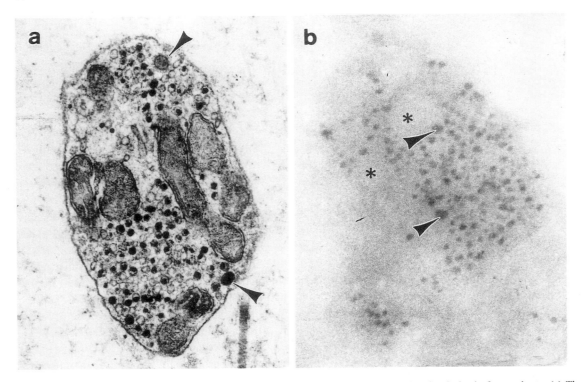

Fig. 1. Electron micrographs of adrenergic nerve terminals in the perivascular space of the pineal gland of normal rats. (a) The tissue has been conventionally processed with aldehyde fixation, followed by osmium tetroxide and lead staining of the thin section. Apart from mitochondria, small dense-cored vesicles are observed as well as some larger vesicles (arrrows) also containing a dense core (×50 000). (b) the tissue was processed with the formaldehyde-glutaraldehyde-dichromate sequence for the demonstration of serotonin storage sites. Small and large deposits corresponding to the cores observed in small and large (arrows) granular vesicles as well as the negative image of mitochondria (asterisk) are observed (×60 000) (from Jaim-Etcheverry and Zieher, 1982).

1972 was memorable. Some colleagues, patient enough to listen to peculiar theories coming from the South, conceded that we were probably dealing with a curiosity of nature.

Such a reaction was not unexpected since the co-existence hypothesis was challenging the accepted dogma of "one neuron, one transmitter". This was formulated by Eccles as "Dale's principle" on the basis of the statement made by Sir Henry Dale in the 1930s that a given class of nerve cells operates at all of its synapses using the same mechanism of transmission (see discussion in Eccles, 1986).

The mechanisms responsible for the co-storage of NA and serotonin

Apart from its significance for the interpretation of the process of peptide hormone storage in endocrine cells, our observations of the co-existence of two active molecules, a peptide and a monoamine in the same vesicle in endocrine cells and later also in peripheral sympathetic nerves (Jaim-Etcheverry and Zieher, 1969a), strengthened the possibility that NA and serotonin found in pineal nerves were in fact present in the same storage organelle. Such a mechanism was suggested by the distribution of the histochemically reactive sites corresponding to the cores of vesicles that occupied almost all the surface of the ending.

These leads prompted the initiation in 1968 of a series of studies aimed at the experimental analysis of the hypothesis of vesicular co-existence. Thus, the major thrust of our subsequent work was an attempt to demonstrate the undemonstrable: that a single nerve vesicle contains at the same time both NA and serotonin (for the detailed description of these studies, see Jaim-Etcheverry and Zieher, 1982).

The first question that we tried to answer was: are the vesicles in pineal sympathetic fibers unique in their ability to store serotonin? We could show that not only pineal fibers but also other sympathetic nerves such as those of the vas deferens, when studied in a condition that mimicked that found around the fibers innervating the pineal gland, have the ability to incorporate exogenous serotonin. The amine can gradually displace endogenous NA from the vesicles in a concentration-dependent manner and thus give a positive cytochemical reaction once it reaches a high intravesicular concentration (Jaim-Etcheverry and Zieher, 1969b; Zieher and Jaim-Etcheverry, 1971).

In 1969, octopamine was identified as a naturally occurring amine in mammalian adrenergic nerves and the possibility that it may serve as a "co-transmitter" was advanced (Molinoff and Axelrod, 1969). This role was similar to that proposed by us for serotonin in pineal nerves. Thus, the presence of octopamine within the vesicles of these nerves was considered feasible. They would contain the NA and octopamine that they synthesize, and serotonin that they take up. We reasoned that if the three amines were sharing storage space in the vesicles, the selective depletion of one of them would leave available intravesicular storage space and, as a consequence, the concentration of the other amines would rise. Figure 2 shows that by using compounds that deplete neuronal serotonin through two entirely different mechanisms, the concentration of NA and octopamine was markedly and selectively increased in the pineal gland. Apparently, as is schematically summarized in Fig. 3, due to the relative lack of specificity of the processes responsible for NA synthesis and reuptake, other molecules may be stored together with the neurotransmitter in the vesicles of adrenergic fibers (Jaim-Etcheverry and Zieher, 1971, 1975).

Consistent with the hypothesis that serotonin shares intravesicular storage space with NA was the finding that when serotonin is depleted from the vesicles, there is a rapid and transient enhancement of the activity of tyrosine hydroxylase due to the incorporation of NA to the vesicles and the release of the negative feedback control that cytoplasmic NA exerts on tyrosine hydroxylase activity (Rubio et al., 1977).

To propose the participation of neuronal serotonin in physiological mechanisms, it is important to demonstrate the release of the amine by nerve stimulation. We could show that when preganglionic nerves to both superior cervical ganglia of the rat were electrically stimulated, the reactive cores characteristic of pineal nerve vesicles almost totally disappear from the small vesicles but remain in the larger ones. Cores reacting cytochemically for serotonin as well as those giving a positive reaction for NA were depleted by

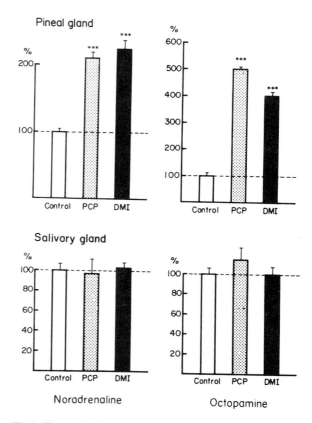

Fig.2. Changes in the content of NA and octopamine in the pineal and salivary glands of rats in which serotonin has been depleted from sympathetic nerves by two different mechanisms, i.e. by inhibiting its synthesis by the pinealocytes with p-chlorophenylalanine (PCP) or by blocking its uptake into the nerves with desmethylimipramine (DMI). Data are expressed as percent change from control values. ***$P < 0.001$ (from Jaim-Etcheverry and Zieher, 1982).

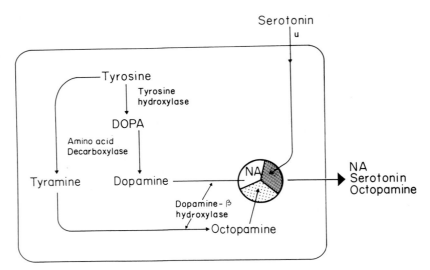

Fig. 3. Diagram showing the processes that can lead to the storage of several monoamines in the same vesicle in pineal adrenergic nerves. Whereas the lack of specificity of the reuptake process (u) is responsible for the accumulation of serotonin in the terminal, the lack of specificty of the enzymes responsible for NA synthesis results in the formation of octopamine. (from Jaim-Etcheverry and Zieher, 1982).

stimulation (Jaim-Etcheverry and Zieher, 1980). Thus, both the transmitter and the co-transmitter seem to be released by nerve impulses, a finding consistent with the hypothesis that they are stored within nerve vesicles.

On the basis of the evidence of these and other studies, we suggested that the presence of serotonin in pineal nerves could provide an efficient mechanism for the regulation of the control exerted by pineal sympathetic nerves on indole metabolism in the pineal parenchyma. The co-transmitter could act simply by modifying the amount of NA released by the nerve impulse, in this case during the 24-h cycle. This could be a special case of co-transmission that does not require the presence of the enzymatic machinery necessary for the synthesis of all the active molecules found in a given ending. This type of co-existence results from the peculiar anatomical and biochemical milieu surrounding a given terminal. Therefore, different endings of the same neuron would not necessarily contain similar active molecules. Moreover, the molecular signalling system of a given ending may change with time, depending on the activity of the surrounding neuronal or non-neuronal elements.

Neuropeptides and the phenomenon of co-existence

The study of transmitter co-existence, particularly in the CNS, poses technical difficulties due to the great heterogeneity of nervous tissue. Since the mid-1970s, the immunocytochemical approach so elegantly and thoroughly developed by Tomas Hökfelt and his group at the Karolinska Institutet in Sweden has provided many powerful insights into the mechanism of neurotransmitter co-existence. The exponential growth in the knowledge about the localization of neuropeptides both in the CNS and in the periphery thus gained, has greatly broadened our views on the possible co-existence in neurons of several molecules active in cellular communication. In this connection, the observation made by Hökfelt in 1977 that a somatostatin-like peptide co-exists with NA in the peripheral nervous system (Hökfelt et al., 1977) and the studies indicating that a substance P-like peptide co-exists with serotonin in the CNS (Hökfelt et al., 1978; Chan-Palay et al., 1978) were of particular significance.

This emerging morphological evidence favoring the mechanism of co-existence, led to a reformulation of

Dale's principle as stating that a neuron releases the same combination of transmitters from all of its terminals (Eccles, 1986). However, we were studying from the beginning a condition in which a set of terminals of a given neuronal population, that of the superior cervical ganglion, stored and released a mixture of substances different from those of terminals from the same neurons innervating other organs. This situation, resulting in our experimental model from the uptake of active substances from the vicinity of the nerve terminals, implies that the postsynaptic cell can infiltrate a "false" transmitter amongst the transmitter molecules of its afferent synapses and thus may control the extent to which it is affected by incoming impulses. A similar phenomenon to that described in the pineal may also occur in the CNS, especially where the serotonin neurons of the raphe are innervated by NA terminals (Bloom, 1974), but there is not yet such evidence probably because this situation is less amenable to experimental study.

There is another example of the heterogeneity of chemical messengers in axons of the same neuron. The invertebrate *Aplysia* was one of the first organisms in which transmitter co-existence was demonstrated (Brownstein et al., 1974; Osborne, 1981). Now there are data indicating that a single *Aplysia* neuron can store and release different neuropeptides from its individual endings (Sossin et al., 1990). This capacity not only depends on the uptake of one of the transmitters from the surrounding medium, as is the case in pineal sympathetic nerves, but rather is the result of the spatial segregation of the various peptides that are targeted to different axonal branches of the same neuron.

Possible physiological significance of transmitter co-existence

At present the phenomena of neurotransmitter co-existence and co-release, seem to provide neurons with important tools for neuronal communication and for its regulation. Different possibilities for co-existence have been described: (1) classical transmitter plus peptide(s); (2) more than one classical transmitter, either metabolically related or unrelated; and (3) more than one peptide, derived from a common prohormone or gene or from different prohormones. Virtually all types of neurons containing classical transmitters may contain one or more peptides. Recently, it has been suggested that, in addition to the biogenic amines and peptides, some neurons may also contain a fast excitatory amino acid as a third transmitter. In this case, the synapse could have the capacity to send fast (amino acid) , moderate (monoamine) and slow (peptide) signals (Nicholas et al., 1990; Hökfelt, 1991).

The particular combination of substances within well defined populations of neurons provides a way of chemically coding these groups. Subsets of neurons within the same nucleus or ganglion can be differentiated on the basis of their peculiar mixture of signalling molecules. The details of the physiological and clinical implications of the mechanism of transmitter co-existence have been extensively reviewed (see for references Hökfelt et al., 1986, 1988; Furness et al., 1989; Hökfelt, 1991).

Once the mechanism of co-existence was firmly established on anatomical grounds, there was a great interest in discovering its possible physiological significance. It has proven extremely difficult to evaluate the roles of these substances and to determine the ways in which more than one substance can participate in the transmission process. The morphological observations led to several questions, including: Are all the messengers present in neurons simultaneously released? Once liberated, are they active in the process of conveying significant signals? Does the anatomical co-existence imply that neurotransmission is plurichemical in nature?

One of the major problems under analysis has been the possible mode of action of multiple messengers. The neurons could release all their active molecules simultaneously and, in this case, the selectivity and specificity would be provided by the nature of the receptors and by their distribution. On the other hand, the selectivity could be presynaptic in nature. This would imply the storage of the messengers in different presynaptic loci. Moreover, both mechanisms may be operating at the same time.

Neuropeptides seem to be localized in the larger vesicles present in nerve terminals (diameter about 1000 Å) while classical transmitters are present in the more abundant smaller vesicles (500 Å in diameter) as well as in the larger ones (see Thureson-Klein and Klein, 1990). This differential localization has led to the speculation that, if the two types of vesicles could be selectively activated, the messenger substances could be differentially released. Such a release has been demonstrated to be dependent on the frequency of impulses and on the pattern of firing. Thus, at low firing rates, classical transmitters would be released from small vesicles at the synaptic cleft whereas at higher frequencies the large vesicles would release the peptides extrajunctionally (Lundberg et al., 1982).

Not much is known about the function of several messengers at the level of the single synapse. In most cases, the classical transmitters seem to be the important messenger but there are examples of a peptide conveying the primary message. There are many examples of the interaction between co-existing transmitters and peptides, these acting as auxiliary messengers with synergistic or antagonistic effects. These actions may be exerted either on the release of the classical transmitter or on its activity on its receptors. For example, in peripheral cholinergic nerves, vasoactive intestinal peptide (VIP) cooperates with acetylcholine (ACh) (Lundberg et al., 1982). Sympathetic fibers contain in many cases neuropeptide Y (NPY) in addition to NA . In some organs, NPY inhibits the release of NA presynaptically while in others both substances cooperate for producing vasoconstriction (Allen et al., 1982; Lundberg and Stjärne, 1984; Lundberg and Hökfelt, 1986) . There are many other situations both in the peripheral and in the central nervous system in which the possible significance of messenger co-existence have been thoroughly explored.

Apart from acting pre- and/or postsynaptically on the release of the classical transmitters, co-secreted peptides have been shown to interact with extracellular enzymes. Such is the case of the calcitonin gene related peptide (CGRP) which, when co-released with SP, seems to potentiate its action by inhibiting the enzyme responsible for SP degradation (see discussion in Hökfelt, 1991).

The interesting possibility has been recently raised that some of the messengers may participate in other forms of cell to cell interactions. They could exert long-term effects on their targets, both neurons or effector cells, acting as trophic factors related to maturation or to chemical differentiation.

The clinical significance of the mechanism of co-transmission in the pathology of the nervous system is being actively explored (see Hökfelt, 1991). For example, the detection of cholecystokinin in the mesencephalic dopaminergic neurons in the brain of schizophrenic patients treated with neuroleptics and the presence of galanin in cholinergic brain neurons, provide interesting examples of such a possibility.

Concluding remarks

Many questions remain unanswered and important details of the co-existence phenomenon are yet to be more clearly understood. Perhaps this mechanism only represents an evolutionary vestige although, as noted, it has been described in molluscs as well as in mammals. Moreover, there are now many indications of its potential role in the strategy that neurons use to communicate.

The alternative model that has emerged in the last decades derived from the study of multiple transmitter neurons is now accepted due to the evidence available for the modulatory interactions of co-transmitters, multiple post-synaptic receptors, multiple second messenger systems and the interactions between them (O'Donohue et al., 1985). During the last 25 years, we have witnessed the process by which this phenomenon has evolved from being an oddity of nature to becoming an established fact beyond discussion albeit its significance is not yet entirely clear. But there is now no doubt that several potentially active molecules coexist in both central and peripheral neurons. The available evidence suggest that their presence contributes to the subtlety and complexity that characterize the chemical signalling between neurons and their targets.

Acknowledgements

The original work reported, carried out together with Professor Luis Maria Zieher, was supported by the Consejo Nacional de Investigaciones Científicas y Técnicas and the Secretaría de Ciencia y Técnica, Argentina.

References

Allen, J., Tatemoto, K., Polak, J., Hughes, J. and Bloom, S. (1982) Two novel related peptides, neuropeptide Y (NPY) and peptide YY (PYY) inhibit the contraction of the electrically stimulated mouse vas deferens. *Neuropeptides*, 3: 71–77.

Bloom, F.E. (1974) Dynamics of synaptic modulation: perspectives for the future. In: F.O. Schmitt and F.G. Worden (Eds.), *The Neurosciences: Third Study Program*, MIT Press, Cambridge, MA, pp. 989–999.

Brownstein, M.J., Saavedra, J.M., Axelrod, J., Zeman, G.H. and Carpenter, D.O. (1974) Coexistence of several putative neurotransmitters in single identified neurons of Aplysia. *Proc. Natl. Acad. Sci. USA*, 7: 4662–4665.

Chan-Palay, V, Jonsson, G. and Palay, S.L. (1978) Serotonin and substance P coexist in neurons of the rat's central nervous system. *Proc. Natl. Acad. Sci. USA*, 75: 1582–1586.

Eccles, J. (1986) Chemical transmission and Dale's principle. In: T. Hökfelt, K. Fuxe and B. Pernow (Eds.) *Coexistence of Neuronal Messengers: A New Principle in Chemical Transmission. Progress in Brain Research*, Vol. 68, Elsevier, Amsterdam, pp. 3–13.

Furness, J.B, Morris, J.L., Gibbins, I.L. and Costa, M. (1989) Chemical coding of neurons and plurichemical transmission. *Annu. Rev. Pharmacol. Toxicol.*, 29: 289–306.

Hökfelt, T. (1991) Neuropeptides in perspective: the last ten years. *Neuron*, 7: 867–879.

Hökfelt, T., Elfvin, L.G., Elde, R., Schultzberg, M., Goldstein, M. and Luft, R. (1977) Occurrence of somatostatin-like immunoreactivity in some peripheral sympathetic noradrenergic neurons. *Proc. Natl Acad. Sci. USA*, 74: 3587–3591.

Hökfelt, T., Ljungdahl, A., Steinbusch, H., Verhofstad, A., Nilsson, G., Pernow, B. and Goldstein, M. (1978) Immunohistochemical evidence of substance P-like immunoreactivity in some 5-hydroxytryptamine-containing neurons in the rat central nervous system. *Neuroscience*, 3: 517–538.

Hökfelt, T., Fuxe, K. and Pernow, B. (Eds.) (1986) *Coexistence of Neuronal Messengers: A New Principle in Chemical Transmission.. Progress in Brain Research*, Vol. 68. Elsevier, Amsterdam, 411 pp.

Hökfelt, T., Meister, B., Melander, T., Schalling, M., Staines, W., Millhorn, D., Seroogy, K., Tsuruo, Y., Holets, V., Ceccatelli, S., Villar, M., Ju, G., Freedman, J., Olson, L., Lindh, B., Bartfai, T., Fisone, G., le Greves, P., Terenius, L., Post, C., Mollenholt, P., Dean, J. and Goldstein, M. (1988) Coexistence of multiple neuronal messengers: new aspects on chemical transmission. In: *Fidia Research Foundation Neuroscience Award Lectures*, pp. 2:61–113.

Jaim-Etcheverry, G. and Zieher, L.M. (1968a) Cytochemistry of 5-hydroxytryptamine at the electron microscope level. I. Study of the specificity of the reaction in isolated blood platelets. *J. Histochem. Cytochem.*, 16:162–171.

Jaim-Etcheverry, G. and Zieher, L.M. (1968b) Cytochemistry of 5-hydroxytryptamine at the electron microscope level. II. Localization in the autonomic nerves of the rat pineal gland. *Z. Zellforsch.*, 86: 393–400.

Jaim-Etcheverry, G. and Zieher, L.M. (1968c) Electron microscopic cytochemistry of 5-hydroxytryptamine (5-HT) in the beta cells of guinea pig endocrine pancreas. *Endocrinology*, 83: 917–923.

Jaim-Etcheverry, G. and Zieher, L.M. (1968d) Cytochemical localization of monoamine stores in sheep thyroid gland at the electron microscope level. *Experientia*, 24:593–595.

Jaim-Etcheverry, G. and Zieher, L.M. (1969a) Selective demonstration of a type of synaptic vesicle by phosphotungstic acid staining. *J. Cell Biol.*, 42: 855–860.

Jaim-Etcheverry, G. and Zieher, L.M. (1969b) Ultrastructural cytochemistry and pharmacology of 5-hydroxytryptamine in adrenergic nerve endings. I. Localization of exogenous 5-hydroxytryptamine in the autonomic nerves of the rat vas deferens. *J. Pharmacol. Exp. Ther.*, 166: 264–271.

Jaim-Etcheverry, G. and Zieher, L.M. (1971) Ultrastructural cytochemistry and pharmacology of 5-hydroxytryptamine in adrenergic nerve endings. III. Selective increase of norepinephrine in the rat pineal gland consecutive to depletion of neuronal 5-hydroxytryptamine. *J. Pharmacol. Exp. Ther.*, 178: 42–48.

Jaim-Etcheverry, G. and Zieher, L.M. (1975) Octopamine probably coexists with noradrenaline and serotonin in vesicles of pineal adrenergic nerves. *J. Neurochem.*, 25: 915–917.

Jaim-Etcheverry, G. and Zieher, L.M. (1980) Stimulation depletion of serotonin and noradrenaline from vesicles of sympathetic nerves in the pineal gland of the rat. *Cell Tissue Res.*, 207: 13–20.

Jaim-Etcheverry, G. and Zieher, L.M. (1982) Coexistence of monoamines in peripheral adrenergic neurons. In: A.C. Cuello (Ed.), *Co-Transmission*, Macmillan, London. pp. 189–206.

Lundberg, J. and Hökfelt, T. (1986) Multiple co-existence of peptides and classical transmitters in peripheral autonomic and sensory neurons – functional and pharmacological implications. In : T. Hökfelt, K. Fuxe and B. Pernow (Eds.) *Coexistence of Neuronal Messengers: A New Principle in Chemical Transmission. Progress in Brain Research*, Vol. 68, Elsevier, Amsterdam, pp. 241–262.

Lundberg, J. and Stjärne, L. (1984) Neuropeptide Y (NPY) depresses the secretion of ^{3}H-noradrenaline and the contractile response evoked by field stimulation in rat vas deferens. *Acta Physiol. Scand.*, 120: 477–479.

Lundberg, J.M., Hedlund, B., Änggärd, A., Fahrenkrug, J., Hökfelt, T., Tatemoto, K. and Bartfai, T. (1982) Costorage of peptides and classical transmitters in neurons. In: S.R. Bloom, J.M. Polak and E. Lindenlaub (Eds.), *Systemic Role of Regulatory Peptides*. Schattauer, Stuttgart, pp. 93–119.

Molinoff, P. and Axelrod, J. (1969) Octopamine: normal occurrence in sympathetic nerves of rats. *Science*, 164: 428–429.

Nicholas, A., Cuello, A., Goldstein, M. and Hökfelt, T. (1990)

Glutamate-like immunoreactivity in medulla oblongata catecholamine/substance P neurons. *NeuroReport*, 1: 235–238.

O'Donohue, T.L., Millington, W.R., Handelmann, G.E., Contreras, P. and Chronwall, B.M. (1985) On the 50th anniversary of Dale's law: multiple neurotransmitter neurons. *Trends Pharmacol.*, 6: 305–308.

Osborne, N.N. (1981) Communication between neurones: current concepts. *Neurochem. Int.*, 3: 3–16.

Pearse, A.G.E. (1969) The cytochemistry and ultrastructure of polypeptide hormone producing cells of the APUD series and the embryologic, physiologic and pathologic implications of the concept. *J. Histochem Cytochem.*, 17: 303–313.

Pellegrino de Iraldi, A., Zieher, L.M. and De Robertis, E. (1963) 5-Hydroxytryptamine content and synthesis of normal and denervated pineal gland. *Life Sci.*, 1: 691–696.

Rubio, M.C., Jaim-Etcheverry, G. and Zieher, L.M. (1977) Tyrosine hydroxylase activity increases in the pineal gland after depletion of neuronal serotonin. N.S. *Arch. Pharmacol.*, 301: 75–78.

Sossin, W.S., Sweet-Cordero, A. and Scheller, R.H. (1990) Dale's hypothesis revisited: different neuropeptides derived from a common prohormone are targeted to different processes. *Proc. Natl. Acad. Sci. USA*, 87: 4845–4848.

Thureson-Klein, A. and Klein, R.L. (1990) Exocytosis from neuronal large dense-cored vesicles. *Int. Rev. Cytol.*, 121:67–126.

Zieher, L.M. and Jaim-Etcheverry, G. (1971) Ultrastructural cytochemistry and pharmacology of 5-hydroxytryptamine in adrenergic nerve endings. II. Accumulation of 5-hydroxtryptamine in nerve vesicles containing norepinephrine in rat vas deferens. *J. Pharmacol. Exp. Ther.*, 178: 30–41.

F. Bloom (Editor)
Progress in Brain Research, Vol. 100
© 1994 Elsevier Science B.V. All rights reserved

Cloning of kappa opioid receptors: functional significance and future directions

H. Akil and S.J. Watson

Mental Health Research Institute, Department of Psychiatry, University of Michigan Medical School, Ann Arbor, MI 48105, USA

Introduction

This review focuses on the molecular and anatomical study of kappa receptors, a class of opioid receptors which mediates unique and distinctive functions, including the modulation of drinking, eating, gut motility, temperature control, and various endocrine functions. Kappa agonists have been proposed to be potentially useful clinical compounds as neuroprotective agents, and as antinociceptive drugs with little drug abuse liability, although they have been reported to produce negative subjective effects. In some instances, the excessive activation of kappa receptors has been deemed harmful, and the use of specific kappa antagonists has been put forth as clinically useful (e.g. in trauma or spinal cord injury). A great deal of the complexity in the field appears to result from the existence of multiple kappa receptors which may mediate different functions. In order to understand the functions of this interesting class of receptors, it is important to first place them in the context of the entire opioid system to which they belong.

Endogenous opioids and their receptors

The study of opioid receptors predated the study of their endogenous ligands by many decades. This fact imparts some unique characteristics to the field. For example, unlike other receptors, opioid receptors are not defined as such on the basis of an endogenous ligand that they recognize, but on the basis of their in-

teraction with certain pharmacological agents, such as heroin, morphine or their congeners. In particular, the antagonist naloxone has become the sine qua non for defining as "opiate" a binding site, a physiological function or a behavioral effect. Furthermore, it is possible for an endogenous opioid peptide to have non-opioid actions (e.g. non-naloxone reversible) and for an opioid binding site to have no identified endogenous ligand. While some of these features of the field may be attributable to historical accident, the nature of the opioid system does not simplify matters. Each receptor interacts with multiple endogenous ligands and each ligand with multiple opioid receptors. For these reasons, it is critical to define, as much as possible, the nature and number of "actors" in this rich and complex system, to identify the molecules involved on both sides of the synapse, and to describe their anatomical relationships and their functional interactions.

The 20 years which have elapsed since the discovery of the enkephalins have yielded a substantial body of knowledge regarding the endogenous opioids: their molecular biology, biogenesis, anatomical distribution, regulation and functions. We now know that three distinct genes encode unique opioid peptide precursors, termed pro-opiomelanocortin, pro-enkephalin and pro-dynorphin which give rise to a wide array of individual opioid and non-opioid peptides. During the same period, we have learned a great deal about the multiplicity of opioid receptors, and evolved many pharmacological tools (e.g. highly selective agonists and antagonists) to study them. Yet, we have no molecular or structural information about the receptors themselves. However, recently, two independent groups (Evans et al., 1992; Kieffer et al., 1992) cloned an opioid receptor of the delta type from a neuroblastoma × glioma cell line (NG-108). This has opened the door to the cloning of other opioid receptors including kappa, and to defining their structure, coupling to signaling pathways, anatomy and regulation.

Multiple opioid receptors

Opioid binding sites were first identified in the brain in the early 1970s. The issue of receptor multiplicity arose shortly thereafter. Martin et al. (1976) postulated the existence of three distinct opiate receptors: a morphine-preferring site termed *mu,* a ketocyclazocine-preferring site termed *kappa,* and an SKF 10, 047 preferring site termed *sigma.* Sigma was subsequently found not to mediate naloxone-reversible effects, and is no longer classified as an opiate site. Meanwhile, Kosterlitz, Hughes and their colleagues (Lord et al., 1977) proposed the existence of an enkephalin-preferring *delta* site. In addition to these three major classes (mu, delta and kappa), a number of receptor types have been proposed, often based on the use of bioassays from different species. The three major classes have been the subject of intense investigation. In the early 1980s, highly selective ligands became available for labeling the multiple receptor types, and the study of their biological functions was also facilitated by the recent syntheses of selective antagonists.

Relationships between multiple opioid peptides and receptors

As mentioned above, there is not a one-to-one correspondence between the endogenous ligands and their receptors, although some general associations do exist. The delta receptor(s) typically recognizes with high affinity the products of the proenkephalin precursor, particularly leucine- and methionine-enkephalin. However, these receptors also interact with excellent affinity with the POMC product β-endorphin 1-31, and with the prodynorphin peptide dynorphin A 1-8. The mu receptors also interact with products of each of the three opioid genes: β-endorphin, almost all pro-enkephalin products, and several products of pro-dynorphin, including dynorphin A. On the other hand, kappa receptors are thought to be somewhat more selective, interacting primarily with products of the prodynorphin family with high affinity and good selectivity. These pharmacological observations in vitro are confirmed by anatomical findings demonstrating that there is no exclusive anatomical relationship between a given opioid peptide family and a specific class of opioid receptors. For instance, prodynorphin products can be found in close proximity to kappa receptors in some sites and mu receptors in other sites.

Kappa receptor heterogeneity

The issue of multiplicity of kappa receptors is genuinely confusing. This is due to a number of reasons. The most fundamental one is the very definition of "kappa". While this receptor was originally identified by Martin (see Martin et al., 1976) on the basis of physiological effects of ethylketocyclazocine (EKC), this definition has been lost in the course of in vitro studies. It was evident from the outset that EKC and other drugs in its class (benzomorphans) interacted with other types of opioid receptors; many of these drugs (e.g. bremazocine) were identified as antagonists at the morphine site, and as agonists or partial agonists at this putative kappa site. Thus, one could not rely on these ligands to selectively label kappa sites in binding studies. Since relatively specific mu and delta ligands existed by the early 1980s, the strategy proposed by Kosterlitz et al. (1981) was to use the high affinity non-specific opiate bremazocine as the labeling compound and to block or suppress delta and mu binding with micromolar concentrations of their most selective ligands. This non-mu, non-delta component was termed kappa. It should be noted however, that such a definition assumes only three major classes of opioid receptors, and also assumes that the blocking drugs will suppress all subtypes of mu and delta receptors; in effect, this approach would cause all opioid sites heretofore not identified in brain to be designated as kappa. On the other hand, Goldstein and James (1984) defined kappa as the dynorphin receptor, due to various observations in bio-assays showing a high selectivity and potency of dynorphin A towards this site. Clearly, the two definitions, as the non-delta/non-mu site, versus the dynorphin A site, would not necessarily be expected to yield identical populations of receptors.

A second source of confusion is the nature of the labeling ligand. The original ligand commonly used was [³H]EKC based on Martin's definition of kappa. However, [³H]bremazocine was used shortly thereafter by numerous groups (Kosterlitz et al., 1981). Finally, as more specific kappa ligands were synthesized, particularly of the benzeneacetamide series, they were used to define kappa, e.g. [³H]U-69 593 (Lahti et al., 1985). Each of these agents is unique in terms of its interactions with multiple types and subtypes of opioid receptors, and may therefore label different populations. A related issue is the exact conditions of the binding, particularly with regards to sodium ion concentration, and temperature, as both these variables are known to differentially affect the ligand binding characteristics of different subtypes of opioid receptors. A final issue is the regional and species differences, which are profound where kappa is concerned. Early studies detected little kappa binding in rat brain or spinal cord, and a great deal more binding in guinea pig brain, monkey and human brain. Different authors have examined kappa binding sites and their subtypes in guinea pig, rat, dog, mouse, calf and human tissue, without necessarily carrying out side-by-side comparisons. Thus, when a subtype is described, it is difficult to determine whether it can be generalized across species, or whether it is unique to that particular species and tissue.

Against this background, the issue of multiplicity of kappa binding sites can be briefly summarized. Reports of heterogeneity began in the early 1980s. For example, in 1981, Herz' laboratory (Pfeiffer et al., 1981) studied a binding preparation from human brain with suppressed mu and delta sites. They noted that dynorphin A was a highly potent ligand at a site that could be classified as kappa; yet this peptide could not displace 50% of the labeled population, which could

be displaced by benzomorphans. This observation essentially contrasted the two definitions of kappa, as the dynorphin A site versus as the non-mu, non-delta site, presaging a great deal of subsequent work. At this point, there is a great deal of consensus about a kappa subtype termed kappa 1, which recognizes with high affinity members of the benzeneacetamide family, such as U-50 488 and U-69 593 synthesized by Upjohn. In addition, this site recognizes most of the products of the pro-dynorphin gene with high affinity, and is readily labeled by EKC, bremazocine and other benzomorphans, as well as by the non-specific antagonist, naloxone and the specific kappa antagonist nor-BNI. Some authors have suggested the existence of subtypes of kappa 1, based on affinity to prodynorphin products. While Dyn A bound both sites with equal affinity, Dyn B and alpha-neoendorphin recognizes the two sites with a 50-fold difference in potency.

The definition of kappa 2 and its subtypes is significantly more problematic. Chang et al. (1981) first suggested the existence of a benzomorphan binding site distinct from mu and delta. Many of the current classifications of the non-mu, non-delta, non-kappa 1 sites are consistent with the existence of such a site(s). Additionally, there is a proposed subdivision within the kappa 2 category, whereby the specific pharmacological profile of kappa 2 and its subtypes have been investigated, and significant differences shown in interactions with endogenous ligands. Taken together the various studies suggest the existence of 3–5 subtypes of benzomorphan binding sites in rat and guinea pig, with substantial species differences. Whether these classifications carry physiological implications remains to be determined. It should be recalled, however, that molecular cloning of other neurotransmitter receptor families has typically uncovered more subtypes than had been anticipated based on binding studies.

The anatomical distribution of kappa 1 versus kappa 2 sites in rat brain was shown to be different (Zukin et al., 1988). Thus, EKC labeling occurs in patches in the striatum, whereas U-69 593 labeling appears homogeneous over this region. EKC labels more lateral regions of the caudate-putamen-accumbens complex, whereas the kappa 1 sites appear to be somewhat more medial. Furthermore, there are a number of sites labeled by EKC but not by the Upjohn compound, such as certain hippocampal regions, habenula, interpeduncular nucleus, locus coeruleus and cerebellum.. However, not all investigators agree on these kappa 1 versus kappa 2 differences in rat, and different anatomical patterns are seen in guinea pig (cf. Mansour and Watson, 1993). These discrepancies are probably due to the various technical and species issues discussed above.

Coupling of kappa receptor to second messenger systems and ion channels

The signal transduction pathway of the kappa receptor(s) has been the subject of some controversy. By analogy to the mu and delta receptor transduction mechanisms, it was expected that kappa receptors would be coupled to G proteins and would produce inhibition of adenylyl cyclase. While some disagreement in the literature exists, there is sufficient evidence to suggest that this, indeed, may be the case. In addition, it has been proposed that kappa receptors may couple to the phospholipase C(PLC)-mediated cascade leading to the formation of IP3 and diacyl glycerol (DAG). The interaction with the PI turnover cascade is rather controversial with reports suggesting an increase and a decrease.

Werz and Macdonald (1982) were the first to show that kappa opioid receptors are coupled to calcium channels. This appeared to be in contrast to the mu and delta receptor coupling. These latter two receptors appeared to cause presynaptic inhibition by increasing potassium conductance (North, 1993), although calcium coupling of the mu receptor has since been also demonstrated. More recently, Macdonald and his co-workers have shown coupling of dynorphin receptors in dorsal root ganglion cultures to a large transient N-type calcium current.

It is clear that kappa receptors, like mu and delta, cause decreased neurotransmitter release via what is termed pre-synaptic inhibition (for review, see Mulder et al., 1984). This process is dependent on extracellular calcium, and given the fact that kappa opioids block calcium entry through the N-channel, it is typically thought that the two mechanisms are linked, i.e. that the inhibition of transmitter release is secondary to the calcium channel blockade, although a strict causal relation has not been established.

Cloning and structural characteristics of kappa receptors

The recent cloning of the mouse delta opioid receptor (Evans et al., 1992; Kieffer et al., 1992) has led to the rapid identification of kappa receptor clones. Bell, Reisine and their colleagues recognized that a mouse brain orphan receptor, previously classified as a member of the somatostatin receptor family, was indeed a member of the opioid family, with pharmacological characteristics consistent with a kappa 1 profile (Yasuda et al., 1993). Our own group, using the polymerase chain reaction (PCR), isolated and identified several opioid receptors from rat brain libraries. One of these clones was demonstrated to be the rat kappa 1 opioid receptor (Meng et al., 1993). The new sequence is most closely related to the mouse delta opioid receptor and to the somatostatin receptor family, with a 62% homology to mouse delta receptor and 49% homology to rat somatostatin receptor at the nucleic acid level. Computer hydrophobicity analysis of the encoded protein indicated that it has seven hydrophobic domains of 22–26 amino acid residues each, suggesting it may be a new member of the seven transmembrane domain G-protein coupled receptor family. Furthermore, its protein sequence possesses other features common to this family of receptors, e.g. two possible N-glycosylation sites in the N-terminal domain, and two putative palmotylation sites in the carboxy terminal region. In addition, it contains putative target sites for protein kinase C phosphorylation, Ca^{2+}/calmodulin dependent kinase, cAMP dependent protein kinase and casein kinase II.

The pharmacological profile exhibited a distinctive signature. The receptor expressed bound all kappa opioid receptor selective ligands tested with high affinity, including all the products of pro-dynorphin and all the arylacetamides (Upjohn compounds). The receptor also bound several non-selective opioid ligands such as bremazocine, EKC and naltrexone with high affinity. Furthermore, it showed high stereospecificity, with good affinity for (–)-naloxone and levorphanol and very poor binding affinity for their chiral isomers, (+)-naloxone and dextrorphan, respectively. It bound neither mu nor delta selective compounds with high affinity. Finally, it exhibited a strong requirement for the N-terminal tyrosine of dynorphin A, as demonstrated by a significant loss of affinity exhibited by Dyn 2-13. Based on this binding profile, and the high affinity to opioids of the arylacetamide family, we identified this clone as a kappa receptor, of the kappa 1 subtype.

To determine how this protein is functionally coupled to the second messenger system, we studied the ability of the expressed receptor (transfected into COS-1 cells) to inhibit adenylyl cyclase stimulation, and elevate IP$_3$ levels. The results showed inhibition of cAMP levels by selective kappa agonists, reversed by a selective antagonist. No effect on PI turnover could be detected. More recently, we have cloned the guinea pig kappa 1 receptor, have characterized its pharmacology and shown its ability to specifically alter calcium influx by using Fura-2 as a detector.

Kappa receptor mRNA distribution is widespread in the CNS with particularly high levels in the more ventral aspects of the basal ganglia, limbic structures and cortex. Within the nigrostriatal and mesolimbic dopamine systems, kappa receptor mRNA appears to be selectively distributed in the mesolimbic system with a localization primarily in the medial caudate-putamen and the medial aspect of the substantia nigra, as well as in the nucleus accumbens and ventral tegmental area. This distribution corresponds well to the distribution of kappa binding sites (both kappa 1 or total kappa), if one considers that some discrepancies are expected due to transport of the receptor proteins to sites distal from the cell bodies where mRNA synthesis occurs (Mansour et al., 1994).

Summary and future directions

The recent cloning of the kappa 1 receptor in mouse, rat, and guinea pig should allow us to answer many questions regarding the nature and unique functions of this receptor. The simplest question regards the existence of multiple members of this branch of the opioid family, i.e. the number of kappa subtypes within and across species. Of great interest at the structural level is how a single receptor molecule binds with great affinity and selectivity both a long peptide (Dyn A) and a compact opioid molecule. A related question is how the entire opioid receptor family achieves such exquisite selectivity between ligands (both endogenous and exogenous) in spite of an exceedingly high level of sequence identity amongst its members. Comparison of the sequences suggests a possible important role of the N-terminal and extracellular loops, as these regions are highly divergent across mu, delta and kappa. In contrast, the intracellular loops, especially loops 1 and 2 and the N-terminal segment of the carboxy-terminal domain, are extremely well conserved across opioid receptors (90%). This suggests very similar patterns of signal transduction. Yet, we know very well that at the functional level, these receptors mediate very distinctive and sometimes physiologically antagonistic functions. The relative importance of molecular events versus more complex neural events (e.g. circuits) in effecting these functions remains to be studied. Finally, the molecular mechanisms involved in desensitization and down regulation of kappa and other opioid receptors can now be elucidated, contributing to our understanding of mechanisms of tolerance and dependence at the whole animal level. Given that kappa receptors mediate very distinctive and clinically relevant functions, these recent breakthroughs promise an accelerated rate of research in the area, with both basic and clinical implications.

References

Chang, K.-J., Hazum, E. and Cuatrecacas, P. (1981) Novel opiate binding sites selective for benzomorphan drugs. *Proc. Natl. Acad. Sci. USA*, 78: 4141–4145.

Evans, C., Keith Jr, D., Morrison, H., Magendzo, K. and Edwards, R. (1992) Cloning of a delta opioid receptor by functional expression. *Science*, 258: 1952–1955.

Goldstein, A. and James, I. (1984) I. Site-directed alkylation of multiple opioid receptors II. Pharmacological selectivity. *Mol. Pharmacol.*, 25: 343–348.

Kieffer, B., Befort, K., Gaveriaux-Ruff, C. and Hirth, C. (1992) The

86

delta opioid receptor: isolation of a cDNA by expression cloning and pharmacological characterization. *Proc. Natl. Acad. Sci. USA*, 89: 12048–12052.

Kosterlitz, H., Paterson and S., Robson, L. (1981) Characterization of the kappa-subtype of the opiate receptor in the guinea pig brain. *Br. J. Pharmacol.*, 73: 939-949.

Lahti, R., Mickelson, M., McCall, J. and Von Voigtlander, P. (1985) [³H]U-69 593 a highly selective ligand for the opioid κ receptor. *Eur. J. Pharmacol.*, 109: 281.

Lord, J., Waterfield, A., Hughes, J. and Kosterlitz, H. (1977) Endogenous opioid peptides: multiple agonists and receptors. *Nature (London)*, 267: 495–499.

Mansour, A and Watson, S. (1993) Anatomical distribution of opioid receptors in mammalians: an overview. In: A. Herz (Ed.), *Opioids I*, Springer-Verlag, Berlin, pp. 79–105.

Mansour, A., Fox, C., Meng, F., Akil, H and Watson, S.J. (1994) Kappa 1 receptor mRNA distribution in the rat CNS: comparison to kappa receptor binding and prodynorphin mRNA. Mol. Cell. Neurosci., in press.

Martin, W., Eades, C., Thompson, J., Huppler, R. and Gilbert, P. (1976) The effects of morphine and nalorphine-like drugs in nondependent and morphine-dependent chronic spinal dog. *J. Pharmacol. Exp. Ther.*, 197: 517–532.

Meng, F., Xie, G., Thompson, R., Mansour, A., Goldstein, A., Watson, S. and Akil, H. (1993) Cloning and pharmacological characterization of a rat κ opioid receptor. *Proc. Natl. Acad. Sci. USA*, 90: 9954–9958.

Mulder, A., Frankhuyzen, A., Stoof, J., Wemer, J. and Schoffelmeer, A. (1984) Catecholamine receptors, opiate receptors and presynaptic modulation of transmitter release in brain. In: E. Usdin (Ed.), *Catecholamines, Neuropharmacology and the Central Nervous System – Theoretical Aspects*, Alan R. Liss, New York, p. 47.

North, R. (1993) Opioid actions on membrane ion channels. In: A. Herz (Ed.), *Opioids I*, Springer-Verlag, Berlin, pp. 773–797.

Pfeiffer, A., Pasi, A., Mehraein, P. and Herz, A. (1981) A subclassification of κ-sites in human brain by use of dynorphin 1–17. *Neuropeptides*, 2: 89–97.

Werz, M. and Macdonald, R. (1982) Opioid peptides decrease calcium-dependent action potential duration of mouse dorsal root ganglion neurons in cell culture. *Brain Res.*, 239: 315–321.

Yasuda, K., Raynor, K., Kong, H., Breder, C.D., Takeda, J., Reisine, T. and Bell, G.I. (1993) Cloning and functional comparison of κ and δ opioid receptors from mouse brain. *Proc. Natl. Acad. Sci. USA*, 90: 6736–6740.

Zukin, R., Eghbali, M., Olive, D., Unterwald, E., Tempel, A. (1988) Characterization and visualization of rat and guinea pig brain kappa opioid receptors: evidence for kappa 1 and kappa 2 opioid receptors. *Proc. Natl. Acad. Sci. USA*, 85: 4061–4065.

F. Bloom (Editor)
Progress in Brain Research, Vol. 100
© 1994 Elsevier Science B.V. All rights reserved

CHAPTER 12

Vasoactive intestinal peptide and noradrenaline regulate energy metabolism in astrocytes: a physiological function in the control of local homeostasis within the CNS

Pierre J. Magistretti

Institut de Physiologie, Faculté de Médecine, Université de Lausanne, CH-1005 Lausanne, Switzerland

Introduction

The normal function of the central nervous system (CNS) depends on proper communication between billions of cells that are heterogeneous in structure and function. The cell types that constitute the CNS include: neurons, astrocytes (fibrous and protoplasmic), oligodendrocytes, microglial cells, ependymal cells, choroid plexus cells and cells of the vasculature, i.e. endothelial cells, pericytes and smooth muscle cells. Communication between neurons has been shown to be mediated by neurotransmitters. These molecules are released in a calcium-dependent manner from the depolarized axon terminal, interact with specific receptors on the postsynaptic membrane and, through elaborate transduction mechanisms, exert their effect(s) on cell function. Some variations on this theme, which greatly enrich the vocabulary of chemical neurotransmission have, however, been discovered in recent years. First, it has become clear that neurotransmitters released from neurons can also interact in a receptor-mediated manner with non-neuronal cells, such as for example astrocytes, choroid plexus cells or cells of the vasculature. Second, non-neuronal cells, in particular astrocytes and the microglia, can release molecules such as interleukins and prostanoids known to play a role in cell–cell communication in the immune system and in inflammatory processes, respectively (Bloom et al., 1993). To summarize, neurotransmitter-mediated neuron–neuron interaction is not the only communication line in the CNS, neurons also communicate with non-neuronal cells.

From the foregoing considerations, we have hypothesized, and in fact found experimental evidence indicating that neurotransmitters, released by neurons, can exert metabolic actions in non-neuronal cells of the CNS. This chapter focuses on the evidence indicating that the neurotransmitters vasoactive intestinal peptide (VIP) and noradrenaline (NA) act on astrocytes to regulate energy metabolism in the cerebral cortex.

Cytological substrate for interactions between neurons and non-neuronal cells

In the cerebral cortex, VIP is contained in a homogeneous population of radially oriented, bipolar interneurons (Magistretti and Morrison, 1988). Because their dendritic arborization diverges only minimally from the main axis of the cell, these intracortical neurons exert very localized input–output functions within radial cortical "columns" (Magistretti and Morrison, 1988) (Fig. 1). VIP neurons are distributed throughout the cortical mantle, with a slight rostro-caudal gradient. In addition, the density of VIP-containing neurons is such that the columnar ensembles that they define partially overlap, meaning that despite their radial nature, VIP neurons can "cover" the entire cerebral cortex (Magistretti and Morrison, 1988). The morphology of the neuronal circuits that contain NA is strikingly

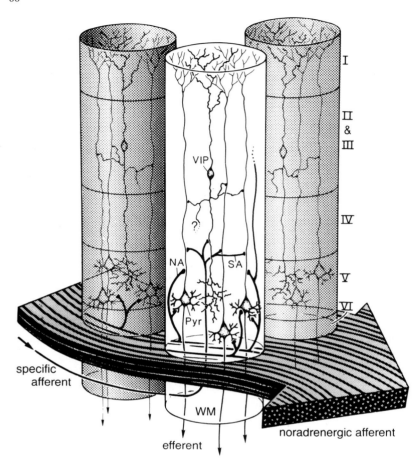

Fig. 1. Columnar organization of vasoactive intestinal peptide (VIP)-containing neurons. VIP, VIP-containing bipolar cells; NA, noradrenergic afferent; Pyr, pyramidal cells furnishing major afferent projections; SA, specific afferent (from the thalamus or from other cortical regions); WM, subcortical white matter. Cortical layers denoted by roman numerals (reproduced with permission from Magistretti and Morrison, 1988).

different from that of VIP intracortical neurons. Thus, noradrenergic axons originate in the locus coeruleus in the brainstem and enter the neocortex rostrally, adopting a tangential trajectory that spans the entire cortical mantle (Fig. 2). These characteristics allow the noradrenergic system to exert its actions globally and simultaneously across functionally distinct cortical areas (Magistretti and Morrison, 1988) (Figs. 1 and 2).

Receptors for VIP and NA have been characterized on astrocytes (Martin et al., 1992; Stone and Ariano, 1989). These receptors are functional, as they are coupled to second messenger systems, in particular the cAMP cascade (Martin et al., 1992; Stone and Ariano,

1989). Since synapses between neurons and astrocytes have not been described in the mammalian brain (Peters et al., 1991), the interaction between VIP- and NA-containing neurons should occur at extrasynaptic sites. In fact the co-existence of synaptic and extrasynaptic release of NA within the neocortex has received experimental support (Beaudet and Descarries, 1978). In the same brain area, the radially-oriented VIP-containing neurons (Figs. 1 and 2)) show an intense labeling of dendrites in immunohistochemical preparations both at the light and electron microscope (Hajòs et al., 1988; Magistretti and Morrison, 1988). In analogy with dopaminergic neurons in the pars reticulata of the substantia nigra and with amacrine cells in the retina, high neurotransmitter content in dendrites may indicate the occurrence of dendritic, possibly extrasynaptic, release (Niéoullon et al., 1977).

In a recent study (Martin et al., 1992) performed in purified preparations of mouse cerebral cortex consisting of primary astrocyte cultures, intraparenchymal microvessels and synaptosomal membranes, respectively, three VIP receptor subtypes, with differential cellular localization, were identified (Table I). The first subtype (VIP 1) is ubiquitous and of high affinity with K_d values of 3.3 nM (astrocytes), 1.4 nM (microvessels) and 4.9 nM (synaptosomes). Secretin does not interact with this site. The second receptor subtype (VIP 2) is exclusively present on synaptosomal membranes. It is a low affinity site, with a K_d of 42.8 nM. Secretin interacts with this site with an IC_{50} of 150 nM. The third subtype (VIP 3) is also of low affinity, with a K_d of 30.3 nM and is exclusively localized in microvessels. Secretin does not interact with this site. In addition to providing a classification for

VIP receptor subtypes, these observations suggest that secretin may represent a useful tool to discriminate between neuronal and non-neuronal VIP binding sites.

Unequivocal evidence at the ultrastructural level indicates the intimate apposition, and in some cases the presence of true synapses, between neurotransmitter-containing profiles and intraparenchymal brain capillaries. In particular this has been demonstrated for VIP, acetylcholine, cholecystokinin and NA (Edvinsson et al., 1993). Figure 3, which has been redrawn from an original micrograph by Rennels and Nelson (1975), is a clear illustration of the cytological substrate for the interaction between (1) an axon terminal (i.e. the site of neurotransmitter release), (2) two elements of an intraparenchymal capillary, i.e. a pericyte and an endothelial cell and (3) an astrocyte. This cytological arrangement clearly provides the substrate for interactions between neurons and three types of non-neuronal cells. In addition, pharmacological studies have demonstrated the presence of receptors for NA and VIP, coupled to cAMP-generating systems in

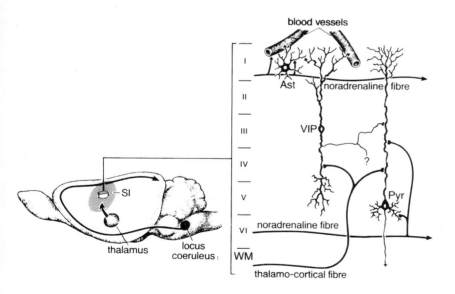

Fig. 2. Anatomical organization and putative targets of the noradrenaline (NA)- and vasoactive intestinal peptide (VIP)-containing neuronal circuits in rat cerebral cortex. Left: Noradrenergic fibers originate in locus coeruleus and project to the cerebral cortex, where they adopt a horizontal trajectory parallel to the pial surface. Right: VIP neurons are intrinsic to the cerebral cortex and are oriented vertically, perpendicular to the pial surface. Astrocytes (Ast), intraparenchymal blood vessels, and neurons such as certain pyramidal cells (Pyr) are potential target cells for VIP neurons. Roman numerals indicate cortical layers. VIP neurons can be activated by specific afferents (e.g.. thalamocortical fibers). SI, primary sensory cortex; WM, white matter (reproduced with permission from Magistretti and Morrison, 1988).

TABLE I

Proposed classification for VIP receptor subtypes in the cerebral cortex

Subtype	Localization	K_d (nM)	Competition by secretin
VIP 1	Astrocytes	3.3	–
	Microvessels	1.4	–
	Neurons	4.9	–
VIP 2	Neurons	42.8	+
VIP 3	Microvessels	30.3	–

intraparenchymal microvessel preparations (Owman and Hardebo, 1986). Similar observations have been made in purified preparations of choroid plexus epithelial cells, where VIP and the β-adrenergic agonist isoproterenol stimulate cAMP formation (Crook and Prusiner, 1986). Furthermore, a very high density of VIP binding sites has been detected in the rat brain by autoradiography, in the subependymal layer at the level of the lateral ventricles (Martin et al., 1987). This observation is favorably correlated with the presence of VIP-immunoreactive neurons in the dentate

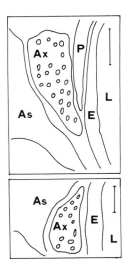

Fig. 3. Cytological substrate for interactions between (1) a neurotransmitter-containing axon terminal, (2) an astrocyte, (3) a pericyte and (4) an endothelial cell. Ax, axon terminal; As, astrocyte endfoot; P, pericyte process; E, endothelial cell; L, capillary lumen. Scale bar: 0.5 μm. (Redrawn and modified from an electron micrograph from Rennels and Nelson, 1975).

gyrus possessing dendrites that extend into the ependyma of the lateral ventricles (Köhler, 1983).

Regulation of glycogen levels by VIP and NA in astrocytes

Glycogen is the single largest energy reserve of the brain (Magistretti et al., 1993). It is predominantly localized in astrocytes, to the point where this cell type can be positively identified at the ultrastructural level by the presence of glycogen granules (for review see Magistretti et al., 1993).

VIP and NA readily promote a concentration-dependent glycogenolysis with EC$_{50}$ values of 3 and 20 nM, respectively (Table II). The pharmacology of NA-induced glycogenolysis indicates both a β- and an α_1-adrenergic component (Sorg and Magistretti, 1991). Thus, both isoproterenol (β-adrenergic agonist) and methoxamine (α_1-adrenergic agonist) promote a concentration-dependent glycogenolysis, with EC$_{50}$ values of 20 and 600 nM, respectively (Table II). A number of other neurotransmitters, for which the presence of receptors has been demonstrated on astrocytes (carbachol, glutamate, GABA) did not promote glycogenolysis (Sorg and Magistretti, 1991).

Peptides sharing sequence homologies with VIP have also been tested. As shown in Table II, PHI, secretin and the recently identified VIP-related peptide PACAP, are glycogenolytic, while the two structurally unrelated peptides somatostatin and neuropeptide Y (NPY) are without effect (Sorg and Magistretti, 1991). To further illustrate the tight regulation of glycogenolysis in astrocytes, adenosine and ATP are also glycogenolytic, with EC$_{50}$ values of 0.8 and 1.3 μM, respectively (Table II). The action of VIP and NA is rapid, with initial rates of hydrolysis of 9.1 and 7.5 nmol/mg protein per min, respectively (Sorg and Magistretti, 1991). Interestingly, this value is close to the rate of ^{3}H-deoxyglucose uptake and phosphorylation by the same culture (Yu et al., 1993) and even by cerebral cortex in situ (Sokoloff et al., 1977). These observations indicate that the glycosyl units released by the neurotransmitter-evoked glycogenolysis can provide energy substrates that match the energy demands of cortical gray matter.

TABLE II

Glycogenolytic neurotransmitters in primary cultures of mouse cortical astrocytes

Substance	EC_{50} (nM)
VIP	3
PACAP	0.08
Secretin	0.5
PHI	6
Noradrenaline	20
– Isoproterenol (β)	20
– Methoxamine (α_1)	600
Adenosine	800
ATP	1300

VIP and NA, in addition to their glycogenolytic action discussed above (Sorg and Magistretti, 1991), which occurs within minutes, also induce a temporally delayed resynthesis of glycogen, resulting, within 9 h, in glycogen levels that are 6–10 times higher than those measured before application of either neurotransmitter (Sorg and Magistretti, 1992). The continued presence of the neurotransmitter is not necessary for this long-term effect since pulses as short as 1 min result in the doubling of glycogen levels 9 h later. The induction of glycogen resynthesis triggered by VIP or NA is dependent on protein synthesis, since both cycloheximide and actinomycin D abolish it entirely. These results indicate that the same neurotransmitter, e.g. VIP or NA, can elicit two actions with different time-courses. Thus, by increasing cAMP levels, VIP or NA simultaneously trigger a short-term effect, i.e. glycogenolysis, as well as a delayed one, i.e. transcriptionally regulated glycogen resynthesis. This longer-term effect ensures that sufficient substrate is available for the continued expression of the short-term action of VIP or NA (Fig. 4).

NA stimulates glucose uptake in astrocytes

Basal glucose uptake by astrocytes calculated from the specific activity of 2-[³H]DG ranges between 3 and 9 nmol/mg protein per min (Yu et al., 1993), a value that compares very favourably with the glucose utilization of the grey matter as determined by the 2-[³H]DG autoradiography technique in rodent cerebral cortex, assuming a protein content of 10% for brain tissue (Sokoloff et al., 1977). This observation would tend to suggest that glucose utilization in the cerebral cortex as measured by the 2-deoxyglucose technique may reflect, at least in part, glucose uptake by astrocytes. NA stimulates in a concentration-dependent manner 2-[³H]DG uptake by astrocytes, with an EC_{50} of 1 μM (Yu et al., 1993). In contrast, VIP is without effect (Yu et al., 1993).

Given its morphological characteristics, the NA-containing neuronal system (see above and Figs. 1 and 2) would be ideally positioned to stimulate glucose uptake globally and simultaneously, throughout the cerebral cortex. In addition, this action, in parallel with the previously described glycogenolytic effect of NA would represent a coordinated regulatory mechanism to provide an adequate supply of metabolic substrates when energy demands of the active neuropil are increased.

Astrocyte end-feet surround intraparenchymal blood vessels (Peters et al., 1991) implying that at

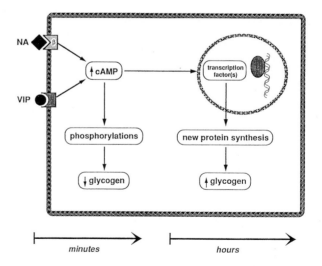

Fig. 4. Bidirectional effects of VIP and NA on glycogen in astrocytes. Short-term effect: within minutes after application, VIP or NA promote glycogenolysis. This effect is due to cAMP-dependent phosphorylation of pre-existing proteins. Long-term effect: within a few hours after application of VIP or NA, glycogen levels are increased 6–10 times above control levels. This effect is due to cAMP-dependent induction of new protein synthesis (reproduced with permission from Sorg and Magistretti, 1992).

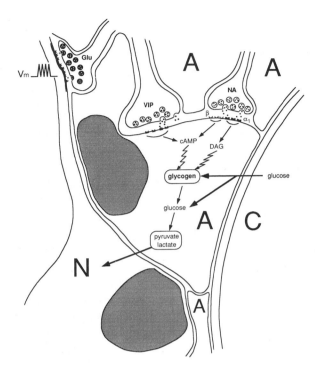

Fig. 5. Cytological substrate for the metabolic trafficking within the brain parenchyma. Glucose is taken up by astrocytic end-feet (A) which surround the capillaries (C). Lactate produced glycolytically from glucose, mobilized in part from glycogen, is released for its utilization by neurons (N). (see text for details). α, β, adrenergic receptor subtypes; cAMP, cyclic AMP; DAG, diacylglycerol; GLU, glutamate; NA, noradrenaline; VIP, vasoactive intestinal peptide; Vm, membrane potential.

least part of the glucose entering the brain parenchyma is taken up by astrocytes. It is therefore conceivable that either glucose crosses the astrocyte barrier unmetabolized or that it is first stored as glycogen and subsequently released by glycogenolytic neurotransmitters such as VIP or NA to provide a readily available metabolic substrate for neurons (Fig. 5).

Lactate is the major metabolic substrate released by astrocytes

In view of the foregoing, the question arises of the metabolic fate for the glucose taken up by astrocytes or for the glycosyl units mobilized from glycogen. Experimental evidence indicates that no glucose is released from astrocyte cultures, even when glucose is absent from the medium (Dringen et al., 1993a), consistent with the view that brain glucose-6-phosphatase activity is very low or not measurable (Sokoloff et al., 1977). It is therefore likely that energy substrates other than glucose are released by astrocytes and utilized by neurons. In vitro studies indicate that quantitatively, lactate is the main metabolic intermediate released by astrocytes at a rate of 15–30 nmol/mg protein per min (Dringen et al., 1993). This rate of release correlates well with the rate of glucose uptake by the grey matter (Sokoloff et al., 1977) or by astrocytes in culture (Yu et al., 1993), which range between 5 and 10 or 3 and 9 nmol/mg protein per min, respectively. Blockade of oxidative phosphorylation by azide or cyanide increases by 1.5–2-fold the release of lactate by astrocytes (Dringen et al., 1993) indicating that part of the glycosyl units mobilized from glycogen are oxidized by astrocytes rather than being exported as lactate. Other, quantitatively less important intermediates released by astrocytes are pyruvate (approximately 10 times less than lactate), α-ketoglutarate, citrate and malate (Shank et al., 1993). Fluxes of endogenous lactate between astrocytes and neurons have been quantified in vitro (Larrabee, 1992) and an avid lactate uptake has been demonstrated in neurons (Larrabee, 1992; Dringen et al., 1993b). It is also well established that lactate and pyruvate are adequate substrates for brain tissue in vitro (McIlwain and Bachelard, 1985; Schurr et al., 1988). In fact, synaptic activity can be maintained in cerebral cortical slices with only lactate or pyruvate as a substrate (McIlwain and Bachelard, 1985; Schurr et al., 1988). Thus, a metabolic compartmentation whereby glucose taken up by astrocytes is metabolized glycolytically to lactate or pyruvate (Fig. 5) which are then released in the extracellular space to be utilized by neurons, is consistent with the available biochemical and electrophysiological observations.

Observations reviewed here show that VIP and NA participate in the regulation of brain energy metabolism, by tightly regulating the glycogen content, and for NA, glucose uptake in astrocytes. In addition, cytological and pharmacological evidence strongly suggest that VIP- and NA-containing neurons interact with intraparenchymal blood vessels. The demonstration of homeostatic functions regulated by neurotransmitters contained in discrete neuronal circuits support the concept that such circuits may represent, within the brain, the counterpart of the autonomic nervous system which regulates, among other functions, blood flow, energy metabolism and local homeostasis in peripheral tissues.

Acknowledgements

This research is supported by a grant of Fonds National Suisse de la Recherche Scientifique (31-26427.89). The author wishes to thank Ms M. Emch for excellent secretarial help.

References

Beaudet, A. and Descarries, L. (1978) The monoamine innervation of rat cerebral cortex: synaptic and nonsynaptic axon terminals. *Neuroscience*, 3: 851–860.

Bloom, F.E., Campbell, I.L. and Mucke, L. (1993) Molecular and cellular mechanisms of neural-immune interactions. *Discussions Neurosci*, IX.

Crook, R.B. and Prusiner, S. (1986) Vasoactive intestinal peptide stimulates cyclic AMP metabolism in choroid plexus epithelial cells. *Brain Res.*, 384: 138–144

Dringen, R., Gebhardt, R. and Hamprecht, B. (1993a) Glycogen in astrocytes: possible function as lactate supply for neighboring cells. *Brain Res.*, 623: 208–214.

Dringen, R., Wiesinger, H. and Hamprecht, B. (1993b) Uptake of L-lactate by cultured rat brain nuerons. *Neurosci. Lett.*, 163: 5–7.

Edvinsson, L., MacKenzie, E.T. and McCulloch, J. (1993) *Cerebral Blood Flow and Metabolism*, Raven Press, New York.

Hajòs, F., Zilles, K., Schleicher, A. and Kalman, M. (1988) Types and spatial distribution of vasoactive intestinal polypeptide (VIP)-containing synapses in the rat visual cortex. *Anat. Embryol.*, 178: 207–217.

Köhler, C. (1983) A morphological analysis of vasoactive intestinal polypeptide (VIP)-like immunoreactive neurons in the area dentata of the rat brain. *J. Comp. Neurol.*, 221: 247–262.

Larrabee, M.G. (1992) Extracellular intermediates of glucose metabolism: fluxes of endogenous lactate and alanine through extracellular pools in embryonic sympathetic ganglia. *J. Neurochem.*, 59:1041–1052.

Magistretti, P.J. and Morrison, J.H. (1988) Noradrenaline- and vasoactive intestinal peptide-containing neuronal systems in neocortex: functional convergence with contrasting morphology. *Neuroscience*, 24: 367–378.

Magistretti, P.J., Sorg, O. and Martin, J.L. (1993) Regulation of glycogen metabolism in astrocytes: physiological, pharmacological, and pathological aspects. In S. Murphy (Ed.), *Astrocytes: Pharmacology and Function*, Academic Press, San Diego, pp. 240–243.

Martin, J.L., Dietl, M.M., Hof, P.R., Palacios, J.M. and Magistretti, P.J. (1987) Autoradiographic mapping of [monoe[^{125}I]iodo-Tyr^{10},MetO^{17}]-vasoactive intestinal peptide binding sites in the rat brain. *Neuroscience*, 23: 539–565.

Martin, J.L., Feinstein, D.L., Yu, N., Sorg, O., Rossier, C. and Magistretti, P.J. (1992) VIP receptors subtypes in mouse cerebral cortex: evidence for a differential localization in astrocytes, microvessels, and synaptosomal membranes. *Brain Res.*, 587: 1–12.

McIlwain, H. and Bachelard H.S. (1985) In *Biochemistry and the Central Nervous System*, Livingstone, Edinburgh, pp. 54–83.

Niéoullon, A., Cheramy, A. and Glowinski, J. (1977) Release of dopamine in vivo from cat substantia nigra. *Nature*, 266: 375–377.

Owman, C. and Hardebo, J.E. (1986) *Neural Regulation of Brain Circulation*, Elsevier, Amsterdam.

Peters, A., Palay, S.L. and Webster, H. de F. (1991) *The Fine Structure of the Nervous System: Neurons and their Supporting Cells*, W.B. Saunders, Philadelphia.

Rennels, M.L. and Nelson, E. (1975) Capillary innervation in the mammalian central nervous system: an electron microscopic demonstration. *Am. J. Anat.*, 144: 233–241.

Schurr, A., West, C.A. and Rigor, B.M. (1988) Lactate-supported synaptic function in the rat hippocampal slice preparation. *Science*, 240:1326–1328.

Shank, R.P., Leo, G.C. and Zielke, H.R. (1993) Cerebral metabolic compartmentation as revealed by nuclear magnetic resonance analysis of D-[1-^{13}C]glucose metabolism. *J. Neurochem.*, 61: 315–323.

Sokoloff, L., Reivich, M., Kennedy, C., Des Rosiers, M.H., Patlak, C.S., Pettigrew, K.D., Sakurada, O. and Shinohara, M. (1977) The [^{14}C]deoxyglucose method for the measurement of local cerebral glucose utilization: theory, procedure, and normal values in the conscious and anesthetized albino rat. *J. Neurochem.*, 28: 897–916.

Sorg, O. and Magistretti, P.J. (1991) Characterization of the glycogenolysis elicited by vasoactive intestinal peptide, noradrenaline and adenosine in primary cultures of mouse cerebral cortical astrocytes. *Brain Res.*, 563: 227–233.

Sorg, O. and Magistretti, P.J. (1992) Vasoactive intestinal peptide and noradrenaline exert long-term control on glycogen levels in astrocytes: blockade by protein synthesis inhibition. *J. Neurosci.*, 12: 4923–4931.

Stone, E.A. and Ariano, M.A. (1989) Are glial cells targets of the central noradrenergic system ? A review of the evidence. *Brain Res. Dev.*, 14: 297–309.

Yu, N., Martin, J.L., Stella, N. and Magistretti, P.J. (1993) Arachidonic acid stimulates glucose uptake in cerebral cortical astrocytes. *Proc. Natl. Acad. Sci. USA*, 90: 4042–4046.

SECTION III

Integrative Brain Research

F. Bloom (Editor)
Progress in Brain Research, Vol. 100
© 1994 Elsevier Science B.V. All rights reserved

CHAPTER 13

Segmental and descending control of the synaptic effectiveness of muscle afferents*

Pablo Rudomin

Department of Physiology, Biophysics and Neurosciences, Centro de Investigación y de Estudios Avanzados, México D.F

Introduction

In 1957, Frank and Fuortes found that conditioning stimulation of group I afferents from flexor muscles depressed the monosynaptic EPSPs elicited in spinal motoneurons by stimulation of muscle spindle afferents (Ia afferents), without changing the membrane properties of the motoneurons or the time course of the Ia-EPSPs. At that time, models of motoneurons assigned practically no role to dendrites in the generation of monosynaptic responses from Ia afferents. That is, physiologically effective Ia synapses were assumed to be located predominantly near the soma (see Eccles, 1953, 1964), and it was therefore postulated that the inhibition resulted from interference with transmission of excitation from Ia afferents to motoneurons, i.e. to presynaptic inhibition.

Following the development of more realistic motoneuron models in which Ia synapses had a significant dendritic location (Rall, 1960; see also Smith et al., 1967), an alternative explanation to presynaptic inhibition was proposed. Namely, that the depression of the Ia EPSPs occurred at the motoneuron distal dendrites (Frank, 1959). Inhibitory conductances produced by the conditioning stimulus at the distal dendrites would not be detected at the motoneuron soma, but would be nevertheless able to depress Ia EPSPs generated in a close vicinity.

Subsequent work was addressed to determine the extent to which the depression of Ia EPSPs was indeed associated with changes in motoneuron membrane properties. The underlying assumption was that presynaptic and postsynaptic inhibition were mutually exclusive. In some cases Ia EPSP depression could not be fully explained by postsynaptic changes and presynaptic inhibition was assumed to be the main cause of EPSP depression (Eccles et al., 1962b; Eide et al., 1968; Cook and Cangiano, 1972; Rudomin et al., 1975b, 1991; Rudomin, 1992). In other cases, there seemed to be an appreciable postsynaptic inhibition and presynaptic inhibition was assumed to have a minor role (Granit et al., 1964; Carlen et al., 1980).

There is now good evidence that presynaptic inhibition is mediated by GABAergic interneurons that make axo-axonic synapses with the intraspinal terminals of the afferent fibers (see below). Electrophysiological studies have further indicated that these GABAergic interneurons also have monosynaptic inhibitory connections with motoneurons (Rudomin et al., 1987) and more recently, direct evidence for the existence of GABAergic boutons that make synapses with identified muscle spindle afferents as well as with the postsynaptic neurons has became available (Fyffe and Light, 1984; Maxwell et al., 1990). The functional implications of the co-existence of pre- and postsynaptic inhibition have been discussed elsewhere (Rudomin et al., 1987; Rudomin, 1990).

---

* This review is dedicated to K. Frank who died on February 25, 1993.

Sources of variability in synaptic transmission

Kuno (1964a,b) found that the monosynaptic potentials produced in a motoneuron by stimulation of a single Ia fiber showed considerable amplitude fluctuations including an appreciable number of failures. He also found that conditioning stimulation of group I fibers from flexors reduced the probabilities of occurrence of the largest EPSPs and increased the number of EPSP failures, without significantly changing the unitary EPSPs. These observations provided a more direct test on the possible existence of presynaptic inhibition. Failures in transmission could be due either to block of impulse conduction in the terminal arborizations of the afferent fibers (Henneman et al., 1984; Lüscher et al., 1990) or to failure in transmitter release (see Redman, 1990). Appraisal of these two possibilities has became an important issue because of their implications in the control of information transfer from Ia afferents to motoneurons.

One of the major problems involved in the analysis of the mechanisms that control the efficacy of synaptic transmission is that the signal to be analyzed occurs in the presence of appreciable noise, most of it of synaptic origin. During the last decade, deconvolution techniques have been used to separate the signal from the noise (Jack et al., 1981; Redman and Walmsley, 1983; see Redman, 1990 for a review). It was found that the amplitude of the noise-free EPSPs produced by stimulation of single Ia fibers varies in discrete steps, each of them with a finite probability. The discrete components appear separated by a constant amplitude interval, suggesting quantal steps in the generation of the single fiber EPSPs. Clements et al. (1987) have further shown that conditioning stimulation of group I fibers from flexors reduces the probabilities of occurrence of the large EPSP components and increases the probabilities of occurrence of the smallest components, without significantly changing the separation between them. Similar results have been obtained after administration of (–)-baclofen, a GABAb agonist (Edwards et al., 1989). These findings have been taken as evidence for the involvement of presynaptic inhibition in the depression of the synaptic potentials.

One assumption in the deconvolution procedure is that signal and noise interact linearly (see Redman, 1990). However, by comparing variance of the directly recorded EPSPs with the variance of the discrete components of the EPSPs obtained with deconvolution techniques, Solodkin et al. (1991) found that even in conditions of low synaptic noise, there is an appreciable non-linear interaction between the signal and noise. Furthermore, the deconvolution procedures require grouping of events of similar size into the same amplitude category (see Wong and Redman, 1980; Redman 1990). In practice, events with amplitudes differing more than 1.5 the standard deviation of the background noise are considered as belonging to a different amplitude category (Clements et al., 1987; Edwards et al., 1989; Kullman et al., 1989), which means that the separation between the discrete components of the noise-free EPSP may depend not only on the statistical properties of the transmitter release mechanisms associated with the generation of the EPSP, but also on the amount of background synaptic noise, even when there is little interaction between signal and noise (see also Solodkin et al., 1991; Clamann et al., 1991).

From the above considerations, it is clear that measurement of the noise-free components of monosynaptic EPSPs is not without problems, particularly in the presence of appreciable background synaptic noise, as it occurs under more physiological conditions. One of the challenges for future research is to seek for new approaches to have more reliable measurements of the signal in the presence of synaptic noise and to assess how the fluctuations of the signal are changed by segmental and descending inputs which are known to affect the synaptic effectiveness of the afferent fibers.

GABAergic origin of presynaptic inhibition

An important step in the understanding of the mechanisms involved in presynaptic inhibition was the discovery that stimulation of segmental and descending pathways depolarizes the intraspinal terminals of afferent fibers (Eccles et al., 1962a; Lundberg, 1964; Rudomin et al., 1983). The available evidence suggests quite strongly that this depolarization (primary afferent depolarization, or PAD) is produced by the activation of GABAergic interneurons that make axo-axonic synapses with the afferent fibers (for review see Schmidt, 1961; Burke and Rudomin, 1977; Davidoff and Hackmann, 1984; Rudomin, 1990, 1991).

It is now known that Ia afferent fibers have at least two different types of GABAergic receptors. Activation of GABAa receptors produces an outward movement of chloride ions and PAD in the afferent fibers. Presynaptic inhibition could result either from the depolarization itself, or from the associated conductance increase and block of conduction of action potentials in the terminal arborizations of the afferent fibers. Activation of GABAb receptors appears to reduce the inward calcium currents generated during the action potential and transmitter release (Gallagher et al., 1978; Curtis and Lodge, 1978; Rudomin et al., 1981; Price et al., 1984; Lev-Tov et al., 1988; Edwards et al., 1989; Peng and Frank, 1989a,b; Jiménez et al., 1991). It also reduces the frequency-dependent depression of monosynaptic EPSPs (Peshori et al., 1991; Pinco and Lev-Tov, 1993).

Quite recently, Sugita et al. (1992) have shown that in single neurons of the lateral amigdala and ventral tegmental area of the rat, GABAa and GABAb receptors are spatially separated and can be activated by independent sets of GABAergic interneurons. A similar segregation of GABAa and GABAb receptors appears to occur in afferent and descending inputs acting on preganglionic sympathetic neurons of newborn rats, which appear to have only GABAb receptors (Wu and Dun, 1992), as well as in the hippocampus where presynaptic inhibition occurs following activation of GABAb and μ-opioid receptors (Thompson et al., 1993).

A separate activation of GABAa and GABAb receptors in afferent fibers would allow, in principle, an independent control of impulse conduction at branch points or of transmitter release frequency behavior. This would increase the capability of the CNS to control information from sensory afferents in the spatial and temporal domain. Although at present time there is no direct evidence for this possibility, the observa-tions of Stuart and Redman (1992) are relevant in this context. These investigators analyzed the effects of iontophoretic application of (–)-baclofen (a GABAb agonist) and of bicuculline and 2-OH-saclofen (GABAa and GABAb antagonists, respectively) on the presynaptic inhibition of Ia EPSPs produced by conditioning stimulation of group I afferents. They concluded that in the Ia afferent-motoneuron synapse, presynaptic inhibition is mediated primarily through the activation of GABAa receptors and that activation of GABAb receptors has a minor role in presynaptic inhibition. They also suggested that existing GABAb receptors in afferent fibers are extrasynaptic.

In contrast, Quevedo et al. (1992) have shown that intravenously applied (–)-baclofen abolishes practi-cally all the PAD produced by stimulation of group I muscle and of cutaneous afferents and also the mono-synaptic PAD that is produced following direct activa-tion, by intraspinal microstimulation, of intermediate nucleus interneurons. They concluded that, in addition to the presence of GABAa and GABAb receptors in the afferent fibers, last-order PAD-mediating interneu-rons have GABAb autoreceptors. This implies that even if GABAb receptors in afferent fibers were extra-synaptic, (–)-baclofen, by acting on the GABAb in-terneuronal autoreceptors would depress the GABAa presynaptic inhibition.

Patterns of primary afferent depolarization

Studies on the PAD produced in single, functionally identified, muscle afferents have indicated that in the normal cat, Ia fibers (from muscle spindles) and Ib fibers (from tendon organs) have different PAD pat-terns (Jiménez et al., 1988). Namely, Ia fibers show PAD following stimulation of group I afferents from flexor muscles as well as by stimulation of the vesti-bular nucleus. Stimulation of cutaneous and joint af-ferents and of the motor cortex, bulbar reticular for-mation, red nucleus and raphe nucleus produces no PAD of Ia fibers, but inhibits the PAD produced in them by other inputs. In contrast, Ib fibers are depolar-ized by group I fibers and by all of the above de-scending inputs (Rudomin et al., 1983; Quevedo et al., 1993a) while cutaneous and joint afferents produce

PAD in a fraction of Ib fibers and inhibit the PAD in another fraction (Rudomin et al., 1986; Jiménez et al., 1988; Quevedo et al., 1993a).

In addition to substantial differences in the patterns of PAD of Ia and Ib fibers, it seems likely that separate last-order interneurons mediate the PAD of Ia and Ib fibers (Rudomin et al., 1983; Rudomin, 1990, 1991). This provides the structural basis for an independent control of the information conveyed by muscle spindles and tendon organs, that is, of muscle length and muscle tension, despite the marked convergence of these afferents on spinal interneurons (Jankowska et al., 1981).

More recently, Enríquez et al. (1991, 1992) recorded intrafiber PAD from functionally identified muscle spindle and tendon organ afferents. Two weeks to three months after crushing the medial gastrocnemius nerve, afferent fibers that became reconnected with receptors "in-parallel" (most likely from muscle spindles) showed increased PAD following stimulation of group I afferents from flexors. Stimulation of cutaneous afferents produced very little PAD, but was nevertheless able to inhibit the PAD produced by group I volleys. Unlike what has been found in normal animals, stimulation of the reticular formation produced a substantial PAD in most muscle spindle afferents. The PAD produced by stimulation of group I and cutaneous fibers in afferents reconnected with receptors "in series" (most likely muscle tendon organs) was also increased. However, in this case, there were no significant changes in the PAD elicited by stimulation of the reticular formation. Assuming that after nerve crush regenerating fibers followed the same path and became reconnected to their original muscle receptors (Barker et al., 1985, 1986), the above results would indicate that the changes in the PAD patterns observed after nerve crush were of central origin.

In humans with chronic spinal lesions, stimulation of cutaneous nerves produces a delayed presynaptic inhibition of Ia afferents (Roby-Brami and Busell, 1992), similar to that seen in the spinal cat after DOPA (Anden et al., 1967). It is therefore possible that the reticular-induced PAD in Ia fibers, regenerated after nerve crush, is also related to changes in the overall excitability of spinal neurons, and that previously inactive pathways became subsequently active.

In this context, it is interesting to mention that in the rat, impulses are conducted rostrally in afferent fibers but fail to penetrate long distances into the caudal branch of long range afferents. Seven to ten days after sectioning the dorsal roots in the area of suspected conduction failure, orthodromic conduction is restored. Failure and release of conduction appears to depend on the control of membrane potential in the primary afferents (Wall and McMahon, 1993).

Selective modulation of presynaptic inhibition

One recent and important advance in studies aimed at disclosing the functional role of presynaptic inhibition has been the development of a non-invasive paradigm to measure presynaptic inhibition (Hultborn et al., 1987a). The changes in the magnitude of Ia-induced heterosynaptic facilitation of H reflexes were used to estimate changes in presynaptic inhibition (see Rudomin et al. (1991) and Rudomin (1992) for additional tests on the validity of this technique). Hultborn et al. (1987a,b) showed that at the onset of a voluntary contraction in humans the background presynaptic inhibition of the Ia fibers arising from the contracting muscle is reduced, whereas the presynaptic inhibition of the Ia fibers innervating heteronymous muscles is increased. Such a differential control of the synaptic effectiveness of the muscle spindle afferents appears to be of supraspinal origin and may probably serve to increase motor contrast.

Further support for a differential control of presynaptic inhibition is provided by Burke et al. (1992) who examined the possibility that facilitation of transmission in the propriospinal-like system during voluntary contraction is due to a decrease in the background presynaptic inhibition of those muscle afferents connected with the propriospinal-like interneurons. They found no evidence of a decreased gating of the afferent input, regardless of whether this input was of muscular or cutaneous origin. In contrast, there was a clear reduction of presynaptic inhibition of the same set of muscle afferents synapsing with forearm motoneurons. In addition, Nielsen and Kagamihara (1992) and Nielsen et al. (1992) found that the changes in presynaptic inhibition that are observed at the onset of a voluntary contraction occur even during ischemic block of afferent input, so they are not due to changes in afferent feedback but are probably of descending origin.

More direct evidence on the selectivity of the cortical control exerted on the synaptic effectiveness of muscle afferents has been obtained by Eguíbar et al. (1993) who analyzed the effects of electrical stimulation of the motor cortex on the intraspinal threshold of two neighboring collaterals of the same muscle spindle or tendon organ afferent fiber in the cat spinal cord. They found that stimulation of the motor cortex was able to suppress the background PAD of muscle spindle afferents produced by group I conditioning volleys in one collateral, practically without affecting the PAD elicited by that same input in the other collateral. They also found that cortical stimulation could produce PAD in one collateral of a tendon organ afferent fiber and very little PAD in a nearby collateral.

These findings support the notion that the cerebral cortex is able to exert a highly selective control of the synaptic effectiveness of muscle afferent fibers. This selectivity is possible because individual collaterals of a single afferent fiber receive synapses from more than one last-order PAD mediating interneuron, and also because there is selectivity in the connections of the PAD-mediating interneurons. Some of these interneurons were found to be connected only with one of the two collaterals examined, while other interneurons were connected with both collaterals (Quevedo et al., 1993b).

Simultaneous measurements of PAD in pairs of single Ia or Ib fibers belonging to the same or to different muscles have further indicated that the most effective cortical regions affecting the PAD of Ia or Ib fibers of the same or of different muscles are distributed in discrete spots surrounded by less effective regions (Eguíbar et al., 1991, 1992). The spatial distribution of the most effective cortical spots affecting the PAD of a single Ia or Ib afferent may change with the amount of background PAD of that particular fiber. This stresses the contribution of segmental pathways in the assessment of cortical modulation of the synap-

tic effectiveness of the afferent fibers. The data also indicate that there is a partial overlap between the most active cortical spots affecting the PAD of single Ia and Ib fibers of the same or different origin. The existence of non-overlapping active regions can be taken as an expression of the selectivity of the cortical control on the synaptic efficacy of Ia and Ib fibers.

Concluding remarks

The information transmitted by the ensemble of Ia fibers will depend not only on the signals provided by the receptor organs, but also on the kind of signals introduced by the interneurons that make axo-axonic synapses with the afferent fibers. In the absence of any correlation in the activity of the PAD mediating interneurons, Ia afferents may function as independent channels. With increasing correlation, the redundancy in the line will also be increased (Rudomin and Madrid, 1972; Rudomin et al. 1975a; Rudomin, 1980). The nature of the redundant information introduced via the axo-axonic synapses has not been elucidated. However, considering the diversity of the segmental and descending inputs received by these interneurons (Jiménez et al., 1988; Rudomin et al., 1983, 1986), it seems unlikely that they convey information pertaining to a single functional parameter (i.e. on muscle length). A more attractive possibility is that by affecting the synaptic effectiveness of a substantial number of Ia fibers in a correlated manner, the interneurons mediating presynaptic inhibition act as a gating system that is able to switch-on or switch-off the information transferred along specific sets of Ia terminal arborizations (Rudomin et al., 1987).

Research in humans and in other vertebrates has now allowed disclosure of the selectivity of the supraspinal control of presynaptic inhibition. It is of particular interest that in humans, changes in presynaptic inhibition occur at the onset of a voluntary contraction and that no afferent feedback is required, suggesting that central structures are able to "select" the kind of sensory information that will be needed for the execution of a particular motor task. It seems likely that the descending commands involved in the selection of the sensory information are part of the cortical loop proposed by Asanuma (1989) to adjust the excitability of the motoneurons that will be involved in a particular movement. The descending control of sensory information may also be involved in the matching of the cortical representation of an intended movement with the movement itself (Georgopoulos, 1992), a situation that ensures that the executed movements are part of a survival strategy.

Acknowledgments

I thank Ismael Jiménez, Ph.D. and Jorge Quevedo, M.D., Manuel Enríquez, M.Sci., and José Ramón Eguíbar, M.D. for their enthusiastic collaboration throughout these years. This work was supported by United States Public Health Service Partly supported by NIH grant NS-09196 and grant 0319 N9197 from the Consejo Nacional de Ciencia y Tecnología, México.

References

Anden, N.E., Jukes, M.G.M. and Lundberg, A. (1967) The effect of DOPA on the spinal cord. I. Influence on transmission from primary afferents. *Acta Physiol. Scand.*, 67: 373–386.

Asanuma, H. (1989) Function of somesthetic input during voluntary movements. In: *The Motor Cortex*, Raven Press, New York, pp. 69–75.

Barker, D., Scott, J.J.A. and Stacey, M.J. (1985) Sensory reinnervation of cat peroneus brevis muscle spindles after nerve crush. *Brain Res.*, 333: 131–138.

Barker, D., Scott, J.J.A. and Stacey, M.J. (1986) Reinnervation and recovery of cat muscle receptors after long-term denervation. *Exp. Neurol.*, 94: 184–202.

Burke, R.E. and Rudomin, P. (1977) Spinal neurons and synapses. In: E.R. Kandel (Ed.), *Handbook of Physiology, Sect I. Vol. I. The Nervous System,* Am. Physiol. Soc., Bethesda, MD, pp. 877–944.

Burke, D., Gracies, J.M., Meunier, S. and Pierrot-Deseilligny, E. (1992) Changes in presynaptic inhibition of afferents to propriospinal-like neurons in man during voluntary contractions. *J. Physiol. (London)*, 449: 673–687.

Carlen, P.L., Werman, R. and Yaari, Y. (1980) Post-synaptic conductance increase associated with presynaptic inhibition in cat lumbar motoneurones. *J. Physiol. (London)*, 298: 539–556.

Clamann, H.P., Rioult-Pedotti M.-S. and Lüscher, H.-R (1991) The influence of noise on quantal EPSP size obtained by deconvolution in spinal motoneurons of the cat. *J. Neurophysiol.*, 65: 67–75.

Clements, J.D., Forsythe, I.D. and Redman, S.J. (1987) Presynaptic inhibition of synaptic potentials evoked in cat spinal motoneu-

rones by impulses in single group Ia axons. *J. Physiol. (London)*, 383: 153–169.

Cook, W.A. and Cangiano, A. (1972) Presynaptic and postsynaptic inhibition of spinal neurons. *J. Neurophysiol.*, 35: 389–403.

Curtis, D.R. and Lodge, D.R. (1978) GABA depolarization of spinal group I afferent terminals. In: R.W. Ryall and J.S. Kelly (Eds.), *Iontophoresis and Transmitter Mechanisms in the Mammalian Central Nervous System*, Elsevier, Amsterdam, pp. 258–260.

Davidoff, R.A. and Hackman, J.C. (1984) Spinal Inhibition. In: R.A. Davidoff (Ed.), *Handbook of the Spinal Cord*. Dekker, New York, pp. 385–459.

Eccles, J.C. (1953) *The Neurophysiological Basis of Mind*, Clarendon Press, Oxford.

Eccles, J.C. (1964) *The Physiology of Synapses*. Academic Press, New York.

Eccles, J.C., Magni, F. and Willis, W.D. (1962a) Depolarization of central terminals of group I afferent fibres from muscle. *J. Physiol. (London)*, 160: 62–93.

Eccles, J.C., Schmidt, R.F. and Willis, W.D. (1962b) Presynaptic inhibition of the spinal monosynaptic reflex pathway. *J. Physiol. (London)*, 161: 282–297.

Edwards, F.R., Harrison, P.J., Jack J.B. and Kullman, D.M. (1989) Reduction by baclofen of monosynaptic EPSPs in lumbosacral motoneurones of the anesthetized cat. *J. Physiol. (London)*, 416: 539–556.

Eguíbar, J.R., Quevedo, J., Jiménez, I. and Rudomin, P. (1991) Selective modulation of the PAD of single Ia and Ib afferents produced by surface stimulation of the motor cortex in the cat. *Soc. Neurosci. Abstr.*, 17: 1024.

Eguíbar, J.R., Quevedo, J., Jiménez, I. and Rudomin, P. (1992) Selective connectivity of last-order interneurons mediating PAD of group I fibers according to the muscle of origin. *Soc. Neurosci. Abstr.*, 18: 524.

Eguíbar, J.R., Quevedo, J., Jiménez, I. and Rudomin, P. (1993) Differential control exerted by the motor cortex on the synaptic effectiveness of two intraspinal branches of the same group I afferent fiber. *Soc. Neurosci. Abstr.*, 19: in press.

Eide, E., Jurna, I. and Lundberg, A. (1968) Conductance measurements from motoneurons during presynaptic inhibition. In: C. Von Euler, A. Skoglund and U. Soderberg (Eds.), *Structure and Function of Inhibitory Neuronal Mechanisms*, Pergamon Press, New York, pp. 215–219.

Enríquez, M., Hernández, O. Jiménez, I. and Rudomin, P. (1991) Is the PAD evoked in Ia fibers related to their responses to stretch? *Soc. Neurosci. Abstr.*, 17: 1024.

Enríquez, M., Jiménez, I. and Rudomin, P. (1992). PAD patterns of regenerated group I afferents after peripheral nerve crush in the cat. *Soc. Neurosc. Abstr.*, 18: 514.

Frank, K. (1959) Basic mechanisms of synaptic transmission in the central nervous system. *Inst. Radio Eng. Trans. Med. Electron.*, 6: 85–88.

Frank, K. and Fuortes, M.G.F. (1957) Presynaptic and postsynaptic inhibition of monosynaptic reflexes. *Fed. Proc.*, 16: 39–40.

Fyffe, R.E.W. and Light, A.R. (1984) The ultrastructure oo group Ia afferent fibre synapses in the lumbosacral spinal cord of the cat. *Brain Res.*, 300: 201–209.

Gallagher, J.P., Higashi, H. and Nishi, S. (1978) Characterization and ionic basis of GABA-induced depolarizations recorded *in vitro* from cat primary afferent neurones. *J. Physiol. (London)*, 275: 263–282.

Georgopoulos, A.P. (1993) Cortical representation of intended movements. In P. Rudomin, M.A. Arbib, F. Cervantes-Pérez and R. Romo (Eds.), *Neuroscience: From Neural Networks to Artificial Intelligence*, Springer-Verlag, Berlin, pp. 398–412.

Granit, R., Kellerth, J.O. and Williams, T.D. (1964) Intracellular aspects of stimulating motoneurones by muscle stretch. *J. Physiol. (London)*, 174: 435–452.

Henneman, E., Lüscher, H.R. and Mathis, J. (1984) Simultaneously active and inactive synapses of single Ia fibres on cat spinal motoneurones. *J. Physiol. (London)*, 352: 147–161.

Hultborn, H., Meunier, S., Morin, C. and Pierrot-Deseilligny, E. (1987a) Assessing changes in presynaptic inhibition of Ia fibres: a study in man and the cat. *J. Physiol. (London)*, 389: 729–756.

Hultborn, H., Meunier, S., Pierrot-Deseilligny E. and Shindo, M. (1987b) Changes in presynaptic inhibition of Ia fibres at the onset of voluntary contraction in man. *J. Physiol. (London)*, 389: 757–772.

Jack, J.J.B., Redman, S.J. and Wong, K. (1981) The components of synaptic potentials evoked in cat spinal motoneurones by impulses in single group Ia afferents. *J. Physiol. (London)*, 321: 65–96.

Jankowska, E., Johannisson, T. and Lipski, J. (1981) Common interneurones in reflex pathways of ankle extensors in cat. *J. Physiol. (London)*, 310: 381–402.

Jiménez, I., Rudomin, P. and Solodkin, M. (1988) PAD patterns of physiologically identified afferent fibers from the medial gastrocnemius muscle. *Exp. Brain. Res.*, 71: 643–657.

Jiménez, I., Rudomin, P. and Enríquez, M. (1991). Differential effects of (-)-baclofen on Ia and descending monosynaptic EPSPs. *Exp. Brain Res.*, 85: 103–113.

Kullman, D.M., Martin, R.L. and Redman, S.J. (1989) Reduction by general anaesthetics of group Ia excitatory postsynaptic potentials and currents in the cat spinal cord. *J. Physiol. (London)*, 412: 277–296.

Kuno, M. (1964a) Quantal components of excitatory synaptic potentials in spinal motoneurons. *J. Physiol. (London)*, 175: 81–89.

Kuno, M. (1964b) Mechanism of facilitation and depression of the excitatory synaptic potential in spinal motoneurones. *J. Physiol. (London)*, 175: 100–112.

Lev-Tov, A., Meyers, D.E.R. and Burke, R.E. (1988) Activation of $GABA_b$ receptors in the intact mammalian spinal cord mimics the effects of reduced presynaptic Ca^{++} influx. *Proc. Natl. Acad. Sci. USA*, 85: 5330–5333.

Lundberg, A. (1964) Supraspinal control of transmission in reflex pathways to motoneurons and primary afferents. In: J.C. Eccles and J.P. Schade (Eds.), *Physiology of Spinal Neurons*, Elsevier, Amsterdam, pp. 197–219.

Lüscher, H.R. (1990) Transmission failure and its relief in the spinal monosynaptic arc. In: M.D. Binder and L.M. Mendell (Eds.), *The Segmental Motor System*, Oxford University Press, New York, pp. 328–348.

Maxwell, D.J., Christie, W.M., Short, A.D. and Brown, A.G. (1990) Direct observations of synapses between GABA-immunoreactive boutons and muscle afferent terminals in lamina VI of the cat's spinal cord. *Brain Res.*, 530: 215–222.

Nielsen, J. and Kagamihara, Y. (1992) The regulation of disynaptic reciprocal Ia inhibition during co-contraction of antagonistic muscles in man. *J Physiol (London)*, 456: 373–391.

Nielsen, J., Kagamihara, Y., Crone, C. and Hultborn, H. (1992) Central facilitation of Ia inhibition during tonic ankle dorsiflexion revealed after blockade of peripheral feedback. *Exp. Brain. Res.*, 88: 651–656.

Peng, Y.Y. and Frank, E. (1989a) Activation of GABA-a receptors causes presynaptic and postsynaptic inhibition at synapses between muscle spindle afferents and motoneurons in the spinal cord of bullfrogs. *J. Neurosci.*, 9: 1516–1522.

Peng, Y.Y. and Frank, E. (1989b) Activation of GABA-b receptors causes presynaptic inhibition at synapses between muscle spindle afferents and motoneurons in the spinal cord of bullfrogs. *J. Neurosci.*, 9: 1502–1515.

Peshori, K.R., Collins III, W.F. and Mendell, L.M. (1991) Change in EPSP amplitude modulation during high frequency stimulation is correlated with changes in EPSP amplitude. A baclofen study. *Soc. Neurosci. Abstr.*, 17: 647.

Pinco, M. and Lev-Tov, A. (1993) Synaptic excitation of alpha motoneurons by dorsal root afferents in the neonatal rat spinal cord. *J. Neurophysiol.*, 70: 406–417.

Price, G.W., Wilkin, G.P., Turnbul, M.J. and Bowery, N.G. (1984) Are baclofen-sensitive $GABA_b$ receptors present on primary afferent terminals of the spinal cord?. *Nature*, 307: 71–72.

Quevedo, J., Eguíbar, J.R., Jiménez, I. and Rudomin, P. (1992) Differential action of (-)-baclofen on primary afferent depolarization produced by segmental and descending inputs. *Exp. Brain. Res.*, 91: 29–45.

Quevedo, J., Eguíbar, J.R., Jiménez, I., Schmidt, R.F. and Rudomin, P. (1993a) Primary afferent depolarization of muscle afferents elicited by stimulation of joint afferents in cats with intact neuraxis and during reversible spinalization. *J Neurophysiol.*, in press.

Quevedo, J., Eguíbar, J.R., Jiménez, I. and Rudomin, P. (1993b) Connectivity patterns of single last-order PAD mediating interneurons with two branches of the same group I fiber. *Soc. Neurosci. Abstr.*, 19: in press.

Rall, W. (1960) Membrane potential transients and membrane time constants. *Exp. Neurol.*, 2: 503–532.

Redman, S.J. (1990) Quantal analysis of synaptic potentials in neurons of the central nervous system. *Physiol. Rev.*, 70: 165–198.

Redman, S.J. and Walmsley, B. (1983) Amplitude fluctuations in synaptic potentials evoked in cat spinal motoneurones at identified group Ia synapses. *J. Physiol. (London)*, 343: 135–145.

Roby-Brami, A. and Bussel, A. (1992) Inhibitory effects on flexor reflexes in patients with a complete spinal cord lesion. *Exp. Brain. Res.*, 90: 201–208.

Rudomin, P. (1980) Information Processing at Synapses in the vertebrate spinal cord: presynaptic control of information transfer in monosynaptic pathways. In: H.M. Pinsker and W.D. Willis (Eds.), *Information Processing in the Nervous System*, Raven Press, New York., pp. 125–155.

Rudomin, P. (1990) Presynaptic control of synaptic effectiveness of muscle spindle and tendon organ afferents in the mammalian spinal cord. In: M.D. Binder and L.M. Mendell (Eds.), *The*

Segmental Motor System, Oxford University Press, New York, pp. 349–380.

Rudomin, P (1991) Presynaptic inhibition of muscle spindle and tendon organ afferents in mammalian spinal cord. *Trends Neurosci.,* 13: 499–505.

Rudomin, P. (1992) Validation of the changes in heterosynaptic facilitation of monosynaptic responses of spinal motoneurons as a test for presynaptic inhibition. In: L. Jami, E. Pierrot-Deseilligny and D. Zytnicki (Eds.), *Muscle Afferents and Spinal Control of Movement,* Pergamon Press, Oxford, pp. 439–455.

Rudomin, P. and Madrid, J. (1972) Changes in correlation between monosynaptic responses of single motoneurons and in information transmission produced by conditioning volleys to cutaneous nerves. *J. Neurophysiol.,* 35: 44–54.

Rudomin, P., Burke, R.E., Núñez, R., Madrid, J. and Dutton, H, (1975a) Control by presynaptic correlation: A mechanism affecting information transmission from Ia fibers to motoneurons. *J. Neurophysiol.,* 38: 267–284.

Rudomin, P., Núñez, R. and Madrid, J. (1975b) Modulation of Synaptic effectiveness of Ia and descending fibers in the cat spinal cord. *J. Neurophysiol.,* 38, 1181–1195.

Rudomin, P., Engberg, I. and Jiménez, I. (1981) Mechanisms involved in presynaptic depolarization of group I and rubrospinal fibers in cat spinal cord. *J. Neurophysiol.,* 46: 532–548.

Rudomin, P., Jiménez, I., Solodkin, M. and Dueñas, S. (1983) Sites of action of segmental and descending control of transmission on pathways mediating PAD of Ia and Ib afferent fibers in the cat spinal cord. *J Neurophysiol.,* 50: 743.

Rudomin, P., Solodkin, M. and Jiménez, I. (1986) Response patterns of group Ia and Ib fibers to cutaneous and descending inputs in the cat spinal cord. *J. Neurophysiol.,* 56: 987–1006.

Rudomin, P., Solodkin, M. and Jiménez, I. (1987) Synaptic potentials of primary afferent fibers and motoneurons evoked by single intermediate nucleus interneurons in the cat spinal cord. *J. Neurophysiol.,* 57: 1288–1313.

Rudomin, P., Jiménez, I. and Enríquez, M. (1991). Effects of stimulation of group I afferents on heterosynaptic facilitation of monosynaptic reflexes produced by Ia and descending inputs: a test for presynaptic inhibition. *Exp. Brain Res.,* 85: 93–102.

Schmidt, R.F. (1971) Presynaptic inhibition in the vertebrate central nervous system. *Ergebn. Physiol.,* 63: 20–101.

Smith, T.G., Wuerker, R.B. and Frank, K. (1967) Membrane impedance changes during synaptic transmission in cat spinal motoneurons. *J. Neurophysiol.,* 30: 1072–1096.

Solodkin, M., Jiménez, I., Collins III, W.F., Mendell, L.M. and Rudomin, P. (1991) Interaction of baseline synaptic noise and Ia EPSPs: evidence for appreciable negative-correlation under physiological conditions. *J. Neurophysiol.,* 65: 927–945.

Stuart, G.J. and Redman S.J. (1992) The role of GABAa and GABAb receptors in presynaptic inhibition of Ia EPSPs in cat spinal motoneurones. *J. Physiol. (London),* 447: 675–692.

Sugita, S., Johnson, S.W. and North, R.A. (1992) Synaptic inputs to GABAa and GABAb receptors originate from discrete afferents neurons. *Neurosci. Lett.,* 134: 207–211.

Thompson, S.M., Capogna, M. and Scanziani, M. (1993) Presynaptic Inhibition in the hippocampus. *Trends Neurosci.,* 16: 222–227.

Wall, P.D. and McMahon, S.B. (1993) Long range afferents in rat spinal cord. III. Failure of impulse transmission in axons and relief of the failure following rhizotomy of dorsal roots. *Philos. Trans. R. Soc. London B.,* in press.

Wong, K. and Redman, S.J. (1980) The recovery of a random variable from a noisy record with application to the study of fluctuations of synaptic potentials. *J. Neurosci. Methods,* 2: 389–409.

Wu, S.Y. and Dun, N.J. (1992) Presynaptic GABAb receptor activation attenuates synaptic transmission to rat sympathetic preganglionic neurons in vitro. *Brain. Res.,* 572: 94–102.

F. Bloom (Editor)
Progress in Brain Research, Vol. 100
© 1994 Elsevier Science B.V. All rights reserved

CHAPTER 14

Noradrenergic control of cerebello-vestibular functions: modulation, adaptation, compensation

O. Pompeiano

Dipartimento di Fisiologia e Biochimica, Via S. Zeno 31, 56127 Pisa, Italy

Introduction

The central nervous system receives noradrenergic (NA) afferents from the locus coeruleus (LC). Although small in size, this dorsal pontine structure gives rise to widespread projections ending within cerebrocortical and subcortical structures, cerebellum, brain stem and spinal cord (cf. Foote et al., 1983). Several lines of evidence indicate that the NA LC neurons control high functions, such as attention, orientation, sleep-waking cycle, learning, memory, and also intervene in development, regeneration and plasticity of the brain (cf. Barnes and Pompeiano, 1991). Moreover, there is evidence that the number of NA LC neurons decreases in humans with age and that a more severe neuron loss in the LC occurs in the senile dementias of the Alzheimer type and Parkinson's disease (Chan-Palay and Asan, 1989).

In an attempt to identify the sensory inputs that could contribute to the low and regular discharge rate of the LC neurons in the animal at rest, we have recently recorded the activity of these neurons in decerebrate cats and found that one of the main sources of tonic activation of the LC originated from macular gravity and neck receptors. In particular, a large proportion of LC complex neurons, including those projecting to the spinal cord, responded not only to static but also to dynamic stimulation of both types of receptors (cf. Pompeiano et al., 1991b). Moreover, these NA neurons contributed to the control of posture as well as to the gain regulation of the vestibulospinal (VSR) and cervicospinal reflexes (cf. Pompeiano et al., 1991a).

The finding that the LC neurons not projecting to the spinal cord are under the control of macular labyrinth and neck receptors raises the question of the possible role that the corresponding inputs exert in the NA regulation of high brain functions. On the other hand, the demonstration that LC neurons, including those projecting to the spinal cord, intervene in the control of postural responses to gravity may be relevant in order to understand the equilibrium disturbances that occur with age, as well as the compensatory mechanisms that appear after labyrinthine lesion or functional inactivation of macular receptors during exposure to microgravity.

The NA influences on posture and VSRs utilize not only coeruleospinal but also coeruleocerebellar projections, which act on Purkinje (P) cell dendrites in the molecular layer and to a lesser extent also on P cell body and superficial granular cell layer through different types of adrenoceptors (cf. Foote et al., 1983; Barnes and Pompeiano, 1991). In the present report, we summarize the results of recent experiments suggesting that the NA signals acting on the cerebellar anterior vermis not only exert a short-term modulatory influence on the VSR, but may also intervene in long-term plastic changes which are at the basis of vestibular adaptation and compensation.

Noradrenergic influences on the cerebellar cortex: modulation of the VSR gain

In decerebrate cats, slow rotation about the longitudinal axis of the whole animal (roll tilt at 0.026–0.15 Hz, ±10°) leading to stimulation of labyrinth receptors, produces a contraction of limb extensors during ipsilateral tilt and a relaxation during contralateral tilt (Lindsay et al., 1976; Schor and Miller, 1981) (Fig. 1*A*). These effects, related to animal position, depend particularly upon activation or inactivation of macular utricular receptors and can be attributed, in part at least, to parallel changes in the firing rate of lateral vestibulospinal (VS) neurons (cf. Pompeiano, 1990), exerting an excitatory influence on ipsilateral limb extensor motoneurons (Lund and Pompeiano, 1968).

We have first shown that the P cells located in the paramedial zone B of the cerebellar anterior vermis, which projects to the lateral vestibular nucleus (Corvaja and Pompeiano, 1979), where they exert an inhibitory influence, respond to roll tilt of the animal with a predominant pattern of simple spike discharge opposite in sign with respect to that of the VS neurons (Denoth et al., 1979). The conclusion of this study, i.e.

that the cerebellar vermis contributes positively to the VSR gain, was proved by the fact that microinjection into zone B of the cerebellar anterior vermis of the GABA-A agonist muscimol or the GABA-B agonist baclofen (0.25 μl in 2–16 μg/μl saline), leading to local inactivation of the P cells, reversibly decreased the amplitude of the VSR recorded from the forelimb extensor triceps brachii during animal tilt (Andre et al., 1992, 1994).

We then investigated the role that the NA afferent input to the cerebellar cortex exerts on the VSRs in decerebrate cats (cf. Andre et al., 1991a–c). Unilateral microinjection into zone B of the cerebellar anterior vermis of small doses of α_1-, α_2- or β-adrenergic agonists (metoxamine, clonidine or isoproterenol, respectively, 0.25 μl at the concentration of 2–16 μg/μl saline) increased the gain of the multiunit electromyogram (EMG) responses recorded from the triceps brachii of both sides during animal tilt (Fig. 2), while opposite results were obtained by injecting the corresponding antagonists (prazosin, yohimbine or propranolol, 0.25 μl at 8–16 μg/μl saline). These effects appeared 5–10 min after the injection, reached peak values after 20 min and disappeared within 2 h.

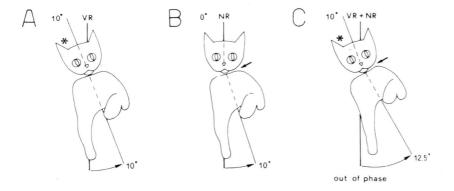

Fig. 1. Schematic representation of different head and/or body displacements, leading to individual or combined stimulation of labyrinth and neck receptors. *A*, Vestibular stimulation: 10° rotation about the longitudinal axis of the whole animal (to the right side, asterisk) produced selective stimulation of labyrinth receptors leading to contraction of the side-down (right) and relaxation of the side-up (left) forelimb extensors. *B*, Neck stimulation: 10° rotation about the longitudinal axis of the body (to the left side, arrow), while maintaining the horizontal position of the head, produced selective stimulation of neck receptors leading to relaxation of the side-down (left) and contraction of the side-up (right) forelimb extensors. *C*, out of phase neck-vestibular stimulation: 10° tilt of the head to the right side (asterisk), leading to stimulation of labyrinth receptors as in *A*, was associated with 12.5° rotation of the body. This produced a 2.5° body-to-head rotation to the left (arrow), which was thus out of phase with respect to head displacement. The resulting neck input increased the postural asymmetry elicited by the pure labyrinth signal (compare with *A*). From Andre et al., 1993.

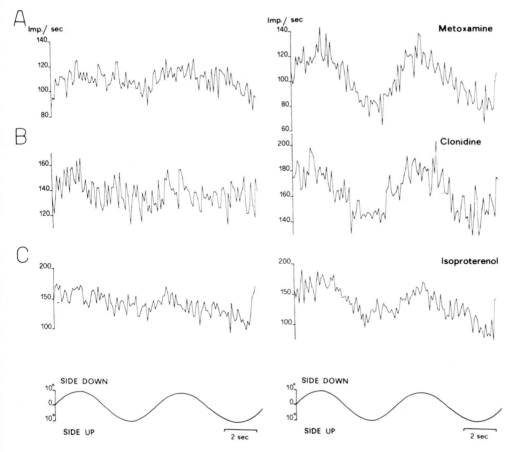

Fig. 2. Increase of the vestibulospinal reflex (VSR) gain elicited by recording the electromyogam (EMG) responses of the triceps brachii to animal tilt after microinjection of an α1- (A), α2- (B) and β- (C) adrenergic agonist into the ipsilateral vermal cortex of the cerebellar anterior lobe (culmen). Precollicular, decerebrate cats. Sequential pulse density histograms (SPDHs) showing the averaged multiunit responses of the triceps brachii of one side to roll tilt of the whole animal at 0.15 Hz, ±10°. Each record is the average of six sweeps, containing the responses to two successive cycles of rotation (128 bins, 0.1 s bin width). The lower traces indicate the animal displacement. The traces on the left side were taken before, while those on the right side after individual or multiple injections of 0.25 μl of metoxamine (4 μg/μl), clonidine (4 μg/μl) and isoproterenol (16 μg/μl) solutions. The response gain increased on average from 0.61 to 2.08 impulses/s per degree in A, from 0.60 to 1.94 impulses/s per degree in B and from 1.24 to 2.72 impulses/s per degree in C. From Andre et al., 1991a,b.

Since activation of VS neurons during ipsilateral tilt depends not only upon an increased discharge of the excitatory labyrinthine afferents, but also on a reduced discharge of the overlying inhibitory P cells, we postulated that the NA system potentiates the gain of the VSR by increasing the amplitude of modulation of the P cells to given parameters of labyrinth stimulation. This conclusion was supported by the results of experiments showing that iontophoretic application of norepinephrine (NE), while depressing the spontaneous activity of P cells, enhanced their responses to both excitatory (mossy fibers and climbing fibers) and inhibitory (basket and stellate cells) inputs, as well as to the corresponding excitatory (glutamate, aspartate) and inhibitory (GABA) transmitters (cf. Woodward et al., 1991). This modulatory action of NE on P cells would act not only by increasing the signal-to-noise ratio of the evoked versus spontaneous activity, but also to gate the efficacy of subliminal synaptic input conveyed by the classical afferent systems, thus improving information transfer within local circuits (cf. Woodward et al., 1991). Second messengers have been implicated in these effects (cf. Waterhouse et al., 1991).

Noradrenergic influences on the cerebellar cortex: adaptation of the VSR gain

Roll tilt of the whole animal increases the contraction not only of the side-down limb extensors but also of the side-up neck extensors (cf. Schor and Miller, 1981), thus stabilizing the position of the head and body in space. In the free-moving condition, this vestibulo-collic reflex generates a proprioceptive neck input, which acts synergistically with the labyrinth input to maintain the postural adjustments during animal tilt. In fact, a contraction of limb extensors can be elicited not only during side-down animal tilt (Fig. 1*A*), but also during side-up neck rotation (Fig. 1*B*) (cf. Lindsay et al., 1976). In decerebrate cats, in which the proprioceptive neck input does not occur due to fixation of the head at the stereotaxic equipment, the VSRs are barely compensatory. We decided, therefore, to investigate whether, in this preparation, a sustained sinusoidal roll tilt of the whole animal performed selectively or associated with appropriate neck rotation produced an adaptive increase in gain of the VSR (Andre et al., 1993) and, if so, whether the NA afferent input to the cerebellar anterior vermis intervened in the regulation of these adaptive changes of the VSR gain (Pompeiano et al., 1992, 1994).

All the experiments started with baseline measurements of VSRs, obtained by recording intermittently groups of averaged multiunit responses of the triceps brachii to 12 cycles of animal tilt at 0.15 Hz, ±10°, performed at regular intervals of 8–10 min for at least 0.5–1 h. After this control period was over, two groups of adaptive experiments were performed. In the first group, a sustained roll tilt of the whole animal at 0.15 Hz, ±10° was applied continuously for 3 h, while the resulting VSRs were recorded on-line from the triceps brachii of one or both sides. In a second group of experiments, a sustained roll tilt of the head at 0.15 Hz, ±10° was associated with a synchronous rotation of the body at 0.15 Hz, ±12.5°. This produced an additional neck input due to 2.5° of out of phase body-to-head displacement (Fig. 1*C*, see arrow),

which exerted a synergistic influence on the postural changes affecting the limb extensors during labyrinth stimulation. This strategy was applied almost continuously for 3 h, being interrupted only every 10–15 min to record the EMG responses to pure labyrinth stimulation. At the end of this adaptive period, the baseline measurements of the pure VSR elicited by animal tilt (at 0.15 Hz, ±10°) were obtained intermittently every 8–10 min for about 1 hour, as during the control period.

The 3-h period of continuous tilt of the whole animal represented a very poor means to induce an adaptive increase in gain of the VSR, which occurred in only one-third of the experiments. However, the gain of the VSR progressively increased in all the experiments submitted to a 3-h period of sustained out of phase head and body rotations, and remained almost unmodified during the first hour of post-adaptation. Figure 3 illustrates the time course of the average increase in gain of the VSR obtained in one of these experiments during the out of phase neck-vestibular stimulation, the dashed line representing the average initial value obtained in the baseline measurements of the VSR before the adaptation of this reflex was started. Moreover, Fig. 4 (dots) illustrates the average curve of adaptation of the VSR recorded from the triceps brachii of one or both sides (11 muscles) in eight experiments. In these instances, the difference between the mean value obtained at the end of the third hour of stimulation and the baseline value was statistically significant ($P < 0.001$, paired t-test). This adaptive change in gain increased by increasing the efficacy of neck rotation. In no instance, however, did the gain of the pure VSR change if tested intermittently in non-adaptation experiments.

The possibility that the neuronal changes, which are at the basis of the VSR adaptation, occurred within the zone B of the cerebellar anterior vermis is indirectly supported by the fact that the corresponding P cells not only showed a mossy fiber discharge to animal tilt as reported in the previous section (Denoth et al., 1979), but also responded with a mossy fiber and a climbing fiber discharge to the neck signals (Denoth et al., 1979, 1980). In particular, the proprioceptive neck input evoked during sustained neck-vestibular stimu-

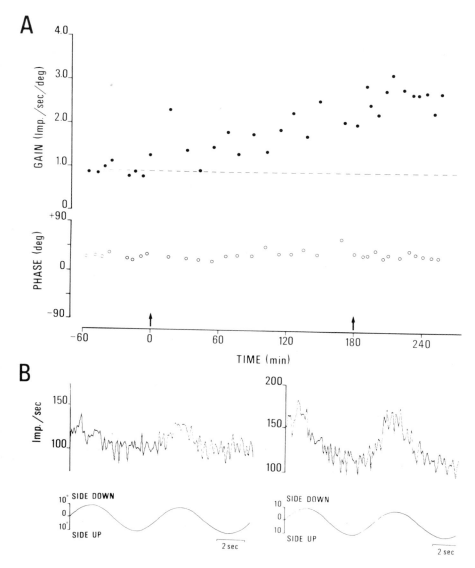

Fig. 3. Adaptive changes of the VSR gain elicited by recording the EMG responses of the triceps brachii to animal tilt during out of phase neck-vestibular stimulation. Precollicular, decerebrate cat. *A*, Changes in gain (upper diagram) and phase angle (lower diagram) of the VSR were obtained by averaging at regular intervals the multiunit responses of the left triceps brachii to roll tilt of the whole animal at 0.15 Hz, ±10° before, during (between 0 and 180 min) and after the adaptive period elicited by a sustained combination of 10° head and 12.5° body rotation at 0.15 Hz. The two arrows indicate the duration of these out of phase head-body rotations, which were briefly interrupted every 13 min to record the VSR. Each symbol represents the averaged response (AR) to 12 cycles of animal tilt at the parameters indicated above. *B*, SPDHs showing AR of the left triceps brachii to animal tilt at 0.15 Hz, ±10° recorded before (left trace) and 50 min after the 3-h period of adaptation (right trace). The response gain increased from 1.01 impulses/s per degree (phase lead of +42.4°) to 2.54 impulses/s per degree (phase lead of +33.3°). From Andre et al., 1993.

lation could, through climbing fibers, not only increase the proportion of P cells showing an out of phase modulatory response to labyrinth stimulation, but also give rise to an efficient process of adaptation, whatever the mechanism at the basis of the adaptive process may be. This model is similar to that proposed to explain the adaptive increase in gain of the vestibulo-ocular reflex (VOR) which occurs during con-

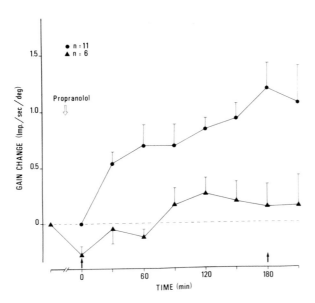

Fig. 4. Effects of unilateral microinjection into the cerebellar anterior vermis of the β-adrenergic antagonist propranolol on adaptive changes of the VSR gain elicited by recording the EMG responses of the triceps brachii to animal tilt during out of phase neck-vestibular stimulation (between arrows). Precollicular decerebrate cats, showing the adaptive changes in gain of the VSR evoked in the triceps brachii of one or both sides by a sustained combination of 10° head rotation and 12.5° body rotation at 0.15 Hz. These adaptive changes were recorded either in the control condition (dots, 8 experiments, 11 periods of adaptation) or after microinjection of propranolol (0.25 μl, 8 μg/μl saline) into zone B of the cerebellar anterior vermis (triangles, 3 experiments, 6 periods of adaptation). Propranolol injection (arrow) was usually performed 1 h prior to the beginning of the adaptive stimulation. The VSRs were elicited during roll tilt of the whole animal at 0.15 Hz, ±10°, and evaluated with respect to the control value (indicated by 0 in the ordinate). In particular, groups of AR to 12 cycles of animal tilt were recorded every 10–15 min after brief interruption of the sustained head-body rotation, as well as during the post-adaptation period. The curves represent the average of the adaptive changes in gain of the VSR obtained in all the experiments during 30-min periods (each symbol indicates mean ± SE values of the responses). From Andre et al., 1993 and Pompeiano et al., 1994.

tinuous sinusoidal rotation of the animal, associated with an out of phase moving screen leading to a synergistic visual-vestibular interaction (cf. Ito, 1982). In these instances, the visual input conveyed through climbing fibers to the specific corticocerebellar area which controls the VOR gain, i.e. the flocculus (see van Neerven et al., 1989 for references), produced a long-term depression of the mossy fiber responses of the P cells to labyrinth stimulation, due to desensitization of the excitatory synapses made by the parallel fibers on the P cell dendrites (Ito, 1990). Experiments are required to find out whether similar cellular mechanisms can be induced by the neck input in the cerebellar anterior vermis during adaptation of the VSR gain.

After the demonstration that adaptive changes affected the gain of the VSR, we investigated whether these changes could be modified by microinjection of β-adrenergic agents into zone B of the cerebellar anterior vermis of decerebrate cats (Pompeiano et al., 1992, 1994). When a 3-h period of continuous roll tilt of the animal was ineffective, microinjection into the cerebellar anterior vermis of the β-adrenergic agonist isoproterenol (0.25 μl at 8 μg/μl saline) performed 30–60 min prior to a second period of sustained stimulation produced not only a small amplitude early increase in the VSR gain, due to a direct modulatory influence of the β-agonist on the P cells activity (cf. Andre et al., 1991b), but also a prominent and delayed increase which reached a peak at the end of the third hour of stimulation and persisted later, thus being attributed to adaptation of the VSR. On the other hand, inactivation of the NA system following intravermal injection of the β-adrenergic antagonists, propranolol or sotalol (0.25 μl at 8 μg/μl saline), either suppressed the adaptive increase in gain following a sustained roll tilt of the animal, or prevented the occurrence of the adaptive increase in the VSR gain which always appeared in the absence of any intravermal injection during a sustained out of phase head and body rotations.

Figure 4 (triangles) illustrates the average changes in gain of the VSR recorded from the triceps brachii of both sides (six muscles) in three adaptation experiments after microinjection of propranolol into zone B of the cerebellar anterior vermis. In these instances, the difference between the baseline value and that obtained at the end of the adaptation period was not statistically significant (paired t-test). Moreover, by using the multifactor analysis of variance, a test which allows the comparison of variables in different groups of animals, it appeared that the changes in gain of the

VSR were severely depressed after microinjection into the cerebellar vermis of the β-adrenergic blocker propranolol with respect to those obtained in the absence of intravermal injections ($P < 0.0001$, MANOVA). Similar results were also obtained in other experiments after intravermal injections of the β-adrenergic antagonist sotalol at the same dose used for propranolol. These findings closely resemble those obtained in previous experiments showing that microinjection into the flocculus of rabbits of isoproterenol increased, while sotalol reduced the adaptation of the VOR to retinal slip (van Neerven et al., 1990).

The modalities by which the NA system contributes to a more efficient process of adaptation of these reflexes are still unknown. It has been postulated that a complex chain of events involving excitatory amino acid receptors and certain second messenger systems at the P cell level underlie the long-term depression that is at the basis of the VOR adaptation (Ito, 1990; Ito and Karachot, 1991). The NA system could potentiate these adaptive processes by acting through β-adrenoceptors.

It is of interest that trans-synaptic signals may elicit not only rapid responses in neurons, ranging from milliseconds (e.g. opening of ligand-gated channels) to seconds and minutes (e.g. second messenger-mediated events), but also slower, long-term responses that are mediated by changes in gene expression (cf. Morgan and Curran, 1991 for references). These genes fall into two general classes: the immediate early genes (IEGs), whose transcription is activated rapidly and transiently within minutes of stimulation and the late response genes, whose expression is induced (or repressed) more slowly, over hours, via a mechanism that is generally dependent on new protein synthesis (cf. Sheng and Greenberg, 1990 for references). It has been demonstrated that many IEGs encode transcription factors that are likely to control the expression of late response genes. The protein products of the latter are then thought to mediate more specific long-term neuronal responses. IEGs may thus function as "third messenger" molecules in signal transduction mechanisms that convert specific stimuli into long-term gene expression of target proteins.

Among the numerous IEGs so far identified, the best known is c-fos. While c-fos transcription, which can be mediated by several second messenger systems, is rapidly induced within minutes of extracellular stimulation, the related Fos proteins, synthesized following mRNA expression, can be detected for several hours (cf. Sheng and Greenberg, 1990; Morgan and Curran, 1991 for references).

There is also evidence that a Fos-like protein binds to a protein product of the Jun family induced by another IEG, the c-jun, to form a heterodimeric transcription factor complex. The resulting Fos/Jun complex moves to the cell nucleus to bind genomic DNA at promoter regions, called AP-1 sites (cf. Doucet et al., 1990). These "activator protein" sites would then control the expression of "downstream" genes that are relevant for long-term responses of neurons to trans-synaptic signals (cf. Curran et al., 1990; Doucet et al., 1990).

With respect to the adaptive experiments reported in this section, we can hypothesize that induction of c-fos and/or other IEGs represents a mechanism by which impulses elicited by sustained neck-vestibular stimulation are transduced into long-term biochemical changes that are required for adaptation of the VSR gain. The NA system could then potentiate the expression of these early genes. This hypothesis receives some indirect support by the evidence that: (1) the NA LC neurons respond to the same modalities of labyrinth and neck stimulation used in our adaptive stimulation (Pompeiano et al., 1991b); (2) an increase in NE release may induce an increase in the c-fos expression in some target regions, as shown in the cerebral cortex of rats (Bing et al., 1992). It appeared also that this effect was predominantly mediated through β-adrenoceptors. Experiments are required to investigate whether the central NA system driven by the labyrinth and neck signals may, through β-adrenoceptors, modify the expression of the c-fos and/or other IEGs and related proteins in the cerebellar anterior vermis and possibly also in other target systems, which could then contribute to the plastic changes underlying adaptation (cf. Ito et al., 1993, for structures involved in VOR adaptation).

Noradrenergic influences on vestibular compensation

Unilateral labyrinthectomy (UL) produces phenomena of deficit, characterized by a decreased postural activity in the ipsilateral limbs and an increased activity in the contralateral limbs, tilting of the head and rolling movements towards the lesioned side and also horizontal nystagmus with the fast phase directed to the intact side. These findings depend upon a reduced discharge in the ipsilateral and an increased discharge in the contralateral vestibular neurons (cf. Smith and Curthoys, 1989).

There are only few data about the possible role of the NA LC system in vestibular compensation. In particular, it appears that intracisternal injection of the NA agonist clonidine in compensated frogs produced decompensation of roll head tilt, whereas the NA antagonist phentolamine caused overcompensation (observation by Abeln and Flohr reported in Flohr and Lüneburg, 1985). Experiments were also performed in unanesthetized cats in which chronically implanted guide tubes allowed microinjection of NA agents in different brain stem structures (see methods in Tononi et al., 1989). In unilaterally labyrinthectomized and compensated animals, microinjection into the dorsal pontine tegmentum of the β-adrenergic antagonist propranolol, which suppressed the inhibitory influence exerted by the NA LC neurons on cholinoceptive pontine reticular structures (d'Ascanio et al., 1989; Pompeiano et al., 1991a), led to the reappearance of the postural and motor deficits induced by the UL (unpublished observations).

Kaufman et al. (1992, 1993) have recently studied the effects of UL on the induction of Fos protein in the brain of Long Evans rats. In these experiments, the animals were killed 24 h and 2 weeks after a lesion performed by injection of sodium arsanilate (5 mg in 50 μl of saline) through the tympanic membrane into the middle ear of one side. The behavioral signs of this lesion appeared slowly within several hours of the arsanilate injections and by 24 h were characterized by a significant head tilt, neck deviation and circling towards the lesioned side. At this time, a bilateral Fos labeling was found in the medial and inferior vestibu-

lar nuclei and the praepositus hypoglossi. However, a greater number of labeled neurons were found in the vestibular nuclei of the ipsilateral side and in the praepositus hypoglossi of the contralateral side. Within the inferior olive, the contralateral β-subnucleus exhibited strong labeling, while the dorsomedial cell column had slight labeling in some rats only. Moreover, ipsilateral labeling was found in the cerebellar uvula and nodulus. Within the midbrain, the dorsolateral periaqueductal gray showed Fos expression that was greater on the ipsilateral side, and there was a bilateral expression in the interstitial nucleus of Cajal and the Darkschewitsch nucleus. These effects were almost gone in rats killed 2 weeks after UL, i.e. when compensation of the vestibular syndrome had already occurred.

Experiments are in progress in our laboratory to investigate: (1) whether the pattern of Fos protein induction following a unilateral *surgical* lesion of the labyrinth closely corresponds to that described by Kaufman et al. (1992, 1993) after a unilateral *chemical* lesion; (2) whether the increase in the Fos protein induction revealed by immunohistochemistry is also associated with a parallel increase in the expression of the c-*fos* mRNA, as detected by using in situ hybridization; finally, (3) whether the time course of the c-*fos* mRNA and Fos protein induction parallels the development of the postural and motor deficits, which occur soon after the surgically induced labyrinthine lesion and largely disappear 24–48 h after this lesion.

Attempts should also be made to find out whether the NA LC system facilitates the c-*fos* expression after UL. This hypothesis is supported by the fact that LC neurons of one side respond to labyrinth stimulation with a predominant response pattern characterized by an increased discharge during contralateral tilt (Pompeiano et al., 1991b), a stimulus which leads to a postural asymmetry similar to that elicited by ipsilateral labyrinthectomy (Lindsay et al., 1976; Schor and Miller, 1981). Since NA efferents project to vestibular nuclei (Schuerger and Balaban, 1993), cerebellar cortex (Foote et al., 1983; Andre et al., 1991a–c) and inferior olive (Powers et al., 1990), asymmetric changes in unit discharge of LC neurons following UL could contribute at least in part to the asymmetric changes in c-*fos* expression observed in these target systems.

The possibility that asymmetric changes in activity of LC neurons determine parallel changes of gene expression in several target systems could be of great significance for the developing brain. It has been asserted that the vestibular system exerts a powerful influence on the development of the brain and behavior (Ornitz, 1993), and that asymmetric prenatal development of the labyrinths, attributed to the position of the human fetus during the final trimester, is probably at the origin of cerebral lateralization (Previc, 1991). The demonstration that changes in the head position leading to macular stimulation produce asymmetric changes in unit discharge in the LC (Pompeiano et al., 1991b) and that this structure may, through ipsilateral ascending projections (Foote et al., 1983), increase the c-*fos* expression in the cerebral cortex (Bing et al., 1992), thus exerting a potential long-term regulation on high brain functions, gives support to these hypotheses.

Acknowledgements

Most of the experiments reported in this review were made in collaboration with Drs. P. Andre, P. d'Ascanio and D. Manzoni. The research was supported by the National Institute of Neurological and Communicative Disorders and Stroke Research grant NS 07685-25 and by grants of the Ministero dell'Università e della Ricerca Scientifica e Tecnologica, and the Agenzia Spaziale Italiana (ASI 91 RS-77 and 92 RS-123), Roma, Italy.

References

Andre, P., d'Ascanio, P., Gennari, A., Pirodda, A. and Pompeiano, O. (1991a) Microinjections of α_1- and α_2-noradrenergic substances in the cerebellar vermis of decerebrate cats affect the gain of vestibulospinal reflexes. *Arch. Ital. Biol.*, 129: 113-160.

Andre, P., d'Ascanio, P., Manzoni, D. and Pompeiano, O. (1991b) Microinjections of β-noradrenergic substances in the cerebellar vermis of decerebrate cats modify the gain of vestibulospinal reflexes. *Arch. Ital. Biol.*, 129: 161-197.

Andre, P., d'Ascanio, P. and Pompeiano, O. (1991c) Noradrenergic agents into the cerebellar anterior vermis modify the gain of the vestibulospinal reflexes in the cat. In C.D. Barnes and O. Pompeiano (Eds.), *Neurobiology of the Locus Coeruleus, Progress in Brain Research*, Vol. 88, Elsevier, Amsterdam, pp. 463-484.

Andre, P., d'Ascanio, P., Manzoni, D. and Pompeiano, O. (1992) Depression of the vestibulospinal reflex by intravermal microinjection of GABA-A and GABA-B agonists in decerebrate cats. *Pflügers Arch.*, 420: R159, n. 51.

Andre, P., d'Ascanio, P., Manzoni, D. and Pompeiano, O. (1993) Adaptive modification of the cat's vestibulospinal reflex during sustained vestibular and neck stimulation. *Pflügers Arch.*, 425: 469-481.

Andre, P., d'Ascanio, P., Manzoni, D. and Pompeiano, O. (1994) Depression of the vestibulospinal reflex by intravermal microinjection of $GABA_A$ and $GABA_B$ agonists in the decerebrate cat. *J. Vestib. Res.*, 4: in press.

Barnes, C.D. and Pompeiano, O. (Eds.) (1991) *Neurobiology of the Locus Coeruleus, Progress in Brain Research*, Vol. 88, Elsevier, Amsterdam, pp. XIV-642.

Bing, G., Stone, E.A., Zhang, Y. and Filer, D. (1992) Immunohistochemical studies of noradrenergic-induced expression of c-fos in the rat CNS. *Brain Res.*, 592: 57-62.

Chan-Palay, V. and Asan, E. (1989) Alterations in catecholamine neurons of the locus coeruleus in senile dementia of the Alzheimer type and Parkinson's disease with and without dementia and depression. *J. Comp. Neurol.*, 287: 373-392.

Corvaja, N. and Pompeiano, O. (1979) Identification of cerebellar corticovestibular neurons retrogradely labeled with horseradish peroxidase. *Neuroscience*, 4: 507-515.

Curran, T., Sonnenberg, J.L., MacGregor, P. and Morgan, J.I. (1990) Transcription factors on the brain-Fos, Jun and the Ap-1 binding site. *Neurotoxicity of Excitatory Amino Acids*, 4: 175-184.

d'Ascanio, P., Horn, E., Pompeiano, O. and Stampacchia, G. (1989) Injections of a β-adrenergic antagonist in pontine reticular structures modify the gain of vestibulospinal reflexes in decerebrate cats. *Arch. Ital. Biol.*, 127: 275-303.

Denoth, F., Magherini, P.C., Pompeiano, O. and Stanojević, M. (1979) Responses of Purkinje cells of the cerebellar vermis to neck and macular vestibular inputs. *Pflügers Arch.*, 381: 87-98.

Denoth, F., Magherini, P.C., Pompeiano, O. and Stanojević, M. (1980) Responses of Purkinje cells of the cerebellar vermis to sinusoidal rotation of neck. *J. Neurophysiol.*, 43: 46-59.

Doucet, J.P., Squinto, S.P. and Basan, N.G. (1990) Fos-jun and the primary genomic response in the nervous system: possible physiological role and pathophysiological significance. In: Bazan, N.G. (Ed.), *Molecular Neurobiology*, Humana Press, Clifton, NJ, pp. 27-55.

Flohr, H. and Lüneburg, U. (1985) Neurotransmitter and neuromodulator systems involved in vestibular compensation. In: A. Berthoz and G. Melvill Jones (Eds.), *Adaptive Mechanisms in Gaze Control: Facts and Theories*. Elsevier, Amsterdam, pp. 269-277.

Foote, S.L., Bloom, F.E. and Aston-Jones, G. (1983) Nucleus locus coeruleus: new evidence of anatomical and physiological specificity. *Physiol. Rev.*, 63: 844-914.

Ito, M. (1982) Cerebellar control of the vestibulo-ocular reflex-around the flocculus hypothesis. *Anun. Rev. Neurosci.*, 5: 275-296.

Ito, M. (1990) Long-term depression in the cerebellum. *Semin. Neurosci.*, 2: 381-390.

Ito, M. and Karachot, L. (1991) Messengers mediating long-term

114

desensitization in cerebellar Purkinje cells. *NeuroReport*, 1: 129–132.

Ito, M., Lisberger, S.G. and Sejnowski, T.J. (1993) Cerebellar flocculus hypothesis. *Nature*, 363: 24–25.

Kaufman, G.D., Anderson, J.H. and Beitz, A.J. (1992) Brainstem Fos expression following acute unilateral labyrinthectomy in the rat. *NeuroReport*, 3: 829–832.

Kaufman, G.D., Anderson, J.H. and Beitz, A.J. (1993) Otolith-brain stem connectivity: evidence for differential neural activation by vestibular hair cells based on quantification of Fos expression in unilateral labyrinthectomized rats. *J. Neurophysiol.*, 70: 117–127.

Lindsay, K.W., Roberts, T.D.M. and Rosenberg, J.R. (1976) Asymmetric tonic labyrinth reflexes and their interaction with neck reflexes in the decerebrate cat. *J. Physiol. (London)*, 261: 583–601.

Lund, S. and Pompeiano, O. (1968) Monosynaptic excitation of alpha-motoneurons from supraspinal structures in the cat. *Acta Physiol. Scand.*, 73: 1–21.

Morgan, J.I. and Curran, T. (1991) Stimulus-transcription coupling in the nervous system: involvement of inducibile proto-oncogenes *fos* and *jun*. *Annu. Rev. Neurosci.*, 14: 421–451.

Ornitz, E.M. (1983) Normal and pathological maturation of vestibular function in the human child. In R. Romand (Ed.), *Development of Auditory and Vestibular Systems*, Academic Press, San Diego, CA, pp. 479–536.

Pompeiano, O. (1990) Excitatory and inhibitory mechanisms involved in the dynamic control of posture during the vestibulospinal reflexes. In: L. Deecke, J.C. Eccles and V.B. Mountcastle (Eds.), *From Neuron to Action*, Springer-Verlag, Berlin, pp. 107–123.

Pompeiano, O., Horn, E. and d'Ascanio, P. (1991a) Locus coeruleus and dorsal pontine reticular influences on the gain of vestibulospinal reflexes. In: C.D. Barnes and O. Pompeiano (Eds.), *Neurobiology of the Locus Coeruleus, Progress in Brain Research*, Vol. 88, Elsevier, Amsterdam, pp. 435–462.

Pompeiano, O., Manzoni, D. and Barnes, C.D. (1991b) Responses of locus coeruleus neurons to labyrinth and neck stimulation. In: C.D. Barnes and O. Pompeiano (Eds.), *Neurobiology of the Locus Coeruleus, Progress in Brain Research*, Vol. 88. Elsevier, Amsterdam, pp. 411–434.

Pompeiano, O., Andre, P., d'Ascanio, P. and Manzoni, D. (1992) Local injections of β-noradrenergic substances in the cerebellar anterior vermis of cats affect adaptation of the vestibulospinal reflex (VSR) gain. *Soc. Neurosci. Abstr.*, 18(1): 508, n. 215.6.

Pompeiano, O., Manzoni, D., d'Ascanio, P. and Andre, P. (1994)

Injections of β-noradrenergic substances in the cerebellar anterior vermis of cats affect adaptation of the vestibulospinal reflex gain. *Arch. Ital. Biol.*, 132: 117–145.

Powers, R.E., O'Connor, D.T. and Price, D.L. (1990) Noradrenergic innervation of human inferior olivary complex. *Brain Res.*, 523: 151–155.

Previc, F.H. (1991) A general theory concerning the prenatal origins of cerebral lateralization in humans. *Psychol. Rev.*, 98: 299–334.

Schor, R.H. and Miller, A.D. (1981) Vestibular reflexes in neck and forelimb muscles evoked by roll tilt. *J. Neurophysiol.*, 46: 167–178.

Schuerger, R.J. and Balaban, C.D. (1993) Immunohistochemical demonstration of regionally selective projections from locus coeruleus to the vestibular nuclei in rats. *Exp. Brain Res.*, 92: 351–359.

Sheng, M. and Greenberg, M.E. (1990) The regulation and function of c-*fos* and other immediate early genes in the nervous system. *Neuron*, 4: 477–485.

Smith, P.F. and Curthoys, I.S. (1989) Mechanisms of recovery following unilateral labyrinthectomy: a review. *Brain Res. Rev.*, 14: 155–180.

Tononi, G., Pompeiano, M. and Pompeiano, O. (1989) Modulation of desynchronized sleep through microinjection of β-adrenergic agonists and antagonists in the dorsal pontine tegmentum of the cat. *Pflügers Arch.*, 415: 142–149.

van Neerven, J., Pompeiano O. and Collewijn, H. (1989) Depression of the vestibulo-ocular and optokinetic responses by intrafloccular microinjection of GABA-A and GABA-B agonists in the rabbit. *Arch. Ital. Biol.*, 127: 243–263.

van Neerven, J., Pompeiano, O., Collewijn, H. and van der Steen, J. (1990) Injections of β-noradrenergic substances in the flocculus of rabbit affect adaptation of the VOR gain. *Exp. Brain Res.*, 79: 249–260.

Waterhouse, B.D., Sessler, F.M., Liu, W. and Lin, C.-S. (1991) Second messenger-mediated actions of norepinephrine on target neurons in central circuits: a new perspective on intracellular mechanisms and functional consequences. In: C.D. Barnes and Pompeiano O. (Eds.), *Neurobiology of the Locus Coeruleus, Progress in Brain Research*, Vol. 88, Elsevier, Amsterdam, pp. 351–362.

Woodward, D.J., Moises, H.C., Waterhouse, B.D., Yeh, H.H. and Cheun, J.E. (1991) The cerebellar norepinephrine system: inhibition, modulation, and gating. In: C.D. Barnes and O. Pompeiano (Eds.), *Neurobiology of the Locus Coeruleus, Progress in Brain Research*, Vol. 88. Elsevier, Amsterdam, pp. 331–341.

F. Bloom (Editor)
Progress in Brain Research, Vol. 100
© 1994 Elsevier Science B.V. All rights reserved

CHAPTER 15

Chemical transmission in the brain: homeostatic regulation and its functional implications

Michael J. Zigmond

Department of Neuroscience, University of Pittsburgh, 570 Crawford Hall, Pittsburgh, PA 15260, USA

Homeostasis of neuronal function

The concept of homeostasis was first applied to organismal physiology and later to cell biology and biochemistry. Over the past 25 years it has become clear that this phenomenon also can be detected in many of the interactions between neurons and their targets, both effectors and other neurons. One of the earliest suggestions of homeostatic regulation of neuronal communication came from the work of Arvid Carlsson who observed that chlorpromazine and haloperidol, which produced a reserpine-like akinesia in rats, also caused an increase in the concentration of its *o*-methylated metabolite, 3-methyoxytyramine (Carlsson and Lindqvist, 1963). Carlsson had already shown that reserpine acted primarily by depleting the brain of dopamine (DA), thus the increase in DA turnover produced by these "neuroleptics" appeared to be a paradox.

Carlsson subsequently proposed that (1) chlorpromazine blocked DA receptors, (2) this action was responsible for the behavioral deficits observed, and (3) the blockade triggered an increase in DA synthesis and release by removing feedback inhibition normally exerted by DA. His innovative hypothesis proved to be correct. In the years to follow it was shown that neuroleptic drugs do act as DA receptor antagonists (Creese et al., 1978), and that a wide variety of negative feedback loops existed which can account for the drug-induced increase in DA metabolism. These feedback loops can be categorized in several ways: local

versus multi-synaptic, synthesis-modulating versus release-modulating, and rapid versus slow (Fig. 1).

Local versus multi-synaptic loops

Some of the regulation of DA synthesis and release occurs at the level of the terminal. For example, once DA is released into the synapse, it can influence dopaminergic activity by acting on receptors located on the terminal from which it was released. Slightly longer loops may also exist. For example, some evidence suggests a local DA-glutamate-DA negative feedback loop through which DA can inhibit glutamate release, thus reducing an inhibitory influence that glutamate can exert on the synthesis and release of DA (Cheramy et al., 1990; but see also Keefe et al., 1993). Although we have labeled these influences as *synaptic homeostasis* (Zigmond and Stricker, 1985), this may be a misnomer as non-synaptic communication may be involved (see below). Furthermore, additional feedback loops also exist, including a neuronal projection from neostriatum back to the level of the cell soma (Bunney, 1979), and input resulting from the release of DA from dendrites (Groves et al., 1975)

Synthesis modulating versus release modulating feedback loops

Although Carlsson focussed on DA release, DA synthesis is also subject to homeostatic regulation; indeed, under normal circumstances, the two processes

116

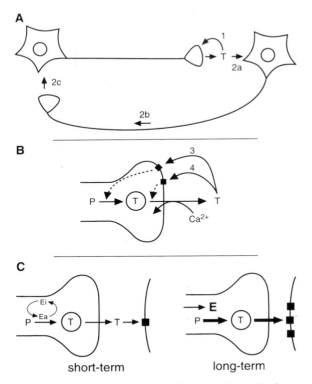

Fig. 1. Categories of feedback loops that can influence the dynamics of transmitter (T) release: (*A*) Local (1) versus multi-synaptic loops (2); (*B*) synthesis-modulating (3) versus release-modulating (4) influences; and (*C*) rapid (e.g. activation of enzyme activity from Ei to Ea, left panel) versus slow (e.g. induction of enzyme levels and synthesis of new receptors, right panel).

are coupled. Thus, whereas regulation of release presumably maintains some constancy in the availability of extracellular transmitter, regulation of synthesis ensures that intracellular transmitter stores are constant even if release is not. Both of these processes can be subject to local as well as long-loop regulation. For example, the synthesis of DA in the neostriatum is increased when impulse flow is elevated (Murrin and Roth, 1976) and when antagonist is applied to the presynaptic terminal (Nybäck and Sedvall, 1968).

Rapid versus slow feedback loops

The Carlsson experiments involved changes that occurred over minutes. However, we now know that the regulation of DA synthesis as well as the transduction of DA into a postsynaptic response via specific receptor proteins are also regulated via processes that develop over several days or weeks. For example, whereas tyrosine hydroxylase, the rate limiting enzyme in catecholamine biosynthesis, can be modulated by phosphorylation of the tyrosine hydroxylase molecule, it is also subject to genomic regulation via induction of new tyrosine hydroxylase protein (see Zigmond and Stricker, 1985).

Homeostatic regulation of neuronal interactions: a widespread phenomenon

Homeostasis is evident in the functioning of a variety of chemically defined neurons, including some that utilize norepinephrine, serotonin, and acetylcholine, both in the peripheral nervous system and in the brain (Zigmond and Stricker, 1985). The homeostatic property of these neuronal systems may have implications for many aspects of neurobiology (Fig. 2). Some examples: the capacity of a neuron to adjust its rate of release to the concentration of transmitter in the adjacent extracellular fluid may permit a few neurons present early in development to exert a disproportionately greater influence on brain function (Fig. 2*A*). Furthermore, the coupling of synthesis to release should enable a neuron to function over a broad range of firing rates without running out of transmitter or generating an excess (Fig. 2*B*). And, the availability of both short- and long-term processes for increasing the capacity for transmitter biosynthesis should permit neurons to respond rapidly to changing demands, and to make more permanent adjustments when the increased demand becomes long-lasting, thereby facilitating a rapid response to still greater challenges (Fig. 2*C*).

Functional response to brain damage

Over the past two decades, my colleagues and I have focussed on the implications of homeostasis of cell–cell interactions for the response to neuronal injury, in particular that associated with Parkinson's disease (for review see Zigmond and Stricker, 1989; Zigmond et al., 1993). We use an animal model of Parkinson's disease in which rats are treated with the neurotoxin 6-

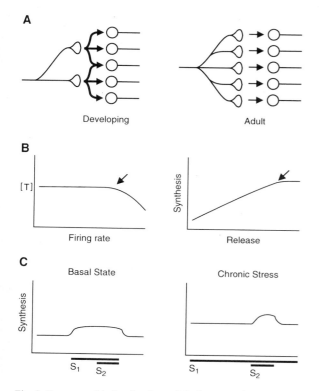

Fig. 2. Some possible implications of the homeostatic properties of neuronal systems: (*A*) during development a small number of initial "pioneer" neurons (left panel) might release transmitter at a higher rate so as to influence a wider field of target neurons than would be predicted by the density of innervation; (*B*) coupling synthesis to release should enable a neuron to function over a broad range of firing rates without running out of transmitter [T] or generating an xcess (until limits of regulation are exceeded, see arrow); and (*C*) short-term processes for increasing the capacity for transmitter biosynthesis (left panel) may permit neurons to respond rapidly to changing demands (S_1) but preclude an additional response to still further demands imposed simultaneously (S_2), whereas long-term processes (right panel) may allow more permanent adjustments when the increased demand becomes long-lasting (S_1), thereby facilitating a rapid response to still greater challenges (S_2).

hydroxydopamine (6-OHDA) in order to produce a selective loss of DA neurons within the brain. Most initial studies of centrally administered 6-OHDA did not detect gross neurological deficits despite the loss of up to 90% of striatal DA. This was curious since previous psychopharmacological studies indicated that disruption of dopaminergic transmission caused a marked reduction in behavioral output, whereas dopaminergic agonists caused behavioral activation. It was soon observed that more extensive bilateral dam-

age to dopaminergic neurons of the nigrostriatal pathway did cause considerable behavioral dysfunction, including impairments of sensorimotor integration, akinesia, and aphasia. Moreover, more subtle behavioral testing indicated functional abnormalities even in partially lesioned animals showing no gross behavioral deficits: when these animals were exposed to a variety of physiological and environmental challenges they exhibited signs of akinesia.

Severely lesioned animals with gross initial neurological deficits often gradually recovered if maintained for a period by intragastric feedings. Why was this? And why were such large lesions required to produce initial deficits? These questions intrigue us because of their possible implications for neuroplasticity, and they also draw our attention to the parallel between this animal model and patients with Parkinson's disease, a disorder involving the degeneration of DA neurons of the nigrostriatal bundle which does not produce obvious clinical deficits until the loss of DA

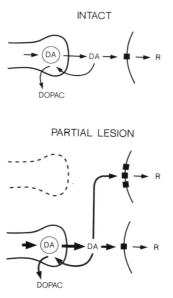

Fig. 3. A model for compensation to partial injury of a projection of dopamine (DA)-containing neurons. It is proposed that the field of influence of those neurons that remain after the lesion is increased due to an increase in the synthesis and release of DA, a decrease in the uptake of DA resulting from the degeneration of neighboring neurons, and an increase in the number of receptors present on denervated targets.

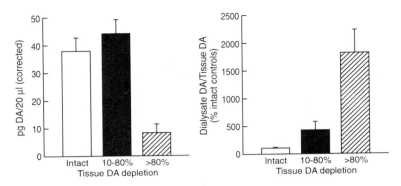

Fig. 4. Extracellular DA concentration in the neostriatum after partial destruction of DA-containing neurons (from Abercrombie et al., 1990). Left panel: The concentration of DA in extracellular fluid as measured by in vivo microdialysis versus the loss of DA in neostriatal tissue, a measure of the extent of terminal degeneration. Right panel: Extracellular DA expressed relative to tissue DA. These results suggest that in lesioned animals the DA terminals that remain are contributing a larger amount of DA to the extracellular pool than in control animals.

neurons is almost complete (Zigmond and Stricker, 1989).

We hypothesize that the capacity to withstand extensive neuronal loss within the dopaminergic nigrostriatal bundle as well as in other neuronal systems derives from homeostatic processes that regulate neuronal interactions. Specifically, we propose that after damage to the dopaminergic system, the remaining DA neurons compensate by increasing their capacity to synthesize and release transmitter (Fig. 3), and this appears to indeed be the case (Zigmond et al., 1993). For example, *in vivo* measurements using microdialysis indicate that the extracellular concentration of DA in striatum remains normal until 80% of the dopaminergic afferents to striatum have been destroyed (Fig. 4) (Abercrombie et al., 1990) and this is accompanied by indicators of increased DA turnover. A detailed analysis of the electrophysiological properties of the residual DA cells do not suggest any changes that might account for this observation: The average firing rate of the cells, the firing pattern, and the apparent number of active cells are within the normal range except under circumstances in which the loss of DA neurons is almost complete.

In contrast to the apparent absence of electrophysiological changes within residual DA neurons, neurochemical evidence suggests that the net amount of DA released per terminal in response to a given set of impulses is increased after the lesion (Fig. 5)

(Stachowiak et al., 1987). This results from an increase in transmitter synthesis and release, and a decrease in transmitter deactivation by high affinity uptake. Several additional observations at both the behavioral and cellular levels support the hypothesis that these changes are compensatory, i.e. they maintain dopaminergic control over striatal function until the loss of DA neurons is extreme (Fig. 6) (Nisenbaum et al., 1986; MacKenzie et al., 1989).

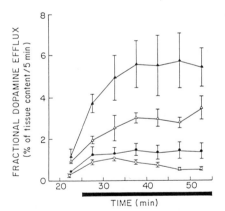

Fig. 5. Fractional DA overflow from neostriatal slices prepared from control (open circles) and rats lesioned with 6-hydroxy-dopamine so as to produce various levels of DA depletion (50–80%, closed circles; 80–96%, open triangles; and >96%, closed triangles). Slices were stimulated at 2 Hz for 30 min (bar) and endogenous DA overflow was expressed as a percent of the DA present in the slices at the outset of the experiment (from Stachowiak et al., 1987).

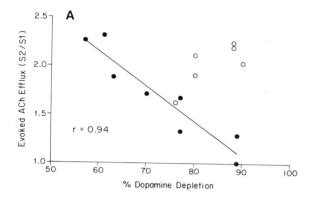
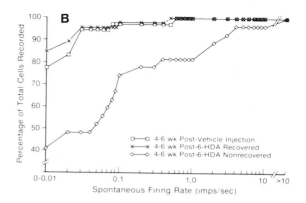

Fig. 6. Evidence that after partial lesions the apparent increase in the availability of DA from residual neurons serves a compensatory role. (*A*) Neostriatal slices were stimulated at 8 Hz for 1 min with standard buffer (S1) and in the presence of the DA receptor antagonist, sulpiride (10 μM; S2), and an estimate of the amount of ACh release was determined in each case. The ratio S2/S1 provides an index of the capacity of endogenous DA to exert an inhibitory influence over ACh release. Shown are results obtained 3 days (closed circles) and 2 months (open circles) after 6-OHDA-induced lesions. Decreases in S2/S1 below the control value of 2.0–2.5 indicate a loss of dopaminergic control (from MacKenzie et al., 1989). (*B*) The cumulative frequency distribution of spontaneous firing rate of a group of neurons in the medial neostriatum of control rats (squares) and rats treated 4–6 weeks earlier with 6-OHDA that have either recovered (crosses) or still show significant behavioral deficits (diamonds). The presence of a large number of neurons firing at relatively high frequencies in the last of these groups suggests the absence of an adequate supply of DA (from Nisenbaum et al., 1986).

Neuroregulatory deficits: lesions without neuropathology?

Consideration of the normal biochemical plasticity of catecholaminergic neurons suggests the existence of a family of disorders that result from neuroregulatory abnormalities caused by a failure of "synaptic homeostasis" (Fig. 7). For example, as discussed above, compensatory hyperactivity appears to allow a small number of DA neurons to perform the functions normally subserved by the full complement of these neurons. If so, it seems reasonable to further propose that deficits in the ability to invoke such compensations may exist in circumstances such as senescence, leading to accelerated rates of behavioral decline (Fig. 7*A*). Furthermore, might such conditions as affective disorders result from an inability of monoaminergic neurons to compensate properly for changes in demand, leading to too much or too little transmitter (Fig. 7*B,C*)? If so, perhaps much of pharmacotherapy actually represents attempts to restore homeostatic mechanisms.

It should be noted that if such neuroregulatory deficits occur in certain disease states, the attendant pathology would not be apparent during any conventional neuropathological examination, either upon imaging the brain or during postmortem analysis. Instead, such disorders would appear to have no organic basis and thus a new generation of tests would be needed to detect neurobiological abnormalities. For example, a deficiency in the autoregulation of transmitter release might require a functional assay, such as an examination of changes in transmitter release after autoreceptor blockade, or an analysis of the presence of the regulatory receptor protein itself.

Some additional implications

Neurochemistry versus electrophysiology

An important implication of the existence of local controls over transmitter release is that the influence of a neuron on its target cannot be fully estimated by monitoring its electrophysiological activity at the soma. Instead, local influences exerted at the terminal region can be expected to modify the impact of action potentials on transmitter release. Indeed, in the extreme case, local influences might actually *trigger* re-

120

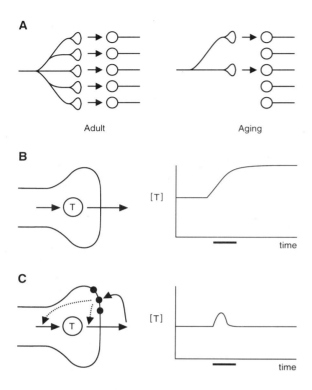

Fig. 7. Models for dysfunction resulting from a breakdown in synaptic homeostasis: (*A*) absence of compensation to the loss of neurons as might occur during senescence (compare with the adaptation postulated to occur during development, shown in Fig. 2*A*); (*B*) reduced compensation of transmitter synthesis and release during a period of increased activity (mania?) compared to the normal case (dashed line); and (*C*) overcompensation of transmitter synthesis and release during a period of increased activity (anhedonia?).

lease in the absence of impulses initiated at the cell soma. There are many examples of this phenomenon occurring at a pharmacological level and there is reason to believe that it can happen under physiological (or at least pathophysiological) conditions (Chesselet, 1984; Abercrombie and Zigmond, 1990). One value of such a scheme would be the conversion of a general system to a more specific one by allowing a cell with multiple terminal branches to deliver different amount of transmitter to different sites.

Neurochemistry versus morphology

A corollary of local regulation of transmitter release is that some influences between neurons can occur in the

absence of conventional synapses. This is because many of the terminals which have receptors on them do not have any axo-axonic synapses. Thus, input to those receptors, if it exists, must occur through a route that is not detectable by conventional morphological criteria. This is hardly a new concept. *Non-synaptic, neurohumoral, paracrine,* and *volume transmission* are all terms that have been applied to interactions between neurons and their targets (Beaudet and Descarries, 1978; Cuello, 1983; Schmitt, 1984; Vizi, 1984; Fuxe and Agnati, 1991). Evidence for such interactions are well documented in the autonomic nervous system and invertebrates. Moreover, application of these concepts to the mammalian CNS has been proposed by many authors on the basis of a considerable body of evidence, including the apparent ability of neurons to influence distant targets (Vizi, 1984; Fuxe and Agnati, 1991), and differences between the distribution of some transmitters and their receptors (Herkenham, 1988) (but see also Bloom, 1991). Of course, if both types of transmission co-exist, the functions subserved by each must of necessity be quite different. Whereas classical synaptic transmission may transfer information from cell to cell with high fidelity and considerable privacy, non-synaptic transmission would be incapable of either of these tasks (Fig. 8).

Neurochemistry versus neurochemistry

No one methodological approach can yield a complete picture; neurochemistry is no exception. What do we measure when we examine "release"? It is not the amount of transmitter released into a synapse, as even the best collection procedure lacks the necessary temporal and the spatial resolution for such a determination. More importantly, virtually every synapse has mechanisms to reduce the spread of transmitter from the synaptic cleft; enzymes like acetylcholine esterase to rapidly degrade the transmitter, and proteins like those in the plasma membranes of monoaminergic neurons which return transmitter into the terminal. These processes presumably sharpen the communication between cells, extending the privacy of axonal conduction to synaptic transmission. It does not follow that *all* transmitter found in extracellular fluid is

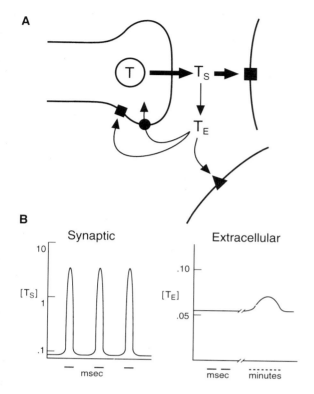

Fig. 8. Some distinctions between synaptic and extrasynaptic communication. Bottom, left: at a resting state the concentration of transmitter in a synaptic space (T_s) would be expected to be very low and to increase rapidly but transiently to a high level in response to an action potential (bars). Bottom, right: in contrast, in the resting state the concentration of transmitter in the surrounding extracellular fluid (T_E) also would be expected to be low, but no significant response to a single action potential would be expected and even extended trains of action potentials should only lead to small and slow changes in transmitter level. Ordinate shows arbitrary units of transmitter concentration. (Note difference in scale.)

merely a faint echo of the biologically significant event. As noted above, cells may communicate with each other through chemical signals that take other than synaptic routes and thus the extracellular pool of a transmitter may be biologically active. Nonetheless, it is clear that a great deal of information is lost by current methods for monitoring transmitter efflux (Finlay and Zigmond, 1994).

Directions for the future

Much has been learned in the 40 years that have

elapsed since Carlsson hypothesized about feedback modulation of neuronal activity. Yet, as always, answers lead to questions:

1. Is transmitter release *really* regulated and if so why? Does this not subvert the objective of chemical transmission, which is to respond faithfully to the electrical impulses that are received from the soma?

2. Do electrophysiological and anatomical methods for evaluating cell–cell interactions fail to disclose critical information about these events? Is transmitter release at the terminal not always reflected by the electrophysiological activity measured in the soma? Do neurons have a field of influence beyond those seen in electronmicrographs? If so what type of information might be transmitted in this non-conventional way?

3. Do deficits of homeostasis occur at the level of chemical communication and do they underlie some of the many psychiatric disorders (depression, anxiety) and neurological disorders (dystonia, Tourettes Syndrome) for which no clear neuropathology is evident? If so, can such regulatory dysfunctions be detected and repaired?

Answers to such questions will require the applications of multiple approaches to the study of neuronal interactions, as well as an increasing dialogue between basic and clinical investigators.

Acknowledgements

Many colleagues have contributed to the research and concepts summarized in this review. Special thanks go to Elizabeth D. Abercrombie, Anthony A. Grace, Janet M. Finlay, and Edward M. Stricker. Thanks also to Beth A. Vojta for her assistance in preparing the manuscript and Blaine Walker for his help in preparing the figures. This work was supported in part by U.S. Public Health Service Grant NS19608, MH43947, MH29670, MH45156 and MH00058.

References

Abercrombie, E.D., and Zigmond, M.J. (1990) Striatal dopamine release: In vivo evidence for local initiation. *Ann. N. Y. Acad. Sci.*, 604: 575–578.

Abercrombie, E.D., Bonatz, A.E. and Zigmond, M.J. (1990) Effects of L-DOPA on extracellular dopamine in striatum of normal and 6-hydroxydopamine-treated rats. *Brain Res.,*. 525: 36–44.

Beaudet, A. and Descarries, L. (1978) The monoamine innervation of rat cerebral cortex: synaptic and non synaptic axon terminals. *Neuroscience,* 3: 851–860.

Bloom, F.E. (1991) An integrative view of information handling in the CNS. In: K. Fuxe and L.F. Agnati (Eds.), *Advances in Neuroscience, Volume 1: Transmission in the Brain: Novel Mechanisms for Neural Transmission*, Raven Press, New York, pp. 11–23.

Bunney, B.S. (1979) The electrophysiological pharmacology of midbrain dopaminergic systems. In: A.S. Horn, J. Korf and B.H.C. Westerink (Eds.), *The Neurobiology of Dopamine*, Academic Press, New York, pp. 417–452.

Carlsson, A. and Lindqvist, J. (1963) Effect of chlorpromazine and haloperidol on formation of 3-methoxytyramine and normetanephrine in mouse brain. *Acta Pharmacol. Toxicol.* 20: 140–144.

Carlsson, A., Kehr, W., Linqvist, M., Magnusson, T., and Atack, C.V. (1972) Regulation of monoamine metabolism in the central nervous system. *Pharmacol. Rev.*, 24: 371–384.

Cheramy, A., Barbeito, L., Godeheu, G., Desce, J.M., Pittaluga, A., Galli, T., Artaud, F., and Glowinski, J. (1990) Respective contributions of neuronal activity and presynaptic mechanisms in the control of the in vivo release of dopamine. *J. Neural. Trans.*, 29: 183–193.

Chesselet, M.-F. (1984) Presynaptic regulation of neurotransmitter release in the brain: facts and hypothesis. *Neuroscience*, 12: 347–375.

Creese, I., Burt, D.R. and Snyder, S.H. (1978) Biochemical actions of neuroleptic drugs: focus on the dopamine receptor. In: L. Iversen, S.D. Iversen, and S.H. Snyder (Eds.), *Handbook of Psychopharmacology, Volume 10: Neuroleptics and Schizophrenia*, Plenum Press, New York.

Cuello, A.C. (1983) Nonclassical neuronal communications. *Fed. Proc.*, 42: 2912–2922.

Finlay, J. and Zigmond, M.J. (1994) A critical analysis of neurochemical methods for monitoring transmitter dynamics in brain. In: F.E. Bloom and D. Kupfer (Eds.), *Psychopharmacology: Fourth Generation of Progress*, Raven Press, New York, in press.

Fuxe, K. and Agnati, L.F. (1991) Two principal modes of electrochemical communication in the brain: Volume versus wiring transmission. In: K. Fuxe and L.F. Agnati (Eds.), *Advances in Neuroscience, Volume 1: Transmission in the Brain: Novel Mechanisms for Neural Transmission*, Raven Press, New York, pp. 11–23.

Groves, P.M., Wilson, C.J., Young, S.J. and Rebec, G.Y. (1975) Self-inhibition by dopaminergic neurons. *Science,* 190: 522–529.

Herkenham, M. (1987) Mismatches between neurotransmitter and receptor localizations in brain: observations and implications. *Neuroscience*, 23: 1–38.

Keefe, K.A., Zigmond, M.J. and Abercrombie, E.D. (1993) In vivo regulation of extracellular dopamine in the neostriatum: influence of impulse activity and local excitatory amino acids. *J. Neural Transm.*, 91: 223–240.

MacKenzie, R.G., Stachowiak, M. and Zigmond, M.J. (1989) Dopaminergic inhibition of striatal acetylcholine release after 6-hydroxydopamine. *Eur. J. Pharmacol.*, 168: 43–52.

Murrin, R.H. and Roth, R.H. (1976) Dopaminergic neurons: effects of electrical stimulation on dopamine biosynthesis. *Mol. Pharmacol.*, 12: 463–475.

Nisenbaum, E.S., Stricker, E.M., Zigmond, M.J. and Berger, T.W. (1986) Long-term effects of dopamine-depleting brain lesions on spontaneous activity of Type II striatal neurons: relation to behavioral recovery. *Brain Res.*, 398: 221–230.

Nybäck, H. and Sedvall, G. (1968) Effect of chlorpromazine on accumulation and disappearance of catecholamines formed from tyrosine-14C in brain. *J. Pharmacol. Exp. Ther.*, 162: 294–301.

Schmitt, F.O. (1984) Molecular regulators of brain function: a new view. *Neuroscience.*, 13: 991–1001.

Stachowiak, M.K., Keller, R.W. Jr., Stricker, E.M., and Zigmond, M.J. (1987) Increased dopamine efflux from striatal slices during development and after nigrostriatal bundle damage. *J. Neurosci.*, 7: 1648–1654.

Vizi, E.S. (1984) *Non-Synaptic Interactions Between Neurons: Modulation of Neurochemical Transmission.*, Wiley, New York.

Zigmond, M.J. and Stricker, E.M. (1985) Adaptive properties of mono-aminergic neurons. In: A. Lajtha (Ed.), *Handbook of Neurochemistry*, Vol. 9, Plenum Press, New York, pp. 87–102.

Zigmond, M.J. and Stricker, E.M. (1989) Animal models of Parkinsonism using selective neurotoxins: Clinical and Basic Implications. In: J.R. Smythies and R.J. Bradley (Eds.), *International Review of Neurobiology*, Vol. 31, Academic Press, New York, pp. 1–79.

Zigmond, M.J., Abercrombie, E.D., Berger, T.W., Grace, A.A. and Stricker, E.M. (1993) Compensatory responses to partial loss of dopaminergic neurons: studies with 6-hydroxydopamine. In: J.S. Schneider and M. Gupta (Eds.), *Current Concepts in Parkinson's Disease Research*, Hogrefe & Huber, Toronto, pp. 99–140.

F. Bloom (Editor)
Progress in Brain Research, Vol. 100
© 1994 Elsevier Science B.V. All rights reserved

CHAPTER 16

Conservation of basic synaptic circuits that mediate GABA inhibition in the subcortical visual system

R. Ranney Mize

Department of Anatomy and the Neuroscience Center, Louisiana State University Medical Center, 1901 Perdido Street, New Orleans, LA 70112, USA

Introduction

Inhibition is fundamental to visual function in the subcortical visual system (SVS). Inhibitory mechanisms are thought to be involved in both spatial and temporal aspects of visual processing. In the spatial domain, inhibition is thought to contribute to center-surround antagonism, to movement and directional selectivity, to binocular inhibition, and to spatial frequency tuning of the receptive fields of single neurons. In the temporal domain, inhibition is thought to play a role in shaping the transient responses of single cells and in controlling levels of adaptation under different illumination conditions. Inhibitory processing is thus involved in a multitude of visual functions (reviewed in Mize et al., 1992).

The inhibitory neurotransmitter, gamma-aminobutyric acid (GABA), is the chief and often the sole neurotransmitter generating intrinsic inhibition in the SVS. Accordingly, GABA inhibition has been invoked to explain each of the above functions. In this chapter, the anatomical organization and physiological processes that underlie GABAergic inhibition in the SVS are reviewed, focusing upon the cell types and synaptic circuitry that have been identified in the SVS. What is known of the physiological actions of GABA in these regions is described briefly. There are three basic types of GABA containing synaptic profile in the SVS. These are relatively homogeneous and form similar synaptic circuits in most of the structures examined. GABA neurons and circuits may therefore be common to a variety of structures and species and represent a highly conserved feature of brain development.

Heterogeneity of SVS function and GABA cell types

The cell types, receptive field characteristics and global functions of the SVS are quite heterogeneous. The lateral geniculate nucleus (LGN) is involved principally in the state-dependent gating of signal transmission from the retina to visual cortex. Retinorecipient nuclei of the pretectum also vary in function. The nucleus of the optic tract (NOT) helps to control the stabilization of gaze and optokinetic nystagmus. The olivary pretectal nucleus (OPN) controls the pupillary light reflex. The principal site of retinal termination in the midbrain, the superior colliculus, is involved in visual attention, detection of moving objects in the visual field and in the generation of saccadic eye movements. SVS functions are therefore remarkably diverse. (for review, see Sherman and Spear, 1982).

The receptive field properties of cells in these regions is equally diverse. Receptive fields in the LGN have a center-surround organization, and may be on or off center and have X, Y, or W receptive fields. The proportion of these cells varies in different regions of the cat LGN. Both X and Y cells are commonly found in the A layers of the dLGN while the parvocellular C layers contain exclusively W cells. The medial interlaminar nucleus (MIN) contains primarily Y cells, while the ventral LGN contains mostly W cells. Cells in the NOT are directionally selective and contribute to optokinetic afternystagmus. OPN cells respond to changes in ambient illumination. Cells within the superior colliculus receive primarily W input from the retina with some Y input located in deeper laminae. Many are directionally selective with silent inhibitory surrounds. Others in the deep layers are multimodal and/or respond in association with saccades (for review, see Sherman and Spear, 1982).

The cells that contain GABA in these SVS structures are correspondingly heterogeneous. The principal local circuit interneuron in the A layers of the dLGN is a type 3 neuron with a small cell body and an exquisite tangle of thin dendrites that form an asymmetric vertically oriented field. These dendrites have complex appendages that contain pleomorphic synaptic vesicles. These cells represent about 25% of all neurons in the A layers (Guillery, 1969; Hamos et al., 1985; Uhlrich and Cucchiaro, 1992). Other GABA containing interneurons in the dLGN are interlaminar cells with larger cell bodies, somatic spines, and stout dendrites that cross laminar boundaries and may not receive retinal input (Montero, 1989). Neurons above the dLGN within the perigeniculate nucleus (PGN) and the thalamic reticular nucleus (TRN) often have horizontally distributed dendrites and axons that dip into the dLGN. Small cells containing GABA are also found throughout the parvocellular C laminae, MIN, and the vLGN (for review, see Uhlrich and Cucchiaro, 1992).

The superior colliculus also has a variety of GABA containing neurons that are about 25–40% of the total population. At least three GABAergic cell types have been described in cat: horizontal cells have oblong, fusiform cell bodies and two stout horizontally oriented presynaptic dendrites that course parallel to the pial surface. They receive limited numbers of synapses, most from visual cortex. Granule 1 type cells are small cells, often with vertically oriented dendrites, that have moderate synaptic input and a definitive axon. Granule 2 neurons also receive moderate synaptic input and have both somatic and dendritic spines that contain synaptic vesicles (Mize, 1992).

The GABA cell types of the OPN and NOT are less well characterized but consist of both small and medium sized neurons with variable morphologies. They may include both interneurons and projection cells (cf. Campbell and Lieberman, 1985; Van der Want et al., 1992).

Homogeneity of GABA synaptic ultrastructure

Despite the heterogeneous and distinctive cell types found to contain GABA, the ultrastructure of synapses established by these cells is surprisingly homogeneous within each of the retinorecipient zones studied. Two and often three GABAergic synaptic types have been identified consistently in the dorsal and ventral lateral geniculate nuclei, medial intralaminar nucleus, two retinorecipient nuclei of the pretectum and the superior colliculus.

The P1 presynaptic dendrite

The best studied of the GABAergic synaptic profiles is a presynaptic dendrite that is one component of the retinal triad. Retinal triads consist of a retinal synaptic terminal (called an R or RT or RLP), a conventional dendrite (D) from a relay cell, and an intermediate synaptic element (referred to as a P or PSD or F2 profile) that is postsynaptic to the RT but presynaptic to the D (Fig. 1). In the dLGN, the retinal triad is surrounded by a glial sheath, which anatomically and functionally segregates it within a structure called a glomerulus. The triad also receives input from acetylcholine fibers from the brainstem and GABA containing fibers from the perigeniculate nucleus (Fig. 1) (Sillito, 1992).

Retinal terminals in these triads contain large, round synaptic vesicles and mitochondria with a pale matrix and broken up cristae (Figs. 2–4). In the A layers of the dLGN, the RT is often the central element with a scallop shape produced by indentations from dendrites that surround it (Fig. 2A). The intermediate presynaptic dendrite, called an F2 in cat LGN (Guillery, 1969), contains a pleomorphic population of round, ovoid, and occasionally flattened synaptic vesicles that are almost always loosely scattered

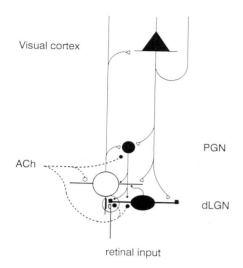

Fig. 1. Synaptic circuitry of the dorsal lateral geniculate nucleus (LGN), illustrating the relationship between retinal afferents, relay cell dendrites and GABA containing interneurons. The units of the retinal triad are outlined by the circle, and include a retinal terminal (open rectangle), a presynaptic dendrite (black square), and a relay neuron (black line), as well as an inhibitory synapse from acetylcholine (ACh) containing synapses from the brainstem. A perigeniculate (PGN) neuron is also shown providing feed backward inhibition to the dLGN (from Sillito, 1992).

Labels in figure: Visual cortex, ACh, PGN, dLGN, retinal input

through the profile (Fig 2A). The triad is a triplicate synapse in which the RT makes synaptic contact with both the D and F2 profiles, while the F2 also contacts the D profile, thus forming a triangular synaptic arrangement (the "triad", Fig. 1).

F2s in dLGN are invariably inhibitory. They are labeled by antibodies to GABA and GAD (glutamic acid decarboxylase, the synthetic enzyme for GABA), contain at least a few distinctively flattened vesicles, and establish symmetric synaptic contacts, all typical features of inhibitory synapses. In the LGN, these profiles can be traced back to their dendrites of origin and are found to be the dendritic spine-like appendages of one class of dLGN interneuron (Hamos et al., 1985).

Synaptic triads between RTs, presynaptic dendrites, and Ds are also found in every other retinorecipient zone of the SVS studied. Presynaptic dendrites receiving retinal input and containing sparse accumulations of pleomorphic synaptic vesicles are found in MIN (Fig. 2B), vLGN (Fig. 2C,D), parvocellular C laminae

of the dLGN (Fig. 2E), the nucleus of the optic tract (Figs. 3A), the olivary pretectal nucleus (Figs. 3B,C), and the superior colliculus (Fig. 4A).

The intermediate elements of these triads, which for consistency are subsequently called P1 profiles, are labeled by antibodies to GABA and establish symmetric synaptic contacts, usually with D profiles. In the cat and monkey superior colliculus, the P1s have also been shown to be the spine-like appendages of GABA containing granule cells (Mize, 1992) and may be spine-like dendritic appendages in the OPN of rat as well (Campbell and Lieberman, 1985).

Although the basic triad synapse and the P1 profile have been identified in every SVS structure examined (Figs. 2–4), their frequency and morphology do differ for different relay cell types and in different nuclei. Triads are frequently associated with X cells in the dLGN, much less frequently with Y cells (where they are estimated to comprise only 10% of the input) (see Uhlrich and Cucchiaro, 1992). Triads are common in MIN, OPN and SC, less common in vLGN, the parvocellular C layers of dLGN, and the NOT. In the vLGN and parvocellular C layers, RTs form synaptic contacts with only about one-third the number of F2 profiles that are contacted by RTs in the dLGN and MIN (Mize and Horner, 1984; Mize et al., 1986). Only about 5–10% of RTs contacting W cells in the parvo C layers form triadic synapses (Raczkowski et al., 1988), a percentage much smaller than that for X cells in the dLGN (see Uhlrich and Cucchiaro, 1992).

The size of triadic profiles also varies in different regions of the SVS. In SC, for example, retinal terminals are often small and P1s are accordingly of smaller diameter than those seen in the dLGN (Fig. 4A). The size of RTs and P1s in both the vLGN and the parvo C layers of dLGN is often less than half that of those in the dLGN and MIN (Figs. 2C–E versus Figs. 2A,B) (Mize and Horner, 1984; Mize et al., 1986).

Despite these differences in frequency and size, the basic triadic arrangement of the synaptic complex is apparent throughout much of the SVS. In addition, the morphology of the P1 is quite similar in all structures examined. It contains a mixed, pleomorphic population of synaptic vesicles that have a characteristic sparse distribution throughout the profile (Figs. 2–4).

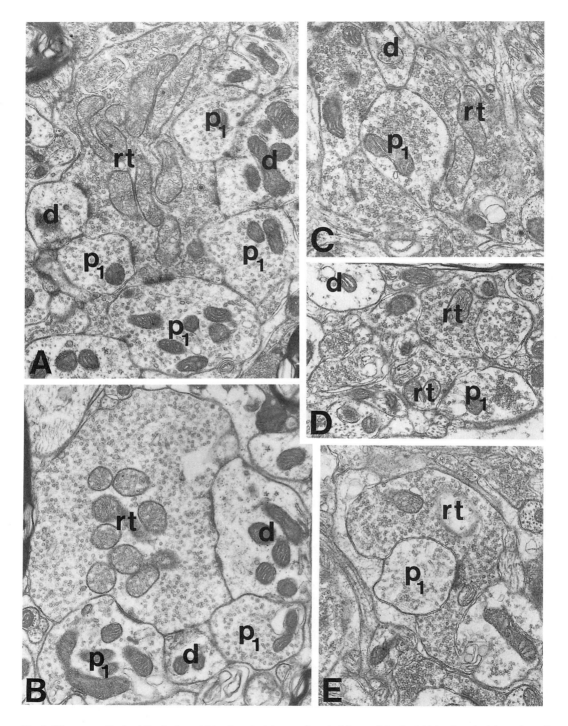

Fig. 2. P1 presynaptic dendrites in the cat lateral geniculate complex. *A*. A layer of the dorsal lateral geniculate nucleus; *B*. medial interlaminar nucleus; *C,D*, ventral lateral geniculate nucleus; *E*, parvocellular C laminae of the dLGN. Retinal terminals (rts) contact these P1s in each structure. Conventional dendrites (d) are also found.

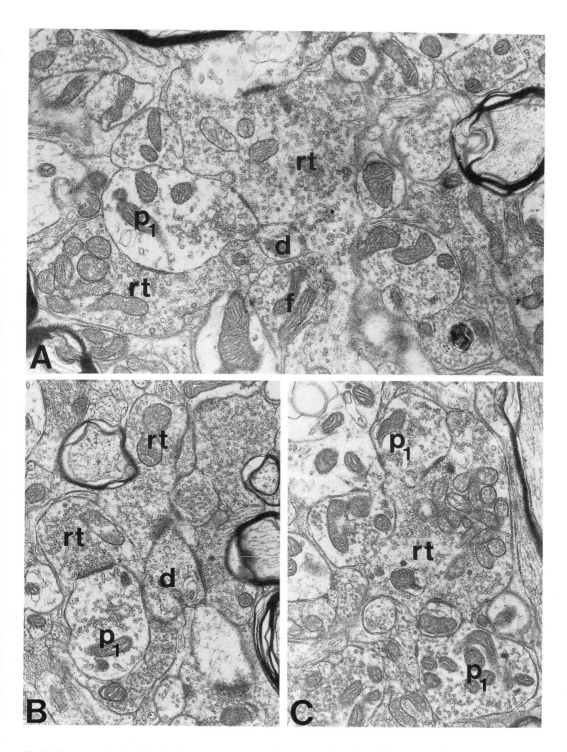

Fig. 3. P1 presynaptic dendrites in the cat pretectum. *A*, olivary pretectal nucleus; *B,C*, nucleus of the optic tract.

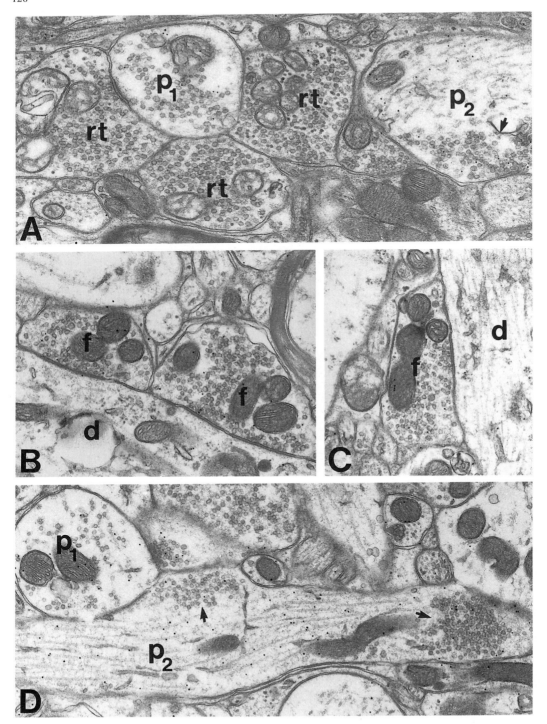

Fig. 4. GABA containing profiles in the rabbit superior colliculus. *A*, P1 presynaptic dendrite surrounded by retinal terminals (rts). *B,C*, F type axon terminals; *D*, P2 presynaptic dendrite. The profiles were labeled by colloidal gold-conjugated GABA antibodies using post-embedding immunocytochemistry.

In fact, the loose clustering of the synaptic vesicles is one "signature" of these profiles that distinguishes them from other GABA containing profiles described below. The P1 and its associated triad is therefore a ubiquitous and fundamental GABAergic circuit in the SVS.

The F axon terminal

A second major class of GABA synapse is formed by F profiles. F profiles are called F1s in dLGN (Guillery) and usually F profiles in other SVS structures (OPN, NOT, SC). F profiles contain pleomorphic synaptic vesicles, some of which are dramatically flattened. These vesicles are densely and uniformly distributed within a dark cytoplasmic ground (Figs. 4B,C). They form symmetric synaptic contacts that have thin post-synaptic densities, often with an apposition area greater than that of P1s (Figs. 4B,C). Fs are easily distinguished from P1 profiles both because of the numbers and density of flattened synaptic vesicles and because they are always presynaptic, not post-synaptic, to other structures. F profiles arise from a variety of extrinsic sources. In the dLGN, they are the terminal axons of neurons in the perigeniculate nucleus, the thalamic reticular nucleus, and the pretectum (Uhlrich and Cucchiaro, 1992). In SC, F profiles in the deep layers arise from the substantia nigra, zona incerta, the pretectum, and a number of brainstem nuclei (Mize, 1992). In the NOT, they arise from the medial terminal nucleus (MTN) of the accessory optic system and probably also from SC (Van der Want et al., 1992). F type terminals also are thought to arise intrinsically from interneurons because some GABAergic local circuit neurons in the LGN, SC and NOT have axons.

The terminal morphology of F profiles is quite homogeneous. F axon terminals have simpler synaptic arrangements than P1s and they are sometimes stacked along the surfaces of proximal and distal dendrites. They rarely participate in serial synapses and are rarely found within glomeruli. There is evidence that F axon terminals are selectively associated with a subunit of the GABAa/benzodiazepine receptor in both the dLGN (Soltesz and Crunelli, 1992) and SC (Mize, 1992).

P2 presynaptic dendrites

The third profile type that contains GABA in the SVS is a second class of presynaptic dendrite, called a P2 in this review. P2s have been most thoroughly characterized in the cat SC. P2s are large calibre dendrites that have small, discrete clusters of densely packed synaptic vesicles often distributed at regular intervals along the dendrite (Fig. 4D) (Mize, 1992). These dendrites have been termed H profiles in SC because reconstructions in cat reveal that they are the dendrites of horizontal cells (Mize, 1992). P2 profiles can be differentiated from P1 profiles by the diameter of the dendrite and the compact but densely packed clustering of their synaptic vesicles. Reconstructions of retinal synaptic islands in monkey SC have shown that P2s receive synaptic input from both P1 and F synapses (Mize, 1992), and thus participate as postsynaptic elements in GABA upon GABA synaptic circuits.

P2 profiles also have been identified in the cat dLGN (Hamos et al., 1985), the tree shrew LGN (called F3 profiles) (see Uhlrich and Cucchiaro, 1992), and in the rabbit NOT (Nunes Cardozo et al., 1993). In cat LGN, they are dendritic shafts with punctate clusters of vesicles that receive mostly Y retinal input and contact Y relay cells (see Uhlrich and Cucchiaro, 1992). Large calibre dendrites with punctate clusters of pleomorphic synaptic vesicles have also been illustrated in the NOT (Fig. 4C of Nunes-Cardozo et al., 1994). Whether this profile type is present in other SVS structures has not yet been established.

Physiological actions of GABA in the SVS

GABA interneurons have been implicated in a variety of inhibitory receptive field properties, including surround antagonism, directional selectivity, movement sensitivity, binocular inhibition and length tuning (see Sillito, 1992, for review). Because the receptive field properties of cells in the LGN, pretectum and SC vary so dramatically in type, the presence of the same three GABAergic synaptic units in all of these regions was unexpected. Recently, however, it has been argued that intrinsic GABA circuits are not involved in directional

horizontal cells that extend up to the surface of that structure (Mize, 1992). Because of the extensive distribution of their dendrites, they have been implicated in lateral and/or remote inhibition that occurs in SC (for review, see Mize, 1992). The large calibre and smooth contour of their dendrites suggests

Acknowledgments

This work was supported by USPHS grant NIH EY-02973 from the National Eye Institute. Grace Butler

A

1 V

2 V

B

134

136

initiates bursting activity (Day, 1989; Renaud and Bourque, 1991). However this is not a simple innervation. Whereas exogenous noradrenaline enhances the excitability of both VP- and OXY-secreting MNCs, the A1 → MNC pathway appears to be selective for VP-secreting MNCs, whereas the A2 → MNC pathway appears to be selective for OT-secreting MNCs (Raby and Renaud, 1989). Moreover, exogenous noradrenaline has an excitatory action when applied in micromolar concentrations, mediated via postsynaptic $\alpha 1$ adrenoreceptors, but a depressant action when applied at higher (millimolar) concentrations, mediated via presynaptic $\alpha 2$ and postsynaptic β adrenergic receptors (Renaud and Bourque, 1991; Khanna et al., 1993). In addition, the neuropeptide NPY, which co-exists within a majority of A1 neurons, appears to have postsynaptic NPY_1 receptors that potentiate the actions of noradrenaline and presynaptic NPY_2 receptors to reduce the input from A1 neurons (Day, 1989). Finally, ATP may contribute to the excitation of SON MNCs evoked by A1 stimulation (Day et al., 1993).

Peptides: focus on angiotensin AT_1 and cholecystokinin B type receptors

Angiotensin II-like immunoreactivity is observed both in MNCs themselves and in their afferents. Exogenously applied angiotensin II induces a slow onset, prolonged membrane depolarization in SON MNCs, involving an AT_1 type receptor and mediated through a non-selective cationic conductance (Yang et al., 1992). A major source for angiotensinergic afferents is the SFO, and electrophysiological data suggest that angiotensin may be the neurotransmitter underlying a long duration increase in excitability in SON MNCs following SFO stimulation (Jhamandas et al., 1989). In the rat, CCK influences MNC function through independent peripheral and central mechanisms. Systemically administered CCK octapeptide (CCK-8) acts at peripheral A type receptors to trigger a vagally mediated and selective increase in the excitability of OT-secreting MNCs (Renaud et al., 1987). The central pathways and transmitters for this response remain undefined. CCK has separate central actions on MNCs. CCK immunoreactivity is present in fibers located near MNCs, CCK

is co-synthesized in a population of MNCs, and exogenous applications of CCK produce membrane depolarizations in both VP- and OT-secreting MNCs, mediated via B-type receptors (Jarvis et al., 1992). Future studies are needed to assess the role(s) of CCK in specific afferent pathways, CCK's role as a co-existing and co-released neurotransmitter, the possibility of local release from somata-dendrites of MNCs and paracrine actions, mechanisms that regulate CCK synthesis and storage in MNCs, its release from neurohypophysial axon terminals and influence on neurosecretion of other peptides.

Comment

As the intrinsic properties and synaptic connectivity of MNCs become more clearly defined and characterized, a profile of the integrative properties of MNCs will emerge. There remains the elucidation of signal transduction mechanisms that govern immediate changes in cell excitability and long-term changes in gene expression and protein synthesis.

Acknowlegement

The author acknowledges the sustained support of the Canadian MRC and Heart and Stroke Foundation.

References

Bourque, C.W. (1990) Intraterminal recordings from the rat neurohypophysis in vitro. *J. Physiol.*, 421: 247–262.

Cunningham, E.T. and Sawchenko, P.E. (1991) Reflex control of magnocellular asopressin and oxytocin secretion. *Trends Neurosci.*, 14: 406–411.

Cunningham, J.T., Nissen, R. and Renaud, L.P. (1992) Catecholamine depletion of the diagonal band reduces baroreflex inhibition of supraoptic neurons. *Am. J. Physiol.*, 263: R363–R367.

Day, T.A. (1989) Control of neurosecretory vasopressin cells by noradrenergic projections of the caudal ventrolateral medulla. *Prog. Brain Res.*, 81: 303–317.

Day, T.A., Sibbald, J.R. and Khanna, S. (1993) ATP mediates an excitatory noradrenergic neuron input to supraoptic vasopressin cells. *Brain Res.*, 607: 341–344.

Decavel, C. and Van Den Pol, A.N. (1992) Converging GABA- and glutamate-immunoreactive axons make synaptic contact with identified hypothalamic neurosecretory neurons. *J. Comp. Neurol.*, 316: 104–116.

Gardiner, G.W., Verbalis, J.G. and Stricker, E.M. (1985). Impaired secretion of vasopressin and oxytocin in rats after lesions of nucleus medianus. *Am. J. Physiol.*, 269: R681–R688.

Jarvis, C.R., Bourque, C.R. and Renaud, L.P. (1992) Depolarizing action of cholecystokinin on rat supraoptic neurones in vitro. *J. Physiol.*, 458: 621–632.

Jhamandas, J.H. and Renaud, L.P. (1986) A gamma aminobutyric acid-mediated baroreceptor input to supraoptic vasopressin neurones in the rat. *J. Physiol.*, 381: 595–606.

Jhamandas, J.H., Lind, R.W. and Renaud, L.P. (1989) Angiotensin II may mediate excitatory neurotransmission from the subfornical organ to the hypothalamic supraoptic nucleus: an anatomical and electrophysiological study in the rat. *Brain Res.*, 487: 52–61.

Khanna, S., Sibbald, J.R. and Day, T.A. (1993) α2-adrenoceptor modulation of A1 noradrenergic neuron input to supraoptic vasopressin cells. *Brain Res.*, 613: 164–167.

Lind, R.W., Swanson, L.W. and Ganten, D. (1985) Organization of angiotensin II immunoreactive cells and fibers in the rat central nervous system. *Neuroendocrinology*, 40: 2–24.

Nissen, R. and Renaud, L.P. (1994) GABA receptors mediate median preoptic nucleus-evoked inhibition of vasopressin and oxytocin neurones in rat supraoptic nucleus. *J. Physiol.*, in press.

Nissen, R., Bourque, C.R. and Renaud, L.P. (1993a) Membrane properties of organum vasculosum lamina terminalis neurons recorded in vitro. *Am. J. Physiol.*, 264: R811–R815.

Nissen, R., Cunningham, J.T. and Renaud, L.P. (1993b) Lateral hypothalamic lesions alter baroreceptor-evoked inhibition of rat supraoptic vasopressin neurones. *J. Physiol.*, 470: 751–766.

Oliet, S.H.R. and Bourque, C.W. (1993) Mechanosensitive channels transduce osmosensitivity in supraoptic neurons. *Nature*, 364: 341–343.

Raby, W.N. and Renaud, L.P. (1989) Nucleus tractus solitarius innervation of supraoptic nucleus: anatomical and electrophysiological studies in the rat suggest differential innervation of oxytocin and vasopressin neurons. *Prog. Brain Res.*, 81: 319–327.

Renaud. L.P. and Bourque, C.W. (1991) Neurophysiology and neuropharmacology of hypothalamic magnocellular neurons secreting vasopressin and oxytocin. *Prog. Neurobiol.*, 36: 131–169.

Renaud, L.P., Tang, M., McCann, M.J., Stricker, E.M. and Verbalis, J.G. (1987) Cholecystokinin and gastric distention activate oxytocinergic cells in rat hypothalamus. *Am. J. Physiol.*, 253: R661–R665.

Swanson, L. E. and Sawchenko, P.E. (1983) Hypothalamic integration: organization of the paraventricular and supraoptic nuclei. *Annu. Rev. Neurosci.*, 6: 269–324.

Yang, C.R., Phillips, M.I. and Renaud. L.P. (1992) Angiotensin II receptor activation depolarizes rat supraoptic neurons in vitro. *Am. J. Physiol.*, 263: R1333–R1338.

Yang, C.R., Senatorov, V.V. and Renaud, L.P. (1994) Organum vasculosum lamina terminalis-evoked post-synaptic responses in rat supraoptic neurones in vitro. *J. Physiol.*, in press.

F. Bloom (Editor)
Progress in Brain Research, Vol. 100
© 1994 Elsevier Science B.V. All rights reserved

Molecular principles from neuroendocrine models: steroid control of central neurotransmission

George Fink

MRC Brain Metabolism Unit, University Department of Pharmacology, 1 George Square, Edinburgh EH8 9JZ, UK

Introduction

Neuroendocrinology, the study of the interactions between the nervous and endocrine systems, has generated several principles crucial for our understanding of chemical neurotransmission. The peripheral neuroendocrine system is comprised mainly of the gastrointestinal system and its innervation, and the adrenal medulla. The pioneering studies of Gaddum, von Euler, Mutt and Gregory on the gastrointestinal system provided the basis for our knowledge of the amino acid residue sequence of many peptides which also have an important role in the central nervous system (Dockray, 1988). The adrenal medulla continues to provide an important model for exocytosis and the intracellular signals involved in the neural control of endocrine secretion (Johnson, 1988).

The central neuroendocrine system is subdivided into the hypothalamo-neurohypophysial system and the hypothalamo-adenohypophysial system. The main function of the hypothalamo-neurohypophysial system is to synthesize and secrete into the systemic circulation, two important nonapeptides, vasopressin and oxytocin. The main physiological role of vasopressin is to reduce the volume of urine produced by the kidneys (hence the synonym, antidiuretic hormone); oxytocin stimulates milk ejection in response to suckling and coordinates and potentiates uterine contractions during parturition. Several properties make the hypothalamo-neurohypophysial system an excellent model system which has generated important principles for neurophysiology, microphysiology, neuropeptide synthesis, axonal transport and exocytosis.

First, vasopressin and oxytocin are synthesized in large (magnocellular) neurons of the hypothalamic paraventricular and supraoptic nuclei (PVN and SON). Their large size and the convenient anatomical location of the PVN and SON magnocellular neurons makes them excellent targets for neurophysiological and microphysiological studies, especially since the readily accessible neurohypophysis facilitates reliable neuronal identification by antidromic stimulation (Cross et al., 1975). Secondly, the rate of synthesis and turnover of AVP and oxytocin is several orders of magnitude greater than that of other transmitters and this makes it relatively easy to use them as models for neuropeptide synthesis and axonal transport (Cross et al., 1975; Sachs et al., 1969). Thirdly, the fact that both peptides contain a cysteine residue allows the use of ^{35}S cysteine as a convenient marker for studies of synthesis, transport and turnover. Fourthly, the neurohypophysis is virtually a "bag" of nerve terminals derived from the PVN and SON and is, therefore, an excellent model for studying the detailed mechanism of neuropeptide release. Finally, the homozygous Brattleboro rat, a mutant which renders AVP mRNA defective so that it cannot be translated, has provided an excellent model for studies of gene transcription and translation and for studies on the effects of AVP gene "knockout" (Sokol and Valtin, 1982; North et al., 1993).

The hypothalamo-adenohypophysial system also provides an excellent model for studying neuropeptide synthesis release and action (Fink, 1976; Fink, 1988; Fink and Sheward, 1989). Both of the two hypothalamo-hypophysial systems have been reviewed extensively (especially in the *Progress in Brain Research* series) and so here attention is focused on the way central neuroendocrine systems can be used to study the profound effects that steroid hormones exert on central neurotransmission by actions on individual brain nuclei and complex neural circuits in which one or more synapses allow for switching of signal sign and thus the mechanism of disinhibition.

Steroids exert either inhibitory or stimulatory effects on neuronal systems. Broadly, the stimulatory actions of steroids have a long latency (hours to days) while the latency of inhibitory actions is short (seconds to minutes) (Fink, 1979a). Membrane (extragenomic) actions of "neurosteroids", mainly pregnenolone and its derivatives, have recently excited considerable interest (Baulieu, 1993). The most compelling evidence for this type of action comes from studies of the steroid anaesthetic alphaxalone which acts through $GABA_A$ receptors (Fink et al., 1982; Majewska, 1987). The present review, however, focuses on the well-established classical action of steroids involving activation of specific steroid receptors which, by way of an action on DNA steroid response elements, perhaps in association with other transcription factors, either stimulate or inhibit gene transcription.

The inhibitory actions of steroids in negative feedback control of the hypothalamic-pituitary-gonadal and adrenal systems have been by far the most well-studied (Fink, 1979a) although the intracellular mechanism of action has yet to be established. Steroids also exert powerful stimulatory actions, examples of which include the facilitation by glucocorticoids of the activity of tyrosine hydroxylase and tryptophan hydroxylase, the rate-limiting enzymes for catecholamine and indolamine synthesis, respectively, and phenylethanolamine *N*-methyl transferase which converts noradrenaline to adrenaline (McEwen et al., 1986). Here attention is focused on two important examples of the stimulatory actions of gonadal steroids illustrating important principles for our understanding of how steroids evoke clear neuroendocrine signals and behaviours through apparently complex actions on brain cells and circuits.

Positive feedback of oestrogen on the hypothalamic-pituitary-gonadotropin system

The spontaneous ovulatory surge of luteinizing hormone (LH) is generated by a positive feedback cascade in which a surge of oestradiol-17β (E_2) acts on the brain to trigger a surge of luteinizing hormone releasing hormone (LHRH), and on the anterior pituitary gland to increase pituitary responsiveness to LHRH (Fink, 1979b, 1988) (Fig. 1). The increase in pituitary responsiveness to LHRH is further potentiated by progesterone. Luteinizing hormone releasing hormone has the unique capacity to increase responsiveness (by at least sevenfold in vivo) to itself. This property of LHRH, which we termed the priming effect of LHRH,

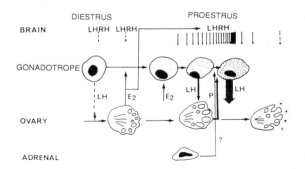

Fig. 1. Schematic diagram which shows the cascade of events which produce the spontaneous ovulatory LH surge in the rat. The increase in plasma concentrations of oestradiol-17β (E_2, the ovarian signal) increases the responsiveness of the pituitary gonadotrophs (increased stippling) to LHRH and also triggers the surge of LHRH. Pituitary responsiveness to LHRH is further increased by progesterone (P) secreted from the ovary in response to the LH released during the early part of the LH surge and by the priming effect of LHRH, the unique capacity of the decapeptide to increase pituitary responsiveness to itself. The priming effect of LHRH coordinates the surges of LHRH with increasing pituitary responsiveness so that the two events reach a peak at the same time. The conditions are thereby made optimal for a massive surge of LH. This cascade, which represents a form of positive feedback, is terminated by destruction of a major component of the system in the form of the rupture of the ovarian follicles (ovulation). From Fink (1979b) with the permission of the British Council.

is probably important to further potentiate pituitary responsiveness to LHRH and to coordinate the increased release of LHRH and pituitary responsiveness to LHRH so that both reach a peak at the same time thereby ensuring a massive spontaneous, ovulatory surge of LH.

Does oestradiol-17β stimulate LHRH biosynthesis?

To determine whether E_2 stimulates the biosynthesis of LHRH, we used the same paradigm as that used to prove that oestradiol stimulated the LHRH surge (Sarkar and Fink, 1979a; Rosie et al., 1990). That is, rats were ovariectomized on the morning of di-oestrus in order to eliminate the spontaneous surge of E_2 and injected s.c. with either oestradiol benzoate (EB) or vehicle (0.2 ml sesame oil). The animals were killed between 1600 and 1700 h of the next day (presumptive pro-oestrus). LHRH mRNA was determined by quantitative in situ hybridization in serial coronal sections of the hypothalamus. The concentrations of LHRH mRNA in perikarya in the medial preoptic area, diagonal band of Broca and medial septum were significantly greater in EB compared with oil-treated control animals (Rosie et al., 1990). Thus, oestradiol in its positive feedback mode stimulates the synthesis of LHRH mRNA. This increased synthesis of LHRH mRNA correlates with increased hypothalamic content of LHRH which can be detected in the adult (Chiappa and Fink, 1977), but is seen much more clearly during the first pro-oestrus (Sarkar and Fink, 1979b).

How does oestradiol stimulate LHRH biosynthesis and release?

Since LHRH neurons do not contain oestradiol receptors (Shivers et al., 1983), the action of E_2 must be mediated by interneurons. Pharmacological and in situ hybridization data show that at least two potent stimulatory and two disinhibitory mechanisms could mediate the positive feedback action of E_2 on LHRH mRNA synthesis and LHRH release. With respect to the stimulatory mechanisms, pharmacological studies (Dow et al., 1994) carried out using the specific α_1 adrenoreceptor antagonist, prazosin, confirmed our

earlier findings with phenoxybenzamine (Sarkar and Fink, 1981) that an α_1 adrenoreceptor mechanism is involved in E_2 stimulation of LHRH and LH release. Prazosin also reduced the total number of LHRH mRNA containing cells in the preoptic area suggesting that an α_1 adrenoreceptor mechanism also mediates E_2 stimulation of LHRH mRNA synthesis (Rosie et al., 1994). Prazosin also blocked the E_2-induced decrease of POMC mRNA expression in the arcuate nucleus (Rosie et al., 1994). Thus, stimulation by E_2 of an α_1 adrenoreceptor mechanism could exert a direct effect on LHRH neurons and, for reasons outlined below, could also stimulate LHRH synthesis and release by the inhibition of arcuate POMC neurons which are known to project to LHRH cell bodies and send projections to the median eminence where they are juxtaposed to and may inhibit LHRH neurons.

Oestradiol-17β stimulation of LHRH biosynthesis and release also involves 5-HT which has been shown to play an important role in stimulating LH release under conditions of high levels of E_2 (Weiner et al., 1988). Guided by our in situ hybridization studies which showed that in our E_2 positive feedback model (Rosie et al., 1990), there was a massive and apparently selective stimulation of $5\text{-}HT_2$ receptor mRNA in the dorsal raphe nucleus (Sumner and Fink, 1993), we focused attention on the role of $5\text{-}HT_2$ receptors, and found that the specific $5\text{-}HT_2$ receptor antagonist, ritanserin, blocked the spontaneous LH surge in pro-oestrous rats (Dow et al., 1994). The mixed $5\text{-}HT_2/\alpha_1$ adrenoreceptor antagonist, ketanserin, not only blocked the LH surge, but also blocked basal LH release. Taken together, these data suggest the E_2 stimulation of LHRH biosynthesis and release is mediated by an α_1 adrenoreceptor and a $5\text{-}HT_2$ receptor mechanism (Fig. 2).

With respect to disinhibitory mechanisms, the most parsimonious hypothesis consists of an opioid and dopaminergic "clamp" whereby arcuate proopiomelanocortin (POMC) containing neurons and dopaminergic (DA) neurons inhibit LHRH neurons (Fig. 3). Both DA and POMC neurons are known to project to the external layer of the median eminence where these terminals are close to those of LHRH neurons. Proopiomelanocortin (β-endorphin) terminals also

142

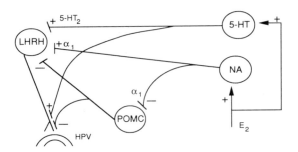

Fig. 2. Schematic diagram illustrating how E_2 could stimulate LHRH biosynthesis and release into the hypophysial portal vessels (HPV) by stimulating noradrenergic (NA) and 5-hydroxytryptamine (5-HT) neurons. The NA and 5-HT neurons (shown schematically in midbrain nuclei) could have a direct action on LHRH neurons by way of α_1 and 5-HT$_2$ receptors, respectively (Dow et al., 1994; Rosie et al., 1994). Our data also suggest that NA neurons could mediate E_2 inhibition of pro-opiomelanocortin (POMC) neurons. Since POMC neurons, at low E_2 levels, normally inhibit LHRH biosynthesis and release, inhibition of POMC neurons would disinhibit LHRH neurons. Other neurotransmitters (e.g. GABA and neuropeptide Y) and more complex neural circuits may also be involved. With respect to circuits, Morello and Taleisnik (1988) and Morello et al. (1989), for example, suggest that dorsal raphe 5-HT neurons stimulate LH release by an adrenergic mechanism involving the locus coeruleus and that medial raphe 5-HT neurons inhibit LH release by way of a GABAergic mechanism. (+, stimulation; —, inhibition).

represent about 9% of all synaptic input to LHRH neurons (Chen et al., 1989). The hypothesis (Fink, 1988) is that in the presence of low levels of oestradiol-17β, arcuate POMC and DA neurons inhibit LHRH biosynthesis and release; when plasma oestradiol-17β concentrations rise to surge levels, POMC and DA neurons are switched off and as a consequence LHRH neurons are disinhibited leading to LHRH biosynthesis and release. Since DA is known to inhibit prolactin release, the inhibition of DA neurons by oestrogen could also result in the spontaneous pre-ovulatory prolactin surge which occurs concurrently with the ovulatory gonadotrophin surge in rat and man (Djahanbakhch et al., 1984; Fink, 1988).

Numerous previous data show that opioids inhibit LH release (Kalra, 1986) and that the selective destruction of tuberoinfundibular DA neurons stimulates LHRH and LH release (Sarkar et al., 1981). With respect to the role of arcuate POMC neurons, E_2 significantly reduced POMC mRNA levels in the anterior region of the arcuate nucleus (Thomson et al., 1990)

and E_2 can significantly reduce POMC transcription within 60 min (Roberts et al., 1986). These results together with those of Wise et al. (1990) are compatible with the possibility that the stimulation of LHRH biosynthesis and release by oestrogen positive feedback may be mediated, in part, by disinhibition of LHRH neurons as a consequence of inhibiting POMC biosynthesis in arcuate neurons that project to and, at low E_2 levels, inhibit LHRH neurons. As pointed out above, the action of E_2 on POMC neurons may be mediated by an α_1 adrenoreceptor mechanism.

This hypothesis is probably grossly oversimplified in that other neurotransmitters, such as GABA, excitatory amino acids and other neuropeptides (e.g. neuropeptide Y) may also modulate LHRH biosynthesis and release. Nonetheless, this hypothesis and the data are important for our understanding of how E_2 regulates LHRH biosynthesis and release, and in addition provide important principles that are relevant to central neurotransmission in general. In particular, the hypothesis focuses attention on inhibitory mechanisms that are common (probably the most common mechanism) within the central nervous system. Corroborative evidence for the role of the inhibitory and disinhibitory mechanisms in LHRH release comes from metabolic studies which showed that 2-[^{14}C]deoxyglucose utilization was markedly reduced in the arcuate nucleus, median eminence and preoptic area around the time of the spontaneous ovulatory LH surge (McQueen and Fink, 1988).

The mechanism of E_2 action: principles from the LHRH priming effect

The priming effect of LHRH is briefly discussed here because recent studies have pointed to a possible common mechanism of action of LHRH and oestrogen. The priming effect of LHRH (for definition see above) differs from the simple releasing action of LHRH in that it (i) cannot be mimicked by K$^+$ depolarization or Ca^{2+} ionophores, (ii) is independent of normal extracellular Ca^{2+} concentrations, (iii) involves an elongation and change in orientation of the microfilaments, (iv) involves the movement of secretory granules towards the plasma membrane of im-

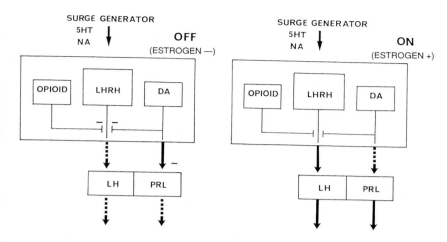

Fig. 3. A highly schematic diagram illustrating the hypothesis of the "opioid and dopamine (DA) clamp". The hypothesis is based on (i) the close juxtaposition of DA, POMC (β-endorphin) and LHRH neurons in the median eminence, (ii) the fact that both DA and opioids inhibit LHRH release, and (iii) that E_2 inhibits POMC gene transcription and reduces POMC mRNA levels in arcuate neurons. Thus, at low E_2 concentrations, the opioid and DA neurons are active and inhibit LHRH release, while at high E_2 concentrations, presumed to reduce opioid (β-endorphin) and DA neuronal activity, LHRH neurons are disinhibited and, therefore, release LHRH. A similar mechanism may operate for LHRH biosynthesis (see text). Neuronal inhibition and disinhibition are powerful and precise control mechanisms which operate widely throughout the nervous system. The diagram also shows that at low E_2 concentrations, the presumed higher release of DA into hypophysial portal blood may inhibit prolactin (PRL) release, while at high E_2 concentrations, DA release is reduced thereby allowing PRL release to occur. This is one of several mechanisms which can explain the concurrence of the LHRH/LH and PRL surges in the rat and the human. From Fink (1988) with permission.

muno-identified gonadotrophs ("margination") and (v) involves the synthesis of a new protein (Fink, 1988).

Our studies on LHRH priming show two important principles for the action of E_2. First, the pI and M_r (70 kDa) of the LHRH-induced protein were identical to those of an E_2-induced protein associated with mating behaviour in the female rat (Mobbs et al., 1990a). The amino acid residue sequences of the N-termini of the LHRH and E_2 induced proteins are identical to one another and with what was originally thought to be phospholipase $C\alpha$ (PLC-α) (Mobbs et al., 1990a,b). However, the existence of PLC-α is controversial and so with the aid of DNA complementary to the LHRH/E_2-induced protein, further studies are now in progress to determine its precise role.

Secondly, it is important to stress that massive changes in pituitary responsiveness cannot simply be attributed to changes in LHRH binding to LHRH receptors (Clayton et al., 1986). That is, the efficacy of

LHRH in evoking the LH surge is dependent upon potentiation of post receptor intracellular signalling events. Thus, for example, we have shown that LHRH priming involves a massive potentiation of (i) the IP_3 released in pituitary tissue in response to LHRH, and (ii) the efflux of Ca^{2+} from pituitary slices (indicative of increased release of Ca^{2+} from intracellular stores) (Mitchell et al., 1988).

LHRH is also known to stimulate lordosis (mating) behaviour about 1 h after injection into the mid brain central grey. Thus, the 70 kDa protein may be an important component of a mechanism common to both LHRH and oestrogen which is involved in massive potentiation of pituitary responsiveness to LHRH and also of lordosis behaviour. In terms of intracellular signalling, the priming effect of LHRH may also provide a useful model for studies of long-term potentiation in brain, in that both phenomena may be dependent on activation of protein kinase C by a "conditioning stimulus" (Johnson et al., 1992).

Long-term reversible effects of steroids

Steroid effects on AVP neurons of the bed nucleus of the stria terminalis (BNST)

De Vries et al. (1986) first demonstrated that there is a marked sex difference in the vasopressinergic innervation of the rat brain outside the classical hypothalamic-neurohypophysial system. These sex steroid-dependent differences are most pronounced in the lateral habenula and lateral septum in which there is a dense plexus of AVP containing fibres which project from BNST perikarya thought to play a crucial role in "social memory" (Dantzer et al., 1988). We confirmed these findings in the mouse and showed that no immunoreactive AVP fibres are present in the lateral habenula of the LHRH deficient mutant hypogonadal (*hpg*) mouse (Mayes et al., 1988). AVP-containing fibres in the lateral habenula can be induced in *hpg* mice by the insertion of a hypothalamic graft from normal mice into the third ventricle. The graft innervates the hypophysial portal vessels with LHRH-containing terminals which stimulate gonadotrophin and thereby testosterone secretion which in turn stimulates the male pattern of AVP-containing fibres in the habenula (Mayes et al., 1988). The administra-

tion of testosterone or oestrogen, but not the non-aromatizable androgen, 5α-dihydrotestosterone, to male *hpg* mice also results in the normal development of AVP fibres in the lateral habenula. The substantially higher concentrations of AVP fibres in male compared with female brain suggests that the amount of oestrogen in the male brain is higher than in the female presumably because the amount of testosterone available for conversion to oestrogen by aromatase exceeds significantly the combined effect of small amounts of androgen and relatively small amounts (by comparison with testosterone in the male) of oestrogen in the female.

Our recent studies were designed to determine whether the action of the gonadal sex steroids was due to stimulation of AVP biosynthesis as assessed by determination of AVP mRNA by in situ hybridization using a ^{35}S-labelled 49 mer oligonucleotide probe complementary to the 5′ end of the glycopeptide coding domain of AVP mRNA (Rosie et al., 1993). Exposure to supraphysiological concentrations of testosterone for 6–12 days induced an exponential, 50-fold increase in the number of cells that expressed AVP mRNA in the BNST in *hpg* mice (Fig. 4). Similar results were obtained in the adult rat (Miller et al., 1989). The action of testosterone is "all-or-none" in

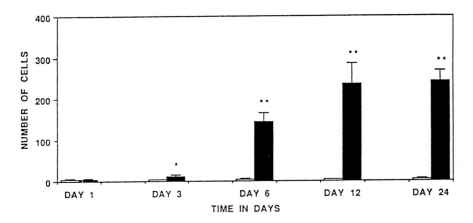

Fig. 4. The mean (±SEM) number of cells expressing AVP mRNA in the BNST of hypogonadal (*hpg*) mice at different times after implanting either empty (open bars) or testosterone-propionate filled (closed bars) silicone elastomer capsules. Note the exponential increase in the number of cells expressing AVP mRNA between days 3 and 6 of implanting the testosterone-propionate filled capsules. Significance of differences (Mann-Whitney *U*-test): *$P < 0.05$; **$P < 0.01$. From Rosie et al. (1993) with permission.

that the level of AVP mRNA in the AVP-positive cells was similar at all times after testosterone implantation and also similar or less than that in the few AVP-positive cells in animals not treated with testosterone (Rosie et al., 1993). The relatively long time taken for testosterone to exert its effect on AVP mRNA in BNST neurons is consistent with its effect on AVP immunoreactivity in the lateral habenula and lateral septum and on behaviour and suggests that the action of testosterone may be mediated by indirect or slow intracellular transduction mechanisms. Relevant to this are the preliminary findings (J Quinn, unpublished) in our laboratory that the $5'$ promoter region of the AVP gene contains a steroid response element, an AP1 site and three E-boxes (members of the helix-loop-helix family of proteins often involved in tissue-specific expression) flanked by CT elements. The latter suggest that the action of E_2 on AVP gene expression may involve a complex interaction of activated E_2 receptor and other transcription factors.

Conclusions

Because of their potent actions on brain-pituitary functions, and because so much is already known about steroid receptors and their interactions with steroid response elements on genes in general, the study of steroid action on brain and pituitary offers a powerful method of establishing key principles about the molecular mechanisms that underlie central neurotransmission. Attention here is focused on acute and longer-term stimulatory effects of gonadal steroids: (i) the stimulation by E_2 of LHRH biosynthesis and the LHRH surge, and (ii) the biosynthesis of AVP in the bed nucleus of the stria terminalis. The action of E_2 is not due to a direct action on LHRH neurons, but is mediated by interneurons involving at least four possibly separate mechanisms; two stimulatory (α_1 adrenoreceptor and 5-HT$_2$ receptor) and at least two disinhibitory (POMC and dopaminergic). Teleologically, the need for four systems to control E_2 induced LHRH biosynthesis and release is probably because the secretion of LHRH is essential for fertility and reproduction of the species. The mechanism of action of oestradiol in increasing pituitary responsiveness to

LHRH is not yet established, but the synthesis of new proteins and the potentiation of post-receptor mechanisms are involved. Oestrogen is also essential for mating behaviour and for increased motor activity that both reach a peak at the time of ovulation early on oestrus (Fink, 1988). There is a remarkable economy in this system in which the same steroid secreted by the ovary activates in a precisely timed manner the mechanisms (amplifier cascades) required for the ovulatory surge of LH and for mating. The stimulation by E_2 of LHRH biosynthesis, the surge-release and action of LHRH, and the stimulation by gonadal steroids of AVP biosynthesis in the BNST provide excellent models for studies of the role of the regulation of gene expression in central neurotransmission which underlies phenomena that involve relatively lengthy (hours to days) biochemical cascades. The two models also provide the basis for precise correlative studies between steroid control of CNS gene expression, central neurotransmission and behaviour.

References

Baulieu, E.E. (1993) Neurosteroids: a function of the brain. In: R. Mornex, C. Jaffiol and J. Leclère (Eds.), *Progress in Endocrinology, 9th Int. Congress of Endocrinology*, Nice, Parthenon Publishing, pp. 147–151.

Chen, W.-P., Witkin, J.W. and Silverman, A.-J. (1989) Beta-endorphin and gonadotropin-releasing hormone synaptic input to gonadotropin-releasing hormone neurosecretory cells in the male rat. *J. Comp. Neurol.*, 286: 85–95.

Chiappa, S.A. and Fink, G. (1977) Hypothalamic luteinizing hormone releasing factor and corticotrophin releasing activity in relation to pituitary and plasma hormone levels in male and female rats. *J. Endocrinol.*, 72: 195–210.

Clayton, R.N., Young, L.S., Naik, S.I., Detta, A. and Abbot, S.D. (1986) Pituitary GnRH receptors – recent studies and their functional significance. In: G. Fink, A.J. Harmar and K.W. McKerns (Eds.), *Neuroendocrine Molecular Biology*, Plenum Press, New York, pp. 429–440.

Cross, B.A., Dyball, R.E.J., Dyer, R.G., Jones, C.W., Lincoln, D.W., Morris, J.F. and Pickering, B.T. (1975) Endocrine neurons. *Recent Prog. Horm. Res.*, 31: 243–286.

Dantzer, R., Koob, G.F., Bluthé, R.-M. and Le Moal, M. (1988) Septal vasopressin modulates social memory in male rats. *Brain Res.*, 457: 143–147.

De Vries, G.J., Duetz, W., Buijs, R.M., van Heerikhuize, J. and Vreeburg, J.T.M. (1986) Effects of androgens and estrogens on the vasopressin and oxytocin innervation of the adult rat brain. *Brain Res.*, 399: 296–302.

Djahanbakhch, O., McNeilly, A.S., Warner, P.M., Swanston, I.A.

and Baird, D.T. (1984) Changes in plasma levels of prolactin, in relation to those of FSH, oestradiol, androstenedione and progesterone around the preovulatory surge of LH in women. *Clin. Endocrinol.*, 20: 463.

Dockray, G.J. (1988) Regulatory peptides and the neuroendocrinology of gut-brain relations. *Q. J. Exp. Physiol.*, 73: 703–727.

Dow, R.C., Williams, B.C., Bennie, J., Carroll, S. and Fink, G. (1994) A central 5-HT$_2$ receptor mechanism plays a key role in the proestrus surge of luteinizing hormone but not prolactin in the rat. *Psychoneuroendocrinology*, in press.

Fink, G. (1976) The development of the releasing factor concept. *Clin. Endocrinol.*, 5: 245s–260s.

Fink, G. (1979a) Feedback actions of target hormones on hypothalamus and pituitary with special reference to gonadal steroids. *Annu. Rev. Physiol.*, 41: 571–585.

Fink, G. (1979b) Neuroendocrine control of gonadotrophin secretion. *Br. Med. Bull.*, 35: 155–160.

Fink, G. (1988) The G.W. Harris Lecture. Steroid control of brain and pituitary function. *Q. J. Exp. Physiol.*, 73: 257–293.

Fink, G. and Sheward, W.J. (1989) Neuropeptide release in vivo: measurement in hypophysial portal blood. In: G. Fink and A.J. Harmar (Eds.), *Neuropeptides: A Methodology*, Wiley, Chichester, UK, pp. 157–188.

Fink, G., Sarkar, D.K., Dow, R.C., Dick, H., Borthwick, N., Malnick, S. and Twine, M. (1982) Sex difference in response to alphaxalone anaesthesia may be oestrogen dependent. *Nature*, 298: 270–272.

Johnson Jr, R.G. (1988) Accummulation of biological amines into chromaffin granules: a model for hormone and neurotransmitter transport. *Physiol. Rev.*, 68: 232–307.

Johnson, M.S., Mitchell, R. and Thomson, F.J. (1992) The priming effect of luteinizing hormone-releasing hormone (LHRH) but not LHRH-induced gonadotropin release, can be prevented by certain protein kinase C inhibitors. *Mol. Cell. Endocrinol.*, 85: 183–193.

Kalra, S.P. (1986) Neural circuitry involved in the control of LHRH secretion: a model for preovulatory LH release. In: W.F. Ganong and L. Martini (Eds.), *Frontiers in Neuroendocrinology*, Raven Press, New York, pp. 31–75.

Majewska, M.D. (1987) Steroids and brain activity: essential dialogue between body and mind. *Biochem. Pharmacol.*, 36: 3781–3788.

Mayes, C.R., Watts, A.G., McQueen, J.K., Fink, G. and Charlton, H.M. (1988) Gonadal steroids influence neurophysin II distribution in the forebrain of normal and mutant mice. *Neuroscience*, 25: 1013–1022.

McEwen, B.S., de Kloet, E.R. and Rostene, W. (1986) Adrenal steroid receptors and actions in the nervous system. *Physiol. Rev.*, 66: 1121–1188.

McQueen, J.K. and Fink, G. (1988) Changes in local cerebral glucose utilization associated with the spontaneous ovulatory surge of luteinizing hormone in the rat. *Neuroendocrinology*, 47: 551–555.

Miller, M.A., Urban, J.H. and Dorsa, D.M. (1989) Steroid dependency of vasopressin neurons in the bed nucleus of the stria terminalis by *in situ* hybridization. *Endocrinology*, 125: 2335–2340.

Mitchell, R., Johnson, M., Ogier, S.-A. and Fink, G. (1988) Facili-

tated calcium mobilization and inositol phosphate production in the priming effect of LH-releasing hormone in the rat. *J. Endocrinol.*, 119: 293–301.

Mobbs, C.V., Fink, G. and Pfaff, D.W. (1990a) HIP-70: a protein induced by estrogen in the brain and LH-RH in the pituitary. *Science*, 247: 1477–1479.

Mobbs, C.V., Fink, G. and Pfaff, D.W. (1990b) HIP-70: An isoform of phosphoinositol-specific phospholipase C-α. *Science*, 249: 566–567.

Morello, H. and Taleisnik, S. (1988) The inhibition of proestrous LH surge and ovulation in rats bearing lesions of the dorsal raphe nucleus is mediated by the locus coeruleus. *Brain Res.*, 440: 227–231.

Morello, H., Caligaris, L., Haymal, B. and Taleisnik, S (1989) Inhibition of proestrous LH surge and ovulation in rats evoked by stimulation of the medial raphe nucleus involves a GABA-mediated mechanism. *Neuroendocrinology*, 50: 81–87.

North, W.G., Moses, A.M. and Share, L. (Eds.) (1993) The neurohypophysis: a window on brain function. *Ann. N. Y. Acad. Sci.*, 689: pp. 701.

Roberts, J.L., Wilcox, J.N. and Blum, M. (1986) The regulation of proopiomelanocortin gene expression by estrogen in the rat hypothalamus. In: G. Fink, A.J. Harmar and K.W. McKerns (Eds.), *Neuroendocrine Molecular Biology*, Plenum Press, New York, pp. 261–270.

Rosie, R., Thomson, E. and Fink, G. (1990) Oestrogen positive feedback stimulates the synthesis of LHRH mRNA in neurons of the rostral diencephalon of the rat. *J. Endocrinol.*, 124: 285–289.

Rosie, R., Wilson, H. and Fink, G. (1993) Testosterone induces an all-or-none, exponential increase in arginine vasopressin mRNA in the bed nucleus of stria terminalis of the *hypogonadal* mouse. *Mol. Cell. Neurosci.*, 4: 121–126.

Rosie, R., Sumner, B.E.H. and Fink, G. (1994) An α_1 adrenergic mechanism mediates estradiol stimulation of LHRH mRNA synthesis and estradiol inhibition of POMC mRNA synthesis in the hypothalamus of the prepubertal female rat. *J. Steroid Biochem. Mol. Biol.*, 49: in press.

Sachs, H., Fawcett, P., Takabatake, Y. and Portanova, R. (1969) Biosynthesis and release of vasopressin and neurophysin. *Recent Prog. Horm. Res.*, 25: 447–484.

Sarkar, D.K. and Fink, G. (1979a) Effects of gonadal steroids on output of luteinizing hormone releasing factor into pituitary stalk blood in the female rat. *J. Endocrinol.*, 80: 303–313.

Sarkar, D.K. and Fink, G. (1979b) Mechanism of the first spontaneous gonadotrophin surge and that induced by pregnant mare serum and effects of neonatal androgen in rats. *J. Endocrinol.*, 83: 339–354.

Sarkar, D.K. and Fink, G. (1981) Gonadotropin-releasing hormone surge: possible modulation through postsynaptic α-adrenoreceptors and two pharmacologically distinct dopamine receptors. *Endocrinology*, 108: 862–867.

Sarkar, D.K., Smith, G.C. and Fink, G. (1981) Effect of manipulating central catecholamines on puberty and the surge of luteinizing hormone and gonadotropin releasing hormone induced by pregnant mare serum gonadotropin in female rats. *Brain Res.*, 213: 335–349.

Shivers, B.D., Harlan, R.E., Morrell, J.E. and Pfaff, D.W. (1983) Absence of oestradiol concentration in cell nuclei of LHRH-immunoreactive neurones. *Nature*, 304: 345–347.

Sokol, H.W. and Valtin, H. (Eds.) (1982) The Brattleboro rat. *Ann. N. Y. Acad. Sci.*, 394: pp. 828.

Sumner, B.E.H. and Fink, G. (1993) Effects of acute estradiol on 5-hydroxytryptamine and dopamine receptor subtype mRNA expression in female rat brain. *Mol. Cell. Neurosci.*, 4: 83–92.

Thomson, E., Rosie, R., Blum, M., Roberts, J.L. and Fink, G. (1990) Estrogen positive feedback reduces arcuate pro-opiomelanocortin mRNA. *Neuroendocrinology*, 52: P3.17.

Weiner, R.I., Findell, P.R. and Kordon, C. (1988) Role of classic and peptide neuromediators in the neuroendocrine regulation of LH and prolactin. In: E. Knobil and J. Neill (Eds.), *The Physiology of Reproduction*, Raven Press, New York, pp. 1235–1281.

Wise, P.M., Scarbrough, K., Weiland, N.G. and Larson, G.H. (1990) Diurnal pattern of proopiomelanocortin gene expression in the arcuate nucleus of proestrous, ovariectomized, and steroid-treated rats; a possible role in cyclic luteinizing hormone secretion. *Mol. Endocrinol.* 4: 886–892.

F. Bloom (Editor)
Progress in Brain Research, Vol. 100
© 1994 Elsevier Science B.V. All rights reserved

Resolving a mystery: progress in understanding the function of adrenal steroid receptors in hippocampus

Bruce S. McEwen, Heather Cameron, Helen M. Chao, Elizabeth Gould, Victoria Luine[1], Ana Maria Magarinos, Constantine Pavlides, Robert L. Spencer, Yoshifumi Watanabe and Catherine Woolley

Laboratory of Neuroendocrinology, Rockefeller University, 1230 York Avenue, New York, NY 10021, USA; and [1]Department of Psychology, Hunter College, New York 10021, NY, USA

Introduction

In 1968, we reported that the adrenal glucocorticoid, corticosterone, was taken up and retained in high levels by the hippocampal formation of adrenalectomized rats (McEwen et al., 1968). The hippocampal localization of corticosterone was a complete surprise, since sex hormones, such as estradiol, were known to be taken up and retained by the hypothalamus and preoptic area of gonadectomized rats. Moreover, the hippocampus was not known to be directly associated with neuroendocrine function, whereas the hypothalamus and preoptic area are designated as the "hypophysiotrophic area" and are involved in control of gonadotrophin secretion and sexual behavior.

The hippocampus is recognized for its involvement in learning and memory, and for its plasticity in relation to spatial orientation and working memory (Eichenbaum and Otto, 1992). It has been only very recently that we have begun to understand some of the significance of adrenal steroid action on the hippocampus. The evolution of this knowledge is the subject of this short review. What we and others have found is that adrenal steroids play multiple roles in the structural and functional plasticity of the hippocampal formation.

Two adrenal steroid receptor types in the brain

Uptake and retention of ^3H steroid hormones by cells is the result of binding of the hormone by intracellular receptors that end up in the cell nuclear compartment, where these receptors bind to specific nucleotide sequences on DNA known as "hormone responsive elements" (Miner and Yamamoto, 1991). The uptake and retention of adrenal steroids by the hippocampus, first found in the rat, has been demonstrated in species as divergent as the duck and the rhesus monkey and this seems to be a widespread and evolutionarily stable trait of the hippocampal region (reviewed in McEwen et al., 1986).

Although it was first thought to reflect a single intracellular receptor type, we now know that two distinct adrenal steroid receptor types are present not only in hippocampus but also in other brain regions and in other tissues of the body. There were four steps in recognizing this fact (for review, see McEwen et al., 1986):

(1) Studies on the kidney in the early 1970s revealed two adrenal steroid receptor types, referred to as Type I and Type II;

(2) Radioimmunoassay of cell nuclear corticosterone in rats exposed in vivo to low, intermediate and

high levels of corticosterone revealed high affinity and lower affinity nuclear retention of the steroid;

(3) Type I and Type II receptors were definitively demonstrated in hippocampus using specific agonist and antagonist steroids in specific binding assays;

(4) The cloning of mineralocorticoid (Type I) and glucocorticoid (Type II) receptors demonstrated each form to be the product of a distinct gene; the mRNA for both receptors can be demonstrated in the hippocampus (Fig. 1). It is the Type I (mineralocorticoid) receptor that is concentrated in the hippocampal formation; this receptor, because of its high affinity for ^{3}H corticosterone, picks up and retains tracer levels of steroid injected into ADX rats, as we found in 1968 (see above).

Receptors in search of a function

Clues to the role of adrenal steroid receptors in hippocampus emerged slowly at first, but progress has accelerated during the past 10 years. The first effects of adrenal steroids concerned destruction of neural tissue, but later findings pointed to additional effects that protect neurons and enhance plasticity.

Neuronal destruction

The first clue regarding an effect of adrenal steroids in the hippocampus was the finding that ACTH or cortisone treatment of guinea pigs caused necrosis of pyramidal neurons of the hippocampus (for review, see

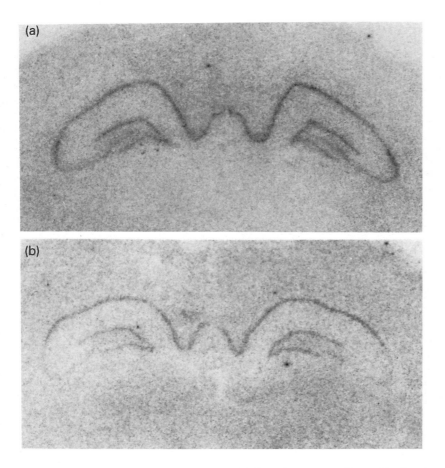

Fig. 1. In situ hybridization to rat hippocampus with riboprobes corresponding to (*A*) mineralocorticoid (Type I) receptor, MR; and (*B*) glucocorticoid (Type II) receptor, GR. Details of the hybridization procedure may be found in Chao et al. (1994).

Sapolsky, 1992). Subsequently, Landfield and co-workers found that aging in the rat results in some pyramidal neuron loss in hippocampus that can be retarded by adrenalectomy in mid-life (Landfield, 1987). Sapolsky then demonstrated that daily corticosterone injections into young adult rats over 12 weeks mimicked the pyramidal neuron loss seen in aging; he went on to demonstrate that excitatory amino acids play an important role in the cell loss by showing, first, that corticosterone exacerbates kainic acid-induced damage to hippocampus, as well as ischemic damage; and, second, that glucocorticoids potentiate excitatory amino acid-killing of hippocampal neurons in culture (Sapolsky, 1992).

In order to examine what actually happens to hippocampal neurons as a result of high levels of glucocorticoids, we have recently used the single section Golgi technique to demonstrate that, after 21 days of daily corticosterone exposure, the apical dendritic tree of CA3 pyramidal neurons has atrophied (Gould et al., 1991) (see Fig. 2). Moreover, this atrophy is prevented by the anti-epileptic drug, phenytoin, given prior to corticosterone each day, thus implicating the release and actions of excitatory amino acids in the process (Watanabe et al., 1992). The effect of corticosterone on dendritic length and branching is not found on basal dendrites of CA3 pyramidal neurons, nor on CA1 pyramidal neurons or dentate gyrus granule neurons; this specificity suggests that the mossy fiber input from the dentate gyrus may be involved (Gould et al., 1991). In this connection, the sensitivity of the CA3 pyramidal neurons is reminiscent of the specific damage to CA3 neurons as a result of kainic acid infusion or of epileptigenic stimulation of the perforant pathway, both of which are attributable to the mossy fiber input to CA3 from the dentate gyrus (for review, see McEwen et al., 1993).

In order to find out if the dendritic atrophy occurs under physiological conditions, we investigated the effects of repeated stress, which is known to induce glucocorticoid secretion. Restraint stress for 21 days produced atrophy that could be blocked by two agents: (1) cyanoketone, which inhibits adrenal steroid formation (Magarinos and McEwen, 1993); and (2) phenytoin, which prevents excitatory amino acid re-

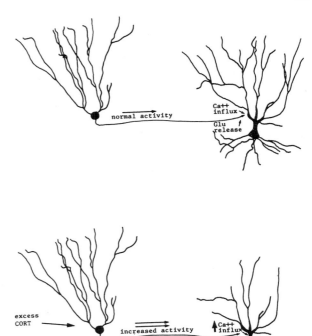

Fig. 2. Schematic diagram showing atrophy of apical dendrites of CA3 pyramidal neurons of hippocampus as a result of the synergistic interaction between excitatory amino acids released by mossy fibers and circulating glucocorticoids released by stress or administered by injection. Reprinted from Gould et al., 1991, by permission.

lease and actions via T-type calcium channels (for data and review, see Watanabe et al., 1992). These findings support the notion that the stress-induced surge of glucocorticoids facilitates the release of excitatory amino acids, which, in turn, produces the morphological changes. Evidence in support of a causal link between adrenocortical secretion and glutamate release, measured indirectly by lactic acid formation, has been provided recently (Krugers et al., 1992).

More severe and prolonged stress (e.g. cold swim; and social, i.e. dominance/subordinance hierarchies in rats) produce actual loss of hippocampal neurons (Mizoguchi et al., 1992; Sapolsky, 1992). We do not yet know the relationship of the dendritic atrophy to cell loss: i.e. whereas it is attractive to suppose that

152

atrophy may represent the first stage of cell damage, the fact that this atrophy is reversible (Magarinos, unpublished data) and that it occurs on apical, but not on basal, dendrites argues that it may be an adaptive process by viable cells.

Death and replacement of dentate gyrus granule neurons

In contrast to pyramidal neurons of Ammons horn, granule neurons of the adult dentate gyrus depend on adrenal steroids for their survival (see Fig. 3). Moreover, continuous replacement of granule neurons oc-

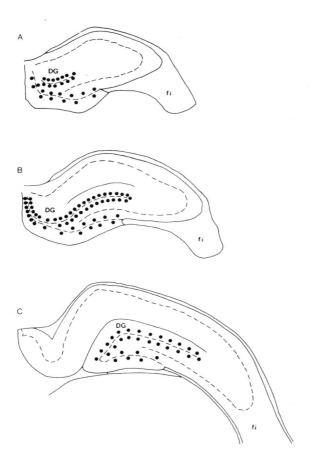

Fig. 3. Pyknotic granule neurons in dentate gyrus are distributed throughout entire hippocampal formation 7 days after bilateral adrenalectomy in adult life. Reprinted from Gould et al. (1990) by permission.

curs in the adult dentate gyrus; and both neurogenesis and cell death increase following adrenalectomy suggesting that it may be the death of neurons that signals the formation of replacement neurons (Gould and McEwen, 1993).

The first clue as to the magnitude of the adrenalectomy effect on neuronal death in dentate gyrus was the finding that, 3 months after ADX of adult rats, some rats showed almost total loss of dentate gyrus granule neurons (Sloviter et al., 1989). This finding attracted much attention because it contrasted with the prevalent view of stress- and glucocorticoid-induced neuronal death in Ammons horn. It was also very puzzling because only some ADX rats showed the effect.

In retrospect, we now understand both of these unusual aspects. First, the selectivity of the ADX effect on killing of dentate gyrus granule neurons has been verified in that it does not occur in other neuronal populations. Moreover, it may be related to the unusual nature of the dentate gyrus, which arises postnatally and continues to generate new neurons in adult life (Gould and McEwen, 1993). Second, the occurrence of cell death only in some rats is related to accessory adrenal tissue; when not removed at the time of ADX, this tissue can supply enough adrenal steroids to prevent neuronal loss; indeed, very low levels of adrenal steroids, sufficient to occupy Type I adrenal steroid receptors (see above) completely blocks dentate gyrus neuronal loss.

Adrenalectomy is not a natural event, and thus one must consider the physiological role of this type of plasticity. One explanation for why the dentate gyrus can make new cells in adult life, as well as get rid of them, is that the hippocampus may change during adult life in relation to its function in spatial orientation and memory (Sherry et al., 1992). Birds that use space around them to hide and locate food, and voles that use their environment to find mates, have larger hippocampal volumes than species that do not; moreover, there are indications that hippocampal volume may change under some circumstances, e.g. with the season of the year (Sherry et al., 1992). It remains to be seen whether it is the dentate gyrus that changes under these changing conditions.

Long-term potentiation

A much more rapid form of plasticity is long-term potentiation. A single burst of high frequency stimulation can immediately alter the responsiveness of neurons to further stimuli, an effect lasting over a time course of many hours to days. A number of in vitro studies have demonstrated, in the hippocampal CA1 field, that acute stress produces an impairment in LTP or in primed-burst potentiation (PBP) (for references, see Diamond et al., 1992; Pavlides et al., 1993a). In these studies, a negative correlation was also seen between the degree of LTP induced and plasma corticosterone levels. More recently, an inverted U-shaped curve was found with regard to induction of PBP in CA1 in relation to circulating glucocorticoid levels (Diamond et al., 1992). That is, both insufficiency as well as high levels of corticosterone had a detrimental effect on PBP; optimal potentiation was obtained at an intermediate level (10–20 μg/dl) of circulating corticosterone.

Within the dentate gyrus, an acute administration of corticosterone has also been shown to produce a decrement in LTP (for data and references, see Pavlides et al., 1993a). The most recent data, however, indicates that LTP can be modulated biphasically by adrenal steroids acting, respectively, via Type I and Type II receptors. In the dentate gyrus, LTP was found to be modulated by adrenal steroids acting via Type I and Type II receptors. Type I receptor stimulation in ADX rats was found to enhance LTP within an hour, whereas Type II receptor stimulation in ADX rats was found to suppress LTP (Pavlides et al., 1993b) (see Fig. 4). These biphasic effects help to explain a biphasic dose response curve with respect to induction of primed-burst potentiation (PBP) in the CA1 region of Ammon's horn, in which low levels of corticosterone within the daily variation of basal secretion facilitate PBP and stress levels of corticosterone inhibit PBP (Diamond et al., 1992).

That the CA1 responds in a similar manner as the dentate gyrus to corticosteroids is not surprising, for two reasons. First, Type I and Type II receptors coexist in pyramidal neurons and dentate gyrus granule neurons (for review, see McEwen et al., 1986). Sec-

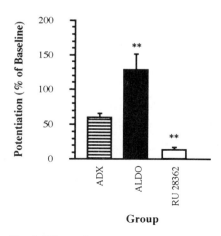

Fig. 4. Effects of Type I and Type II adrenal steroid receptors on dentate gyrus long-term potentiation. Extracellular field potentials were recorded in the dentate gyrus granule cell layer with stimulation of the medial perforant pathway. Animals were ADX (2 days prior to the experiment) and received an acute peripheral injection of either vehicle, the Type I agonist, aldosterone (100 μg/kg) or the Type II agonist, Ru 28362 (100 μg/kg). In comparison to the ADX controls, high frequency stimulation in the aldosterone injected animals produced a significant ($p < 0.001$) enhancement of long-term potentiation. In contrast, Ru 28362 elicited a pronounced suppression of LTP. Specific Type I and Type II antagonists reversed these effects (data not shown; see Pavlides et al., 1993a).

ond, in CA1 pyramidal neurons, corticosteroids biphasically modulate excitability: i.e. Type I receptor stimulation facilitates excitability by disinhibiting a 5HT1A receptor input; while Type II receptor stimulation inhibits excitability by suppressing a beta receptor-mediated noradrenergic input (for review, see Joels and DeKloet, 1992).

Conclusions

It appears that adrenal steroid receptors in the hippocampus are not an enigma, after all, and that they mediate at least three types of morphological and functional changes in the hippocampus. Thus, the role of the hippocampus in learning and memory processes may be subject to regulation by circulating adrenal steroids over both short and long time periods. What is the possible physiological or pathophysiological significance of each of these types of plasticity?

Long-term potentiation and primed-burst potentiation, as noted above, are biphasically regulated by adrenal steroids, with basal levels of corticosterone facilitating, and stress levels of corticosterone inhibiting, the potentiation of the response. Type I and Type II receptors appear to mediate the rising and falling limbs, respectively. Based on the work of Diamond et al. (1992), it is tempting to relate the rising limb of the biphasic curve to the increase in basal corticosterone secretion that precedes waking activity and the falling limb to the response to stressful stimuli. Since LTP or PBP may be related to learning and memory, it is important to note that there are indications that both adrenocortical insufficiency and exposure to excess adrenal steroids adversely affect cognitive function in experimental animals and humans (Martigioni et al., 1992; Conrad and Roy, 1993) and that the waking period is associated with greater sensitivity as far as hippocampal evoked responses than the sleeping phase of the diurnal cycle (for review, see McEwen et al., 1992).

However, the effects of adrenocortical excess or insufficiency may not be due to acute actions of the hormone, but rather to the longer-term changes in hippocampal morphology that have also been described. Repeated restraint stress, which causes atrophy of apical dendrites of CA3 pyramidal neurons, impairs the initial learning of an 8-arm radial maze (Villegas et al., 1993); and Cushing's disease has been linked to a reduction in hippocampal volume, which, in turn, is correlated with decreased verbal memory function (Starkman et al., 1992). These two preliminary studies need to be followed up by extensive investigations of glucocorticoid effects on both rodent spatial maze learning and human cognitive function.

Adrenalectomy, which causes increased turnover of dentate granule neurons, has been shown to result in impaired spatial learning (Armstrong et al., 1993; Conrad and Roy, 1993; Vaher et al., 1993). However, it is not yet clear whether neuronal loss per se is responsible for the behavioral deficits. At the same time, acute effects of adrenal steroid replacement on spatial learning have been described, involving differential effects mediated by Type I and Type II receptors, indicating that rapid actions of adrenal steroids must always be reckoned with (Oitzl and DeKloet, 1992).

Thus the story of adrenal steroid receptors in the hippocampus continues to unfold in ever-widening circles that encompass other aspects of neuroscience and other aspects of neuroendocrinology. The adult hippocampus is also the site of two other types of hormonally directed plasticity. Estradiol and progesterone regulate the cyclic formation and breakdown of excitatory synapses on CA1 pyramidal neurons (Woolley and McEwen, 1992, 1993); and excess thyroid hormone promotes a reduction in dendritic spines on CA1 pyramidal neurons, whereas transient elevation of thyroid hormone neonatally produces a long-term increase of dendritic branching and spine density in the CA3 region of the hippocampal formation (for review, see Gould et al., 1991). It remains to be seen what interactive roles thyroid hormone balance, sex hormones and gender play, together with the actions of adrenal steroids, in determining the ability of the hippocampus to change its structure and function in response to the external environment.

Acknowledgments

Research support for work described in this review was obtained from NIH Grants NS 07080 and MH41256 to BMc and MH49184 to EG, as well as Air Force Grant F 49620 to BMc and CP. AMM was supported by Fogarty Fellowhship F05TW04499.

References

Armstrong, J.D., McIntyre, D.C., Neubort, S. and Sloviter, R.S. (1993) Learning and memory after adrenalectomy-induced hippocampal dentate granule cell degeneration in the rat. *Hippocampus*, 3: 359–371.

Chao, H., Blanchard, D.C., Blanchard, R.J., McEwen, B.S. and Sakai, R.R. (1994) The effect of social stress on hippocampal gene expression. *Mol. Cell. Neurosci.*, 4: 543–548.

Conrad, C.D. and Roy, E.J. (1993) Selective loss of hippocampal granule cells following adrenalectomy: implications for spatial memory. *J. Neurosci.*, 13: 2582-2590.

Diamond, D.M., Bennet, M.C., Fleshner, M. and Rose, G.M. (1992) Inverted-U relationship between the level of peripheral corticosterone and the magnitude of hippocampal primed burst potentiation. *Hippocampus*, 2: 421–430.

F. Bloom (Editor)
Progress in Brain Research, Vol. 100
© 1994 Elsevier Science B.V. All rights reserved

CHAPTER 20

Neural-immune interactions

Suzanne Y. Felten and David L. Felten

Department of Neurobiology and Anatomy, Box 603, University of Rochester School of Medicine and Dentistry, 601 Elmwood Avenue, Rochester, NY. 14642, USA

Introduction

At the heart of the emerging discipline of psycho-neuroimmunology is the contention that the nervous system can modulate the actions of the immune system. Further implications of this assumption are that stimuli from the environment of the organism that impact on and are processed by the nervous system, such as sensory stimuli, stress, and various psychosocial factors, can be translated by the nervous system into signals that may modulate the function of the immune system, thereby affecting health and potential illness from pathogens or tumors. Because the sum of experience, emotion, and environment come together in the CNS (limbic and cortical processing), the most provocative implication is that the "mind" (brain) may be able to influence health related to immunologic function.

Behavioral studies

Conditioning

In 1975, Ader and Cohen (reviewed in Ader and Cohen, 1991) reported that immune suppression caused by the drug cyclophosphamide could be conditioned using classical behavioral conditioning. This was not simply a conditioned stress response caused by glucocorticoid release, because it also could be elicited in adrenalectomized animals. Ader and colleagues further demonstrated that conditioned immunosuppression could be used to maintain autoimmune mice into old age with far less immunosuppressive drug than was required to keep unconditioned autoimmune mice alive. This work provides evidence that the CNS can detect immunologic reactivity of some types and can, in turn, generate immunoregulatory signals to the periphery. For these reasons, their work became one of the cornerstones of the emerging discipline of psychoneuroimmunology.

Stress

A variety of physical and psychological stressors have been found to alter cellular and humoral immunity (reviewed in Ader et al., 1990); sometimes positively, and often negatively, depending upon the nature and timing of the stressor. Some models of disease have shown a poorer response to challenge following stress (e.g. influenza challenge in C57BL/6 mice). In some models, stress-induced alterations in specific measures of immune response appear to act through glucocorticoid interactions, some appear to act through sympathetic noradrenergic signaling, and others appear to act through neurotransmitter or hormonal systems not yet fully identified (e.g. Cunnick et al., 1990). Subtle variations in the timing and nature of the stressor can alter the pattern of outflow of neurotransmitters and hormones from the CNS, which in turn, can differentially influence a variety of measures of immunologic responsiveness. The most important questions yet to be answered are to what extent these altered measures of immunologic responsiveness can effect an animal in a given state when challenged by a virus, other pathogens, tumors, or autoimmune challenge, and to what extent we can intervene during a stressor with pharmacologic agents modulating the relevant mediators to block adverse immunologic consequences of the stressor.

Endocrine system

Since the early demonstration that hypophysectomy can alter the development and function of the immune system, neurohormones have been investigated for immunomodulatory activity. Physicians have been using glucocorticoids as anti-inflammatory agents for decades. The observations that many autoimmune diseases are more prevalent in women than in men suggests an interaction of the sex hormones in this process. Virtually all anterior pituitary hormones, and most peripheral target organ hormones can alter specific immunologic activity, sometimes profoundly. These complexities are well beyond this review, and are summarized in many chapters in *Psychoneuroimmunology*, 2nd edition (Ader et al., 1991). Some cells of the immune system, including T lymphocytes, can produce classical anterior pituitary hormones in response to viral stimulation or releasing factor challenge, further blurring the boundaries between cytokines and neurotransmitters/neurohormones. An important unanswered question regarding this novel production of classical hormones by cells of the immune system is the extent of their involvement in ongoing immune response to a disease challenge.

The most commonly acknowledged hormonal system that influences immunologic reactivy is the hypothalamo-pituitary-adrenal (HPA) axis via glucocorticoids. Although glucocorticoids inhibit a variety of macrophage, T cell, and B cell functions, they are not universally inhibitory (Munck and Guyre, 1991). They can activate latent viruses, and shift the CD4 cell response from cellular (T_{H1}) to humoral immunity (T_{H2} predominant). This may be an important factor in the progression of HIV infection. Recent evidence indicates that immune responses to virus and other challenges (mainly via IL-1 and perhaps other cytokines such as IL-6 and TNF-α) can themselves induce CRF-ACTH-glucocorticoid secretion (Besedovsky and del Rey, 1991). This may act as a counter-regulatory signal to dampen proliferation and other immunologic activation that could be damaging to the organism (e.g. autoimmune provoking). The role of the HPA axis in autoimmunity, viral infections, and the balance between cellular and humoral immunity is an important area of clinical interest in neural-immune signaling. The balance between immunologically induced and CNS stress-induced HPA axis activation may be critical in the progression and severity of relevant diseases.

A further system that has provoked interest is growth hormone (GH). GH administration to old mice can restore the weight and cellularity to the involuted thymus, and can restore T cell proliferation, cytokine production and functioning (Kelley, 1991).

Autonomic nervous system

Sympathetic innervation

Both primary (bone marrow and thymus) and secondary (spleen, lymph nodes, mucosal associated) lymphoid organs are innervated by noradrenergic (NA) and peptidergic nerve fibers. Fluorescence histochemical studies of spleen and thymus innervation done in our laboratories (e.g. Williams and Felten, 1981) found NA innervation present in smooth muscle compartments such as the vascular, and capsular/trabecular areas and also in the parenchyma with no clear vascular association. Immunocytochemical studies in the rat revealed that, NA innervation was associated primarily with areas occupied by T cells (e.g. the periarteriolar lymphatic sheath in the spleen, the paracortical zone of the lymph node, and the thymic cortex), and areas with many macrophages (e.g. the marginal zone of the spleen, the medullary cords of the lymph node), but tended to avoid B cell zones (lymphoid follicles) (Felten et al., 1987a; reviewed in Felten and Felten, 1991).

Examination of the innervation of the spleen at the electron microscopic level revealed tyrosine hydroxylase positive nerve terminals in direct contact with T lymphocytes (Felten and Olschowka, 1987; Felten and Felten, 1991; Felten et al., 1992), in both adventitial zones and deeper regions populated by lymphoid cells. NE released from more distant terminals can diffuse and interact with receptors on lymphocytes, resulting in modulation of their function. The role of these close neuro-effector contacts on a small subset of lymphoid cells is unclear. It has not yet been determined whether these lymphocytes have special characteristics that cause them to have contact with nerve terminals. It is possible that they serve as intermediates in translating neuronal signals into lymphocyte signals (cytokines), but it is equally likely that they are in contact with neurons to provide cytokine signals to regulate release of neurotransmitters (e.g. IL-1 or IL-2 influencing NE release) from local nerve terminals.

Parasympathetic and peptidergic innervation

Although parasympathetic (cholinergic) innervation has been reported in the thymus, its extent is not clear, nor has it been demonstrated in other lymphoid organs (reviewed in Felten and Felten, 1991). However, extensive substance P, calcitonin gene-related peptide, vasoactive intestinal peptide, neuropeptide Y (often co-localized with NE) and other peptides have been found in nerves in the parenchyma of bone marrow, thymus, spleen, lymph nodes and mucosal-associated lymphoid tissues (for reviews, see *Brain, Behavior, and Immunity* Special Issue, and Bellinger et al., 1990).

Receptors

Lymphocytes and macrophages have receptors for a number of neurotransmitters (reviewed in Ader et al., 1990; Carr and Blalock, 1991), including α and β adrenergic receptors, muscarinic cholinergic receptors and receptors for vasoactive intestinal polypeptide (VIP), somatostatin, and substance P. Other receptors have been suggested, but are not yet well characterized.

Perhaps the best receptor characterization is of the β_2-adrenergic receptor, which has been demonstrated on both T and B lymphocytes and on macrophages. β-receptor agonists have been shown to increase cAMP production (reviewed in Roszman and Carlson, 1991)

as would be expected. However, such agonists can also act synergistically with activators of lymphocytes such as phytohemagglutinin (PHA) which alone does not increase cAMP, to greatly augment cAMP production in T lymphocytes. β-Agonists also can synergize cAMP generation in T lymphocytes activated by T cell receptor stimulation with anti-CD3 antibody.

Functional significance

Two major strategies have been used to investigate the functional role of neurotransmitters in immunomodulation: (1) pharmacologic interventions; and (2) denervation of lymphoid organs. The NA sympathetic system has been studied in greatest detail. Following the transmitter or nerve manipulation, immunologic responses have been measured (reviewed in Felten et al., 1993), including: (1) individual cellular functions of specific subsets (mainly T cells and B cells), including proliferation, differentiation, production and release of specific products (immunoglobulin isotypes, cytokines), or trafficking; (2) collective cellular interactions such as primary and secondary antibody responses, cytotoxic T cell responses, delayed type hypersensitivity responses, natural killer responses; and (3) response of the organism to challenge by viruses, bacteria, tumors, or autoimmunity. This hierarchical approach has permitted investigation of the role of neurotransmitters in modulating disease-relevant immune functions, while pursuing more mechanistic and molecular aspects of such interactions.

In vitro studies have shown that NE or other β-agonists, when present at the beginning of cell culture, can enhance primary antibody responses and cellular immune responses (e.g. cytotoxic T cell responses), probably through enhancement of the initiative phase of immune responses (reviewed in Madden and Livnat, 1991). In contrast, when NE or β-agonists are added at the effector cell phase, these effector cells are inhibited (e.g. antibody production, cytotoxic T cell activity are decreased). NE can stimulate the pre-B cells that develop into IgM-producing cells. Thus, timing of the signal is very important, and both the cell subset and its stage of activation can determine the response to the signal.

Denervation of non-immune (i.e. non-stimulated murine lymph nodes of NE nerve fibers with 6-hydroxydopamine results in increased cell proliferation, altered cellularity (diminished T cells, enhanced B cells) and mitogen responses, and an immunoglobulin isotype switch (in the absence of antigen challenge) from IgM to IgG, accompanied by increased secretion of IFN-γ by T_{H1} T helper cells (Madden et al., 1994a,b). In challenged mice, NA denervation results in diminished primary antibody responses (80% decrease in spleen challenged systemically, 97% decrease in LNs challenged in the draining site), enhanced secondary antibody responses, diminished cytotoxic T lymphocyte responses (50%) and IL-2 secretion, diminished delayed-type hypersensitivity responses, and enhanced natural killer cell responses (for review, see Bellinger et al., 1992). Thus, it appears that NE stimulates T_{H1} responses (cellular immunity) while NA denervation diminishes them. However, humoral immunity is also affected, perhaps with additional signaling to B cells, with NE favoring IgM responses and NA denervation shifting away from IgM towards IgG. These studies suggest that NE signaling is neither simplistic nor unidirectional, but may differentially influence multiple cell types at multiple stages during a reaction. Working out the nature and timing of these interactions is one of the major challenges of the field. Further, during an infection, neurotransmitters may influence three separate sites: (1) the site of initial presentation and continuing presentation as a replicating antigen; (2) the site of generation of an immune response (usually a secondary lymphoid organ); and (3) the site of inflammation or response to the infection.

Other neurotransmitters have also been studied for immunomodulatory activity. For example, substance P can stimulate T cell proliferation, enhance antibody production of IgA and IgM, enhance cellular immune responses, and stimulate macrophage chemotaxis (Payan, 1992). During an ongoing behavior, many sets of nerve fibers, releasing many neurotransmitters differentially at a variety of sites of immunologic reactivy, may simultaneously impinge on many subsets of lymphoid cells to achieve a collective effect. Sorting out this signaling will be as complex as sorting out cytokine influences on immune responses.

Autoimmune disease

Although denervation studies have demonstrated that the absence of NE is often related to a decreased immune response, especially of T cells, studies using several models of autoimmune disease demonstrate that sympathetic denervation also may exacerbate the development of experimental autoimmune disease (such as experimental allergic encephalomyelitis or experimentally induced arthritis) in susceptible animals (reviewed in Levine et al., 1991; Bellinger et al., 1993). Although this could be interpreted superficially as indicating that NE has an inhibitory effect on immune responses that is removed with sympathectomy, thereby causing augmented responses leading to autoimmunity, it is much more accurate to view sympathectomy as removing an important regulatory influence that normally promotes an optimal response. Autoimmune disease should not be viewed as an increased immune response, but rather as an inappropriate response. The ability of NE to suppress this abnormal response should be seen as an enhancement of normal function.

Aging

Our investigations of sympathetic innervation of lymphoid organs in aging Fischer 344 rats (Felten et al., 1987b; reviewed in Ackerman et al., 1991; Bellinger et al., 1993), have shown that the spleen and lymph nodes of 27-month-old rats has greatly diminished sympathetic innervation compared with their younger counterparts. These aging rats showed diminished T cell proliferation, IL-2 secretion, and cellular immune responses. The similarity of immune response in normal aging (with age-related loss of NE nerves) and younger rats experimentally denervated of NA nerve fibers, suggests that some aspects of immunosenescence (mainly diminished T cell responses) may be causally related to loss of NA innervation of secondary organs.

Conclusions

Although we have learned much about neurotransmitter and neurohormone influences on immune responses, we have just scratched the surface. We view the following areas of investigation to be important steps in further expanding our understanding of neural modulation of immune responses. (1) Further identification of chemically specific nerve fibers that distribute to lymphoid organs and tissues, the specific cell types with which they associate, the receptor expression for those neurotransmitters on specific subsets of lymphoid cells, and variability by gender, age, strain, and other characteristics. (2) Dermination of the specific immunologic responses, in vitro and in vivo, that are induced by each neurotransmitter or neurohormone in question (dose-response studies necessary, for physiological correlations). This includes looking at synergistic interactions of these molecules with each other and with cytokines. (3) Determination of the pattern of neurotransmitters and neurohormones resulting from specific behavioral paradigms (and how those patterns change with time), thereby cataloging "stress" responses according to the pattern of efferent signaling rather than the sensory characteristics of the stimulus. (4) Determination of the role of these signal molecules, both singly and in combination, during ongoing challenges from viruses, bacteria, tumors, autoimmune reactivity, and other immunologic challenges. (5) Use of neurotransmitter agonists or antagonists to deliberately enhance or inhibit specific reactions of specific cells of the immune system during a specific immunologic challenge, with the prospect of intervening for the benefit of patients. (6) Investigation of immunologic development and neurotransmitter or neurohormone signaling, continuing throughout adulthood into immunosenescence. (7) Distribution of cytokines (constituitive and inducible) and cytokine receptors in the nervous system. (8) Effects of cytokines on specific CNS structures and influences on subsequent outflow back to the immune system, studied both as individual cytokines and collective groups of cytokines that occur during infections or other immunologic reactions. (9) Pathways in the CNS utilized during stressors, conditioning, or other immunologically relevant states, to achieve signaling to the immune system. (10) A complete mapping of any specific neural-immune interactions from the initial behavior, to the CNS cells and reactions induced by that behavior, to the pathways activated by that behavior, to the collective timing and output of the signal molecules secreted or released, to the interactions with specific cells of the immune system at specific sites, to the altered collective interactions of those cells, to the influence exerted by these cells on health and illness during a specific challenge to the immune system. With this type of comprehensive sequential understanding of specific neural-immune interactions, we will be at the threshold of explaining psychoneuroimmunology at the level of biological signaling. However, the important extension of these observations to intervention with neural agents in infections, tumors, autoimmunity, and other immune-relevant diseases will depend on a better understanding of how individual cell responses contribute to the overall reactivity of the immune system. Perhaps one of the most important contributions of neural-immune signaling is the conspicuous necessity of requiring a hierarchical understanding of the immune system itself from the molecular and cellular level through collective cellular interactions, to the overall immunophysiology of the entire system in a challenged host.

Acknowledgements

This work was supported in part by NS 25223 from the National Institutes of Health, and MH 00899, P50 MH 40381, and MH 42076 from the National Institutes of Mental Health.

References

Ackerman, K.D., Bellinger, D.L., Felten, S.Y. and Felten, D.L. (1991) Ontogeny and senescence of noradrenergic innervation of the rodent thymus and spleen. In: R. Ader, D.L. Felten and N. Cohen (Eds.), *Psychoneuroimmunology*, 2nd edition, Academic Press, San Diego, pp. 72–125.

Ader, R. and Cohen, N. (1991) The influence of conditioning on immune responses. In: R. Ader, D.L. Felten and N. Cohen (Eds.), *Psychoneuroimmunology*, 2nd edition, Academic Press, San Diego, pp. 611–646.

Ader, R., Felten, D.L. and Cohen, N. (1990) Interactions between the brain and the immune system. *Annu. Rev. Pharmacol. Toxicol.*, 30: 561–602.

Ader, R., Felten, D.L. and Cohen, N. (Eds.) (1991) *Psychoneuroimmunology*, 2nd edition, Academic Press, San Diego.

162

Bellinger, D.L., Lorton, D., Romano, T., Olschowka, J.A., Felten, S.Y. and Felten, D.L. (1990) Neuropeptide innervation of lymphoid organs. *Ann. N. Y. Acad. Sci.*, 594: 17–33.

Bellinger, D.L., Felten, S.Y. and Felten, D.L. (1992) Neural-immune interactions: Neurotransmitter signaling of cells of the immune system. In: A. Tasman and M.B. Riba (Eds.), *Review of Psychiatry*, American Psychiatric Press, Washington, DC, pp. 127–144.

Bellinger, D.L., Felten, S.Y., Ackerman, K.D., Lorton, D., Madden, K.S. and Felten, D.L. (1993) Noradrenergic sympathetic innervation of lymphoid organs during development, aging, and in autoimmune disease. In: F. Amenta (Ed.), *Aging of the Autonomic Nervous System*, CRC Press, Boca Raton, FL, pp. 243–284.

Besedovsky, H.O. and del Rey, A. (1991) Physiological implications of immune-neuro-endocrine network. In: R. Ader, D.L. Felten and N. Cohen (Eds.), *Psychoneuroimmunology*, 2nd edition, Academic Press, San Diego, pp. 589–608.

Carr, D.J.J. and Blalock, J.E. (1991) Neuropeptide hormones and receptors common to the immune and neuroendocrine systems: Bidirectional pathway of intersystem communication. In: R. Ader, D.L. Felten and N. Cohen (Eds.), *Psychoneuroimmunology*, 2nd edition, Academic Press, New York, pp. 573–588.

Cunnick, J.E., Lysle, D.T., Kucinski, B.J. and Rabin, B.S. (1990) Evidence that shock-induced immune suppression is mediated by adrenal hormones and peripheral b-adrenergic receptors. *Pharmacol. Biochem. Behav.*, 36: 645–651.

Felten, S.Y. and Felten, D.L. (1991) Innervation of lymphoid tissue. In: R. Ader, D.L. Felten and N. Cohen (Eds.), *Psychoneuroimmunology*, 2nd edition, Academic Press, New York, pp. 27–68.

Felten, S.Y. and Olschowka, J.A. (1987) Noradrenergic sympathetic innervation of the spleen: II. Tyrosine hydroxylase (TH)-positive nerve terminals form synaptic-like contacts on lymphocytes in the splenic white pulp. *J. Neurosci. Res.*, 18: 37–48.

Felten, D.L., Ackerman, K.D., Wiegand, S.J. and Felten, S.Y. (1987a) Noradrenergic sympathetic innervation of the spleen: I. Nerve fibers associate with lymphocytes and macrophages in specific compartments of the splenic white pulp. *J. Neurosci. Res.*, 18: 28–36.

Felten, S.Y., Bellinger, D.L., Collier, T.J., Coleman, P.D. and Felten, D.L. (1987b) Decreased sympathetic innervation of spleen in aged Fischer 344 rats. *Neurobiol. Aging*, 8: 159–165.

Felten, S.Y., Felten, D.L., Bellinger, D.L. and Olschowka, J.A. (1992) Noradrenergic and peptidergic innervation of lymphoid organs. In: J.E. Blalock (Ed.), *Chemical Immunology: Neuroimmunoendocrinology*, 2nd edition, S. Karger, Basel, pp. 25–48.

Felten, D.L., Felten, S.Y., Bellinger, D.L. and Madden, K.S. (1993) Fundamental aspects of neural-immune signaling. *Psychother. Psychosom.*, 60: 46–56.

Kelley, K.W. (1991) Growth hormone in immunobiology. In: R. Ader, D.L. Felten and N. Cohen (Eds.), *Psychoneuroimmunology*, 2nd edition, Academic Press, San Diego, CA, pp. 337–402.

Levine, J.D., Goetzl, E.J. and Basbaum, A.I. (1991) Contribution of the nervous system to the pathophysiology of rheumatoid arthritis and other polyarthritides. *Rheum. Dis. Clin. N. Am.*, 13: 369–383.

Madden, K.S. and Livnat, S. (1991) Catecholaminergic influences on immune reactivity. In: R. Ader, D.L. Felten and N. Cohen (Eds.), *Psychoneuroimmunology*, 2nd edition, Academic Press, San Diego, CA, pp. 283–310.

Madden, K.S., Felten, S.Y., Felten, D.L., Hardy, C.A. and Livnat, S. (1994a) Sympathetic nervous system modulation of the immune system. II. Induction of lymphocyte proliferation and migration in vivo by chemical sympathectomy. *J. Neuroimmunol.*, 49: 67–75.

Madden, K.S., Moynihan, J.a., Brenner, G.J., Felten, S.Y., Felten, D.L. and Livnat, S. (1994b) Sympathetic nervous system modulation of the immune system. III. Alterations in T and B cell proliferation and differentiation in vitro following chemical sympathectomy. *J. Neuroimmunol.*, 49: 77–87.

Munck, A. and Guyre, P.M. (1991) Glucocorticoids and immune function. In: R. Ader, D.L. Felten and N. Cohen (Eds.), *Psychoneuroimmunology*, 2nd edition, Academic Press, San Diego, CA, pp. 447–474.

Payan, D.G. (1992) The role of neuropeptides in inflammation. In: J.I. Gallin, I.M. Goldstein and R. Snyderman (Eds.), *Inflammation: Basic Principles and Clinical Correlates*, 2nd edition, Raven Press, New York, pp. 177–192.

Roszman, T.L. and Carlson, S.L. (1991) Neurotransmitters and molecular signaling in the immune response. In: R. Ader, D.L. Felten and N. Cohen (Eds.), *Psychoneuroimmunology*, 2nd edition, Academic Press, San Diego, CA, pp. 311–335.

Special Issue (1991) Peptidergic localization and innervation of lymphoid tissue. *Brain Behav. Immun.*, 5: 1–147.

Williams, J.M. and Felten, D.L. (1981) Sympathetic innervation of murine thymus and spleen: a comparative histofluorescence study. *Anat. Rec.*, 199: 531–542.

F. Bloom (Editor)
Progress in Brain Research, Vol. 100
© 1994 Elsevier Science B.V. All rights reserved

CHAPTER 21

Human cortical functions revealed by magnetoencephalography

Riitta Hari

Low Temperature Laboratory, Helsinki University of Technology, 02150 Espoo, Finland

Introduction

Magnetoencephalography, MEG, complements the traditional microlevel and macrolevel approaches to unravelling the functions of the human brain. MEG recordings are based on non-invasive detection of weak magnetic fields produced by cerebral electric currents. Signals from various cortical regions can be differentiated with good temporal and spatial resolution. MEG studies have so far focused on functional mapping of the healthy human cerebral cortex but some clinical applications are also emerging. For details of the MEG method, see previous reviews (Hari and Lounasmaa, 1989; Sato, 1990; Hämäläinen et al., 1993).

MEG is closely related to EEG, the recording of electric potential differences on the scalp. MEG patterns caused by multiple simultaneous sources are often more straightforward to interpret than the corresponding EEG distributions. One reason for this is that concentric electric inhomogeneities do not affect the magnetic field. A combination of MEG and EEG is necessary for identifying all active brain areas and all orientations of the source currents (cf. Wikswo et al., 1993).

Measurements

Electric currents flowing in the brain generate weak magnetic signals, typically 100–1000 fT (fT = femto-Tesla = 10^{-15} T), i.e. only one part in 10^9 or 10^8 of the Earth's geomagnetic field. The signals are first picked up by superconducting flux transformers (Fig. 1A) and then detected by SQUIDs (Superconducting QUantum Interference Devices), which are extremely sensitive to magnetic fields. The configuration of the flux transformer (a magnetometer, axial gradiometer, or a planar gradiometer; Fig. 1B) affects the instrument's sensitivity to various brain versus noise sources.

To localize the underlying neural activity, the field pattern outside the head must be determined in detail. Instead of earlier time-consuming sequential mapping with (1–37)-channel instruments, it is now possible to record signals simultaneously over the entire cortex. The first whole-head helmet-type magnetometers were constructed recently by Neuromag Ltd (Espoo, Finland; 122 channels, Fig. 1C) and by CTF Systems Inc. (Vancouver, Canada; 64 channels).

Origin and interpretation of MEG signals

An inherent limitation of the MEG (and EEG) method is the non-uniqueness of the inverse problem. This means that, in principle, several current distributions may produce identical signal patterns outside the brain. Therefore, source models are used for data interpretation. The most common model of a local source is a tangential current dipole within a sphere. The orientation, strength and three-dimensional location of the equivalent current dipole (ECD), which best explains the measured field pattern, are determined by means of a least-squares fit to the data. The

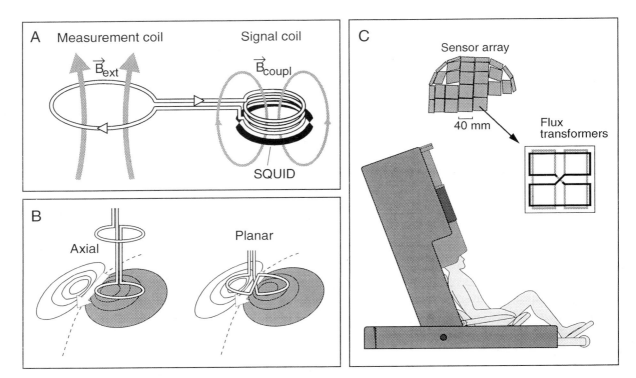

Fig. 1. *A*, Principle of MEG signal detection. The external magnetic field induces into the superconducting flux transformer a current that couples the magnetic field from the signal coil to the SQUID. *B*, Two flux transformer configurations above a schematic magnetic field pattern produced by a current dipole. The axial gradiometer picks the maximum signal at both field extrema whereas the planar figure-of-eight transformer senses the strongest signal (gradient) just above the dipole. *C*, Schematic illustration of a whole-head neuromagnetometer. The subject's head is inside the dewar, which contains the SQUID sensors immersed in liquid helium. With this 122-channel device (Neuromag-122^{TM}), the gradient of the magnetic field is picked up outside the head simultaneously at 61 locations of the helmet-shaped sensor array (upper insert); at each location, two orthogonal field gradients are measured with planar flux transformers of figure-of-eight configuration (lower insert). The experiments are carried out inside a magnetically shielded room.

MEG signals are caused mainly by intracellular synaptic currents in the fissural cortex (cf. Hämäläinen et al., 1993). Physiologically, the ECD reflects the centre of gravity of an active cortical layer smaller than 2 cm in diameter. Multiple simultaneous sources can be modelled with time-varying multidipole models.

The solutions can be improved considerably by incorporating the anatomical constraints obtained, for example, from magnetic resonance images (MRIs). Such a combination of structural (MRI) and functional (MEG) information is especially useful for clinical purposes. Future developments will also include integration of MEG and positron emission tomography (PET) data.

Examples

Auditory responses and sensory memory

Figure 2*A* shows auditory evoked magnetic fields elicited by short tones. The most prominent deflection, N100m, peaks about 100 ms after sound onset and has dipolar field patterns over both temporal lobes (Fig. 2*B*). The signals are slightly larger and earlier in the left (contralateral) than the right hemisphere. A two-dipole model, one ECD in each supratemporal cortex, explained the signal distribution satisfactorily. Superposition of the ECDs on the 3D-MRI reconstruction (Fig. 2*C*) implies that N100m may receive a contribution from Heschl's gyrus (cf. Tissari et al., 1993), although its main source is probably in the cortex of planum temporale.

Sensory memory in its simple form can be studied by determining recovery cycles of different MEG responses. The N100m amplitude increases with the interstimulus interval (ISI) and reaches a plateau at ISIs

of about 8 s. As shown in Fig. 2D, the ISI dependence is similar in the left and right hemispheres, implying that tones leave traces of similar duration into auditory cortices of both hemispheres. The storage of auditory information for a few seconds can also be demonstrated by presenting infrequent deviant sounds among a series of monotonously repeated standard sounds.

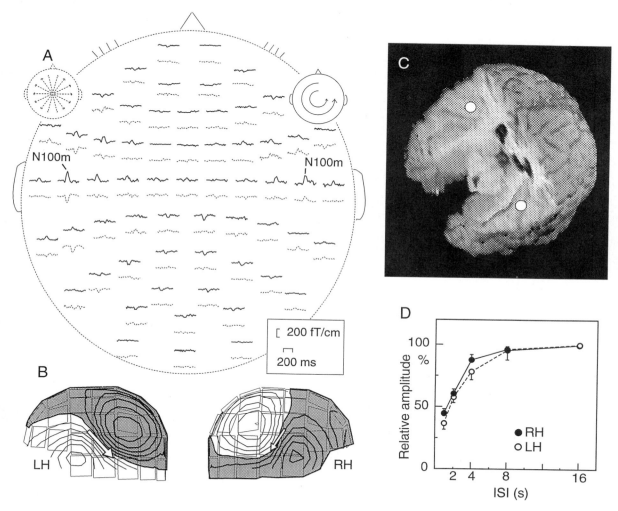

Fig. 2. *A*, AEFs to 50-ms tones presented to the right ear once every 4 s. In each response pair, the upper (solid) curves indicate the azimuthal and the lower (dotted) ones the polar derivatives (illustrated in the right- and left-sided insert heads, respectively); the relative amplitudes of the two traces indicate the direction of the source current at each location. The head is viewed from above, with the nose pointing to the top of the figure. The traces start 50 ms before the tone onset. Passband is 0.03–40 Hz. *B*, Field patterns during N100m over the left (LH) and right (RH) hemispheres. The maps have been drawn over the helmet-shaped sensor array. The shadowed areas indicate magnetic flux out of the skull. The arrows show the sites and orientations of the equivalent current dipoles best explaining the signal patterns. The isocontours are separated by 100 fT. *C*, 3-D MRI reconstruction of the subject's brain. The frontal lobes have been removed to expose the surfaces of the temporal lobes. The white circles indicate the sources of N100m. Adapted from Tissari et al. (1993). *D*, Mean (± SEM; 9 subjects) relative amplitudes of N100m over the left and right hemispheres to contralateral stimulation. Adapted from Mäkelä et al. (1993).

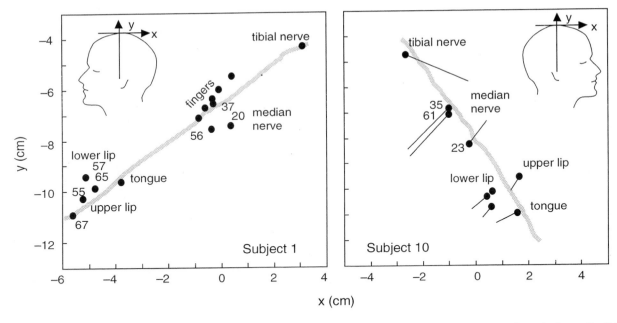

Fig. 3. ECD locations for stimulation of different parts of the body in two subjects. The numbers indicate response latencies in ms. For Subject 10, dipole orientations are also shown. The thick grey line illustrates the approximate course of the Rolandic fissure, determined on the basis of ECD locations and orientations. Adapted from Hari et al. (1993b).

Such recordings suggest that the auditory sensory memory lasts about 10 s (Sams et al., 1993).

Somatosensory responses and somatotopy

Recordings of somatosensory evoked fields (SEFs) can be employed to study functional organization of the somatosensory cortices. In the contralateral primary somatosensory cortex SI, a clear somatotopical order is evident, with different body parts represented at different locations (Fig. 3). The non-invasively identified Rolandic fissure is an important functional landmark in studies of epileptic foci and in preoperative planning of epilepsy surgery.

SEF recordings also indicate activation of other cortical areas. At 100–140 ms, signals peak in the secondary somatosensory cortices SII of both hemispheres, with slightly longer latencies for the ipsi- than the contralateral stimuli (Hari et al., 1993b). A novel source area was recently found in the posterior parietal cortex, medial and posterior to the SI hand area (Forss

et al., 1994); this source was most active 70–110 ms after the stimulus.

Signals following voluntary blinking

The eye acts as a strong electric dipole and eye movements and blinks are serious sources of artefacts in EEG and MEG recordings. EEG responses have been observed in the posterior parts of the brain about 200 ms after blink artefacts; the signals were interpreted as visual evoked responses caused by luminance changes (Heuser-Link et al., 1992).

Figure 4 (left) shows magnetic field patterns associated with voluntary blinking (Hari et al., 1994); the magnetic signals were averaged using the vertical electro-oculogram as the trigger. Strong signals occur close to both orbits during a blink. About 200 ms later, another signal with a dipolar field pattern emerges in the posterior head areas. Superposition of its ECD on the brain surface (Fig. 4, right; white circles) indicates activation of the parieto-occipital midline. The signals disappeared when blinking occurred in complete darkness. However, since the source location was clearly distinct from that of early visually evoked fields (Fig. 4, right; black circle), the blink-related posterior response does not seem to be an ordinary visual evoked response but rather a sign of activation of the posterior parietal cortex (PPC).

The PPC is known to be strongly associated with the control of eye movements and fixation. In monkey, eye-movement-related neurons in this area react preferentially to large, salient stimuli which "signal the presence of an important stimulus in the visual environment" (Goldberg and Robinson, 1977). Interestingly, the PPC is strongly connected to prefrontal cortical areas underlying spatial working memory (Wilson et al., 1993). The observed response in the human PPC might thus be related to updating of the spatial working memory, necessary for maintaining a continuous image of the environment, despite interruption of the visual input for a tenth of a second during each blink.

Clinical perspectives and conclusions

During preoperative evaluation of epileptic patients, irritative foci have been located in relation to functional landmarks at cortical projection areas, determined on the basis of magnetic evoked responses. A good agreement has been reported in several patients between MEG foci and intraoperative corticographic findings. Determining the temporal relationships between several foci may also be clinically important. For example, in some patients, it is possible to find the callosal conduction time between foci in homologous

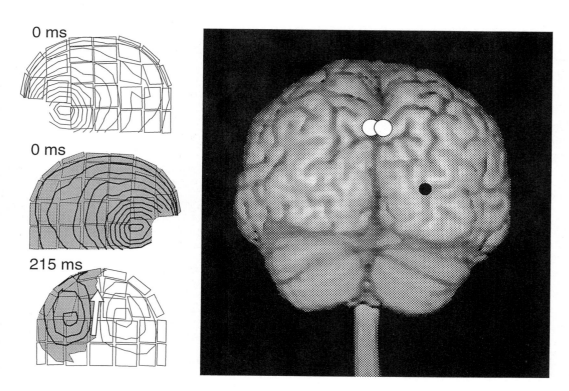

Fig. 4. *Left*: Field patterns over the left and right hemispheres during the maximum blink signal (0 ms) and over the back of the head during the peak of the posterior response (215 ms). The isocontours are separated by 200 fT (upper two patterns) and by 100 fT (the lowest pattern). *Right*: ECDs superimposed on a MRI surface reconstruction of the brain, viewed from the back. The white circles indicate ECDs for the blink-associated signals, determined from two measurements; the dipole orientations are perpendicular to the course of the parieto-occipital sulcus. The black circle shows the ECD for visual evoked field. Modified from Hari et al. (1994).

areas of the two hemispheres (Hari et al., 1993a). Other clinical applications aim at a better understanding of the pathophysiology of different neurological diseases (Hari, 1993). More extensive clinical applications necessitate installation of high-quality multi-channel instruments into hospital environments.

MEG complements information obtained from other brain imaging methods in studying human cortical functions. The MEG approach lacks the accuracy of single-cell recordings but is non-invasive and gives information on an analysis level that is relevant for an understanding of the macroscopic functional organization of the cerebral cortex.

Whole-head MEG recordings allow comparison of hemispheric differences in the processing of complex stimuli, such as speech sounds. This is of paramount importance for research into the neural basis of cognitive activity in humans, such as studies of brain dynamics and related disorders during complex problem solving. One recent whole-head MEG study revealed the activation sequence of several cortical areas associated with overt and covert picture naming (Salmelin et al., 1994). In addition to evoked response recordings, the whole-head neuromagnetometers provide a global picture of ongoing spontaneous activity, which is of great interest for both basic neuroscience and for clinical applications.

Acknowledgments

This study has been financially supported by the Academy of Finland and by the Sigrid Jusélius Foundation. The MRIs were obtained at the Department of Radiology, Helsinki University Central Hospital. I thank Olli V. Lounasmaa, Linda McEvoy and Riitta Salmelin for comments on the manuscript.

References

Forss, N., Hari, R., Salmelin, R., Ahonen, A., Hämäläinen, M., Kajola, M., Knuutila, J. and Simola, J. (1994) Activation of the human parietal cortex by median nerve stimulation. *Exp. Brain Res.*, in press.

Goldberg, M. and Robinson, D. (1977) Visual mechanisms underlying gaze: function of the cerebral cortex. In: R. Baker and A. Berthoz (Eds.), *Control of Gaze by Brain Stem Neurons. Developments in Neuroscience*, Vol. 1, Elsevier, pp. 469–476.

Hämäläinen, M., Ahonen, A., Hari, R., Ilmoniemi, R., Knuutila, J. and Lounasmaa, O.V. (1993) Magnetoencephalography – theory, instrumentation, and applications to noninvasive studies of the working human brain. *Rev. Modern Phys.*, 41: 413–497.

Hari, R. (1993) Magnetoencephalography as a tool of clinical neurophysiology. In: E. Niedermeyer and F. Lopes da Silva (Eds.), *Electroencephalography. Basic Principles, Clinical Applications and Related Fields*, 3rd edition, Williams & Wilkins, Baltimore, pp. 1035–1061.

Hari, R. and Lounasmaa, O.V. (1989) Recording and interpretation of cerebral magnetic fields. *Science*, 244: 432–436.

Hari, R., Ahonen, A., Forss, N., Granström, M.-L., Hämäläinen, M., Kajola, M., Knuutila, J., Mäkelä, J.P., Paetau, R., Salmelin, R. and Simola, J. (1993a) Parietal epileptic mirror focus detected with a whole-head neuromagnetometer. *NeuroReport*, 5: 45–48.

Hari, R., Karhu, J., Hämäläinen, M., Knuutila, J., Salonen, O., Sams, M. and Vilkman, V. (1993b) Functional organization of the human first and second somatosensory cortices: a neuromagnetic study. *Eur. J. Neurosci.*, 5: 724–734.

Hari, R., Salmelin, R., Tissari, S., Kajola, M. and Virsu, V. (1994) Visual stability during eyeblinks. *Nature*, 367: 121–122.

Heuser-Link, M., Dirlich, G., Berg, P., Vogl, L. and Scherg, M. (1992) Eyeblinks evoke potentials in the occipital brain region. *Neurosci. Lett.*, 143: 31–34.

Mäkelä, J., Ahonen, A., Hämäläinen, M., Hari, R., Ilmoniemi, R., Kajola, M., Knuutila, J., Lounasmaa, O.V., McEvoy, L., Salmelin, R., Sams, M., Simola, J., Tesche, C. and Vasama, J.-P. (1993) Functional differences between auditory cortices of the two hemispheres revealed by whole-head neuromagnetic recordings. *Human Brain Mapping*, 1: 48–56.

Salmelin, R., Hari, R., Lounasmaa, O.V. and Sams, M. (1994) Dynamics of brain activation during picture naming. *Nature*, in press.

Sams, M., Hari, R., Rif, J. and Knuutila, J. (1993) The human auditory sensory memory trace persists about 10 s: neuromagnetic evidence. *J. Cogn. Neurosci.*, 5: 363–370.

Sato, S. (Ed.) (1990) *Magnetoencephalography. Advances in Neurology*, Vol. 54, Raven Press, New York.

Tissari, S., Hämäläinen, M., Hari, R. and Mäkelä, J. (1993) Sources of auditory evoked fields superimposed on 3D-reconstruction of temporal lobes. In: *9th Int. Conf. Biomagnetism*, Vienna, 1993, Volume of Abstracts, pp. 138–139.

Wikswo, J.J., Gevins, A. and Williamson, S. (1993) The future of EEG and MEG. *Electroencephalogr. Clin. Neurophysiol.*, 87: 1–9.

Wilson, F.A.W., Ó Schalaidhe, S.P. and Goldman-Rakic, P.S. (1993) Dissociation of object and spatial processing domains in primate prefrontal cortex. *Science*, 260: 1955–1958.

F. Bloom (Editor)
Progress in Brain Research, Vol. 100
© 1994 Elsevier Science B.V. All rights reserved

CHAPTER 22

The prefrontal system: a smorgasbord

Ivan Divac

Department of Medical Physiology, Panum Institute, University of Copenhagen, Blegdamsvej 3C, DK-2200 Copenhagen, Denmark

Introduction

Three decades ago, Rosvold[1] and Szwarcbart (1964) published a paper in which they argued that in addition to sensory and motor systems, there is the prefrontal system (PFS) in the brain consisting of the prefrontal cortex (PFC) and a set of anatomically and functionally related formations. The concept of PFS was based mainly on the results of neurobehavioral and anatomical studies on rhesus monkeys. Joint functioning of the components of PFS was inferred from impaired performance in delayed response-type tasks following lesions or electrical stimulation anywhere in the system. The neostriatal region innervated by PFC was one such component.

This notion was just hatched when I arrived to Rosvold's laboratory in early 1963, a short time after my graduation. In retrospect, it is obvious that I became "imprinted" in Rosvold's laboratory since a large portion of my work has been devoted to the PFS, especially to relations between PFC and the neostriatum. During my stay at NIH, we obtained evidence that PFS can be divided in subsystems (Divac et al., 1967).

In 1965, I came to the Nencki Institute in Warsaw where Konorski and his group had been studying functions of the PFC in cats and dogs. There, I acquired my second major line of interest: the comparative approach.

Comparisons of PFS demand a definition of PFC that is useful across species. Attempts at such a definition are as old as the term PFC itself (Divac, 1988).

According to the definition I accepted, PFC is the cortical projection area of the thalamic mediodorsal nucleus (MD) (to appreciate the complexity of this issue, see Divac and Öberg (1990) and Divac et al. (1993)). This definition of PFC obviously requires in turn a useful definition of MD. Neither topography, currently the main criterion, nor presently available chemical markers are reliable (Regidor and Divac, 1987) but hodology seems promising. A discussion of what is an entity in the thalamus has been discussed elsewhere (Divac, 1979).

Our work on the rat demonstrated the usefulness of defining PFC by MD projections to the cortex: The cortical area in rats outlined by Leonard[2] on the basis of thalamo-cortical connections was shown to mediate delayed response-type behavior, just as cortical areas, defined in the same way, do in any tested species, e.g. monkeys, dogs and cats (Divac, 1971).

My studies of the PFS provided data relevant for the neostriatum as well as the PFC. The studies which focused on the neostriatum have been reviewed elsewhere (Divac, 1984). Presently, I would like to review my work that focused on PFC. The decision to get involved in any of the studies reviewed here was made on the basis of existing data and opportunities. Opportunities mostly arose when I encountered people who shared my interest, usually with the contribution of a technical expertise that I did not possess. Availability of funds often determined certain undertakings. Thanks to generous donors I have been able to study

---

[1] This paper is dedicated to H.E. Rosvold.

[2] The influential studies from other laboratories will not be cited here; they are accessible in the relevant papers discussed in this review.

feral cats in Norway, wild rats on Hawaii, pigeons in Italy and echidnas in Australia. Predictably, sometimes the available data and opportunities caused whimsical turns in this line of my research.

My early neuropsychological studies in cats (Divac, 1968, 1972) and rats (Divac, 1971; Wikmark et al., 1973) established the generality of the concept of PFS across mammalian species. Much later, 2-deoxyglucose was used to visualize the PFS in rats (Divac and Diemer, 1980). The results of that study showed coactivation of the PFC and many subcortical structures listed by Rosvold and Szwarcbart (1964). In a related experiment, delayed alternation impairment was observed after neostriatal lesions made by kainic acid. In these animals, PFC connections remained demonstrably preserved and functionally viable (Divac et al., 1978c). These two experiments dispersed (at least my) doubt that behavioral impairments seen after neostriatal lesions could be the consequence of accidental damage to cortical connections. In conclusion, the PFC and a part of the neostriatum do share the same functions and therefore do belong to the same system.

Anatomy of the prefrontal cortex

Good agreement between morphological and functional data obtained in the rat and the exciting discovery of dopaminergic innervation of the cortical area described by Leonard as prefrontal, suggested a study in which American opossums, tree shrews and rats were compared. The results showed a good overlap of the projection from the thalamic mediodorsal nucleus and dopamine-containing fibers originating in the ventral tegmental area in each species. Interestingly, the cortical area which receives this overlapping projection has different topography in each of these species (Divac et al., 1978a). These observations suggested that a dense dopaminergic innervation might be used to outline the prefrontal cortex instead of the projection from MD. On the basis of this generalization, an attempt was made to identify the bird equivalent of the PFC. Histochemical (Divac and Mogensen, 1985), biochemical (Divac et al., 1985) and behavioral data (Mogensen and Divac, 1982, 1993a) suggested

that the postero-dorso-lateral "neostriatum" in pigeons could be considered equivalent to the PFC in mammals.

A later discovery, by immunohistochemical techniques, of a dense network of tyrosine hydroxylase- and dopamine-containing fibers also in non-prefrontal cortical areas in primates has restricted the use of cortical dopamine as an indicator of the presence and position of the PFC to the species with a steep gradient of distribution of dopamine in the cortex. Thus far, high density of dopaminergic innervation of the prefrontal area remains unchallenged as an indicator of PFC in non-primate brains. (The perirhinal and entorhinal areas, also densely innervated with dopamine-containing fibers, are not neocortical areas.) Although *density* of dopamine-containing fibers in the motor area of primates appears higher than in the PFC, biochemical measurements in samples of cortical tissue indicate that both the *amount* of dopamine (e.g. Björklund et al., 1978), and binding of spiroperidol to dopamine receptors (Divac et al., 1981) are at the highest level in the PFC. The differences in dopaminergic innervation of the cerebral cortex might offer a test of evolutionary position of a particular species, e.g. among prosimians.

One line of my research aimed to establish the localization and size of PFC in different species. We used mainly horseradish peroxidase as the tracer. This approach confirmed results from other laboratories that, in rats (Divac et al., 1978b, 1993), and probably in hedgehogs (I. Divac and J. Regidor, unpublished), the PFC is split into mesial and suprarhinal parts by a ventral cortical strip innervated by thalamic nucleus submedius and dorsally by cortex innervated by the nucleus ventralis lateralis. This "primitive" arrangement differs from the fronto-polar position of PFC found in tree shrews (Divac et al., 1978a; Divac and Passingham, 1980) and cats (Markowitsch et al., 1978). The same fronto-polar localization, but with a larger relative size of the PFC, exists in dogs and simians. Some evidence suggests that the same arrangement exists in echidnas (*Tachyglossus aculeatus*), the species with proportionally the largest PFC among mammals, including humans (Divac et al., 1987a,b). In bush-babies, PFC has a unique position and shape:

MD projects to the ventral surface of the frontal lobe and to the mesial, fronto-polar and lateral surfaces. A large part of the lateral frontal surface, reaching far rostrally, is not innervated by MD (Markowitsch et al., 1980). These observations suggest that PFC has undergone considerable changes during the evolution. Unfortunately, the sample of different species available so far is too small for a reliable and revealing typology.

Further anatomical studies on PFS revealed: (a) intricate patterns of numerous subcortico-cortical connections to the PFC in rats (Divac et al., 1978b, Divac, 1979) and cats (Markowitsch et al., 1978); (b) sources of cortical projections to the PFC in cats (Markowitsch et al., 1979); and (c) sources of afferents to the MD in tree shrews (Sapawi and Divac, 1978). Since MD projections define PFC, information about inputs to MD is expected to contribute to understanding the functional role of PFC.

In a few experiments, neurochemical techniques revealed interesting features of PFC: First, the capacity of glia to take up glutamate varied with the brain region from which the glia was cultured; the glia cultured from PFC showed a stronger uptake rate than that cultured from the visual cortex or cerebellum (Schousboe and Divac, 1979). Second, the performance of behaviors mediated by PFS did influence the turnover of synapses in rat PFC (Mogensen et al., 1982) but not the turnover of dopamine (Divac et al., 1984a; Mogensen et al., 1992).

Functional analysis of the prefrontal cortex

My studies of functional properties of PFC had the following general objectives: (i) to map PFS neurobehaviorally in different species; (ii) to analyze the relations between the PFC and its related neostriatal region; and (iii) to improve understanding of behavioral roles played by PFS.

A part of the neurobehavioral work on mapping PFS in cats, rats and pigeons has been reviewed above. Other experiments showed that in monkeys, the same small part of the PFC is essential for delayed responding and delayed alternation (Warren and Divac, 1972). Later, we showed that also in rats only a part of

the PFC mediates delayed alternation (Larsen and Divac, 1978).

Neurobehavioral comparisons of different species showed essentially the same functions of PFS in such widely different animals as nocturnal omnivores (rats), solitary hunters (cats), pack hunters (dogs) and aboreal, daylight fruit gatherers (monkeys). Yet, one difference is striking: rats, dogs and cats can relearn delayed response type behavior, whereas monkeys do not. We showed that this difference cannot be attributed to differences either in test situations (Divac and Warren, 1971) or in completeness of the prefrontal ablations (Divac, 1973).

In some experiments, I attempted to see whether cats with PFC ablations succeed in relearning delayed responding by positioning and/or "sustained attention" in the presumed absence of short-term memory. In this attempt, two approaches were taken. In the first, lesioned cats which relearned delayed responding were trained under the following modifications of the task: during the delay period, the wire cage was covered with an opaque cylinder which had a small hole turned towards the experimenter. Through this hole, a syringe with meat paste was inserted into the cage and the cat was allowed to lick the food for about 10 s in the middle of the 30 s delay. The visual isolation and distraction had a negligible effect; no drastic and long-lasting relapse of impairment was seen (Divac, 1968). In the second approach, cats were blinded by bilateral transection of the optic nerve and after 10 weeks taught delayed responding. Retest after ablations of PFC produced the same degree of impairment as seen in cats with preserved vision. This result did not support either the hypothesis of distractibility as an important element in the impairment (blind cats would be less distracted and thus perform better than sighted cats) nor the hypothesis of compensation by visual imagery (blind cats should be more impaired in the absence of the possibility to make use of visual spatial orientation) (Divac, 1969).

In rats, we looked for a brain formation which takes over the functions after PFC ablations and established that the brain formation which mediates the performance in rats with PFC ablations is neither the parietal cortical area (Wörtwein et al., 1993) nor the entire dorsolateral isocortex (Wörtwein et al., 1994). The latter study also shows that PFC can mediate delayed alternation in absence of the cortico-cortical input.

In several experiments on cats (reviewed in more detail in Divac, 1984), it was shown that PFC and the associated part of the neostriatum are serially related. Once a cat relearns delayed responding after a lesion of either of these two structures, additional lesion of the remaining structure has no effect on the performance (Wikmark and Divac, 1973; Divac, 1974). Furthermore, combined lesion of the two formations did not induce a larger impairment than a lesion of either of them alone (Divac, 1968).

The roles of PFC in situations that mimic real life of some species were studied neurobehaviorally. Ablations of mesial PFC did not affect fear behavior in wild rats (Divac et al., 1984b) nor flight and defence behaviors in feral cats (Ursin and Divac, 1975). These results should be reconciled with the effects of frontal lesions on "emotional behaviors" in humans. Other experiments showed that no lesion in the rat frontal lobes had an effect on sexual performance of male rats (Larsson et al., 1980); that ablation only of the ventral part of the PFC in rats induced transient aphagia without adipsia (Mogensen and Divac, 1993b); and that ablation of the pigeon equivalent of the mammalian PFC impaired homing from unfamiliar sites, but not from familiar sites (Gagliardo and Divac, 1993).

In rats, the mesial, but not suprarhinal, PFC lesions impaired spontaneous alternation behavior (Divac et al., 1975b). A later experiment showed an interaction between the lesion localization and behavioral situation; the impairment was found only in animals with dorsal mesial lesions and only if the arms of the T-maze were made different by black or white walls (Mogensen and Divac, 1993b). The impairment in spontaneous alternation, when compared to that of delayed spatial alternation, demonstrates that neither the type of reinforcement nor the kind of learning interact essentially with PFC functioning.

Nauta has suggested that PFC mediates "interoceptive gnosis". This hypothesis was tested by taste aversion conditioning. No ablation within PFC affected taste aversion (Divac et al., 1975a; Mogensen and Divac 1993b).

Ablation of the orbital part of the PFC in monkeys and dogs induces "response disinhibition". We replicated the experiment using rats in which orbital cortex was removed. We saw no sign of any response disinhibition (Mogensen and Divac, 1993b).

Efforts to understand the function of the PFC have often emphasized the role of the spatial factor (as in egocentric orientation) in the tasks that reveal impairments after PFC lesions. We tested such hypotheses first by applying differential reinforcement for low response rates to rats with PFC ablations. The task does not require differential spatial responding but only withholding responses for a predetermined interval. Ablation of the PFC did impair performance in this task thus showing that PFC also plays a role in situations where the spatial factor is considerably reduced if not entirely eliminated (Rosenkilde and Divac, 1975).

Another study along the same lines led to the design of a task in which the informing cue had no spatial localization; cats were supposed to guide their responses to spatially separated feeders on the basis of the duration of confinement under a cage. Again, ablations of the PFC induced a clear impairment (Rosenkilde and Divac, 1976). This result confirms the conclusion that PFC also plays a role in behaviors with reduced spatial requirements.

Some authors postulated involvement of PFC in sequential behaviors. Instead of observing a complex behavior such as maternal, we trained animals to manipulate two objects sequentially in an operant test chamber. Against the prediction, orbital ablation impaired sequencing much more strongly than did a dorsomedial lesion (Mogensen and Divac, 1984). It is likely that the essential part of the PFC for sequential behavior is the medial part of the orbital area (ventral part of the mesial PFC in rats).

Conclusions

Demonstration of the existence of the PFC in a number of species from different orders offers a solid basis for extrapolation to other species, including humans. An extrapolation based on results obtained in a single species is more risky even when this species is considered to be closely related to humans. Indeed, participation of a part of the neostriatum in prefrontal functions inferred from animal studies, has also been found in humans studied with PET and functional MR scanning.

In my attempts to study functions of PFC, negative results were obtained at least as frequently as positive ones. We know now that the entire dorsolateral neocortex in rats plays *no* role in the recovery of delayed response-type behavior (Wörtwein et al., 1994); that cats after PFC lesions do *not* relearn delayed responding through body positioning or "sustained attention" (Divac, 1968); that the PFC does *not* mediate "visceral gnosis" (Divac et al., 1975a); that the PFC is *un*necessary for sexual performance of rats (Larsson et al., 1980); that large parts of the PFC either in cats (Ursin and Divac, 1975) or rats (Divac et al., 1984b) are *not* essentially involved in "emotional behaviors".

On the other hand, no species with lesions in the PFC has escaped impairment of delayed response-type behaviors. Across species, this lesion consequence is more reliable than limb paralysis after motor cortical lesions. Unfortunately, no stringent a priori description of such tasks is available. Sometimes a task which apparently belongs to this group is performed successfully by animals with lesions in the PFS (Mogensen et al., 1987). In the long run, careful analysis of task differences sensitive or insensitive to PFS lesions may provide hints about critical features of situations in which PFS lesions induce impairments.

The presence of the impairments in delayed response-type tasks by all species tested so far with PFC lesions contrasts with the different effects of the same lesions in other behavioral situations. Some conspicuous examples are first, as already mentioned, the inability of monkeys to relearn this performance after PFS lesions. Secondly, following prefrontal ablations, an exceptionally high behavioral activity is seen in Old World monkeys in comparison with other species, including squirrel monkeys. Thirdly, an established "response disinhibition" found after orbital PFC lesions in Old World monkeys could not be replicated in rats in spite of efforts to create similar behavioral requirements (Mogensen and Divac, 1993b). Of course, one can always wonder whether the identical situation

in the judgement of humans is also the same for two other different species.

These few examples illustrate the problems of neurobehavioral analysis of PFC. A partial explanation of apparent inconsistencies and contradictions probably lies in the different functions of different subdivisions of PFC. This requires a parcellation of the PFC (and MD) comparable across species.

References

Björklund. A., Divac, I. and Lindvall, O. (1978) Regional distribution of catecholamines in monkey cerebral cortex. Evidence for a dopaminergic innervation of the primate prefrontal cortex. *Neurosci. Lett.*, 7: 115–119.

Divac, I. (1968) Effects of prefrontal and caudate lesions on delayed response in cats. *Acta Biol. Exp. (Warsaw)*, 28: 149–167.

Divac, I. (1969) Delayed response in blind cats before and after prefrontal ablation. *Physiol. Behav.*, 4: 795–800.

Divac, I. (1971) Frontal lobe system and spatial reversal in the rat. *Neuropsychologia*, 9: 175–183.

Divac, I. (1972) Delayed alternation in cats with lesions of the prefrontal cortex and the caudate nucleus. *Physiol. Behav.*, 8: 519–522.

Divac, I. (1973) Delayed response in cats after frontal lesions extending beyond the gyrus proreus. *Physiol. Behav.*, 10: 717–720.

Divac, I. (1974) Caudate nucleus and relearning of delayed alternation in cats. *Physiol. Psychol.*, 104–106.

Divac, I. (1979) Patterns of subcortico-cortical projections as revealed by somatopetal horseradish peroxidase tracing. *Neuroscience*, 4: 455–461.

Divac, I. (1984) The neostriatum viewed orthogonally. In: *Functions of the Basal Ganglia, CIBA Foundation Symposium 107*, Pitman, London, pp. 201–215.

Divac, I. (1988) A note on the history of the term 'prefrontal'. *IBRO News*, 16: No 2.

Divac, I. and Diemer, N.H. (1980) The prefrontal system in the rat visualized by means of labelled deoxyglucose. Further evidence for functional heterogeneity of the neostriatum. *J. Comp. Neurol.*, 190: 1–13.

Divac, I. and Mogensen, J. (1985) The prefrontal 'cortex' in the pigeon. Catecholamine histofluorescence. *Neuroscience*, 15: 677–682.

Divac, I. and Öberg, R.G.E. (1990) Prefrontal cortex: The name and the thing. In: W. Schwerdtfeger and P. Germroth (Eds.), *Structure and Development of the Forebrain in Lower Vertebrates, Experimental Brain Research Series*, Springer-Verlag, Berlin, pp. 213–220.

Divac, I. and Passingham, R.E. (1980) Connections of the mediodorsal nucleus of the thalamus in the tree shrew. II. Efferent connections. *Neurosci. Lett.*, 19: 21–26.

Divac, I. and Warren, J.M. (1971) Delayed response by frontal monkeys in the Nencki Testing Situation. *Neuropsychologia*, 9: 209–217.

Divac, I., Rosvold H.E., Szwarcbart, M. (1967) Behavioral effects of selective ablation of the caudate nucleus. *J. Comp. Physiol.Psychol.*, 63: 184–190.

Divac, I., Gade, A. and Wikmark, R.G.E. (1975a) Taste aversion in rats with lesions in the frontal lobes: no evidence for interoceptive agnosia. *Physiol. Psychol.*, 3: 43–46.

Divac, I., Wikmark, R.G.E. and Gade, A. (1975b) Spontaneous alternation in rats with lesions in the frontal lobes. An extension of the frontal lobe syndrome. *Physiol. Psychol.*, 3: 39–42.

Divac, I., Björklund, A., Lindvall, O. and Passingham, R.E. (1978a) Converging projections from the mediodorsal thalamic nucleus and mesencephalic dopaminergic neurons to the neocortex in three species. *J. Comp. Neurol.*, 180: 59–72.

Divac, I., Kosmal, A., Björklund, A. and Lindvall, O. (1978b) Subcortical projections to the prefrontal cortex in the rat as revealed by the horseradish peroxidase technique. *Neuroscience*, 3: 785–796.

Divac, I., Markowitsch, H.J. and Pritzel, M. (1978c) Behavioral and anatomical consequences of small intrastriatal injections of kainic acid in the rat. *Brain Res.*, 151: 523–532.

Divac, I., Bræstrup, C. and Nielsen, M. (1981) Spiroperidol, naloxone, diazepam and QNB binding in the monkey cerebral cortex. *Brain Res. Bull.*, 7: 469–477.

Divac, I., Lichtensteiger, W. and Gade, A. (1984a) Catecholamine microfluorometry of nigral perikarya and tyrosine hydroxylase assay in some telencephalic structures of rats exposed to different behavioral situations. *Acta Neurobiol. Exp.*, 44: 263–272.

Divac, I., Mogensen, J., Blanchard, R.J. and Blanchard, D.C. (1984b) Mesial cortical lesions and fear behavior in the wild rat. *Physiol. Psychol.*, 12: 271–274.

Divac, I., Mogensen, J. and Björklund, A. (1985) The prefrontal 'cortex' in the pigeon. Biochemical evidence. *Brain Res.*, 332: 365–368.

Divac, I., Holst, M.-C., Nelson, J., McKenzie, J.S (1987a) Afferents of the frontal cortex in the echidna (*Tachyglossus aculeatus*). Indication of an outstandingly large prefrontal area. *Brain Behav. Evol.*, 30: 303–320.

Divac, I., Pettigrew, J.D., Holst, M.-C. and McKenzie, J.S. (1987b) Efferent connections of the prefrontal cortex of echidna (*Tachyglossus aculeatus*). *Brain Behav. Evol.*, 30: 321–327.

Divac, I., Mogensen, J., Petrovic-Minic, B., Zilles, K., Regidor, J. (1993) Cortical projections of the thalamic mediodorsal nucleus in the rat. Definition of the prefrontal cortex. *Acta Neurobiol. Exp.*, 53: 425–429.

Gagliardo, A. and Divac, I. (1993) Effects of ablation of the presumed equivalent of the mammalian prefrontal cortex in pigeon homing. *Behav. Neurosci.*, 107: 280–288.

Larsen, J.K. and Divac, I. (1978) Selective ablations within the prefrontal cortex of the rat and performance of delayed alternation. *Physiol. Psychol.*, 6: 15–17.

Larsson, K., Öberg, R.G.E. and Divac, I. (1980) Frontal cortical ablations and sexual performance in male albino rats. *Neurosci. Lett.*, Suppl. 5: 319.

Markowitsch, H.J., Pritzel, M. and Divac, I. (1978) The prefrontal cortex of the cat: anatomical subdivisions based on retrograde labelling of cells in the mediodorsal thalamic nucleus. *Exp. Brain Res.*, 32: 335–344.

Markowitsch, H.J., Pritzel, M. and Divac, I. (1979) Cortical afferents to the prefrontal cortex of the cat: a study with the horseradish peroxidase technique. *Neurosci. Lett.*, 11: 115–120.

Markowitsch, H.J., Pritzel, M., Wilson, M. and Divac, I. (1980) The prefrontal cortex of a prosimian (*Galago senegalensis*) defined as cortical projection area of the thalamic mediodorsal nucleus. *Neuroscience*, 5: 1771–1779.

Mogensen, J. and Divac, I. (1982) The prefrontal 'cortex' in the pigeon. Behavioral evidence. *Brain Behav. Evol.*, 21: 60–66.

Mogensen, J. and Divac, I. (1984) Sequential behavior after modified prefrontal lesions in the rat. *Physiol. Psychol.*, 12: 41–44.

Mogensen, J. and Divac, I. (1993a) Behavioural effects of ablation of the pigeon-equivalent of the mammalian prefrontal cortex. *Behav. Brain Res.*, 55: 101–107.

Mogensen, J. and Divac, I. (1993b) Behavioural changes after ablation of subdivisions of the rat prefrontal cortex. *Acta Neurobiol. Exp.*, 53: 439–449.

Mogensen, J., Jørgensen, O.S. and Divac, I. (1982) Synaptic proteins in frontal and control brain regions of rats after exposure to spatial problems. *Behav. Brain Res.*, 5: 375–386.

Mogensen, J., Iversen, I.H. and Divac, I. (1987) Neostriatal lesions impaired rats' delayed alternation performance in a T-maze but not in a two-key operant chamber. *Acta Neurobiol. Exp.*, 47: 45–54.

Mogensen, J., Björklund, A. and Divac, I. (1992) Catecholamines and DOPAC in cortical and neostriatal regions during rats' learning of delayed alternation. *Acta Neurobiol. Exp.*, 52: 49–56.

Regidor, J. and Divac, I. (1987) Architectonics of the thalamus in echidna (*Tachyglossus aculeatus*): search for the mediodorsal nucleus. *Brain Behav. Evol.*, 30: 328–341.

Rosenkilde, C.E. and Divac, I. (1975) DRL performance following anteromedial cortical ablations in rats. *Brain Res.*, 95: 142–146.

Rosenkilde, C.E. and Divac, I. (1976) Time discrimination performance in cats with lesions in the prefrontal cortex and the caudate nucleus. *J. Comp. Physiol. Psychol.*, 90: 343–352.

Rosvold, H.E. and Szwarcbart, M.K. (1964) Neural structures involved in delayed-response performance. In: J.M. Warren and K. Akert (Eds.), *The Frontal Granular Cortex and Behavior*, McGraw-Hill, New York, pp. 1–15.

Sapawi, R.R. and Divac, I. (1978) Connections of the mediodorsal nucleus of the thalamus in the tree shrew. I. Afferent connections. *Neurosci. Lett.*, 7: 183–189.

Schousboe, A. and Divac, I. (1979) Differences in glutamate uptake in astrocytes cultured from different brain regions. *Brain Res.*, 177: 407–409.

Ursin, H. and Divac, I. (1975) Emotional behavior in feral cats with ablations of the prefrontal cortex and subsequent lesions in amygdala. *J. Comp. Physiol. Psychol.*, 88: 36–39.

Warren, J.M. and Divac, I. (1972) Delayed response performance by rhesus monkeys with midprincipalis lesions. *Psychonomic Sci.*, 8: 146–147.

Wikmark, R.G.E. and Divac, I. (1973) Absence of effect of caudate lesions on delayed responses acquired after large frontal ablations in cats. *Israeli J. Med. Sci.*, 9: 92–97.

Wikmark, R.G.E., Divac, I. and Weiss, R. (1973) Retention of spatial delayed alternation in rats with lesions in the frontal lobes. Implications for a comparative neuropsychology of the prefrontal system. *Brain Behav. Evol.*, 8: 329–339.

Wörtwein, G., Mogensen, J. and Divac, I. (1993) Retention and relearning of spatial delayed alternation in rats after combined or sequental lesions of the prefrontal and parietal cortex. *Acta Neurobiol. Exp.*, 53: 357–366.

Wörtwein G, Mogensen J, Divac, I. (1994) Retention and relearning of spatial delayed alternation in rats after ablation of the prefrontal cortex or total nonprefrontal isocortex. *Behav. Brain Res.*, in press..

SECTION IV

Neuroplasticity

F. Bloom (Editor)
Progress in Brain Research, Vol. 100
© 1994 Elsevier Science B.V. All rights reserved

CHAPTER 23

A comparison of the mechanistic relationships between development and learning in *Aplysia*

Emilie A. Marcus[1], Nigel J. Emptage[2], René Marois[3] and Thomas J. Carew[1-3]

Departments of [1]Biology, [2]Psychology and the [3]Interdepartmental Neuroscience Program, Yale University, New Haven, CT, USA

Introduction

At the turn of the century, Ramón y Cajal (1911) articulated the hypothesis that growth processes involved in the development of the nervous system persist into the adult where they subserve learning and memory. Since Cajal's seminal suggestion, considerable experimental attention has been aimed at elucidating the cellular and molecular mechanisms of both learning and neuronal development. Historically, however, preparations that have been favored by developmental neurobiologists have not been preferred for studying mechanisms of learning; likewise the systems that are best understood with respect to adult learning and memory have not been well-characterized developmentally. Consequently, to date no single experimental system has been extensively studied from both a developmental and a learning perspective. For this reason, comparisons between the mechanisms of learning and development often resort to analogies and inferences drawn across diverse systems. Ultimately, an assessment of the mechanistic commonalities between development and learning will require an analysis of similarities and differences within the same experimental system. Towards that end, in this review, we focus our attention on the marine mollusc *Aplysia californica* (with references to other systems where appropriate) with the goal of bringing together what is known about the relationship between development and learning in a single experimental system.

The principal advantage of *Aplysia* as a system in which to examine the relationship between develop-

mental and adult plasticity stems from the fact that mechanisms of learning in the adult CNS have been extensively characterized at the cellular and molecular level (for review, see Kandel and Schwartz, 1982; Kandel and Hawkins, 1992). One general principle that has emerged from this work, as well as from related work in vertebrate systems, is that learning occurs through the modulation of synaptic efficacy. Perhaps the best understood form of learning in *Aplysia* is sensitization, which is defined as an increase in reflex response amplitude following the presentation of a noxious stimulus. By varying the number and magnitude of noxious stimuli, it is possible to produce sensitization of defensive withdrawal reflexes that lasts minutes to hours (short-term), or days to weeks (long-term). In both cases, the increase in reflex responsiveness is produced at least in part by presynaptic facilitation of a monosynaptic connection between the sensory and motor neurons that mediate the reflex. Presynaptic facilitation is in turn produced by release of the neuromodulatory transmitter serotonin (5HT) from interneurons which fire in response to the noxious stimulus. The short-term effects of 5HT on transmitter release are mediated by cAMP-dependent and protein kinase C-dependent reduction of specific potassium conductances; this results in a broadening of the sensory neuron action potential which permits an increase in intracellular calcium in the presynaptic terminals. The long-term effects on transmitter release involve modulation of the biophysical properties of sensory neurons described above, as well as morphological changes such as an increase in the number of synapses onto motor neurons, a process that requires gene transcription and protein synthesis (Bailey, 1991; Montarolo et al., 1986). Thus, in summary, considerable progress has been made in elucidating the mechanisms of short-term and long-term plasticity in adult *Aplysia*. In this review, we use this understanding of the cellular and molecular mechanisms of learning in *Aplysia* as a basis for comparison with the three principle stages of neuronal development: differentiation, neurite outgrowth and synapse formation.

Differentiation

The term differentiation refers to the process by which a cell acquires a specific identity. It is generally considered to be the first step in a developmental program during which a proliferative pleuripotent cell gives rise to a post-mitotic cell committed to a particular fate. In the development of the nervous system, the commitment to a neuronal cell fate typically is a prerequisite step for further elaboration, such as neurite outgrowth, axonal path finding and synapse formation. Thus, it might seem rather surprising to look for comparisons between this initial step of neuronal development and the cellular processes of learning and memory since the presumptive neurons have yet to become integrated in a functional neural circuit. However, the evidence described below suggests that both the cellular and molecular processes that lead to neuronal differentiation in *Aplysia* (as well as in the mammalian hippocampus) may have intriguing parallels to the mechanisms underlying the neural basis of learning and memory.

In *Aplysia* as in other systems, a cell generated from the proliferation of progenitor cells will follow a particular differentiation pathway in response to intrinsic and/or extrinsic factors. Whether intrinsic or extrinsic, the signal must ultimately be transduced in the nucleus where it initiates a cascade of molecular interactions that transform the phenotype of the cell. In this way, differentiation and long-term plasticity may share a fundamental common principle in that they both involve the transduction of a transient instructive biochemical signal into a self-sustained molecular process in order to retain cell-specific infor-

mation. Below, we provide examples at both the cellular, transducing step and at the molecular, genomic level that illustrate the possible convergence of the mechanistic bases of differentiation and long-term plasticity.

Role of axosomatic contacts in differentiation and plasticity

Schacher et al. (1979) have shown that neuronal differentiation in the anlage of the abdominal ganglion of *Aplysia* appears to be triggered by an extrinsic signal in the form of a synaptic contact from a neuronal process that travels in the pleuro-abdominal connective. Following a transient synaptic contact by this fiber on their cell bodies, abdominal neurons appear to undergo major ultrastructural changes suggestive of a differentiative process: relaxation of the nuclear chromatin, proliferation of cytoplasmic constituents, and initiation of an axonal projection at precisely the site where the contact was previously established (Schacher et al., 1979). Although the identity of the pre-synaptic fiber is still unknown, recent work by Marois et al. (1992) has shown that serotonergic cells that have their cell bodies near the cerebral ganglion send processes in the pleuro-abdominal connective to the anlage of the abdominal ganglion where they make contact with presumptive neuronal cell bodies at a time that is consistent with their having a role in differentiation. These results raise the possibility that serotonergic neurons make appropriate synaptic contact with abdominal neurons, triggering their differentiation.

In parallel to the proposed role of axosomatic contacts in neuronal differentiation, there is also increasing evidence suggesting a role for serotonergic axosomatic contacts in the induction of long-term synaptic plasticity in *Aplysia*. For example, the somata of sensory neurons in the abdominal and pleural ganglia of adult *Aplysia* receive serotonergic contacts (Kistler et al., 1985; Zhang et al., 1991). Recently, Emptage and Carew (1993) have shown that exogenous application of 5HT to the cell body (and proximal synaptic region) of pleural sensory cells produces long-term synaptic facilitation of distant synapses that were never

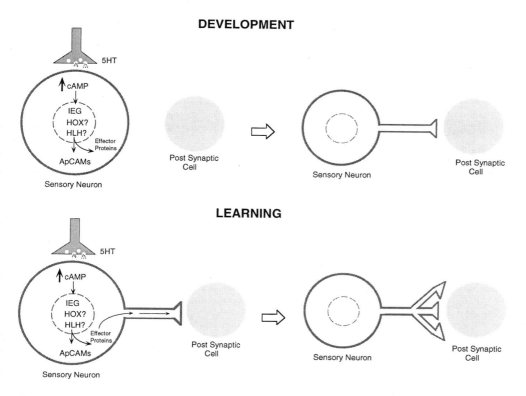

Fig. 1. A schematic representation of similarities in the cellular and molecular mechanisms of development and learning in *Aplysia*. The specific points of convergence include: (i) the role of serotonergic axosomatic contacts; (ii) the activation of transcription factors including immediate early genes and perhaps differentiation-inducing genes; (iii) the necessity of an appropriate post-synaptic target; (iv) the role of cAMP as a second messenger in the signal transduction cascade; and (v) the common role of cell adhesion molecules and other growth related proteins. During development, activation of these pathways leads to differentiation and neurite outgrowth; in adult learning, reactivation of these same pathways results in a growth-mediated increase in synaptic strength. See text for details.

exposed to 5HT (for similar findings in abdominal sensory neurons, see also Clark and Kandel, 1993). This raises the possibility that the somatic serotonergic input might be ideally situated to affect genomic (long-term) changes. If this were the case, then this system in the adult might correspond to that described above in development in which axosomatic contacts are involved in triggering the differentiation of neurons. Moreover, if the differentiation-inducing axosomatic contacts in developing *Aplysia* prove to be serotonergic, this may indicate that the serotonergic system impinges on the cell body region of neurons throughout the life of the animal to specifically activate genomic machinery; initially to trigger differentiation of a cell during development, and later to reactivate the genomic program in the context of long-term synaptic enhancement (Fig. 1).

Role of identified transcription factors

It is more difficult to pursue a comparison of differentiation and learning at the molecular level in *Aplysia* because, although the molecular events in long-term synaptic facilitation are being increasingly elucidated, the molecular basis of neuronal differentiation in *Aplysia* is virtually unexplored. However, the molecular basis of differentiation, as described in *Mus*, *Drosophila* and *C. elegans* shows a high degree of conservation, to the point where one can begin to consider a universal plan for differentiation of any cell, regardless of tissue type or animal species (see Anderson, 1992). The current model for understanding how information contained in the cytoplasm ultimately affects the nucleus centers on activation of two main sets of transcription factor genes. One set, the immediate-early genes (IEGs), is expressed rapidly and transiently, prior to or at the onset of differentiation. Based on the temporal pattern of expression, the IEGs have generally been regarded as serving as a rapid and amplifying nuclear signal to regulate and orchestrate the expression of downstream genes responsible for making the decision to either differentiate or re-enter the cell cycle (Sheng and Greenberg, 1990). The second class of transcription factor genes (which includes genes with homeobox or helix-loop-helix DNA-binding domains) are typically expressed over a long period of the differentiation process. This second class of genes tends to be seen as directing the cell's differentiation by orchestrating the expression of downstream effector genes that will endow the cell with its particular molecular identity (Gehring, 1987; Garrell and Campuzano, 1991).

Although still at an early stage, the study of the molecular basis of learning and memory already hints at interesting parallels with the molecular program of differentiation described above. For instance, changes in the expression of immediate-early proteins (IEPs) have been detected in paradigms involving the induction of long-term synaptic plasticity in *Aplysia* (Barzilai et al., 1989). The involvement of IEPs in the induction of long-term synaptic plasticity is further supported by the requirement for protein and RNA synthesis during and immediately following 5HT application, a time window that is consistent with the temporal expression of the IEPs (Montarolo et al., 1986; Barzilai et al., 1989; Castellucci et al., 1989). Specific IEGs are also differentially expressed in the mammalian hippocampus following the induction of long-term synaptic plasticity (Cole et al., 1989; Wisden et al., 1990; Nedivi et al., 1993; Qian et al., 1993). Although no genes belonging to the second class of nuclear proteins have yet been shown to be expressed differentially with long-term synaptic plasticity, the recent findings that genes of this class may regulate neurite outgrowth (LeRoux et al., 1993) and the ex-

pression of neural cell adhesion molecules (Jones et al., 1993; see below) suggest that such genes may also be implicated in neuronal plasticity. Thus, the activation of these two classes of transcription factors may prove to be central to the molecular basis of long-term synaptic changes accompanying long-term memory. These genes would be responsible for orchestrating the new levels of expression of an array of downstream effector genes that in turn would underlie the physiological and structural alterations associated with learning (Bailey, 1991; Madison et al., 1991; Bailey and Kandel, 1993). From this perspective, the molecular basis of long-term plasticity can be viewed as a reactivation of at least a portion of the molecular program for cell differentiation (Fig. 1).

Neurite outgrowth

Once a proliferative cell is committed to becoming a neuron, it enters the second stage in its development, the growth of neuronal processes. The nature of this growth is stringently regulated since it underlies the highly specific and reproducible patterns of neuronal connectivity that are characteristic of the adult nervous system. One principle that has emerged recently in the study of mechanisms of adult plasticity in both invertebrates and vertebrates, is that long-term changes in synaptic efficacy are associated with growth-dependent structural changes (Bailey and Kandel, 1993). For example, a detailed examination of learning-related morphological changes in neurons has been performed by Bailey and colleagues in *Aplysia* (Bailey, 1991). They found that behavioral training that produces long-term sensitization of the gill and siphon withdrawal reflex also produces long-lasting morphological changes in the sensory neurons that mediate this reflex. These changes include increases in the number and size of active zones, the number and distribution of synaptic vesicles, and the total number of presynaptic varicosities per sensory neuron. These findings raise the possibility that the same mechanisms which regulate outgrowth during development may be re-utilized during learning to mediate long-term changes in neuronal morphology. Within this general framework of growth-related processes during development and learning, below we discuss several specific examples that demonstrate possible points of convergence between the mechanisms of neurite outgrowth and long-term plasticity.

Role of post-synaptic targets

Glanzman et al. (1989) analyzed *Aplysia* sensory neurons growing in culture and found that the presence of a postsynaptic cell appears to be critical for normal neuronal growth. Sensory neurons grown alone had neurites with few branches that tended to aggregate together into thick bundles. In contrast, sensory neurons grown in co-cultures with the appropriate postsynaptic cell had many finer neurites and numerous varicosities and thus appeared more comparable to sensory neurons observed in vivo. Moreover, if sensory neurons were co-cultured with inappropriate postsynaptic target cells (i.e. cells onto which they would not normally synapse) then the neuritic structure of the sensory neurons was similar to that seen for sensory neurons grown alone. It therefore appears that complex growth of the sensory neurons is not simply dependent on the presence of another neuron, but on the ability of the sensory neurons to recognize and form viable synaptic contacts with their appropriate post-synaptic target. However, it is important to note that these experiments have been carried out in regenerating neurons isolated from the mature CNS and grown in culture. In light of the as yet unclear relationship between development and regeneration, similar experiments will ultimately need to be carried out with embryonic neurons.

Glanzman et al. (1990) have also examined the role of the post-synaptic cell in mediating the effects of 5HT-induced growth in mature sensory neurons. 5HT repeatedly applied to co-cultures of sensory and motor neurons produced significant increases in the number of varicosities of the siphon sensory neurons. This cell growth was correlated with long-term synaptic enhancement, providing support for the idea that growth may be critical for production of long-term memory. In experiments where the postsynaptic target cell was not cultured with the sensory neuron, repeated presentations of 5HT did not produce morphological changes

in the sensory neurons, suggesting that the presence of the postsynaptic cell is critical for these morphological changes to occur. Thus, the post-synaptic cell may be required not only for establishing appropriate sensory neuron morphology in development but also for the plasticity-associated growth induced by 5HT in the adult. It is therefore possible that the postsynaptic neuron subserves a similar mechanistic role for both types of growth processes (Fig. 1).

Role of second messengers

A second point of convergence that has come to light from work in developing and mature *Aplysia* neurons is the involvement of cAMP as a second messenger in both neuritic outgrowth and long-term synaptic plasticity. Direct support for a role for cAMP in development comes from studies examining the structural and biophysical consequences of manipulating cAMP concentrations in developing neurons. At the structural level, Forscher et al. (1987) have demonstrated that elevation of cAMP serves as the inductive agent in promoting growth cone differentiation into secretory terminals in cultured *Aplysia* bag cell neurons. In another mollusc, *Helisoma*, Mattson et al. (1988) have also shown that 5HT-induced elevation of cAMP can regulate neurite outgrowth. At the biophysical level, Belardetti et al. (1986) have demonstrated that 5HT-induced modulation of the 5HT-sensitive potassium current (an effect that is known to be mediated by activation of cAMP), is present in growth cones of cultured *Aplysia* sensory neurons. In addition, recent work examining the development of the biophysical properties of sensory neurons in vivo has shown that the effects of 5HT that are known to be mediated by cAMP in adults emerge early in development relative to other modulatory effects of 5HT (Marcus and Carew, 1990). Moreover, biochemical assays have revealed that 5HT is able to stimulate adenylate cyclase and elevate cAMP levels in the isolated central nervous system at the earliest stages of juvenile development (Chang et al., 1989). Taken collectively, these data demonstrate that a subcellular signaling pathway involving the elevation of cAMP as a second messenger is present and can be functionally triggered early in development and suggest that the role of this pathway may be to mediate neuritic outgrowth.

From the perspective of adult plasticity, there are now several lines of evidence implicating cAMP as an essential step in the intracellular cascade that mediates the long-term enhancement of synaptic efficacy associated with behavioral long-term sensitization in adult *Aplysia*. Recently, Nazif et al. (1991) have shown that cAMP can itself induce morphological changes (increases in the number of varicosities and the number of branch points) in *Aplysia* sensory neurons similar to those induced by 5HT and by sensitization training. Physiologically, elevation of cAMP in the sensory neurons produces a long-term decrease in the magnitude of the 5HT-sensitive potassium current (Scholz and Byrne, 1987) and an enhancement of the EPSP onto the motor neuron that persists for at least 24 h (Schacher et al., 1988). It has also recently been demonstrated that elevation of cAMP mimics the effects of long-term sensitization training on the expression and phosphorylation of specific proteins (Sweatt and Kandel, 1989; Noel et al., 1991). Finally, perhaps the most convincing demonstration of a role for cAMP in mediating long-term changes in synaptic efficacy in adult *Aplysia* comes from recent molecular analyses demonstrating a requirement for cAMP-dependent transcription factors in the induction of long-term synaptic plasticity (Dash et al., 1990). Thus, it appears that cAMP may be an important second messenger in the signal transduction cascades that regulate neurite outgrowth during development and mediate the reactivation of growth processes that accompany long-term plasticity (Fig. 1).

Regulation of specific proteins

Important advances have recently been made in the study of the molecular mechanisms that contribute to neurite outgrowth in *Aplysia*. Specifically, a family of proteins, designated ApCAMs, that are closely related to the cell adhesion molecules NCAM and fasciclin II, have recently been identified in the cells of developing *Aplysia* (Schacher et al., 1990). ApCAMs are found on the surface of all cells in the early blastula and with further development, their expression becomes re-

stricted to the CNS (Schacher et al., 1990). That ApCAM proteins may be important in the growth of developing neurons has recently been demonstrated by Keller and Schacher (1990) who found that antibodies raised against ApCAM proteins disrupt fasciculation of growing axons in vitro, consequently altering neuronal cell morphology.

With regard to adult plasticity, Mayford et al. (1992) have shown that ApCAM expression decreases in the adult CNS in a protein synthesis-dependent manner following multiple applications of 5HT or cAMP. Since the level of cell adhesion molecules on the surface of the neuronal substrate has been shown to dramatically affect neurite outgrowth (Doherty et al., 1990), it has been suggested that a reduction in the level of ApCAM expression in adult *Aplysia* sensory neurons is the initial step in the process of neuritic outgrowth and the formation of new synaptic contacts between sensory and motor neurons that accompanies long-term plasticity. Thus, these results support the idea that a common set of adhesion molecules may be used during neural development and then re-utilized during learning-related growth at mature *Aplysia* synapses (Fig. 1).

Formation and modulation of synapses

A third critical step in the development of the nervous system is the establishment of functional synaptic connections between the individual elements of a neural circuit. In light of the current appreciation for the role of modulation of synaptic efficacy in mediating adult plasticity, it is reasonable to ask whether the cellular processes that underlie the modulation of synaptic strength in adult animals are the same processes that underlie the formation of synaptic connections during development. This question cannot yet be addressed in *Aplysia* because little is known about the mechanisms of synapse formation in this system.

Thus, although we have implicated mechanisms of long-term synaptic facilitation as playing a role in both differentiation and neurite outgrowth, it remains to be demonstrated whether these same mechanisms also play a role in synapse formation. There is reason, however, to be optimistic that such a comparison will be fruitful since it is known from work in vertebrate systems that there is considerable overlap between the mechanisms of synapse formation and long-term synaptic facilitation in the hippocampus (for review, see Kelly, 1992; Pffenninger et al., 1992)

One way in which to address the issue of whether mechanisms of synaptic facilitation contribute to synapse formation is to examine when different forms of synaptic plasticity first emerge developmentally. There are already several examples in *Aplysia* indicating that one form of synaptic modulation, short-term facilitation, emerges developmentally well after the formation of synaptic connections. It is therefore not likely that the mechanisms of short-term facilitation are involved in the initial development of synaptic connectivity.

Support for this view is provided by Ohmori (1982) who have examined the developmental expression of post-tetanic potentiation (a short-lasting form of homosynaptic facilitation) at identified inhibitory and excitatory synapses and have found that in both cases, short-term modulation of synaptic efficacy emerges at a distinct and later phase than the establishment of a functional synaptic connection.

In addition, Rayport and Camardo (1984) and Nolen and Carew (1988) have found a similar sequence for the developmental emergence of short-term heterosynaptic facilitation. Finally, Marcus and Carew (1990) have shown that spike broadening in *Aplysia* sensory neurons, an effect that has been strongly implicated in short-term synaptic facilitation in adult animals, emerges at the very end of the juvenile phase of development, well after functional synaptic connections have been made between sensory and motor neurons.

To date, the developmental expression of long-term synaptic facilitation has not been examined; however, based on our observations that elements of the mechanism of long-term facilitation play a role in differentiation and neurite outgrowth, we expect that some of these elements may also be involved in synapse formation. Thus, one further prediction of the early developmental role for the mechanisms of long-term synaptic facilitation is that long-term synaptic facilitation itself might develop earlier than short-term facilitation.

Concluding remarks

Our comparison of development and learning in *Aplysia* has revealed a striking number of mechanistic similarities between these two processes. These observations lend substantial support to Cajal's hypothesis that growth mechanisms involved in the development of the nervous system persist into the adult where they subserve learning and memory. It is particularly intriguing that growth processes were the focus of Cajal's attention in view of the finding that short-term synaptic plasticity, a process that does not involve growth but rather is dependent on the covalent modification of pre-existing proteins, emerges developmentally well after functional neuronal circuitry has been established. It therefore appears that the adaptive properties of the adult nervous system represent a combination of two classes of mechanisms, one that includes retained developmental processes, and a second class that appears to be specifically related to adult plasticity; the distinguishing feature between the two classes is the dependence on cell growth.

Where do we go from here? For studies in *Aplysia*, there are some clear avenues that warrant further investigation. For example, if we are correct in thinking that long-term plasticity involves the reactivation of at least part of the molecular program for differentiation, it will be important to look for regulation of differentiation genes such as homeobox and helix-loop-helix transcription factors in long-term synaptic plasticity. This is an avenue of research that remains virtually unexplored and may provide valuable insights into the molecular nature of long-term memory.

From the perspective of neurite outgrowth, important insights may come from an analysis of the role of ion channel modulation in the regulation of growth cone motility and axon guidance. In particular, the critical role that Ca^{2+} plays in these processes makes this an obvious focus for investigation. Specifically, it is known that in adult *Aplysia*, 5HT can modulate Ca^{2+} channels that do not contribute to normal synaptic transmitter release (Edmonds et al., 1990); perhaps it is through the modulation of these or related conductances in the growth cone that 5HT exerts an effect on neurite outgrowth.

Finally, with respect to synapse formation, recent advances have been made in vertebrate systems where synapse-specific proteins and their role in the development of connectivity and transmitter release are currently being elucidated (Kelly, 1992; DeCamilli, 1993). Thus, it may be useful to look for counterparts to these proteins in *Aplysia* where learning is well-characterized and determine whether they play comparable roles in synapse formation and modulation.

At a more general level, the real test of the relationship between development and learning will ultimately come from studies that ask whether the same process is *required* for both neuronal development and synaptic plasticity. Important advances in this direction have already been made with genetic manipulation in vertebrates and invertebrates. For example, it has been possible using homologous recombination technology in mice to demonstrate that knocking out the gene for a specific kinase can produce both developmental abnormalities in the CNS and a deficiency in long-term synaptic plasticity in the adult (Grant et al., 1992; Silva et al., 1992).

Likewise, in *Drosophila*, Drain et al. (1991) have used heat inducible promoters to control the temporal expression of inhibitors of the cAMP-dependent protein kinase and have shown that kinase activity in the adult fly is required for learning and memory. Therefore, the use of inducible promoters that allow selective spatial and temporal activation of downstream genes may provide a powerful strategy for specifying the developmental and adult requirement for the expression of specific processes and may in the future permit a means of directly testing the relationship between development and learning.

In summary, considerable progress has recently been made in the analysis of cellular and molecular mechanisms of both development and learning and there are now several points of convergence between these two fields. Thus, it appears that the ideas underlying the original development and formulation of Cajal's hypothesis have been retained through the intervening century and have helped to shape and guide our contemporary view of the mechanistic relationship between development and learning.

Acknowledgments

We thank Laura Stark for helpful comments on an earlier draft of the manuscript. Supported by NIMH post-doctoral training fellowship 5T332MH18397-07 to E.A.M., SERC-NATO post-doctoral fellowship to N.J.E., predoctoral NSERC and FCAR fellowships (Canada) to R.M. and NIH grant R01-MH-1083 and AFOSR award F49620-93-1-0273 to T.J.C.

References

Anderson, D.J. (1992) Molecular control of neural development. In: Z. Hall (Ed.), *Molecular Neurobiology*, Sinauer Associates, MA.

Bailey, C.H. (1991) Morphological basis of short- and long-term memory in *Aplysia*. In: R. Lister and H. Weingartner (Eds.), *Perspectives on Cognitive Neuroscience*, Oxford University Press, New York.

Bailey, C.H. and Kandel, E.R. (1993) Structural changes accompanying memory storage. *Annu. Rev. Physiol.*, 55: 397–426.

Barzilai, A., Kennedy, T.E., Sweatt, J.D. and Kandel, E.R. (1989) 5-HT modulates protein synthesis and the expression of specific proteins during long-term facilitation in *Aplysia* sensory neurons. *Neuron*, 2: 1577–1586.

Belardetti, F., Schacher, S., Kandel, E.R. and Siegelbaum, S.A. (1986) The growth cones of *Aplysia* sensory neurons: modulation by serotonin of action potential duration and single potassium currents. *Proc. Natl. Acad. Sci. USA*, 83: 7094–7098.

Cajal, S.R. (1911) Histologie du système nerveux de l'homme et des vertébrés.

Castellucci, V.F., Blumenfeld, H., Goelet, P. and Kandel, E.R. (1989) Inhibitor of protein synthesis blocks long-term behavioral sensitization in the isolated gill-withdrawal reflex of *Aplysia. J. Neurobiol.*, 20: 1–9.

Chang, T.N., Marcus, E.A., Dudai, Y. and Carew, T.J. (1989) Developmental analysis of adenylate cyclase activity and its modulation by 5-HT in the CNS of *Aplysia. Soc. Neurosci. Abstr.*, 15: 1019.

Clark, G.A. and Kandel, E.R. (1993) Induction of long-term facilitation in *Aplysia* sensory neurons by local application of 5HT to remote synapses. *Proc. Natl. Acad. Sci. USA*, 90: 11411–11415.

Cole, A.J., Saffen, D.W., Baraban, J.M. and Worley, P.F. (1989) Rapid increase of an immediate early gene messenger RNA in hippocampal neurons by synaptic NMDA receptor activation. *Nature*, 340: 474–476.

Dash, P.K., Hochner, B. and Kandel, E.R. (1990) Injection of the cAMP-responsive element into the nucleus of *Aplysia* sensory neurons blocks long-term facilitation. *Nature*, 345: 718–721.

DeCamilli, P. (1993) Exocytosis goes with a SNAP. *Nature*, 364: 387–388.

Doherty, P., Fruns, M., Seaton, P., Dickson, G., Barton, C.H., Sears, T.A. and Walsh, F.S. (1990) A threshold effect of the major isoforms of NCAM on neurite outgrowth. *Nature*, 343: 464–466.

Drain, P., Folkers, E. and Quinn, W.G. (1991) cAMP-dependent protein kinase and the disruption of learning in transgenic flies. *Neuron*, 6: 71–82.

Edmonds, B., Klein, M., Dale, N. and Kandel, E.R. (1990) Contributions of two types of calcium channels to synaptic transmission and plasticity. *Science*, 250: 1142–1147.

Emptage, N.J. and Carew T.J. (1993) Long-term synaptic facilitation in the absence of short-term synaptic facilitation in *Aplysia* neurons. *Science*, 262: 253–256.

Forscher, P., Kaczmarek, L.K., Buchanan, J. and Smith, S.J. (1987) Cyclic AMP induces changes in distribution and transport of organelles within growth cones of *Aplysia* bag cell neurons. *J. Neurosci.*, 7: 3600–3611.

Garrell, J. and Campuzano, S. (1991) The helix-loop-helix domain: a common motif for bristles, muscles and sex. *Bioessays*, 13: 493–498.

Gehring, W.J. (1987) Homeo boxes in the study of development. *Science*, 236: 1245–1252.

Glanzman, D.L., Kandel, E.R. and Schacher, S. (1989) Identified target motor neuron regulates neurite outgrowth and synapse formation of *Aplysia* sensory neurons *in vitro*. *Neuron*, 3: 441–450.

Glanzman, D.L., Kandel, E.R. and Schacher, S. (1990) Target dependent structural changes accompanying long-term synaptic facilitation in *Aplysia* neurons. *Science*, 249: 799–802.

Grant, S.G., O'Dell, T.J., Karl, K.A., Stein, P.L., Soriano, P. and Kandel, E.R. (1992) Impaired long-term potentiation. spatial learning, and hippocampal development in *fyn* mutant mice. *Science*, 258: 1903–1910.

Jones, F.S., Holst, B.D., Minowa, O.., DeRobertis, E.M. and Edelman, G.M. (1993) Binding and transcriptional activation of the promoter for the neural cell adhesion molecule by HoxC6 (Hox-3.3). *Proc. Natl. Acad. Sci. USA*, 90: 6557–6561.

Kandel, E.R. and Hawkins, R.D. (1992) The biological basis of learning and individuality. *Sci. Am.*, 267: 78–86.

Kandel, E.R. and Schwartz, J.H. (1982) Molecular biology of learning: Modulation of transmitter release. *Science*, 218: 433–443.

Keller, F. and Schacher, S. (1990) Neuron-specific membrane glycoproteins promoting neurite fasciculation in *Aplysia californica*. *J. Cell Biol.*, 111: 2637–2650.

Kelly, P.T. (1992) Calmodulin-dependent protein kinase II. *Mol. Neurobiol.*, 5: 153–177.

Kistler, H.B., Jr., Hawkins, R.D., Koester, J., Steinbusch, H.W., Kandel, E.R. and Schwartz, J.H. (1985) Distribution of serotonin-immunoreactive cell bodies and processes in the abdominal ganglion of mature *Aplysia*. *J. Neurosci.*, 5: 72–80.

LeRoux, I., Joliot, A.H., Bloch-Gallego, E., Prochiantz, A. and Volovitch, M. (1993) Neurotrophic activity of the Antennapedia homeodomain depends on its specific DNA-binding properties. *Proc. Natl. Acad. Sci.*, 90: 9120–9124.

Madison, D.V., Malenka, R.C. and Nicoll, R.A. (1991) Mechanisms underlying long-term potentiation of synaptic transmission. *Annu. Rev. Neurosci.*, 14: 379–397.

Marcus, E.A. and Carew, T.J. (1990) Differential modulation of excitability and spike duration in the tail sensory neurons of developing *Aplysia*. *Soc. Neurosci. Abstr.*, 16: 19.

Marois, R., Kelly, G.M., Hockfield, S. and Carew, T.J. (1992) An ultrastructural study of serotonergic cells in the CNS of embryonic and larval *Aplysia*. *Soc. Neursci. Abstr.*, 18: 1471.

Mattson, M.P., Taylor-Hunter, A. and Kater, S.B. (1988) Neurite outgrowth in individual neurons of a neuronal population is differentially regulated by calcium and cyclic AMP. *J. Neurosci.*, 8: 1704–1711.

Mayford, M., Barzilai, A., Keller, F., Schacher, S. and Kandel, E.R. (1992) Modulation of an NCAM-related adhesion molecule with long-term synaptic plasticity in *Aplysia*. *Science*, 256: 638–644.

Montarolo, P.G., Goelet, P., Castellucci, V.F., Morgan, J., Kandel, E.R. and Schacher, S. (1986) A critical period for macromolecular synthesis in long-term heterosynaptic facilitation in *Aplysia*. *Science*, 234: 1249–1254.

Nazif, F.A, Byrne, J.H and Cleary, L.J. (1991) cAMP induces long-term morphological changes in sensory neurons of *Aplysia*. *Brain Res.*, 539: 324–327.

Nedivi, E., Hevroni, D., Naot, D., Israeli, D. and Citri, Y. (1993) Numerous candidate plasticity-related genes revealed by differential cDNA cloning. *Nature*, 363: 718–721.

Noel, F., Scholz, K.P., Eskin, A. and Byrne, J.H. (1991) Common set of proteins in *Aplysia* sensory neurons affected by an in vitro analogue of long-term sensitization training, 5-HT and cAMP. *Brain Res.*, 568: 67–75.

Nolen T.G. and Carew, T.J. (1988) The cellular analog of sensitization emerges at the same time in development as behavioral sensitization in *Aplysia*. *J. Neurosci.*, 8: 212–222.

Ohmori, H. (1982) Development of post-tetanic potentiation at identified inhibitory and excitatory synapses in *Aplysia*. *J. Physiol.*, 322: 223–240.

Pfenninger, K.H., de la Houssaye, B.A., Helmke, S.M. and Quiroga, S. (1992) Growth-regulated proteins and neuronal plasticity. *Mol. Neurobiol.*, 5: 143–151.

Qian, Z., Gilbert, M.E., Colicos, M.A., Kandel, E.R. and Kuhl, D. (1993) Tissue-plasminogen activator is induced as an immediate-early gene during seizure, kindling, and long-term potentiation. *Nature*, 361: 453–457.

Rayport, S.G. and Camardo, J.S. (1984) Differential emergence of cellular mechanisms mediating habituation and sensitization in the developing *Aplysia* nervous system. *J. Neurosci.*, 4: 2528–2532.

Schacher, S., Kandel, E.R. and Wooley, R. (1979) Development of neurons in the abdominal ganglion of *Aplysia californica*: axosomatic synaptic contacts. *Dev. Biol.*, 71: 163–175.

Schacher, S., Castellucci, V.F. and Kandel, E.R. (1988) cAMP evokes long-term facilitation in *Aplysia* sensory neurons that requires new protein synthesis. *Science*, 240: 1667–1669.

Schacher, S., Glanzman, D., Barzilai, A., Dash, P., Grant, S.G.N., Keller, F., Mayford, M. and Kandel, E.R. (1990) Long-term facilitation in *Aplysia*: persistent phosphorylation and structural changes. *Cold Spring Harbor Symp. Quant. Biol.*, 55: 187–202.

Scholz, K.P. and Byrne, J.H. (1987) Intracellular injection of cAMP induces a long-term reduction of neuronal potassium currents. *Science*, 240: 1664–1666.

Sheng, M. and Greenberg, M.E. (1990) The regulation and function of c-*fos* and other immediate early genes in the nervous system. *Neuron*, 4: 477–485.

Silva, A.J., Stevens, C.F., Tonegawa, S. and Wang, Y. (1992) Deficient hippocampal long-term potentiation in α-calcium-calmodulin kinase II mutant mice. *Science*, 257: 210–206.

Sweatt, J.D. and Kandel, E.R. (1989) Persistent and transcripionally-dependent increase in protein phosphorylation in long-term facilitation of *Aplysia* sensory neurons. *Nature*, 339: 51–54.

Wisden, W., Errington, M.L., Williams, S., Dunnett, S.B., Waters, C., Hitchcock, D., Evan, G., Bliss, T.V.P. and Hunt, S.P. (1990) Differential expression of immediate early genes in the hippocampus and spinal cord. *Neuron*, 4: 603–614.

Zhang, Z.S., Fang, B., Marshak, D.W., Byrne, J.H. and Cleary, L.J. (1991) Serotoninergic varicosities make synaptic contacts with pleural sensory neurons of *Aplysia*. *J. Comp. Neurol.*, 311: 259–270.

F. Bloom (Editor)
Progress in Brain Research, Vol. 100
© 1994 Elsevier Science B.V. All rights reserved

CHAPTER 24

Synapse-activated protein synthesis as a possible mechanism of plastic neural change

I.J. Weiler[1,2], X. Wang[3] and W.T. Greenough[1–4]

[1]Beckman Institute, [2]Department of Psychology, [3]Neuroscience Program and [4]Department of Cell and Structural Biology, University of Illinois, Urbana, IL, USA

There has been considerable interest for the last several decades in the extent of involvement of the metabolic machinery of the cell, and particularly de novo RNA and protein synthesis, in plastic neural change, including learning and memory. Much of current experimental work employs long-term potentiation (LTP) as a model (Bliss and Lomo, 1973); the term refers to long-lasting increased postsynaptic responses following presynaptic tetanization. Following LTP induction, both presynaptic alterations (e.g. modulation of transmitter release) and postsynaptic modifications (e.g. channel sensitivity or synaptic architecture changes) have been proposed to mediate the altered synaptic efficacy. In this review, we consider postsynaptic modifications.

There appear to be at least three sequential phases in the establishment of this altered response (Bliss and Collingridge, 1993): (a) a kinase-dependent, protein synthesis-independent stage, which is seen even in the presence of protein synthesis inhibitors such as anisomycin; (b) a protein synthesis-dependent stage, affected by anisomycin and other translation blockers; and (c) an mRNA transcription-dependent stage, blocked by actinomycin D. Although the first stage may last up to 3 h, it is followed by rapid decay if a protein translation inhibitor has been present during tetanization or during the first 15 min thereafter (Krug et al., 1984; Otani et al., 1989). Thus, during the first 15 min after tetanization, synthesis of key proteins which will prevent this rapid decay must be initiated. Finally, long-term effects are associated with the induction of immediate early genes such as *zif-268*, which are believed to induce a program of activation of specific genes which will be ultimately responsible for changes in cellular architecture (e.g. Worley et al., 1993).

There is evidence for involvement of dendritic protein synthesis in behaviorally driven neural plasticity. Rats reared in complex environments have, in the visual cortex, neurons with larger dendritic fields and more synapses than rats reared in pairs or individually in standard laboratory cages (e.g. Turner and Greenough, 1983). Greenough et al. (1985) reported that rats reared in a complex environment had a greater percentage of synapses with polyribosomal aggregates (PRA) in dendritic spines, relative to cage-housed groups.

An ambitious survey of protein changes in the dentate gyrus of the hippocampus, after LTP induction in anesthetized intact rats by tetanic stimulation, was made by Fazeli et al. (1993). Three hours after induction, eleven spots on two-dimensional protein gels were found to have altered densities; these included reductions as well as increases in spot intensity, suggesting that complex patterns of changes are occurring.

Since the transcriptional inhibitor actinomycin D does not initially affect LTP decay, the maintenance of LTP during at least the first 3–6 h depends on protein synthesis from pre-existing mRNA. Since a neuron may have over ten thousand synapses (Turner and Greenough, 1983; Harvey and Napper, 1991), a con-

190

siderable degree of local control over rapid production of proteins would be required for specific, localized structural changes; and the mRNA must be targeted to specific cellular locations. Ca^{2+}-imaging techniques demonstrate that the Ca^{2+} elevation induced by tetanus is in fact localized to regions near dendritic spines (Mueller and Connor, 1991); there is increasing evidence for a complex interplay of calcium release from intracellular stores and influx of extracellular calcium (e.g. van den Pol et al., 1993).

Several laboratories have found evidence for cellular targeting of a few specific mRNAs to dendritic areas (e.g. Steward and Banker, 1992). Rao and Steward (1991) have shown that proteins can be synthesized within synaptosomes; and Torre and Steward (1992), employing an elegant tissue culture system in which dendrites can be definitively separated from cell somata, have demonstrated protein synthesis in isolated dendrites. In a recent report, Miyashiro et al. (1993), using poly-A primed cDNA amplification followed by PCR amplification of mRNA from single neurites of hippocampal neurons in tissue culture, presented evidence that in fact many species of mRNA may be present in neurites; identification of mRNA translated in or near dendritic spines will be harder to come by.

With regard to the more precise localization of mRNA in dendrites, Steward and Levy (1982) made the important observation that PRAs were more frequently found in postsynaptic spines during reactive synaptogenesis. Hwang and Greenough (1986) subsequently found, examining the repeatedly identifiable population of synapses on visual cortical layer V pyramidal neuron apical dendrites in layer IV, that PRAs were more frequently found postsynaptically during the period of peak synaptogenesis (days 13–20) than subsequently ($\geq$25).

Because any attempt to examine synaptically associated PRA-related protein synthesis was likely to be masked by the vastly greater somatic protein synthesis, we have adapted a synaptoneurosome preparation (Hollingsworth et al, 1985) from the occipital-parietal cortex of 14–16-day-old Long-Evans rats, for further study of what we believe may be the same phenomenon. Synaptoneurosomes, depicted in Fig. 1, consist of pinched-off and resealed presynaptic terminals con-

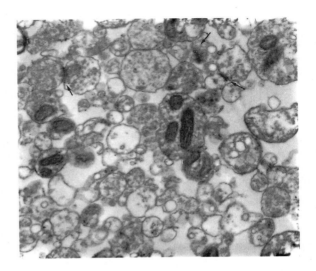

Fig. 1. Electron micrograph of synaptoneurosomal preparation, after filtration and pelleting, immersion fixation in 2.5% glutaraldehyde, followed by osmium tetroxide, sectioning and staining with uranyl acetate. Several complete synaptoneurosomes can be seen; some other profiles may also represent synaptoneurosomes in which the plane of section fails to include characteristic morphological components. Used with permission of Academic Press, copyright 1991.

nected to pinched-off and resealed postsynaptic compartments that appear to be larger, on average, than typical dendritic spines. They exhibit normal presynaptic neurotransmitter release in response to depolarization as well as apparently normal postsynaptic responses (Dunkley and Robinson, 1986; Recasens et al., 1987; Gorelick et al., 1988; Verhage et al., 1992). In a series of investigations of the biochemical events (see Fig. 2; numbers in bold refer to steps we have documented in this sequence) following in vitro depolarization by 40 mM K^+ (**1**), we have found a rapid aggregation of ribosomes with mRNA, which we have shown to be associated with accelerated synthesis of some new proteins (Weiler and Greenough, 1991). Furthermore, we found that the effect is mediated by glutamate release (**2**), which triggers protein synthesis via metabotropic glutamate receptors (mGluR) (Weiler and Greenough, 1993).

In this system we measured, at short intervals, the fraction of total synaptoneurosomal RNA trapped in the form of polyribosomal aggregates, selected by

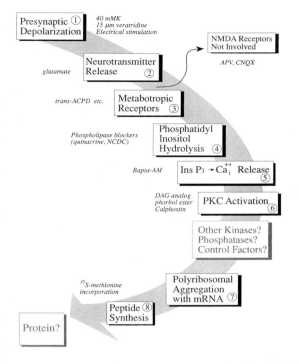

Fig. 2. Schematic description of probable cascade of intermediaries leading from presynaptic depolarization to postsynaptic protein synthesis. Numbers in circles correspond to references in text, where experimental documentation is available.

centrifugation through 1 M sucrose. We found that a rapid (1–2 min) loading of ribosomes onto mRNA was accompanied (**7,8**) by an accelerated rate of incorporation of [^{35}S]methionine into TCA-precipitable polypeptides. Entry of extracellular calcium appears not to be necessary to this process, since it was not prevented by calcium chelators in the buffer (0.04 mM BAPTA) and not weakened by co-application of 2-amino-5-phosphonovalerate (APV, a competitive NMDA receptor antagonist, **3**). An internal calcium buffer blocked the effect, however (**5**). Nifedipine, a blocker of voltage-sensitive calcium channels, also does not prevent the response. The susceptibility of the effect to a series of glutamate analogues (quisqualate, ibotenate and *trans*-aminocyclopentane-1*S*,3*R*-dicarboxylic acid, ACPD, **3**) matched that of mGluR receptors 1 and 5 (Schoepp et al., 1990).

Metabotropic receptors trigger the hydrolysis of membrane phosphatidyl inositol; in accord with this we found (**4**) that phospholipase blockers (quinacrine or 2-nitro-4-carboxyphenyl-*N*,*N*-dephenylcarbamate, NCDC) reduced the response. This hydrolysis leads to the production of inositol triphosphate (which releases Ca^{2+} from internal stores) and diacylglycerol which activates protein kinase C (PKC). We used phorbol ester and a diacylglycerol analogue (1-oleoyl-2-acetyl-glycerol) to activate PKC (**6**), and found a similar rapid increase of polyribosome aggregation. Calphostin C, a highly specific inhibitor which reacts with the regulatory domain of PKC, effectively blocked (80%) the response to ACPD. Within the same experiments, however, calphostin did not block the polyribosomal aggregation triggered by 40 mM K^+, suggesting that more than one activation system may be triggered by depolarization.

The induction of LTP involves both NMDA and metabotropic glutamate receptors. Activation of second messengers via metabotropic neurotransmitter receptors has been shown to play a crucial role in some forms of LTP (Aniksteijn et al., 1992; Zheng and Gallagher, 1992; Bashir et al., 1993). Indeed, induction of LTP by application of the metabotropic agonist trans-ACPD alone has recently been reported (Bortolotto and Collingridge, 1993). Furthermore, protein synthesis has been demonstrated directly by Feig and Lipton (1993), pairing patterned electrical stimulation of hippocampal CA1 pyramidal cells, in an acute slice preparation, with exposure to 50 μM carbachol (a metabotropic cholinergic agonist). Neither electrical stimulation nor carbachol alone caused increased protein synthesis; but paired stimulation gave rise to a threefold increase of [^{3}H]leucine incorporation into dendrites, strongly suggesting de novo protein synthesis. This pairing has not been shown to produce LTP, although the metabotropic agonist *trans*-ACPD can induce LTP in hippocampal slices when it is coupled with a weak subthreshold presynaptic tetanus (Otani and Ben-Ari, 1991).

Initiation of protein synthesis is not likely to be a simple response; it is likely that several competing processes participate in regulation of the response to synaptic activation. In recent experiments we have found that Ca^{2+} entry (caused for example by stimulation with NMDA as well as by the calcium ionophore ionomycin) prior to mGluR activation markedly depresses the polyribosome aggregation (unpublished results). Thus, the threshold for polyribosomal aggregation in response to metabotropic glutamate receptor activation may be continuously adjusted according to the recent history of the postsynaptic Ca^{2+} level regulated by NMDA receptor activation or other sources. Similarly, the threshold for LTP induction is also closely regulated by the recent history of NMDA receptor activation (Huang et al., 1992). It is known that the activation of the NMDA receptors elicits a Ca^{2+} dependent release of nitric oxide (Garthwaite et al., 1988), which has been proposed as a retrograde messenger to affect presynaptic aspects of LTP, either in a positive or negative modulatory role (Izumi et al, 1992).

In recent work, we have been investigating the effects of electrical stimulation on synaptoneurosome suspensions. A polyribosome aggregation response is dependent on voltage (2 V, under these conditions about 1 mA), on burst length (20 ms), on frequency (100–200 Hz), and on the interval between bursts of stimuli (200 ms). These frequency parameters are similar to those defined as optimal for "prime burst" or "theta burst" potentiation (Larson and Lynch, 1986; Rose and Dunwiddie, 1986). Thus, there are, in addition to neurotransmitter responsiveness, a number of aspects in which experimental requirements for LTP parallel those we find for polyribosomal aggregation and initiation of protein synthesis. While there are tantalizing pharmacological links between the phospholipase-triggered second messenger effects and the initiation of protein synthesis in synaptoneurosomes, a direct link with LTP cannot yet be established.

There are several plausible candidates for alterations which would support the earliest phase of LTP, which can be maintained for 1–3 h without protein synthesis. The conformational state of NMDA and AMPA channels is known to be changed upon phosphorylation, such that Ca^{2+} entry is expedited (e.g. Reymann, 1993). Depending on which kinases are activated, either serine/threonine or tyrosine residues are phosphorylated. Some translational factors might require coordinate activation of both kinds of phosphorylation sites (e.g. Tuazon et al., 1989). Synaptic activation of protein phosphatases has also been shown to be an important element in regulation of synaptic strength (e.g. Mulkey et al., 1993). Calcium-calmodulin dependent kinase II (CaMKII) becomes autophosphorylated as a result of competing phosphorylating and dephosphorylating activities regulated in part by Ca^{2+}; the autophosphorylated form is then independent of calcium for some time. A biochemical model for storage of synaptic information based on this equilibrium in the state of phosphorylation of CaMKII has been suggested by Lisman (1989).

When we come to more permanent synaptic changes, requiring protein synthesis, there may simply be a shift in amount of proteins already present, but also some new proteins, such as PKM, the constitutively active form of PKC (Sacktor et al., 1993); this important question is still open to investigation. Geinisman (1993) and others have described a complex process of synaptic remodelling in hippocampal spines; a considerable array of proteases, structural proteins, and enzymatic complexes must be mobilized to implement these new structures, so that in addition to rapid synthesis of proteins from messages already present, we may expect delivery of new mRNA, and centrally synthesized proteins, also to play an important role.

Thus, an array of mechanisms is available which could maintain an altered postsynaptic state for minutes or hours on the basis of an altered phosphorylation state of pre-existing proteins; but altered phosphorylation may well also serve as a finely tuned regulatory device for stopping or starting the translation of proteins from localized RNA messages, held poised awaiting the proper combination of signals, which may be activated both by finely tuned Ca^{2+} oscillations and, as we have shown, by phospholipase-activated second messenger cascades which are triggered by metabotropic receptors. As in the case of growth factors, a complex interdigitation of interacting pathways could facilitate rapid information storage in a multifacetted way at the level of synapses. Given the number of intermediaries that the various pathways have in common, some sort of functional compartmentalization must exist to limit their interactions. Increasingly sophisticated techniques are being used to probe the finely tuned interplay between receptors, localized calcium ion flux, and a restricted, targeted set of messenger RNAs which might, under the appropriate conditions, be translated to effect a structural synaptic change. Which proteins these are, and how their translation is regulated, will be a challenging subject for future research.

Acknowledgement

The research reported here was supported by MH35321, NSF BNS 8821219, the Kiwanis Spastic Paralysis Foundation, and the Office of Naval Research.

References

Aniksztejn, L., Otani, S. and Ben-Ari, Y. (1992) Quisqualate metabotropic receptors modulate NMDA currents and facilitate induction of long-term potentiation through protein kinase C. *Eur. J. Neurosci.*, 4: 500–505.

Bashir, Z.I., Bortolotto, Z.A., Davies, C.H., Berretta, N., Irving, A.J., Seal, A.J., Henley, J.M., Jane, D.E., Watkins, J.C. and Collingridge, G.L. (1993) Induction of LTP in the hippocampus needs synaptic activiation of glutamate metabotropic receptors. *Nature*, 363: 347–350.

Bliss, T.V.P. and Collingridge, G.L. (1993) A synaptic model of memory: long-term potentiation in the hippocampus. *Nature*, 361: 31–39.

Bliss, T.V.P. and Lomo, T. (1973) Long-lasting potentiation of synaptic transmission in the dentate area of the anesthetized rabbit following stimulation of the perforant path. *J. Physiol. (London)*, 232: 331–356.

Bortolotto, Z.A. and Collingridge, G.L. (1993) Characterisation of LTP induced by the activation of glutamate metabotropic receptors in area CA1 of the hippocampus. *Neuropharmacology*, 32: 1–9.

Dunkley, P.R. and Robinson P.J. (1986) Depolarization-dependent protein phosphorylation in synaptosomes: mechanisms and significance. In: W.H. Gispen and A. Routtenberg (Eds.), *Progress in Brain Research*, Vol. 69, Elsevier, Amsterdam, pp. 273–293.

Fazeli, M.S., Corbet, J., Dunn, M.J., Dolphin, A.C. and Bliss, T.V.P. (1993) Changes in protein synthesis accompanying long-term potentiation in the dentate gyrus *in vivo*. *J. Neurosci.*, 13: 1346–1353.

Feig, S. and Lipton, P. (1993) Pairing the cholinergic agonist carbachol with patterned Schaffer collateral stimulation initiates protein synthesis in hippocampal CA1 pyramidal cell dendrites via a muscarinic, NMDA-dependent mechanism. *J. Neurosci.*, 13: 1010–1021.

Garthwaite, J., Charles, S.L. and Chess-Williams, R. (1988) Endothelium-derived relaxing factor release   relaxing factor release on activation of NMDA receptors suggests role as intercellular messenger in the brain. *Nature*, 336: 385–388.

Geinisman, Y. (1993) Perforated axospinous synapses with multiple, completely partitioned transmission zones: probable structural intermediates in synaptic plasticity. *Hippocampus*, 3: 417–434.

Gorelick, F.S., Wang, J.K.T., Lai, Y., Nairn, A.C. and Greengard, P. (1988) Autophosphorylation and activation of Ca^{2+}/calmodulin-dependent protein kinase II in intact nerve terminals. *J. Biol. Chem.*, 263: 17209–17212.

Greenough, W.T., Hwang, H.-M.F. and Gorman, C. (1985) Evidence for active synapse formation or altered postsynaptic metabolism in visual cortex of rats reared in complex environments. *Proc. Natl. Acad. Sci. USA*, 82: 4549–4552.

Harvey, R.J. and Napper, R.M.A. (1991) Quantitative studies on the mammalian cerebellum. *Prog. Neurobiol.*, 36: 437–463.

Hollingsworth, E.B., McNeal, E.T., Burton, J.L., Williams, R.J., Daly, J.W. and Creveling, C.R. (1985) Biochemical characterization of a filtered synaptoneurosome preparation from guinea pig cerebral cortex: cyclic adenosine 3′:5′-monophosphate-generating systems, receptors, and enzymes. *J. Neurosci.*, 5: 2240–2253.

Huang, Y-Y., Colino, A., Selig, D.K. and Malenka, R.C. (1992) The influence of prior synaptic activity on the induction of long-term potentiation. *Science*, 255: 730–733.

Hwang, H.M. and Greenough, W.T. (1984) Spine formation and synaptogenesis in rat visual cortex: a serial section developmental study. *Soc. Neurosci. Abstr.*, 10: 579.

Izumi, Y., Clifford, D.B. and Zorumski, C.F. (1992) Inhibition of long-term potentiation by NMDA-mediated nitric oxide release. *Science*, 257: 1273–1275.

Krug, M., Loessner, B. and Ott, T. (1984) Anisomycin blocks the late phase of long-term potentiation in the dentate gyrus of freely moving rats. *Brain Res. Bull.*, 13: 39–42.

Larson, J. and Lynch, G. (1986) Induction of synaptic potentiation in hippocampus by patterned stimulation involves two events. *Science*, 232: 985–988.

Lisman, J. (1989) A mechanism for the Hebb and the anti-Hebb processes underlying learning and memory. *Proc. Natl. Acad. Sci. USA*, 86: 9574–9578.

Miyashiro, K., Dichter, M. and Eberwine, J. (1993) Presence of multiple mRNA products in hippocampal neurites. *Soc. Neurosci. Abstr.*, 327: 16.

Mueller, W. and Connor, J.A. (1991) Dendritic spines as individual neuronal compartments for synaptic Ca^{2+} responses. *Nature*, 354: 73–76.

Mulkey, R.M., Herron, C.E. and Malenka, R.C. (1993) An essential role for protein phosphatases in hippocampal long-term depression. *Science*, 261: 1051–1055.

Otani, S. and Ben-Ari, Y. (1991) Metabotropic receptor-mediated long-term potentiation in rat hippocampal slices. *Eur. J. Pharmacol.*, 205: 325–326.

Otani, S., Marshall, C.J., Tate, W.P., Goddard, G.V. and Abraham, W.C. (1989) Maintenance of long-term potentiation in rat dentate gyrus requires protein synthesis but not messenger RNA synthesis immediately post-tetanization. *Neuroscience*, 28: 519–526.

Rao, A. and Steward, O. (1991) Evidence that protein constituents of postsynaptic membrane specializations are locally synthesized: analysis of proteins synthesized within synaptosomes. *J. Neurosci.*, 11: 2881–2895.

Recasens, M., Sassetti, I., Nourigat, A., Sladeczek, F. and Bockaert, J. (1987) Characterization of subtypes of excitatory amino acid receptors involved in the stimulation of inositol phosphate synthesis in rat brain synaptoneurosomes. *Eur. J. Pharmacol.*, 141: 87–93.

Reymann, K.G. (1993) Mechanisms underlying synaptic long-term potentiation in the hippocampus: focus on postsynaptic glutamate receptors and protein kinases. *Funct. Neurol.* 8 (Suppl. 5): 7–32.

Rose, G.M. and Dunwiddie, T.V.(1986) Induction of hippocampal long-term potentiation using physiologically patterned stimulation. *Neurosci. Lett.*, 69: 244–248.

Sacktor, T.C., Osten, P., Valsamis, H., Jiang, X., Naik, M.U. and Sublette, E. (1993) Persistent activation of the ζ isoform of protein kinase C in the maintenance of long-term potentiation. *Proc. Natl. Acad. Sci. USA*, 90: 8342–8346.

Schoepp, D., Bockaert, J. and Sladeczek, F. (1990) Pharmacological and functional characteristics of metabotropic excitatory amino acid receptors. *Trends Pharmacol. Sci.*, 111: 508–515.

Steward, O. and Banker, G.A. (1992) Getting the message from the gene to the synapse: sorting and intracellular transport of RNA in neurons. *Trends Neurosci.*, 15: 180–186.

Steward, O. and Levy, W. (1982) Preferential localization of polyribosomes under the base of dendritic spines in granule cells of the dentate gyrus. *J. Neurosci.*, 2: 284–291.

Torre, E.R. and Steward, O. (1992) Demonstration of local protein synthesis within dendrites using a new cell culture system that permits the isolation of living axons and dendrites from their cell bodies. *J. Neurosci.*, 12: 762–772.

Tuazon, P.T., Merrick, W.C. and Traugh, J.A. (1989) Comparative analysis of phosphorylation of translational initiation and elongation factors by seven protein kinases. *J. Biol. Chem.*, 264: 2773–2777.

Turner, A.M. and Greenough, W.T. (1983) Synapses per neuron and synaptic dimensions in occipital cortex of rats reared in complex, social or isolation housing. *ACTA Stereol.*, 2 (Suppl I): 239–244.

Van den Pol, A., Finkbeiner, S.M. and Cornell-Bell, A.H. (1993) Calcium excitability and oscillations in suprachiasmatic nucleus neurons and glia in vitro. *J. Neurosci.*, 12: 2648–2664.

Verhage, M., Sandman, H., Mosselveld, F., van de Velde, M., Hengst, P.A., Lopes da Silva, F.H. and Ghijsen, W.E.J.M. (1992) Perfusion of immobilized isolated nerve terminals as a model for the regulation of transmitter release: release of different, endogenous transmitters, repeated stimulation, and high time resolution. *J. Neurochem.*, 58: 1313–1320.

Weiler, I.J. and Greenough, W.T. (1991) Potassium ion stimulation triggers protein translation in synaptoneurosomal polyribosomes. *Mol. Cell. Neurosci.*, 2: 305–314.

Weiler, I.J. and Greenough, W.T. (1993) Metabotropic glutamate receptors trigger postsynaptic protein synthesis. *Proc. Natl. Acad. Sci. USA*, 90: 7168–7171.

Worley, P.F., Bhat, R.V., Baraban, J.M., Erickson, C.A., McNaughton, B.L. and Barnes, C.A. (1993) Thresholds for synaptic activation of transcription factors in hippocampus: correlation with long-term enhancement. *J. Neurosci.*, 13: 4776–4786.

Zheng, F. and Gallagher, J.P. (1992) Metabotropic glutamate receptors are required for the induction of long-term potentiation. *Neuron*, 9: 163–172.

F. Bloom (Editor)
Progress in Brain Research, Vol. 100
© 1994 Elsevier Science B.V. All rights reserved

CHAPTER 25

Plasticity of adult central fibre tracts

G. Raisman

*Norman and Sadie Lee Research Centre, Laboratory of Neurobiology, National Institute for Medical Research,
The Ridgeway, Mill Hill, London NW7 1AA, UK*

Introduction

When axons are severed in the adult brain or spinal cord they are unable to grow back to their original targets. Until we solve this problem, stroke and spinal cord injury will remain irreparable.

A number of observations suggest that the reason for the failure of regeneration of cut central axons lies in the white matter of the myelinated fibre tracts rather than in the grey matter of the neuropil:

(1) New short range synaptic connections readily form within denervated adult neuropil after partial deafferentation (Raisman, 1969, 1985),

(2) Embryonic transplants placed directly into neuropil both give and receive specific patterns of synaptic connections with an adult host brain (e.g. Zhou et al., 1985; Field et al., 1991; Björklund, 1992), and

(3) Peripheral nerve grafts induce cut central adult axons to regenerate for long distances and reinnervate their original targets (Villegas-Pérez et al., 1988; Carter et al., 1989; Thanos, 1992).

Thus, cut adult axons do have the power of regeneration, and the adult CNS retains the ability to mediate complex patterns of synaptic reconnection in neuropil after injury. Such observations sustain the hope that one day it may be possible to repair axon injuries in the brain and spinal cord, and they focus the next stages of the search for repair on the question of axon growth in central adult myelinated fibre tracts.

We have therefore directed our investigations towards the analysis of adult central fibre tracts: their glial structure and its development, their ability to incorporate additional transplanted glia and Schwann cells, and their capacity to permit the growth of embryonic and adult axons.

The glial organization of central fibre tracts

We have examined the arrangement of the glia in the adult rat fimbria, and found that the tract has a complex and regular organization (Fig. 1) (Suzuki and Raisman, 1992). The macroglial cell bodies are assembled in largely unicellular rows, which can be of great length, and which are aligned along the longitudinal, axonal axis of the tract. Although the regularity is not perfect, the arrangement of the glia can be described by a set of average dimensions. Sections along the longitudinal axis of the tract show that the cells consist of solitary astrocytes, interspersed singly at a repeat distance of about $40-80\,\mu m$ between stretches of about 6–10 contiguous oligodendrocytes (Fig. 1a). In the transverse axis of the tract, the rows form an equidistant array, separated by about $10-20\,\mu m$. Each row is surrounded by about 1000–1400 axons, of which 600–1000 are myelinated.

Both oligodendrocytes and astrocytes each give rise to two different types of processes which lie in the radial and longitudinal planes of the tract. The oligodendrocytes (Fig. 1a) each have about 20–40 fine radial processes which cross the axons, and each process gives rise to a myelin internode which ensheathes a stretch of about $150-250\,\mu m$ of axon in the longitudinal axis of the tract. The astrocytic cell bodies (Fig.

196

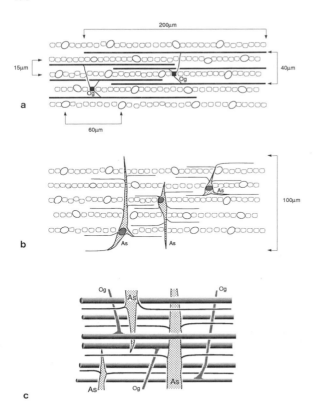

Fig. 1. (a) Radial (stem) and longitudinal (myelinating) processes of two oligodendrocytes (Og, black squares) shown against a background of the interfascicular glial nuclear rows in a horizontal section of the adult rat fimbria. (b) Three astrocytes (As) with radial and longitudinal processes. (c) Higher magnification of the meshwork of oligodendrocytic (Og) and astrocytic (As) processes. Typical dimensions: core-to-core distance between interfascicular glial rows, 15μm; interastrocytic distance within a row, 60μm; oligodendrocytic radial span, 40μm; length of internode, 200μm; astrocytic radial span, 100μm.

1b) are prolonged into tapering radial processes which cross the axons and generate large numbers of fine, untapering longitudinal processes which run parallel to and among the axons (Fig. 2a). Thus, the radial and longitudinal processes of the oligodendrocytes and the astrocytes are interwoven to form a rectilinear network through which the tract axons run (Fig. 1c).

We have found similar glial arrangements in the descending corticospinal tract and in the ascending sensory columns of the dorsal horn of the cervical spinal cord (Y. Ajayi et al., unpublished observations; see also Matthews and Duncan, 1971). Thus, despite their

very different fibre compositions and times of formation (the sensory tracts very early in embryonic CNS development, the fimbria after the 15th day of embryonic life in the rat, and the corticospinal tract postnatally), the glial frameworks of each of these tracts are qualitatively alike, differing only in quantitative parameters such as the numbers of axons per interfascicular glial row, the dimensions of the glial cells, their spacing, or the lengths of their processes.

Compared with the ability of peripheral axons to regenerate in the Schwann cell environment of peripheral nerves, the complexity of the glial framework may be a reason why axons do not regenerate in adult central tracts. During the developmental period when axons are growing, the future central fibre tracts have a

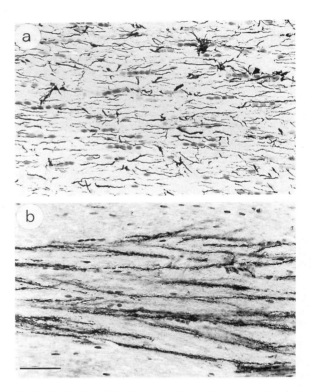

Fig. 2. (a) Section of the fimbria cut along its horizontal axis to show the parallel array of longitudinal processes of the astrocytes. GFAP immunohistochemistry. (b) An adjacent serial section showing a loose fascicle of axons running parallel to the longitudinal axis of the host tract. The axons belong to neurons from a suspension of E18 embryonic mouse neocortical cells micro-transplanted into the adult rat fimbria. M6 immunohistochemistry, 6 days after transplantation. Scale bar (for both), 50μm.

simple structure consisting of radial glia whose cell bodies are confined to the ventricular layer, so that the developing axons grow through a region occupied by radial glial processes which lie at right angles to the axons and which run from the ventricular zone to the pial surface (Rickmann et al., 1987; Sievers et al., 1992).

At birth, the fimbria is still at the radial glial stage, and the postnatal formation of the definitive glial skeleton (M. Suzuki and G. Raisman, unpublished observations) is associated with the migration of glial cells out of the ventricular layer (finally leaving only the inert, adult unicellular lining ependyma). The first interfascicular glia are scattered, solitary cells. Over the first 10 days of postnatal life, cell division (and accompanying cell death) leads to a continuous increase in the numbers of glial cells, which become assembled into longer and longer rows, which themselves gradually become aligned into the regular adult pattern of evenly spaced unicellular interfascicular glial rows. The oligodendrocytes are formed entirely postnatally. Myelination is a multifocal process, starting by simultaneous differentiation of regularly scattered individual cells, and taking several months to reach adult density.

Axons are present in the fimbria from the 15th day of embryonic life (Valentino and Jones, 1982), when the glial skeleton still consists only of the radial processes of cells in the ventricular layer. It is not known when axon growth ceases in the fimbria, but it certainly continues for some time into the postnatal period, since some of the hippocampal pyramidal cells which will subsequently send axons into the fimbria do not have their final birthdays until around the time of birth (Schlessinger et al., 1978). It is also possible that, as has been demonstrated for the corpus callosum (Innocenti and Clarke, 1984), there may be considerable remodelling of axonal pathways in the postnatal period.

Growth of embryonic axons in adult fibre tracts

That the adult glial tract skeleton is not universally inhibitory to axon growth has recently been shown by the use of embryonic transplants (e.g. Wictorin et al., 1990). We have developed a minimally traumatic approach (Emmett et al., 1990) to transplant small volumes of suspensions of late embryonic hippocampal neurons directly into the adult fimbria (Davies et al., 1993). The effect of this form of transplantation was that the host tract astrocytes did not form reactive scars, and the longitudinal processes of the tract astrocytes continued undeflected into the transplants, which themselves developed an internal glial skeleton whose astrocytic processes flowed out in smooth continuity with the longitudinal astrocytic processes of the host tract.

From as little as 2 days after operation, the neurons extended a beam of abundant axons through the fimbria (Fig. 2b) at a rate of at least 1 mm per day. This is equivalent to the rate of regeneration of peripheral nerve axons. The axons grew for at least 10 mm in the tract, and reached the contralateral hippocampus by 10 days. Thus, adult myelinated central tracts retain the capacity to direct profuse and rapid growth of axons from embryonic donor neurons.

The donor axons formed a loose bundle, but did not fasciculate with each other. The donor projections travelled in both directions in the host fimbria, and did not seem to require any appreciable degree of destruction of host axons. Both for the host and the donor axons, a characteristic mode of exit from the tract was by the formation of collaterals at right angles to the parent axonal stem. The donor intrafimbrial axons projected to the septal nuclei, and the ipsilateral and contralateral hippocampi, where they diffusely invaded terminal fields appropriate to hippocampal projection fibres.

We have compared the pattern of axon growth after transplanting donor cell suspensions taken from three different brain areas (hippocampus, neocortex and superior colliculus) into two different host tracts: the fimbria and the corpus callosum (Davies et al., 1994). In both tracts the speed and density of the intrafascicular axon projection was the same for all three types of donor tissue. The pattern of distribution of the donor projections was determined not by the type of donor tissue, but by its position in the host tract. This formation of inappropriate types of projection is in marked contrast to the situation in neuropil, where embryonic transplants usually only form correct specific patterns of projection (e.g. Björklund and Stenevi, 1984; Zhou et al., 1990). We do not know whether the projections we have observed after transplantation of incorrectly matched donor tissue into fibre tracts would be permanent. Our observations were based on a mouse-specific axonal marker, M6, which was only suitable for following projections for a few weeks, so that it is possible that what we were detecting was an initial "exuberant" formation of temporary projections which might, if inappropriate to the postsynaptic targets, later be retracted (e.g. Innocenti and Clarke, 1984; O'Leary et al., 1990).

Regardless of the donor cell type, the intrafascicular projections followed rigidly controlled routes through the host tracts. The common feature of these routes was that they were parallel to the host tract axons and to the longitudinal processes of the host tract astrocytes, and they respected the boundaries between fibre tracts. When a transplant occupied only part of a tract, the projection was also restricted to a band which did not occupy the full width of the tract, and whose distribution was restricted to the part of the terminal field reached by that band.

That adult myelinated central fibre tracts are facilitatory for axon growth from embryonic transplants was confirmed in a series of experiments in which we micro-transplanted embryonic hippocampal cells into the dorsal columns of the adult rat spinal cord (Li and Raisman, 1993). The donor axons grew at a similar rate to those in the fimbria, and also strictly in alignment with the longitudinal axis of the host tracts. The donor axons grew equally in the rostral and in the caudal directions in both the descending corticospinal tract and the ascending sensory dorsal column tracts. The axons showed a marked preference for white (rather than grey) matter, and they were neither stopped nor deflected by an adjacent transplant of hippocampal tissue which would have contained their normal postsynaptic targets.

Because of the transformation of the glial skeleton of central fibre tracts from radial glia (the structure present during the developmental stage when most axon growth occurs) to the complex astro/oligodendrocytic meshwork of adult tracts, the growth of embryonic axons along adult fibre tracts involves a series of axon/glial interactions which cannot be regarded as a simple recapitulation of the events of normal development. It is possible that the ability of the embryonic axons to grow along adult tracts is due to some special property of immature axons (e.g. that they do not have a receptor to respond to an axon growth-inhibitory molecule expressed on oligodendrocytes (Schwab et al., 1993). Another possible factor preventing regeneration could be the response of the glia in the adult tracts: thus, the axons from our minimally traumatic intra-tract embryonic transplants were growing in a tract whose glial orientation was relatively undisturbed, and which was continuous with the glial orientation in the transplants. In contrast, adult axons attempting to regenerate after a traumatic tract lesion are faced with reactive tract astrocytes which become rearranged into "scar" formations (Reier, 1986) which may have the effect of distorting what otherwise might be growth permissive astrocytic surfaces into an impenetrable tangle.

Migration of glia and Schwann cells into central tracts

Surprisingly, although the glial processes form a dense meshwork in adult tracts, the glial array remains permissive to the ingrowth of additional glia from embryonic transplants, and also transplanted cultured Schwann cells.

When either solid embryonic grafts (Lindsay and Raisman, 1984) or suspensions of purified astrocytes (Emmett et al., 1991) were injected into the hippocampus in the vicinity of the fimbria or alveus, donor astroglial cells migrated for considerable distances out of the transplants. While these migrating glial cells were capable of traversing neuropil, and also leaving the brain and entering the subarachnoid space, their preferred routes of migration were along blood vessels or fibre tracts. In some cases, we found that the donor astrocytes had inserted themselves into the interfascicular glial rows of the host at some distance from the contact with the graft and in regions of the tract that showed no detectable damage.

The use of peripheral nerve grafts to bring about regenerative growth of cut adult central axons (Villegas-

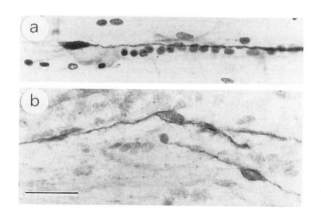

Fig. 3. (a),(b) Ribbon-like elongated Schwann cells from a micro-transplanted suspension of cultured adult peripheral nerve Schwann cells migrating along the longitudinal axis of the adult rat fimbria. Low affinity NGF receptor immunohistochemistry (MC192 monoclonal antibody), (a) 10 and (b) 22 days after transplantation. Scale bar (for both), 50 μm.

Pérez et al., 1988; Carter et al., 1989; Thanos, 1992), and the demonstration that this effect depends on the presence of viable Schwann cells (Berry et al., 1988; Smith and Stevenson, 1988) has led to experiments designed to explore whether injections of suspensions of purified cultured Schwann cells can also be used to induce regenerative axon growth (Neuberger et al., 1992; Brook et al., 1994).

We have found (Brook et al., 1993) that transplanted cultured Schwann cells were able to migrate rapidly through the adult brain. Within 1–2 days of injecting a small volume of a suspension of cultured Schwann cells into the adult fimbria, the donor cells started to disperse from the injection site. Initially the cells migrated as cuffs along the blood vessels of the transplant region. By 4–5 days, however, individual cells had detached themselves from the perivascular cuffs, and had become transformed into ribbon-like, bipolar cells (Fig. 3) which entered the host fibre tract and migrated as dispersed single cells along the longitudinal axis of the tract.

Schwann cells and adult central axons

When suspensions of cultured Schwann cells were injected into the long tracts of the dorsal columns of the spinal cord, they induced sprouting of both cut and uncut axons in both the corticospinal tract and the ascending sensory dorsal columns (Li and Raisman, 1994). This sprouting occurred both at the cut ends of the axons and also at intervals (probably at myelin internodes) along the axonal shafts of both cut and uncut axons. In these experiments, the sprouts formed branching terminal plexuses with presynaptic-like varicosities.

In order to convey axon sprouts across a lesion site and into distant deafferented terminal territories, it would be necessary to induce elongative growth. In the case of peripheral nerve grafts, a directional factor is provided by the basal lamina and the fibroblastic/collagenous framework of the nerve, as well as by the aligned bands of Bungner formed by the reactive dividing Schwann cells. We have now found (Brook et al., 1994) that a similar, highly effective directional

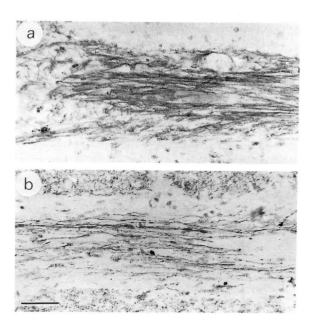

Fig. 4. (a) Parallel fascicles of cultured adult rat peripheral nerve Schwann cells transplanted as a column by continuous extrusion from a micropipette which was gradually withdrawn along a vertical track through the thalamus. Low affinity NGF receptor immunohistochemistry, 11 days after transplantation. (b) Adjacent serial section showing parallel fascicles of adult host axons induced to grow along the Schwann cell column. Neurofilament immunohistochemistry (RT97 monoclonal antibody). Scale bar (for both), 50 μm.

effect can be produced by "extrusion grafting" of suspensions of Schwann cells.

A suspension of donor Schwann cells was continuously extruded from a micropipette tip which was placed in the ventral thalamus/subthalamic region and gradually withdrawn dorsally through the thalamus and overlying forebrain during expulsion. Within 1–2 days, the donor Schwann cells became aligned to form a columnar track along the axis of retraction (Fig. 4a). Host axons progressively invaded the Schwann cell column, and became aligned along its vertical axis (Fig. 4b), where they extended for considerable distances (up to 4 mm). The extrusion grafts were able to carry axons through a perforation of the pial surface, so that regenerating fibres were carried out of the dorsal surface of the thalamus, across the choroid fissure and back into the brain at the ventral surface of the hippocampus.

Conclusions

Although adult central myelinated fibre tracts have a complex and regular glial structure, with densely interwoven processes, the tracts show considerable plasticity. Thus:

(1) embryonic axons grow readily in adult fibre tracts, and follow the orientation of the elements of the glial skeleton, and

(2) adult central fibre tracts allow the incorporation of additional cells, both embryonic glia and also cultured Schwann cells.

The incorporation of Schwann and/or other cells into adult tracts provides a possible future method to encourage the regeneration of cut adult fibres along these tracts.

References

Berry, M., Rees, L., Hall, S., Yiu, P. and Sievers, J. (1988) Optic axons regenerate into sciatic nerve isografts only in the presence of Schwann cells. *Brain Res. Bull.*, 20: 223–231.

Björklund, A. (1992) Dopaminergic transplants in experimental parkinsonism: cellular mechanisms of graft-induced functional recovery. *Curr. Opinions Neurobiol.*, 2: 683–689.

Björklund, A. and Stenevi, U. (1984) Intracerebral neural implants: neuronal replacement and reconstruction of damaged circuitries. *Annu. Rev. Neurosci.*, 7: 279–308.

Brook, G.A., Lawrence, J.M. and Raisman, G. (1993) Morphology and migration of cultured Schwann cells transplanted into the fimbria and hippocampus in adult rats. *Glia*, 9: 292–304.

Brook, G.A., Lawrence, J.M., Shah, B. and Raisman, G. (1994) Extrusion transplantation of Schwann cells into the adult rat thalamus induces directional host axon growth. *Exp. Neurol.*, in press.

Carter, D.A., Bray, G.M. and Aguayo, A.J. (1989) Regenerated retinal ganglion cell axons can form well-differentiated synapses in the superior colliculus of adult hamsters. *J. Neurosci.*, 9: 4042–4050.

Davies, S.J.A., Field, P.M. and Raisman, G. (1993) Long fibre growth by axons of embryonic mouse hippocampal neurons micro-transplanted into the adult rat fimbria. *Eur. J. Neurosci.*, 5: 95–106.

Davies, S.J.A., Field, P.M. and Raisman, G. (1994) Long interfascicular axon growth from embryonic neurons transplanted into adult myelinated tracts. *J. Neurosci.*, 14: 1596–1612.

Emmett, C.J., Jaques-Berg, W. and Seeley, P.J. (1990) Microtransplantation of neural cells into adult rat brain. *Neuroscience*, 38: 213–222.

Emmett, C.J., Lawrence, J.M., Raisman, G. and Seeley, P.J. (1991) Cultured epithelioid astrocytes migrate after transplantation into the adult rat brain. *J. Comp. Neurol.*, 310: 330–341.

Field, P.M., Seeley, P.J., Frotscher, M. and Raisman, G. (1991) Selective innervation of embryonic hippocampal transplants by adult host dentate granule cell axons. *Neuroscience*, 41: 713–727.

Innocenti, G.M. and Clarke, S. (1984) The organization of immature callosal connections. *J. Comp. Neurol.*, 230: 287–309.

Li, Y. and Raisman, G. (1993) Long interfascicular axon growth from embryonic mouse hippocampal neurons transplanted into the myelinated corticospinal tracts and dorsal columns of immunosuppressed adult rat hosts. *Brain Res.*, 629: 115–127.

Li, Y. and Raisman, G. (1994) Schwann cells induce sprouting in motor and sensory axons in the adult rat spinal cord. *J. Neurosci.*, in press.

Lindsay, R.M. and Raisman, G. (1984) An autoradiographic study of neuronal development, vascularization and glial cell migration from hippocampal transplants labelled in intermediate explant culture. *Neuroscience*, 12: 513–530.

Matthews, M.A. and Duncan, D. (1971) A quantitative study of morphological changes accompanying the initiation and progress of myelin production in the dorsal funiculus of the rat spinal cord. *J. Comp. Neurol.*, 142: 1–22.

Neuberger, T.J., Cornbrooks, C.J. and Kromer, L.F. (1992) Effects of delayed transplantation of cultured Schwann cells on axonal regeneration from central nervous system cholinergic neurons. *J. Comp. Neurol.*, 315: 16–33.

O'Leary, D.D.M., Bicknese, A.R., De Carlos, J.A., Heffner, C.D., Koester, S.I., Kutka, L.J. and Terashima, T. (1990) Target selection by cortical axons: alternative mechanisms to establish axonal connections in the developing brain. *Cold Spring Harbor Symp. Quant. Biol.*, 55: 453–468.

Raisman, G. (1969) Neuronal plasticity in the septal nuclei of the adult rat. *Brain Res.*, 14: 25–48.

Raisman, G. (1985) Synapse formation in the septal nuclei of adult rats. In: C.W. Cotman (Ed.), *Synaptic Plasticity*, Guilford Press, New York, pp. 13–38.

Reier, P.J. (1986) Gliosis following CNS injury: the anatomy of astrocytic scars and their influences on axonal elongation. In: S. Fedoroff and A. Vernadakis (Eds.), *Astrocytes*, Vol. 3, Raven Press, New York, pp. 163–196.

Rickmann, M., Amaral, D.G. and Cowan, W.M. (1987) Organization of radial glial cells during the development of the rat dentate gyrus. *J. Comp. Neurol.*, 264: 449–479.

Schlessinger, A.R., Cowan, W.M. and Swanson, L.W. (1978) The time of origin of neurons in Ammon's horn and the associated retrohippocampal fields. *Anat. Embryol.*, 154: 153–173.

Schwab, M.E., Kapfhammer, J.P. and Bandtlow, C.E. (1993) Inhibitors of neurite growth. *Annu. Rev. Neurosci.*, 16: 565–595.

Sievers, J., Hartmann, D., Pehlemann, F.W. and Berry, M. (1992) Development of astroglial cells in the proliferative matrices, the dentate granule cell layer, and the hippocampal fissure of the hamster dentate gyrus. *J. Comp. Neurol.*, 320: 1–32.

Smith, G.V. and Stevenson, J.A. (1988) Peripheral nerve grafts lacking viable Schwann cells fail to support central nervous system axonal regeneration. *Exp. Brain Res.*, 69: 299–306.

Suzuki, M. and Raisman, G. (1992) The glial framework of central white matter tracts: segmented rows of contiguous interfascicular oligodendrocytes and solitary astrocytes give rise to a continuous meshwork of transverse and longitudinal processes in the adult rat fimbria. *Glia*, 6: 222–235.

Thanos, S. (1992) Adult retinofugal axons regenerating through peripheral nerve grafts can restore the light-induced pupilloconstriction reflex. *Eur. J. Neurosci.*, 4: 691–699.

Valentino, K.L. and Jones, E.G. (1982) The early formation of the corpus callosum: a light and electron microscopic study in foetal and neonatal rats. *J. Neurocytol.*, 11: 583–609.

Villegas-Pérez, M.P., Vidal-Sanz, M., Bray, G.M. and Aguayo, A.J. (1988) Influences of peripheral nerve grafts on the survival and regrowth of axotomized retinal ganglion cells in adult rats. *J. Neurosci.*, 8: 265–280.

Wictorin, K., Brundin, P., Gustavii, B., Lindvall, O. and Björklund, A. (1990) Reformation of long axon pathways in adult rat central nervous system by human forebrain neuroblasts. *Nature*, 347: 556–558.

Zhou, C.F., Raisman, G. and Morris, R.J. (1985) Specific patterns of fibre outgrowth from transplants to host mice hippocampi, shown immunohistochemically by the use of allelic forms of Thy-1. *Neuroscience*, 16: 819–833.

Zhou, C.F., Li, Y., Morris, R.J. and Raisman, G. (1990) Accurate reconstruction of three complementary laminar afferents to the adult hippocampus by embryonic neural grafts. *Neurosci. Res.*, 13(Suppl.): S43–S53.

F. Bloom (Editor)
Progress in Brain Research, Vol. 100
© 1994 Elsevier Science B.V. All rights reserved

CHAPTER 26

Brain damage and recovery

Donald G. Stein

Institute of Animal Behavior, Rutgers, The State University of New Jersey, Newark, NJ 07102, USA

Introduction

Although clinical neurologists and neuropsychologists have known for a long time that some recovery after damage to the brain and spinal cord is possible, it has only been within the last two decades that a serious and consistent effort has been made to understand its physiological bases. Now there are many dozens of laboratories interested in studying the mechanisms of recovery from brain and spinal cord damage, but back in the mid-1960s, when I began my career, there were only a handful of people working on the problem.

Rather than provide yet another traditional review of the pharmacology of recovery mechanisms (there are now many excellent and comprehensive papers available), the editors of this commemorative volume asked me to give a personal retrospective. So, in this essay I would like to start with a very brief background of the area and then highlight some of the conceptual and practical issues that I suggest require further thought and study. However, given what I have to say, I would guess that those of you with no interest in behavioral neuroscience would probably be happier skipping to one of the other articles in this volume.

Research on functional recovery may actually have begun in the early part of the 19th century. In the 1840s, the physiologist, Pierre Flourens, was probably one of the first experimentalists to manipulate brain damage and observe recovery of function in laboratory animals. He mutilated the brains of pigeons and despite the massive damage, Flourens noted that the birds gradually re-acquired all of their sensory and motor functions (Finger and Stein, 1982). Although

there were other reports on recovery from brain damage, it was Karl Lashley's pioneering work (1929, see also Finger, 1994 for more) from the 1920s to the 1950s, which provided the most convincing data demonstrating that laboratory rats could suffer massive brain injuries and yet show dramatic sparing of function on a variety of behavioral tasks.

Lashley was less interested in studying recovery of function for its clinical implications than in demonstrating that the idea of discrete localization of associative and cognitive functions to specific brain regions, was not the best way to describe cerebral organization (Finger, 1994). Except for a few devoted followers, most of Lashley's work was not welcomed because it did not fit the prevailing paradigm in which behavioral deficits following specific lesions were used to infer the functions of the damaged tissue. At the time, cortical cartography was capturing the imagination and talents of many investigators and great amounts of empirical data could be generated with little concern for theoretical implications. Defining cortical and subcortical regions of the brain also fit very well with the idea that all behaviors could be represented or "mediated" by a specific cerebral organ. By the 1960s, the focus on map-making and localization of function had become so strong that the leading neuroanatomist, Walle Nauta, had to express his concern as follows:

"It seems that if we try to discover the ways in which any part of the brain functions, it is only logical to try to find out in what way it acts within the brain as a whole. There is evidence that whatever the frontal lobe does must in some way affect the reticular formation, hypothalamus, limbic system, and a number of other structures about which we do not know very much. I think the point should be made that no part of the brain functions on its own, but only through the other parts of the brain with which it is connected." (Nauta, 1964)

The overemphasis on cartography that disturbed Walle Nauta is not one that now can simply be consigned to the history textbooks because it is still being taught in many places. For example, as recently as 1981, the editors (Kandel and Schwartz, 1981) of a major textbook in neuroscience stated the argument as follows:

> "Clinical studies and their counterparts in experimental animals suggest that all behavior, including higher (cognitive as well as affective) mental functions, is localizable to specific regions or constellations of regions within the brain." p. 11

The case for inferring function from damage to brain regions was made more strongly as a result of testing the large numbers of head-injured veterans returning from World War II, and a few years later, the Korean war. In the clinical literature, much of what was written about brain–behavior relationships and cerebral organization derived from studies in patients with bullet and shrapnel wounds to the head. Yet, very little of this extensive literature concerned itself with how, or whether, the victims of head injury would ever recover.

Head-injured veterans were entitled to receive comprehensive rehabilitation but there was nothing available in the way of early intervention or treatment to promote cognitive or functional recovery. Many patients simply languished in VA hospitals or were discharged to a life of dependency. For the most part, neuropsychologists focused on defining and precisely measuring the nature and severity of the deficits caused by the trauma rather than in providing "therapy" to the patients.

During the post-war period and up until the 1960s, one of the few people writing on recovery in humans was Alexander Luria. Luria was one of the Soviet Union's most distinguished neurologists and he wrote extensively on recovery and cerebral organization (Luria, 1966). He thought that direct localization of complex cerebral functions to circumscribed areas of the brain did not make much sense. In that regard, he

antedated the notions of serial and parallel processing. He believed that the "performance of a given function necessitates the integrity of far more extensive and far more structurally varied zones of the cortex than was assumed by classical neurology." (p. 13)

Indeed, it would not have been possible for Luria to stress recovery of function after massive trauma, if the functions were permanently lost as a result of damage to specific regions thought to mediate them. Although Luria clearly had a few strong followers here and abroad, most of his theories of cerebral organization and approaches to treatment were generally ignored because they also did not fit with the prevailing localization paradigm.

Hans-Lukas Teuber, who helped introduce Luria's work to American neuropsychologists, was one of the first post-World War II neuropsychologists to examine the residual capacities of brain-damaged patients and investigate the role of cerebral shock (diaschisis) in blocking recovery of function. Teuber (1975) did long-term follow-up studies with young, brain-damaged patients and was able to show remarkable recovery that required years to develop . He was one of the first to highlight clinical research on recovery and the role of early versus late brain damage. His studies gave credence to the idea that recovery of function in human patients merited further study and reflection.

Working independently in the late 1950s and 1960s, the physiological psychologists, Donald and Patricia Meyer (Meyer et al., 1963) Walter Isaac (1964) and Louis Petrinovich (Petrinovich and Carew, 1969), began to examine some of the factors contributing to functional recovery from cortical injuries in laboratory animals. These investigators looked at how specific types of training and control of environmental conditions before and after injury, could promote functional recovery. They were also interested in studying whether stimulant drugs like amphetamine could enhance recovery from cortical damage (Meyer, 1972). In their studies, the benefits conferred by drug treatments, seemed to last only while the animals were intoxicated. Once the drug wore off, the deficits returned so that recovery was not sustained.

My own work in the area of brain injury began as a straightforward examination of the role of the hippocampus in learning and the consolidation of memory traces (Stein and Kimble, 1966). In the course of my experiments, I created almost total, bilateral aspiration hippocampectomies in rats and then tested the animals on a variety of maze tasks. Although I obtained the expected deficits, I also noticed that some of the animals in the lesion groups performed almost as well as normal controls. Some might attribute the sparing to the typical "variability" that one sees in all living systems. However, when I did the lesion reconstructions and found that some animals had no behavioral deficits despite the fact that they also had no hippocampus, it became more difficult for me to think that the hippocampus was "necessary" for short-term memory functions. I was very puzzled by these data and by the few reports on recovery that were appearing at the time. However, I really wanted to get my PhD and get on with my life so I did not try to pursue the question of sparing of function and its theoretical implications until I began my first job at Clark University. At Clark, I was able to return to the work of John Adametz (1959), a neurosurgeon who showed that if one slowly damaged the rostral reticular formation in cats by doing staged surgeries, spaced 3 weeks apart, the animals would show normal sleep-wake cycles, groom normally and maintain themselves quite well. In contrast, if the same kind of lesions were made in a single sitting, all of the cats lapsed into coma and died within a few weeks. Adametz did not perform any systematic, cognitive testing of his animals, so my students and I decided to perform staged lesions in a number of different brain areas and then test our animals on a variety of behavioral tasks.

To make a long story short, we were able to show that, if complete bilateral injuries to different brain structures were done in stages (i.e. with about 2 weeks between each surgical operation), the animals were able to perform as well as intact controls on all of our behavioral tests. In contrast, animals with the same bilateral lesions inflicted in one sitting, demonstrated all of the deficits typically associated with that type of injury. In a number of different experiments, we examined what we then called the "serial lesion effect" in the frontal cortex (Stein et al., 1969), hippocampus (Isseroff et al., 1976), amygdala (McIntyre and Stein,

1973), motor cortex (Gentile et al., 1978), caudate nucleus (Schultze and Stein, 1975), lateral hypothalamus (Fass et al., 1975), and superior colliculus (Weinberg and Stein, 1978). In each case, we obtained essentially the same results. One-stage injuries produced the "expected" deficits, whereas the same damage inflicted in stages permitted the animals to escape the impairments and perform as well as controls.

In collaboration with Nelson Butters and Jeffrey Rosen (Rosen et al., 1971, 1975; Butters et al., 1974; Stein et al., 1977), we did a series of studies to replicate our findings in adult monkeys. We were able to demonstrate that multiple stage removals (i.e. in four operations removing one bank of the *sulcus principalis* at a time) of the frontal cortex led to spared performance on spatial learning performance. Monkeys with two stage lesions, spaced 4 weeks apart, were in turn, significantly better than those with one-stage lesions. What was interesting to note was that the recovered monkeys with four-stage lesions actually had more extensive damage and more gliosis than their one-stage counterparts who were very impaired. At the time we had no idea that glia might actually have contributed to the recovery process by serving as a source of trophic factors that could support the survival of remaining, damaged or dysfunctional neurons (Ermakova et al., 1993).

Around the same time, Stanley Finger was reproducing similar results in tactile discrimination after bilateral removal of the somatosensory cortex (Finger et al., 1971). Similar recovery was also being observed after staged damage to other sensory systems. For example, Dru et al. (1975) and Spear and Barbas (1975) were showing that, under appropriate conditions, serial lesions of the visual cortex would lead to functional sparing of visual discrimination performance. These and many other additional findings made it clear that the serial lesion effect was very robust and generalizable to different areas of the brain, different types of injuries and different species. The only problem was that no one really had a good explanation of why staged lesions almost always led to better outcomes that when the same damage was inflicted in a single setting (but see reference to Bulsara et al., 1992 for attempts to address this question).

To this day there is no completely satisfactory answer to what is inherently a very fundamental problem: why should the context in which an injury occurs, that is, "how" you remove a structure determine whether its "function" is lost or preserved? Also, the implications of this work for theories of cerebral organization have not been given much serious consideration in the neuroscience community. This is due to the fact that the serial lesion results simply do not fit easily with reductionist/localizationist theories implying that each and every structure has a specific function and that damage to the structure should result in the permanent loss of the specific function.

One way to dismiss the problem of what type of reorganization in response to bilateral injury can mediate recovery, is to propose that there are both "serial and parallel systems" involved in behavior and any one component can "take over" for the lost parts through some type of vicariation (see Slavin et al., 1988 for more discussion of this issue). This idea has become very tempting, especially in the light of newer imaging techniques which can show the brain areas that become metabolically active by measuring blood flow or glucose utilization. How much predictive power do we gain from talking about serial and parallel processing in recovery? Not a lot. Recently, Douglas and Martin (1991) discussed how map making based on the neuron doctrine needs to be reexamined. They presented a figure showing that, in 1983, the wiring diagram for cortical visual areas consisted of ten structures with a number of reciprocal connections. By 1990, the number of structures just "devoted" to processing cortical visual information had grown to 43 with reciprocal connections numbering in the hundreds. In applying the same logic to complex associative functions like learning and memory, which involve the processing of motor, sensory, kinesthetic and proprioceptive cues, one can easily begin to understand why the concept of mapping the structures in "parallel processing" begins to lose much of its explanatory value.

This is why working with isolated neurons or in vitro preparations, is so much more captivating; the issues are easier to deal with and can be explained with much more mechanistic concepts. In times of serious fiscal constraint, no study section wants to award research dollars to examine old theoretical constructs that do not fit well with established paradigms. So, to be more practical, our laboratory put aside the serial lesion puzzle and turned to the investigation of using newly developed pharmacological agents to promote functional recovery. We never did get back to the serial lesion effect.

By the mid-1980s things changed for the better. Policy makers, patients and their families, and pharmaceutical companies grew to recognize that head injury is a significant medical problem that needs more focused attention and better funding. Extramural support for work on neural plasticity became available and a whole new field of research developed. As a result, research on traumatic brain injury entered a new stage as changes in both conceptual thinking about the brain and exciting discoveries about mechanisms, began to appear almost on a daily basis.

The traditional notion of the brain as a static, genetically determined, collection of structures, each with a specific function, has (grudgingly?) given way to a much more dynamic view based on principles of plasticity, and capacity for rapid change in response to trauma. In addition, there is a much more comprehensive understanding of the immediate and long-lasting biochemical and anatomic changes that occur in response to cerebral trauma (for detailed reviews, see for example, Feeney and Sutton, 1988; Ziven and Choi, 1991; Stein and Glasier, 1992; Brodkey et al., 1993; Povlishock, 1993).

These last ten years have witnessed a "revolutionary" paradigm shift in thinking about brain injury repair. It is now accepted that functional recovery after traumatic injury to the brain can be obtained once the cascade of injury processes that accompanies trauma is properly controlled. We know much more about the mechanisms of injury-induced, neuronal sprouting; the role of glial cells and trophic factors in promoting the rescue of neurons; the effects of blocking high levels of excitatory amino acids; the role of free radicals in the injury process, and a host of other mechanistic factors that can determine the success or failure of the organism to survive and recover from brain damage. The problem is to figure out what do and when to do it at the biochemical, morphological and behavioral levels of analysis.

Like most other laboratories concerned with head trauma and recovery, we have focused our efforts on examining the specific molecular and anatomic variables that we can manipulate to enhance recovery. But this reductionistic approach provides only one part of the answer. A problem that must also be addressed if we are to move from laboratory research on recovery using animals as subjects, to the clinical rehabilitation of patients, is: what do we mean by the term "recovery"? Why is recovery so clearly seen in some laboratories and clinics and not others? Are the tests of clinical recovery relevant to what the patient really needs to accomplish? Why do certain drugs seem to have such dramatic and beneficial effects in some cases and fail just as dramatically in others? Are there surgical alternatives to promoting recovery? Why do some groups report highly successful instances of fetal brain tissue grafts in the clinical treatment of Parkinson's disease while others using the same surgical techniques fail to get benefits? Should grafts also be used to aid victims of head trauma?

One reason for the discrepancy is that scientists and clinicians do not often agree about how they would define "recovery". Different groups often have their own definitions for recovery of function, rehabilitation outcomes and clinical restoration. For example, in discussing recovery from brain injury, Laurence and Stein (1978) stressed that the phrase, "recovery of function" can refer to the straightforward accomplishment of certain goals by the subject (achieving an "end") or it can refer to the strategies (or "means") by which organisms accomplish their goals.

On the one hand, in the laboratory, recovery may mean only that after a specific injury, a particular drug or treatment causes neurotransmitter levels in one area of the brain to return or exceed pre-injury levels. On the other hand, for therapists and their patients, the more important issue is to improve quality of life; there is less concern about the particular mechanisms or underlying, physiological substrates. Thus, the question of "how" may be less important than "whether" a clinical goal is obtained. Yet, if each laboratory or rehabilitation clinic sets its own arbitrary

definition of "recovery", it is not surprising that there are so many differences of opinion concerning whether or not a given function is said to be "recovered"; not to mention what might satisfy the patients or their families.

A parallel question to that of defining what is meant by recovery, is what is meant by the term, "function". Do we really know how is the function of a given brain area is defined, or even what the "function" is in the first place? In the past, functions of brain regions were defined by observing and describing the loss or impairments of behaviors that accompanied damage to the structure in question.

Ernst Poppel (1989) recently defined (CNS) functions "as those that, in principle, can be lost after circumscribed injuries of the brain." (p. 6). But, as I have discussed above, there are numerous cases in which "circumscribed injuries" do not lead to significant, functional impairments. As I mentioned earlier, there is a substantial literature demonstrating that slow growing, bilateral injuries to the brain (e.g. serial lesions), often spare the complex behaviors thought to be mediated by the injured structures (Finger et al., 1973; Finger and Stein, 1982). In these cases involving rats, cats monkeys and people, slowly occurring bilateral damage does not always lead to behavioral symptomatology or to the same severity of impairments.

Recently, Anderson et al. (1990) carefully examined patients with neuropsychological deficits associated with lesions caused by tumors or stroke. They carefully matched the patients on the locus and the extent of their brain injuries. The neuropsychologists found that all of the patients with stroke in the left hemisphere (i.e. rapid onset of injury) have more severe language impairments than did their counterparts with slowly forming tumors (which had larger areas of damage). In fact, most of the tumor patients were normal on all of the language tests. What constitutes an adequate definition of an injury and a "deficit" in the context I have just described? What is the appropriate behavioral test to identify when and how a function is lost? For example, although Poppel (1989) has argued that "the integrity of local neuronal structures is essential for the availability of specific psychological functions," (p. 222) the serial lesion data and the tumor/stroke data argue against that view.

In addition, in the clinic, Poppel et al. (1973) and others (e.g. Zihl, 1981; Pommerenke and Markowitsch, 1989) have demonstrated that patients with cerebral "blindness" following posterior cortical injuries, have residual vision and can make limited visual discriminations if they are properly trained; a phenomenon they refer to as "blindsight". In this case are visual functions lost or are they suppressed or 'blocked' by the neural insult? Animal research on this topic as well as the blindsight data, can be taken to indicate that "inhibition" of function rather than loss, may be one result of "localized" brain injury. Under the circumstances, the problem becomes how to "unlock" or "unmask" the repressed function.

I mentioned above that about 20 years ago, Donald Meyer (1972) and his colleagues showed that cats with massive, bilateral, posterior cortical lesions could be rendered almost totally blind. However, following an injection of amphetamine, a potent neuroleptic, the "blind" cats were able to make visually guided placing responses as long as they were under the effects of the drug. Meyer argued that the lesions blocked access to the visual "engrams" which could be "derepressed" by the activating properties of the amphetamine. More recently, Feeney and Sutton (1988), showed that cats and rats could recover almost normal limb movements and gait following bilateral sensorimotor cortex lesions if they were given a single injection of amphetamine at the time of the injury. Without recourse to any drugs, Held et al. (1985) were able to show that enriched sensory activity and opportunity to explore the environment, could lead to better (although not complete) recovery of gait in adult rats which had received extensive injury to the sensorimotor cortex. In combination, these studies reveal that the "functions" of a given area may be altered (or determined?) by the organism's experience and post-traumatic environment and not just by its genetically "fixed" neuronal connections (or their disruption).

William Jenkins' research most directly speaks to this important issue. He, Michael Merzenich and their colleagues (Jenkins et al., 1990) have repeatedly demonstrated that the classical view suggesting that maturation of neuronal connections determines their "functions" is simply not true. Using precise, electrophysiological recording of single neurons in the sensorimotor cortex to map their receptive fields, Jenkins and his colleagues have shown that such fields can be modeled and remodeled by experience and training. More importantly for this discussion, following loss of sensory inputs, these same neurons may change their receptive fields dramatically (i.e. skin surface representation shifts). In some cases after cortical damage, the representation of skin sensory areas may shift to undamaged, previously unused portions of the remaining cortex. Likewise, as animals are trained on a sensory discrimination task, there are continuous shifts in the locus of the field as in their size and shape characteristics. This means that environment and training can model and alter neuronal properties in an adaptive manner.

The functional reorganization seen in Jenkins' work occurs far more rapidly than could be explained by the physical regeneration of nerve pathways themselves. The findings suggest that there are "latent" or "silent" pathways that occur in the normal development of the CNS. Such pathways can be unmasked and modified by experience or injury and later play a role in the recovery process. Although there are many questions that could be addressed in more detail, two with particular clinical relevance will close my review. The first is concerned with how soon after injury, the treatment should begin. Thanks to a large body of recent laboratory research, it is now quite clear that early and aggressive intervention and therapy may lead to the best prognosis for recovery. It has to be emphasized, here again, that brain injury and the concomitant neuronal loss is not a single, unitary event. Rather, a cascade of processes, some of which may last for years, is the complex result of neural damage. For example, in the first stage(s) of injury, substances in the brain itself are produced which are toxic to neurons and which diffuse beyond the immediate area of the injury to kill or damage vulnerable cells (Nieto-Sampedro, 1988; McIntosh, 1993). Toxic substances can also enter through the blood supply or through a compromised blood–brain barrier, leading to inflammation and immune reactions. As a result, neurons initially spared by the trauma could begin to die in massive numbers resulting in cell loss more devastating to the patient than the initial injury itself.

This is one reason why research on how much time should be devoted to rehabilitation or other forms of post-injury "therapy" is another area that needs careful investigation. Norman Geschwind (1985), felt that most clinicians not only did not pay sufficient attention to "seeking the right maneuvers" to elicit recovery, they also did not give enough attention to the time necessary for the processes leading to recovery to become manifest. Referring to the aphasias, He said that:

"Most neurologists are gloomy about the prognosis of severe adult aphasias after a few weeks and pessimism is reinforced by a lack of prolonged follow-up in most cases. I have, however, seen patients severely aphasic for over one year, who then made excellent recovery. One patient returned to work as a salesman, the other as a psychiatrist. Furthermore, there are patients who continue to improve over many years, for example, the patient whose aphasia is still quite evident six years after onset, cleared up substantially by 18 years." (p. 3)

I take Geschwind's observations to suggest that perhaps we are not doing enough to provide long-term therapy and rehabilitation to patients whose progress through the spectrum of recovery may be arduous and long. There is no principle of neuronal and behavioral organization that demands that functional and behavioral recovery occur immediately or not at all. The decision to withhold or terminate either pharmacological treatments or rehabilitation therapy is probably based more on economic (i.e. it would cost too much to continue) and social factors (let's get on to something with a more rapid, personal payoff; i.e. seeing a quick recovery) than it is on purely physiologic grounds; i.e. what we know about how the nervous system actually works.

The long time-course of neuronal recovery also means that the specifics of the therapy itself should change as the brain's endogenous response to the trauma progresses. As the underlying brain chemistry and morphology change over time, so should the course and type of therapy. Thus, for example, in the earliest stages, it might be appropriate to give drugs which block edema and reduce excitotoxicity, then shortly follow this regimen with injection of neurotrophic factors that could enhance new neuronal growth or reduce neuronal loss by repairing damaged cell membranes. It is important to emphasize that pharmacologic therapy alone may not likely be sufficient to ensure complete and long-lasting functional recovery in patients with serious brain damage. Systematic, physical rehabilitation and cognitive therapy will continue to play a critical role in returning the patient to full health. Psychological and emotional aspects of recovery should be considered and manipulated in a combined program of medical and psychosocial management.

Much more research needs to be done to determine what specific types of cognitive and behavioral rehabilitation should be provided. Paul Bach-y-Rita, a well known physiatrist, has often stated that:

"there is little or no demonstrated scientific basis for most of the (rehabilitation) procedures, and few of these procedures have been validated by controlled studies. The importance of the intervention of the various therapies has not been demonstrated."

For rehabilitation to be fully accepted by the medical and scientific community, rigorous controlled studies will have to demonstrate that the procedures employed are those that are, indeed, beneficial and appropriate to the patient's complete recovery.

Although a contextual approach to "recovery of function" is a new paradigm in the process of its own development, it is worthy of serious consideration and study. This approach puts emphasis on a more holistic approach to patients and their potential therapy. It is a view which leads to specifically testable hypotheses and proposes new alternatives for therapy and rehabilitation. Given the rapid progress being made these last few years, it is certain that brain-injured patients, who only too recently had nothing to hope for, may soon expect to participate more fully in all of the range of activities that are part of daily life.

By now, everyone working in the field of neural plasticity knows that Santiago Ramon y Cajal (1928), the Nobel prize-winning neuroanatomist, expressed initial pessimism about the possibility for regenerative growth in the adult central nervous system. He stated that:

"Once development was ended, the fonts of growth and regeneration of the axon and dendrites dried up irrevocably. In adult centers, the nerve paths are something fixed and immutable; everything may die, nothing may be regenerated." (p. 750)

However, Cajal was not ready to give up on the question of how one might go about unlocking or promoting neural plasticity. He also stated that:

"It is the duty of future scientists … with the inspiration of high ideals … to continue working to avoid or modulate the gradual and continuous decay of neurons, the almost invincible rigidity of their connections and, finally, to obtain the establishment of new neuronal pathways when diseases untie the intimately associated populations of neurons." (cited in Portera-Sanchez, 1987)

In looking back on the last 25 years of research and teaching, I believe that we are well on the way to realizing Cajal's dreams and aspirations.

References

Adametz, J. (1959) Rate of recovery of functioning in cats with rostral reticular lesions. *J. Neurosurg.*, 16: 85–98.

Anderson, S.W., Damasio, H. and Tranel, D. (1990) Neuropsychological impairments associated with lesions caused by tumor or stroke. *Arch. Neurol.*, 47: 397–405.

Bach-y-Rita, P. (1994) Applications of principles of brain plasticity and training to restore function. In: R.R. Young and P.J. Delwaide (Eds.), *Principles of Restorative Neurology*, Butterworths, London, in press.

Brodkey, J.A., Gates, M.A., Laywell, E.D. and Steindler, D.A. (1993) The complex nature of interactive neuroregeneration-related molecules. *Exp. Neurol.*, 123: 251–270.

Bulsara, K.R., Manibo, J.F. and Ramirez, J.J. (1992) Progressive entorhinal lesions accelerate hippocampal sprouting in rats. *Soc. Neurosci. Abstr.*, 18: 345.

Butters, N., Rosen, J.J. and Stein, D.G. (1974) Recovery of behavioral functions after sequential ablations of the frontal lobes of monkeys. In: D.G. Stein et al. (Eds.), *Plasticity and Recovery of Function in the Central Nervous System*, Academic Press, New York, pp. 429–466.

Douglas, R.J. and Martin, K.A.C. (1991) Opening the grey box. *Trends Neurosci.*, 14: 286–293.

Dru, D.O., Walker, J.P. and Walker, J.B. (1975) Recovery of CNS function:sSelf produced locomotion restores visual capacity after striate lesions. *Science*, 187: 265–266.

Ermakova, L., Fulop, Z., Geller, H.M., Chachaj, J., Mody, N. and Stein, D.G. (1993) Cultured astrocytes implanted into damaged NBM 48 hours after ibotenic acid lesions facilitate passive avoidance performance in rats. *Soc. Neurosci. Abstr.*, 19: 447.

Fass, B., Jordan, H., Rubman, A., Seibel, S. and Stein, D.G. (1975) Recovery of function after serial or one-stage lesions of the lateral hypothalamic area in rats. *Behav. Biol.*, 14: 283–294.

Feeney, D.M. and Sutton, R.L. (1988), Catecholamines and recovery of function after brain damage. In: D.G. Stein and B.A. Sabel (Eds.), *Pharmacological Approaches to the Treatment of Brain and Spinal Cord Injury*, Plenum Press, New York, pp. 121–142.

Finger, S. (1994) Origins of Neuroscience, New York, Oxford University Press.

Finger, S. and Stein, D.G. (1982) Brain Damage and Recovery: Research and Clinical Perspectives, Academic Press, New York.

Finger, S., Marshak, R.A., Cohen, M., Scheff, S. Trace, R. and Niemand, D. (1971) Effects of successive and simultaneous lesions of somatosensory cortex on tactile discrimination in the rat. *J. Comp. Physiol. Psychol.*, 77: 221–227.

Finger, S., Walbran, B., and Stein, D.G. (1973) Brain damage and behavioral recovery: serial lesion phenomena. *Brain Res.*, 63: 1–18.

Gentile, A.M., Green, S., Nieburgs, A., Schmelzer, W. and Stein, D.G. (19??) Disruption and recovery of locomotor and manipulatory behavior following cortical lesions in rats. *Behav. Biol.*, 22: 417–455.

Geschwind, N. (1985) Mechanisms of change after brain lesions. In: F. Nottebohm. (Ed.), Hope for a new neurology. *Ann. N. Y. Acad. Sci.*, 457: 1–11.

Held, J.M., Gordon, J. and Gentile, A.M. (1985) Environmental influences on locomotor recovery following cortical lesions in rats. *Behav. Neurosci.*, 99: 678–690.

Isaac, W. (1964) Role of stimulation and time in the effects of spaced occipital ablations. *Psychol. Rep.*, 14: 151.

Isseroff, A., Leveton, L., Freeman, G., Lewis, M.E. and Stein, D.G. (1976) Differences in the behavioral effects of single stage and serial lesions of the hippocampus. *Exp. Neurol.*, 53: 339–354.

Jenkins, W.M., Merzenich, M.M. and Recanzone, G. (1990) Neocortical representational dynamics in adult primates: implications for neuropsychology. *Neuropsychologia*, 23: 573–584.

Kandel, E.R. and Schwartz, J.H. (1981) *Principles of Neural Science*, Elsevier, Amsterdam, p. 11.

Lashley, K. (1929) *Brain Mechanisms and Intelligence*, University of Chicago Press, Chicago, IL.

Laurence, S., and Stein, D.G. (1978), Recovery after brain damage and the concept of localization of function. In: S. Finger (Ed.), *Recovery from Brain Damage: Research and Theory*, Plenum Press, New York, pp. 369–407.

Luria, A.R. (1966) Human Brain and Psychological Processes, Harper and Row, New York, p. 13.

McIntosh, T.K (1993) Novel pharmacologic therapies in the treatment of experimental traumatic brain injury: a review. *J. Neurotrauma*, 10: 215–262.

McIntyre, M. and Stein, D.G. (1973) Differential effects of one versus two-stage amygdaloid lesions on activity, exploratory and avoidance behavior in the albino rat. *Behav. Biol.*, 9: 451-465.

Meyer, D.R. (1972) Access to engrams. *Am. Psychol.*, 27: 124–33.

Meyer, P.M., Horel, J.A. and Meyer, D.R. (1963) Effects of dl-amphetamine upon placing responses in neodecorticate cats. *J. Comp. Physiol. Psychol.*, 56: 402–404.

Nauta, W.J.H. (1964) Discussion of Stamm, J.S., Retardation and facilitation in learning by stimulation of frontal cortex in monkeys. In: M. Warren and K.A. Akert (Eds.), *The Frontal Granular Cortex and Behavior*, McGraw-Hill, New York.

Nieto-Sampedro, M. (1988) Growth factor induction and order of events in CNS repair. In: D.G. Stein and B.A. Sabel (Eds.), *Pharmacological Approaches to the Treatment of Brain and Spinal Cord Injury*. Plenum Press, New York, pp. 301–338.

Petrinovich, L. and Carew, T.J. (1969) Interaction of neocortical lesion size and interoperative experience in retention of a learned brightness discrimination. *J. Comp. Physiol. Psychol.*, 68: 451–454.

Pommerenke, K. and Markowitsch, H.J. (1989) Rehabilitation training of homonymous visual field defects in patients with postgeniculate damage of the visual system. *Restor. Neurol. Neurosci.*, 1: 47–64.

Poppel, E. (1989) Taxonomy of the subjective: an evolutionary perspective. In: J.W. Brown (Ed.), *Neuropsychology of Visual Perception*, Lawrence Earlbaum, New Jersey, pp. 219–232.

Poppel, E., Held, R. and Frost, D. (1973) Residual visual function after brain wounds involving the central visual pathways in man. Nature (London), 243: 295–296.

Portera-Sanchez, A. (1987) Cajal's concepts on plasticity in the central nervous system revisited: a perspective. In: R.L. Masland, A. Portera-Sanchez and G. Toffano (Eds.), *Neuroplasticity: A New Therapeutic Tool in the CNS Pathology*, Springer-Verlag, Berlin, pp. 9–30.

Povlishock, J.T. (1993) Traumatic brain injury: the pathobiology of injury and repair. In: A. Gorio (Ed.), *Neuroregeneration*, New York, Raven Press, pp. 185–216.

Ramon y Cajal, S. (1928) *Degeneration and Regeneration of the Nervous System*, translated by R.M. May, Oxford University Press, London.

Rosen, J.J., Stein, D.G. and Butters, N. (1971) Recovery of function after serial ablation of prefrontal cortex in the monkey. *Science*, 173: 353–355.

Rosen, J., Butters, N., Soeldner, C. and Stein, D.G. (1975) Effects of one stage and serial ablations of the middle third of sulcus principalis on delayed alternation performance in monkeys. *J. Comp. Physiol. Psychol.*, 89: 1077–1082.

Schultze, M.J. and Stein, D.G. (1975) Recovery of function in the albino rat following either simultaneous or seriatim lesions of the caudate nucleus. *Exp. Neurol.*, 46, 291–301.

Slavin, M.D., Laurence, S. and Stein, D.G. (1988) Another look at vicariation. In: S. Finger, T.E. LeVere, C.R. Almli and D.G. Stein (Eds.), *Brain Injury and Recovery: Theoretical and Controversial Issues*, Plenum Press, New York, pp. 165–168.

Spear, P.D. and Barbas, H. (1975) Recovery of pattern discrimination ability in rats receiving serial or one-stage visual cortex lesions. *Brain Res.*, 94: 337–346.

Stein, D.G. and Glasier, M. (1992) An overview of developments in research on recovery from brain injury. *Adv. Exp. Med. Biol.*, 325: 1–22.

Stein, D.G. and Kimble, D.P. (1966) Effects of hippocampal lesions and post-trial strychnine administration on maze behavior in the rat. *J. Comp. Physiol. Psychol.*, 62: 243–249.

Stein, D.G., Rosen, J.J., Graziadei, J., Mishkin, D. and Brink, J.J. (1969) Central nervous system: recovery of function. *Science*, 166: 528–530.

Stein, D.G., Butters, N. and Rosen, J.J. (1977) A comparison of two and four-stage ablations of sulcus principalis on recovery of spatial performance in the monkey. *Neuropsychologia*, 15: 179–182.

Teuber, H.-L. (1975) Recovery of function after brain injury in man. In: Outcome of Severe Damage to the CNS, Ciba Foundation Symposium, Elsevier, Amsterdam, pp. 159–186.

Weinberg, D. and Stein, D.G. (1978) Impairment and recovery of visual functions after bilateral lesions of superior colliculus. Physiol. Behav., 20: 323–329.

Zihl, J. (1981) Recovery of visual field associated with specific training in patients with cerebral damage. In: M.W. van Hof and G. Mohn (Eds.), *Functional Recovery from Brain Damage*, Elsevier, Amsterdam, pp. 189–202.

Ziven, J. and Choi, D.W. (1991) Stroke therapy. *Sci. Am.*, 265: 56–63.

F. Bloom (Editor)
Progress in Brain Research, Vol. 100
© 1994 Elsevier Science B.V. All rights reserved

CHAPTER 27

Trophic factor therapy in the adult CNS: remodelling of injured basalo-cortical neurons

A. Claudio Cuello

McGill University, Department of Pharmacology and Therapeutics, McIntyre Medical Building, 3655 Drummond Street, Suite 1325, Montreal, Quebec, Canada H3G 1Y6

Introduction

It is a great pleasure to contribute to the 100th volume of *Progress in Brain Research* with some thoughts on one of the most exciting developments in the neurosciences. For me, this is a great satisfaction as this collection has accompanied my career since one of the first volumes was lent to me in the early 1960s, in Buenos Aires, by Professor Eduardo De Robertis. Much has changed in neurobiology since those early years.

The concept that future neurology might resort to pharmacological intervention, to attenuate or even reverse neurological processes leading to neuronal cell death or loss of synaptic connections, would have been an untenable proposition just over a decade ago. However, scientific advances have provided strong foundations for this proposition. Presently, not only academic units are investigating potential avenues for the pharmacological treatment of neurodegenerative processes, but also well established pharmaceutical industries, as well as newly born biotechnological enterprises. Indeed, the neurosciences are becoming one of the most exciting scientific areas with challenging advances comparable to those of developmental biology and cancer research.

Two important factors have contributed significantly to this. One is the demonstration that the neurons of the CNS possess a capacity of recovery well beyond that assumed by the traditional "medical culture". The successful neuronal grafting within the CNS

and the offering of adequate "milieu" to central neurons for the growth of axonal processes have done much to question traditional concepts on the immutability of the CNS. Another crucial aspect which contributed to the generation of this new scenario has been the realization that neurotrophic factors (NTFs) known to elicit fundamental phenotypic changes in neurons during development were also capable of profoundly affecting these cells in mature, fully differentiated animals (for reviews see Hefti et al., 1989; Thoenen, 1991; Cuello, 1993).

A concept which is emerging from such experimentation is that NTFs (or their derivatives) can be used as *drugs* to elicit trophic responses in damaged neurons of the CNS. Figure 1 represents in schematic fashion the circumstances in which exogenously applied NTFs to the adult and fully differentiated CNS might elicit trophic responses leading to the re-establishment or compensation of neural function lost by damage of cell bodies or processes. The hypothetical scheme assumes that diverse NTFs are produced in relatively large amount during development, securing the differentiation and connectivity of neurones in a programmed temporal-spatial fashion. During the developmental period, distinct sets of neurons are probably dependent on these factors for their survival; a situation that can closely be reproduced in tissue culture conditions. The levels of NTFs decrease considerably during early post-natal stages to "basal" levels during adulthood. Although this is an issue of some controversy, we can tentatively assume that the main conse-

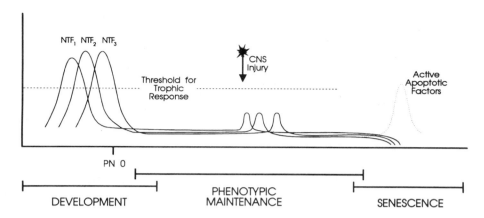

Fig. 1. Hypothetical circumstances in which the production of neurotrophic factors (NTFs) might control the survival, development and specific connections of distinct neuronal populations. During development, relatively high levels of NTFs are produced at various stages to secure differentiation of specific sets of neurons. During adulthood, basal levels of NTFs are produced presumably to maintain the differential phenotypic characteristics of mature CNS neurons and probably their pattern of synaptic connections. The enhanced production of NTFs consequent to neural injury during this ontogenic phase is apparently insufficient to reach the threshold for trophic responses, which can be evoked by exogenous NTFs. It is as yet unclear if CNS senescence with the loss of neurons and connections is due, to some extent, either to a diminution in the expression of NTFs and their receptors or to de novo expression of presumptive apoptotic factors (from Cuello et al., 1993).

quence of this basal production of NTFs during adulthood is the maintenance of phenotypic characteristics of mature neurons, their arborization and synaptic connectivity.

Experimental injury of the CNS in adult mammals results in upregulation of the synthesis of some NTFs. Is this an attempt of the mature injured CNS to recapitulate the embryonic growth of neural cells? If so, this would fulfil Ramon y Cajal's assertion that "...the central axons, and in a less measure the dendrites, possess, *ab initio*, the capacity inherent in the constitution itself of the nervous protoplasm, of increasing their mass intrinsically and extrinsically, that is, of rebuilding their structure and of expanding into new projections" (Ramon y Cajal, 1928).

It is clear, however, that these surges in the production of NTFs are insufficient in adulthood to recover the ab initio properties of neurons. The episodic increase in endogenous NTFs is unable to re-establishing neuronal phenotypic characteristics and connectivity following a major injury of the CNS. The experimental exogenous application of NTFs is proving to be capable of doing precisely that for certain subsets of CNS neurons. Much of this knowledge and cur-

rent excitement derives from studies in which the application of neurotrophins (nerve growth factor (NGF), brain derived neurotrophic factor (BDNF), neurotrophin 3 (NT3)) importantly redresses the neuronal cell loss or atrophy which follows from lesions of the CNS of adult animals. Some of these aspects, centering on our experience with cholinergic neurons of the nucleus basalis magnocellularis, are discussed below.

The rescue of cholinergic neurons of the nucleus basalis magnocellularis

In the past decade we have been interested in the capacity of recovery of the cholinergic neurons of nucleus basalis magnocellularis (nbm). These neurons are particularly interesting in that they provide the bulk of the cholinergic innervation to neocortex. They constitute the "basalo-cortical" cholinergic pathway. Their transmitter (acetylcholine: ACh) has been associated with higher functions such as memory, attention and learning. Some of the symptoms of Alzheimer's disease (AD) have been attributed to the failure of cortical cholinergic function. Indeed, this transmitter and its biosynthetic enzyme (choline acetyltransferase: ChAT) are depleted to an important extent (albeit not exclusively) in this disease.

The cortical pathology of AD is accompanied in the basal forebrain by severe loss and atrophy of the cells of the nbm (nucleus magnocellularis of Meynert in the human species). From the experimental viewpoint, these cells provide an excellent opportunity to investigate CNS plasticity as they are clearly well endowed (as is also the case for cholinergic medial septum neurons) with both the low (p75^{LNGFR}) and the high (p140^{trk}, the proto-oncogen product: tyrosine kinase A) affinity receptor to NGF (for review, see Bothwell, 1991).

The abundance of NGF receptor (low and high affinity) mRNAs in the nbm of the rat is illustrated in Fig. 2. The lesion model in which we have explored extensively the responsiveness of nbm neurons consists of partial, unilateral cortical infarctions involving mainly the parietal cortex and adjacent portions of the neocortex (see Fig. 3). This ischemic injury deprives a

large portion of the nbm of their normal target sites and the resulting lesion engulfs the *terminal* portion of these forebrain cholinergic neurons. The experimental procedure is such that it spares the main axonal shaft of these neurons and, in consequence, it is not an *axotomy* lesion model.

The outcome of this lesion is a gradual retrograde degeneration of nbm cholinergic neurons, ending with a marked and prolonged atrophy of these cells. Ostensibly, cell death does not occur, since the ChAT immunoreactive neurons persist unchanged in number. However, they appear considerably shrunken (Sofroniew et al., 1983), with important retraction of their dendritic processes in the nbm area and axonal networks in the remaining cortex of the lesioned side (Garofalo et al., 1992). These changes are accompanied by a marked depletion in ChAT enzymatic activity in the microdissected region of the nbm (Stephens et al., 1985). The intracerebro-ventricular administration of relatively low amounts of NGF completely redresses the biochemical and morphological signs for

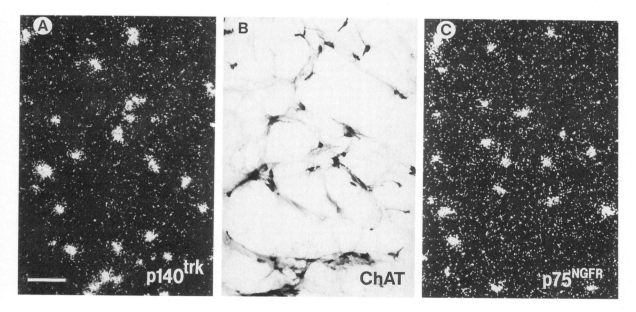

Fig. 2. Typical distribution of neurons at the level of the middle portion of the nucleus basalis magnocellularis of the rat. (*A*) and (*C*) Dark-field photomicrographs of neurons expressing p140^{trk} and p75^{NGFR} mRNAs, respectively. In situ hybridization experiments were performed with 10-μm-thick coronal sections using radioactive antisense DNA oligoprobes. Note the close correspondence in the pattern of distribution of the low and high affinity of NGF receptors with the nbm cholinergic neurons. (*B*) Photomicrograph of 50-μm thick coronal section at the same level as *A* and *B*, displaying ChAT-immunopositive neurons. Bar, 100 μm (*A–C*) (from Figueiredo, Skup, Bedard, Tetzlaff and Cuello, unpublished).

216

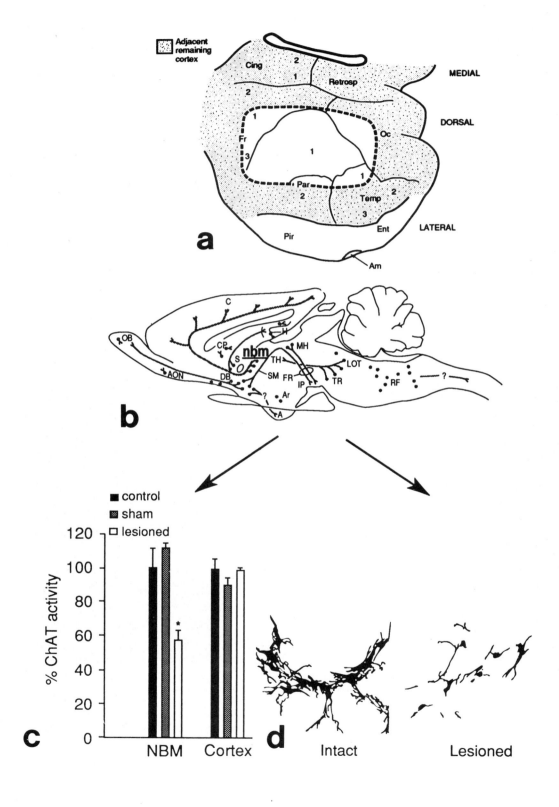

the retrograde degeneration in the nbm (Cuello et al., 1989).

Other NTFs such as acidic fibroblast growth factor can achieve the same effect (Figueiredo et al., 1993) while the neurotrophins BDNF and NT3 are seemingly ineffective in the same experimental circumstances (Skup et al., 1994). Interestingly, the application of NGF in this experimental basalo-cortical lesion model not only protects cholinergic cell somata but also results in supranormal levels of ChAT activity in the terminal field, i.e. in the remaining cortex ipsilateral to the lesion (Cuello et al., 1989).

Does this imply that NTFs are capable of provoking changes compensatory to the deficits provoked by the infarction? Indeed, the neurotrophic therapy results in a marked increase in high affinity choline uptake sites in synaptosomes obtained from rat cortices bearing lesions and treated with neurotrophins (Garofalo and Cuello, 1993) and in a facilitated spontaneous output of endogenous ACh, recorded in vivo with micro-dialysis probes implanted in the remaining cortex of lesioned, neurotrophin-treated animals (Maysinger et al., 1992).

Neurotrophin-induced synaptic remodelling of the cerebral cortex

Are the structural cholinergic terminal elements also altered by the trophic factor therapy? The immunocytochemical investigation combined with computerized image analysis of these fine cholinergic cortical fibres revealed important modifications in the terminal network of the basalo-cortical pathway induced by the experimental neurotrophic therapy (Garofalo et al., 1992). Thus, a significant retraction of cholinergic fibers terminating in the neocortex occurs in the ipsilateral cortex to an ischemic lesion.

Administration of small amounts of NGF for 7 days suffice to correct this retrenchment of the cholinergic network and increase above normal the number of identifiable varicosities along these axons. These varicosities were further investigated at electron microscopic level concentrating the analysis in lamina 5, which is a prominent area of termination of basalo-cortical cholinergic fibers. At the ultrastructural level, it was seen that, concomitantly with the retraction of the fiber network and the diminution of the number of cholinergic varicosities, a contraction of the size of ChAT immunoreactive boutons occurs in lesioned animals. This contraction in the size of the individual ChAT immunoreactive boutons is not only corrected by the NGF administration but this neurotrophin provokes a considerable hypertrophy of these presynaptic cholinergic elements in lesioned animals.

These consequences of neurotrophic factor therapy are illustrated in Fig. 4. Furthermore (also illustrated in Fig. 4), the NGF application provoked a remarkable incidence in the number of synaptic differentiations as revealed by high resolution immunocytochemistry. Interestingly, none of these changes were noticed in unoperated animals receiving NGF. These observations demonstrate that NGF is capable of provoking profound remodelling of the cortical synaptic circuitry and, furthermore, by increasing the number of varicosities and synaptic differentiations of generating additional synapses, i.e. "synaptogenesis". Synaptic remodelling and synaptogenesis have in the past been identified in the adult CNS. For example, synaptic changes occur as a consequence of considerable deafferentation of the affected nuclei while pre- and post-synaptic alterations have been shown to develop in the hippocampal formation after long-term potentiation (for review, see Cotman, 1985). However, the NGF-induced synaptogenesis (Garofalo et al., 1992) is the first direct demonstration that a *drug* (a NTF in this case), is capable of inducing remodelling of the terminal network and synapses in mature, fully differentiated animals.

Fig. 3. Schematic representation of the cortical devascularizing lesion model. (*a*) Planimetric representation of the rat cerebral cortex from the medial aspects to the piriform (Pir) cortex; Fr, frontal; Oc, occipital; temp, temporal cortices. The removing of pial vessels in the framed, empty area causes an infarct of the frontal-parietal rat cortex. The shaded areas depict the remaining neocortex after infraction. This lesion leads to retrograde and anterograde degeneration of cholinergic neurons of the nbm. The basalo-cortical cholinergic pathway is indicated in (*b*). The depletion of ChAT enzymatic activity in the microdissected nbm is indicated in (*c*), and the extent of cell shrinkage and retraction of neurites is illustrated in (*d*) (Camera lucida drawing) (from Cuello, 1993).

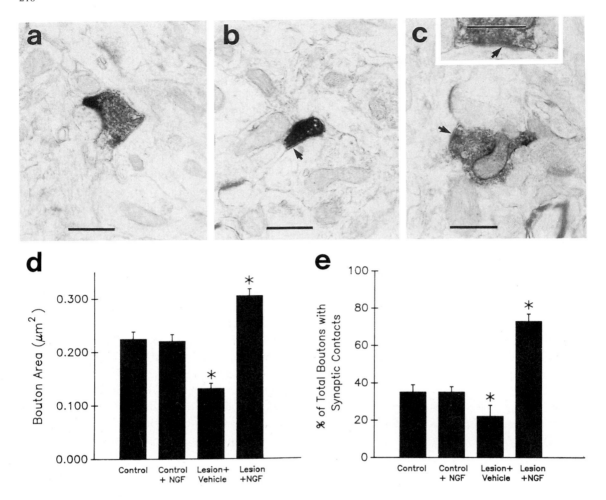

Fig. 4. Electron micrographs of cortical ChAT-IR boutons from layer V of rat somatosensory cortex. Representative profiles of cholinergic presynaptic terminal boutons of control (*a*), lesioned vehicle-treated (*b*), and lesioned NGF-treated (*c*) rats. Scale bars = 0.5 μm.) (*d*) Cross-sectional area of ChAT immunoreactive boutons in cortical layer V. (*e*) Percentage of varicosity profiles quantified with visible synaptic contacts. *$P < 0.01$ from control (analysis of variance post hoc Tukey test) (from Garofalo et al., 1992).

The trophic factor therapy in primates

It is obviously essential that before embarking on neu-rotrophic therapies in the clinical scenario, that these agents are exhaustively investigated in subhuman pri-mates. The thorough knowledge of the organization of the two main basal forebrain cholinergic projections (the septo-hippocampal and the basalo-cortical path-ways) have greatly facilitated this task. The therapeu-tic capabilities of NGF in the *axotomy* lesion model in primates (unilateral fimbria-fornix sections resulting in

"loss" of cholinergic neurons of the medial septum) have proven its efficacy. Thus, Tuszynski et al. (1990, 1991) and Koliatsos et al. (1990, 1991) have shown in *Macaca fascicularis*, utilizing either mouse or human recombinant NGF, that they were able to prevent cho-linergic cell loss in the medial septum. They have even demonstrated a NGF-induced hypertrophy of forebrain cholinergic cell somata. The survival time of these le-sioned-treated animals was 2–4 weeks.

We were able to reproduce in *Cercopithecus aethiops* the rodent model of retrograde degeneration of basolo-cortical cholinergic neurons. This was done by producing unilateral, ischemic, infarctions of the most superficial gyri in a region of the neocortex analogous to the rodent lesion model (Pioro et al., 1993). The ischemic lesion comprised portions of posterior frontal, superior temporal, parietal and anterior occipital cortices while sparing Brodmann area 4. Human-recombinant NGF (Genentech) was applied to these animals in the form of a gelatin implant in the area of the affected cortex in amounts comparable to those previously applied in rodents.

These investigations demonstrated that a retrograde cholinergic degeneration of cells of the nucleus basalis of Meynert (nbM) occurred, exclusively restricted to its intermediate region, that is the Ch4i group according to the classification of Mesulam et al. (1986). This region of the nbM is the sole region responsible for the cholinergic innervation of the affected areas of the neocortex. Shrunken cholinergic neurons in the intermediate nbM (Ch4i) were apparent some 6 months after surgical intervention (Liberini et al., 1993; Pioro et al., 1993). The morphology and dimensions of these

cholinergic nbM cells appeared normal after 6 months survival time and more than 5 months after the complete dissolution of the gel containing the human-recombinant NGF (Liberini et al., 1993).

In addition, the deficits in ChAT enzymatic activity observed in the microdissected nbM were corrected by the NGF application (Liberini et al., 1993). Furthermore, a supranormal enzymatic activity of ChAT was found in samples of cortical tissue adjacent to the infarcted area. This upregulation of the activity of the acetyl choline synthesising enzyme is reminiscent of the biochemical changes observed in rodents (Cuello et al., 1989) which occur concomitantly with the remodelling of cortical synaptic elements (Garofalo et al., 1992).

It is therefore, very possible that profound plasticity of forebrain cholinergic neurons can be achieved in subhuman primates with the therapeutic administration of NTFs. Table I summarizes the results obtained with the application of neurotrophins in primates in two different lesion models after short and long survival times.

TABLE I

Effects of trophic agent treatment in different primate lesion models affecting the cholinergic system (from Cuello et al., 1993)

Lesion model	Species	Treatment	Survival time	Effects	Ref.[b]
FF transection	*Macaca fascicularis*		**Short survival**		
		Mouse-NGF (360 μg i.c.v.)	4 weeks	Cell loss prevention Neuronal hypertrophy	1
		Mouse-NGF (5 mg i.c.v.)	2 weeks	Cell loss prevention	2
		Human-NGF (360 μg i.c.v.)	4 weeks	Cell loss prevention	3
		Human-NGF (5 mg i.c.v.)	2 weeks	Cell loss prevention Neuronal hypertrophy	4
Cortical devascularization	*Cercopithecus aethiops*		**Long survival**		
		GMl (175 mg/gel)	6 months	Rescue from cell atrophy ChAT decrease prevention[a]	5
		Human NGF (2.8 mg/gel)	6 months	Rescue from cell atrophy ChAT decrease prevention[a]	6
		GM1 + human NGF (175 mg + 2.8 mg/gel)	6 months	Rescue from cell atrophy Dendritic expansion Supranormal ChAT increase[a]	6

[a]ChAT assay was performed in the nbM ipsilateral to the lesion side and in cortex surrounding the devascularized area.
[b]1, Tuszynski et al. (1990); 2, Koliatsos et al. (1990); 3, Tuszynski et al. (1991); 4, Koliatsos et al. (1991); 5, Pioro et al. (1993); 6, Liberini et al. (1993).

Significance of CNS trophic factor therapy and future possibilities

Does trophic factor therapy have a clinical significance or it is merely an approach to acquire further knowledge on brain plasticity? The two quests, individually, are each important enough to concentrate our attention in the working hypothesis that most CNS neurons can be rescued from atrophy, and further that this therapy might lead to compensatory remodelling of synaptic circuitry. The minimal outcome from these studies will be a better understanding of brain function and dysfunction. The optimal outcome will be the designing of novel neurological therapies directly based on experience gathered with the experimental application of diverse NTFs (or their derivatives) in a variety of animal models, reproducing as closely as possible traumatic and neurodegenerative conditions.

The outstanding questions largely exceed the number of answers already assembled. The spectrum of NTFs' specificity, the receptors responsible for their biological actions as well as their intermediate intracellular messengers are yet to be established in most cases. This information, and that of the responsiveness of distinct CNS neuronal sets to the application of NTFs in a variety of experimental circumstances, will be gathered in the coming years. By then, the question of the right indication in the clinical setting will be paramount. At this point in time it is tempting to speculate that the cortical synaptic remodelling of cholinergic fibers might be a desirable therapeutic goal in AD.

Our confidence in bridging the experimental to clinical gap will be, among other factors, based on the fidelity with which animal models reproduce neuropathological conditions. The path to clinical application is full of potential drawbacks. One of the most immediate is the thought that NTFs might additionally activate undesired genes. Thus, the possibility has been raised of the potential overproduction of beta-amyloid or the generation of neuritic plaques in the case of Alzheimer's disease (for review, see Butcher and Woolf, 1989).

Age might also be a factor for consideration. It is clear from present information that the CNS of younger animals responds better to experimental trophic therapy. However, sustained application of NGF has shown to improve cholinergic markers and some behavioral responses in aged, impaired animals (for review, see Williams et al., 1993). Would the NTF-induced neuronal remodelling provoke disorganized connectivity? It is possible. We do not have enough information in this regard. It is, nonetheless, rewarding to note that this therapy in the lesioned basalo-cortical model resulted in correction of the deficient behaviors (Garofalo and Cuello, 1993).

Assuming that trophic factor therapy gathers sufficient momentum for clinical application, pharmaceutical issues will become crucial. For instance, should NTFs be administered directly into the CNS and, if so, how? Experimentally both permanent cannulae linked to mini-pumps and the grafting of microcapsule containing NTFs have proven successful. Adaptation of these procedures are possible but also cumbersome.

The possibility that future pharmacology might resort to the utilization of other active molecules capable of crossing the blood–brain barrier is on the horizon. These can be agents which either act cooperatively with endogenous NTFs (as might be the case for the sialogangliosides), substances which interfere with the cellular mechanisms involved in the trophic response (secondary, tertiary cellular messengers' responses) or tailored peptide "mimetics" able to activate specific NTF receptors. In the not so distant future it is conceivable that neurologists will consider the grafting of genetically transformed cells producing specific NTFs. This is a path that has been successfully pioneered by Gage et al. (1991) and which we have found of value in the basalo-cortical lesion model (Piccardo et al., 1992). Beyond that, the in vivo somatic cell transgenesis in the CNS could be an exciting prospect if the means for directing DNA material coding for NTFs is specifically incorporated by the desired cells and in the desired region of the CNS. All these options are full of unknowns but will certainly be explored in years to come.

Acknowledgements

The author gratefully acknowledges the support from

the MRC (Canada), the fruitful interactions with present and past collaborators, the secretarial assistance of Ms. Dawn Torsein and Ms. Oralia Mackprang and Dr. Paul Clarke and Dr. Bonald Figueiredo for their critical reading of the manuscript.

References

Bothwell, M. (1991) Keeping track of neuropeptide receptors. *Cell*, 65: 915–918.

Butcher, L.L. and Woolf, N.J. (1989) Neurotrophic agents may exacerbate the pathologic cascade of Alzheimer's disease. *Neurobiol. Aging*, 10: 557–570.

Cotman, C.W. (1985) Growth factor induction and temporal order in central nervous system repair. In: C.W. Cotman (Ed.), *Synaptic Plasticity*, Guilford Press, New York, pp. 407–456.

Cuello, A.C. (1993) Trophic responses of forebrain cholinergic neurons: a discussion. In: A.C. Cuello (Ed.), *Cholinergic Function and Dysfunction, Progress in Brain Research*, Vol. 98, Elsevier, Amsterdam, pp. 265–277.

Cuello, A.C., Garofalo, L., Kenigsberg, R.L. and Maysinger, D. (1989) Gangliosides potentiate in vivo and in vitro effects of nerve growth factor on central cholinergic neurons. *Proc. Natl. Acad. Sci. USA*, 86: 2056–2060.

Cuello, A.C., Liberini, P. and Piccardo, P. (1993) Atrophy and regrowth of CNS forebrain neurons. Models of study and clinical significance. In: A.C. Cuello (Ed.), *Neuronal Cell Death and Repair*, Elsevier, Amsterdam, pp. 173–191.

Figueiredo, B.C., Piccardo, P., Maysinger, D., Clarke, P.B.S. and Cuello, A.C. (1993) Effects of acidic fibroblast growth factor on cholinergic neurons of nucleus basalis magnocellularis and in a spatial memory task following cortical devascularization. *Neuroscience*, 56: 955–963.

Gage, F.H., Kawaja, M.D. and Fisher, L.J. (1991) Genetically modified cells: applications for intracerebral grafting. *Trends Neurosci.*, 14: 328–333.

Garofalo, L, and Cuello, A.C. (1993) Nerve growth factor and the monosialoganglioside GM1: analogous and different in vivo effects on biochemical, morphological and behavioral parameters of adult cortically lesioned rats. *Exp. Neurol.*, 125: 195–217.

Garofalo, L., Ribeiro-da-Silva, A. and Cuello, A.C. (1992) Nerve growth factor-induced synaptogenesis and hypertrophy of cortical cholinergic terminals. *Proc. Natl. Acad. Sci. USA*, 89: 2639–2643.

Hefti, F., Hartikka, J. and Knusel, B. (1989) Function of neurotrophic factors in the adult and aging brain and their possible use in the treatment of neurodegenerative diseases. *Neurobiol. Aging*, 10: 515–533.

Koliatsos, V.E, Martin, L.J., Walker, L.D., Richardson, R.T., DeLong, M.R. and Price, D.L. (1990) Mouse nerve growth factor prevents degeneration of axotomized basal forebrain cholinergic neurons in the monkey. *J. Neurosci.*, 10: 3801–3813.

Koliatsos, V.E., Clatterbuck, R.E., Nauta, H.J.W., Knüsel, B., Burton, L.E., Hefti, F.F., Mobley, W.C. and Price, D.L. (1991) Human nerve growth factor prevents degeneration of basal forebrain cholinergic neurons in primates. *Ann. Neurol.*, 30: 831–840.

Liberini, P., Pioro, E.P., Maysinger, D., Ervin, F.R. and Cuello, A.C. (1993) Long-term protective effects of human recombinant nerve growth factor and monosialoganglioside GM1 treatment on primate nucleus basalis cholinergic neurons after neocortical infarction. *Neuroscience*, 53: 625–637.

Maysinger, D., Herrera-Marschitz, M., Goiny, M., Ungerstedt, U. and Cuello, A.C. (1992) Effects of nerve growth factor on cortical and striatal acetylcholine and dopamine release in rats with cortical devascularizing lesions. *Brain Res.*, 577: 300–305.

Mesulam, M.M., Mufson, E.J. and Wainer, B.H. (1986) Three-dimensional representation and cortical projection topography of the nucleus basalis (CH4) in the macque: current demonstration of choline acetyltransferase and retrograde transport with a stabilized tetramethybenzidine method for horse radish peroxidase. *Brain Res.*, 367: 301–308.

Piccardo, P., Maysinger, D. and Cuello, A.C. (1992) Recovery of nucleus basalis cholinergic neurons by grafting NGF secretor fibroblasts. *Neurosci. Rep.*, 3: 353–356.

Pioro, E.P., Maysinger, D., Ervin, F.R., Desypris, G. and Cuello, A.C. (1993) Primate nucleus basalis of Meynert p75^{NGFR}-containing cholinergic neurons are protected from retrograde degeneration by the ganglioside GM$_1$. *Neuroscience*, 53: 49–56.

Ramon y Cajal, S. (1928) *Degeneration and Regeneration of the Nervous System*, translated by Raoul M. May, Oxford University Press, London.

Skup, M., Figueiredo, B.C. and Cuello, A.C. (1994) Intraventricular application of BDNF and NT-3 failed to protect NBM cholinergic neurons. *NeuroReport*, in press.

Sofroniew, M.V., Pearson, R.C., Eckenstein, F., Cuello, A.C. and Powell T.P. (1983) Retrograde changes in cholinergic neurons in the basal forebrain of the rat following cortical damage. *Brain Res.*, 289: 370–374.

Stephens, P.H., Cuello, A.C., Sofroniew, M.V., Pearson, R.C. and Tagari, P. (1985) Effect of unilateral decortication on choline acetyltransferase activity in the nucleus basalis and other areas of the rat brain. *J. Neurochem.*, 45: 1021–1026.

Thoenen, H. (1991) The changing scene in neurotrophic factors. *Trends Neurosci.*, 14: 165–170.

Tuszynski, M.H., Sang, U.H., Amaral, D.G. and Gage, F.H. (1990) Nerve growth factor infusion in the primate brain reduces lesion-induced neural degeneration. *J. Neurosci.*, 10: 3604–3614.

Tuszynski, M.H., Sang, U.H., Yoshida, K. and Gage, F.H. (1991) Recombinant human nerve growth factor infusions prevent cholinergic neuronal degeneration in the adult primate brain. *Ann. Neurol.*, 30 625–636.

Williams, L.R., Rylett, R.J., Ingram, D.K., Joseph, J.A., Moises, H.C., Tang, A.H. and Mervis, R.F. (1993) NGF affects the cholinergic neurochemistry and behavior of aged rats. In: A.C. Cuello (Ed.), *Cholinergic Function and Dysfunction, Progress in Brain Research*, Vol. 98, Elsevier, Amsterdam, pp. 251–256.

F. Bloom (Editor)
Progress in Brain Research, Vol. 100
© 1994 Elsevier Science B.V. All rights reserved

CHAPTER 28

ACTH/MSH-derived peptides and peripheral nerve plasticity: neuropathies, neuroprotection and repair

Willem Hendrik Gispen[1], Joost Verhaagen[1] and Dop Bär[2]

[1]Department of Medical Pharmacology and [2]Department of Neurology, Rudolf Magnus Institute for Neurosciences, Utrecht University, Universiteitsweg 100, 3584 CG Utrecht, The Netherlands

Introduction

The regenerative capacity of the peripheral nervous system is limited. Since mature neurons do not have the ability to divide, the recovery of function depends completely on the potential of injured neurons to repair damaged nerve fibres. Numerous humoral and structural factors of neuronal, glial or target cell origin, most of which are active during development, appear to facilitate nerve repair by governing different stages of the repair process. Moreover, such factors may be of significance under conditions when neuronal function is compromised as a result of metabolic disturbance or neurointoxication. Restoring the balance between regenerative and degenerative forces may aid the neuron to cope with noxious stimuli. In this chapter, we review some of the evidence concerning the putative efficacy of neurotrophic peptides related to ACTH and MSH in animal and human disorders of the peripheral nervous system. As their neurotrophic or protective efficacy is manifest irrespective of the nature of the threatening conditions, eventual application may involve many disorders that have the dysfunction of neurons in common (for more extensive reviews, see Strand et al. (1991) and Bär et al. (1990)).

Mechanical trauma

Various laboratories have shown in animal experiments that treatment with peptides related to ACTH and MSH improves post-lesion repair of the sciatic nerve as illustrated by morphological, neurophysiological and functional evidence. Structure-activity studies pointed to the significance of the amino acid sequence ACTH/MSH-(4–10) (Met-Glu-His-Phe-Arg-Trp-Gly). This sequence lacks the classical corticotrophic activity and thus its neurotrophic property is not due to adrenal steroid release but acts rather by a direct effect on neural tissue. Although steroids are often used in the treatment of central or peripheral nervous system diseases, the rationale behind that treatment refers to their anti inflammatory or immunosuppressive action and seldom to their presumed neurotrophic or protective effect. Peptide dose response curves display an inverted U-shape. Effective routes of administration are subcutaneous injection (repeated), implantation (osmotic micropumps, biodegradable microspheres) or local administration at the site of injury whereas oral or nasal administration so far have been unsuccessful. Treatment must commence shortly following the injury of the nerve and should last at least 8 days in order to initiate an improvement in the recovery process (Bär et al., 1990).

Diabetic neuropathy

Diabetic neuropathy is defined by the American Diabetics Association as a demonstrable disorder, evident either clinically or subclinically, that occurs in the setting of diabetes mellitus in the absence of other possible causes for the peripheral neuropathy. Prevalence of the neuropathy varies between 5 and 80% and increases with both age and duration of diabetes mellitus. There is considerable uncertainty about the pathogenesis of the neural disorder. Roughly three working hypotheses can be distinguished. Firstly, the "metabolic" hypothesis suggests that chronic hyperglycaemia causes activation of the polyol pathway at the cost of myoinositol, resulting in a reduced neural Na^+/K^+ ATP-ase activity and consequently in a reduced nerve conduction velocity. Secondly, high blood glucose levels would lead to glycation of neural proteins and hence disturbing neuronal function. Lastly, chronic hyperglycaemia is known to lead to pathology of the endoneurial vessels resulting in decreased blood flow in the peripheral nerve. The subsequent anoxia is thus taken as the primary cause in nerve degeneration. However, it may well be that a combination of these pathological factors underlies the development of diabetic neuropathy (Dyck et al., 1987).

In two different experimental models of diabetic neuropathy, the efficacy of chronic treatment with the ACTH-(4–9) analog was determined. The first model involved the single administration of the cytostatic drug streptozotocin, which is known to kill the β-cells in the islets of Langerhans and thus to increase blood glucose. No insulin therapy was applied. The second model employed the BB/Wor rat, a strain of rats that genetically develop an autoimmune disease resulting in hyperglycaemia. Insulin therapy is required to maintain the rats that develop this disease. Longitudinal measurement of nerve conduction velocities was used to assess the onset and development of the peripheral neuropathy. In the streptozotocin model subcutaneous treatment with 75 μg/kg ACTH-(4–9) analog every 48 h improved peripheral nerve function both in a preventive and in an interventive protocol (Van der Zee et al., 1989; Bravenboer et al., 1993). Histological examination of sciatic nerves revealed a normal fiber size distribution in peptide-treated diabetic rats. In the BB/Wor rat, peptide treatment of animals with an existing neuropathy resulted in a marked improvement in neuronal function without a major demonstrable effect on histological parameters (Bravenboer et al., 1992b). The peptide treatment did not affect parameters indicative of the diabetic disease as such in any of the experiments. Preliminary studies revealed that peptide treatment may also interfere with the development of autonomic neuropathies as evidenced by improved presynaptic regulation of peripheral blood pressure (Van der Zee et al., 1990). Based on these promising animal data, a first clinical double blind study on the efficacy of chronic treatment with the ACTH-(4–9) analog in diabetic neuropathy was performed involving 62 patients suffering from Type 1 diabetes mellitus randomly divided over a placebo and a peptide treatment group. During the treatment period of 12 months, a number of parameters for peripheral and autonomic neuropathy were assessed. The peptide treatment was effective in lowering the vibration threshold in patients with diabetic neuropathy. There were no differences in any other parameter studied (Bravenboer et al., 1992a). Currently a dose finding study is being performed to optimize the efficacy of peptide treatment in diabetic neuropathy.

Chemotherapy related neuropathies

Peripheral nerve intoxication due to oncolytic treatment is among the most prominent side effects encountered in the treatment of various cancers. Peripheral neurotoxicity as a dose-limiting factor and discontinuation of the oncolytic treatment may profoundly interfere with adequate treatment of the malignancy. Therefore, prevention or diminishing of the neurotoxic side effects is of the utmost significance in the chemotherapy of cancer.

Cisplatin

The cytotoxic drug cisplatin (cis-diamine dichloroplatinum) has shown particular efficacy against bladder, testicular and ovarian cancer. Its neurotoxicity is manifested by a primarily sensory neuropathy leading to diminished proprioception and sensory ataxia. This selective neurotoxicity points to a particular sensitivity of dorsal root ganglia, although the neurotoxic action of cisplatin in these sensory neurons is poorly understood (Hamers et al., 1991a).

In rats, as in humans, repeated injections with cisplatin result in a selective decrease in the sensory nerve conduction velocity of the sciatic nerve. Various studies have demonstrated that co-treatment with the ACTH-(4–9) analog nearly completely counteracted this cisplatin-induced decrease in sensory conduction velocity. The protective effect was evident in both young adult and fullgrown rats and during relatively mild and severe cisplatin treatment regimens (Hamers et al., 1991b, 1993a). Notably, in two different models to evaluate antitumor efficacy of cisplatin, the peptide treatment did not interfere with the oncolytic action of the drug. In view of the close resemblance between cisplatin neurotoxicity in rats and humans, a randomized, double blind, placebo-controlled study was initiated to assess the efficacy of peptide treatment in the prevention of cisplatin neurotoxicity in women suffering from ovarian cancer. Fifty-four women were treated with a cisplatin based therapy and received either placebo, a low (0.25 mg/m^2) or a high (1 mg/m^2) dose of ACTH-(4–9). The principle measure of neurotoxicity was the vibration perception threshold, although a number of neurological signs and symptoms were also recorded. After six cycles of chemotherapy, the perception threshold in cisplatin-placebo treated women showed an increase over 8-fold from the baseline whereas the patients treated with the high dose peptide regimen displayed a non-significant increase of less than 2-fold. Similarly, the peptide-treated group showed significantly less clinical signs and symptoms than the placebo-treated patients (Gerritsen van der Hoop et al., 1990). Although patients from all groups showed a progression of the neuropathy following discontinuation of all treatment, such progression was smaller in patients originally belonging to the high peptide dose regimen group (Hovestadt et al., 1992). These results are a first indication that treatment with a neurotrophic peptide can prevent or diminish cisplatin neuropathy in the clinic.

Vincristine and taxol

Both *Vinca* alkaloids and taxol are known to interact with microtubules. Undoubtedly, the interference with microtubular kinetics is responsible for their oncolytic action and perhaps also for their neurotoxicity as the cytoskeleton is essential for proper neuronal function.

Again, clinical use is threatened by their neurotoxic side effects. Taxol is a novel oncolytic drug with a major indication in cisplatin refractory carcinomas. Recently, it was demonstrated that, in rats, taxol-induced sensory peripheral neuropathy can be counteracted by chronic co-treatment with the ACTH-(4–9) analog (Hamers et al., 1993b) (Fig. 1).

Vinca alkaloids such as vincristine are widely used in the treatment of leukemia and malignant lymphomas. Using neurons of the snail *Lymnea stagnalis* as a model to study neurotoxic effects of cytostatic compounds, it was reported that the ACTH-(4–9) analog greatly diminishes the severity of vincristine neurotoxicity (Müller et al., 1992). In a randomized, double-blind placebo-controlled pilot study, the effect of the peptide was studied on neurotoxicity in 28 patients with lymphoma, who were treated with vincristine and vinblastine. Thirteen patients received the ACTH-(4–9) analog and 15 patients received placebo treatment. The placebo-treated patients had more autonomic complaints, motor deficits and sensory disturbances than the peptide-treated patients. The authors warrant some caution, however, as the average age of the peptide-treated patients was significantly lower than that of the placebo-treated patients (Van Kooten et al., 1992).

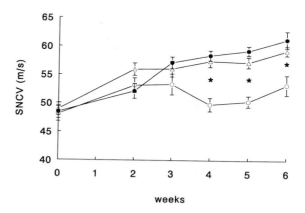

Fig. 1. Effects of taxol treatment on the sensory nerve conduction velocity (SNCV). (Δ) Age controls, (O) taxol/saline, (●) taxol/Org 2766. Values are given as means ± SEM. Taxol was injected weekly i.p. in a dose of 9 mg/kg. Org 2766 was injected s.c. every 48 h in a dose of 75 μg/kg during the whole experimental period. (*p < 0.02; age controls and taxol/Org 2766 versus taxol/saline).

The Guillain-Barré syndrome

Demyelinating diseases form an important group of life-threatening neurological disorders that await effective pharmacotherapy. The underlying mechanism appears to be a cell-mediated immune response directed against myelin components. Current therapeutic strategies are based on the use of anti-inflammatory and immunosuppressive drugs. As under demyelinating conditions neurons are in despair and their function compromised, it was hypothesized that neurotrophic or neuroprotective agents might be of benefit in improving neuronal function in these disorders. An established model of the human demyelinating syndrome of the peripheral nervous system (Guillain-Barré syndrome) is experimental allergic neuritis induced in the Lewis rat by peripheral myelin components. Recently, we were able to demonstrate that chronic treatment of such rats with the ACTH-(4–9) analog markedly suppresses the clinical symptoms (Fig. 2), protects against loss of motor coordination and prevents the degeneration of myelinated axons in the affected peripheral nerve. Subsequently, it was demonstrated that peptide treatment was also effective when the treatment commenced at the first appearance of clinical symptoms indicative of experimental allergic neuritis. These data were taken to illustrate that treatment with a neurotrophic peptide may provide a new approach in the therapy of peripheral demyelinating polyneuropathies (Duckers et al. in Vaudry and Eberle, 1993).

Mechanism of action of melanocortins

The mechanism by which melanocortins exert their beneficial effect is still largely unknown. However, several observations concerning the mode of action of melanocortins have been made.

(1) In vitro experiments show that melanocortins stimulate nerve outgrowth of cultured primary sensory and motoneurons, suggesting that melanocortins exert a direct trophic effect on one or more of the cell types present in these cultures (Van der Neut et al., 1992). Peptide signal transduction involves the activation of adenylate cyclase and c-fos (Hol et al., 1993). Tissue culture experiments also revealed putative binding sites for melanocortins in non-neuronal cells (Dyer et al. in Vaudry and Eberle, 1993) in the nervous system suggesting the significance of neuron–glia interaction in peptide induced nerve repair and protect. The neuroprotective effect of melanocortins in cisplatin neuropathy was confirmed in cultured dorsal root ganglia (Bär et al. in Vaudry and Eberle, 1993; Hol et al., 1994).

(2) Treatment schedules have demonstrated that melanocortins stimulate peripheral nerve regeneration only during a restricted period early following the lesion.

(3) Experiments in which different routes of melanocortin administration were tested demonstrated that local application at the site of injury is effective in facilitating nerve regeneration, implying that melanocortins act at the damaged nerve site (Bär et al., 1990).

Studies demonstrating an increase in POMC-derived peptides at the damaged nerve site following nerve injury are in line with the idea of a physiological role of endogenous ACTH/MSH-like peptides in the process of nerve regeneration (Bär et al., 1990). Firstly, it has been demonstrated with an in vitro bioassay for α-MSH that degenerating nerve portions contain agents with MSH-like activity, whereas intact nerves do not (Edwards and Gispen, 1985). Secondly, following nerve transection, increased α-MSH and β-endorphin immunoreactivity has been detected in the damaged nerve (Hughes and Smith, 1988). Increased immunoreactivity for ACTH/MSH-like peptides has also been demonstrated in rodents with neuromuscular disorders, such as inherited motoneuron disease in the wobbler mouse and inherited muscular dystrophy in C57BL/6J or REF/129 mice (Haynes and Smith, 1985). Rats treated with $\beta\beta'$-iminodiproprionitrile (IDPN), a neurotoxin that affects motoneurons, and mice with streptozotocin-induced diabetes have been shown to express increased levels of POMC-derived peptides in motoneurons (Hughes et al., 1992). These results collectively suggest that increased immunoreactivity for ACTH/MSH-like peptides is present whenever neuropathic changes occur in motor nerves, whether this is due to a neurological disorder, to neurotoxicity or to mechanical damage. We have sug-

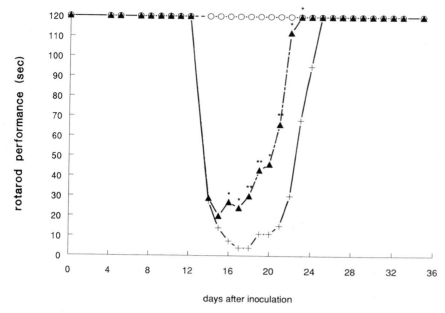

Fig. 2. Rotarod performance test. Rotarod performance scores are presented as medians. Solid line ($n = 10$) represents Lewis rats with EAN treated with 0.5 ml saline; dashed line (closed triangle, $n = 10$) represents Lewis rats with EAN treated with 75 μg Org 2766/kg body wt. in 0.5 ml saline; dashed line with open circles represents age-matched, control rats treated with 0.5 ml saline ($n = 10$). Saline and the peptide were administered by subcutaneous injections in the neck every 48 h. Statistics: Kruskal–Wallis test followed by Mann–Whitney U-tests (EAN-saline group versus EAN-Org 2766 group): *$p < 0.05$, **$p < 0.01$.

gested that exogenous melanocortins mimic or amplify a naturally occurring ACTH/MSH-like peptide signal early in the repair process that is part of the regenerative repertoire.

Two different working hypotheses have been put forward to explain the source and the nature of the naturally occurring endogenous melanocortins after nerve damage (Edwards and Gispen, 1985). Firstly, mature neurons might re-express proopiomelanocortin (POMC), the large precursor peptide from which ACTH and α-MSH derive, in their cell bodies after peripheral nerve damage. POMC mRNA is expressed in the developing spinal cord of rat embryos and is subsequently downregulated, although immunoreactivity for the POMC-derived peptides β-endorphin, α-MSH and ACTH has been demonstrated in a small portion of the motor nerves of the normal adult mouse and rat (Hughes and Smith, 1988). However, no increase in the expression of POMC mRNA has been detected in dorsal root ganglia, spinal cord or in the damaged nerve after sciatic nerve crush (Plantinga et

al., 1992). Therefore, at this point it is not clear whether POMC mRNA expression in the nerve cell bodies and in the nerve contribute to the physiological stimulus leading to regeneration following nerve injury.

The second hypothesis on the nature and source of endogenous melanocortin production following nerve injury suggests that ACTH/MSH-like peptides are derived from the degenerating distal nerve stump (Edwards and Gispen, 1985). Immunoblotting and immunohistochemistry have demonstrated epitopes shared by α-MSH and the 150 kDa neurofilament protein (NF150). Since NF150 in the distal nerve stump is rapidly degraded after injury, we suggested that breakdown of NF150 results in the formation of an α-MSH-like peptide substance. Current research is aimed at further characterizing that peptide.

The work on the mechanism of action of melanocortins has been hampered by the fact that no receptor for Org 2766 has been identified. Putative binding sites of [³H]Org 2766 have been demonstrated in spinal cord sections, but the binding of radiolabeled peptide was poorly displaceable by unlabeled Org 2766 (Dekker and Tonnaer, 1989). Recently, three different members of the ACTH/MSH receptor family have been cloned (Mountjoy et al., 1992; Gantz et al., 1993a,b). The human melanocortin-1 receptor has been identified as an α-MSH receptor and is expressed in melanoma cells, whereas the melanocortin-2 receptor comprises an ACTH receptor and is localized in the adrenal tissue. The third member of this group, the melanocortin-3 receptor, appears to be an MSH receptor that also recognizes the ACTH-(4-10) heptapeptide core common to ACTH, α-, β- and γ-MSH. It is expressed in brain, placenta, and gut but not in melanocytes or in the adrenal gland. Low stringency hybridization of human genomic DNA has indicated the existence of additional melanocortin receptors. Identification of the receptor for melanocortins involved in the neurotrophic action of these peptides will have a significant impact on advances in understanding the molecular mechanisms underlying the stimulatory effect of ACTH/MSH-like peptides on nerve regeneration.

References

Bär, P.R.D., Schrama, L.H. and Gispen, W.H. (1990) Neurotrophic effects of the ACTH/MSH-like peptides in the peripheral nervous system. In: D. de Wied (Ed.), *Neuropeptide Concept*, Elsevier, Amsterdam, pp. 175–211.

Bravenboer, B., Hendriksen, P.H., Oey, P.L., Van Huffelen, A.C., Gispen, W.H. and Erkelens, D.W. (1992a) ACTH$_{4-9}$ analogue in a randomized, double-blind, placebo-controlled trial in diabetic patients with neuropathy. *Diabetologia*, 35 (suppl. 1): 50.

Bravenboer, B., Kappelle, A.C., Van Buren, T., Erkelens, D.W. and Gispen, W.H. (1992b) ACTH4–9-analogue ORG 2766 improves existing diabetic neuropathy in the BB/Wor model. *Diabetes*, 41 (suppl 1): 491.

Bravenboer, B., Kappelle, A.C., Buren van, T., Erkelens, D.W. and Gispen, W.H. (1993) ACTH$_{4-9}$ analogue ORG 2766 can improve existing neuropathy in streptozocin-induced diabetic rats. *Acta Diabetol.*, 30: 21–24.

Dekker, A.J.A.M. and Tonnaer, J.A.D.M. (1989) Binding of the neurotrophic peptide Org 2766 to rat spinal cord sections is affected by a sciatic nerve crush. *Brain Res.*, 477: 327–331.

Dyck, P.J., Thomas, P.K., Asbury, A.K., Winegrad, A.I. and Porte, D. (1987) *Diabetic Neuropathy*, W.B. Saunders, Philadelphia.

Edwards, P.M. and Gispen, W.H. (1985) Melanocortin peptides and neural plasticity. In: J. Traber and W.H. Gispen (Eds.), *Senile Dementia of the Alzheimer's Type: Early Diagnosis, Neuro-*

pathology and Animal Models, Springer-Verlag, Heidelberg, pp. 231–240.

Gantz, I., Konda, Y., Tashiro, T., Shimoto, H., Miwa, H., Munzert, G., Watson, S.J., DelValle, J. and Yamada, T. (1993a) Molecular cloning of a novel melanocortin receptor. *J. Biol. Chem.*, 268: 8246–8250.

Gantz, I., Miwa, H., Konda, Y., Shimoto, Y., Tashiro, T., Watson, S.J., DelValle, J. and Yamada, T. (1993b) Molecular cloning, expression, and gene localization of a fourth melanocortin receptor. *J. Biol. Chem.*, 268: 15174–15179.

Gerritsen van der Hoop, R., Vecht, C.J., Van der Burg, M.E.L., Elderson, A., Boogerd, W., Heimans, J.J., Els, D., Vries, P., Van Houwelingen, J.C., Jennekens, F.G.I., Gispen, W.H. and Neijt, J.P. (1990) Prevention of cisplatin neurotoxicity with an ACTH(4-9) analogue in patients with ovarian cancer. *N. Engl. J. Med.*, 322: 89–94.

Hamers, F.P.T., Gispen, W.H. and Neijt, J.P. (1991a) Neurotoxic side-effects of cisplatin. *Eur. J. Cancer*, 27: 372–376.

Hamers, F.P.T., Gerritsen van der Hoop, R., Steerenburg, P.A., Neijt, J.P. and Gispen, W.H. (1991b) Putative neurotrophic factors in the protection of cisplatin-induced peripheral neuropathy in rats. *Toxicol. Appl. Pharmacol.*, 111: 514–522.

Hamers, F.P.T., Pette, C., Bravenboer, B., Vecht, C.J., Neijt, J.P. and Gispen, W.H. (1993a) Cisplatin-induced neuropathy in mature rats. Effects of the melanocortin-like peptide ORG 2766. *Cancer Chemother. Pharmacol.*, 32: 162–166.

Hamers, F.P.T., Pette, C., Neijt, J.P. and Gispen, W.H. (1993b) The ACTH(4-9) analog ORG 2766, prevents taxol-induced neuropathy in rats. *Eur. J. Pharmacol.*, 233: 177–178.

Haynes, L.W. and Smith, M.E. (1985) Presence of immunoreactive α-melanotropin and β-endorphin in spinal motor neurons of the dystrophic mouse. *Neurosci. Lett.*, 53: 13–18.

Hol, E.M., Hermens, W.T.J.M.C., Verhaagen, J., Gispen, W.H. and Bär, P.R. (1993) α-MSH but not ORG 2766 induces expression of c-fos in cultured rat spinal cord cells. *NeuroRep.*, 4: 651–654.

Hol, E.M., Mandys, V., Sodaar, P., Gispen, W.H. and Bär, P.K. (1994) Protection by an ACTH$_{4-9}$ analogue against the toxic effects of cisplatin and taxol on sensory neurons and glial cells in vitro. *J. Neurosci. Res.*, in press.

Hovestadt, A., Van der Burg, M.E.L., Verbiest, H.B.C., Van Putten, W.L.J. and Vecht, Ch.J. (1992) The course of neuropathy after cessation of cisplatin treatment, combined with Org 2766 or placebo. *J. Neurol.*, 239: 143–146.

Hughes, S. and Smith, M.E. (1988) Effect of nerve transection on β-endorphin and α-melanotropin immunoreactivity in motor nerves of normal and dystrophic mice. *Neurosci. Lett.*, 92: 1–7.

Hughes, S., Smith, M.E., Simpson, M.G. and Allen, S.L. (1992) Effect of EDPN on the expression of POMC-derived peptides in rat motoneurons. *Peptides*, 13: 1021–1023.

Mountjoy, K.G., Robbins, L.S., Mortrud, M.T. and Cone, R.D. (1992) The cloning of a family of genes that encode the melanocortin receptors. *Science*, 257: 1248–1251.

Müller, L.J., Moorer-van Delft, C.M. and Boer, H.H. (1992) The ACTH(4-9) analog ORG 2766 stimulates microtubule formation in axons of the central nervous system of the snail *Lymnea stagnalis*. *Peptides*, 13: 769–774.

Plantinga, L.C., Verhaagen, J., Edwards, P.M., Schrama L.H., Burbach, J.P.H. and Gispen, W.H. (1992) Expression of the pro-opiomelanocortin gene in dorsal root ganglia, spinal cord and sciatic nerve after sciatic nerve crush in the rat. *Mol. Brain Res.*, 16: 135–142.

Strand, F.L., Rose, K.J., Zuccarelli, L.A., Kume, J., Alves, S.E., Antonawich, F.J. and Garrett, L.Y. (1991) Neuropeptide hormones as neurotrophic factors. *Physiol. Rev.*, 71: 1017–1046.

Van der Neut, R., Hol, E.M., Gispen, W.H. and Bär, P.R. (1992) Stimulation by melanocortins of neurite outgrowth from spinal and sensory neurons in vitro. *Peptides*, 13: 1109–1115.

Van der Zee, C.E.E.M., Gerritsen van der Hoop, R. and Gispen, W.H. (1989) Beneficial effect of Org 277 in the treatment of peripheral neuropathy in streptozocin-induced diabetic rats. *Diabetes,* 38: 225–230.

Van der Zee, C.E.E.M., Van den Buuse, M. and Gispen, W.H. (1990) Beneficial effect of an ACTH-(4–9) analog on peripheral neuropathy and blood pressure response to tyramine in streptozocin diabetic rats. *Eur. J. Pharmacol.,* 117: 211–213.

Van Kooten, B., Van Diemen, H.A.M., Groenhout, K.M., Huijgens, P.C., Ossenkoppele, G.I., Nauta, J.J.P. and Heimans, J.J. (1992) A pilot study on the influence of a corticotropin (4–9) analogue on *Vinca* alkaloid-induced neuropathy. *Arch. Neurol.,* 49: 1027–1031.

Vaudry, H. and Eberle, A.N. (1993) *The Melanotropic Peptides*, The New York Academy of Sciences, New York.

SECTION V

Neuro-Psychiatric Conditions

F. Bloom (Editor)
Progress in Brain Research, Vol. 100
© 1994 Elsevier Science B.V. All rights reserved

CHAPTER 29

Enhancement of action potential conduction following demyelination: experimental approaches to restoration of function in multiple sclerosis and spinal cord injury

S.G. Waxman, D.A. Utzschneider and J.D. Kocsis

Department of Neurology, Yale University School of Medicine, New Haven, CT 06510; and PVA/EPVA Neuroscience Research Center, VA Hospital, West Haven, CT 06516, USA

Introduction

Restoration of function is a major goal of current research on demyelinating diseases. Multiple sclerosis (MS) represents a prototype demyelinating disorder of the CNS, in which axons usually maintain continuity through the lesions, but myelin is damaged. Researchers have been especially interested in restoration of function in MS since its course can include partial or complete remissions characterized by clinical recovery; moreover, subclinical demyelinated plaques (i.e. demyelinated lesions that are not accompanied by an appropriate clinical deficit) are well documented in MS, and may account for more than 50% of the lesions in many patients with this disorder (for review, see Waxman, 1988).

Non-penetrating spinal cord injury and spinal cord compression provide other examples of disorders in which there can be significant demyelination. Histological and electron microscopic studies have demonstrated demyelination in spinal cord white matter in experimental compressive and contusive spinal cord injury (Gledhill et al., 1973; Harrison and McDonald, 1977; Griffiths and McCulloch, 1983). Moreover, electron microscopic studies have provided evidence suggesting that myelin may be stripped from spinal cord axons following contusive injury, as a result of delayed invasion by inflammatory cells (Blight, 1985). There is also evidence for demyelination in spinal cord white matter following spinal cord injury and spinal cord compression in man (Byrne and Waxman, 1990; Bunge et al., 1993). These observations provide a pathological correlate for the presence, in some patients in whom spinal cord injury has been judged to be clinically complete, of residual descending influences on spinal reflex activity, a situation that has led to the concept of "dyscomplete" injury (Sherwood et al., 1992). Although a relapsing-remitting course is not usually observed after spinal cord injury, in some patients who were initially judged to have "complete" spinal cord injury, careful serial examinations have demonstrated improvements in neurological status that can occur over time periods extending at least as long as 1 year (Young, 1989). This delayed clinical improvement, together with the evidence for demyelination cited above, suggests the possibility that restoration of conduction in previously demyelinated axons may provide a basis for functional recovery following spinal cord injury.

This chapter briefly reviews recent studies which have explored two approaches aimed at restoration of function following demyelination of central axons.

Pharmacologic manipulation of ionic conductances in demyelinated axons

The distribution of voltage-sensitive ion channels within the axon membrane of myelinated axons is dis-

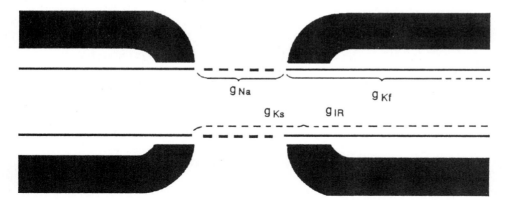

Fig. 1. Model showing putative localization of voltage-sensitive ion channels in the mammalian myelinated fiber. Abbreviations: g_{Na}, Na^+ channels; g_{Kf}, fast K^+ channels; g_{Ks}, slow K^+ channels; g_{IR}, inward rectifier. Sodium channels are clustered in high density in the axon membrane at the node of Ranvier and are present in much lower densities in the internode. Fast K^+ channels, present in the axon membrane under the myelin, are normally masked by myelin but are unmasked by demyelination. Slow Na^+ channels may be co-localized with rapidly-inactivating Na^+ channels, although a differential distribution has not been excluded.

tinctly heterogeneous, and includes a non-uniform distribution of Na^+ and K^+ channels. Figure 1 shows the current model of ion channel organization of the mammalian myelinated fiber. Na^+ channels are clustered in high density ($\sim 1000/\mu m^2$) in the axon membrane at the node of Ranvier, which is the site of action potential generation in normal myelinated axons (Ritchie and Rogart, 1977; Waxman, 1977). Within the internodal axon membrane (i.e. the axon membrane under the myelin sheath), the Na^+ channel density is much lower ($<25/\mu m^2$). At least three types of K^+ channels are present in the axon membrane in mammalian myelinated fibers: a "fast" K^+ channel, a "slow" K^+ channel, and an inward rectifier (for reviews, see Kocsis et al., 1993; Waxman and Ritchie, 1993). Fast K^+ channels display a distribution that is complementary to that of the Na^+ channels that are clustered in the nodal axon membrane and are expressed in highest density in the axon membrane under the myelin, but only in low densities in the axon membrane at the node (Chiu and Ritchie, 1981; Foster et al., 1982; Kocsis et al., 1982; Ritchie, 1982). Voltage-clamp studies indicate that the density of fast K^+ channels is maximal in the paranodal axon membrane, decreasing to 1/6 of the paranodal value in the node and internode (Röper and Schwarz, 1989).

Fast K^+ channels can be blocked by 4-amino-pyridine (4-AP) when it is applied externally if it is given access to these channels (Kocsis et al., 1986; Baker et al., 1987). In normal non-myelinated fibers, application of 4-AP leads to delayed repolarization and prolongation of the action potential in both the PNS (Sherratt et al., 1980; Bostock et al., 1981) and CNS (Malenka et al., 1981; Preston et al., 1983); these results indicate that fast K^+ channels contribute to action potential repolarization in these fibers.

In contrast, in myelinated axons within the adult mammalian PNS and CNS, fast K^+ channels do not appear to play a significant role in action potential repolarization, and as shown in Fig. 2B (Kocsis et al., 1982), the action potential is not prolonged by exposure to 4-AP (Bostock et al., 1981; Kocsis and Waxman, 1980). This does not imply, however, that fast K^+ channels are not present in mature myelinated fibers. These channels are expressed in the internodal axon membrane, and are masked by the overlying myelin. This can be seen in developmental studies, which show a significantly larger effect of 4-AP on action potential duration in premyelinated axons, compared to mature myelinated fibers after the maturation of myelin (Fig. 2A) (Eng et al., 1988; Foster et al., 1982; Kocsis et al., 1982; Ritchie, 1982). The fast K^+ chan-

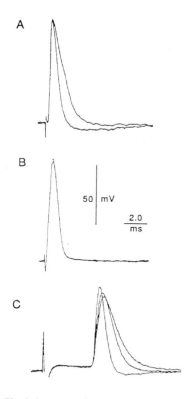

Fig. 2. Intra-axonal recordings showing the effect of 4-aminoyridine (0.5 mM) on action potential configuration in (A) preyelinated axon in regenerating sciatic nerve after nerve crush, (B) myelinated axon in adult rat sciatic nerve, and (C) demyelinated (lysophosphatidyl-choline) ventral root axon. Note the conduction slowing after demyelination as evidenced by the long spike onset latency of the demyelinated ventral root axon. Extracellular application of 4-AP results in substantial prolongation of the action potential in pre-myelinated and demyelinated axons but not in mature myelinated axons where fast K$^+$ channels are masked. (A, B reproduced with permission from Kocsis et al. (1982); C reproduced with permission from Bowe et al. (1987)).

nels can also be seen following acute demyelination (Targ and Kocsis, 1986); when 4-AP is applied to de-myelinated fibers where it has access to the exposed (formerly internodal) axon membrane, it produces a significant delay in repolarization of the action potential (Fig. 2C).

Since safety factor is decreased in demyelinated axons, it might be expected that maneuvers that prolong the action potential, thereby increasing the time integral of inward current, might improve conduction (Schauf and Davis, 1974). Bostock and co-workers

(Sherratt et al., 1980; Bostock et al., 1981) demonstrated that 4-AP increases the temperature at which conduction failure occurs in demyelinated ventral root axons, in some cases reversing conduction block at physiologic temperatures. Experiments at the single fiber level have also demonstrated reversal of conduction block, with restoration of secure impulse conduction, following treatment of experimentally demyelinated sciatic nerve axons with 4-AP (Targ and Kocsis, 1985).

Figure 3 shows an example of reversal of conduction block in an experimentally demyelinated (lyso-phosphatidyl choline-treated) axon following application of 4-AP (Targ and Kocsis, 1985). Stimulating electrodes were positioned on both ends of the nerve, and recordings from single axons were obtained with

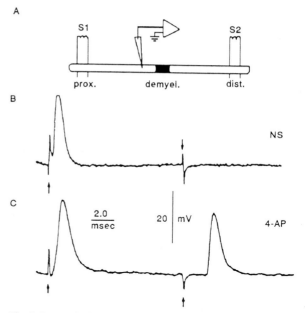

Fig. 3. Reversal of conduction block in demyelinated sciated nerve fiber with 4-AP (1.0 mM). The fiber was focally demyelinated by injection of lysophosphatidyl choline. (A) Experimental design permits examination of conduction through normal (stimulation at S_1) or demyelinated (stimulation at S_2) regions. (B) Stimulation at S_1 leads to an action potential, but conduction block occurs following S_2 stimulation, when the demyelinated zone is interposed between stimulation and recording site. (C) Following application of 4-AP, conduction block is overcome and the action potential propagates, with increased latency, through the demyelinated zone. Note the increased action potential duration, due to blockade of fast K$^+$ channels which tend to repolarize the fiber in demyelinated regions. NS = normal solution (modified from Targ and Kocsis, 1985).

microelectrodes positioned intra-axonally on one side of the lesion (Fig. 3A). Following stimulation proximal to the lesion (so that the conduction block did not include the demyelinated region), a propagated action potential could be recorded in normal Ringer solution. In contrast, following stimulation on the contralateral side of the lesion (so that conduction had to cross the zone of demyelination), an action potential could not be recorded since conduction block had occurred (Fig. 3B). The nerve was then exposed to 4-AP and, as shown in Fig. 3C, action potential duration was increased and conduction through the lesion was restored.

These observations have now been extended to the clinical arena. A number of clinical studies have been carried out with 4-AP, and with the related drug 3,4-diaminopyridine (3,4-DAP), to examine the effects of these agents on neurological status in patients with MS (see e.g. Jones et al., 1983; Stefoski et al., 1987; Davis et al., 1990). These studies have demonstrated improvements in motor function, improved brainstem function (e.g. improvement in extraocular movements), reduction in the size of scotomata, and improved critical flicker fusion in patients with MS. Similar studies have been carried out in the Lambert-Eaton myasthenic syndrome (on the basis of the rationale that prolongation of the action potential by blockade of fast K^+ channels in the preterminal axon will lead to an increase in acetylcholine release) and have shown improved motor function (Lundh et al., 1984; Murray and Newsom-Davis 1981).

Recently, Hansebout et al. (1993) reported a preliminary clinical study, in which 4-AP was administered to eight patients with chronic spinal cord injury. Beneficial effects were not detected in the two patients with complete paraplegia who were studied. However, in five of the six patients with incomplete spinal cord injury, there appeared to be significant transient neurologic improvement. This included improvement in sensory scores, as well as reduction in spasticity and in chronic pain and dysesthesias in the lower extremities. There was a tendency towards improvement in motor scores, although this did not reach a statistically significant level in this initial study of a small number of cases.

Further, systematic studies on larger numbers of patients with spinal cord injury are clearly needed. Hansebout et al. (1993) noted a decrease in vibratory sensation in some spinal cord injured patients following treatment with 4-AP, and this may provide some clues about the mechanism of this drug's action in spinal cord injury; in this regard, it is now well-established that there are differences in ion channel organization of mammalian sensory versus motor axons (Bowe et al., 1985) and between different types of sensory fibers (Honmou et al., 1994). Recent studies suggest that the repertoire of ion channels expressed by mammalian axons may be more complex than previously suspected (Kampe et al., 1992; Scholz et al., 1992; Kocsis et al., 1993; Stys et al., 1993). If axons in different CNS tracts display differences in ion channel expression, it may be possible to develop targeted pharmacologic interventions that will specifically alter conduction in a given pathway; this strategy would allow selective treatment of symptoms such as pain, spasticity and sensory loss.

Transplantation of myelin-forming cells

Theoretical studies demonstrate that remyelination with even thin, or short, myelin segments can support the conduction of action potentials through previously demyelinated fibers, if the remyelinated nodes of Ranvier develop membrane properties similar to those in normal fibers (Koles and Rasminsky, 1972; Waxman and Brill, 1978). The development of relatively normal Na^+ channel densities at remyelinated nodes of Ranvier is, in fact, suggested by cytochemical studies in the spinal cord, which show that newly formed nodes along remyelinated axons develop normal properties (Weiner et al., 1980), and by saxitoxin-binding experiments in sciatic nerve, which show an increase in the number of Na channels that is proportional to the increase in nodal membrane area imposed by the shorter spacing between remyelinated nodes (Ritchie, 1982).

In peripheral nerves demyelinated with lysophosphatidyl choline, increased conduction velocity and restoration of the ability to conduct high-frequency impulse trains are observed in association with remye-

plant region (Fig. 5C,D), and fibers within the transplant region could follow tetanic stimuli at frequencies up to 100 Hz, similar to fibers outside the transplant zone.

To further assess the physiological consequences of cell transplantation, intracellular recordings were obtained from single dorsal root ganglion (DRG) neurons, following antidromic stimulation of dorsal columns. These experiments demonstrated a significant increase (~3-fold faster) in conduction velocity within the transplant region. Conduction of the action potential from the transplant region, into non-transplanted areas, indicated that action potentials were securely conducted through the zone of potential impedance mismatch from the myelinated to non-myelinated parts of the host nervous system (Fig. 5A).

These results demonstrate that myelination of CNS axons, by exogenous CNS glial cells, is associated with significantly increased conduction velocities. Axons myelinated by the transplanted cells have refractory periods and frequency-following characteristics similar to those of axons in non-transplanted regions. Moreover, action potentials can be initiated outside the transplant region, propagate into the transplant area, and continue beyond the transplanted zone. Transplantation of exogenous glial cells into the amyelinated spinal cord thus can result in myelination that is associated with an enhancement of conduction properties.

While detailed biophysical data are not yet available, it is likely that the increased conduction velocity is due to myelination by the transplanted cells. The conduction velocity of axons in the transplanted zone increased approximately threefold relative to the non-transplant region, and is significantly greater than the conduction velocity of normal CNS non-myelinated axons (Waxman and Bennett, 1972). A very large increase (~9-fold) in axon diameter would be required to account for this increased conduction velocity in the absence of myelination. Saltatory conduction in normal myelinated axons requires a nodal Na^+ channel density (~$1000/\mu m^2$) that is much higher than in normal non-myelinated axons (Ritchie and Rogart, 1977). While Na^+ channel densities at the newly formed nodes along transplanted axons have not yet been measured, increased Na^+ channel densities have been demonstrated in chronically demyelinated spinal cord axons following the injection of ethidium bromide and X-irradiation (Black et al., 1991), and at the newly formed nodes along remyelinated axons following viral-induced demyelination in the mouse spinal cord (Weiner et al., 1980). The increased conduction velocity and normal frequency-following properties of axons in the transplanted zone suggest that relatively normal nodes of Ranvier are formed in association with myelination by exogenous glial cells following transplantation.

Since there is a fourfold reduction in conduction velocity in md spinal cord axons (Utzschneider et al., 1992), the threefold increase in conduction velocity demonstrates a significant return toward normal function following transplantation of myelin-forming glial cells in the amyelinated spinal cord. This provides a demonstration that functional properties, as well as morphological characteristics, of pathological white matter tracts can be favorably altered by transplantation of glial cells.

In these initial studies, the electrophysiological

Fig. 4. Increased conduction velocity in dorsal column axons of myelin-deficient (md) rat 16 days following transplantation of myelin-forming cells. Field potentials from transplant and non-transplant regions of the dorsal columns are shown. (A) A schematic showing the longitudinal extent of the transplant region (~3 mm). Two stimulation sites (S_1 and S_2) provide recording tracks within the transplant region and more rostrally outside the transplant region. The recording interval is 0.5 mm for both tracks. (B) Field potentials outside the transplant region usually show a single main negativity with occasional early or late components (fifth trace from top). (C) Field potentials from transplant region of the same animal show two separate negativities (N_1 and N_2) with increasingly distinct latencies as the recording electrode is moved further away from the stimulus site. Conduction velocity for the N_1 component is increased. The stimulus site is outside the transplant region, indicating propagation of the impulse across the amyelinated-myelinated junction. (D) Aggregate conduction latencies in non-transplant (upper graph) and transplant regions (lower graph) in the md dorsal columns. The upper graph shows the latency of the main N negativity (from 100 recording sites from 17 recording tracks) outside the transplant region. The slope of the linear regression indicates an average conduction velocity of 0.9 ± 0.03 m/s. The lower graph shows a significantly smaller increase in latency with increasing conduction distance in the transplant region, with an average conduction velocity of 3.2 ± 0.23 m/s (modified from Utzschneider et al., 1993).

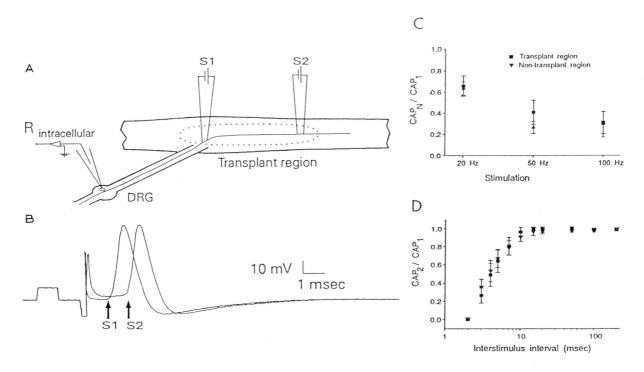

Fig. 5. (*A*) Single-cell recording of action potential conduction through the transplant region. The schematic shows the placement of two stimulating electrodes in the transplant zone and an intracellular recording electrode in a dorsal root ganglion cell. (*B*) Action potentials recorded from dorsal root ganglion cell following stimulation at two sites (S_1, S_2) in the transplant region. Propagation of the action potential from stimulating electrode S_2 to the dorsal root ganglion cell demonstrates that conduction occurred through the zone of potential impedance mismatch, from the transplant zone to non-transplanted parts of the host nervous system. From the latency shift and interstimulus distance, a conduction velocity of 2.6 m/s within the transplant zone can be calculated. (*C*) The ability of axons to follow tetanic stimuli is similar inside and outside the transplant region. The graph shows the ratio of the amplitudes of the first and last compound action potentials (CAPs) for repetitive stimuli of 20 Hz (10 s), 50 Hz (10 s), and 100 Hz (2 s). (*D*) Double-shock experiments showing the ratio of test CAP to control CAP for interstimulus intervals of 2–200 ms. The time-course of recovery for impulse conduction is similar inside and outside the transplant region.

consequences of transplantation of myelin-forming glial cells into immature (5-day-old) rats was studied within 3 weeks of transplantation; this strategy focused on examining the effects of glial cell transplantation during the normal period of myelination. Future studies will examine the long-term effects of glial cell transplantation and the effects of transplantation into adult recipients.

It is also possible that the transplantation strategy may be applicable to the development of new immunotherapies for inflammatory demyelinating diseases such as MS. A relatively new approach to controlling the immune response in MS involves attempts to downregulate T-cell-mediated activity directed against myelin antigens by using protein and peptide-based immunotherapy. Antigen-specific tolerization could result from a downregulation of self-reactive T-cells or a vaccination-like approach that would upregulate the capacity of regulatory T-cells to control self-reactive T-cells (Adorini, 1993; Hafler et al., 1993). Weiner et al. (1993) recently suggested, from an initial study in MS patients, that oral tolerization with bovine myelin may result in a significant reduction in myelin-basic-protein (MBP)-reactive T-cells associated with clinical improvement; the tolerization regimen with the bovine myelin did not result in apparent toxicity or side-effects. On the basis of our observations of appropriate function by transplanted glial cells, we are led to speculate that glial cell transplantation may provide an effective means of providing antigen-specific immunotherapy. The ability to genetically modify the MBP and proteolipid protein (PLP) epitopes expressed by the transplanted myelin-forming glial cells and to specify the localization of the newly expressed myelin may represent a uniquely effective method for presenting antigen to self-reactive T-cells and inducing tolerance. Thus, myelin-forming transplants may have a role in antigen-specific, peptide-based *immunotherapy* as well as in the *physiological restoration* of conduction.

Concluding remarks

As described above, several experimental strategies have demonstrated, in experimental models, that it is possible to improve conduction of action potentials along previously demyelinated axons. In the case of K^+ channel blockade with 4-AP and 3,4-DAP, transient beneficial effects have been well documented in some patients with MS. Initial studies in a small number of patients with spinal cord injury have provided provocative results, and further studies are underway. The observation of relatively long-lasting (48 h or more) changes in sensory symptoms in spinal cord injury patients following treatment with 4-AP (Hansebout et al., 1993) raises important questions about the mechanism of action of this drug. The multiplicity of K^+ channel subtypes that are expressed in different types of axons (Honmou et al., 1994; Vogel and Schwarz, 1994) suggests that it may be possible to develop ion channel blocking agents that selectively alter the conduction properties of demyelinated axons in specific pathways or tracts.

Much work remains to be done on transplantation of myelin-forming cells. Recently, it has been demonstrated that transplanted O2-A glial progenitor cells can differentiate and form myelin around myelin-deprived axons in the CNS (Groves et al., 1993), and it is possible that engineered cells may also be developed, as a source for transplantation. The presently available data are promising in that they indicate, in genetically amyelinated axons, that myelination by exogenous glial cells after transplantation can enhance axonal conduction. Nevertheless, considerable work will be needed before transplantation can be considered in the clinical domain, particularly for disorders such as MS, where demyelination is multi-focal and progressive. The occurrence of demyelination in spinal cord injury (where the pathology is presumably static rather than progressive) may present a situation that is especially appropriate for further study, in terms of restoration of action potential conduction via repair of demyelinated axons by transplantation.

Acknowledgments

Work in the authors' laboratories has been supported in part by grants from the National Multiple Sclerosis Society and the NINCDS, and by the Medical Research Service, US Department of Veterans Affairs. DAU was supported in part by the Medical Scientist Training Program, and by an EPVA Multiple Sclerosis Fellowship.

References

Adorini, L. (1993) Selective inhibition of T cell responses by protein and peptide-based immunotherapy. *Clin. Exp. Rheumatol.*, 11(Suppl. 8): S41–S44.

Baker, M., Bostock, H., Grafe, P. and Martins, P. (1987) Function and distribution of three types of rectifying channel in rat spinal root myelinated axons. *J. Physiol. (London)*, 383: 45–67.

Black, J.A., Felts, P., Smith, K.J., Kocsis, J.D. and Waxman, S.G. (1991) Distribution of sodium channels in chronically demyelinated spinal cord axons: immuno-ultrastructural localization and electrophysiological observations. *Brain Res.*, 544: 59–70.

Blight, A.R. (1985) Delayed demyelination and macrophage invasion: a candidate for secondary cell damage in spinal cord injury. *CNS Trauma*, 2: 299–314.

Blight, A.R. and Young, W. (1989) Central axons in injured cat spinal cord recover electrophysiological function following remyelination by Schwann cells. *J. Neurol. Sci.*, 91: 15–34.

Bostock, H., Sears, T.A. and Sherratt, R.M. (1981) The effects of 4-aminopyridine and tetraethylammonium ions on normal and demyelinated mammalian nerve fibers. *J. Physiol. (London)*, 313: 301–315.

Bowe, C.M., Kocsis, J.D. and Waxman, S.G. (1985) Differences between mammalian ventral and dorsal spinal roots in response to blockade of potassium channels during maturation. *Proc. R. Soc. London, Ser. B*, 224: 355–366.

Bowe, C.M., Kocsis, J.D., Targ, E.F. and Waxman, S.G. (1987) Physiological effects of 4-aminopyridine on demyelinated mammalian motor and sensory fibers. *Ann. Neurol.*, 22: 264–268.

Bunge, R.P., Puckett, W.R., Becerra, J.L., Marcillo, A. and

Quencer, R.M. (1993) Observations on the pathology of human spinal cord injury. A review and classification of 22 new cases with details from a case of chronic cord compression with extensive focal demyelination. In: F.J. Seil (Ed.), *Advances in Neurology*, Vol. 59. *Neural Injury and Regeneration*, Raven Press, New York, pp. 75–89.

Byrne, T.N. and Waxman, S.G. (1990) *Spinal Cord Compression*, F.A. Davis, Philadelphia.

Chiu, S.Y. and Ritchie, J.M. (1981) Evidence for the presence of potassium channels in the paranodal region of acutely demyelinated mammalian nerve fibres. *J. Physiol. (London)*, 313: 415–437.

Davis, F.A., Stefoski, D. and Rush, J. (1990) Orally administered 4-aminopyridine improves clinical signs in multiple sclerosis. *Ann. Neurol.*, 27: 186–192.

Duncan, I.D., Hammang, J.P., Jackson, K.F., Wood, P.M., Bunge, R.P. and Langford, L. (1988) Transplantation of oligodendrocytes and Schwann cells into the spinal cord of the myelin-deficient rat. *J. Neurocytol.*, 17: 351–360.

Duncan, I.D., Archer, D.R. and Wood, P.M. (1992) Functional capacities of transplanted cell-sorted adult oligodendrocytes. *Dev. Neurosci.*, 14: 114–122.

Eng, D.L., Gordon, T.R., Kocsis, J.D. and Waxman, S.G. (1988) Development of 4-AP and TEA sensitivities in mammalian myelinated nerve fibers. *J. Neurophysiol.*, 60: 2168–2179.

Felts, P.A. and Smith, K.J. (1991) Conduction properties of central nerve fibers remyelinated by Schwann cells. *Brain Res.*, 574: 178–192.

Foster, R.E., Connors, B.W. and Waxman, S.G. (1982) Rat optic nerve: electrophysiological, pharmacological, and anatomical studies during development. *Dev. Brain Res.*, 3: 361–376.

Gledhill, R.F., Harrison, B.M. and McDonald, W.I. (1973) Demyelination and remyelination after acute spinal cord compression. *Exp. Neurol.*, 38: 472–487.

Gout, O., Gansmuller, A., Baumann, N. and Gumpel, M. (1988) Remyelination by transplanted oligodendrocytes of a demyelinated lesion in the spinal cord of the adult shiverer mouse. *Neurosci. Lett.*, 87: 195–199.

Griffiths, I.R. and McCulloch, M.C. (1983) Nerve fibers in spinal cord impact injuries. 1. Changes in the myelin sheath during the initial five weeks. *J. Neurol. Sci.*, 58: 335–345.

Groves, A.K., Barnett, S.C., Franklin, R.J.M., Crang, A.J., Mayer, M., Blakemore, W.F. and Noble, M. (1993) Repair of demyelinated lesions by transplantation of purified O-2A progenitor cells. *Nature*, 362: 453–456.

Hafler, D.A., Zharg, J.W., LaSalle, J., Donnelly, C., Webster, H.L. and Wucherpfeffnig, K. (1993) The development of antigen-specific therapies for autoimmune diseases; investigations in multiple sclerosis as a paradigm for rheumatoid arthritis. *Clin. Exp. Rheumatol.*, 11(Suppl. 8): S39–S40.

Hansebout, R.R., Blight, A.R., Fawcett, S. and Reddy, K. (1993) 4-Aminopyridine in chronic spinal cord injury: a controlled, double-blind, crossover study in eight patients. *J. Neurotraum.*, 10: 1–18.

Harrison, B.M. and McDonald, W.I. (1977) Remyelination after transient experimental compression of the spinal cord. *Ann. Neurol.*, 1: 542–551.

Hirano, A. and Dembitzer, H.M. (1978) Morphology of normal central myelinated axons. In: S.G. Waxman (Ed.), *Physiology and Pathobiology of Axons*, Raven Press, New York, pp. 68–82.

Honmou, O., Utzschneider, D.A., Rizzo, M.A., Bowe, C.M., Waxman, S.G. and Kocsis, J.D. (1994) Delayed depolarization and slow sodium currents in cutaneous afferents. *J. Neurophysiol*, in press.

Jones, R.E., Heron, J.R., Foster, D.H., Snelgar, R.S. and Mason, R.J. (1983) Effects of 4-aminopyridine in patients with multiple sclerosis. *J. Neurol. Sci.*, 60: 353–362.

Kampe, K., Safronov, B. and Vogel, W. (1992) A Ca-activated and three voltage-dependent K channels identified in mammalian peripheral nerve. *Pflügers Arch., Eur. J. Physiol.*, 420(Suppl. 1): R28.

Kocsis, J.D. and Waxman, S.G. (1980) Absence of potassium conductance in central myelinated axons. *Nature*, 287: 348–349.

Kocsis, J.D., Waxman, S.G., Hildebrand, C. and Ruiz, J.A. (1982) Regenerating mammalian nerve fibres: changes in action potential waveform and firing characteristics following blockage of potassium conductance. *Proc. R. Soc. London Ser. B*, 217: 277–287.

Kocsis, J.D., Gordon, T.R. and Waxman, S.G. (1986) Mammalian optic nerve fibers display two pharmacologically distinct potassium channels. *Brain Res.*, 393: 357–361.

Kocsis, J.D., Black, J.A. and Waxman, S.G. (1993) Pharmacological modification of axon membrane molecules and cell transplantation as approaches to the restoration of conduction in demyelinated axons. In: S.G. Waxman (Ed.), *Molecular and Cellular Approaches to the Treatment of Neurological Disease*, Raven Press, New York, pp. 265–292.

Koles, Z.J. and Rasminsky, M. (1972) A computer simulation of conduction in demyelinated nerve fibres. *J. Physiol. (London)*, 227: 351–364.

Lundh, H., Nilsson, O. and Rosen, I. (1984) Treatment of Lambert-Eaton syndrome: 3,4-di-aminopyridine and pyridostigmine. *Neurology*, 34: 1324–1330.

Malenka, R.C., Kocsis, J.D., Ransom, B.R. and Waxman, S.G. (1981) Modulation of parallel fiber excitability by postsynaptically mediated changes in extracellular potassium. *Science*, 214: 339–341.

Murray, N.M. and Newsom-Davis, J. (1981) Treatment with oral 4-aminopyridine in disorders of neuromuscular transmission. *Neurology*, 31: 265–271.

Preston, R.J., Waxman, S.G. and Kocsis, J.D. (1983) Effects of 4-aminopyridine on rapidly and slowly conducting axons of rat corpus callosum. *Exp. Neurol.*, 79: 808–820.

Ritchie, J.M. (1982) Sodium and potassium channels in regenerating and developing mammalian myelinated nerves. *Proc. R. Soc. London Ser. B*, 215: 273–287.

Ritchie, J.M. and Rogart, R.B. (1977) The density of sodium channels in mammalian myelinated nerve fibers and the nature of the axonal membrane under the myelin sheath. *Proc. Natl. Acad. Sci. USA*, 74: 211–215.

Röper, J. and Schwarz, J.R. (1989) Heterogeneous distribution of fast and slow potassium channels in myelinated rat nerve fibers. *J. Physiol. (London)*, 416: 93–110.

Rosenbluth, J., Hasegawa, M., Shirasaki, N., Rosen, C.L. and Liu, Z. (1990) Myelin formation following transplantation of normal fetal glia into myelin-deficient rat spinal cord. *J. Neurocytol.*, 19: 718–730.

Schauf, C.L. and Davis, F.A. (1974) Impulse conduction in multiple sclerosis: a theoretical basis for modification by temperature and pharmacological agents. *J. Neurol. Neurosurg. Psychiatry*, 37: 152–161.

Scholz, A., Reid, G., Bostock, H. and Vogel, W. (1992) Na and K channels in human axons. *Pflügers Arch., Eur. J. Physiol.*, 420 (Suppl. 1): R28.

Sears, T.A., Bostock, H. and Sherratt, M. (1978) The pathophysiology of demyelination and its implications for the symptomatic treatment of multiple sclerosis. *Neurology*, 28: 21–26.

Sherratt, R.M., Bostock, H. and Sears, T.A. (1980) Effects of 4-aminopyridine on normal and demyelinated mammalian nerve fibers. *Nature*, 283: 570–572.

Sherwood, A.M., Dimitrijevic, M.R. and McKay, W.B. (1992) Evidence of subclinical brain influence in clinically complete spinal cord injury: discomplete SCI. *J. Neurol Sci.*, 110: 90–98.

Smith, K.J. and Hall, S.M. (1980) Nerve conduction during peripheral demyelination and remyelination. *J. Neurol. Sci.*, 48: 201–219.

Smith, K.J., Blakemore, W.F. and McDonald, W.I. (1983) Central remyelination restores secure conduction. *Nature*, 280: 395–396.

Stefoski, D., Davis, F.A., Faut, M. and Schauf, C.L. (1987) 4-Aminopyridine improves clinical signs in multiple sclerosis. *Ann. Neurol.*, 21: 71–77.

Stys, P.K., Sontheimer, H., Ransom, B.R. and Waxman, S.G. (1993) Non-inactivating, TTX-sensitive Na$^+$ conductance in rat optic nerve axons. *Proc. Natl. Acad. Sci. USA*, 90: 6976–6980.

Targ, E.F. and Kocsis, J.D. (1985) 4-Aminopyridine leads to restoration of conduction in demyelinated rat sciatic nerve. *Brain Res.*, 328: 358–361.

Targ, E.F. and Kocsis, J.D. (1986) Action potential characteristics of demyelinated rat sciatic nerve following application of 4-aminopyridine. *Brain Res.*, 363: 1–9.

Utzschneider, D., Black, J.A. and Kocsis, J.D. (1992) Conduction properties of spinal cord axons in the myelin-deficient rat mutant. *Neuroscience*, 49: 221–228.

Utzschneider, D.A., Archer, D.R., Kocsis, J.D., Waxman, S.G. and Duncan, I.D. (1994) Transplantation of glial cells enhances action potential conduction of amyelinated spinal cord axons in the myelin-deficient rat. *Proc. Natl. Acad. Sci. USA*, 91: 53–57.

Vogel, W. and Schwarz, J.R. (1994) Voltage-clamp studies in frog, rat, and human axons: macroscopic and single channel currents. In: S.G. Waxman, J.D. Kocsis and P.K. Stys (Eds.), *The Axon*, Oxford University Press, New York, in press.

Waxman, S.G. (1977) Conduction in myelinated, unmyelinated, and demyelinated fibers. *Arch. Neurol.*, 34: 585–590.

Waxman, S.G. (1978) Prerequisites for conduction in demyelinated fibers. *Neurology*, 28: 27–34.

Waxman, S.G. (1988) Clinical course and electrophysiology of multiple sclerosis. In: S.G. Waxman (Ed.), *Functional Recovery in Neurological Disease*, Raven Press, New York, pp. 157–184.

Waxman, S.G. and Bennett, M.V.L. (1972) Relative conduction velocities of small myelinated and non-myelinated fibers in the central nervous system. *Nat., New Biol.*, 238: 217–219.

Waxman, S.G. and Brill, M.H. (1978) Conduction through demyelinated plaques in multiple sclerosis: computer simulations of facilitation by short internodes. *J. Neurol. Neurosurg. Psychiatry*, 41: 408–417.

Waxman, S.G. and Ritchie, J.M. (1993) Molecular dissection of the myelinated axon. *Ann. Neurol.*, 33: 121–136.

Weiner, L.P., Waxman, S.G., Stohlman, S.A. and Kwan, A. (1980) Remyelination following viral-induced demyelination: ferric ion-ferrocyanide staining of nodes of Ranvier within the CNS. *Ann. Neurol.*, 8: 580–583.

Weiner, H.L., Mackin, G.A., Matsui, M., Orav, E.J., Khoury, S.J., Dawson, D.M. and Hafler, D.A. (1993) Double-blind pilot trial of oral tolerization with myelin antigens in multiple sclerosis. *Science*, 259: 1321–1324.

Young, W. (1989) Recovery mechanisms in spinal cord injury: implications for regenerative therapy. In: F.J. Seil (Ed.), *Neural Regeneration and Transplantation*, Alan R. Liss, New York, pp. 157–169.

F. Bloom (Editor)
Progress in Brain Research, Vol. 100
© 1994 Elsevier Science B.V. All rights reserved

CHAPTER 30

Functional integrity of neural systems related to memory in Alzheimer's disease

Nancy A. Simonian, G. William Rebeck and Bradley T. Hyman

Neurology Service, Massachusetts General Hospital and Harvard Medical School, Boston, MA 02114, USA

Memory impairment is a hallmark of Alzheimer's disease

The initial symptom of the disease is most frequently loss of memory function, as exemplified by losses on short-term delayed recall tasks. Memory impairment, in one form or another, remains at the core of the clinical syndrome and dominates the illness as it progresses for the next 5–10 years, until death. The underlying pathophysiology of this progressive and relentless memory impairment remains unknown. When we began our studies of the causes of memory impairment in Alzheimer's disease 10 years ago, we were interested in knowing the functional status of the neural systems that subserve memory in the human brain. As a first approximation we began a systematic study of structural changes that occur in memory-related brain areas.

Anatomic basis for memory impairment in Alzheimer's disease

Structures whose integrity is crucial for normal memory function have been defined on the basis of lesion experiments in animals and as a result of surgical or pathological lesions in the human. A review of this literature is beyond the scope of this chapter, but certainly a neural system whose components include the hippocampus, entorhinal cortex (anterior parahippocampal gyrus), the cholinergic basal forebrain, and likely contributions from the amygdala, midline and anterior thalamic nuclei, mammillary bodies, and pro-isocortical areas surrounding the medial temporal lobe are implicated. The pathological changes of Alzheimer's disease seem to specifically affect this memory-related neural system, along with the neocortical association cortices that are crucial for information processing.

Histopathologically, the Alzheimer disease brain shows intraneuronal inclusions of cytoskeletal elements (neurofibrillary tangles) and extraneuronal deposits of β/A4 amyloid protein as senile plaques. Our initial studies (Hyman et al., 1984) showed that a specific set of neurons within the hippocampal formation consistently developed neurofibrillary tangles, while other anatomic fields were consistently spared. Layer II of the entorhinal cortex, layer IV of the entorhinal cortex, and the CA1/subicular field of the hippocampus were the most vulnerable regions for neuronal loss.

We interpreted these data in the context of known neuroanatomical connections as derived from studies in the non-human primate (for review, sees Rosene and Van Hoesen, 1987). Afferents from limbic areas, and unimodal, and multimodal association cortices converge on the entorhinal cortex rather than projecting directly to the hippocampus. The stellate neurons of layer II of entorhinal cortex give rise to the perforant pathway, which "perforates" across the subiculum and across the hippocampal fissure to terminate on the distal dendrites of pyramidal cells throughout the hippocampus and, most strongly, in the outer portion of the molecular layer of the dentate gyrus (Fig. 1). A series of intrinsic intrahippocampal projections lead from the dentate gyrus to CA3 (mossy fibers), from CA3 to CA1 (Schaeffer collaterals), and from CA1 to the subiculum (ammonic-subicular pathway). Cortically directed hippocampal output arises in great part from the pyramidal neurons of the CA1/subicular field. One of the major projections of these neurons is a reciprocal projection back to layer IV of entorhinal cortex, which in turn gives rise to widespread cortical projections. Thus neuronal lesions in the neurons of layer II of entorhinal cortex would disrupt the flow of information from the cortex, via the perforant pathway, to the hippocampus, and neuronal lesions in CA1/subiculum and layer IV of entorhinal cortex would disrupt the flow of information from the hippocampal formation back towards the cortex. We postulated that these lesions would isolate the hippocampus from the cortex, and, together with the already known loss of cholinergic projections to the hippocampus, contribute to the memory impairment of Alzheimer's disease.

These observations, based in part on the studies of Ball (1978) and Kemper (1978), have since been confirmed and expanded. We later demonstrated that senile plaques often occur in the terminal zones of neurons that contain neurofibrillary tangles (Hyman et al., 1986, 1990). A detailed study of the amygdala showed that it, too, was severely affected in Alzheimer's dis-

ease in a fashion somewhat analogous to the way the hippocampus was affected. Specific nuclei (e.g. accessory basal nucleus) that had strong projections with the hippocampus tended to accumulate neurofibrillary tangles and senile plaques, whereas other nuclei were consistently spared (Hyman et al., 1990; Kromer Vogt et al., 1990). A survey of degree of pathological change in each of 49 cytoarchitectural fields in 17 hemispheres of individuals with Alzheimer's disease revealed a striking, consistent hierarchical pattern of involvement of various brain areas, with neurofibrillary tangles most severe in the entorhinal cortex, hippocampus, amygdala, and adjacent anatomically closely related perirhinal cortex, temporal pole, and posterior parahippocampal gyrus (Arnold et al., 1991). We confirmed the observation that high order association areas were more severely affected than unimodal association cortices, which in turn were more affected than the primary sensory and motor areas (Brun and Gustafson, 1976; Arnold et al., 1991; Braak and Braak., 1991). Moreover, within association cortex, the neurons of layers V and III were preferentially affected. These neurons are large pyramidal neurons that give rise to many cortico-cortical projections, and their loss was interpreted as leading to a widespread disconnection syndrome (Hof and Morrison, 1990; Hyman et al., 1990; Lewis et al., 1987; Arnold et al., 1991).

Our recent studies have shown that the hierarchical pattern of vulnerability seems to reflect the temporal order of various brain areas developing neurofibrillary tangles or senile plaques. We examined a cohort of Alzheimer patients who had been followed clinically and with neuropsychometric testing for 1–16 years. All these individuals had marked changes in the entorhinal cortex and CA1/subicular hippocampal fields. With increasing duration or severity of illness, the degree of pathological changes in neocortical and subcortical ascending neurotransmitter specific areas increased, and this increase, especially in the high order association cortices, was the factor that was best correlated with clinical parameters (Arriagada et al., 1992a). We have also examined a cohort of 25 presumed normal, non-demented individuals and found that many of them had small numbers of neurofibril-

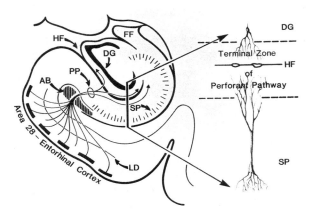

Fig. 1. Line drawing of the perforant pathway and its disruption in Alzheimer's disease. Reprinted from Hyman et al., 1986.

lary tangles and senile plaques. When these were present, they were invariably in the cytoarchitectural fields and lamina predicted by the hierarchical vulnerability scheme we had defined in Alzheimer's disease itself, again with entorhinal cortex layer II being most vulnerable (Arriagada et al., 1992b; see also Hof et al., 1992; Price et al., 1991). Finally, an ongoing study of individuals with Down's syndrome of various ages also demonstrates this same pattern of vulnerability of projection neurons in these cytoarchitectural fields, and again emphasizes entorhinal lesions as an early signature of the disease (Hyman and Mann, 1991).

The perforant pathway in Alzheimer's disease as a model of deafferentation

As noted above, layer II of the entorhinal cortex provides nearly all the cortical afferents to the outer two-thirds of the molecular layer of the dentate gyrus via the perforant pathway. In Alzheimer's disease, these neurons invariably develop neurofibrillary tangles, and senile plaques frequently occur in the terminal zone (Fig. 2). Synaptic loss and re-innervation have also

been demonstrated, presumably as a result of neurofibrillary tangles in the cells of origin, or senile plaques in the terminal zone, of this major projection. Evidence of dentate gyrus deafferentation in Alzheimer's disease has been established in several ways: there is a plasticity response analogous to that seen after entorhinal lesions in experimental animals in kainate receptors and acetylcholinesterase staining (Geddes et al., 1985; Hyman et al., 1987a); there is loss of the putative neurotransmitter glutamate in the terminal zone (Hyman et al., 1987b), and there is loss of immunoreactive synaptic markers in the terminal zone (Hamos et al., 1989; Masliah et al. 1991; Cabalka et al., 1992). Moreover, senile plaques have been implicated in the pathogenesis of altered synaptic transmission. Reduced axonal numbers and disrupted morphology have been found both within and around plaques and synaptic loss as determined by synaptophysin staining has been demonstrated in "mature" plaques (Masliah et al., 1990). These studies suggest that SPs through local pathogenetic mechanisms related to plaque formation, may disrupt axons en passage and contribute to deafferentation.

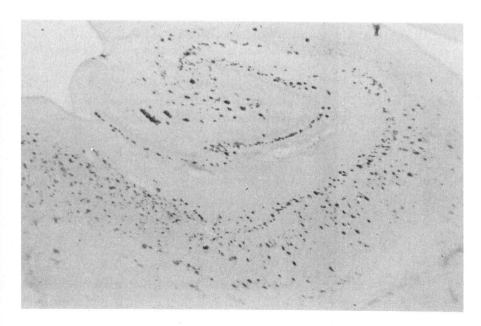

Fig. 2. Senile plaques frequently occupy the middle and outer portions of the molecular layer of the dentate gyrus, the terminal zone of the perforant pathway.

Markers of diminished afferent activity in experimental systems

Intact neuronal projections clearly play a crucial role in the early development of the nervous system and in the establishment of neural systems. Although it is widely believed that the adult central nervous system has a much more limited repertoire of responses to changes in the level of afferent activity, recent studies have shown that a remarkable degree of plasticity is still present in the adult. Deafferentation of the visual system, the somatosensory system, and the hippocampal formation (Geddes et al., 1985) in the adult animal result in alterations in the expression of a variety of gene products. In several instances, the effects are seen not only in neurons that are directly deafferented by a lesion but also trans-synaptically, sometimes several synapses away. For example, after monocular deprivation by eyelid suture or injection of tetrodotoxin, effects are seen most prominently in layer IV (which receives the major thalamic relay input) but also extend to other layers within the vertical organization of the ocular dominance columns (Jones, 1990).

Cytochrome oxidase decreases as a functional marker of deafferentation

Cytochrome oxidase, or complex IV, is the terminal enzyme of the electron transport chain and is one of the energy-generating enzymes most strongly correlated with neuronal functional activity (Wong-Riley, 1989). Cytochrome oxidase activity is highest in dendrites and cell bodies and can easily be detected in tissue using diaminobenzidine histochemistry (Kageyama and Wong-Riley, 1982). This method provides precise localization of reaction product at the regional, laminar, cellular and subcellular levels and relative changes in enzymatic activity can be quantitated by optical densitometry. The intensity of reaction product detected by optical density in rat brain is closely correlated with cytochrome oxidase measured spectrophotometrically in punch biopsies of brain (Darriet et al., 1986).

Cytochrome oxidase activity in the outer two-thirds of the molecular layer of the dentate gyrus is signifi-

cantly reduced after disruption of the perforant pathway by entorhinal cortex lesions in rats (Borowsky and Collins, 1989). Similarly, in monkey, cytochrome oxidase activity is reduced within 24 h in neurons in ocular dominance columns in area 17 deprived of visual input by lid suture or enucleation (Horton and Hubel, 1981).

Cytochrome oxidase abnormalities in Alzheimer's disease

While evidence is emerging that alterations in energy metabolism exist in Alzheimer's disease (Beal, 1992), the pathophysiologic basis for these changes is not known. Hypometabolism of higher order association areas has been demonstrated by positron emission tomography (Duara et al., 1986) and reduced cytochrome oxidase activity has been reported in brain homogenates of frontal cortex (Kish et al., 1992) in Alzheimer's disease. Cytochrome oxidase histochemistry and in situ hybridization provide a tool to measure changes in energy metabolism in individual neurons in specific cytoarchitectural areas and to address whether these changes are primary or secondary. Based on our deafferentation model, we predicted that cytochrome oxidase activity would be decreased in the terminal zone of the perforant pathway, and polysynaptically in neurons downstream in the circuit. In support of this, Chandrasekaran et al. (1992) recently reported significantly decreased mRNA for two mitochondrial encoded cytochrome oxidase subunits in the dentate gyrus, CA3 and CA1 of Alzheimer's disease patients.

We recently studied the distribution and intensity of cytochrome oxidase activity in the human hippocampal formation using the Wong–Riley histochemical technique (Simonian and Hyman, 1993). Overall, in control individuals, the hippocampal formation is fairly intensely stained compared to other cortical regions. By contrast, however, in Alzheimer's disease there is a marked diminution in staining. This loss is specific for certain areas. For example, the loss of staining is greater in the outer than in the inner molecular layer of the dentate, likely because of the loss of perforant path afferents to the outer portion of the

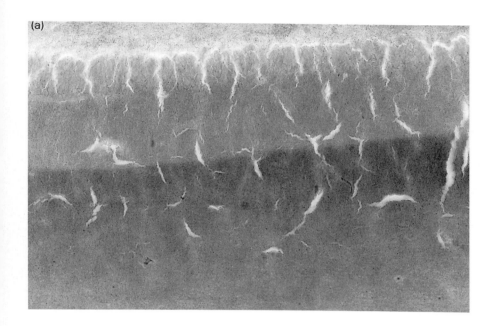

Fig. 3. Cytochrome oxidase histochemical staining on a hippocampal section from a non-demented control patient (a) and a patient with Alzheimer's disease (b). In the control brain, a dark band of cytochrome oxidase staining is seen in the outer two-thirds of the molecular layer of the dentate gyrus (DG) (arrow marks border). In the Alzheimer brain, there is a decrease in staining in the dentate molecular layer and loss of demarcation between the outer and inner layers (b). Magnification bar = 100 μm.

TABLE I

Cytochrome oxidase activity is reduced in the hippocampal formation, but not visual cortex, in Alzheimer's disease (from Simonian and Hyman, 1993)

	Diffuse density ($X \pm$ SEM)	
	Control	Alzheimer's disease
Dentate gyrus: outer 2/3	0.88 ± 0.10	0.60 ± 0.05*
Dentate gyrus: inner 1/3	0.78 ± 0.07	0.62 ± 0.05*
CA4	0.83 ± 0.08	0.62 ± 0.05*
CA3	0.86 ± 0.07	0.65 ± 0.05*
CA1	0.85 ± 0.08	0.65 ± 0.05*
Area 17	0.69 ± 0.10	0.71 ± 0.05

*$p < 0.05$.

molecular layer (Fig. 3). In addition, CA3, CA1 and subiculum also contain diminished activity. This may be due to a transynaptic effect, with diminished excitatory input to the dentate gyrus reflected by diminished activity throughout the hippocampal projection fields. By contrast, examination of the primary visual cortex in Alzheimer's disease showed no difference in cytochrome oxidase staining compared to controls, consistent with the clinical and anatomical observations suggesting that primary visual input is not affected in Alzheimer's disease (Table I).

Glut 3 glucose transporter isoform is the primary neuronal glucose transport protein: loss in the perforant pathway terminal zone in Alzheimer's disease may reflect diminished energy metabolism

At least five glucose transport proteins have been identified that provide the molecular basis for facilitated glucose transport across cell membranes. Of these, two appear to be predominant in brain: Glut 1 in brain capillaries, responsible for transporting glucose across the tight junctions of the blood–brain barrier, and Glut 3, present on neurons, presumably responsible for regulating glucose uptake to neurons (Mantych et al., 1992). Neurons are dependent on glucose for most of their energy needs, and functional activity in

creases glucose utilization. It is of course this principle that underlies the use of 2-deoxyglucose for PET studies.

Mantych et al., (1992) showed that the Glut 3 transporter molecule is located principally in neurons in the human brain. We have taken advantage of this to examine whether or not alterations in the pattern or level of expression occur in Alzheimer's disease. We hypothesized that deafferented areas would downregulate the amount of Glut 3 that was expressed. Our preliminary analyses suggest that there is a loss of Glut 3 immunoreactivity (East Acres Biologicals, Southbridge, MA, diluted 1:500) in the Alzheimer's disease hippocampal formation that in many ways parallels the type of changes we have seen for cytochrome oxidase. In particular, the outer portion of the molecular layer of the dentate gyrus, i.e. the perforant pathway terminal zone, shows a dramatic loss of Glut 3 immunoreactivity in each of the eight Alzheimer brains we have examined to date.

NADPH diaphorase (nitric oxide synthase) activity is diminished in the perforant pathway terminal zone in Alzheimer's disease

We have recently examined the population of nitric oxide synthase containing neurons in Alzheimer's disease to determine whether this population of neurons, which are resistant to a variety of metabolic insults, NMDA excitotoxicity, and to degeneration in the striatum in Huntington's disease, was also spared from degeneration in Alzheimer's disease. Indeed, in the hippocampal formation, the number of nitric oxide synthase immunoreactive neurons was unchanged in Alzheimer's disease (Hyman et al., 1992).

However, we noticed that the processes of these neurons appeared to be distorted and somewhat atrophic. We therefore examined the distribution and intensity of staining of NADPH diaphorase (a histochemical stain that identifies nitric oxide synthase). Again, there was an alteration in the pattern of staining, with the staining in the perforant pathway terminal zone depleted in Alzheimer's disease (Rebeck et al., 1993).

Alteration of substance P in the perforant pathway terminal zone in Alzheimer's disease

Substance P levels are known to inversely reflect levels of afferent activity in the visual cortex in models of acute deprivation (Jones, 1990). We postulated that the same may be true in the hippocampal formation in Alzheimer's disease. There have been relatively few prior studies of substance P immunoreactivity in Alzheimer's disease. Bouras et al. (1990) describe "significantly reduced substance P like immunoreac-

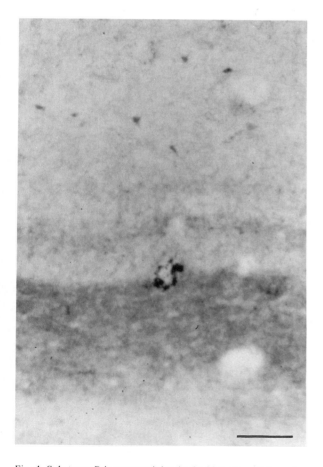

Fig. 4. Substance P immunostaining in the hippocampal formation reveals three bands of terminal-like staining in the molecular layer of the dentate gyrus: an intense supragranular band, a somewhat lighter band in the inner one-third of the molecular layer, and a heavier band in the outer two-thirds of the molecular layer. Magnification bar = 100 μm.

tivity in the neocortical areas and in the hippocampus". Quigley and Kowall (1991) also reported that substance P neurons are depleted in Alzheimer's disease and noted a band of terminal like staining in the molecular layer of the dentate gyrus.

We used substance P immunohistochemistry (Accurate Immunochemicals, 1:5000) to assess the pattern of substance P immunostaining in the hippocampal formation. We also found a distinct band of immunoreactivity in the dentate gyrus molecular layer in both control and Alzheimer individuals. There is an intense supragranular band, a light stain in the inner one-third of the dentate molecular layer, and a more intense band in the outer two-thirds (Fig. 4). We used a Bioquant image analysis system to quantitate the amount of immunostaining in these bands. Surprisingly, in contrast to Bouras' description, our quantitative analysis of 10 Alzheimer and 10 control individuals shows an increase in staining intensity in all three bands in Alzheimer's disease (Fig. 5). This may reflect reinnervation of the deafferented areas by remaining intact afferents, such as the substance P positive neurons of the hilus.

This type of remodelling of afferents has also been noted for acetylcholinesterase activity (Geddes et al., 1985; Hyman et al., 1987a) and for some glutamate receptor binding (Geddes et al., 1985). However, we have recently demonstrated by immunohistochemistry that at least some types of glutamate receptors (GluR1, GluR2,3 and GluR4) are unaltered in the dentate gyrus molecular layer in Alzheimer's disease (Hyman et al., 1994). Thus, neurotransmitter system remodelling occurs in several, but not all inputs to the deafferented hippocampus in Alzheimer's disease.

Conclusion

Anatomical evidence suggests loss of projection neurons and widespread disconnection of the hippocampal formation and association cortices in Alzheimer's disease. This is perhaps most pronounced in the perforant pathway, the projection from the entorhinal cortex to the dentate gyrus which is uniformly destroyed in Alzheimer's disease. We have recently developed new methodologies to examine the functional

252

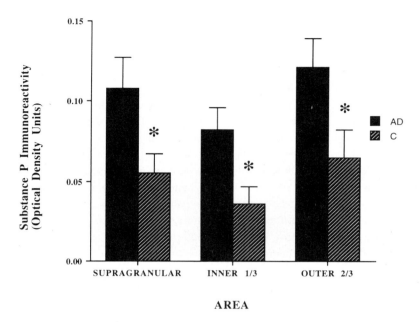

Fig. 5. Substance P immunoreactivity increases in the dentate gyrus in Alzheimer's disease. Optical density measurements of substance P immunoreactivity was measured using a Bioquant image analysis system in the supragranular, inner one-third, and outer two-thirds of the molecular layer of the dentate gyrus. Ten Alzheimer and 10 control individuals were studied. There is a statistically significant increase in staining in each area in Alzheimer's disease ($p < 0.05$).

integrity of hippocampal projections in the post mortem human brain, and have found that there is impairment both of neural elements that are directly affected by the disease process (i.e. by neurofibrillary tangles) as well as "downstream" of the pathological changes. These results highlight the effect of the disease process in disrupting neural systems, no doubt causing the impairment of memory function that is so prominent in patients with Alzheimer's disease.

Acknowledgments

We thank Ted Elvhage and Steven Harr for excellent technical assistance. Supported by NIH AG08487, and grants from the Brookdale Foundation and the Alzheimer Association. We thank the Massachusetts Alzheimer Disease Research Center Brain Bank (Dr. E.T. Hedley-Whyte, Director) for tissue used in these studies, S. Melanson for assistance with the manuscript and H. West for photographic expertise.

References

Arnold, S.E., Hyman, B.T., Flory, J., Damasio, A.R. and Van Hoesen, G.W. (1991) The topographical and neuroanatomical distribution of neurofibrillary tangles and neuritic plaques in the cerebral cortex of patients in Alzheimer's disease. *Cerebral Cortex*, 1: 103–116.

Arriagada, P.V., Growdon, J.H., Hedley-White, E.T. and Hyman, B.T. (1992a) Neurofibrillary tangles but not senile plaques parallel duration and severity of Alzheimer's disease. *Neurology*, 42: 631–639.

Arriagada, P.V., Marzloff, K.M. and Hyman, B.T. (1992b) The distribution of Alzheimer type pathological changes in nondemented elderly individuals matches the pattern in Alzheimer disease. *Neurology*, 42: 1681–1688.

Ball, M.J. (1978) Topographic distribution of neurofibrillary tangles and granulovacuolar degeneration in hippocampal cortex of aging and demented patients. *Acta Neuropathol.*, 42: 73–80.

Beal, M.F. (1992) Does impairment of energy metabolism result in excitotoxic neuronal death in neurodegenerative illnesses? *Ann. Neurol.*, 31: 119–130.

Borowsky, W. and Collins, R.C. (1989) Histochemical changes in enzymes of energy metabolism in the dentate gyrus accompany deafferentation and synaptic reorganization. *Neuroscience*, 33: 253–262.

Bouras, C., Vallet, P.G., Hof, P.R., Charnay, Y., Golaz, J. and Constantinidis, J. (1990) Substance P immunoreactivity in Alzheimer disease: a study in cases presenting symmetric or asymmetric cortical atrophy. *Alzheimer Dis. Assoc. Disord.*, 4: 24–34.

Braak, H. and Braak, E. (1991) Neuropathological staging of Alzheimer-related changes. *Acta Neuropathol.*, 82: 239–259.

Brun, A. and Gustafson, L. (1976) Distribution of cerebral degeneration in Alzheimer's disease. *Arch. Psychiatr. Nervenk,* 223: 15–33.

Cabalka, L.M., Hyman, B.T., Goodlett, C.R., Ritchie, T.C. and Van Hoesen, G.W. (1992) Alteration in the pattern of nerve terminal protein immunoreactivity in the perforant pathway in Alzheimer's disease and in rats after entorhinal lesions. *Neurobiol. Aging*, 13: 283–291.

Chandrasekaran, K., Stoll, J., Brady, D.R., and Rapoport, S.I. (1992a) Distribution of cytochrome oxidase(COX) activity and mRNA in monkey and human brain: COX mRNA distribution correlates with neurons vulnerable to Alzheimer pathology. *Neuroscience*, 557 (Abstr).

Darriet, D., Der, T. and Collins, R.C. (1986) Distribution of cytochrome oxidase in rat brain: studies with diaminobenzidine histochemistry in vitro and [^{14}C] cyanide tissue labeling in vivo. *J. Cereb. Blood Flow. Metab.*, 6: 8–14.

Duara, R., Grady, C., Haxby, J., Sundaram, M., Cutler, N.R., Heston, L., Moore, A., Schlageter, N., Larson, S. and Rapoport, S.I. (1986) Positron emission tomography in Alzheimer's disease. *Neurology*, 36: 879–887.

Geddes, J.W., Monaghan, D.T. and Cotman, C.W. (1985) Plasticity of the hippocampal circuitry in Alzheimer's disease . *Science*, 230: 1179–1181.

Hamos, J.E., DeGennaro, L.J. and Drachman, D.A . (1989) Synaptic loss in Alzheimer's disease and other dementias. *Neurology*, 39: 355–361.

Hof, P.R. and Morrison, J.H. (1990) Quantitative analysis of a vulnerable subset of pyramidal neurons in Alzheimer's disease: II. Primary and secondary visual cortex. *J. Comp. Neurol.*, 301: 55–64.

Hof, P.R., Bierer, L.M., Perl, D.P., Delacourte, A., Buee, L., Bouras, C. and Morrison, J.H. (1992) Evidence of early vulnerability of the medial and inferior aspects of the temporal lobe in an 82 year old patient with preclinical signs of dementia. *Arch. Neurol.*, 49: 946–953.

Horton, J.C. and Hubel, D.H. (1981) Regular patchy distribution of cytochrome oxidase staining in primary visual cortex of macque monkey. *Nature*, 292: 762–764.

Hyman, B.T. and Mann, D.M.A. (1991) Alzheimer type pathological changes in Down's syndrome individuals of various ages. In: K. Iqbal, D.R.C. McLachlan, B. Winblad and H.M. Wisniewski (Eds.), *Alzheimer's Disease: Basic Mechanisms, Diagnosis, and Therapeutic Strategies*, Wiley New York, pp. 105–113.

Hyman, B.T., Damasio, A.R., Van Hoesen, G.W. and Barnes, C.L. (1984) Alzheimer's disease: cell specific pathology isolates the hippocampal formation. *Science*, 298: 83–95.

Hyman, B.T., Van Hoesen, G.W., Kromer, L.J. and Damasio, A.R. (1986) Perforant pathway changes and the memory impairment of Alzheimer's disease. *Ann. Neurol.*, 20: 472–481.

Hyman, B.T., Kromer, L.J. and Van Hoesen, G.W. (1987a) Reinnervation of the hippocampal perforant pathway zone in Alzheimer's disease. *Ann. Neurol.* 21: 259–267.

Hyman, B.T., Van Hoesen, G.W. and Damasio, A.R. (1987b) Alzheimer's disease: glutamate depletion in perforant pathway terminals. *Ann. Neurol.*, 22: 37–40.

Hyman, B.T., Van Hoesen, G.W., Kromer, L.J. and Damasio, A.R. (1990) Memory-related neural systems in Alzheimer's disease: an anatomic study. *Neurology*, 40: 1721–1730.

Hyman, B.T., Marzloff, K.M., Wenniger, J.J., Dawson, T.M., Bredt, D.S. and Snyder, S.H. (1992) Relative sparing of nitric oxide synthase containing neurons in the hippocampal formation in Alzheimer's disease. *Ann. Neurol.*, 32: 818–821.

Hyman, B.T., Penney, J.B., Blackstone, C.D. and Young, A.B. (1994) Localization of non-*N*-methyl-D-aspartate glutamate receptors in normal and Alzheimer hippocampal formation. *Ann. Neurol.*, 35: 31–37.

Jones, E.G. (1990) The role of afferent activity in the maintenance of primate neocortical function. *J. Exp. Biol.*, 153: 155–176.

Kageyama, G.H. and Wong-Riley, M.T.T. (1982) Histochemical localization of cytochrome oxidase in the hippocampus: correlation with specific neuronal types and afferent pathways. *Neuroscience*, 7: 2337–2361.

Kemper, T.L. (1978) Senile dementia: a focal disease in the temporal lobe. In: K. Nandy (Ed.), *Senile Dementia: A Biomedical Approach*, Elsevier, Amsterdam, pp. 105–113.

Kish, S.J., Bergeron, C., Rajput, A., Dozie, S., Mastrogiacomo, F., Chang, L.J., Wilson, J.M., DiStefano, L.M. and Nobrega, J.N. (1992) Brain cytochrome oxidase in Alzheimer's disease. *J. Neurochem.*, 59: 776–779.

Kromer Vogt, L.J., Hyman, B.T., Van Hoesen, G.W. and Damasio, A.R. (1990) Pathological alterations in the amygdala in Alzheimer's disease. *Neuroscience*, 37: 377–385.

Lewis, D.A., Campbell, J.M., Terry, R.D. and Morrison, J.H. (1987) Laminar and regional distributions of neurofibrillary tangles and neuritic plaques in Alzheimer's disease: a quantitative study of visual and auditory cortices. *J. Neurosci.*, 7: 1799–1808.

Mantych, G.J., James, D.E., Chung, H.D. and Devaskar, S.U. (1992) Cellular localization and characterization of Glut 3 glucose transporter isoform in human brain. *Endocrinology*, 131: 1270–1278.

Masliah, E., Terry, R.D., Mallory, B.S., Alford, M. and Hansen, L. (1990) Diffuse plaques do not accentuate synaptic loss in Alzheimer's disease. *Am. J. Pathol.*, 137: 1293–1297.

Masliah, E., Terry, R.D., Alford, M., DeTeresa, R. and Hansen, L.A. (1991) Cortical and subcortical patterns of synaptophysin immunoreactivity in Alzheimer's disease. *Am. J. Pathol.*, 138: 235–246.

Price, J.L., David, P.B., Morris, J.C. and White, D.L. (1991) The distribution of tangles, plaques and related immunohistochemical markers in healthy aging and Alzheimer's disease. *Neurobiol. Aging*, 12: 295–312.

Quigley, B.J., Jr. and Kowall, N.W. (1991) Substance P-like immunoreactive neurons are depleted in Alzheimer's disease cerebral cortex. *Neuroscience*, 41: 41–60.

Rebeck, G.W., Marzloff, K.M. and Hyman, B.T. (1993) The pattern of NADPH-diaphorase staining, a marker of nitric oxide synthase activity, is altered in the perforant pathway terminal zone in Alzheimer's disease. *Neurosci. Lett.*, 152: 165–168.

Rosene, D.L. and Van Hoesen, G.W. (1987) The hippocampal formation of the primate brain. In: E.G. Jones and A. Peters (Eds.), *The Cerebral Cortex*, Vol. 6, Plenum, New York, pp. 345–456.

Simonian, N.A. and Hyman, B.T. (1993) Functional alterations in Alzheimer's disease: diminution of cytochrome oxidase in the hippocampal formation. *J. Neuropathol. Exp. Neurol.*, 52: 580–585.

Wong-Riley, M.T.T. (1989) Cytochrome oxidase: an endogenous metabolic marker of neuronal activity. *Trends Neurosci.*, 12: 94–101.

F. Bloom (Editor)
Progress in Brain Research, Vol. 100
© 1994 Elsevier Science B.V. All rights reserved

CHAPTER 31

The search for a manic depressive gene: from classical to molecular genetics

J. Mendlewicz

Department of Psychiatry, Free University Clinics of Brussels, Erasme Hospital, route de Lennik 808, 1070 Brussels, Belgium

A growing number of researchers in the last decade have addressed the issue of genetic factors in affective illness and its various subtypes (for review see Mendlewicz et al., 1993). The twin method allows comparison of concordance rates for a trait between sets of monozygotic (MZ) and dizygotic (DZ) twins in bipolar manic depression. The concordance rates in MZ twins vary between 50 and 90% (mean 70%) as compared to 0–39% in DZ twins (mean 20%). These results strongly support the presence of a genetic factor in the etiology of bipolar disorder (BP). Among pairs of identical twins who had been reared apart since early childhood and who were characterized by at least one of the twins being diagnosed as affectively ill, eight out of 12 pairs were concordant for the disease, an observation suggesting that the predisposition to BP will usually express itself regardless of the early environment.

In adoption studies, depressive disorders in adulthood are significantly more frequent in adopted away offspring of affectively ill biological parents compared to adoptees whose biological parents were well or had other psychiatric conditions (Cadoret, 1978). Similarly, psychopathology of the affective spectrum is found more frequently in biological parents of bipolar adoptees than in their adoptive parents (Mendlewicz and Rainer, 1977).

Most of the early studies on BP have shown that this illness tends to be familial. The lifetime risk for the disease in relatives of bipolar probands is significantly higher than the risk in the general population (about ten times higher).

Bipolar patients show a greater genetic loading for affective disorders with more hypomanic temperaments in relatives. Moreover, bipolar and unipolar illnesses are present in the relatives of bipolar patients whereas only unipolar illnesses were present in the relatives of unipolar patients. After reviewing all family studies, the risk for manic depressive illness in the relatives of bipolar patients can be estimated at somewhere between 15 and 35%. There is, however, a large proportion of relatives of bipolar probands who exhibit unipolar illness only.

Linkage analysis is a promising method to study the genetics of manic depressive illness (BPI). It explores a major single genetic transmission, and evaluates the degree of co-segregation between genetic markers, including deoxyribonucleic acid (DNA) polymorphisms and illness traits in informative pedigrees. This method tests the hypothesis of a potential linkage relationship between a known genetic marker and a trait known to be genetically determined, but not yet mapped on the chromosome. DNA polymorphisms in various regions of the human genome are being explored using the DNA recombinant method and, more recently, the polymerase chain reaction (PCR) for gene amplification is also being used.

Unfortunately, several factors limit the results of linkage analysis. BP is a complex disorder lacking clear-cut mendelian patterns of inheritance. Although the true mode of inheritance may involve the interaction of alleles at more than one locus, the major contributing loci may still be detected by assuming a single mendelian locus model in the linkage analysis.

Assumptions are also to be made on numerous parameters such as gene frequency, penetrance, genetic heterogeneity, variable age of onset and diagnostic uncertainties. Since the underlying genetic model is not known, penetrance and allele frequency may be mispecified and may reduce the linkage results. Lack of replication between studies is often attributed to genetic heterogeneity. The latter occurs when one disease phenotype is caused by different mutant alleles at different loci.

The vulnerability to affective illness could be linked to more that one gene, and for such common disorders as affective illness, phenocopies (or false positive) may also be present in large pedigrees. Because of variable age of onset, relatives of probands may be diagnosed as unaffected at the time of study, and may become affectively ill in follow-up studies, resulting in a significant change in linkage scores. Moreover, co-morbidity of other psychiatric disorders with depressive illness may modify the expression of the affective disorder which may result in misclassification. Other factors such as assortative mating, the change in the rate of mental illness over time (cohort effect) and laboratory errors may also bias the results.

Linkage analysis results may be improved by defining age-specific and cohort-specific penetrances. Because of assortative mating, spouses and their relatives should be evaluated systematically, and families with evidence of illness on both paternal and maternal sides should be excluded from linkage analysis or should be analyzed separately. Notwithstanding these limitations, linkage with DNA markers in manic depression has been studied in three distinct chromosomal regions: the subterminal region of the long arm of the X chromosome (Xq26–28), and regions of the short (11p15) and long (11q21–23) arms of chromosome 11. So far, two main hypotheses of genetic transmission for affective illness have been tested: an X-linked and an autosomal dominant transmission.

Besides X-linked transmission, a major autosomal dominant gene with reduced penetrance for bipolar illness has been postulated. Indeed, a preponderance of affected females, as compared to males in first-degree relatives has not been found in some studies, and a male to male transmission of the disease is pres-

ent in some families (Mendlewicz et al., 1993). Although it is nevertheless a rare event in the kindreds of bipolar probands, it has been observed in about 10% of most samples. The hypothesis of an autosomal transmission has been investigated in association studies with the O blood group located on chromosome 9, as well as linkage studies on chromosome 6 with the human leucocyte antigen (HLA) haplotypes and on chromosome 11 with DNA markers for the following genes: D2 dopamine receptor, tyrosinase, C-Harvey-Ras-A (HRAS) oncogene, insulin (ins), and tyrosine hydroxylase (TH).

The O blood group has been found to be more frequent in BP patients in some studies. Although poorly understood, the association between a blood group factor and a major psychosis indicates that the ABO genotype located on 9q34 may play a role in the predisposition to BP. Although a linkage to HLA genes located on the short arm of chromosome 6 has been proposed for affective illness, it has not been confirmed. On the long arm of chromosome 11, a balanced translocation from 11q23.3 to chromosome 9p22 was described in some bipolar patients and in some others, a translocation from region 11q21–22 to region q43 of chromosome 1 was reported suggesting, a linkage between psychiatric illness and genes at the site of the translocation. The human D2 dopamine receptor gene located on 11q22–23, and the tyrosinase gene also located on the long arm of chromosome 11 may be close to the translocation point observed. Consequently, linkage analysis between these markers and BP was performed. However, no evidence of linkage has been found so far. Concerning the short arm of chromosome 11, a positive linkage between BP and the HRAS oncogene as well as the INS marker on the short arm of chromosome 11 (11p15) was reported in studying a large pedigree of the old order Amish Community (Egeland et al., 1987). However, linkage analysis in American bipolar pedigrees of non-Amish origin, in other European pedigrees of bipolar disorders, and in pedigrees of unipolar disorder could not confirm these results. Additionally, the probability of linkage of affective illness to the 11p15 region of chromosome 11 was almost excluded by a re-analysis of the original Amish pedigree with two lateral extensions (Kelsoe et al., 1989). Because of a close link between the genes coding for TH, INS and HRAS loci on chromosome 11, linkage between BPI and the TH locus has also been investigated in BP, but with negative results so far (Mendlewicz et al., 1991b). In association studies, positive results between the TH gene and affective illness have been reported but not yet confirmed.

Rosanoff et al. (1934) first postulated a chromosome X transmission for bipolar illness, which was also suggested by studies reporting a sex ratio of two females to one male in the distribution of bipolar illness and an observed excess of females over males in the relatives of bipolar probands. Colour blindness (CB) and glucose-6-phosphate dehydrogenase (G6PD) deficiency are two loci known to be located in the region Xq28 on the long arm of the X chromosome.

Previous studies have provided evidence of a linkage between these loci and a dominant gene involved in the transmission of manic depressive illness in some families (Mendlewicz et al., 1992). Additionally (Mendlewicz et al., 1987, 1991a), in 11 informative pedigrees, Lucotte et al. (1992) in one French pedigree, reported DNA results suggestive of a linkage between MDI and blood coagulation factor 9 (F9) in the Xq27 region. In addition, Gill et al. (1992) and Craddock and Owen (1992) reported segregation of affective disorders with Christmas disease and new

data from Berretini (personal communication) indicated the presence of an X-linked gene in some MDI families proximal of the F9 gene. However, the logarithm of the odds ratio (LOD scores) for F9 and MDI were not very robust in our study (Mendlewicz et al., 1991a). A subsequent study using additional pedigrees could not confirm linkage with factors 9 as was also the case in the study of Bredbacka et al. (1993). Nevertheless, the results suggested the presence of a MDI dominant gene located in the region Xq27–Xq28 (Mendlewicz et al., 1987). However, X-linked transmission has not been observed in all families studied with classical markers (Gershon et al., 1979) or DNA polymorphisms (Berretini et al., 1990; Gejman et al., 1990; Baron et al., 1993; Bredbacka et al., 1993). Moreover, a possible linkage between the fragile X syndrome (Fra-x) and affective illness has been observed (Mendlewicz and Hirsch, 1991).

These contradictory findings are usually attributed to genetic heterogeneity. Accordingly, only a subgroup of bipolar pedigrees will show close linkage to the X chromosome and thus carry the X-linked gene.

Another hypothesis about these inconsistent findings is the presence of diagnostic uncertainties, and the possibility of spurious linkage has also been discussed (Mendlewicz et al., 1991c).

In order to address the issue of diagnostic uncertainties, previous X-linkage data of our group were re-

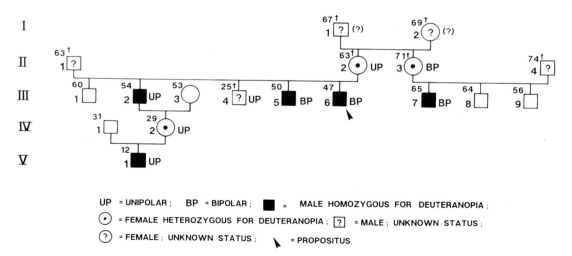

Fig. 1. Pedigree indicative of X-linkage of manic depressive illness.

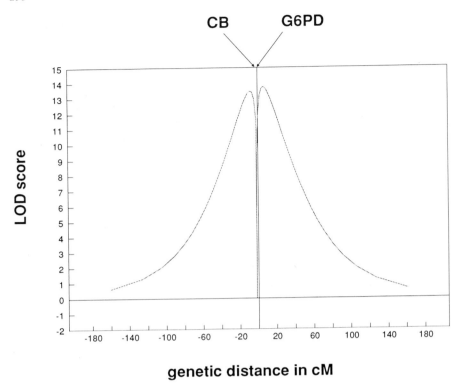

Fig. 2. Linkage of MDI to the X-chromosome: model BP + UP.

analysed by using narrow and broad definitions of MDI.

Thirty-five families of bipolar probands informative for X-linked transmission who participated in previous studies were included in the linkage re-analysis: 23 pedigrees had been analyzed for color blindness, 1 pedigree for glucose-6-phosphate dehydrogenase and 11 pedigrees for F9 linkage. A section of a pedigree illustrating the co-segregation of deuteranopia and bipolar-unipolar illness in successive generations of a family informative for linkage analysis is provided in Fig. 1.

Analyses were performed using two models (M1 and M2). M1 assumes that unipolar (UP) and bipolar (BP) individuals are affected. M2 is more conservative than M1 and assumes that only BP individuals are affected.

The sum of the two-point LOD scores with CB and G6PD genes under classification M1 (BP + UP) gives a maximum LOD score of 13.8 at 6.2 centiMorgan

(cM) to the left of the CB gene and a maximum LOD score of 13.8 at 6.2 cM to the right of the G6PD gene (Fig. 2).

Two-point linkage analyses results thus confirm our previous finding of a conclusive linkage between the MDI and the CB-G6PD genes.

The present re-analysis confirms the X-linked hypothesis of a MDI genetic transmission, but this susceptibility gene may probably account for only a fraction of bipolar patients, and may represent one of the major genes involved in the genetic vulnerability to bipolar disorder. In a recent study, an X-linked susceptibility gene in the transmission of affective disorders has also been postulated by Vailland et al. (1992) who demonstrated an association between affective disorders in males and early mortality in their maternal grandfathers.

Although non-X-linked forms of the illness are most likely to be present, a major susceptibility gene for BP on chromosome 11 is at present not confirmed.

Nevertheless, results of linkage studies are limited by several factors such as uncertainty in mode of inheritance, genetic heterogeneity, methodological and statistical problems originating from the use of several disease definitions and genetic models, ascertainment bias, number of marker loci, assortative mating, nongenetic environmental factors and cohort effect. Hence, the linkage results should be interpreted with caution to avoid making premature claims of linkage because of the possibility of a spurious linkage especially when dealing with selective ascertainment of frequent disorders and common genetic traits, as seems to be the case in the area of psychiatric disorders. Because of the complex nature and the heterogeneity of MDI, replication of results and re-analysis of existing data will have to be emphasized in future studies through collaborative efforts in such projects as carried out by the European Science Foundation (ESF) or the National Institute for Mental Health (NIMH) in the United States. Hopefully, a major susceptibility locus for BP can be detected through a systematic screen covering the whole human genome together with non-parametric tests (sib pair method, affected pedigree member method), and population based association studies.

Acknowledgments

The support of the Association for Mental Health Research is acknowledged.

References

Baron, M., Freimer, N.F., Risch, N., Lerer, B., Alexander, J.R., Straub, R.E., Asokan, S., Das, K., Peterson, A., Amos, J., Endicott, J. and Gilliam, C. (1993) Diminished support for linkage between manic depressive illness and X-chromosome markers in three Israeli pedigrees. *Nature Genet.*, 3: 49–55.

Berretini, W.H., Goldin, L.R., Gelernter, J., Gejman, P.V., Gershon, E.S. and Detera-Wadleigh, S. (1990) X-Chromosome markers and manic depressive illness: rejection of linkage to Xq28 in nine bipolar pedigrees. *Arch. Gen. Psychiatry*, 47: 366–373.

Bredbacka, P.E., Pekkarinen, P., Peltonen, L. and Lönnqvist, J. (1993) Bipolar disorder in an extended pedigree with a segregation pattern compatible with X-linked transmission: exclusion of the previously reported linkage to F9. *Psychiatric Genet.*, 3: 79–87.

Cadoret, R.J. (1978) Evidence for genetic inheritance of primary affective disorders in adoptees. *Am. J. Psychiatry*, 134: 463–466.

Craddock, N. and Owen, M. (1992) Christmas disease and major affective disorder. *Br. J. Psychiatry*, 160: 715.

Egeland, J.A., Gerhard, D.S., Paul, D.C., Sussex, J.N., Kidd, K.K., Allen, C.R., Hostetter, A.M. and Housman, D.E. (1987) Bipolar affective disorder linked to DNA markers on chromosome 11. *Nature*, 325: 783–787.

Gejman, P.V., Detera-Wadleigh, S., Martinez, M.M., Berretini, W.H., Goldin, L.R., Gelernter, J., Hsieh, W.-T. and Gershon, E.S. (1990) Manic depressive illness not linked to factor IX region in an independent series of pedigrees. *Genomics*, 8: 648–655.

Gershon, E.S., Targum, S.D., Matthysse, S. and Bunney, W.E. (1979) Color blindness not closely linked to bipolar illness. *Arch. Gen. Psychiatry*, 36: 1423–1430.

Gill, M., Castle, D. and Duggan, C. (1992) Cosegregation of Christmas disease and major affective disorder in a pedigree. *Br. J. Psychiatry*, 160: 112–114.

Kelsoe, J.R., Ginns, E.I., Egeland, J.A., Gerhard, D.S., Gostein, A.M., Bale, S.J., Pauls, D.L., Long, R.J., Kidd, K.K., Conte, G., Housman, D.E. and Paul, S.M. (1989) Re-evaluation of the linkage relationship between chromosome 11p loci and the gene for bipolar affective disorder in the Old Order Amish. *Nature*, 342: 238–243.

Lucotte, G., Landoulsi, A., Berriche, S., David, F. and Babron, M.C. (1992) Manic depressive illness is linked to factor IX in a french pedigree. *Ann. Génét.*, 35: 93–95.

Mendlewicz, J. and Hirsch, D. (1991) Bipolar manic depressive illness and X-fragile syndrome. *Biol. Psychiatry*, 29: 295–308.

Mendlewicz, J. and Rainer, J.D. (1977). Adoption study supporting genetic transmission in manic depression illness. *Nature*, 268: 327–329.

Mendlewicz, J., Simon, P., Sevy, S., Charon, F., Brocas, H., Legros, S. and Vassart, G. (1987) A polymorphic DNA marker on X chromosome and manic depression. *Lancet*, i: 1230–1232.

Mendlewicz, J., Leboyer, M., De Bruyn, A., Malafosse, A., Sevy, S., Hirsch, D., Van Broeckhoven, C. and Mallet, J. (1991a) Absence of linkage between chromosome 11p15 markers and manic depressive illness in a Belgian pedigree. *Am. J. Psychiatry*, 148: 12.

Mendlewicz, J., Sevy, S., Charon, F. and Legros, S. (1991b) Manic depressive illness and X chromosome. *Lancet*, 338: 1213.

Mendlewicz, J., Sandkuyl, L.A., De Bruyn, A., Van Broeckhoven, C. (1991c) X-linkage in bipolar illness (letter). *Biol. Psychiatry*, 29: 730–734.

Mendlewicz, J., Sevy, S. and Mendelbaum, K. (1993) Molecular genetics in affective illness. *Life Sci.*, 52: 231–242.

Rosanoff, A.H., Handy, L.M. and Rosanoff-Plesset, I.B.A. (1934) The etiology of manic depressive syndromes with special reference to their occurrence in twins. *Am. J. Psychiatry*, 91: 725–762.

Vaillant, G.E., Roston, D. and McHugo, G.J. (1992) An intriguing association between ancestral mortality and male affective disorder. *Arch. Gen. Psychiatry*, 49: 709–715.

F. Bloom (Editor)
Progress in Brain Research, Vol. 100
© 1994 Elsevier Science B.V. All rights reserved

261

CHAPTER 32

Age, sex and light: variability in the human suprachiasmatic nucleus in relation to its functions

D.F. Swaab and M.A. Hofman

Graduate School of Neurosciences Amsterdam, Netherlands Institute for Brain Research, Meibergdreef 33,
1105 AZ Amsterdam, The Netherlands

Introduction

In the last decade, when dealing with the subject of the human brain, the major research effort has undoubtedly been the clinically highly relevant comparison of material from neurological patients with that of controls. For such studies, controls are generally matched with the pathological cases for a few factors, e.g. postmortem interval, age and sex. However, the possibility of extracting fundamental information from the controls has generally attracted little or no attention. On the contrary, studies on human brain structures in controls are generally discouraged in view of the large variability often obtained in these investigations. Our 10 years of experience in studying human hypothalamic nuclei using a combination of immunocytochemistry and morphometrics have confirmed the presence of a considerable variability in functional-anatomical parameters. However, it has also been shown that this variability is not necessarily of a disturbing nature. Quite the reverse, it may bear important functional information. In this chapter, the idea is presented that variability of data on the human brain may become an increasingly useful tool in research on the relationship between structure and function.

As an example, we present data on the suprachiasmatic nucleus (SCN) of the human hypothalamus, a small structure (0.25 mm^3) on top of the optic chiasm. It is one of the few brain structures for which a main function is known. The SCN generates and coordinates circadian rhythms (Moore, 1992), but this is certainly not its only function (see below). It is not possible to reliably localize the SCN in conventionally stained human brain sections (Swaab et al., 1990), but it shows up clearly following staining of its peptidergic neurotransmitters, e.g. vasopressin (VP) (Swaab et al., 1985) or vasoactive intestinal polypeptide (VIP) (Moore, 1992). These peptides are stable in postmortem material. The number of SCN neurons expressing them varies widely in relation to age, sex and stage of rhythms providing information on the functional involvement of the SCN in these processes.

Age and SCN structure-function

Circadian rhythms are already present in the fetus, i.e. in rest-activity, breathing movements, hormone levels and heart rate variability. In addition, a circadian rhythm is found in the pattern of birth in humans, with a peak at approximately 0300–0400 h and a nadir at 1700–1800 h. These rhythms are probably mainly driven by the mother and not by the fetus (Honnebier et al., 1989). Yet, circadian rhythms in body temperature are found in 50% of low risk "healthy" premature infants with a gestational age of 29–35 weeks (Mirmiran and Kok, 1991). However, in contrast to adult rhythms, these preterm rhythms are more variable and not synchronized to the time of day, possibly through a lack of functional SCN afferents and efferents.

In order to assess the maturity of the human SCN at the moment of birth, the number of neurons expressing

262

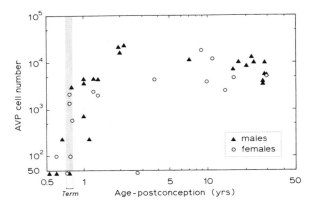

Fig. 1. Development of vasopressin (VP) cell number in the human suprachiasmatic nucleus (SCN) of the hypothalamus. Log–log scale. The period at term (38–42 weeks of gestation) is indicated by the vertical bar (from Swaab et al. (1990) with permission).

VP were determined (Fig. 1). VP staining in the SCN was present from 31 weeks onwards. However, most cells only start to express VP after birth. At term (38–42 weeks of gestation), only 13% of the adult numbers of VP-expressing neurons was present. VP cell numbers rose rapidly in the first neonatal months and at the same time overt sleep-wakefulness, temperature and *N*-acetyltransferase rhythms developed (Swaab et al., 1990) (Fig. 1). The presence of an immature SCN in premature children and the fact that normally the mother guides the circadian rhythms of the fetus has practical consequences. Exposure of premature children in the neonatal care unit to a light-dark environment improves their development (Mann et al., 1986; Fajardo et al., 1990).

In addition, at the other end of our lifespan, the SCN shows clear changes that can be related to, e.g. a fragmentation of sleep/wakefulness patterns in senescence. The neurological basis for these sleep changes may be found in the SCN and its input. A marked decrease in the number of SCN cells expressing VP was found in subjects older than 80 years, and even more so in Alzheimer patients (Fig. 2) (Swaab et al., 1985). Of practical importance in this respect may be the observation of Witting et al. (1993) that similar circadian disturbances in the aged rat can be countered by increasing the SCN input, i.e. by increasing the environmental light intensity. This way the circadian am-

plitude of sleep-wakefulness in old rats reached the level of young rats. Current research shows that circadian disturbances in Alzheimer patients can also be improved by light therapy (Okawa et al., 1991; Satlin et al., 1992).

Sex and SCN structure-function

Although the exact role of the SCN in sexual behaviour and reproduction has not yet been crystallized, data on various species strongly indicate the existence of such a role. Neuronal activity in the SCN increases around puberty, whereas circadian functions mature much earlier. The ovarian cycle of the rat is controlled by the SCN, and in the female rabbit, postcoital ultrastructural changes have been observed in the SCN (for references, see Swaab et al., 1994). In addition, neonatal castration of gerbils results in a 62% decrease in SCN volume (Holman and Hutchison, 1991).

With respect to the possible role of the SCN in sexual behaviour and reproduction, differences in the human SCN in relation to gender and sexual orientation are of interest. So far, two sex differences have been

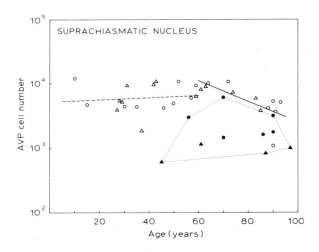

Fig. 2. Linear regression between VP cell numbers in the human SCN and age. A statistically significant decrease was observed in controls after 60 years of age (*P* < 0.05). Triangles represent males and circles represent females. Values of Alzheimer patients (closed symbols) are delineated by a minimum convex polygon and were reduced as compared to age-matched controls (*P* < 0.01). Redrawn using data from Swaab et al. (1985, 1987).

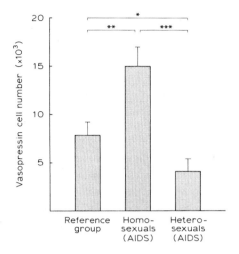

Fig. 3. The number of VP neurons in the human SCN in homosexuals contains 1.9 times more VP-producing neurons than the reference group and 3.6 times as many VP neurons as the SCN of heterosexual AIDS patients (from Swaab and Hofman (1990) with permission).

found in the human SCN. A sex difference in shape is present in the VP compartment of the SCN as the shape of the SCN is more spherical in men and more elongated in women (Swaab et al., 1985). Another, remarkable, recent finding is the sex difference in cell number in the VIP population of SCN neurons; between 10 and 30 years of age, twice as many VIP-expressing neurons were observed in males as in females (Swaab et al., 1994). Regarding sexual orientation, at least twice as many cells were found in the VP compartment of the SCN of homosexual as in heterosexual men (Swaab and Hofman, 1990) (Fig. 3).

What the exact functional meaning of the variability of the SCN is in relation to gender and sexual orientation is currently being studied. The observation of an enlarged SCN in homosexual men shows that male homosexuals do not have a "female hypothalamus", as was proposed by Dörner (1988).

Rhythms and SCN structure-function

Strong circannual and circadian fluctuations have been observed in the human SCN. The season in which the patients died appeared to be responsible for a consid-

erable amount of variation in the SCN. The volume of the VP cell population of the SCN was 2.5 times larger in October–November than in May–June, and contained 2.7 times as many VP-immunoreactive neurons in the autumn period (Hofman and Swaab, 1992; Hofman et al., 1993) (Fig. 4). The annual cycle of the human SCN showed a non-sinusoidal pattern, reaching maximum values in early autumn, a lower plateau in winter and a deep trough in late spring and early summer. The VP neurons in the PVN did not show such changes over the year, which is an indication of the specificity of the SCN rhythm. The annual SCN rhythms appeared to depend on the photoperiod cycle rather than on the annual temperature cycle, and these data, therefore, indicate that human beings are much more influenced by photoperiodic changes than is generally assumed. The annual variations in VP immunoreactivity in the human SCN coincide with (1) variations in plasma testosterone levels which are high during late summer and early autumn and low during spring, (2) the amount of sleep per 24-h period, which is the lowest in May–June and the highest in September–October, and (3) annual reproductive differences (see Hofman et al., 1993).

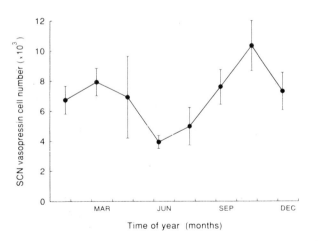

Fig. 4. VP cell number of the human SCN as a function of time of year. The values represent the mean ± SEM The seasonal variation in the cell number of the SCN is statistically significant (Kruskal–Wallis multiple comparisons test, $P = 0.05$). The human SCN contains, on average, 2.7 times as many cells in October–November as in May–June (from Hofman et al. (1993) with permission).

Since the environmental light-dark cycle is the main Zeitgeber for the biological clock, it will probably not come as too much of a surprise that the human SCN also shows clear fluctuations over the 24-h period, i.e. in relation to the hour of the day when the patient died. The volume of the VP cell population was, on average, 1.4 times larger during the day than during the night, and contained 1.8 times as many VP-immunoreactive neurons in subjects between 6 and 47 years of age (Hofman and Swaab, 1993).

Such changes are, of course, consistent with the circadian clock function of the SCN. A lesion in the suprachiasmatic region of the anterior hypothalamus, e.g. as the result of a tumour, indeed results in disturbed circadian rhythms in humans (Schwartz et al., 1986; Cohen and Albers, 1991). Totally blind people may show free-running temperature, cortisol and melatonin rhythms. In addition, they may suffer from sleep disturbances (Sack et al., 1992). The circadian variability in the SCN emphasizes the importance of the light-dark cycle for synchronization and of the SCN for the generation and coordination of circadian rhythms in humans.

The data discussed show that the variation in number of hypothalamic neurons expressing a certain neuropeptide may reveal a wealth of data on processes in which such neurons are involved. A practical consequence of the finding that structural characteristics of hypothalamic nuclei are to a large extent determined by age, gender, sexual orientation, season, hour of the day, and other factors that have not even been discussed, such as agonal state, lateralization and postmortem delay (Ravid et al., 1992), is that the marginal matching procedure generally used in neuropathology have to be greatly extended. Careful and systematic documentation of premortem and postmortem factors that might influence the later outcome of brain research are absolute prerequisites, which, in turn, demand a well-organized brain bank (Ravid et al., 1992).

As the factors influencing the morphometry of our brain are gradually becoming known, the unexplained variation remaining is comparable to the variation that occurs in similar structures in the hypothalamus of rats that have been inbred for generations and kept under well-standardized conditions. The unexplained varia-

tion remaining in the human SCN (age, season and hour of the day having been accounted for) is comparable to that of studies in rat.

Of course, observations on the human brain are primarily of a correlative nature, showing a relationship, for instance, between the number of SCN cells expressing a certain peptide and age, sex, season or hour of death. Animal experiments are, in principle, best suited for the study of the causality of such relationships, although human pathological conditions affecting a particular system in the human brain and interference studies may also provide such causal relationships. However, this last possibility usually demands more time and effort. Examples of such observations in the human hypothalamus are: (1) the degenerative changes in the SCN in Alzheimer's disease (Swaab et al., 1985) in relation to the functional circadian changes (Witting et al., 1990); (2) lesions in the SCN area, caused by tumours, that result in circadian rhythm disturbances (Schwartz et al., 1986; Cohen and Albers, 1991); (3) the free-running system in blind people (Sack et al., 1992), and (4) the disappearance of circadian behavioral disturbances in Alzheimer patients by exposure to bright light (Okawa et al., 1991; Satlin et al., 1992).

In conclusion, the large variability generally found in data on human brain structures in controls is not necessarily a disturbing factor. It may provide useful functional information on such structures in relation to, e.g. development, reproduction and aging. Such information will become more and more useful in the coming years now that powerful modern neurobiological techniques have been developed that can be applied to human postmortem brain tissue.

Acknowledgements

The authors would like to express their thanks to Ms. W.T.P. Verweij and Ms. O. Pach for their secretarial help. Brain material was obtained from the Netherlands Brain Bank (coordinator Dr. R. Ravid).

References

Cohen, R.A. and Albers, H.E. (1991) Disruption of human circadian and cognitive regulation following a discrete hypothalamic lesion: a case study. *Neurology*, 41: 726–729.

Dörner, G. (1988) Neuroendocrine response to estrogen and brain differentiation in heterosexuals, homosexuals, and transsexuals. *Arch. Sexual Behav.*, 17: 57–75.

Fajardo, B., Browning, M., Fisher, D. and Paton, J. (1990) Effect of nursery environment on state regulation in very-low-birth-weight premature infants. *Inf. Behav. Dev.*, 13: 287–303.

Hofman M.A. and Swaab, D.F. (1992) Seasonal changes in the suprachiasmatic nucleus of man. *Neurosci. Lett.*, 139: 257–260.

Hofman M.A. and Swaab, D.F. (1993) Diurnal and seasonal rhythms of neuronal activity in the suprachiasmatic nucleus of humans. *J. Biol. Rhythms*, 8: 283–295.

Hofman, M.A., Purba, J.S. and Swaab, D.F. (1993) Annual variations in the vasopressin neuron population of the human suprachiasmatic nucleus. *Neuroscience*, 53: 1103–1112.

Holman, S.D. and Hutchison, J.B. (1991) Differential effects of neonatal castration on the development of sexually dimorphic brain areas in the gerbil. *Dev. Brain Res.*, 61: 147–150.

Honnebier, M.B.O.M., Swaab, D.F. and Mirmiran, M. (1989) Diurnal rhythmicity during early human development. In: S.M. Reppert (Ed.), *Development of Circadian Rhythmicity and Photoperiodism in Mammals*, Perinatology Press, Ithaca, NY, pp. 83–103.

Mann, N.P., Haddow, R., Stokes, L., Goodley, S. and Rutter, N. (1986) Effect of night and day on pre-term infants in a newborn nursery: randomised trial. *Br. Med. J.*, 293: 1265–1267.

Mirmiran, M. and Kok, J.H. (1991) Circadian rhythms in early human development. *Early Hum. Dev.*, 26: 121–128.

Moore, R.Y. (1992) The organization of the human circadian timing system. In: D.F. Swaab, M.A. Hofman, M. Mirmiran, R. Ravid and F.W. Van Leeuwen (Eds.), *The Human Hypothalamus in Health and Disease, Progress in Brain Research,* Vol. 93, Elsevier, Amsterdam, pp. 99–117.

Okawa, M., Hishikawa, Y., Hozumi, S. and Hori, H. (1991) Sleep-wake rhythm disorder and phototherapy in elderly patients with dementia. In: G. Racagni et al. (Eds.), *Biological Psychiatry,* Vol. 1, Elsevier, Amsterdam, pp. 837–840.

Ravid, R., Van Zwieten, E.J. and Swaab, D.F. (1992) Brain banking and the human hypothalamus - factors to match for, pitfalls and potentials. In: D.F. Swaab, M.A. Hofman, M. Mirmiran, R. Ravid and F.W. Van Leeuwen (Eds.), *The Human Hypothalamus in Health and Disease, Progress in Brain Research,* Vol. 93, Elsevier, Amsterdam, pp. 83–95.

Sack, R.L., Lewy, A.J., Blood, M.L., Keith, L.D. and Nakagawa, H. (1992) Circadian rhythm abnormalities in totally blind people: incidence and clinical significance. *J. Clin. Endocrinol. Metab.*, 75: 127–134.

Satlin, A., Volicer, L., Ross, V., Herz, L. and Campbell, S. (1992) Bright light treatment of behavioral and sleep disturbances in patients with Alzheimer's disease. *Am. J. Psychiatry*, 149: 1028–1032.

Schwartz, W.J., Bosis, N.A. and Hedley-Whyte, E.T. (1986) A discrete lesion of ventral hypothalamus and optic chiasm that disturbed the daily temperature rhythm. *J. Neurol.*, 233: 1–4.

Swaab, D.F. and Hofman, M.A. (1990) An enlarged suprachiasmatic nucleus in homosexual men. *Brain Res.*, 537: 141–148.

Swaab, D.F., Fliers, E. and Partiman, T.S. (1985) The suprachiasmatic nucleus of the human brain in relation to sex, age and senile dementia. *Brain Res.*, 342: 37–44.

Swaab, D.F., Roozendaal, B., Ravid, R., Velis, D.N., Gooren, L. and Williams, R.S. (1987) Suprachiasmatic nucleus in aging, Alzheimer's disease, transsexuality and Prader-Willy syndrome. In: R. de Kloet, V.M. Wiegany and D. de Wied (Eds.), *Neuropeptides and Brain Function. Progress in Brain Research,* Vol. 72, Elsevier, Amsterdam, pp. 301–310.

Swaab, D.F., Hofman. M.A. and Honnebier, M.B.O.M. (1990) Development of vasopressin neurons in the human suprachiasmatic nucleus in relation to birth. *Dev. Brain Res*, 52: 289–293.

Swaab, D.F., Zhou, J.N., Ehlhart, T. and Hofman M.A. (1994) Development of vasoactive intestinal polypeptide (VIP) neurons in the human suprachiasmatic nucleus (SCN) in relation to birth and sex. *Dev. Brain Res.*, in press.

Witting, W., Kwa, I.H., Eikelenboom, P., Mirmiran, M. and Swaab, D.F. (1990) Alterations in the circadian rest-activity rhythm in aging and Alzheimer's disease. *Biol. Psychiatry*, 27: 563–572.

Witting, W., Mirmiran, M., Bos, N.P.A. and Swaab, D.F. (1993) Effect of light intensity on diurnal sleep-wake distribution in young and old rats. *Brain Res. Bull.*, 30: 157–162.

F. Bloom (Editor)
Progress in Brain Research, Vol. 100
© 1994 Elsevier Science B.V. All rights reserved.

CHAPTER 33

Schizophrenia: neurobiological perspectives

C.N. Stefanis

Department of Psychiatry, Athens University Medical School, Eginition Hospital, 72–74 Vas Sophias Ave., 115 28 Athens, Greece

Introduction

Schizophrenia despite recent advances, undoubtedly still remains the most enigmatic and elusive of all psychopathological conditions. The present revSwaab, D.F., piew cannot be extensive enough to include all the available information, derived from clinical, neuropsycological, psychosocial, neurogenetic and neuroscience research areas, on its etiology and pathogenesis. It is rather limited to surveying the field from a combined clinical and neurobiological perspective and more specifically, recent findings are presented supporting the author's view that schizophrenia, as an aberrant emotional, cognitive and behavioral state rather than a homogeneous distinct entity, is closely related to (determined by) a dysfunction of the brain's information processing system involving the associative cortical areas, limbic system, prefrontal cortex loop and primarily arising from a defective signal gating and signal modulating mechanism in limbic structures (mainly in hippocampus and parahippocampal cortex). The proposition lies in a three-dimensional conceptual framework comprising neurodevelopmental, activity dependent neuroplastic and functional connectivity processes interacting in an integrative fashion.

The profile of schizophrenia

A unified neurobiological model of schizophrenia should be capable of accounting, partly or in full, for the following features of the illness (Kales et al., 1990). It is a condition recognized only by a variety of affective, cognitive and behavioral manifestations defined only on phenomenological grounds by operational-clinical criteria.

The diversity of the symptoms is enormous and a distinction is currently made between positive (hallucinations, delusions etc) and negative (apathy, poor thought and speech, inattention, etc.) symptoms often co-occurring and overlapping with other psychiatric disorders.

The course is variable. The first episode usually presents with positive symptoms accompanied by agitation, while in long-standing cases the positive symptoms tend to be attenuated and the negative prevail. The peak of onset is 18–30 years. In a percentage of cases, some signs of cognitive dysfunction and social maladjustment are retrospectively detected to precede the onset of the first episode. Current treatments, be they pharmacological or psychosocial are symptom-oriented.

Although, almost immediate and full occupancy of DA receptors is accomplished by low dose neuroleptics treatment, duration exceeding 3 weeks is usually required for the core clinical symptoms to be modified.

Neuroanatomical and neurophysiological correlations

Among the limbic structures, endorhinal cortex (EC) is considered to play a crucial role as a relay and integrative station of the sensory information converging on the hippocampal formation. EC receives inputs from widespread parts of the somatosensory, auditory, visual, olfactory, gustatory and nociceptive cortical areas, either directly or by way of the paralimbic and perirhinal cortex.

Apart from the strong projections from the subiculum and the EC to the nucleus accumbens, all limbic areas have reciprocal connections with widespread parts of the telencephalic isocortex. The projections from primary sensory areas to the EC are very weak compared with those of the multimodal association areas. The EC may thus receive highly processed information that is committed to several modalities.

Because the most massive afferent projection to the hippocampus originates in the endorhinal cortex, it is clear that lesions of the parahippocampal cortex deprive the hippocampus from its main input. It is, therefore, to be expected that the behavioral deficits found after such lesions are essentially similar to those obtained after damage to the hippocampus.

According to a proposed model (Teyler and Di-Scenna, 1984), the hippocampus is considered to represent a coordinate system capable of reciprocally addressing neocortical loci in space and time.

Although there is no indication, as yet, that neuronal responses in the limbic cortical areas are elicited by specific features of sensory stimuli, responses in these areas are invariably dependent on the behavioral meaning of the stimulus, namely when the applied stimulus is used as a conditioned one in a discrimination task. Experimental findings suggest that the changes in firing rate of hippocampal cells in response to CS signal the formation of hippocampus memory traces and that the hippocampal neuronal populations process combinations of stimulus features that animals use in memory tasks (Lopes Da Silva et al., 1990).

It may thus be concluded that the limbic cortical areas (a) receive multimodal sensory information and form associations between stimuli of different kinds and (b) are involved in the formation of the substrate for temporary storage of information effected by the strong plastic properties of the synapses in the circuitry, namely initiating LTP-like processes.

The role of the reticular slow activity (RSA) seems to be pertinent. In all limbic cortical areas, RSA is present and appears to modulate the fast synaptic transmission and the long-term changes in synaptic strength (LTP). It largely depends on the brain stem inputs that are related to arousal and motivation.

The hippocampal circuit (perforant path, dentate gyrus, CA_3, CA_1, subiculum) subserves the function of a selector. Each synapse of the hippocampal trisynaptic circuit represents a gate, the state of which depends on the behavior of the organism and the RSA.

Structural changes in schizophrenia

Post mortem studies on brains of schizophrenics have shown: (a) a substantial increase in the total volume of the ventricular system mainly of the temporal horn (Brown et al., 1986); (b) a considerable volume reduction of temporal lobe structures (hippocampal formation, amygdala, parahippocampal gyrus) (Bogerts et al., 1985); and (c) a reduction of neuronal cells in the hippocampal formation, pyramidal cell bands, hippocampal segments and endorhinal cortex. In all cases, the number of neuronal cells were reduced, but there was no evidence of gliosis (Falkai and Bogerts, 1986).

Morphological changes in the temporal lobe of schizophrenics included alterations in the sulcogyral pattern of the cortex and cell loss from the cortical lamina of the ventral insula (claustro-cortex) and parahippocampal gyrus. The cytoarchitecture of the remaining temporal cortex was normal. The abnormalities were more conspicuous in the left hemisphere and were considered to indicate abnormal ontogenetic development of a small part of the endorhinal cortex.

Thus, alterations to the cellular organization of the parahippocampal gyrus and hippocampus appear to be a primary and central feature of the cellular biology of schizophrenia.

Neuroimaging findings

Both computed tomography (CT) and magnetic resonance (MR) studies yielded results comparable to those obtained from post mortem studies.

Two neuroimaging techniques to visualize the functional state of the brain, single photon emission computed tomography (SPECT) and positron. emission tomography (PET) have extensively been used recently to assess possible physiological abnormality in schizophrenia. Metabolic activity measured at the resting state as well as during a cognitive challenge suggested "hypofrontality" frequently associated with negative symptoms of schizophrenia (Andreassen et al., 1992). Conversely, "hyperfrontality" during the resting state was observed in drug-naive, recent onset schizophrenic patients by a Canadian group of investigators (Gleghorn et al., 1990). The use of PET for the investigation of DA activity in the brain yielded conflicting results by two groups of investigators and failed to either definitely refute or support the dopamine hypothesis.

Synaptic transmitters and modulators in schizophrenia

In the hippocampal formation, a large number of neurotransmitters and modulators of synaptic transmission are involved. Cardinal among them are the amino acids, glutamate and aspartate, that are present not only in all intrinsic pathways (mossy fibers, schaffer collaterals), but also in the major input pathway, the perforant path. Their direct effects are mainly excitatory through membrane depolarization, although the different types of receptors are activated in different ways and have a specific regional distribution. An important feature of these receptors (mainly the NMDA type) is that their activation depends critically on the state of neuronal membrane potential, i.e. on the immediate past history of the neuronal circuit. In this way, they play a crucial role in synaptic plasticity through the regulation of the influx of Ca^{2+}. In the hippocampus, NMDA receptors are not involved directly in normal excitatory transmission but appear to mediate synaptic potentiation such as long-term potentiation (LTP).

The excitatory amino acids (EAA) have recently been implicated in the pathogenesis of schizophrenia either as excitotoxic agents accounting for the observed structural abnormalities or as hyper or hypoactivators of an aberrant neurotransmission in schizophrenia. The latter has to be viewed in relation to the long standing dopaminergic hypothesis in schizophrenia. The validity of a dopaminergic overactivity hypothesis rests on the induction of some of the symptoms by DA receptor agonists and, conversely, on their amelioration by DA receptor blockers. However, both of these pharmacological findings do not necessarily imply that the apparent DA overactivity constitutes the primary chemical abnormality. It may very well reflect a state of imbalance brought about by a primary abnormality in another neurotransmission system, much like the Ach/DA imbalance of Parkinson's disease for which an Ach relative hyperactivity was postulated in the past. The glutamatergic system deficiency, more specifically in glutamatergic projections from the prefrontal cortex and hippocampal regions to the nucleus accumbens with their modifying and reciprocal effect on DA activity is the likely candidate of such an imbalance.

Other aminergic systems, and particularly, the 5-HT system have also to be considered as evidenced by the established efficacy of the new atypical neuroleptics with antiserotonergic action. Moreover, the observation that D_2 and D_1 receptor blockers, if at all effective, modify the negative symptoms for the worse and it takes weeks before their clinical effects are manifested, as well as the observation that patients with tardive dyskinesia with their D_2 receptors presumably fully occupied still present with psychotic symptoms, argues against the primary and sole pathogenetic factor of DA hyperactivity in schizophrenic symptomatology.

The reciprocal function of the glutamatergic and DAminergic system at the neurotransmission and at the circuit level has been adequately documented in the past few years. It has been shown that: glutamate regulates DA release from DAminergic neuron terminals in the frontal cortex, NMDA receptors modulate striatal cortex DA–D_2 transmission and neuroleptics, typical and atypical in addition to their antidopaminergic activity also exert a direct effect on the NMDA receptor function.

Plasticity of limbic neuronal networks

Limbic cortical neuronal networks are characterized by their readiness to undergo plastic changes dependent on the past experience of the organism. This explains why they are involved in learning and memory processes and also why they are prone to epileptic seizures. A form of synaptic plasticity that received considerable attention in recent years is the phenomenon of long-term potentiation (LTP), defined as an increase in the efficacy of synaptic transmission, lasting >15 min, even hours or days, following a short-lasting high-frequency stimulation. LTP has been induced in hippocampal and several other limbic structures. Polysynaptic LTP (pp-dentate gyrus, CA_3, CA1) has also been produced, while the induction of LTP in the output pathway from the hippocampus to the prefrontal cortex, may provide a useful model for a functional analysis of hippocampo-neocortical communication in learning and behavior.

In the induction stage of LTP, glutamate by binding to the AMPA receptor depolarizes the neuron and activates the *N*-methyl-D-aspartate (NMDA) receptor, to allow Na^+ and Ca^{++} to pass through its ionic channel. Fast transmission is mediated by the AMPA receptor but during intense synaptic activity, NMDA receptor is activated and triggers long-term changes. Drugs blocking the NMDA receptor also abolish synaptic plasticity as well as all forms of LTP.

LTP was regarded at first as a unitary process, but accumulating data indicate that at least two stages can be differentiated: induction and maintenance (Ben-Ari et al., 1992). The induction phase, during which a cascade of events triggers synaptic potentiation includes a NMDA component. The maintenance phase results in long-lasting and selective enhancement of the synaptic responses mediated by AMPA receptors. In the presence of D-2-amino-5-phosphonovalerate (APV) the specific antagonist of the NMDA receptor or Ca^{2+} chelators (PCP and MK-801), a tetanic stimulation fails to enhance the synaptic response. In the presence of protein kinase C inhibitors, a tetanic stimulation enhances the synaptic response, but it is accompanied by a smaller slope of the rising phase and faster early decay of the potentiation to the control level. Other than glutamate neurotransmitters active in the region and known for their modulatory functions may contribute to modifying the neuronal mechanisms underlying the late and long-lasting maintenance phase of LTP as the NE input to the dentate.

Dopamine receptor-mediated signals may also contribute to the production of the late, maintenance LTP since DA receptor blockers during tetanization prevent the occurrence of the late LTP maintenance. Moreover, in addition to enhancing protein synthesis a dopamine (D_1) mediated increase in glycoprotein fucosylation was shown to be necessary for the maintenance of the late stage of LTP.

An interesting aspect of the hippocampal LTP is its relationship with the typical rhythmic slow activity (RSA) (Larson and Lynch, 1986). In the dentate gyrus and the CA1 field, LTP induction is optimal when the time interval between stimuli is approximately 200 ms, corresponding to the frequency band of the spontaneously occurring RSA in the hippocampus. It appears that brief high-frequency stimulation elicits a weak NMDA receptor response that is amplified when the bursts are delivered in a pattern within the frequency range of the RSA.

In a recent study, non-linear mathematical analysis of hippocampal EEG epochs recorded during the maintenance phase of hippocampal LTP, have shown a relative reduction in the correlation dimension compared to the values estimated prior to the LTP induction. This suggests that the physiological mechanisms underlying the plastic neuronal changes occurring in the process of the LTP, behave as a non-linear deterministic system with lower degrees of freedom (Koutsoukos et al., 1993).

Evidence for involvement of glutamatergic system in schizophrenia

Interest in the search for more direct evidence implicating glutamatergic system involvement in schizophrenia was mainly initiated by the observation that phencyclidine (PCP), as well as ketamine, both noncompetitive NMDA receptor antagonists evoke in normals and exacerbate in schizophrenics, psychotomimetic symptoms most characteristic of schizophrenia. Consistent with these clinical observations are the results obtained in recent years from the administrations of the MK-801, the highly selective noncompetitive antagonist of the PCP binding site of the NMDA-ion channel to experimental animals. Overall, the PCP receptor blockers in animals exhibit amphetamine-like behavioral effects on a variety of tasks usually employed in psychosis-simulation experiments.

A number of recent post mortem studies on brains of schizophrenics have demonstrated changes in EAA and NMDA receptor complex such as presynaptic and postsynaptic upregulation of glutamate receptors in frontal and temporal cortex (Deakin et al., 1989), elevated binding to NMDA receptor PCP sites in the hippocampus and endorhinal cortex (Kornhuber et al., 1989), a significant reduction in the mRNA that encodes the KA/AMPA-R non-NMDA glutamate receptor within the CA_3 hippocampal field (Harrison et al., 1991) and significantly higher concentrations of serine glycine in the medial temporal lobe (Waziri et al., 1992).

Concluding remarks

At the present state of knowledge, no single brain mechanism can be invoked to account for the multiformity and highly complicated clinical and biological profile of schizophrenia. It would suffice to state that several brain mechanisms subserved by multiregional, multineuronal, multisynaptic, multitransmitional, multiansportational, multitranductional and multieffectorial systems are involved. To reduce this complexity to a primary and single cause initiating the cascade of phenomena observed in the clinical setting and in the experimental laboratory seems at present an impossible task. However, the data presented deriving from seemingly disparate observations seem to converge in a fashion that may be used as inferential evidence to formulate empirically testable hypotheses. It is in this frame that our three-dimensional proposition involving neurodevelopmental, neuroplastic and functional neuroconnectivity processes has been articulated. The available morphological findings are consistent with the view advanced recently by several authors, that the observed structural abnormalities exist in schizophrenia as residues of a neurodevelopmental deficit either of genetic or environmental origin (during the perinatal period of development) mainly affecting the temporolimbic cortical areas and taxing them with an increased functional vulnerability to subsequent (in adulthood) adverse stimuli. The strategic position within the brain's neuronal network of the hippocampus and of the parahippocampal complex with their vast incoming and outgoing connections makes them the most likely candidates for the distributor's and amplifier's role of any disturbance in the patterning of the neuronal signals that may occur. That in schizophrenia such a disturbance may originate or be amplified in the hippocampal-endorhinal complex is inferred from this structure's neuroplastic properties displayed by its marked capacity to gate, process, encode and temporarily store information through LTP-like NMDA receptor mediated cascade of synaptic and intercellular events. Such an inference derives empirical support from the psychotomimetic behavioral effects of PCP receptor blocking agents.

Consequent to the above, an altered state of functional connectivity with other brain areas, such as the prefrontal lobe in which information fine tuning and storage occur, follows a sequential logic. Considering further the observation already mentioned that LTP or LTP-like processes subserving learning and mneumonic functions behave as non-linear deterministic systems with lower degrees of freedom, we may speculate that the altered functional connectivity of hippocampo-cortical networks may develop irregularities in the neurocognitive substrate either by the efficacious reproduction of the same pattern of information, as in the case of LTD, or with erroneous association of the information, results in disturbances in the plasticity process that may affect the integration process of information in schizophrenia.

Acknowledgements

I am indebted to my co-workers E. Angelopoulos and E. Koutsoukos for their helpful advice and comments.

References

Andreassen, N.C., Rezai, K., Alliger, R., Swayze, V.W., Falum, M., Kirchener, P., Cohen, G. and O'Leary, D.S. (1992) Hypofrontality in neuroleptic-naive patients and in patients with chronic schizophrenia. Assessment with xenon 133 single-photon emission computed tomography and the Tower of London. *Arch. Gen. Psychiatry*, 49: 943–958.

Ben-Ari, Y., Aniksztejn, L. and Bregestovski, P. (1992) Protein kinase C modulation of NMDA currents: an important link for LTP induction. *Trends Neurosci.*, 15: 333–339.

Bogerts, B., Meertz, E. and Schoenfeldt-Bausch, R. (1985) Basal gaglia and limbic system pathology in schizophrenia. A morphometric study of brain volume and shrinkage. *Arch. Gen. Psychiatry*, 42: 784–791.

Brown, R., Colter, N., Corsellis, J.A.N. et al. (1986) Postmortem evidence of structural brain changes in schizophrenia. Differences in brain weight, temporal horn area, and parahippocampal gyrus compared with affective dis*order. Arch. Gen. Psychiatry*, 43: 36–42.

Deakin, J.F.W., Slater, P., Simpson, M.D.C., Gilchrist, A.C., Skan, W.J., Royston, M.C., Reynolds, G.P. and Cross, A.J. (1989) Frontal cortical and left temporal glutamatergic dysfunction in schizophrenia. *J. Neurochem.*, 52: 1781–1786.

Falkai, P. and Bogerts, B. (1986) Cell loss in the hippocampus of schizophrenics. *Eur. Arch. Psychol. Neurol. Sci.*, 236: 154–161.

Gleghorn, J.M., Garnett, E.S., Nahmias, C., Brown, G.M., Kaplan, R.D., Szetchman, H., Szechtman, B., Franco, S., Dermer, S.W. and Cook, P. (1990) Regional brain metabolism during auditory hallucinations in chronic schizophrenia. *Br. J. Psychiatry*, 157: 562–570.

Harrison, P.J., McLaughin, D. and Kerwin, R.W. (1991) Decreased hippocampal expression of a glutamate receptor gene in schizophrenia. *Lancet*, 337: 450–452.

Kales, A., Stefanis, C. and Talbot J. (1990) Recent advances in schizophrenia. In: A. Kales and C. Stefanis (Eds.), *Int. Perspective Series: Psychiatry, Psychology and Neurosciences,* ??Publisher???

Kornhuber, J., Mack-Burkhardt, F., Riederer, P., Hebenstreit, G.F., Reynolds, G.P., Andrews, H.B. and Beckmann, H. (1989) [^{3}H]MK-801 binding sites in postmortem brain regions of schizophrenic patients. *J. Neural Transmission*, 77: 231–236.

Koutsoukos, E., Angelopoulos, E., Maillis, A. and C. Stefanis (1993) Does learning mean more order in the CNS? *9th World Congress of Psychiatry Abstract Book*, 1893, p. 482.

Larson, J. and Lynch, G. (1986) Induction of synaptic potentiation in hippocampus by patterned stimulation involves two events. *Science*, 232: 986–988.

Lopes da Silva, F.H., Witter, M.P., Boeijninga, P.H. and Lohman, A.H.M. (1990) Anatomical organization and physiology of the limbic cortex. *Physiol. Rev.*, 70: 453–511.

Teyler, T.J. and Discenna, R. (1984) The topological anatomy of the hippocampus: a clue to its function. *Brain Res. Bull.*, 12: 711–719.

Waziri, R., Baruah, S. and Sherman, A.D. (1992) Abnormal serine-glycine metabolism in the brains of schizophrenics. *Schizophrenia Res.*, 8: 233–243.

Informatics and Progress in Brain Research

F. Bloom (Editor)
Progress in Brain Research, Vol. 100
© 1994 Elsevier Science B.V. All rights reserved

New solutions for neuroscience communications are still needed

Floyd E. Bloom and Warren G. Young

Department of Neuropharmacology, The Scripps Research Institute, La Jolla, CA, USA

Introduction

More than 15 years ago, Bloom and Melnechuk (1978) asserted that "even the most active neuroscientist spends more working hours in reading, reviewing and writing scientific reports than on direct experimental effort". The dilemma continues: to do or to read? In 1994, it seems nearly impossible to maintain an active ongoing comprehension of the scientific literature in any special corner of neuroscience research, let alone a broad awareness of new discoveries, or an in-depth awareness of any but the most narrowly defined field . The explosions of data about the brain, its cells and their molecules that startled us in the late 1970s and 1980s have grown unwaveringly throughout this first half of the Decade of the Brain. Yet the fact remains that there have been only a few changes in the habits of scientific information gathering, sharing and analysing that have been the traditional standards of neuroscientists: namely reading research journals and travelling to scientific meetings. This despite the obvious recognition by all participants in the profession of neuroscience that the data they are reading or hearing are months to years behind the actual state of experimental progress at the bench tops of our field.

For this milestone volume in the *Progress of Brain Research*, we note here some of the steps we are taking to begin to harness the flow of scientific data and to develop within the community of neuroscientists some means of information handling that rival the so-phistication of the instruments and methods by which we acquire our data.

A database of the brain

For the past 5 years, we have devoted considerable effort towards the development of a complex hierarchical, relational, object oriented database of published neuroscience information, built around the orientation of a brain atlas template (see Bloom, 1990) for additional background on neuroscience databases). We have taken this path as our initial approach to an eventual superhighway of neuroscience information traffic control. We describe here how we plan to use such an information handling system to establish the normative parameters of molecular, cellular and behavioral data (in terms composed of genetic, metabolic, physiologic and structural details of chemistry, circuitry and physiology), which could then be used for the detection and definition of pathological variations. It is our perspective that a comprehensive neuronal circuitry database for each of the major vertebrate central nervous systems is an essential tool for understanding the known molecular, cellular and macroscopic features of vertebrate brains and their interspecies relationships.

We also take the pragmatic position that such a data management system is necessary to illuminate essential missing elements of information. As a consequence, our efforts have been dedicated to the development of a technology to combine informatics (the science of data collection, organization and interpretation) with neuroscience with the goal of improved management and distribution of neuroscience information. A program to encourage such research efforts has recently been promulgated by several of the NIH institutes with ultimate international applications in mind (see Huerta et al., 1993).

We should note in passing that neuroscience is not alone among active areas of biomedical science in recognizing the need for such information handling tools. For example, those several hundred scientists involved in the Human Genome Project (see Pearson and Söll 1991; Cuticchia et al., 1993) have acknowledged comparable problems with the acquisition, analysis, and sharing of information on an essentially linear, but extremely long two-dimensional dataset consisting of alternations in four nucleic acid bases, and a far cry from the sort of complexities to be faced in developing a brain database (see below). Nevertheless, despite the differences in the complexity of the information sets being studied, those involved in the Human Genome Project have been explicit in advocating for informatics investments, and have stated that "the success of the genome project will depend in large part on the ease with which biologists can gain access to and use the information produced". Therefore, increased emphasis on data handling, its organization and its distribution remain major elements of the second 5 years of planning for the Genome Project (Collins and Galas, 1993).

The growth of neuroscience information

Scientific interest in the neurosciences has grown enormously over the past several years, as witnessed by the growth in membership of the national societies of neurosciences throughout the world, by the proliferation of scientific journals and magazines focused on the neurosciences, and by the programmatic interests of a wide range of governmental and nongovernmental agencies. The sheer volume of accumulated published original reviewed articles in the neurosciences over the past 5 years probably rivals that over the entire previous history of neuroscience research. This increased level of activity has in part been fueled by the development of large series of scientific technologies (many of which are described in other chapters of this volume) for the rapid acquisition of rigorous data that were in the past elusive and capricious. At present, one can expect to reveal in rich detail far more reliable information on the detailed connections and mechanisms of interaction of neuronal circuitry at the cellular and molecular levels of understanding.

Although there can be little doubt that high quality data have expanded explosively in the neurosciences, there are several implicit barriers to the optimal utilization of this information, and in particular to the practical convergence of these myriad observations into testable hypotheses of normal brain function or the pathogenesis of the major human brain disorders such as Alzheimer's, Huntington's and Parkinson's diseases (see Morrison et al., 1985; Rogers and Morrison, 1985; Love et al., 1989; Masliah et al., 1990a,b; Morrison et al., 1991; Ludwig, 1993) or those with more subtle forms of pathology (e.g. schizophrenia, Andreasen et al., 1986; Benes and Bird, 1987; Benes et al., 1987a,b; Benes 1988; Andreasen, 1989; Beckmann, 1992; Akbarian et al., 1993a,b) or HIV-associated neurocognitive disorders (e.g. Masliah et al., 1992a–c; Wiley et al., 1992).

Aside from these pathological considerations, there is a striking need for serious scholarly attempts to model human cognitive operations through incorporation of rigorous data from chemical neuroanatomy and neurophysiology into modeling algorithms. However, when one seeks to do so, there is an immediate awareness that we lack reliable quantitative information on most aspects of human and experimental neuroanatomy. As noted by Cherniak (1990), estimates published by highly regarded neuroscientists for such elemental factual considerations as the actual area or volume of the human cortex, the density of the neurons within this sheet, and the average number of synapses within the cortical neuropil differ by orders of magnitude. Some estimates are clearly incompatible with known quantitative details such as the volume of the skull and the actual assembly of the predicted numbers of synapses with their afferent axons and target dendrites onto the predicted numbers and volumes of neurons within the predicted cortical volume. While there have been quantitative estimates of some such features of the human brain published years ago (Blinkov and Glezer, 1968), these data are not well known, and clearly antedate the major advances in defining neurochemical markers of interest or the advances in non-invasive imaging.

When one considers further the differences in brain shape between individuals, the difficulties in applying rigorously cytoarchitectonic and cortical connectivity criteria to define specific cortical regions, and the inability now to apply to human brain the connectivity tracing tools of experimental neuroanatomy (see Crick and Jones, 1993), details of the structure and function of the human brain may appear unapproachable. However, one promising path through these technical complexities may be through the development of principles to relate human brain structure and function to non-human primates, as well as to be able to develop procedures by which variations in brain shapes available from non-invasive imaging of the human brain (see Pfefferbaum et al., 1988; Gazzaniga 1989; Oppenheim et al., 1989) can be employed to assist in such inferential linkages. However, even with animal brains, there have been few attempts at objective identification of nuclear or laminar boundaries, or the areal boundaries of cortical regions; see Fleischhauer et al. (1980), Rehkamper et al. (1984), Rehkamper et al. (1985) and Ahrens et al. (1990) for examples of attempts to do so, but which lack actual volumetric parameters for cells or layers using partially automated discrimination of Nissl-stained neuronal packing densities.

Quite apart from these pathological and quantitative correlates, there appear to be finite limits on the ability of any individual scientist to absorb, digest and interpret the existing studies and to monitor, evaluate and incorporate new data into one's appreciation for a given brain region, system, or question. The characteristic motif of "neuroscience", namely the interdisciplinary merging of data acquired by anatomists, chemists and physiologists working at their preferred levels of resolution from the molecular to the organismic constitutes its own a major barrier to substantive intellectual consolidation of the data.

Neuroscience tools for organized data gathering

Paralleling the data explosion in the neurosciences comes frustration: While it is generally possible to retrieve relevant reliable information on brain molecules one may be quickly stymied for information to understand the cell systems which express these genes and then to relate those genes and cells to the pertinent behaviors governed by these cells and cell systems. One hungers for a means to perform such vertical integrations of information (from the molecular to the behavioral) in a manner that would meet rigorous scientific standards and yet permit individual scholars the intellectual opportunity to conduct investigation of the accumulated data for their own specific relationships and for hypothesis generation. In our view, several sorts of information management tools are most needed and therefore motivate our efforts in this activity.

High on our list is an integrated software system for the quantitative acquisition, display and analysis of cellular and subcellular morphological information from the microscope, in a manner that can be integrated with a textual database management system (i.e. the literature awareness library of individual or working groups of scientists) and a structural icon of the places in the brain of the species of animals to which those pieces of textual information are connected (we use the generic term "templates of atlases" to symbolize the graphical counterpart to the designated structural linkage dataset). Although the application of such a tool to structural information may be readily visualized, comparable tools are also required for the data obtained by neurochemical and neurophysiological research strategies, similarly tied to the cells and regions in which those facts are acquired.

One eventual goal for such tools is to provide the neuroscience scholar, regardless of prior experience, with access to a computer or microscope system of their selection and the capability to move from the synaptic level, through cellular, multi-cellular (like layers of specific cortical areas or nuclei of defined subcortical locations), and regional microscopic levels up to the macroscopic framework of our atlases and databases within a quantitatively accurate, and platform (i.e. computer type) independent graphic display environment.

Concentrating for purposes of illustration strictly on structural information, we are developing a set of graphical software to merge and analyze existing whole brain macro-structural data sets (section data in experimental animals and MRIs in humans) to understand the volumetric and spatial variations in defined brain macro-structures according to age, gender and experimental or health status; such software would permit the development of statistically definable volumetric and stereotaxic properties for specific macroscopically defined brain regions of interest, and allow for within- and between-species comparisons.

Since experimental verification of detailed structural and functional information on human brains is unlikely to be obtainable, we look to the non-human primate brain as a likely experimental route through which human brain scholars could access the much richer database of neuronal circuitry, chemistry and cellular function in other species. However, this approach is not fully dependable, given the growing number of situations in which monkey and rodent (or other non-primate) differ substantially; see Lewis et al. (1986, 1987, 1988) and Campbell et al. (1987) for aminergic differences between primate and rodent.

A realistic brain database

We are also actively developing software to create and distribute an interactive Brain Object Database of the nervous system oriented within species on the templates representing the "pages" (electronically speaking) of a classical brain structural atlas. Comparisons of datasets across species are made with reference to the definable homologies between brain regional structures. Our working model, is composed of many of the standard classes of objects that are encountered in Neurosciences, namely, neuroanatomic structures at various levels of resolution (from the top down: areas, regions, groups, nuclei, cells, cellular organelles and macromolecules), neurochemical objects (from gene and mRNA sequences "upwards" (in size) to proteins, organelles and the regulatory molecular machinery for intracellular metabolic maintenance and intercellular transductive signaling) neurofunctional objects (cells, synapses, receptors, transductive mechanisms including ion channels, and their interactions on membrane properties) providing for cell–cell interactions in the sense of defined circuits.

Realistic classes of generic neurons are initially encoded with the actual known details of their generalized features, and enhanced by their exceptional properties, which may be defined when determined. Such biologically based neurons may then be collected into defined assemblies of neurons which represent any of the several defined functional systems. This collection can be applied to both normal and pathological states and carried from the molecular specifications up to the behavioral levels. We also envision such a data representational system to encode other neurodata objects (classical data renditions EEG, and event-related potentials) as well as imaging modalities (MRI, PET, CAT, MEG). This Brain Object Database will be constantly extendible in the classes of objects (molecules, organelles, neurons, neuronal subtypes, etc.) and derived classes (circuits, circuit operations) based upon the latest research information. Because the classes of objects and their relationships will be linked as lifelike metaphors to their biological structures, the system can be suitable not only for encoding and comparing data across levels of analysis and species, but should also be suitable for work at the theoretical level of cellular or systems simulations.

In this manner, we are working to establish a truly comprehensive database that can link graphic image sets as well as textually defined qualitative characteristics, based upon progressively accumulated and refined (and eventually quantitatively established) data. The data would range from the level of whole brains down to the level of DNA and protein sequence, along with archival reference lists to papers containing those and other data and would lend itself to other online commentary forums. Eventually one can envision an ongoing global neuroscience forum for informal and cooperative data analysis and concept formulation among those collecting the data and those hungry for data to interpret.

Attracting the users and data producers

Ultimately the users of this or some subsequent iteration of a whole brain database may decide to create an online intellectual community. Such a User Group would share their common interest in linking human brain data pertinent to neurological and psychiatric diseases with the collected wisdom deducible from experimental brain research. To build such a group of users, and more particularly to convince them that the overall database effort is sufficiently attractive to invest their own time in getting their data into a form that can be entered into the database will require a community-debated and harmoniously formulated database masterplan, and with community-accepted standard descriptors as well as standards of rigor for data inclusion.

Our experience with prior efforts to develop even primitive databases of this type for the rat (see Bloom et al., 1989) is that widespread user acceptance is essential to the effective participation of the community to get data analyzed in ways suitable for inclusion in a database, and that the only way to achieve effective and active user participation is through progressive iteration and modification with potential users.

Thus, a driving justification for establishing a Brain Object Database of realistic and modifiable objects representing real molecules in real linkages with other molecules, organelles, cells, circuits and functions is that it will be realistic enough to attract data producers and data analysts. It should take on the significance of a "deep" knowledge system in which the pieces are not just mechanically linked, but rather contain realistic intellectual connections based on defined properties. Furthermore, the Brain Object Database can lead to a shared conceptual view of the brain, and of specific brains as a databased suprastructure onto which new data, new linkages and new concepts can be superimposed/incorporated.

The necessity for user acceptance, motivation and participation also means to us that one cannot coerce users to any single form of computer platform. Thus, users should be free to use the device with which they are most comfortable, and in which they may already have substantial capital and intellectual investment.

For that reason, we intend to use software that is portable across heterogeneous computer platforms, starting with the Macintosh and Windows based computer systems, and then developing it for UNIX/Motif systems. This developmental environment would make the entire database and its class structures executable on virtually any computer presently used by neuroscientists.

The database environment we envision should also provide means to integrate the efforts of many individual neuroscientists, regardless of where they work. There is no question that research institutions are already well connected via the Internet, and that having tasted this new communication, capacity has generated a boundless demand for higher speeds on new data superhighways. We envision the databases as being distributed among the neuroscientists such that database actions (such as searching for a specific combination of facts or diseases) will automatically be empowered to reach out into the worldwide network to retrieve the desired data with no more delay than if those data were already present within the network of the local research laboratory.

A more informed future?

Perhaps in this fashion, one may begin to change the information gathering habits of the neuroscientific community and allow the science to rise to even more powerful means to capture the information residing within today's data and to ask more heuristic questions tomorrow.

In addition to establishing a user-friendly "deep knowledge" database of brain information across levels of resolution (molecules to cells to systems to behaviors) and across grouped members of a species of brain, the Brain Object Database should also be operated in conjunction with an intelligent data filtering, indexing and database entry system such that the interested users can in fact be on top of current information that matches their user-defined profiles of interest and to which new interest elements can later be defined, dropped or re-assigned. Both parts of this neuroscientific communications solution are necessary to solve the current information problem. While we have only spoken here about the database tool, the development of data gathering tools cannot lag far behind.

Acknowledgment

This work is supported by HBP Grant MH52154.

References

Ahrens, P., Schleicher, A., Zilles, K. and Werner, L. (1990) Image analysis of Nissl-stained neuronal perikarya in the primary visual cortex of the rat: automatic detection and segmentation of neuronal profiles with nuclei and nucleoli. *J. Microsc.,* 157(Pt 3): 349–365.

Akbarian, S., Bunney Jr., W.E., Potkin, S.G., Wigal, S.B., Hagman, J.O., Sandman, C.A. and Jones, E.G. (1993a) Altered distribution of nicotinamide-adenine dinucleotide phosphate-diaphorase cells in frontal lobe of schizophrenics implies disturbances of cortical development. *Arch. Gen. Psychiatry,* 50: 169–177.

Akbarian, S., Vinuela, A., Kim, J.J., Potkin, S.G., Bunney Jr., W.E. and Jones, E.G. (1993b) Distorted distribution of nicotinamide-adenine dinucleotide phosphate-diaphorase neurons in temporal lobe of schizophrenics implies anomalous cortical development. *Arch. Gen. Psychiatry,* 50: 178–187.

Andreasen, N.C. (1989) Neural mechanisms of negative symptoms. *Br. J. Psychiatry,* 7(Suppl.): 93–98.

Andreasen, N., Nasrallah, H.A., Dunn, V., Olson, S.C., Grove, W.M., Ehrhardt, J.C., Coffman, J.A. and Crossett, J.H. (1986) Structural abnormalities in the frontal system in schizophrenia. A magnetic resonance imaging study. *Arch. Gen. Psychiatry,* 43: 136–144.

Beckmann, H. (1992) Temporal lobe cytoarchitectural neuropathology in schizophrenia. *Clin. Neuropharmacol.,* 15: 493A–494A.

Benes, F.M. (1988) Post-mortem structural analyses of schizophrenic brain: study designs and the interpretation of data. *Psychiatr. Dev.,* 6: 213–226.

Benes, F.M. and Bird, E.D. (1987) An analysis of the arrangement of neurons in the cingulate cortex of schizophrenic patients. *Arch. Gen. Psychiatry,* 44: 608–616.

Benes, F.M., Majocha, R., Bird, E.D. and Marotta, C.A. (1987a) Increased vertical axon numbers in cingulate cortex of schizophrenics. *Arch. Gen. Psychiatry,* 44: 1017–1021.

Benes, F.M., Matthysse, S.W., Davidson, J. and Bird, E.D. (1987b) The spatial distribution of neurons and glia in human cortex based on the poisson distribution. *Anal. Quant. Cytol. Histol.,* 9: 531–534.

Blinkov, S. and Glezer, I. (1968) *The Human Brain in Figures and Tables: A Quantitative Handbook.* Plenum, New York.

Bloom, F.E. (1990) *Databases of Brain Information. Three-Dimensional Neuroimaging.* Raven Press, New York, 273–306.

Bloom, F.E. and Melnechuk, T. (1978) New solutions for science communication problems needed now. *Trends Neurosci.,* 1: I–II.

Bloom, F.E., Young, W.G. and Kim, Y. (1989) *Brain Browser.* Academic Press, San Diego, CA.

Campbell, M.J., Lewis, D.A., Foote, S.L. and Morrison, J.H. (1987)

Distribution of choline acetyltransferase-, serotonin-, dopamine-beta-hydroxylase-, tyrosine hydroxylase-immunoreactive fibers in monkey primary auditory cortex. *J. Comp. Neurol.,* 261: 209–20.

Cherniak, C. (1990) The bounded brain: toward quantitative neuroanatomy. *J. Cognitive Neurosci.,* 2: 58–68.

Collins, F. and Galas, D. (1993) A new five-year plan for the U.S. human genome project. *Science,* 262: 43–46.

Crick, F. and Jones, E.G. (1993) Backwardness of human neuroanatomy. *Nature,* 361: 109–110.

Cuticchia, A.J., Chipperfield, M.A., Porter, C.J., Kearns, W. and Pearson, P.L. (1993) Managing all those bytes: the human genome project. *Science,* 262: 47–48.

Fleischhauer, K., Zilles, K. and Schleicher, A. (1980) A revised cytoarchitectonic map of the neocortex of the rabbit (*Oryctolagus cuniculus*). *Anat. Embryol.,* 161: 121–143.

Gazzaniga, M.S. (1989) Organization of the human brain. *Science,* 245: 947–952.

Huerta, M.F., Koslow, S.H. and Leshner, A.I. (1993) The human brain project: an international resource. *Trends Neurosci.,* 16: 436–438.

Lewis, D.A., Campbell, M.J., Foote, S.L. and Morrison, J.H. (1986) The monoaminergic innervation of primate neocortex. *Hum. Neurobiol.,* 5: 181–188.

Lewis, D.A., Campbell, M.J., Foote, S.L., Goldstein, M. and Morrison, J.H. (1987) The distribution of tyrosine hydroxylase-immunoreactive fibers in primate neocortex is widespread but regionally specific. *J. Neurosci.,* 7: 279–290.

Lewis, D.A., Foote, S.L., Goldstein, M. and Morrison, J.H. (1988) The dopaminergic innervation of monkey prefrontal cortex: a tyrosine hydroxylase immunohistochemical study. *Brain Res.,* 449: 225–243.

Love, S., Burrola, P., Terry, R.D. and Wiley, C.A. (1989) Immunoelectron microscopy of Alzheimer and Pick brain tissue labelled with the monoclonal antibody Alz-50. *Neuropathol. Appl. Neurobiol.,* 15: 223–231.

Ludwig, F.C. (1993) Pathology in historical perspective. *The Pharos,* 56(2): 5–10.

Masliah, E., Iimoto, D.S., Saitoh, T., Hansen, L.A. and Terry, R.D. (1990a) Increased immunoreactivity of brain spectrin in Alzheimer disease: a marker for synapse loss? *Brain Res.,* 531: 36–44.

Masliah, E., Terry, R.D., Alford, M. and DeTeresa, R. (1990b) Quantitative immunohistochemistry of synaptophysin in human neocortex: an alternative method to estimate density of presynaptic terminals in paraffin sections. *J. Histochem. Cytochem.,* 38: 837–844.

Masliah, E., Achim, C.L., Ge, N., DeTeresa, R., Terry, R.D. and Wiley, C.A. (1992a) Spectrum of human immunodeficiency virus-associated neocortical damage. *Ann. Neurol.,* 32: 321–329.

Masliah, E., Ge, N., Achim, C.L., Hansen, L.A. and Wiley, C.A. (1992b) Selective neuronal vulnerability in HIV encephalitis. *J. Neuropathol. Exp. Neurol.,* 51: 585–593.

Masliah, E., Ge, N., Morey, M., DeTeresa, R., Terry, R.D. and Wiley, C.A. (1992c) Cortical dendritic pathology in human immunodeficiency virus encephalitis [see comments]. *Lab. Invest.,* 66: 285–291.

Morrison, J.H., Rogers, J., Scherr, S., Benoit, R. and Bloom, F.E.

(1985) Somatostatin immunoreactivity in neuritic plaques of Alzheimer's patients. *Nature*, 314: 90–92.

Morrison, J.H., Hof, P.R. and Bouras, C. (1991) An anatomic substrate for visual disconnection in Alzheimer's disease. *Ann. N. Y. Acad. Sci.*, 640: 36–43.

Oppenheim, J.S., Skerry, J.E., Tramo, M.J. and Gazzaniga, M.S. (1989) Magnetic resonance imaging morphology of the corpus callosum in monozygotic twins. *Ann. Neurol.*, 26: 100–104.

Pearson, M.L. and Söll, D. (1991) The human genome project: a paradigm for information management in the life sciences. *FASEB J.*, 5: 35–39.

Pfefferbaum, A., Zipursky, R.B., Lim, K.O., Zatz, L.M., Stahl, S.M. and Jernigan, T.L. (1988) Computed tomographic evidence for generalized sulcal and enlargement in schizophrenia. *Arch. Gen. Psychiatry*, 45: 633–640.

Rehkamper, G., Zilles, K. and Schleicher, A. (1984) A quantitative approach to cytoarchitectonics. IX. The areal pattern of the hyperstriatum ventrale in the domestic pigeon, *Columba livia* f.d. *Anat. Embryol.*, 169: 319–327.

Rehkamper, G., Zilles, K. and Schleicher, A. (1985) A quantitative approach to cytoarchitectonics. X. The areal pattern of the neostriatum in the domestic pigeon, *Columba livia* f.d. A cyto- and myeloarchitectonical study. *Anat. Embryol.*, 171: 345–355.

Rogers, J. and Morrison, J.H. (1985) Quantitative morphology and regional and laminar distributions of senile plaques in Alzheimer's disease. *J. Neurosci.*, 5: 2801–2808.

Wiley, C.A., Johnson, R.T. and Reingold, S.C. (1992) Neurological consequences of immune dysfunction: lessons from HIV infection and multiple sclerosis. *J. Neuroimmunol.*, 40: 115–119.

Subject Index

286